Seventh Edition

# Understanding Canadian Business

**William G. Nickels**
University of Maryland

**James M. McHugh**
St. Louis Community College at Forest Park

**Susan M. McHugh**
Applied Learning Systems

**Rita Cossa**
McMaster University

**Bob Sproule**
University of Waterloo

**McGraw-Hill Ryerson**
*Connect. Learn. Succeed.*

**Understanding Canadian Business**
**Seventh Edition**

Statistics Canada information is used with the permission of Statistics Canada. Users are forbidden to copy the data and redisseminate them, in an original or modified form, for commercial purposes, without permission from Statistics Canada. Information on the availability of the wide range of data from Statistics Canada can be obtained from Statistics Canada's Regional Offices, its World Wide Web site at www.statcan.gc.ca, and its toll-free access number: 1-800-263-1136.

ISBN-13: 978-0-07-097027-4
ISBN-10: 0-07-097027-0

1 2 3 4 5 6 7 8 9 0  TCP  1 9 8 7 6 5 4 3 2 1 0

Printed in Canada.

Vice-President and Editor-in-Chief: Joanna Cotton
Senior Sponsoring Editor: Kim Brewster
Marketing Manager: Cathie Lefebvre
Developmental Editor: Lori McLellan
Supervising Editor: Kara Stahl
Senior Editorial Associate: Christine Lomas
Copy Editor: Cat Haggert
Team Lead, Production: Paula Brown
Cover and Interior Design: Sarah Orr/ArtPlus Design & Communications
Page Layout: Heather Brunton/ArtPlus Design & Communications
Printer: Transcontinental Printing Group

**Library and Archives Canada Cataloguing in Publication**

Understanding Canadian business / William G. Nickels ... [et al.]. — 7th ed.

Includes bibliographical references and index.
ISBN 978-0-07-097027-4

1. Industrial management—Textbooks.   2. Business—Textbooks.   I. Nickels, William G

HD31.U5135 2010          650          C2009-906965-2

## Dedication

*To my daughters, Mattia and Leila. Your hugs, kisses, smiles, and artwork make all the effort worthwhile.*

**Rita Cossa**

*To my wife and children, who endured an absentee husband and father. Thank you for your support and encouragement. To my students, who provide me with the opportunity to support their learning.*

**Bob Sproule**

*To Marsha, Joel, Casey, Dan, Molly, Michael, and Colin—you have been our strength in the past, our joy in the present, and our hope for the future.*

**Bill Nickels, Jim McHugh, Susan McHugh**

# About the Authors

**Bill Nickels** is professor emeritus of business at the University of Maryland, College Park. He has over 35 years' experience teaching graduate and undergraduate business courses, including introductory courses in business, marketing, and promotion. He has won the Outstanding Teacher on Campus Award four times and was nominated for the award many other times. He received his MBA degree from Western Reserve University and his PhD from The Ohio State University. He has written a marketing communications text and two marketing principles texts in addition to many articles in business publications. He has taught many seminars to business people on subjects such as power communications, marketing, non-business marketing, and stress and life management.

**Jim McHugh** holds an MBA degree from Lindenwood University and has had broad experience in education, business, and government. As chairman of the Business and Economics Department of St. Louis Community College/Forest Park, Jim coordinated and directed the development of the business curriculum. In addition to teaching several sections of Introduction to Business each semester for nearly 30 years, Jim taught in the marketing and management areas at both the undergraduate and graduate levels. Jim enjoys conducting business seminars and consulting with small and large businesses. He is actively involved in the public service sector and served as chief of staff to the St. Louis County Executive.

**Susan McHugh** is a learning specialist with extensive training and experience in adult learning and curriculum development. She holds an MEd degree from the University of Missouri and completed her coursework for a PhD in education administration with a specialty in adult learning theory. As a professional curriculum developer, she has directed numerous curriculum projects and educator training programs. She has worked in the public and private sectors as a consultant in training and employee development.

**Rita Cossa** is a faculty member at the DeGroote School of Business at McMaster University, where she teaches the undergraduate introduction to business and marketing courses. Teaching highlights include a nomination to TVOntario's Best Lecturer Competition and notations in the *Maclean's Guide to Universities* as a Popular Prof for Marketing. She has authored various instructor and student supplements, including two marketing study guides. Prior to the completion of her MBA, Rita held several management-level positions in the financial services industry.

**Bob Sproule** is a faculty member in the School of Accounting and Finance at the University of Waterloo. He is a CMA who completed an MBA, majoring in Human Resource Management. Bob spent 30 years in industry working in various accounting and senior management positions before making his passion for teaching a full-time occupation. He has taught Introductory Financial and Management Accounting courses, but has found his true niche in teaching Introductory Business to over 1000 students annually. He is recognized within the University community for his innovative use of technology. Bob's scholarly work in teaching and learning included the development of a learning tool, "Preparing a Cash Flow Statement Using the Indirect Method," which received an Innovation in Accounting Education award from the Canadian Academic Accounting Association. Within the university he has facilitated the Teaching Excellence Academy and is a member of the Teaching Excellence Council. He maintains leadership positions in the Canadian Academic Accounting Association, Society for Teaching and Learning in Higher Education, and Multi-Media Resources for Learning and On-Line Teaching (MERLOT), and has received both national and international awards.

# Brief Contents

# Contents

# PART 2
## BUSINESS OWNERSHIP AND SMALL BUSINESS *168*

## CHAPTER 6
### Forms of Business Ownership  *168*

## CHAPTER 7
### Entrepreneurship and Starting a Small Business  *198*

## CHAPTER 13
## Understanding Employee–Management Issues and Relations 388

# PART 5
# MARKETING: DEVELOPING AND IMPLEMENTING CUSTOMER-ORIENTED MARKETING PLANS 420

## CHAPTER 14
## Marketing: Building Customer and Stakeholder Relationships 420

## CHAPTER 17
### Financial Management  *510*

## APPENDIX D
### Risk Management  *540*

# Preface

*Understanding Canadian Business*, by Nickels, McHugh, McHugh, Cossa, and Sproule has been the number-one textbook in the introductory business market for several editions for three reasons: (1) The commitment and dedication of an author team that teaches this course and believes in the importance and power of this learning experience, (2) authors who listen to our customers, and (3) the quality of our supplements package. We consistently look to the experts—full-time faculty members, adjunct instructors, and of course students—to drive the decisions we make about the text itself and the ancillary package. Through a series of focus groups, as well as full-book, single-chapter, and revised manuscript reviews of both text and key ancillaries, we have heard the stories of more than 500 professors over our seven editions. Their insights and experiences are evident on every page of this revision and in every supplement. As teachers of the course and users of our own materials, this author team is dedicated to the principles of excellence in business education. By providing the richest, most current topical coverage, using dynamic pedagogy that puts students in touch with today's real business issues, and creating groundbreaking and market-defining ancillary items for professors and students alike, *Understanding Canadian Business* leads the way.

As authors, it is thrilling to see the results of the work we love be embraced by colleagues in colleges and universities across Canada. *Understanding Canadian Business* has been designed to introduce students to the exciting topic of business. It also provides insight into career choices and opportunities, as well as a look at the ethical dilemmas businesses and managers face.

This book marks the seventh edition of the most popular introductory business text in Canada. This edition has undergone major revisions to reflect today's marketplace. Most of the examples cited are Canadian companies or transnational companies operating in Canada. The number of chapters, 18, was decided on after careful thought and discussion. This number takes into consideration the limitations of the 13- to 15-week semester or term commonly found in Canada, and students' capacity to absorb information.

Many instructors provided us with in-depth evaluations for this seventh edition. Their suggestions for improvement are reflected on every page of this edition. Once the final draft was written, another group of instructors critiqued our initial effort, which led to more important refinements. While this is an extensive product development process, we consider this sharing of ideas with colleagues and students critical if we are to produce a text that reflects what students should be learning about business in Canada and around the world.

# Student-Friendly Approach

"Easy to read and at the same time motivating in a sense that makes entering business intriguing."

—**John Fakouri, Algonquin College**

"Great information on start-ups and micro businesses; superb Canadian examples and success stories."

—**Peter Mombourquette, Mount Saint Vincent University**

"A strength of this textbook is how it outlines various types of entrepreneurs and how it specifically highlights the female entrepreneur."

—**Randy Delorey, St. Francis Xavier University**

As evidenced by the above quotations, *Understanding Canadian Business* has developed an excellent reputation among Canadian instructors and students as a text that delivers key concepts in a student-friendly style without watering down the material. This Seventh Edition continues to be characterized by

- *A high-engagement style*—an easy-to-read, high-involvement, interactive writing style that engages students through active learning techniques, timely and interesting examples, and challenging applications.
- *Personalized business*—a vivid and accurate description of business, business professionals, and entrepreneurs (through cases, exercises, and testimonials) that allows students to personalize business and identify possible career interests and role models.
- *Emphasis on critical thinking*—the use of extended examples, cases, and videos involving people making business decisions, which students can easily relate to text concepts.
- *A strong pedagogical framework*—a rigorous pedagogical framework in the text, based on the use of learning objectives, progress assessments, key terms, photo and illustration essays, and interactive summaries, along with supportive student supplements, appeal to a wide range of learning styles.

Before students can begin to understand today's business world, you have to provide them with the most up-to-date and relevant material. With help from reviews and focus groups, *Understanding Canadian Business* provides a unified collection of educational tools. This combination of text and visual media works to teach students everything they should know before entering the real world of business.

This special walkthrough section was developed to highlight the new and retained features that have made this text the clear market leader. If you still have questions after reading through this material, please contact your local McGraw-Hill Ryerson *i*Learning Sales Specialist.

# Integration of Important Concepts throughout the Text

Based on research and the preferences expressed by both users and non-users of *Understanding Canadian Business*, the following key topics are incorporated as themes throughout the text:

- Constant and dynamic change
- Small business and entrepreneurship
- Ethics and social responsibility
- "Green" business in the new "Green Box" features
- Global business
- Technology and change
- Pleasing customers
- Teams
- Quality
- E-commerce
- Cultural diversity

These themes reflect a strong consensus among instructors of introductory business courses that certain topics deserve and need special emphasis. Among these, instructors encouraged us to add particular focus in the areas of small business/entrepreneurship, ethics, global business, and e-commerce. In response, this edition includes many small business, global, and Internet examples throughout. It continues to feature boxes titled "Spotlight on Small Business," "Making Ethical Decisions," "Reaching Beyond Our Borders," "Dealing with Change," and introduces the new "Green Box."

## Learning Objectives ▶

Tied directly to the summaries at the end of the chapter and to the Test Bank questions, the Learning Objectives help students preview what they should know after reading the chapter, and then test that knowledge by answering the questions in the summary.

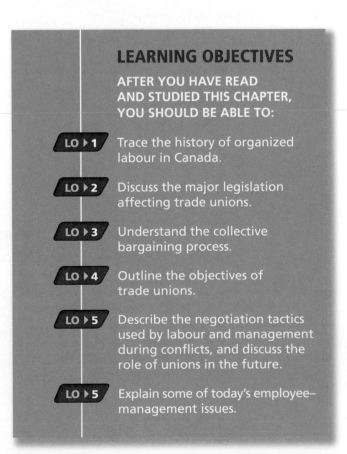

### LEARNING OBJECTIVES

**AFTER YOU HAVE READ AND STUDIED THIS CHAPTER, YOU SHOULD BE ABLE TO:**

**LO▶1** Trace the history of organized labour in Canada.

**LO▶2** Discuss the major legislation affecting trade unions.

**LO▶3** Understand the collective bargaining process.

**LO▶4** Outline the objectives of trade unions.

**LO▶5** Describe the negotiation tactics used by labour and management during conflicts, and discuss the role of unions in the future.

**LO▶5** Explain some of today's employee–management issues.

# Getting to Know Business Professionals

Each chapter begins with a profile of a business person whose career relates closely to the material covered in that chapter. Not all of the personalities are famous, since many of them work in small businesses and non-profit organizations. Getting to know these business professionals provides the perfect transition to the text material.

▼

## Micropreneurs and Home-Based Businesses

Not every person who starts a business has the goal of growing it into a mammoth corporation. Some are interested in simply enjoying a balanced lifestyle while doing the kind of work they want to do. The smallest of small businesses are called **micro-enterprises**, most often defined as having fewer than five employees.[11] While other entrepreneurs are committed to the quest for growth, **micropreneurs** (owners of micro-enterprises) know they can be happy even if their companies never appear on a list of top-ranked businesses.

Many micropreneurs are owners of home-based businesses. According to Industry Canada, approximately 55 percent of all employer businesses (597,432 in number) were micro-enterprises, with almost 43 percent of these businesses operating in the service sector.[12] Micropreneurs include writers, consultants, video producers, architects, bookkeepers, and such. In fact, the development of this textbook involved many home-based business owners. The authors, the developmental editors, the copy editor, and even the text designer operate home-based businesses.

Many home-based businesses are owned by people who are trying to combine career and family.[13] Don't misunderstand and picture home-based workers as female childcare providers; men also run home-based businesses. In addition to helping business owners balance work and family, other reasons for the growth of home-based businesses include the following:[14]

- *Computer Technology.* Computer technology has levelled the competitive playing field, allowing home-based businesses to look and act as big as their corporate competitors. Broadband Internet connections, fax machines, and other technologies are so affordable that setting up a business takes a much smaller initial investment than it used to.

- *Corporate Downsizing.* Downsizing has made workers aware that there is no such thing as job security, leading some to venture out on their own. Meanwhile, the work of the downsized employees still needs to be done and corporations are outsourcing much of the work to smaller companies; that is, they are contracting with small companies to temporarily fill their needs.

- *Change in Social Attitudes.* Whereas home-based entrepreneurs used to be asked when they were going to get a "real" job, they are now likely to be asked instead for "how-to-do-it" advice.

Working at home has its challenges, of course. In setting up a home-based business, you could expect the following major challenges:[15]

- *Getting New Customers.* Getting the word out can be difficult because you don't have signs or a storefront, especially if the business does not have a Web presence.

**micro-enterprise**
A small business defined as having fewer than five employees.

**micropreneurs**
Small-business owners with fewer than five employees who are willing to accept the risk of starting and managing the type of business that remains small, lets them do the kind of work they want to do, and offers them a balanced lifestyle.

Chef Michael Smith, Canada's best-known chef, is host of several cooking shows on Food Network Canada and in 26 other countries. He is an award-winning cookbook author, newspaper columnist, restaurant chef, and home cook who works from his home. His third series, *Chef At Home*, features some of his home cooking.

## ◀ Photo and Illustration Essays

More and more students have expressed that they are visually oriented learners; therefore, increased emphasis on the pedagogical value of illustrations is essential. Some photos and illustrations in the text are accompanied by a short essay that highlights the relevance of the visuals to the material in the text.

# Progress Assessments

To ensure that students are understanding and retaining the material, Progress Assessments stop them and show them that they need to review before proceeding. The Progress Assessment is a proven learning tool that helps students comprehend and retain material.

## Progress Assessment

- What is the difference between materials resource planning (MRP) and enterprise resource planning (ERP)?
- What is just-in-time inventory control?
- How does flexible manufacturing differ from lean manufacturing?
- What are CAD, CAM, and CIM?

# Interactive Summaries

The end-of-chapter summaries are directly tied to the learning objectives and are written in a question-and-answer format.

## SUMMARY

**LO ▸ 1** Trace the history of organized labour in Canada.

1. Organized labour in Canada dates back to the 1800s. Early unions on the wharves of Halifax, St. John's, and Quebec existed during the War of 1812 to profit from labour scarcity. Craft unions represented shoemakers and printers. Many of the early labour organizations were local or regional in nature.

**Describe some of the main objectives of labour and whether they were achieved.**
Unions hoped to improve workers' poor conditions and wages by forming unions that would fight for workers' rights. This has largely been achieved, and many early demands are now entrenched in law.

**Describe some of the unions in existence today.**
The Canadian Union of Public Employees (CUPE) and the Canadian Auto Workers (CAW) are two of the largest unions in Canada. They represent workers from different sectors in the economy. Many unions in Canada are national in nature. Many also belong to international organizations. The Canadian Labour Congress, which represents over 3 million unionized workers, is the national voice of the labour movement in Canada.

**LO ▸ 2** Discuss the major legislation affecting trade unions.

2. Much labour legislation has been passed by federal and provincial governments.

**What is the major piece of labour legislation?**
The Canada Labour Code outlines labour legislation as it applies to federal government employees, who represent approximately 10 percent of all workers in Canada. Each provincial jurisdiction in Canada has its own labour legislation and employment standards that apply to workers within its borders.

**LO ▸ 3** Understand the collective bargaining process.

3. Collective bargaining is the process by which a union represents employees in relations with their employer.

**What is included in collective bargaining?**
Collective bargaining includes how unions are selected, the period prior to a vote, certification, ongoing contract negotiations, and behaviour while a contract is in force.

**What are the steps in the collective bargaining process?**
Refer to Figure 13.4 for the steps in the collective bargaining process.

**LO ▸ 4** Outline the objectives of trade unions.

4. The objectives of trade unions shift in response to changes in social and economic trends.

**What topics typically appear in labour–management agreements?**
Labour–management agreements may include issues such as management rights, union security clauses, hours of work, vacation policies, job rights and seniority principles, and employee benefits. See Figure 13.5 for a more exhaustive list.

# Key Terms ▶

Important terms, highlighted in bold face throughout the text with an accompanying definition in the margin, are listed in alphabetical order with their corresponding page numbers for ease of reference.

**KEY TERMS**

assembly process 314
computer-aided design (CAD) 319
computer-aided manufacturing (CAM) 319
computer-integrated manufacturing (CIM) 320
continuous process 314
economic order quantity 315
enterprise resource planning (ERP) 316
facility layout 306
facility location 302
flexible manufacturing 318
form utility 314

intermittent process 314
ISO 9000 310
ISO 14000 311
just-in-time (JIT) inventory control 317
lean manufacturing 318
logistics 311
mass customization 319
materials requirement planning (MRP) 316
operations management 300
process manufacturing 314
production 300

production management 300
purchasing 317
quality 307
research and development (R&D) 397
robot 318
six sigma quality 307
statistical process control (SPC) 308
statistical quality control (SQC) 308
supply chain 311
supply chain management 311

**CRITICAL THINKING**

1. People on the manufacturing floor are being replaced by robots and other machines. On the one hand, that is one way in which companies compete with cheap labour from other countries. No labour at all is less expensive than cheap labour. On the other hand, automation eliminates many jobs. Are you concerned that automation may increase unemployment or under-employment in Canada and around the world? Why?

2. Computer-integrated manufacturing (CIM) has revolutionized the production process. Now everything from cookies to cars can be designed and manu-

factured much more cheaply than before. Furthermore, customized changes can be made with very little increase in cost. What will such changes mean for the clothing industry, the shoe industry, and other fashion related industries? What will they mean for other consumer and industrial goods industries? How will you benefit as a consumer?

3. One way to create new jobs in Canada is to have more innovation. Much innovation comes from new graduates from engineering and the sciences. What could Canada do to motivate more students to major in those areas?

# ◀ Critical Thinking Questions

Found in each chapter, Critical Thinking questions ask students to pause and think about how the material they are reading applies to their own lives.

# Developing Workplace Skills ▶

The Developing Workplace Skills section has activities designed to increase student involvement in the learning process. Some of these mini-projects require library or Internet searches, while others can be used as team activities either in or out of the classroom.

**DEVELOPING WORKPLACE SKILLS**

1. Debate the following statement with several classmates: Non-union firms are better managed (or perform better) than unionized firm. To get a better feeling for the other side's point of view, take the opposite side of this issue from the one you normally would. Include information from outside sources to support your position.

2. Top executives' high pay creates tremendous incentives for lower-level executives to work hard to get those jobs. Their high pay also creates resentment among workers, shareholders, and members of the general public. Debate the following in class: Business executives receive a total compensation package that is far beyond their value. They should not earn more than twenty times the compensation of the lowest-

paid worker at the firm. Take the opposite side of the issue from your normal stance to get a better feel for the other point of view.

3. Find the latest information on federal and provincial legislation related to child care, parental leave, and elder care benefits for employees. In what direction are the trends pointing? What will be the cost to businesses for these new initiatives? Do you favour such advancements in workplace legislation? Why or why not?

4. Examine an actual collective agreement and identify the constraints set upon workers and management by its provisions.

**TAKING IT TO THE NET 1**                    www.mcgrawhillconnect.ca

**Purpose**
To learn more about a Government of Canada resource that highlights labour topics.

**Exercise**
The Department of Human Resources and Skills Development Canada develops labour policies through one of its programs, the Labour Program. Visit this site at http://www.hrsdc.gc.ca/eng/labour/index.shtml.

1. What are some of the topics that are covered on this site? (Hint: Look at the tabs on the left-hand side of the page.) Search through each of these topics to learn more about them.

2. Input 'union membership' in the Search box. Looking at Table 1, what is the trend in union membership in Canada? In Table 2, state the top five organizations that have the largest membership. Have you heard of these organizations?

3. Visit the Newsroom tab and search for recent News Releases that relate to Labour. What is in the news right now?

# ◀ Taking It to the Net Exercises

Each chapter contains Taking It to the Net exercises that ask students to research topics and issues on the Web and make decisions based on their research.

## ANALYZING MANAGEMENT DECISIONS

**Why Big Companies Fail to Innovate**

Matthew Kiernan, based in Unionville, Ontario, is a management consultant whose views command attention. He has a PhD degree in strategic management from the University of London and was a senior partner with an international consulting firm, KPMG Peat Marwick. Subsequently, he founded his own firm, Innovest Group International, with a staff operating out of Geneva, London, and Toronto. He was also a director of the Business Council for Sustainable Development based in Geneva.

His book *Get Innovative or Get Dead* took aim at big corporations for their poor record on innovation. Any five-year-old could tell you that companies must innovate to survive, he said, so what's the problem? According to Kiernan, it's one thing to understand something in your head but quite another thing to really feel it in your gut. This is further complicated by the difficulty of getting a big company to shift gears, to turn its culture around so that innovation becomes the norm rather than the special effort.

Kiernan called for a company to develop a style and atmosphere that favours individual risk-taking, the intrapreneurial approach discussed in Chapter 7. That means

that if a team tries something that doesn't work, you don't shoot it down. Encouraging innovation, which inevitably involves taking risks with the unknown, means accepting the fact that it may take two or three attempts before something useful is developed. Recently, Matthew has applied this principle to sustainable development, including the topic of carbon finance.

The 3M company is often used as a great example of a company that encourages creativity. Its policy dictates that 30 percent of annual sales come from products less than four years old. However, 3M wasn't always that progressive. When the now legendary Post-it Notes were first developed by an employee, he had a hard time getting the company to see the potential in his idea. This ultimately triggered a major change in the company's policy. Kiernan pointed out that most companies give lip service to the necessity of innovation but do not act in a credible way as far as their employees are concerned. If you mean business, you must take that "bright guy out of the basement, [the one] everybody knows is a genius, but whose last two enterprise efforts came to grief, and visibly promote him."

**Discussion Questions**

1. Do large companies find it difficult to innovate because they resist change? Is it because they are big or because they are afraid of the unknown? Why is that?

2. Do smaller companies do better at innovation because they are not so risk-averse? Is that because most of

them are private companies and not accountable to outside stakeholders?

3. If you were a vice-president in charge of operations management at a big corporation, how would you encourage innovation?

◀ # Analyzing Management Decisions

Each chapter concludes with a case that allows students to analyze management decision making. These cases are intentionally brief and are meant to initiate discussion rather than require the entire class period.

# Video Cases ▶

Video cases from CBC programs and custom segments from the McGraw-Hill Management Library are provided for each chapter. They feature companies, processes, practices, and managers that highlight and bring to life the key concepts, and especially the themes, of the Seventh Edition.

## Video Cases

### CHAPTER 1   No Clowning Around—*Cirque du Soleil*

Several themes were introduced in this first chapter, including the importance of entrepreneurship to the success of the overall economy, the need for entrepreneurs to take risks (and the greater the risk, the higher the profit may be), and the dynamic business environment and the challenges it presents. Few organizations in today's society are more indicative of the new challenges than *Cirque du Soleil*.

First, Guy Laliberté took a huge risk by challenging the established circus tradition. The elaborate shows are expensive to start, and the talent must be the best in the world. But the risk paid off big time with sales of almost a billion dollars per year. *Cirque du Soleil* creates thousands of new jobs and contributes greatly to the communities it serves. It does this not only through the taxes it pays, but also through community outreach programs. Because of its entertainment value, *Cirque* contributes to both the standard of living (through the taxes it pays) and the quality of life (the fun it provides for citizens of all ages).

Like all organizations, *Cirque du Soleil* has many stakeholders. They include the owners, the employees, and the local community. The organization is especially focused on the stakeholder group called customers. It wants to put on the best show possible, and that means providing the best talent in the best locations. To reach as many people as possible, many of the shows go on the road. You can even watch some of the shows on TV.

The business environment presents many challenges for *Cirque du Soleil*, as it does for all businesses. The

economic and legal environment of Canada greatly supports entrepreneurs like Laliberté.

The technological environment in Canada and the United States is also supportive of new business ventures. No circus in the past came close to the elaborate technological devices used by *Cirque du Soleil*. The stage for one of the *Cirque* productions in Las Vegas, for example, is a huge pool that delights the audience with its ability to change from a place where the actors can seem to walk on water to one where they can dive from many feet above it.

The social environment is also conducive to new businesses. The diversity of the Canadian population has contributed greatly to the ability of the circus to find diverse acts and to recruit such acts from around the world. The ability of the organization to adapt to many cultures is shown by its success in various cities throughout the world.

Of course, success is likely to breed much competition, and *Cirque* has its share. Even traditional circuses are tending to offer more exciting programs that reflect what *Cirque* has been doing for years. Competition is good for business, as it prompts all businesses to offer the best products possible.

One of the best things about this video is that it allows you to see part of *Cirque du Soleil* in action. If you have never seen the show, search it out—if only on TV. It is exciting and fun, and it shows that entrepreneurship is alive and well and providing wonderful new services. The result is profits for the owners and a better quality of life for us.

**Discussion Questions**

1. What lessons can you take from Guy Laliberté about how to be a successful entrepreneur?

2. What are some of the challenges and opportunities you can identify for *Cirque du Soleil* in today's dynamic business environment?

3. How would you compare the excitement and fun of working for a new entrepreneurial venture like *Cirque du Soleil* with working for a large, traditional business? What are the risks? The rewards? The challenges?

## RUNNING CASE

**Attraction, Retention, and Engagement at Canadian Tire Financial Services (CTFS)**

Canada's population will undergo considerable aging in the twenty-first century. This, along with a fertility rate below replacement and increased life expectancy due to improvements in public health, will create challenges and opportunities for Canadian companies to attract, retain, and engage high-performing employees.

At Canadian Tire Financial Services (CTFS), being an employer of choice is no accident. One advantage that CTFS has is that it can draw on the strong brand image of its parent company, Canadian Tire Corporation, Limited. But this is only the beginning. To be attractive to candidates, companies need to evaluate recruiting channels (e.g., speak with recruiters), research the competition, conduct informal focus groups, and review existing employee opinion data.

Employees usually choose to pursue opportunities elsewhere because they are dissatisfied with their pay, with their career development, with management, or with a combination of these. To retain and engage employees, efforts are made to differentiate pay (base and variable) to keep key talent. In addition, profit-sharing, stock purchase, and long-term incentives (e.g., stock options plan) may be offered.

Career development efforts include formal training and development programs, job enrichment, and succession planning. Participation in performance management programs, mentoring, and sharing 360-degree feedback are other examples of how CTFS effectively applies some of the techniques discussed in Chapter 12.

Senior managers at CTFS are expected to model their behaviour on CTFS's core values (enterprise-wide core beliefs) of honesty, integrity, dignity, and respect. These managers not only need to understand the business strategy and business drivers, but they must also know the impact of their own role in the business. To achieve their performance metrics, they need to inspire the trust of their subordinates and, in turn, motivate them to succeed. Company values, a well-communicated business strategy, strong leadership, and alignment with human resources practices all contribute to a performance culture. In the words of Lou Gerstner, retired chairman of IBM, "Culture isn't just one aspect of the game. It is the game."

Sources: Sharon Patterson, Vice-President Human Resources, Canadian Tire Financial Services, in-person interview, 5 April 2006; and Sharon Patterson, "Why Culture and Human Resources Practices Are a Competitive Advantage," Canadian Tire Financial Services, 6 November 2003.

**Discussion Questions**

1. At what step of the selection process might new hires be surveyed about their level of satisfaction?

2. Consider Maslow's hierarchy of needs. What level of needs are unmet if employees leave because they are dissatisfied with their career development?

3. Efforts are made to decrease the level of dissatisfaction as an attempt to retain and engage employees. What theorist tried to answer the question, "What creates enthusiasm for workers and makes them work to full potential?"

◀ # End-of-Part Running Case

This six-part running case, found at the end of each text Part, provides realistic business scenarios based on Canadian Tire Financial Services. The discussion questions at the end of the case encourage students to consider how this company has applied some of the concepts that were introduced in the chapter.

# Current, Streamlined Coverage

*Understanding Canadian Business*, Seventh Edition, is substantially revised, updated, and filled with new examples of business in Canada and around the world. Each chapter begins with a focus on a business professional. Take some time to consider their career choices and how they spend their time applying the business principles that are introduced in the subsequent pages. New to this edition are *Green Boxes* in each chapter. They illustrate environmental issues that are being evaluated by organizations of all sizes. You will learn how some companies are implementing organizational changes in response to stakeholder demands for more socially-responsible business practices. The following lists some of the additional changes that you will find in this edition.

## Detailed List of Changes

### Chapter 1: Managing Within the Dynamic Business Environment

New terms (e.g., "global footprint") were introduced, while some other terms (e.g., "e-commerce" and "e-business") were clarified. The business environment discussion includes the economic downturn in the late 2000s as well as some recent federal government census data. New boxes—"Cirque du Soleil Tumbles to Success" (*Dealing with Change*) and "Social Entrepreneurship" (*Spotlight on Small Business*)—are examples of theory application.

### Chapter 2: How Economic Issues Affect Business

The *Spotlight on Small Business* box shares how the Kalikori owners understand supply and demand when running their business. The sections on the mixed economy and the unemployment rate have been expanded. Look in particular to the report "Exposed: Revealing Truths About Canada's Recession."

### Chapter 3: Competing in Global Markets

There are three notable additions, namely the *Analyzing Management Decisions* discussion ("The Challenge of Offshoring"), the *Reaching Beyond Our Borders* box ("How Does Canada Shape Up as an International Competitor?"), and the *Dealing with Change* box ("Canada's Auto Sector"). You will learn about Canada's priority markets, while some examples are taken from PROFIT's "Hot 50: Canada's Emerging Growth Companies" list.

### Chapter 4: The Role of Government in Business

Economic conditions require the introduction of new topics: Canada's first budget deficit in ten years, the subprime mortgage crisis, auto company bailouts, and the "Buy American" policy. The section on education looks at changes to the student loan program. "Free Trade Between Provinces" (*Dealing with Change*) and "Ink Isle" (*Spotlight on Small Business*) are new boxes.

### Chapter 5: Ethics and Social Responsibility

Sustainable development, the impact of employee larceny, and the move toward triple-bottom line reporting are introduced. The section on responsibility to investors has been expanded. Two new boxes are "The Federal Accountability Initiative for Reform" (*Dealing with Change*) and "An Assessment of Action on Anti-Corruption Commitments" (*Reaching Beyond Our Borders*).

## Chapter 6: Forms of Business Ownership

Founder Inder Bedi of matt & nat (*Reaching Beyond Our Borders*) has developed a vegan line of handbags and wallets. Information has been added to the discussion on each form of business, including taxation implications for Canadian-controlled private corporations.

## Chapter 7: Entrepreneurship and Starting a Small Business

Differences between entrepreneurial ventures and small businesses are listed. A section has been created on family businesses. New boxes include "Riding the Tracks to Otter Valley Railroad" (*Spotlight on Small Business*) and "Some Unique Challenges of Family Business" (*Dealing with Change*). You can learn how to write a business plan in the *Taking it to the Net* exercise.

## Chapter 8: Management and Leadership

New boxes include: "We Need Managers Over Here" (*Reaching Beyond Our Borders*), "I Would Rather Be Blue" (*Spotlight on Small Business*), and "Are You Responsible for Your Boss's Success?" (*Making Ethical Decisions*). "Hitting the Retail Bull's Eye" (*Dealing with Change*), as well as many areas of the planning and leadership sections have been updated.

## Chapter 9: Adapting Organizations to Today's Markets

The *Reaching Beyond our Borders* box ("The Internet Assists with Decision Making") and the *Dealing with Change* box ("Hurd to the Rescue at Hewlett-Packard Company") have been updated. The *Spotlight on Small Business* box ("Getting the Word Out") is new. A discussion on change management has been added, along with updates to some of the end-of-chapter exercises.

## Chapter 10: Producing World-Class Goods and Services

The *Making Ethical Decisions* box ("Financial Support or Not") is new to this edition. Video links have been added to supplement the discussions of the Canadian auto industry and supply chain management. Numerous updates have been made to the discussion of quality control.

## Chapter 11: Motivating Employees

This chapter starts with the definition of motivation and it includes discussion of some of the costs associated with losing employees. More detail has been added to some of the theories to clarify their history and value. The Job Characteristics Model and the *Dealing with Change* box ("Applying Open Communication in Self-Managed Teams") are new additions.

## Chapter 12: Human Resource Management: Finding and Keeping the Best Employees

Studies identify critical human resources management challenges. A discussion of costs-per-hire, including costs associated with benefits plans, has been added. The topics of empowering workers and a list of human resources information site have also been added.

## Chapter 13: Understanding Employee-Management Issues and Relations

The *Dealing with Change* box ("Industrial Relations Outlook: Managing Expectations in Uncertain Times") summarizes the expectations that both management and labour can expect given some of the current environmental challenges. Students can learn about some of the services of the Department of Human Resources and Skills Development Canada as they relate to labour topics.

### Chapter 14: Marketing: Building Customer and Stakeholder Relationships

The term "green marketing" and its importance are introduced. The *Reaching Beyond Our Borders* box ("Canada—Your Vacation Destination") shares how the Canadian Tourism Commission is trying to promote Canada as a destination for global travellers. You can learn how much car you can afford in the *Taking it to the Net* exercise.

### Chapter 15: Managing the Marketing Mix: Product, Price, Place, and Promotion

Direct marketing is included in the promotion discussion. New boxes include "Reaching High with lululemon athletica" (*Reaching Beyond Our Borders*), "Have You Been 'Buzzed'?" (*Spotlight on Small Business*), and "The Personal Information Protection and Electronic Documents Act" (*Dealing with Change*). The Analyzing Management Decisions discussion ("The Fox40® Sonik Whistle: Breaking the Sound Barrier!") expands on what students learned in the chapter profile.

### Chapter 16: Understanding Accounting and Financial Information

Updates to this chapter include discussions of managerial accounting, the fundamental accounting equation, forensic accounting, profitability ratios, and the Sarbanes-Oxley Act. New boxes include "The Accounting Shot Heard Around the World" (*Reaching Beyond Our Borders*) and "Accounting for What's Coming and Going in a Small Business" (*Spotlight on Small Business*). End-of-chapter exercises investigate a mid-level accounting position and the loan application process. Links to two award-winning online learning objects have been added to reinforce understanding of the basic financial statements and ratios.

### Chapter 17: Financial Management

Numerous updates have been made to this chapter as a result of the global financial crisis of 2008–2009. Updates have been made to the information on monthly cash budgets, the need for funds, commercial paper, and debt financing. New boxes include: "Financial Restructuring for Canwest Global Communications" (*Dealing with Change*) and "Sharing the Wealth" (*Reaching Beyond Our Borders*).

### Chapter 18: The Financial Services Industry in Canada

The banking crisis of 2008–2009 has been the impetus for a number of new boxes including: "The Banking Crisis Goes Global" (*Reaching Beyond Our Borders*) and "How the Banking Crisis Affected Small Business" (*Spotlight on Small Business*). New information has been provided on pension plans, and updates have been made to the Canadian Tire Financial Services running case. Numerous end-of-chapter exercises have also been changed.

# Student Support

## Student Supplements

**Connect™ (www.mcgrawhillconnect.ca):** Developed in partnership with Youthography, a Canadian youth research company, and hundreds of students from across Canada, McGraw-Hill Connect™ embraces diverse study behaviours and preferences to maximize active learning and engagement.

With McGraw-Hill Connect™, students complete pre- and post-diagnostic assessments that identify knowledge gaps and point them to concepts they need to learn. McGraw-Hill Connect™ provides students the option to work through recommended learning exercises and create their own personalized study plan using multiple sources of content, including a searchable e-book, multiple-choice and true/false quizzes, chapter-by-chapter learning objectives, interactivities, personal notes, videos, and more. Using the copy, paste, highlight, and sticky note features, students collect, organize, and customize their study plan content to optimize learning outcomes.

*McGraw-Hill Connect™ — helping instructors and students **Connect, Learn, Succeed!***

**E-STAT:** E-STAT is an educational resource designed by Statistics Canada and made available to Canadian educational institutions. Using 450,000 current CANSIM (Canadian Socio-economic Information Management System) Time Series and the most recent—as well as historical—census data, E-STAT allows you to bring data to life in colourful graphs and maps. Access to E-STAT is made available to purchasers of this book, via Connect™, by special agreement between McGraw-Hill Ryerson and Statistics Canada.

# Instructor Support

*Understanding Canadian Business*, Seventh Edition, offers a complete, integrated supplements package for instructors to address all of your needs.

## Instructor Supplements

**Connect™ (www.mcgrawhillconnect.ca):** McGraw-Hill Connect™ assessment activities don't stop with students! There is material for instructors to leverage as well, including a personalized teaching plan where instructors can choose from a variety of quizzes to use in class, assign as homework, or add to exams. They can edit existing questions and add new ones; track individual student performance—by question, assignment, or in relation to the class overall—with detailed grade reports; integrate grade reports easily with Learning Management Systems such as WebCT and Blackboard; and much more. Instructors can also browse and search teaching resources and text-specific supplements and organize them into customizable categories. All your teaching resources are now located in one convenient place.

*McGraw-Hill Connect™ — helping instructors and students **Connect, Learn, Succeed!***

Connect also offers instructors downloadable supplements, including an Instructor's Manual, Microsoft® PowerPoint® slides, streaming video cases, as well as access to the Integrator and PageOut, the McGraw-Hill Ryerson Web site development centre. Also included on Connect is a sample of the **Group-Video Resource Manual**. This online matrix and accompanying manual is available to adopters and contains everything an instructor needs to successfully integrate McGraw-Hill technology and additional group activities into the classroom.

**Instructor's Manual:** Prepared by the text authors, this contains a short topic outline of the chapter and a listing of learning objectives and key terms, a resource checklist with supplements that correspond to each chapter, a detailed lecture outline including marginal notes recommending where to use supplementary cases, lecture enhancers, and critical thinking exercises.

**Computerized Test Bank:** In response to market feedback, the test bank has undergone a complete revision for the seventh edition. Various instructors contributed to this development over the past few years, and Thomas McKaig of the University of Guelph and the University of Guelph-Humber has authored the new edition's version, which includes alignment to all learning objectives, as well as new levels of learning and additional questions.

The computerized Brownstone version allows instructors to add and edit questions, save and reload multiple test versions, select questions based on type, difficulty, or key word and use password protection. True/False questions test three levels of learning: (1) knowledge of key terms, (2) understanding of concepts and principles, and (3) application of principles. Both multiple-choice and short-answer questions now include a fourth level of learning.

**Microsoft® PowerPoint® Presentations:** Prepared by Valerie Miceli of Seneca College of Applied Arts and Technology (basic presentation) and Tim Richardson of Seneca College of Applied Arts and Technology and the University of Toronto (enhanced presentation), the slideshows for each chapter are based around the learning objectives and include many of the figures and tables from the textbook, as well as some additional slides that support and expand the text discussions. Slides can be modified by instructors with PowerPoint®.

**Videos for all Chapters:** Complementary videos from CBC programs and customized business segments from the McGraw-Hill Management Library are available on DVD and also can be accessed on the password-protected area of Connect. Detailed teaching notes written by the text authors are available in the Instructor's Manual and on the instructor area of Connect.

**Manager's Hot Seat Videos:** In today's workplace, managers are confronted daily with issues such as ethics, diversity, working in teams, and the virtual workplace. The Manager's Hot Seat is an online resource that allows students to watch as 15 real managers apply their years of experience to confront these issues. These videos are available as a complementary instructor supplement or for bundling with student textbooks.

**The Integrator:** Keyed to the chapters and learning objectives of *Understanding Canadian Business*, Seventh Edition, the Integrator is prepared by Michael Wade of Seneca College of Applied Arts and Technology. This tool ties together all of the elements in your resource package, guiding you to where you will find corresponding coverage in each of the related support package components—be it the Instructor's Manual, Computerized Test Bank, PowerPoint® slides, or videos. Link to the Integrator via Connect at www.mcgrawhillconnect.ca.

**Business Plan Pro:** The Business Plan Pro is available as a bundled option that includes more than 250 sample business plans and 400 case studies to give you a wide variety of examples as you create your own plan. It helps you set up your business by answering questions that help the software customize your plan. Then you enter your financial data to generate financial worksheets and statements.

**New Business Mentor:** For instructors who incorporate a business plan project into their class, the New Business Mentor software can be bundled upon request with student textbooks and includes sample business plans, resources to help you as you start your business, business planning and feasibility planning software, and the "mentor," who will walk you through each step of the business plan. Teaching notes are available.

**Create Online:** McGraw-Hill's Create Online gives you access to the most abundant resource at your fingertips—literally. With a few mouse clicks, you can create customized learning tools simply and affordably. McGraw-Hill Ryerson has included many of our market-leading textbooks within Create Online for e-book and print customization as well as many licensed readings and cases.

## WebCT and Blackboard

In addition, content cartridges are available for these course management systems. These platforms provide instructors with user-friendly, flexible teaching tools. Please contact your local McGraw-Hill Ryerson iLearning Sales Specialist for details.

## eInstruction's Classroom Performance System (CPS)

**CPS** is a student response system using wireless connectivity. It gives instructors and students immediate feedback from the entire class. The response pads are remotes that are easy to use and engage students.

- **CPS** helps you increase **student preparation, interactivity, and active learning** so you can receive immediate feedback and know what students understand.
- **CPS** allows you to administer quizzes and tests, and provide **immediate grading**.
- With **CPS** you can create lecture questions that can be multiple-choice, true/false, and subjective. You can even create questions on-the-fly as well as conduct group activities.

- Not only does **CPS** allow you to **evaluate classroom attendance, activity, and grading** for your course as a whole, but CPSOnline allows you to provide students with an immediate study guide. All results and scores can easily be imported into Excel and can be used with various classroom management systems.

CPS-ready content is available for use with *Understanding Canadian Business*, Seventh Edition. Please contact your iLearning Sales Specialist for more information on how you can integrate CPS into your classroom.

## Superior Service

Service takes on a whole new meaning with McGraw-Hill Ryerson and *Understanding Canadian Business*. Rather than just bringing you the textbook, we have consistently raised the bar in terms of innovation and educational research—both in the study of business and in education in general. These investments in learning and the educational community have helped us understand the needs of students and educators across the country and allow us to foster the growth of truly innovative, integrated learning.

*i***Learning Sales Specialist:** Your Integrated Learning Sales Specialist is a McGraw-Hill Ryerson representative who has the experience, product knowledge, training, and support to help you assess and integrate any of the above-noted products, technology, and services into your course for optimum teaching and learning performance. Whether it's how to use our test bank software, helping your students improve their grades, or how to put your entire course online, your *i*Learning Sales Specialist is there to help. Contact your local *i*Learning Sales Specialist today to learn how to maximize all McGraw-Hill Ryerson resources!

*i***Learning Services Program:** McGraw-Hill Ryerson offers a unique *i*Services package designed for Canadian faculty. Our mission is to equip providers of higher education with superior tools and resources required for excellence in teaching. For additional information, visit www.mcgrawhill.ca/highereducation/iservices/.

# Acknowledgements

## Development of the Text and Supplements Package

To ensure continuous improvement of our product, we have used an extensive review and development process for each of our editions. Building on that history, the development process for this seventh edition included several phases of evaluation by a broad panel of instructors, and several focus groups where new ideas on content and technology were exchanged. Thank you to all of our reviewers and participants—your suggestions to improve the quality, coverage, and the supplements package are invaluable. We extend our deepest thanks for your time and involvement.

Reviewers who were vital in helping us develop this edition include:

Laura Allan, *Wilfrid Laurier University*
James Appleyard, *University of Toronto Mississauga*
Edith Callaghan, *Acadia University*
Lezlie Cunningham, *University of Guelph*
Randy Delorey, *St. Francis Xavier University*
Shawna DePlonty, *Sault College*
Tony Dunn, *British Columbia Institute of Technology*
John Fakouri, *Algonquin College*
Kathy Falk, *University of Toronto Mississauga*
Jai Goolsarran, *Centennial College*
Brent Groen, *Trinity Western University*
Don Hill, *Langara College*
Sunil Kaplash, *University of Victoria*
Brooke Klassen, *University of Saskatchewan*
Ed Leach, *Dalhousie University*
Puneet Luthra, *Seneca College of Applied Arts and Technology*
Carolyn McGregor, *University of Ontario Institute of Technology*
Carolan McLarney, *Dalhousie University*
Valerie Miceli, *Seneca College of Applied Arts and Technology*
Peter Mombourquette, *Mount Saint Vincent University*
Paul Myers, *St. Clair College*
Kayrod Niamir, *Dawson College*
Glenn Planert, *Conestoga College*
John Purcell, *Sheridan College*
Al Ruggero, *Seneca College of Applied Arts and Technology*
Frank Saccucci, *Grant MacEwan College*
Lewis Silvestri, *Niagara College*
Cindy Stewart, *University of British Columbia*
Julie Wong, *Dawson College*

Many thanks are also due to the following people who worked hard to make this book a reality: Kim Brewster, Senior Sponsoring Editor; Lori McLellan, Developmental Editor; Kara Stahl, Supervising Editor; Margaret Henderson, Manager, Editorial Services; Paula Brown, Team Lead, Production; Cat Haggert, Copy Editor; Alison Derry, Permissions and Photo Researcher; and Sarah Orr of ArtPlus, Designer.

# PART 1

# CHAPTER 1

# Managing Within the Dynamic Business Environment

## LEARNING OBJECTIVES

AFTER YOU HAVE READ
AND STUDIED THIS CHAPTER,
YOU SHOULD BE ABLE TO:

**LO ▶ 1** Describe the relationship of businesses' profit to risk assumption.

**LO ▶ 2** Discuss the importance of stakeholders and non-profit organizations to business activities.

**LO ▶ 3** Explain how entrepreneurship is critical to the wealth of an economy, and list the five factors of production that contribute to wealth.

**LO ▶ 4** Review the six elements that make up the business environment and explain why the business environment is important to organizations.

**LO ▶ 5** Understand how the service sector has replaced manufacturing as the principal provider of jobs, but why manufacturing remains vital for Canada.

## PROFILE

## Getting to Know Mike Lazaridis of Research In Motion Ltd.

Mike Lazaridis is known in the global wireless community as a visionary, innovator, and engineer of extraordinary talent. He traces his passion for his work to his hometown of Windsor, Ontario, where his love of science and fascination with electronics were nurtured in supportive family and school environments. Lazaridis studied electrical engineering at the University of Waterloo but dropped out two months before graduation. Using a small loan from his parents and a contract with General Motors, he founded Research In Motion Ltd. (RIM) in 1984.

RIM is a competitor in the ICT (information and communications technology—or technologies) sector. ICT is an umbrella term that includes any communication device or application encompassing radio, television, cellular phones, computer and network hardware and software, satellite systems and so on, as well as the various services and applications associated with them, such as videoconferencing and distance learning. The ICT sector contributed $57 billion to Canada's gross domestic product in 2007, accounting for 4.7 percent of Canadian output. Research and development (R&D) spending in the ICT sector has been steadily increasing over the years and is now at $6.0 billion, representing 38 percent of total Canadian private sector R&D expenditures. ICT sector employment is characterized by a highly educated workforce. The top three industries that employ the largest share of university-educated personnel are communications equipment, software and computer services, and computer equipment.

As RIM's President and Co-CEO, Lazaridis is responsible for product strategy, research and development, product development, and manufacturing. In fiscal 2009 (ended 28 February 2009), the company generated approximately US$11 billion in revenues. Today, RIM is a leading designer, manufacturer, and marketer of innovative wireless solutions for the worldwide mobile communications market. Through the development of integrated hardware, software, and services that support multiple wireless network standards, RIM provides platforms and solutions for seamless access to time-sensitive information. RIM technology also enables a broad array of third-party developers and manufacturers to enhance their products and services with wireless connectivity. RIM's portfolio of award-winning products, services, and embedded technologies are used by thousands of organizations around the world and include the BlackBerry wireless platform, the RIM BlackBerry Smartphone product line, software development tools, radio-modems, and software/hardware licensing agreements. The brand is becoming more global with products increasingly being introduced in new markets such as Vietnam, Malawi, and Egypt. Students and professionals alike have embraced the products. For example, do you know that a secure BlackBerry Smartphone was developed for U.S. President Barack Obama after he insisted on keeping a BlackBerry?

Lazaridis advocates for education and scientific research. He is a member of the Natural Sciences and Engineering Research Council of Canada (NSERC), the Ontario Research and Innovation Council, and a Governor of the Information Technology Association of Canada. He supports his community and country through generous philanthropic gifts made possible by his success in business. He has donated $100 million to the University of Waterloo to help establish the Institute for Quantum Computing. His gift of $150 million established the Perimeter Institute for Theoretical Physics. As a result of his leadership and tireless effort, more than $100 million has been generated in additional private and public sector funding for this world centre of excellence, based in Waterloo and affiliated with more than 30 Canadian universities.

In recognition of his contributions, Lazaridis has won many awards. Some examples include sharing Canada's most prestigious innovation prize, The Ernest C. Manning Principal Award. He was named an Officer to the Order of Canada in 2006, chosen as Canada's Outstanding CEO of the Year in 2006, listed on the *TIME* 100 List of Most Influential People in 2005, previously recognized as Canada's Nation Builder of the Year and was a recipient of Ontario's Entrepreneur of the Year award. He has been inducted into both the Canadian Business Hall of Fame and Canada's Telecommunications Hall of Fame.

The purpose of this text is to introduce you to the exciting and challenging world of business. Each chapter will begin with a story similar to this one. You will meet more successful entrepreneurs who have started a business. You will also learn about people who work for companies and have succeeded far beyond their original expectations. You will learn about all aspects of business: management, human resource management, marketing, accounting, finance, and more. You will also learn about businesses of all sizes. We begin by looking at some key terms and exploring the rapidly changing business environment so that you can prepare to meet tomorrow's challenges today.

Sources: "RIM's Executive Team – Mike Lazaridis," Research In Motion Ltd., 2009, http://www.rim.net/newsroom/ media/executive/index.shtml; "RIM 2008 Annual Report," Research in Motion Ltd., 2009, http://www. shareholder.com/visitors/DynamicDoc/document.cfm?DocumentID=2259 &CompanyID=RIMM; "Canadian ICT Sector Profile," Industry Canada, 10 July 2008, http://www.ic.gc.ca/epic/site/ict-tic.nsf/en/h_it07229e.html; Brian Banks and Mark Evans, "Two Men and Their Baby," *Financial Post Business*, November 2006, 35; and "ICT Definition," SearchCIO-Midmarket. com, 14 January 2004, http://searchcio-midmarket.techtarget.com/ sDefinition/0,,sid183_gci 928405,00.html#.

**business**
Any activity that seeks to provide goods and services to others while operating at a profit.

**profit**
The amount a business earns above and beyond what it spends for salaries and other expenses.

**entrepreneur**
A person who risks time and money to start and manage a business.

**For an up-to-date list of the world's wealthiest citizens, visit www.forbes. com/billionaires/. Who is Canada's wealthiest person?**

**revenue**
The total amount of money a business takes in during a given period by selling goods and services.

**loss**
When a business's expenses are more than its revenues.

# BUSINESS AND ENTREPRENEURSHIP: REVENUES, PROFITS, AND LOSSES

Thousands of people have learned that one of the best ways to become a success in Canada, or almost anywhere else in the world, is to have a career in business. A **business** is any activity that seeks to provide goods and services to others while operating at a profit. **Profit** is the amount of money a business earns above and beyond what it spends for salaries and other expenses. Since not all businesses make a profit, starting a business can be risky. An **entrepreneur** is a person who risks time and money to start and manage a business.

Businesses provide people with the opportunity to become wealthy. *Forbes* magazine reports that in 2009 there were 790 billionaires around the world, of which 20 were of Canadian citizenship.[1] American business person and philanthropist Bill Gates, founder and Chairman of Microsoft Corporation, was said to be worth US$40 billion, making him the richest person in the world.[2] Maybe someday you will be a billionaire!

Businesses don't just make money for entrepreneurs. Businesses provide all of us with necessities such as food, clothing, housing, medical care, and transportation, as well as other goods and services that make our lives easier and better.

## Matching Risk with Profit

Profit, remember, is the amount of money a business earns *above and beyond* what it pays out for salaries and other expenses. For example, if you were to start a business selling hot dogs in the summer, you would have to pay for the cart rental, for the hot dogs and other materials, and for someone to run the cart while you were away. After you paid your employee and yourself, paid for the food and materials you used, paid the rent on the cart, and paid your taxes, any money left over would be profit. Keep in mind that profit is over and above the money you pay yourself in salary. You could use any profit you make to rent or buy a second cart and hire other employees. After a few summers, you might have a dozen carts employing dozens of workers.

**Revenue** is the total amount of money a business takes in during a given period by selling goods and services. A **loss** occurs when a business's expenses are more than its revenues. If a business loses money over time, it will likely have to close, putting its employees out of work. In fact, approximately 125,000 businesses exit the marketplace

How well do you know yourself? Are you more excited at the prospect of starting your own small business or would you prefer to work for a large- or medium-sized business? The answer to this question may start with understanding your personal risk tolerance.

each year.³ Some owners close down one business to start another one or to retire. Even though such closings are not failures, they are reported as exits by Industry Canada. Only a small proportion of firms that exit the marketplace end up filing for *bankruptcy*, which refers to the liquidation of the business debtor's assets and the end of the commercial entity's operations.⁴ As discussed later in this textbook, most business failures are due to poor management or problems associated with cash flow.

Starting a business involves risk. **Risk** is the chance an entrepreneur takes of losing time and money on a business that may not prove profitable. Even among companies that do make a profit, not all make the same amount. Those companies that take the most risk may make the most profit. Decades ago, there was a lot of risk involved in, for example, producing automobiles to replace horse-drawn carriages. Today, we see investors betting on information highway pioneers such as Google as a way to prosper. Such is the nature of risk and reward in business.

As a potential business owner, you need to do research (e.g., talk to other business people and read business publications) to find the right balance between risk and profit for you. Different people have different tolerances for risk. To decide which is the best choice for you, you have to calculate the risks and the potential rewards of each decision. The more risks you take, the higher the rewards may be. In Chapter 7, you will learn more about the risks and rewards that come with starting a business.

**risk**
The chance an entrepreneur takes of losing time and money on a business that may not prove profitable.

## Responding to the Various Business Stakeholders

**Stakeholders** are all of the people who stand to gain or lose by the policies and activities of a business. As noted in Figure 1.1, stakeholders include many different groups such as customers, employees, financial institutions (e.g., banks and credit unions), investors (e.g., stockholders), environmentalists, and government (e.g., federal, provincial, and municipal). All of these groups are affected by the products, policies, and practices of businesses, and their concerns need to be addressed. Don't forget that businesses can also influence government policies through the activities and efforts of their associations, lobbyists, and trade unions.

**stakeholders**
All the people who stand to gain or lose by the policies and activities of a business.

## STAKEHOLDERS

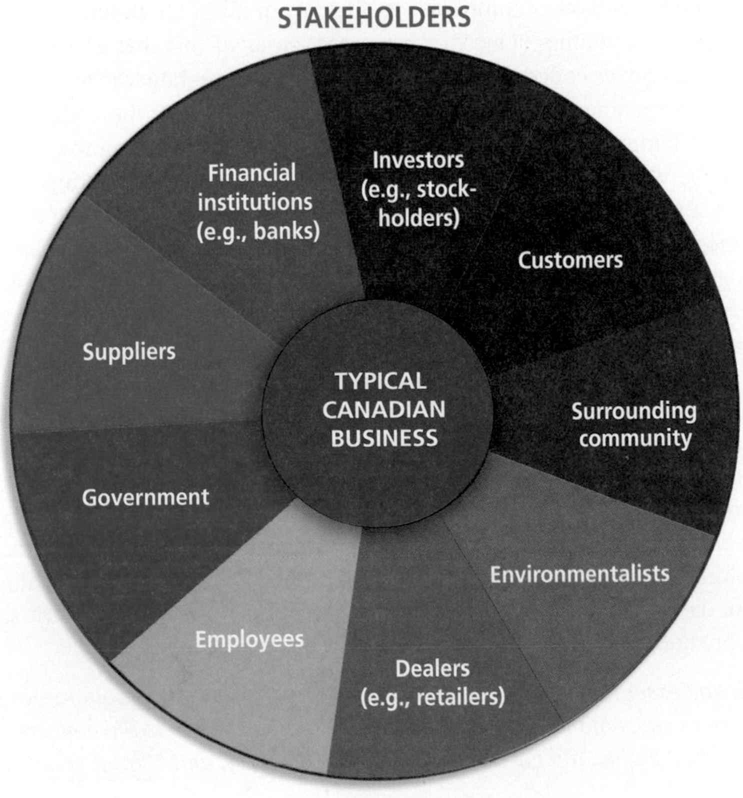

**FIGURE 1.1**

**A Business and Its Stakeholders**
Often the needs of a firm's various stakeholders will conflict. For example, paying employees more may cut into stockholders' profits. Balancing such demands is a major role of business managers.

## DEALING with CHANGE

### *Cirque du Soleil* Tumbles to Success

With annual sales of more than US$700 million and nearly 10 million visitors a year, *Cirque du Soleil* is a Canadian (and international) success story. The company was formed in 1984 by a group of street performers that had a dream to create a Quebec circus and take it around the world. Since that time, it has become an international entertainment organization, growing to 18 shows in over 200 cities on five continents. Each show is a theatrical blend of circus arts and street performance, with spectacular costumes and fairyland sets. Due to its fast-paced growth and the complexity of staging shows around the world, *Cirque du Soleil* has outsourced its information technology needs in a $130-million, 10-year contract with Montreal-based CGI Group Inc. As part of this contract, CGI hired 84 of Cirque's employees that already were doing the job. CGI will help Cirque with everything from payroll to managing costume inventory to its Internet cafés that are set up when its shows travel.

Guy Laliberté is the founder, majority owner, and CEO of *Cirque du Soleil*. A former street performer himself, he guides the company that has a mission to invoke the imagination, provoke the senses, and evoke the emotions of people around the world. Creativity is the cornerstone of the organization's identity. Every concept and scenic element is created at the Studio, a training facility in Montreal. There, more than 1,000 employees work together to create new shows and costumes. Laliberté juggles the demands of creative and financial types and walks a tightrope among the almost 4,000 employees from over 40 different countries. With such diversity, you can see why the company's great strength is its ability to develop material that resonates with audiences worldwide.

Sources: Lori McLeod and Gordon Pitts, "From Quebec's Streets to Dubai," *The Globe and Mail*, 7 August 2008, B4; "Cirque du Soleil At a Glance," Cirque du Soleil, 26 July 2008 http://www.cirquedusoleil.com/cirquedusoleil/pdf/pressroom/en/cds_en_bref_en.pdf; Telios Demos, "Cirque du Balancing Act," *Fortune*, 12 June 2006, http://money.cnn.com/magazines/fortune/fortune_archive/2006/06/12/8379232/index.htm; and Shirly Won, "Cirque Faces New Balancing Act," *The Globe and Mail*, 7 April 2006, B3.

The challenge of the twenty-first century will be for organizations to balance, as much as possible, the needs of all stakeholders. For example, the need for the business to make profits must be balanced against the needs of employees for sufficient income. The need to stay competitive may call for offshoring jobs to other countries, recognizing that this sound business strategy might do harm to the community because jobs would be lost.[5] **Offshoring** entails sourcing part of the purchased inputs outside of the country.[6] **Outsourcing** means contracting with other companies to do some or all of the functions of a firm, such as production or accounting.[7] One of the major themes of this text is managing change. There are special boxes called "Dealing with Change" throughout the text that discuss the rapidly changing business environment and the need to adjust to these changes. This first Dealing with Change box discusses how *Cirque du Soleil* is adapting to change.

You may be wondering, how are the terms outsourcing and offshoring that different? A Statistics Canada report highlights the distinction. As stated, "Outsourcing decisions affect the boundaries of the firm—what production takes place within the firm and what is purchased from outside the firm. Changes in offshoring may be, but are not necessarily, related to changes in outsourcing. They involve decisions both to purchase outside of the firm and to do so from abroad. Considerations to do the latter are at the heart of the study of international trade. Interest in outsourcing arises because it may foretell changes in industrial structure. Interest in offshoring arises because it may signify changes in international trading patterns."[8]

Companies have gone from outsourcing production jobs to offshoring research and development and design functions. Such decisions may prove disastrous to these firms doing the offshoring if the overseas companies use the information to produce their own competitive products.[9] In Canada, most of the offshoring that occurs is with the United States, though there has been some increase over the last decade with developing countries.[10] Canada is also an attractive offshoring location for U.S.-based firms, says Peter McAdam, president and CEO of Everest Group Canada:

> *Canada has essentially the same culture and many of the same companies have locations on both sides of the border. Education is similar and so is the concern for privacy and individual rights. You get all this plus polite, friendly, and helpful people at less cost.*

**offshoring**

Sourcing part of the purchased inputs outside of the country.

**outsourcing**

Assigning various functions, such as accounting, production, security, maintenance, and legal work to outside organizations.

*Companies are comfortable offshoring to Canada and callers/users are comfortable calling there. They find little difference between Canadians and American counterparts.[11]*

This is especially true in the areas of software development related to business intelligence, industry-specific applications, business process outsourcing, and customer service-oriented call centres.

It is legal to outsource and offshore, but is that best for all stakeholders, including workers? Business leaders must make decisions based on all factors, including the need to make a profit. As you can see, pleasing all stakeholders is not easy and it calls for trade-offs that are not always pleasing to one or another stakeholder. Keep in mind that regardless of temptations, company officials do have a responsibility to their stakeholders.

Such trade-offs are also apparent in the political arena. As will be discussed in Chapter 4, governments make policies that affect many stakeholders. However, budget limitations force governments to make difficult choices, and these decisions are often not popular. Consequently, after years of insufficient funding, any changes in the areas of the environment, health care, and education generate a lot of attention. As you will learn, balancing the demands of stakeholders is not limited to for-profit businesses.

**non-profit organization**
An organization whose goals do not include making a personal profit for its owners or organizers.

**For more information about non-profit organizations, visit the Charity Village Web site at www.charityvillage.com. This site is dedicated to supporting Canada's charities and non-profit organizations as well as the stakeholders who support them.**

## Using Business Principles in Non-Profit Organizations

Despite their efforts to satisfy all of their stakeholders, businesses cannot do everything that is needed to make a community all it can be. Non-profit organizations—such as schools, hospitals, and charities—also make a major contribution to the welfare of society. A **non-profit organization** is an organization whose goals do not include making a personal profit for its owners or organizers.[12] Non-profit organizations often do strive for financial gains, but such gains are used to meet the stated social or educational goals of the organization rather than personal profit.[13]

*Social entrepreneurs* are people who use business principles to start and manage non-profit organizations and help countries with their social issues.[14] Canadian-born Jeff Skoll, eBay's first president, is one example. He left eBay to focus on philanthropic activities. The Skoll Foundation supports social entrepreneurs and innovative non-profit organizations around the world. The Spotlight on Small Business box features the Canadian Social Entrepreneurship Foundation. Would you consider becoming a social entrepreneur?

Your interests may lead you to work for a non-profit organization. Millions of professionals, staffers, volunteers, and donors work for Canada's approximately 200,000 charities and non-profit organizations.[15] This doesn't mean, however, that you shouldn't study business. If you want to start or work in a non-profit organization, you'll need to learn business skills such as information management, leadership, marketing, and financial management. Therefore, the knowledge and skills you acquire in this and other business courses will be useful for careers in any organization, including non-profits.

Starting any business, profit or non-profit, can be risky. Once an entrepreneur has started a business, there is usually a need for good managers and other workers to keep the business going. Not all entrepreneurs are skilled at being managers. We shall explore entrepreneurship right after the Progress Assessment.

Non-profit organizations use for-profit business principles to achieve results. Canadian Blood Services is a national not-for-profit charitable organization whose mission is to manage the blood and blood products supply for Canadians. Did you know that approximately every minute of every day, someone in Canada needs blood? The good news is that one blood donation—in just one hour—can save up to three lives. This is a poster that has been used in schools across Canada with the purpose of encouraging people to donate blood.

That's the beauty of giving blood.

Call 1 888 2 DONATE    www.blood.ca

Canadian Blood Services
*it's in you to give*

Share your vitality

## SPOTLIGHT ON Small Business

### Social Entrepreneurship

The Canadian Social Entrepreneurship Foundation (CSEF) site, sixty percent a virtual organization, was created in 2004 by Jason Carvalho to spur innovation and "bridge the gap" that was developing between the non-profit, business, and government sectors. Carvalho is an entrepreneur focused on creating sustainable value in a changing global economy. The motto of the CSEF is taken from a famous line which is as follows: "Some men and women see things as they are and say, 'Why?' I dream things that never were and say, 'Why not?'"

To begin to bridge this gap, the CSEF looks for social entrepreneurs who are under the age of 40 that want to develop and take a new service or product to market. Although social entrepreneurs share some characteristics and techniques with traditional business entrepreneurs—for example, an emphasis on innovation and the utilization of time-tested business theories and practices—their work and impact span the private, non-profit, and governmental sectors.

The CSEF provides access to funding, provincial/national/international networks, a wide variety of start-up resources, mentorship, and evaluation resources. It invests in Canadian social enterprises that focus on specific areas such as children and youth (e.g., employing at-risk youth), human rights, environment (e.g., clean technologies and energy efficiency), and economic development. Social economy enterprises are organizations that are run like businesses, producing goods and services, but which manage their operations on a not-for-profit basis. Instead, they direct any surpluses to the pursuit of social and community goals.

Can you see yourself as a social entrepreneur? You could become a small-business owner in Canada, but you could also use the business skills you learn in this course to be a social entrepreneur in Canada and other countries. Think of the possibilities.

Source: The Canadian Social Entrepreneurship Foundation. Copyright 2009, http://www.csef.ca. Used with permission.

### Progress Assessment

- What is the difference between revenue and profit?
- What is risk, and how is it related to profit?
- What do the terms *stakeholders*, *offshoring*, and *outsourcing* mean?

## ENTREPRENEURSHIP VERSUS WORKING FOR OTHERS

There are two ways to succeed in business. One is to rise up through the ranks of large companies such as Royal Bank of Canada or Manulife Financial. The advantage of working for others is that somebody else assumes the entrepreneurial risk and provides you with benefits such as paid vacation time and health insurance. Most people choose that option, which can lead to a happy and prosperous life.

The other, riskier path, is to start your own business and become an entrepreneur. When you consider Canada's wealthiest citizens, you will find that they arrived at their wealth as a result of this entrepreneurial spirit. Some well known billionaires and their companies include the Thomson family (Thomson-Reuters), Ted Rogers Jr. (Rogers Communications), Galen Weston (Loblaw Cos. Ltd.), and Paul Desmarais Sr. (Power Corp.).[16] Mike Lazaridis, the focus of this chapter's profile, also ranks in the top ten list of most affluent Canadians.[17] While you may hear about the success stories, keep in mind that many small businesses fail each year; thus, it takes a brave person to start a small business or to turn a business around. Furthermore, as an entrepreneur you don't receive any benefits such as paid vacation time and health insurance. You have to provide them for yourself!

Before you take on the challenge of entrepreneurship it makes sense to study the experiences of those who have succeeded to learn the process. Consider the example of Ron Joyce, who in 1963 purchased a Dairy Queen outlet. Two years later, he invested $10,000 to become a franchisee in the first Tim Hortons. (We will discuss franchising in Chapter 6.) By 1967, he became a full partner in the company with Tim Horton. In the early years, both partners worked on expanding the business. When Horton died in 1974, Joyce became the sole owner of the chain. In the following years, he continued to develop the business, spending hundreds of hours piloting his plane in search of new franchise opportunities and doing everything from training new store owners to baking donuts. When Joyce sold the chain to Wendy's for US$450 million in 1995, there were more than 1,000 Tim Hortons restaurants. Today, Tim Hortons is Canada's largest national chain in the coffee and fresh-baked goods segment, with 3,238 systemwide restaurants, including 2,930 in Canada and 527 in the United States.[18] What you can learn from successful entrepreneurs like Ron Joyce and Mike Lazaridis is that you need to find something that you love to do. Before he became an entrepreneur, Joyce was a police officer. He started to get experience in business with his Dairy Queen outlet, and from there went on to great success with his Tim Hortons restaurants. While there were many challenges along the way, he was willing to put in the long hours needed to be successful. In addition to the original coffee and donut offerings, he continuously added new products to the restaurants to meet his customers' needs.

Small businesses and entrepreneurs contribute enormously to the Canadian economy. While these terms have been briefly mentioned in this chapter, be aware that more time will be spent discussing their significance in Chapters 6 and 7. After all, without the initial ideas and risks taken by entrepreneurs, we would not have successful businesses today.

Charles Chang started Sequel Naturals Ltd. in his basement in 2001. Today the company, which manufactures premium natural health products and nutritional supplements (including the award-winning Vega brand of plant-based whole food products) is the eighth fastest-growing company in Canada with over 2,000 retailers carrying the company's products. Do you have a new product idea that could be turned into a successful business?

## The Importance of Factors of Production to the Creation of Wealth

Have you ever wondered why some countries are relatively wealthy and others are poor? Economists have been studying the issue of wealth creation for many years. They began the process by studying potential sources of wealth to determine which are the most important. Over time, they came up with five factors that seemed to contribute to wealth, which they called **factors of production**. Figure 1.2 describes those five factors, which are:

1. Land (or natural resources)
2. Labour (workers)
3. Capital Goods (This includes machines, tools, buildings, or whatever else is used in the production of goods. It does not include money. Money is used to buy factors of production—it is not a factor itself.)
4. Entrepreneurship
5. Knowledge

**factors of production**
The resources used to create wealth: land, labour, capital goods, entrepreneurship, and knowledge.

Traditionally, business and economics textbooks have emphasized only four factors of production: land, labour, capital, and entrepreneurship. But management expert and business consultant Peter Drucker says that the most important factor of production in our economy is and always will be knowledge. The young workers in the high-tech industries are sometimes called *knowledge workers*. When high-tech businesses began

**FIGURE** | **1.2**

**The Five Factors
of Production**

| | |
|---|---|
| **LAND:** | Land and other natural resources are used to make homes, cars, and other products. |
| **LABOUR:** | People have always been an important resource in producing goods and services, but many people are now being replaced by technology. |
| **CAPITAL GOODS:** | Capital includes machines, tools, buildings, and other means of manufacturing. |
| **ENTREPRENEURSHIP:** | All the resources in the world have little value unless entrepreneurs are willing to take the risk of starting businesses to use those resources. |
| **KNOWLEDGE:** | Information technology has revolutionized business, making it possible to quickly determine wants and needs and to respond with desired products. |

to fail in the early 2000s, many knowledge workers had to find new jobs in other parts of the country, but their education and experience made this transition easier. Today, the environment is more competitive as new graduates are increasingly being sought by tech companies, such as Research In Motion Ltd. and Google Inc., looking to expand their operations domestically and internationally.[19]

Such results should motivate today's students to get as much education as possible to prepare themselves for knowledge-oriented jobs and to be prepared to change jobs as the economy demands.[20] Note that information is not the same as knowledge. There is usually too much information available and information management is critical. We will study the importance of using technology to manage information in the appendix at the end of this chapter.

If you were to analyze rich countries versus poor countries to see what causes the differences in the levels of wealth, you'd have to look at the factors of production in each country. Such analyses have revealed that some relatively poor countries often have plenty of land and natural resources. Russia and China, for example, both have vast areas of land with many resources, but they are not rich countries (yet). In contrast, Japan and Hong Kong are relatively rich countries but are poor in land and other natural resources. Therefore, land isn't the critical element for wealth creation.

Most poor countries have many labourers, so labour is not the primary source of wealth today. Labourers need to find work to make a contribution; that is, they need entrepreneurs to provide jobs for them. Furthermore, capital—machinery and tools—is now becoming available in world markets, so capital isn't the missing ingredient. Capital is not productive without entrepreneurs to put it to use.

What makes countries rich today is a combination of entrepreneurship and the effective use of knowledge. Together, lack of entrepreneurship and the absence of knowledge among workers, along with lack of freedom, contribute to keeping countries poor. The Reaching Beyond Our Borders box discusses the importance of freedom to economic development.

Entrepreneurship also makes some provinces and cities in Canada rich while others remain relatively poor. The business environment either encourages or discourages entrepreneurship. In the following section, we'll explore what makes up the business environment and how to build an environment that encourages growth and job creation.

## Progress Assessment

- What are some of the advantages of working for others?
- What benefits do you lose by being an entrepreneur, and what do you gain?
- What are the five factors of production? Which factors are key to wealth?

### Reaching Beyond Our Borders

#### Freedom Equals Prosperity

Recent studies have found that the freer a country is, the wealthier its citizens are. Freedom includes freedom from excess taxation, government regulations, and restrictions on trade. The average per capita gross domestic product (GDP)—the total value of all final goods and services produced in a country divided by the number of people in the country—for the freest countries greatly exceeds that in less-free countries. For example, Hong Kong is considered the freest country, and it has a per capita GDP of $39,062. Singapore, the second freest country, has a per capita GDP of $49,708. Canada's per capita GDP is $36,713. At the other end of the scale (less-free countries), you will find Libya with a per capita GDP of $11,622. Some countries make even less than that per capita: Haiti, for example, has a per capita GDP of $1,224 and Burundi's is just $333. As more countries become free (e.g., freedom from corruption), the standard of living around the world increases. And this is a good thing.

The 2009 Index of Economic Freedom covers 183 countries across 10 specific freedoms which include business freedom, trade freedom, fiscal freedom, government size, monetary freedom, investment freedom, financial freedom, property rights, freedom from corruption, and labour freedom. Canada's seventh place ranking was 0.3 percentage points higher than the year before, partly as a result of improved competitiveness in fiscal freedom accompanied by a reduced perception of corruption. Canada scores very high in seven of the 10 economic freedoms, especially business freedom, property rights, and freedom from corruption. The process for conducting a business is straightforward and encourages entrepreneurial activity. Overall, regulation is thorough but transparent. A strong rule of law ensures property rights, a low level of corruption, and transparent application of the commercial code. Canada trails the world average only in size and expense of government. Its elaborate social programs raise government spending. However, it has been able to establish sound fiscal management and federal budget surpluses in recent years, providing a competitive edge.

Numbers are always a good starting point when beginning to understand a situation. Keep in mind that the wealth of a country does not necessarily equate to health and happiness for all citizens, or even equity among citizens. Other sources, such as the Human Development Index or Genuine Progress Indicators, may shed more light on these issues.

Source: 2008 Index of Economic Freedom, Kim R. Holmes et al., eds., The Heritage Foundation and Dow Jones & Co., Inc., Washington, DC, 2008.

# THE BUSINESS ENVIRONMENT

The **business environment** consists of the surrounding factors that either help or hinder the development of businesses. Figure 1.3, which summarizes some of the points discussed in this chapter, shows the six elements in the business environment:

**business environment**
The surrounding factors that either help or hinder the development of businesses.

1. The legal and regulatory environment
2. The economic environment
3. The technological environment
4. The competitive environment
5. The social environment
6. The global environment

Businesses grow and prosper in a healthy environment. The results are job growth and the wealth that makes it possible to have a high quality of life. The wrong environmental conditions, in contrast, lead to business failure, job losses, and a poor quality of life. In short, creating the right business environment is the foundation for social progress of all kinds, including good schools, clean air and water, good health care, and low rates of crime.

Companies should be aware of these elements and make it a practice to continuously assess the business environment for changes in trends. These trends could affect the organization's ability to achieve its objectives, steer clear of threats, or take advantage of new opportunities.

**FIGURE** **1.3**

**Today's Dynamic Business Environment**

## The Legal and Regulatory Environment

People are willing to start new businesses if they believe that the risk of losing their money isn't too great. Part of that decision is affected by how governments work with businesses. Governments can do a lot to lessen the risk of starting and running a business through the laws (also known as Acts) that are passed by its elected officials. The Constitution Act defines the powers that can be exercised by the different levels of government (i.e., federal and provincial). In Chapter 4, we will review some of the responsibilities of these different levels.

An important piece of legislation is the Competition Act. The purpose of the Competition Act is to:

> … *maintain and encourage competition in Canada in order to promote the efficiency and adaptability of the Canadian economy, in order to expand opportunities for Canadian participation in world markets while at the same time recognizing the role of foreign competition in Canada, in order to ensure that small- and medium-sized enterprises have an equitable opportunity to participate in the Canadian economy and in order to provide consumers with competitive prices and product choices.*[21]

Other examples of laws include the Canada Small Business Financing Act, the Consumer Packaging and Labelling Act, and the Trade Unions Act. As you can imagine, these laws are relevant to many businesses.

Each legislation authorizes an agency (such as Industry Canada) to write regulations that interpret the law in more detail and indicate how it will be implemented and enforced. Consequently, **regulations** are rules or orders made by government to carry out the purposes set out in statutes.[22] These regulations exist to protect consumers as well as businesses. In Chapter 4, you will be introduced to some government departments that deal with businesses.

**regulations**
Rules or orders made by government to carry out the purposes set out in statutes.

## Laws Affect Business

Businesses need to be aware of the laws that are in place (or may be passed) that will affect their business. For example, a government can keep taxes and regulations to a minimum, thereby encouraging entrepreneurship and increasing wealth. Entrepreneurs are looking for a high return on investment (ROI), including the investment of their time. If the government takes away much of what the business earns through high taxes, ROI may no longer be worth the risk. Provinces and territories that have high taxes and restrictive regulations tend to drive entrepreneurs out, while areas with low taxes and less restrictive regulations can attract entrepreneurs.

The government can also lessen the risks of entrepreneurship by passing laws that enable business people to write contracts that are enforceable in court. You can read more about the importance of business law in Canada in the appendix at the end of Chapter 4.

There are many laws in Canada that are intended to minimize corruption, and businesses can flourish when these laws are followed. Nonetheless, corrupt and illegal activities at some companies do negatively affect the business community and the economy as a whole.[23] You hear about sports scandals (e.g., the taking of performance-enhancing drugs), church scandals, government scandals, and business scandals. In one high-profile case, a jury convicted media baron Conrad Black of obstructing justice and defrauding shareholders of his former newspaper company, Hollinger International Inc. As a result, he was sentenced to a 6½-year sentence. His three co-accused, namely John Boultbee, Peter Atkinson, and Mark Kipnis, were also convicted of mail fraud.[24]

Such scandals cross borders and organizations. (Think of the sub-prime mortgage scandal.) Ethics is so important to the success of businesses and the economy as a whole that we feature ethics boxes in each chapter and devote Chapter 5 to the subject. The Making Ethical Decisions box highlights the importance of individual ethical decision making.

## The Economic Environment

The economic environment affects businesses as well as consumers. For our discussion, the focus will be on businesses. The economic environment looks at income, expenditures, and resources that affect the cost of running a business. Businesses review the results of major economic indicators such as consumer spending, employment levels, and productivity. This analysis will give them a sense of what is happening in the marketplace and what actions they may need to take. Since Chapter 2 is dedicated to how economic issues affect businesses, the discussion here will be very brief.

The movement of a country's currency relative to other currencies also pertains to this environment. Currency movements are especially critical for countries, such as Canada, that generate a great deal of business activity from exports. For instance, a lower Canadian dollar value relative to the U.S. dollar makes our exports cheaper and more attractive to the U.S. market, as consumers can buy more products with their higher-valued currency. The opposite is also true. For example in the late 2000s, the Ontario economy was negatively impacted as a result of the strong Canadian dollar, which surpassed parity with the U.S. dollar in the fall of 2007. The province lost tens of thousands of manufacturing jobs in just a few years as manufacturers shifted operations overseas. Some of the province's flagship employers, like General Motors, closed factories and trimmed production at others.[25]

Starting a business in some countries is much harder than in others. In India, for example, a person has to go through an extraordinary and time-consuming bureaucratic process to get permission to start a business—and with no certainty of success. Nonetheless, those businesses that do get started can become a major source of wealth and employment. This jewellery business is one example. Can you imagine the opportunities and wealth that might be created with just a little more freedom in this country of over one billion people?

## Making Ethical Decisions

### How Ethical Are You?

Despite the fact that the vast majority of business people are ethical, television, movies, and the print media all paint a dismal picture of ethics among business people, government officials, and citizens in general. It is easy to criticize the ethics of people whose names appear in the headlines. It is more difficult to see the moral and ethical misbehaviour of your own social group. Do you find some of the behaviours of your friends to be morally or ethically questionable? Some students have been known to tear out pages from books in the library or hide materials that are needed by classmates to complete an assignment. Other examples include cheating on tests and reusing work from someone else's assignment or from the Internet.

In the workplace, some employees call in sick when they are not sick. Rather than working, others have been seen completing their personal banking or visiting their Facebook account. One of the major trends in business today is that many companies are creating ethics codes to guide their employees' behaviour. We believe that this trend toward improving ethical behaviour is so important that we've made it a major theme of this book. Throughout the text you'll see boxes, like this one, called Making Ethical Decisions. The boxes contain short descriptions of situations that pose ethical dilemmas and ask what you would do to resolve them. The idea is for you to think about the moral and ethical dimensions of every decision you make.

Here is your ethical dilemma. You are doing a home project that requires paper, pens, and other materials available at work. You have noticed other employees taking home such materials, and are thinking about doing the same. What is the problem in this situation? What are your alternatives? What are the consequences of each alternative? Which alternative will you choose? Is your choice ethical?

One way for governments to actively promote entrepreneurship is to allow private ownership of businesses. In some countries, the government owns most businesses; thus, there's little incentive for people to work hard or create a profit. All around the world today, various countries in which the government formerly owned most businesses are selling those businesses to private individuals to create more wealth. In Chapter 2, we will discuss the different economic systems around the world.

You should soon realize, as we continue with our brief introduction to the other business environments, that the activities occurring in one environment have an impact on the others. In short, all of the environments are linked. For example, if a new government regulation decreases business taxes, then the impact will be seen in the economic environment when one considers expenditures. Therefore, as a business person you need to scan all of the environments to make good business decisions.

## The Technological Environment

**technology**
Inventions or innovations from applied science or engineering research.

**Technology** refers to inventions or innovations from applied science or engineering research.[26] Technology can include (but is not limited to) everything from phones and copiers to computers, medical imaging devices, personal digital assistants, and the various software programs that make business processes` more effective, efficient, and productive. New technologies are dramatically changing business practices and the way businesses and customers buy and sell.[27]

Since prehistoric times, humans have felt the need to create tools that make their jobs easier. Few technological changes have had a more comprehensive and lasting impact on businesses than the emergence of information technology (IT), which includes computers, modems, cellular phones, and so on. The appendix at the end of this chapter considers how you can use technology to manage information. We also discuss the Internet's impact on businesses throughout the text. In addition, we provide Internet exercises at the end of each chapter to give you some hands-on experience with various Internet sites.

Rogers Wireless is Canada's largest wireless provider. It provides wireless voice and data services to more than seven million customers. Are you a customer?

## How Technology Benefits Workers and You

One of the advantages of working for others is that the company often provides the tools and technology to make your job more productive. **Productivity** is the amount of output you generate given the amount of input (e.g., hours worked). The more you can produce in any given period of time, the more money you are worth to companies. *Effectiveness* means producing the desired result. *Efficiency* means producing goods and services using the least amount of resources. Note that effectiveness is more important than efficiency. Companies look to technology to allow them to be more efficient, effective, and productive.

## The Growth of Electronic Commerce (E-Commerce)

One of the more important changes of recent years is the growth of **e-commerce**, which encompasses the buying and selling of goods and services over the Internet.[28] There are two major types of e-commerce transactions: business-to-consumer (B2C) and business-to-business (B2B). As important as the Internet has been in the consumer market, it has become even more important in the B2B market, which consists of selling goods and services from one business to another. Such is the case for Richmond, British Columbia-based Talent Technology Corporation (considered one of Canada's fastest growing companies), whose largest clients, such as Oracle and SAP, pay up to $50,000 a year for its hosted recruitment software.[29] Traditional businesses have been learning how to deal with the competition from B2B and B2C firms. As discussed in Appendix A, there are issues (e.g., security) surrounding such sites that companies need to consider and regularly monitor.

Do not confuse e-commerce with electronic business (e-business). Mostly done with Web technologies, the term **e-business** refers to any information system or application (e.g., business software) that empowers business processes.[30] While e-commerce is frequently mixed up with the term e-business, e-commerce only covers one aspect of e-business (i.e., the use of an electronic support for the commercial relationship between a company and individuals).[31]

**productivity**
The amount of output that is generated given the amount of input.

**e-commerce**
The buying and selling of goods and services over the Internet.

**e-business**
Any information system or application that empowers business processes.

According to the Survey of Electronic Commerce and Technology (SECT), the value of total online Canadian Internet sales in 2007 was $62.7 billion. For updated statistics on the digital economy, visit http://e-com.ic.gc.ca.

## Using Technology to Be Responsive to Customers

Another major theme of this text is that businesses succeed or fail largely because of the way they treat their customers. The businesses that are most responsive to customer wants and needs will succeed, and those that do not respond to customers will not be as successful. One way that traditional retailers can respond to the Internet revolution is to use technology to become much more responsive to customers. For example, businesses mark goods with Universal Product Codes (bar codes)—those series of lines and numbers that you see on most consumer packaged goods. Bar codes can be used to tell retailers what product you bought, in what size and colour, and at what price. A scanner at the checkout counter can read that information and put it into a database. A **database** is an electronic storage file in which information is kept. One use of databases is to store vast amounts of information about customers. For example, a retailer may ask for your name, address, and telephone number so it can put you on its mailing list. The information you give the retailer is added to the database. Using that information, the company can send you catalogues and other direct mail advertising that offers the kind of products you might want, as indicated by your past purchases. The use of databases enables stores to carry only the merchandise that the local population wants.

**database**

An electronic storage file in which information is kept; one use of databases is to store vast amounts of information about customers.

**identity theft**

Obtaining personal information about a person and using that information for illegal purposes.

Alvin Amparo displays a selection of some of the paper shredders available at a Toronto office supply store. Whenever a TV show airs anything on identity theft, a flood of shoppers comes in to buy paper shredders, one of the best ways to guard against the crime, which is considered the fastest growing scam in North America. Once an identity thief has obtained your social insurance number, credit card number, address, and other such information, he or she can charge goods and services to your account. Do you know the limit you are liable for?

Unfortunately, gathering personal information about people has led to identity theft. **Identity theft** is the act of obtaining personal information about a person, such as social insurance number and/or credit card number, and using that information for illegal purposes, such as buying things with them. In response to consumer complaints, federal privacy laws have been created. The Personal Information Protection and Electronic Documents Act (PIPEDA) sets out ground rules for how private sector organizations may collect, use, or disclose personal information in the course of commercial activities.[32] If you think an organization covered by the Act is not living up to its responsibilities under the law, you have the right to lodge an official complaint.

To find out more about privacy legislation, visit the Office of the Privacy Commissioner of Canada's Web site at www.privcom.gc.ca.

## Progress Assessment

- List the six elements of the business environment.
- What are four ways in which the government can foster entrepreneurship?
- How does technology benefit workers and customers?

## The Competitive Environment

Competition among businesses has never been greater than it is today. Some companies have found a competitive edge by focusing on quality. The goal for many companies is zero defects—no mistakes in making the product.[33] However, simply making a high-quality product isn't enough to allow a company to stay competitive in world markets.

## Components of Competition[34]

When developing their strategies, companies must consider the factors that drive competition: entry, bargaining power of buyers and suppliers, existing rivalries, and substitution possibilities. Scanning the competitive environment requires a look at all of these factors.

**Entry**   In considering the competition, a firm must assess the likelihood of new entrants. Additional producers increase industry capacity and tend to lower prices. *Barriers to entry* are business practices or conditions that make it difficult for new firms to enter the market. Barriers to entry can be in the form of capital requirements, product identity, distribution access, or switching costs. The higher the expense of the barrier, the more likely it will deter new entrants, and vice versa (e.g., barriers to exit).

**Power of Buyers and Suppliers**   Powerful buyers exist when they are few in number, there are low switching costs, or the product represents a significant share of the buyer's total costs. This last factor leads the buyer to exert significant pressure for price competition. A supplier gains power when the product is critical to the buyer and when it has built up switching costs.

**Existing Competitors and Substitutes**   Competitive pressure among existing firms depends on the rate of industry growth. In slow-growth settings, competition is more heated for any possible gains in market share. High fixed costs also create competitive pressures for firms to fill production capacity. (We will discuss production in Chapter 10.) For example, airlines offer discounts for making early reservations and charge penalties for changes or cancellations in an effort to fill seats, which represent a high fixed cost.

## Competing by Exceeding Customer Expectations

Manufacturers and service organizations throughout the world have learned that today's customers are very demanding. Companies have to offer both high-quality products and outstanding service at competitive prices (value). Business is becoming customer-driven, not management-driven as in the past. This means that customers' wants and needs must come first.

Customer-driven organizations include Disney amusement parks (the parks are kept clean and appeal to all ages) and Moto Photo (it does its best to please customers with fast, friendly service). Such companies can successfully compete against Internet firms if they continue to offer better and friendlier service. Successful organizations must now listen more closely to customers to determine their wants and needs, then adjust the firm's products, policies, and practices to meet those demands. We will explore these concepts in more depth in Chapter 14.

## Competing by Restructuring and Empowerment

To meet the needs of customers, firms must give their front-line workers (office clerks, front-desk people at hotels, salespeople, etc.) the responsibility, authority, freedom, training, and equipment they need to respond quickly to customer requests and to make other decisions essential to producing quality goods and providing good service. This is called **empowerment**, and we'll be talking about that process throughout this book. To implement a policy of empowerment, managers must train front-line people to make decisions within certain limits, without the need to consult managers.

Empowering employees leads to developing entirely new organizational structures to meet the changing needs of customers and employees. As many companies have discovered, it sometimes takes years to restructure an organization so that managers are willing to give up some of their authority and employees are willing to assume more responsibility. We'll discuss such organizational changes and models in Chapter 9.

**empowerment**
Giving front-line workers the responsibility, authority, and freedom to respond quickly to customer requests.

# The Social Environment

**demography**
The statistical study of the human population with regard to its size, density, and other characteristics such as age, race, gender, and income.

**Demography** is the statistical study of the human population with regard to its size, density, and other characteristics such as age, race, gender, and income. In this book, we're particularly interested in the demographic trends that most affect businesses and career choices. The Canadian population is going through major changes that are dramatically affecting how people live, where they live, what they buy, and how they spend their time. Furthermore, tremendous population shifts are leading to new opportunities for some firms and to declining opportunities for others.

## The Aging Population

The Canadian population has been aging for several decades. More people are living longer due to better medical knowledge and technology and better health habits, including proper nutrition, more exercise, and a reduction in the number of people who smoke. The portion of the population that is very young continues to decrease because of declining birth rates since the mid-1960s. Although the rate is low, the actual number of children being born is still large because of the baby-boom echo. The **baby-boom echo** (those born in the period from 1980 to 1995) represents the children of the large number of **baby boomers** (those born in the period from 1947 to 1966).[35] Most students are part of this echo generation.

**baby-boom echo**
A demographic group of Canadians that were born in the period from 1980 to 1995; the children of the baby boomers.

Figure 1.4 shows the population projections for Canada. You will notice that the 5 to 19 age group is declining, while the 65 years and over age group is increasing steadily. Based on these projections, it is expected that seniors will become more numerous than children sometime around 2015.

The projections use the 2005 population estimate as their base. The underlying assumption is that Canada will experience medium growth and recent migration trends. The median age of Canada's population will continue to rise as a direct result of the pronounced baby boom.

**baby boomers**
A demographic group of Canadians that were born in the period from 1947 to 1966.

What do such demographics mean for you and for businesses in the future? In his book *Boom Bust & Echo: Profiting from the Demographic Shift in the 21st Century*, economist and demographer David Foot writes that demographics play a pivotal role in the economic and social life of our country. According to Foot, demographics explain about two-thirds of everything—including which products will be in demand in five years.[36]

Think of the goods and services that the middle-aged and elderly will need—anything from travel and recreation to medicine, assisted-living facilities, and smaller apartments. Don't forget the impact of aging baby boomers; more grandparents with more money in their pockets will be buying more gifts for their grandchildren. We will discuss some of the human resource management issues related to an aging population in Chapter 12.

**FIGURE | 1.4**

**Population Distribution by Age Group**

| Year | 0–4 | 5–19 | 20–34 | 35–64 | 65 and Above |
|------|-----|------|-------|-------|--------------|
| 2006 | 5% | 19% | 21% | 42% | 13% |
| 2011 | 5% | 17% | 21% | 43% | 14% |
| 2016 | 5% | 16% | 20% | 42% | 16% |
| 2021 | 5% | 16% | 19% | 41% | 19% |
| 2026 | 5% | 15% | 18% | 40% | 21% |
| 2031 | 5% | 15% | 17% | 39% | 23% |

Source: Adapted from "Population Projections for Canada, Provinces and Territories 2005–2031," Cat. No. 91-520- XIE, December 2005.

## Managing Diversity[37]

Canada has a strong multicultural population. Since the 1980s, it has welcomed 5.1 million immigrants. Between 2001 and 2006 alone, 1.4 million newcomers—or an annual average of 242,000 individuals—were admitted as permanent residents. Looking at Canada's overall population, 19.8 percent of the entire population (6,186,950) is made up of people who were born outside of Canada. The high level of annual admission of immigrants and the relatively slow rate of natural growth of the population explain why the proportion of the foreign-born in the Canadian population has been increasing since the 1990s. Companies have responded to this diverse customer base by hiring a more diversified workforce to serve them. For example, one of NAV CANADA's goals as an employer is to recruit and retain people who have not only talent and skill but a range of backgrounds and perspectives. Company officials believe that diversity in the workplace makes everyone a higher performer and it makes the company stronger by promoting new ideas and new ways of thinking. This generates creativity and adaptability, which are basic elements in at least two areas critical to NAV CANADA's future as a global leader: problem solving and innovation.[38]

## The Family Portrait (Census 2006)[39]

Approximately 54 percent of all families in Canada are supported by two income earners. Factors that have contributed to the growth in two-income families include the high costs of housing and of maintaining a comfortable lifestyle, and more women wanting a career outside of the home. Families with a single parent, on the other hand, represented 15.9 percent of all census families, which was a slight increase from 2001 (15.7 percent). Companies have implemented a host of programs in response to such trends. For example, employee plans may include parental leave, flexible work schedules, and referral services for child care or elder care.

There were also several "firsts" recorded with the 2006 Census results. For example, there were more families comprised of couples without children (42.7 percent) than with children (41.4 percent). There were also more unmarried people aged 15 and over in Canada than legally married people. That is, just over one-half of Canada's population aged 15 and over was unmarried (i.e., never been legally married, were divorced, widowed, or separated). The proportion of young adults aged 20 to 29 who lived in the parental home continued to increase. In 2006, 43.5 percent of young adults lived at home, up substantially from 32.1 percent two decades earlier. Provincially, Newfoundland and Labrador (52.2 percent) and Ontario (51.5 percent) had the highest proportions of young adults in their twenties living in the parental home in 2006 while Alberta (31.7 percent) and Saskatchewan (31.8 percent) had the lowest proportions.

While this information is not exhaustive, it should give you an idea of some of the demographic trends that business people track as they develop their products and services. Can you think of some opportunities that are not currently being met as a result of some of these trends?

Kids & Company Ltd. is Canada's fastest growing company. Its business is providing backup and full-time child care to employees of dozens of corporate clients such as AGF, BP, and CIBC. The services are promoted as an employee benefit and an employee-retention tool.

## Progress Assessment

- Describe the components of competition.
- What is empowerment?
- What social trends are evident in Canada?

# The Global Environment

The global environment of business is so important that we show it as surrounding all other environmental influences (refer to Figure 1.3). Two important environmental changes in recent years have been the growth of international competition and the increase of free trade among nations. Two things that have led to more trade are the improvements in transportation and communication. These changes include more efficient distribution systems (we'll talk about this in Chapter 15) and communication advances such as the Internet. World trade (sometimes called *globalization*) has greatly improved living standards around the world. For example, the number of East Asian people living on less than $1 a day has declined from 56 percent to less than 16 percent.[40]

Better technology, machinery, tools, education, and training enable each worker to be more productive. It is the primary responsibility of businesses to focus on these areas to ensure success. Government support also contributes to domestic and global success. For example, the federal government has developed a science and technology (S&T) strategy, called *Mobilizing Science and Technology to Canada's Advantage*, that will foster a business environment by encouraging innovations that will provide solutions to environmental, health, and other important social challenges, while also improving the country's economic competitiveness. The government plans to do this by creating a policy environment that will encourage an entrepreneurial advantage, a knowledge advantage, and a people advantage.[41] Other government initiatives to support Canadian businesses will be discussed in Chapter 4.

Companies such as Bombardier Inc. (manufacturer of innovative transportation solutions, from commercial aircraft and business jets to rail transportation equipment, systems, and services) and CAE Inc. (provider of simulation and modelling technologies and integrated training solutions for the civil aviation industry and defence forces around the globe), as well as many smaller companies, are as good as or better than competing organizations anywhere in the world. But some businesses have gone beyond simply competing with organizations in other countries by learning to co-operate with international firms. Co-operation among businesses has the potential to create rapidly growing world markets that can generate prosperity beyond most people's expectations. The challenge is tremendous, but so is the will to achieve.

World trade has its benefits and costs. You'll read much more about the importance of global business in Chapter 3 and in the Reaching Beyond Our Borders boxes throughout the text.

There are an increasing number of terms that recognize today's preoccupation with how individual and business actions impact us nationally and internationally. Some examples include *carbon footprint* (defined as the impact of human activity measured in terms of the amount of carbon dioxide it causes to be emitted into the atmosphere), *food miles* (the distance travelled from the place where food is produced to the place where it is eaten, considered in terms of the environmental damage that transporting it entails), *green tax* (a tax imposed with the intention of discouraging activities that may damage the environment), and *eco-village* (a small-scale, environmentally friendly settlement designed for sustainable living).[42] In the Green Boxes throughout the text you will read about companies that recognize the importance in making changes as the planet's climate worsens. The first box highlights the activities of Global Footprint Network.

## GreenBOX

### Global Footprint Network, Advancing the Science of Sustainability

Global Footprint Network is non-profit organization established to enable a sustainable future where all people have the opportunity to live satisfying lives within the means of one planet. A focus is on advancing the scientific rigour and practical application of the Ecological Footprint, a resource accounting tool that measures how much nature we have, how much we use, and who uses what. Conceived in 1990 by Mathis Wackernagel and William Rees at the University of British Columbia, the Ecological Footprint is now in wide use by scientists, businesses, governments, agencies, individuals, and institutions working to monitor ecological resource use and advance sustainable development.

Global Footprint Network, through its numerous programs, aims to influence decision makers and create a critical mass of powerful institutions using the Footprint to put an end to ecological overshoot and get economies back into balance. The key to achieving this is to make the Ecological Footprint as prominent a metric as the gross domestic product. By 2015, through its flagship Ten-In-Ten campaign, Global Footprint Network aims to have at least ten key national governments managing their ecological wealth in the same way they manage their finances—by the numbers.

Since its inception in 2003, Global Footprint Network has made significant progress toward its goals. Over 90 organizations, spanning six continents, have become formal Global Footprint Network partners. Currently, six nations and numerous municipalities have adopted the Footprint to benchmark progress towards sustainability, make informed infrastructure and investment decisions, and identify solutions that will make a true difference to the ecological bottom line.

Source: Global Footprint Network, 22 June 2009, http://www.footprintnetwork.org.

# THE EVOLUTION OF CANADIAN BUSINESS

Many managers and workers are losing their jobs in major manufacturing firms. Businesses in Canada have become so productive that, compared to the past, fewer workers are needed in industries that produce goods. **Goods** are tangible products such as computers, food, clothing, cars, and appliances. Due to the increasing impact of technology and global competition, shouldn't we be concerned about the prospect of high unemployment rates and low incomes? Where will the jobs be when you graduate? These important questions prompt us to look briefly at the manufacturing and service sectors.

**goods**
Tangible products such as computers, food, clothing, cars, and appliances.

## Progress in the Agricultural and Manufacturing Industries

Canada has seen strong economic development since the nineteenth century. The agricultural industry led the way, providing food for Canadians and people in other parts of the world. Inventions such as the harvester and cotton gin did much to make farming successful, as did ongoing improvements to such equipment. The modern farming industry has become so efficient through the use of technology that the number of farms has dropped. Due to increased competition, many of the farms that existed even 50 years ago have been replaced by some huge farms, some merely large farms, and some small but highly specialized farms. The loss of farm workers over the past century is not a negative sign. It is instead an indication that Canadian agricultural workers are more productive.

Most farmers who lost their jobs went to work in factories. The manufacturing industry, much like agriculture, used technology to become more productive. The consequence, as in farming, was the elimination of many jobs. Again, the loss to society is minimal if the wealth created by increased productivity and efficiency creates new jobs elsewhere. This is exactly what has happened over the past 50 years. Many workers in the industrial sector found jobs in the service sector. Most of those who can't find work today are people who need retraining and education to become qualified for jobs that now exist.

## Canada's Manufacturing Industry

The goods-producing sector includes the manufacturing, construction, utilities, agriculture, forestry, fishing, and mining industries. Of this sector, manufacturing employs a little over 7 percent of Canada's working population, as noted in Figure 1.5.

Tens of thousands of Canadian jobs were lost in the late 2000s. The rising Canadian dollar and increasing global competition were two of the reasons for these losses. Despite such losses, manufacturing still remains an important contributor to the Canadian economy. The Canadian Manufacturing Coalition highlights some of the reasons why this sector is important to Canada:

- Manufacturing directly accounts for 17 percent of the Canadian economy;

- Every $1 of manufacturing output in Canada generates $3.05 in total economic activity; and

- Manufacturing accounts for two-thirds of Canada's total exports of goods and services.[43]

While the manufacturing sector is much smaller today than it was 25 years ago, it is still clearly an integral part of our business economy. We will discuss the manufacturing sector and production in more detail in Chapter 10.

**FIGURE | 1.5**

**The Importance of the Goods-Producing and Services-Producing Sectors in Canada**
Canada is a service economy, where the majority of jobs are generated in the services-producing sector. This excerpt from Statistics Canada's *Employment by Industry* for 2008 highlights the importance of manufacturing and agriculture (the two largest-employer industries in the goods-producing sector) to Canadians.

|  | Number of Employed (thousands) | Total Workforce (percent) |
|---|---|---|
| **Total employed in Canada** | 17,125.8 | 100.0 |
| **Goods-producing sector** | 4,021.3 | 23.5 |
| **Agriculture** | 326.0 | 1.9 |
| **Manufacturing** | 1,970.3 | 7.2 |
| **Services-producing sector** | 13,104.5 | 76.5 |

Source: "Employment by Industry," Statistics Canada, CANSIM Table 282-0008. Retrieved from http://www40.statcan.ca/l01/cst01/econ40.htm?sdi=employment, (9 August 2008). Last modified 10 January 2008.

Agriculture is an important industry in Canada. The entire process of growing food and getting it to our tables is so smooth that it's easy to take for granted. But behind those well-stocked supermarkets is an army of farmers and distributors who supply our needs. Use of technology has led to increased productivity and made farmers more efficient, resulting in larger farms. This trend has meant less expensive food for us, but a continual reduction in the number of small, family-run farms. Is it still possible for small farms to be successful, and if so, how?

## Progress in Service Industries

The service sector is distinct from the goods-producing sector. **Services** are intangible products (i.e., products that cannot be held in your hand) such as education, health care, insurance, recreation, and travel and tourism. In the past, the dominant industries in Canada produced goods such as steel, railroads, and machine tools. Over the last 30 years, the service sector in Canada and around the world has grown dramatically.

The shift in Canada's employment makeup began slowly early in the twentieth century, and has accelerated rapidly since the 1950s. Today, the leading firms are in services (such as legal, health, telecommunications, entertainment, financial services, etc.). As noted in Figure 1.5, the services-producing sector employs a little more than 76 percent of the working population.

There are several reasons why there has been growth in this sector. First, technological improvements have enabled businesses to reduce their payrolls while increasing their output. Since staffing has been downsized by many companies, business has become more complex and specialized companies have relied more heavily on outside services firms. Secondly, as large manufacturing companies seek to become more efficient, they contract out an increasing number of services, creating more opportunities for business people. Other service firms have risen or expanded rapidly to provide traditional services that used to be performed by women at home. Since many women have entered the workforce, there is increased demand for food preparation, child care, and household maintenance, to name just a few.

## Your Future in Business

Despite the growth in the service sector, the service era now seems to be coming to a close as a new era is beginning. We're now in the midst of an information-based global revolution that will alter all sectors of the economy. It's exciting to think about the role you'll play in that revolution. You may be a leader; that is, you may be one of the people who will implement the changes and accept the challenges of world competition based on world quality standards. This book will introduce you to some of the concepts that will make such leadership possible.

Remember that most of the concepts and principles that make businesses more effective and efficient are also applicable to government agencies and non-profit organizations. This is an introductory business text, so we will focus on business. Business cannot prosper in the future without the co-operation of government and social leaders throughout the world.

**services**
Intangible products (i.e., products that can't be held in your hand) such as education, health care, insurance, recreation, and travel and tourism.

Visit http://jobfutures.ca to find out what the future's most promising jobs will be.

### Progress Assessment

- What are two changes that have affected the global environment?
- Why is the manufacturing sector important to the economy?
- What is the major factor that caused people to move from farming to industry and from industry to the service sector?

## SUMMARY

**LO ▸ 1** Describe the relationship of businesses' profit-to-risk assumption.

1. A business is any activity that seeks to provide goods and services to others while operating at a profit.

   **What are the relationships between risk, profit, and loss?**
   Profit is money a business earns above and beyond the money it spends for salaries and other expenses. Business people make profits by taking risks. Risk is the chance an entrepreneur takes of losing time and money on a business that may not prove profitable. A loss occurs when a business's costs and expenses are more than its revenues.

**LO ▸ 2** Discuss the importance of stakeholders and non-profit organizations to business activities.

2. Stakeholders include customers, employees, investors (e.g., stockholders), suppliers, dealers, people in the local community, environmentalists, and government.

   **Which stakeholders are most important to a business?**
   The goal of business leaders is to try to balance the needs of all stakeholders and still make a profit. Some businesses put the needs of stockholders above the other interests, but most businesses today seek a balance among the needs of the various stakeholders.

**LO ▸ 3** Explain how entrepreneurship is critical to the wealth of an economy, and list the five factors of production that contribute to wealth.

3. Entrepreneurs are people who risk time and money to start and manage a business.

   **What importance does entrepreneurship hold in the list of the five factors of production?**
   Businesses use five factors of production: land (natural resources), labour (workers), capital goods (buildings and machinery), entrepreneurship, and knowledge. Of these, the most important are entrepreneurship and knowledge (managed information), because without them land, labour, and capital are not of much use.

**LO ▸ 4** Review the six elements that make up the business environment and explain why the business environment is important to organizations.

4. The business environment consists of the surrounding factors that either help or hinder the development of businesses. The six elements are the legal and regulatory environment, the economic environment, the technological environment, the competitive environment, the social environment, and the global environment.

   **Explain why the business environment is important to organizations.**
   Scanning the business environment on a continual basis is important to organizations so that they can take advantage of trends. These trends could affect the organization's ability to achieve its objectives, steer clear of threats, or take advantage of new opportunities.

**LO ▸ 5** Understand how the service sector has replaced manufacturing as the principal provider of jobs, but why manufacturing remains vital for Canada.

5. Canada has evolved from an economy based on manufacturing to one based on services.

   **Why is manufacturing still a vital industry for Canada?**
   While the services-producing sector employs a little more than 76 percent of the working population, the manufacturing industry employs a little over 7 percent of workers. Every $1 of manufacturing in Canada generates $3.05 in total economic activity. Directly, manufacturing accounts for 17 percent of economic activity, and two-thirds of Canada's exports of goods and services.

## KEY TERMS

baby-boom echo 18

baby boomers 18

business 4

business environment 11

database 16

demography 18

e-business 15

e-commerce 15

empowerment 17

entrepreneur 4

factors of production 9

goods 21

identity theft 16

loss 4

non-profit organization 7

offshoring 6

outsourcing 6

productivity 15

profit 4

regulations 12

revenue 4

risk 5

services 23

stakeholders 5

technology 14

## CRITICAL THINKING

Imagine that you are thinking of starting a restaurant in your community and answer the following questions.

1. You need to consider whether you will purchase using locally-grown produce versus foreign-grown produce. What are the advantages and disadvantages of using either, especially if the foreign-grown produce is cheaper or of better quality?

2. What are some of the things you could do to benefit your community other than provide jobs and generate tax revenue?

3. You are considering paying your employees the minimum wage. Do you think that you would attract better employees if your wages were higher?

4. How might you be affected by the six environmental factors outlined in this chapter? Which factor(s) might have the biggest impact on your business?

## DEVELOPING WORKPLACE SKILLS

1. Make a list of non-profit organizations in your community that might offer you a chance to learn some of the skills you'll need in the job you hope to have when you graduate. How could you make time in your schedule to volunteer or work at one or more of those organizations? Write a letter to a non-profit organization to inquire about such opportunities.

2. Reading the news or surfing the Internet, find two examples of top executives who have disregarded their stakeholders. Present your findings to the class.

3. Imagine that you are a local business person who has to deal with the various issues involved with outsourcing.

You want to begin with the facts. How many jobs have been lost to outsourcing in your area, if any? Are there any foreign firms in your area that are creating jobs (insourcing)? You may want to use the Internet to find the data you need.

4. Form into teams of four or five and discuss the technological and e-commerce revolutions. How many students now shop for goods and services online? What have been their experiences? What other high-tech equipment (e.g., cellphones, personal digital assistants, etc.) do they use?

## TAKING IT TO THE NET 1

### Purpose

To gather data regarding trends in population and the social environment and to understand how this information affects Canadian businesses.

### Exercise

To access this information, you will need to visit the Statistics Canada site at www.statcan.gc.ca.

1. Who is responsible for collecting the information found on this site? How is this information collected?

2. Statistics Canada conducts a census every five years. Why is the Census important? Who is included in the Census? Who will use this Census information? (To help answer these questions, click on Census on the bar on the left-hand side of the Statistics Canada home page.)

3. Return to the Statistics Canada home page. What is the population of Canada right now? How can businesses use this information?

## TAKING IT TO THE NET 2

### Purpose

To understand what influences tween spending.

### Exercise

Tweens are Canadians aged 9 to 14. Visit YTV's Annual Tween Report site at www.corusmedia.com/ytv/research. asp.

1. What key topics are covered by the YTV Annual Tween Report?

2. How much money do tweens spend each year?

3. In what areas do tweens have a high level of influence?

4. What opportunities for product sales exist for businesses if they wish to target this group?

## ANALYZING MANAGEMENT DECISIONS

### Canada's Fastest-Growing Companies— PROFIT 100

Every year, *PROFIT* magazine publishes a list of Canada's 100 fastest-growing companies. The importance of many of the points we discussed in this chapter is evident in a recent issue, especially when one considers the breakdown among the types of companies. Services providers dominate the marketplace, which reinforces that Canada is a service economy. Here is a breakdown of the Top 100:

| Focus | Number of Firms |
| --- | --- |
| Business services | 42 |
| Manufacturing | 19 |
| Software development | 12 |
| Consumer services | 7 |
| Construction | 6 |
| Natural resource production and services | 6 |
| Wholesale/distribution | 5 |
| Retail | 3 |

While the companies were located across Canada, Ontario continued to support the largest share of these companies:

| | |
| --- | --- |
| Ontario | 42 |
| Alberta | 23 |
| British Columbia | 19 |
| Quebec | 12 |
| Manitoba | 2 |
| Atlantic Canada | 2 |

Clearly, great teams start with great people. Interesting statistics about the Top 100 company leaders include:

1. The age ranges from 27 to 67, with an average age of 43 years.

2. A substantial share (28 percent) are foreign-born.

3. An overwhelming 94 percent are male.

4. The average yearly compensation was $398,000.

What makes these companies leaders is that they grew rapidly, with a minimum explosive growth of 627 percent over the past five years. It does not matter whether they are high-tech or old-economy companies, manufacturing or service companies, they all were exceptional. A remarkable assortment of products and services are offered by these companies. Examples include child-care centres, IT staffing services, smoothies, air purifiers, custom clothing, and organic cranberries and blueberries. Seventy-five of the companies are exporters with 69 percent of sales ($7.9 billion) being thus generated. The top export markets are the United States, the United Kingdom, other Western European countries, Australia, the Pacific Rim (excluding China and Japan), Africa, the Middle East, and Eastern Europe (excluding Russia).

Source: Jim McElgunn, "Sights for Sore Eyes," *PROFIT*, June 2008, 38–58.

## Discussion Questions

1. Which of these data support the information discussed in the chapter? Explain your answer.

2. Why do certain provinces or regions have so many (e.g., Ontario) or few (e.g., Atlantic Canada) companies?

3. Visit www.canadianbusiness.com/entrepreneur to see the latest information on the PROFIT 100 companies. How much has changed since these results were posted?

# Using Technology to Manage Information

## THE ROLE OF INFORMATION TECHNOLOGY

Throughout this text, we emphasize the need for managing information flows among businesses and their employees, businesses and their suppliers, businesses and their customers, and so on. Since businesses are in a constant state of change, those managers who try to rely on old ways of doing things will simply not be able to compete with those who have the latest in technology and know how to use it.

Business technology has often changed names and roles. In the 1970s, business technology was known as data processing (DP). (Although many people use the words *data* and *information* interchangeably, they are different. Data are raw, unanalyzed, and unorganized facts and figures. Information is the processed and organized data that can be used for managerial decision making.) DP was used to support an existing business; its primary purpose was to improve the flow of financial information. DP employees tended to be hidden in a back room and rarely came in contact with customers.

In the 1980s, business technology became known as information systems (IS). These IS moved out of the back room and into the centre of the business. Their role changed from supporting the business to doing business. Customers began to interact with a wide array of technological tools, from automated teller machines (ATMs) to voice mail. As business increased its use of information systems, it became more dependent on them. Until the late 1980s, business technology was just an addition to the existing way of doing business. Keeping up to date was a matter of using new technology on old methods.

But things started to change as the 1990s approached. Businesses shifted to using new technology on new methods. Business technology then became known as **information technology (IT)**, and its role became to change business.

Obviously, the role of the information technology staff has changed as the technology itself has evolved. The chief information officer (CIO) has moved out of the back room and into the boardroom. Because improved hardware and software keep computers running more smoothly than in the past, the average CIO can spend less time worrying about keeping the systems running and more time finding ways to use technology to boost business by participating in purchasing decisions, operational strategy, and marketing and sales.[1] Today the role of the CIO is to help the business use technology to communicate better with others while offering better service and lower costs.[2]

**information technology (IT)**
Technology that helps companies change business by allowing them to use new methods.

## How Information Technology Changes Business

Time and place have always been at the centre of business. Customers had to go to the business during certain hours to satisfy their needs. We went to the store to buy clothes. We went to the bank to arrange for a loan. Businesses decided when and where we did business with them. Today, IT allows businesses to deliver goods and services whenever and wherever it is convenient for the customer. Thus, you can order clothes from the Home Shopping Network, arrange a home mortgage loan by phone or computer, or buy a car on the Internet at any time you choose.

Consider how IT has changed the entertainment industry. If you wanted to see a movie 35 years ago, you had to go to a movie theatre. Thirty years ago, you could wait for it to be on television. Twenty years ago, you could wait for it to be on cable television. Fifteen years ago, you could go to a video store and rent it. Now you can order video on demand by satellite or cable, or download the movie over the Internet to watch on your TV, computer, or even cellphone or iPod, whenever and wherever you wish.[3]

As IT breaks time and location barriers, it creates organizations and services that are independent of location. For example, the TSX Venture Exchange is an electronic stock exchange without trading floors. Buyers and sellers make trades by computer.

Being independent of location brings work to people instead of people to work. With IT, data and information can flow thousands of kilometres in a second, allowing businesses to conduct work around the globe continuously. We are moving toward what is called **virtualization**, which is accessibility through technology that allows business to be conducted independently of location.[4] For example, you can carry a virtual office in your pocket or purse. Such tools as cellular phones, pagers, laptop computers, and personal digital assistants (PDAs) allow you to access people and information as if you were in an actual office. Likewise, people who otherwise would not have met are forming virtual communities through computer networks.

**virtualization**
Accessibility through technology that allows business to be conducted independent of location.

The way people do business drastically changes when companies increase their technological capabilities. Electronic communications can provide substantial time savings whether you work in an office, at home, or on the road. E-mail ends the tedious games of telephone tag and is far faster than paper-based correspondence. Instant messaging (IM), best known as the preferred way for millions of teenagers to communicate, is now a favourite business real-time communication tool. For example, you may turn on your computer first thing in the morning to see who else is logged on. You may participate in half a dozen IM conversations at once through a cascade of pop-up windows. You might try to respond to a client in one window and agree to meet a colleague for lunch in another. Canadians are also sending each other more than 49 million text messages every day.[5]

This is an opportunity for companies to generate additional revenues. For example, in 2008, two of Canada's wireless carriers, Bell Mobility and Telus Corp., announced that they would charge subscribers 15 cents for each incoming text message. One of the chief reasons the two companies gave for the new charge was the need to accommodate a larger volume of traffic. One day's worth of text messages was equivalent to a year's worth of text messages five years previously, Jim Johannsson, a Telus spokesman, wrote in an e-mail. "That requires ongoing investment in our network to carry the ever-increasing loads."[6]

Internet and intranet communication using shared documents and other methods allow contributors to work on a common document without time-consuming meetings. See Figure A.1 for other examples of how information technology changes business.

## Moving from Information Toward Knowledge and Business Intelligence

In the mid-1990s, we started to move away from information technology and toward knowledge technology (KT). Knowledge is information charged with enough intelligence to make it relevant and useful. KT adds a layer of intelligence to filter appropriate information and deliver it when it is needed.

KT changes the traditional flow of information; instead of an individual going to the database, the data come to the individual. For example, using KT business training software, AT&T can put a new employee at a workstation and then let the system take over everything from laying out a checklist of the tasks required on a shift to answering questions and offering insights that once would have taken up a supervisor's time. Knowledge databases may one day replace the traditional mentors who helped workers up the corporate ladder.

KT "thinks" about the facts according to an individual's needs, reducing the time that a person must spend finding and getting information. As KT became more sophisticated

| Organization | Technology is breaking down corporate barriers, allowing functional departments or product groups (even factory workers) to share critical information instantly. |
|---|---|
| Operations | Technology shrinks cycle times, reduces defects, and cuts waste. Service companies use technology to streamline ordering and communication with suppliers and customers. |
| Staffing | Technology eliminates layers of management and cuts the number of employees. Companies use computers and telecommunication equipment to create "virtual offices" with employees in various locations. |
| New products | Information technology cuts development cycles by feeding customer and marketing comments to product development teams quickly so that they can revive products and target specific customers. |
| Customer relations | Customer service representatives can solve customers' problems instantly by using companywide databases to complete tasks from changing addresses to adjusting bills. Information gathered from customer service interactions can further strengthen customer relationships. |
| New markets | Since it is no longer necessary for customers to walk down the street to get to stores, online businesses can attract customers to whom they wouldn't otherwise have access |

in the mid-2000s it became better known as business intelligence systems (BI). BI refers to a variety of software applications that analyze an organization's raw data and take useful insights from it. BI activities include data mining (which we will discuss later in this appendix), online analytical process, querying, and reporting.[7]

Business people that use BI can focus on what's important: deciding about how to react to problems and opportunities. For example, imagine you are a sales rep who just closed a big deal. While you celebrate your success, someone in the finance department is upset because your customer never pays on time, which costs the company a lot of money. By using BI that provides the right information to the right person at the right time, you could have negotiated different payment terms with the customer, thus connecting the sales activity to the financial requirements in a seamless process.[8]

Businesses that build flexible information infrastructures will have a significant competitive advantage. Constant changes in technology interact with each other to create more change. Maintaining the flexibility to successfully integrate these changes is crucial to business survival.[9] History is filled with stories of once-mighty companies that couldn't keep up with the challenge of change: Packard Bell and RCA once dominated their industries but failed to compete effectively and have lost market share. They had size and money, but not flexibility. Knowledge sharing is at the heart of keeping pace with change.

## TYPES OF INFORMATION

Today, information flows into and through an organization from many different directions. The types of information that are available to businesses today include the following:[10]

- *Business Process Information.* This includes all transaction data gathered at the point of sale as well as information gained through operations such as enterprise resource planning, supply chain management (these will be discussed in Chapter 10), and customer relationship management systems. It is estimated that the amount of corporate data available doubles every six months.

- *Physical-World Observations.* These observations result from the use of radio frequency identification devices (RFID), miniature cameras, wireless access, global positioning systems (GPS), and sensor technology that record where people or items are located and what they are doing. Computer chips cost pennies apiece and can be found in a wide range of products including credit cards, printer ink cartridges, baseballs, tire valves, running shoes, and vacuum cleaners. For example, Montreal's Metropolitan Transit Authority has installed RFID readers in several terminal entrances and exits.[11] As soon as a bus enters the terminal, a large electronic display board is updated so that waiting passengers know their bus is about to pull up; if a bus doesn't pass the entrance on time, the board indicates that it is delayed.[12]

- *Biological Data.* Forms of identification include fingerprinting, which, while not new, can now be taken and shared more easily. Biometric devices can scan retinas, recognize faces and voices, and analyze DNA data. Although such information is usually used for security purposes, it may be used to customize products and services in the future.

- *Public Data.* This includes information in databases that are free and accessible. This includes electronic traces that people leave when posting to the Internet, sending e-mail, and using instant messaging. More and more, these public data are stored, shared, or sold.

- *Data that Indicate Personal Preferences or Intentions.* Internet shoppers leave a trail of information that can reveal personal likes and dislikes. You can imagine how valuable this information is. The volume and complexity of all of this information are staggering. While it appears in all forms and formats including text, numbers, audio, and video, computing systems have been developed that can search through the data and identify, categorize, and refine relevant opinions on any topic.[13]

## Managing Information

Even before the use of computers, managers had to sift through mountains of information to find what they needed to help them make decisions. Today, business people are deluged with so much data that this information overload is referred to as *infoglut*. Too much information can confuse issues rather than clarify them. How can managers keep from getting buried in the infoglut? Stepping back to gain perspective is the key to managing the flood of information.

The most important step toward gaining perspective is to identify the four or five key goals you wish to reach. Eliminating the information that is not related to those top priorities can reduce the amount of information flowing into your office by half. For example, as we were gathering information to include in this appendix, we collected several hundred journal articles. Feeling the pressure of information overload, we identified the goals we wanted the appendix to accomplish and eliminated all of the articles that didn't address those goals. As we further refined our goals, the huge stack of paper gradually dropped to a manageable size.

Obviously, not all of the information that ends up on your desk will be useful. The usefulness of management information depends on four characteristics:

1. *Quality.* Quality means that the information is accurate and reliable. When the clerk at a fast-food restaurant enters your order into the cash register, it may be automatically fed to a computer, and the day's sales and profits can be calculated as soon as the store closes. The sales and expense data must be accurate, or the rest of the calculations will be wrong. This can be a real problem when, for example, a large number of calculations are based on questionable sales forecasts rather than actual sales.

2. *Completeness.* There must be enough information to allow you to make a decision but not so much as to confuse the issue. Today, as we have noted, the problem is often too much information rather than too little.

3. *Timeliness.* Information must reach managers quickly. If a customer has a complaint, that complaint should be handled instantly if possible and certainly within no more than one day.

4. *Relevance.* Different managers have different information needs. Again, the problem today is that information systems often make too much data available. Managers must learn which questions to ask to get the answers they need.

The important thing to remember when facing information overload is to relax. You can never read everything that is available. Set goals for yourself, and do the best you can.

## Storing and Mining Data

It doesn't matter how interesting your information is if nobody's paying attention or can't get to the information when it is needed. Storing, sorting, and getting useful information to the right people at the right time are the goals in managing information. How do businesses organize a data glut into useful information? The answer for many companies is a data warehouse. A *data warehouse* stores data on a single subject over a specific period of time.

The whole purpose of a data warehouse is to get data out. *Data mining* is looking for hidden patterns in a data warehouse. Data mining software discovers previously unknown relationships among the data. For example, Walmart has massive data warehouses that track sales on a minute-by-minute basis and can reveal regional and local sales trends. Using this information, Walmart customizes each store's offerings on the basis of local demand, keeping it and its suppliers informed about how each of the 70,000 products in the stores is selling and what it anticipates will sell next.

The success of data mining depends on a number of factors, but perhaps the most important is access to data to mine in the first place. Frequently, organizations have a multitude of data storage systems that run on incompatible platforms. The divergent systems must be integrated in some way before the data can be connected. Such integration is possible today, but getting departments and divisions to hand over the keys to their data can be difficult, as seen in this example:

> *Canada Post transformed its systems in order to become more competitive. This did not happen overnight as it took six years and $442 million to accomplish this task. According to Aaron Nichols, general manager of Canada Post Corp.'s internal IT department, "...those custom-built systems were so unwieldy that every time we wanted to raise the price of stamps, it took a year to make the changes to all the systems." Surprisingly, the greatest resistance to Canada Post's transformation was from middle management: hoarding knowledge was previously a source of power for this group, and they were unused to providing all levels of staff with access to operating information.[14]*

# THE ROAD TO KNOWLEDGE: THE INTERNET, INTRANETS, EXTRANETS, AND VIRTUAL PRIVATE NETWORKS

The importance of business knowledge is nothing new; what is new is the recognition of the need to manage it like any other asset. To manage knowledge, a company needs to learn how to share information throughout the organization and to implement systems for creating new knowledge. This need is leading to new technologies that support the exchange of information among staff, suppliers, and customers. Who wins and who loses will be decided by who harnesses the technology that provides the pipeline of interaction and information flows between individuals and organizations. At the heart of this technology are the Internet, intranets, extranets, and virtual private networks.

You already know that the Internet is a network of computers. The Internet has evolved from a tool that only allowed one-to-one communications (usually through e-mail) to a one-to-many broadcast communications tool. Today the Internet allows many-to-many communication through such things as file sharing, blogs, wikis, and social networking services (e.g., Facebook) that connect masses of people to each other at once.[15]

Internet users can point and click their way from site to site with complete freedom. But what if you don't want just anybody to have access to your Web site? You might create an intranet. An **intranet** is a companywide network, closed to public access, that uses Internet-type technology. To prevent unauthorized outsiders (particularly the competition) from accessing their sites, companies can construct a firewall between themselves and the outside world to protect corporate information from unauthorized users. A firewall can consist of hardware, software, or both. Firewalls allow only authorized users to access the intranet. Some companies use intranets only to publish information for employees, such as phone lists and employee policy manuals. These companies do not enjoy as high a return on their investment as other companies that create interactive intranet applications. Such applications include allowing employees to update their addresses or submit company forms such as supply requisitions, time sheets, or payroll forms online. These applications save money or generate revenue increases because they eliminate paper handling and enable decision making.

Many businesses choose to open their intranets to other, selected companies through the use of extranets. An **extranet** is a semi-private network that uses Internet technology and allows more than one company to access the same information or allows people on different servers to collaborate. One of the most common uses of extranets is to extend an intranet to outside customers. Extranets change the way we do business. No longer are the advantages of electronic data interchange (EDI) available only to the large companies that can afford such a system. Now almost all companies can use extranets to share data and process orders, specifications, invoices, and payments.

Notice that we described an extranet as a semi-private network. This means that outsiders cannot access the network easily; but since an extranet does use public lines, knowledgeable *hackers* (people who break into computer systems for illegal purposes such as transferring funds from someone's bank account to their own without authorization) can gain unauthorized access. Companies want a network that is as private and secure as possible. One way to increase the probability of total privacy is to use *dedicated lines* (lines reserved solely for the network). There are two problems with this method: (1) it's expensive, and (2) it limits use to computers directly linked to those lines. What if your company needs to link securely with another firm or individual for just a short time? Installing dedicated lines between companies in this case would be too expensive and time-consuming. Virtual private networks are a solution.

A **virtual private network (VPN)** is a private data network that creates secure connections, or "tunnels," over regular Internet lines.[16] The idea of the VPN is to give the company the same capabilities at much lower cost by using shared public resources rather than private ones. This means that companies no longer need their own leased lines for wide-area communication but can instead use public lines securely. Just as phone companies provide secure shared resources for voice messages, VPNs provide the same secure sharing of public resources for data. This allows for on-demand networking: an authorized user can join the network for any desired function at any time, for any length of time, while keeping the corporate network secure.

**intranet**
A companywide network, closed to public access, that uses Internet-type technology.

**extranet**
A semi-private network that uses Internet technology and allows more than one company to access the same information or allows people on different servers to collaborate.

**virtual private network (VPN)**
A private data network that creates secure connections, or "tunnels," over regular Internet lines.

## The Front Door: Enterprise Portals

How do users log on to an organization's network? Frequently, through an enterprise portal that centralizes information and transactions. Portals serve as entry points to a variety of resources, such as e-mail, financial records, schedules, and employment and benefits files. They can even include streaming video of the company's daycare centre.

Portals are more than simply Web pages with links. They identify users and allow them access to areas of the intranet according to their roles: customers, suppliers, employees, and so on. They make information available in one place so that users don't have to deal with a dozen different Web interfaces. The challenge to the CIO is to integrate resources, information, reports, and so on—all of which may be in a variety of places—so that they appear seamless to the user and save money for the firm.

## Broadband Technology

**broadband technology**

Technology that offers users a continuous connection to the Internet and allows them to send and receive mammoth files that include voice, video, and data much faster than ever before.

As traffic on the Internet increases, the slower the connection becomes. New technologies unlock many of the traffic jams on the Internet. For example, **broadband technology** offers users a continuous connection to the Internet and allows them to send and receive mammoth files that include voice, video, and data much faster than ever before. The more bandwidth, the bigger the pipe for data to flow through—and the bigger the pipe, the faster the flow. Whether the broadband connection is by cable modem, digital subscriber lines (DSL), satellite, or fixed wireless, the impact is much the same. With broadband, data can reach you more than 50 times faster than with a dial-up connection using a 56K modem (the kind that came with most computers in the early 2000s).[17] About 25 out of every 100 Canadians subscribe to broadband.[18]

Even with broadband technology, the traffic on the Internet has become so intense that early Net settlers—scientists and other scholars—have found themselves being squeezed off the crowded Internet and thus unable to access, transmit, and manipulate complex mathematical models, data sets, and other digital elements of their craft. Their answer? Create another Internet, reserved for research purposes only.

**Internet2**

The new Internet system that links government supercomputer centres and a select group of universities; it runs more than 22,000 times faster than today's public infrastructure and supports heavy-duty applications.

The new system, **Internet2**, runs more than 22,000 times faster than today's public infrastructure and supports heavy-duty applications such as videoconferencing, collaborative research, distance education, digital libraries, and full-body simulations known as teleimmersion. A key element of Internet2 is a network called very-high-speed backbone network service (vBNS), which was set up in 1995 as a way to link government supercomputer centres and a select group of universities. The power of Internet2 makes it possible for a remote medical specialist to assist in a medical operation over the Internet without having to contend with deterioration of the connection as, say, home users check sports scores.

Although Internet2 initially became available to only a few select organizations, there are now more than 300 member organizations including universities, corporations, government research agencies, and non-profit networking organizations.[19] Whereas the public Internet divides bandwidth equally among users (if there are 100 users, they each get to use 1 percent of the available bandwidth), Internet2 is more capitalistic. Users who are willing to pay more can use more bandwidth.

Cynics say that soon Internet2 itself will be overrun by networked undergrads engaged in song swapping and other resource-hogging pursuits. However, the designers of Internet2 are thinking ahead. Not only do they expect Internet history to repeat itself, but they are counting on it. They are planning to filter the Internet2 technology out to the wider Internet community in such a way that there is plenty of room on the road for all of us—at a price, of course.

## THE ENABLING TECHNOLOGY: HARDWARE

We hesitate to discuss the advances that have been made in computer hardware because what is powerful as we write this may be obsolete by the time you read it. Rather than add potentially outdated facts to your information overload, we offer you a simple overview of the current computer technology.

Hardware includes computers, pagers, cellular phones, printers, scanners, fax machines, PDAs, and so on. The mobile worker can find travel-size versions of computers, printers, and fax machines that are almost as powerful and feature-laden as their big brothers.

All-in-one devices that address the entire range of your communications needs are also available. For example, there are handheld units that include a wireless phone, camera, fax and e-mail capabilities, Web browsers, and a personal information manager (PIM).

## Cutting the Cord: Wireless Information Appliances

Some experts think we have entered the post-PC era—that is, they believe we are moving away from a PC-dominant environment and toward an array of Internet appliance options. Internet appliances are designed to connect people to the Internet and to e-mail. They include equipment such as PDAs (e.g., smart phones/mobile phones such as BlackBerry and iPhone), two-way paging devices, and in-dash computers for cars. "We are entering a golden age of mobility," says Bob Ianucci, chief technology office for Nokia Corp. "Web 1.0 made lots of information available to a lot of people. Web 2.0 democratized information. Web 3.0 is about all that, anywhere, where mobility and connectivity converge in our lifestyle."[20] Last year, Nokia surveyed 200 million advanced users in Europe and Asia about their mobile habits, and it turns out that making phone calls accounted for just 12 percent of their usage. They spent about 37 percent of their time text messaging, 16 percent using multimedia (watching videos or listening to music), 14 percent delving into their contact directory and calendar, 8 percent browsing, and 4 percent playing games.[21]

The standardization of wireless networking has set the common PC free as well. No longer chained to their desks, laptop computer users find it liberating to have the mobility and flexibility to work on the Internet or company network anywhere they can tap into a wireless network. Wireless networks use a technology called Wi-Fi, from the term *wireless fidelity*. (Techies call Wi-Fi by its official name, 802.11.) Wireless local-area networks in hotel rooms, coffee shops, and airport lounges allow users with laptops outfitted with wireless modems to connect to the Web and download at 50 times the speed of typical dial-up connections. People are taking the Internet with them, tapping in anytime and anywhere to gather information and transact business.

## Computer Networks

Perhaps the most dynamic change in business technology has been the move away from mainframe computers that serve as the centre of information processing and toward network systems that allow many users to access information at the same time. In an older system, the mainframe performed all tasks and sent the results to a "dumb" terminal that could not perform those tasks itself. In a **network computing system** (also called **client/server computing**), personal computers (clients) can obtain needed information from huge databases in a central computer (the server). Networks connect people to people and people to data; they provide companies with the following benefits:

* save time and money,
* provide easy links across functional boundaries, and
* allow employees to see complete information.

**network computing system (client/server computing)** Computer systems that allow personal computers (clients) to obtain needed information from huge databases in a central computer (the server).

Networks have their drawbacks as well. Maintaining a fleet of finicky desktop PCs can be expensive. The cost of the computer itself is just the down payment. Computing costs go up with productivity losses as you upgrade and troubleshoot equipment and train employees to use it. By the time you've recouped your costs, it's time for another upgrade. A large part of PC support costs comes from adding software that causes conflicts or disables other software on the system. Making upgrades to two or three PCs in a small home office is annoying; making them to dozens or hundreds of PCs in a corporation is daunting. Using networks requires so many organizational changes and incurs such high support and upgrade costs that some companies that tried networking PCs are now looking at other options.

One option is a hybrid of mainframe and network computing. In this model, applications and data reside on a server, which handles all of the processing needs for all of the client machines on the networks. The client machines look like the PCs that most people

**FIGURE | A.2**

**Types of Popular Computer Software**

| | |
|---|---|
| **Word processing programs** | With word processors, standardized letters can be personalized quickly, documents can be updated by changing only the outdated text and leaving the rest intact, and contract forms can be revised to meet the stipulations of specific customers. The most popular word processing programs include Corel WordPerfect, Microsoft Word, and Lotus WordPro. |
| **Desktop publishing (DTP) software** | DTP combines word processing with graphics capabilities that can produce designs that once could be done only by powerful page-layout design programs. Popular DTP programs include Microsoft Publisher, Adobe PageMaker Plus, and Corel Print Office. |
| **Spreadsheet programs** | A spreadsheet program is simply the electronic equivalent of an accountant's worksheet plus such features as mathematical function libraries, statistical data analysis, and charts. Using the computer's speedy calculations, managers have their questions answered almost as fast as they can ask them. Some of the most popular spreadsheet programs are Lotus 1-2-3, Corel Quattro Pro, and Microsoft Excel. |
| **Database programs** | A database program allows users to work with information that is normally kept in lists: names and addresses, schedules, inventories, and so forth. Using database programs, you can create reports that contain exactly the information you want in the form you want it to appear in. Leading database programs include Q&A, Access, Approach, Paradox, PFS: Professional File, PC-File, R base, and FileMaker Pro for Apple computers. |
| **Personal information managers (PIMs)** | PIMs or contact managers are specialized database programs that allow users to track communication with their business contacts. Such programs keep track of everything—every person, every phone call, every e-mail message, every appointment. Popular PIMs include Goldmine, Lotus Organizer, ACT!, and ECCO Pro. |
| **Graphics and presentation programs** | Computer graphics programs can use data from spreadsheets to visually summarize information by drawing bar graphics, pie charts, line charts, and more. Inserting sound clips, video clips, clip art, and animation can turn a dull presentation into an enlightening one. Some popular graphics programs are Illustrator and Freehand for Macintosh computers, Microsoft PowerPoint, Harvard Graphics, Lotus Freelance Graphics, Active Presenter, and Corel Draw. |
| **Communications programs** | Communications software enables a computer to exchange files with other computers, retrieve information from databases, and send and receive electronic mail. Such programs include Microsoft Outlook, ProComm Plus, Eudora, and Telik. |
| **Message centre software** | Message centre software is more powerful than traditional communications packages. This new generation of programs has teamed up with fax/voice modems to provide an efficient way of making certain that phone calls, e-mail, and faxes are received sorted, and delivered on time, no matter where you are. Such programs include Communicate, Message Centre, and WinFax Pro. |
| **Accounting and finance programs** | Accounting software helps users record financial transactions and generate financial reports. Some programs include online banking features that allow users to pay bills through the computer. Others include "financial advisers" that offer users advice on a variety of financial issues. Popular accounting and finance programs include Peachtree Complete Accounting, Simply Accounting, Quicken, and QuickBooks Pro. |
| **Integrated programs** | Integrated software packages (also called suites) offer two or more applications in one package. This allows you to share information across applications easily. Such packages include word processing, database management, spreadsheet, graphics, and communications. Suites include Microsoft Office, Lotus SmartSuite, and Corel WordPerfect Office. |
| **Groupware** | Groupware is software that allows people to work collaboratively and share ideas. It runs on a network and allows people in different areas to work on the same project at the same time. Groupware programs include Lotus Notes, Frontier's Intranet Genie, MetaInfo Sendmail, and Radnet Web Share. |

use, but they lack the processing power to handle applications on their own. Called *thin-client networks,* these networks may resemble the ill-tempered dumb terminals of the 1980s, but the execution is much better. Users can still use the Windows applications they had been using. In a thin-client network, software changes and upgrades need to be made only on the server, so the cost of ownership can be reduced by 20 percent.

Another option is to rent software and hardware access by way of the Internet as needed instead of trying to maintain your own network. During the Web boom, companies called application service providers (ASPs) ran software at data centres and rented access to these functions to customers who didn't want to buy expensive servers and software. Most ASPs went out of business because CIOs were slow to hand over their critical data to companies with no track record or little experience in their specific industries. However, the fall of little ASPs didn't stop the flow of outsourcing IT functions to big service providers such as IBM. IBM offers pay-as-you go computing, even hourly rentals, involving all types of IT, from server access to supply-chain-management software.

# SOFTWARE

Computer software provides the instructions that enable you to tell the computer what to do. Although many people looking to buy a computer think first of the equipment, it is important to find the right software before finding the right hardware. The type of software you want dictates the kind of equipment you need.

Some programs are easier to use than others. Some are more sophisticated and can perform more functions than others. A business person must decide what functions he or she wants the computer system to perform and then choose the appropriate software. That choice will help determine what brand of computer to buy, how much power it should have, and what other peripherals it needs.

Although most software is distributed commercially through suppliers such as retail stores or electronic retailers, there is some software (called **shareware**) that is copyrighted but distributed to potential customers free of charge. The users are asked to send a specified fee to the developer if the program meets their needs and they decide to use it. The shareware concept has become very popular and has dramatically reduced the price of software. **Public domain software (freeware)** is software that is free for the taking. The quality of shareware and freeware varies greatly. To get an idea of the quality of such programs, find a Web site that rates shareware and freeware programs. For example, Sharewarejunkies.com lists the programs downloaded most often, editors' picks, and links to downloadable programs.

Business people most frequently use software for (1) writing (word processors), (2) manipulating numbers (spreadsheets), (3) filing and retrieving data (databases), (4) presenting information visually (graphics), (5) communicating (e-mail and instant messaging), and (6) accounting. Today's software can perform many functions in a kind of program known as integrated software or a software suite. Another class of software program, called groupware, is used on networks. Figure A.2 describes these types of software. Be aware that all of the software cited is either copyrighted, trademarked, or both.

**shareware**
Software that is copyrighted but distributed to potential customers free of charge.

**public domain software (freeware)**
Software that is free for the taking.

# EFFECTS OF INFORMATION TECHNOLOGY ON MANAGEMENT

The increase of information technology has affected management greatly and will continue to do so. Four major issues arising out of the growing reliance on information technology are human resource changes, security threats, privacy concerns, and stability.

# Human Resource Issues

By now, you may have little doubt that computers are increasingly capable of providing us with the information and knowledge we need to do our daily tasks. The less creative the tasks, the more likely they will be managed by computers. For example, many telemarketing workers today have their work structured by computer-driven scripts. That process can apply to the work lives of customer service representatives, stockbrokers, and even managers. Technology makes the work process more efficient as it replaces many bureaucratic functions. In Chapter 9, we will discuss tall versus flat organization structures. Computers often eliminate middle management functions and thus flatten organization structures.

One of the major challenges technology creates for human resource managers is the need to recruit employees who know how to use the new technology or train those who already work in the company. Often companies hire consultants instead of internal staff to address these concerns. Outsourcing technical training allows companies to concentrate on their core businesses.

Perhaps the most revolutionary effect of computers and the increased use of the Internet and intranets is that of **telecommuting**, also known as **telework**. Mobile employees, using computers linked to the company's network, can transmit their work to the office and back from anywhere as easily as (and sometimes more easily than) they can walk into the boss's office.[22] Info-Tech Research Group now classifies nearly 40 percent of all workers in Canada and the United States as "mobile," meaning that they routinely do at least 20 percent of their "core business functions" remotely.[23] International Data Corp. predicts the number of mobile workers will soar to more than 850 million worldwide in 2009.[24]

Naturally, such work decreases travel time and overall costs, and often increases productivity. Telecommuting helps companies save money by allowing them to retain valuable employees during long pregnancy leaves or to tempt experienced employees out of retirement. Companies can also enjoy savings in commercial property costs, since having fewer employees in the office means a company can operate with smaller, and therefore less expensive, offices than before.[25] For additional information about home-based workers and telecommuting, see Chapters 7 and 12.

Electronic communication can never replace human communication for creating enthusiasm and esprit de corps. Efficiency and productivity can become so important to a firm that people are treated like robots. In the long run, such treatment decreases efficiency and productivity. Computers are a tool, not a total replacement for managers or workers, and creativity is still a human trait. Computers should aid creativity by giving people more freedom and more time. Often they do, but unfortunately many North Americans take the results of their productivity gains not in leisure (as do the Europeans), but in increased consumption, making them have to work even harder to pay for it all. Information technology allows people to work at home, on vacation, and in the car at any time of the day.

# Security Issues

One current problem with computers that is likely to persist in the future is data security breaches. Average annual costs associated with these breaches are shooting up rapidly, costing Canadian public companies $637,000, government organizations $320,000, and private companies $294,000.[26] "Secure" information is typically stolen by hackers who break into companies' networks, employees who steal it, or companies who lose it through incompetence, poor gatekeeping, or bad procedures.[27] Computer security is more complicated than ever before. When information was processed on mainframes, the single data centre was easier to control because there was limited access to it. Today, however, computers are accessible not only in all areas within the company but also in all areas of other companies with which the firm does business. While companies are getting much better at preventing people from getting unauthorized access to data, people who want to penetrate security systems are getting much more sophisticated, so it is really an ongoing competition.[28]

**telecommuting
(telework)**
Occurs when paid workers reduce their commute by carrying out all, or part, of their work away from their normal place of business.

Some of the most common security breaches involve viruses and phishing. A **virus** is a piece of programming code inserted into other programming to cause some unexpected and, for the victim, usually undesirable event. Viruses are spread by downloading infected programming over the Internet or by sharing an infected disk. Often the source of the file you downloaded is unaware of the virus. The virus lies dormant until circumstances cause its code to be executed by the computer. Some viruses are playful ("Kilroy was here!"), but some can be quite harmful, erasing data or causing your hard drive to crash. There are programs, such as Norton AntiVirus, that "inoculate" your computer so it doesn't catch a known virus. But because new viruses are being developed constantly, antivirus programs may have only limited success. Therefore, you should keep your antivirus protection program up to date and, more important, practise "safe computing" by not downloading files from unknown sources and by using your antivirus program to scan disks before transferring files from them.[29]

**Phishing** involves e-mails embellished with a stolen logo for a well-known enterprise (often from financial institutions) that make the messages look authentic. The messages often state something like "Dear Customer" (rather than your name), "Account activation required" or "Your account will be cancelled if you do not verify." When the victims click the link contained in the message, they are sent to phony Web sites that take personal data and use it to commit fraud. The best way to avoid this scam is to never access a Web site through a link in an e-mail message. Instead open a new window and go to the Web site directly.[30] Canadian banks are working together through the Canadian Bankers Association to share information to fight back against threats to online commerce, and phishing is on top of the group's list because attackers have targeted bank customers directly. "We're able to shut these things down within one to three hours by working closely with the RCMP," says Mark Saunders, senior vice-president of enterprise infrastructure at the Bank of Montreal. "But these threats come in every hour and they're not selective, so they'll go after all the financial institutions, which is likely why we've been seeing a lot of phishing over the last year or two."[31]

Cybercrimes cost companies billions of dollars a year. Companies that insure businesses against security breaches are demanding that strong measures be put in place, and it's also becoming the law.[32] Privacy regulations such as Sarbanes-Oxley in the United States (discussed in Chapter 5) and the European Data Protection Act stipulate that organizations doing business in their jurisdiction have systems in place to protect and preserve data from misuse, alteration, or destruction.[33]

Existing laws do not address all of the problems with today's direct, real-time communication. As more and more people log on to the Internet, the number of legal issues likely will increase. Today, copyright and pornography laws are crashing into the virtual world. Other legal questions—such as those involving intellectual property and contract disputes, online sexual and racial harassment, and the use of electronic communication to promote crooked sales schemes—are being raised as millions of people log on to the Internet.

## Privacy Issues

The increasing use of technology creates major concerns about privacy. For example, e-mail is no more private than a postcard. You don't need to be the target of a criminal investigation to have your e-mail snooped. Companies today scan employee e-mail regularly and legally. Just as employers can log and listen to employees' telephone conversations, they can track e-mail in a search for trade secrets, non-work-related traffic, harassing messages, and conflicts of interest. Also, most e-mail travels over the Internet in unencrypted plain text. Any hacker with a desire to read your thoughts can trap and read your messages. Some e-mail systems, such as Lotus Notes, can encrypt messages so that you can keep corporate messages private. If you use browser-based e-mail, you can obtain a certificate that has an encryption key from a company such as VeriSign; the cost is about $10 a year. Of course, legitimate users who want to decrypt your mail need to get an unlocking key.

**virus**
A piece of programming code inserted into other programming to cause some unexpected and, for the victim, usually undesirable event.

**phishing**
E-mails embellished with a stolen logo for a well-known enterprise (often from financial institutions) that make the messages look authentic, but which are used to collect personal data and use it to commit fraud.

The Internet presents increasing threats to your privacy, as more and more personal information is stored in computers and people are able to access that data, legally or illegally. The Internet allows Web surfers to access all sorts of information about you. For example, some Web sites allow people to search for vehicle ownership from a licence number or to find individuals' real estate property records. One key question in the debate over protecting our privacy is: Isn't this personal information already public anyway? Civil libertarians have long fought to keep certain kinds of information available to the public. If access to such data is restricted on the Internet, wouldn't we have to re-evaluate our policies on public records entirely? The privacy advocates don't think so. After all, the difference is that the Net makes obtaining personal information too easy. Would your neighbours or friends even consider going to the appropriate local agency and sorting through public documents for hours to find your driving records or to see your divorce settlement? Probably not. But they might dig into your background if all it takes is a few clicks of a button.

Average PC users are concerned that Web sites have gotten downright nosy. In fact, many Web servers track users' movements online. Web surfers seem willing to swap personal details for free access to online information. This personal information can be shared with others without your permission. Web sites often send **cookies** to your computer that stay on your hard drive. These are pieces of information, such as registration data or user preferences, sent by a Web site via the Internet to a Web browser that the browser is expected to save and send back to the server whenever the user returns to that Web site. These cookies often contain simply your name and a password that the Web site recognizes so that you don't have to re-enter the same information every time you visit. Other cookies track your movements around the Web and then blend that information with a database so that a company can tailor the ads you receive. Some software, known as *spyware*, can be installed on your computer without your knowledge. The spyware can then infect your system with viruses and track your online behaviour.[34]

Do you mind someone watching over your shoulder while you're on the Web? Tim Berners-Lee, the researcher who invented the World Wide Web, led the development of a way to prevent you from receiving cookies without your permission. His Platform for Privacy Preferences, or P3, allows a Web site to automatically send information on its privacy policies. With P3 you can set up your Web browser to communicate only with those Web sites that meet certain criteria.[35] You need to decide how much information about yourself you are willing to give away. Remember, we are living in an information economy, and information is a commodity—that is, an economic good with a measurable value.

## Stability Issues

Although technology can provide significant increases in productivity and efficiency, instability in technology also has a significant impact on business. For example, candy maker Hershey discovered the Halloween trick was on itself when the company couldn't get its treats to the stores on time. Failure of its new $115-million computer system disrupted shipments, and retailers were forced to order Halloween treats from other companies. Consequently, Hershey suffered a 12 percent decrease in sales that quarter. The list of computer glitches that have caused delays, outages, garbled data, and general snafus could go on and on.

What's to blame? Experts say it is a combination of computer error, human error, malfunctioning software, and an overly complex marriage of software, hardware, and networking equipment. Some systems are launched too quickly to be bug-proof, and some executives are too naive to challenge computer specialists. As critical as technology is to business, some of it is not built for rigorous engineering, and people aren't properly trained to use it. As things become more complex, we will probably be prone to more errors.

**cookies**

Pieces of information, such as registration data or user preferences, sent by a Web site over the Internet to a Web browser that the browser software is expected to save and send back to the server whenever the user returns to that Web site.

# TECHNOLOGY AND YOU

If you are beginning to think that being computer illiterate may negatively affect your career, you are getting the point. Workers in every industry come in contact with computers to some degree. As information technology eliminates old jobs while creating new ones, it is up to you to learn and maintain the skills you need to be certain you aren't left behind.

## KEY TERMS

broadband technology  34

cookies  40

extranet  33

information technology (IT)  28

Internet2  34

intranet  33

network computing system (client/server computing)  35

phishing  39

public domain software (freeware)  36

shareware  36

telecommuting (telework)  38

virtual private network (VPN)  33

virtualization  29

virus  39

# CHAPTER 2

# How Economic Issues Affect Business

## LEARNING OBJECTIVES

**AFTER YOU HAVE READ AND STUDIED THIS CHAPTER, YOU SHOULD BE ABLE TO:**

**LO ▶ 1** Explain what capitalism is and how free markets work. As part of this discussion, define supply and demand and explain the relevance of the equilibrium point.

**LO ▶ 2** Define socialism and its benefits and negative consequences.

**LO ▶ 3** Understand communism and the challenges of such a system.

**LO ▶ 4** Describe the mixed economy of Canada.

**LO ▶ 5** Discuss the significance of key economic indicators and the business cycle.

## PROFILE

## Getting to Know Hernando de Soto: Economist for the Poor

A crowd of anxious fans pushes to get a glimpse of a celebrity visiting a poor community in Peru. Who is this person who has the town so excited? A rock singer, a famous athlete, a movie star? No. Would you believe he's an economist? Hernando de Soto, a noted economist, wrote one of Peru's bestselling books and the crowds were eager to hear his ideas about improving the country's economy—and thus their own lives.

Hernando de Soto was born in Peru. He went on to study in Canada, the United States, and Switzerland. Eventually he earned a graduate degree in international economics and law at the University of Geneva. He was successful enough to become managing director of Universal Engineering Corporation, a Swiss consulting firm. He made enough money to retire, but instead decided to devote his time to studying what makes some countries rich and others poor. He returned to Peru and studied the entrepreneurs there to see what held them back. What he learned was that the business owners were locked out of the formal, legal economy because there were no laws that provided property titles. That is, people could have houses, but no titles to them; farms, but no deeds to them; and businesses, but no statutes of incorporation. The lack of formal titling prevented owners from using their property as collateral, and thus prevented the capital embedded in these assets to be used for other purposes. This meant that entrepreneurs could not sell their property and use the money to invest. They also could not borrow money from banks to expand or improve their businesses. De Soto's book *The Other Path* outlined his findings.

De Soto found that another barrier to wealth in Peru and other less developed countries is government bureaucracy. It took de Soto and others 6.5 years and 207 administrative steps in 52 government offices to obtain legal authorization to build a house on state-owned land. It took 289 six-hour days and $1,231 (about 31 times the monthly minimum wage) in fees to legally open a garment workshop. In short, it is often very difficult and very expensive to become an entrepreneur in less developed countries.

De Soto estimates that the value of real estate held, but not owned, by the poor in less developed countries is at least $9.3 trillion. That's a lot of money that could be used to start or expand businesses, hire more people, and create wealth. De Soto's second book, *The Mystery of Capital*, goes into more detail about how property ownership leads to the creation of wealth.

De Soto is now the president of the Institute for Liberty and Democracy, a Lima, Peru–based think tank. He says that two-thirds of humanity is not in a position to participate in a modern market economy, and that is his biggest challenge. De Soto finds this to be true around the world and in countries such as Peru, Egypt, Russia, Africa, and the Philippines. He found, for example, that it takes 25 years of red tape to gain through legal means the kind of home in Manila that people now obtain through squatting. Roughly half of the world's people live in makeshift homes in squatter settlements and work in shadow economics. In many countries, more than 80 percent of all homes and businesses are unregistered. In the Philippines, the figure is 65 percent and in Tanzania, 90 percent. More than one-third of the developing world's GDP is generated in the underground economy, a figure that has increased steadily

over the past decade. He cites Switzerland and Japan as two countries that went from relative poverty to wealth by modifying their property laws.

As you can imagine, de Soto has his share of detractors. Articles have been written challenging his thinking, and his life has been threatened. But such challenges only help him bring the issue of poverty to the forefront and urge countries to change their laws to make prosperity a reality.

Many people don't realize the importance of the economic environment to the success of business. That is what this chapter is all about. You will learn to compare different economic systems to see the benefits and drawbacks of each. You will learn that the mixed economy is the system in Canada. By the end of the chapter, you should understand the direct effect that economic systems have on the wealth and happiness of communities throughout the world.

Sources: Madeleine Albright, "Giving The Poor Their Rights," *Time*, 5 July 2007, http://www.ild.org.pe/en/hernando-de-soto/blog/time/jul07; Hernando de Soto, *The Mystery of Capital: Why Capitalism Triumphs in the West and Fails Everywhere Else* (New York: Basic Books, 2003); Hernando de Soto, *The Other Path: The Invisible Revolution in the Third World* (New York: Harper and Row, 1989); "Hernando de Soto's Biography," www.Cato.org/special/friedman/desoto/; Jeremy Main, "How to Make Poor Countries Rich," *Fortune*, 16 January 1989; and N. Stephan Kinsella (ed.), book review, Journal of Libertarian Studies, Winter 2002; and www.nytimes.com/books/00/12/24/reviews/00124.24skidelt.html.

# HOW ECONOMIC CONDITIONS AFFECT BUSINESS

If you want to understand the underlying situation and conditions in which Canadian businesses operate, it is essential that you (1) have some grasp of economics, (2) be aware of the impact of the global environment, and (3) understand the role of the federal and provincial governments in Canada.

The Canadian economy is an integral part of the world economy. Business firms use labour from other countries, export to and import from other countries, buy land in other countries for their facilities, and receive money from foreign investors. To understand events in the Canadian economy, therefore, one has to understand the world economy.

Why is South Korea comparatively wealthy and North Korea suffering economically, with many of its people starving? Why is China's annual gross domestic product per capita (PPP) of $6,757 much less than Switzerland's $35,633?[1] Such questions are part of the subject of economics. In this chapter, we explore the various economic systems of the world and how they either promote or hinder business growth, the creation of wealth, and a higher quality of life for all.

A major part of business success is due to an economic and social climate that allows businesses to operate freely. Foreign investors like Canada because we have a stable economic and political environment. Investing is risky enough without having to worry about unpredictable governments, massive corruption, and weak laws. Therefore, any change in our economic or political system can have a major influence on businesses.

## What Is Economics?

**economics**

The study of how society chooses to employ resources to produce goods and services and distribute them for consumption among various competing groups and individuals.

**Economics** is the study of how society chooses to employ resources to produce goods and services and distribute them for consumption among various competing groups and individuals. Remember from Chapter 1 that these resources (land, labour, capital goods, entrepreneurship, and knowledge) are called *factors of production* .

Businesses may contribute to an economic system by inventing products that greatly increase available resources. For example, businesses may discover new energy sources, new ways of growing food, and new ways of creating needed goods and services.[2] Ballard Power Systems, a global leader in the design, development and manufacture of hydrogen fuel cells, is doing just this. Among other initiatives, Ballard is working with auto manufacturers to develop the next generation of efficient and clean engines for buses, automobiles, and trucks.[3]

Your buying behaviour falls under the study of macroeconomics. How does understanding spending patterns benefit a country's economy?

This is a close-up of a salmon farm in British Columbia. Environmental groups are concerned that some current mariculture practices create negative environmental impacts such as water pollution (e.g., due to chemicals used to control diseases), transfer of disease from caged species to wild populations, and the death of sea birds, turtles and marine mammals due to entanglement in nets.

There are two major branches of economics: **macroeconomics** looks at the operation of a nation's economy as a whole, and **microeconomics** looks at the behaviour of people and organizations in particular markets. For example, while macroeconomics looks at how many jobs exist in the whole economy, microeconomics examines how many people will be hired in a particular industry or a particular region of the country. Topics discussed in this chapter that are part of macroeconomics include gross domestic product, unemployment rate, and price indexes. Chapter topics that deal with microeconomic issues include pricing and supply and demand.

Some economists define economics as the allocation of "scarce" resources. They believe that resources are scarce and that they need to be carefully divided among people, usually by the government. There's no way to maintain peace and prosperity in the world by merely dividing the resources we have today among the existing nations. There aren't enough known resources available to do that. **Resource development** is the study of how to increase resources and to create the conditions that will make better use of those resources (e.g., recycling and oil conservation).[4] Outside of government, businesses may contribute to an economic system by inventing products that greatly increase available resources such as discovering new energy sources (e.g., hydrogen), new ways of growing food, and new ways of creating needed goods and services.[5] For example, people are starting to raise more fish in pens out in the ocean.[6] Such *mariculture* (the farming of aquatic plants and animals in land-based tanks and ponds or in sea cages) could lead to more food for everyone and more employment. The Green Box recognizes one company for its eco-winery philosophy.

**macroeconomics**
The part of economic study that looks at the operation of a nation's economy as a whole.

**microeconomics**
The part of economic study that looks at the behaviour of people and organizations in particular markets.

**resource development**
The study of how to increase resources and the creation of the conditions that will make better use of those resources (e.g., recycling).

## Growth Economics and Adam Smith

Adam Smith was one of the first people to imagine a system for creating wealth and improving the lives of everyone. Rather than believing that fixed resources had to be divided among competing groups and individuals, Smith envisioned creating more resources so that everyone could become wealthier. The year was 1776. Adam Smith's book, *An Inquiry into the Nations and Causes of the Wealth of Nations* (simply called *The Wealth of Nations*), was later considered the foundation of the study and understanding of the newly developing capitalist industrial society.

## GreenBOX

### Stratus Winery Is LEEDing the Way

There are close to 500 wineries in Canada that provide jobs, preserve valuable agricultural land, and create tourist destinations. The sale of just one litre of Canadian wine provides over $4 in economic value to the Canadian economy. Wine sales in Canada are approaching $5 billion annually, and 40 percent of this total comes from Canadian brands. Canada's wine industry is characterized by new investments in world-class wineries, aggressive new plantings of vinifera varietals, diversified wine offerings, new technology, expanding exports, and greater recognition of the industry's ability to produce fine wines at competitive prices.

Stratus Vineyards, established in 2000, is one company that is achieving success with its eco-winery philosophy. Committed to responsible stewardship of the land, environmental sustainability is a core value of all involved in the design and operation of Stratus. Stratus is a sustainable, innovative winery located in Niagara-on-the-Lake. Its goal is to make limited quantities of premium wine with as minimal a carbon footprint as possible. The winery is the first building in Canada to achieve LEED® (Leadership in Energy and Environmental Design) certification from the Canada Green Building Council and it is the only winery worldwide to achieve this designation fully.

To qualify for LEED certification, the winery had to meet numerous criteria that reduced the negative impact on the environment both during construction and on a permanent, operational basis. Primary features include geothermal technology to heat and cool the building, the use of recycled materials in the construction and design, resource and energy-efficient electrical and plumbing systems, a toxin-free waste management program, herbicide-free vineyards, and a landscape plan that is organic and based on indigenous grasses and plants. For example, it estimated that 80 percent of the energy that is used is free. The company also uses a hybrid, gas-electric vehicle for winery deliveries.

Stratus is a strong example of the sustainable "triple bottom-line": plant, people, and profit. Its wines are critically acclaimed and have become benchmarks of quality within the Canadian wine industry.

Sources: Frederick G. Crane et al., *Marketing*, 7th Canadian ed. (Toronto: McGraw-Hill Ryerson Ltd., 2008), 5–6; Terri Meyer, "Case Studies in Canadian Sustainable Design: Stratus Winery," University of Waterloo, 27 June 2006, http://www.architecture.uwaterloo.ca/faculty_projects/terri/sustain_casestudies/stratus_gallery.html; and "Stratus Vineyards Becomes First Winery Worldwide to Achieve LEED Certification," CSRwire, 15 May 2005, http://www.csrwire.com/News/3943.html.

Adam Smith believed that freedom was vital to the survival of any economy, especially the freedom to own land or property and the freedom to keep profits from working the land or owning a business. He believed that people will work hard if they have incentives for doing so—that is, if they know that they will be rewarded.

He made the desire for improving one's condition in life the basis of his theory. According to Smith, as long as farmers, labourers, and business people (entrepreneurs) could see economic rewards for their efforts (i.e., receive enough money in the form of profits to support their families), they would work long hours and work hard. As a result of these efforts, the economy would prosper—with plenty of foods and all kinds of products available to everyone.

## How Businesses Benefit the Community

Under Adam Smith's theory, business people don't necessarily deliberately set out to help others. They work primarily for their own prosperity and growth. Yet as people try to improve their own situation in life, Smith said, their efforts serve as an "invisible hand" that helps the economy grow and prosper through the production of needed goods, services, and ideas. Thus, the **invisible hand** turns self-directed gain into social and economic benefits for all.

**invisible hand**
A phrase coined by Adam Smith to describe the process that turns self-directed gain into social and economic benefits for all.

How is it that people working in their own self-interest produce goods, services, and wealth for others? The only way farmers in a given area can become wealthy is to sell some of their crops to others. To become even wealthier, farmers would have to hire workers to produce more food. As a consequence, people in that area would have plenty of food available and some would have jobs on the farms. So the farmers' self-centred efforts to become wealthy lead to jobs for some and food for almost all. Stop and think

## Making Ethical Decisions

### Helping After Natural Disasters

Natural disasters have highlighted the need to look beyond ourselves. The 2004 series of tsunamis that were triggered by the Indian Ocean earthquake, the flooding of New Orleans by Hurricane Katrina in 2005, and the 2008 Sichuan earthquake in Sichuan Province, China, are just some of the global events that you may recall. These disasters prompted worldwide efforts to help victims, with billions of dollars raised for disaster relief. While Canadian natural disasters do not generate such attention, examples have included wildfires in British Columbia (e.g., the 2003 wildfires in Okanagan Mountain Provincial Park) and floods in Manitoba (e.g., the 2009 Red River Flood).

Imagine you live in an area where the homes are medium priced. You have plenty of food to eat and spare rooms in your house. A deadly flood hits your neighbouring province. There has not been a national call for you to help out, but you know that the need is great and the ethical thing is for everyone to do his or her part. "We are all Canadians," the news media are saying, and you understand all that such a message means. You can send money to the Red Cross, the Salvation Army, or other charities; you can go to the endangered areas and try to help; or you can offer your home for protection and aid until things get better. What are the potential consequences of each action? What action are you most likely to take, if any? And why? What can ethical business people do to help?

Sources: Anna Mulrine, "To the Rescue," *U.S. News and World Report*, 12 September 2005, 20-26; "The Lost City," *Newsweek*, 12 September 2005, 40-52; various news reports on TV and radio, 2005; and "2004 Indian Ocean Earthquake," Wikipedia, 20 June 2006, http://en.wikipedia.org/wiki/2004_Indian_Ocean_earthquake.

about that process for a minute because it is critical to your understanding of economic growth in Canada and other countries in the world. The same principle applies to other products as well—everything from clothing to iPods.

Smith assumed that as people became wealthier, they would naturally reach out to help the less fortunate in the community.[7] This has not always happened, which is why government regulation in the public interest has always been required. Today, more business people are becoming concerned about social issues and their obligation to return to society some of what they've earned. Worldwide charitable donations in 2007 from Canadian banks totalled approximately $197.2 million, of which approximately $145.3 million remained within Canada.[8] Entrepreneur Bill Gates (the co-founder of Microsoft) and his wife Melinda set up the largest foundation in history, worth some $35.9 billion.[9] Among other initiatives, the Bill and Melinda Gates Foundation works to improve world health by providing vaccines (at least 700,000 lives in poor countries have been saved), training people in health matters, and more.[10] As we mentioned in Chapter 1, it is important for businesses to be ethical as well as generous. Unethical practices undermine the whole economic system; therefore, there needs to be more emphasis on ethics at all stages in business education. You can explore your own ethical position regarding responses to people in need by looking at the Making Ethical Decisions box.

## Progress Assessment

- What is the difference between macroeconomics and microeconomics?
- What does Adam Smith's term *invisible hand* mean? How does the invisible hand create wealth for a country?

# UNDERSTANDING FREE-MARKET CAPITALISM

Basing their ideas on free-market principles, such as those of Adam Smith, business people began to create more wealth than had ever been created before. They hired others to work on their farms and in their factories and nations began to prosper as a result. Business people soon became the wealthiest people in society. While there were great disparities between the wealthy and the poor, there was always the promise of opportunities to become wealthy.

A free market system is evident at a farmer's market. As a buyer, what can you do to ensure that you pay the best price for produce?

**capitalism**

An economic system in which all or most of the factors of production and distribution are privately owned and operated for profit.

The economic system that has led to wealth creation in much of the world is known as capitalism. **Capitalism** is an economic system in which all or most of the factors of production and distribution (e.g., land, factories, railroads, and stores) are privately owned (not owned by the government) and are operated for profit. In capitalist countries, business people decide what to produce, how much to pay workers, how much to charge for goods and services, where to sell these goods and services, and so on. Capitalism is the popular term used to describe free-market economies.

No country is purely capitalist, however. Often the government gets involved in issues such as determining minimum wages and subsidizing certain sectors, as the federal government does in Canada for the agriculture sector. Today, capitalism is the foundation for the economies of Canada, England, Australia, the United States, and most other developed nations. We will discuss Canada's mixed economy in some detail later in this book.

## How Free Markets Work

The free market is one in which decisions about what to produce and in what quantities are made by the market—that is, by buyers and sellers negotiating prices for goods and services. Consumers (such as you and I) send signals to tell producers what to make, how many, in what colours, and so on. We do that by choosing to buy (or not to buy) certain goods and services. Note that just as no country is purely capitalist, no market is truly free. "Free" markets work not just from the interaction of buyers and sellers, but also from government signals (e.g., laws and regulations, taxes, warnings, advice, etc.).

## How Prices Are Determined

In a free market, prices are not determined by sellers; they are determined by buyers and sellers negotiating in the marketplace. A seller may want to receive $50 for a T-shirt, but the quantity demanded at that price may be quite low. If the seller lowers the price,

With 75,000 hotel rooms and an estimated 300,000 visitors, some Vancouverites rented out their homes during the 2010 Vancouver Olympics. Would you pay $36,000 for a two-bedroom condo for one month?

the quantity demanded is likely to increase. How is a price that is acceptable to both buyers and sellers determined? The answer is found in the microeconomic concepts of supply and demand.

## The Economic Concept of Supply

**Supply** refers to the quantity of products that manufacturers or owners are willing to sell at different prices at a specific time. Generally speaking, the amount supplied will increase as the price increases because sellers can make more money with a higher price.

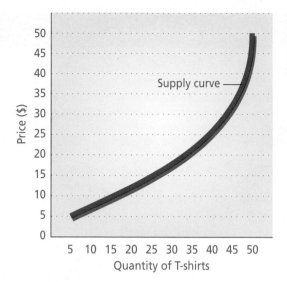

**FIGURE 2.1**

**The Supply Curve at Various Prices**
The supply curve rises from left to right. Think it through. The higher the price of T-shirts goes (the left margin), the more sellers will be willing to supply.

**supply**
The quantity of products that manufacturers or owners are willing to sell at different prices at a specific time.

Economists show this relationship between quantity supplied and price on a graph. Figure 2.1 shows a simple supply curve for T-shirts. The price of the T-shirts in dollars is shown vertically on the left of the graph. The quantity of T-shirts that sellers are willing to supply is shown horizontally at the bottom of the graph. The various points on the curve indicate how many T-shirts sellers would provide at different prices. For example, at a price of $5 a T-shirt, a vendor would provide only five T-shirts, but at $50 a T-shirt the vendor would supply 50 shirts. The supply curve indicates the relationship between the price and the quantity supplied. All things being equal, the higher the price, the more the vendor will be willing to supply. The Spotlight on Small Business box highlights how small businesses especially need to be aware of their capabilities when supplying customers.

## The Economic Concept of Demand

**Demand** refers to the quantity of products that people are willing to buy at different prices at a specific time. Generally speaking, the quantity demanded will increase as the price decreases. Again, the relationship between price and quantity demanded can be shown in a graph. Figure 2.2 shows a simple demand curve for T-shirts. The various points on the graph indicate the quantity demanded at various prices. For example, at a price of $45, the quantity demanded is just five T-shirts, but if the price were $5, the quantity demanded would increase to 35 T-shirts. The line connecting the dots is called a demand curve. It shows the relationship between quantity demanded and price. The Dealing with Change box highlights some challenges when changes occur faster than a company is able to adapt.

**demand**
The quantity of products that people are willing to buy at different prices at a specific time.

## The Equilibrium Point and the Market Price

It should be clear to you after reviewing Figures 2.1 and 2.2 that the key factor in determining the quantity supplied and the quantity demanded is *price*. Sellers prefer a high price, and buyers prefer a low price. If you were to lay one of the two graphs on top of the other, the supply curve and

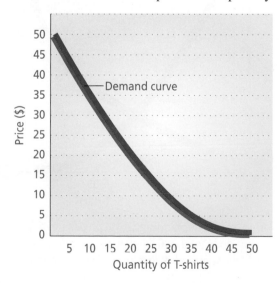

**FIGURE 2.2**

**The Demand Curve at Various Prices**
This is a simple demand curve showing the quantity of T-shirts demanded at different prices. The demand curve falls from left to right. It is easy to understand why. The lower the price of T-shirts, the higher the quantity demanded.

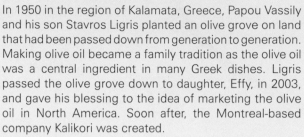

## SPOTLIGHT ON Small Business

### Pressing on with Kalikori

In 1950 in the region of Kalamata, Greece, Papou Vassily and his son Stavros Ligris planted an olive grove on land that had been passed down from generation to generation. Making olive oil became a family tradition as the olive oil was a central ingredient in many Greek dishes. Ligris passed the olive grove down to daughter, Effy, in 2003, and gave his blessing to the idea of marketing the olive oil in North America. Soon after, the Montreal-based company Kalikori was created.

All year long, the olive grove is nurtured. The olives are harvested in November, before all the olives are ripe. They are picked by hand, just as it's been done for hundreds of years. Then the olives are sent to the pressing machine, which washes and sorts the olives and extracts the oil. Within a year, Effy Ligris and partner Spyros Bourboulis imported their first batch of L'Olivier de Vassily Olive Oil. This is a single-variety, cold-pressed olive oil named after Ligris' grandfather.

Because of the early harvest, the amount of oil that is produced is small but of premium quality. The high quality is partly due to the rocky soil of the mountainous Kalamata region. The small green olives produced in the grove are the only ones used, as the overall product is not a blend. L'Olivier de Vassily was an instant success, so much so that the 4,000 units Kalikori imported sold out to specialty food shops within a few months, without any chance of restocking until the next year's harvest.

"Stocking too little or too much is a serious problem facing many startups," says Bakr Ibrahim, director of the Centre for Small Business and Entrepreneurial Studies at Concordia University. "But in the first year, they were only trying to test the market. Good entrepreneurs will test the market and use their gut feeling."

In 2007 the business partners knew that their business was in trouble when fire spread across Greece. While the olive grove that produced the olives for their cold-pressed olive oil wasn't torched, there were concerns about an insufficient harvest. To its credit, the company also imported red wine vinegar and handpicked sea salt. Ibrahim believes that this kind of diversification is the best way to combat impending olive oil supply problems. By increasing its vinegar production and choosing other complementary products, all of the company's products may not be affected by the same weather conditions.

Ligris believes there is a growing market for her rather expensive specialty product. "The small estate olive oils that are produced by the family are usually the real deal, the good stuff," she says. At $23 to $27 for a 375-millilitre bottle (compared with $6 to $9 for a bottle double that size of standard supermarket-variety oil), they are premium-priced to reflect the quality. Consumers seem to buy into Ligris' belief. Kalikori's sales more than doubled in the second year, and in the third year, sales were five times the first, at 20,000 units. In 2008, the company was seeking U.S. distributors to bring its products to the United States.

Sources: "L'Olivier de Vassily Olive Oil," Kalikori, 9 August 2008, http://kalikorioliveoil.com/en/about.html; and Regan Ray, "Slippery Business," *Canadian Business Magazine*, 24 September 2007, http://www.canadianbusiness.com/managing/strategy/article.jsp?content=20070918_19919_19919.

---

| **FIGURE** | **2.3** |
|---|---|

**The Equilibrium Point**
The place where quantity demanded and supplied meet is called the equilibrium point. When we put both the supply and demand curves on the same graph, we find that they intersect at a price where the quantity supplied and the quantity demanded are equal. In the long run, the market price will tend toward the equilibrium point.

**market price**
The price determined by supply and demand.

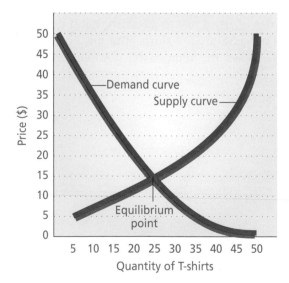

the demand curve would cross. At that crossing point, the quantity demanded and the quantity supplied are equal. Figure 2.3 illustrates that point. At a price of $15, the quantity of T-shirts demanded and the quantity supplied are equal (25 shirts). That crossing point is known as the *equilibrium point* or the *equilibrium price*. In the long run, that price would become the market price. **Market price**, then, is determined by supply and demand.

Supporters of a free market would argue that, because supply and demand interactions determine prices, there is no need for government involvement or government planning. If surpluses develop (i.e., if quantity supplied exceeds quantity demanded), a signal is sent to sellers to lower the price. If shortages develop (i.e., if quantity supplied is less than quantity demanded), a signal is sent to sellers to increase

## DEALING with CHANGE

### Adapting to Swings in Demand

Imagine that your local professional hockey team has not been winning many games in the last few years. We're sure that many of you can identify with that. Ticket prices are set and the season begins. Because of a few new people on the team, the team begins winning game after game and the demand for tickets goes up. The owners cannot raise the prices without creating great tumult among the fans, so the price remains stable. But an informal market (among fans) grows for tickets, often on the Internet. Prices for these tickets usually go up because interested purchasers may be willing to pay more than the ticket's face value. Revenue also goes up for the owners because they sell a lot more hot dogs and beverages.

But what happens if the team starts losing again? Demand for tickets falls. The owners begin losing money at the concession stand. What can the owners do to adjust? You can see how adapting to changes in demand are often difficult to do.

The same is true with auto sales. When gas prices go up dramatically, as they did in 2008, auto dealers find themselves with many large SUVs and light trucks in their inventories. This created opportunities as sales of subcompacts, compacts, and small sport utility vehicles jumped dramatically when consumers shifted sharply to more fuel-efficient models because of the gas-price shock. Toyota Canada Inc., for example, smashed a company record for July 2008 as sales shot up 18.3 percent. Business for the Corolla compact jumped 36 percent and sales for its hybrid Prius soared 137 percent. What other examples could you cite that show the lag between changes in supply and/or demand and the reaction by business people?

Sources: Tony Van Alphen, "Canadian Auto Sales Back in Gear," *The Toronto Star*, 2 August 2008, http://www.thestar.com/article/471543; and Victoria Murphy, "Seattle's Best Kept Secret," *Forbes*, 25 April 2005, 86–88.

---

the price. Eventually, supply will again equal demand if nothing interferes with market forces. Such price swings were evident when the oil supply was cut because of Hurricane Katrina. When supplies were low because of the hurricane, the price of gasoline went up (dramatically). When supplies were again plentiful, the price of gas fell.

In countries without a free market, there is no such mechanism to reveal to businesses (via price) what to produce and in what amounts, so there are often shortages (not enough products) or surpluses (too many products). In such countries, the government decides what to produce and in what quantity, but the government has no way of knowing what the proper quantities are. Furthermore, when the government interferes in otherwise free markets, such as when it subsidizes farm goods, surpluses and shortages may also develop.

## Competition Within Free Markets

Economists generally agree that four different degrees of competition exist: (1) perfect competition, (2) monopolistic competition, (3) oligopoly, and (4) monopoly.

**Perfect competition** exists when there are many sellers in a market and no seller is large enough to dictate the price of a product. Under perfect competition, sellers produce products that appear to be identical. Agricultural products (e.g., apples, corn, potatoes) are often considered to be the closest examples of such products. You should know, however, that there are no true examples of perfect competition. Today, government price supports and drastic reductions in the number of farms make it hard to argue that even farming is an example of perfect competition.

**Monopolistic competition** exists when a large number of sellers produce products that are very similar but are perceived by buyers as different (e.g., hot dogs, candy, and T-shirts). Under monopolistic competition, product differentiation (the creation of real or perceived product differences) is a key to success. The fast-food industry, in which there are often promotional battles between hamburger restaurants, offers a good example of monopolistic competition.

An **oligopoly** occurs when a few sellers dominate a market. Oligopolies exist in industries that produce products in the areas of oil and gas, tobacco, automobiles, aluminum, and

**perfect competition**
The market situation in which there are many sellers in a market and no seller is large enough to dictate the price of a product.

**monopolistic competition**
The market situation in which a large number of sellers produce products that are very similar but that are perceived by buyers as different.

**oligopoly**
A form of competition in which just a few sellers dominate the market.

Although WestJet Airlines Ltd. operates within an oligopoly in Canada, it still has to listen to the needs of its customers and try to be innovative. Check-in choices include traditional counter, Web, mobile, self-service kiosks, and flow-through check-in.

aircraft. One reason some industries remain in the hands of a few sellers is that the initial investment required to enter the business is tremendous. In an oligopoly, prices for products from different companies tend to be close to the same. The reason for this is simple. Intense price competition would lower profits for all competitors, since a price cut on the part of one producer would most likely be matched by the others. As in monopolistic competition, product differentiation, rather than price, is usually the major factor in market success.

**monopoly**
A market in which there is only one seller for a product or service.

A **monopoly** occurs when there is only one seller for a good or service, and that one seller controls the total supply of a product and the price. Traditionally, monopolies were common in areas such as water, electricity, and telephone services that were considered essential to a community.[11] As a result of continuing deregulation (this will be discussed in more detail in Appendix B), there are fewer examples in Canada of a monopoly. Figure 2.4 highlights where these forms of free-market competition fall when one considers the number of sellers (i.e., competitors) in the marketplace.

| FIGURE | 2.4 |

**Free-Market Competition**

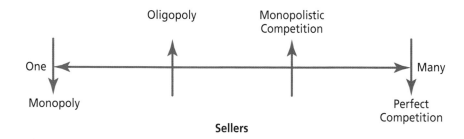

## Benefits and Limitations of Free Markets

The free market—with its competition and incentives—was a major factor in creating the wealth that industrialized countries now enjoy. Free-market capitalism, more than any other economic system, provides opportunities for poor people to work their way out of poverty.

The free market allows open competition among companies. Businesses must provide customers with quality products at fair prices with good service. Otherwise, they will lose customers to those businesses that do provide good products, good prices, and good service.

Yet even as free-market capitalism has brought prosperity, it has brought inequality as well. Business owners and managers make more money and have more wealth than workers. There is much poverty, unemployment, and homelessness. People who are old, disabled, or sick may not be able to support themselves.

Smith assumed that as people became wealthier, they would naturally reach out and help the less fortunate in the community. As was discussed earlier, while this has not always happened, business people are becoming more concerned about social issues and their obligation to return to society some of what they've earned. For example, Warren Buffet, CEO of Berkshire Hathaway and ranked as one of the world's wealthiest people, has pledged to give away most of his money to the Bill and Melinda Gates Foundation.[12] In another example, Cirque du Soleil dedicates one percent of its revenues to social and cultural programs in the community.[13]

One of the dangers of free markets is that business people and others may let greed dictate how they act. Recent charges made against some big businesses indicate the scope of this danger. We hear more and more examples of business people deceiving the public about their products and others deceiving their shareholders about the value of their stock.[14] All of this was done to increase the executives' personal assets.

Clearly, some government rules and regulations are necessary to make sure that all of a business's stakeholders are protected and that people who are unable to work get the basic care they need. To overcome the limitations of capitalism, some countries have adopted an economic system called socialism. It, too, has its good and bad points. We explore the advantages and disadvantages of socialism after the Progress Assessment questions.

## Progress Assessment

- How do business people know what to produce and in what quantity?
- How are prices determined?
- Describe the four degrees of competition.
- What are some of the limitations of free markets?

# UNDERSTANDING SOCIALISM

**Socialism** is an economic system based on the premise that some, if not most, basic businesses—such as steel mills, coal mines, and utilities—should be owned by the government so that profits can be evenly distributed among the people.[14] Entrepreneurs often own and run the smaller businesses, but private businesses and individuals are taxed relatively steeply to pay for social programs.

Socialists acknowledge the major benefit of capitalism—wealth creation—but believe that wealth should be more evenly distributed than occurs in free-market capitalism. They believe that the government should be the agency that carries out the distribution. The major benefit of socialism is supposed to be social equality as income is taken from the wealthier people, in the form of taxes, and redistributed to the poorer members of the population through various government programs. Free education, health care, child care, and unemployment insurance are some of the benefits evident in socialist countries.

Socialism may create more equality than capitalism, but it takes away some of business people's incentives to work hard, as their profits will be heavily taxed. For example, tax rates in some nations once reached 85 percent. Socialism also results in fewer inventions and less innovation because those who come up with new ideas usually don't receive as much reward as they would in a capitalist system. Generally speaking, over the past decade or so, most socialist countries have simply not kept up with more capitalist countries in new inventions, job creation, or wealth creation.[15]

Communism may be considered an advanced version of socialism. We shall explore that system next.

**socialism**
An economic system based on the premise that some, if not most, basic businesses should be owned by the government so that profits can be evenly distributed among the people.

Socialism has been much more successful in some countries than in others. The photo on the left of Denmark's modern and clean transportation systems reflects the relative prosperity of that country. India (right photo) is not doing nearly as well, but it is experiencing economic growth as a result of a move away from agriculture toward more services and industrial firms. What other factors could account for this disparity in the economic success of these two socialist countries?

# UNDERSTANDING COMMUNISM

The nineteenth-century German political philosopher Karl Marx saw the wealth created by capitalism, but he also noted the poor working and living conditions of labourers in his time. He decided that workers should take ownership of businesses and share in the wealth. In 1848, he wrote *The Communist Manifesto*, outlining the process, thus becoming the father of communism.

**communism**

An economic and political system in which the state (the government) makes all economic decisions and owns almost all of the major factors of production.

**Communism** is an economic and political system in which the state (the government) makes *almost all* economic decisions and owns almost all of the major factors of production. Communism affects personal choices more than socialism does. For example, some communist countries have not allowed their citizens to practise certain religions, change jobs, or move to the town of their choice.

One problem with communism is that the government has no way of knowing what to produce because prices don't reflect supply and demand as they do in free markets. As a result, shortages of many items may develop, including shortages of food and basic clothing. Another problem with communism is that it doesn't inspire business people to work hard, because the government takes most of their earnings. Therefore, although communists once held power in many nations around the world, communism is slowly disappearing as an economic form.

Most communist countries today are suffering economic depression, and some people (for example, in North Korea) are starving. Some parts of the former Soviet Union remain under communist concepts, but the movement there, until recently, was toward free markets. The trend toward free markets is also appearing in Vietnam and parts of China.[16]

# THE TREND TOWARD MIXED ECONOMIES

The nations of the world have largely been divided between those that followed the concepts of capitalism and those that adopted the concepts of communism or socialism. Thus, to sum up the preceding discussion, the two major economic systems vying for dominance in the world today can be defined as follows:

1. **Free-market economies** exist when the market largely determines what goods and services are produced, who gets them, and how the economy grows. *Capitalism* is the popular term used to describe this economic system.

2. **Command economies** exist when the government largely decides what goods and services are produced, who gets them, and how the economy will grow. *Socialism* and *communism* are the popular terms used to describe variations of this economic system.

**free-market economy**
An economy in which the market largely determines what goods and services are produced, who gets them, and how the economy grows.

**command economy**
An economy in which the government largely decides what goods and services are produced, who gets them, and how the economy will grow.

Experience has shown that neither of these systems has resulted in optimum economic conditions. Free-market mechanisms haven't been responsive enough to the needs of the poor, the old, or the disabled. Some people also believe that businesses in free-market economies have not done enough to protect the environment. Over time, voters in free-market countries, such as Canada, have therefore elected officials who have adopted social and environmental programs such as medicare, unemployment compensation, and various clean air and water acts.

Socialism and communism, for their part, haven't always created enough jobs or wealth to keep economies growing fast enough. As a consequence, communist governments are disappearing and socialist governments have been cutting back on social programs and lowering taxes for businesses and workers. The idea is to generate more business growth and thus generate more revenue.[17]

The trend, then, has been for so-called socialist countries (e.g., France) to move toward more capitalism. We say "so-called" because no country in the world is purely capitalist or purely socialist. All countries have some mix of the two systems. Thus, the long-term global trend is toward a blend of capitalism and socialism. This trend likely will increase with the opening of global markets as a result of the Internet.[18] The net effect of capitalist systems moving toward socialism and socialist systems moving toward capitalism is the emergence throughout the world of mixed economies.

**Mixed economies** exist where some allocation of resources is made by the market and some is made by the government. Most countries don't have a name for such a system. If the dominant way of allocating resources is by free-market mechanisms, then the leaders of such countries still call their system capitalism. If the dominant way of allocating resources is by the government, then the leaders call their system socialism. Figure 2.5 compares the various economic systems.

**mixed economies**
Economic systems in which some allocation of resources is made by the market and some by the government.

## Progress Assessment

- What led to the emergence of socialism?
- What are the benefits and drawbacks of socialism?
- What are the characteristics of a mixed economy?

| | Capitalism | Socialism | Communism | Mixed Economy |
|---|---|---|---|---|
| **Social and economic goals** | Private ownership of land and business. Freedom and the pursuit of happiness. Free trade. Emphasis on freedom and the profit motive for economic growth. | Public ownership of major businesses. Some private ownership of smaller businesses and shops. Government control of education, health care, utilities, mining, transportation and media. Very high taxation. Emphasis on equality. | Public ownership of all businesses. Government-run education and health care. Emphasis on equality. Many limitations on freedom, including freedom to own businesses, change jobs, buy and sell homes, and assemble to protest government actions. | Private ownership of land and business with government regulation. Government control of some institutions (e.g., mail). High taxation for the common welfare. Empasis on a balance between freedom and equality. |
| **Motivation of workers** | Much incentive to work efficiently and hard, because profits are retained by owners. Workers are rewarded for high productivity. | Capitalist incentives exist in private businesses. Government control of wages in public institutions limits incentives. | Very little incentive to work hard or to produce quality products. | Incentives are similar to capitalism except in government-owned enterprises, which have few incentives. |
| **Control over markets** | Complete freedom of trade within and among nations. No government control of markets. | Some markets are controlled by the government and some are free. Trade restrictions among nations vary and include some free trade agreements. | Total government control over markets except for illegal transactions. | Some government control of trade within and among nations (trade protectionism). |
| **Choices in the market** | A wide variety of products is available. Almost no scarcity or oversupply exists for long because supply and demand control the market. | Variety in the marketplace varies considerably from country to country. Choice is directly related to government involvement in markets. | Very little choice among competing products. | Similar to capitalism, but scarcity and oversupply may be caused by government involvement in the market (e.g., subsidies for farms). |

**FIGURE** | **2.5**

Comparisons of Key Economic Systems

# CANADA'S MIXED ECONOMY

Like most other nations of the world, Canada has a mixed economy. The degree of government involvement in the economy today—in areas such as health care, education, and business regulation, just to name a few—is a matter of some debate. (In Chapter 4, we will discuss the role of government in more detail.) The government's perceived goal is to grow the economy while maintaining some measure of social equality. The goal is very hard to attain. Nonetheless, the basic principles of freedom and opportunity should lead to economic growth that is sustainable.

Several features have played a major role in Canada becoming an independent economic entity with high government involvement in the economy. First, we are one of the largest countries in the world geographically, but we have a small population (approximately 33.6 million in early 2009).[19] We have one of the lowest population densities in the world.

Most important, our neighbour to the south has ten times the population and an economy even greater than that proportion, speaks our language, is very aggressive economically, and is the most powerful country in the world. The United States exerts a very powerful influence on Canada as our largest trading partner. (We will discuss details in Chapter 3.)

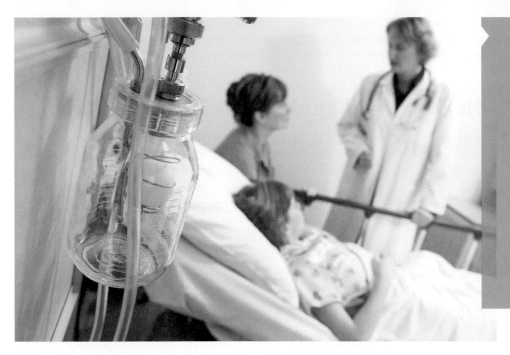

Governed by the Canada Health Act, public care is designed to make sure that all eligible people in the country have reasonable access to insured health services on a prepaid basis, without direct charges at the point of service. Private care covers anything beyond what the public system will pay for. Who would benefit from private health coverage? What happens if someone is not eligible for private coverage?

To control our destiny, Canadian governments have passed many laws and regulations to ensure that significant economic and cultural institutions, such as banks, insurance companies, and radio and TV stations, remain under Canadian control. (Even powerful countries like the United States and Japan have similar regulations.)

All of these factors led to the Canadian capitalist system taking on many characteristics of a mixed economy. Massive government support was necessary to build our first national rail line, the CPR, in the 1880s. When air transport was beginning in the 1930s no company wanted to risk investing heavily in such a large country with only 10 million people spread thinly across the land. So the government set up Air Canada (then called Trans Canada Airlines) to transport mail, people, and freight. There are many such examples of government action to protect the national interest.

In the 1980s, many countries, including Canada, began to reduce government involvement in, and regulation of, the economy. This trend toward deregulation was widespread. In Canada, airlines, banks, and the trucking industry have all seen a marked reduction in regulatory control.

This trend continues today as groups lobby the government to relax regulations to allow them to be more competitive. For example, to encourage competitiveness, the Competition Policy Review Panel recommends lowering barriers to foreign investment in a number of industries, including telecommunications and air transportation.[20] The Conference Board of Canada has released a report that warns that Canadian industries need to do a better job competing for global investment dollars, attracting foreign investors, and establishing new investments overseas.[21]

There are also many new players entering the Canadian marketplace that are competing with publicly funded (i.e., government-funded) institutions. One such industry is health care. Canada's health care spending in 2007 was expected to reach $160.1 billion, with public-sector spending representing $113.0 billion (70.6 percent) and private-sector spending (including privately insured and out-of-pocket expenses) representing the balance.[22] Private health care supporters continue to lobby for a greater presence in Canada. In the years to come, we can expect to see more examples of our mixed economy moving toward a more capitalist system, as the private sector will play a greater role in delivering some goods and services (e.g., health care) that have historically been managed by public institutions. Keep in mind that during tough economic times, voters demand more government involvement. Thus, it is a traditional and desirable role of government to increase expenditures (e.g., provide financial aid to industries, increase spending on infrastructure, etc.) to support and stabilize the economy. The question is how much involvement, debt, etc. is appropriate.

# UNDERSTANDING CANADA'S ECONOMIC SYSTEM

The strength of the economy has a tremendous effect on business. When the economy is strong and growing, most businesses prosper and almost everyone benefits through plentiful jobs, reasonably good wages, and sufficient revenues for the government to provide needed goods and services. When the economy is weak, however, businesses are weakened, employment and wages fall, and government revenues decline as a result.

Because business and the economy are so closely linked, business literature is full of economic terms and concepts. It is virtually impossible to read business reports with much understanding unless you are familiar with the economic concepts and terms being used. One purpose of this chapter is to help you learn additional economic concepts, terms, and issues—the kinds that you will be seeing daily if you read the business press, as we encourage you to do.

## Key Economic Indicators

Three major indicators of economic conditions are (1) the gross domestic product (GDP), (2) the unemployment rate, and (3) the price indexes. Another important statistic is the increase or decrease in productivity. When you read business literature, you'll see these terms used again and again. It will greatly increase your understanding if you learn the terms now.

### Gross Domestic Product

**gross domestic product (GDP)**
The total value of goods and services produced in a country in a given year.

**Gross domestic product (GDP)** is the total value of final goods and services produced in a country in a given year. Either a domestic company or a foreign-owned company may produce the goods and services included in the GDP as long as the companies are located within the country's boundaries. For example, production values from Japanese auto-maker Toyota's factory in Cambridge, Ontario, would be included in the Canadian GDP. Likewise, revenue generated by the Ford Motor Company car factory in Mexico would be included in Mexico's GDP, even though Ford Motor Company is a U.S.-owned company.

If GDP growth slows or declines, there are often many negative effects on business. As noted in Figure 2.6, GDP growth has been slowing down in recent years. According to Statistics Canada, "2008 marked the first decline in exports since 2003 as trade of manufactured goods, particularly related to forestry and automotive products, were hard hit. Domestic demand grew at a slower pace than 2007, as growth of personal spending

**FIGURE | 2.6**

**Canadian Real GDP, 2003–2008**

Source: Economic Accounts Key Indicators, Canada, Statistics Canada, Provincial and Territorial Economic Accounts Review, Catalogue Number 13-016-X, www. statcan.gc.ca/pub/13-016-x/ 2009001/t/tab0101-eng.htm.

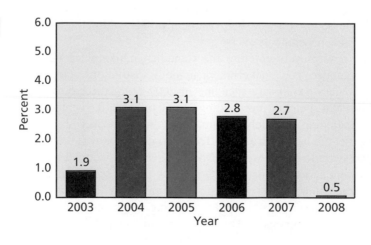

decelerated and housing construction slowed. Growth in services industries generally slowed."[23] An Economist Intelligence Unit report forecast that the real GDP would fall by 2.9 percent in 2009, driven by falls in real private consumption and investment. As well, it expected that weak global trade would cause a trade deficit in 2009.[24] Was this report accurate?

What can account for increases in GDP? A major influence on the growth of GDP is how productive the workforce is—that is, how much output workers create with a given amount of input. This is linked to the combination of creating jobs, working longer hours, or working smarter. Working smarter means being more productive through the use of better technology and processes and a more educated and efficient workforce. In the past, GDP growth has been affected by rising employment (to be discussed soon), low inflation, and low interest rates.[25]

The more you produce, the higher the GDP and vice versa. The economy benefits from a strong GDP. Money that is earned from producing goods and services goes to the employees that produce them in the form of wages. People who own the business generate a return on their investment, and government benefits from tax collection. A strong economy usually leads to a high standard of living for Canadians. The term **standard of living** refers to the amount of goods and services people can buy with the money they have. This includes homes, cars, trips, and the like.

Note that this is different from quality of life. **Quality of life** refers to the general well-being of a society in terms of political freedom, a clean natural environment, education, health care, safety, free time, and everything else that leads to satisfaction and joy. In your opinion, have too many people in Canada sacrificed their quality of life to have a higher standard of living by working more? Since productivity is central to a country's GDP, we will look at this next.

## Productivity in Canada

**Productivity** is measured by dividing the total output of goods and services of a given period by the total hours of labour required to produce them. An increase in productivity means that a worker can produce more goods and services in the same period of time than before, usually through the use of machinery or other equipment.

Labour cost measures the same equation in dollars. The dollar value of outputs is divided by the dollar value of the work hours to arrive at the labour cost per unit. Anything that increases productivity or reduces labour costs makes a business, and a country, more competitive because prices can be lower. Productivity has gone up in recent years because computers and other technology have made the process of production faster and easier for many workers.[26] The higher productivity is, the lower costs are in producing products and the lower prices can be. Therefore, business people are eager to increase productivity. For example, the installation of self-serve registers in stores such as Home Depot and Zellers are attempts to decrease the number of cashiers and as a result, decrease labour costs. Do you prefer to deal with a cashier or check out your own purchases?

Starbucks, like all companies, is concerned about productivity. The faster an employee can make a venti-sized cold beverage, the more profits the store can make and the more productive the employee becomes. When someone discovered that it took two scoops of ice to make a venti-sized drink, a new scoop was invented to cut the production time by 14 seconds. A tall black drip coffee can be made in less than 20 seconds, while a venti Double Chocolate Chip Frappuccino Blended Crème takes closer to 90 seconds.[27] Which drink is more profitable for the store?

Since Canada is a service economy, productivity is an issue because firms are so labour-intensive. As a result of foreign competition, productivity in the manufacturing sector has been rising over the years. However, in the service sector, productivity is growing more slowly because there are fewer new technologies available to assist service workers (e.g., teachers, clerks, lawyers, and personal service providers such as barbers) than there are to assist factory workers. Computers, word processors, and other

**standard of living**
The amount of goods and services people can buy with the money they have.

**quality of life**
The general well-being of a society in terms of political freedom, a clean natural environment, education, health care, safety, free time, and everything else that leads to satisfaction and joy.

**CANADIAN ECONOMY ONLINE, found at http://canadianeconomy.gc.ca, is a one-stop guide to the national economy that provides statistics, federal government facts, and more about economic concepts and events.**

**productivity**
The total output of goods and services in a given period divided by the total hours of labour required to provide them.

| REPORT CARD | | | | | | |
|---|---|---|---|---|---|---|
| | **Economy** | **Innovation** | **Environment** | **Education and Skills** | **Health** | **Society** |
| Australia | B | D | D | B | B | C |
| Austria | C | D | C | C | B | B |
| Belgium | B | C | C | B | n.a. | B |
| Canada | B | D | C | B | B | B |
| Denmark | B | C | C | C | D | A |
| Finland | B | C | A | A | B | B |
| France | D | C | B | C | B | B |
| Germany | D | B | C | B | B | B |
| Ireland | A | A | C | C | C | C |
| Italy | D | D | B | D | B | C |
| Japan | C | B | C | B | A | D |
| Netherlands | A | B | C | B | C | A |
| Norway | A | D | A | C | B | A |
| Sweden | A | B | A | B | B | A |
| Switzerland | A | A | A | B | A | B |
| U.K. | B | B | B | C | D | C |
| U.S. | B | A | D | C | D | D |

Note: Data for the most recent year available used.
Source: Used with permission of the Conference Board of Canada.

According to the Conference Board of Canada, businesses need to work smarter to improve productivity. This includes producing higher-value-added products and services that are worth more in the marketplace. This report card summarizes country ratings in a variety of areas.

technological innovations have contributed to worker productivity. However, one problem is that an influx of machinery may add to the *quality* of the service provided but not to the *output per worker* (productivity).

For example, you've probably noticed that many computers have been installed on your campus. They add to the quality of education but don't necessarily boost professors' productivity. The same is true of some new equipment in hospitals, such as CAT scanners and PET scanners (more modern versions of the X-ray machine). They improve patient care but don't necessarily increase the number of patients that can be seen. In other words, today's productivity measures fail to capture the increase in quality caused by new technology.

Clearly Canada and other countries need to develop new measures of productivity for the service economy, measures that include quality as well as quantity of output. Productivity is extremely important to a country, as it is a measure of its economic prosperity. Canadian businesses are criticized for not spending enough on research and development, relative to other advanced countries. By not doing so, these businesses will fall behind in the fierce global competitive battle. We will discuss the importance of research and development in Chapter 10.

Of course, technological advances usually lead to people being replaced by machines, often contributing to unemployment. We will now examine this important issue.

## The Unemployment Rate

**unemployment rate**
The percentage of the labour force that actively seeks work but is unable to find work at a given time.

The **unemployment rate** refers to the percentage of the labour force that actively seeks work but is unable to find work at a given time.[28] Figure 2.7 describes different types of employment and highlights Canada's unemployment rate over the past six years. The real rate is higher because Statistics Canada does not include people who have given up looking for jobs, those who are working at part-time or temporary jobs, those who stay in or return to school because they cannot find full-time work, and various other categories of

**FIGURE** | **2.7**

**Canadian Unemployment Rate, 2003–2008**

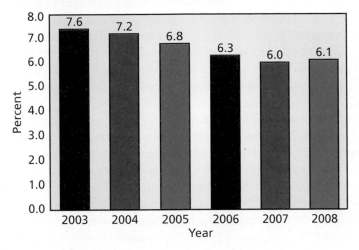

Source: "Labour Force Characteristics," Statistics Canada, 8 January 2009, http://www40.statcan.ca/l01/cst01/econ10.htm.

**The types of unemployment are:**

- *Frictional unemployment* refers to those people who have quit work because they didn't like the job, the boss, or the working conditions and who haven't yet found a new job. It also refers to those people who are entering the labour force for the first time (e.g., new graduates) or are returning to the labour force after significant time away (e.g., parents who raised children). There will always be some frictional unemployment because it takes some time to find a first job or a new job.
- *Structural unemployment* refers to unemployment caused by the restructuring of firms or by a mismatch between the skills (or location) of job seekers and the requirements (or location) of available jobs (e.g., coal miners in an area where mines have been closed).
- *Cyclical unemployment* occurs because of a recession or a similar downturn in the business cycle (the ups and downs of business growth and decline over time). This type of unemployment is the most serious.
- *Seasonal unemployment* occurs where demand for labour varies over the year, as with the harvesting of crops.

people. The unemployment rate is a key indicator of the health of the economy and of society more generally. That is, when economic growth is strong, the unemployment rate tends to be low and a person who wants a job is likely to experience little trouble finding one. On the other hand, when the economy is stagnating or in recession, unemployment tends to be higher.[29]

People are unemployed in Canada for various reasons. Perhaps their employer goes out of business or their company cuts staff. Young persons enter the job market looking for their first job and other employees quit their jobs but have trouble finding new ones. Companies merge and jobs are consolidated or trimmed. Companies transfer their operations to another country, or a branch of a foreign company is closed down. Of course, in a period of economic recession, such as the early 1980s, the early 1990s, and the end of 2008, unemployment increases. When a job is lost, not only is it a loss to society and the economy, but the loss of income can also create hardship for individuals and families.

Armine Yalnizyan, Chief Economist for the Canadian Centre for Policy Alternatives, has written a report titled, *Exposed: Revealing Truths About Canada's Recession*. In this report, he shares that Canada took four years to restore the full-time jobs lost in the 1980s recession and seven years to restore the 1990s recession job losses. Recovery from the 2008 recession could take years. He cites that Canadians are more vulnerable to financial ruin than in any recession since the Great Depression for the following reasons: Canadians have the weakest unemployment insurance system since the 1940s; their personal savings rates are low and comparable to those of the 1930s; and household debt levels were at a record high even before the recession began. The report recommends improving benefits for the unemployed, given that six of out ten unemployed Canadians don't get jobless benefits today. In the last recession, only two out of ten unemployed had no income protection.[30]

One industry that has been particularly hard hit is the manufacturing industry where in 2008 alone, 84,800 jobs were lost.[31] Foreign demand continued to weaken due to the global downturn which, in part, continued to be impacted by the sub-prime mortgage situation and declining consumer confidence. As well, Canadian industries that were driven by discretionary consumer spending, such as motor vehicles and wood products (e.g., for residential construction), also saw a decrease in sales throughout much of 2008.[32] In Chapter 3, you will learn how countries are influenced by what is happening globally.

## The Price Indexes

**inflation**
A general rise in the prices of goods and services over time.

The price indexes help measure the health of the economy by measuring the levels of inflation, disinflation, deflation, and stagflation. **Inflation** refers to a general rise in the prices of goods and services over time. Rapid inflation is scary. If the cost of goods and services goes up by just 7 percent a year, everything will double in cost in just ten years or so. Inflation increases the cost of doing business. When a company borrows money, interest costs are higher, employees demand increases to keep up with the rise in the cost of living, suppliers raise their prices, and as a result the company is forced to raise its prices. If other countries succeed in keeping their inflation rates down, then Canadian companies will become less competitive in the world market.

**disinflation**
A situation in which price increases are slowing (the inflation rate is declining).

**Disinflation** describes a condition where price increases are slowing (the inflation rate is declining). **Deflation** means that prices are actually declining.[33] It occurs when countries produce so many goods that people cannot afford to buy them all. That is, too few dollars are chasing too many goods. **Stagflation** occurs when the economy is slowing but prices are going up regardless.[34]

**deflation**
A situation in which prices are declining.

**stagflation**
A situation in which the economy is slowing but prices are going up regardless.

The **consumer price index (CPI)** is a monthly statistic that measures the pace of inflation or deflation. To calculate the Consumer Price Index, costs of a "basket" of about 600 goods and services for an average family—including housing, food, apparel, medical care, and education—are calculated to see if they are going up or down. For example, Canadian consumers paid, on average, 0.4 percent more in April 2009 than in April 2008 for the products included in the CPI basket.[35] According to Statistics Canada, some of the contributors to the increase were price increases for food and household operations and furnishings, which rose 7.1 percent and 2.8 percent respectively during the 12-month period. Price declines were reported for energy, natural gas prices, and transportation costs (which fell in the wake of year-over-year declines in prices for both gasoline and passenger vehicles).[36] The CPI is an important figure because it affects nearly all Canadians, either directly or indirectly. For example, government benefits (such as Old Age Security and Canada Pension Plan), rental agreements, some labour contracts, and interest rates are based on it.

**consumer price index (CPI)**
Monthly statistic that measures the pace of inflation or deflation.

Other indicators of the economy's condition include housing starts, retail sales, motor vehicle sales, consumer confidence, and changes in personal income. You can learn more about such indicators by reading business periodicals, contacting government agencies, listening to business broadcasts on radio and television, and exploring the Internet. In the Taking It to the Net exercise near the end of this chapter, you will learn that Statistics Canada (www.statcan.gc.ca) is an excellent source of economic information.

## The Business Cycle

**business cycles (economic cycles)**
The periodic rises and falls that occur in economies over time.

**Business cycles** (also known as **economic cycles**) are the periodic rises and falls that occur in economies over time.[37] These fluctuations are often measured using the real gross domestic product.[38] Economists look at a number of types of cycles, from seasonal cycles that occur within a year to cycles that occur every 48 to 60 years. Economist Joseph Schumpeter identified the four phases of long-term business cycles as boom, recession, depression, recovery:

1. An economic boom is just what it sounds like—business is booming. Periods of economic boom bring jobs, growth, and economic prosperity. In Canada this was evidenced in the late 1990s and early 2000s.[39]

**recession**
Two or more consecutive quarters of decline in the GDP.

2. **Recession** is two or more consecutive quarters of decline in the GDP. In a recession, prices fall, people purchase fewer products, and businesses fail. A recession has many negative consequences for an economy: high unemployment, increased business failures, and an overall drop in living standards. The most recent recession was reported at the end of 2008 when the economy reflected two consecutive quarters of GDP decline. How long did this recession last?

3. A **depression** is a severe recession usually accompanied by deflation. Business cycles rarely go through a depression phase. In fact, while there were many business cycles during the twentieth century, there was only one severe depression (1929–1933).

**depression**
A severe recession.

4. A recovery occurs when the economy stabilizes and starts to grow. This eventually leads to an economic boom, starting the cycle all over again.

The goal of economists is to predict such ups and downs. That is very difficult to do. Business cycles are based on facts, but what those facts describe can be explained only by using theories. Therefore, one cannot say with certainty what will happen next. One can only theorize. But one thing is for sure: the economy will rise and fall.[40]

Since dramatic swings up and down in the economy cause all kinds of disruptions to businesses, the government tries to minimize such changes. The government uses fiscal policy and monetary policy to try to keep the economy from slowing too much or growing too rapidly. We will discuss both of these policies in Chapter 4.

## Progress Assessment

- What factors have contributed to the decision to have a mixed economy in Canada?
- Name three economic indicators and describe how well Canada is doing using each one.
- What's the difference between a recession and a depression?

## SUMMARY

1. Capitalism is an economic system in which all or most of the means of production and distribution (e.g., land, factories, railroads, and stores) are privately owned and operated for profit.

**LO ▶ 1** Explain what capitalism is and how free markets work. As part of this discussion, define supply and demand and explain the relevance of the equilibrium point.

### Who decides what to produce under capitalism?
In capitalist countries, business people decide what to produce; how much to pay workers; how much to charge for goods and services; whether to produce certain goods in their own countries, import those goods, or have them made in other countries; and so on.

### How does the free market work?
The free market is one in which decisions about what to produce and in what quantities are made by the market—that is, by buyers and sellers negotiating prices for goods and services. Buyers' decisions in the marketplace tell sellers what to produce and in what quantity. When buyers demand more goods, the price goes up, signalling suppliers to produce more. The higher the price, the more goods and services suppliers are willing to produce. Price, then, is the mechanism that allows free markets to work.

### What is supply and demand?
Supply refers to the quantity of products that manufacturers or owners are willing to sell at different prices at a specific time. Demand refers to the quantity of products that people are willing to buy at different prices at a specific time. The key factor in determining the quantity supplied and the quantity demanded is price.

### What is the relevance of the equilibrium point?
The equilibrium point, also referred to as the equilibrium price, is the point where the quantity demanded is the same as the quantity supplied. In the long run, that price becomes the market price.

**LO ▶ 2**  Define socialism and its benefits and negative consequences.

2.  Socialism is an economic system based on the premise that some businesses should be owned by the government.

    **What are the advantages and disadvantages of socialism?**
    Socialism creates more social equity. Compared to workers in capitalist countries, workers in socialist countries not only receive more education and health care benefits but also work fewer hours, have longer vacations, and receive more benefits in general, such as child care. The major disadvantage of socialism is that it lowers the profits of owners and managers, thus cutting the incentive to start a business or to work hard. Socialist economies tend to have a higher unemployment rate and a slower growth rate than capitalist economies.

**LO ▶ 3**  Understand communism and the challenges of such a system.

3.  Under communism, the government owns almost all major production facilities and dictates what gets produced and by whom.

    **How else does communism differ from socialism?**
    Communism is more restrictive when it comes to personal freedoms, such as religious freedom. With communism, one can see shortages in items such as food and clothing, and business people may not work as hard as the government takes most of their earnings. While many countries practise socialism, only a few (e.g., North Korea) still practise communism.

**LO ▶ 4**  Describe the mixed economy of Canada.

4.  A mixed economy is one that is part capitalist and part socialist. That is, some businesses are privately owned, but taxes tend to be high to distribute income more evenly among the population.

    **What countries have mixed economies?**
    Canada has a mixed economy, as do most other countries of the world.

    **What does it mean to have a mixed economy?**
    A mixed economy has most of the benefits of wealth creation that free markets bring plus the benefits of greater social equality and concern for the environment that socialism offers.

**LO ▶ 5**  Discuss the significance of key economic indicators and the business cycle.

5.  Three major indicators of economic conditions are (1) the gross domestic product (GDP), (2) the unemployment rate, and (3) the price indexes.

    **What are the key terms used to describe the Canadian economic system?**
    Gross domestic product (GDP) is the total value of goods and services produced in a country in a given year. The unemployment rate represents the number of unemployed persons expressed as a percentage of the labour force. The Consumer Price Index (CPI) measures changes in the prices of about 600 goods and services that consumers buy. It is a monthly statistic that measures the pace of inflation (consumer prices going up) or deflation (consumer prices going down). Productivity is the total volume of goods and services one worker can produce in a given period. Productivity in Canada has increased over the years due to the use of computers and other technologies.

    **What are the four phases of business cycles?**
    In an economic boom, businesses do well. A recession occurs when two or more quarters show declines in the GDP, prices fall, people purchase fewer products, and businesses fail. A depression is a severe recession. Finally, recovery is when the economy stabilizes and starts to grow.

## KEY TERMS

business cycles
(economic cycles)  62

capitalism  48

command economy  55

communism  54

consumer price index (CPI)  62

deflation  62

demand  49

depression  63

disinflation  62

economics  44

free-market economy  55

gross domestic product (GDP)  58

inflation  62

invisible hand  46

macroeconomics  45

market price  50

microeconomics  45

mixed economies  55

monopolistic competition  51

monopoly  52

oligopoly  51

perfect competition  51

productivity  59

quality of life  59

recession  62

resource development  45

socialism  53

stagflation  62

standard of living  59

supply  49

unemployment rate  60

## CRITICAL THINKING

Many say that business people do not do enough for society. Some students choose to work for non-profit organizations instead of for-profit organizations because they want to help others. However, business people say that they do more to help others than non-profit groups because they provide jobs for people rather than giving them charity, which often precludes them from searching for work. Furthermore, they believe that businesses create all the wealth that non-profit groups distribute. Can you find some middle ground in this debate that would show that both business people and those who work for non-profit organizations contribute to society and need to work together more closely to help people? Could you use the concepts of Adam Smith to help illustrate your position?

## DEVELOPING WORKPLACE SKILLS

1. Show your understanding of the principles of supply and demand by looking at the employment market today. Consider the high salaries that computer scientists are getting. Explain why some PhDs are being paid less than computer scientists who, in comparison, only have college diplomas or undergraduate degrees. Also consider the comparison in pay between graduates from a business program and those who have a skilled trade, such as electricians.

2. This exercise will help you understand socialism from different perspectives. Form three groups. Each group should adopt a different role in a socialist economy: one group will be the business owners, another group will be workers, and the third will be government leaders. Within your group, discuss and list the advantages and disadvantages to you of lowering taxes on businesses. Then have each group choose a representative to debate the tax issue with the representatives from the other groups.

3. Draw a line and mark one end "capitalism" and the other end "socialism." Mark where Canada is now on that line. Explain why you marked the spot you did. Students from other countries may want to do this exercise for their own countries and explain the differences to the class.

4. Break into small groups. In your group, discuss how the following changes have affected people's purchasing behaviour and attitudes toward Canada and its economy: the war in Iraq; new illnesses such as listeriosis; the growth of the Internet; and the numerous charges against big business behaving illegally and unethically. Have a group member prepare a short summary for the class.

# TAKING IT TO THE NET 1

www.mcgrawhillconnect.ca

### Purpose

To familiarize yourself with recent economic indicators that are important to business decision-makers.

### Exercise

Statistics Canada (StatsCan) produces statistics that help Canadians better understand their country. If you want to find out about Canada's population, resources, economy, government, society, and culture, it is likely that StatsCan can help you. Go to the StatsCan Web site at www.statcan.gc.ca and answer the following questions as they pertain to Canada.

1. What is the latest CPI indicator? What percentage change was there from the previous year? What products reflected an increase in price since last year?

What products reflected a decrease in price since last year? What products make up the eight most volatile components?

2. What is the latest unemployment rate indicator? How many new full-time jobs were created? How many part-time jobs were created? What sectors created these new jobs? What sectors laid off employees? What province saw the greatest increase in jobs? What province reflects the largest unemployment rate for this past quarter?

3. What is the latest GDP indicator? What percentage change was there from the previous month? What sectors contributed to an increase in production from the previous month? What is the dollar value of all products that were produced last month?

# TAKING IT TO THE NET 2

www.mcgrawhillconnect.ca

### Purpose

To become familiar with forecasting and analyzing tools.

### Exercise

1. Analyses of the constantly changing economy are made regularly by various experts and government departments. See if you can find some forecasts for the Canadian economy, using the keywords "Canadian economic

forecasts" to search Web sites such as those offered by the *Globe and Mail* (www.theglobeandmail.com), the *National Post* (www.nationalpost.com), and *Canadian Business* magazine (www.canadianbusiness.com).

2. Visit www.td.com/economics and review the Latest Releases. What are the latest economic forecasts? Is Canada's economic outlook positive? Explain.

# ANALYZING MANAGEMENT DECISIONS

## Canada's Non-Profit Sector

You may recall from Chapter 1 that non-profit organizations are those whose goals do not include making a personal profit for their owners or organizers. Often referred to interchangeably as "civil society," the "voluntary," "third," or "independent" sector, this group of organizations plays a critical role in society and is central to community engagement and to the building of social capital. This sector encompasses service delivery organizations in areas such as health, education, social services, community development, and housing, as well as those that serve "expressive" functions in arts and culture, religion, sports, recreation, civic advocacy, environmental protection, and through business, labour, and professional associations.

**Non-Profit Organizations in 2004:** Non-profit organizations continue to make a significant contribution to the economic and social well-being of Canada. In 2004, the value added, or gross domestic product, of the overall non-profit sector amounted to $83.4 billion, accounting for 6.9 percent of the total Canadian economy. This sector is over seven times larger than the motor vehicle manufacturing industry, and over three times larger than each of the agriculture and the accommodation and food services industry. It also exceeded the value of the entire retail trade industry. Economic activity is dominated by hospitals (42.7 percent), and universities and colleges (21.8 percent).

During this time, $135.5 billion was collected in income. A little over half (55.5 percent on average) was received by hospitals, universities and colleges. From this, 95 percent originated from only two sources: government transfers and sales of goods and services. For the other core non-profit organizations, the situation was quite different. Sales of goods and services were, by far, the most important source of revenue, accounting for 41.7 percent of the total. Government transfers were significant at 20.3 percent. In addition to these funds, core non-profit organizations derived more than one-third of their revenue from three additional sources: membership fees (17.2 percent), transfers from households (13.7 percent), and investment income (5.3 percent).

### Volunteering in 2000 (Most Recent Data Available):

Because the non-profit sector relies heavily on volunteers to undertake its activities, the value of volunteer work is based on the replacement cost approach. That is, it represents how much it would cost to replace volunteer effort if the same services were purchased on the paid labour market. The replacement cost value of work was approximately $14.0 billion, compared to $55.9 billion for paid labour. Put another way, volunteering continues to represent a considerably larger resource to the non-profit sector than monetary and in-kind donations from households. The replacement cost value of volunteering was estimated at $14.0 billion, which was more than double the $6.6 billion of donations received from households.

The use of volunteers relative to paid labour varies considerably by type of organization. The majority of volunteer work is concentrated in three fields of activity: culture and recreation, social services, and religion, with these three groups accounting for nearly three-quarters of the total in the core segment. Large service providers in health and education rely more heavily on paid labour, as do business and professional associations.

The value of volunteer work declined between 1997 and 2000, due to a drop in hours volunteered. While a million fewer Canadians offered volunteer services, those who did invested more hours on average, partially mitigating this decline. Non-profit and voluntary organizations appear to be experiencing difficulties fulfilling their missions or achieving their organizational objectives. Just over one-half report having problems planning for the future, recruiting the types of volunteers needed, and obtaining Board members.

Sources: "Satellite Account of Non-profit Institutions and Volunteering: 1997 to 2004," Statistics Canada, 10 July 2008, http://www.statcan.ca/english/freepub/13-015-XIE/13-015-XIE2007000.pdf; and Michael H. Hall et al., "The Canadian Nonprofit and Voluntary Sector in Comparative Perspective," The John Hopkins Institute for Policy Studies, 2005, http://nonprofitscan.imaginecanada.ca/files/en/misc/jhu_report_en.pdf.

## Discussion Questions

1. If Canada followed a pure capitalist system, how would the non-profit sector be affected?

2. Do you agree with the standard measure of GDP for non-profit organizations (i.e., to include a replacement cost value of volunteer work)? Explain.

3. Why do you think these organizations are experiencing difficulties in recruiting volunteers? How could you be encouraged to volunteer?

## CHAPTER 3

# Competing in Global Markets

## LEARNING OBJECTIVES

**AFTER YOU HAVE READ AND STUDIED THIS CHAPTER, YOU SHOULD BE ABLE TO:**

**LO ▶ 1** Discuss the growing importance of the global market and the roles of comparative advantage and absolute advantage in global trade.

**LO ▶ 2** Explain the importance of importing and exporting and understand key terms used in global business.

**LO ▶ 3** Illustrate the strategies used in reaching global markets and explain the role of multinational corporations in global markets.

**LO ▶ 4** Evaluate the forces that affect trading in global markets.

**LO ▶ 5** Debate the advantages and disadvantages of trade protectionism, define tariff and non-tariff barriers, and give examples of common markets.

**LO ▶ 6** Discuss the changing landscape of the global market.

## Getting to Know Lisa Olfman and Joy Rosen of Portfolio Entertainment Inc.

It all started in a spare bedroom with a borrowed typewriter, a $15,000 bank loan, and a determination to produce and export world-class television programs. Portfolio Entertainment Inc. was founded by co-presidents Lisa Olfman and Joy Rosen in 1991 after the production/distribution firm where they both worked stopped operating. Both partners had relevant experience in the industry. Rosen was formerly Head of Distribution and Marketing for Venture Entertainment Group. She also served in international sales and marketing positions at Sullivan Entertainment (where she was responsible for the worldwide sales of *Anne of Green Gables*). Olfman formerly served as the General Manager and Executive Producer for Venture Entertainment Group. Prior to her work at Venture she was the Supervising Producer for the Emmy Award–winning television series, *Lorne Greene's New Wilderness*. She launched her television career as an Associate Producer on a number of Canadian game shows, and created one of the first trivia-based game shows for CTV called *You Tell Us*.

The company is now one of Canada's leading independent producers and distributors of bold, award-winning television programs for kids, tweens, teens, and adults. Portfolio's newest projects include the preschool animated series *The Cat In The Hat Knows A Lot About That*, featuring Dr. Seuss's iconic "Cat" character; *Hood*, an animated adventure/comedy; and *Chinatown Cops*, a prime time animated comedy. Successful productions include Teletoon's hit series, *Carl*, which has been sold to Nickelodeon in Germany, Jetix in the Netherlands, and ABC in Australia; *Roboroach* for Teletoon, Animania in the United States, and Jetix internationally; *Stolen Miracle*, a Gemini Award–nominated movie of the week for Lifetime in the United States and CTV in Canada; and *Something from Nothing*, a film festival and perennial TV favourite. Offering an ambitious catalogue that consists of more than 2,000 episodes of programming, the company produces and exports over $20 million worth of programming each year. Its distribution arm, Portfolio International, sells to over 100 territories worldwide.

According to Olfman, the company's export success lies in its strong relationships. "We have developed a very strong network of contacts in every country we deal with," says Olfman. "And we don't wait for our phone to ring," adds Rosen. Instead, they're regularly in touch with foreign clients and contacts via telephone and e-mail, and maintain an up-to-date database to keep track of industry changes, such as personnel moves, industry trends, and new channel openings.

The company also advertises in trade magazines and takes booth space at each of the four major international trade shows each year. "That's our opportunity to sit down face-to-face with our clients and talk to them," says Rosen. "Our goal is also to meet new ones and increase our base of contacts. Without having those eyes and ears on the ground in other places, we'd be doing a lot of walking around in the dark."

Due to open markets and global trade, there are many opportunities for Canadian companies beyond our borders. This chapter will introduce some of the topics that explain the opportunities that exist in global markets and the challenges that business people such as Lisa Olfman and Joy Rosen face as they continue to look globally for growth and success.

Sources: Portfolio Entertainment Inc., 31 March 2009, http://www.portfolio entertainment.com/; and Susanne Baillie, "Secrets of an entertainment exporter," Canadian Business Online, 11 December 2003, http://www. canadianbusiness.com/entrepreneur/exporting/article.jsp?content=200312 11_131146_2932.

# THE DYNAMIC GLOBAL MARKET

Have you ever dreamed of travelling to exotic cities such as Paris, Tokyo, Rio de Janeiro, or Cairo? In times past, the closest most Canadians ever got to working in such cities was in their dreams. Today, the situation has changed. It's hard to find a major Canadian company that does not cite global expansion as a link to its future growth.

If a career in global business has never crossed your mind, maybe a few facts will make the possibility of such a career interesting: Canada is a market of more than 33.6 million people, but there are almost 6.8 billion potential customers in the 195 countries that make up the global market.[1] (See Figure 3.1 for a map of the world and important statistics about the world's population.[2]) Perhaps more interesting is that a little less than 74 percent of the world's population lives in developing areas where technology, education, and per capita income still lag considerably behind those of developed (or industrialized) nations such as Canada.[3]

Canadian companies, both large and small, continuously look for opportunities to grow their businesses. For example, Scotiabank's acquisition of E*TRADE Canada from U.S.-based parent E*TRADE Financial Corporation "demonstrates our commitment to pursuing opportunities to grow our wealth management business and drive revenue growth," said Rick Waugh, President and CEO, Scotiabank. "This is consistent with our overall strategic focus on growing our wealth management business in Canada and around the world," he added.[4] Small-business Lija Style Inc. was started by Linda Hipp after she became frustrated with the unflattering golfwear available for women. The company employs 19 people and its products are sold in pro shops, resorts, and department stores. Today, exports (to be discussed soon) represent 80 percent of the company's sales.[5] Canadian companies also scan the marketplace to get ideas on what is working well elsewhere. The Green Box shares one example of how Paris's Velib program is influencing new programs being developed nationally.

Companies also continuously review their global operations to ensure that they are operating at a profit. One Canadian industry that has been particularly hard hit as a result of global trends is the auto industry. Factors such as the increasing price of gas and weakening demand for trucks and sport utility vehicles (SUVs) have forced companies to consider restructuring plans. As a result, thousands of Canadian jobs have been eliminated. Layoffs have occurred at General Motors Canada, Chrysler Canada, Ford Motor

**FIGURE  3.1**

**World Population
By Continent**

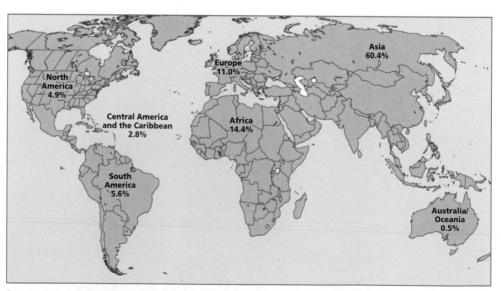

Source: Nations Online, "Current World Population, 2009," www.nationsonline.org/oneworld/world_population.htm.

# GreenBOX

## Rent Your Wheels

The city of Toronto is rolling out a high-tech rent-a-bike program in 2009, similar to a successful one in Paris. Launched in Paris in 2006, Paris's Velib program already has more than 211,000 subscribers who have taken 31 million trips. The Paris program has about 20,000 bikes and 1,400 self-serve rental kiosks. For the equivalent of approximately $45 a year, cyclists can swipe their credit card at a kiosk, unlock a bike, ride it across town and drop it off at another kiosk. The first 30 minutes are free with fees starting at about $1.60 (1 euro) for each additional half hour. The bikes have a distinct appearance that makes them hard to steal, and a penalty is applied for lost or damaged bikes.

According to Councillor Adrian Heaps, head of Toronto's Cycling Committee, the city plans to emulate the best aspects of programs in other jurisdictions and would include automated stations with swipe-card access. A subscription would give users access to a bicycle that is a one-speed or three-speed, with a kind of mousetrap rack on the back where you can put books or a briefcase. At this stage of the planning, there are still some questions that need to be answered. What are the best locations for hubs? How many bicycles could work? Do we do it in the downtown core? Do we do it where there are subways and intermodal transportation hubs?

Such programs are gaining in popularity around the world with the rise of gas prices and environmental consciousness. Montreal and other U.S. cities (e.g., Denver, Minneapolis, and San Francisco) are kicking off similar programs, while Copenhagen, Lyon ,and Barcelona already have bike-sharing programs in place.

Source: Reprinted with permission—Torstar Syndication Services. Adapted from an article that originally appeared in the *Toronto Star* on 21 August 2008; and www.footprintnetwork.org/.

Company of Canada, and many parts suppliers, such as Polywheels Manufacturing and Progressive Moulded Products Ltd.[6] The global market is truly dynamic, and progressive companies continuously scan the business environment to ensure that they take advantage of the opportunities and minimize the impact of threats.

Canada is a large exporting nation. **Exporting** is selling goods and services to another country. **Importing** is buying goods and services from another country. Competition in exporting is very intense and Canadian companies face aggressive competition from exporters based in countries such as Germany, China, and Japan.

**exporting**
Selling goods and services to another country.

The purpose of this chapter is to familiarize you with the potential of global business, including its many challenges. The demand for students with training in global business is almost certain to grow as the number of businesses competing in global markets increases.[7] You might decide that a career in global business is your long-term goal. If you make that choice, prepare yourself to work hard and always be ready for new challenges.[8]

**importing**
Buying goods and services from another country.

# Why Trade with Other Nations?

There are several reasons why countries trade with other countries. First, no country, not even a technologically advanced one, can produce all of the products that its people want and need. Second, even if a country did become self-sufficient, other nations would seek to trade with that country to meet the needs of their own people. Third, some nations have an abundance of natural resources and a lack of technological know-how (e.g., China and Russia), while other countries have sophisticated technology but few natural resources (e.g., Japan and Switzerland). Global trade enables a nation to produce what it is most capable of producing and to buy what it needs from others in a mutually beneficial exchange relationship. This happens through the process of free trade. **Free trade** is the movement of goods and services among nations without political or economic trade barriers. It is often a hotly debated concept. Figure 3.2 offers some of the pros and cons of free trade.

**free trade**
The movement of goods and services among nations without political or economic obstruction.

| Pros | Cons |
|---|---|
| • The global market contains more than 6 billion potential customers for goods and services.<br>• Productivity grows when countries produce goods and services in which they have a comparative advantage.<br>• Global competition and less-costly imports keep prices down, so inflation does not curtail economic growth.<br>• Free trade inspires innovation for new products and keeps firms competitively challenged.<br>• Uninterrupted flow of capital gives countries access to foreign investments, which helps keep interest rates low. | • Domestic workers (particularly in manufacturing-based jobs) can lose their jobs due to increased imports or production shifts to low-wage global markets.<br>• Workers may be forced to accept pay cuts from employers who can threaten to move their jobs to lower-cost global markets.<br>• Moving operations overseas because of intense competitive pressure often means the loss of service jobs and white-collar jobs.<br>• Domestic companies can lose their comparative advantage when competitors build advanced production operations in low-wage countries. |

**FIGURE 3.2**

**The Pros and Cons of Free Trade**

**comparative advantage theory**
Theory that states that a country should sell to other countries those products that it produces most effectively and efficiently, and buy from other countries those products that it cannot produce as effectively or efficiently.

**absolute advantage**
The advantage that exists when a country has the ability to produce a particular good or service using fewer resources (and therefore at a lower cost) than another country.

# The Theories of Comparative and Absolute Advantage

Global trade is the exchange of goods and services across national borders. Exchanges between and among countries involve more than goods and services, however. Countries also exchange art, sports, cultural events, medical advances, space exploration, and labour. Comparative advantage theory, suggested in the early nineteenth century by English economist David Ricardo, was the guiding principle that supported this idea of free economic exchange.[9]

**Comparative advantage theory** states that a country should sell to other countries those products that it produces most effectively and efficiently, and buy from other countries those products it cannot produce as effectively or efficiently. Japan has shown this ability with cars and electronic items. Canada has such an advantage with certain forestry products, aluminum, and various minerals. In practice, it does not work so neatly. For various reasons, many countries decide to produce certain agricultural, industrial, or consumer products despite a lack of comparative advantage. To facilitate this plan, they restrict imports of competing products from countries that can produce them at lower costs. The net result is that the free movement of goods and services is restricted. We will return to the topic of trade protectionism later in the chapter.

A country has an **absolute advantage** if it has the ability to produce a particular good or service using fewer resources (and therefore at a lower cost) than another country.[10] Trade with other countries permits specialization, which allows resources to be used more productively.[11] For instance, Zambia has an absolute advantage over many countries in the production of copper due to its copper ore reserves.

Canada became a diamond producer in 1998 when the Ekati diamond mine opened about 300 kilometres northeast of Yellowknife. Here you see the Diavik Diamond Mine, located on a 20-square-kilometre island in the same area. Today Canada is the world's third largest diamond producer on a value basis, after Botswana and Russia.

# GETTING INVOLVED IN GLOBAL TRADE

People interested in finding a job in global business often think of firms like Bombardier, IBM, and Sony, which have large multinational accounts. The real job potential, however, may be with small businesses. In Canada, small businesses account for 48 percent of the total private labour force and about 85 percent of exports.[12] With the help of government agencies, such as Foreign Affairs and International Trade Canada and Export Development Canada (EDC), many small businesses are becoming more involved in global markets.

Getting started globally is often a matter of observation, determination, and risk. What does that mean? First, it is important to observe and study global markets. Your library, the Internet, and your fellow classmates are good starting points for doing your research. Second, if you have the opportunity, travelling to different countries is a great way to observe foreign cultures and lifestyles and see if doing business globally appeals to you.

## Importing Goods and Services

Imports for goods and services reached $529.4 billion in 2008, as noted in Figure 3.3. Services imports represented 16.3 percent of total imports, or almost one out of every six dollars of total imports. When considering merchandise trade, you will see that three categories (machinery and equipment, industrial goods and materials, and automotive products) represent almost 65 percent of imports. If imports keep increasing as they have, how might this affect our standard of living and quality of life?

Nickelback began as a cover band in Hanna, Alberta, and to date has sold millions of records worldwide. Other Canadian musicians who have exported their music and have global appeal include Avril Lavigne, Celine Dion, and Finger Eleven, just to name a few. Do you prefer to support Canadian talent?

## Exporting Goods and Services

You may be surprised at what you can sell in other countries. The fact is, you can sell just about any good or service that is used in Canada to other countries—and often the competition is not nearly as intense for producers in global markets as it is at home. You can, for example, sell snowplows to the Saudi Arabians. Don't forget that services can be exported as well.

While Canada has a small population, it produces vast quantities of products, ranking high in terms of nations that export. Why is trade so important? Trade with other countries enhances the quality of life for Canadians and contributes to our country's economic well-being. Exports alone account for one in five Canadian jobs and generate 30 cents out of every dollar earned.[13]

Sales abroad by affiliates of Canadian companies are an important means by which Canadian companies engage in international business and are equivalent to almost 85 percent of the value of exports of goods and services.[14] Goods comprise the largest component of trade, being more than seven times as great as services on the export side (and about five times as great on the import side).[15] As highlighted in Figure 3.3, exports of goods and services were approximately $560.5 billion, which included service exports of approximately $70.5 billion. Industrial goods and materials, and machinery and equipment represented the two largest export categories for merchandise trade.

Spend some time reviewing Figure 3.3. By understanding these categories and their impact on our exports (as well as imports), you will realize why you hear so much about specific industries in the news. After all, such activities are vital to our economy. It's important for businesses to be aware of these great opportunities. But don't be misled: Selling in global markets is not by any means easy. Adapting goods and services to specific global markets is potentially profitable but can be very difficult. We shall discuss a number of forces that affect global trading later in this chapter.

 **Visit the Foreign Affairs and International Trade Canada site at http://www.international.gc.ca for updated statistics and information on Canada's state of trade.**

**FIGURE 3.3**

Canada's Merchandise and Service Trade, 2008

| CATEGORIES | EXPORTS | | IMPORTS | |
|---|---|---|---|---|
| | $ Billions | % | $ Billions | % |
| **MERCHANDISE TRADE** | | | | |
| **Industrial Goods and Materials** (incl. metals and metal ores, chemicals and plastics, other industrial goods and materials) | 111.5 | 22.8 | 91.6 | 20.7 |
| **Machinery and Equipment** (incl. industrial and agricultural machinery, aircraft and other transportation equipment, and other machinery and equipment) | 93.0 | 19.0 | 122.6 | 27.7 |
| **Energy Products** (incl. crude petroleum and other energy products such as natural gas and petroleum and coal products) | 125.8 | 25.7 | 53.1 | 12.0 |
| **Automotive Products** (incl. passenger autos and chassis, trucks and other motor vehicles, and motor vehicle parts) | 61.1 | 12.5 | 72.0 | 16.3 |
| **Agricultural and Fishing Products** (incl. wheat, fruits and vegetables, and other agricultural and fishing products such as live animals, feed, beverages, and tobacco) | 40.9 | 8.3 | 28.5 | 6.4 |
| **Forestry Products** (incl. lumber and sawmill products, wood pulp and other wood products, and newsprint and other paper products) | 25.7 | 5.2 | 2.9 | 0.7 |
| **Other Consumer Goods** (incl. apparel and footwear, and miscellaneous consumer goods such as watches, sporting goods and toys, television and radio sets) | 18.2 | 3.7 | 57.5 | 13.0 |
| **Special Transactions Trade and Unallocated Adjustments** | 13.8 | 2.8 | 14.8 | 3.3 |
| **Merchandise Trade Total** | **490.0** | **100.0** | **443.0** | **100.0** |
| **SERVICE TRADE** | | | | |
| **Other Services** (incl. government services such as military activities and commercial services such as accounting, legal, and financial services) | 41.8 | 59.3 | 39.8 | 42.7 |
| **Travel** (incl. business travel and personal travel) | 16.1 | 22.8 | 26.6 | 28.7 |
| **Transportation Services** (incl. air transport services, water transport services, land and other transport services) | 12.6 | 17.9 | 20.0 | 21.6 |
| **Service Trade Total** | **70.5** | **100.0** | **86.4** | **100.0** |
| **Merchandise and Service Trade Total** | **560.5** | | **529.4** | |

Sources: "Canada's Merchandise and Service Trade, 2007," adapted from Statistics Canada Web site "Exports of Goods on a Balance-of-Payments Basis, by Product," Statistics Canada, 13 August 2008, http://www40.statcan.ca/l01/cst01/gblec04.htm; "Imports of Goods on a Balance-of-Payments Basis, by Product," Statistics Canada, 13 August 2008, http://www40.statcan.ca/l01/cst01/gblec05.htm; and "Canada's Balance of International Payments," Statistics Canada, 29 May 2008, http://www40.statcan.ca.libaccess.lib.mcmaster.ca/l01/cst01/econ01a.htm?sdi=services.

## Measuring Global Trade

In measuring the effectiveness of global trade, nations carefully follow two key indicators: balance of trade and balance of payments. The **balance of trade** is a nation's ratio of exports to imports. A favourable balance of trade, or trade surplus, occurs when the value of the country's exports exceeds that of its imports. Overall, Canada has a favourable balance of trade. Since 1990, three of the seven major categories of goods—agricultural and fishing products, forestry, and energy products—have consistently posted trade surpluses and remain in surplus.[16] Two other categories—machinery and consumer goods—have always posted trade deficits.[17] An **unfavourable balance of trade**, or **trade deficit**, occurs when the value of the country's imports exceeds that of its exports. It is easy to understand why countries prefer to export more than they import. If I sell you $200 worth of goods and buy only $100 worth, I have an extra $100 available to buy other things. However, I'm in an unfavourable position if I buy $200 worth of goods from you and sell you only $100.

The **balance of payments** is the difference between money coming into a country (from exports) and money leaving the country (for imports) plus money flows coming into or leaving a country from other factors such as tourism, foreign aid, military expenditures, and foreign investment. The goal is always to have more money flowing into the country than flowing out of the country; in other words, a *favourable* balance of payments. Conversely, an *unfavourable* balance of payments is when more money is flowing out of a country than coming in.

**balance of trade**
A nation's ratio of exports to imports.

**trade deficit (unfavourable balance of trade)**
Occurs when the value of a country's imports exceeds that of its exports.

**balance of payments**
The difference between money coming into a country (from exports) and money leaving the country (for imports) plus money flows from other factors such as tourism, foreign aid, military expenditures, and foreign investment.

## Trading in Global Markets: The Canadian Experience

At first glance, Canada's foreign trade statistics are impressive. As a country, we rank eleventh in the world as both exporter and importer in world merchandise trade.[18] While our abundant natural resources are a major area for exports, developing countries continue to give Canada stiff competition in these areas. When we look carefully at the numbers, we see that we are dependent on one country, the United States. Figure 3.4 shows that over 73 percent of our exports and a little under 69 percent of our imports are with the United States. No other modern industrialized country is so dependent on one country for trade and investments.

Trade in automotive products, for example, stems from agreements that have been signed between the two countries over the years, starting with the 1965 Automotive Products Trade Agreement (also known as the "Auto Pact") and reinforced by the North American Free Trade Agreement (NAFTA) in 1994. The Dealing with Change box highlights the importance of the auto sector to the Canadian economy. In recent years, Canada has been diversifying its trade away from the United States and focusing on other countries. Read the next section to learn about these priority markets.

**FIGURE 3.4**

**Regional Shares of Canada's Trade in Goods and Services, 2007**

|  | Exports % | Imports % |
|---|---|---|
| United States | 73.5 | 68.8 |
| European Union | 9.9 | 10.7 |
| Japan | 2.2 | 2.6 |
| Other OECD | 4.4 | 5.1 |
| Non-OECD | 10.0 | 12.9 |

Source: Statistics Canada, CANSIM database, http://cansim2.statcan.ca/, Table 228-0003.

## Canada's Priority Markets[19]

Technological advances in most fields, primarily in the area of transmission and storage of information, have shattered the archaic notions of how things ought to function, from production and trade to war and politics. The new ways of communicating, organizing, and working are inviting the most remote corners of the world to be actors on the global economic stage. These *emerging economies* are enjoying high growth rates, rapid increases in their living standards, and a rising global prominence. Tapping into these markets is crucial. For example, in thirty years a gain of just 0.1 percent in the Canadian share of the import markets of Brazil, Russia, India, and China (BRIC countries) would mean an export gain of $29 billion.

## DEALING with CHANGE

### Canada's Auto Sector

The automotive sector is a key player in Canada's economy. It is the single biggest contributor to Canada's manufacturing GDP at 12 percent nationally, and regionally it contributes over 20 percent in Ontario alone. One in seven Canadians is either directly or indirectly employed in the automotive industry. It supports hundreds of thousands of high-wage, high-skill manufacturing jobs across the country in 11 light-duty and 3 heavy-duty assembly plants, over 540 Original Equipment (OEM) parts manufacturers, thousands of dealerships (3,949) and many other directly related industries. It is estimated that every $1 billion in exports creates or maintains 11,000 jobs.

Canada's automotive manufacturers have made nearly $40 billion in direct investment in Canada since 1990. The positive impact on the Canadian economy is significant given the automotive sector's 3:1 economic multiplier. This means that for every dollar spent in the industry, three more are spent in the economy.

The sector has a huge export orientation, with roughly 85 percent of vehicle production and 60 percent of all parts production being exported. In fact, Canada is the ninth largest vehicle producer in the world. The Canadian vehicle assemblers are highly competitive, accounting for 3.7 percent of total world production of 68.6 million units and a global trade surplus in finished vehicles of more than $13.8 billion. This accounted for 31.4 percent of Canada's 2007 global trade surplus. Automotive exports totalled roughly $70 billion in 2007, with over $67 billion sent to the United States. This maintained the automotive sector as one of Canada's most significant export industries.

Despite all these positive points, Canada's assembly industry is shrinking due to globalization and environmental changes. Global automotive growth is shifting from the mature markets of North America and Western Europe to emerging markets. In the next five years, China will account for 39 percent of the growth in automobile sales, while India will account for 15 percent. North America will account for only 3 percent of the growth. Automobile assemblers are global in their reach, but they rationalize their production and investments on a regional basis. Over time, they will establish their plants where they sell the most vehicles.

At the time this box was written, the auto industry was undergoing a major transformation. In 2008, auto analysts had forecast that over the next several years, for every plant that opened in North America, another two were expected to close as a result of market shifts. (In emerging countries, in contrast, for every automotive plant that closes, another three are expected to open.) Other environmental trends that also contributed to the recent closure of plants included the rising Canadian dollar, rising fuel prices, and weakening U.S. demand for vehicles. Weakening demand in Canada has also been impacted by poor management decisions. That is, poor management decisions that have produced cars that do not meet the expectations of consumers.

Fast forward to 2009. Both the Canadian and U.S. governments spent billions of dollars bailing out both Chrysler LLC (it filed for bankruptcy protection in April) and General Motors Corporation (it filed for bankruptcy in June). In exchange for an 11.7 percent equity stake in General Motors (GM), the federal and Ontario provincial governments paid $10.5 billion. Equity stakes were also owned by the U.S. government (60 percent), the United Auto Workers (17.5 per cent), and unsecured bondholders (10 percent.) It is expected that once GM is up and running, the government can sell its stake in the company. It was feared that not approving the bailout loan would have forced the company out of Canada.

Do you agree with the government bailout? Why should taxpayers be paying for poor management decisions? As a condition of the bailout, union members were told to go back to the table several times to re-negotiate labour contract conditions to lower overall payroll costs. Was this fair given that there was already a contract in place that had been agreed upon by both management and labour? Why do you think the government did not mandate that management also be forced to take a pay cut? After all, poor management decisions also contributed greatly to the company's overall financial situation. What were the implications for Canada if the government did not get involved in these negotiations? Do you think the cost outweighs the benefits?

Sources: "GM Hoping for Speedy Sale and Exit from Chapter 11," Sympatico.msn. 2 June 2009, http://news.sympatico.msn.ctv.ca/abc/home/contentposting.aspx?isfa=1&feedname=CTV-TOPSTORIES_V3&showbyline=True&date=true&newsitemid=CTVNews%2f20090602%2fGM_sale_090602; "Canada, Ontario Commit $10.5B to Revamped GM," CBC News, 1 June 2009, http://www.cbc.ca/money/story/2009/06/01/harper-mcguinty-gm.html; "The Automotive Industry in Canada," Canadian Vehicles Manufacturers' Association, 2008, http://www.cvma.ca/eng/industry/industry.asp; "Strategic Automotive Policy," Canadian Vehicles Manufacturers' Association, 2008, http://www.cvma.ca/eng/issues/strategicauto.asp; "Role," Canadian Vehicles Manufacturers' Association, 2008, http://www.cvma.ca/eng/industry/role.asp; and "Notes for an Address by the Honourable Jim Prentice, PC, QC, MP, Minister of Industry," Industry Canada, 29 February 2008, http://www.ic.gc.ca/epic/site/ic1.nsf/en/01926e.html.

One objective of the federal government's Science and Technology program is to identify and incorporate world leading research into the development of innovative processes, goods, and services in Canada. What are some other benefits of such collaboration?

Based on extensive consultation with government, academic, and Canadian business and industry representatives, the federal government has identified 13 priority markets around the world where Canadian opportunities and interests have the greatest potential for growth. The priority markets are as follows: the Association of South East Asian Nations (Brunei Darussalam, Burma, Cambodia, Indonesia, Laos, Malaysia, Philippines, Singapore, Thailand, Vietnam), Australia and New Zealand, Brazil, China, Europe, Gulf Cooperation Council (Saudi Arabia, United Arab Emirates, Kuwait, Qatar, Bahrain and Oman), India, Japan, Korea, Latin America and the Caribbean, Mexico, Russia, and the United States. China and India are of particular interest as they are growing and emerging markets due to their size and economic transformation. A Conference Board of Canada report notes that by 2050, India will be the world's third-largest economy, with a GDP approaching US$30 trillion, behind only the United States and China, which will top the list. Steps already taken to encourage a stronger Canadian presence in the global marketplace include tax cuts, increased support for research and development, and critical investments in infrastructure at Canada–U.S. border crossings and Canada's Asia-Pacific Gateway. The federal government is investing $50 million a year to advance Canada's Global Commerce Strategy. Some specific initiatives include the International Science & Technology Partnerships Program and the Going Global Fund, which are programs that encourage research projects between Canada and China/India that have the potential for commercialization. Visit www.international.gc.ca/commerce/strategy-strategie/r.aspx to get an update on Canada's priority markets.

To learn about the recent global export forcecast, visit Export Development Canada's site at www.edc.ca.

## Progress Assessment

- How do world population and market statistics support the expansion of Canadian businesses into global markets?
- What is comparative advantage? How does this differ from absolute advantage?
- How are a country's balance of trade and balance of payments determined?

# STRATEGIES FOR REACHING GLOBAL MARKETS

Businesses use many different strategies to compete in global markets. The key strategies include exporting, licensing, franchising, contract manufacturing, creating international joint ventures and strategic alliances, and engaging in foreign direct investment. Each of these strategies provides opportunities for becoming involved in global markets, along with specific commitments and risks. Figure 3.5 places the strategies discussed on a continuum showing the amount of commitment, control, risk, and profit potential associated with each one. Take a few minutes to look over Figure 3.5 before you continue.

## Exporting

The simplest way of going international is to export your goods and services (e.g., call centres, IT consultants, and cultural and performing artists). As you will see in the chapters on marketing, many decisions have to be made when a company markets a new product or goes into new markets with existing products. Often the first export sales occur as a result of unsolicited orders received. Regardless of how a company starts exporting, it must develop some goals and strategies for achieving those goals.

Canadian firms may be reluctant to go through the trouble of establishing foreign trading relationships. In such cases, specialists called export-trading companies (or export-management companies) are available to step in and negotiate and establish the trading relationships desired. An export-trading company not only matches buyers and sellers from different countries but also provides needed services (such as dealing with foreign customs offices, documentation requirements, even weights and measures) to ease the process of entering global markets. Export-trading companies also help exporters with a key and risky element of doing business globally: getting paid. If you are considering a career in global business, export-trading companies often provide internships or part-time opportunities for students. In Chapter 4 we will illustrate how governments aid exporters.

Success in exporting often leads to licensing with a foreign company to produce the product locally to better serve the local market.

## Licensing

A firm (the licensor) may decide to compete in a global market by **licensing** the right to manufacture its product or use its trademark to a foreign company (the licensee) for a fee (a royalty). A company with an interest in licensing generally needs to send company representatives to the foreign producer to help set up the production process. The licensor may also assist or work with a licensee in such areas as distribution, promotion, and consulting.

**licensing**
A global strategy in which a firm (the licensor) allows a foreign company (the licensee) to produce its product in exchange for a fee (a royalty).

**FIGURE** **3.5**

**Strategies for Reaching Global Markets**

A licensing agreement can be beneficial to a firm in several different ways. Through licensing, an organization can gain additional revenues from a product that it normally would not have generated in its home market. In addition, foreign licensees must often purchase start-up supplies, component materials, and consulting services from the licensing firm. Such agreements have been very profitable for companies such as Disney, Coca-Cola,

The sun never sets on Mickey and the gang, which is making the Disney Company very happy. The firm has had great success licensing the famous mouse and his cast of characters in Europe and Asia. Here Mickey welcomes visitors to Tokyo Disneyland. What challenges does a company like Disney face in global markets?

and PepsiCo. These firms often enter foreign markets through licensing agreements that typically extend into long-term service contracts. For example, Oriental Land Company and the Hong Kong government have licensing agreements with Walt Disney Company. Oriental Land Company owns and operates Tokyo Disneyland and Tokyo Disney Sea Park under a licensing agreement; Disney also collects management and consulting fees.[20]

A final advantage of licensing worth noting is that licensors spend little or no money to produce and market their products. These costs come from the licensee's pocket. Therefore, licensees generally work very hard to see that the product they license succeeds in their market. However, licensors may also experience some problems. One major problem is that often a firm must grant licensing rights to its product for an extended period, maybe 20 years or longer. If a product experiences remarkable growth and success in the foreign market, the bulk of the revenues earned belong to the licensee. Perhaps even more threatening is that a licensing firm is actually selling its expertise in a product area. If a foreign licensee learns the company's technology or product secrets, it may break the agreement and begin to produce a similar product on its own. If legal remedies are not available, the licensing firm may lose its trade secrets, not to mention the agreed-on royalties.

## Franchising

A variation of licensing is franchising. Franchising is an arrangement whereby someone with a good idea for a business sells the rights to use the business name and sell a product or service to others in a given territory. In Canada, there are thousands of franchise units—such as Canadian Tire, Molly Maid, Boston Pizza, and Japan Camera 1 Hour Photo—in many categories of business. Franchising is popular both domestically and internationally and will be discussed in depth in Chapter 6.

Franchisors, however, have to be careful to adapt their good or service in the countries they serve. For example, KFC's first eleven Hong Kong outlets failed within two years. Apparently the chicken was too greasy, and eating with fingers was too messy for the fastidious people of Hong Kong. McDonald's made a similar mistake when entering the Netherlands market. It originally set up operations in the suburbs, as it does in North America, but soon learned that the Dutch mostly live in the cities. Pizza Hut originally approached the global market using a strategy of one-pie-fits-all. The company found out the hard way that Germans like small individual pizzas, not the large pies preferred in North America. Preferences in pizza toppings also differ globally. Japanese customers, for example, enjoy squid and sweet mayonnaise pizza.

## Contract Manufacturing

**Contract manufacturing** involves a foreign company's production of private-label goods to which a domestic company then attaches its own brand name or trademark. The practice falls under the broad category of *outsourcing*, which we introduced in Chapter 1 and

**contract manufacturing**
A foreign country's production of private-label goods to which a domestic company then attaches its brand name or trademark; also called outsourcing.

will discuss in more depth in Chapter 10. For example, Dell Computer contracts with Quanta Computer of Taiwan to make notebook PCs, on which it then puts the Dell brand name, while Nike has almost 700 contract factories around the world that manufacture its footwear and apparel.[21]

Contract manufacturing enables a company to experiment in a new market without incurring heavy start-up costs such as a manufacturing plant. If the brand name becomes a success, the company has penetrated a new market with relatively low risk. A firm can also use contract manufacturing temporarily to meet an unexpected increase in orders and, of course, labour costs are often very low. One company, featured in *PROFIT* magazine's ranking of Canada's emerging growth companies, used contract manufacturing successfully. FouFou Dog is a dog apparel company whose collection includes canine track suits, hoodies, jewelled collars and leashes, as well as iChew and Fouberry chew toys. In 2004 and at the age of 24, Cheryl Ng, owner of a Maltese dog named Ernie, started the company because she liked how Paris Hilton dressed her dog. Today, the company exports 95 percent of its products. According to Ng, "All our stuff is made in Argentina. In China, quality control can be hit-and-miss or downright sloppy—you could have a disaster on your hands—but it's been consistently good from my suppliers." And she has other reasons for heading south instead of east: "My suppliers will make me a small quantity if I want to try something out. You can't get that from China anymore, and I don't want to be stuck with a colour or style nobody wants; besides, they let me check out the textiles before I buy and they always have good stuff." She also likes the shorter flights and the fact that she only has to cross two time zones.[22]

## International Joint Ventures and Strategic Alliances

**joint venture**

A partnership in which two or more companies (often from different countries) join to undertake a major project or to form a new company.

A **joint venture** is basically a partnership in which two or more companies (often from different countries) join to undertake a major project or to form a new company. For example, to design a new biofuel engine British manufacturer Lotus has teamed up with Jaguar and Queen's University, who will help with every step of the development process.[23] Joint ventures can be mandated by governments, such as China where entry is difficult, as a condition of doing business in their country. It's often hard to gain entry into a country like China, but agreeing to a joint venture with a Chinese firm can help a company gain such entry. Such was the case for Volkswagen and General Motors, who have both had joint ventures with Shanghai Automotive Industrial Corporation to build cars in China.[24]

Joint ventures are developed for different business reasons as well. In the early 2000s, Campbell Soup Company formed a joint venture with Japan's Nakano Vinegar Company, called Campbell Nakano Inc., to expand its rather low share of the soup market in Japan. Nestlé and L'Oreal formed a joint venture to develop a line of inner-beauty products to improve the quality of a person's skin, hair, and nails.[25]

The benefits of international joint ventures are clear:

1. Shared technology and risk.

2. Shared marketing and management expertise.

3. Entry into markets where foreign companies are often not allowed unless goods are produced locally.

4. Shared knowledge of the local market, including local customs, government connections, access to local skilled labour and supplies, and awareness of domestic laws and regulations.

The Bank of Nova Scotia will pay US$15-million for 33 percent of a new mutual fund company in China that will be formed with the Bank of Beijing. The new joint venture, Bank of Beijing Scotiabank Asset Management Co. Ltd., will market mutual funds to retail and institutional customers through the Chinese bank's national branch network.

The drawbacks are not as obvious, but they are important. One partner can learn the other's technology and practices, then go off and use what has been learned. Also, over time, a shared technology may become obsolete or the joint venture may become too large to be as flexible as needed.

The global market is also fuelling the growth of strategic alliances. A **strategic alliance** is a long-term partnership between two or more companies established to help each company build competitive market advantages. Unlike joint ventures, however, they do not typically involve sharing costs, risks, management, or even profits. Such alliances can provide access to markets, capital, and technical expertise, causing executives and global consultants to predict that few companies in the future will succeed globally by going alone.[26] Plus, because of their flexibility, they can effectively link firms from different countries and firms of vastly different sizes.

Air Canada is expanding its access to overseas destinations by forming a strategic alliance with Continental Airlines Corp., clearing the way for the two airlines to work co-operatively on everything from ticketing to check-in to baggage transfer. Passengers benefit from coordinated frequent-flier rewards and access to each other's airport lounges around the world.[27] Continental, the fourth-largest airline in the United States, is a major player in the New York region with its hub at Newark, New Jersey, offering flights to Europe and Asia, while its Houston hub is a busy take-off point to Central and South America.[28] In another example, Consilient Technologies Corporation, a mobile software developer, and GroupM, a leading global media investment management operation, have created an alliance to enable both companies to cross promote their services and offerings to clients, end-users, and mobile operators throughout Asia Pacific.[29] GroupM will promote Consilient's Push™ e-mail advertising service as an advertising channel to their agencies in the region and Consilient will provide support and preferred access for GroupM's clients within their Push advertising service, which is commercially available through leading mobile operators in Asia Pacific.[30] For more information about Consilient Technologies, see the Spotlight on Small Business box.

**strategic alliance**
A long-term partnership between two or more companies established to help each company build competitive market advantages.

## SPOTLIGHT ON Small Business

### Newfoundland's Consilient Technologies Corporation

Founded in 2000, Consilient Technologies Corporation was formed by Trevor Adey (President and CEO) and Rod White (Senior Director). Consilient is a leading developer of wireless push e-mail for mobile devices and phones. Push e-mail means that e-mail travels directly to a customer's mobile phone or device—there's no need to pull the e-mail from a server or use desktop forwarding because e-mail is automatically pushed to the mobile phone or device.

The company's customer base comprises Global Fortune 500 companies, network operators, service providers, and government agencies. To meet the needs of its customers, Consilient has established strategic alliances with IT solution developers, network carriers, handheld device manufacturers (e.g., Research In Motion), system integrators, and application developers. Technology partners include industry leaders such as Oracle, Nokia, and Sun Microsystems.

People ask the St. John's entrepreneurs: Why would you build a software company in Newfoundland? Adey replies, "It's where I want to live. I don't have to rationalize it." Even so, he does: cheap office costs and, most of all, proximity to Memorial University. A Memorial University graduate himself, Adey believes that "what allows us to

build a company in St. John's like this is having a world-class university right here with students who want to stay in Newfoundland and Labrador, but don't think they can."

In recognition of its impact in the industry, Consilient was awarded the top Asian Mobile Innovation Award in 2007. "It is fitting that Consilient won the award, as our offering is the first of its kind that enables people to get free mobile services on their phones through brand advertising," said Adey. "Our approach and advanced mobile marketing platform has introduced a brand new business model for operators and advertisers. With this success under our belt, we will continue to partner with more mobile operators and market brands around the globe to bring free mobile applications, data, and advertising to the world's 2.5 billion mobile phone users."

Sources: "Consilient Wins Top Mobile Innovation Award in Asia," Consilient Technologies Corporation, 15 November 2007, http://www.consilient. com/media/press/top-mobile-innovation-award-winner.php; Simon Avery, "RIM's next rival may be an upstart from St. John's," *Report on Business*, 14 March 2006, http://global.factiva.com//aa/default.asp; Gordon Pitts, "Newfoundland Duo Battle Image Problem," *The Globe and Mail*, 25 November 2002, http://www.theglobeandmail.com; and Roy MacGregor, "And Not a Rubber Boot in Sight," *The Globe and Mail*, 18 October 2003, A11.

# Foreign Direct Investment

Economists measure a nation's economic strength by comparing several factors. They calculate the amount of money a nation owes to foreign creditors and the value of what foreign creditors own in a particular country, referred to as foreign direct investment. **Foreign direct investment (FDI)** is buying permanent property and businesses in foreign nations. FDI provides benefits to Canadian firms through the transfer of knowledge, technology and skills, and increased trade related to investment, all of which contribute to productivity growth and competitiveness.[31] Some research in necessary before such an investment. For example, Simply Audiobooks Inc., an audiobook e-tailer, entered the U.S. market only after its test Web site attracted more U.S. than Canadian clients by 15 to 1. The company opened its first shipping facility in Buffalo, New York, about a month later, and today the U.S. market accounts for 90 percent of revenue. "When you're a startup, you can't afford a high risk/reward ratio," says CEO Sean Neville. "You can't think you're going to get 50 customers and only get one. This helped us narrow the deviation of what could be."[32]

Foreign direct investment is compared to how much money foreign creditors owe to a nation and the value of what a nation owns in other countries. Increasingly, economists and trade analysts have come to agree that a high amount of foreign direct investment in a nation is not necessarily a bad sign. In fact, the amount of foreign direct investment in a country means that other nations perceive that country as a strong economic leader. Figure 3.6 lists the countries with the largest direct foreign investment in Canada, as well as Canadian direct investment abroad.

As the size of a foreign market expands, many firms increase foreign direct investment and establish a foreign subsidiary. A **foreign subsidiary** is a company that is owned in a foreign country by another company (called the *parent company*). Such a subsidiary would operate much like a domestic firm, with production, distribution, promotion, pricing, and other business functions under the control of the foreign subsidiary's management.

The legal requirements of both the country where the parent firm is located (called the *home country*) and the foreign country where the subsidiary is located (called the *host country*) have to be observed. The primary advantage of a subsidiary is that the company maintains complete control over any technology or expertise it may possess. The major shortcoming of a subsidiary is that the parent company commits a large amount of funds and technology within foreign boundaries. Should relations with the host country falter, the firm's assets could be taken over by the foreign government. Such a takeover is called *expropriation*.

Canadian subsidiaries of American companies have played a major role in developing the Canadian economy. As noted in Figure 3.6, in 2008 U.S. companies alone invested more than $290 billion in Canada. There are, however, several disadvantages to foreign investment. One is that Canada has been criticized for having a "branch plant economy." This occurs when many subsidiaries are owned by foreign companies and profits are returned to the home country rather than reinvested in Canada. There are concerns that decisions made by the parent company are not primarily based on the needs of Canadians. For example, if a U.S. company decides to reduce its workforce or close a plant, it may more readily do that to a subsidiary than in its home country.

**FIGURE 3.6**

Foreign Direct Investment in 2008

| Canadian Direct Investment Abroad | 2008 ($ Billions) |
| --- | --- |
| United States | 310.7 |
| United Kingdom | 54.0 |
| Barbados | 45.0 |
| Bermuda | 22.3 |
| Ireland | 20.5 |
| Cayman Islands | 19.2 |
| France | 18.7 |
| Hungary | 10.8 |
| Germany | 10.5 |
| Brazil | 9.2 |
| All other countries | 116.5 |
| **Total** | **637.4** |

| Foreign Direct Investment in Canada | |
| --- | --- |
| United States | 293.6 |
| United Kingdom | 54.4 |
| Netherlands | 33.9 |
| France | 18.5 |
| Switzerland | 15.3 |
| Japan | 13.0 |
| Brazil | 11.9 |
| Germany | 9.4 |
| Luxembourg | 5.7 |
| All other countries | 49.1 |
| **Total** | **504.9** |

Source: "Foreign Direct Investment 2008," Statistics Canada, 8 April 2009, http://www.statcan.gc.ca/daily-quotidien/090408/dq090408a-eng.htm.

In the early 1990s, Michael Porter, the competition guru from Harvard University Business School, released a report titled *The Competitive Advantage of Nations* that was commissioned by the Canadian government. While this report is now more than 20 years old, some of his points still ring true today:

> *One of Canada's competitive problems is the high concentration of foreign-owned firms that perform little sophisticated production or R&D. It matters a lot where a multinational calls home, because a company's home base is where the best jobs exist, where core R&D is undertaken, and where strategic control rests... Home bases are important to an economy because they support high productivity and productivity growth.*

Regardless of these concerns, more countries are welcoming subsidiaries as a way to develop their economies.

Swiss-based Nestlé is an example of a major firm with many foreign subsidiaries. The consumer-products giant spent billions of dollars acquiring foreign companies such as Ralston Purina, Chef America (maker of Hot Pockets), Dreyer's Ice Cream, and Perrier in France. All told, Nestle has approximately 283,000 employees in factories or operations in almost every country in the world.[33]

Nestlé is also an example of a multinational corporation. A **multinational corporation** is an organization that manufactures and markets products in many different countries; it has multinational stock ownership and multinational management. Multinational corporations are typically extremely large corporations, but not all large firms involved in global business are multinationals. For example, a business could literally be exporting everything it produces, deriving 100 percent of its sales and profits globally, and still not be considered a multinational corporation. Only firms that have *manufacturing capacity* or some other physical presence in different nations, such as Magna International Inc., can truly be called multinational.

Getting involved in global business requires selecting an entry strategy that best fits the goals of the business. The different strategies discussed reflect different levels of ownership, financial commitment, and risk that a company can assume. However, this is just the beginning. It's important to be aware of key market forces that affect a business's ability to trade in global markets. After the Progress Assessment, we will discuss these forces.

**foreign direct investment (FDI)**
The buying of permanent property and businesses in foreign nations.

**foreign subsidiary**
A company owned in a foreign country by the parent company.

**multinational corporation**
An organization that manufactures and markets products in many different countries and has multinational stock ownership and multinational management.

Bombardier Transportation won a contract to supply Bombardier Flexity Swift high-floor light rail vehicles to the Bursa Metropolitan Municipality, Turkey. The vehicles will be built at Bombardier's manufacturing facility in Bautzen, Germany. Bodies will come from the Siegen site, while the electrical equipment will be supplied by the Mannheim plant.

## Progress Assessment

- What services are usually provided by an export-trading company?
- What are the advantages to a firm of using licensing as a method of entry in global markets? What are the disadvantages?
- What are the key differences between a joint venture and a strategic alliance?
- What is a multinational corporation?

# FORCES AFFECTING TRADING IN GLOBAL MARKETS

Succeeding in any business takes work and effort due to the many challenges that exist in all markets. Unfortunately, the hurdles are higher and more complex in global markets than in domestic ones. This is particularly true when dealing with differences in sociocultural forces, economic forces, legal and regulatory forces, and technological forces. (Recall that these were introduced in Chapter 1.) Let's take a look at each of these global market forces to see how they challenge even the most established and experienced global businesses.

## Sociocultural Forces

**culture**
The set of values, beliefs, rules, and institutions held by a specific group of people.

**ethnocentricity**
An attitude that one's own culture is superior to all others.

Canada is a multicultural country, yet understanding cultural diversity remains one of the true business challenges of the twenty-first century. The word **culture** refers to the set of values, beliefs, rules, and institutions held by a specific group of people.[34] Culture can also include social structures, religion, manners and customs, values and attitudes, language, and personal communication. An attitude that one's own culture is superior to all others is known as **ethnocentricity**. If you hope to get involved in global trade, it's critical to be aware of the cultural differences among nations.

Different nations have very different ways of conducting business. Canadian businesses that wish to compete globally must adapt to those ways. In North America, we like to do things quickly. We tend to call each other by our first names and try to get friendly even on the first encounter. In Japan, China, and other countries these actions would be considered surprising and even rude. Canadian negotiators will say no if they mean no, but Japanese negotiators usually say maybe when they mean no.

Religion is an important part of any society's culture and can have a significant impact on business operations. Consider the violent clashes between religious communities in India, Northern Ireland, and the Middle East—clashes that have wounded these areas' economies. Unfortunately, companies at times do not consider the religious implications of business decisions. Both McDonald's and Coca-Cola offended Muslims in Saudi Arabia by putting the Saudi Arabian flag on their packaging. The flag's design contains a passage from the Quran (Islam's sacred scripture), and Muslims feel that their holy writ should never be wadded up and thrown away.

Successful companies are those that can understand these differences and develop goods and services accordingly. The focus may be on a large global market or a smaller, yet profitable global market.

Understanding sociocultural differences can also be important when managing employees. In Latin American countries, workers believe that managers are placed in positions of authority to make decisions and be responsible for the well-being of their workers. Consider what happened to one North American manager in Peru who was unaware of this characteristic and believed that workers should participate in managerial functions. This manager was convinced that he could motivate his workers to higher levels of productivity by instituting a more democratic decision-making style than the one already in place. Soon workers began quitting their jobs in droves. When asked why, the workers said the new manager did not know his job and was asking the workers what to do. All stated that they wanted to find new jobs, since obviously this company was doomed due to incompetent managers.

The truth is that many companies still fail to think globally. A sound philosophy to adopt in global markets is: Never assume that what works in one country will work in another. Companies such as

After learning to fit in at this dinner table (one saves the eyes for last), the local enterprise system was an easily acquired taste. In parts of southern Asia, flavors can be exotic. And the same can be said for currencies, tax laws, and financial systems. Understanding exactly what's going on locally in 187 countries is the key to our success. And it's one reason why we've provided 25% of the Fortune 500® with financial software solutions that are scaleable, complementary to existing systems, and effective in every corner of the globe. Whatever the language. Whatever the currency. Whatever the menu. We're there.

SunSystems

Can you think of anything more appetizing than a tasty fish head? No? Well, the cheeseburgers and "finger-licking-good" chicken we devour in Canada often get similar reactions in other cultures. Understanding different sociocultural perspectives related to time, change, natural resources, and even food can be important in succeeding in global markets. How do you think companies can help employees being assigned to global markets adapt to the different cultures they will encounter and avoid culture shock?

| |
|---|
| PepsiCo attempted a Chinese translation of "Come Alive, You're in the Pepsi Generation" that read to Chinese customers as "Pepsi Brings Your Ancestors Back from the Dead." |
| Coor's Brewing Company put its slogan "Turn It Loose" into Spanish and found it translated as "Suffer from Diarrhea." |
| Perdue Chicken used the slogan "It Takes a Strong Man to Make a Chicken Tender," which was interpreted in Spanish as "It Takes an Aroused Man to Make a Chicken Affectionate." |
| KFC's patented slogan "finger-lickin' good" was understood in Japanese as "Bite Your Fingers Off." |

**FIGURE 3.7**

**Oops, Did We Say That?** A global marketing strategy can be very difficult to implement. Look at the problems these well-known companies encountered in global markets.

Roots, Nike, and Toyota have developed brand names with widespread global appeal and recognition. However, even these successful global marketers often face difficulties. To get an idea of the problems companies have faced with translations, take a look at Figure 3.7. "Think global, act local" is a valuable motto to follow.

# Economic Forces

Economic differences can also make entering global markets more challenging. Surely it's hard for us to imagine buying chewing gum by the stick instead of by the package. Yet this buying behaviour is commonplace in economically depressed nations such as Haiti, because customers there have only enough money to buy small quantities. You might suspect that with more than 1 billion people, India would be a dream market for companies such as Hershey's, Skippy Peanut Butter, and Coca-Cola.[35] However, Indians annually consume an average of only three soft drinks per person, and the vast majority of people cannot afford chocolate or peanut butter due to their low per capita income level. So for these products, what seems like an unbelievable global opportunity is not viable due to economic conditions. Keep in mind that there may be opportunities for other goods and services. The challenge is to tailor products and strategies for local market conditions.

Global financial markets unfortunately do not have a worldwide currency. Mexicans shop with pesos, South Koreans with won, Japanese with yen, and Canadians with dollars. Globally, the U.S. dollar is considered the world's dominant and most stable form of currency. This doesn't mean, however, that the dollar always retains the same market value. In an international transaction today, one dollar may be exchanged for eight pesos; tomorrow, you may only get seven pesos for the same dollar. The **exchange rate** is the value of one nation's currency relative to the currencies of other countries.

Changes in a nation's exchange rates can have important implications in global markets. A *high value of the dollar* means that a dollar would be traded for more foreign currency than normal. The products of foreign producers would be cheaper because it takes fewer dollars to buy them, but the cost of Canadian-produced goods would become more expensive to foreign purchasers because of the dollar's high value. Conversely, a *low value of the dollar* means that a dollar is traded for less foreign currency than normal. Therefore, foreign goods become more expensive because it takes more dollars to buy them, but Canadian goods become cheaper to foreign buyers because it takes less foreign currency to buy Canadian goods.[36]

Global financial markets operate under a system called *floating exchange rates*, in which currencies "float" according to the supply and demand in the global market for the currency. This supply and demand is created by global currency traders, who develop a market for a nation's currency based on the perceived trade and investment potential of the country. Changes in currency values cause many problems globally. Consider a multinational corporation like Nestlé. Costs for labour, raw materials, and machinery can vary considerably as currency values shift, causing production to be juggled from one country to another.[37]

Currency valuation problems can be especially harsh on developing economies. At certain times a nation's government will intervene and adjust the value of its currency,

**exchange rate**
The value of one nation's currency relative to the currencies of other countries.

**devaluation**
Lowering the value of a nation's currency relative to other currencies.

**countertrading**
A complex form of bartering in which several countries may be involved, each trading goods for goods or services for services.

often to increase the export potential of its products. **Devaluation** is lowering the value of a nation's currency relative to other currencies. In other instances due to a nation's weak currency, the only possibility of trade in many developing nations is through one of its oldest forms: *bartering*, which is the exchange of merchandise for other merchandise or service for other service with no money involved.[38] **Countertrading** is a complex form of bartering in which several countries may be involved, each trading goods for goods or services for services. It has been estimated that countertrading accounts for more than 20 percent of all global exchanges, especially deals involving developing countries. For example, let's say that a developing country such as Jamaica wants to buy vehicles from Ford Motor Company in exchange for Jamaican bauxite. Ford, however, does not have a need for Jamaican bauxite but does have a need for computer monitors. In a countertrade agreement, Ford may trade vehicles to Jamaica, which then trades bauxite to another country—say, India—which then exchanges computer monitors with Ford. This countertrade is thus beneficial to all three parties. Trading products for products helps businesses avoid some of the financial problems and currency constraints that exist in global markets. Understanding economic conditions, currency fluctuations, and countertrade opportunities is vital to a company's success in global markets.

## Legal and Regulatory Forces

In any economy, both the conduct and the direction of business are firmly tied to the legal and regulatory environment. In Canada, federal, provincial, and municipal laws and regulations heavily affect business practices. In global markets, no central system of law exists, so several groups of laws and regulations may apply. This makes the task of conducting global business extremely difficult as business people find myriad laws and regulations in global markets that are often inconsistent. Important legal questions related to antitrust rules, labour relations, patents, copyrights, trade practices, taxes, child labour, product liability, and other issues are written and interpreted differently country by country.[39]

Canadian businesses are required to follow Canadian laws and regulations in conducting business globally. For example, bribery is not considered legal in Canada. The problem is that this runs contrary to beliefs and practices in many countries where corporate or government bribery not only is acceptable, but also may be the only way to secure a lucrative contract.[40] Members of the Organisation for Economic Co-operation and Development (OECD) have been urged to lead a global effort to fight corruption and bribery in foreign markets. In Transparency International's annual Corruption Perceptions Index, Finland, Denmark, and New Zealand are perceived to be the world's least corrupt countries.[41] For the purposes of this Index, corruption is defined as the misuse of public power for private benefit. "Despite some gains, corruption remains an enormous drain on resources sorely needed for education, health and infrastructure," said Huguette Labelle, Chair of Transparency International. At the same time, deeply troubled states such as Afghanistan, Iraq, Myanmar, Somalia, and Sudan remain at the very bottom of the Index, with a strong correlation between corruption and poverty being evident. "Countries torn apart by conflict pay a huge toll in their capacity to govern. With public institutions crippled or non-existent, mercenary individuals help themselves to public resources and corruption thrives," said Labelle.[42]

It's important to remember that to be successful in global markets, it's often useful to contact local business people in the host countries and gain their co-operation and sponsorship. Such local contacts can help a company penetrate the market and deal with what can be imposing bureaucratic barriers. Local business people are also familiar with laws and regulations that could have an important impact on a foreign firm's business in their country.

# Technological Forces

Certain technological forces can also have an important impact on a company's ability to conduct business in global markets. In fact, technological constraints may make it difficult given the nature of exportable products. For example, houses in most developing countries do not have electrical systems that match those of Canadian homes, in kind or in capacity. How would the differences in electricity available (110 versus 220 volts) affect a Canadian appliance manufacturer wishing to export?

Also, computer and Internet usage in many developing countries is rare or non-existent. You can see how this would make for a tough business environment in general and would make e-commerce difficult, especially as this is becoming a critical element of business. After the Progress Assessment, we will explore how trade protectionism affects global business.

## Progress Assessment

- What are the major hurdles to successful global trade?
- What does *ethnocentricity* mean?
- Which cultural and social differences are most likely to affect global trade efforts? (Name at least two.)

# TRADE PROTECTIONISM

As we discussed in the previous section, sociocultural, economic, legal and regulatory, and technological forces are all challenges to trading globally. What is often a much greater barrier to global trade, however, is trade protectionism. **Trade protectionism** is the use of government regulations to limit the import of goods and services. Supporters of trade protectionism believe that it allows domestic producers to survive and grow, producing more jobs. Those against trade protectionism argue that it not only impedes global trade, but that it also adds millions of dollars to the price of products, costing consumers billions of dollars.

Countries often use protectionist measures to guard against practices such as dumping. **Dumping** is the practice of selling products in a foreign country at lower prices than those charged in the producing country. Companies sometimes use this tactic to dispose of surplus products in foreign markets or to gain a foothold in a new market by offering products for lower prices than domestic competitors do. Dumping benefits foreign firms, as it generates more sales by intentionally charging lower prices. Dumping also benefits purchasers, as they can buy products at a lower price. However, domestic producers do not benefit. Dumping usually leads to a lower share of the market if they do not lower their prices. Lower prices may damage the domestic industry by leading to less revenues and potential job losses. It can take time to prove accusations of dumping, however. There's also evidence that some governments offer financial incentives to certain industries to sell goods in global markets for less than they sell them at home. To understand how trade protectionism affects global business, let's briefly review some global economic history.

Business, economics, and politics have always been closely linked. What we now call economics was once referred to as *political* economy, indicating the close ties between politics (government) and economics. In the seventeenth and eighteenth centuries, business people and governments advocated an economic principle called *mercantilism*. The overriding idea of mercantilism was for a nation to sell more goods to other nations than it bought from them; that is, to have a favourable balance of trade.[43] According to the mercantilists, this resulted in a flow of money to the country that sold the most globally. This philosophy led governments to implement **tariffs**, which are basically taxes on imports, thus making imported goods more expensive to buy.

**trade protectionism**
The use of government regulations to limit the import of goods and services.

**dumping**
Selling products in a foreign country at lower prices than those charged in the producing country.

**tariff**
A tax imposed on imports.

Generally, there are two different kinds of tariffs: protective and revenue. *Protective tariffs* (import taxes) are designed to raise the retail price of imported products so that domestic products will be more competitively priced. These tariffs are meant to save jobs for domestic workers and to keep industries (especially *infant industries*, which consist of new companies in the early stages of growth) from closing down entirely because of foreign competition. Such tariffs are usually met with resistance. After the Canada Border Service Agency ruled that grain was being subsidized in the United States and then sold in Canada below its true cost, the federal government imposed a duty of US$1.65 a bushel on U.S. corn imports.[44] In another instance, Canada, the United States, and the European Union successfully lodged a complaint to the World Trade Organization (to be discussed soon) arguing that China was imposing a 40 percent tariff on auto parts when it had promised not to treat parts as whole cars.[45] If it had been upheld, such a tariff would have forced manufacturers to source 40 percent of an auto's parts by value in China to avoid the tax on cars as the Chinese government considered auto parts as a complete vehicle if they accounted for 60 percent or more of the value of a final vehicle.[46]

*Revenue tariffs* are designed to raise money for the government. They are commonly used by developing countries to help infant industries compete in global markets.

An **import quota** limits the number of products in certain categories that a nation can import. Canada has import quotas on a number of products including textiles and clothing, agricultural products, steel products, and weapons and munitions.[47] Overall, the goal is to protect companies to preserve jobs. An **embargo** is a complete ban on the import or export of a certain product or the stopping of all trade with a particular country. Political disagreements have caused many countries to establish embargoes, such as Canada's embargo against the Burmese regime, reflecting its condemnation of the Burmese regime's complete disregard for human rights and ongoing repression of the democratic movement.[48]

*Non-tariff barriers* are not as specific or formal as tariffs, import quotas, and embargoes but can be as detrimental.[49] It's common for nations to set restrictive standards that detail exactly how a product must be sold in a country. For example, Denmark requires companies to sell butter in cubes, not tubs. For many years Japan argued it had some of the lowest tariffs in the world and welcomed foreign exports, yet business found it difficult to establish trade relationships with the Japanese. A Japanese tradition called *keiretsu* (pronounced "care-yet-sue") built "corporate families" (such as Mitsui and Mitsubishi)

**import quota**
A limit on the number of products in certain categories that a nation can import.

**embargo**
A complete ban on the import or export of a certain product or the stopping of all trade with a particular country.

Canada's long dispute with the United States over softwood lumber cost the economy billions of dollars and thousands of jobs. In 2002, the United States imposed duties of 27 percent on Canadian softwood lumber, arguing that Canada unfairly subsidized producers of spruce, pine, and fir lumber. While international trade tribunals sided with Canada, it was not until July 2006 that an agreement between both countries was signed. The United States agreed to return over $4.5 billion in duties it had collected and remove tariffs on lumber.

that forged semi-permanent ties with suppliers, customers, and distributors with full support of the government.[50] The Japanese believed that corporate alliances would provide economic payoffs by nurturing long-term strategic thinking and mutually beneficial co-operation.

Other non-tariff barriers include safety, health, and labelling standards. The United States has stopped some Canadian goods from entering because it said that the information on the labels was too small. The discovery of mad cow disease resulted in a temporary import ban of Canadian beef by the United States, Japan, South Korea, Australia, and other countries.[51]

It would be easy for would-be exporters to view the trade barriers discussed above as good reasons to avoid global trade. Still, wherever you stand on the tariff issue, it's obvious that overcoming trade constraints creates business opportunities. Next, we'll look at organizations and agreements that attempt to eliminate trade barriers among nations.

## The GATT and the WTO

In 1948, government leaders from 23 nations throughout the world formed the **General Agreement on Tariffs and Trade (GATT)**, which established an international forum for negotiating mutual reductions in trade restrictions. In short, the countries agreed to negotiate to create monetary and trade agreements that might facilitate the exchange of goods, services, ideas, and cultural programs. In 1986, the Uruguay Round of the GATT was convened to specifically deal with the renegotiation of trade agreements. After eight years of meetings, 124 nations at the Uruguay Round voted to modify the GATT. Under the agreement, tariffs were lowered an average of 38 percent worldwide, and new trade rules were expanded to areas such as agriculture, services, and the protection of patents.

The Uruguay Round also established the **World Trade Organization (WTO)** to assume the task of mediating future trade disputes. The WTO, headquartered in Geneva, Switzerland, is an independent entity now composed of 153 member nations, and its purpose is to oversee cross-border trade issues and global business practices among those nations.[52] It's the world's first attempt at establishing a global mediation centre. Trade issues are expected to be resolved within 12 to 15 months instead of languishing for years, as was the case in the past.

It would be a mistake to assume that the WTO has solved all problems in global trade. Legal and regulatory problems (discussed earlier) often impede trade expansion. Also, a wide divide exists between developed (e.g., Canada) and developing, or least-developed nations, which comprise over three quarters of the WTO membership.[53] "Few would contest the benefits that globalization and trade have brought in terms of greater prosperity for hundreds of millions, as well as greater stability among nations. But many individuals in different societies across the world have shared little or not at all in the benefits. The challenges facing governments in managing globalization are formidable, and success in spreading prosperity more widely requires a strong common purpose" says WTO Director-General Pascal Lamy.[54] WTO challenges will likely persist throughout the current decade.

**General Agreement on Tariffs and Trade (GATT)**
A 1948 agreement that established an international forum for negotiating mutual reductions in trade restrictions.

**World Trade Organization (WTO)**
The international organization that replaced the General Agreement on Tariffs and Trade, and was assigned the duty to mediate trade disputes among nations.

The WTO has been trying since 2001 to secure a deal on the rules governing trade. But there have been continual disagreements between Western nations and emerging economic powers, such as India and China, over manufacturing and agricultural import rules.

## The IMF and the World Bank

The **International Monetary Fund (IMF)** was created in 1944. The IMF is an international bank supported by its members that usually makes short-term loans to countries experiencing problems with their balance of trade. The IMF's basic objectives are to promote exchange stability, maintain orderly exchange arrangements, avoid competitive currency depreciation, establish a multilateral system of payments, eliminate exchange

**International Monetary Fund (IMF)**
An international bank that makes short-term loans to countries experiencing problems with their balance of trade.

restrictions, and create standby reserves. The IMF makes long-term loans at low interest rates to the world's most destitute nations to help them strengthen their economies. The function of the IMF is very similar to that of the World Bank.

The **World Bank** (also known as the **International Bank for Reconstruction and Development**), an autonomous United Nations agency, is concerned with developing infrastructure (e.g., roads, schools, hospitals, power plants) in less-developed countries. The World Bank borrows from more prosperous countries and lends at favourable rates to less-developed countries. In recent years, the IMF and the World Bank have forgiven some loans to highly indebted countries, such as Mozambique. To qualify for the program, numerous macroeconomic policies (such as inflation and poverty reduction) have to be implemented. These new requirements allow the lending organizations to continue to fulfill their objectives.

Some countries believe that their economies will be strengthened if they establish formal trade agreements with other countries. Some of these agreements, involving forming producers' cartels and common markets, are discussed next.

> **World Bank (International Bank for Reconstruction and Development)**
> An autonomous United Nations agency that borrows money from the more prosperous countries and lends it to less-developed countries to develop their infrastructure.

## Producers' Cartels

**Producers' cartels** are organizations of commodity-producing countries. They are formed to stabilize or increase prices, optimizing overall profits in the long run. The most obvious example today is Organization of the Petroleum Exporting Countries (OPEC). Similar attempts have been made to manage prices for copper, iron ore, bauxite, bananas, tungsten, rubber, and other important commodities. These cartels are all contradictions to unrestricted free trade and letting the market set prices.

> **producers' cartels**
> Organizations of commodity-producing countries that are formed to stabilize or increase prices to optimize overall profits in the long run.

## Common Markets

An issue not resolved by the GATT or the WTO is whether common markets create regional alliances at the expense of global expansion. A **common market** (also called a **trading bloc**) is a regional group of countries that have a common external tariff, no internal tariffs, and the coordination of laws to facilitate exchange among member countries. Two examples are the North American Free Trade Agreement and the European Union (EU). Let's look briefly at both.

> **common market (trading bloc)**
> A regional group of countries that have a common external tariff, no internal tariffs, and a coordination of laws to facilitate exchange; also called a trading bloc.

### The North American Free Trade Agreement (NAFTA)

A widely debated issue of the early 1990s was the ratification of the **North American Free Trade Agreement (NAFTA)**, which created a free-trade area among Canada, the United States, and Mexico. On 1 January 1993 NAFTA came into effect, replacing the previous Free Trade Agreement between Canada and the United States. The objectives of NAFTA were to (1) eliminate trade barriers and facilitate cross-border movement of goods and services among the three countries; (2) promote conditions of fair competition in this free-trade area; (3) increase investment opportunities in the territories of the three nations; (4) provide effective protection and enforcement of intellectual property rights (patents, copyrights, etc.) in each nation's territory; (5) establish a framework for further regional trade co-operation; and (6) improve working conditions in North America.

> **North American Free Trade Agreement (NAFTA)**
> Agreement that created a free-trade area among Canada, the United States, and Mexico.

NAFTA was driven by the desire of Mexico to have greater access to the U.S. market. Improved access would spur growth, provide more employment for Mexicans, and raise the low standard of living in Mexico. The U.S. government was hoping to create jobs in Mexico and stop the flow of illegal immigrants that were entering its border. Canada was really a minor player in this deal; the Canadian government was concerned that it would be left out or penalized indirectly unless it joined the bloc. Canadians do have something to gain by having freer access to the growing Mexican market, but the country is still a minor customer for Canada.

Today, the three NAFTA countries have a combined population of over 445 million and a gross domestic product of more than $15.7 trillion.[55] The agreement permits all three countries to reduce trade barriers with one another while maintaining independent trade agreements with other countries.

There is continuing concern by some groups (e.g., unions) in Canada and the United States that NAFTA has contributed to employment losses and that economic benefits were not realized. Some Canadian business people remain opposed because they did not like many of the details in NAFTA. In addition, Mexico has a poor policy on environmental problems, bad working conditions, and a poor record on human rights and political freedom. The country has repeatedly been condemned by many organizations in North America and abroad for serious flaws on all these counts. Others believe that NAFTA will force Mexico to gradually improve these conditions. This has been happening, but at a very slow pace.

## The European Union (EU)

The EU began in the late 1950s as an alliance of six trading partners (then known as the Common Market and later the European Economic Community). Today the EU is a group of 27 member nations, located primarily in Europe, with a population of almost 500 million citizens and an estimated 30 percent share of the world's nominal gross domestic product (US$18.4 trillion in 2008).[56] Today, the EU is the world's biggest trading power and member nations see this economic integration as the major way to compete for global business, particularly with the United States, China, and Japan.[57]

Officially, almost all trade in the NAFTA region now flows tariff-free. But several major areas of dispute have yet to be resolved including trucking, immigration, the environment, and agricultural tariffs.

The path to European unification was not easy, but a significant step was taken in 1999, when the EU officially launched its joint currency, the euro. The formal EU transition to the euro occurred three years later, when 12 of the 15 member nations at that time agreed to a single monetary unit. (EU members Great Britain, Sweden, and Denmark elected not to convert to the euro at that time.) EU businesses saved billions each year with the entry of the euro, as currency conversions that were required prior to the euro were eliminated. Globally, the euro is certainly a worthy challenger to the U.S. dollar's dominance in global markets due to the economic strength and size of the EU.

To learn more about the countries that belong to the EU, visit http://europa.eu/abc/european_countries/index_en.htm.

A Canada-European Union Trade Agreement was being negotiated in 2009. A study estimated that Europe would gain $18.5 billion a year and Canada about $13 billion by cutting restrictions on services trade, removing tariffs, and reducing non-tariff barriers.[58] Was this agreement successfully negotiated and implemented?

The issues surrounding common markets and free-trade areas will extend far into the twenty-first century. Many fear that poor and developing countries that don't fit in the plans of the trading blocs will suffer. After the Progress Assessment, we'll look at the future of global trade.

## Progress Assessment

- What are the advantages and disadvantages of trade protectionism?
- What is the difference between protective tariffs and revenue tariffs?
- What is the primary purpose of the WTO?
- State four objectives of NAFTA.
- What is the primary objective of a common market like the EU?

# GLOBALIZATION AND YOUR FUTURE

Global trade opportunities grow more interesting, yet challenging, each day. New and expanding markets present great potential for trade and development. Changes in technology, especially through the Internet, have changed the landscape of business. Internet usage and advances in e-commerce enable companies worldwide to bypass historical distribution channels to reach a large market that is only a mouse click away. Take New England Potter Company, for example. Using the Internet, the company was able to speed up the flow of information between buyers and its manufacturing partners in Europe, South America, and Asia. The company became the world's largest vendor in the garden pottery industry.

The lure of more than 6 billion customers is hard to pass up, especially since the Internet makes the global market instantly accessible. With more than 600 million people worldwide now plugged into the Net, the global market is where opportunities exist.[59] However, nowhere on this planet is the lure to global markets keener than in the world's most populous country, China. With more than 1.2 billion people, China is an economy in high gear since shifting its philosophy from central planning to free markets.

Not long ago, foreign direct investment in China was considered risky and not worth the effort, but today this is not the case. Many view China as the fulfillment of a free trader's dream, where global investment and entrepreneurship are leading the nation to wealth and economic interdependence with the rest of the world. However, concerns remain about China's one-party political system, human rights policies, and growing trade imbalance.[60] Product piracy and counterfeiting are also significant problems. China's underground economy is still actively counterfeiting everything from Calloway golf clubs to Kiwi shoe polish to Louis Vuitton bags.[61] However, since its admission to the WTO in 2001, China has been more receptive to dealing with piracy and counterfeiting. Still, few expect problems to disappear anytime soon. Economists have warned that profits will take a long time to materialize for most companies doing business in China. Nonetheless, in a relatively short period of time, China has become an economic phenomenon. With its openness to trade and investment, educated workforce, and stable infrastructure, China is expected to be a key driver of the world economy.

While China clearly attracts most of the attention in Asia, it's important not to forget the rest of the continent. For example, India's 1.1 billion population (600 million of whom are under 25 years of age) and Russia's 150 million potential customers represent opportunities too good to pass up. Both nations are emerging markets that present business opportunities. India has seen huge growth in information technology, pharmaceuticals, and biotechnology.[62] Still, it remains a nation with extreme poverty and difficult trade laws. Russia is an industrialized nation with large reserves of oil, gas, and gold.[63] Unfortunately, political, currency, and social problems still persist in Russia. The developing nations of Asia, including Indonesia, Thailand, Singapore, the Philippines, Korea, Malaysia, and Vietnam also offer great potential for businesses—and possibly for you.

As you learned in Chapter 1, outsourcing means contracting with other companies to do some of all of the functions of a firm, rather than providing them within the company. In Canada, companies have outsourced payroll functions, accounting, and some manufacturing operations for many years. However, the shift in outsourcing manufacturing and services from domestic businesses to primarily low-wage markets outside of Canada is getting more attention. This shift is referred to as offshoring. The Making Ethical Decisions box offers an example of this practice.

## Making Ethical Decisions

### How Much Information Is Necessary?

Imagine that you're having a problem with your computer. Not able to fix the problem yourself, you take out the operator's manual and dial customer service. Your call is answered by a service technician who identifies himself as Jeff. You explain to Jeff the problem you are having and wait for his reply. Unfortunately, Jeff cannot solve your problem and transfers your call to his colleague Jennifer. Jennifer analyzes the situation and promptly provides a suggestion that fixes your computer. Impressed, you ask Jennifer for her direct line so you can call her if you have additional questions. She says she is unable to give you her direct number, according to company policy. Upset, you call customer relations and inquire why a service technician cannot give her direct number to a customer. The company representative says, in a rather disgusted tone, "Because the service centre is overseas. You were talking to people trained to identify themselves as Jeff and Jennifer." Should a company let customers know if its service facilities are being outsourced? Should service people be required to give their real names when dealing with customers? What are the consequences of each alternative?

To remain competitive, Canada must stay aware of the global challenge and focus on innovation and entrepreneurship. It's increasingly important for Canadian workers to get the proper education and training needed to stay ahead in the future.[64] The key thing to remember as you progress through this text is that globalization is for real, and competition promises to intensify. The Reaching Beyond Our Borders box highlights how Canada shapes up as a global competitor.

Whether you aspire to be an entrepreneur, a manager, or some other type of business leader, it's becoming increasingly important to think globally in planning your career. As this chapter points out, global markets offer many opportunities, yet they are laced with significant challenges and complexities. By studying foreign languages, learning about foreign cultures, and taking business courses (including a course in global business), you can develop a global perspective on your future.[65] But remember, the potential of global markets does not belong only to large, multinational corporations. Small- and medium-sized businesses are often better prepared to take the leap into global markets and react quickly to opportunities than are large firms saddled with bureaucracies. Also don't forget the global potential of franchising, which we will examine in more detail in Chapter 6.

## Progress Assessment

- What are the economic risks of doing business in countries like China?
- What might be some important factors that will have an impact on global trading?
- What can you do in the next few years to ready yourself for a career in global business?

## Reaching Beyond Our Borders

### How Does Canada Shape Up as an International Competitor?

How does Canada rank when compared to other industrialized countries? Canadian businesses have been criticized for not being more productive, because pro ductivity leads to competitiveness. However, productivity is just one important component. Assessing international competitiveness is complex and open to varying opinions.

There are several indexes that attempt to measure competitiveness, and different criteria and weightings are used by the agencies that produce them. You will notice the importance of economic conditions and the role of government when evaluating a country's attractiveness. The prestigious World Economic Forum (WEF) produces the annual Global Competitiveness Report. According to the WEF, one of its indexes—the Growth Competitiveness Index—is based on estimates of each country's ability to grow over the next five to ten years. Thus, economic conditions and institutions (e.g., government and financial markets) are reviewed. Canada's high tax rates, tax regulation, and inefficient government bureaucracy are cited as the most problematic factors for doing business in this country.

The International Institute for Management Development (IMD) produces the World Competitiveness Yearbook, which ranks the ability of a nation to provide an environment that sustains the competitiveness of enterprises. The ranking considers four criteria: economic performance, government efficiency, business efficiency, and infrastructure. While Canada ranks well on government policies conducive to competitiveness, IMD analysts

suggest Canada would rank higher if it had a more enterprising business community.

| YEAR | WEF'S GROWTH COMPETITIVENESS INDEX | IMD'S OVERALL COUNTRY RANKING |
|---|---|---|
| 2009 | 10 | 8 |
| 2008 | 13 | 8 |
| 2007 | 12 | 10 |
| 2006 | 14 | 5 |
| 2005 | 15 | 3 |

It is clear that there is no one conclusive authority that is able to answer the question of how productive, and therefore how competitive, Canada is. These rankings, however, should give you an idea of how the business environment can change quickly and how challenging it is to be consistently competitive.

Sources: "The World Competitiveness Scoreboard 2009," IMD International, 20 May 2009, http://www.imd.ch/research/publications/wcy/upload/scoreboard.pdf; "The Global Competitiveness Report 2008–2009," World Economic Forum, 8 October 2008, http://www3.weforum.org/en/initiatives/gcp/Global%20Competitiveness%20Report/index.htm; and "David Crane, "Innovation: Management Gap Means Canada Is Falling Behind," *The Montreal Gazette*, 22 May 2008, B5.

## SUMMARY

**LO ▶ 1**   **Discuss the growing importance of the global market and the roles of comparative advantage and absolute advantage in global trade.**

1.  Canada has a population of more than 33 million people. The world market for trade is huge. Some 99 percent of the people in the world live outside Canada. Major Canadian companies routinely cite expansion to global markets as a route to future growth.

    **Why should nations trade with other nations?**
    Nations should trade globally as (1) no country is self-sufficient, (2) other countries need products that prosperous countries produce, and (3) natural resources and technological skills are not distributed evenly around the world.

    **What is the theory of comparative advantage?**
    The theory of comparative advantage contends that a country should make and then sell those products it produces most efficiently but buy those it cannot produce as efficiently.

### What is absolute advantage?

Absolute advantage means that a country has the ability to produce a particular good or service using fewer resources (and therefore at a lower cost) than another country. For example, Zambia has an absolute advantage over many countries in the production of copper due to its copper ore reserves.

2. Anyone can get involved in world trade through importing and exporting. Business people do not have to work for big multinational corporations.

**LO ▸ 2** Explain the importance of importing and exporting and understand key terms used in global business.

### What kinds of products can be imported and exported?

Just about any kind of product can be imported and exported. Companies can sometimes find surprising ways to succeed in either activity. Selling in global markets is not necessarily easy, though.

### What terms are important in understanding world trade?

Exporting is selling goods and services to other countries. Importing is buying goods and services from other countries. The balance of trade is the relationship of exports to imports. The balance of payments is the balance of trade plus other money flows such as tourism and foreign aid. Dumping is selling products for less in a foreign country than in your own country. Trade protectionism is the use of government regulations to limit the importation of products.

3. A company can participate in world trade in a number of ways.

**LO ▸ 3** Illustrate the strategies used in reaching global markets and explain the role of multinational corporations in global markets.

### What are some ways in which a company can get involved in global business?

Ways of entering world trade include exporting, licensing (which includes franchising), contract manufacturing, joint ventures and strategic alliances, and direct foreign investment.

### How do multinational corporations differ from other companies that participate in global business?

Unlike other companies that are involved in exporting or importing, multinational corporations also have manufacturing facilities or some other type of physical presence in different nations.

4. Many forces affect foreign trade.

**LO ▸ 4** Evaluate the forces that affect trading in global markets.

### What are some of the forces that can discourage participation in global business?

Potential stumbling blocks to global trade include sociocultural forces (e.g., religion), economic forces (e.g., disposable income), legal and regulatory forces (e.g., law on bribery), and technological forces (e.g., Internet usage).

5. Political differences are often the most difficult hurdles to international trade.

**LO ▸ 5** Debate the advantages and disadvantages of trade protectionism, define tariff and nontariff barriers, and give examples of common markets.

### What is trade protectionism?

Trade protectionism is the use of government regulations to limit the import of goods and services. Advocates believe that it allows domestic producers to survive and grow, producing more jobs. The key tools of protectionism are tariffs, import quotas, and embargoes.

### What are tariff and non-tariff barriers?

Tariffs are taxes on foreign products. There are two kinds of tariffs: (1) protective tariffs, which are used to raise the price of foreign products, and (2) revenue tariffs, which are used to raise money for the government. Non-tariff barriers include safety, health, and labelling standards.

**What are some examples of trade organizations that try to eliminate trade barriers and facilitate trade among nations?**

The World Trade Organization (WTO) replaced the General Agreement on Tariffs and Trade (GATT). The purpose of the WTO is to mediate trade disputes among nations. The International Monetary Fund (IMF) is an international bank that makes short-term loans to countries experiencing problems with their balance of trade. The World Bank is a United Nations agency that borrows money from the more prosperous countries and lends it to less-developed countries to develop their infrastructures.

**What is a common market? State some examples.**

A common market is a regional group of countries that have a common external tariff, no internal tariff, and a coordination of laws to facilitate exchange. The idea behind a common market is the elimination of trade barriers that existed prior to the creation of this bloc. Examples include the North American Free Trade Agreement (NAFTA) and the European Union (EU).

**LO ▶ 6**  Discuss the changing landscape of the global market.

6. The landscape of global business is changing.

**What countries offer opportunities for Canadian businesses?**

Expanding markets such as China, India, and Russia present great potential for trade and development.

**What is outsourcing and how have companies used this business strategy?**

Outsourcing is the purchase of goods and services from outside a firm rather than providing them inside the company. It has been a large part of business for many years. Today, more businesses are outsourcing manufacturing and services offshore.

## KEY TERMS

absolute advantage  72

balance of payments  75

balance of trade  75

common market (trading bloc)  90

comparative advantage theory  72

contract manufacturing  79

countertrading  86

culture  84

devaluation  86

dumping  87

embargo  88

ethnocentricity  84

exchange rate  85

exporting  71

foreign direct investment (FDI)  82

foreign subsidiary  82

free trade  71

General Agreement on Tariffs and Trade (GATT)  89

import quota  88

importing  71

International Monetary Fund (IMF)  89

joint venture  80

licensing  78

multinational corporation  83

North American Free Trade Agreement (NAFTA)  90

producers' cartels  90

strategic alliance  81

tariff  87

trade deficit (unfavourable balance of trade)  75

trade protectionism  87

World Bank (International Bank for Reconstruction and Development)  90

World Trade Organization (WTO)  89

## CRITICAL THINKING

1. You have read that global financial markets operate under a system called floating exchange rates. China is an exception as its exchange rate does not float. Research how this policy impacts the country's balance of trade. What is the reaction of other countries to this decision?

2. Countries like Canada that have a high standard of living are referred to as industrialized nations. Countries with a low standard of living and quality of life are called developing countries (terms formerly used were *underdeveloped* or *less-developed countries*). What prevents developing nations from fully industrializing? Consider economic indicators and political decisions as a starting point.

3. Two different types of tariffs—revenue and protective—are used by government to protect a country's trade. How would you justify the use of either a revenue or a protective tariff in today's global market?

## DEVELOPING WORKPLACE SKILLS

1. Call, e-mail, or visit a business involved with importing foreign goods (perhaps a wine or specialty foods importer). Check with the owner or manager about the problems and joys of global trade and compile a list of advantages and disadvantages. Compare notes with your classmates about what they found in their research.

2. Prepare a short list of the advantages and disadvantages of trade protectionism. Share your ideas with others in the class and debate the following statement: Canada should increase trade protection to save Canadian jobs and companies.

3. The economies of Ontario and British Columbia depend heavily on exports. Ontario relies primarily on trade to the United States and Europe, while British Columbia relies heavily on trade with Asia. In a group of four, research these statements. Develop on Excel two graphs that break down the exporting countries that trade with each of these provinces. Present your findings to the class.

4. In a group of four, list the top ten Canadian-based multinationals. When researching, create a table that will include the following pieces of information: the company names, the year each was created, the number of global employees, the industry or industries in which they operate, annual revenues, and number of countries in which they have offices. Present your findings to the class.

 ## TAKING IT TO THE NET 1

**www.mcgrawhillconnect.ca**

### Purpose
To discover the role the federal government plays in helping Canadian businesses compete successfully in international trade.

### Exercise
Visit Foreign Affairs and International Trade Canada (www.international.gc.ca/). Answer the following questions:

1. What is the mandate for this federal department?

2. What are some of the services available for doing business abroad?

3. What are some of the most recent trade negotiations and agreements?

# TAKING IT TO THE NET 2

## Purpose

To identify those nations with high export potential and those with low export potential (except for basic goods such as food).

## Exercise

Imagine that your company is ready to expand its products to foreign countries. Which countries are most likely to buy your products? The potential to export to a specific country is based on a number of factors, including the size of its population and the strength of its GDP.

1. From the population data given on the United Nations Population Information Network Web site (www.un.org/popin), prepare a list of the 20 countries with the largest populations.

2. Go to the InfoNation section of the UN's Cyber School Bus Web site (www.un.org/Pubs/CyberSchoolBus) and find the GDP per person for each of the nations on your population list. Rate each of the nations on your list for its export potential. Using the GDP per capita and the population size, place each of those nations into the following categories:

a. High export potential (those nations whose population is one of the ten largest and whose GDP per capita is greater than $20,000).

b. Medium-high export potential (those nations whose population is ranked 11 to 21 and whose GDP per capita is greater than $20,000).

c. Medium export potential (those nations whose population is one of the ten largest and whose GDP per capita is between $3,000 and $20,000).

d. Low export potential (those nations whose population is ranked 11 to 21 and whose GDP per capita is less than $3,000).

# ANALYZING MANAGEMENT DECISIONS

## The Challenge of Offshoring

The truth is that Canadian companies such as Bombardier and Celestica have outsourced manufacturing offshore for years. Fundamentally, as lower-level manufacturing became more simplified, Canadian companies shifted focus from assembling products to design and architecture. Today, economists agree that we are moving into the "second wave" of offshoring that involves sizable numbers of skilled, well-educated middle-income workers in service-sector jobs such as accounting, law, financial and risk management, health care, and information technology that were thought to be safe from foreign market competition. This shift is potentially more disruptive to the Canadian job market than was the first, which primarily involved manufacturing jobs. To take a look at the pros and cons of offshoring, review the following table.

| PROS | CONS |
|---|---|
| 1. Less strategic tasks can be outsourced globally so companies can focus on where they can excel and grow. | 1. Jobs are lost permanently and wages fall due to low-cost competition offshore. |
| 2. Outsource work allows companies to create efficiencies that in fact let them hire more workers. | 2. Offshoring may reduce product quality, which can cause permanent damage to a company's reputation. |
| 3. Consumers benefit from lower prices generated by effective use of global resources and developing nations grow, thus fuelling global economic growth. | 3. Communication within the company, with its suppliers, and with its customers becomes much more difficult. |

China and India are oftentimes named as country providers of offshoring. Currently, China is primarily involved with manufacturing at the low end of the technology scale, and India focuses on call centres, telemarketing, data entry, billing, and low-end software development. However, China is intent on developing advanced manufacturing technology and India has a deep pool of scientists, software engineers, chemists, accountants, lawyers, and physicians. The technology talent in these nations also keeps growing: China graduates 250,000 engineers each year and India about 150,000.

When you consider the impact of offshoring on Canada, research supports that more than two-thirds of imported services are from the United States, not China and India. A Statistics Canada paper calculates a number of corre-lations and finds that services offshoring doesn't seem to affect productivity or employment. It does seem to reduce wages in the service sector, though not in the goods-producing sector. Finally, on an industry-by-industry basis, rising offshoring of services seems to be associated with rising value-added. In the financial sector, for instance, low value-added activities such as general accounting are outsourced while high value-added activities such as strategizing are kept in-house and in-country.

Sources: William Watson, "Myth-Busting Offshoring," *National Post*, 30 May 2008, http://network.nationalpost.com/np/blogs/fpcomment/archive/2008/5/30/myth-busting-offshoring.aspx; Pete Engardio, "The Future of Outsourcing," *BusinessWeek*, 30 January 2006, 50–58; and Richard Ernsberger, "The Big Squeeze: A 'Second Wave' of Offshoring Could Threaten Middle-Income, White-Collar and Skilled Blue-Collar Jobs," *Newsweek International*, 30 May 2005.

## Discussion Questions

1. Why are more Canadian companies investigating offshoring as a possible business strategy?

2. Do you think that offshoring is detrimental to the Canadian economy? Explain.

3. In your opinion, what are some business activities that should not be offshored? Explain.

# CHAPTER 4

# The Role of Government in Business

## PROFILE

## Getting to Know Melody Dover of Fresh Media Inc.

Melody Dover founded Fresh Media Inc. in 2003 after working as a professional graphic designer for more than ten years. Prior to opening this business, she broke her right wrist while working for a graphic designer, which prompted her to rethink her career. She decided to enrol in the Interactive Multimedia course at Holland College offered in partnership with Sheridan College. With her newly gained skills, she entered an Atlantic region animation and web design competition, Animediafest, where she took first prize. "People started contacting me to do work for them, and so in June of 2003 I registered the business," says Dover.

Fresh Media is a advertising and branding agency based in Charlottetown, Prince Edward Island (P.E.I.). A creative company with eight employees, it is focused on giving other businesses the best design solutions for their promotional and branding needs. Fresh Media started out with only three clients, but within a year business "just started to swell," says Dover. "Word of mouth was incredible." Now, Fresh Media's clients include a broad range of P.E.I. businesses as well as some off-Island, and sales have continued to increase steadily. As a successful entrepreneur, Dover speaks to students interested in becoming entrepreneurs. "I tell them you have to have passion, because that's what drives you to reach your goal," she says. "Being an entrepreneur is a lifestyle. Your business is a living, breathing creature that you have to take care of . . . When you're an entrepreneur, you have to be prepared for the unknown. You have to be really flexible and ready to accommodate whatever comes along, whether it's a challenge, a catastrophe, or something positive." Dover's company also contributes to the community. Fresh Media adopts one charitable organization each year and provides services free of charge to help promote it. "The community side of the business is really important to me," says Dover. "I believe everyone deserves quality material—even if they can't afford it."

There are many government agencies mandated to provide support for entrepreneurs, and we will discuss several of them in this chapter. One example is the Business Development Bank of Canada (BDC), a financial institution wholly owned by the Government of Canada. This Crown corporation plays a leadership role in delivering financial, investment, and consulting services to Canadian small business, with a particular focus on the technology and export sectors of the economy.

BDC also supports young entrepreneurs. Winner of the 2005 BDC Young Entrepreneur of the Year Award for Prince Edward Island, "Melody is an example of the best of Canada's young entrepreneurs," says BDC President and CEO Jean-René Halde. "The energy and commitment with which she runs her business have resulted in success for herself and generated opportunities for others. She has shown that creativity, passion, and dedication make for a powerful combination and drive the Canadian economy."

Sources: "The Fresh Family," Fresh Media Inc., 28 March 2009, www.fresh media.ca/fresh_family.php?MELODY%20DOVER; and "Melody Dover Takes Creative Leap into Business," Business Development Canada, 18 October 2005, http://www.bdc.ca/en/about/mediaroom/news_releases/2005/2005101805.htm.

# GOVERNMENT AFFECTS BUSINESS

Government activities that affect business may be divided into six categories: Crown corporations, laws and regulations, taxation and financial policies, government expenditures, purchasing policies, and services. Because all of these activities are scattered among different levels of government and many departments, agencies, and corporations, it is not possible to present this information in such neatly divided categories. However, as you make your way through the rest of the chapter you will be able to see elements of these different aspects of government actions affecting business.

Since the focus of this chapter is on the role of government in business, there will be limited discussion on how business affects government. It should become obvious as you read that governments are trying to respond to business needs. This can be anything from creating laws that create a level playing field to providing services that support business initiatives. Reviewing Figure 4.1 will give you a sense of the scope of this relationship.

| FIGURE | 4.1 |
|--------|-----|

**Government Involvement with Business**
Government activities that affect business can be divided into six categories.

1. **Crown Corporations.** There are hundreds of such companies, and they play an important role in the economy. Crown corporations sometimes compete with for-profit businesses.

2. **Laws and Regulations.** These cover a wide range, from taxation and consumer protection to environmental controls, working conditions, and labour–management relations.

3. **Taxation and Financial Policies.** All levels of government collect taxes—income taxes, the GST, sales taxes, and property taxes. Taxation is also fine-tuned by government to achieve certain goals or to give effect to certain policies. This is called fiscal policy.

4. **Government Expenditures.** Governments pay out billions of dollars to Canadians. When these recipients spend this money, businesses benefit. All levels of government provide a host of direct and indirect aid packages as incentives to achieve certain goals. These packages consist of tax reductions, grants, loans, and loan guarantees.

5. **Purchasing Policies.** Governments are very large purchasers of ordinary supplies, services, and materials to operate the country. Because the federal government is the single largest purchaser in Canada, its policies regarding where to purchase have a major effect on particular businesses and the economy.

6. **Services.** These include a vast array of direct and indirect activities, among them helping companies go international, bringing companies to Canada, training and retraining the workforce, and providing a comprehensive statistics service through Statistics Canada.

# GOVERNMENT INVOLVEMENT IN THE ECONOMY

As noted in Chapter 2, the Canadian economic system is described as a mixed economy—that is, an economic system in which some allocation of resources is made by the market and some is made by the government. If you look at the Government of Canada section (and equivalent provincial government sections) in a city telephone directory, you will get some idea of the degree of government involvement in our economy today. Every country's government is involved in its economy, but the specific ways in which the governments participate vary a great deal. There are particular historical reasons why Canada developed into a nation in which governments play very important roles.

When Canada was formed as a country in 1867, the federal government was given the power to "regulate trade and commerce." When the western provinces later joined this Confederation, it became clear that it would take special efforts to build a unified Canada. The very small population was scattered across a huge country, and there was no railway to connect it. Trading patterns were in a north to south configuration because, like today, most people lived near the U.S. border.

The United States developed much faster and with a much larger population and a bigger economy—which provided products not available in the provinces, either because they were not made in Canada or because there was no transportation to distribute them.

This led the Canadian governments, starting with our first prime minister, Sir John A. Macdonald, to develop what was called a **National Policy**. The Policy placed high tariffs on imports from the United States to protect Canadian manufacturing, which had higher costs. (Since that time, trade agreements such as the North American Free Trade Agreement, discussed in Chapter 3, the Canada-Peru Free Trade Agreement, and the Canada-European Free Trade Association have focused on eliminating such tariffs between countries. Note that in 2009, Canada was discussing the creation of a Canada–European Union Trade Agreement.) In addition, the government began to grapple with the difficult question of building a costly rail line to the west coast.

These two issues set the tone for the continuing and substantial involvement of Canadian governments in developing and maintaining the Canadian economy. As you make your way through this chapter and see their complex activities, you should not be surprised to learn that the different levels of government are large employers in the country. The federal government and the provinces with the largest populations and levels of economic activity—namely, Ontario, Quebec, British Columbia, and Alberta—in particular have been excellent sources of employment for graduates in the past.

As you will see in this chapter, we also have an interventionist government that through its activities (e.g., monetary policy and expenditures) tries to create a stable economy for businesses. Before we go into more detail, let us briefly review how government affects business. You never know, one day you may have a job in one of these areas.

**I WANT** to work for the Public Service of Canada

**FEDERAL STUDENT WORK EXPERIENCE PROGRAM**

Canada

The Federal Student Work Experience Program provides full-time students with work experience related to their field of study as well as learning opportunities. With only one application, students can access the more than 8,000 student jobs in the federal government.

**National Policy**
Government directive that placed high tariffs on imports from the United States to protect Canadian manufacturing, which had higher costs.

# CROWN CORPORATIONS

In Canada, an important aspect of the role of government is expressed through **Crown corporations**, which are companies that are owned by the federal or provincial governments. Review Figure 4.2 for a brief list of the top Crown corporations in Canada. Crown corporations were set up for several reasons. They provided services that were not being provided by businesses, which is how Air Canada came into being in the 1930s. Crown corporations were created to bail out a major industry in trouble, which is how the Canadian National Railway was put together in 1919. Lastly, they provided some special services that could not otherwise be made available, as in the case of the Bank of Canada.

Each province also owns a variety of Crown corporations. Typically, a Crown corporation owns the province's electric power company. Some examples are New Brunswick's Power Corporation, Sask-Power, and Hydro-Québec. Alberta owns a bank called Alberta Treasury Branches (ATB), originally set up to help farmers in bad times. Two other examples in Alberta and Quebec are discussed next.

**Crown corporation**
A company that is owned by the federal or provincial government.

Set up in 1978, VIA Rail Canada Inc. serves some 450 Canadian communities throughout the country. Have you ever taken advantage of the student savings offered by VIA Rail?

| Rank | Company | 2008 Revenue ($ Billions) |
|:---:|---|:---:|
| 1 | Hydro-Québec | 12.7 |
| 2 | Canada Mortgage and Housing Corporation | 9.6 |
| 3 | Canadian Wheat Board | 8.4 |
| 4 | Canada Post Corp. | 7.5 |
| 5 | Ontario Lottery and Gaming Corp. | 6.2 |

Source: "Largest Crown Corporations," *Financial Post Business*, 2 June 2009, p. 82. Material reprinted with the express permission of The National Post Company.

## The Financial Role of Two Special Provincial Crown Corporations

The Alberta Heritage Savings Trust Fund was established in the 1970s, when the Alberta economy was prospering as a result of the oil boom. The government set aside a part of its oil royalty revenue to start the fund. In 2008 the Fund's assets totalled $14.5 billion.[1] It must operate on a sound financial basis, but, as much as possible, it makes investment decisions that will benefit Alberta.

Quebec has the Caisse de dépôt et placement du Québec (which means Quebec Deposit and Investment Fund), a giant fund that was established to handle the funds collected by the Quebec Pension Plan. With $220.4 billion in total assets under management in 2008, it is one of the largest pools of funds in North America.[2] This plan was set up parallel to the Canada Pension Plan in 1966. The fund also handles other Quebec government funds, and it is a very powerful investment vehicle that is used to guide economic development in Quebec. Although it, too, must operate on a sound financial basis, it has a lot of scope to make decisions that will benefit the Quebec economy.

## The Role for Government

Since the 1990s, federal and provincial governments have embarked upon a series of measures designed to reduce the role of government in the economy. Over the years, former large corporations like Teleglobe Canada, Air Canada, and Canadian National Railway (CNR) were sold. The national system of air traffic control, the management of airports, hundreds of ports and ferries, and other maritime installations were also sold.

**privatization**
The process of governments
selling Crown corporations.

This disposal of government assets and companies signalled a minor revolution in Canadian history. The whole process of selling publicly-owned corporations is called **privatization**. As well, during this time, industries that had been regulated, such as airlines, oil and gas, and trucking, were partially or completely deregulated. Review Appendix B for a discussion on deregulation.

Similar activities were undertaken by provincial governments. Alberta privatized its liquor board. Ontario sold the toll-road Highway 407 and its share in a land-registry firm. Saskatchewan reduced its interest in giant uranium producer Cameco Corporation and the British Columbia provincial government sold BC Rail Ltd.

Municipal governments are also looking to privatize services such as water systems, garbage collection, and cleaning. Everywhere you look, government agencies, like for-profit organizations, are looking at ways to lower costs and improve efficiencies.

The federal government sold its remaining stake in Petro-Canada, an oil and gas company, in 2005. Here you see the Hanlan Robb gas plant near Edson, Alberta.

## Progress Assessment

- What are the six categories of government involvement with business?
- What are Crown corporations? Why were they created?
- What does privatization refer to? Can you cite any examples?

# LAWS AND REGULATIONS

In Chapter 1 you were introduced to the importance of the legal and regulatory environment. These laws and regulations are created by the politicians who, for the most part, have been elected by Canadians. Consequently, the political parties in power can greatly affect the business environment. This is also why it is important to be aware of the beliefs of the different parties. Some think the government should have more say in business, while others think that less government intervention is best.

The power to make laws is based on the British North America Act, 1867 (BNA Act). The BNA Act was passed by the British Parliament in 1867. It is the law that created the Canadian Confederation and it sets the legal ground rules for Canada. In 1982, the BNA Act became part of the new Constitution and was renamed the Constitution Act, 1867.

Laws are derived from four sources: the Constitution, precedents established by judges, provincial and federal statutes, and federal and provincial administrative agencies.[3] As a business person, you will be affected by current (and potential) laws and regulations. The appendix at the end of this chapter considers the importance of working within the legal environment of business.

Canada has a legislature in each province and territory to deal with local matters. The Parliament in Ottawa makes laws for all Canadians. The Constitution defines the powers that can be exercised by the federal and provincial governments. In the event of a conflict, federal powers prevail.

The Supreme Court of Canada has the final decision on constitutional questions and on important cases of civil and criminal law. It deals also with appeals from decisions of the provincial courts of appeal.

## Federal Government Responsibilities

The federal government is responsible for issues that affect citizens across Canada. Its primary responsibility is to ensure and support the country's economic performance. Some other responsibilities that may have an impact on business operations include:

- trade regulations (interprovincial and international)
- incorporation of federal companies
- taxation (both direct and indirect)
- the banking and monetary system
- national defence
- unemployment
- immigration
- criminal law
- fisheries

In addition to the above-noted areas, the federal government also oversees such industries as aeronautics, shipping, railways, telecommunications, and atomic energy.[4]

As noted in Chapter 1, competition has never been greater than it is today, both internationally and domestically. For example, despite trade agreements, new government policies (e.g., the "Buy American" provisions of U.S. President Obama's massive economic stimulus package, which encourages priority for contracts with U.S. firms) can create barriers to trade.[5] The federal government lobbies other country governments to decrease such trade barriers in an attempt to create business opportunities for Canadian firms. This flip side to this is that these countries may request the same of Canada.

Domestically, the Competition Bureau listens to business and consumer complaints and, in some instances, launches investigations to ensure fair competition. You may recall that Industry Canada is the federal agency that administers a variety of laws affecting businesses trends and consumers. One of the most relevant pieces of legislation is the Competition Act, which aims to ensure that mergers of large corporations will not restrict

Canadian Agricultural Products Standards Act covers a wide range of farm products, such as meat, poultry, eggs, maple syrup, honey, and dairy products.

Consumer Packaging and Labelling Act applies to all products not specifically included in other acts.

Food and Drugs Act covers a whole range of regulations pertaining to quality, testing approval, packaging and labelling.

Hazardous Products Act covers all hazardous products.

Textile Labelling Act includes apparel sizing and many other special areas.

Weights and Measures Act applies to all equipment that measures quantities (scales, gas pumps, and so forth).

**FIGURE** | **4.3**

**Some Major Federal Consumer Protection Laws**
These laws all provide consumers with information and protection in various ways. There are also provincial consumer protection laws.

competition and that fair competition exists among businesses. (Some of the major consumer protection laws are shown in Figure 4.3.) The Act covers many laws, including discriminatory pricing, price fixing, misleading advertising, and the refusal to deal with certain companies. Let us look at some examples. The first considers price fixing and the second considers a concern (unproven at the time this chapter was being written) of unfair competition:

- In 2008, the Competition Bureau of Canada laid charges against 11 gas companies and 13 individuals associated with them for conspiring to fix prices in four Quebec municipalities. Three of the firms pleaded guilty on the spot. The other accused faced trial later that year—and, if found guilty, faced fines up to $10 million or five years in jail for individuals. Newly released court documents show that investigators who have been plowing through the wiretap evidence from the investigation have found references to pricing in half a dozen other towns, including Montreal. The Bureau says more charges might come of the continuing investigation, and that similar investigations are under way in other parts of the country.[6]

*How Canadians Govern Themselves* is a publication that describes Canada's Constitution, the judicial system, and government powers.

- The Competition Bureau of Canada is reviewing a proposed search engine partnership between Yahoo Inc. and Google Inc. amid concerns the deal will lead to rising costs for Canadian companies that advertise online. If the Bureau were to determine that the deal violates the Competition Act, it could force the companies to alter the terms of the partnership or squash it altogether. Google controls nearly 80 percent of the search market in Canada, while Yahoo controls less than 4 percent. Keyword prices on Yahoo could rise as much as 22 percent if the company decides to pursue a "profit maximization strategy," according to a recent report from search engine marketing firm SearchIgnite.[7]

Consider the clothes you wear. They are required to have a label showing the country of origin, size, type of fabric, and washing instructions. When you buy 25 litres of gasoline, you can feel confident that you have received a true measure because of the sticker on the equipment showing when it was last inspected. There are laws that give consumers the right to cancel contracts or return goods within a certain period of time. It is not possible to go through a day and not find an instance where laws have helped you in some way. The appendix at the end of this chapter will highlight the importance of working within the legal environment of business.

## Marketing Boards

In Canada, we have a special system of **marketing boards** that control the supply or pricing of certain agricultural products. Consequently, they often control trade. This supply

**marketing boards**
Organizations that control the supply or pricing of certain agricultural products in Canada.

management is designed to give some stability to an important area of the economy that is normally very volatile. Farmers are subject to conditions that are rather unique and that have a great effect on their business and on our food supply. Weather and disease are major factors in the operation of farms and are beyond the control of the individual farmer. So are unstable prices and changes in supply resulting from uncoordinated decision making by millions of farmers around the world, or the exercise of market power by concentrated business organizations.

In the past farmers have experienced periods of severe drought, flooding, severe cold, and diseases that affected crops, livestock, and poultry. The situation regarding international markets and supply has a serious impact on Canada's grain farmers, since Canada exports much more wheat than it consumes domestically. This market fluctuates greatly depending on the supply in other major grain-exporting countries such as the United States, Argentina, and Australia. The market also depends on demand from major importers such as China and Russia, whose abilities to meet their own requirements are subject to wide variation. Often the Canadian government (like other governments) grants substantial loans with favourable conditions to enable these countries to pay for their imports of our wheat and other agricultural products.

Because we export billions of dollars of agricultural products annually, the ability to hold our own in international markets has a major impact on the state of the Canadian economy. When farmers are flourishing, they buy new equipment and consumer goods and their communities feel the effects of ample cash flow. So does the transportation industry. Conversely, when farmers are suffering, all of these sectors hurt as well.

To smooth out the effects of these unusual conditions on this sector of our economy, and to ensure a steady supply of food to consumers at reasonable prices, six government agencies have been set up to control wheat and barley, dairy products, and poultry. The Canadian Wheat Board operates in the three Prairie provinces. (Read the Reaching Beyond Our Borders box for more details.) The Canadian Dairy Commission controls the output and pricing of milk and other dairy products. The Canadian Egg Marketing Agency, Chicken Farmers of Canada, the Canadian Turkey Marketing Agency, and the Canadian Broiler Hatching Egg Marketing Agency consist of representatives from the provinces that produce these items.

All of these bodies, except the Canadian Wheat Board, control the amount of production for all of the products under their supervision by allocating quotas to each province that produces them. Provincial agencies administer these quotas and set prices for their province. Each agency controls products that are sold only in its province.

The Canadian system of marketing boards has been under attack by various organizations because it does not permit normal competitive conditions to operate in this field. This, they argue, distorts the whole industry and raises prices to Canadian consumers. Defenders of the system argue that other countries have different systems that have the same effect as our marketing boards but are just less visible. The European Union spends billions of dollars on subsidies for their farmers. The United States, which often complains about other countries' unreasonable trade barriers, has its own restrictions, such as on sugar imports.

In Chapter 3, we referred to the World Trade Organization, whose main purpose is to reduce barriers to trade among countries. If the organization is successful, we may see a very different picture emerging worldwide over the next decade: limited protection for domestic markets, reduced tariffs and other restrictions, and the market having a much greater impact on prices and production. The effect on Canadian farmers and on the agricultural industry in general would be enormous, as everyone would be trying to cope with the necessary adjustments to such new conditions.

## Provincial Government Responsibilities[8]

Each province has its own government, while the territories are still governed federally. Issues that affect provincial residents but do not necessarily affect all Canadians are

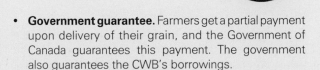

## Reaching Beyond Our Borders

### The Canadian Wheat Board

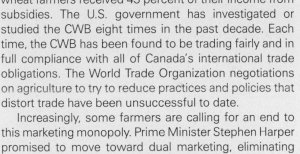

While some erroneously believe that the Canadian Wheat Board (CWB) provides and receives subsidies from the Government of Canada, in fact it is a farmer-controlled organization that markets wheat and barley grown by western Canadian producers. Based in Winnipeg, the CWB is one of the world's largest grain-trading companies, marketing 22 to 24 million tonnes of wheat and barley annually both domestically and to over 70 countries worldwide. Annual sales revenues average between US$3 to $4 billion. While farmers decide what to produce, the role of the CWB is to sell these grains for the best possible price. Sales revenues earned, less marketing costs, are passed back to farmers.

Western Canadian farmers control their marketing organization through the election of ten fellow farmers to the board of directors. The board also includes five directors that are appointed by the federal government. It is up to these 15 directors to oversee the management of the CWB. The CWB's value to farmers is based on three pillars:

- **Single-desk selling.** Instead of competing against one another for sales, these farmers sell as one through the CWB and can therefore command a higher return for their grain. Single-desk selling is the mainstay of the CWB. Without it, customers could choose to buy their products from several different competitors. Farmers would be left with an open market where customers could choose to deal with whoever gives them the lowest price, resulting in lower returns for all farmers.
- **Price pooling.** Price pooling means that all CWB sales during an entire crop year (August 1 to July 31) are deposited into pool accounts. This ensures that all farmers delivering the same grade of wheat or barley receive the same return at the end of the crop year, regardless of when their grain is sold during the year.

- **Government guarantee.** Farmers get a partial payment upon delivery of their grain, and the Government of Canada guarantees this payment. The government also guarantees the CWB's borrowings.

There is a perception that Canadian farmers are more subsidized than farmers in other countries. According to information gathered by the Organisation for Economic Co-operation and Development (OECD), Canadian farmers received 17 percent of their income from subsidies. American wheat producers received 49 percent of their income from subsidies, while European Union wheat farmers received 43 percent of their income from subsidies. The U.S. government has investigated or studied the CWB eight times in the past decade. Each time, the CWB has been found to be trading fairly and in full compliance with all of Canada's international trade obligations. The World Trade Organization negotiations on agriculture to try to reduce practices and policies that distort trade have been unsuccessful to date.

Increasingly, some farmers are calling for an end to this marketing monopoly. Prime Minister Stephen Harper promised to move toward dual marketing, eliminating the monopoly. Under this model, farmers could market their wheat without having to go through the CWB. Since this box was written, what changes have been imposed as a result of WTO negotiations (Doha round)? Has Parliament altered the role of the CWB?

Sources: "About Us," Canadian Wheat Board, 29 June 2009 and 7 September 2008, www.cwb.ca; "Canadian Wheat Board Gag Order Unconstitutional, Court Rules," CBC.ca, 20 June 2008, http://www.cbc.ca/canada/saskatchewan/story/2008/06/20/cwb-ruling.html; and "Strahl Must Defend Canadian Wheat Board and Supply Management," Liberal Party of Canada, 15 March 2006, www.liberal.ca/news_e.aspx? id=11502.

governed at the provincial level. Provincial governments are responsible for the following areas:

- regulation of provincial trade and commerce
- natural resources within their boundaries
- direct taxation for provincial purposes
- incorporation of provincial companies
- licensing for revenue purposes
- the administration of justice
- health and social services
- municipal affairs
- property law
- labour law
- education

## DEALING with CHANGE

### Free Trade Between Provinces

While interprovincial trade is a $300-billion industry in Canada, many Canadian companies and individuals face obstacles when trying to do business outside of their home province or territory. Some trade barriers exist because governments created them to protect their economies from outside competition. Governments also put policies in place to protect the environment, establish workforce standards, or achieve other regulatory purpose. Estimates on the costs of these interprovincial barriers in Canada are $14 billion per year. Interprovincial trade barriers are damaging to the economy and to Canadians' standard of living. These protectionist barriers discourage competition, distort market forces, and reduce efficiency.

The Agreement on Internal Trade (AIT) was signed in 1995 by the first ministers of Canada to allow freer trade between the provinces so that all may benefit. Its purpose is to foster improved interprovincial trade by addressing obstacles to the free movement of persons, goods, services, and investments within Canada. The objective is to reduce extra costs to Canadian businesses by making internal trade more efficient, increasing market access for Canadian companies, and facilitating work mobility for tradespeople and professionals. For example, the Certified General Accountants of New Brunswick successfully appealed to the Internal Trade Secretariat to have the government of Quebec stop restricting access to those that were recognized as qualified to practise accounting in that province.

In 2008, Canada's provincial premiers finally reached a deal to remove barriers that have made it difficult, and sometimes impossible, for workers from one province or territory to work in another. While it is not expected that the amendments will address all barriers, it is a step in the right direction. Amendments to the AIT will lead to full labour mobility for workers and professionals, except where protection of public health or safety justifies barriers. They will also provide for an effective dispute resolution mechanism, including monetary penalties for ignoring a trade panel ruling. Penalties will range from a maximum of $250,000 for the smallest provinces and territories to $5 million for Quebec and Ontario. The issue is especially important to British Columbia, where a shortage of 350,000 workers is forecast between now and 2015. Alberta Premier Ed Stelmach estimates that Alberta will create 400,000 jobs over the next decade. Labour mobility is seen as key to filling these jobs.

Sources: "Certified General Accountants Applaud Movement on Labour Mobility and Resolving Disputes," Certified General Accountants Association of Canada, 30 July 2008, www.cga-canada.org/en-ca/MediaCentre/CurrentMediaReleases/Pages/ca_mdr_2008-07-30.aspx; "Labour Mobility Deal Will Enhance Competitiveness: B.C.'s Campbell and Alberta's Stelmach Deserve Praise for Getting Other Premiers to Sign Up," *Vancouver Sun*, 22 July 2008, A10; "Improving Internal Trade: A Bold Approach," Certified General Accountants Association of Canada, 2008, www.cga-canada.org/en-ca/DiscussionPapers/ca_rep_internal_trade_position-paper2008.pdf; "Overview of the Agreement on Internal Trade, 2009" Internal Trade Secretariat, www.intrasec.mb.ca/index_en/ait.htm; and Paul Vieira, "Internal Barriers an Obstacle," *National Post*, 26 April 2006.

The participation of all provincial governments in federal–provincial, shared-cost arrangements for hospital insurance and medicare has helped ensure nationwide standards of service, despite some differences in their modes of financing and program coverage. While the federal government is responsible for health care, it is still up to the provinces to implement these policies, and their co-operation is critical for success. In contrast, the retention of a high degree of provincial autonomy in the provision of elementary and secondary school education and the accommodation of religious and linguistic preferences has resulted in a variation in school systems. Both government levels also fund programs for post-secondary education. Some changes that are being implemented by the federal and one provincial government with respect to student loans are examined below. The Dealing with Change box highlights provincial decisions that have an impact on the Canadian economy.

### Education[9]

Both the federal and provincial governments run their own student loan programs. The federal government plans to phase out interest and other debt relief options for borrowers under the Canada Student Loans Program. Under the new program, known as the Repayment Assistance Plan (RAP), payments will be geared to income and no payments on federal loans will be required for those individuals with a gross annual income of $20,000 or less. Borrowers who are not eligible for RAP will be able to apply to extend their repayment period to reduce their monthly loan payments. This is especially good news for those that owe thousands of dollars in student loans. Statistics Canada reports that about 27 percent of 2005 graduates with bachelor's degrees still owed an average of $16,200 in government loans two years later, another 15 percent owed an average of $31,600 in government and other loans. Fully 43 percent of those owing more than $25,000 reported having difficulty paying their loans, although fewer than 11 percent were unemployed.

Provincially, the Newfoundland and Labrador government has made an effort to improve its post-secondary education policies. Changes to the student loan program include it being the first province to eliminate interest on student loans and extending a long-running freeze on tuition fees at Memorial University and other post-secondary institutions. "We're extremely excited about this," Daniel Smith, the provincial chair of the Canadian Federation of Students said after the program was revealed. This is going to ease the burden of student debt for students of Newfoundland and Labrador. Almost 50,000 people who currently fall under the student loan portfolio here in the province are going to be in a much better situation coming out of this."

## Municipal Government Responsibilities[10]

Municipal governments—cities, towns, villages, counties, districts, and metropolitan regions—are set up by the provincial legislatures. Their authority is defined by the specific province in which they operate. There are roughly 4,000 municipal governments in Canada that provide a variety of services.

Municipalities also play a role in consumer protection. For example, they have regulations and laws regarding any establishment that serves food. Inspectors regularly examine the premises of all restaurants for cleanliness. Local newspapers often publish lists of restaurants fined for failing to maintain required standards. There are similar laws (called zoning laws) about noise, odours, signs, and other activities that may affect a neighbourhood. Certain zones are restricted to residences, and others permit only certain quiet businesses to operate.

Zoning requirements also limit the height of buildings and define how far they must be set back from the road. Most Canadian cities require that all high-rise buildings have a certain ratio of garage space so that cars have off-street parking spots. Parking problems in residential areas due to overflow of vehicles from adjacent businesses have led to parking being limited to residential permit holders on certain streets, so that stores and other places of business must offer commercial parking lots for their customers. And, of course, there are speed limits set by municipal or provincial authorities.

Municipalities provide services such as water supply, sewage and garbage disposal, roads, sidewalks, street lighting, building codes, parks, playgrounds, libraries, and so forth. Schools are generally looked after by school boards or commissions elected under provincial education Acts

All businesses usually must obtain a municipal licence to operate so the appropriate department can track them to ensure they are following regulations. Many municipalities also have a business tax and a charge for water consumption.

In summary, each level of government has its own roles and responsibilities. Sometimes there is overlap and in other instances, there is downloading of responsibilities. Such is the case with some municipal services. An understanding of these responsibilities will contribute to a better understanding of who is responsible for developing, implementing, and overseeing policies that are important to business.

# TAXATION AND FINANCIAL POLICIES

Mention the word taxes and most people frown. That's because taxes affect almost every individual and business in the country. Taxes are how all levels of government redistribute wealth. The revenue that is collected allows governments to discharge their legal obligations. This revenue is used to pay for public services (e.g., fire, police, and libraries), pay down debt, and fund government operations and programs. Taxes have also been used as a method of encouraging or discouraging taxpayers. For example, if the government wishes to reduce the use of certain classes of products (e.g., cigarettes, alcohol, etc.), it passes what is referred to as a sin tax. It is hoped that the additional cost of the product from increased taxes discourages additional consumption.

In other situations, the government may encourage business to hire new employees or to purchase new equipment by offering a tax credit. A tax credit is an amount that can be deducted from a tax bill. Research In Motion (RIM) opened a technical support operations centre in Halifax that is expected to create 1,200 jobs over five years. As an incentive, the Nova Scotia government offered RIM $19 million in subsidies (some consider this a tax credit), including $14 million in payroll rebates and $5 million for training and recruitment.[11]

Taxes are levied from a variety of sources. Income (personal and business), sales, and property are the major bases of tax revenue. The federal government receives its largest share of taxes from personal income. Figure 4.4 illustrates the impact that taxation has on the price of gasoline.

| FIGURE 4.4 | |
| --- | --- |

**What Goes Into the Price of Gasoline?**
Gasoline prices are impacted by the cost of crude oil (approximately 50 percent of cost), taxes, and refining and marketing costs. They are also subject to market forces (e.g., supply of crude oil). This breakdown is based on gas costing $1.24 per litre, the average price in Canada in May 2008.

| Factor | Cost per Litre |
| --- | --- |
| Crude Oil Barrel Cost | 78¢ |
| Taxes | 32¢ – 33¢ |
| Federal Excise Tax* | 10¢ |
| Provincial Tax | ranges from 6.2¢ in Yukon to 16.5¢ in Newfoundland and Labrador |
| Goods and Services Tax | 5% |
| or Harmonized Sales Tax | 13% in Newfoundland and Labrador, Nova Scotia, and New Brunswick |
| Provincial Sales Tax | in Quebec only |
| Municipal Taxes in Three Cities | 1.5¢ in Montreal, 12.0¢ in Vancouver, and 3.5¢ in Victoria |
| Refining, Marketing Costs, and Margins | 13¢ |

*The federal government raises $4 billion a year.

Source: Based on "What Goes into the Price of Gasoline?" CBC News, 14 May 2009, http://www.cbc.ca/consumer/story/2009/05/14/f-gas-prices-oil.html.

## Progress Assessment

- What are four responsibilities of the federal government?
- What are responsibilities of the provincial governments?
- Why are there interprovincial trade barriers?

# Stabilizing the Economy Through Fiscal Policy

**Fiscal policy** refers to the federal government's effort to keep the economy stable by increasing or decreasing taxes or government spending. The first half of fiscal policy involves taxation. Theoretically, high tax rates tend to slow the economy because they draw money away from the private sector and are remitted to the government. High tax rates may discourage small business ownership because they decrease the profits businesses can make, and this can make the effort less rewarding. It follows then that, theoretically, low tax rates would tend to give the economy a boost.[12] The government can use taxation to help move the economy in a desired direction. For example, taxes may be lowered to stimulate the economy when it is weak. Similarly, taxes may be raised when the economy is booming to cool it off and slow down inflation.

Federal and provincial governments constantly use the lever of fiscal policy to stimulate specific geographic and industrial areas. They offer special tax credits to companies that open plants in areas of chronically high unemployment, such as Cape Breton or Newfoundland and Labrador. All companies that invest in specific activities considered desirable by the government (such as the technology sector) receive a tax credit that reduces the income tax they have to pay. Unfortunately, many of these programs have been scaled back or eliminated due to budget constraints.

The second half of fiscal policy involves government spending. The government spends money in many areas including social programs, highways, the environment, and so on. If the government spends over and above the amount it gathers in taxes for a specific period of time (namely, a fiscal year), then it has a **deficit**.

One way to lessen annual deficits is to cut government spending. This is difficult to do. Every year, there is demand by the provinces (to be discussed later) and territories for increased transfer payments, the need for funds due to unexpected situations (such as the massive flooding in New Brunswick), more pressure from international bodies to increase peacekeeping support, and so on. Some people believe that spending by the government helps the economy grow. Others believe that the money the government spends comes out of the pockets of consumers and business people—especially when taxes have been increased—and that this slows growth. What do you think? Let us look at government actions that have been taken over the past decade.

## The National Debt (Federal Debt)

For many years, the Canadian government spent more than it received in revenues, and it had to borrow heavily. However, it did not reduce spending when times were good to pay back these loans. In Canada, 25 years of annual deficits, starting in the mid-1970s, resulted in a huge (net) national debt of $588 billion by 1997.[13] The **national debt** (also known as the **federal debt**) is the accumulation of government surpluses and deficits over time. This debt was approximately $458 billion in 2008.[14]

After relentless pressure from business organizations and right-wing political groups, the Canadian government decided in 1996 that the only way out of that recession was to eliminate annual deficits and stop the debt from growing. This plan meant cutting expenses and cash outlays as much as possible, including reducing transfers to the provinces to pay for health care, education, and welfare. The government reduced employment insurance payments by raising eligibility standards, paying for shorter periods, and paying smaller amounts. The government also laid off thousands of people and reduced pension payments to wealthier senior citizens.

**fiscal policy**
The federal government's effort to keep the economy stable by increasing or decreasing taxes or government spending.

**deficit**
Occurs when a government spends over and above the amount it gathers in taxes for a specific period of time (namely, a fiscal year).

**national debt (federal debt)**
The accumulation of government surpluses and deficits over time.

## Making Ethical Decisions

### Tackling the Deficit

In the late 1990s the federal government was under strong pressure from the business community to reduce or wipe out the annual deficit in the annual budget. Business was convinced that these constant deficits and the resulting accumulated debt were dragging the Canadian economy down and making Canada uncompetitive with other major countries. To arrive at the surpluses that we have seen since, the federal government drastically cut its expenditures.

This resulted in significant reductions in funding to the provinces for health care, post-secondary education, and other important activities. Combined with other budget-cutting measures that have led to lower and fewer payments to the unemployed, the result has been an increase in poverty levels, especially among children and women.

These facts lead to some ethical questions. How could such severe budget cuts have been avoided? Does the business community bear some responsibility for the increase in poverty in Canada? In other words, was it ethical for business to allow our national debt to grow so large and not challenge the government's annual deficits much earlier? What do you think?

These reductions in spending contributed to Canada's slow recovery from the recession. Increased government borrowing and spending stimulates an economy, while cuts in spending have the opposite effect—they slow down the economy.

The drastic slashing of government spending in the 1990s was strongly opposed by left-wing political groups and many organizations such as churches, unions, welfare groups, food banks, and other community-centred groups because of the hardship these cuts inflicted on many people. Reduced employment insurance and welfare payments, a reduction in hospital funding, the closing of hospitals, and so on, affected many poor and sick people. Cuts to post-secondary education funding resulted in fewer instructors and more students per class, higher fees, increased costs for some services, and a reduction of other services. Food banks across Canada reported a jump in the number of people seeking food. When economic problems become severe, attempts to remedy them can be difficult and painful. Part of budget surpluses since that time were used to restore some of the funding cuts to health and education. The Making Ethical Decisions box highlights the results of the drastic cuts during this time.

Why is it important to control the debt? Financial security is critical to a country's investment in its people and businesses. A lower debt means that less money will need to go toward paying down the national debt and any outstanding interest. Reducing government spending on interest charges will allow the government to spend more money on social programs or to lower taxes. Lower taxes will stimulate the economy, as companies and individuals will have more disposable income.

With a lower debt, Canada could also be considered a more attractive country to invest in—a healthy and educated workforce is able to work and buy products. In addition, employers like well-funded social programs, as there is less risk that they will be asked to increase employee benefits. A lower debt load also means that in times of economic slowdown or when unexpected events occur (such as SARS) the government may have funds available to alleviate the ensuing pressures. Of course, if the debt is high, there is less money that can be dedicated to social programs and initiatives to assist businesses in becoming more competitive.

**surplus**
An excess of revenues over expenditures.

Reductions in the national debt have been the result of surpluses—a **surplus** is an excess of revenues over expenditures. As the debt comes down, the annual interest costs are also reduced. This reduction in the national debt has translated into a savings of billions of dollars each year on debt interest payments. In the mid-1990s, this number was as high as 37.6 cents of each revenue dollar.[14]

## The Federal Budget

In late February of most years the federal finance minister releases a blueprint for how the government wants to set the country's annual economic agenda. This document, called the **federal budget**, is a comprehensive report that reveals government financial policies for the coming year. This political document shows how much revenue the government expects to collect, any changes in income and other taxes, and whether a deficit or a surplus is expected. The federal budget answers questions that affect businesses and Canadians, such as: How much money will go to pay down the debt? How much money will go to social programs such as health care? Will there be more money for research and development? and, Will taxes go up or down?

The budget is reviewed carefully by businesses, consumers, and other countries because the information it contains affects all of these stakeholders. It reflects revenues (from taxation) and expenditures (e.g., Canada Pension Plan payments) for the past year. In addition, the government will communicate program changes for the future, as well as forecasted growth projections. From this document, stakeholders can get an idea of what issues are important to the government.

Keep in mind that promises made by the federal government in a budget are not necessarily permanent. If a new political party is elected, it can reverse these decisions and announce its own initiatives. This is why the first budget after an election is critical. It clearly communicates to the population whether a new government will support its campaign promises. As well, it sends strong signals to businesses and international markets about the government's priorities.

Provincial governments also release their own budgets. A province's financial stability affects political decisions and, ultimately, the business environment within the province's boundaries.

**federal budget**
A comprehensive report that reveals government financial policies for the coming year.

## The Reversal of a Trend: Federal Budget Deficits[16]

After over ten years of budget surpluses, Canada will experience a budget deficit in 2009–2010. Projected to be $50 billion, three factors that have contributed to the projected deficit include a falling world GDP, a continuing U.S. recession, and a drop in commodities prices. (You can see how an understanding of economics and global business is critical when reviewing the federal budget.) As a result of these economic conditions the federal government has been trying to stimulate the economy through initiatives such as increased spending (e.g., infrastructure) and lowering taxes. While the federal government has predicted that the budget will be balanced by 2013–2014, Toronto-Dominion Bank economists Derek Burleton and Don Drummond disagree. They predict that over the next five years, Ottawa will rack up $170 billion in new debt. Increased pressure will come from an aging population that will demand more health-care spending. The baby boom generation is the largest single group in Canada's population and its aging will drive up hospital bills and long-term care costs for taxpayers. "On average, somebody over the age of 65 costs double in terms of somebody under the 65," says Drummond. What are the implications for you, as a young adult, of this growing deficit? What social programs do you think may be cut in order to decrease expenditures?

# Using Monetary Policy to Keep the Economy Growing

Have you ever wondered who lends the federal government money when it spends more than it collects in taxes? One source is the Bank of Canada, a Crown corporation. Its role is to "promote the economic and financial well-being of Canada." The day-to-day administration of monetary policy is the responsibility of the Bank of Canada, in co-operation and in consultation with the federal finance minister.

**Monetary policy** is the management of the money supply and interest rates. It is controlled by the Bank of Canada. When the economy is booming, the Bank of Canada tends to raise interest rates in an attempt to control inflation. This makes money more

**monetary policy**
The management of the money supply and interest rates.

expensive to borrow. Businesses thus borrow less, and the economy slows as business people spend less money on everything, including labour and machinery. The opposite is true when the Bank of Canada lowers interest rates. When this happens, businesses tend to borrow more, and the economy improves. Raising and lowering interest rates should therefore help control the business cycles.

The Bank of Canada also controls the money supply. A simple explanation of how this works is that the more money the Bank of Canada makes available to business people and others, the faster the economy grows. To slow the economy, the Bank of Canada lowers the money supply. If you are eager to learn more about the money supply, you can turn to Chapter 18 now. A recent example of the Canadian government stepping in to stimulate the economy is its reaction to the U.S. subprime crisis that impacted the global economy. Read about this in the next section.

In summary, the government makes two major efforts to control the economy: fiscal policy (taxes and spending) and monetary policy (control over interest rates and the money supply). The economic goal is to keep the economy growing so that more people can rise up the economic ladder and enjoy a satisfying quality of life.[17]

## The Subprime Mortgage Crisis[18]

Subprime mortgages are loans targeted at people who couldn't qualify for regular mortgages because their credit records were not good enough or they did not have a credit history. Some mortgages were also interest-only loans and lower in cost as no principal was being paid down. Initially, these loans came with very low rates (thus, subprime). At the end of this term (e.g., two years), interest rates were much higher and people couldn't afford to make their payments. As housing prices started to fall, they often found they could not longer afford to sell the home either. The fallout has seen decreasing home sales and prices, and rising foreclosures. The resulting crisis contributed to approval of a US$700 billion bank bailout by the U.S. Congress in October 2008 to stabilize the financial sector and reinforce hundreds of financial institutions. The U.S. bailout was not sufficient for its intended purpose. In 2009, President Obama anticipated a new US$750 billion bank bailout. Bank bailouts soon followed in England, Germany, France, Italy, and Spain.

While Canadian financial institutions did not face the high default rates experienced in the United States, they were having trouble borrowing money because banks and other lenders in other countries were more cautious. This credit squeeze sent stock markets (read more about this in Chapter 17) crashing and there were worries of a global meltdown. The federal government announced in October 2008 that it would take over $25 billion worth of bank-held mortgages to ease the growing liquidity problems faced by the country's financial institutions. This would provide more money to financial institutions. To further stimulate the economy and encourage banks to continue lending money, the Bank of Canada continued to lower its lending rate, effectively hitting 0.25 percent, the lowest it can go using conventional monetary policy.

The government did not agree with critics who characterized this action as a bailout of an industry that generated record profits. "This is not a bailout; this is a market transaction that will cost the government nothing," said Prime Minister Harper. "We are not going in and buying bad assets. What we're doing is simply exchanging assets that we already hold the insurance on and the reason we're doing this is to get out in front. The issue here is not protecting the banks." He believes that the problem the country's financial institutions face is not solvency but the availability of credit. It is expected that this action will make loans and mortgages more available and more affordable for ordinary Canadians and businesses. One month later, another $50 billion allocation was announced. Do you agree that this is not a bailout? What would have been the implications for business people and consumers if more money had not been made available by financial institutions?

The Bank of Canada is Canada's central bank. It is not a commercial bank and it does not offer banking services to the public. Rather, it has the responsibilities for Canada's monetary policy, bank notes, financial system, funds management, and retail debt.

## Progress Assessment

- How does the government manage the economy using fiscal policy?
- What is Canada's national debt? Has it been increasing or decreasing over the past six years?
- Explain the purpose of the federal budget.
- What does the term *monetary policy* mean? What organization is responsible for Canada's monetary policy?

# GOVERNMENT EXPENDITURES

Governments in Canada help disburse tens of billions of dollars annually in old-age pensions, allowances to low-income families or individuals, employment insurance, welfare, workers' compensation, and various other payments to individuals. These transfers give Canadians more purchasing power and, therefore, the creation of a more viable market for businesses.

As people spend their money, large numbers of Canadian companies and their employees benefit as a result of this purchasing power. Increasing or lowering the rates or eligibility for these payments results in further fine-tuning of the economy. Again, government cutbacks have resulted in the reduction of such payments in recent years.

Governments also spend huge sums of money on education, health, roads, ports, waterways, airports, and various other services required by businesses and individuals. They also provide aid through direct and indirect government programs designed to help businesses. The Canadian Subsidy Directory lists more than 3,200 sources of financing and government programs for anyone searching for Canadian grants, loans, and government programs.[19] Governments also intervene on an ad hoc (special or unplanned) basis in important cases. Aid to Saskatchewan and Alberta farmers and Newfoundland and B.C. fishers when their industries faced severe hardships are examples.

A visit to Atlantic Canada Opportunities Agency (www.acoa.ca) will introduce you to projects that facilitate development in this region. See if you can find other Web sites for parallel agencies.

# Financial Aid

All levels of government offer a variety of direct assistance programs to businesses, including grants, loans, loan guarantees, consulting advice, information, and other aids that are designed to achieve certain purposes. For example, the Northwest Territories government gave a $34-million loan to Discovery Air to refinance its existing debt. Said Finance Minister Michael Miltenberger, "We have to look at this, because this is a big outfit, has lots of northern content, hundreds and hundreds of jobs."[20] In another example, the Newfoundland government created a program worth up to $18 million to help crab workers affected by the late start to the fishery; the program focused on employment projects to help the approximately 8,500 workers.[21]

Some government aid is designed to help industries or companies that are deemed to be very important—at the cutting edge of technology, providing highly skilled jobs, and oriented toward exports. Bombardier, which makes the Learjet, plans to use $315 million in aid from the United Kingdom, $350 million from Canada, and further help from Quebec authorities, to create a new commercial jet to compete with the smaller offerings of Boeing and Airbus. The company said that plants in Belfast, Northern Ireland, Saint-Laurent and Mirabel in Quebec, and Kansas City, Missouri, will be involved in designing and constructing the new aircraft.[22]

Major companies often hint or announce outright that they are planning to close a plant that they claim is not efficient enough to be competitive. They often suggest that they will consolidate operations with other plants in Canada or the United States. These announcements naturally result in a flurry of efforts by all affected parties to prevent the closure. Unions, municipalities, and provincial and federal governments all work to save the jobs and economies of the area. Such examples are evident in a variety of businesses, including auto plants, pulp and paper mills, food processing plants, oil refineries, shipbuilding yards, meat-packing plants, and steel mills.

While in many cases the closures could not have been prevented, some have been saved by such concerted action. For example, in 2009 GM Canada received an auto bailout of $10.8 billion ($7.1 billion from the federal government and $3.5 billion from Ontario provincial government). What Canada gets is five GM plants in Ontario remaining

Ford Motor Company invested $1 billion to redevelop its Oakville, Ontario, plant as a state-of-the-art flexible manufacturing system. Project Centennial also received $200 million from the Ontario provincial government and from the Government of Canada. The Government of Canada's $100-million contribution is part of a larger commitment to the automotive industry that was supported with the creation of a $1-billion, five-year incentive fund for other automakers and manufacturers. What are the benefits of such government support?

open, while GM is shutting down many plants in the United States, and a guarantee that at least 16 percent of its North America assembly will be done in this country, including a new hybrid, as well as a promise of $2.2 billion in new investments over the next seven years. All this to save less than 5,000 jobs in the assembly plants. This works out to an investment of $1.4 million to save each job. However, in addition to saving these auto assembly jobs, auto parts suppliers can also continue to remain in Canada.[23]

Some of these rescue efforts end in costly failures. For example, in 2004 the P.E.I. government bought Polar Foods, as its bankruptcy put at risk tens of millions of dollars in government investments and brought into question where Island lobsters would be sold.[24] It was estimated that the government lost close to $27 million when it later sold the company. To assist the approximately 800 unemployed fish plant workers, the government set aside close to $1 million in an aid package. Was it worthwhile to spend such sums to provide hundreds of jobs in chronically depressed areas? Was it the best way to help the unemployed in areas of high unemployment? How do you decide what businesses or industries to help and which ones to ignore? These questions are constantly being asked in Canada.

## Equalization of Transfer Payments[25]

Canada is a very large country with uneven resources, climate, and geography, which has led to uneven economic development. Ontario and Quebec, with large populations, proximity to the United States, an abundance of all kinds of natural resources, and excellent rail and water transport, were the earliest to develop industrially.

Nova Scotia and New Brunswick began to suffer when wooden ships gave way to metal ships in the last half of the nineteenth century and their lumber industries declined. The west was sparsely populated until well into the twentieth century. Alberta and British Columbia became strong industrially only in the last 30 years as oil, gas, coal, hydroelectric power, and forestry became significant competitive resources for them. Saskatchewan and Manitoba are essentially tied to the volatile agricultural industry. Newfoundland, which became part of Canada in 1949 and was far below the average Canadian living standard, has relied mainly on fisheries and pulp and paper. With the collapse of the cod fishery, Newfoundland and Labrador now looks to Hibernia and other offshore oil fields to become major factors in its economic growth in the twenty-first century. Nova Scotia is counting on the development of the huge gas fields off Sable Island. The three territories—Yukon, the Northwest Territories, and Nunavut—are very lightly populated and have difficult climates. The Northwest Territories is rich in diamonds and gas exploration.

**Transfer payments** are direct payments from governments to other governments or to individuals. Federal transfer payments to individuals include elderly benefits and employment insurance. Such payments provide social security and income support. **Equalization** is a federal government program for reducing fiscal disparities among provinces. These payments enable less prosperous provincial governments to provide their residents with public services that are roughly comparable to those in other provinces, at roughly comparable levels of taxation. While provinces are free to spend the funds on public services according to their own priorities, these payments are intended to fund medicare, post-secondary education, and smaller programs.

In 2009–2010, Ottawa distributed $14.2 billion in equalization payments to six provinces (P.E.I., Nova Scotia, New Brunswick, Quebec, Ontario, and Manitoba). Introduced in 1957, this system of payments (transfers) to poorer provinces is financed by wealthier ones, such as Alberta. While traditionally Ontario has been considered a "have" province, it received equalization payments for the first time due to a downturn in the manufacturing sector. This was also the first time Newfoundland and Labrador did not receive payments. According to Premier Willians, this can be attributed to Newfoundland and Labrador "operating on its own resources and its own monies because of oil revenues, corporate income taxes, commodity prices, and retail sales."

**transfer payments**
Direct payments from governments to other governments or to individuals.

**equalization**
A federal government program for reducing fiscal disparities among provinces.

The Taking It to the Net exercise near the end of this chapter will encourage you to become more familiar with the details of this program. Note that the Territorial Formula Financing program provides territorial governments with funding to support public services, in recognition of the higher cost of living in the north.

---

## Progress Assessment

- Explain how governments in Canada spend tax dollars to help Canadians.
- Give two examples of how government has provided financial aid to businesses.
- What two groups benefit from equalization transfer payments?

# PURCHASING POLICIES

Most governments are very large purchasers and consumers of goods and services; indeed, in Canada they are the largest buyers. The federal and provincial governments use this enormous purchasing power to favour Canadian companies. The provinces favour these companies in their own territories and have even set up trade barriers between provinces (as discussed earlier). When advanced technology items—civilian or military—must be obtained from foreign companies, our governments usually insist that a certain minimum portion be manufactured in Canada. This enables Canadian companies to acquire advanced technology know-how and to provide employment.

Contracts are awarded most often to help Canadian businesses even if they are sometimes more expensive than bids by non-Canadian companies. This is particularly true in the military acquisitions programs. Whatever can be produced or serviced in Canada—ships, electronics, trucks, artillery, ammunition—is acquired from Canadian companies. These federal and provincial policies are being modified as a result of the general movement to freer trade due to NAFTA. See the Spotlight on Small Business box for an example of a company that benefits from a government contract.

---

## SPOTLIGHT ON **Small Business**

### Ink Isle

Located in Charlottetown, Prince Edward Island (P.E.I.), Ink Isle is the only business of its kind in the province that remanufactures inkjet cartridges and resells other generic inkjet and toner cartridges. This is an environmentally-friendly alternative to throwing out unused inkjet and toner cartridges.

A proud Mi'kmaq member of the Abegweit First Nation, entrepreneur Jacob Jadis discovered his business idea during several exciting travel opportunities for Aboriginal youth across Canada, Australia, and the United States. During these trips he noticed several seemingly successful ink refilling kiosks located mostly in malls. This was a type of business that had not yet reached P.E.I., and with further research it became evident that he could create a better business by remanufacturing, instead of just refilling, ink cartridges. Jadis spent a year on business planning activities including researching the industry, writing a business plan, seeking start-up funding, receiving specialized

training in Colorado, searching for a storefront location and finally purchasing the equipment and products he needed to start Ink Isle. Not only is he fulfilling one of his lifetime goals of being an entrepreneur, but he is also enjoying it because the future is in his hands.

Since he started his business in 2005, Jadis has been receiving orders for toners from a large federal government agency on the Island. As you can infer, the different levels of government not only provide funding for small businesses, but they are also a good source of potential revenue generation. Jadis has also been recognized as the 2007 Prince Edward Island Best Business Award Winner, Winner of the 2006 Aboriginal Entrepreneur of the Year Award for Prince Edward Island, and second place for Atlantic Canada Youth Aboriginal Entrepreneur of the Year.

Source: © Thomas I. White.

# SERVICES

The federal government has departments that provide services to businesses and consumers. We will look at two of these important departments: Industry Canada and Foreign Affairs and International Trade Canada. There are corresponding departments in many of the provinces, especially the four largest and most developed ones (British Columbia, Alberta, Ontario, and Quebec).

## Industry Canada

For many years, the federal government has implemented a variety of programs to help small businesses get started. These programs are part of a larger one that involves setting up Canada Business service centres in every province and territory. These centres are operated jointly with provincial governments and certain local organizations. Industry Canada publishes brochures, booklets, and guides informing business people of the help available and how and where to get it. Industry Canada also participates in the production of publications to promote Canadian businesses internationally.

Other programs are designed to encourage businesses to establish themselves or expand in economically depressed areas of the country. These are populated regions that are industrially underdeveloped, have high unemployment, and have lower standards of living. The programs include help for the tourism industry and for Aboriginal residents of remote areas who want to establish businesses.

## The National Research Council

The National Research Council (NRC) is a federal agency that began in 1916. It reports to Parliament through Industry Canada. The NRC plays a significant role in research that helps Canadian industry remain competitive and innovative. It has been mandated to provide substantial resources to help Canada become one of the world's top five R&D performers by 2010.[26]

This organization of some 4,000 scientists, researchers, and technicians represents Canada's principal science and technology agency. NRC also benefits from the efforts of guest workers, drawn from Canadian and foreign universities, companies, and public- and private-sector organizations. Located in every province, areas of research and industry support are aerospace, biotechnology, engineering and construction, fundamental sciences, information and communications technologies, and manufacturing.

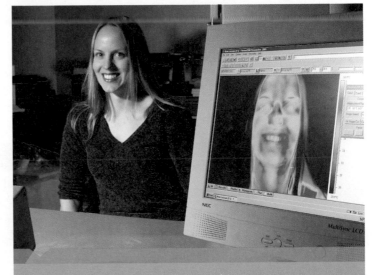

NRC researchers are using thermographic cameras to design tools for physicians to rapidly identify tissue damage. Thermographic video cameras record infrared radiation, or heat, rather than visible light. This heat-imaging camera is thus able to identify differences in blood flow. Warmer areas have greater blood flow, and areas of tissue damage will register abnormally low levels of flow and thus heat. Here, a healthy subject's nose has less blood flow and is cooler (bluer) than her cheeks and the sides of her neck, which are warmer (redder).

## Foreign Affairs and International Trade Canada

Because exports are particularly important to Canada's economic well-being, the government has a very large and elaborate system to assist companies in their exporting and foreign-investment activities. The federal government and most provincial and all large municipal governments have various ministries, departments, and agencies that provide a variety of such services. These include information, marketing, financial aid, insurance and guarantees, publications, and contracts. All major trading countries provide similar support to their exporters.

**FIGURE 4.5**

**Some Government Sources Available to Assist Canadian Businesses**

| Government Source | Mission | Web Site |
|---|---|---|
| Business Development Bank of Canada (BDC) | BDC provides small- and medium-sized businesses with flexible financing, affordable consulting services, and venture capital. BDC has a particular focus on the emerging and exporting sectors of the economy. | www.bdc.ca |
| Export Development Canada (EDC) | EDC provides Canadian exporters with financing, insurance, and bonding services as well as foreign market expertise. | www.edc.ca |
| Industry Canada | The Department's mission is to foster a growing, competitive, knowledge-based Canadian economy. Program areas include developing industry and technology capability, fostering scientific research, and promoting investment and trade. | www.ic.gc.ca/ic_wp-pa.htm |
| National Research Council Canada (NRC) | NRC helps turn ideas and knowledge into new processes and products. Businesses work with partners from industry, government, and universities. | www.nrc-cnrc.gc.ca |
| Canada Business | Canada Business is a government information service for businesses and start-up entrepreneurs in Canada. It serves as a single point of access for federal and provincial/territorial government services, programs, and regulatory requirements for business. | www.canadabusiness.ca |

See Figure 4.5 for a list of government sources that are available to assist Canadian businesses. All of them also provide some support for those that wish to succeed in global markets. We have discussed some of these organizations already in this textbook.

## Progress Assessment

- Why do federal and provincial governments tend to favour Canadian companies when contracts are approved?
- How does the NRC contribute to technology advancement in Canada?
- List four organizations that aim to help exporters.

# ROLE OF THE CANADIAN GOVERNMENT— SOME FINAL THOUGHTS

**industrial policy**

A comprehensive, coordinated government plan to guide and revitalize the economy.

What should be clear is that government always has a critical role to play. Some people believe that the best way to protect the Canadian economy is for the federal government to reverse its current direction of privatization. Instead of withdrawing from active direction and participation in the economy, it should develop a long-term industrial policy of leadership and an active role in shaping the future of the economy. An **industrial policy** is a comprehensive, coordinated government plan to guide and revitalize the economy. An industrial policy requires close consultation with business and labour to develop a comprehensive program for long-term sustainable industrial development.

Others are opposed in principle to such government involvement. As mentioned earlier in this chapter, the 1980s witnessed the start of a movement toward deregulation, privatization, and less government involvement within Canada and other countries. Some believe that these were the right steps for the government to take, and that it should continue with these activities. One organization that supports less government involvement is the Fraser Institute. You will be asked to investigate some of its opinions in the Developing Workplace Skills section of this chapter. Interestingly enough, when events such as SARS or a recession appear, some groups that normally lobby for less government involvement in their industries suddenly believe that government should step in and provide financial assistance. While this is contrary to free-market principles, troubled times are usually followed by calls for more government involvement.

The Constitution Act outlines the powers of all levels of government. Each level of government is focused on creating a competitive environment for businesses of all sizes. As we move forward, the federal government will continue to focus on international trade initiatives to provide opportunities for Canadian businesses. This chapter has highlighted some of the resources that are available to businesses to assist them in their operations.

It is natural for disputes to arise as industries and countries attempt to act in their best interests. These disputes arise even between established trading partners such as Canada and the United States, as evidenced by the long-running lumber dispute. However, in most instances, trade agreements create opportunities. Did you know, for example, that 95 percent of Canada–U.S. trade due to NAFTA is problem-free?[27] While disputes will not be resolved overnight, they are being addressed in a global arena, and this is at least a step in the right direction. Since Canada is a large exporter of goods and services, it must also be aware how its policies on the environment may impact future trade. Read the Green Box for more information.

## Green BOX

### The Environment and the Economy

Governments have many policy options available to reduce greenhouse gas emissions. Some are more politically acceptable and easier to implement than others, and not all approaches are likely to be equally effective. Experience in addressing other environmental issues has shown that using a mix of policy measures is more likely to succeed and to spread the responsibility around fairly. It has been a challenge for governments in Canada to come up with effective policy options to address climate change, partly because all three levels of government (federal, provincial, and municipal) have a stake in this issue as well as responsibilities and opportunities. Not all policy options are suitable for all levels of government, so co-operation and collaboration will be important to make sure that effective measures are put in place without overlap and duplication.

The National Round Table on the Environment and the Economy has recommended that Canada immediately put in place a hard cap regime on emissions by 2015, with auctioning of carbon permits to businesses by 2020. To do otherwise would face dire environmental and economic consequences. Round table chairman Bob Page says the United States is moving quickly on capping emissions and will penalize Canadian exports if Canada does not follow suit. "It is the most serious protectionist challenge we've had to face. Now we're going to see in place of the softwood lumber issue, we're going to see the issue that cuts right across manufacturing in Ontario and Quebec, and natural resource products like the oil sands in Alberta and Saskatchewan ... those products will be subject to a carbon intensity surcharge at the American border" unless Canada meets new American standards." Alberta won't like it, but will likely agree, since the oil sands producers are likely concerned about being shut out of the United States and possibly world markets, said Page, a professor of sustainable development at the University of Calgary.

The Report says it is imperative that Canada move from the patchwork approach adopted by different provinces and for Ottawa to have a unified policy with identical standards across jurisdictions and industries. And it says it is critical that Canadian policy be compatible with that of its largest trading partners, particularly the United States. The cap-and-trade system is designed to put a price on pollution, but instead of taxing energy use by individuals directly, the cost is borne first by large emitters, who are expected to pass it on to consumers. Emissions permits can be traded on an open market between firms that need extra quota and those who have quota to sell.

While this system will involve a major transformation on the cost, the usage, and even the nature of energy in Canada, it is expected that the Canadian economy will continue to grow through the transformation period and that new industries will be created.

Sources: "Control Greenhouse Emissions or Face Trade Sanctions, Panel Tells Governments," The Canadian Press, 16 April 2009, www.cbc.ca/news/story/2009/04/16/tech-090416-cap-and-trade-greenhouse-gas.html; and "Government Policy Options," The Pembina Foundation, 2009, www.greenlearning.ca/climate/policy/canadian-policy-directions/2.

## SUMMARY

**LO ▶ 1** Understand the six categories of government activities that can affect business.

1. There are six categories of government involvement in Canada.

### What are the government activities that affect business?

The six categories of government activities are Crown corporations, laws and regulations, taxation and financial policies, government expenditures, purchasing policies, and services. See Figure 4.1 for a brief description of each activity.

### What is the relationship between Canada's economic system and government involvement?

As noted in Chapter 2, Canada has a mixed economy, which is an economic system in which some allocation of resources is made by the market and some by the government. As a result of the Constitution Act, the different levels of government (federal, provincial, and municipal) have responsibilities and jurisdiction over certain matters of the economy and population.

**LO ▶ 2** Trace the historical role of government in the Canadian economy and understand why Crown corporations were created.

2. The Canadian government played a key role from the beginning of the country in 1867 in protecting young manufacturing industries and getting the railroad built to the west coast, helping to bind the country together.

### Why did the government have to do what it did?

It had the legal power and responsibility to do so, as a result of the Constitution Act. The United States threatened to overwhelm our industry, which was not strong enough by itself to resist or to build the railway.

### Why were Crown corporations necessary?

Companies were not willing or able to assume certain responsibilities or fill some needs in the marketplace. The CNR, Air Canada, Hydro-Québec, and Atomic Energy of Canada Ltd. are some important examples. (The CNR and Air Canada are no longer Crown corporations.)

### What is the recent trend with Crown corporations?

In recent years, we have seen an increasing trend where governments (both federal and provincial) have been selling Crown corporations. This is called privatization. Some examples include the sale of remaining Petro-Canada shares and the sale of BC Rail Ltd.

**LO ▶ 3** Discuss why understanding laws and regulations at all levels of government is critical to business success.

3. Businesses need to understand the laws and regulations that affect them. The Constitution Act defines the powers that can be exercised by the federal government and provincial governments. In the event of a conflict, federal powers prevail.

### What are some federal government responsibilities?

The federal government's responsibilities include trade regulations, the incorporation of federal companies, national defence, immigration, and the fisheries.

### What are some provincial government responsibilities?

Among other areas, provincial governments oversee natural resources within their boundaries, the administration of justice, municipal affairs, and education.

### What are some municipal government responsibilities?

Municipal governments—cities, towns, villages, counties, districts, metropolitan regions—are set up by the provincial legislatures. Municipalities provide services such as water supply, sewage and garbage disposal, roads, sidewalks, street lighting, building codes, parks, playgrounds, libraries, and so forth. They play a role in consumer protection (e.g., inspectors examine restaurants) and the establishment of zoning requirements.

4. Each level of government collects taxes from companies. These taxes allow governments to discharge their legal obligations and to fund social programs.

**LO ▶ 4** Explain how taxation and financial policies affect the Canadian economy.

**What is fiscal policy?**
Fiscal policy refers to the federal government's effort to keep the economy stable by increasing or decreasing taxes or government spending.

**What is the national debt?**
The national debt is the accumulation of past government surpluses and deficits. Since the late 1990s, the national debt has been decreasing. In 2008, it was approximately $458 billion.

**How is monetary policy different from fiscal policy?**
Controlled by the Bank of Canada, monetary policy is the management of the money supply and interest rates. When the economy is booming, the Bank of Canada tends to raise interest rates in an attempt to control inflation. Since money is more expensive to borrow, businesses borrow less, and the economy slows as business people spend less money on everything.

5. Government expenditures benefit consumers and businesses alike.

**LO ▶ 5** Describe how government expenditures benefit consumers and businesses alike.

**How do governments assist consumers with their tax dollars?**
Governments disburse tens of millions of dollars annually in social program spending (e.g., old-age pensions, employment insurance, allowances to low-income families, etc.). These transfers give consumers more purchasing power.

**How do businesses benefit from government expenditures?**
All levels of government provide direct and indirect aid packages as incentives to achieve certain goals. These packages can consist of tax reduction, tariffs and quotas on imports, grants, loans, and loan guarantees.

6. Purchasing policies and services assist Canadian businesses.

**LO ▶ 6** Illustrate how purchasing policies and services assist Canadian businesses

**Why is preferential treatment given to Canadian companies when they bid for a government contract?**
Contracts are awarded most often to help Canadian businesses. This way, Canadians are employing and contributing to a strong economy.

**What are two government departments that are particularly focused on assisting Canadian businesses?**
Industry Canada and the Department of Foreign Affairs and International Trade assist businesses domestically and internationally.

## KEY TERMS

| | | |
|---|---|---|
| Crown corporation  103 | industrial policy  122 | National Policy  103 |
| deficit  113 | marketing boards  107 | privatization  104 |
| equalization  119 | monetary policy  115 | surplus  114 |
| federal budget  115 | national debt (federal debt)  113 | transfer payments  119 |
| fiscal policy  113 | | |

## CRITICAL THINKING

1. The issue of how much government should be involved in the economy has been the subject of much debate in Canada. In the United States, ideology has played a major role in influencing Americans to believe that,

in principle, government should "butt out." This thinking ignores the significant role that the U.S. government has played and continues to play in the country's economy. In Canada, we are less negative and perhaps more pragmatic: If it works, let's do it. But where do we go from here? Do we need less or more government involvement? Is it a question of the quality of that involvement? Could it be smarter rather than just less? How can the cost of government involvement decrease?

2. What are the implications of a minority federal government to the Canadian political scene? Explain. (A minority government exists when no one party has a majority of seats in a legislative assembly. To pass legislation and other measures, that government would need the support of at least some members of other parties in the assembly.[28])

3. If you represented the federal government, how would you respond to industries that have been seeking government action (e.g., bailout money or changes to policies) but to no avail? (For example, take the position of the forestry industry in Canada which in the past six years has lost about 130,000 jobs in Canada.[29]) Keep in mind that the other industries (e.g., auto) have received such support (i.e., bailout money).

## DEVELOPING WORKPLACE SKILLS

1. Scan your local newspapers, the *Globe and Mail*, the *National Post*, or a Canadian magazine such as *Canadian Business* for references to government programs that help Canadian businesses or have assisted a specific company. Bring these articles to class and discuss.

2. Many U.S. states and foreign governments have developed strong marketing campaigns to attract Canadian businesses. They also offer many incentives (including financial ones) to lure businesses to move there. Should anything be done about this? Most provincial governments have similar programs to attract foreign companies to their jurisdictions. Check out your provincial government's Web site to see what it is doing in this regard. Bring your information to class to discuss this kind of government expenditure.

3. The Fraser Institute is a Canadian think tank that believes in a competitive marketplace, lower taxes, and less regulation. It supports a limited role for government in the marketplace. In a group of four, review some of its research. Some possibilities are economic freedom, government spending, privatization, and trade. Present your findings to the class. (Hint: You can find information at www.fraserinstitute.ca.)

4. Although unemployment remains high, especially among young people, business people complain that they cannot find trained employees to fill existing vacancies. Job candidates lack math and science backgrounds and their written English-language skills are weak. (In Quebec, there are similar complaints, but the language problems are with French.) Further, too many candidates are high school dropouts. What can be done about this serious problem? Should business or government be working on it? What exactly should they be doing? Discuss this in a group of three.

## TAKING IT TO THE NET 1

www.mcgrawhillconnect.ca

### Purpose

To become familiar with the financial budget and Canada's fiscal balance.

### Exercise

Visit the Department of Finance Canada's Web site at www.fin.gc.ca. Click on Budget Info and answer the following questions.

1. What was the largest component of budgetary expenditures for last year's budget, as communicated in the most recent budget? How was this different from the previous year's budget?

2. What was the largest component of budgetary revenues for last year's budget, as communicated in the most recent budget? How was this different from the previous year's budget?

3. Common revenue sources for provincial (and federal) governments include personal income taxes, corporate income taxes, sales taxes (except in Alberta), and payroll taxes. List other provincial revenue sources.

4. Did Canada experience a deficit or a surplus last year?

## TAKING IT TO THE NET 2

While still on the Department of Finance Canada's site, click on Transfer Payments to Provinces. Answer the following questions.

1. What is the estimated equalization entitlement for next year?

2. How are equalization payments calculated?

3. What provinces are scheduled to receive equalization payments?

## ANALYZING MANAGEMENT DECISIONS

### Gambling: A Cash Cow for Provincial Governments

Starting slowly in Quebec in the late 1960s, but catching on quickly across the country, lotteries, casinos, bingo, video-lottery terminals (VLTs), and other forms of gambling had become, by the end of the twentieth century, a major source of revenue for many provincial governments.

You can get some idea of how large the gambling business has become by looking at the revenues and profits for the Ontario and Quebec governments. For the year ended 31 March 2008, the Ontario Lottery and Gaming Corporation generated $3.7 billion in economic activity. Total revenue at Loto-Québec was a little over $3.8 billion. Over the years, both organizations have generated billions of dollars for their respective governments. Both operations also allot millions of dollars to help gamblers whose obsession with gambling has proven destructive to themselves or their families.

Sources: "2008 Annual Report," Loto-Québec, 2008, www.loto-quebec. com, http://www.loto-quebec.com/corporatif/pdf/2008_annual_report.pdf# page=1; and "OLG Gives Back," Ontario Lottery and Gaming Corporation, 2008, http://www.olg.ca/about/economic_benefits/index.jsp.

### Discussion Questions

1. Some people and organizations argue that governments should not be in the gambling business, that encouraging gambling is a bad idea. Others argue that private enterprise should run that kind of business, and argue further that companies would generate more profit for governments. Governments reply that they want to prevent organized crime from controlling gambling, so they must own and run such operations. What do you think? Is it okay for governments to be in the gambling business?

2. Governments seem to believe that gambling is a great way to raise money because Canadians don't seem to mind creating revenue by having some fun, and a chance at big winnings, instead of just paying higher taxes. Besides, they argue, nobody is forced to gamble, so it's a kind of voluntary tax. How do you feel about that? Do you buy that argument? Explain.

3. Some churches and other institutions concerned with personal and family welfare point to the rising number of family and personal breakdowns caused by people becoming gambling addicts. Also, easy access to VLTs is very bad for young persons. Do you agree with either of these concerns? Why? What can be done to improve the situation?

4. Suppose that you agree with those who are totally opposed to governments encouraging gambling. Wouldn't taxes have to be raised to replace these revenues? Would you mind paying more taxes? Do you think your parents or family members would mind? Do you have any other suggestions?

# Working Within the Legal Environment of Business*

## THE NEED FOR LAWS

Imagine a society without laws. Just think, no speed limits to control how fast we drive, no age restrictions on the consumption of alcoholic beverages, no limitations on who can practise medicine—a society in which people are free to do whatever they choose, with no interference. Obviously, the more we consider this possibility, the more unrealistic we realize it is. Laws are an essential part of a civilized nation. Over time, though, the direction and scope of the body of laws must change to reflect changes in the needs of society.

In the Canadian system of government, which uses the English model, there are three branches of government. Each has a distinct role in the legal system, though sometimes the lines get blurred. The primary function of the legislative branch, composed of the Parliament of Canada and the legislatures of the provinces, is to make the laws. Municipal councils also make laws, but their legislative power is limited to the scope delegated to them by their provincial legislature. The executive branch (e.g., government departments, administrative boards, and police departments) administers the laws, putting them into practice. The judicial branch (i.e., the courts) applies the law and interprets it when there is a dispute.

The Canadian court system has both federal and provincial courts, with jurisdiction that parallels the constitutional division of power between the central and provincial governments. The courts hear cases involving both criminal and civil law. **Criminal law** defines crimes, establishes punishments, and regulates the investigation and prosecution of people accused of committing crimes. **Civil law** involves legal proceedings that do not involve criminal acts; it includes laws regulating marriage, payment for personal injury, and so on. There are also appeal courts that hear appeals of decisions made at the initial trial, brought by the losing party in the case. Appeal courts can review and overturn decisions made by the trial court. The highest level appeal court for all matters is the Supreme Court of Canada.

The law also governs the activities and operations of business in general. In fact, business people often complain that the government is stepping in more and more to govern the behaviour of business. We have laws and regulations regarding sexual harassment on the job, hiring and firing practices, leave for family emergencies, environmental protection, safety, and more. As you may suspect, business people prefer to set their own standards of behaviour. However, the business community has not been perceived as implementing acceptable practices quickly enough. To hasten the process, governments have expanded their control and enforcement procedures. In this appendix we will look at some of the laws and regulations now in place and how they affect business.

**Business law** refers to rules, statutes, codes, and regulations that are established to provide a legal framework within which business may be conducted and that are enforceable by court action. A business person should be familiar with laws regarding product liability, sales, contracts, fair competition, consumer protection, taxes, and bankruptcy. Let's start at the beginning and discuss the foundations of the law. It's hard to understand the law unless you know what the law is.

---

**criminal law**
Defines crimes, establishes punishments, and regulates the investigation and prosecution of people accused of committing crimes.

**civil law**
Legal proceedings that do not involve criminal acts.

**business law**
Rules, statutes, codes, and regulations that are established to provide a legal framework within which business may be conducted and that are enforceable by court action.

---

* Written by Ray Klapstein, Dalhousie University

# STATUTORY AND COMMON LAW

There are two major kinds of law: statutory law and common law. Both are important for business people.

**Statutory law** includes the laws that are made by the Parliament of Canada and the provincial legislatures, international treaties, and regulations and bylaws—in short, written law established by or through the legislative branch of government. You can read the statutes that make up this body of law, but they are often written in language whose meaning must be determined in court. That's one reason why there are so many lawyers in Canada! **Common law** is the body of law that comes from decisions handed down by judges. Common law is often referred to as unwritten law because it does not appear in any legislative enactment, treaty, or other such document. Under common law principles, what judges have decided in previous cases is very important to today's cases. Such decisions are called **precedents**, and they guide judges in the handling of new cases. Common law evolves through decisions made in trial courts, appellate courts, and special courts. Lower courts (trial courts) must abide by the precedents set by higher courts (appeal courts) such as the Supreme Court of Canada. In law classes, therefore, students study case after case to learn about common law as well as statutory law.

The Canadian legal system is complicated by the fact that federal law and provincial (including municipal) law in nine provinces operate under the English common law system, while provincial law in the Province of Quebec operates under the French civil law system. The difference lies more in principle than in practice: the common law system recognizes that courts actually make law through their decisions, while the civil law system restricts courts to interpreting the law that is provided by leglislation that takes the form of the provincial civil code.

**statutory law**
Federal and provincial legislative enactments, treaties of the federal government, and bylaws/ordinances—in short, written law.

**common law**
The body of law that comes from decisions handed down by judges; also referred to as unwritten law.

**precedent**
Decisions judges have made in earlier cases that guide the handling of new cases.

## Laws Made Under Delegated Authority: Administrative Agencies

Different organizations within the government issue many rules, regulations, and orders. **Administrative agencies** are federal or provincial institutions and other government organizations created by Parliament or provincial legislatures with delegated power to pass rules and regulations within their mandated area of authority. Legislative bodies can both create administrative agencies and dissolve them. Some administrative agencies hold quasi-legislative, quasi-executive, and quasi-judicial powers. This means that an agency is allowed to pass rules and regulations within its area of authority, conduct investigations in cases of suspected rule violations, and hold hearings to determine whether the rules and regulations have been violated.

Administrative agencies actually issue more rulings affecting business and settle more disputes than courts do. There are administrative agencies at the federal, provincial, and local levels of government. For example, these include:

**administrative agencies**
Federal or state institutions and other government organizations created by Parliament or provincial legislatures with delegated power to pass rules and regulations within their mandated area of authority.

1. *At the federal level:* The CRTC (Canadian Radio-television and Telecommunications Commission) regulates the use of the airwaves, OSFI (Office of the Superintendent of Financial Institutions) regulates the operation of banks and other financial institutions, and the Commissioner of Competition is responsible for investigating complaints that the Competition Act has been violated.

2. *At the provincial level:* Public utility commissions and boards regulate prices for services such as electricity, licensing boards set the qualifications required for practising trades and professions (e.g., the practice of medicine or law), and labour relations boards oversee the certification of unions and relations between employers and unionized employees.

3. *At the local level:* Zoning boards and planning commissions control land use and development, and there are school boards and police commissions.

# TORT LAW

The tort system is an example of common law at work. A **tort** is a wrongful act that causes injury to another person's body, property, or reputation. This area of law comes within provincial jurisdiction, so legislation dealing with the topic comes from the provincial legislatures.

Criminal law focuses its attention on punishing and rehabilitating wrongdoers. Tort law, though, focuses on the compensation of victims. There are two kinds of torts. An intentional tort is a wilful act that results in injury. On the other hand, the unintentional tort of **negligence** provides compensation when the wrongdoer should have acted more carefully even though the harm or injury was unintentional. Decisions involving negligence can often lead to huge judgments against businesses. In a highly publicized U.S. case, McDonald's lost a lawsuit to a person severely burned by its hot coffee. The jury felt the company failed to provide an adequate warning on the cup, and awarded a very large amount as compensation. Product liability is another example of tort law that's often very controversial. This is especially true regarding torts related to business actions. Let's look briefly at this issue.

## Product Liability

Few issues in business law raise as much debate as product liability. Critics believe that product liability laws have gone too far and deter product development. Others feel that these laws should be expanded to include products such as software and fast food. **Product liability**, covered under tort law, holds businesses liable for harm that results from the production, design, sale, or use of products they market. At one time, the legal standard for measuring product liability was whether a producer knowingly placed a hazardous product on the market. Today, many provinces have extended product liability to the level of **strict product liability**. Legally, this means without regard to fault. Thus, a company could be held liable for damages caused by placing a defective product on the market even if the company did not know of the defect at the time of sale. In such cases, the company is required to compensate the injured party financially.

The rule of strict liability has caused serious problems for businesses. For example, companies that produced lead-based paint in the past could be subject to expensive legal liabilities even though lead paint has not been sold for many years. The manufacturers of chemicals and drugs are also often susceptible to lawsuits under strict product liability. A producer may place a drug or chemical on the market that everyone agrees is safe. Years later, a side effect or other health problem could emerge. Under the doctrine of strict liability, the manufacturer could still be held liable. Businesses and insurance companies have called for legal relief from huge losses awarded in strict product liability suits. They have lobbied to set limits on the amounts of damages for which they are liable should their products harm consumers.

## Intellectual Property: Patents, Copyrights, and Trademarks

Many people, perhaps including you, have invented products that may have commercial value. The question that obviously surfaces is what to do next. One step may be to apply for a patent. A **patent** gives inventors exclusive rights to their inventions for 20 years from the date they file their patent application. The Canadian Intellectual Property Office (http://cipo.gc.ca) receives the application and grants the patent. In addition to filing forms, the inventor must ensure that the product is truly unique. Most inventors rely on lawyers who specialize in the field to manage the filing process.

Patent owners have the right to sell or license the use of a patent to others. Foreign companies are also eligible to file for Canadian patents. Recent changes in the Patent Act and an international patent co-operation treaty permit any inventor who applies within 12 months of filing in his or her own country to obtain a uniform filing date in all participating countries.

The penalties for violating a patent can be very severe, but the defence of patent rights is solely the job of the patent holder. In a rather famous U.S. case (where the law regarding patents is much the same as in Canada), the camera and film company Polaroid was able to force Kodak to recall all of its instant cameras because Polaroid had several patents that Kodak violated. Kodak lost millions of dollars, and Polaroid maintained market leadership in instant cameras for many years. The possible remedies for patent infringement include compensation in the form of money damages, injunctions prohibiting further infringements, and an accounting for all profits gained from the infringement.

Just as a patent protects an inventor's right to a product or process, a **copyright** protects a creator's rights to materials such as books, articles, photos, paintings, and cartoons. Copyright is protected by the Copyright Act, a federal statute. The protection of a copyright extends for the life of the original author plus 50 years after his or her death. Registration of the copyright is not required, but provides the benefit of public notice of its existence and provides proof of the copyright holder's ownership of the work.

A **trademark** is a brand that has been given legal protection for both the brand name and the pictorial design. Trademarks generally belong to the owner forever, as long as they are properly registered and renewed every 15 years. Some well-known trademarks include the Pillsbury Doughboy, the Disney Company's Mickey Mouse, the Nike swoosh, and the golden arches of McDonald's. Like a patent, a trademark is protected from infringement. Companies fight hard to protect trademarks, especially in global markets where pirating can be extensive. Like patents, there are specific requirements imposed by the Trademarks Act, the most difficult one being that the trademark must be "distinctive."

The fourth type of intellectual property protected by federal legislation in Canada is an **industrial design**. Industrial designs differ from things that can be copyrighted by the fact that they are produced by an industrial process. For example, fine china dinnerware would be a product that would fall into this category. As with the other types of intellectual property, the design of the subject matter must be original.

**copyright**
A form of intellectual property that protects a creator's rights to materials such as books, articles, photos, and cartoons.

**trademark**
A brand that has been given exclusive legal protection for both the brand name and the pictorial design.

**industrial design**
A form of intellectual property that protects the owner's exclusive right to use the visible features of a finished product that identify it.

## THE SALE OF GOODS

Each of Canada's provinces has a statute called the Sale of Goods Act. With limited exceptions (i.e., contracts where the price is below the minimum set by the individual province's Act), this Act applies to all contracts for the sale of goods. A sale contract is different from others in that there must be a transfer of ownership of goods in return for money consideration. Except in Ontario and British Columbia, a contract for the sale of goods must be written. There are exceptions, though, where part of the goods have actually been received by the buyer, there has been partial payment of the price, or an "earnest" has been given to demonstrate sincerity. The Sale of Goods Act establishes the rules and requirements associated with the deal, establishing the respective rights and obligations of the parties of the contract.

## Warranties

A warranty guarantees that the product sold will be acceptable for the purpose for which the buyer intends to use it. There are two types of warranties. **Express warranties** are specific representations by the seller that buyers rely on regarding the goods they purchase. The warranty you receive in the box with a clock, toaster, or DVD player is an express warranty. **Implied warranties** are legally imposed on the seller. It is implied, for example, that the product will conform to the customary standards of the trade or industry in which it competes. For example, it's expected that a toaster will toast your bread to your desired degree (light, medium, dark) or that food bought for consumption off an establishment's premises is fit to eat.

**express warranties**
Specific representations by the seller that buyers rely on regarding the goods they purchase.

**implied warranties**
Guarantees legally imposed on the seller.

Warranties offered by sellers can be either full or limited. A *full warranty* requires a seller to replace or repair a product at no charge if the product is defective, whereas a *limited warranty* typically limits the defects or mechanical problems that are covered. Many of the rights of buyers, including the acceptance and rejection of goods, are spelled out in the Sale of Goods Act, so both buyers and sellers should be familiar with its provisions.

# NEGOTIABLE INSTRUMENTS

**negotiable instruments**
Forms of commercial paper (such as cheques) that are transferable among businesses and individuals and represent a promise to pay a specified amount.

**Negotiable instruments** are forms of commercial paper, and come in three types: promissory notes, cheques, and bills of exchange. A *promissory note* is a written contract with a promise to pay a sum of money in the future. A *cheque* is an instruction to a bank to make a payment. A *bill* (or *draft*) is an order to make a payment. All three types are regulated by the federal Bills of Exchange Act. All three types are transferable among businesses and individuals and represent a promise to pay a specified amount. They must be (1) written and signed by the maker or drawer, (2) payable on demand or at a certain time, (3) payable to the bearer (the person holding the instrument) or to a specific order, and (4) contain an unconditional promise to pay a specified amount of money. Negotiable instruments are transferred (negotiated for payment) when the payee signs the back. The payee's signature is referred to as an endorsement.

# CONTRACT LAW

If I offer to sell you my bike for $35 and later change my mind, can you force me to sell the bike, saying we had a contract? If I lose $120 to you in a poker game, can you sue in court to get your money? If I agree to sing at your wedding for free and back out at the last minute, can you claim that I violated a contract? These are the kinds of questions that contract law answers.

**contract**
A legally enforceable agreement between two or more parties.

A **contract** is a legally enforceable agreement between two or more parties. **Contract law** specifies what constitutes a legally enforceable agreement. Basically, a contract is legally binding if the following conditions are met:

**contract law**
Set of laws that specify what constitutes a legally enforceable agreement.

1. *An offer is made.* An offer to do something or sell something can be oral or written. If I agree to sell you my bike for $35, I have made an offer. That offer is not legally binding, however, until other conditions are met.

2. *There is a voluntary acceptance of the offer.* Both parties to a contract must voluntarily agree on the terms. If I used duress in getting you to agree to buy my bike, the contract would not create enforceable rights and obligations. Duress occurs if there is coercion through force or threat of force. You couldn't use duress to get me to sell my bike, either. Even if we both agree, though, the contract is still not legally binding without the next four conditions.

**consideration**
Something of value; consideration is one of the requirements of a legal contract.

3. *Both parties give consideration.* **Consideration** means something of value, and there must be a flow of consideration in both directions. If I agree to sell you my bike for $35, the bike and the $35 are consideration, and we have a legally binding contract. If I agree to sing at your wedding and you do not agree to give me anything in return (consideration), we have no contract.

4. *Both parties are competent.* A person under the influence of alcohol or drugs, or a person of unsound mind (e.g., one who has been legally declared incompetent), cannot be held to a contract. In many cases, a minor may not be held to a contract either. For example, if a 15-year-old agrees to pay $10,000 for a car, the seller will not be able to enforce the contract due to the buyer's lack of competence.

5. *The contract must be legal.* A contract to do something illegal cannot be enforced. For example, a contract for the sale of illegal drugs or stolen merchandise would not be enforceable, since both types of sales are violations of criminal law.

6. *The contract is in proper form.* Provincial legislation in each province requires that an agreement for the sale of goods for more than a fixed amount (e.g., $200) must be in writing. Contracts that cannot be fulfilled within one year and contracts regarding real property (land and everything attached to it) must be in writing as well.

## Breach of Contract

**Breach of contract** occurs when one party fails to follow the terms of a contract. Both parties may voluntarily agree to end a contract. While in force, however, if one person violates the contract, the following remedies may be available.

1. *Specific performance.* The person who violated the contract may be required to live up to the agreement if money damages would not be adequate. For example, if I legally offered to sell you a rare painting, I may be required to actually sell you that painting.

2. *Payment of damages.* The term **damages** refers to the monetary settlement awarded by the court to a person who is injured by a breach of contract. If I fail to live up to a contract, you can sue me for damages, usually the amount you would lose from my non-performance. If we had a legally binding contract for me to sing at your wedding, for example, and I failed to come, you could sue me for the cost of hiring a new singer of the same quality and reputation.

3. *Discharge of obligation.* If I fail to live up to my end of a contract, you could agree to drop the matter. Generally you would not have to live up to your end of the agreement either.

Lawyers would not be paid so handsomely if the law were always as simple as implied in these rules of contracts. In fact, it is always best to have a contract in writing even if not required under law. The offer and consideration in a contract should be clearly specified, and the contract should be signed and dated. A contract does not have to be complicated as long as it has these elements: it is in writing, mutual consideration is specified, and there is a clear offer and agreement to accept it.

**breach of contract**
When one party fails to follow the terms of a contract.

**damages**
The monetary settlement awarded to a person who is injured by a breach of contract.

# LAWS TO PROMOTE FAIR AND COMPETITIVE PRACTICES

One objective of legislators is to pass laws that the courts will enforce to ensure a competitive atmosphere among businesses and promote fair business practices. In Canada, the Competition Bureau and other government agencies serve as watchdogs to ensure that competition among sellers flows freely and that new competitors have open access to the market. The scope of the governments' approach on this is broad and extensive.

There was a time when big businesses were able to drive smaller competitors out of business with little resistance; however, governments have responded to these troubling situations and continue to establish new rules to govern how businesses must deal with the new challenges facing them today.

The changing nature of business from manufacturing to knowledge technology has called for new levels of regulation on the part of both federal and provincial agencies. For example, Microsoft's competitive practices have been the focus of intense investigation in countries around the globe. One of the major accusations against the computer software firm has been that it has hindered competition by refusing to sell the Windows operating system to computer manufacturers unless they agree to sell Windows-based computers exclusively. This requirement has forced computer manufacturers to make a difficult choice: buy only Windows or don't buy Windows at all! Given that many consumers wanted Windows, the computer companies had little choice but to agree.

# LAWS TO PROTECT CONSUMERS

**Consumerism** is a social movement that seeks to increase and strengthen the rights and powers of buyers in relation to sellers. Although consumerism is not a new movement, it has taken on new vigour and direction in the early twenty-first century because of the corporate scandals and greed involving companies such as Enron and WorldCom. Consumers have been particularly critical of government for its lack of oversight and action in the securities markets.

The protection of consumers has only recently come into vogue as a suitable topic for legislation. In earlier times, legislators deemed it appropriate to leave this to the common law, supplemented by the provisions of the Sale of Goods Act. The modern phenomenon of concentration of economic power in large manufacturing and distributing companies and in financial institutions has dramatically eroded the relative bargaining power of the consumer. The technical sophistication of modern products makes it impossible for consumers to detect product defects in advance. Price, quality, and safety have become matters that are often not negotiable: the consumer's choice is to accept or not accept the product, as is. Because of the inequality of bargaining power held by consumers in comparison to large retailers, manufacturers, and financial institutions, legislators have deemed it appropriate to intervene, readjusting the balance by protecting the consumer. The topics that have received the most attention are product performance and business practices.

## Product Performance

The Parliament of Canada has enacted several major statutes dealing with consumer safety and product performance. The Consumer Packaging and Labelling Act establishes requirements for disclosing ingredients and quantities, and includes provision for some standardization of package sizes. The Textile Labelling Act requires disclosure of the fabrics and fibres in wearing apparel, together with recommended cleaning procedures. The Weights and Measures Act establishes a uniform system for weighing and measuring goods sold to consumers. The Food and Drugs Act provides for inspection and regulation of food and drugs, requires purity and sanitary storage, and restricts the distribution of potentially harmful substances. The Hazardous Products Act establishes a list of dangerous products that it is illegal to manufacture, and regulations governing the manufacture, packaging, and distribution of other products that can be harmful. The Motor Vehicle Safety Act and the Aeronautics Act establish national standards, specifying safety features that must be provided in motor vehicles and aircraft.

This federal legislation is supplemented by provincial legislation in all provinces. Some provinces have been much more active in this regard than others. In most, this legislation appears in a provincial Consumer Protection Act, but provisions designed to protect consumers appear in other Acts as well.

## Business Practices

With respect to door-to-door sales, most provinces have legislation permitting the consumer to rescind a purchase contract within a specified "cooling off" period. All provinces also have registration and licensing requirements for door-to-door sellers and collection agencies, designed to prevent the use of harassment and pressure. Most also provide that a consumer who receives unsolicited goods through the mail is not liable to pay for them, or even to return them. Most provinces have also established statutory warranties with regard to contracts for the purchase and sale of consumer durables, voiding attempts to negate the warranties implied by the Sale of Goods Act.

## Misleading Advertising

One of the major topics addressed by the Competition Act, mentioned earlier in this appendix, is misleading advertising. False or misleading representations about the characteristics of a product are prohibited. These include statements, warranties, and guarantees about the performance, efficacy, or length of life of a product that are not based upon adequate or proper testing, and by placing the onus on anyone making such representations to prove that they are based on testing. Misleading representations about the "ordinary" price of a product are also prohibited, as is the advertising of products for sale at a "bargain" price when the advertiser does not have reasonable quantities available for sale.

Most provinces supplement the federal legislation in this area, in much the same way as they do with regard to product performance requirements. The Ontario Business Practices Act, for example, prohibits false representations about product performance.

# DOING BUSINESS AS A CORPORATION

A company or corporation is a person, separate from its owners (who are called shareholders or stockholders), in the eyes of the law. The shareholders elect a small group of individuals (called directors) who are given ultimate decision-making authority for the corporation. In turn, the directors appoint the officers (e.g., president, CEO), who are placed in charge of the day-to-day management of the corporation. Shareholders do not participate in the normal management processes of the corporation.

The rules for how a corporation is governed and the nature of its rights and obligations are established by statute law (e.g., The Canada Business Corporations Act) and by the principles of common law and equity. The directors and officers of a corporation have obligations to the shareholders, but also have responsibilities to non-shareholder groups, including employees, creditors, customers, and the public at large. Issues in the area of corporate governance have gained much attention in recent years. Notable cases such as Enron and WorldCom (discussed in Chapter 5) have demonstrated clearly the need for corporate officers and directors to act with utmost good faith in discharging their obligations.

# BANKRUPTCY AND INSOLVENCY

The **bankruptcy** process recognizes that a debtor can reach a point where he or she will never be able to meet all obligations to creditors. The process is designed to minimize the negative impact of this situation for both debtor and creditor. The Bankruptcy and Insolvency Act, a federal statute, establishes a uniform national system for dealing with the problem. It is designed to achieve a reasonable and fair distribution of the debtor's assets among creditors, and to release the honest debtor in this position from ongoing obligations that cannot possibly be met, allowing him or her to resume productive business activity without them.

The provinces continue to have jurisdiction over an individual's financial affairs until he or she becomes insolvent or bankrupt. Once a person becomes bankrupt, the central government has jurisdiction to enact laws governing the rights and obligations of bankrupts and their creditors.

Bankruptcy can be either voluntary or involuntary. In **voluntary bankruptcy** cases the debtor applies for bankruptcy, whereas in **involuntary bankruptcy** cases the creditors start legal procedures against the debtor. Most bankruptcies today are voluntary because creditors often want to wait in hopes that they will be paid all of the money due them rather than settle for only part of it.

**bankruptcy**
The legal process by which a person, business, or government entity unable to meet financial obligations is relieved of those obligations by a court that divides debtor assets among creditors, allowing creditors to get at least part of their money and freeing the debtor to begin anew.

**voluntary bankruptcy**
Legal procedures initiated by a debtor.

**involuntary bankruptcy**
Bankruptcy procedures filed by a debtor's creditors.

The Bankruptcy and Insolvency Act establishes the scheme of distribution to be followed by the trustee in settling the claims of a bankrupt person's creditors. There are three basic categories of creditors for these purposes.

The highest priority is given to *secured creditors*, who have a direct claim against a specified asset of the debtor. When a debtor goes through bankruptcy proceedings, secured creditors are entitled to the entire proceeds realized on the sale of the asset in which they hold security, up to the secured amount owed to them by the debtor.

The second class of creditors is *preferred creditors*, and they have priority over general or unsecured creditors. This category includes trustees and lawyers involved in the process, unpaid employees of the bankrupt individual, and unpaid taxes.

The third group is the *unsecured creditors*, who do not have a direct claim against any asset and are not given preferred treatment by the Act. Unsecured claims include amounts owed to secured or preferred creditors that are in excess of the amount secured or preferred. All unsecured claims are treated equally by the Act, with each entitled to receive the same amount per dollar owed from the trustee in settlement of the amount claimed.

The bankrupt's contractual obligations to his or her creditors are discharged once he or she has complied fully with the terms of the arrangement that has been made by the trustee and accepted by the court. Payment of the established proportion of unsecured obligations, rather than payment in full, is sufficient to discharge all obligations. However, the discharge of a bankrupt is not automatic; it is a matter within the court's discretion. Whether a discharge is granted depends on matters like whether the person is a first-time bankrupt. Also, a discharge doesn't cover absolutely all obligations. Some obligations continue anyway. These include fines, child support payments, and amounts gained through fraud.

## The Companies' Creditors Arrangement Act

The Companies' Creditors Arrangement Act (CCAA) is a federal statute that provides a second option in the commercial context for insolvent debtors to avoid bankruptcy proceedings. It makes provision for the restructuring of business debt when a company is unable to meet its financial obligations. The CCAA enables a company to submit a proposal to its creditors for an arrangement without bankruptcy proceedings. It permits a company to remain in business even though insolvent, and protects it from proceedings by creditors who might wish to force it into bankruptcy. The benefit to creditors is orderly conduct of the debtor's affairs, by maintaining the status quo while the debtor attempts to gain its creditors' approval of the plan and, if the plan is approved, payment by its terms. The attempts to financially restructure Air Canada and Stelco in the early years of this decade have been made under the CCAA.

The CCAA and the Bankruptcy and Insolvency Act work in concert with each other. The Bankruptcy and Insolvency Act expressly provides that it does not affect the operation of the CCAA, and allows the court to order continuation of a proposal made under the Bankruptcy and Insolvency Act under the CCAA.

# DEREGULATION

**deregulation**
Government withdrawal of certain laws and regulations that seem to hinder competition.

Canada now has laws and regulations covering almost every aspect of business. In recent years, public concern that there are too many laws and regulations, and that these laws and regulations cost the public too much money, has developed. Thus began the movement toward deregulation. **Deregulation** means that the government withdraws certain laws and regulations that seem to hinder competition. Perhaps the most publicized examples of deregulation were those in the airline and telecommunications industries. Government used to severely restrict airlines with regard to where they could land and fly. When such restrictions were lifted, the airlines began competing for different routes and charging lower prices. This has provided a clear benefit to consumers, but puts tremendous pressure on the airlines to be competitive. Airlines such as WestJet have taken advantage of the opportunities, while Air Canada has had difficulty adapting. Similar deregulation in telecommunications has given consumers a flood of options in the telephone service market.

It seems that some regulation of business is necessary to ensure fair and honest dealings with the public. Still, businesses have adapted to the laws and regulations, and have done much toward producing safer, more effective products. However, corporate scandals since the turn of the century have soured what appeared to be better dialogue and co-operation between business and government. Many in government and society called for even more government regulation and control of business operations to protect investors and workers. With global competition increasing and small- and medium-sized businesses striving to capture selected markets, business and government need to continue to work together to create a competitive environment that is fair and open. If businesses do not want additional regulation, they must accept their responsibilities to all their stakeholders.

## KEY TERMS

administrative agencies  129

bankruptcy  135

breach of contract  133

business law  128

civil law  128

common law  129

consideration  132

consumerism  134

contract  132

contract law  132

copyright  131

criminal law  128

damages  133

deregulation  136

express warranties  131

implied warranties  131

industrial design  131

involuntary bankruptcy  135

negligence  130

negotiable instruments  132

patent  130

precedent  129

product liability  130

statutory law  129

strict product liability  130

tort  130

trademark  131

voluntary bankruptcy  135

# CHAPTER 5

# Ethics and Social Responsibility

## LEARNING OBJECTIVES

AFTER YOU HAVE READ
AND STUDIED THIS CHAPTER,
YOU SHOULD BE ABLE TO:

**LO ▶ 1** Explain why legality is only one step in behaving ethically.

**LO ▶ 2** Describe management's role in setting ethical standards and distinguish between compliance-based and integrity-based ethics codes.

**LO ▶ 3** List the six steps that can be considered when setting up a corporate ethics code.

**LO ▶ 4** Define corporate social responsibility and examine corporate responsibility to various stakeholders.

**LO ▶ 5** Discuss the responsibility that business has to customers, investors, employees, society, and the environment.

## Getting to Know Mary Dawson, Canada's Conflict of Interest and Ethics Commissioner

In 2006, the Federal Accountability Act was implemented to help strengthen accountability and increase transparency and oversight in government operations. The Federal Accountability Act created the Conflict of Interest Act. As Canada's Conflict of Interest and Ethics Commissioner, Mary Dawson is responsible for administering the Conflict of Interest Act ("Act") and helping public office holders avoid conflicts of interest. The Act sets out clear conflict of interest and post-employment rules applicable to public office holders. Public office holders are ministers, parliamentary secretaries, full- and part-time ministerial staff and advisors, and Governor in Council and ministerial appointees (deputy ministers, heads of agencies and Crown corporations, members of federal boards and tribunals).

The main responsibilities of the Office in administering the Act are to advise public office holders on their obligations under the Act; to receive confidential reports of assets, liabilities, and activities of certain public office holders; to maintain confidential files of required disclosures; to maintain a public registry for publicly declarable information; and to conduct examinations into alleged contraventions of the Act. In her role, Dawson is also responsible for administering the Conflict of Interest Code for Members of the House of Commons.

Dawson holds a Bachelor of Arts (Philosophy) and a Bachelor of Civil Law from McGill University, a Bachelor of Laws from Dalhousie University and a post-graduate degree in Public Law from the University of Ottawa. She began her career in the public service in 1967 as a researcher with the Department of National Revenue. Joining the Department of Justice in 1968, she subsequently held positions of increasing scope and responsibility.

To highlight some of her roles, Dawson held the position of Associate Chief Legislative Counsel from 1980 to 1986 and was the Assistant Deputy Minister of the Public Law Sector of Justice from 1986 to 1995. She was personally involved in the drafting of numerous pieces of legislation, including key statutes such as the Constitution Act, 1982, as well as the Meech Lake Accord and the Charlottetown Accord. In 1987 she was appointed as Chairperson of the Statute Revision Commission, a legislative body responsible for revising and consolidating the public general statutes of Canada. In 1995, Dawson became Associate Deputy Minister with responsibility for the Constitutional Affairs and Canadian Unity Section and, as such, supported the Minister of Justice, the Minister of Intergovernmental Affairs and the Prime Minister, through the Clerk of the Privy Council, on all constitutional matters. Since her retirement from the Department of Justice, Dawson has acted as a consultant on a variety of projects, both in the public and the private sectors. She often speaks to university classes and other groups and participates from time to time on panels. In 2007, she was named a member of the Order of Canada.

This chapter introduces you to the importance of ethical behaviour. With the media saturated by stories of high-profile business and government failures, why do we open this chapter on ethics with a profile of Mary Dawson and the Office of the Conflict of Interest and Ethics Commissioner? Because by attempting to improve oversight in government operations, the Office plays a key role in promoting good governance and accountability, the key to which is a high standard of ethical behaviour. The need for improved governance and better accountability to stakeholders has recently assumed increasing prominence in the private sector as well.

In this chapter, we explore the responsibility of businesses to all of their stakeholders: customers, investors, employees, and society. We also look at the responsibilities of individuals. After all, responsible business behaviour depends on the responsible behaviour of each individual in the organization.

Sources: "About the Office," Office of the Conflict of Interest and Ethics Commissioner, 31 July 2008, http://ciec-ccie.gc.ca/Default.aspx?pid=8&lang=en; "About the Commissioner," Office of the Conflict of Interest and Ethics Commissioner, 24 July 2008, http://ciec-ccie.gc.ca/Default.aspx?pid=3&lang=en; and "Prime Minister Welcomes New Conflict of Interest and Ethics Commissioner," Office of the Prime Minister, 9 July 2007, http://www.pm.gc.ca/eng/media.asp?category=1&id=1740.

# ETHICS IS MORE THAN LEGALITY

It is not uncommon to hear of instances where business people are involved in unethical behaviour. Some examples of Canadian companies that have been caught in such scandals include Livent, CIBC World Markets, Nortel, and WestJet. After two years of denying accusations, WestJet Airlines Ltd. admitted to spying on Air Canada. In a news release, WestJet apologized for accessing a confidential Air Canada Web site designated for reservations: "This practice was undertaken with the knowledge and direction of the highest management levels of WestJet and was not halted until discovered by Air Canada. This conduct was both unethical and unacceptable and WestJet accepts full responsibility for such misconduct."[1] As part of the settlement, WestJet paid Air Canada's investigation and litigation costs of $5.5 million and it made a $10 million donation in the name of both airlines to children's charities across Canada.[2] The Canadian business environment has also been impacted by notable scandals in other countries such as Enron, Arthur Andersen, Tyco, and Parmalat, just to name a few.

It is not just for-profit business people that exhibit unethical behaviour. In the mid-2000s, Canadians were shocked to learn of the Auditor General's findings related to the advertising and sponsorship program run by the federal Public Works Department. It was disclosed that "senior government officials running the federal government's advertising and sponsorship contracts in Quebec, as well as five Crown corporations—the Royal Canadian Mounted Police (RCMP), Via Rail, Canada Post, the Business Development Bank of Canada, and the Old Port of Montreal—wasted money and showed disregard for rules, mishandling millions of dollars since 1995."[3] In 2007, the Atlantic Lottery Corporation announced it was turning over its files to police over concerns of retailers stealing winning tickets from customers.[4] This was soon followed by the British Columbia government's audit announcement of the province's lottery system following the Ombudsman report that found the lottery system was open to fraud.[5] In Figure 5.1, you will see a brief summary of some of the most-publicized corporate scandals in recent years.

Given the ethical lapses that are so prevalent today, what can be done to restore trust in the free-market system and leaders in general? First, those who have broken the law need to be punished accordingly. Arresting business leaders and sending them to jail may seem harsh, but it is a first step toward showing the public that it is time to get serious about legal and ethical behaviour in business. No one should be above the law: not religious people, not government people, and not business people. New laws making accounting records more transparent (easy to read and understand) and more laws making business people and others more accountable may help. But laws don't make people honest, reliable, or truthful. If laws alone were a big deterrent, there would be much less crime than exists today.

The danger in writing new laws to correct behaviour is that people may begin to think that any behaviour that is within the law is also acceptable. The measure of behaviour, then, becomes: "Is it legal?" A society gets in trouble when it considers ethics and legality to be the same. Ethics and legality are two very different things. Although following the law is an important first step, ethical behaviour requires more than that. Ethics reflects people's proper relations with one another: How should people treat others? What responsibility should they feel for others? Legality is more narrow. It refers to laws we have written to protect ourselves from fraud, theft, and violence. Many immoral and unethical acts fall well within our laws.[6]

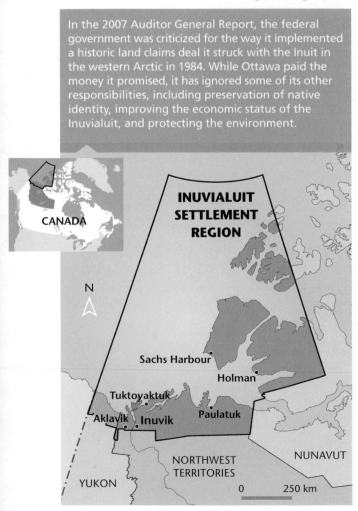

In the 2007 Auditor General Report, the federal government was criticized for the way it implemented a historic land claims deal it struck with the Inuit in the western Arctic in 1984. While Ottawa paid the money it promised, it has ignored some of its other responsibilities, including preservation of native identity, improving the economic status of the Inuvialuit, and protecting the environment.

CANADA

INUVIALUIT SETTLEMENT REGION

N

Sachs Harbour

Holman

Tuktoyaktuk

Aklavik   Inuvik   Paulatuk

NORTHWEST TERRITORIES    NUNAVUT

YUKON

0     250 km

**Lottery Corporations:** In March 2007, Ontario Ombudsman Andre Marin's Report blasted the Ontario Lottery and Gaming Corporation for not cracking down on retailers who collected tens of millions of dollars in jackpots between 1999 and 2006, some of them fraudulently. Police began probing allegations of fraudulent lottery prize claims by retailers after Marin accused the Corporation of "coddling" ticket sellers and playing "games" with customers who complained they had been cheated of their jackpots. In May 2007, the Atlantic Lottery Corporation announced it was turning over its files to police over similar concerns of retailers stealing winning tickets from customers. Also in May, the British Columbia government announced an audit of the province's lottery system following a negative report by the ombudsman that found it was open to fraud.

**Research In Motion (RIM) Stock Option Scandal:** An Ontario court approved a settlement between the company and the Ironworkers of Ontario Pension Fund over allegations RIM had backdated stock options to company executives. Under terms of the settlement, RIM's co-founders Jim Balsillie and Mike Lazaridis agreed to pay $2.5 million each (in addition to the $5 million the executives had each agreed to repay earlier). The company has also ceased giving stock options to directors, added more independent directors to the board and tightened up its executive compensation practices. Both the Ontario Securities Commission and the U.S. Securities and Exchange Commission announced they are looking at allegations of stock options backdating at the company.

**Federal Government Sponsorship Scandal:** The Auditor General's 2004 Report found that $100 million was paid to a variety of communications agencies in the form of fees and commissions, and said that the program was basically designed to generate commissions for these companies rather than to produce any benefit for Canadians. Implicated in this scandal were high-level officials. Charles Guité, a former senior bureaucrat, was sentenced to 42 months in prison for defrauding the federal government. Other scandal participants who received prison sentences, and whose advertising agencies benefited from these funds, include Jean Brault (30 months) and Paul Coffin (18 months). Gilles-André Gosselin, who headed Gosselin Communications, was charged in 2008 with nineteen criminal charges, including fraud.

**Hollinger International Inc.:** Conrad Black, who once headed the Hollinger International Inc. media empire, was convicted of obstruction of justice in 2007. In addition to three other former Hollinger executives, he was also found guilty of fraud for funneling US$6.1 million from the media company. Black was sentenced to 6½ years in federal prison and ordered to pay a small six-figure fine plus restitution of $6.1 million. Throughout the trial, Black has maintained his innocence. Before he was sentenced, he voiced his "deep regret" for the $1.2 billion in shareholder value lost to the company by the inept management of his successors. Three former Hollinger executives also received sentences: Jack Boultbee (27 months), Peter Atkinson (24 months), and Mark Kipnis (placed on probation with six months of house arrest). David Radler, one-time CEO of Hollinger International, pleaded guilty to mail fraud. He received a 29-month sentence and agreed to pay a US$250,000 fine.

Sources: Mark Steyn, "Conrad Black Trial," *Maclean's*, 24 December 2008, http://forums.macleans.ca/advansis/ ?mod=for&act=dis&eid=52&so=1&sb=1&ps=5; "Former Sponsorship Ad Exec Facing Criminal Charges," CBC News, 17 December 2008, http://www.cbc.ca/canada/story/2008/12/17/gosselin-charges.html; "Chicago Judges Reject Request to Reconsider Conrad Black's Appeal," CBC News, 21 August 2008, http://www.cbc.ca/money/ story/2008/08/21/black.html; "Police Probe in Lottery Scandal not Over Yet," CBC News, 20 December 2007, http:// www.cbc.ca/canada/toronto/story/2007/12/20/lottery-investigation.html; "Forgive and (Maybe) Forget," Canadian Business Online, 6 November 2007, http://www.canadianbusiness.com/columnists/john_gray/article.jsp?conte nt=20071106_153800_5340; "Lotto 6/49 Bonus Rounds Coincided with Lottery Scandals," CBC News, 30 May 2007, http://www.cbc.ca/canada/toronto/story/2007/05/30/lotto649-bonus-rounds.html; "U.S. Judge Decides not to Revoke Black's Bond," CTV.ca, 26 June 2006, http://www.ctv.ca/servlet/ArticleNews/story/CTVNews/20060626/ black_bond_060626/20060626/; Ross Marowits, "Guite Sentenced to 3 1/2 Years in Prison," Canoe Inc., 19 June 2006, http://CNRews.canoe.ca/CNREWS/Law/2006/03/29/1511103-cp.html; and "Federal Sponsorship Scandal," CBC News Online, 19 June 2006, http://www.cbc.ca/news/background/groupaction/.

**FIGURE 5.1**

**Brief Summary of Some Corporate Scandals**

# Ethical Standards Are Fundamental

**ethics**

Standards of moral behaviour; that is, behaviour that is accepted by society as right versus wrong.

We define **ethics** as the standards of moral behaviour; that is, behaviour that is accepted by society as right versus wrong. Many people today have few moral absolutes. Many decide situationally whether it's okay to steal, lie, or drink and drive. They seem to think that what is right is whatever works best for the individual, that each person has to work out for himself or herself the difference between right and wrong. That is the kind of thinking that has led to the recent scandals in government and business. This isn't the way it always was. However, in the past decade there has been a rising tide of criticism in Canada (and other countries) of various business practices that many Canadians consider unacceptable.

In a country like Canada, with so many diverse cultures, you might think it would be impossible to identify common standards of ethical behaviour. However, among sources from many different times and places—such as the Bible, Aristotle's *Ethics*, William Shakespeare's *King Lear*, the Quran, and the *Analects* of Confucius—you'll find the following basic moral values: integrity, respect for human life, self-control, honesty, courage, and self-sacrifice are right; cheating, cowardice, and cruelty are wrong. Furthermore, all of the world's major religions support a version of the Golden Rule: Do unto others as you would have them do unto you.[7]

# Ethics Begins with Each of Us

It is easy to criticize business and political leaders for their moral and ethical shortcomings, but we must be careful in our criticism to note that ethics begins with each of us. Ethical behaviour should be exhibited in our daily lives, not just in a business environment.

The Fraser Institute's annual Generosity Index measures the propensity to give to charitable donations. Based on the 2008 Generosity Index, and as highlighted in Figure 5.2, the Institute found that 24.7 percent of Canadian tax filers donated to registered charities in 2006. The average annual donation was $1,470. Manitoba and Ontario rank as leaders in both the percentage of tax filers who donate and the percentage of income donated. Though the extent of charitable giving in almost every province from 1996 to 2006 has decreased, the percentage of aggregate personal income donated in Canada has increased.[8] What do you think accounts for this trend?

Young people learn from the behaviour of others. In a study conducted on one college campus, 80 percent of the students surveyed admitted to cheating. At the University

Downloading from the Internet is the most common form of cheating today. Have you ever been tempted to take credit for someone else's work?

of Maryland, a group of instructors conducted a "techno sting" by posting false answers to an accounting exam on a Web site. Twelve students used the false answers, including a few who admitted to getting the answers from the site during the exam itself by using their cellphones. To fight the problem of plagiarism, many instructors now use services such as Turnitin.com, which scans students' papers against over 64 million student papers in the Student Paper Database.[9] Have you seen students cheat on assignments or exams? How did this make you feel? Students use many reasons to rationalize such behaviour, such as "Everyone else is doing it" or "I ran out of time to prepare, but I will do all my own work next time." What do you think of these reasons?

Two studies found that there is a strong relationship between academic dishonesty among undergraduate students and dishonesty later when these same students were in the working world.[10] In response, many schools are adopting stricter

**FIGURE | 5.2**

**The Fraser Institute's 2008 Generosity Index**

| Province | Percent of Returns with Charitable Donations (%) | Rank for Percent of Returns with Charitable Donations | Percent of Income Donated (%) | Rank for Percent of Income Donated | Average Charitable Donation ($) | Rank for Average Charitable Donation |
|---|---|---|---|---|---|---|
| British Columbia | 23.4 | 7 | 0.84 | 5 | 1,713 | 4 |
| Alberta | 25.0 | 5 | 0.86 | 4 | 2,057 | 1 |
| Saskatchewan | 26.0 | 4 | 0.91 | 3 | 1,440 | 6 |
| Manitoba | 28.1 | 1 | 1.14 | 1 | 1,734 | 3 |
| Ontario | 26.7 | 2 | 0.92 | 2 | 1,746 | 2 |
| Quebec | 22.3 | 9 | 0.33 | 11 | 613 | 13 |
| New Brunswick | 22.9 | 8 | 0.76 | 6 | 1,291 | 7 |
| Nova Scotia | 23.9 | 6 | 0.73 | 8 | 1,263 | 8 |
| Prince Edward Island | 26.4 | 3 | 0.76 | 7 | 1,075 | 11 |
| Newfoundland & Labrador | 21.6 | 10 | 0.49 | 9 | 944 | 12 |
| Yukon | 20.7 | 11 | 0.38 | 10 | 1,174 | 10 |
| Northwest Territories | 17.3 | 12 | 0.29 | 12 | 1,213 | 9 |
| Nunavut | 10.8 | 13 | 0.25 | 13 | 1,549 | 5 |
| **Canada** | **24.7** | | **0.76** | | **1,470** | |

Sources: "Generosity in Canada and the United States: The 2008 Generosity Index," The Fraser Institute, December 2008, http://www.fraserinstitute.org/Commerce.Web/product_files/Generosity_Index_2008.pdf; Canada Revenue Agency, 2008a; and Statistics Canada, 2008a.

honour policies that provide serious consequences for cheating. Do you think that such policies make a difference to student behaviour?

It is always healthy when discussing moral and ethical issues to remember that ethical behaviour begins with you and me. We cannot expect society to become more moral and ethical unless we as individuals commit to becoming more moral and ethical ourselves.

The purpose of the Making Ethical Decisions boxes you see throughout the text is to demonstrate to you that it is important to keep ethics in mind whenever you are making a business decision. The choices are not always easy. Sometimes the obvious solution from an ethical point of view has drawbacks from a personal or professional point of view. For example, imagine that your supervisor at work has asked you to do something you feel is unethical. You have just taken out a mortgage on a new house to make room for your first baby, due in two months. Not carrying out your supervisor's request may get you fired. What would you do? Sometimes there is no desirable alternative. Such situations are called ethical dilemmas because you must choose between equally unsatisfactory alternatives. It can be very difficult to maintain a balance between ethics and other goals such as pleasing stakeholders or advancing in your career. It is helpful to ask yourself the following questions when facing an ethical dilemma:[11]

1. *Is it legal?* Am I violating any law or company policy? Whether you are thinking about having a drink and then driving home, gathering marketing intelligence, designing

a product, hiring or firing employees, planning on how to get rid of waste, or using a questionable nickname for an employee, it is necessary to think about the legal implications of what you do. This question is the most basic one in behaving ethically in business, but it is only the first.

2. *Is it balanced?* Am I acting fairly? Would I want to be treated this way? Will I win everything at the expense of another party? Win–lose situations often end up as lose–lose situations. There is nothing like a major loss to generate retaliation from the loser. You can see this in the stock market today. Many companies that were merely suspected of wrongdoing have seen their stock drop dramatically. Not every situation can be completely balanced, but it is important to the health of our relationships that we avoid major imbalances over time. An ethical business person has a win–win attitude. In other words, such a person tries to make decisions that benefit all parties involved.

3. *How will it make me feel about myself?* Would I feel proud if my family learned of my decision? My friends? Would I be able to discuss the proposed situation or action with my immediate supervisor? The company's clients? How would I feel if my decision were announced on the evening news? Will I have to hide my actions or keep them secret? Has someone warned me not to disclose my actions? Am I feeling unusually nervous? Decisions that go against our sense of right and wrong make us feel bad—they corrode our self-esteem. That is why an ethical business person does what is proper as well as what is profitable.

It is important to note that there are no easy solutions to ethical dilemmas. Individuals and companies that develop a strong ethics code and use the three ethics-check questions presented above have a better chance than most of behaving ethically. If you would like to know which style of recognizing and resolving ethical dilemmas you favour, fill out the ethical orientation questionnaire in Figure 5.3.

---

**FIGURE | 5.3**

**Ethical Orientation Questionnaire**

Please answer the following questions.

1. Which is worse?
   A. Hurting someone's feelings by telling the truth.
   B. Telling a lie and protecting someone's feelings.

2. Which is the worse mistake?
   A. To make exceptions too freely.
   B. To apply rules too rigidly.

3. Which is it worse to be?
   A. Unmerciful.
   B. Unfair.

4. Which is worse?
   A. Stealing something valuable from someone for no good reason.
   B. Breaking a promise to a friend for no good reason.

5. Which is it better to be?
   A. Just and fair.
   B. Sympathetic and feeling.

6. Which is worse?
   A. Not helping someone in trouble.
   B. Being unfair to someone by playing favourites.

7. In making a decision you rely more on
   A. Hard facts.
   B. Personal feelings and intuition.

8. Your boss orders you to do something that will hurt someone. If you carry out the order, have you actually done anything wrong?
   A. Yes.
   B. No.

9. Which is more important in determining whether an action is right or wrong?
   A. Whether anyone actually gets hurt.
   B. Whether a rule, law, commandment, or moral principle is broken.

To score: The answers fall in one of two categories, J or C. Count your number of J and C answers using this key:
1. A = C, B = J; 2. A = J, B = C; 3. A = C, B = J; 4. A = J, B = C; 5. A = J, B = C; 6. A = C, B = J; 7. A = J, B = C; 8. A = C;
B = J; 9. A = C, B = J

(continued)

What your score means: The higher your J score, the more you rely on an ethic of *justice*. The higher your C score, the more you prefer an ethic of *care*. Neither style is better than the other, but they are different. Because they appear so different they may seem opposed to one another, but they're actually complementary. In fact, your score probably shows you rely on each style to a greater or lesser degree. (Few people end up with a score of 9 to 0.) The more you can appreciate both approaches, the better you'll be able to resolve ethical dilemmas and to understand and communicate with people who prefer the other style.

An ethic of justice is based on principles such as justice, fairness, equality, or authority. People who prefer this style see ethical dilemmas as conflicts of rights that can be solved by the impartial application of some general principle. The advantage of this approach is that it looks at a problem logically and impartially. People with this style try to be objective and fair, hoping to make a decision according to some standard that's higher than any specific individual's interests. The disadvantage of this approach is that people who rely on it might lose sight of the immediate interests of particular individuals. They may unintentionally ride roughshod over the people around them in favour of some abstract ideal or policy.

An ethic of care is based on a sense of responsibility to reduce actual harm or suffering. People who prefer this style see moral dilemmas as conflicts of duties or responsibilities. They believe that solutions must be tailored to the special details of individual circumstances. They tend to feel constrained by policies that are supposed to be enforced without exception. The advantage of this approach is that it is responsive to immediate suffering and harm. The disadvantage is that, when carried to an extreme, this style can produce decisions that seem not simply subjective, but arbitrary.

To learn more about an ethic of justice, consult the writings of Lawrence Kohlberg. To learn more about an ethic of care, consult the research of Carol Gilligan.

Source: © Thomas I. White.

## Progress Assessment

- What is ethics?
- How does ethics differ from legality?
- When faced with ethical dilemmas, what questions can you ask yourself that might help you make ethical decisions?

# MANAGING BUSINESSES ETHICALLY AND RESPONSIBLY

It cannot be stressed enough that organizational ethics begin at the top. Ethics is caught more than it is taught. That is, people learn their standards and values from observing what others do, not from hearing what they say. This is as true in business as it is at home. The leadership and example of strong top managers can help instill corporate values in employees. The majority of CEOs surveyed recently attributed unethical employee conduct to the failure of the organization's leadership in establishing ethical standards and culture.[12]

Any trust and co-operation between workers and managers must be based on fairness, honesty, openness, and moral integrity. (This can be challenging as there is less mutual loyalty and trust given the increasing focus on profits at the expense of jobs.) The same can be said about relationships among businesses and among nations. A business should be managed ethically for many reasons: to maintain a good reputation; to keep existing customers; to attract new customers; to avoid lawsuits; to reduce employee turnover; to avoid government intervention (the passage of new laws and regulations controlling business activities); to please customers, employees, and society; and simply to do the right thing.

Some managers think that ethics is a personal matter—that individuals either have ethical principles or they don't. These managers feel that they are not responsible for an individual's misdeeds and that ethics has nothing to do with management. But a growing number of people think that ethics has everything to do with management. Individuals do not usually act alone; they need the implied, if not direct, co-operation of others to behave unethically in a corporation.

# Setting Corporate Ethical Standards

Formal corporate ethics codes are popular these days. Eighty-nine percent of the organizations surveyed have written codes of ethics.[13] Figure 5.4 offers a sample from one company's code of ethics.

Although ethics codes vary greatly, they can be classified into two major categories: compliance-based and integrity-based. **Compliance-based ethics codes** emphasize preventing unlawful behaviour by increasing control and by penalizing wrongdoers. Whereas compliance-based ethics codes are based on avoiding legal punishment, **integrity-based ethics codes** define the organization's guiding values, create an environment that supports ethically sound behaviour, and stress a shared accountability among employees. See Figure 5.5 for a comparison of compliance-based and integrity-based ethics codes.

The following six-step process can help improve business ethics:

1. Top management must adopt and unconditionally support an explicit corporate code of conduct.

2. Employees must understand that expectations for ethical behaviour begin at the top and that senior management expects all employees to act accordingly.

3. Managers and others must be trained to consider the ethical implications of all business decisions.

4. An ethics office must be set up. Phone lines to the office should be established so that employees who don't necessarily want to be seen with an ethics officer can inquire about ethical matters anonymously. **Whistleblowers** (people who report illegal or unethical behaviour) must feel protected from retaliation as oftentimes this exposure can lead to great career and personal cost.

5. Outsiders such as suppliers, subcontractors, distributors, and customers must be told about the ethics program. Pressure to put aside ethical considerations often comes from the outside, and it helps employees to resist such pressure when everyone knows what the ethical standards are.

6. The ethics code must be enforced. It is important to back any ethics program with timely action if any rules are broken. This is the best way to communicate to all employees that the code is serious.[14]

This last step is perhaps the most critical. No matter how well intended a company's ethics code is, it is worthless if it is not enforced. Enron had a code of ethics. However, by ignoring this code, Enron's board and management sent employees the message that rules could be shelved when they were inconvenient.[15]

**compliance-based ethics codes**
Ethical standards that emphasize preventing unlawful behaviour by increasing control and by penalizing wrongdoers.

**integrity-based ethics codes**
Ethical standards that define the organization's guiding values, create an environment that supports ethically sound behaviour, and stress a shared accountability among employees.

**whistleblowers**
People who report illegal or unethical behaviour.

---

| **FIGURE** | **5.4** |
| --- | --- |

**Overview of Johnson & Johnson's Code of Ethics**
Johnson & Johnson calls this code of ethics its Credo.

Written in 1943 by long-time Chairman General Robert Wood Johnson, the Johnson & Johnson Credo serves as a conscious plan that represents and encourages a unique set of values. Our Credo sums up the responsibilities we have to the four important groups we serve:

- Our customers—We have a responsibility to provide high-quality products they can trust, offered at a fair price.
- Our employees—We have a responsibility to treat them with respect and dignity, pay them fairly and help them develop and thrive personally and professionally.
- Our communities—We have a responsibility to be good corporate citizens, support good works, encourage better health and protect the environment.
- Our stockholders—We have a responsibility to provide a fair return on their investment.

The deliberate ordering of these groups—customers first, stockholders last—proclaims a bold business philosophy: If we meet our first three responsibilities, the fourth will take care of itself ... To ensure our adherence to Credo values, we periodically ask every employee to evaluate the company's performance in living up to them. We believe that by monitoring our actions against the ethical framework of Our Credo, we will best ensure that we make responsible decisions as a company.

| Features of Compliance-Based Ethics Codes | | Features of Integrity-Based Ethics Codes | |
|---|---|---|---|
| Ideal: | Conform to outside standards (laws and regulations) | Ideal: | Conform to outside standards (laws and regulations) and chosen internal standards |
| Objective: | Avoid criminal misconduct | Objective: | Enable responsible employee conduct |
| Leaders: | Lawyers | Leaders: | Managers with aid of lawyers and others |
| Methods: | Education, reduced employee discretion, controls, and penalties | Methods: | Education, leadership, accountability, decision processes, controls, and penalties |

**FIGURE | 5.5**

**Strategies for Ethics Management**
Both codes have a concern for the law and use penalties as enforcement. Integrity-based ethics codes move beyond legal compliance to create a "do-it-right" climate that emphasizes core values such as honesty, fair play, good service to customers, a commitment to diversity, and involvement in the community. These values are ethically desirable, but not necessarily legally mandatory.

An important factor in the success of enforcing an ethics code is the selection of the ethics officer. The most effective ethics officers set a positive tone, communicate effectively, and relate well with employees at every level of the company. They are equally comfortable serving as counsellors or as investigators. While many ethics officers have backgrounds in law, it is more important that they have strong communication skills than a background in specific rules, regulations, and risks. Effective ethics officers are people who can be trusted to maintain confidentiality, can conduct objective investigations and ensure that the process is fair, and can demonstrate to stakeholders that ethics is important in everything that the company does.

As more organizations are recognizing the importance of this role, associations are also providing support for those in these roles. One such example is the Ethics Practitioners' Association of Canada (EPAC). EPAC's mission is "to enable individuals to work successfully in the field of ethics in organizations by enhancing the quality and availability of ethics advice and services across Canada." This organization supports ethics officers, consultants, educators, students, and others who are interested in the field of ethics as applied to organizations of all kinds.

## The Sarbanes-Oxley Act of 2002 (SOX)[16]

The major corporate and accounting scandals in the United Sates in the early 2000s (e.g., Enron, Tyco, Adelphia, and WorldCom) gave rise to the implementation of U.S. federal legislation known as the Sarbanes-Oxley Act (SOX). The legislation established stronger standards to prevent misconduct and improve corporate governance practices. SOX applies to all publicly-traded companies whose shares are listed on the stock exchanges under the jurisdiction of the U.S. Securities and Exchange Commission. The goal of SOX is to ensure the accuracy and reliability of published financial information, and therefore the main part of the legislation requirements deal with the proper administration routines, procedures, and control activities. In response to SOX, Canada also implemented similar corporate governance legislation.

As Vice President for Corporate Development at Enron, Sherron Watkins sensed that something was rotten with the company's financial reporting. She "blew the whistle" on her bosses, who hid billions of dollars of debt and operating losses from investors and employees. Watkins said she would have come forward sooner, but she was afraid of losing her job. SOX now also protects whistleblowers like Watkins from any company retaliation as it requires that all public corporations provide a system that allows employees to submit concerns regarding accounting and auditing issues both confidentially and anonymously. Obviously, the purpose is to motivate employees to

As the office manager, Linda Merk discovered that the president and business manager of Ironworkers Union Local 771 were double dipping on their travel expenses. She was fired when she went to the police after the union's international office ignored her concerns. In a precedent-setting decision, the Supreme Court of Canada ruled in her favour. Merk received a settlement and was reinstated to her position.

report any wrongdoing. For example, the legislation provides for reinstatement and back pay to people who were punished by their employers for passing information about frauds to authorities.

## Whistleblowing Legislation in Canada[17]

Clearly, one might suggest that for the six steps mentioned earlier to work, there must first be protection in place for the whistleblower. Otherwise, how effective can such a process be? Bill C-11: The Public Servants Protection Disclosure Act is Canada's only national whistleblower legislation. Passed in 2005, Bill C-11 applies to almost the entire public sector. It provides for significant powers to investigate wrongdoing, it contains a clear legal prohibition of reprisal against those who make good-faith allegations of wrongdoing, and it proposes measures to protect the identity of persons making disclosures.

As noted in the chapter profile, the Federal Accountability Act was implemented to help strengthen accountability and increase transparency and oversight in government operations. Reforms include a five-year lobbying ban on former ministers, their aides, and senior public servants (i.e., to communicate in an attempt to influence), the elimination of corporate and union donations to political parties and candidates, and protection for whistleblowers. Critics condemn the Act as they believe that loopholes have actually weakened government accountability. For example, Democracy Watch (Canada's leading citizen group advocating democratic reform, government accountability, and corporate responsibility) points out that one year after the Act was passed, despite a staff of 21 and a budget of $6.5 million, the Public Service Integrity Commissioner did not report a single instance of wrongdoing or a single case of reprisal against a whistleblower in the entire federal public sector. Review the Dealing with Change box for more information on another organization, the Federal Accountability Initiative for Reform, that also believes that Canada needs stronger legislation.

Both of these Acts protect public sector workers but there is no provision to protect private-sector whistleblowers. In a KPMG survey on private corporations' policies on whistleblowers, almost two-thirds of respondents to the business ethics survey stated that they have a written policy requiring employees to report fraud or misconduct in the workplace. However, only 40 percent of respondents reported having formal systems designed to protect whistleblowers from retaliation. One-fifth of respondents lacked any type of protection system.

Petro-Canada communicates its Whistleblower Protection Policy on its Web site (www.petro-canada.ca). This policy includes the implementation of an anonymous 1-800 "whistleblowing line." A third-party service provider answers the telephone line and reports all calls to the appropriate members of Petro-Canada's executive or audit committee, depending on the nature of the call. Employees are informed that they will not be discharged, demoted, suspended, threatened, harassed, or in any other manner discriminated against in the terms and conditions of employment, or otherwise, because of any lawful act done by an employee in the provision of information to superiors, or to appropriate government agencies, regarding conduct that the employee reasonably believes violates the Petro-Canada Code of Business Conduct or any applicable governmental laws, rules, and regulations, or in assisting in an investigation of these types of violations.

## Progress Assessment

- How are compliance-based ethics codes different from integrity-based ethics codes?
- What are the six steps to follow in establishing an effective ethics program in a business?
- What protection is being offered to whistleblowers in the public sector?

# DEALING with CHANGE

## Federal Accountability Initiative for Reform

Founded in 1998, the Federal Accountability Initiative for Reform (FAIR) promotes integrity and accountability within government by empowering employees to speak out without fear of reprisal when they encounter wrongdoing. Its aim is to support legislation and management practices that will provide effective protection for whistleblowers and hence occupational free speech in the workplace. A registered Canadian charity, it is Canada's only public interest organization dedicated to protecting employees who blow the whistle on government misconduct.

Many public service scandals have come to light in Canada over the past several years. A few notable examples are the tainted blood scandal (in which 60,000 Canadians were infected with hepatitis C, many of them fatally), the gun registry scandal (in which a program with a budget of $2 million spent $1 billion without authorization or reporting of the cost overrun to Parliament), and the sponsorship scandal (in which millions of dollars of public money were diverted illegally to government-favoured advertising agencies). While these cases received extensive media coverage, there was very little media coverage or public debate regarding what Canada could do to prevent such abuses in the future.

Since these cases, the federal government implemented several key pieces of legislation. One example is the Public Servants Disclosure Protection Act (PSDPA), which purports to protect Canadians who blow the whistle on federal government wrongdoing. A central part of the Federal Accountability Act, the PSDPA establishes a process for whistleblowers' allegations of wrongdoing to be investigated, and for whistleblowers to seek protection from reprisals. FAIR believes that the "ironclad" protection provided for whistleblowers by this legislation is misleading. For example, it believes that the legislation provides no assurance that any wrongdoing reported by the whistleblower will be corrected. On another point, it denies whistleblowers access to our normal system of public courts.

FAIR has developed five points for judging any whistleblower legislation. Meeting all these in full will ensure that the legislation can be made to work effectively. Failing to meet any of these will create loopholes that may render the entire system useless. In the opinion of FAIR, there is still much work to be done with whistleblower legislation in Canada today. The five points are as follows:

1. *Full Free Speech Rights*—Whistleblowers must be able to blow the whistle on wrongdoing anywhere, anytime, and to any audience unless release of the information is specifically prohibited by statute, in which case disclosure must still be permitted to law enforcement and/or to Parliament.

2. *Right to Disclose All Illegality and Misconduct*—Disclosure must extend to any illegality, gross waste, gross mismanagement, abuse of authority, substantial and specific danger to public health or safety, as well as the contravention of any workplace policy, regulation, rule, professional statement, directive, or code of conduct.

3. *No Harassment of Any Kind*—Any harassment must be banned.

4. *Forum for Adjudication, with Realistic Burden of Proof and Appropriate Remedies*—Whistleblowers must have access to an effective judicial process, which includes access to the courts. Whistleblowers also require realistic burdens of proof. The law must therefore provide a reverse onus whereby once the whistleblower has shown that the whistleblowing was a contributing factor in the action taken against them (i.e., a short time frame between the whistleblowing and the retaliation), the burden shifts to the employer to show by clear and convincing evidence that the employer had other legitimate reasons for taking the action. Finally, if the whistleblower prevails, the relief must be comprehensive to cover all direct, indirect, and future consequences of the reprisal. This may mean relocation, medical bills, and compensation in lieu of salary.

5. *Mandatory Corrective Action*—Employees remain silent for two key reasons: one, they have no faith that anything will change; and two, fear of reprisal. To promote true accountability, persons who engage in harassment against an employee must be held personally responsible. As well, ministers must be required to take remedial action on the wrongdoing.

Source: "Our Mission," Federal Accountability Initiative for Reform, 22 December 2008, http://fairwhistleblower.ca/. Used with permission.

# CORPORATE SOCIAL RESPONSIBILITY

**corporate social responsibility (CSR)**
A business's concern for the welfare of society as a whole.

Just as you and I need to be good citizens, contributing what we can to society, corporations need to be good citizens as well. **Corporate social responsibility (CSR)**, also known as *corporate responsibility*, is the concern businesses have for the welfare of society. It is based on a company's concern for the welfare of all of its stakeholders, not just the owners. CSR goes well beyond merely being ethical. It is based on a commitment to such basic principles as integrity, fairness, and respect.[18]

There is discussion in this chapter about ethics and CSR. It is important to note that both of these are often judgement calls, depending on which side of the issue you are on. To clarify, one person's unethical behaviour can be considered another person's sound business decision. Also, do not underestimate the impact of cultural values. Differences from country to country also contribute to varying perspectives on the same issue. This can result in decision making that is not in line with one's personal values but is congruent with what is considered ethical in a country.

Not everyone thinks that CSR is a good thing. Some critics of CSR believe that a manager's sole role is to compete and win in the marketplace. Economist Milton Friedman made a classic statement when he said that the only social responsibility of business is to make money for stockholders. He thought that doing anything else was moving dangerously toward socialism.[19] CSR critics believe that managers who pursue CSR are doing so with other people's money—money they invested to make more money, not to improve society. They view spending money on CSR activities as stealing from their investors.

CSR defenders, on the other hand, believe that businesses owe their existence to the societies they serve. Businesses cannot succeed in societies that fail. They are given access to society's labour pool and its natural resources, things that every member of the society has a stake in. Even Adam Smith, the father of capitalism, believed that the self-interested pursuit of profit was wrong. He argued that benevolence was the highest virtue. CSR defenders acknowledge that businesses have deep obligations to investors, and that businesses should not attempt government-type social responsibility projects. However, they also argue that CSR makes more money for investors in the long run. They base their arguments on studies that have shown that companies with good ethical reputations attract and retain better employees, draw more customers, and enjoy greater employee loyalty. Very simply, CSR is simply good business because it is what society demands. What do you think?

The social performance of a company has several dimensions:

**corporate philanthropy**
Dimension of social responsibility that includes charitable donations.

Tim Horton Children's Foundation is a private organization that is supported by Tim Hortons. Every year, thousands of children from economically challenged homes participate in camps that are run by the Foundation.

- **Corporate philanthropy** includes charitable donations to non-profit groups of all kinds. Strategic philanthropy involves companies making long-term commitments to one cause, such as the Canadian Tire Foundation for Families. Since its launch in 1999, the Foundation has donated more than $30 million to charitable organizations that support families in local communities by helping to ensure that life's basic needs are met.[20] The Spotlight on Small Business box highlights how CanadaHelps.org provides a channel for those that wish to make charitable donations.

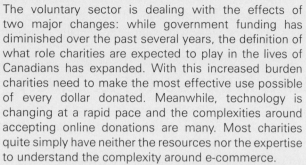

## SPOTLIGHT ON Small Business

### Giving Online Through E-philanthropy

The voluntary sector is dealing with the effects of two major changes: while government funding has diminished over the past several years, the definition of what role charities are expected to play in the lives of Canadians has expanded. With this increased burden charities need to make the most effective use possible of every dollar donated. Meanwhile, technology is changing at a rapid pace and the complexities around accepting online donations are many. Most charities quite simply have neither the resources nor the expertise to understand the complexity around e-commerce.

CanadaHelps.org believes that charities should focus on their core activities, such as protecting the environment, educating the population, or providing relief to the less fortunate. CanadaHelps is Canada's only donation portal that provides access to all of Canada's 80,000 charities, from larger organizations such as national cancer charities to smaller groups such as local animal shelters and soup kitchens. It provides information and ideas about how people can help their communities.

Three university students—Ryan Little, Matthew Choi, and Aaron Pereira—launched CanadaHelps.org in December 2000. They recognized the opportunity that e-commerce presented to the voluntary sector to increase efficiency. Together with a diverse group of volunteers and a committed board of advisers and directors and staff, the company has gained the support of individuals and organizations in the charitable and corporate sectors.

"Because of Canadians' increasingly hectic lifestyles, making charitable donations online has clicked in a big way," says Little. This service is available in both official languages to all Canadians, living domestically and abroad, who wish to make a donation to a Canadian charity. Making your donation is simple. You search/browse for the charity you wish to donate to, add it to your "Giving Basket" and then pay for the gift. One of the newest options is the CanadaHelps Give the Gift of Giving™ program. This gift card service allows donors to give a charitable donation to friends and family. Donors purchase a gift card in a certain amount, and the gift recipient chooses which charity receives the donation amount.

Once the donation has been paid, the donor receives an immediate, secure PDF tax receipt, issued by CanadaHelps via e-mail. CanadaHelps then disburses the funds (less a 3 percent transaction fee) to the designated charity.

Not only is donating online convenient and efficient for donors, but charities are benefiting as well. CanadaHelps provides a cost-effective alternative to setting up their own online donations facilities: there is no set-up fee or annual charge, and charities receive immediate notification when a donation is received. Charities are only charged when a donation is actually made, thereby ensuring that a charity does not pay for a service that is not being used. (Raising funds through the Internet is estimated to cost about 20 percent less than direct mail or telemarketing.) Today, CanadaHelps facilitates more than $10 million in donations to Canadian charities annually.

Sources: "How It Works," CanadaHelps.org, 21 December 2008, www.canadahelps.org; "Giving Just Got Easier," 3 November 2003, St. John's: Community Services Council Newfoundland and Labrador, http://www.envision.ca/templates/news.asp?ID=4718; and "Volunteers of the Year Awards 2001," Toronto: City of Toronto, http://www.city.toronto.on.ca/volunteer_awards/winners_2001.htm.

- **Corporate social initiatives** include enhanced forms of corporate philanthropy that are more directly related to the company's competencies. For example, as part of the 2004 Asian tsunami disaster relief, UPS and FedEx shipped emergency relief supplies for free from all over the world, Johnson & Johnson sent medical supplies, and other pharmaceutical companies sent antibiotics, nutritional supplements, and baby formula.[21]

- **Corporate responsibility** includes everything from hiring minority workers to making safe products, minimizing pollution, using energy wisely, and providing a safe work environment—that is, everything that has to do with acting responsibly within society and toward employees. We will discuss this in more detail later in the chapter.

- **Corporate policy** refers to the position a firm takes on social and political issues.

So much news coverage has been devoted to the problems caused by corporations that people tend to develop a negative view of the impact that companies have on society. If the news were more balanced, much more could be said about the positive contributions that businesses make. Few people know, for example, that Xerox has a program called Social Service Leave, which allows employees to take a leave of absence for up to a year to work for a non-profit organization. While on Social Service Leave, the Xerox employee

**corporate social initiatives**
Dimension of social responsibility that includes enhanced forms of corporate philanthropy that are more directly related to the company's competencies.

**corporate responsibility**
Dimension of social responsibility that includes everything from hiring minority workers to making safe products.

**corporate policy**
Dimension of social responsibility that refers to the position a firm takes on social and political issues.

receives full salary and benefits, including job security.[22] Microsoft Canada belongs to the I CAN Program. The I Volunteer element of this program permits employees to volunteer 40 hours during regular Microsoft work hours.[23]

Two-thirds of the MBA students surveyed by a group called Students for Responsible Business said they would take a lower salary to work for a socially responsible company. But when the same students were asked to define a socially responsible company, things got complicated. It appears that even those who want to be socially responsible can't agree on what it involves.

## Corporate Responsibility in the Twenty-First Century

What should be the guiding philosophy for business in the twenty-first century? For most of the twentieth century, there was uncertainty regarding the position top managers should take, and this question is still being debated today. How a company answers this question depends on its fundamental belief of how stakeholders should be treated and its responsibility to society. There are two different views of corporate responsibility to stakeholders:

1. *The Strategic Approach.* The strategic approach requires that management's primary orientation be toward the economic interests of shareholders. The rationale is this: as owners, shareholders have the right to expect management to work in their best interests; that is, to optimize profits. Furthermore, Adam Smith's notion of the invisible hand suggests that the maximum social gain is realized when managers attend only to their shareholders' interests.

   Friedman and others argue that since (in their view), only people can have social responsibilities, corporations are only responsible to their shareholders and not to society as a whole. Although they accept that corporations should obey the laws of the countries within which they work, they assert that corporations have no other obligation to society.[24] For example, when John Akers was the CEO of IBM, he said that an IBM decision about whether to cease operations in a country would be a business decision: "We are not in business to conduct moral activity; we are not in business to conduct socially responsible action. We are in business to conduct business." The strategic approach encourages managers to consider an actions' effects on stakeholders other than owners, but asserts that others' interests are secondary. Often those interests are considered only when they would adversely affect profits if ignored.

2. *The Pluralist Approach.* This approach recognizes the special responsibility of management to optimize profits, but not at the expense of employees, suppliers, and members of the community. This approach recognizes the moral responsibilities of management that apply to all human beings. Managers don't have moral immunity when making managerial decisions. This view says that corporations can maintain their economic viability only when they fulfill their moral responsibilities to society as a whole. When shareholders' interests compete with those of the community, as they often do, managers must decide, using ethical and moral principles.

The guiding philosophy for the twenty-first century will be some version of the pluralist approach. Managerial decision making won't be easy, and new ethical guidelines may have to be drawn. But the process toward such guidelines has been started, and a new era of more responsible and responsive management is under way. Perhaps it would be easier to understand social responsibility if we looked at the concept through the eyes of the stakeholders to whom businesses are responsible: customers, investors, employees, society in general, and the environment.

Imperial Tobacco Canada promotes itself as a socially responsible company. Among other programs, it supports Operation I.D., a youth smoking prevention program. Overall, what view of corporate responsibility to stakeholders do you believe this company supports?

# Responsibility to Customers

One responsibility of business is to satisfy customers by offering them goods and services of real value. A recurring theme of this book is the importance of pleasing customers. This responsibility is not as easy to meet as it seems. Keep in mind that more than half of new businesses fail—perhaps because their owners failed to please their customers. One of the surest ways of failing to please customers is not being totally honest with them. For example, a consumer magazine reported that the Suzuki Samurai was likely to roll over if a driver swerved violently in an emergency. When Suzuki executives denied there was a problem, sales plummeted.

In contrast, Daimler-Benz suffered a similar problem during a test simulating a swerve around a wayward elk, when its A-class Baby Benz rolled over. The company quickly admitted a problem, came up with a solution, and committed the money necessary to put that solution into action. In addition, company representatives continued to answer questions in spite of aggressive press coverage. Daimler took out full-page ads that read: "We should like to thank our customers most warmly for their loyalty. You have given us the chance to remedy a mistake." Following the test flip, only 2 percent of the orders for the vehicle were cancelled. The solution cost the company $59 million in the first year and $118 million in the next. Analysts say those costs probably eliminated any profit on the vehicle. However, the quick resolution of the problem protected the company's reputation, thus allowing its other models to become such hits that Daimler's net earnings remained the same.[25]

The payoff for socially conscious behaviour could result in new business as customers switch from rival companies simply because they admire the company's social efforts—a powerful competitive edge. Consumer behaviour studies show that, all else being equal, a socially conscious company is likely to be viewed more favourably than less socially responsible companies. The important point to remember is that customers prefer to do business with companies they trust and who share their values. This means that they do not want to do business with companies they don't trust.

# Responsibility to Investors[26]

Some people believe that before you can do good, you must do well (i.e., make a lot of money); others believe that by doing good, you can also do well. What we do know is that ethical behaviour is good for shareholder wealth. It doesn't subtract from the bottom line, but rather adds to it. On the other hand, unethical behaviour does cause financial damage. Those cheated by financial wrongdoing are the shareholders themselves. Unethical behaviour may seem to work for the short term, but it guarantees eventual failure. The following are two examples:

- In the early 2000s, accounting irregularities reported at Nortel Networks Corp., once the most-traded stock in Canada, damaged investor trust and subsequently the company's share value. Years later, the company was still being scrutinized amid rumours of bankruptcy when its share price was under $1. In early 2009, the company declared bankruptcy.

- Co-founders Garth Drabinsky and Myron Gottlieb, of the theatre company Livent Inc., were found guilty in 2009 of defrauding investors of about half a billion dollars. It was found that both deliberately misrepresented their company's finances before the company went public in the early 1990s. Both men pleaded not guilty to all charges, arguing that they were victims of collusion by a group of former employees who sought to frame them. The verdict came more than 10 years after police began probing what they called one of the biggest fraud cases in Canadian history. The convictions on two counts each of fraud and one of forgery carry respective maximum sentences of 10 and 14 years.[27]

Unfortunately, we continue to read of individual business people who abuse the trust that individual investors have placed in them. Some high-profile examples in recent years include Bernard Madoff and Earl Jones. Financier Bernard Madoff is serving a 150-year sentence after admitting he squandered tens of billions of dollars in investors' money. Madoff's crimes have left many investors impoverished and some charities decimated. At the time this chapter was written, an investigation was underway against financier Earl Jones. He was accused by between 100 and 150 investors of cheating them out of millions of dollars. Quebec's financial securities regulator has alleged the amount could be as high as $50 million. What was the resolution of these charges?

Many people believe that it makes financial as well as moral sense to invest in companies that are planning ahead to create a better environment. By choosing to put their money into companies whose goods and services benefit the community and the environment, investors can improve their own financial health while improving society's health. In the 2005 Canada's Most Respected Corporations survey, 89 percent of Canadian CEOs agreed with the statement that "companies that are more respected by the public enjoy a premium in their share price," while only 9 percent disagreed. The same survey also confirmed that 65 percent of CEO respondents agree with the statement that they are "finding a greater part of his/her job these days involves building respect for his/her company among the general public."

## Insider Trading[28]

**insider trading**
An unethical activity in which insiders use private company information to further their own fortunes or those of their family and friends.

A few investors, known as inside traders, have chosen unethical means to improve their own financial health. **Insider trading** involves insiders using private company information to further their own fortunes, or those of their family and friends. For example, Andrew Rankin, a former executive with RBC Dominion Securities, was charged by the Ontario Securities Commission (OSC) with ten counts of tipping his friend, Daniel Duic. Investigators found that Rankin had alerted Duic to upcoming mergers and acquisitions before they were publicly known. The OSC alleges that, based on this information, Duic bought and sold investments in ten companies and saw his investment increase following the release of the merger and acquisition news. Duic agreed to pay just over $3 million in the form of a penalty, taxes, and lawyer's fees and to testify against Rankin. Under the Ontario Securities Act, Rankin was sentenced to six months in jail for Canada's first conviction for illegal stock tipping.

## Responsibility to Employees

Businesses have several responsibilities to employees. First, they have a responsibility to create jobs if they want to grow. It's been said that the best social program in the world is a job. Once a company creates jobs, it has an obligation to ensure that hard work and talent are fairly rewarded. Employees need realistic hope of a better future, which comes only through a chance for upward mobility. People need to see that integrity, hard work, good-will, ingenuity, and talent pay off. Studies have shown that the factor that most influences a company's effectiveness and financial performance is human resource management.

High-risk groups lined up for hours at public clinics when the H1N1 vaccine was released in October 2009, while many non-high-risk Canadians (e.g., some professional athletes and private-clinic members) received the vaccine courtesy of their employers. For weeks following the initial rollout, thousands of those on the priority list did not receive the vaccine due to the shortage. Were the actions of these employers ethical?

If a company treats employees with respect, they usually will respect the company as well. That respect can make a huge difference in a company's bottom line. In their book *Contented Cows Give Better Milk*, Bill Catlette and Richard Hadden compared "contented cow" companies with "common cow" companies. The companies with the contented employees outgrew their counterparts by four to one for more than ten years. The "contented cow" companies outearned the "common cow" companies by nearly $40 billion and generated 800,000 more jobs. The authors attribute this difference in performance to the commitment and caring that the companies demonstrate for their employees.[29]

When employees feel they've been treated unfairly, they often strike back. Getting even is one of the most powerful incentives for good people to do bad things. Not many disgruntled workers are desperate enough to resort to violence in the workplace, but a great number do relieve their frustrations in more subtle ways, such as blaming mistakes on others, not accepting responsibility for decision making, manipulating budgets and expenses, making commitments they intend to ignore, hoarding resources, doing the minimum needed to get by, making results look better than they are, or even stealing. The loss of employee commitment, confidence, and trust in the company and its management can be very costly indeed. Employee larceny costs Canadian businesses billions of dollars every year. According to the Association of Certified Fraud Examiners, fraud and theft cost employers an average of $9 a day per employee, with the average organization losing about five percent of its total annual revenue to thieves.[30] On average, most victimized firms lose around $159,000, up more than one-third since 2002.[31] Canadian retailers alone are relieved of approximately $8 million of merchandise every day, with employees outstealing the shoplifters.[32] You will read more about issues that affect employee–management relations in Chapter 13.

# Responsibility to Society

One of business's responsibilities to society is to create new wealth, which is disbursed to employees, suppliers, shareholders, and other stakeholders. But if businesses don't create wealth, who will? Non-profit organizations play an important role in distributing the funds they receive from donors, governments, and even their own investments in billions of shares in publicly-held companies. As those stock prices increase, more funds are available to benefit society. However, for stock prices to increase, the publicly-held company must be successful. For companies to prosper, they need to provide customers with safe products. Businesses today, more than ever before, need to develop long-term profitable relationships with their customers. There is no question that repeat business is based on buying safe and value-laden goods and services, at reasonable prices.

Businesses are also partially responsible for promoting social justice. Business is perhaps the most crucial institution of civil society. For its own well-being, business depends on its employees being active in politics, law, churches and temples, arts, charities, and so on. Many companies believe that business has a role in building a community that goes well beyond giving back. To them, charity is not enough. Their social contributions include cleaning up the environment, building community toilets, providing computer lessons, caring for the elderly, and supporting children from low-income families.[33] Samsung, a Korean electronics conglomerate, emphasizes volunteer involvement. For example, a busload of Samsung employees and managers are transported each month to a city park, where they spread out to pick up garbage, pull weeds, and plant saplings. Managers even volunteer to help spruce up employee homes. Local employees feel such loyalty to the company that in the height of an unrest that destroyed many businesses in Indonesia, local employees and their neighbours pulled together to protect Samsung's refrigerator factory there and shielded foreign managers from violence. With the help of relatives in the countryside, the local employees set up a food supply network that helped protect their colleagues from skyrocketing prices for food staples such as rice and palm oil.

The focus of this book is on business; however, one should not forget that government decisions also affect business and society. The Walkerton, Ontario, E. coli tragedy that killed seven people and made half of the town's 5,000 residents ill from contaminated water is one such example. After hearing testimony from more than 100 witnesses over nine months, Justice O'Connor concluded that the catastrophe could have been prevented if brothers Stan and Frank Koebel, who ran Walkerton's water system, had properly chlorinated the water and if the Ontario government had heeded warnings that cuts to the provincial environment ministry were resulting in ineffective testing.[34] Clearly, the Koebel brothers were responsible for their individual decisions.

## Responsibility to the Environment[35]

Businesses are often criticized for their role in destroying the environment. Such was the case when images of the slow death of 500 ducks on a toxic oil sands tailings pond in northern Alberta flashed around the world. This led to federal and provincial charges against Syncrude Canada Ltd., which was charged under the Alberta Environmental Enhancement and Protection Act and the federal Migratory Birds Convention Act. While Syncrude attempted to rescue some of the ducks that landed in the tailings pond, only a handful were taken out of the water for cleaning and none survived.

We are seeing more efforts being made to reverse years of neglect to the environment. For example, the Sydney Tar Ponds in Nova Scotia are North America's largest hazardous waste site. More than 80 years of discharges from the steel-producing coke ovens near the harbour have filled Muggah Creek with contaminated sediments. By 1983, Environment Canada had pinpointed the coke ovens as the major source of pollution in the Sydney area. Fishing was banned and the Sydney lobster fishery was closed. Statistics show significantly higher levels of cancers and other debilitating diseases than anywhere else in Canada. The disposal of the toxic waste has been slow. Two decades later, there have been several attempts and more than $100 million spent to clean up this toxic site. In May 2004, the governments of Canada and Nova Scotia committed $400 million to the cleanup. It is expected that this cleanup will take ten years.

This is not the only example of government getting involved with business. The Great Lakes—lakes Superior, Michigan, Huron, Erie, and Ontario—span more than 1,200 kilometres. The Great Lakes basin is home to more than one-quarter of Canada's population and more than one-tenth of the U.S. population. Some of the world's largest concentrations of industrial capacity are located in the Great Lakes region. In spite of their large size, the Great Lakes are sensitive to the effects of a wide range of pollutants, including runoff of soils and farm chemicals from agricultural lands, waste from cities, and discharges from industrial areas.

One hot spot is Sarnia's Chemical Valley. There have been hundreds of spills in the St. Clair River since 1986. Chemical Valley is home to dozens of chemical and petroleum companies. They account for about 40 percent of Canada's chemical production and 20 percent of the nation's refineries. Thousands of residents in the area are concerned about spills because they draw their drinking water from the river. Efforts since 1987 were supposed to have reduced the spills into the river to virtually zero. In the Sarnia area, Health Canada

The Ethical Funds Company selects investments based on financial as well as social and environmental criteria. The company does not invest in corporations that derive a significant portion of their income from military weapons, tobacco, or nuclear power. Would you invest in companies on the basis of their environmental, social, and governance performance?

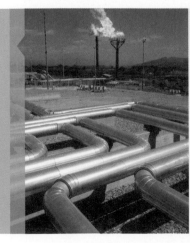

statistics show that residents have a higher rate of illnesses than in the rest of Canada, ranging from cancer to birth defects. Despite these efforts and the fact that companies have been heavily fined, spills still occur. What do you think should be the next step to stop these spills? Is it realistic to expect zero spills? The Analyzing Management Decisions case near the end of this chapter discusses the implications of an oil spill in Alberta.

Some governments are taking more responsibility for improving the environment, as highlighted in the Green Box. Businesses are also taking more responsibility for helping to make their own environment a better place. Environmental efforts may increase the company's costs, but they also may allow the company to charge higher prices, to increase market share, or both. For example, Ciba Specialty Chemicals, a Swiss textile-dye manufacturer, developed dyes that require less salt than traditional dyes. Since used dye solutions must be treated before they are released into rivers or streams, having less salt and unfixed dye in the solution means lower water-treatment costs. Patents protect Ciba's low-salt dyes, so the company can charge more for its dyes than other companies can charge for theirs. Ciba's experience illustrates that, just as a new machine enhances labour productivity, lowering environmental costs can add value to a business.

Environmental practices are of interest to many stakeholders, including investors. Jantzi Research Inc. has developed the Canadian Social Investment Database™, which contains social and environmental profiles of approximately 300 Canadian companies and income trusts. Institutional investors that incorporate social and environmental criteria—such as corporate governance, environmental performance, ethical business practices, human rights issues, and tobacco and weapons-related production—into their investment decisions use this tool. According to Michael Jantzi, President, "Companies that look at social and environmental issues in a consistent, clear way do better than their counterparts."

Environmental quality is a public good; that is, everyone gets to enjoy it regardless of who pays for it. The challenge for companies is to find the right public good that will appeal to their target market. Many corporations are publishing reports that document their net social contribution. To do that, a company must measure its positive social contributions and subtract its negative social impacts. We will discuss that process next.

## Social Auditing

It is nice to talk about having organizations become more socially responsible. It is also encouraging to see some efforts made toward creating safer products, cleaning up the environment, designing more honest advertising, and treating women and minorities fairly. But is there any way to measure whether organizations are making social responsibility an integral part of top management's decision making? The answer is yes, and the term that represents that measurement is *social auditing*.

A **social audit** is a systematic evaluation of an organization's progress toward implementing programs that are socially responsible and responsive. One of the major problems of conducting a social audit is establishing procedures for measuring a firm's activities and its effects on society. What should be measured? Many social audits consider such things as workplace issues, the environment, product safety, community relations, and respecting the rights of local people.[36] See Figure 5.6 for an outline of business activities that could be considered socially responsible.

A commitment to corporate social responsibility implies a commitment to some form of **triple-bottom line** ("**TBL**," "**3BL**," or "**People, Planet, Profit**") reporting.[37] TBL is used as a framework for measuring and reporting corporate performance against economic, social, and environmental parameters.[38] Such corporations focus on the economic value they add, but also on the environmental and social value they add and destroy.[39]

There is some question as to whether positive actions should be added (e.g., charitable donations and pollution control efforts) and negative effects subtracted (e.g., layoffs and overall pollution levels) to get a net social contribution. Or should only positive actions be recorded? In general, social responsibility is becoming one of the aspects of corporate success that business evaluates, measures, and develops.

**social audit**
A systematic evaluation of an organization's progress toward implementing programs that are socially responsible and responsive.

**triple-bottom line (TBL, 3BL, or People, Planet, Profit)**
A framework for measuring and reporting corporate performance against economic, social, and environmental parameters.

# GreenBOX

## To Carbon Tax or Not?

The carbon tax, sometimes called a green tax, can refer to any number of measures designed to increase the cost of burning fossil fuels like oil, gas, and coal. In basic terms, it is a tax on greenhouse gas emissions levied with the aim of reducing pollution to combat climate change. Those emissions spewing from exhaust pipes or industrial smokestacks are made up primarily of carbon dioxide, which is produced when fossil fuels containing carbon—such as coal, natural gas, or diesel—are burned. "It's a really important tool for fighting climate change," says Clare Demerse, a senior policy analyst with the Pembina Institute. "It's a way to make sure pollution carries a cost."

A carbon tax would provide an incentive to stop the social harm and move to more positive alternatives. The idea is both to change behaviour (e.g., turn people and businesses away from "bad" fossil fuels and toward "good" clean alternatives) and to set aside a fund to help smooth the transition to a cleaner economy.

A carbon tax can be (1) an across-the-board levy on all fuels based on $CO_2$ (carbon dioxide) emissions, (2) applied to just the businesses that produce carbon emissions, leaving it up to them whether or not to pass costs along to consumers, or (3) directly levied on consumers. Another alternative is a "revenue-neutral carbon tax" in which any levies extracted from a particular sector (e.g., transportation) would be given back in some other form of subsidy or tax break, that would reward more fuel-efficient behaviour. The most common form of this has been the fairly modest tax breaks on small and hybrid cars.

The tax is described in terms of a dollar value per tonne of gas produced. This can then be translated into a cost on the fuel that emits the greenhouse gases (e.g., 10 cents a litre on gasoline). The Pembina Institute and the David Suzuki Foundation say that Canada needs a carbon tax of $30/tonne immediately, at least $50/tonne by 2015 and $75/tonne by 2020 for the country to do its part in cutting greenhouse gas pollution.

Opposition to carbon taxes includes suggestions that they are merely a cash grab to bolster government revenue and will just push jobs and business to cheaper jurisdictions. In Alberta, for example, where oil and gas production are such a strong segment of the economy, there is little support for any kind of across-the-board carbon tax. Depending on how the tax is introduced, and whether it is accompanied by tax cuts, financial assistance for people with lower incomes or other incentives to encourage consumers to make choices that reduce pollution, its costs may not be distributed evenly in the economy.

Quebec was the first province to introduce a carbon tax in 2007. The levy was just under one cent for a litre of gas, with funds to pay for energy-saving initiatives such as improvements to public transit. British Columbia followed in 2008, taxing carbon-based fuels such as gasoline, diesel, natural gas, and home heating fuel, at a rate of $10 per tonne of greenhouse gases generated. The carbon tax will reach $30 per tonne in 2012. This works out to an extra 2.4 cents a litre on gasoline, increasing to 7.24 cents per litre by 2012. The provincial government has said that all carbon tax revenue—about $1.8 billion over three years—will be returned to British Columbians through reductions to income and business taxes. To soften the impact of the carbon tax, the government gave a $100 climate action dividend to each British Columbian.

Compare these taxes to those imposed in Finland, where drivers pay a carbon surtax of about eight Canadian cents per litre. In Sweden, people pay almost 40 cents extra per litre in carbon taxes at the pumps. What do you think? Could governments, businesses, and consumers be doing more? Do you agree or disagree with a green tax?

Sources: "Just What Is a Carbon Tax?" CBC News, 29 September 2008, http://www.cbc.ca/news/canadavotes/story/2008/09/19/f-carbontaxprimer.html; "Carbon Taxes: Cash Grab or Climate Saviour?" CBC News, 19 June, 2008, http://www.cbc.ca/canada/story/2008/06/18/f-carbon-tax.html; and "B.C. Carbon Tax Kicks in on Canada Day," CBC News, 1 July 2008, http://www.cbc.ca/canada/british-columbia/story/2008/06/30/bc-carbon-tax-effective.html.

| FIGURE 5.6 | |
|---|---|
| **Socially Responsible Business Activities** | Community-related activities such as participating in local fundraising campaigns, donating employee time to various non-profit organizations (including local government), and participating in urban planning and development. |
| | Employee-related activities such as establishing equal opportunity programs, offering flextime and other benefits, promoting job enrichment, ensuring job safety, and conducting employee development programs. (You'll learn more about these activities in Chapter 12.) |
| | Political activities such as taking a position on nuclear safety, gun control, pollution control, consumer protection, and other social issues; and working more closely with local, provincial, and federal government officials. |
| | Support for higher education, the arts, and other non-profit social agencies. |
| | Consumer activities such as ensuring product safety, creating truthful advertising, handling complaints promptly, setting fair prices, and conducting extensive consumer education programs. |

In addition to the social audits conducted by the companies themselves, there are four types of groups that serve as watchdogs regarding how well companies enforce their ethical and social responsibility policies:

1. *Socially conscious investors* who insist that a company extend its own high standards to all its suppliers. Social responsibility investing (SRI) is on the rise. Be aware that SRI is highly subjective. Different people have different values, so what's ethically appropriate for one is not for another.
2. *Environmentalists* who apply pressure by naming names of companies that don't abide by the environmentalists' standards.
3. *Union officials* who hunt down violations and force companies to comply to avoid negative publicity.
4. *Customers* who take their business elsewhere if a company demonstrates unethical or socially irresponsible practices.

What these groups look for constantly changes as the world view changes. One important thing to remember is that it isn't enough for a company to be right when it comes to ethics and social responsibility. It also has to *convince* its customers and society that it's right.

## Sustainable Development[40]

**Sustainable development** means implementing a process that integrates environmental, economic, and social considerations into decision making. This reinforces the World Commission on Environment and Development's conclusion that development should be sustainable for the benefit of current and future generations. Such a focus has created opportunities for new ventures such as Revive. Corporations that wish to eliminate no-longer-needed facility assets (e.g., chairs, desks, etc.) can deal with Revive, which provides a cost-effective alternative to having these items removed. These items are then redistributed to needy non-profit organizations, schools, and health clinics then receive critically needed equipment and supplies, and planet Earth is given relief from the pressures of expanding population and waste.

> **sustainable development**
> Implementing a process that integrates environmental, economic, and social considerations into decision making.

In another example, Canada's two largest grocery chains, Loblaw Companies Limited and Sobeys, are gradually eliminating free plastic bags at their checkout counters. The plastic bags will be available only on request, and will cost five cents each. "It represents the next natural step forward as we continue to acknowledge and respond to Canadians' desire to support environmental initiatives," Loblaw executive chairman Galen Weston Jr. said. Most of the proceeds from the sale of Loblaw's bags will be used to cover the cost of its plastic bag reduction program. As well, "we'll take some of the money and invest it in lower food prices ... [and] in our sustainability projects and a couple of environmental charities," said Weston.

Other companies have also implemented similar actions. The Liquor Control Board of Ontario (LCBO) has ended its use of plastic shopping bags, offering shoppers paper bags instead. Furniture retailer IKEA Canada charges five cents for plastic bags, donating proceeds to Tree Canada to help plant trees throughout the country. Would you shop more at a retailer that supports such initiatives?

## Progress Assessment

- What is corporate social responsibility, and how does it relate to each of a business's major stakeholders?
- How does the strategic approach differ from the pluralist approach?
- What is a social audit, and what kinds of activities does it monitor?

# INTERNATIONAL ETHICS AND SOCIAL RESPONSIBILITY

Ethical problems and issues of social responsibility are not unique to Canada. Top business and government leaders in Japan were caught in a major "influence-peddling" (read bribery) scheme in Japan. Similar charges have been brought against top officials in South Korea, the People's Republic of China, Italy, Brazil, Pakistan, and Zaire. What is new about the moral and ethical standards by which government leaders are being judged? They are much stricter than in previous years. The Reaching Beyond Our Borders box highlights some areas that require improvement in reducing corruption.

Government leaders are not the only ones being held to higher standards. Many businesses are demanding socially responsible behaviour from their international suppliers by ensuring that suppliers do not violate domestic human rights and environmental standards. For example, Sears will not knowingly import products made by Chinese prison labour. The clothing manufacturer Phillips–Van Heusen said it would cancel orders from suppliers that violate its ethical, environmental, and human rights code. McDonald's denied rumours that one of its suppliers grazed cattle on cleared rain forest land, but wrote a ban on the practice anyway.

In contrast to companies that demand that their suppliers demonstrate socially responsible behaviour are those that have been criticized for exploiting workers in less developed countries. Nike, the world's largest athletic shoe company, has been accused by human rights and labour groups of treating its workers poorly while lavishing millions of dollars on star athletes to endorse its products. Nike is working to improve its reputation, in part by joining forces with Patagonia, Gap, and five other companies and six leading anti-sweatshop groups to create a single set of labour standards with a common factory-inspection system. The goal of the Joint Initiative on Corporate Accountability & Workers' Rights, as the project is called, is to replace the current multitude of approaches with something that is easier and cheaper to use, in the hope that more companies will adopt the standards as well.[41] Nike has established key targets to be met by 2011: eliminate excessive overtime in its contract factories; implement tailored human resource management systems and educational training for workers in its focus factories; implement Freedom of Association Educational Programs in 100 percent of its focus factories; and lead multi-brand collaboration on compliance issues in 30 percent of its supply chain.[42]

Ethical responsibility does not stop at North American borders. Many colleges and universities have adopted standards that prohibit their schools' names or logos from being displayed on apparel made in foreign sweatshops. Sweatshops are factories with very low pay and poor health and safety standards. Would you be willing to buy products from a manufacturer that produces its goods in substandard facilities in foreign nations?

The justness of requiring international suppliers to adhere to domestic ethical standards is not as clear-cut as you might think. For example, what could be considered a gift in one culture is considered a bribe in another.[43] Is it always ethical for companies to demand compliance with the standards of their own countries? What about countries in which child labour is an accepted part of the society and families depend on the children's salaries for survival? What about foreign companies doing business in Canada? Should these companies have to comply with Canadian ethical standards? What about multinational corporations? Since they span different societies, do they not have to conform to any one society's standards? None of these questions are easy to answer, but they give you some idea of the complexity of social responsibility issues in international markets. The Reaching Beyond Our Borders box highlights one external body that can assist countries in developing laws and regulations to fight corruption. The UN Global Compact (the focus of a Taking It To The Net exercise) is another organization that provides a practical framework for companies that are committed to sustainability and responsible business practices around the world.

## Reaching Beyond Our Borders

### An Assessment of Action on Anti-Corruption Commitments

Transparency International (TI) is the global civil society organization leading the fight against corruption. TI raises awareness of the damaging effects of corruption and works with partners in government, business, the private sector, and civil society to develop and implement effective measures to tackle corruption.

A recent report assessed commitments made by the Group of Eight (G8) since 2002 with respect to reducing corruption and found that overall, they had fallen short. While there has been significant enforcement of anti-bribery laws in France, Germany, and the United States, this has not been the case with Canada, Japan, and the United Kingdom. For example, for Canada there has been only one minor case against a company for a small payment allegedly made to a U.S. immigration official to gain access to the United States for business purposes.

Furthermore, Canada is the only Organisation for Economic Co-Operation and Development (OECD) country not to have adopted nationality jurisdiction in its legislation through the Corruption of Foreign Public Officials Act. Canadian courts apply "territorial" jurisdiction in almost all criminal matters and do not interpret it broadly. It has been recommended that the Government of Canada amend this Act to clarify that it applies extraterritorially to Canadian nationals. As it now stands, permitting nationals to pay foreign bribes as long as they do outside Canada creates an easy loophole that should be closed.

Experts have called on the Canadian government to do more to promote anti-bribery compliance programs among small- and medium-sized businesses and to make greater efforts within those agencies engaged in other countries and with foreign trade initiatives to report bribery allegations "up the line" and ultimately, to enforcement authorities.

In a positive development, following Canada's ratification of the United Nations Convention Against Corruption, the Royal Canadian Mounted Police established two International Anti-Corruption Teams that focus on the detection, investigation, and prevention of international corruption such as bribery, embezzlement, and money laundering.

Source: Reprinted from Transparency International, "2008 G8 Progress Report." Copyright 2009 Transparency International: The Global Coalition Against Corruption. Used with permission. For more information, visit www.transparency.org.

## SUMMARY

1. Ethics goes beyond obeying laws. It also involves abiding by the moral standards accepted by society.

**LO ▶ 1** Explain why legality is only one step in behaving ethically.

### How is legality different from ethics?
Ethics reflects people's proper relation with one another. Legality is more limiting; it refers only to laws written to protect people from fraud, theft, and violence.

### What influences our ethical decision making?
Ethical behaviour begins with you and me. We are influenced by our society and what it considers to be ethical, the behaviour of others (both socially and in a work setting), and by our own personal values and beliefs.

### How can we tell if our business decisions are ethical?
There is no universally-accepted approach when answering this question. One suggestion is to ask yourself three questions: (1) Is it legal? (2) Is it balanced? and (3) How will it make me feel? Companies (and individuals) that develop strong ethics codes and use these three questions have a better chance than most of behaving ethically.

**LO ▶ 2** Describe management's role in setting ethical standards and distinguish between compliance-based and integrity-based ethics codes.

2. Some managers think that ethics is an individual issue that has nothing to do with management, while others believe that ethics has everything to do with management.

**What is management's role in setting ethical standards?**

Managers often set formal ethical standards, but more important are the messages they send through their actions. Management's tolerance or intolerance of ethical misconduct influences employees more than written ethics codes do.

**What's the difference between compliance-based and integrity-based ethics codes?**

Whereas compliance-based ethics codes are concerned with avoiding legal punishment, integrity-based ethics codes define the organization's guiding values, create an environment that supports ethically sound behaviour, and stress a shared accountability among employees.

**LO ▶ 3** List the six steps that can be considered when setting up a corporate ethics code.

3. Business ethics can be improved if companies follow a six-step process.

**What are the six steps that can improve business ethics?**

The six steps are as follows: (1) top management must adopt and support an explicit corporate code of conduct; (2) employees must understand that expectations for ethical behaviour begin at the top and that senior management expects all employees to act accordingly; (3) managers and others must be trained to consider the ethical implications of all business decisions; (4) an ethics office must be set up, and phone lines to the office should be established; (5) outsiders such as suppliers, subcontractors, distributors, and customers must be told about the ethics program; and (6) the ethics code must be enforced.

**Which step is the most critical in this six-step process?**

The last step is most critical because a company's ethics policy must be enforced to be taken seriously.

**LO ▶ 4** Define corporate social responsibility and examine corporate responsibility to various stakeholders.

4. Corporate social responsibility goes beyond merely being ethical.

**Define *corporate social responsibility*.**

Corporate social responsibility is the concern businesses have toward stakeholders.

**What are the dimensions of corporate social responsibility?**

The social performance of a company has several dimensions. Corporate philanthropy includes charitable donations to non-profit groups. Corporate responsibility includes everything from hiring minority workers to making safe products. Corporate policy refers to the position a firm takes on social and political issues.

**Discuss the two views of corporate responsibility to stakeholders.**

The strategic approach requires that management's primary orientation be toward the economic interests of shareholders. This approach encourages managers to consider an actions' effects on stakeholders other than owners, but ultimately others' interests are secondary. Often these interests are considered only when they would adversely affect profits if ignored. The pluralist approach recognizes the special responsibility of management to optimize profits, but not at the expense of employees, suppliers, and members of the community. This approach recognizes the moral responsibilities of management that apply to all human beings. The guiding philosophy for the twenty-first century will be some version of the pluralist approach.

**LO ▶ 5** Discuss the responsibility that business has to customers, investors, employees, society, and the environment

5. Business has a responsibility to many stakeholders.

**What responsibility does business have to customers?**

Business's responsibility to customers is to satisfy them with goods and services of real value.

**What responsibility does business have to investors?**

Business is responsible for making money for its investors. Implicit is that decisions are good not only for the economic bottom line but also for the social responsibility bottom line.

**What responsibility does business have to employees?**

Business has several responsibilities to employees: to create jobs, to maintain job security, and to see that hard work and talent are fairly rewarded. This should be accomplished within a safe work environment.

**What responsibility does business have to society?**

Business has several responsibilities to society: to create new wealth, to promote social justice, and to contribute to making its own environment a better place.

**What responsibility does business have to the environment?**

Business has the responsibility to minimize its negative impact on the environment.

**How are a company's social responsibility efforts measured?**

A corporate social audit measures an organization's progress toward social responsibility. Some people believe that the audit should sum the organization's positive actions and then subtract the negative effects of business to get its net social benefit.

## KEY TERMS

compliance-based ethics codes 146

corporate philanthropy 150

corporate policy 151

corporate responsibility 151

corporate social initiatives 151

corporate social responsibility (CSR) 150

ethics 142

insider trading 154

integrity-based ethics codes 146

social audit 157

sustainable development 159

triple-bottom line (TBL, 3BL, or People, Planet, Profit) 157

whistleblowers 146

## CRITICAL THINKING

1. Think of a situation you have been involved in that tested your ethical behaviour. For example, perhaps your best friend forgot about a term paper due the next day and asked you if he could copy and hand in a paper you wrote for another instructor last semester. What are your alternatives, and what are the consequences of each one? Would it have been easier to resolve the dilemma if you had asked yourself the three questions in the ethics check? Try answering them now and see if you would have made a different choice.

2. In Chapter 4 we discussed how the granting of subprime mortgages contributed to a crisis in the financial markets. Was it ethical for firms to provide mortgages to individuals that were unlikely to be able to afford them? How about for investors? How about for the homeowners?

3. Companies appear to act with corporate responsibility but the underlying motive seems to be to increase profits. Does this motive undermine the value of corporate responsibility or is it only the actions that are important? That is, do you think less of a company if you know it is being responsible only to increase its profits?

## DEVELOPING WORKPLACE SKILLS

1. Newspapers and magazines are full of stories about individuals and businesses that are not socially responsible. What about those individuals and organizations that do take social responsibility seriously? We don't normally read or hear about them. Do a little investigative reporting of your own. Identify a public interest group in your community and identify its officers, objectives, sources and amount of financial support, and size and characteristics of membership. List some examples of its recent actions and/or accomplishments. Consider environmental groups, animal protection groups, political action committees, and so on. Call your local Chamber of Commerce, the Better Business Bureau, or local government agencies for help. Try using one of the Internet search engines to help you find more information.

2. You are the manager of a coffee house called the Morning Cup. One of your best employees wants to be promoted to a managerial position; however, the owner is grooming his son for the promotion your employee seeks. The owner's act of nepotism may hurt a valuable employee's chances for advancement, but complaining may hurt your own chances for promotion. What do you do?

3. You are a salesperson at a clothing store. You walk into the storage room to start ticketing some clothes that came in that morning and see a co-worker quickly take some pants from a box and put them into her knapsack. Your colleague does not see you enter the room. What do you do? Do you leave and not say anything to your employer? Do you say something to your colleague? Do you tell your employer about this incident? Is your responsibility to your organization, your colleague, or both? What might be the implications of your decision?

4. Contact a local corporation and ask for a copy of its written ethics code. Would you classify its code as compliance-based or integrity-based? Explain.

 ## TAKING IT TO THE NET 1

### Purpose

To learn about a corporate social responsibility (CSR) resource available to support business decisions that will improve performance and contribute to a better world.

### Exercise

Canadian Business for Social Responsibility (CBSR) is a non-profit, member-led organization that is committed to corporate social responsibility. Go to www.cbsr.ca and answer the following questions.

1. What is the CSBR approach?
2. Looking at the Resources tab, what are some of the recent CSR trends?
3. What is the focus of the next Summit? (Hint: Visit the Conferences & Events tab.) What are some of the workshop themes?

 ## TAKING IT TO THE NET 2

### Purpose

To be aware of an external body that can help firms develop ethical codes of conduct.

### Exercise

The UN Global Compact has the mandate to be both a policy platform and to provide a practical framework for companies that are committed to sustainability and responsible business practices. Visit the site (http://www.unglobalcompact.org/) and answer the following questions:

1. What are the two complementary objectives that the UN Global Compact aims to advance?
2. What are companies that voluntarily join the Global Compact expected to do?
3. Considering human rights, labour, the environment, and anti-corruption, what are the ten principles of the UN Global Compact?

## ANALYZING MANAGEMENT DECISIONS

### CNR Charged with Spill

Canadian National Railway (CNR) was charged by Alberta Environment with failing to take all reasonable measures to remedy and confine the spill from a train derailment into a northern Alberta lake in August 2005. In the incident, 43 cars derailed next to Wabamun Lake, west of Edmonton, spilling almost 800,000 litres of heavy fuel and a potentially cancer-causing wood preservative. The environmental offence is punishable by a maximum fine of $500,000.

Alberta Environment spokeswoman Kim Hunt said the charges were laid by Alberta Justice after a review. "It's the law in Alberta that the polluter pays," Hunt told the Canadian Press. After the spill, Alberta Environment issued an Environmental Protection Order to CNR. The company was ordered to clean up the spill, begin long-term environmental planning and monitoring of the area, and keep the public informed on its progress. Residents of Wabamun were told in June 2006 that they could use the lake again for swimming and boating, but not for washing dishes, cleaning vegetables, or bathing. At that time, CNR said in a statement that it was committed to the monitoring and testing of the lake, and announced that the cleanup was expected to be completed by the end of the month.

The spill initially left a slick on the surface of the lake and coated migrating waterfowl. While most of the oil has been removed, residents claim that balls of tar still occasionally wash up onshore. Wabamun Lake residents' committee chairman Doug Goss said that while CNR has already spent $75 million removing the mess, he hopes in future that the provincial government will clean up spills immediately and send the bill to the company responsible.

CNR offered nearly $7.5 million on a sliding scale to the area's 1,600 residents. The payments, which ranged from $1,500 to $27,000 for those closest to the spill, were in recognition of loss of property use as a result of the derailment. The Paul First Nation, whose reserve is on the western shore of the lake, also filed a multi-million-dollar lawsuit against CNR, Ottawa, and the province, alleging that the spill destroyed its traditional way of life. In September 2008, CNR reached a $10 million settlement with the band. "This money will play a major part in implementing the band's business development plan, which we are confident will result in a much stronger economic situation for our people," said Chief Daniel Paul. Earlier in 2008, three charges were laid by Environment Canada and Fisheries and Oceans Canada against CNR: one for allegedly depositing a substance harmful to migratory birds into a lake and the other two for alleged disruption of a fish habitat.

Sources: "Canadian National Railway to Pay $10M to Alta. Band in Derailment Along Lake," CANOE Inc., 12 September 2008, http://cnews.canoe.ca/CNEWS/Politics/2008/09/12/6751421-cp.html; "Oil Spill Nets CN Rail Three Charges from Feds," *Canadian Geographic*, 18 March 2008, http://www.canadiangeographic.ca/cea/archives/news_item.asp?articleid=493; Gordon Kent and Kelly Cryderman, "Wabamun Residents Unhappy with CN Charge," CanWest News Service, 6 June 2006, http://www.canada.com/topics/news/national/story.html?id=14a77881-cc1b-4ec0-90a7-fd86af5a9c7c&k=58041; and "CN Rail Charged in Oil Spill at Alta. Lake," The Canadian Press, 6 June 2006, http://sympaticomsn.ctv.ca/servlet/ArticleNews/story/CTVNews/20060605/cn_wabamun_060506.

### Discussion Questions

1. What stakeholders were impacted by this incident?

2. Conduct some research into this story. As a result of this derailment, what changes were implemented by CNR and Environment Alberta?

3. Do you feel that the costs associated with this incident are excessive? Explain.

## RUNNING CASE

### Canadian Tire Financial Services: Adapting to the Business Environment

As the financial arm of Canadian Tire Corporation, Ltd. (Canadian Tire), Canadian Tire Financial Services (CTFS) primarily engages in financing and managing the Canadian Tire Options® MasterCard for more than five million card members. CTFS also markets related financial products and services to retail and petroleum customers including personal loans, insurance and warranty products, and emergency roadside assistance through the Canadian Tire Auto Club. A banking pilot is currently underway at Canadian Tire Bank offering high-interest savings accounts, guaranteed investment certificates, residential mortgages, and the One-and-Only™ account.

CTFS originated in 1961 as Midland Shoppers Credit Limited, a small financial services company offering third-party credit processing for local retailers. During the 1960s, the Canadian Tire Associate Stores became clients. In 1968, Midland became a subsidiary of Canadian Tire Corporation and was renamed Canadian Tire Acceptance Limited (CTAL). In the decades that followed, CTAL continued to provide credit processing. In 1995, it became the first non-deposit-taking financial institution worldwide to launch a MasterCard. In 2000, it expanded the Canadian Tire "Money" loyalty program by launching Canadian Tire "Money" On The Card. People could accumulate Canadian Tire "Money" On The Card by using their MasterCard anywhere in the world and redeem Canadian Tire "Money" On The Card in any Canadian Tire store on merchandise, auto parts, or auto labour.

Changes to the Bank Act in 2001 created opportunities for non-traditional banks to enter the Canadian industry. During this time, a project group was formed and consultants were hired to investigate the benefits of creating a bank. A major benefit would be that CTFS would need to comply with one set of federal rules and legislation rather than to the individual provincial and territorial government rules and legislation. As well, CTFS would be able to compete with what banks could offer. Third, a bank structure would change the terms and conditions of existing products. In 2002, CTAL's name was changed to Canadian Tire Financial Services to better reflect the company's stronger and broader position within the financial services industry. In 2003, CTFS established Canadian Tire Bank to enable greater marketing flexibility for its card operations, and to facilitate continued expansion into the high growth bank card market. Canadian Tire Bank is a federally chartered, federally regulated bank. Operating the credit card business under Canadian Tire Bank enables the company to offer customers credit card services consistently across the country.

As part of its 2007–2012 Strategic Plan, CTFS continues its focus on growth in the areas of insurance and warranty, the credit card portfolio, and its retail banking products. Approximately 46 percent of Canadian Tire's 2009 first quarter earnings were generated by CTFS's activities. Looking at 2009 alone, CTFS will be relaunching credit cards with PayPass® capability, testing new credit cards, and providing select investments in balance transfer offers.

Each year, corporate donations to the community exceed $1 million. CTFS believes that a portion of its earnings should be reinvested into the community from which they are derived. Overarching CTFS committees work to support different charities and worthy causes. For example, the Corporate Donations Committee sets aside an annual budget with a third allocated to sports (e.g., employee and youth teams), a third allocated to the arts (e.g., Niagara Symphony, local theatres, etc.), and a third allocated to the community (e.g., Welland Food Festival). Employees contribute to some of these causes as evidenced by the annual Employee Giving Campaign. In 2008, more than $286,000 was raised for local charities through this endeavour. More recently, and in partnership with Canadian Tire Jumpstart Charities, CTFS raised $300,000 in support of Goodwill's Stokes Community Village and the Niagara-area Canadian Tire Jumpstart Chapter.

Sources: "Canadian Tire Corporation Overview," Canadian Tire Corporation, Ltd., 9 June 2009, http://corp.canadiantire.ca/EN/Pages/default.aspx; Lara V. Strebul, Senior Communications Consultant Corporate Communications, Canadian Tire Financial Services, interview, 9 June 2009; Marco Marrone, President, Canadian Tire Financial Services, interviews, 13 August 2008 and 10 March 2006; and *Canadian Tire Financial Times*, Spring 2008 and Fall/Winter 2007.

## Discussion Questions

**1.** List some stakeholders that must be considered when top executives at CTFS develop policies and strategies.

**2.** How does CTFS incorporate social responsibility in its business practices? How does the company benefit as a result of this community involvement?

**3.** Consider the elements in the business environment. What are some trends that must be analyzed as CTFS moves forward with its growth strategy?

# PART 2

# CHAPTER 6

# Forms of Business Ownership

## LEARNING OBJECTIVES

**AFTER YOU HAVE READ AND STUDIED THIS CHAPTER, YOU SHOULD BE ABLE TO:**

**LO ▶ 1** List the advantages and disadvantages of sole proprietorships.

**LO ▶ 2** Describe the advantages and disadvantages of partnerships. Include the differences between general and limited partners.

**LO ▶ 3** Discuss the advantages and disadvantages of corporations.

**LO ▶ 4** Define and give examples of three types of corporate mergers, and explain the role of leveraged buyouts and taking a firm private.

**LO ▶ 5** Outline the advantages and disadvantages of franchises, and discuss the challenges of global franchising.

**LO ▶ 6** Describe the role of co-operatives in Canada.

## Getting to Know Michelle Strum and David Eisnor, Co-Owners of Halifax Backpackers Hostel

Michelle Strum and David Eisnor have been friends for all of their lives. They have travelled extensively and lived for many months in various hostels around the world. With the number of travellers visiting Halifax growing, they felt that there would be a need for more budget accommodations in the city.

Their first business expense was a personal computer. On the day after they made this purchase, they registered their business name, Halifax Backpackers Hostel. The hostel provides budget accommodation for travellers who can share rooms or come together in common areas, such as the kitchen where they can prepare their own meals or the café that is run by another local entrepreneur. Guests also have access to the Internet and laundry facilities.

From the day they opened Halifax Backpackers Hostel in August 2001, Strum and Eisnor knew it was going to take off. "We were full from that day right into the middle of October," says Strum. "It was quite amazing." Since opening, they bought the building that houses the hostel, doubled the accommodation it provides, and continue to focus on efforts to help revitalize the neighbourhood.

Getting started required a lot of elbow grease and hard work by the partners, who quickly learned about doing renovations themselves and the challenges of financing the business. They received two $15,000 young entrepreneur loans, applied for a bunch of credit cards and did a lot of bartending to pay for drywall! "We've had to be creative," explains Eisnor. "For example, in the summertime, we share employees with the café owner to cut down on payroll costs."

Whether you dream of going into business for yourself, starting a business with a friend, or someday leading a major corporation, it's important to know that each form of business ownership has advantages and disadvantages. You will learn more about them in this chapter.

Sources: "History—Our Story," Halifax Backpackers Hostel, 13 September 2008, www.halifaxbackpackers.com; Bonnie Schiedel, "Spirit: A Hundred Grand," *Chatelaine*, November 2005, http://www.northstarwriting.ca/articles/article_100K.html; and "Co-owners David Eisnor and Michelle Strum Win BDC's Young Entrepreneur Award for Nova Scotia," Business Development Bank of Canada, 19 October 2004, http://www.bdc.ca/en/about/mediaroom/news_releases/2004/2004101903.htm.

# STARTING A SMALL BUSINESS

Like Michelle Strum and David Eisnor, thousands of people start new businesses in Canada every year. Chances are, you have thought of owning your own business or know someone who has. One key to success in starting a new business is understanding how to get the resources you need. You may have to take on partners or find other ways of obtaining money. To stay in business, you may need help from someone with more expertise than you have in certain areas, or you may need to raise more money to expand. How you form your business can make a tremendous difference in your long-term success. You can form a business in one of several ways. The three major forms of business ownership are (1) sole proprietorships, (2) partnerships, and (3) corporations.

It can be easy to get started in your own business. You can begin a word-processing service out of your home, open a car repair centre, start a restaurant, develop a Web site, or go about meeting other unmet wants and needs in your community. A **sole proprietorship** is one person owning and operating a business, without forming a corporation.[1] (We will discuss corporations soon.) In a sole proprietorship, the business and the owner are a single entity. As noted in Figure 6.1, almost 24 percent of all registered businesses in Canada fall under this form of ownership.

Many people do not have the money, time, or desire to run a business on their own. They prefer to have someone else or a group of people get together to form the business. When two or more people legally agree to become co-owners of a business, the organization is called a **partnership**.

There are advantages to creating a business that is separate and distinct from the owners. A legal entity with authority to act and have liability separate from its owners is called a **corporation**. There are more than 1.5 million corporations in Canada, and they have the largest share of business revenue by far, as noted in Figure 6.1.

As you will learn in this chapter, each form of business ownership has advantages and disadvantages. It is important to understand these advantages and disadvantages before attempting to start a business. Keep in mind that just because a business starts in one form of ownership, it doesn't have to stay in that form. Many companies start out in one form, then add (or drop) a partner or two, and eventually may become corporations. The advantages and disadvantages that are highlighted in this chapter may give you an idea of why there may be a change in ownership form as the business grows.

Another thing that must be looked at before proceeding is the meaning of the term *liability*. **Liability** is often just another word for debt, but it also has a wider and important meaning, as you will see in the following pages. Liability for a business includes the responsibility to pay all normal debts and to pay:

1. Because of a court order
2. Because of a law

**sole proprietorship**
A business that is owned and operated by one person, without forming a corporation.

**partnership**
A legal form of business with two or more parties.

**corporation**
A legal entity with authority to act and have liability separate from its owners.

**liability**
For a business, it includes the responsibility to pay all normal debts and to pay because of a court order or law, for performance under a contract, or payment of damages to a person or property in an accident.

**FIGURE | 6.1**

**Business Distribution by Type, Number, and Revenue**
The category of *partnerships/joint ventures* represents unincorporated businesses.

| Business Type | Number of Businesses | Business (%) | Revenue (%) |
|---|---|---|---|
| Incorporations | 1,576,866 | 69.1 | 88.9 |
| Sole Proprietorships | 544,858 | 23.9 | 2.9 |
| Partnerships/Joint Ventures | 100,860 | 4.4 | 5.4 |
| Other/Unknown | 51,646 | 2.3 | 0.9 |
| Government | 7,413 | 0.3 | 1.4 |
| Trust and Special Funds | 1,328 | 0.1 | 0.5 |
| **Total** | **2,282,971** | | **100.0** |

Source: "Business Distribution by Type, Number, and Revenue," adapted from Statistics Canada, special tabulation, unpublished data (Business Register Database), June 2008.

3. For performance under a contract (recall this from Appendix B)

4. For damages to a person or property

Let's begin our discussion by looking at the most basic form of ownership—the sole proprietorship.

# SOLE PROPRIETORSHIPS

## Advantages of Sole Proprietorships

Sole proprietorships are the easiest kind of businesses for you to explore in your quest for an interesting career. Every town has sole proprietors you can visit. Talk with some of these business people about the joys and frustrations of being on their own. Most will mention the benefits of being their own boss and setting their own hours. Other advantages they mention may include the following:

Tammy Beese started *What's Up Yukon*, a free weekly magazine that features 100 percent local content. Printed on newsprint, the magazine covers Yukon news about arts and culture, sports and recreation, and "all things fun and entertainment."

1. *Ease of starting and ending the business.* All you have to do to start a sole proprietorship is buy or lease the needed equipment (e.g., a saw, a word processor, a tractor, a lawn mower) and put up some announcements saying you are in business. It is just as easy to get out of business; you simply stop. There is no one to consult or to disagree with about such decisions. You may have to get a permit or licence from the local government, but often that is no problem.

2. *Being your own boss.* As noted earlier, this is one of the most common reasons cited for starting a sole proprietorship. Working for others simply does not have the same excitement as working for yourself—at least, that's the way sole proprietors feel. You may make mistakes, but they are your mistakes—and so are the many small victories encountered each day.

3. *Pride of ownership.* People who own and manage their own businesses are rightfully proud of their work. They deserve all the credit for taking the risks and providing needed products.

4. *Retention of company profit.* Other than the joy of being your own boss, there is nothing like the pleasure of knowing that you can earn as much as possible and not have to share that money with anyone else (except the government, in taxes).

5. *No special taxes.* All profits of a sole proprietorship are taxed as the personal income of the owner, and the owner pays the normal personal income tax on that money. Another tax advantage for sole proprietors is that they can claim any business losses against other earned income. These losses would decrease the personal taxes they would need to pay. Understanding tax planning is an important factor in choosing the appropriate form of business organization and often requires the advice of professional accountants. Accounting will be discussed in Chapter 16.

6. *Less regulation.* While proprietorships are regulated by the provincial/territorial governments, and the proprietorship may have to be registered, overall they are less regulated than corporations.[2] As well, the administration of a proprietorship is less costly than that of a corporation.

## Disadvantages of Sole Proprietorships

Not everyone is equipped to own and manage a business. Often it is difficult to save enough money to start a business and keep it going. The costs of inventory, supplies, insurance, advertising, rent, computers, utilities, and so on may be too much to cover alone. Other disadvantages of owning your own business are listed on the next page.

**unlimited liability**
The responsibility of business owners for all of the debts of the business.

1. *Unlimited liability—the risk of personal losses.* When you work for others, it is their problem if the business is not profitable. When you own your own business, you and the business are considered one. You have **unlimited liability**; that is, any debts or damages incurred by the business are your debts and you must pay them, even if it means selling your home, your car, or whatever else you own. This is a serious risk, and one that requires not only thought but also discussion with a lawyer, an insurance agent, an accountant, and others.

2. *Limited financial resources.* Funds available to the business are limited to the funds that the one (sole) owner can gather. Since there are serious limits to how much money one person can raise, partnerships and corporations have a greater probability of obtaining the needed financial backing to start a business and keep it going.

3. *Management difficulties.* All businesses need management; that is, someone must keep inventory records, accounting records, tax records, and so forth. Many people who are skilled at selling things or providing a service are not so skilled at keeping records. Sole proprietors often find it difficult to attract good, qualified employees to help run the business because they cannot compete with the salary and benefits offered by larger companies.

4. *Overwhelming time commitment.* Though sole proprietors may say they set their own hours, it's hard to own a business, manage it, train people, and have time for anything else in life. This is true of any business, but a sole proprietor has no one with whom to share the burden. The owner often must spend long hours working. The owner of a store, for example, may put in 12 hours a day, at least six days a week—almost twice the hours worked by a non-supervisory employee in a large company. Imagine how this time commitment affects the sole proprietor's family life. Tim DeMello, founder of the successful company Wall Street Games Inc., echoes countless other sole proprietors when he says, "It's not a job, it's not a career, it's a way of life."

5. *Few fringe benefits.* If you are your own boss, you lose the fringe benefits that often come from working for others. You have no paid health insurance, no paid disability insurance, no sick leave, and no vacation pay. These and other benefits may add up to approximately 30 percent of a worker's income.[3]

6. *Limited growth.* Expansion is often slow since a sole proprietorship relies on its owner for most of its creativity, business know-how, and funding.

7. *Limited lifespan.* If the sole proprietor dies, is incapacitated, or retires, the business no longer exists, unless it is sold or taken over by the sole proprietor's heirs. While the net business assets pass to the heirs, valuable leases and contracts may not.[4]

8. *Possibly pay higher taxes.* If the business's income exceeds $400,000, it will usually be paying higher taxes than if it was incorporated as a Canadian Controlled Private Corporation (CCPC).[5] That is, tax rates are more advantageous if the business is incorporated. We will expand on this point later on in the chapter under the corporations discussion.

Talk with a few local sole proprietors about the problems they have faced in being on their own. They are likely to have many interesting stories to tell about problems in getting loans from the bank, problems with theft, problems simply keeping up with the business, and so on. These problems are also reasons why many sole proprietors choose to find partners to share the load.

## Progress Assessment

- What are the three forms of business ownership?
- Most people who start businesses in Canada are sole proprietors. What are the advantages and disadvantages of sole proprietorships?
- Why would unlimited liability be considered a major drawback of sole proprietorships?

# PARTNERSHIPS

A partnership is a legal form of business with two or more parties. The business can be a partnership of individuals, corporations, trusts, other partnerships, or a combination of these.[6] Two types of partnerships are general partnerships and limited partnerships. A **general partnership** is a partnership in which all owners share in operating the business and in assuming liability for the business's debts. A **limited partnership** is a partnership with one or more general partners and one or more limited partners.

A **general partner** is an owner (partner) who has unlimited liability and is active in managing the firm. Every partnership must have at least one general partner. A **limited partner** is an owner who invests money in the business but does not have any management responsibility or liability for losses beyond the investment. **Limited liability** means that limited partners are not responsible for the debts of the business beyond the amount of their investment—their liability is limited to the amount they put into the company; therefore, their personal assets are not at risk.

## Advantages of Partnerships

There are many advantages to having one or more partners in a business, as we will list for you next. Some professionals who enjoy the advantages of partnerships today are physicians, lawyers, dentists, and accountants. The advantages of a partnership include the following:

1. *More financial resources.* When two or more people pool their money and credit, it is easier to pay the rent, utilities, and other bills incurred by a business. A limited partnership is specially designed to help raise capital (money). As mentioned earlier, a limited partner invests money in the business but cannot legally have any management responsibility and has limited liability. Read the Reaching Beyond Our Borders box for how taking on a partner has allowed Inder Bedi to grow his business.

2. *Shared management and pooled/complementary skills and knowledge.* It is simply much easier to manage the day-to-day activities of a business with carefully chosen partners. Partners give each other free time from the business and provide different skills and perspectives. Some people find that the best partner is a spouse. That is why you see so many husband-and-wife teams managing restaurants, service shops, and other businesses.

3. *Longer survival.* One study that examined 2,000 businesses started since 1960 reported that partnerships were four times as likely to succeed as sole proprietorships. Being watched by a partner can help a business person become more disciplined.

4. *Shared risk.* A partnership shares the risk among the owners. This includes financial risk in starting the business and ongoing risks as the business grows.

5. *No special taxes.* As with sole proprietorships, all profits of partnerships are taxed as the personal income of the owners, and the owners pay the normal income tax on that money. Similarly, any business losses can be used to decrease earned income from other sources.

6. *Less regulation.* Like a sole proprietorship, a partnership is less regulated than a corporation.

## Disadvantages of Partnerships

Any time two people must agree, there is the possibility of conflict and tension. Partnerships have caused splits among families, friends, and marriages. Let's explore the disadvantages of partnerships:

1. *Unlimited liability.* Each general partner is liable for the debts of the firm, no matter who was responsible for causing those debts. You are liable for your partners' mistakes as well as your own. Like sole proprietors, general partners can lose their homes, cars, and everything else they own if the business loses a lawsuit or goes bankrupt.

**general partnership**
A partnership in which all owners share in operating the business and in assuming liability for the business's debts.

**limited partnership**
A partnership with one or more general partners and one or more limited partners.

**general partner**
An owner (partner) who has unlimited liability and is active in managing the firm.

**limited partner**
An owner who invests money in the business but does not have any management responsibility or liability for losses beyond the investment.

**limited liability**
The responsibility of a business's owners for losses only up to the amount they invest; limited partners and shareholders have limited liability.

## Reaching Beyond Our Borders

### Bags That Travel

It started with a challenge to forgo animal products for thirty days. Today, matt & nat's line of vegan handbags and wallets for men and women is known to an ever-growing number of consumers across Canada, the United States, and Europe. Celebrity followers include Brad Pitt, Eva Mendes, and Natalie Portman. Founded eleven years ago by Inder Bedi, 35, the company has expanded to include 18 employees, an office in the United Kingdom, and revenues that have grown 1,000 percent from 2001 to 2007.

Bedi started matt & nat fresh out of university. "I dreamed of something that no one else in the market was doing: a lifestyle brand that embraces a philosophy of positivity and is environmentally conscious," he says. "Being a vegetarian, I wanted the line to be cruelty-free, using no animal products. But beyond that, I wanted the product to reflect a philosophy, which is why there is a positivity message stamped on all bags, something that has universal appeal."

When he began, Bedi lived with family until he saved enough money to fund the business start-up, while learning everything he could about design and the trade. "In the first years of the company, the line was produced locally in Montreal," says Bedi. "I got to the point where I wanted to bring the business to the next level. Seven years ago, I brought in a business partner and we took production to Asia. This allowed us to make the line more affordable, while maintaining our designer appeal. Due to the attention we give to design and details, we have managed to maintain the perception of a high-end line while taking it to mass market."

matt & nat has successfully distinguished itself in the crowded fashion accessories industry with three key factors: fashion-forward designs, a philosophy, and reasonable pricing. The company targets boutique businesses and has, over time, defined a recognizable matt & nat style that appeals to a wide range of people. "We keep our designs as practical as possible without compromising style. Our strategy is to carefully select who we sell to and be the most affordable line in high-end stores," says Bedi. matt & nat has garnered attention in the fashion media for its distinctive message tags and eco-conscious offerings. "We have specifically chosen not to advertise through traditional ways," adds Bedi. "We want the brand and the product to speak for themselves."

The company opened an office in London, England, three years ago and is developing its presence internationally with sales representatives throughout Canada, as well as in the United States, Germany, Poland, and Dubai. Distribution agreements are in the works with Japan, Korea, and Sweden. "Long-term, we would be looking to open our own showrooms as well as matt & nat concept stores throughout North America," says Bedi.

Sources: "About Us," matt & nat, 2008, http://www.mattandnat.ca/about_us; and "Inder Bedi Wins BDC's Young Entrepreneur Award for Québec," Business Development Bank of Canada, 16 October 2007, http://www.bdc.ca/en/about/mediaroom/news_releases/2007/2007101603.htm.

2. *Division of profits.* Sharing risk means sharing profits, and that can cause conflicts. There is no set system for dividing profits in a partnership, so profits are not always divided evenly. For example, two people form a partnership in which one puts in more money and the other puts in more hours working the business. Each may feel justified in asking for a bigger share of the profits. Imagine the resulting conflict.

3. *Disagreements among partners.* Disagreements over money are just one example of potential conflict in a partnership. If things are going badly, one partner may blame the other. Who has final authority over employees? Who hires and fires employees? Who works what hours? What if one partner wants to buy expensive equipment for the firm and the other partner disagrees? Potential conflicts are many. All too often, not enough effort is spent at the creation of the partnership delineating the nature of the relationship through a partnership agreement. Because of such problems, all the terms of the partnership should be spelled out in writing to protect all parties and to minimize misunderstandings.[7] Figure 6.2 gives you some ideas about what should be included in a partnership agreement. The Spotlight on Small Business offers some suggestions on what to consider when choosing the right partner.

4. *Difficult to terminate.* Once you have committed yourself to a partnership, it is not easy to get out of it (other than by death, which immediately terminates the partnership). Sure, you can end a partnership just by quitting. However, questions about who gets what and what happens next are often very difficult to solve when the partnership ends. Surprisingly, law firms often have faulty **partnership agreements** (legal documents that specify the rights and responsibilities of each partner) and find that breaking up is hard to do. How do you get rid of a partner you don't like? It is best to decide such questions up front in the partnership agreement. In the absence of an agreement, or if certain provisions are not addressed in the agreement, provincial or territorial laws will determine some or all of the terms of the partnership.[8]

5. *Possibly pay higher taxes.* Similar to a sole proprietorship, if the partnership is very profitable, it may be paying higher taxes than if it was incorporated as a Canadian Controlled Private Corporation (CCPC).[9]

**partnership agreement**
Legal document that specifies the rights and responsibilities of each partner

The best way to learn about the advantages and disadvantages of partnerships is to interview several people who have experience with such agreements. They will give you insights and hints on how to avoid problems. The Making Ethical Decisions box leaves you with a dilemma to consider when it comes to making decisions in a partnership.

One common fear of owning your own business or having a partner is the fear of losing everything you own if the business loses a lot of money or someone sues the business. Many business people try to avoid this and the other disadvantages of sole proprietorships and partnerships by forming corporations. We discuss this basic form of business ownership in the next section.

## Progress Assessment

- What is the difference between a limited partner and a general partner?
- What are some of the advantages and disadvantages of partnerships?
- State four provisions usually included in a partnership agreement.

## SPOTLIGHT ON Small Business

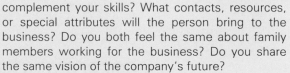

### Choose Your Partner

Suppose you need money and want help running your business, and you decide to take on a partner. You know that partnerships are like marriages and that you won't really know the other person until after you live together. How do you choose the right partner? Before you plunge into a partnership, do three things:

1. Talk to people who have been in successful—and unsuccessful—partnerships. Find out what worked and what didn't. Ask them how conflicts were resolved and how decisions were made.
2. Interview your prospective partner very carefully. Do you share the same goals? What skills does the person have? Are they the same as yours, or do they complement your skills? What contacts, resources, or special attributes will the person bring to the business? Do you both feel the same about family members working for the business? Do you share the same vision of the company's future?
3. Evaluate your prospective partner as a decision maker. Ask yourself, "Is this someone with whom I could happily share authority for all major business decisions?"

As in a good marriage, the best way to avoid major conflicts is to begin with an honest communication of what each partner expects to give and get from the partnership.

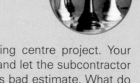

## Making Ethical Decisions

### Outsourcing or Outsmarting?

Imagine that you and your partner own a construction company. You receive a bid from a subcontractor that you know is 20 percent too low. Such a loss to the subcontractor could put him out of business. Accepting the bid will certainly improve your chances of winning the contract for a big shopping centre project. Your partner wants to take the bid and let the subcontractor suffer the consequences of his bad estimate. What do you think you should do? What will be the consequences of your decision?

---

**FIGURE | 6.2**

**Partnership Agreement Provisions**

It's not hard to form a partnership, but it's wise for each prospective partner to get the counsel of a lawyer experienced with such agreements. Lawyers' services are usually expensive, so would-be partners should read all about partnerships and reach some basic agreements before calling a lawyer.

For your protection, be sure to put your partnership agreement in writing. The following provisions are usually included in a partnership agreement:

1. The name of the business. All provinces require the firm's name to be registered with the province if the firm's name is different from the name of any of the partners.
2. The names and addresses of all partners.
3. The purpose and nature of the business, the location of the principal offices, and any other locations where business will be conducted.
4. The date the partnership will start and how long it will last. Will it exist for a specific length of time, or will it stop when one of the partners dies or when the partners agree to discontinue?
5. The contributions made by each partner. Will some partners contribute money, while others provide real estate, personal property, expertise, or labour? When are the contributions due?
6. The management responsibilities. Will all partners have equal voices in management, or will there be senior and junior partners?
7. The duties of each partner.
8. The salaries and drawing accounts of each partner.
9. Provision for sharing of profits or losses.
10. Provision for accounting procedures. Who'll keep the accounts? What bookkeeping and accounting methods will be used? Where will the books be kept?
11. The requirements for taking in new partners.
12. Any special restrictions, rights, or duties of any partner.
13. Provision for a retiring partner.
14. Provision for the purchase of a deceased or retiring partner's share of the business.
15. Provision for how grievances will be handled.
16. Provision for how to dissolve the partnership and distribute the assets to the partners.

# CORPORATIONS

Although the word *corporation* makes people think of big businesses such as the Bank of Montreal or Irving Oil, it is not necessary to be big to incorporate (start a corporation). Obviously, many corporations are big. However, incorporating may be beneficial for small businesses also.

A corporation is a federally or provincially chartered legal entity with authority to act and have liability separate from its owners. The corporation's owners (called stockholders/shareholders, as they hold stock/shares of ownership in the company) are not liable for the debts or any other problems of the corporation beyond the money they invest. Corporate stockholders do not have to worry about losing their houses, cars, and other personal property if the business cannot pay its bills—a very significant benefit. A corporation not only limits the liability of owners, but it also enables many people to share in the ownership (and profits) of a business without working there or having other commitments to it. We will discuss the rights of stockholders in Chapter 17.

In Canada, corporations are divided into two classes: public and private. A **public corporation** has the right to issue stock (ownership in the company through shares) to the public, which means its shares may be listed on a stock exchange. This offers the possibility of raising large amounts of capital, regardless of the size of the company. That is, public corporations can be small and large companies.

A **private corporation** is not allowed to issue stock to the public, so its shares are not listed on a stock exchange, and it is limited to 50 or fewer stockholders. This greatly reduces the costs of incorporating. Many small corporations are in the private category. This is the vehicle employed by individuals or partners who do not anticipate the need for substantial financing but want to take advantage of limited liability. Private corporations can be very large. Examples include Sun Life Assurance of Canada, Katz Group, and Honda Canada.

There are several advantages that Canadian-owned private corporations have over public corporations, especially from a taxation perspective. For example, a Canadian controlled private corporation (CCPC) pays a much lower rate of federal tax (small business rate) on the first $400,000 (in 2007) of active business income than would be paid by an unincorporated business, due to the small business deduction.[10] The combined federal and provincial small business tax rate varies from approximately 16 percent to 22 percent, depending on the province, and the threshold amount subject to the lower rate also varies between provinces.[11] With each federal and provincial budget, accountants study the impact of changes to corporate taxes. Such was the case when the 2006 federal budget reduced the general corporate tax rate from 21 percent to 19 percent, effective 1 January 2010.[12]

Another important advantage for the owner of a private corporation is that he or she can issue stock to a daughter, a son, or a spouse, making them co-owners of the company. This procedure is not available to a sole proprietor. It is a simple and useful way of recognizing the contribution of these or other family members, or employees, to the company. This procedure may also be a good way for the owner to prepare for retirement by gradually transferring ownership and responsibility to those who will be inheriting the business.

Keep in mind that with any kind of succession planning in private corporations, conflict may arise. In the mid-1990s, brothers Wallace and Harrison McCain of McCain Foods were bitterly divided over who should be picked to lead the company when they were gone. Wallace wanted his son Michael to take over, while Harrison preferred outside management. The fight ultimately wound up in a New Brunswick court, which sided with Harrison. Ousted from the company, Wallace ended up in Toronto, where he took over Maple Leaf Foods with sons Michael and Scott.[13] The Dealing with Change box discusses some of the challenges associated with taking over a family business.

**public corporation**
Corporation that has the right to issue shares to the public, so its shares may be listed on a stock exchange.

**private corporation**
Corporation that is not allowed to issue stock to the public, so its shares are not listed on stock exchanges; it is limited to 50 or fewer shareholders.

Chapman's Ice Cream is a private corporation. Started in 1973 by David and Penny Chapman, it is now Canada's largest independent ice cream manufacturer. Did you know that vanilla is the world's most popular ice cream flavour?

To find out the details on how one would set up a corporation, visit the Business Start-Up Assistant site at http://bsa.canadabusiness.ca.

There is a formal procedure for forming a corporation that involves applying to the appropriate federal or provincial agency. It is always recommended that company owners seek the services of a competent lawyer and accountant prior to proceeding with any incorporation. The procedure for large or public corporations is much more complex and expensive and definitely requires hiring a legal firm. These costs can easily run into the thousands of dollars.

## Advantages of Corporations

Most people are prepared to risk some pre-determined amount when they invest in a business, but are not willing to risk everything to go into business. Yet, for businesses to grow and prosper and create economic opportunity, many people need to invest their money. One way to manage the risk is to create an artificial being, an entity that exists only in the eyes of the law—a corporation. A corporation has a separate legal identity from the owners—the stockholders—of the company. The corporation files its own tax returns. This entity is a technique for involving people in business without risking their other personal assets. Advantages include:

1. *Limited liability.* A major advantage of corporations is the limited liability of owners. Many corporations in Canada have the letters *Ltd.* after their name. This stands for "limited liability," probably the most significant advantage of corporations. Remember, limited liability means that the owners of a business are responsible for losses only up to the amount they invest. Corporations can also end their names with *Inc.* or *Corp.* to indicate their status.

   Be aware that you should not incorporate if it is your intention to use this ownership form as a way to avoid your debts. As a sole proprietorship or partnership, the debts the business incurs remain personal liabilities even after they are taken over by a corporation. Legally, it is the status existing at the time the debts were incurred that governs, not what happens subsequently.

2. *More money for investment.* To raise money, a corporation can sell ownership (stock) to anyone who is interested. This means that thousands of people can own part of major companies such as Rogers Communications Inc., TD Bank Financial Group, Manulife Financial Corp., EnCana Corp., Canadian National Railway Co., Loblaw Companies Ltd., and smaller companies as well. If a company sold 1 million shares for $50 each, it would have $50 million available to build plants, buy materials, hire people, manufacture products, and so on. Such a large amount of money would be difficult to raise any other way.

The TDL Group (owner of the Tim Hortons chain) was a private corporation owned by Wendy's International, Inc. In 2006, Wendy's sold 15 percent of the TDL Group to raise approximately $671 million. This money was used to repay debt owed by Wendy's. Today, Tim Hortons is considered the fourth largest publicly traded quick service restaurant chain in North America.

| Rank | Company | 2008 Revenue ($ Billions) | Industry Group |
|------|---------|---------------------------|----------------|
| 1 | Royal Bank of Canada | $37.6 | Financial Services |
| 2 | Power Corp. of Canada | $37.1 | Conglomerates |
| 3 | Manulife Financial | $33.0 | Insurance |
| 4 | George Weston Ltd. | $32.1 | Retail Services |
| 5 | EnCana Corp. | $31.2 | Major Integrated Oil and Gas |

**FIGURE | 6.3**

**Canada's Largest Publicly Traded Corporations**

Source: "Canada's 500 Largest Corporations 2009," *Financial Post Business Magazine*, 2 June 2009, 42. Material reprinted with the express permission of The National Post Company.

Corporations can also borrow money from individual investors by issuing bonds. Corporations may also find it easier to obtain loans from financial institutions, since lenders find it easier to place a value on the company when they can review how the shares are trading. Many small or individually owned corporations that do not trade actively may not have such opportunities, however. You can read about how corporations raise funds through the sale of stock and bonds in Chapter 17.

3. *Size.* That one word summarizes many of the advantages of some corporations. Because they have the ability to raise large amounts of money to work with, corporations can build modern factories or software development facilities with the latest equipment. They can also hire experts or specialists in all areas of operation. Furthermore, they can buy other corporations in other fields to diversify their risk. (What this means is that a corporation can be involved in many businesses at once so that if one is not doing well, the negative impact on the total corporation is lessened.) In short, a large corporation with numerous resources can take advantage of opportunities anywhere in the world.

  When one considers size, different criteria can be used. This can include the number of employees, revenues, assets, and profits. Note that corporations do not have to be large to enjoy the benefits of incorporation. Professionals (such as physicians and lawyers) can incorporate, as will soon be highlighted in the discussion of professional corporations. Other individuals and partnerships can also incorporate. Figure 6.3 lists some of Canada's largest publicly traded corporations.

4. *Perpetual life.* Because corporations are separate from those who own them, the death of one or more owners does not terminate the corporation.

5. *Ease of ownership change.* It is easy to change the owners of a corporation. All that is necessary is to sell the stock to someone else.

6. *Ease of drawing talented employees.* Corporations can attract skilled employees by offering benefits such as a pension plan, dental plan, and stock options (the right to purchase shares of the corporation for a fixed price). To be competitive, sole proprietorships and partnerships may offer money or other benefits to compete with such plans. Benefits will be discussed in some detail in Chapter 12.

7. *Separation of ownership from management.* Corporations are able to raise money from many different investors without getting them involved in management. A corporate hierarchy is shown in Figure 6.4.

  The pyramid in Figure 6.4 shows that the owners/stockholders are separate from the managers and employees. The owners/stockholders elect a board of directors. The directors hire the officers of the corporation and oversee major policy issues. The owners/stockholders thus have some say in who runs the corporation, but they have no control over the daily operations.

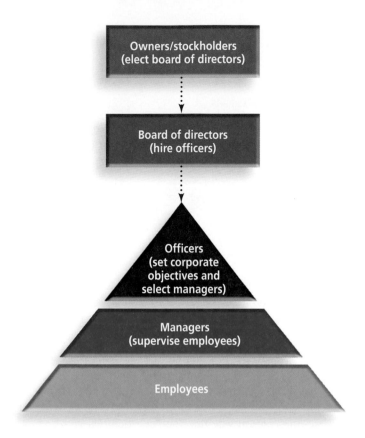

## Disadvantages of Corporations

There are so many sole proprietorships and partnerships in Canada that clearly there must be some disadvantages to incorporating. Otherwise, more people would incorporate their businesses. The following are a few of the disadvantages:

1. *Extensive paperwork.* The paperwork filed to start a corporation is just the beginning. Tax laws demand that a corporation prove that all of its expenses and deductions are legitimate. Corporations must therefore process many forms. A sole proprietor or a partnership may keep rather broad accounting records; a corporation, in contrast, must keep detailed financial records, the minutes of meetings, and more.

2. *Double taxation.* Corporate income is taxed twice. First the corporation pays tax on income before it can distribute any to stockholders. Then the stockholders pay tax on the income (dividends) they receive from the corporation. While this is *double* taxation, it is not *excessive* taxation, as the tax system is designed to provide some offsetting credits such as the dividend tax credit for investors.

3. *Two tax returns.* If an individual incorporates, he or she must file both a corporate tax return and an individual tax return. Depending on the size of the corporation, a corporate return can be quite complex and require the assistance of an accountant.

4. *Size.* Size may be one advantage of corporations, but it can be a disadvantage as well. Large corporations sometimes become too inflexible and too tied down in red tape to respond quickly to market changes.

5. *Difficulty of termination.* Once a corporation is started, it's relatively difficult to end. Legal procedures are costly and more complex than for unincorporated companies.

6. *Possible conflict with stockholders and board of directors.* Some conflict may brew if the stockholders elect a board of directors that disagrees with the present management.

**FIGURE 6.5**

**Comparison of Forms of Business Ownership**

| | Sole Proprietorship | Partnerships | | Corporation | |
|---|---|---|---|---|---|
| | | General Partnership | Limited* Partnership | Public Corporation | Private Corporation |
| **Documents Needed to Start Business** | None, may need permit or licence | Partnership agreement (oral or written) | Written agreement; must file certificate of limited partnership | Articles of incorporation, bylaws | Articles of incorporation, bylaws; must meet criteria |
| **Ease of Termination** | Easy to terminate: just pay debts and quit | May be hard to terminate, depending on the partnership agreement | Same as general partnership | Hard and expensive to terminate | Not difficult; pay off debts, sell off assets, withdraw cash, and pay taxes |
| **Length of Life** | Terminates on the death of owner, sale, or retirement | Terminates on the death or withdrawal of partner | Same as general partnership | Perpetual life | Perpetual life |
| **Transfer of Ownership** | Business can be sold to qualified buyer | Must have agreement of other partner(s) | Same as general partnership | Easy to change owners; just sell stock | Easy—just sell stock† |
| **Financial Resources** | Limited to owner's capital and loans | Limited to partners' capital and loans | Same as general partnership | More money to start and operate: sell stock and bonds; loans | Owners' capital and loans; no public stock issue allowed |
| **Risk of Losses** | Unlimited liability | Unlimited liability | Limited liability | Limited liability | Limited liability |
| **Taxes** | Taxed as personal income | Taxed as personal income | Same as general partnership | Corporate, double taxation | Same as public corporation |
| **Management Responsibilities** | Owner manages *all* areas of the business | Partners share management | Can't participate in management | Separate management from ownership | Owners usually manage all areas |
| **Employee Benefits** | Usually fewer benefits and lower wages | Often fewer benefits and lower wages; promising employee could become a partner | Same as general partnership | Usually better benefits and wages, advancement opportunities | Same as public corporation |

* There must be at least one general partner who manages the partnership and has unlimited liability.
† Unless the agreement specifies otherwise.

Since the board of directors chooses the company's officers, entrepreneurs could find themselves forced out of the very company they founded. This is what happened to Rod Canion, one of the founders of Compaq Computer.

7. *Initial cost.* Incorporation may cost thousands of dollars and involve the services of expensive lawyers and accountants.

Many people are discouraged by the costs, paperwork, and special taxes that corporations must pay. However, many other business people believe that the challenges of incorporation outweigh the advantages. Figure 6.5 compares the three main types of organizations.

## Other Types of Corporations

When reading about corporations, you will find that there are variations of private and public corporations.

### Professional Corporations[14]

Not all corporations are large organizations with hundreds of employees or thousands of stockholders. Individuals can also incorporate. A *professional corporation* is a Canadian-controlled private corporation engaged in providing professional services. The member must be part of a profession that is governed by a professional body that allows its members to practise through a corporation, as opposed to a sole proprietorship or partnership. Each province has different laws and rules as to which professions have these governing bodies. Professions that can incorporate include accountants, architects, lawyers, physicians, dentists, and engineers. Normally, individuals who incorporate do not issue shares to those outside of their business or family; therefore, they do not share all of the same advantages and disadvantages of large public corporations (such as more money for investment and size). Limited liability is a benefit, depending on your professional service. For example, all legislation relating to physician practices in Canada specifically prohibits any limitation of personal liability. The major benefit of professional corporations is tax advantages: professional corporations can benefit from the Small Business Deduction (discussed earlier), income splitting with family members, and the capital gains exemption for qualifying small business corporation shares (if shares are later sold).

### Non-Resident Corporations

A *non-resident corporation* conducts business in Canada but has its head office outside Canada. For example, most foreign airlines are non-resident corporations.

### Non-Profit Corporations

A *non-profit corporation* is formed for charitable or socially beneficial purposes. As mentioned in Chapter 1, it is not run for profit. It has many features of business corporations, but it pays no income taxes and it does not issue shares. In short, it does not have owners or stockholders. In some towns, property is tax exempt if it belongs to a non-profit organization such as a religious institution, hospital, college, museum, YMCA, or athletic, artistic, or charitable organization.

### Crown Corporations

Note that this chapter does not discuss another type of corporation that we reviewed in Chapter 4. You will recall that *Crown corporations* are companies that only the federal or a provincial government can set up.

## Corporate Governance

**corporate governance**
The process and policies that determine how an organization interacts with its stakeholders, both internal and external.

**Corporate governance** refers to the process and policies that determine how an organization interacts with its stakeholders—both internal and external. Rules outline how the organization is to be managed by the board of directors and the officers. Corporate governance is necessary because of the evolution of public ownership. In public corporations, unlike sole proprietorships and partnerships, there is a separation between ownership and management.[15] As a result, the board of directors was created.

The pyramid in Figure 6.4 shows that the owners/stockholders elect a board of directors. These board members have the responsibility of representing the best interests of the stockholders. The board assumes many of the same responsibilities that would typically rest with the sole proprietors, partners, or owners of a private corporation. Board members are often chosen based on their business experience and level of expertise. They have responsibilities such as hiring the officers of the corporation and overseeing major policy

issues. Be aware that those who serve on boards (both for-profit and non-profit) may be held personally liable for the misconduct of the organization. Having directors insurance is one way to try to limit this risk. Risk will be discussed in more detail in Appendix D.

The owners/stockholders thus have some say in who runs the corporation but they have no control over the daily operation. This is up to the officers and their management team. We will discuss the levels of management in Chapter 8.

In the past, many boards were made up of officers of the company. It was not uncommon to have the chief executive officer hold the chairman of the board position. In the wake of corporate scandals, companies and their boards of directors are being scrutinized. Is the board independent from officers? Does the company have a statement of corporate governance practices? To truly represent the stockholders, are directors elected every year? These are just some of the questions that are being addressed by boards across Canada.

The annual *Report on Business* Board Games ranking of Canadian companies' corporate governance practices assesses a variety of governance issues including board composition, compensation, shareholder rights, and disclosure practices.[16] A trend reveals that Canadian companies are giving shareholders a growing volume of information about their executive compensation and their boards of directors as shareholders have particularly demanded greater information to explain and justify growing executive pay packages.[17] Bill Mackenzie, director of special projects for the powerful Canadian Coalition for Good Governance, says the expanded disclosure is a reform particularly championed by shareholders: "If we paid a whole lot of money for this CEO, the idea is to be able to figure out if we got the value we paid for or not," he says. "The key is to tell us how you got there, so we can figure out if it makes sense over the long term."[18]

## Business Regulations

Companies that wish to operate in Canada must follow federal and provincial business laws and regulations. Among other things, this applies to registration and to reporting and information.

### Registration

Governments need to know what businesses are in operation to ensure that a wide range of laws and regulations are being followed. Guaranteeing that the names of businesses are not duplicated is important to avoid confusion. Additionally, governments have to be sure that taxes are being paid. To ensure these and other goals, every company must register its business. This is a simple, routine, and inexpensive procedure.

Companies wanting to incorporate must fill out articles of incorporation and file these with the appropriate provincial/territorial or federal authority. **Articles of incorporation** are a legal authorization from the federal or provincial/territorial government for a company to use the corporate format. The main advantage of being a federally incorporated company is that incorporation gives the company name added protection and guarantees its usage across Canada. Depending on the type of business you are considering, you may be required to incorporate federally.

**articles of incorporation**
A legal authorization from the federal or provincial/territorial government for a company to use the corporate format.

## Reporting and Information

Businesses receive many documents from governments during the course of a year. Some are just information about changes in employment insurance, the Canada or Quebec Pension Plan, or tax legislation as it affects them or their employees. Then there are various forms that all companies must complete so that governments can compile statistical reports that businesses, individuals, research organizations, and governments need to operate effectively. Statistics Canada maintains vast databases and creates useful reports from this information.

All public corporations must file annual reports containing basic data about themselves. An annual report should include the name of the officers, how many shares have been issued, and the head office location. Of course, every corporation must also file an annual tax return containing financial statements and pay the necessary taxes during the year.

## Progress Assessment

- What are the major advantages and disadvantages of incorporating a business?
- What is the role of owners (stockholders) in the corporate hierarchy?
- If you buy stock in a corporation and someone is injured by one of the corporation's products, can you be sued? Why or why not?

# CORPORATE EXPANSION: MERGERS AND ACQUISITIONS

The last decade saw considerable corporate expansion. It was not uncommon to read of a new merger or acquisition on a weekly basis. It seemed as though each deal was intended to top the one before it. Most of the new deals involved companies trying to expand within their own fields to save costs, enter new markets, position for international competition, or adapt to changing technologies or regulations. Those proved to be unattainable goals for many of the merged giants. Read the Dealing with Change box for some examples.

**merger**
The result of two firms forming one company.

**acquisition**
One company's purchase of the property and obligations of another company.

**vertical merger**
The joining of two companies involved in different stages of related businesses.

**horizontal merger**
The joining of two firms in the same industry.

What's the difference between mergers and acquisitions? A **merger** is the result of two firms forming one company. It is similar to a marriage joining two individuals as one. An **acquisition** is one company's purchase of the property and obligations of another company. It is more like buying a house than entering a marriage.

There are three major types of corporate mergers: vertical, horizontal, and conglomerate. A **vertical merger** is the joining of two firms involved in different stages of related businesses. Think of a merger between a soft drink company and a company that produces artificial sweetener. Such a merger would ensure a constant supply of sweetener needed by the soft drink manufacturer. It could also help ensure quality control of the soft drink company's products. A **horizontal merger** joins two firms in the same industry and allows them to diversify or expand their products. An example of a hori-

## DEALING with CHANGE

### The Urge to Merge

Two-thirds of the merged giants of the late 1990s failed to meet their goals. The greatest merger mania in history unravelled before our eyes. These failing corporate giants lost trillions of dollars in market value. The once high-flying WorldCom filed for bankruptcy. The 2000 AOL/Time Warner marriage was so rocky that the company's stock lost two-thirds of its value in 2001. In 2009, AOL separated from Time Warner.

Why did CEOs have the urge to merge if so many land mines lay in the way? The booming markets in the mid-1990s convinced many CEOs that they needed to beef up to compete and to achieve the double-digit growth that Wall Street expected. The stock market's remarkable upward spiral gave dot-com entrepreneurs rising stock prices. They used that high-priced stock to buy other companies, which increased their earnings, which raised their stock prices higher, which allowed them to buy more and bigger businesses. Of course, if the CEOs got a big bonus for merger deals no matter what happened to the share price, they were even more eager to merge. Joseph Nacchio, CEO of Qwest Communications, received a $26 million "growth payment" when Qwest bought US West, and Solomon Trujillo of US West got $15 million for selling. (The deal was not as profitable for the company's shareholders. Qwest's value fell $20 to $30 billion in late 2000 when the merger was completed and continued to free-fall for the next two years. If you had bought 100 shares of the stock at its height in mid-2000, you'd have paid $8,500. If you still held the stock in 2005, the shares would have been worth a mere $400—that's a 95 percent loss.)

Some economists see merger waves in terms of games that CEOs play. When one company merges with another, its competitors ask themselves what their next move should be to get not the best outcome, but the least bad outcome. Since they fear being left behind, the first deal inspires others. For example, after Daimler bought Chrysler, Ford and GM each bought other carmakers. But which carmakers have remained the most profitable? BMW, Porsche, and Toyota—all of which stayed out of the mania.

Following Competition Bureau approval, Petro-Canada and Suncor Energy Inc. merged under the Suncor name. Both company CEOs have emphasized the benefits of being huge: The merged company will be "able to compete with global supermajors," it "will have a commanding presence as Canada's largest energy company and the fifth largest in North America," it will be "large enough to compete in the top tier of global energy companies," and the combination would make for a more efficient player in Canada's oil patch, which will insulate the new Canadian firm from potential foreign takeovers. Have these predictions come to fruition?

Change is constant, of course, so every merger wave is followed by a counterwave. More than a third of the largest international mergers completed in the preceding decade are now being "demerged." For example, luxury goods giant LVMH sold bits of the empire it accumulated in the 1990s. However, after avoiding big deals for more than three years, a new wave of mergers surged in early 2005 as corporations announced 48 deals of $1 billion or more, totalling $357 billion in just three months. Procter & Gamble paid $57 billion for Gillette. Will P&G's shares collapse as has happened with many of the mega mergers of the past? According to analysts, P&G must increase profits from Gillette's razor, batteries, and other businesses by 12 percent each year for the next five years to cover the costs of the merger. In the past five years, Gillette's profits have risen at only one-third that rate. So, meeting that goal may be a close shave.

Sources: "Merged Suncor, Petro-Canada Ready to Compete with 'Global Supermajors'," CBC News, 4 June 2009, http://www.cbc.ca/canada/calgary/story/2009/06/04/suncor-petrocanada-merger.html; "Time Warner Inc. Announces Plan to Separate AOL," Time Warner Inc., 28 May 2009, http://www.timewarner.com/corp/newsroom/pr/0,20812,1901397,00.html; Gregory Zuckerman and Ian Mcdonald, "Time to Slice the Mergers," The Wall Street Journal, 10 January 2006, C; Harry Berkowitz. "Time Warner Pays $2.4B to Settle Class-Action Suit," Newsday, 4 August 2005; Robert Barker, "P&G's $57 Billion Bargain," BusinessWeek, 25 July 2005; and Shawn Tully, "The Urge to Merge," Fortune, 21 February 2005.

---

zontal merger is the merger of a soft drink company and a mineral water company. The business can now supply a variety of drinking products. A **conglomerate merger** unites firms in completely unrelated industries. The primary purpose of a conglomerate merger is to diversify business operations and investments. The merger of a soft drink company and a snack food company would be an example of a conglomerate merger. Figure 6.6 illustrates the differences between the three types of mergers.

There are many benefits to a merger. One of them is that a merger may allow regional players to work together and compete more effectively. This is the case with the merger of salted snack food companies Old Dutch Foods Ltd. and Humpty Dumpty Snack Foods Inc. The combined entity will have $300 million in annual sales and about 25 percent of

**conglomerate merger**
The joining of firms in completely unrelated industries.

**FIGURE** | **6.6**

**Types of Mergers**

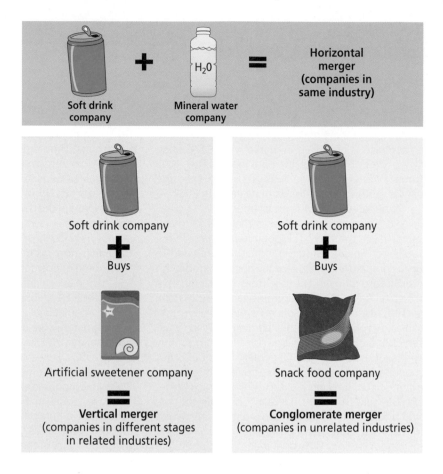

the Canadian market, says Steve Aanenson, president, CEO, and co-owner of Old Dutch Foods Inc.[19] It is estimated that the market leader, Frito-Lay (a division of PepsiCo. Inc.), has more than 60 percent of the Canadian market. The newly merged company will also have new clout when negotiating with national retailers and undertaking marketing and promotional activities, an important consideration given ongoing consolidation in the food retail and consumer products industries.[20]

Rather than merge or sell to another company, some corporations decide to maintain control, or in some cases regain control, of a firm internally. Years ago, the former owners of Cara Operations Limited, the largest operator of full-service restaurants in Canada, decided to take the firm private. Taking a firm private involves the efforts of a group of stockholders or management to obtain all of the firm's stock for themselves.[21] Cara's wholly owned businesses include Swiss Chalet, Harvey's, Second Cup, Kelsey's Neighbourhood Bar & Grill, Montana's Cookhouse, Milestone's Grill and Bar, Cara Air Terminal Restaurant Division, Cara Airport Services Division, and Summit Food Service Distributors Inc. Prior to going private in 2004, the company's annual system sales were in excess of $1.8 billion.[22]

Suppose the employees in an organization feel there is a good possibility they may lose their jobs. Or what if the managers believe that corporate performance could be enhanced if they owned the company? Do either of these groups have an opportunity to take ownership of the company? Yes—they might attempt a leveraged buyout. A **leveraged buyout (LBO)** is an attempt by employees, management, or a group of investors to purchase an organization primarily through borrowing. The funds borrowed are used to buy out the stockholders in the company. The employees, managers, or investors now become the owners of the firm. LBOs have ranged in size from millions to billions of dollars and have involved everything from small family businesses to giant corporations such as R.J.R. Nabisco and Toys "R" Us.[23]

**leveraged buyout (LBO)**
An attempt by employees, management, or a group of investors to purchase an organization primarily through borrowing.

# FRANCHISING

Some people are not comfortable starting their own business from scratch. They would rather join a business with a proven track record through a franchise agreement. A **franchise agreement** is an arrangement whereby someone with a good idea for a business (the **franchisor**) sells the rights to use the business name and to sell a good or service (the **franchise**) to others (the **franchisee**) in a given territory. As you might suspect, both franchisors and franchisees have a stake in the success of the franchise.

A franchise can be formed as a sole proprietorship, partnership, or corporation. Business students often mistakenly identify franchising as an industry. It is important to stress a few things before we go any further. Franchising is a method of distributing a good or service, or both, to achieve a maximum market impact with a minimum investment. It is not a separate form of business ownership from those already discussed in Figure 6.5 and it does not replace a form of business. How the franchisee sets up the franchise business (i.e., sole proprietorship, partnership, or corporation) and operates it, however, is dependent on the advantages and disadvantages of each form of business ownership.

Often, what looks like a chain of stores—Canadian Tire, Quiznos Sub, Buck or Two—is usually a franchise operation with each unit owned by a different person or company. Sometimes one person or group may own and operate more than one franchise unit. Regardless of the form of business ownership (e.g., sole proprietorship), all units are part of a franchise operation. In the following pages you will see the advantages and disadvantages of this type of business operation, and you will learn what to consider before buying a franchise unit.

Canada has the second largest franchise industry in the world, led only by the United States.[24] As noted in Figure 6.7, franchises employ more than 1.5 million people and generate annual sales of more than $100 billion. Of the franchises that opened in Canada within the last five years, 86 percent are still under the same ownership and 97 percent are still in business.[25]

Canadian food franchises that you may be familiar with are Booster Juice, Mr. Sub, Crabby Joe's Tap & Grill, and Edo Japan. Keep in mind that there are also non-food

**franchise agreement**
An arrangement whereby someone with a good idea for a business sells the rights to use the business name and sell its goods and services in a given territory.

**franchisor**
A company that develops a product concept and sells others the rights to make and sell the products.

**franchise**
The right to use a specific business's name and sell its goods or services in a given territory.

**franchisee**
A person who buys a franchise.

# SupperWorks™
### Taking the work out of supper

## A fresh concept with all the ingredients for success!

In our kitchen, customers move through several food stations, complete with raw, prepped ingredients and recipes. In less than two hours they'll assemble twelve freezable dinners, while enjoying a social and relaxed environment. Recipes are designed to provide nutritious, delicious meals. *All for about $4 a serving!*

For franchise information visit www.SupperWorks.com or call 905-849-1550

SupperWorks is a meal preparation business that has been helping families and students save time while providing nutritious, cost-effective meals. Would you consider using this company's services?

**FIGURE 6.7**

**Franchising in Canada**

| Total franchise units | 75,809 |
|---|---|
| Annual sales | Over $100 billion |
| Rate of new franchises | One opens every 2 hours, 365 days a year |
| Employment | More than 1.5 million people |
| Average franchise fee | $25,000 |
| Average franchisee investment | $166,600 |

Source: "Interesting Facts," CANAM Franchise Development Group, 2008, http://www.canamfranchise.com/interestingfacts.cfm. Used with permission.

franchises, such as Shoppers Drug Mart, Molly Maid, Oxford Learning, 1-800-GOT-JUNK?, Home Hardware, and Budget Brake & Muffler. Have you ever considered owning one of these?

A growing number of companies, including franchise systems, deliver goods and services that directly or indirectly protect the environment. The Green Box highlights some of these examples.

## GreenBOX

### Franchises Going Green

According to Barry Young, President and CEO of Lord & Partners Holdings, a franchisor specializing in environmentally friendly commercial cleaning agents, the Canadian environmental business sector represents $30 billion each year. The global sector generates $900 billion annually. Lord & Partners is a worldwide venture with more than 100 cleaning agents and solvents that are developed in two plants in Huntsville, Ontario, and the list is growing as increasingly stringent regulatory guidelines force industries to seek alternatives to hazardous chemicals.

Two years before regulations required it to do so, Maaco Systems Canada's owners of the company's 36 franchises started using water-based paints, as opposed to those containing solvents. They had to invest in new spray guns as well as oscillation equipment. The cost of converting ran anywhere from $6,000 to $75,000, depending on the age of the equipment. A volatile organic compound (VOC) is a class of chemicals that produces ground-level ozone, commonly known as smog. The company's reduction in VOCs emissions was equivalent to taking 1,000 cars off the road. "If our small chain of stores can do that," says Gary Dohring, President and CEO, "imagine the effect if the country's 6,500 body shops changed their ways."

Harvey's Restaurants, a division of Cara Operations, is overhauling its 280 stores across the country. Each of its locations will either be extensively renovated or rebuilt from scratch, says company President Rick McNabb. Over the next five years, Harvey's will build 100 stores and most will occupy about 2,200 square feet versus the typical 2,300 square feet of today. For starters, this smaller footprint will consume fewer building materials. New store features will include an added layer of insulation around the exterior of the building, cold cathode compact fluorescents (which are 90 percent more efficient than conventional incandescent lights), and awnings over the windows to reduce solar heat gain during the warm weather months.

Banks that provide franchising financing are also looking to become more environmental. TD Canada Trust became the first Canadian bank to pledge that it would become carbon neutral by 2010. While it can never eliminate emissions entirely, it can reduce consumption through better lighting practices, among other things, and by acquiring green energy. Through its Friends of the Environment Foundation, which was set up in 1990 to support community-based, eco-friendly initiatives, TD Canada Trust has funded over 16,000 green initiatives.

Sources: Roma Ihnatowycz, "Ecology Economics," *Franchise Canada Magazine*, July/August 2008, 22–24; and D'Arcy Jenish, "Going Green," *Franchise Canada Magazine*, July/August 2008, 34–39. Reprinted with permission from *Franchise Canada Magazine*, published by the Canadian Franchise Association.

## Advantages of Franchises

Franchising has penetrated every aspect of Canadian and global business life by offering goods and services that are reliable, convenient, and competitively priced. The world-wide growth of franchising could not have been accomplished by accident. Franchising clearly has some advantages:

1.  *Management and marketing assistance.* Compared with someone who starts a business from scratch, a franchisee (the person who buys a franchise) has a much greater chance of succeeding because he or she is selling an established product (e.g., Domino's pizza). As well, the franchisor provides assistance in all phases of the operation. This assistance can include help in choosing a location, setting up an accounting system, training staff, and marketing. It is like having your own store with full-time consultants available when you need them.

    Franchisors provide intensive management training, since they want the franchisees to succeed. For example, franchisor Boston Pizza International offers its franchisees eight weeks of training and support in its corporate training centre, one week of business management sessions, and ongoing training as needed.[26] McDonald's sends all new franchisees to Hamburger University. To be eligible as franchisees, applicants are also required to complete 1,600 hours of on-the-job training.

    Some franchisors are helping their franchisees succeed by helping with local marketing efforts rather than having franchisees depend solely on national advertising. Furthermore, franchisees have a network of fellow franchisees that face similar problems and can share their experiences. For example, The UPS Store provides its franchisees with a software program that helps them build data banks of customer names and addresses. The company also provides one-on-one phone support and quick e-mail access through its help desk. The help desk focuses on personalizing contact with the company's franchisees by immediately addressing their questions and concerns.

2.  *Personal ownership.* A franchise operation is still your store, and you enjoy many of the incentives and profit of any sole proprietor. You are still your own boss, although you must follow more rules, regulations, and procedures than you would with your own privately owned store.

3.  *Nationally recognized name.* It is one thing to open a gift shop or ice cream store. It is quite another to open a new Hallmark store or a Baskin-Robbins. With an established franchise, you get instant recognition and support from a product group with established customers around the world.

4.  *Financial advice and assistance.* A major problem with small businesses is arranging financing and learning to keep good records. Franchisees get valuable assistance and periodic advice from people with expertise in these areas. In fact, some franchisors will even provide financing to potential franchisees they believe will be valuable partners of the franchise system.

5.  *Lower failure rate.* Historically, the failure rate for franchises has been lower than that of other business ventures. Some experts say that independent businesses fail eight times more often than franchised businesses.[27] However, franchising has grown so rapidly that many weak franchises have entered the field, so you need to be careful and invest wisely.

*Canadian Business Franchise* is a bimonthly magazine that features articles on franchise advice from bankers, lawyers, and franchise specialists. Visit www.cgb.ca for advice and to view profiles on individual franchises.

## Disadvantages of Franchises

It almost sounds like franchising is too good to be true. There are, however, some potential pitfalls. You must be sure to check out any such arrangement with present franchisees and possibly discuss the idea with a lawyer and an accountant. Disadvantages of franchises are listed on the next page.

Canadian Tire is Canada's most-shopped retailer. To own a franchise, candidates must be willing to make a personal and financial investment. A minimum of $125,000 of accessible capital is needed to become an associate dealer. In addition, successful dealer candidates will be charged a dealer training and development fee of $100,000 upon receiving their first store.

1. *Large start-up costs.* Most franchises will demand a fee just for the rights to the franchise. Fees for franchises can vary considerably. Start-up costs for a Kumon Math and Reading Centre include $1,000 for the franchise fee and a minimum investment ranging from $10,000 to $20,000.[28] But if you want to own a Keg Restaurant, you will need more money. The franchise fee is $50,000 and capital requirements range from $2.0 to $3.25 million.[29]

2. *Shared profit.* The franchisor often demands either a large share of the profits in addition to the start-up fees or a percentage commission based on sales rather than profit. This share demanded by the franchisor is generally referred to as a royalty. For example, if a franchisor demands a 10-percent royalty on a franchise's sales, 10 cents of every dollar collected at the franchise (before taxes and other expenses) must be paid to the franchisor.

3. *Management regulation.* Management "assistance" has a way of becoming managerial orders, directives, and limitations. Franchisees feeling burdened by the company's rules and regulations may lose the spirit and incentive of being their own boss with their own business. One of the biggest changes in franchising in recent years has been the banding together of franchisees to resolve their grievances with franchisors rather than each fighting their battles alone.

4. *Coattail effects.* What happens to your franchise if fellow franchisees fail? Quite possibly you could be forced out of business even if your particular franchise has been profitable. This is often referred to as a *coattail effect*. The actions of other franchisees clearly have an impact on your future growth and level of profitability. If customers have a negative experience at one franchise location, this may destroy the reputation of other franchisees. Franchisees must also look out for competition from fellow franchisees. For example, TCBY franchisees' love for frozen yogurt melted as the market became flooded with new TCBY stores. McDonald's franchisees complain that due to the McDonald's Corporation's relentless growth formula, some of the new stores have cannibalized (taken away) business at existing locations, squeezing franchisees' profits.

5. *Restrictions on selling.* Unlike owners of private businesses who can sell their companies to whomever they choose on their own terms, many franchisees face restrictions in the reselling of their franchises. To control the quality of their franchisees, franchisors often insist on approving the new owner, who must meet their standards.

6. *Fraudulent franchisors.* Contrary to common belief, most franchisors are not large systems like McDonald's or Subway. Most franchisors are honest, but there has been an increase in complaints about franchisors that deliver little or nothing of what they promised.[30]

If you are interested, Figure 6.8 provides some tips on evaluating a franchise.

## Home-Based Franchises

Home-based businesses offer many obvious advantages, including relief from the stress of commuting, extra time for family activities, and low overhead expenses.

For example, when Henry and Paula Feldman decided to quit sales jobs that kept them on the road for weeks, they wanted to find a business to run at home together. The Feldmans started their home-based franchise, Money Mailer, Inc. (a direct mail advertiser), with nothing more than a table and a telephone. Five years later, they owned 15 territories, which they ran from an office full of state-of-the-art equipment. They grossed more than $600,000 during their fifth year. Henry says that the real value of being in a franchise is that the systems are in place: "You don't have to develop them yourself. Just be willing to work hard, listen, and learn. There's no greater magic than that."

**FIGURE** 6.8

**Buying a Franchise**

Since buying a franchise is a major investment, be sure to check out a company's financial strength before you get involved.

**CHECKLIST FOR EVALUATING A FRANCHISE**

**The franchise**

Did your lawyer approve the franchise contract you're considering after he or she studied it paragraph by paragraph?

Does the franchise give you an exclusive territory for the length of the franchise?

Under what circumstances can you terminate the franchise contract and at what cost to you?

If you sell your franchise, will you be compensated for your goodwill (the value of your business's reputation and other intangibles)?

If the franchisor sells the company, will your investment be protected?

**The franchisor**

How many years has the firm offering you a franchise been in operation?

Does it have a reputation for honesty and fair dealing among the local firms holding its franchise?

Has the franchisor shown you any certified figures indicating exact net profits of one or more going firms that you personally checked yourself with the franchisee? Ask for the company's disclosure statement.

Will the firm assist you with

    A management training program?

    An employee training program?

    A public relations program?

    Capital?

    Credit?

    Merchandising ideas?

Will the firm help you find a good location for your new business?

Has the franchisor investigated you carefully enough to assure itself that you can successfully operate one of its franchises at a profit both to itself and to you?

**You, the franchisee**

How much equity capital will you need to purchase the franchise and operate it until your income equals your expenses?

Does the franchisor offer financing for a portion of the franchising fees? On what terms?

Are you prepared to give up some independence of action to secure the advantages offered by the franchise? Do you have your family's support?

Does the industry appeal to you? Are you ready to spend much or all of the remainder of your business life with this franchisor, offering its good or service to the public?

**Your market**

Have you conducted any studies to determine whether the good or service that you propose to sell under the franchise has a market in your territory at the prices you'll have to charge?

Will the population in the territory given to you increase, remain static, or decrease over the next five years?

Will demand for the good or service you're considering be greater, about the same, or less five years from now than it is today?

What competition already exists in your territory for the good or service you contemplate selling?

Sources: U.S. Department of Commerce, *Franchise Opportunities Handbook*; and Rhonda Adams, "Franchising Is No Simple Endeavour," Gannett News Services, 14 March 2002.

But one of the disadvantages of owning a business based at home is the feeling of isolation. Compared to home-based entrepreneurs, home-based franchisees feel less isolated. Experienced franchisors share their knowledge of building a profitable enterprise with franchisees.

# E-Commerce in Franchising

We've already talked about how e-commerce is revolutionizing the way we do business. Online business is not limited to those with technical knowledge and the desire to take on the challenge of starting their own business from scratch. Today, Internet users are able to obtain franchises to open online retail stores stocked with merchandise made in all parts of the world. Before you jump online and buy a web-based franchise, however, make certain that you check out the facts fully.

PropertyGuys.com is an example of a franchise that uses e-commerce as an important component of the service it offers. Formed in 1998 in Moncton, New Brunswick, PropertyGuys.com has built on the "For Sale by Owner (FSBO)" Internet concept. The

Holiday Inn's InterContinential Amstel hotel in Amsterdam has been celebrated as the Netherlands' most beautiful and luxurious hotel. Holiday Inn franchises try to complement the environment of the area they serve. This hotel is on the crossroads of Amsterdam's financial and exclusive shopping districts. What do you think would have been the reaction if Holiday Inn built the typical American-style hotel in this area?

service is a no-commission, low-cost alternative to pricey real estate commissions. PropertyGuys.com has been used to list homes, land, apartments, commercial buildings, and cottages. According to company literature, what differentiates this company from other FSBO sites is its personal touch. Company representatives will set up clients, install signage, take photos, and make themselves available during the process. Furthermore, the company does not rely solely on the Internet to display properties. Packages include a combination of print advertising, direct mail, electronic mail, seller's documentation, a "For Sale" sign, a Web site listing, and a phone answering service.

Some franchisees with existing brick-and-mortar stores are expanding their businesses online. Franchisees that started with a limited territory are now branching out globally. Other franchisors prohibit franchisee-sponsored Web sites. Conflicts between franchisors and franchisees can erupt if the franchisor then creates its own Web site. The franchisees may be concerned that the site will pull sales from their brick-and-mortar locations. Sometimes the franchisors send "reverse royalties" to outlet owners who feel that their sales were hurt by the franchisor's Internet sales, but that doesn't always bring about peace. Before buying a franchise, you would be wise to read the small print regarding online sales.

## Franchising in International Markets[31]

What makes franchising successful in international markets is what makes it successful domestically: convenience and a predictable level of service. Because of proximity and language, the United States is by far the most popular target for Canadian-based franchises. Let us look at some examples.

In 1986, brothers Michael and Aaron Serruya, then aged 19 and 20, wanted to buy a franchise, but no one would take a chance on them. So, they started their own frozen yogurt shop, Yogen Früz. Today, Yogen Früz has grown to be a world leader in the frozen yogurt category, with over 1,100 locations operating in 20 countries around the world.

Montreal-based Couche-Tard Inc. is the largest convenience store operator in Canada with a network of over 2,000 stores in Canada as well as a considerable presence in the United States, with more than 3,000 additional stores. The stores are primarily operated under the Couche-Tard® and Mac's® trademarks in Canada and the Circle K® trademark in the United States. In addition to the North American Couche-Tard network, there are approximately 3,500 Circle K licensed stores located in seven other regions worldwide (Japan, Hong Kong, China, Indonesia, Guam, Macao, and Mexico).

Beavertails Pastry is another successful franchisor story. First introduced in Ottawa in 1978, there are now more than 130 locations in seven countries. One of the company's products is a hot pastry treat that resembles—you guessed it—a beaver tail. Expansion opportunities exist in amusement parks, sports venues, tourist destinations, and ski hills.

Not only is the United States an attractive market for our franchisors, but Canada is also an attractive market for American franchisors. Taco Del Mar, a Seattle-based quick-service restaurant chain specializing in Baja style "mondo burritos and rippin' tacos," has inked a deal with B.C.-based TDM Federal Holdings, Inc. to develop restaurants across Canada. The deal could produce 600 Taco Del Mar franchises in Canada by 2014.

## CO-OPERATIVES[32]

Some people dislike the notion of having owners, managers, workers, and buyers as separate individuals with separate goals. They envision a world where people co-operate with one another more fully and share the wealth more evenly. These people have formed a different type of organization that reflects their social orientation. This is called a co-operative, or co-op. A **co-operative** is an organization owned by members and customers who pay an annual membership fee and share in any profits (if it is a profit-making organization). Often the members work in the organization for a certain number of hours per month as part of their duties.

Co-operatives in Canada represent a large and diverse heritage of Canadians working together to build better communities based upon co-operative principles. Collectively, there are over 10,000 co-operatives and credit unions, providing products and services to over 10 million Canadians. Co-operatives employ over 150,000 Canadians and they can be found in many sectors of the economy, including the finance, insurance, and service sectors. They are especially significant in rural and remote regions of the country, where they meet the economic needs of producers in agriculture, the fisheries, arts and crafts production, and manufacturing. Some co-ops are listed in Canada's top 500 companies and several financial co-operatives have been rated the best places to work in Canada.

Co-operatives differ from other businesses principles in several ways:

OUR TIMING WAS PERFECT. MADELYN WAS TOO YOUNG TO WALK AWAY OR CRAWL OVERBOARD. [LANNY, MEC MEMBER]

Mountain Equipment Co-op is Canada's largest retailer co-operative. With your $5 lifetime membership, you become part owner, and you have a voice in the governance of the company. Have you shopped at a store?

- *A different purpose.* The primary purpose of co-operatives is to meet the common needs of their members. Most investor-owned businesses have a primary purpose to maximize profit for their stockholders.

- *A different control structure.* Co-operatives use the one-member/one-vote system, not the one-vote-per-share system used by most businesses. This helps the co-operative serve the common need rather than the individual need.

- *A different allocation of profit.* Co-operatives share profits among their member-owners on the basis of how much they use the co-op, not on how many shares they hold. Profits tend to be invested in improving services for the members.

**co-operative**
An organization that is owned by members and customers, who pay an annual membership fee and share in any profits.

Because co-ops distribute their profits to members as a reduction in members' costs, these profits are not subject to income tax. From time to time, various business organizations assert that many co-ops are now more like large businesses and should be taxed. So far, this viewpoint does not appear to have extensive support.

## WHICH FORM OF OWNERSHIP IS BEST FOR YOU?

As you can see, you may participate in the business world in a variety of ways. You can start your own sole proprietorship, partnership, and/or corporation. You can purchase a franchise and structure your business as a sole proprietorship, partnership, or corporation. Co-operatives are corporations that usually have a different motivation than traditional for-profit businesses. There are advantages and disadvantages to each. However, there are risks no matter which form you choose. Before you decide which form is best for you, you need to evaluate all of the alternatives carefully.

### Progress Assessment

- What are some of the factors to consider before buying a franchise?
- What opportunities are available for starting a global franchise?
- What is a co-operative?

# SUMMARY

**LO ▶ 1** List the advantages and disadvantages of sole proprietorships.

1. The major forms of business ownership are sole proprietorships, partnerships, and corporations.

**What are the advantages and disadvantages of sole proprietorships?**

The advantages of sole proprietorships include ease of starting and ending the business, being your own boss, pride of ownership, retention of profits, no special taxes, and less regulation than for corporations. The disadvantages include unlimited liability, limited financial resources, difficulty in management, overwhelming time commitment, few fringe benefits, limited growth, limited lifespan, and the possibility of paying higher taxes depending on the level of income.

**LO ▶ 2** Describe the advantages and disadvantages of partnerships. Include the differences between general and limited partners.

2. The three key elements of a general partnership are common ownership, shared profits and losses, and the right to participate in managing the operations of the business.

**What are the main differences between general and limited partners?**

General partners are owners (partners) who have unlimited liability and are active in managing the company. Limited partners are owners (partners) who have limited liability and are not active in the company.

**What are the advantages and disadvantages of partnerships?**

The advantages include more financial resources, shared management and pooled knowledge, longer survival, and less regulation than for corporations. The disadvantages include unlimited liability, division of profits, possible disagreements among partners, difficulty of termination, and the possibility of paying higher taxes depending on the level of income.

**LO ▶ 3** Discuss the advantages and disadvantages of corporations.

3. A corporation is a legal entity with authority to act and have liability separate from its owners.

**What are the advantages and disadvantages of corporations?**

The advantages include more money for investment, limited liability, size, perpetual life, ease of ownership change, ease of drawing talented employees, and separation of ownership from management. The disadvantages include initial costs, paperwork, size, difficulty of termination, double taxation, and possible conflict with a board of directors.

**What is a professional corporation?**

A professional corporation is a Canadian-controlled private corporation engaged in providing professional services. The member must be part of a profession that is governed by a professional body that allows its members to practise through a corporation, as opposed to a sole proprietorship or partnership. Members may include physicians and lawyers.

**LO ▶ 4** Define and give examples of three types of corporate mergers, and explain the role of leveraged buyouts and taking a firm private.

4. This decade has witnessed increased activity in the area of mergers.

**What is a merger?**

A merger is the result of two firms forming one company. The three major types of mergers are vertical mergers, horizontal mergers, and conglomerate mergers. A vertical merger is the joining of two companies involved in different stages of related businesses. A horizontal merger is the joining of two firms in the same industry. A conglomerate merger is the joining of firms in completely unrelated industries.

**What are leveraged buyouts, and what does it mean to take a company private?**

Leveraged buyouts are attempts by managers and employees to borrow money and purchase the company. Individuals who, together or alone, buy all of the stock for themselves are said to take the company private.

5. A person can participate in the entrepreneurial age by buying the rights to market a new product innovation in his or her area.

**What are the benefits and drawbacks of being a franchisee?**

The benefits include a nationally recognized name and reputation, a proven management system, promotional assistance, and pride of ownership. Drawbacks include high franchise fees, managerial regulation, shared profits, and transfer of adverse effects if other franchisees fail.

**What is the major challenge to global franchises?**

It may be difficult to transfer an idea or product that worked well in Canada to another culture. It is essential to adapt to the region.

**LO ▶ 5** Outline the advantages and disadvantages of franchises, and discuss the challenges of global franchising.

6. Co-operatives have a different purpose, control structure, and allocation of profit than traditional for-profit businesses.

**What is the role of a co-operative?**

Co-operatives are organizations owned by members/customers. Some people form co-operatives to give members more economic power than they would have as individuals. Small businesses often form co-operatives to give them more purchasing, marketing, or product development strength.

**What types of co-operatives are found in the economy?**

Co-operatives can be found in many sectors of the economy, including the finance, insurance, agri-food and supply, wholesale and retail, housing, health, and service sectors.

**LO ▶ 6** Describe the role of co-operatives in Canada.

## KEY TERMS

acquisition  184

articles of incorporation  184

conglomerate merger  185

co-operative  193

corporate governance  182

corporation  170

franchise  187

franchise agreement  187

franchisee  187

franchisor  187

general partner  173

general partnership  173

horizontal merger  184

leveraged buyout (LBO)  186

liability  170

limited liability  173

limited partner  173

limited partnership  173

merger  184

partnership  170

partnership agreement  175

private corporation  177

public corporation  177

sole proprietorship  170

unlimited liability  172

vertical merger  184

## CRITICAL THINKING

1. Have you ever dreamed of opening your own business? If so, what kind of business? Could you start such a business in your own home? How much would it cost to start? Could you begin the business part-time while you attended school? What satisfaction and profit could you get from owning your own business? What could you lose? (Be aware that you must be careful not to use a name for your business that has already been used or registered by someone else. You may face some local restrictions and license requirements if you operate from your residence such as number of parking spaces, size and type of vehicle and signage, noise by-laws, etc.)

2. Is it fair to say that franchisees have the true entrepreneurial spirit? Could you see yourself as a franchisee or franchisor? Which one? Do you have an idea that you think could eventually grow into a franchise? Explain.

# DEVELOPING WORKPLACE SKILLS

1. Research businesses in your area and identify two companies that use the following forms of ownership: sole proprietorship, partnership, and corporation. Arrange interviews with managers from each form of ownership and get their impressions about their business. (If you are able to work with a team of fellow students, divide the interviews among team members.) Some questions that you might ask include: How much did it cost to start this business? How many hours do you work? What are some drawbacks that you have encountered with the way your business is set up (i.e., business form), if any? What are the specific benefits of this business? Share the results with your class.

2. Have you thought about starting your own business? What opportunities seem attractive? Think of a friend or friends whom you might want as a partner or partners in the business. List all of the financial resources and personal skills you will need to launch the business. Then make separate lists of the personal skills and the financial resources that you and your friend(s) might bring to your new venture. How much capital and what personal skills do you need but lack? Develop an action plan to obtain them.

3. Let's assume you want to open one of the following new businesses. What form of business ownership would you choose for each business? Why?
   a. Video game rental store
   b. Wedding planning service
   c. Software development firm
   d. Computer hardware manufacturing company
   e. Online bookstore

4. Find out how much it costs to incorporate a company in your province or territory. Then compare it to the cost of a federal incorporation. Is there a significant difference? Why might you choose not to incorporate federally?

## TAKING IT TO THE NET 1

www.mcgrawhillconnect.ca

### Purpose

To find information about co-operatives.

### Exercise

There are several sources of information for Canadian co-operatives. The Canadian Co-operative Association (www.coopscanada.coop) is a national umbrella organization representing co-operatives and credit unions. The Co-operative Secretariat (www.agr.gc.ca/ rcs-src/coop/) was established in 1987 to help the federal government respond more effectively to the concerns and needs of co-operatives.

1. Visit each of these sites. What are some recent statistics about co-operatives in Canada?
2. Profile how co-operatives affect a sector of the economy.
3. Describe the history and relevance of co-operatives in your province.

## TAKING IT TO THE NET 2

www.mcgrawhillconnect.ca

### Purpose

To explore current franchising opportunities and to understand more about the challenges of starting a franchise.

### Exercise

Go to BeTheBoss Canada (www.betheboss.ca).

1. On the home page, click on the Franchise Directory tab. Choose Browse by Company Name. Key in some franchise names that you recognize. Are you surprised by any of the information (e.g., start-up cost, level of franchisor support, etc.)? Click on Browse by Investment Level. Would you be interested in any of the franchises in the $0 to $10,000 range? How about in any of the other ranges such as the $200,001 to $500,000 range?

2. Visiting Sponsored Links (lower left-side of the home page), what sources can you review to get more information on franchising?

3. On the home page, click on the Resources tab (near the top of the page). Clicking on Introduction to Franchising, list the Ten Golden Rules (found under Franchising Basics). Review the Worksheets. If you were interested in franchising, would you consider completing them?

## ANALYZING MANAGEMENT DECISIONS

### Going Public

George Zegoyan and Amir Gupta face a difficult decision. Their private auto parts manufacturing company has been a great success—too quickly. They cannot keep up with the demand for their product. They must expand their facilities, but have not had time to accumulate sufficient working capital, nor do they want to acquire long-term debt to finance the expansion. Discussions with their accountants, lawyers, and stockbrokers have confronted them with the necessity of going public to raise the required capital.

Zegoyan and Gupta are concerned about maintaining control if they become a public company. They are also worried about loss of privacy because of the required reporting to various regulatory bodies and to their stockholders. Naturally, they are also pleased that the process will enable them to sell some of their shareholdings to the public and realize a fair profit from their past and expected future successes. They will be able to sell 40 percent of the shares for $500,000, which is ten times their total investment in the company. It will also allow them to raise substantial new capital to meet the needs of their current expansion program.

The proposed new structure will allow them to retain 60 percent of the outstanding voting shares, so they will keep control of the company. Nevertheless, they are somewhat uneasy about taking this step, because it will change the nature of the company and the informal method of operating they are used to. They are concerned about having "partners" in their operations and profits. They are wondering whether they should remain as they are and try to grow more slowly, even if it means giving up profitable orders.

### Discussion Questions

1. Are Zegoyan and Gupta justified in their concerns? Why?

2. Do they have any other options besides going public? Is the franchise route a viable option? Explain?

3. Do you think they should try to limit their growth to a manageable size to avoid going public, even if it means forgoing profits now? Why?

4. Would you advise them to sell their business now if they can get a good price and then start a new operation? Explain.

## CHAPTER 7

# Entrepreneurship and Starting a Small Business

## LEARNING OBJECTIVES

**AFTER YOU HAVE READ AND STUDIED THIS CHAPTER, YOU SHOULD BE ABLE TO:**

**LO ▸ 1** Explain why people are willing to become entrepreneurs, and describe the attributes of successful entrepreneurs.

**LO ▸ 2** Discuss the importance of small business to the Canadian economy.

**LO ▸ 3** Summarize the major causes of small-business failure.

**LO ▸ 4** List ways to learn about how small businesses operate.

**LO ▸ 5** Analyze what it takes to start and run a small business.

**LO ▸ 6** Outline the advantages and disadvantages that small businesses have in entering global markets.

## Getting to Know Marlene Ross of Marlene Ross Design

Marlene Ross has changed the face of hockey around the world. She has designed and painted original pieces of "Mask Art" for Martin Brodeur, Roberto Luongo, J.S. Giguere, Marc-Andre Fleury, Grant Fuhr, and Ron Hextall, just to name a few. For over twenty years, she has been the premier artist for goalies in the NHL, international and Olympic competition, NCAA and CIS Leagues, major motion pictures, and for amateurs in minor hockey around the world.

Ross didn't have much to do with hockey when she was growing up in Merrickville, southwest of Ottawa. The self-taught painter began her career as a cartoonist and serious portrait artist. She soon developed a reputation for being able to paint on any medium. When she was 19, a goalie playing in an adult recreational league offered her $225 to paint his mask to look like the face of Batman's nemesis, the Joker. At a hockey tournament, the mask caught the eye of everyone who saw it—including Gerry Wright, of the Chicago hockey company Itech, which makes goalie helmets. For a while, Ross painted masks for Itech, and she was offered a contract. But she wanted to remain independent, so she turned the offer down. It has proved to be the right decision. Ross owns the rights to all of her designs and collects royalties from Pinnacle hockey trading cards, McDonald's restaurants, EA sports video games, and Corinthian mini masks.

There is an eight-week wait to have a mask custom painted, each of which takes about 25 to 30 hours to paint. Each goalie is provided with detailed preliminary drawings with custom design for approval. Ross might spend anywhere from 20 to 80 hours brainstorming one idea. She listens to people, helps them flesh out their ideas and then follows inspiration through to design the original custom mask. The artistic process is the same for all of her art, as amateur players and professionals receive the same quality work.

Stories about people like Marlene Ross who take risks are commonplace in this age of the entrepreneur. As you read about such risk-takers in this book, maybe you will become inspired to become an entrepreneur yourself!

Sources: "Behind the Mask," Marlene Ross Design, 2008, http://www.marlene rossdesign.com/aboutus.html; and Jody Kingsbury, "The Woman Behind the Mask," Capital Arts Online, 1 February 2006, http://www.carleton.ca/sjc/ capitalarts/2006/s10.shtml.

# ENTREPRENEURSHIP AND SMALL BUSINESS[1]

The 2.6 million people in Canada who are self-employed represent approximately 15 percent of all employed workers in the Canadian economy. Increasingly, young people are considering starting a small business when they graduate. Others, like Marlene Ross, start even earlier. "The perception is out there among young people that a job with an IBM for 30 years is not likely to happen," said Bruce Phillips, a senior fellow in regulatory studies at the National Federation of Independent Business Research Foundation. "Thus, working in or starting a small business has increased appeal...where there is a feeling that you control more of your own destiny."

Schools are responding to this trend by offering more courses on the subject of entrepreneurship. **Entrepreneurship** is accepting the challenge of starting and running a business. The word entrepreneur originates from the French word, *entreprendre*, which means "to undertake." In a business context, it means to start a business. You can imagine how the concept of entrepreneurship has a wide variety of meanings. On the one extreme, an entrepreneur is a person of very high aptitude who pioneers change, possessing characteristics found in only a very small fraction of the population. On the other extreme of definitions, anyone who wants to work for himself or herself is considered an entrepreneur. It is for this reason that we discuss both topics in this chapter.

While many people use the terms entrepreneurship and small business interchangeably, there are significant differences. Entrepreneurial ventures differ from small businesses in the following four ways:[2]

1. *Amount of Wealth Creation.* Rather than simply generating an income stream that replaces traditional employment, a successful entrepreneurial venture creates substantial wealth, typically in excess of several million dollars of profit.

2. *Speed of Wealth Creation.* While a successful small business can generate several million dollars of profit over a lifetime, entrepreneurial wealth creation often is rapid. For example, this may occur within five years.

3. *Risk.* The risk of an entrepreneurial venture must be high. Otherwise, with the incentive of sure profits, many people would pursue the idea of entrepreneurship, making business ventures impossibly competitive.

4. *Innovation.* Entrepreneurship often involves substantial innovation beyond what a small business might exhibit. This innovation gives the venture the competitive advantage that results in wealth creation. Innovation may be in new products, new production methods, new markets, and new forms of organizations.

From this list, you can quickly gather that entrepreneurship is not always small and small business is not always entrepreneurial.

While most businesses start small, it's the intent to stay small that separates them from entrepreneurship. Explore this chapter and think about the possibilities. That is, the possibility of entrepreneurship and the possibility of starting a small business in your future. Or, the possibility of working for an entrepreneur or an agency that supports entrepreneurship.

## Well-Known Canadian Entrepreneurs[3]

Entrepreneurs have played a major role in developing the Canadian economy. Consider just a few of the many entrepreneurs who have created companies that are now household names in Canada:

- Jim Pattison acquired a Pontiac Buick dealership in Vancouver in 1961 and started Jim Pattison Lease. In 1965, he was awarded a license to operate Vancouver AM radio station CJOR. In subsequent years he continued acquisitions across the country until today the Jim Pattison Group is the third largest private company in Canada. Headquartered in Vancouver, British Columbia, it is comprised of over 410 locations

**entrepreneurship**
Accepting the challenge of starting and running a business.

worldwide focusing on the automotive, media, packaging, food sales and distribution, magazine distribution, entertainment, export, and financial industries.

- In 1922, two brothers, John W. and Alfred J. Billes, with a combined savings of $1,800, bought Hamilton Tire and Garage Ltd. Today, nine out of ten adult Canadians shop at Canadian Tire at least twice a year, and 40 percent of Canadians shop at Canadian Tire every week. Canadian Tire Corporation, Limited, is engaged in retail (which includes PartSource and Mark's Work Wearhouse), financial services, and petroleum.

- Ablan Leon began his career selling clothing from a suitcase door-to-door. When he had enough money, he bought a small building in Welland, Ontario, in 1909 and the A. Leon Company was established. When he died in 1942, operation of the family business became the responsibility of his children. Today, Leon's Furniture Limited is Canada's largest retailer of home furnishings.

In 1957, brothers Harrison and Wallace McCain began producing frozen french fries in Florenceville, New Brunswick. Today, privately-owned McCain Foods Limited is the world's largest french fry manufacturer. The company's products, which include green vegetables, desserts, pizzas, juices and beverages, oven meals, entrees, and appetizers, are sold in more than 125 countries.

- In 1969, Jean Coutu (founder of The Jean Coutu Group) and his associate at the time, Louis Michaud, opened a discount pharmacy in Montreal. They offered a large array of products, high-quality professional services, and longer store-opening hours. By 1973, there were five branches of the "Jean Coutu Discount Pharmacies" and a franchise system was established. Today, The Jean Coutu Group is a leading pharmacy franchisor in Canada with 353 stores in Quebec, Ontario, and New Brunswick. It also holds a significant interest in Rite Aid Corporation, an American national drugstore chain with more than 4,900 drugstores.

- In 1907, J. W. Sobey started a meat delivery business in Stellarton, Nova Scotia. With a horse-drawn meat cart, he purchased and collected livestock from local farmers for resale. The first modern Sobeys supermarket opened in 1947. Today, Sobeys Inc. is one of Canada's two national retail grocery and food distributors. Sobeys owns or franchises more than 1,300 corporate and franchised stores in all ten provinces under retail banners that include Sobeys, IGA, and Price Chopper.

- Kenneth Colin Irving opened Bouctouche, New Brunswick's first garage and service station in 1924. That same year, he opened a Ford dealership in Saint John and established Irving Oil. He was 25 years old. Today, Irving Oil is a regional energy processing, transporting, and marketing company. It sells a range of finished energy products including gasoline, diesel, home heating fuel, jet fuel, and complementary products.

These stories are all very much the same: one entrepreneur or a couple of entrepreneurs had a good idea and started a business. Each one now employs thousands of people and helps the country prosper.

## WHY PEOPLE TAKE THE ENTREPRENEURIAL CHALLENGE

Taking the challenge of starting a business can be scary and thrilling at the same time. One entrepreneur described it as almost like bungee jumping. You might be scared, but if you watch six other people do it and they survive, you're then able to do it yourself. There are many triggers to why people become entrepreneurial and some reasons may include unexpected structural unemployment, a sudden inheritance that allows them to try something different, a change in health that forces a career path adjustment, a change in family responsibility that sparks a search to increase income, or even disliking a supervisor so much that being self-employed is an attractive option. Other reasons why people are willing to take the challenge of starting a business are described in more detail below:

- *New Idea, Process, or Product.* Some entrepreneurs are driven by a firm belief, perhaps even an obsession, that they can produce a better product, or a current product at a lower cost, than anybody else. Perhaps they have gotten hold of a new widget or have conceived of an improvement that they are convinced has a large potential market. That's how Travel CUTS (Canadian Universities Travel Service) started. In 1969, Canadian students established a national travel bureau to provide travel opportunities for students. Travel CUTS, co-owned and operated by the Canadian Federation of Students Society and the Canadian Student Horizons Group, is Canada's only national student travel bureau that provides unique student-oriented products in over 70 locations on or near Canadian university and college campuses.[4] The Spotlight on Small Business highlights another business that was started by a student while he was still in school.

- *Independence.* Many entrepreneurs simply do not enjoy working for someone else. They like doing things their own way without someone standing over them. This type of person gets a great deal of satisfaction out of what he or she achieves. Some corporate managers get tired of big-business life and quit their jobs to start their own small businesses. They bring with them their managerial expertise and their enthusiasm.

- *Challenge.* Closely related to the previous factors are the excitement and the challenge of doing something new or difficult. Many people thrive on overcoming challenges. These people welcome the opportunity to run their own business.

- *Family Pattern.* Some people grow up in an atmosphere in which family members have started their own businesses, perhaps going back several generations. The talk at the dinner table is often about business matters. This background may predispose young men or women to think along the same lines. Sometimes there is a family business, and the next generation grows up expecting to take its place there in due course.

  For example, the Anne of Green Gables Museum in Prince Edward Island is on a 110-acre property. The property includes the museum, an antique shop, a craft shop that sells Anne of Green Gables products, a tearoom, and a variety of activities for families. The Campbell home was built in 1872 by author L. M. Montgomery's uncle and aunt. Montgomery often visited this location, and it has become popular with tourists from around world. Campbells first settled on the property in 1776 and it is still in the Campbell family after two hundred years.[5]

- *Profit.* It's natural for people to benefit monetarily from their ideas and dedication and to be rewarded for the money they risk and their hard work when they run a business. Yet long after a business has produced substantial profits and amassed personal fortunes for its owners, many continue to enjoy the challenge of overcoming the endless problems that every business faces and the satisfaction of continued success.

*Company's Coming*, Canada's most popular name in cookbooks, began in the home of Jean Paré in Vermilion, Alberta. Since 1981, Paré has sold more than 28 million cookbooks. *Company's Coming* has turned into a family business. Grant Lovig, Jean's son and co-founder of *Company's Coming*, is the president. Jean's daughter, Gail, is responsible for marketing and distribution. Do you know of any other successful family businesses?

## SPOTLIGHT ON Small Business

### Riding the Tracks to Otter Valley Railroad at www.ovrtrains.com

Lorne James started Otter Valley Railroad with his father, Roger, while he was in the third year of his undergraduate Commerce program at the DeGroote School of Business at McMaster University. The name is derived from Otter Valley, an area in southern Ontario along Lake Erie, where generations of Jameses have lived. James's passion for trains started when his father gave him his first model train at the age of eight. Wanting to do something fun with his son, it was not long before a small train table led to a home layout. Over the years, father and son went to hobby shops and trade shows as they built their layout. Along the way, they met other modellers and joined some groups and associations.

There are several reasons why James started his business: "Over the years, I was getting tired of the poor service, lack of support, and the high prices that traditional local hobby stores were charging other hobby enthusiasts. After scanning the business environment, I realized that there was a market for a new player, and coupled with my father's support and the ease of starting a business, Otter Valley Railroad was created in May 2003."

To develop his business, James made connections with several manufacturers, wholesalers, and distributors to ensure the availability of products at competitive prices. He began to build his client base by promoting the company at local and regional trade shows. He, his father, and mother, Cheryl, became the face of Otter Valley Railroad. As they met other modellers, they stressed the company's products, services (e.g., layout consultation), convenience, and especially their great prices. Due to low overhead and high product turnover, they are able to offer prices 10 to 20 percent lower than traditional local hobby stores.

While the Jameses attend 12 to 15 trade shows in Ontario each year and a few out-of-province trade shows, they feel that they have saturated the mid-West Ontario market. So, what are the future plans for Otter Valley Railroad? James wishes to become a leader in the Canadian market and have one of the biggest catalogues in the country. In the meantime, he is working toward becoming a Chartered Accountant. While studying for his School of Accountancy examination, he developed the marketing plan and Web site for the company's new e-commerce site. His strategy is to gain market share of the Canadian e-commerce market, eventually ship coast-to-coast, and offer unique custom runs. It will also allow him to serve U.S. customers with a goal to eventually ship anywhere in the world. In addition, new products and suppliers are being brought on board.

Another growth area is creating digital custom control sound. There are customers who wish to have sound-equipped locomotives that are customized to their locomotives and specific routes. This is an alternative to factory sound, which is purchased from a manufacturer. To create the custom sound, James researches the locomotive history on the Internet (versus going through old books) and collects sounds digitally from different sources (e.g., videos, the Internet, his recordings, and modellers around the world). Then, he modifies the sound based on locomotive matches. This "sound detailing" allows customers to have a realistic, trackside sound.

Is there a hobby that you have that can be turned into a business? Could you make the time to develop such as business while you are in school? What are some of the sacrifices and rewards that one would face if such a "track" was followed?

Sources: Lorne James, co-owner, Otter Valley Railroad, personal interviews, 3 August 2008 and 6 May 2006.

- *Immigrants.* Some immigrants who come to Canada lack education. This, combined with no Canadian job experience and weak language skills, makes it difficult for them to find employment. However, they often have the drive and desire to succeed, and if they can obtain the capital, they can start their own business. We see this in the many immigrants who run convenience stores (called dépanneurs in Quebec) as well as other types of businesses, such as importing and manufacturing. Other immigrants arrive with capital, skills, and strong entrepreneurial backgrounds. Vancouver, and British Columbia in general, have been major beneficiaries of such immigrants from Hong Kong.

## What Does It Take to Be an Entrepreneur?

Would you succeed as an entrepreneur? You can learn about the managerial and leadership skills needed to run a firm. However, you may not have the personality to assume the risks, take the initiative, create the vision, and rally others to follow your lead. Those traits are harder to learn or acquire. The following page lists some important entrepreneurial attributes. Do you have them?[6]

- *Self-directed.* You should be a self-starter, with a lot of confidence in yourself. You do not hesitate to step into any situation. You should be comfortable and self-disciplined, even though you are your own boss. You will be responsible for your success or possible failure. The best lesson Rebecca MacDonald, Executive Chair and co-CEO of Energy Savings Income Fund, ever learned is "to believe in yourself, because business throws you curveballs on a minute-to-minute basis. If you start second-guessing yourself, your confidence can be shaken very quickly, and lack of confidence is going to create lack of performance."

- *Determined.* Closely related to self-direction is the drive you need to see you through all of the obstacles and difficulties you will encounter. You have to believe in your idea even when no one else does, and be able to replenish your own enthusiasm. In short, you have to keep going when others would give up. This often accompanies the high degree of self-confidence mentioned earlier.

- *Action-Oriented.* Great business ideas are not enough. The most important thing is a burning desire to realize, actualize, and build your dream.

- *Highly Energetic.* It's your own business and you must be emotionally, mentally, and physically able to work long and hard. For example, when starting Extreme Pita, brothers Mark and Alex Rechichi were so consumed with work that they often slept on cots in the shop's backroom after their evening shift. That way, the entrepreneurs could get a few hours of sleep before starting all over again the next morning.

- *Tolerant of Uncertainty.* Successful entrepreneurs take only calculated risks (if they can help it). On a day-to-day basis, you must make decisions that involve varying degrees of risk. Remember, entrepreneurship is not for anyone who is squeamish or bent on security.

- *Able to Learn Quickly.* Making errors is inevitable. Only those who do nothing make no mistakes. What is important is what you learn from them. Good entrepreneurs are quick to learn such lessons. They adapt and change direction as required instead of letting pride stand in the way of admitting a mistake.

While courage is not considered a skill, it is nevertheless an important element of an entrepreneur. Courage is required to challenge the status quo, to see an opportunity, and then most importantly, to try to do something about it. Entrepreneurs are doers. They don't just think and talk about an idea, they act on it! Also be aware that even if you possess many (or even all) of these attributes, there is no guarantee that you will be successful with every endeavour.

It is important to know that most entrepreneurs don't get the ideas for their goods and services from some flash of inspiration. Rather than a flash, the source of innovation is more like a flashlight. Imagine a search party, walking around in the dark, shining lights, looking around, asking questions, and looking some more. The late Sam Walton used such a flashlight approach. He visited his stores and those of competitors and took notes. He'd see a good idea on Monday, and by Tuesday every Walmart manager in the country knew about it. He expected his managers to use flashlighting too. Every time they travelled on business, they were expected to come back with at least one idea worth more than the cost of their trip. "That's how most creativity happens," says business author Dale Dauten. "Calling around, asking questions, saying 'What if?' 'till you get blisters on your tongue."

Keep in mind that necessity isn't always the mother of invention. Entrepreneurs don't always look for what customers need—they look for what they *don't* need as well. Aaron Lapin thought we didn't need the hassles of the touchy process of whipping heavy cream to top our pies. He made millions selling his invention: Reddi Wip. Although we'd rather reach for a can in the refrigerator than whip our own cream, Reddi Wip isn't a necessity. If you think you may have the entrepreneurial spirit in your blood, complete the Entrepreneur Readiness Questionnaire that appears in the appendix at the end of this chapter. There is also some advice for would-be entrepreneurs in Figure 7.1.

**Advice for Potential Entrepreneurs**

- Work for other people first and learn on their money.
- Research your market, but don't take too long to act.
- Start your business when you have a customer. Maybe try your venture as a sideline at first.
- Set specific objectives, but don't set your goals too high. Remember, there's no easy money.
- Plan your objectives within specific time frames.
- Surround yourself with people who are smarter than you—including an accountant and an outside board of directors who are interested in your well-being and who'll give you straight answers.
- Don't be afraid to fail. Former football coach Vince Lombardi summarized the entrepreneurial philosophy when he said, "We didn't lose any games this season, we just ran out of time twice." New entrepreneurs must be ready to run out of time a few times before they succeed.

Sources: Kathleen Lynn, "Entrepreneurs Get Tips on Weathering Recession," *Bergen County (New Jersey) Record*, 5 March 2002, l5; and Keith Lowe, "Setting Clear Goals," Entrepreneur.com, 5 August 2002.

## Women Entrepreneurs[7]

A major phenomenon since the late 1970s is the large number of women who have gone into business for themselves. Throughout this book, you will see examples of such enterprises. Statistics Canada's *Labour Force Survey* reports that there were 877,000 self-employed women in Canada in 2006, accounting for about one-third of all self-employed persons. Between 1996 and 2006 (the most recent data available), the number of self-employed women grew by 18 percent, compared with 14 percent growth in male self-employment. It was estimated that 47 percent of small and medium-sized enterprises (SMEs) have some degree of female ownership: 16 percent of SMEs were majority-owned by women, 20 percent were owned in equal partnerships between male and female owners, and 11 percent have a minority female ownership. The term **SME** refers to all businesses with fewer than 500 employees. CIBC predicts that 1 million Canadian women will own a small business by 2010.

Women owners of SMEs tend to operate in the wholesale, retail, and professional services industry. One such example is Rachel Arseneau-Ferguson, president of Centre Transmed Center Inc. in Campbellton, New Brunswick. While teaching bilingual medical transcription at a local college, Arseneau-Ferguson started her business after her research revealed that there was no other company in Canada providing bilingual medical transcriptions. Transmed provides bilingual medical transcription and translation for large hospital corporations, private clinics, and doctors' offices throughout central and eastern Canada. Doctors dictate medical reports into a digital voice system to be transcribed for patient files. The company's software can link to any hospital and download voice files with medical reports. Doctors can also punch in codes and dictate reports directly into Transmed's system. "We can do work for anyone, anywhere in the world. It's just a matter of having a phone line," says Arseneau-Ferguson.

Studies have shown a variety of reasons for the significant emergence of female entrepreneurs:

- *Financial Need.* The previous decade saw the average real incomes of Canadian employees drop and unemployment fluctuate. This has forced many women to support the family budget by starting a business.
- *Lack of Promotion Opportunities.* Most positions in higher management are still dominated by men. In a recent survey conducted by Toronto-based Rosenzweig & Co., only 5 percent

**small and medium-sized enterprises (SMEs)**
Refers to all businesses with fewer than 500 employees.

Visit http://www.canadianbusiness.com/rankings/w100/ for a list of Canada's top women entrepreneurs.

Christine Magee started Sleep Country Canada with partners Steve Gunn and Gord Lownds based on their dream to give customers what they want. Today, the company is the number one mattress specialist in Canada.

of the top 500 senior executives in Canada are women.[8] Although the situation is improving, the pace is extremely slow. Many women who are frustrated by this pace take the entrepreneurial route.

- *Women Returning to the Workforce.* Many women who return to the job market after raising a family find that their skills are outdated. They also encounter subtle age discrimination. These factors encourage many to try self-employment.

- *Family and Personal Responsibility.* The high rate of divorced women and single mothers in recent years has created a situation in which many women find themselves with children and little or no financial support. Some even refuse such support to be more independent. The development of affordable personal computers and other modern technology has made it possible for women to start home-based businesses.

- *Public Awareness of Women in Business.* As more publicity highlights the fact that growing numbers of women have started their own ventures, the idea catches on and gives others the confidence to try. Often two or more women will team up to form a partnership.

- *Part-Time Occupations.* Often women with some particular talent—for example, publicity, writing, designing, making clothes, cooking, organizing, or human relations—are encouraged to develop their hobby or skills on a part-time basis to see how far they can go with it. This focus has resulted in many notable success stories, some of which are reported in this book.

- *Higher Rate of Success for Women.* Women entrepreneurs seem to have a better success rate than men. Various factors may account for this. Women feel less pressured than men to achieve quick results. They are a little more cautious, so they make fewer mistakes. They also accept advice more readily than men, who may have a macho image of having to know it all. It will be interesting to follow this process to see if women continue to start ventures at the same rate and maintain their remarkable track record.

There are many resources available to help women entrepreneurs network and get general support. Some examples include Canadian Women's Business Network (www.cdnbizwomen.com), Women Entrepreneurs of Canada (www.wec.ca), and Canadian Association of Women Executives & Entrepreneurs (www.cawee.net). Financial institutions also offer small business products and services, which can be accessed on their sites. One example is www.rbcroyalbank.com/sme/women/.

## Entrepreneurial Teams

**entrepreneurial team**
A group of experienced people from different areas of business who join together to form a managerial team with the skills needed to develop, make, and market a new product.

An **entrepreneurial team** is a group of experienced people from different areas of business who join together to form a managerial team with the skills needed to develop, make, and market a new product.[9] A team may be better than an individual entrepreneur because team members can combine creative skills with production and marketing skills right from the start. Having a team also can ensure more co-operation and coordination among functions.

When you think of Apple Computers, the name Steven Jobs may spring to mind. However, while Jobs was the company's charismatic folk hero and visionary, it was Steve Wozniack who invented the first PC model and Mike Markkula who offered the business expertise and access to venture capital.[10] The key to Apple's early success was that the company was built around this "smart team" of entrepreneurs. The team wanted to combine the discipline of a big company with an environment where people could feel they were participating in a successful venture. The trio of entrepreneurs recruited seasoned managers with similar desires. All of the managers worked as a team. Everyone worked together to conceive, develop, and market products.

## Progress Assessment

- What are key differences between entrepreneurial ventures and small businesses?
- Why are people willing to become entrepreneurs?
- What are the advantages of entrepreneurial teams?

## Micropreneurs and Home-Based Businesses

Not every person who starts a business has the goal of growing it into a mammoth corporation. Some are interested in simply enjoying a balanced lifestyle while doing the kind of work they want to do. The smallest of small businesses are called **micro-enterprises**, most often defined as having fewer than five employees.[11] While other entrepreneurs are committed to the quest for growth, **micropreneurs** (owners of micro-enterprises) know they can be happy even if their companies never appear on a list of top-ranked businesses.

Many micropreneurs are owners of home-based businesses. According to Industry Canada, approximately 55 percent of all employer businesses (597,432 in number) were micro-enterprises, with almost 43 percent of these businesses operating in the service sector.[12] Micropreneurs include writers, consultants, video producers, architects, bookkeepers, and such. In fact, the development of this textbook involved many home-based business owners. The authors, the developmental editors, the copy editor, and even the text designer operate home-based businesses.

Many home-based businesses are owned by people who are trying to combine career and family.[13] Don't misunderstand and picture home-based workers as female childcare providers; men also run home-based businesses. In addition to helping business owners balance work and family, other reasons for the growth of home-based businesses include the following:[14]

- *Computer Technology.* Computer technology has levelled the competitive playing field, allowing home-based businesses to look and act as big as their corporate competitors. Broadband Internet connections, fax machines, and other technologies are so affordable that setting up a business takes a much smaller initial investment than it used to.

- *Corporate Downsizing.* Downsizing has made workers aware that there is no such thing as job security, leading some to venture out on their own. Meanwhile, the work of the downsized employees still needs to be done and corporations are outsourcing much of the work to smaller companies; that is, they are contracting with small companies to temporarily fill their needs.

- *Change in Social Attitudes.* Whereas home-based entrepreneurs used to be asked when they were going to get a "real" job, they are now likely to be asked instead for "how-to-do-it" advice.

Working at home has its challenges, of course. In setting up a home-based business, you could expect the following major challenges:[15]

- *Getting New Customers.* Getting the word out can be difficult because you don't have signs or a storefront, especially if the business does not have a Web presence.

**micro-enterprise**

A small business defined as having fewer than five employees.

**micropreneurs**

Small-business owners with fewer than five employees who are willing to accept the risk of starting and managing the type of business that remains small, lets them do the kind of work they want to do, and offers them a balanced lifestyle.

Chef Michael Smith, Canada's best-known chef, is host of several cooking shows on Food Network Canada and in 26 other countries. He is an award-winning cookbook author, newspaper columnist, restaurant chef, and home cook who works from his home. His third series, *Chef At Home*, features some of his home cooking.

---

**FIGURE | 7.2**

**Some Home-Based Business Ideas**

Starting your own business at home can be a viable business opportunity. It is important to note that some home-based businesses may be subject to the approval of local authorities (e.g., health, zoning, etc.).

Look for a business that meets these important criteria: (1) Pick a business that interests you, for which you have a talent or expertise, for which there is a need, and which you can afford to finance; (2) Do your market research; (3) Complete a business plan; (4) Check on and obtain all necessary licences, permits, and registrations; and (5) Advertise. The following are examples of ideas for home-based businesses.

1. Antique refinishing and repair
2. Music/dance lessons
3. Bed and breakfast
4. Accounting
5. Consulting
6. Research
7. Catering
8. Gift basket service
9. Trade (e.g., electrician)
10. Clothing design

Source: "Home-Based Business Ideas," Government of Canada, 2008, http://www.canadabusiness.ca.

- *Managing Time.* Of course, you save time by not commuting, but it takes self-discipline to use that time wisely.
- *Keeping Work and Family Tasks Separate.* Often it is difficult to separate work and family tasks. It's great to be able to throw a load of laundry in the washer in the middle of the workday if you need to, but you have to keep such distractions to a minimum. It is also difficult to leave your work at the office if the office is your home. Again, it takes self-discipline to keep work from trickling out of the home office and into the family room.
- *Abiding by City Ordinances.* Government ordinances restrict the types of businesses that are allowed in certain parts of the community and how much traffic a home-based business can attract to the neighbourhood.
- *Managing Risk.* Home-based entrepreneurs should review their homeowner's insurance policy, since not all policies cover business-related claims. Some even void the coverage if there is a business in the home.

Those who wish to get out of an office building and into a home office should focus on finding opportunity instead of accepting security, getting results instead of following routines, earning a profit instead of earning a paycheque, trying new ideas instead of avoiding mistakes, and creating a long-term vision instead of seeking a short-term pay-off. Figure 7.2 lists ten ideas for potentially successful home-based businesses. You can find a wealth of online information about starting a home-based business at http://sbinfocanada.about.com and www.entrepreneur.com.

## Web-Based Businesses

The Internet has sprouted a world of small Web-based businesses that sell everything from staplers to refrigerator magnets to wedding dresses. These small businesses compete with other small businesses as well as large Web-based and bricks-and-mortar businesses. Take a moment and ponder the opportunities that have been created by eBay alone for entrepreneurs. This has been such a powerful channel for part-time and full-time entrepreneurs that a book has been developed, titled *eBay for Dummies,* to teach people how to successfully use this Web site (www.ebay.ca) to buy and sell products and services.

While 87 percent of firms used the Internet in 2007, only 41 percent reported having a Web site.[16] A Statistics Canada report highlights some of the recent trends. Internet sales, including not only retailers but all enterprises in the private and public sectors, grew to an estimated $62.7 billion in 2007, up 26 percent over the year before. The private sector constituted the largest part of that, with sales of $58.2 billion, which was a 25 percent increase over 2006. Nevertheless, Statistics Canada said "e-commerce still represents a relatively small fraction of total economic activity. In 2007, online sales of private-sector firms accounted for just under 2 percent of total operating revenue." In the private sector, business-to-business sales made up 62 percent of online sales, down from 68 percent in 2006. Statistics Canada's report also shows Canadian enterprises are more inclined to be consumers than creators of online commerce: 48 percent of private-sector firms were reported to be purchasers of goods and services online versus only 8 percent who were sellers.[17]

KEH Camera Brokers began as a hobby, grew into a mail-order business, and is now a flourishing Web-based business (www.keh.com). More than 57 percent of the store's sales are made online. Customers have found that the Web site is an efficient pipeline for buying and selling cameras. The far reach of the Web was a natural fit for the company. "The Web is a much better vehicle for our customers [compared with a mail-order catalogue]," store manager Pat Mulherin said. "They want to be able to see our inventory." When KEH's first Web page went active, it was an immediate success. "Within two months it was accounting for 35 percent of our business, then quickly went up." Prior to the Web, the small store produced mail-order catalogues listing used cameras for sale. Creating and mailing the catalogues was a slow process; by the time a customer saw a product and tried to order it, another customer could have already purchased it. The KEH Web site's listing of available cameras is updated every four hours. A used camera is listed for sale on the Web site a few hours after it enters KEH's inventory.

Don't get the idea that a Web-based business is always a fast road to success. It can sometimes be a shortcut to failure. Hundreds of high-flying dot-coms crashed after promising to revolutionize the way we shop.[18] That's the bad news. The good news is that you can learn from someone else's failure and spare yourself some pain. Startupfailures.com serves as a community for those who have tried and failed. To help future Web-based entrepreneurs understand online-business fundamentals and how to avoid the failed dot-coms' mistakes, visit www.businessplanarchive.org. There, you will see a database of dot-com business plans and marketing documents.

**intrapreneurs**
Creative people who work as entrepreneurs within corporations.

## Entrepreneurship Within Firms

Entrepreneurship in a large organization is often reflected in the efforts and achievements of intrapreneurs. **Intrapreneurs** are creative people who work as entrepreneurs within corporations. The idea is to use a company's existing resources—human, financial, and physical—to launch new products and generate new profits.[19]

At 3M, which produces a wide array of products from adhesives (Scotch tape) to non-woven materials for industrial use, managers are expected to devote 15 percent of their time to thinking up new products or services.[20] You know those brightly coloured Post-it Notes that people use to write messages on just about everything? That product was developed by Art Fry, a 3M employee. He needed to mark the pages of a hymnal in a way that wouldn't damage or fall out of the book. He came up with the idea of the self-stick, repositionable paper. The 3M labs soon produced a sample, but distributors thought the product wasn't important and market surveys were inconclusive. Nonetheless, 3M kept sending samples to secretaries of top executives. Eventually, after launching a major sales and marketing program, the orders began pouring in, and Post-it Notes became a big winner. The company continues to update the product; making the notes from recycled paper is just one of many innovations. Post-it Notes have gone international as well—the notepads sent to Japan are long and narrow to accommodate vertical writing. Now you can even use Post-it Notes electronically—the software program Post-it Software Notes allows you to type messages onto brightly coloured notes and store them on memo boards, embed them in documents, or send them through e-mail.

When you come up with a winning idea, stick with it. That's certainly been the motto of the 3M company, the maker of Post-it Notes. 3M encourages intrapreneurship among its employees by requiring them to devote at least 15 percent of their time to thinking about new products. How has this commitment to innovation paid off for the company and its employees?

# ENCOURAGING ENTREPRENEURSHIP: WHAT GOVERNMENT CAN DO[21]

The different levels of government provide many services to help entrepreneurs and small businesses to succeed. Canada Business (http://canadabusiness.gc.ca) is a federal government information service for entrepreneurs that serves as a single point of access for federal and provincial/territorial government services, programs, and regulatory requirements for business. Canada Business's mandate is to serve as the primary source of up-to-date and accurate business-related information and to provide referrals on government programs, services, and regulations—without charge—in all regions of Canada. The mission of Canada Business is to improve the start-up, survival, and growth rates of small and medium-sized enterprises. This includes assisting with sound business planning, market research, and the use of strategic business information.

There are also specialized programs. For example, the Aboriginal Business Service Network (ABSN) provides Aboriginal entrepreneurs with information and resources to improve their access to capital and to establish or develop their business. ABSN is one element of the Aboriginal Business Development Initiative.

Industry Canada's Small Business Research and Policy Web site is designed to encourage small business researchers and policy analysts across Canada to share information. It includes an extensive database of research literature on small business and entrepreneurship, recent reports on small-business financing, small-business statistics, and lists of researchers and policy development offices across Canada. The *Small Business Quarterly* (*SBQ*) provides a quick and easy-to-read snapshot of the recent performance of Canada's small-business sector. (For additional government sources, review the Services section in Chapter 4.)

Entrepreneurs and new start-ups can also find assistance from incubators. Incubators were first developed to be centres that offered new businesses low-cost offices with basic business services such as accounting, legal advice, and secretarial help. Since then, the "networked" incubator has emerged with the creation of innovation centres. The networked incubator goes beyond the simple provision of office space and provides entrepreneurs and new companies with access to more services. According to the Canadian Association of Business Incubation (www.cabi.ca), **incubators** today provide hands-on management assistance, education, information, technical and vital business support services, networking resources, financial advice, as well as advice on where to go to seek financial assistance. In fact, the average survival rate of companies in Canada that go through business incubation has been shown to be higher than 80 percent after five years.

The goal of an incubator is not only to ensure that the small business survives the start-up period, but also to produce confident, successful graduates who will run a productive business in the future. One example of an incubator that has received worldwide recognition is the Quebec Biotechnology Innovation Centre (QBIC) in Laval. It provides start-ups in the health, environment, agri-food, and forestry sectors with lab space, scientific equipment, and mentoring services. Located in Laval's Biotech City, QBIC is just one organization that fosters entrepreneurship.

According to the National Incubation Association, there are over 1,400 business incubators in North America (including 120 in Canada) and about 5,000

**incubators**
Centres that provide hands-on management assistance, education, information, technical and vital business support services, networking resources, financial advice, as well as advice on where to go to seek financial assistance.

The National Research Council (NRC) supports Industrial Partnership Facilities (IPFs). Similar to incubators, each IPF has a focus on a different technology sector, depending on the specialization of its host institute. IPFs offer start-ups access to specialized laboratory space and equipment, regular interaction with researchers, and the opportunity to benefit from a range of NRC technology-transfer initiatives. The NRC Plant Biotechnology Institute in Saskatoon (viewed here) strengthens the region's agricultural biotechnology cluster.

worldwide. The government can also have a significant effect on entrepreneurship by offering investment tax credits that give tax breaks to businesses that make the kind of investments that create jobs. For example, the Biotechnology Development Centre is a tenant in Laval's Biotech City. This Centre is supported by the Canadian and Quebec governments in addition to the City of Laval. These government bodies encourage research and development by granting corporations and individuals tax incentives that foster scientific and technological development. One incentive includes a 30 percent refundable tax credit on capital or rental costs for eligible equipment (up to three years).

While the government provides a great deal of assistance, it is still primarily up to the entrepreneur to make a success of the new business.

Visit http://www.canadaone. com/magazine/loan_programs. html for a list of Canadian grant and loan programs for young entrepreneurs.

## Progress Assessment

- How do micropreneurs differ from other entrepreneurs?
- What are some of the opportunities and risks of Web-based businesses?
- List some services for entrepreneurs provided by the federal government.

# STARTING A SMALL BUSINESS

Let's suppose you have a great idea for a new business, you have the attributes of an entrepreneur, and you are ready to take the leap into business for yourself. How do you start a business? How much paperwork is involved? That is what the rest of this chapter is about. We will explore small businesses, their role in the economy, and small-business management. It may be easier to identify with a small neighbourhood business than with a giant global firm, yet the principles of management are similar. The management of charities, government agencies, churches, schools, and unions is much the same as the management of small and large businesses. So, as you learn about small-business management, you will make a giant step toward understanding management in general. All organizations demand capital, good ideas, planning, information management, budgets (and financial management in general), accounting, marketing, good employee relations, and good overall managerial know-how. We shall explore these areas as they relate to small businesses and then, later in the book, apply the concepts to large firms, even to global organizations.

## Small Versus Big Business[22]

The Business Registrar of Statistics Canada maintains a count of business establishments. A **business establishment** must have at least one paid employee, have annual sales revenue of $30,000, or be incorporated and have filed a federal corporate income tax return at least once in the previous three years. While there are a little over 2.3 million business establishments in Canada, approximately 1.1 million of them are employer businesses. An **employer business** meets one of the business establishment criteria and usually maintains a payroll of at least one person, possibly the owner. The rest are classified as "indeterminate." Figure 7.3 breaks down the number of businesses by sector and number of employees.

It would be helpful to define what is meant by the term *small business*. Giant companies like Telus Corporation or Magna International may look at most companies as small. A **small business** is often defined as a business that is independently owned and operated, is not dominant in its field, and meets certain standards of size in terms of employees or annual revenues.

Many institutions define small business according to their own needs. For example, the Canadian Bankers Association classifies a loan authorization of less than $250,000 as small. Industry Canada often uses a definition based on the number of employees: goods-producing firms are considered small if they have fewer than 100 employees, while services-

**business establishment**
Has at least one paid employee, annual sales revenue of $30,000, or is incorporated and has filed a federal corporate income tax return at least once in the previous three years.

**employer business**
Meets one of the business establishment criteria and usually maintains a payroll of at least one person, possibly the owner.

**small business**
A business that is independently owned and operated, is not dominant in its field, and meets certain standards of size in terms of employees or annual revenues.

**FIGURE | 7.3**

**Number of Business Establishments by Sector and Firm Size (Number of Employees)**
A little over 95 percent of Canadian companies are considered small businesses.

| | | No. of Business Establishments | | |
| --- | --- | --- | --- | --- |
| | Percentage of Employer Businesses | Total | Goods-Producing Sector | Service-Producing Sector |
| Indeterminate[1] | | 1,300,594 | 315,798 | 984,796 |
| Employer Businesses | | 1,085,719 | 238,279 | 847,440 |
| Small businesses (1–49 employees) | 95.2 | 1,033,803 | 225,266 | 808,447 |
| Medium-sized businesses (50–499 employees) | 4.5 | 48,976 | 12,444 | 36,622 |
| Large businesses (500+ employees) | 0.3 | 2,940 | 569 | 2,371 |
| **Total** | | **2,386,313** | **554,077** | **1,832,236** |

Note 1: The "indeterminate" category consists of incorporated or unincorporated businesses that do not have a Canada Revenue Agency (CRA) payroll deductions account. The workforce of such businesses may consist of contract workers, family members, and/or owners.

Source: "Number of Business Establishments by sector and size (Number of Employees)," adapted from Statistics Canada, special tabulation, unpublished data, (Business Register Database), June 2008.

producing firms with 50 employees or less are considered small. Generally speaking, 50 employees is the upper limit most used when defining a small business based on the number of employees. Medium-sized businesses have 50 to 499 employees, while large businesses employ more than 500 people. In Figure 7.3, of the approximately 1.1 million employer businesses in Canada, 0.3 percent have more than 500 employees. Businesses employing fewer than 50 employees account for the vast majority (95.2 percent) of all employer businesses.

As you can see, small business is really a big part of the Canadian economy. How big a part? We'll explore that question next.

## Importance of Small Businesses[23]

The small-business sector is a dynamic part of the Canadian economy. Nearly all small businesses are Canadian-owned and -managed. This is in contrast to large businesses, of which many are foreign-owned and -managed. Small business thus plays a major role in helping to maintain the Canadian identity and Canadian economic independence.

Small businesses also continue to be feeders for future large businesses. As they prosper and develop new goods and services, they are often bought out by large companies, which in turn become more competitive. Alternatively, after small businesses establish a good track record, some of them convert from private to public companies, enabling them to obtain significant financing and become larger companies.

Here are some quick facts about small businesses (defined by Industry Canada as firms that have fewer than 100 employees):

- On average, 130,000 new small businesses are created in Canada each year.
- Small businesses employ approximately 5 million individuals in Canada, or 48 percent of the total private labour force.
- Small businesses account for almost 98 percent of all employer businesses.

*Key Small Business Statistics* is a semi-annual publication that provides baseline data on the small-business sector in Canada. Visit the Web site (http://www.ic.gc.ca/eic/site/sbrp-rppe.nsf/eng/h_rd01252.html) to find up-to-date information.

- On average, small businesses that have fewer than 50 employees contributed about 26 percent to Canada's gross domestic product.

- Approximately 15 percent (2.6 million) of all employed workers in the Canadian economy were self-employed.

Since most of Canada's jobs are in small businesses, there is a very good chance that you will either work in a small business some day or start one. One-quarter of small businesses list "lack of qualified workers" as one of their biggest obstacles to growth. In addition to providing employment opportunities, small firms believe that they offer other advantages that larger companies do not. Owners of small companies report that their greatest advantages over big companies are their more personal customer service and their ability to respond quickly to opportunities.

Bigger is not always better. Picture a hole in the ground. If you fill it with big boulders, there are many empty spaces between them. However, if you fill it with sand, there is no space between the grains. That's how it is in business. Big businesses don't serve all the needs of the market. There is plenty of room for small companies to make a profit filling those niches.

# Wide Diversification

Another significant aspect of small business is the wide diversification of its activities. If you look, you will find small businesses in many sectors:

1. *Service Businesses.* You are already familiar with the services provided by car mechanics, dry cleaners, travel agencies, lawn care firms, salons, and other services that cater to you and your family. In your career search, be sure to explore opportunities provided by hotels and motels, health clubs, amusement parks, income tax preparation organizations, employment agencies, accounting firms, rental firms of all kinds, management consulting, repair services (e.g., computers, DVD players), insurance agencies, real estate firms, stockbrokers, and so on. A growth area is in computer consulting and the knowledge-based industries.

2. *Retail Businesses.* You only have to go to a major shopping mall to see the possibilities in retailing. There are stores selling shoes, clothes, hats, skis, housewares, sporting goods, ice cream, groceries, and more. Much more. Watch the trends and you will see ideas such as fancy popcorn stores and cafés with Internet access areas.

3. *Construction Firms.* Drive through any big city and you will see huge cranes towering over major construction sites. Would you enjoy supervising such work? Visit some areas where construction firms are building bridges, roads, homes, schools, buildings, and dams. There is a feeling of power and creativity in such work that excites many observers. How about you? Talk to some of the workers and supervisors and learn about the risks and rewards of small construction firms.

4. *Wholesalers.* Have you ever visited a wholesale food warehouse, jewellery centre, or similar wholesale firm? If not, you are missing an important link in the small-business chain, one with much potential. Wholesale representatives often make more money, have more free time, travel more, and enjoy their work more than similar people in retailing. Wholesaling will be discussed in Chapter 15.

5. *Manufacturing.* Of course, manufacturing is still an attractive career for tomorrow's graduates. Surveys show that manufacturers make the most money among small-business owners. There are careers for designers, machinists, mechanics, engineers, supervisors, safety inspectors, and a host of other occupations. Visit some small manufacturers in your area and inquire about such jobs to get some experience before starting your own manufacturing business. Today's high-tech world opens up many opportunities, if you are interested.

There are also thousands of small farmers who enjoy the rural life and the pace of farming. Small farms have been in great trouble for the last few years, but some that specialize in exotic or organic crops do quite well. Similarly, many small mining operations attract college and university students who have a sense of adventure. People who are not sure what career they would like to follow have a busy time ahead. They need to visit service firms, construction firms, farms, mines, retailers, wholesalers, and all other kinds of small and large businesses to see the diversity and excitement available in Canadian business.

# Small-Business Success and Failure

You can't be naive about business practices, or you will go broke. There is some debate about how many new small businesses fail each year. There are many false signals about entries and exits. When small-business owners go out of business to start new and different businesses, they may be included in the "failure" category when obviously this is not the case. Similarly, when a business changes its form of ownership from partnership to corporation, it may be counted as a failure. Retirements of sole owners may also be in this category.

As mentioned in Chapter 1, thousands of businesses enter and exit the marketplace throughout the year. Statistics Canada reports that about 96 percent of small businesses that enter the marketplace survive for one full year, 85 percent survive for three years, and 70 percent survive for five years.[24] Figure 7.4 lists reasons for small-business failure. Managerial incompetence and inadequate financial planning are two of the biggest reasons for these failures.

Choosing the right type of business is critical. Many of the businesses with the lowest failure rates require advanced training to start—veterinary services, dental practices, medical practices, and so on. While training and degrees may buy security, they do not tend to produce much growth. If you want to be both independent and rich, you need to go after growth. Often high-growth businesses, such as technology firms, are not easy to start and are even more difficult to keep going.

In general, it seems that the easiest businesses to start are the ones that tend to have the least growth and the greatest failure rate (e.g., restaurants). The easiest businesses to keep alive are difficult ones to get started (e.g., manufacturing). And the ones that can

---

**FIGURE | 7.4**

**Causes of Small-Business Failure**

The following are some of the causes of small-business failure:
- Plunging in without first testing the waters on a small scale.
- Underpricing or overpricing goods or services.
- Underestimating how much time it will take to build a market.
- Starting with too little capital.
- Starting with too much capital and being careless in its use.
- Going into business with little or no experience and without first learning something about the industry or market.
- Borrowing money without planning just how and when to pay it back.
- Attempting to do too much business with too little capital.
- Not allowing for setbacks and unexpected expenses.
- Buying too much on credit.
- Extending credit too freely.
- Expanding credit too rapidly.
- Failing to keep complete, accurate records, so that the owners drift into trouble without realizing it.
- Carrying habits of personal extravagance into the business.
- Not understanding business cycles.
- Forgetting about taxes, insurance, and other costs of doing business.
- Mistaking the freedom of being in business for oneself for the liberty to work or not, according to whim.

**Situations for Small-Business Success**

The following factors increase the chances of small-business success:
- The customer requires a lot of personal attention, as in a beauty parlour.
- The product is not easily made by mass-production techniques (e.g., custom-tailored clothes or custom auto-body work).
- Sales are not large enough to appeal to a large firm (e.g., a novelty shop).
- A large business sells a franchise operation to local buyers. (Don't forget franchising as an excellent way to enter the world of small business.)
- The owner pays attention to new competitors.
- The business is in a growth industry (e.g., computer services or Web design).

make you rich are the ones that are both hard to start and hard to keep going. See Figure 7.5 to get an idea of the business situations that are most likely to lead to success.

When you decide to start your own business, you must think carefully about what kind of business you want. You are not likely to find everything you want in one business—easy entry, security, and reward. Choose those characteristics that matter the most to you; accept the absence of the others; plan, plan, plan; and then go for it!

# LEARNING ABOUT SMALL-BUSINESS OPERATIONS

Hundreds of would-be entrepreneurs of all ages have asked the same question: How can I learn to run my own business? Many of these people had no idea what kind of business they wanted to start; they simply wanted to be in business for themselves. That seems to be a major trend among students today.

There are several ways to get into your first business venture:

1. Start your own company.
2. Buy an existing business.
3. Buy a franchise unit (see Chapter 6).
4. Inherit / takeover a family business.

Here are some hints for learning about small business.

## Start Your Own Company

Your search for small-business knowledge might begin by investigating your local area schools for classes on the subject. There are entrepreneurship programs in post-secondary schools throughout Canada. One of the best things about such courses is that they bring together entrepreneurs from diverse backgrounds. (Many entrepreneurs have started businesses as students—see the Analyzing Management Decisions case near the end of the chapter for an example.) An excellent way to learn how to run a small business is to talk to others who have already done it. They will tell you that location is critical. They will caution you not to be undercapitalized; that is, not to start without enough money. They will warn you about the problems of finding and retaining good workers. And, most of all, they will tell you to keep good records and hire a good accountant and lawyer before you start. Free advice like this is invaluable.

## Get Some Experience

There is no better way to learn small-business management than by becoming an apprentice or working for a successful entrepreneur. Many small-business owners got the idea for their businesses from their prior jobs. An industry standard is to have three years' experience in a comparable business.

MBAs Without Borders (MWB) was co-founded by Tal Dehtiar (seen here meeting with some Masai in Kenya) and Michael Brown. MWB gives MBAs experience by helping to promote enterprise in developing nations. According to Dehtiar, "The classroom and office are great environments for education, but MWB forces MBAs to not only think outside of the box, but out of this world."

Many new entrepreneurs come from corporate management. They are tired of the big-business life or are being laid off because of corporate downsizing. Such managers bring their managerial expertise and enthusiasm with them. Such was the case with Tom Heintzman and Greg Kiessling, co-founders of Bullfrog Power, the focus of this chapter's Green Box. Prior to starting the company, Heintzman had experience in the private and non-governmental organizations sectors as a consultant and more recently, as the director of corporate development for Zenon Environmental. Kiessling had 18 years of private sector experience leading high-growth, entrepreneurial organizations.

By running a small business part-time during your off hours or on weekends, you can experience the rewards of working for yourself while still enjoying a regular paycheque. This is what John Stanton, founder of the Running Room, did when he first started his company. He kept his full-time job as a vice-president in the grocery sector and he opened the Running Room in a house in Edmonton. At first, he only sold cotton T-shirts and running shoes. Four years later, he was confident that the company had growth potential. He quit his job and concentrated on building the Running Room chain. Today, there are more than 92 locations from coast to coast with expansion plans for Canada and the United States.

# GreenBOX

## Are You Interested in Becoming Bullfrog-Powered?

Conventional electricity production is among the largest industrial sources of carbon dioxide, a primary greenhouse gas that is linked to climate change. Electricity production is also a major source of pollutants including nitric oxide, sulphur dioxide, mercury, and particulates that contribute to poor air quality and smog conditions.

Founded in 2005 by Tom Heintzman and Greg Kiessling, Bullfrog Power is a leading provider of 100 percent green electricity, with service available to Ontario and Alberta residents and businesses. Bullfrog Power provides customers with a convenient way to support locally generated renewable power as all of Bullfrog's power comes from clean, green sources like wind power and low-impact water power.

When customers switch to Bullfrog Power, they continue to draw their power from the province's grid in the same way that they always have. They don't need any special equipment or wiring and there is no change in the reliability of the service. Bullfrog Power injects green power onto the grid to match the amount of power a customer's home (or office building) uses. Customers receive estimates of their emission/waste reductions on their billing statements.

So while greening a building's electricity costs a little extra, customers have the comfort of knowing that their electricity dollars are supporting clean, renewable power instead of polluting and carbon-intensive sources like coal. To date, thousands of Canadian homeowners and hundreds of businesses have made the decision to become "bullfrogpowered." What's more, this support helps the company bring more new, renewable power online in Canada. For example, new wind turbines have already been commissioned in Canada as a direct result of support from Bullfrog Power customers.

Source: "About Bullfrog Power," Bullfrog Power, 22 September 2008, http://www.bullfrogpower.com/about/about.cfm.

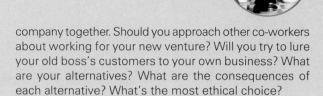

## Making Ethical Decisions

### Sabotaging Your Employer

Suppose you've worked for two years in a company and you see signs that the business is beginning to falter. You and a co-worker have ideas about how to make a company similar to your boss's succeed. Rather than share your ideas with your boss, you and your friend are considering quitting your jobs and starting your own company together. Should you approach other co-workers about working for your new venture? Will you try to lure your old boss's customers to your own business? What are your alternatives? What are the consequences of each alternative? What's the most ethical choice?

---

Learning a business while working for someone else may also save you money because you are less likely to make "rookie mistakes" when you start your own business. (See the Making Ethical Decisions box, though, for a scenario that raises a number of questions.)

## Buy an Existing Business

Small-business management takes time, dedication, and determination. Owners work long hours and rarely take vacations. After many years, they may feel stuck in their business. They may think they can't get out because they have too much time and effort invested. Consequently, there are some small-business owners out there eager to get away, at least for a long vacation.

This is where you come in. Find a successful business person who owns a small business. Tell him or her that you are eager to learn the business and would like to serve an apprenticeship—that is, a training period. State that at the end of the training period (one year or so), you would like to help the owner or manager by becoming assistant manager. As assistant manager, you would free the owner to take off weekends and holidays, and to take a long vacation—a good deal for him or her. For another year or so, work very hard to learn all about the business—suppliers, inventory, bookkeeping, customers, promotion, and so on. At the end of two years, make the owner this offer: he or she can retire or work only part-time and you will take over the business. You can establish a profit-sharing plan for yourself plus a salary. Be generous with yourself; you will earn it if you manage the business. You can even ask for 40 percent or more of the profits.

The owner benefits by keeping ownership in the business and making 60 percent of what he or she earned before—without having to work. You benefit by making 40 percent of the profits of a successful firm. This is an excellent deal for an owner about to retire—he or she is able to keep the firm and a healthy profit flow. It is also a clever and successful way to share in the profits of a successful small business without any personal investment of money. If you think that this is not realistic, be aware that nearly half of Canada's small-business owners plan to retire before 2020—and 500,000 are set to leave the workforce by 2011.[25]

If profit-sharing doesn't appeal to the owner, you may want to buy the business outright. How do you determine a fair price for a business? Value is based on (1) what the business owns, (2) what it earns, and (3) what makes it unique. Naturally, your accountant will need to help you determine the business's value.

If your efforts to take over the business through either profit-sharing or buying fail, you can quit and start your own business fully trained.

## Franchising

In Chapter 6, you were introduced to franchising. Many business people first get into business via franchising. Recall that franchising is a method of distributing a good or service, or both, to achieve a maximum market impact with a minimum investment. From

## Reaching Beyond Our Borders

### Canadian Franchisor Cleans Up

Molly Maid International Inc. set out to provide domestic cleaning services in Mississauga, Ontario, in 1979. The company is built on the fact that families are now busier than ever and need time-saving, convenient services to help manage their responsibilities at home. Since that time, Molly Maid has performed more than 6 million home cleanings across Canada and more than 12 million around the world. This year alone, the company is expecting to perform 2 million home cleanings.

Molly Maid's success should not be surprising when you scan the business environment. Much of the company's growth results from the increased participation of women in the workforce. While the majority of women between the ages of 18 and 65 now hold jobs outside the home, most are still responsible for the majority of the housework. Statistics reveal that working mothers spend as much as five hours each day on household chores—in addition to the almost eight hours spent working for employers.

Independent market research shows that Molly Maid is the most recognized brand in the cleaning industry. Eight of ten Canadians are familiar with the Molly Maid name and four of ten Canadians mention it first when asked to name a cleaning service. Today, Molly Maid is the largest Canadian-based cleaning company in the world with over 500 franchises and global sales in excess of $200 million. It has a presence on three continents and can be found in seven countries including Canada, the United States, the United Kingdom, Portugal, and Japan.

Franchise owners have received numerous industry awards. For example, *Success* magazine ranked Molly Maid first in residential cleaning and fourth in the franchising industry overall in its annual Franchise Gold 200. *Income Opportunities* magazine ranked Molly Maid first in residential cleaning and second in the franchising industry overall. *Entrepreneur* magazine has ranked Molly Maid in the top 100 of their Franchise 500 for over six years.

Sources: "History," Molly Maid International Inc., 22 October 2008, http://www.mollymaid.ca/news/index.php; "The Real Dirt on Canadians and Their Homes," Canada NewsWire, 19 March 2007, http://proquest.umi.com; "Molly Maid Still Cleaning Up in Canada After 25 years," *Canadian Business Franchise*, March/April 2004, 80–81; and "Pioneer in Home Cleaning Business Continues to Meet the Needs of the Modern Family," Canada NewsWire, 13 April 2004, http://proquest.umi.com.

your investment perspective, you are not creating a product or service from scratch. Rather, you are benefiting from the experience of the franchisor. In addition to the two methods mentioned earlier, franchising is a way that you can start a business venture, especially if you are more comfortable doing so with an established product and process. When deciding which method is best for you in terms of getting into your first business venture—whether it be starting your own company from scratch, buying an existing business, or franchising—be sure to weigh the advantages and disadvantages of each option before proceeding. One example a successful franchise business is Molly Maid International Inc., a leader in the cleaning industry. The Reaching Beyond Our Borders introduces you to this company.

## INHERIT OR TAKE OVER A FAMILY BUSINESS[26]

It is not uncommon for the dream of one to evolve into a family business. Some examples highlighted in this textbook include Company's Coming and Irving Oil. Husband and wife teams (such as Timothy Snelgrove and Teresa Snelgrove, founders of Timothy's World Coffee, and David and Penny Chapman, founders of Chapman's Ice Cream) are also quite common when you review the Canadian landscape of family businesses.

There are a number of factors that make family businesses unique. One is ownership. Public companies are typically owned by a large number of shareholders whose primary interest in ownership is generating the best return on investment. However, family businesses are often owned by a much smaller group whose ownership often has elements of personal identity, family legacy, and community responsibility entwined

## DEALING with CHANGE

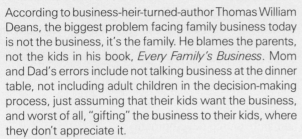

### Some Unique Challenges of Family Businesses

According to business-heir-turned-author Thomas William Deans, the biggest problem facing family business today is not the business, it's the family. He blames the parents, not the kids in his book, *Every Family's Business*. Mom and Dad's errors include not talking business at the dinner table, not including adult children in the decision-making process, just assuming that their kids want the business, and worst of all, "gifting" the business to their kids, where they don't appreciate it.

Management problems in a family-owned business are somewhat different from similar problems in non-family businesses. When close relatives work together, emotions often interfere with business decisions. When you put up your own money and operate your own business, you prize your independence. "It's my business," you tell yourself. However, "It's our business" in a family company.

Conflicts sometimes abound because relatives look upon the business from different viewpoints. Those relatives who are silent partners, shareholders, and directors may only see dollar signs when judging capital expenditures, growth, and other major matters. Relatives who are engaged in daily operations judge major matters from the viewpoint of the production, sales, and personnel necessary to make the company successful. Obviously, these two viewpoints may conflict in many instances. This natural conflict can be aggravated by family members who have no talent for money or business.

While the majority of family business owners would like to see their business transferred to the next generation, it is estimated that 70 percent will not survive into the second generation and 90 percent will not survive into the third generation. With 90 percent of businesses being family businesses, and half of all business owners planning to retire over the next decade, Canada's economic health clearly hinges on creating more successful successions.

One factor that might contribute to a successful transfer is governance. The key to effective governance for a family business is recognizing when the family business is moving from one stage to another, such as from the controlling owner (i.e., the original entrepreneur) to a sibling partnership where siblings have an ownership interest and/or some family shareholders are not working in the business. By designing revisions to the governance structure that will meet the needs of the owners for the next stage, expectations and responsibilities are likely to be clearer, contributing to a more successful business venture.

Sources: "Problems in Managing a Family-Owned Business," *Canada Business*, 5 October 2005, http://www.canadabusiness.ca/servlet/Content Server?cid=1081945276597&pagename=CBSC_FE%2Fdisplay&lang=en&c=GuideFactSheet; "Governance for the Family Business," KPMG in Canada, 2008, http://www.kpmg.ca/en/services/enterprise/issuesGrowth Governance.html; "The Parent Trap," *PROFIT*, October 2008, 13; and Grant Walsh, Family Business Succession, KPMG Enterprise™, 2008, http://www.kpmg.ca/en/services/enterprise/documents/3468_Succession.pdf.

with its economic interests. This "emotional ownership" often results in family businesses having a longer-term view. Another factor that tends to separate successful family firms from their public counterparts is the concept of stewardship. Many family businesses have a clear understanding that the business is something to be preserved and grown for future generations. As Bill Ford, the chairman of Ford Motor Company once said, "I'm working for my children and grandchildren and feel I'm working for our employees' children and grandchildren as well."

As with any form of business, there are some challenges associated with a family business, as highlighted in the Dealing with Change box. Regardless of such challenges, inheriting or taking over a family business is another way that one can learn about small business.

## Progress Assessment

- Why are small businesses important to Canada?
- What are causes of small-business failure?
- How can one get into a business venture?

# MANAGING A SMALL BUSINESS

The number-one reason for small-business failure is poor management. Keep in mind, though, that the term *poor management* covers a number of faults. It could mean poor planning, poor record keeping, poor inventory control, poor promotion, or poor employee relations. Most likely it would include poor capitalization.[27] To help you succeed as a business owner, in the following sections we explore the functions of business in a small-business setting:

- planning your business
- financing your business
- knowing your customers (marketing)
- managing your employees (human resource development)
- keeping records (accounting).

Although all of the functions are important in both the start-up and management phases of the business, the first two functions—planning and financing—are the primary concerns when you start your business. The remaining functions are the heart of the actual operations once the business is started.

## Begin with Planning

**business plan**

A detailed written statement that describes the nature of the business, the target market, the advantages the business will have in relation to competition, and the resources and qualifications of the owner(s).

It is amazing how many people are eager to start a small business but have only a vague notion of what they want to do. Eventually, they come up with an idea for a business and begin discussing the idea with professors, friends, and other business people. It is at this stage that the entrepreneur needs a business plan. A **business plan** is a detailed written statement that describes the nature of the business, the target market, the advantages the business will have in relation to competition, and the resources and qualifications of the owner(s). A business plan forces potential owners of small businesses to be quite specific about the goods or services they intend to offer. They must analyze the competition, calculate how much money they need to start, and cover other details of operation. A business plan is also mandatory for talking with bankers or other investors. Put another way, a business plan is a tool that is used to transition the entrepreneur from having an idea to actually developing a strategic and operational framework for the business.

If you are looking for bank financing, here are some tips. First, pick a bank that serves businesses the size of yours, have a good accountant prepare a complete set of financial statements and a personal balance sheet, and make an appointment before going to the bank. Second, go to the bank with an accountant and all of the necessary financial information and demonstrate to the banker that you're a person of good character: civic minded and respected in business and community circles. Finally, ask for all the money you need, be specific, and be prepared to personally guarantee the loan.

## Writing a Business Plan

A good business plan takes a long time to write, but you've got to convince your readers (e.g., prospective lenders and investors) in five minutes not to throw it away. While there is no such thing as a perfect business plan, prospective entrepreneurs do think out the smallest details. Jerrold Carrington of Inroads Capital Partners advises that one of the most important parts of the business plan is the executive summary. The summary has to catch the reader's interest. Bankers receive business plans every day. "You better grab me up front," says Carrington. Figure 7.6 gives you an outline of a comprehensive business plan.

Getting the completed business plan into the right hands is almost as important as getting the right information into the plan. Finding proper funding requires research. Next, we will discuss some of the many sources of money available to new business ventures. All of them call for a comprehensive business plan. The time and effort you invest before starting a business will pay off many times over. With small businesses, the big payoff is survival.

**FIGURE** | **7.6**

**Sample Outline of a Business Plan**

**LENGTH OF A COMPREHENSIVE BUSINESS PLAN**

A good business plan is between 25 and 50 pages long and takes at least six months to write.

**Cover letter**

Only one thing is certain when you go hunting for money to start a business: You won't be the only hunter out there. You need to make potential funders want to read your business plan instead of the hundreds of others on their desks. Your cover letter should summarize the most attractive points of your project in as few words as possible. Be sure to address the letter to the potential investor by name. "To Whom It May Concern" or "Dear Sir" is not the best way to win an investor's support.

**Section 1—Executive Summary**

Begin with a two-page or three-page management summary of the proposed venture. Include a short description of the business, and discuss major goals and objectives.

**Section 2—Company Background**

Describe company operations to date (if any), potential legal considerations, and areas of risk and opportunity. Summarize the firm's financial condition, and include past and current balance sheets, income and cash-flow statements, and other relevant financial records. (You will learn about these financial statements in Chapter 16.) It is also wise to include a description of insurance coverage. Investors want to be assured that death or other mishaps do not pose major threats to the company.

**Section 3—Management Team**

Include an organization chart, job descriptions of listed positions, and detailed resumés of the current and proposed executives. A mediocre idea with a proven management team is funded more often than a great idea with an inexperienced team. Managers should have expertise in all disciplines necessary to start and run a business. If not, mention outside consultants who will serve in these roles and describe their qualifications.

**Section 4—Financial Plan**

Provide five-year projections for income, expenses, and funding sources. Don't assume the business will grow in a straight line. Adjust your planning to allow for funding at various stages of the company's growth. Explain the rationale and assumptions used to determine the estimates. Assumptions should be reasonable and based on industry/historical trends. Make sure all totals add up and are consistent throughout the plan. If necessary, hire a professional accountant or financial analyst to prepare these statements.

Stay clear of excessively ambitious sales projections; rather, offer best-case, expected, and worst-case scenarios. These not only reveal how sensitive the bottom line is to sales fluctuations but also serve as good management guides.

**Section 5—Capital Required**

Indicate the amount of capital needed to commence or continue operations, and describe how these funds are to be used. Make sure the totals are the same as the ones on the cash-flow statement. This area will receive a great deal of review from potential investors, so it must be clear and concise.

**Section 6—Marketing Plan**

Don't underestimate the competition. Review industry size, trends, and the target market segment. Discuss strengths and weaknesses of the good or service. The most important things investors want to know are what makes the product more desirable than what's already available and whether the product can be patented. Compare pricing to the competition's. Forecast sales in dollars and units. Outline sales, advertising, promotion, and public relations programs. Make sure the costs agree with those projected in the financial statements.

**Section 7—Location Analysis**

In retailing and certain other industries, the location of the business is one of the most important factors. Provide a comprehensive demographic analysis of consumers in the area of the proposed business as well as a traffic-pattern analysis and vehicular and pedestrian counts.

**Section 8—Manufacturing Plan**

Describe minimum plant size, machinery required, production capacity, inventory and inventory-control methods, quality control, plant personnel requirements, and so on. Estimates of product costs should be based on primary research.

**Section 9—Appendix**

Include all marketing research on the good or service (off-the-shelf reports, article reprints, etc.) and other information about the product concept or market size. Provide a bibliography of all the reference materials you consulted. This section should demonstrate that the proposed company won't be entering a declining industry or market segment.

**FIGURE** | **7.7**

**Sources of Financing for SMEs**
Many companies use multiple sources of financing. Half of all SMEs rely on financial services firms to provide them with business debt financing. Beyond business credit, however, SMEs also make use of other sources of financing such as:

- supplier credit (51.9%)
- personal savings (56.9%)
- personal credit cards (50.0%)
- retained earnings (53.7%)
- business credit cards (48.4%)
- personal lines of credit (45.2%)
- leasing (30.4%)
- personal loans (33.2%)
- loans from friends and relatives (24.2%)
- government lending agencies (20.9%)
- angel investment (15.1%)

Source: "Where Does the Money Come From?" Canadian Bankers Association, 2008, www.cba.ca.

**venture capitalists (VCs)**
Individuals or companies that invest in new businesses in exchange for partial ownership of those businesses.

**angel investors**
Private individuals who invest their own money in potentially hot new companies before they go public.

# Getting Money to Fund a Small Business

An entrepreneur has several potential sources of capital for a small business, as listed in Figure 7.7. Half of all SMEs rely on financial services firms to provide them with business financing. While banks provide 54 percent of this financing, credit unions and caisses populaires, finance companies, insurance companies, and venture capital/ investment funds also play a significant role in financing SMEs.[28]

Investors known as **venture capitalists (VCs)** may finance your project—for a price. Venture capitalists may ask for a hefty stake (as much as 60 percent) in your company in exchange for the cash to start your business. If the VC demands too large a stake, you could lose control of the business. This may have been the case with Chris & Larry's Clodhoppers. Chris Emery and Larry Finnson started Krave's in 1996. Their Clodhopper treats are bite-sized pieces of graham wafer and chocolate candy. By the mid-2000s, they had accepted venture capital financing and management advice when their sales kept growing but they were still broke. In October 2005, Finnson stepped down as president and he and Emery turned the running of the company over to a management company so they could focus on marketing. Five months later, the assets of the company were sold to Brookside Foods. Harold Heide, vice-president of investments at ENSIS Growth Fund, which owned about 45 percent of Krave's, said the deal made sense: "The time had simply come in ENSIS's investing cycle to sell its position in Krave's."[29]

According to *PROFIT*'s "Financing Guide," financing from VCs ranges from $500,000 to $20 million.[30] In 2008, the average amount invested per company was $3.6 million, with total venture capital investment in Canada reaching $1.3 billion.[31] If you are interested in finding out more, visit Canada's Venture Capital & Private Equity Association (www.cvca.ca), which represents Canada's venture capital and private equity industry.

An alternate source of funds, if you cannot get venture capital, is to consider finding an angel investor. **Angel investors** are private individuals who invest their own money in potentially hot new companies before they go public.[32] Angel investors usually target their support (generally $20,000 to $500,000) to pre-start-up and early-stage companies with high growth prospects.[33] If your proposed venture does require millions of dollars to start, experts recommend that you talk with at least five investment firms and their clients to find the right VCs.

There are many information sources for financing. You can visit government sites such as the Business Development Bank of Canada or Industry Canada's Financing Web site. The Industry Canada site provides information aimed at helping small- and medium-sized businesses, companies, and entrepreneurs in Canada find financing from public- and private-sector sources. You can also find a listing of federal and provincial government assistance programs, tax incentives for small businesses, and a listing of financial providers, including

*Dragon's Den* is a CBC production where aspiring entrepreneurs pitch their business concepts and products to a panel of Canadian business moguls. If you can convince them to lend you money, they will expect ownership in the business in exchange.

VCs. Examples of government grants and programs include the Scientific Research and Experimental Development program, the National Research Council's Industrial Research Assistance Program, and Ontario Centres of Excellence Investment Accelerator Fund.[34] Another useful source is www. canadianbusiness.com/entrepreneur/financing.

Obtaining money from banks, VCs, and government sources can be a challenge for most small businesses. (You will learn more about financing in Chapter 17.) Those who do survive the planning and financing of their new ventures are eager to get their businesses up and running. Your success in running a business depends on many factors. Three important factors for success are knowing your customers, managing your employees, and keeping efficient records. These topics will be discussed next.

## Knowing Your Customers

One of the most important elements of small-business success is knowing the market. In business, a **market** consists of people with unsatisfied wants and needs who have both the resources and the willingness to buy. For example, we can confidently state that many of our students have the willingness to own a brand new car. However, few of them have the resources necessary to satisfy this want. Would they be considered a good market for a luxury car dealer to pursue?

Cervélo Cycles is the world's largest manufacturer of time trial and triathlon bikes. Cervélo founders and co-owners Phile White (left) and Gerard Vroomen (right) have launched their own Cervélo TestTeam. In 2008, the Tour de France was won aboard a Cervélo bike.

Once you have identified your market and its needs, you must set out to fill those needs. The way to meet your customers' needs is to offer top quality at a fair price with great service. Remember, it isn't enough to get customers—you have to keep them. Everything must be geared to bring the customers the satisfaction they deserve. Gérard Vroomen and Phil White founded Cervélo Cycles Inc. when they were engineering students and wished to market the new time-trial bikes they were developing. Today, the company produces road and triathlon racing bikes, and Cervélo is internationally recognized as one of the most innovative bike manufacturers. According to Vroomen, "Our basic philosophy is that we start by having very strong products. It's much easier to market a good product than a bad one."[35]

**market**
People with unsatisfied wants and needs who have both the resources and the willingness to buy.

One of the greatest advantages that small businesses have over larger ones is the ability to know their customers better and to adapt quickly to their ever-changing needs. You will gain more insights about marketing in Chapters 14 and 15. Now let's consider the importance of effectively managing the employees who help you serve your market.

## Managing Employees

As a business grows, it becomes impossible for an entrepreneur to oversee every detail, even if he or she is working 60 hours per week. This means that hiring, training, and motivating employees are critical.

It is not easy to find good, qualified help when you offer less money, fewer benefits (if any), and less room for advancement than larger firms do. That is one reason why employee relations is such an important part of small-business management. Employees of small companies are often more satisfied with their jobs than are their counterparts in big business. Why? Quite often they find their jobs more challenging, their ideas more accepted, and their bosses more respectful.

Often entrepreneurs reluctantly face the reality that to keep growing, they must delegate authority to others. Nagging questions such as "Who should be delegated authority?" and "How much control should they have?" create perplexing problems.

This can be a particularly touchy issue in small businesses with long-term employees, and in family businesses. As you might expect, entrepreneurs who have built their companies from scratch often feel compelled to promote employees who have been with them from the start—even when those employees aren't qualified to serve as managers. Common sense probably tells you this could be detrimental to the business.

The same can be true of family-run businesses that are expanding. Attitudes such as "You can't fire family" or "You must promote certain workers because they're family" can hinder growth. Entrepreneurs can best serve themselves and the business if they gradually recruit and groom employees for management positions. By doing this, entrepreneurs can enhance trust and the support of the manager among other employees and themselves.

When Heida Thurlow of Chantal Cookware suffered an extended illness, she let her employees handle the work she once had insisted on doing herself. The experience transformed her company from an entrepreneurial one into a managerial one. She says, "Over the long run that makes us stronger than we were." You'll learn more about managing employees in Chapters 11 to 13.

## Keeping Records

Small-business owners often say that the most important assistance they received in starting and managing the business involved accounting. A business person who sets up an effective accounting system early will save much grief later. Computers simplify record keeping and enable a small-business owner to follow the progress of the business (sales, expenses, profits) on a daily basis. An inexpensive computer system can also help owners with other record-keeping chores, such as inventory control, customer records, and payroll.

A good accountant is invaluable in setting up such systems and showing you how to keep the system operating smoothly. Many business failures are caused by poor accounting practices. A good accountant can help make decisions such as whether to buy or lease equipment and whether to own or rent the building. Help may also be provided for tax planning, financial forecasting, choosing sources of financing, and writing up requests for funds.[36]

Other small-business owners may tell you where to find an accountant experienced in small business. It pays to shop around for advice. You'll learn more about accounting in Chapter 16.

## Looking for Help

Small-business owners have learned, sometimes the hard way, that they need outside consulting advice early in the process. This is especially true of legal, tax, and accounting advice but may also be true of marketing, finance, and other areas. Most small- and medium-sized firms cannot afford to hire such experts as employees, so they must turn to outside assistance. As a start, ask friends, other entrepreneurs, or family to recommend someone.

A necessary and invaluable aide is a competent, experienced lawyer—one who knows and understands small businesses. Partners have a way of forgetting agreements unless the contract is written by a lawyer and signed. Lawyers can help with a variety of matters, including leases, contracts, and protection against liabilities.

Marketing decisions should be made long before a product is produced or a store is opened. An inexpensive marketing research study may help you determine where to locate, whom to select as your target market, and what would be an effective strategy for reaching those people. Thus, a marketing consultant with small-business experience can be of great help to you.

Given the marketing power of the Internet, your business will benefit from a presence on the Internet, even if you do not sell products or services directly from the Web. This applies to both small and large companies. For example, while the Forzani Group Ltd. is the largest and only national sporting goods retailer in Canada, you can visit its site to view products but you cannot buy anything online.[37]

Two other invaluable experts are a commercial account officer and an insurance agent. The commercial account officer can help you design an acceptable business plan and give you valuable financial advice as well as lend you money when you need it. An insurance agent will explain the risks associated with a small business and how to cover them most efficiently with insurance and other means (e.g., safety devices, sprinkler systems).

Often, local schools have business professors who will advise small-business owners for a small fee or for free. Some universities have clubs or programs that provide consulting services by master of business administration (MBA) candidates for a nominal fee. Does your school provide such services?

It also is wise to seek the counsel of other small-business owners. Other sources of counsel include local chambers of commerce, the Better Business Bureau, national and local trade associations (such as the Canadian Federation of Independent Business), the business reference section of your library, and many small business-related sites on the Internet. Some have been noted in this chapter.

# GOING INTERNATIONAL: SMALL-BUSINESS PROSPECTS

As we noted in Chapter 3, the world market is a much larger, much more lucrative market for small businesses than Canada is alone. In spite of that potential, most small businesses still do not think internationally, and only a small percentage of small businesses export.

Why are so many companies missing the boat to the huge global markets? Primarily because the voyage involves a few major hurdles: (1) financing is often difficult to find, (2) many would-be exporters don't know how to get started, (3) potential global business people do not understand the cultural differences of prospective markets, and (4) the bureaucratic paperwork can threaten to bury a small business. See the Reaching Beyond Our Borders box for a story about how one company has become a leader in its field.

Besides the fact that most of the world's market lies outside of Canada, there are other good reasons for going international. For instance, exporting products can absorb excess inventory, soften downturns in the domestic market, and extend product lives. It can also spice up dull routines.

Jen Kluger and Suzie Orol met while studying for their business degrees. They set out to build their company, Foxy Originals, with a vision: high-style fashion jewellery accessible to young women. Upon graduation, they focused full-time on their business. Their products are found in hundreds of stores across North America and they are quickly expanding beyond. What are some challenges they might have encountered in global markets?

Small businesses have several advantages over large businesses in international trade:

- overseas buyers enjoy dealing with individuals rather than with large corporate bureaucracies
- small companies usually can begin shipping much faster
- small companies provide a wide variety of suppliers
- small companies can provide more personal service and more undivided attention, because each overseas account is a major source of business.

The growth potential of small businesses overseas is phenomenal. This is why there are many organizations that offer assistance. Some of these have been cited in this chapter as well as in Chapter 4. Web-based business applications are helping small businesses cross boundaries like never before and, in some instances, levelling some of the advantages that large businesses traditionally have had.

## Progress Assessment

- What are the five functions of business?
- There are nine sections in the business plan outline in this chapter. Can you describe at least five of those sections now?
- What are some of the advantages that small businesses have over large businesses in selling in global markets?

## SUMMARY

**LO ▶ 1** Explain why people are willing to become entrepreneurs, and describe the attributes of successful entrepreneurs.

1. There are many reasons why people are willing to take the risks of entrepreneurship.

**What are significant differences between the entrepreneurial venture and the small business?**
Entrepreneurial ventures differ from small businesses in four ways: amount of wealth creation, speed of wealth creation, risk, and innovation.

**What are a few of the reasons people start their own businesses?**
Reasons include profit, independence, opportunity, and challenge.

**What are the attributes of successful entrepreneurs?**
Successful entrepreneurs are self-directed, determined, action-oriented, highly energetic, tolerant of uncertainty, and able to learn quickly.

**LO ▶ 2** Discuss the importance of small business to the Canadian economy.

2. Businesses employing fewer than 50 employees account for approximately 95 percent of all employer businesses.

**What does the "small" in small business mean?**
A small business is often defined as a business that is independently owned and operated, is not dominant in its field, and meets certain standards of size in terms of employees or annual revenues. Many institutions define small business according to their own needs.

**Why are small businesses important to the Canadian economy?**
Small business that have fewer than 100 employees contribute approximately 26 percent to Canada's gross domestic product. Perhaps more important to tomorrow's graduates, small businesses employ a large portion of the total private labour force.

3. Thousands of businesses enter and exit the marketplace throughout the year.

**LO ▶ 3** Summarize the major causes of small-business failure.

**How many small businesses fail each year?**

Statistics Canada reports that 60 percent of micro-enterprises fail within their first four years, with a slightly lower percentage (58 percent) for businesses with five to ninety-nine employees.

**Why do so many small businesses fail?**

Many small businesses fail because of managerial incompetence and inadequate financial planning. See Figure 7.4 for a list of causes of small-business failure. Some of these causes include attempting to do too much business with too little capital, underestimating how much time it will take to build a market, and not allowing for setbacks and unexpected expenses.

**What factors increase the chances for success?**

Figure 7.5 outlines some situations for small-business success. This includes whether the product is not easily made by mass-production techniques, whether sales are not large enough to appeal to a large firm, and whether the owner pays attention to new competitors.

4. Most people have no idea how to go about starting a small business.

**LO ▶ 4** List ways to learn about how small businesses operate.

**What hints would you give someone who wants to learn about starting a small business?**

An entrepreneur can improve the odds by learning from others. First, take courses and talk with some small-business owners. Second, get some experience working for others. Third, take over a successful firm. Finally, study the latest in small-business management techniques, including the use of computers for things such as payroll, inventory control, and mailing lists.

5. Writing a business plan is the first step in organizing a business.

**LO ▶ 5** Analyze what it takes to start and run a small business.

**What goes into a business plan?**

See Figure 7.6 to see what goes into a business plan. A business plan includes a section on company background, the financial plan, and the location analysis.

**What sources of funds should someone wanting to start a new business consider investigating?**

A new entrepreneur has several sources of capital: personal savings, relatives, banks, finance companies, venture capital organizations, government agencies, angel investors, and more.

**What are some of the special problems that small-business owners have in dealing with employees?**

Small-business owners often have difficulty finding competent employees and grooming employees for management responsibilities.

**Where can potential entrepreneurs find help in starting their businesses?**

Help can be found from many sources: accountants, lawyers, marketing researchers, loan officers, insurance agents, the Business Development Bank of Canada, and even professors.

**What online sources are available to assist entrepreneurs?**

Entrepreneurs can start by visiting government sources, such as the Industry Canada Web site. Financial services providers, such as RBC Financial Group and CIBC, also have sites dedicated to small businesses.

**LO ▸ 6** Outline the advantages and disadvantages that small businesses have in entering global markets.

6. The future growth of some small businesses is in foreign markets.

**What are some advantages small businesses have over large businesses in global markets?**
Foreign buyers enjoy dealing with individuals rather than large corporations because (1) small companies provide a wider variety of suppliers and can ship products more quickly and (2) small companies give more personal service.

**Why don't more small businesses start trading internationally?**
There are several reasons: (1) financing is often difficult to find, (2) many people don't know how to get started, (3) many do not understand the cultural differences in foreign markets, and (4) the bureaucratic red tape is often overwhelming.

## KEY TERMS

angel investors  222

business establishment  211

business plan  220

employer business  211

entrepreneurial team  206

entrepreneurship  200

incubators  210

intrapreneurs  209

market  223

micro-enterprise  207

micropreneurs  207

small and medium-sized enterprises (SMEs)  205

small business  211

venture capitalists (VCs)  222

## CRITICAL THINKING

1. There was mention in the chapter that small businesses continue to be feeders for future large businesses. As they prosper and develop new goods and services, they are often bought out by large companies. Is this good or bad? Should we do anything about it? If so, what?

2. Are there any similarities between the characteristics demanded of an entrepreneur and those of a professional athlete? Would an athlete be a good prospect for entrepreneurship? Why or why not? Could teamwork be important in an entrepreneurial effort?

3. Imagine yourself starting a small business. What kind of business would it be? How much competition is there? What could you do to make your business more attractive than those of competitors? Would you be willing to work 60 to 70 hours a week?

## DEVELOPING WORKPLACE SKILLS

1. Find issues of *Canadian Business*, *Canadian Business Franchise*, and *PROFIT* magazines in the library, your local bookstore, or on the Internet. Read about the entrepreneurs who are heading today's dynamic new businesses. Write a profile about one entrepreneur.

2. Select a small business that looks attractive as a career possibility for you. Talk to at least one person who manages such a business. Ask how he or she started the business. Ask about financing, personnel problems (hiring, firing, training, scheduling), accounting problems, and other managerial matters. Prepare a summary of your findings, including whether the job was rewarding, interesting, and challenging—and why or why not.

3. Contact a government agency such as Export Development Canada or Business Development Bank of Canada. Write a brief summary of the services that they provide for small businesses. (Hint: Each organization has a Web site: www.edc.ca and www.bdc.ca.)

4. Contact a local bank and make an appointment to speak with a commercial accounts officer. Ask this person what a small business owner should consider if she or he is looking for financing. Discuss other sources of financing that might be available to an entrepreneur. Find out what resources this bank has available to assist small-business owners. Bring this information to class and share it with your peers.

5. There has been some discussion in this chapter about entrepreneurship and traits of entrepreneurs. In a group, highlight the differences between a business person and an entrepreneur.

## TAKING IT TO THE NET 1

www.mcgrawhillconnect.ca

### Purpose

To assess your potential to succeed as an entrepreneur.

### Exercise

Go to www.bizmove.com/other/quiz.htm and take the interactive entrepreneurial quiz to find out if you have the qualities needed to be a successful entrepreneur.

## TAKING IT TO THE NET 2

www.mcgrawhillconnect.ca

### Purpose

To write a business plan.

### Exercise

Sometimes one of the most difficult tasks in writing a business plan is knowing where to start. One source is *Canadian Business*'s Interactive Business Planner, which assists entrepreneurs in preparing a three-year business plan for their new or existing business.

Go to http://www.canadabusiness.ca/ibp/eng/intro.cfm. How will this tool assist an entrepreneur in preparing a business plan? What are the key features in this tool?

## ANALYZING MANAGEMENT DECISIONS

### Starting a Small Business While in School

Milun Tesovic, co-founder and owner of Metroleap Media Inc., was named the 2009 national CIBC Student Entrepreneur of the Year by Advancing Canadian Entrepreneurship Inc. (ACE). The company won over the judges because of the accomplishments Tesovic has achieved as a small-business owner while attending Simon Fraser University as a full-time student. Started in 2004, the company hosts a music lyric Web site (www.metrolyrics.com) that provides music lovers with the written lyrics of their favourite songs. In creating a market and revenue stream for the music industry, Metroleap Media Inc. was named the second-largest music Web site online (as of January 2009 by Hitwise), reaching 32 million visitors per month. It has been growing 8 percent month over month.

Tesovic competed at the national level against five other regional champions, to a panel of 30 top executives.

In addition to the national title, he received a $10,000 cash prize. "You always hear people say that the youth of today are the future," says Tesovic. "...this Student Entrepreneur Competition puts that saying into perspective. I am proud to be representing Canada at the Global Student Entrepreneur Awards so I can demonstrate the amazing accomplishments students can do alongside a full course load. For me, ACE's Student Entrepreneur Competition has been a great source of publicity and recognition. Most importantly, it has put me in touch with other young entrepreneurs from across Canada."

Sources: "Milun Tesovic Named 2009 National Student Entrepreneur Competition Champion," Advancing Canadian Entrepreneurship Inc., 7 May 2009, http://www.acecanada.ca/news/newsItem.cfm?cms_news_id=32105.07.2009; and "British Columbia Student Entrepreneur Provincial Champion Named," Advancing Canadian Entrepreneurship Inc., 24 February 2009, http://www.acecanada.ca/news/newsItem.cfm?cms_news_id=277.

## Discussion Questions

1. What are the advantages and potential problems of starting a business while in school?

2. What kinds of entrepreneurs are operating around your school? Talk to them and learn from their experiences.

3. What opportunities exist for satisfying student needs at your school? Pick one idea, write a business plan, and discuss it in class (unless it is so good you don't want to share it; in that case, good luck).

## RUNNING CASE

### Canadian Tire Corporation, Ltd.: Then and Now

In 1913, there were only 23,700 cars in Canada, but by 1922, the number had jumped to 210,333 in Ontario alone. That year, with a combined savings of $1,800, two brothers, John W. Billes and Alfred J. Billes, bought Hamilton Tire and Garage Ltd. in Toronto's east end. The brothers stocked a small range of repair parts for the two most popular car makes, tires, batteries, and a homemade brand of antifreeze at a time when Toronto's 40,000 cars were being accepted as transportation. A big part of their early earnings came from renting out parking spaces in their heated garage—a necessity in those days if a car was to start on a cold morning.

In 1927, Canadian Tire Corporation, Limited, was officially incorporated. "We chose Canadian Tire," A.J. Billes later recalled, "because it sounded big." From across the country, people began writing to the store, looking for automotive parts that were hard to find in more isolated areas. In 1928, to serve this market, the brothers produced their first catalogue featuring tire values on one side, and a handy road map of Ontario on the back.

Today, Canadian Tire Corporation, Limited, is Canada's most-shopped general merchandise retailer. As a public corporation, it generated net earnings of approximately $374.2 billion in 2008. Reporting to the parent corporation are five interrelated businesses: Canadian Tire Retail (CTR), PartSource, Canadian Tire Petroleum (CTP), Canadian Tire Financial Services (CTFS), and Mark's Work Wearhouse.

CTR operates 475 stores from coast to coast through its network of entrepreneurial associate dealers. Together, these stores offer customers a unique mix of products and services through three specialty categories: automotive parts, accessories, and service; sports and leisure products; and home products. Its Web site, www.canadiantire.ca, offers Canadians the opportunity to shop online and is among the country's busiest e-commerce sites.

PartSource is an automotive parts specialty chain with 86 stores designed to meet the needs of major purchasers of automotive parts. This includes professional automotive installers and serious do-it-yourselfers.

CTP is one of the country's largest and most productive independent retailers of gasoline, operating 273 gas bars, 266 convenience stores and kiosks, and 74 car washes. Petroleum is an important component of the company's total offering, giving customers discounts on store merchandise as well as loyalty rewards with every purchase.

As the financial arm of Canadian Tire Corporation, Ltd. (Canadian Tire), Canadian Tire Financial Services (CTFS) primarily engages in financing and managing the Canadian Tire Options® MasterCard for more than five million card members. CTFS also markets related financial products and services to retail and petroleum customers including personal loans, insurance and warranty products, and emergency roadside assistance through the Canadian Tire Auto Club. A banking pilot is currently underway at Canadian Tire Bank offering high-interest savings accounts, guaranteed investment certificates, residential mortgages, and the One-and-Only™ account.

Mark's Work Wearhouse is one of the country's leading apparel retailers, operating 372 stores in Canada. Under the Clothes that Work™ marketing strategy, Mark's sells apparel and footwear in work, work-related, casual, and active-wear categories, as well as health-care and business-to-business apparel. Its Web site, www.marks.com, offers Canadians the opportunity to shop for Mark's products online.

Source: "Corporate Profile," Canadian Tire Corporation, Limited, 2009, http://corp.canadiantire.ca/EN/AboutUs/Pages/CorporateProfile.aspx.

## Discussion Questions

1. Entrepreneurs have played a major role in developing the Canadian economy. Visit http://corp.canadiantire.ca/EN/BusinessOpportunities/RetailOwnership/Pages/FAQs.aspx to learn read some commonly-asked questions by those considering applying for a store. How much does it cost to invest in an CTR store? What qualifications are needed in a Dealer? (Note that this term is used in the place of franchisee.)

2. What are some advantages and disadvantages to becoming an Associate Dealer?

3. What are some advantages and disadvantages of being a wholly owned subsidiary, as is the case for Canadian Tire Financial Services?

# Entrepreneur Readiness Questionnaire

Not everyone is cut out to be an entrepreneur. The fact is, though, that all kinds of people with all kinds of personalities have succeeded in starting small and large businesses. There are certain traits, however, that seem to separate those who'll be successful as entrepreneurs from those who may not be. The following questionnaire will help you determine in which category you fit. Take a couple of minutes to answer the questions and then score yourself at the end. Making a low score doesn't mean you won't succeed as an entrepreneur. It does indicate, however, that you may be happier working for someone else.

Each of the following items describes something that you may or may not feel represents your personality or other characteristics about you. Read each item and then circle the response (1, 2, 3, 4, or 5) that most nearly reflects the extent to which you agree or disagree that the item seems to fit you.

## Scoring:

Give yourself one point for each 1 or 2 response you circled for questions 1, 2, 6, 8, 10, 11, 16, 17, 21, 22, 23.

Give yourself one point for each 4 or 5 response you circled for questions 3, 4, 5, 7, 9, 12, 13, 14, 15, 18, 19, 20, 24, 25.

### Add your points to see how you rate in the following categories:

21–25 Your entrepreneurial potential looks great if you have a suitable opportunity to use it. What are you waiting for?

16–20 This is close to the high entrepreneurial range. You could be quite successful if your other talents and resources are right.

11–15 Your score is in the transitional range. With some serious work you can probably develop the outlook you need for running your own business.

6–10 Things look pretty doubtful for you as an entrepreneur. It would take considerable rearranging of your life philosophy and behaviour to make it.

0–5 Let's face it. Entrepreneurship isn't really for you. Still, learning what it's all about won't hurt anything.

| | RESPONSE | | | | |
|---|---|---|---|---|---|
| **Looking at my overall philosophy of life and typical behaviour, I would say that …** | Agree Completely (1) | Mostly Agree (2) | Partially Agree (3) | Mostly Disagree (4) | Disagree Completely (5) |
| 1. I am generally optimistic. | 1 | 2 | 3 | 4 | 5 |
| 2. I enjoy competing and doing things better than someone else. | 1 | 2 | 3 | 4 | 5 |
| 3. When solving a problem, I try to arrive at the best solution first without worrying about other possibilities. | 1 | 2 | 3 | 4 | 5 |
| 4. I enjoy associating with co-workers after working hours. | 1 | 2 | 3 | 4 | 5 |
| 5. If betting on a horse race I would prefer to take a chance on a high-payoff "long shot." | 1 | 2 | 3 | 4 | 5 |
| 6. I like setting my own goals and working hard to achieve them. | 1 | 2 | 3 | 4 | 5 |
| 7. I am generally casual and easy-going with others. | 1 | 2 | 3 | 4 | 5 |
| 8. I like to know what is going on and take action to find out. | 1 | 2 | 3 | 4 | 5 |
| 9. I work best when someone else is guiding me along the way. | 1 | 2 | 3 | 4 | 5 |
| 10. When I am right I can convince others. | 1 | 2 | 3 | 4 | 5 |
| 11. I find that other people frequently waste my valuable time. | 1 | 2 | 3 | 4 | 5 |
| 12. I enjoy watching football, baseball, and similar sports events. | 1 | 2 | 3 | 4 | 5 |
| 13. I tend to communicate about myself very openly with other people. | 1 | 2 | 3 | 4 | 5 |
| 14. I don't mind following orders from superiors who have legitimate authority. | 1 | 2 | 3 | 4 | 5 |
| 15. I enjoy planning things more than actually carrying out the plans. | 1 | 2 | 3 | 4 | 5 |
| 16. I don't think it's much fun to bet on a "sure thing." | 1 | 2 | 3 | 4 | 5 |
| 17. If faced with failure, I would shift quickly to something else rather than sticking to my guns. | 1 | 2 | 3 | 4 | 5 |
| 18. Part of being successful in business is reserving adequate time for family. | 1 | 2 | 3 | 4 | 5 |
| 19. Once I have earned something, I feel that keeping it secure is important. | 1 | 2 | 3 | 4 | 5 |
| 20. Making a lot of money is largely a matter of getting the right breaks. | 1 | 2 | 3 | 4 | 5 |
| 21. Problem solving is usually more effective when a number of alternatives are considered. | 1 | 2 | 3 | 4 | 5 |
| 22. I enjoy impressing others with the things I can do. | 1 | 2 | 3 | 4 | 5 |
| 23. I enjoy playing games like tennis and handball with someone who is slightly better than I am. | 1 | 2 | 3 | 4 | 5 |
| 24. Sometimes moral ethics must be bent a little in business dealings. | 1 | 2 | 3 | 4 | 5 |
| 25. I think that good friends would make the best subordinates in an organization. | 1 | 2 | 3 | 4 | 5 |

Source: Kenneth R. Van Voorhis, *Entrepreneurship and Small Business Management* (New York: Allyn & Bacon, 1980).

# PART 3

# CHAPTER 8

# Management and Leadership

## LEARNING OBJECTIVES

AFTER YOU HAVE READ
AND STUDIED THIS CHAPTER,
YOU SHOULD BE ABLE TO:

**LO ▸ 1** Explain how the changes that are occurring in the business environment are affecting the management function.

**LO ▸ 2** Describe the four functions of management.

**LO ▸ 3** Describe the different types of planning and the importance of decision making in choosing the best alternative.

**LO ▸ 4** Describe the organizing function of management and the three categories of skills needed by managers.

**LO ▸ 5** Explain the differences between leaders and managers, and describe the various leadership styles.

**LO ▸ 6** Summarize the five steps of the control function of management.

## PROFILE

## Getting to Know Richard (Rick) George of Suncor Energy

Suncor pioneered the commercial development of the oil sands. Suncor is a major North American energy producer and marketer with a team of over 6,500 employees. Operating an upgrader near Fort McMurray, Alberta, Suncor extracts and upgrades oil sands into high-quality, refinery-ready crude oil products. They also explore for and develop natural gas and sell refined products in Ontario and Colorado. Suncor is also investing in clean renewable energy sources. They have a number of wind power projects in operation with a total capacity of over 150 megawatts of renewable energy. In addition, they operate ethanol production facilities developing ethanol from non-food sources such as wood residues.

Rick George is the President and Chief Executive Officer of Suncor. Rick was named Canada's "Outstanding CEO of the Year" after leading a remarkable business turnaround at Suncor, lifting the company from an underperformer to a leader in Canada's energy industry. Since Rick took the company public in 1992, Suncor's market capitalization has increased to more than $40 billion from less than $1 billion.

Rick received the Canadian Business Leader Award in 2000 and served as chairperson of the Canadian Council of Chief Executives from 2003 to 2006. He has been a member of the North American Competitiveness Council since 2006 and was appointed an Officer of the Order of Canada in December 2007. He was a member of the Calgary Committee to End Homelessness in 2007 and chair of the 2008 Governor General's Canadian Leadership Conference. Originally from Brush, Colorado, Rick spent 10 years with Sun Company both in the United States and the United Kingdom. During this time he held various positions in project planning, production evaluation, exploration and production, and in the international oil business.

Rick led Suncor's move to new technologies and processes that propelled the oil sands from the margins of viability to a major Canadian energy source. Investment in technology to improve productivity and reduce environmental impacts has remained central to Rick's business philosophy. Suncor is one of Canada's top 20 research and development spenders, and putting technology into action forms a substantial part of the company's planned capital spending.

Under his leadership, Suncor has also invested outside the oil and gas industry to adopt a "parallel path" approach to reaching sustainable energy objectives: developing hydrocarbon resources responsibly to meet current needs while supporting the long-term diversification of energy sources. He talks about his concern for the environment both from the standpoint of current tar sands extraction and investment in renewable energy in the CEO messages on the Suncor Web site, which you are encouraged to visit.

With the majority of Suncor's business operations in northern Alberta, Rick has also taken a lead role in working with Canada's Aboriginal communities and leadership to build opportunities for aboriginals to participate in the growing economy. Under Rick's leadership, Aboriginal participation in Suncor's oil sands workforce has grown from less than 3 per cent to nearly 10 percent by 2005. From 2001 to 2003, Rick was co-chair of the Taking Pulse Initiative of the national Aboriginal Achievement Foundation.

In this chapter, you will read about management and the changes occurring in this area. Like George, most managers today are flexible and open to new ideas. They see opportunity and act much faster than they did in the past. They tend to give their workers more responsibility and authority and act more like leaders (visionaries) and coaches than hands-on managers who tell people what to do and how to do it.

Source: Suncor, 22 August 2008, www.suncor.com; and The Governor General's Canadian Leadership Conference, 22 August 2008, www.leadershipcanada.ca.

# MANAGERS' ROLES ARE EVOLVING

**resources**
A general term that incorporates human resources, natural resources, and financial resources.

Managers must practise the art of getting things done through organizational resources. **Resources** is a general term that incorporates human resources (e.g., employees), natural resources (e.g., raw materials), and financial resources (e.g., money). Resources include the factors of production, which were introduced in Chapter 1. Every business has scarce resources, and management is about deciding how to effectively use these scarce resources. It is for this reason that you will be introduced to the study of management and how the different functional areas of business (operations, human resources, and marketing are the first three covered in this book) must work together.

At one time, managers were called bosses, and their job consisted of telling people what to do and watching over them to be sure they did it. They were typically more proficient and knew more than the employees they supervised. Bosses tended to reprimand those who didn't do things correctly, and generally were impersonal. Many managers still behave that way. Perhaps you've witnessed such behaviour.

Today, management is becoming more progressive. Managers are educated to guide, train, support, motivate, and coach employees rather than tell them what to do.[1] When coaching, managers are trying to get the best out of their employees. Management is an assignment; coaching is a choice.[2]

Managers of high-tech firms realize that workers often know much more about technology than they do. Thus, most modern managers emphasize teamwork and co-operation rather than discipline and giving orders.[3] Managers in some high-tech firms and in progressive firms of all kinds tend to be friendly and generally treat employees as partners rather than unruly workers.

In the past, an employee would expect to work for the same company for many years, maybe even a lifetime. Similarly, companies would proudly acknowledge employees who achieved milestones in terms of duration of employment. Today, many companies don't hesitate to lay off employees, and employees don't hesitate to leave if their needs are not being met. Today's top leaders of Fortune 100 companies are younger, and more of them are female. They tend to move from one company to another as their careers unfold.[4] Traditional long-term contracts between management and employees—and the accompanying trust—are often no longer there. This increases the difficulty of the management task because managers must earn the trust of their employees, which includes rewarding them and finding other ways to encourage them to stay in the firm.

**management**
The process used to accomplish organizational goals through planning, organizing, leading, and controlling people and other organizational resources.

In general, management is studied more and more. Managers in the future are likely to be working in teams and assuming completely new roles in the firm. Further, they'll have to deal with a different set of issues in developing nations—see the Reaching Beyond Our Borders box.

**planning**
A management function that includes anticipating trends and determining the best strategies and tactics to achieve organizational goals and objectives.

What this means for you and other graduates of tomorrow is that successful management will demand a new kind of person: a skilled communicator and team player as well as a planner, coordinator, organizer, and supervisor. These trends will be addressed in the next few chapters to help you decide whether management is the kind of career you would like.

# FUNCTIONS OF MANAGEMENT

**organizing**
A management function that includes designing the structure of the organization and creating conditions and systems in which everyone and everything work together to achieve the organization's goals and objectives.

Well-known management consultant Peter Drucker says that managers give direction to their organizations, provide leadership, and decide how to use organizational resources to accomplish goals.[5] Such descriptions give you some idea of what managers do. In addition to those tasks, managers today must deal with conflict resolution, create trust in an atmosphere where trust has been badly shaken, and help create balance between work lives and family lives.[6] Managers look at the big picture, and their decisions make a major difference in organizations.[7] The following definition of management provides the outline of this chapter: **Management** is the process used to accomplish organizational goals through planning, organizing, leading, and controlling people and other organizational resources.

## Reaching Beyond Our Borders

### We Need Managers Over Here

OK, so there are many opportunities for growing a business overseas. What is keeping Canadian companies from expanding rapidly in global markets? Jack Welch, former CEO of General Electric, says the problem is not a lack of engineers or scientists; the problem is a lack of professional managers. Top managers from many companies are complaining that they can't find people to run their operations. That includes managers in all areas, from human resource management to finance. That means lots of opportunity for today's college graduates. If they can broaden their perspective to think of global markets, the potential is awesome.

The challenges are pretty daunting, however. Here is what the *Sloan Management Review* said in 2008: "Village roads can be impassable, home cooking is still a way of life, product prices can be below the cost of production . . . and local products often have generations

of loyal customers." Flexibility is a key to conquering such challenges. For example, companies are using motorcycles to get through on those supposedly impassible roads. Developing products that appeal to local markets is another strategy. That may mean selling cigarettes one by one instead of in packs. It may mean selling crank-up radios that run without electricity. The challenges can be fun as well as daunting. Sure, you'll have to learn how to negotiate with the government. Sure, you'll face all the issues discussed in this chapter. But the payoff is a rewarding managerial position in a growing country. Often the rewards far outstrip the costs.

Sources: Jack Welch and Suzy Welch, "Red Flags for the Decade Ahead," *BusinessWeek*, 19 May 2008; and Satish Shankar, Charles Ormiston, Nicolas Bloch, Robert Schaus and Vijay Vishwanath, "How to Win in Emerging Markets," *Sloan Management Review*, Spring 2008.

---

(Figure 8.1 provides a comprehensive listing of all the critical tasks in this process.)

**Planning** includes anticipating trends and determining the best strategies and tactics to achieve organizational goals and objectives. One of those objectives is to please customers.[8] The trend today is to have *planning teams* to help monitor the environment, find business opportunities, and watch for challenges. Planning is a key management function because the other management functions depend heavily on having a good plan.

**Organizing** includes designing the structure of the organization and creating conditions and systems in which everyone and everything work together to achieve the organization's goals and objectives.[9] Many of today's organizations are being designed around the customer. The idea is to design the firm so that everyone is working to please the customer at a profit. Thus, organizations must remain flexible and adaptable because customer needs change, and organizations must either change along with them or risk losing their business. General Motors, for example, has lost much of its customer base to more fuel-efficient cars.[10] It hopes to win them back by offering hydrogen-powered vehicles that could save consumers much money in fuel.[11]

Many managers today are working in teams, and this means working *with* employees rather than simply directing them. These teams are likely to be ethnically diverse and include people of varied ages and backgrounds. Since managers will function primarily as trainers, coaches, and motivators of teams, it is expected that member of the team will do year-end evaluations of the manager and vice versa. How do you think most managers will react to having lower-level employees evaluate *their* effectiveness?

**Leading** means creating a vision for the organization and communicating, guiding, training, coaching, and motivating others to work effectively to achieve the organization's goals and objectives. Researchers have spent a considerable amount of time studying motivation, given the direct relationship between motivation and output. This subject is explored further in Chapter 11. The trend is to empower employees, giving them as much freedom as possible to become self-directed and self-motivated. This function was once known as *directing*; that is, telling employees exactly what to do. In many smaller firms, that is still the role of managers. In most large modern firms, however, managers no longer tell people exactly what to do because knowledge workers and others often know how to do their jobs better than the manager. Nonetheless, leadership is necessary to keep employees focused on the right tasks at the right time along with training, coaching, motivating, and the other leadership tasks.[12]

**leading**
Creating a vision for the organization and guiding, training, coaching, and motivating others to work effectively to achieve the organization's goals and objectives.

**What Managers Do**
Some modern managers perform all of these tasks with the full co-operation and participation of workers. Empowering employees means allowing them to participate more fully in decision making.

**Planning**
- Setting organizational goals.
- Developing strategies to reach those goals.
- Determining resources needed.
- Setting precise standards.

**Organizing**
- Allocating resources, assigning tasks, and establishing procedures for accomplishing goals.
- Preparing a structure (organization chart) showing lines of authority and responsibility.
- Recruiting, selecting, training, and developing employees.
- Placing employees where they'll be most effective.

**Leading**
- Guiding and motivating employees to work effectively to accomplish organizational goals and objectives.
- Giving assignments.
- Explaining routines.
- Clarifying policies.
- Providing feedback on performance.

**Controlling**
- Measuring results against corporate objectives.
- Monitoring performance relative to standards.
- Rewarding outstanding performance.
- Taking corrective action when necessary.

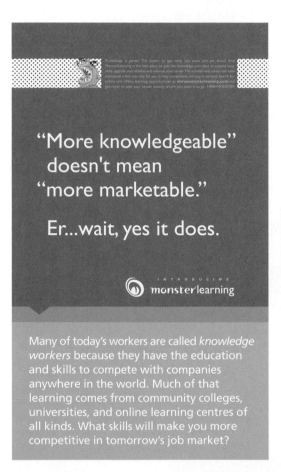

"More knowledgeable" doesn't mean "more marketable."

Er...wait, yes it does.

INTRODUCING
monster learning

Many of today's workers are called *knowledge workers* because they have the education and skills to compete with companies anywhere in the world. Much of that learning comes from community colleges, universities, and online learning centres of all kinds. What skills will make you more competitive in tomorrow's job market?

**controlling**
A management function that involves establishing clear standards to determine whether or not an organization is progressing toward its goals and objectives, rewarding people for doing a good job, and taking corrective action if they are not.

**Controlling** involves establishing clear standards to determine whether an organization is progressing toward its goals and objectives, rewarding people for doing a good job, and taking corrective action if they are not. Basically, it means measuring whether what actually occurs meets the organization's goals.

The four functions—planning, organizing, leading, and controlling—are the heart of management, so let's explore them in more detail. The process begins with planning; we'll look at that right after the Progress Assessment.

### Progress Assessment

- What is the definition of management used in this chapter?
- What are the four functions of management?

# PLANNING: CREATING A VISION BASED ON VALUES

Planning, the first managerial function, involves setting the organizational vision, values, goals, and objectives. Executives rate planning as the most valuable tool of their workbench. Part of the planning process involves the creation of a vision for the organization. A **vision** is more than a goal; it's an encompassing explanation of why the organization exists and where it's trying to head. A vision gives the organization a sense of purpose. **Values** are a set of fundamental beliefs that guide a business in the decisions they make. Values guide strategic planning through to day-to-day decisions by being mindful of how all stakeholders will be treated. Vision informs values, while values come alive through vision. Together, they unite workers in a common destiny. Managing an organization without first establishing a vision can be counterproductive. It's like motivating everyone in a rowboat to get really excited about going somewhere, but not telling them exactly where. As a result, the boat will just keep changing directions rather than speeding toward an agreed-on goal. Without a set of values, an organization has no basis for determining how their employees should interact with stakeholders. As a result, sustainable long-term relationships will be difficult.

Suncor's vision is "to become a sustainable energy company and so we manage our business to deliver superior shareholder returns, while providing social and economic benefits to our stakeholders and reducing the environmental impact of our operations and products." Notice the reference to corporate social responsibility, as discussed in Chapter 5, and to the environment, as seen in each chapter's Green Boxes. Their values include reference to safety, people and relationships, high performance, sustainability, and accountability.

A **mission statement** is an outline of the organization's fundamental purposes.[13] Mission statements are usually developed by top management, with some input from employees, depending on the size of the company. A meaningful mission statement should address:

- the organization's self-concept
- company philosophy and goals
- long-term survival
- customer needs
- social responsibility
- the nature of the company's product or service

Figure 8.2 contains Canadian Tire Financial Services' mission statement. How well does this mission statement address all of the issues listed above?

The mission statement becomes the foundation for setting specific goals and selecting and motivating employees. **Goals** are the broad, long-term accomplishments an organization wishes to attain. Goals need to be mutually agreed on by workers and management. Thus, goal setting is often a team process.

**Objectives** are specific, short-term statements detailing how to achieve the organization's goals. One of your goals for reading this chapter, for example, may be to learn basic concepts of management. An objective you could use to achieve this goal is to answer the chapter's Progress Assessment questions correctly. Objectives must be measurable. For example, you can measure your progress in answering questions by determining what percentage you answer correctly over time.

Planning is a continuous process. It's unlikely that a plan that worked yesterday would be successful in today's market. Most planning follows a pattern. The procedure you would follow in planning your life and career is basically the same as that used by businesses for their plans. Planning answers several fundamental questions for businesses:

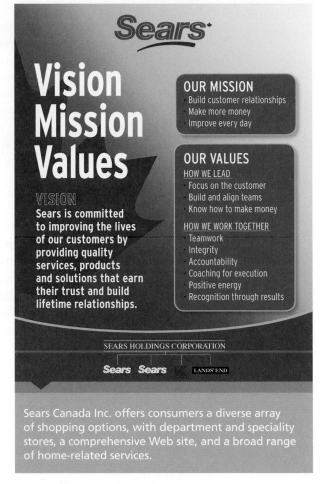

**OUR MISSION**
- Build customer relationships
- Make more money
- Improve every day

**OUR VALUES**
HOW WE LEAD
- Focus on the customer
- Build and align teams
- Know how to make money

HOW WE WORK TOGETHER
- Teamwork
- Integrity
- Accountability
- Coaching for execution
- Positive energy
- Recognition through results

VISION
Sears is committed to improving the lives of our customers by providing quality services, products and solutions that earn their trust and build lifetime relationships.

SEARS HOLDINGS CORPORATION

Sears Canada Inc. offers consumers a diverse array of shopping options, with department and speciality stores, a comprehensive Web site, and a broad range of home-related services.

**vision**
An encompassing explanation of why the organization exists and where it's trying to head.

**values**
A set of fundamental beliefs that guide a business in the decisions they make.

**mission statement**
An outline of the fundamental purposes of an organization.

**goals**
The broad, long-term accomplishments an organization wishes to attain.

**objectives**
Specific, short-term statements detailing how to achieve the organization's goals.

---

| FIGURE | 8.2 |
|---|---|

**Canadian Tire Financial Services' Mission Statement**

| Canadian Tire's vision comes to life through our Team Values: |
|---|
| We are *learners* … who thrive in a challenging and fast-paced environment. |
| We are *committed* … to operate with honesty, integrity and respect. |
| We are *owners* … with a passion to continuously improve. |
| We are *driven* … to help customers achieve their goals. |
| We are *accountable* … to ourselves and each other. |
| We are *leaders* … who perform with heart. |
| The Canadian Tire Way is our foundation and inspiration that will continue to guide our future growth and success. |

Source: Marco Marrone, president of Canadian Tire Financial Services.

1. What is the situation now? What trends are being observed in the business environment? What opportunities exist for meeting customers' needs? What products and customers are most profitable or will be most profitable? Why do people buy (or not buy) our products? Who are our major competitors? What threats are there to our business? These questions frame the **SWOT analysis**. This is an analysis of an organization's **S**trengths, **W**eaknesses, **O**pportunities, and **T**hreats—how can strengths be used and capitalized on, how can weaknesses be improved, how can opportunities be exploited, and how can threats be mitigated. Soliciting input from all key stakeholders, a company begins such a process with a general review of the business situation. Then it identifies its internal strengths and weaknesses, relative to its competitors. These strengths and weaknesses are for the most part within the control of the organization. They include elements that are referred to as PRIMO-F: people, resources, innovation and ideas, marketing, operations, and finance. Next, a business environment analysis (you were introduced to some elements, such as the legal environment, in Chapter 1) is conducted. Opportunities and threats in the marketplace are identified—and, while they cannot always be controlled or anticipated, they most definitely affect the organization. Opportunities and threats include concepts referred to as PESTLE: political, economic, social, technological, legal, and environmental. Given all of this information gathered in the SWOT analysis, a company can then create an action plan to address the business situation identified. Figure 8.3 lists some of the potential issues companies consider when conducting a SWOT analysis: Where do we want to go? How much growth do we want? What is our profit goal? What are our social objectives? What are our personal development objectives? A SWOT analysis is framed by the vision and when completed may result in the vision being revisited. The Dealing With Change box highlights how a large department store chain has used the results of such an analysis to plan a successful course of action.

2. How can we get there from here? This is the most important part of planning. It takes four forms: strategic, tactical, operational, and contingency. See Figure 8.4 for a visual of this. Notice the continuous connection between the four forms. Not only does this illustrate the relationship between them, but also that planning is a continuous process, which each of the forms being informed by another of the forms.

**Strategic planning** outlines how the company will meet its objectives and goals. It provides the foundation for the policies, procedures, and strategies for obtaining and using resources to achieve those goals. In this definition, policies are broad guides to action,

---

**SWOT analysis**
A planning tool used to analyze an organization's strengths, weaknesses, opportunities, and threats.

**strategic planning**
The process of determining the major goals of the organization and the policies and strategies for obtaining and using resources to achieve those goals.

---

| **FIGURE** | **8.3** |

**SWOT Analysis**
This figure identifies potential strengths, weaknesses, opportunities, and threats that organizations may discover in a SWOT analysis.

**Potential Internal Strengths**
- an acknowledged market leader
- core competencies in key areas
- proven and respected management team

**Potential Internal Weaknesses**
- no clear strategic direction
- weak market image
- subpar profitability

**Potential External Opportunities**
- falling trade barriers in attractive foreign markets
- new government policies (e.g., incentives for R&D, lower taxes, industry deregulation)
- increases in market demand (due to changing buyer needs and tastes, growing incomes)

**Potential External Threats**
- recession and changing (negative) economic conditions
- introduction of substitute products (by competitors)
- costly regulatory requirements

## DEALING with CHANGE

### Hitting the Retail Bull's Eye

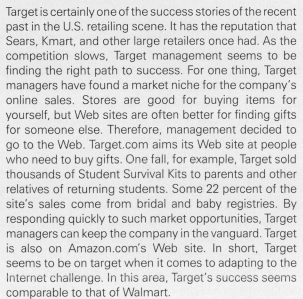

Target is certainly one of the success stories of the recent past in the U.S. retailing scene. It has the reputation that Sears, Kmart, and other large retailers once had. As the competition slows, Target management seems to be finding the right path to success. For one thing, Target managers have found a market niche for the company's online sales. Stores are good for buying items for yourself, but Web sites are often better for finding gifts for someone else. Therefore, management decided to go to the Web. Target.com aims its Web site at people who need to buy gifts. One fall, for example, Target sold thousands of Student Survival Kits to parents and other relatives of returning students. Some 22 percent of the site's sales come from bridal and baby registries. By responding quickly to such market opportunities, Target managers can keep the company in the vanguard. Target is also on Amazon.com's Web site. In short, Target seems to be on target when it comes to adapting to the Internet challenge. In this area, Target's success seems comparable to that of Walmart.

Target management has been less successful in competing with Walmart in the area of superstores. Target's superstores are less productive than its regular stores. Was it a mistake to go after Walmart's super-centres? Walmart has its own grocery warehouses,

giving it a cost advantage. Target could create its own distribution centres to become more competitive, but that is dangerous ground. Such centres are costly. Adapting to change is never easy, but adapting to Walmart is truly daunting. Target has its own image and its own customer base. Sometimes change is good and sometimes it's not. By listening to its customer base and responding appropriately, Target's managers should be able to expand and increase profits. That may mean sticking to what Target knows best and not venturing into Walmart's strengths. Or, it may not. That's the future challenge for Target's managers.

Walmart has entered the Canadian market, first with smaller scale department stores and a number of Sam's Club Wholesale outlets. More recently, they are focusing their expansion on their SuperStore format, aggressively expanding their produce offerings including grocery products. Target continues to stay away from the Canadian marketplace. There has been no public talk in the past few years about them coming to Canada, even with the continuing problems at The Bay.

Sources: Jim Collins, "Bigger, Better, Faster," *Fast Company*, June 2003, 74–78; www.target.com, 2005; and Michael Barbaro, "Pinch Me—Is That a Wal-Mart?" *The Washington Post*, 7 August 2005, F1, F6.

and strategies determine the best way to use resources. At the strategic planning stage, the company decides which customers to serve, what goods or services to sell, and the geographic areas in which the firm will compete.[14] For example, GM is going through the painful process of deciding which products to keep and which to cut.[15] Poor decision making in the past has had disastrous consequences on this company.

In today's rapidly changing environment, strategic planning is becoming more difficult because changes are occurring so fast that plans—even those set for just months into the future—may soon be obsolete.[16] Therefore, some companies are making shorter-

**FORMS OF PLANNING**

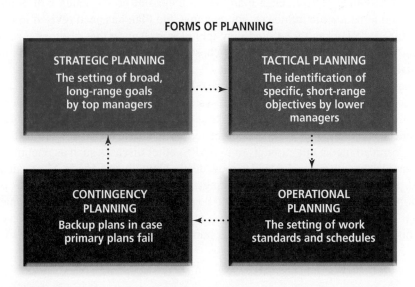

STRATEGIC PLANNING
The setting of broad, long-range goals by top managers

TACTICAL PLANNING
The identification of specific, short-range objectives by lower managers

CONTINGENCY PLANNING
Backup plans in case primary plans fail

OPERATIONAL PLANNING
The setting of work standards and schedules

**FIGURE | 8.4**

**Planning Functions**
Very few firms bother to make contingency plans. If something changes the market, such companies may be slow to respond. Most organization do strategic, tactical, and operational planning.

term plans that allow for quick responses to customer needs and requests.[17] The goal is to be flexible and responsive to the market.

**tactical planning**
The process of developing detailed, short-term statements about what is to be done, who is to do it, and how it is to be done.

**Tactical planning** is the process of developing detailed, short-term statements about what is to be done, who is to do it, and how it is to be done. Tactical planning is normally the responsibility of managers or teams of managers at *lower* levels of the organization, whereas strategic planning is the responsibility of the *top* managers of the firm (e.g., the president and vice-presidents of the organization). Tactical planning, for example, involves setting annual budgets and deciding on other details and activities necessary to meet the strategic objectives. If the strategic plan of a truck manufacturer, for example, is to sell more trucks in northern Canada, the tactical plan might be to fund more research of northern truck drivers' wants and needs, and to plan advertising to reach those customers.

**operational planning**
The process of setting work standards and schedules necessary to implement the company's tactical objectives.

**Operational planning** is the process of setting work standards and schedules necessary to implement the company's tactical objectives. Operational planning focuses on the specific responsibilities of supervisors, department managers, and individual employees. Operational plans can include operational budgets. You will read about budgets in more detail in Chapter 17. Or, The operational plan is the department manager's tool for daily and weekly operations. An operational plan could also include, say, the specific dates for certain truck parts to be completed and the quality specifications those parts must meet. You will read about operations management in more detail in Chapter 10.

**contingency planning**
The process of preparing alternative courses of action that may be used if the primary plans don't achieve the organization's objectives.

**Contingency planning** is the process of preparing alternative courses of action that may be used if the primary plans don't achieve the organization's objectives. The economic and competitive environments change so rapidly that it's wise to have alternative plans of action ready in anticipation of such changes. For example, if an organization doesn't meet its sales goals by a certain date, the contingency plan may call for more advertising or a cut in prices at that time. The global outbreak of SARS in 2003 forced many health agencies around the world to develop contingency plans to respond to this atypical pneumonia. The SARS experience (estimated to have cost the business community $50 billion) and mad cow disease ($7 billion and growing) have also forced companies in the private sector to develop contingency plans.[18]

Some believe that the H5N1 type of avian flu, which started in Korea in 2003 and has spread to other countries, or the H1N1 strain, sometimes referred to as swine flu, which gained prominence in 2009, is a pandemic-in-waiting. While no one knows conclusively when the next pandemic will occur, the World Health Organization warns that the global spread of a pandemic can't be stopped—but preparing properly will reduce its impact.[19] In response, the Public Health Agency of Canada, together with federal government departments and provincial and territorial governments, has taken many steps to protect Canadians from a possible influenza (flu) pandemic.[20] This includes maintaining the Canadian Pandemic Influenza Plan, which maps out how Canada will prepare for and respond to pandemic influenza. For example, the Plan has been revised in response to the 2009 H1N1 virus threat, and now includes an Annex that outlines a suggested planning framework for addressing the psychosocial implications of a pandemic influenza or any large-scale public health emergency.[21]

Some companies see opportunities where others see threats. Morneau Sobeco provides global benefits consulting, administration systems, and outsourcing services. It encourages companies to re-evaluate their thinking regarding contingency planning and the importance of anticipating health care–related emergencies (HREs). While there has been widespread media attention given to SARS, other diseases such as pneumonia and influenza (also known as the flu) lead to more deaths annually in Canada. Morneau Sobeco believes that most companies view contingency planning solely as a tool to prevent operational shutdowns. A company should be able to mitigate the potential damage and financial loss resulting from an unforeseen emergency or catastrophe. The benefits of developing an HRE contingency plan are numerous. However, the main goals of such

## I'd Rather Be Blue

Some of the best-managed organizations can be found in the most unusual situations. Consider, for example, three entrepreneurs whose product involved shaving their heads, slathering themselves with blue paint, and drumming on homemade instruments such as PVC pipe. Enter the Blue Man Group. Today the original Blue Men—Matt Goldman, Phil Stanton, and Chris Wink—manage an organization of over 500 employees, 70 of whom appear nightly as Blue Men in 12 cities around the world. Their Megastar World Tour included a number of shows in central Canada featuring their unique music, comedy, and multimedia theatrics.

Like the founders of any other company, the Blue Man Group creators knew they had to tinker with their product if they wanted to expand and be successful. Planning and organization were critical. The partners locked themselves away for several days to write a detailed 132-page Blue Man operating manual. Writing the manual made the partners realize the vast market potential for their concept, but it also taught them the importance of managing the product's growth and everyday operations. They decided that company decisions would not be made on a majority vote but rather by consensus among the three of them. That policy continues today.

Sources: Liz Welch, "How We Did It: The Blue Man Group," *Inc.*, August 2008; and Blue Man Group, www.blueman.com, accessed 29 January 2009.

initiatives are ensuring business continuity, reducing risk to employees and their dependants, and maintaining productivity, as well as minimizing the possibility of litigation.[22]

Crisis planning is a part of contingency planning. **Crisis planning** involves reacting to sudden changes in the environment. At the 16th World Conference on Disaster Management, Peter Power, a veteran of the anti-terrorism branch of the London Metropolitan Police, stated that "nowhere near enough" Canadian companies are ready to deal with the fallout from an environmental, accidental, technological, or terrorist-driven catastrophe.[23] Crisis planning can be especially challenging to medium-sized and smaller companies due to fewer resources, said Carolee Birchall, vice-president and senior risk officer of technology and solutions at BMO Bank of Montreal.[24] In short, crisis planning is a critical component of contingency planning that requires understanding and acceptance throughout the whole organization, regardless of its size. You will read more about risk management in Appendix D.

Planning is a key management function because the other management functions depend on having good plans. Starting with a directional plan based on broad business objectives and performance targets over three to five years, companies can then focus their efforts through strategic planning. The idea is to stay flexible, listen to customers, and seize opportunities when they come, whether or not those opportunities were expected.[25] The opportunities, however, must fit into the company's overall goals and objectives or the company could lose its focus. Clearly, then, much of management and planning involves decision making.

Before we consider decision making, let us summarize some of the points in this chapter. A vision ("WHERE we are going..."), in combination with values (HOW we will treat our stakeholders...) ..."), and the mission statement ("Our purpose IS ..."), provides direction for the company. A company's objectives (WHAT we want to accomplish) are linked to its strategy (HOW we will accomplish the objectives). So, there is a progression from vision and values, to mission, to objectives, and to strategy. Once the strategy has been established, plans must be developed and implemented to ensure that objectives are met. There is never a strategy without there first being an objective. A SWOT analysis alone is almost useless unless you match it to the company's strategy and plan.

Clearly, then, much of management and planning requires decision making. The Spotlight on Small Business box illustrates how one unique small business handles planning and decision making.

**crisis planning**
Involves reacting to sudden changes in the environment.

**The following YouTube video talks about car sharing in Kitchener-Waterloo:**
http://www.youtube.com/watch?v=43rEQzbk-c8.

## GreenBOX

### How About Car Sharing?

Car sharing is affordable for people who do not need a car every day. "When you want a glass of milk, do you buy a cow?" Cars are located in convenient locations, near bus lines. Members of a car share not-for-profit corporation do not pay for gas, repairs, or insurance; just a flat fee based on length of use (which could be as short as one hour) and a fixed cost per kilometre. Car sharing creates a culture of a more caring, respectful community, given that these are co-operative organizations. Car sharing has proven to reduce auto emissions by over 50 percent per member.

Considerable planning is required to initiate this business, which is so contrary to the norm for car ownership. It was in the early 1990s that car sharing started to take hold on a global basis, with the first North American location being in Quebec City. The concept needed to build a public profile. Local car shares operate as a co-operative, so funding continually needs to be planned for. Common sources of funding are government agencies and charitable foundations. In each of these applications, car sharing co-operatives need to demonstrate a thorough plan. The co-operative must start with the basics of a plan, including vision, values, and mission statements. Then it must produce operational plans showing how the not-for-profit entity is going to achieve financial stability. On an ongoing basis, contingency plans need to be in place to respond to the membership levels. Given the incremental increasing costs of car ownership and the concern for the environment, car sharing appears to be more than a passing phenomenon.

Source: Grand River Carshare and Hamilton Carshare, 20 October 2009, www.peoplescar.org.

## DECISION MAKING: FINDING THE BEST ALTERNATIVE

**decision making**
Choosing among two or more alternatives.

All management functions involve some kind of decision making. **Decision making** is choosing among two or more alternatives. It sounds easier here than it is in practice. In fact, decision making is the heart of all management functions. The rational decision-making model is a series of steps that managers often follow to make logical, intelligent, and well-founded decisions.[26] These steps can be thought of as the seven Ds of decision making:

1. Define the situation.
2. Describe and collect needed information.
3. Develop alternatives.
4. Develop agreement among those involved.
5. Decide which alternative is best.
6. Do what is indicated (begin implementation).
7. Determine whether the decision was a good one and follow up.

**problem solving**
The process of solving the everyday problems that occur. Problem solving is less formal than decision making and usually calls for quicker action.

Managers don't always go through this seven-step process. Sometimes decisions have to be made on the spot—with little information available. Managers must make good decisions in all such circumstances.

**Problem solving** is the process of solving the everyday problems that occur. It is less formal than the decision-making process and usually calls for quicker action. Problem-solving teams are made up of two or more workers who are given an assignment to solve a specific problem (e.g., Why are customers not using our service policies?). Problem-solving techniques that companies use include **brainstorming** (i.e., coming up with as many solutions as possible in a short period of time with no censoring of ideas) and **PMI** (i.e., listing all the **P**luses for a solution in one column, all the **M**inuses in another, and the **I**nteresting in a third column). PMI is an tool developed by Edward de Bono as part of his work on lateral and creative thinking strategies. You can practise using the PMI system on almost all of your decisions. For example, should you stay home and study tonight? You would list all benefits of your choice (Pluses) in one column: better grades,

**brainstorming**
Coming up with as many solutions to a problem as possible in a short period of time with no censoring of ideas.

**PMI**
Listing all the pluses for a solution in one column, all the minuses in another, and the interesting in a third column.

improved self-esteem, more responsible, and so forth. In the other column, you would put the negatives (Minuses): boredom, less fun, etc. We hope that the pluses outweigh the minuses most of the time, and that you study often, but sometimes it is best to go out and have fun. In that case, the Interesting would be that having fun would not hurt your grades or job prospects.

## Progress Assessment

- What's the difference between goals and objectives?
- What does a company analyze when it does a SWOT analysis?
- What's the difference between strategic, tactical, and operational planning?
- What are the seven Ds in decision making?

## ORGANIZING: CREATING A UNIFIED SYSTEM

After managers have planned a course of action, they must organize the firm to accomplish their goals. Operationally, organizing means allocating resources (such as funds for various departments), assigning tasks, and establishing procedures for accomplishing the organizational objectives. When organizing, a manager develops a structure or framework that relates all workers, tasks, and resources to each other. That framework is called the organization structure. In Chapter 9, we will look at examples of several organizational structures and will review some of the challenges in developing an organization structure.

Most organizations draw a chart showing these relationships. This tool is called an organization chart. An **organization chart** is a visual device that shows relationships among people and divides the organization's work; it shows who is accountable for the completion of specific work and who reports to whom. Figure 8.5 shows a simple one. Each rectangle indicates a position (and usually who holds this position) within the organization. The chart plots who reports to whom (as indicated by the lines) and who is responsible for each task.

**organization chart**
A visual device that shows relationships among people and divides the organization's work; it shows who is accountable for the completion of specific work and who reports to whom.

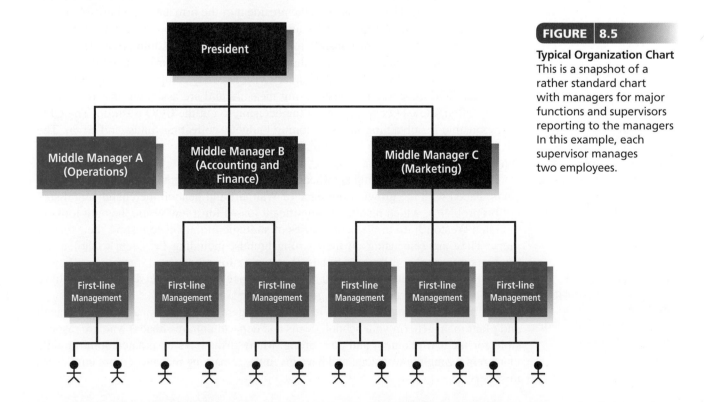

**FIGURE | 8.5**

**Typical Organization Chart**
This is a snapshot of a rather standard chart with managers for major functions and supervisors reporting to the managers In this example, each supervisor manages two employees.

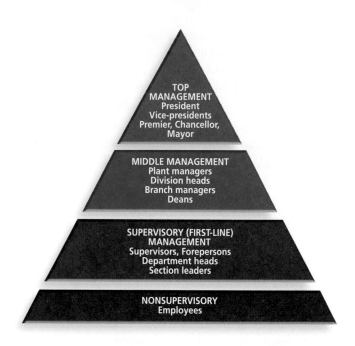

**FIGURE | 8.6**

**Levels of Management**
This figure shows the three levels of management. In many firms, there are several levels of middle management. Recently, some firms have been eliminating middle-level managers because fewer are needed to oversee self-managed teams of employees.

**top management**
Highest level of management, consisting of the president and other key company executives, who develop strategic plans.

**middle management**
The level of management that includes general managers, division managers, and branch and plant managers, who are responsible for tactical planning and controlling.

For example, in Figure 8.5, Manager B is the accounting and finance manager, and this middle manager reports directly to the president. Reporting directly to the accounting and finance manager are two first-line supervisors; two employees report directly to each of these first-line supervisors. The corporate hierarchy illustrated on the organization chart includes top, middle, and first-line managers. The problems involved in developing an organization structure will be discussed later in the text. For now, it's important to know that the corporate hierarchy usually includes three levels of management (see Figure 8.6).

**Top management** (the highest level of management) consists of the president and other key company executives who develop strategic plans. Terms you're likely to see often are chief executive officer (CEO), chief operating officer (COO), chief financial officer (CFO), and chief information officer (CIO), or in some companies, chief knowledge officer (CKO). The CEO is often the president of the firm and is responsible for all top-level decisions in the firm. CEOs are responsible for introducing change into an organization. The COO is responsible for putting those changes into effect. His or her tasks include structuring work, controlling operations, and rewarding people to ensure that everyone strives to carry out the leader's vision. Many companies today are eliminating the COO function as a cost-cutting measure and are assigning that role to the CEO.[27] Often, the CFO participates in the decision to cut the COO position. The CFO is responsible for obtaining funds, planning budgets, collecting funds, and so on. The CIO or CKO is responsible for getting the right information to other managers so they can make correct decisions.

Loblaws has been making significant changes in their operations over the past few years. Faced with the growing presence of Walmart and general merchandising distribution problems, which resulted in significant losses for a few years, they are looking to Galen Weston Jr. to implement a series of strategic initiatives to restore their former glory. They are refocusing on their strong brands, including President's Choice, re-pricing some staple products to provide best-value-for-money, and improving efficiencies in their supply chain. Time will tell what impact these strategic decisions will have on Loblaws' place in the Canadian grocery world.[28]

**Middle management** includes general managers, division managers, and branch and plant managers (in your school, deans and department/area heads) who are responsible for tactical planning and controlling. Many firms have eliminated some middle managers through downsizing, and have given the remaining managers more employees to supervise.

**Supervisory management** includes those who are directly responsible for supervising workers and evaluating their daily performance; they're often known as first-line managers (or supervisors) because they're the first level above workers.[29]

## Tasks and Skills at Different Levels of Management

Few people are trained to be good managers. Usually a person learns how to be a skilled accountant or sales representative or production-line worker, and then—because of his or her technical skills—is selected to be a manager. Once someone becomes a manager they spend more of their time in supporting those people they supervise, showing them how to do things, helping them, supervising them, and generally being very active in the operating task. Robert Katz developed a model to explain the types of skills and the mix of these skills through the various management levels.

The further up the managerial ladder a person moves, the less important his or her original job skills become. At the top of the ladder, the need is for people who are visionaries, planners, organizers, coordinators, communicators, morale builders, and motivators.[30] Figure 8.7 shows that a manager must have three categories of skills:

1. **Technical skills** involve the ability to perform tasks in a specific discipline (such as selling a product or developing software) or department (such as marketing or information systems).

2. **Human relations skills** involve communication and motivation; they enable managers to work through and with people. Such skills also include those associated with leadership, coaching, morale building, delegating, training and development, and help and supportiveness.

3. **Conceptual skills** involve the ability to picture the organization as a whole and the relationships among its various parts. Conceptual skills are needed in planning, organizing, controlling, systems development, problem analysis, decision making, coordinating, and delegating.

While it is not specifically stated, you can see how time management skills are a necessary component of each one of these categories of skills. Good managers must be able to effectively handle the daily points of contact that require their attention. This includes a lot of phone calls, interruptions, meetings, and numerous e-mails.

Looking at Figure 8.7, you'll notice that first-line managers need to be skilled in all three areas. However, most of their time is spent on technical and human relations tasks (assisting operating personnel, giving directions, etc.). First-line managers spend little time on conceptual tasks. Top managers, in contrast, need to use few technical skills. Instead, almost all of their time is devoted to human relations and conceptual tasks. A person who is competent at a low level of management may not be competent at higher levels, and vice versa. The skills needed are different at each level of management.

**supervisory management**
Managers who are directly responsible for supervising workers and evaluating their daily performance.

**technical skills**
Skills that involve the ability to perform tasks in a specific discipline or department.

**human relations skills**
Skills that involve communication and motivation; they enable managers to work through and with people.

**conceptual skills**
Skills that involve the ability to picture the organization as a whole and the relationships among its various parts.

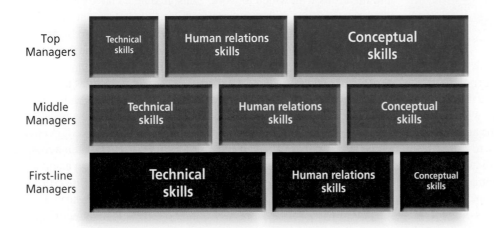

**FIGURE** | **8.7**

**Skills Needed at Various Levels of Management**
All managers need human relation skills. At the top, managers need strong conceptual skills and rely less on technical skills. First-line managers need strong technical skills and rely less on conceptual skills. Middle managers need to have a balance between technical and conceptual skills.

# The Stakeholder-Oriented Organization

A dominating question of the past 20 years or so has been how to best organize a firm to respond to the needs of its stakeholders. Remember, stakeholders include customers, employees, suppliers, dealers, environmental groups, and the surrounding communities. The consensus seems to be that smaller organizations are more responsive than larger organizations. Therefore, many large firms are being restructured into smaller, more customer-focused units.

The point is that companies are no longer organizing to make it easy for managers to have control. Instead, they're organizing so that customers have the greatest influence. The change to a customer orientation is being aided by technology. For example, establishing a dialogue with customers on the Internet enables some firms to work closely with customers and respond quickly to their wants and needs. For instance, by allowing customers the option to book flights via the Web, WestJet Airlines not only generated cost savings (a cost of $2 for online booking compared with as much as $20 when a travel agent booked the flight), but customers could collect Air Miles and get a small discount off any round trip fare.[31]

There's no way an organization can provide high-quality goods and services to customers unless suppliers provide world-class parts and materials with which to work. Thus, managers have to establish close relationships with suppliers, including close Internet ties.[32] To make the entire system work, similar relationships have to be established with those organizations that sell directly to consumers—namely retailers. To continue to serve the travel agency market, as well as to acquire more of corporate Canada's business, WestJet increased the size and scope of its sales team.[33]

In the past, the goal of the organization function in the firm was to clearly specify who does what within the firm. Today, the organizational task is much more complex because firms are forming partnerships, joint ventures, and other arrangements that make it necessary to organize the whole system; that is, several firms working together, often across national boundaries.[34] One organization working alone is often not as effective as many organizations working together. Creating a unified system out of multiple organizations will be one of the greatest management challenges of the twenty-first century. This discussion will be re-visited in Chapter 10, when we look at operations management.

Canadian Securities Registration Systems (CSRS) is a Canadian registry agent that offers registration and search services across Canada. A winner in Canada's 50 Best Managed Companies program, it attributes its successes to its vision, which is "to be a dynamic, innovative and responsive organization focused on building relationships with our clients and employees." Would you consider researching other companies that have been recognized with this award when looking for a job?

# LEADING: PROVIDING CONTINUOUS VISION AND VALUES

In business literature there's a trend toward separating the notion of management from that of leadership. One person might be a good manager but not a good leader. Another might be a good leader without being a good manager. One difference between managers and leaders is that managers strive to produce order and stability, whereas leaders embrace and manage change. Leadership is creating a vision for others to follow, establishing corporate values and ethics, and transforming the way the organization does business to improve its effectiveness and efficiency. Good leaders motivate workers and create the environment for workers to motivate themselves.[35] *Management is the carrying out of the leadership's vision.*

Can we identify the characteristics of successful leaders? In looking at leaders in entrepreneurial situations, Murray Johannsen (a leading consultant on transformational leadership) identified nine characteristics: self-esteem, need to achieve, screening for opportunity, internal locus of control, goal orientation, optimism, courage, tolerance to ambiguity, and strong internal motivation. Leaders are motivated by intrinsic values: needs, desires, motive and will power: as opposed to extrinsic values: rewards and recognition.[36] We will talk more about motivation in Chapter 11.

Transformational leadership has been another focus.[37] A famous quote from Robert Kennedy, when he was Attorney General of the United States, in 1961, illustrates this concept very well, " Some people see things the way they are and ask why, I see things as they could be and ask why not." Put another way, transformational leadership occurs where the leader takes a visionary position and inspires people to follow. Nine spheres of influence, at play when this type of leadership is at play, include authority, charisma, expertise, punishment, positive reinforcement, persuasion, coaching, relationship, and vision.

Now and in the future, all organizations will need leaders who can supply the vision as well as the moral and ethical foundation for growth. You don't have to be a manager to be a leader. All employees can lead. That is, any employee can contribute to producing order and stability and can motivate others to work well. All employees can also add to a company's ethical environment and report ethical lapses when they occur.

Companies can expect negative consequences if leaders do not behave in an ethical manner. For years, Clive Beddoe (former president and CEO of WestJet Airlines) had been recognized for his leadership. Under his management, WestJet had become Canada's second-largest airline. He won several awards, including Alberta's Most Respected Leader

Canada's Top 40 Under 40 honours Canadians who have reached a significant level of success before the age of 40. Winners have demonstrated excellence in areas such as vision and leadership, innovation, and community involvement. For a list of winners, visit www. top40awardcanada.org.

According to a Conference Board of Canada report titled *Creating High-performance Organizations: Leveraging Women's Leadership*, organizations with diverse executive teams—reflecting different genders, ages, and ethnicity—achieve superior corporate performance. However, a study by research firm Catalyst shows that only 12 percent of corporate director positions are held by women. What can companies do to change this?

## Making Ethical Decisions

### Are You Responsible for Your Boss's Success?

First-line managers assist in the decisions made by their department heads. The department heads retain full responsibility for the decisions—if a plan succeeds, it's their success; if a plan fails, it's their failure. Now picture this: As a first-line manager, you have new information that your department head hasn't seen yet. The findings in this report indicate that your manager's recent plans are sure to fail. If the plans do fail, the manager will probably be demoted and you're the most likely candidate to fill the vacancy. Will you give your department head the report? What will the consequences be of your decision?

(2004) and Top CEO in Canada (2003). In the Eleventh Annual Survey of Canada's Most Respected Corporations (2005), he was ranked third as the most respected leader in Canada. In 2006, WestJet admitted that the company was involved in corporate espionage against Air Canada (recall Chapter 5) and that it was "undertaken with the knowledge and direction of the highest management levels of WestJet." Some questioned whether Beddoe should be allowed to continue as CEO as the admission "raises a lot of questions about leadership and appropriateness of behaviour either in a complicit sense or supervisory sense that the board cannot ignore."[38] It remains to be seen, however, what the long-term impact will be on WestJet's corporate culture. "When the leader of a strong-culture organization admits wrongdoing—it's devastating," said Marc-David Seidel, a professor at the University of British Columbia's Sauder School of Business.[39] Do you agree? In 2007, the board of directors accepted Clive's resignation, and appointed him Chairperson of the Board. Since then, the company has performed very well.

Organizations will need workers and managers who share a vision and know how to get things done co-operatively. The workplace is changing from an environment in which a few dictate the rules to others to an environment in which all employees work together to accomplish common goals. Furthermore, managers must lead by doing, not just by saying. In summary, leaders must:

- *Communicate a vision and rally others around that vision.* In doing so, the leader should be openly sensitive to the concerns of followers, give them responsibility, and win their trust. They should ensure that employees get the message, through quality communication.

- *Establish corporate values.* These values (as discussed earlier in this chapter) include a concern for employees, for customers, for the environment, and for the quality of the company's products. When companies set their business goals today, they're defining the values of the company as well.

- *Promote corporate ethics.* Ethics include an unfailing demand for honesty and an insistence that everyone in the company is treated fairly. That's why we stress ethical decision making throughout this text. See the *Making Ethical Decisions* box for a scenario. Many business people are now making the news by giving away huge amounts to charity, thus setting a model of social concern for their employees and others.

- *Embrace transformational change.* A leader's most important job may be to transform the way the company does business so that it's more effective (does things better) and efficient (uses fewer resources to accomplish the same objectives).

Over the past ten years, there has been an increasing trend in compensation packages. These packages have been justified as necessary to attract and keep good leaders. McGill University's Henry Mintzberg has been vocal on his disagreement with the increasing

CEO compensation packages. In his view, many CEOs focus solely on the short-term increase in the share value of the company and their bonuses. "Find me a chief executive who refuses those bonuses, who takes the long-term view and says his team will share the spoils of their mandate in 10 years time, and I'll show you a leader," he said.[40] Do you agree that top executives should receive such lucrative packages in today's environment?

## The Importance of Middle Managers to Leadership[41]

The Conference Board of Canada released a report on the changing role of middle managers, "Leading from the Middle: Managers Make the Difference." Researcher Carolyn Farquahar wrote, "A decade ago, senior managers viewed middle managers poorly— they thought middle managers blocked change and prevented the transfer of authority to front-line employees... A fundamental shift has occurred, and middle managers are now considered an essential link to making change throughout the organization and a training ground for executives of the future."

Carolyn Clark, vice-president of human resources for Fairmont Hotels & Resorts Inc., said that a growing body of research shows "people don't quit their companies, they quit their managers. Therefore, leadership quality is of critical importance at all levels of the company." Dofasco Inc. has also elevated the role of middle managers as key players "in repositioning the company for a new group of leaders." According to the Conference Board report, the greatest challenge facing Dofasco is its aging workforce. Most of the executive team will be gone in the next five to seven years, and over the next decade up to one-third of the workforce will turn over. Middle management will help ensure that Dofasco's unique culture is retained, even with the influx of a large number of new employees.

The Conference Board of Canada report notes that not all organizations recognize the importance of middle managers. However, there are more examples seen today than in the past. This is indeed positive news for those middle managers who survived the downsizing of the past five years and were left with heavy workloads. According to the report, opportunities for middle managers to do challenging and rewarding work are increasing. "In just a few years, middle managers have moved from traditional roles of planning, monitoring, and controlling, to assuming additional roles relating to strategy and process."

The Conference Board of Canada's mission is to build leadership capacity for a better Canada by creating and sharing insights on economic trends, public policy, and organizational performance. Visit www. conferenceboard.ca to review some of its more recent findings.

## Leadership Styles

Nothing has challenged researchers in the area of management more than the search for the "best" leadership traits, behaviours, or styles. Thousands of studies have been undertaken of successful businesses to identify a common style. Intuitively, you would conclude about the same thing that researchers have found: leadership styles are hard to pin down. In fact, results of most studies on leadership have been neither statistically significant nor reliable. Some leaders are well groomed and tactful, while others are unkempt and abrasive—yet the latter may be just as effective as the former.

There's also no one style of leadership that works best in all situations. Even so, we can look at a few of the most commonly recognized leadership styles (see Figure 8.8) and see how they may be effective:

1. **Autocratic leadership** involves making managerial decisions without consulting others. Such a style is effective in emergencies and when absolute "followership" is needed— for example, when fighting fires. Autocratic leadership is also effective sometimes with new, relatively unskilled workers who need clear direction and guidance.

2. **Participative (democratic) leadership** consists of managers and employees working together to make decisions. Research has found that employee participation in decisions may not always increase effectiveness, but it usually increases job satisfaction. Many progressive organizations are highly successful at using a democratic style of leadership that values traits such as flexibility, good listening skills, and empathy.

**autocratic leadership**
Leadership style that involves making managerial decisions without consulting others.

**participative (democratic) leadership**
Leadership style that consists of managers and employees working together to make decisions.

**FIGURE** | **8.8**

**Various Leadership Styles**

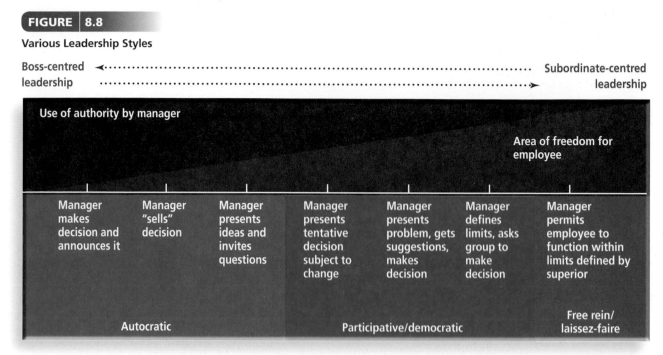

Source: Reprinted by permission of the *Harvard Business Review*. An exhibit from "How to Choose a Leadership Pattern" by Robert Tannenbaum and Warren Schmidt (May/June 1973). Copyright © 1973 by the President and Fellows of Harvard College, all rights reserved.

At meetings in such firms, employees discuss management issues and resolve those issues together in a democratic manner. That is, everyone has some opportunity to contribute to decisions. Many firms have placed meeting rooms throughout the company and allow all employees the right to request a meeting.

**free-rein (laissez-faire) leadership**

Leadership style that involves managers setting objectives and employees being relatively free to do whatever it takes to accomplish those objectives.

3. **Free-rein (laissez-faire) leadership** involves managers setting objectives and employees being relatively free to do whatever it takes to accomplish those objectives. In certain organizations, where managers deal with doctors, engineers, or other professionals, often the most successful leadership style is free rein. The traits needed by managers in such organizations include warmth, friendliness, and understanding. More and more firms are adopting this style of leadership with at least some of their employees.

Individual leaders rarely fit neatly into just one of these categories. Researchers illustrate leadership as a continuum with varying amounts of employee participation, ranging from purely boss-centred leadership to subordinate-centred leadership.

Which leadership style is best? Research tells us that successful leadership depends largely on what the goals and values of the firm are, who's being led, and in what situations. It also supports the notion that any leadership style, ranging from autocratic to free-rein, may be successful depending on the people and the situation. In fact, a manager may use a variety of leadership styles, depending on a given situation. A manager may be autocratic but friendly with a new trainee, democratic with an experienced employee who has many good ideas that can only be fostered by a flexible manager who's a good listener, and free-rein with a trusted, long-term supervisor who probably knows more about operations than the manager does.

There's no such thing as a leadership style that always works best. A truly successful leader has the ability to use the leadership style most appropriate to the situation and the employees involved. Figure 8.9 lists some rules of leadership.

**FIGURE 8.9**

**The Rules of Leadership**

| The 12 Rules of Leadership | The 7 Don'ts of Leadership |
|---|---|
| 1. *Set a good example.* Your subordinates will take their cue from you. If your work habits are good, theirs are likely to be too. | On the other hand, these items can cancel any constructive image you might try to establish. |
| 2. *Give your people a set of objectives and a sense of direction.* Good people seldom like to work aimlessly from day to day. They want to know not only what they're doing but why. | 1. *Trying to be liked rather than respected.* Don't accept favours from your subordinates. Don't do special favours in trying to be liked. Don't try for popular decisions. Don't be soft about discipline. Have a sense of humour. Don't give up. |
| 3. *Keep your people informed of new developments of the company and how they'll affect them.* Let people know where they stand with you. Let your close assistants in on your plans at an early stage. Let people know as early as possible of any changes that will affect them. Let them know of changes that won't affect them but about which they may be worrying. | 2. *Failing to ask subordinates for their advice and help.* |
| | 3. *Failing to develop a sense of responsibility in subordinates.* Allow freedom of expression. Give each person a chance to learn his or her superior's job. When you give responsibility, give authority too. Hold subordinates accountable for results. |
| 4. *Ask your people for advice.* Let them know that they have a say in your decisions whenever possible. Make them feel a problem is their problem too. Encourage individual thinking. | 4. *Emphasizing rules rather than skill.* |
| 5. *Let your people know that you support them.* There's no greater morale killer than a boss who resents a subordinate's ambition. | 5. *Failing to keep criticism constructive.* When something goes wrong, do you tend to assume who's at fault? Do you do your best to get all the facts first? Do you control your temper? Do you praise before you criticize? Do you listen to the other side of the story? |
| 6. *Don't give orders.* Suggest, direct, and request. | |
| 7. *Emphasize skills, not rules.* Judge results, not methods. Give a person a job to do and let him or her do it. Let an employee improve his or her own job methods. | 6. *Not paying attention to employee gripes and complaints.* Make it easy for them to come to you. Get rid of red tape. Explain the grievance machinery. Help a person voice his or her complaint. Always grant a hearing. Practise patience. Ask a complainant what he or she wants to do. Don't render a hasty or biased judgment. Get all the facts. Let the complainant know what your decision is. Double-check your results. Be concerned. |
| 8. *Give credit where credit is due.* Appreciation for a job well done is the most appreciated of fringe benefits. | |
| 9. *Praise in public.* This is where it will do the most good. | |
| 10. *Criticize in private.* | 7. *Failing to keep people informed.* |
| 11. *Criticize constructively.* Concentrate on correction, not blame. Allow a person to retain his or her dignity. Suggest specific steps to prevent recurrence of the mistake. Forgive and encourage desired results. | |
| 12. *Make it known that you welcome new ideas.* No idea is too small for a hearing or too wild for consideration. Make it easy for them to communicate their ideas to you. Follow through on their ideas. | |

Sources: "To Become an Effective Executive: Develop Leadership and Other Skills," *Marketing News*, April 1984, 1; and Brian Biro, *Beyond Success* (New York: Berkley, 2001).

# Managing Knowledge

There's an old saying that still holds true today: "Knowledge is power." Empowering employees means giving them knowledge—that is, getting them the information they need to do the best job they can. Finding the right information, keeping the information in a readily accessible place, and making the information known to everyone in the firm together constitutes **knowledge management**.[42] For example, Canadian Tire was the

**knowledge management**
Finding the right information, keeping the information in a readily accessible place, and making the information known to everyone in the firm.

first major Canadian retailer to use an Internet-based eLearning program. eLearning is an online training and education program that delivers product knowledge and skills training on everything from plumbing to paint mixing. The program is credited with improved customer and employee satisfaction levels. According to Janice Wismer, former vice-president of human resources, "People say the lessons have increased their confidence, that they're happier working here because the company is committing to their growth and development."[43] This is good news for store sales.

The first step to developing a knowledge management system is determining what knowledge is most important. Do you want to know more about your customers? Do you want to know more about competitors? What kind of information would make the company more effective or more efficient or more responsive to the marketplace? Once you have decided what you need to know, you set out to find answers to those questions.

Knowledge management tries to keep people from reinventing the wheel—that is, duplicating the work of gathering information—every time a decision needs to be made. A company really progresses when each person in the firm asks continually, "What do I still not know?" and "Whom should I be asking?" It's as important to know what's not working as what is working. Employees and managers now have e-mail, fax machines, intranets, and other means of keeping in touch with each other, with customers, and with other stakeholders. The key to success is learning how to process that information effectively and turn it into knowledge that everyone can use to improve processes and procedures. That is one way to enable workers to be more effective. (Recall that there is a brief discussion in Appendix A on information technology and knowledge management.)

## Progress Assessment

- What are some characteristics of leadership today that make leaders different from traditional managers?
- Explain the differences between autocratic and democratic leadership styles.
- What is the first step in developing a knowledge management system?

# CONTROLLING: MAKING SURE IT WORKS

The control function involves measuring performance relative to the planned objectives and standards, rewarding people for work well done, and then taking corrective action when necessary. Thus, the control process (see Figure 8.10) is the heart of the management system because it provides the feedback that enables managers and workers to adjust to any deviations from plans and to changes in the environment that have affected performance. Controlling consists of five steps:

1. Establishing clear performance standards. This ties the planning function to the control function. Without clear standards, control is impossible.
2. Monitoring and recording actual performance (results).
3. Comparing results against plans and standards.
4. Communicating results and deviations to the employees involved.
5. Taking corrective action when needed and providing positive feedback for work well done.

**FIGURE** **8.10**

**The Control Process**
The whole control process is based on clear standards. Without such standards, the other steps are difficult, if not impossible. With clear standards, performance measurement is relatively easy and the proper action can be taken.

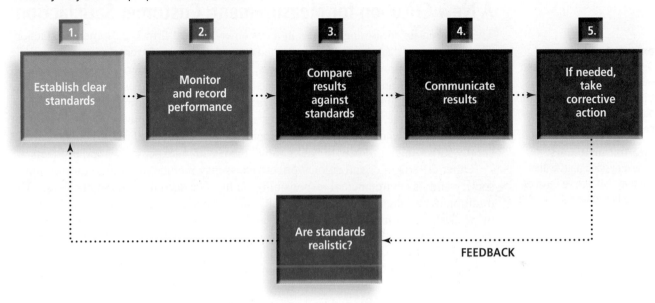

This control process is ongoing throughout the year. Continuous monitoring ensures that if corrective action is required, there is enough time to implement changes. When corrective action is necessary, the decision-making process is a useful tool to apply (recall the seven Ds of decision making). Simply, managers are encouraged to review the situation and, based on collected information, develop alternatives with their staff and implement the best alternative. Or, in some circumstances, if significant changes have occurred, management can implement a contingency plan (as discussed earlier in the chapter). The focus is to meet the standards that were initially established during the planning stage or the standards that have since been modified. This process is also ongoing. It may take several attempts before standards are successfully met.

The control system's weakest link tends to be the setting of standards. To measure results against standards, the standards must be specific, attainable, and measurable. Vague goals and standards such as "better quality," "more efficiency," and "improved performance" aren't sufficient because they don't describe what you're trying to achieve. For example, let's say you're a runner and you want to improve your distance. When you started your improvement plan last year, you ran 2 kilometres a day. Now you run 2.1 kilometres a day. Did you meet your goal? You did increase your distance, but certainly not by very much. A more appropriate goal statement would be: To increase running distance from 2 kilometres a day to 4 kilometres a day by January 1. It's important to establish a time period for when specific goals are to be met. Here are examples of goals and standards that meet these criteria:

- Cut the number of finished-product rejects from 10 per 1,000 to 5 per 1,000 by March 31.

- Increase the number of times managers praise employees from 3 per week to 12 per week by the end of the quarter.

- Increase sales of product X from $10,000 per month to $12,000 per month by July 31.

One way to make control systems work is to establish clear procedures for monitoring performance. Accounting and finance are often the foundation for control systems because they provide the numbers management needs to evaluate progress. We shall explore both accounting and finance in detail later in the text.

## A New Criterion for Measurement: Customer Satisfaction

The criterion for measuring success in a customer-oriented firm is customer satisfaction. This includes satisfaction of both external and internal customers. **External customers** include dealers, who buy products to sell to others, and ultimate customers (also known as end users) such as you and me, who buy products for their own personal use. **Internal customers** are individuals and units within the firm that receive services from other individuals or units. For example, the field salespeople are the internal customers of the marketing research people who prepare research reports for them. One goal today is to go beyond simply satisfying customers to "delighting" them with unexpectedly good products.

Other criteria of organizational effectiveness may include the firm's contribution to society and its environmental responsibility in the area surrounding the business.[44] The traditional measures of success are usually financial; that is, success is defined in terms of profits or return on investment. Certainly these measures are still important, but they're not the whole purpose of the firm. The purpose of the firm today is to please employees, customers, and other stakeholders. Thus, measurements of success must take all of these groups into account. Firms have to ask questions such as: Do we have good relations with our employees, our suppliers, our dealers, our community leaders, the local media, our shareholders, and our bankers? What more could we do to please these groups? Are the corporate needs (such as making a profit) being met as well?

Let's pause now, review, and do some exercises. Management is doing, not just reading.

**external customers**
Dealers, who buy products to sell to others, and ultimate customers (or end users), who buy products for their own personal use.

**internal customers**
Individuals and units within the firm that receive services from other individuals or units.

## Progress Assessment

- What are the five steps in the control process?
- What's the difference between internal and external customers?

# SUMMARY

1. Many managers are changing their approach to corporate management.

   **LO ▶ 1** Explain how the changes that are occurring in the business environment are affecting the management function.

   **What reasons can you give to account for these changes in management?**
   Business people are being challenged to be more ethical and to make their accounting practices more visible to investors and the general public. Change is now happening faster than ever, and global competition is just a click away. Managing change is an important element of success, particularly in light of today's emphasis on speed in the global marketplace. National borders mean much less now than ever before, and co-operation and integration among companies have greatly increased. Within companies, knowledge workers are demanding managerial styles that allow for freedom, and the workforce is becoming increasingly diverse, educated, and self-directed.

   **How are managers' roles changing?**
   Managers are being educated to guide, train, support, and teach employees rather than tell them what to do.

2. Managers perform a variety of functions.

   **LO ▶ 2** Describe the four functions of management.

   **What are the four primary functions of management?**
   The four primary functions are (1) planning, (2) organizing, (3) leading, and (4) controlling.

   **Describe each of the four functions.**
   Planning includes anticipating trends and determining the best strategies and tactics to achieve organizational goals and objectives. Organizing includes designing the structure of the organization and creating conditions and systems in which everyone and everything works together to achieve the organization's goals and objectives. Leading involves creating a vision for the organization and guiding, training, coaching, and motivating others to work effectively to achieve the organization's goals and objectives. Controlling involves establishing clear standards to determine whether an organization is progressing toward its goals and objectives, rewarding people for doing a good job, and taking corrective action if they are not.

3. The planning function involves the process of setting objectives to meet the organizational goals. Goals are broad, long-term achievements that organizations aim to accomplish.

   **LO ▶ 3** Describe the different types of planning and the importance of decision making in choosing the best alternative.

   **What are the four types of planning, and how are they related to the organization's goals and objectives?**
   Strategic planning is broad, long-range planning that outlines the goals of the organization. Tactical planning is specific, short-term planning that lists organizational objectives. Operational planning is part of tactical planning and involves setting specific timetables and standards. Contingency planning involves developing an alternative set of plans in case the first set doesn't work out.

   **What are the steps involved in decision making?**
   Decision making is choosing among two or more alternatives and it is the heart of all management functions. The seven Ds of decision making are (1) define the situation, (2) describe and collect needed information, (3) develop alternatives, (4) develop agreement among those involved, (5) decide which alternative is best, (6) do what is indicated (begin implementation), and (7) determine whether the decision was a good one and follow up.

**LO ▶ 4** Describe the organizing function of management and the three categories of skills needed by managers.

4. Organizing means allocating resources (such as funds for various departments), assigning tasks, and establishing procedures for accomplishing the organizational objectives.

### What are the three levels of management in the corporate hierarchy?

The three levels of management are (1) top management (highest level consisting of the president and other key company executives who develop strategic plans); (2) middle management (general managers, division managers, and plant managers who are responsible for tactical planning and controlling); and (3) supervisory management (first-line managers/supervisors who evaluate workers' daily performance).

### What skills do managers need?

Managers must have three categories of skills: (1) technical skills (ability to perform specific tasks such as selling products or developing software), (2) human relations skills (ability to communicate and motivate), and (3) conceptual skills (ability to see organizations as a whole and how all the parts fit together). Managers at different levels need different skills.

**LO ▶ 5** Explain the differences between leaders and managers, and describe the various leadership styles.

5. Executives today must be more than just managers; they must be leaders as well.

### What's the difference between a manager and a leader?

A manager plans, organizes, and controls functions within an organization. A leader has vision and inspires others to grasp that vision, establishes corporate values, emphasizes corporate ethics, and doesn't fear change.

### Which leadership style is most effective?

Figure 8.8 shows a continuum of leadership styles ranging from boss-centred to subordinate-centred leadership. The most effective leadership style depends on the people being led and the situation.

**LO ▶ 6** Summarize the five steps of the control function of management.

6. The control function of management involves measuring employee performance against objectives and standards, rewarding people for a job well done, and taking corrective action if necessary.

### What are the five steps of the control function?

Controlling incorporates (1) setting clear standards, (2) monitoring and recording performance, (3) comparing performance with plans and standards, (4) communicating results and deviations to employees, and (5) providing positive feedback for a job well done and taking corrective action if necessary.

### What qualities must standards possess to be used to measure performance results?

Standards must be specific, attainable, and measurable.

## KEY TERMS

autocratic leadership  251

brainstorming  244

conceptual skills  247

contingency planning  242

controlling  238

crisis planning  243

decision making  244

external customers  256

free-rein (laissez-faire)
leadership  252

goals  239

human relations skills  247

internal customers  256

knowledge management  253

leading  237

management  236

middle management  246

mission statement  239

objectives  239

operational planning  242

organization chart  245

organizing  237

participative (democratic)
leadership  251

planning  237

PMI  244

problem solving  244

resources  236

strategic planning  240

supervisory management  247

SWOT analysis  240

tactical planning  242

technical skills  247

top management  246

values  238

vision  238

## CRITICAL THINKING

1.  Is the democratic management style most appropriate in all situations? Why or why not? Can you see a manager getting frustrated when he or she can't control others? Can someone who's trained to give orders (e.g., a military sergeant) be retrained to be a democratic manager? What problems may emerge? What kind of manager would you be? Do you have evidence to show that?

2.  Sometimes when working in a team, one team member habitually overloads themselves with team requirements, while another deftly dodges everything the team asks them to do. What would you do in this situation? How would you frame the discussion? If you are aware of these traits, before assigning team work, how would you approach the assignment? How would you make team members responsible?

## DEVELOPING WORKPLACE SKILLS

1.  Allocate some time to do some career planning by doing a SWOT analysis of your present situation. What does the marketplace for your chosen career(s) look like today? What skills do you have that will make you a winner in that type of career? What weaknesses might you target to improve? What are the threats to that career choice? What are the opportunities? Prepare a two-minute presentation for the class.

2.  Bring several decks of cards to class and have the class break up into teams of four or so members. Each team should then elect a leader. Each leader should be assigned a leadership style: autocratic, participative, or free-rein. Have each team try to build a house with a given design. The team that complete the task the most quickly wins. Each team member should then report his or her experience under that style of leadership.

3.  Review Figure 8.8 and discuss managers you have known, worked for, or read about who have practised each style. Students from other countries may have interesting experiences to add. Which management style did you like best? Why? Which were most effective? Why?

4.  Because of the illegal and unethical behaviour of a few managers, managers in general are under suspicion for being greedy and dishonest. Discuss the fairness of such charges, given the thousands of honest and ethical managers, and what could be done to improve the opinion of managers among the students in your class.

## TAKING IT TO THE NET 1

### Purpose

To discover some of Canada's leaders and find out what makes them great leaders.

### Exercise

Many national awards are given out each year to recognize Canadian business leaders. Go on the Web and see if you can find some of these leaders. Two sites you may wish to visit are www.canadianbusiness.com/allstars and www.top40award-canada.org.

1. What are some common characteristics in these leaders?

2. Analyze the criteria used to choose these leaders. Are these measures reflective of the theory discussed in this chapter?

3. Referring back to your answer to the first question, what characteristics do you personally need to develop further and how do you plan on doing so?

4. Visit www.robmagazine.com and review the best-paid executives in Canada. Did you find some of Canada's top leaders on this list? Is salary reflective of a great leader? Explain.

## TAKING IT TO THE NET 2

### Purpose

To perform a simple SWOT analysis.

### Exercise

Go to www.marketingteacher.com/ and then click on SWOT Analysis. Complete the SWOT analysis for the Highly Brill Leisure Center (click on Exercise).

1. What are the company's strengths, weaknesses, opportunities, and threats?

2. Analyze the company's weaknesses. How do you think the company's strengths might be used to overcome some of its weaknesses?

3. Analyze the opportunities and threats. What additional opportunities can you suggest? What additional threats can you identify?

## ANALYZING MANAGEMENT DECISIONS

### Leading in a Leaderless Company

In an issue of *Business Week* devoted to the future of business, writer John Byrne speculated about the future of leadership. He said that the twenty-first century would be unfriendly to leaders who try to run their companies by sheer force of will, and that success would come instead to companies that are "leaderless"—or companies whose leadership is so widely shared that they resemble ant colonies or beehives. In a world that is becoming more dependent on brainpower, having teams at the top will make more sense than having a single top manager. The Internet enables companies to act more like beehives because information can be shared horizontally rather than sent up to the top manager's office and then back down again. Decisions can be made instantly by the best people equipped to make them.

In the past, uniform thinking from the top could cripple an organization. Today, however, team leadership is ideally suited for the new reality of fast-changing markets. Urgent projects often require the coordinated contribution of many talented people working together. Such thinking does not happen at the top of the organization; it takes place down among the workers.

In the future, therefore, managers are more likely to be chosen for their team experience and their ability to delegate rather than make all key decisions themselves. Companies in the future, it is said, will be led by people who understand that in business, as in nature, no one person can be really in control.

Sources: John A. Byrne, "The Global Corporation Becomes a Leaderless Corporation," *Business Week*, 30 August 1999, 88–90; and Etienne C. Wenger and William M. Synder, "Communities of Practice: The Organizational Frontier," *Harvard Business Review*, January–February 2000, 139–145.

## Discussion Questions

1. What would you look for on a resumé that would indicate that a candidate for work was a self-motivated team player? Are you that type? How do you know?

2. Given your experience with managers in the past, what problems do you see some managers having with letting employees decide for themselves the best way to do things and giving them the power to obtain needed equipment?

3. What would happen if all businesses in your area had their employees mix with customers to hear their comments and complaints? Would that be a good or bad thing? Why?

4. What are the various ways you can think of for companies to pay bonuses to team members? One way is to divide the money equally. What are other ways? Which would you prefer as a team member?

# CHAPTER 9

# Adapting Organizations to Today's Markets

## LEARNING OBJECTIVES

**AFTER YOU HAVE READ AND STUDIED THIS CHAPTER, YOU SHOULD BE ABLE TO:**

**LO ▶ 1** Explain the historical organizational theories of Henri Fayol and Max Weber.

**LO ▶ 2** Discuss the various issues involved in structuring organizations.

**LO ▶ 3** Describe and differentiate the various organizational models.

**LO ▶ 4** Understand how organizations are connecting with their external environment

**LO ▶ 5** Explain how restructuring, organizational culture, and informal organizations can help businesses adapt to change.

## Getting to Know Heather Reisman of Indigo Books & Music Inc.

The goal of this chapter is to introduce you to the terms and concepts involved in organizing companies (and reorganizing them as well). Few challenges in business are greater than moving an established company from the slow-moving, management-oriented style of the past to the fast-moving, team-oriented, Internet-based, and customer-based firms that most of today's markets demand.

No one understands the fast-paced business environment better than Heather Reisman, founder and CEO of Indigo Books & Music Inc., Canada's largest book retailer. Indigo operates 300 bookstores across the country under the names Indigo Books Music & More, Chapters, The World's Biggest Book Store, and Coles. Indigo also operates www.chapters.indigo.ca, an online retailer of books, gifts, music, videos, and jewellery.

Reisman has more than 25 years of business experience. For the first 16 years of her career, she was managing director of Paradigm Consulting, the strategy and change management firm she co-founded in 1979. Paradigm was the world's first strategic change consultancy and it pioneered many organizational change strategies in use today. Reisman left Paradigm to become president of Cott Corporation. During her tenure, Cott grew from a regional bottler to the world's largest retailer-branded beverage supplier.

Reisman created Indigo Books & Music in 1996. Launching Indigo was the culmination and integration of a lifelong passion for books and music, and an entire career focused on understanding and building new-age organizations. By 2000, the chain had expanded to 14 locations across Canada. Indigo was the first book retail chain to add music, gifts, and licensed cafés to its store locations.

During this time, Indigo's closest competitor was Chapters. In 1996, Chapters Inc. opened its first two book superstores, and from there it grew to become the largest book retailer in Canada, operating bookstores in all provinces. In November 2000, Trilogy

Retail Enterprises L.P. (co-owned by Reisman and her husband, Gerry Schwartz) announced its intent to purchase a controlling interest in Chapters. "We are truly excited by the prospects of this merger," Reisman said in an interview. "It makes great sense. It allows us to take advantage of a broader base of expertise, substantial cost savings, synergies and efficiencies, all of which will have a positive impact on our customers, shareholders, and suppliers." In August 2001, Chapters and Indigo legally merged under the corporate name Indigo Books & Music Inc.

Since the merger, Indigo has successfully integrated the two companies and continues to outperform every other book chain in the English-speaking world. Indigo opened a "green" retail chain called Pistachios in the fall of 2008. This company is the focus of the Green Box later in this chapter.

Sources: CBC News, "Chapters, Indigo Unveil Merger Details," 13 June 2001, http://www.cbc.ca/stories/2001/06/13/business/ chapters_ 010611; Nancy Carr, "Indigo Sees Itself as Purveyor of Lifestyle," *The Toronto Star*, 15 September 2004, http://www.thestar.com/NASApp/cs/ContentServer?pagename=thestar/ Layout/Article_Type1&call_pageid=9713586371776c=Article&cid= 1095199811221; and www.chapters.indigo.ca, 5 May 2006.

# ORGANIZATION FROM THE BOTTOM UP

The principles of management are much the same, no matter the size of the business. Management, as you learned in Chapter 8, begins with planning. Let's say, for example, that you and two of your friends plan to start a lawn-mowing business. One of the first steps is to organize your business. Organizing, or structuring, begins with determining what work needs to be done (mowing, edging, trimming, etc.) and then dividing up tasks among the three of you; this is called a *division of labour*. One of you, for example, might have a special talent for trimming bushes, while another is better at mowing. Dividing tasks into smaller jobs is called *job specialization*. The success of a firm often depends on management's ability to identify each worker's strengths and assign the right tasks to the right person. Often a job can be done quickly and well when each person specializes.

If your business is successful, you will probably hire more workers to help. You might then organize them into teams or departments to do the various tasks. One team, for example, might mow the lawn while another team uses blowers to clean up the leaves and cut grass. If you are really successful over time, you might hire an accountant to keep records for you, various people to do your marketing (e.g., advertising), and repair people to keep the equipment in good shape. You can see how your business might evolve into a company with several departments: operations (mowing the lawns and everything related to that), marketing, accounting, and repair. The process of setting up individual departments to do specialized tasks is called *departmentalization*. Finally, you would need to assign authority and responsibility to people so that you could control the whole process. If something went wrong in the accounting department, for example, you would know who was responsible.

Structuring an organization, then, consists of devising a division of labour (sometimes resulting in specialization), setting up teams or departments to do specific tasks (e.g., human resources and accounting), and assigning responsibility and authority to people. Part of the process would include allocating resources (such as funds for various departments), assigning specific tasks, and establishing procedures for accomplishing the organizational objectives. Right from the start, you have to make some ethical decisions about how you will treat your workers (see the Making Ethical Decisions box). Finally, as you learned in Chapter 8, you may develop an organization chart that shows relationships among people: it shows who is accountable for the completion of specific work and who reports to whom. Finally, you have to monitor the environment to see what competitors are doing and what customers are demanding. Then, you must adjust to the new realities. For example, a major lawn care company may begin promoting its services in your area. You might have to make some organizational changes to offer even better service at competitive prices. What would be the first thing you would do if you began to lose business to competitors?

This photo shows women sewing parachutes during the Second World War while being carefully monitored by their manager. How have organizations changed since this time? How have they remained the same?

# The Changing Organization

Never before in the history of business has so much change been introduced so quickly—sometimes too quickly.[1] As you learned in earlier chapters, much of that change is due to the dynamic business environment, including more global competition and faster technological change.[2] Equally important to many businesses is the change in customer expectations. Customers today expect high-quality products and fast, friendly service—at a reasonable cost.[3] *Managing change*, then, has become a critical managerial function. That sometimes includes changing the whole organizational structure. Many organizations in the past were designed more to facilitate management than to please the customer. Managers were typically the only members of an organization who had some level of training, and possessed most of the knowledge needed to run the business. Companies designed many rules and regulations to give managers control over employees. As you will learn later, that is called bureaucracy. Where did bureaucracy come from? What are the alternatives? To understand where we are, it helps to know where we've been.

# The Development of Organizational Design

Until the twentieth century, most businesses were rather small, the processes for producing goods were relatively simple, and organizing workers was fairly easy. Organizing workers is still not too hard in most small firms, such as a lawn-mowing service or a small shop that produces custom-made boats. Not until the 1900s and the introduction of *mass production* (efficiently producing large quantities of goods) did business production processes and organization become complex. Usually, the bigger the plant, the more efficient production became.

Business growth led to what was called **economies of scale**. This term refers to the fact that companies can reduce their production costs if they can purchase raw materials in bulk and develop specialized labour, resulting in the unit cost of goods going down

**economies of scale**
The situation in which companies can reduce their production costs if they can purchase raw materials in bulk and develop specialized labour; resulting in the average cost of goods going down as production levels increase.

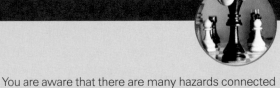

## Making Ethical Decisions

### Safety and Environmental Concerns Versus Profit

Imagine that you have begun a successful lawn-mowing service in your neighbourhood. You have talked to your neighbours and established several long-term agreements to mow lawns, trim hedges, and do other yardwork as necessary. It occurs to you that this could be a great long-term career for you. You would have to sign up more customers, hire people to help, and buy the appropriate equipment to do the work. That equipment might include lawn mowers of different sizes, gas-powered blowers for removing leaves, a shredder to get rid of tree branches, and more. You may even buy a machine to spray liquid fertilizer on the lawns.

To get some input on what is needed, you observe other lawn-mowing services in the area. Several seem to hire untrained workers, many of them from other countries. The companies pay the workers minimum wage or slightly more. Most obviously, however, the owners often provide no safety equipment. Workers don't have ear protection against the loud mowers and blowers. Most don't wear goggles when operating the shredder. Very few workers wear masks when spraying potentially harmful fertilizers.

You are aware that there are many hazards connected with yardwork. You also know that safety gear can be expensive and that workers often prefer to work without such protection. You are interested in making as much money as possible, but you also are somewhat concerned about the safety and welfare of your workers. Furthermore, you are aware of the noise pollution caused by blowers and other equipment and would like to keep noise levels down, but quiet equipment is expensive.

Clearly, most other lawn services don't seem too concerned about safety and the environment. On the one hand, you know that the corporate culture you create as you begin your service will last for a long time. If you emphasize safety and environmental concern from the start, your workers will adopt your values. On the other hand, you can see the potential for making faster profits by ignoring as many safety rules as you can and by paying as little attention as you can to the environment. What are the consequences of each choice? Which would you choose?

and production levels increasing. The cost of building a car, for example, got much cheaper when the automobile companies went to mass production. You may have noticed the same benefits of mass production with houses and computers. It was during this era that the huge factories that produce GM and Ford cars were introduced. While economies of scale focus on the supply side of a business, **economies of scope** focus on the demand side. This term refers to efficiencies that can be realized through product bundling and family branding, which well be covered in our discussion of marketing.

During the era of mass production, organization theorists emerged. In France, Henri Fayol published his book *Administration industrielle et générale* in 1919. It was popularized in North America in 1949 under the title *General and Industrial Management*.

**economies of scope**
Efficiencies associated with the demand side of a business where more products are promoted or a broader media is used to increase the potential customers reached with each dollar spent.

## Fayol's Principles of Organization

Fayol introduced such principles as the following:

- *Unity of command.* Each worker is to report to one, and only one, boss. The benefits of this principle are obvious. What happens if two different bosses give you two different assignments? Which one should you follow? Reporting to only one manager prevents such confusion. Just think about what happens in a family when each parent gives different directions to their child.

- *Hierarchy of authority.* All workers should know to whom they should report. Managers should have the right to give orders and expect others to follow.

- *Division of labour.* Functions are to be divided into areas of specialization such as production, marketing, and finance. This principle, as you will read later, is now being questioned or modified.

- *Subordination of individual interests to the general interest.* Workers are to think of themselves as a coordinated team. The goals of the team are more important than the goals of individual workers.

- *Authority.* Managers have the right to give orders and the power to enforce obedience. Authority and responsibility are related: whenever authority is exercised, responsibility arises. This principle is also being modified as managers are beginning to empower employees.

- *Degree of centralization.* The amount of decision-making power vested in top management should vary by circumstances. In a small organization, it's possible to centralize all decision-making power in the top manager. In a larger organization, however, some decision-making power should be delegated to lower-level managers and employees on both major and minor issues.

- *Clear communication channels.* All workers should be able to reach others in the firm quickly and easily.

- *Order.* Materials and people should be placed and maintained in the proper location.

- *Equity.* A manager should treat employees and peers with respect and justice.

- *Esprit de corps.* A spirit of pride and loyalty should be created among people in the firm.

These principles became synonymous with the concept of management. Organizations were designed so that no person had more than one boss, lines of authority were clear, and everyone knew to whom they were to report. Naturally, these principles tended to be written down as rules, policies, and regulations as organizations grew larger. That process of rule making often led to rather rigid organizations that didn't always respond quickly to consumer requests. So, where did the idea of bureaucracy come from? We talk about that next.

## Max Weber and Organizational Theory

Sociologist Max Weber (pronounced "Vay-ber") was writing about organization theory in Germany around the same time Fayol was writing his books in France. Weber's book *The*

*Theory of Social and Economic Organizations*, like Fayol's, also appeared in North America in the late 1940s. He studied the hierarchy of many significant historical organizations, including the Roman Empire. It was Weber who promoted the pyramid-shaped organization structure that became so popular in large firms. Weber put great trust in managers and felt that the firm would do well if employees simply *did what they were told*. The less decision making employees had to do, the better. Clearly, this is a reasonable way to operate if you're dealing with relatively uneducated and untrained workers. *Where are you likely to find such workers today?* Often, such workers were the only ones available at the time Weber was writing; most employees did not have the kind of educational background and technical skills that today's workers generally have.

Weber's principles of organization were similar to Fayol's. In addition, Weber emphasized:

- job descriptions
- written rules, decision guidelines, and detailed records
- consistent procedures, regulations, and policies
- staffing and promotion based on qualifications

At one time, less-educated workers were best managed, it was believed, by having them follow many strict rules and regulations monitored by managers or supervisors. Max Weber's rules and regulations could explain why you go to a store and the clerk says, "I'm sorry I can't do that, it's against company policy." Are there industries or businesses today where you think it would be desirable or necessary to continue to use such controls?

Weber believed that large organizations demanded clearly established rules and guidelines that were to be followed precisely. In other words, he was in favour of *bureaucracy*. Although his principles made a great deal of sense at the time, the practice of establishing rules and procedures sometimes was so rigid in some companies that it became counterproductive. However, some organizations today still thrive on Weber's theories. United Parcel Service (UPS), for example, still has written rules and decision guidelines that enable the firm to deliver packages quickly because employees don't have to pause to make decisions. The procedures to follow are clearly spelled out for them. Other organizations are not as effective because they don't allow employees to respond quickly to new challenges. That is clearly the case with disaster relief in many areas, as was the case when Hurricane Katrina hit New Orleans. Later, we shall explore what can be done to make organizations more responsive. First, let's look again at some basic terms and concepts.

## Turning Principles into Organizational Design

Following the concepts of theorists like Fayol and Weber, managers in the latter part of the 1900s began designing organizations so that managers could *control* workers. Many organizations are still organized that way, with everything set up in a hierarchy. A **hierarchy** is a system in which one person is at the top of the organization and there is a ranked or sequential ordering from the top down of managers and others who are responsible to that person. Since one person can't keep track of thousands of workers, the top manager needs many lower-level managers to help. The **chain of command** is the line of authority that moves from the top of the hierarchy to the lowest level. (Review Figure 8.5 for a traditional organization structure.)

Some organizations have a dozen or more layers of management between the chief executive officer (CEO) and the lowest-level employees. If employees want to introduce work changes, they ask a supervisor (the first level of management), who asks his or her manager, who asks a manager at the next level up, and so on. Eventually a decision is made and passed down from manager to manager until it reaches the employees. Such decisions can take weeks or months to be made. Max Weber used the word *bureaucrat* to describe a middle manager whose function was to implement top management's orders. Thus, **bureaucracy** came to be the term used for an organization with many layers of managers who set rules and regulations and oversee all decisions. It is such bureaucracy that

**hierarchy**
A system in which one person is at the top of the organization and there is a ranked or sequential ordering from the top down of managers who are responsible to that person.

**chain of command**
The line of authority that moves from the top of a hierarchy to the lowest level.

**bureaucracy**
An organization with many layers of managers who set rules and regulations and oversee all decisions.

forces employees to say to customers, "I will have to get back to you. I can't make that decision." Recently, many companies, including IBM, went through major reorganizations eliminating thousands of jobs. They wanted to reduce bureaucracy and move more of their people and resources out to the field (closer to the customer).[4]

When employees have to ask their managers for permission to make a change, the process may take so long that customers become annoyed. Such consumer discontent may happen either in a small organization such as a flower shop or in a major organization such as an automobile dealership or a large construction firm. The employee has to find the manager, get permission to make the requested change, return to the customer, explain the management decision, and so on. Has this happened to you in a department store or some other organization? Since many customers want efficient service—and they want it *now*—slow service is simply not acceptable in many of today's competitive firms.

To make customers happier, some companies are reorganizing to give employees power to make more decisions on their own. Rather than always having to follow strict rules and regulations, they are encouraged to please the customer no matter what. As you will see in Chapter 11, giving employees such authority and responsibility to make decisions and please customers is called *empowerment*. Remember that empowerment works only when employees are given the proper training and resources to respond.

It is important to note that well-run bureaucratic organizations can be extremely effective in certain contexts—when there is little innovation in the marketplace, consistency in demand, low-skilled workers, and a lot of time to weigh the consequences of decisions. If firms do not operate under these conditions, there is a need to reorganize.

## Progress Assessment

- What do the terms division of labour and specialization mean?
- What are the principles of management outlined by Fayol?
- What did Weber add to Fayol's principles?

# ISSUES INVOLVED IN STRUCTURING ORGANIZATIONS

What decisions are involved in structuring an organization? Since the turn of the century, many business leaders believed that there was one best way to structure an organization. However, this is changing. A starting point is the vision, values, and mission of the organization, as discussed in Chapter 8. These directives will affect the firm's structure, as employees must be organized so that they can achieve results. Structuring begins here, and also includes the goals and objectives.

Henry Mintzberg supports the current view that there is no single structure that will lead to success for all organizations. "Structure should reflect the organization's situation—for example, its age, size, type of production system, and the extent to which its environment is complex and dynamic. Small businesses with up to five employees do not need to spend time on how to structure themselves. However, the effectiveness of larger organizations or those experiencing significant change is impacted by structure. As well, a firm's design decisions (such as span of control, centralization versus decentralization, and matrix structures) need to be chosen so they can work within the chosen structure and design."[5] These design decisions will be discussed in this chapter. He has also written a book on MBA programs entitled, *Managers Not MBAs*,[6] which is a hard look at the soft practice of managing and management development.

By their nature, many organizational structures today are slow and unwieldy. One Canadian management consultant reported that research shows that 85 to 95 percent of service, quality, or productivity problems stem from the organization's structure and processes. Ask the question: For whose convenience are systems designed? Too often they serve accountants, technocrats, or management. Get the cart behind the horse. Your systems should serve your customers or those producing, delivering, or supporting your products.[7] Remember you can't generate a profit unless you first sell a good or provide a service.

That is why current trends are toward smaller, more flexible structures that let companies react more quickly to today's fast-changing, technologically competitive business climate. They also unleash employees' initiative and enable them to participate in decision making.

When designing responsive organizations, firms have had to deal with several organizational issues: (1) centralization versus decentralization, (2) span of control, (3) tall versus flat organization structures, and (4) departmentalization. The process they use is called change management. This strategic approach starts by preparing for the change, then managing the change, and concludes with re-enforcing the change. Given the risk involved with this type of change, this formal process increases the likelihood of success.

## Centralization Versus Decentralization of Authority

Imagine for a minute that you're a top manager for a retail company such as Roots. Your temptation may be to preserve control over all of your stores to maintain a uniform image and merchandise. You've noticed that such control works well nationally for McDonald's; why not for Roots? The degree to which an organization allows managers at the lower levels of the managerial hierarchy to make decisions determines the degree of decentralization that an organization practises.

When a company needs radical changes, centralized decision making is often necessary, at least for a while. On the other hand, computer and printer maker HP (Hewlett Packard) may be moving in the opposite direction. Its former CEO, Carly Fiorina, changed what was once a decentralized organization structure into a more centralized form. The new CEO, Mark Hurd, is likely to go back to a more decentralized form of management to get more ideas from his various divisions, because there are regional opportunities.[8]

**Centralized authority** occurs when decision-making authority is maintained at the top level of management at the company's headquarters. **Decentralized authority** occurs when decision-making authority is delegated to lower-level managers and employees who are more familiar with local conditions than headquarters' management could be. Figure 9.1 lists some advantages and disadvantages of centralized versus decentralized authority.

Roots customers in Kelowna, for example, are likely to demand clothing styles different from those demanded in Charlottetown or Lethbridge. It makes sense, therefore, to give store managers in various cities the authority to buy, price, and promote merchandise appropriate for each area. Such delegation of authority is an example of decentralized management. Magna International has a decentralized operating structure. Magna's manufacturing divisions operate as independent profit centres aligned by geographic region in each of the company's product areas. This decentralized structure prevents bureaucracy and makes Magna more responsive to customer needs and changes within the global automotive industry as well as within specific regions.[9]

**centralized authority**
An organization structure in which decision-making authority is maintained at the top level of management at the company's headquarters.

**decentralized authority**
An organization structure in which decision-making authority is delegated to lower-level managers more familiar with local conditions than headquarters management could be.

| Advantage | Disadvantage |
|---|---|
| **Centralized** | |
| • Greater top-management control | • Less responsiveness to customers |
| • More efficiency | • Less empowerment |
| • Simpler distribution system | • Interorganizational conflict |
| • Consistent brand/corporate image | • Lower morale away from headquarters |
| **Decentralized** | |
| • Better adaptation to customer wants | • Less efficiency |
| • More empowerment of workers | • Complex distribution system |
| • Faster decision making | • Less top-management control |
| • Higher morale | • Diverse corporate image |

**FIGURE 9.1**

**Advantages and Disadvantages of Centralized Versus Decentralized Management**

## Reaching Beyond Our Borders

### The Internet Assists with Decision Making

Nothing has had a bigger impact on organizations throughout the world than the emergence of the Internet. The Internet is a ready-made marketplace that consists of more than $1 trillion worth of computer power, network connections, and databases stuffed with information about individual consumers and groups. What's more amazing is that it's available to anyone with a personal computer, a modem, and an Internet connection—and it's open 24 hours a day, seven days a week. This may sound wonderful to you, but it is a tremendous challenge to traditional organizations organized in traditional ways. They simply cannot respond quickly enough to marketplace changes or reach global markets as quickly and efficiently as new companies can—companies designed to take advantage of the Internet. What are they to do? How do they reorganize to match such competition?

The CEO of Ford Motor Company says that traditional companies must become more nimble and more closely attuned to consumers. One source at Ford says, "You've got to break down the business into the smallest possible units to give the employees in them authority and accountability." (Throughout this text, we call that empowerment.) In the past, Ford centralized worldwide responsibility for functions such as product development, purchasing, design, and manufacturing. The new model decentralizes such decisions so that managers in Canada, Europe, and South America can readily adapt to consumers in those markets.

Did you know that Ford owns Volvo? To appeal to consumers, Ford is developing more fuel-efficient cars. You can see how the company is trying to make cars that will appeal to almost everyone everywhere.

Like Chrysler and General Motors, all is not well at Ford today. With the drastic reduction in automobile sales starting at the end of 2008, all three companies were facing very serious financial problems. (In Canada, Chrysler and General Motors received loans from the Federal and Ontario governments.) All three have negotiated major reductions in their Canadian labour costs.

Ford was one of the first of the Big Three to embark on a major restructuring; announcing plant closures and job cuts to slash production costs. Other than the already mentioned changes in vehicles, at the same time Ford was able to convince major debt holders to convert their debt to equity. As you can see, adapting organizations to today's markets is an ongoing challenge but one that Ford believes it will be able to do successfully.

Sources: Kathleen Kerwin and Jack Ewing, "Nasser: Ford Be Nimble," *Business Week*, 27 September 1999, 42–43; "Ambitious Ford Aims High as It Sets Targets," *Birmingham Post*, 12 January 2001, 22; John D. Wolpert, "Breaking Out of the Innovation Box," *Harvard Business Review*, August 2002, 77–83; CBC News Online, "The Not-so-Big Three," 22 March 2006, http://www.cbc.ca/news/background/autos/bigthree.html; and CBC News Online, "The Used-to-Be Big Three," 8 May 2009, http://www.cbc.ca/money/story/2009/02/17/f-bigthreeupdate.html.

In contrast, McDonald's feels that purchasing, promotion, and other such decisions are best handled centrally. There's usually little need for each McDonald's restaurant to carry different food products. McDonald's would therefore lean toward centralized authority. However, today's rapidly changing markets, added to global differences in consumer tastes, tend to favour more decentralization and thus more delegation of authority, even at McDonald's. Its restaurants in England offer tea, those in France offer a Croque McDo (a hot ham-and-cheese sandwich), those in Japan offer rice, those in China offer taro and red bean desserts, and so on.[10] Rosenbluth International is a service organization in the travel industry. It too has decentralized so that its separate units can offer the kinds of services demanded in each region while still getting needed resources from corporate headquarters. The Reaching Beyond Our Borders box describes how Ford Motor Company used the Internet to decentralize decision making.

## Choosing the Appropriate Span of Control

**span of control**
The optimum number of subordinates a manager supervises or should supervise.

**Span of control** refers to the optimum number of subordinates a manager supervises or should supervise. There are many factors to consider when determining span of control. At lower levels, where work is standardized, it's possible to implement a wide span of control (15 to 40 workers). For example, one supervisor can be responsible for 20 or more workers who are assembling computers or cleaning up movie theatres. However, the number gradually narrows at higher levels of the organization because work is less

| Advantage | Disadvantage |
|---|---|
| **Narrow**<br>• More control by top management<br>• More chances for advancement<br>• Greater specialization<br>• Closer supervision | • Less empowerment<br>• Higher costs<br>• Slower decision making<br>• Less responsiveness to customers |
| **Wide**<br>• Reduced costs<br>• More responsiveness to customers<br>• Faster decision making<br>• More empowerment | • Fewer chances for advancement<br>• Overworked managers<br>• Loss of control<br>• Less specific management expertise |

**FIGURE 9.2**

**Advantages and Disadvantages of a Narrow Versus a Wide Span of Control**

standardized and there's more need for face-to-face communication. Variables in span of control include the following:

- *Capabilities of the manager.* The more experienced and capable a manager is, the broader the span of control can be. (A large number of workers can report to that manager.)
- *Capabilities of the subordinates.* The more the subordinates need supervision, the narrower the span of control should be. Employee turnover at fast-food restaurants, for example, is often so high that managers must constantly be training new people and thus need a narrow span of control.
- *Geographical closeness.* The more concentrated the work area is, the broader the span of control can be.
- *Functional similarity.* The more similar the functions are, the broader the span of control can be.
- *Need for coordination.* The greater the need for coordination, the narrower the span of control might be.
- *Planning demands.* The more involved the plan, the narrower the span of control might be.
- *Functional complexity.* The more complex the functions are, the narrower the span of control might be.

Other factors to consider include the professionalism of superiors and subordinates and the number of new problems that occur in a day.

In business, the span of control varies widely. The number of people reporting to a company president may range from 1 to 80 or more. The trend is to expand the span of control as organizations reduce the number of middle managers and hire more educated and talented lower-level employees. That is all included in the idea of *empowerment*. It's possible to increase the span of control as employees become more professional, as information technology makes it possible for managers to handle more information, and as employees take on more responsibility for self-management. More companies could expand the span of control if they trained their employees better and were willing to trust them more. Figure 9.2 lists some advantages and disadvantages of a narrow versus a wide span of control.

## Tall Versus Flat Organization Structures

In the early twentieth century, organizations grew bigger and bigger, adding layer after layer of management until they came to have what are called tall organization structures. A **tall organization structure** is one in which the pyramidal organization chart would be quite tall because of the various levels of management. Some organizations had as many as 14 levels, and the span of control was small (that is, there were few people reporting to each manager). You can imagine how a message would be distorted, and how long it

**tall organization structure**
An organization structure in which the pyramidal organization chart would be quite tall because of the various levels of management.

**FIGURE 9.3**

**Narrow Versus Wide Span of Control**
This figure describes two ways to structure an organization with the same number of employees. The tall structure with a narrow span of control has two managers who supervise four employees each. Changing to a flat surface with a wide span of control, the company could eliminate two managers and perhaps replace them with one or two employees, but the top manager would have to supervise ten people instead of two.

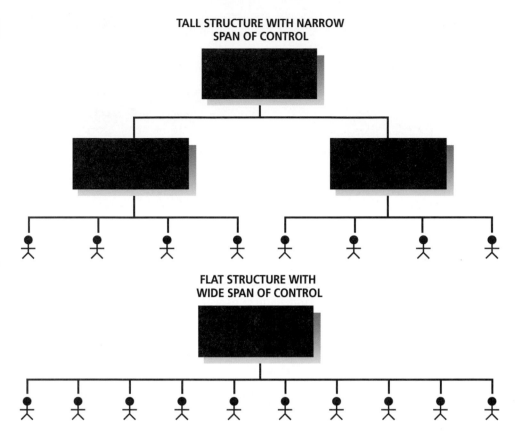

would take, as it moved up the organization from manager to manager and then back down. When viewing such a tall organization, you saw a huge complex of division, department, and area managers, management assistants, secretaries, assistant secretaries, supervisors, trainers, and so on. The cost of keeping all of these managers and support people was quite high. The paperwork they generated was enormous, and the inefficiencies in communication and decision making often became intolerable.

**flat organization structure**
An organization structure that has few layers of management and a broad span of control.

The result was the movement toward flatter organizations. A **flat organization structure** is one that has few layers of management (see Figure 9.3) and a broad span of control (that is, there are many people reporting to each manager). Such structures can be highly responsive to customer demands because authority and responsibility for making decisions may be given to lower-level employees and managers can be spared certain day-to-day tasks. Chrysler has eliminated 6,000 white-collar jobs for just that reason.[11]

In a bookstore that has a flat organization structure, employees may have the authority to resolve customer complaints, process special orders for customers, and so on. In many ways, large organizations were trying to match the service of small firms, whose workers have the authority to deal with customer issues. The flatter organizations became, the larger the span of control became for most managers, and many management positions were eliminated. However, for the new structure to work, many of the issues identified in the previous discussion of span of control had to be in place.

## Advantages and Disadvantages of Departmentalization

**departmentalization**
Dividing an organization into separate units.

**Departmentalization** is dividing an organization into separate units. The traditional way to departmentalize organizations is by function. Functional structure is the grouping of workers into departments based on similar skills, expertise, or resource use. A company might have, for example, a production department, a human resources department, and a finance department. Departmentalization by function enables employees to specialize and work together efficiently. It may also save costs. Other advantages include the following:

1. Employees can develop skills in depth and can progress within a department as they master those skills.
2. The company can achieve economies of scale in that it can centralize similar resources in one area.
3. There's good coordination within the function, and top management can easily direct and control various departments' activities.

As for disadvantages of departmentalization by function,

1. There may be a lack of communication among the different departments. For example, production may be so isolated from marketing that the people making the product do not understand customer needs.
2. Individual employees may begin to identify with their department and its goals rather than with the goals of the organizaion as a whole. For example, the purchasing department may find a good value somewhere and buy a huge volume of goods that have to be stored at a high cost to the firm and may become obsolete or spoil, if not used in a timely manner. Such a deal may make the purchasing department look good, but it hurts the overall profitability of the firm.
3. The company's response to external changes may be too narrow.
4. People may not be trained to take broad-based senior managerial responsibilities; rather, they tend to become narrow specialists.
5. People in the same department tend to think alike (engage in groupthink) and may need input from outside the department to become more creative.

## Alternative Ways to Departmentalize

Functional separation isn't always the most responsive form of organization. So what are the alternatives? Figure 9.4 shows five ways a firm can departmentalize. One form of departmentalization is by product. Heinz has seven divisions, including food service, infant foods, and condiments. Each division resembles a separate business in producing and marketing its products. They believe this type of structure better positions them to respond to their customers, so separate development and marketing processes must be created for each product. Such product-focused departmentalization usually results in differentiated customer relations.

It makes more sense in some organizations to departmentalize by customer group. A pharmaceutical company, for example, might have one department that focuses on the consumer market, another that calls on hospitals (the institutional market), and another that targets doctors. You can see how the customer groups might benefit from having specialists satisfying their needs.

Some firms group their units by geographic location because customers vary so greatly by region. Japan, Europe, and Korea may involve separate departments. Again, the benefits are the same. Geographic locations may also be on a smaller scale; for example, by province or by city.

The decision about which way to departmentalize depends greatly on the nature of the product and the customers served. A few firms find that it's most efficient to separate activities by process. For example, a firm that makes leather coats may have one department cut the leather, another dye it, and a third sew the coat together. Such specialization enables employees to do a better job because they can focus on a few critical skills.

Loblaw Companies Limited, Canada's largest food distributor, operates a number of supermarket chains across Canada including Atlantic Cash & Carry, Dominion, Fortinos, Loblaws, Provigo, and Real Canadian Superstore. They have operated since the 1960s and have developed many excellent brands, including the President's Choice line of products. Over the last three years they have gone through a series of senior management shake-ups as they gear up for direct competition from Walmart. Consolidating their distribution centres resulted in serious problems with their supply chain, costing them millions of dollars. These issues were followed up with significant job cuts in head office, as they moved to a centralized model. Whether this move to a more "responsive organization structure" will foster effective competition with the retail Goliath is yet to be seen.

**Ways to Departmentalize**
A computer company may want to departmentalize by geographic location, a manufacturer by function, a pharmaceutical company by customer group, a leather manufacturer by process, and a publisher by product. In each case the structure must fit the firm's goals.

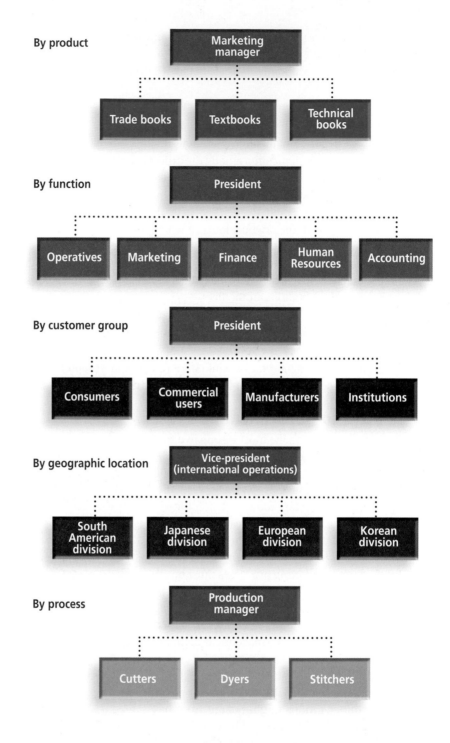

Some firms use a combination of departmentalization techniques; they would be called *hybrid forms*. For example, a company could departmentalize simultaneously among the different layers by function, by geography, and by customers.

The development of the Internet and intranets has created whole new opportunities for reaching customers. Not only can you sell to customers directly over both channels, but you can also interact with them, ask them questions, and provide them with any information they may want. Companies must now learn to coordinate the efforts made by their traditional departments and their technology people to create a friendly, easy-to-use process for accessing information and buying goods and services.[12] The firms that have implemented such coordinated systems for meeting customer needs are winning market share.

## Progress Assessment

- What is bureaucracy? What challenges do bureaucratic organizations face in a time of rapid change?
- Why are organizations becoming flatter?
- What are some reasons for having a narrow span of control in an organization?
- What are the advantages and disadvantages of departmentalization?
- What are the various ways a firm can departmentalize?

# ORGANIZATION MODELS

Now that we've explored the basic issues of organizational design, we can explore in depth the various ways to structure an organization. We'll look at four models: (1) line organizations, (2) line-and-staff organizations, (3) matrix-style organizations, and (4) self-managed teams. You'll see that some of these models violate traditional management principles. The business community is in a period of transition, with some traditional organizational models giving way to new structures. Not only can such transitions be painful, but they can also be fraught with problems and errors. It will be easier for you to understand the issues involved after you have learned the basics of organizational modelling.

## Line Organizations

A **line organization** has direct two-way lines of responsibility, authority, and communication running from the top to the bottom of the organization, with all people reporting to only one supervisor. The military and many small businesses are organized in this way. For example, Mario's Pizza Parlour has a general manager and a shift manager. All general employees report to the shift manager, and he or she reports to the general manager or owner. A line organization does not have any specialists who provide managerial support. For example, there would be no legal department, no accounting department, no personnel department, and no information technology (IT) department. Such organizations follow all of Fayol's traditional management rules. Line managers can issue orders, enforce discipline, and adjust the organization as conditions change.

In large businesses, a line organization may have the disadvantages of being too inflexible, having few specialists or experts to advise people along the line, having lines of communication that are too long, and being unable to handle the complex decisions involved in an organization with thousands of sometimes unrelated products and literally tonnes of paperwork. Such organizations usually turn to a line-and-staff form of organization.

**line organization**
An organization that has direct two-way lines of responsibility, authority, and communication running from the top to the bottom of the organization, with all people reporting to only one supervisor.

## Line-and-Staff Organizations

To minimize the disadvantages of simple line organizations, many organizations today have both line and staff personnel. A couple of definitions will help. **Line personnel** are part of the chain of command that is responsible for achieving organizational goals. Included are production workers, distribution people, and marketing personnel. **Staff personnel** advise and assist line personnel in meeting their goals (e.g., marketing research, legal advising, information technology, ethics advising, and human resource management). See Figure 9.5 for a diagram of a line-and-staff organization. One important difference between line and staff personnel is authority. Line personnel have formal authority to make policy decisions. Staff personnel have the authority to advise the line personnel and make suggestions that might influence those decisions, but they can't make policy changes themselves. The line manager may choose to seek or to ignore the advice of staff personnel.

Many organizations have benefited from the expert advice of staff assistants in areas such as ethics, safety, legal issues, quality control, database management, motivation, and investing.

**line personnel**
Employees who are part of the chain of command that is responsible for achieving organizational goals.

**staff personnel**
Employees who advise and assist line personnel in meeting their goals.

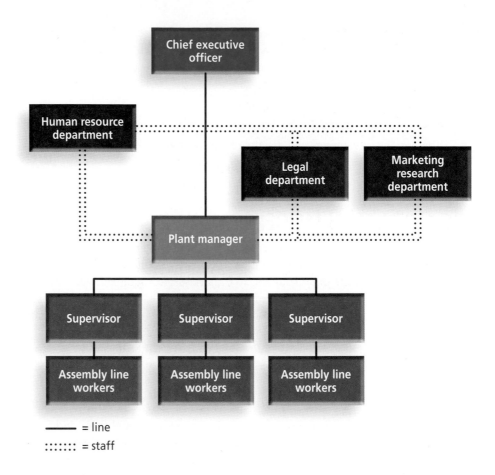

Staff positions strengthen the line positions and are not inferior or lower paid. Having people in staff positions is like having well-paid consultants on the organization's payroll.

## Matrix-Style Organizations

Both line and line-and-staff organization structures suffer from certain inflexibility. Both allow for established lines of authority and communication, and both work well in organizations with a relatively unchanging environment and slow product development, such as firms selling consumer products like toasters and refrigerators. In such firms, clear lines of authority and relatively fixed organization structures are assets that ensure efficient operations.

Today's economic scene, however, is dominated by high-growth industries (e.g., telecommunications, nanotechnology, robotics, and biotechnology) unlike anything seen in the past. In such industries, competition is stiff and the life cycle of new ideas is short. Emphasis is on product development, creativity, special projects, rapid communication, and interdepartmental teamwork.[13] The economic, technological, and competitive environments are rapidly changing.

**matrix organization**
An organization in which specialists from different parts of the organization are brought together to work on specific projects but still remain part of a line-and-staff structure.

From those changes grew the popularity of the matrix organization. In a **matrix organization**, specialists from different parts of the organization are brought together to work on specific projects but still remain part of a line-and-staff structure. (See Figure 9.6 for a diagram of a matrix organization.) In other words, a project manager can borrow people from different departments to help design and market new product ideas.

Matrix organization structures were first developed in the aerospace industry at firms such as Boeing and Lockheed Martin. The structure is now used in banking, management consulting firms, accounting firms, ad agencies, and school systems. Advantages of a matrix organization structure include the following:

- It gives flexibility to managers in assigning people to projects.

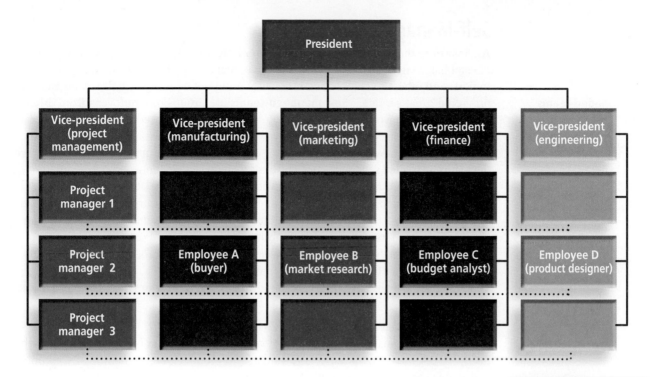

**FIGURE** 9.6

- It encourages intcrorganizational co-operation and teamwork.
- It can result in creative solutions to problems such as those associated with product development.
- It provides for efficient use of organizational resources.

Although it works well in some organizations, the matrix style doesn't work well in others. As for disadvantages,

- It's costly and complex.
- It can cause confusion among employees as to where their loyalty belongs—to the project manager or to their department.
- It requires good interpersonal skills and co-operative employees and managers; communication problems can emerge.
- It may be only a temporary solution to a long-term problem.

If it seems to you that matrix organizations violate some traditional managerial principles, you're right. Normally a person can't work effectively for two bosses. Who has the real authority? Which directive has the first priority: the one from the project manager or the one from the employee's immediate supervisor? In reality, however, the system functions more effectively than you might imagine. To develop a new product, a project manager may be given temporary authority to "borrow" line personnel from production, marketing, and other line functions. Together, the employees work to complete the project and then return to their regular positions. Thus, no one really reports to more than one manager at a time. The effectiveness of matrix organizations in high-tech firms has led to the adoption of similar concepts in many firms, including such traditional firms as Rubbermaid. During the past decade, Rubbermaid turned out an average of one new product every day using the team concept from matrix management.

A potential problem with matrix management, however, is that the project teams are not permanent. They are formed to solve a problem or develop a new product, and then they break up. There is little chance for cross-functional learning because experts from each function are together for such little time.

**A Matrix Organization**
In a matrix organization, project managers are in charge of teams made up of members of several departments. In this case, project manager 2 supervises employees A, B, C, and D. These employees are accountable not only to project manager 2 but also to the head of their individual departments. For example, employee B, a market researcher, reports to project manager 2 and to the vice-president of marketing.

# Self-Managed Teams

**self-managed teams**
Groups of employees from different departments who work together on a long-term basis.

An answer to the disadvantage of the *temporary* teams created by matrix management is to establish *long-lived teams* and to empower them to work closely with suppliers, customers, and others to quickly and efficiently bring out new, high-quality products while providing great service.[14] **Self-managed teams** are groups of employees from different departments who work together on a long-term basis (as opposed to the temporary teams established in matrix-style organizations).[15] Usually the teams are empowered to make decisions on their own without having to seek the approval of management.[16] That's why the teams are called self-managed. The barriers between design, engineering, marketing, distribution, and other functions fall when interdepartmental teams are created. One Smooth Stone (a company featured in the Video Case) is a corporate events company. They put together large, one-time functions for corporate clients. They have a team of highly skilled and trained staff that go from the planning and execution of one corporate function to another. Sometimes the teams are interfirm. Toyota, for example, works closely with teams at other firms to produce its cars.

Figure 9.7 lists the advantages and disadvantages of these four types of organizations.

# Going Beyond Organizational Boundaries

Self-managed teams work best when the voice of the customer is brought into organizations.[17] Customer input is especially valuable to product development teams. Suppliers and distributors should be included on the team as well. A self-managed team that includes customers, suppliers, and distributors goes beyond organizational boundaries.

Some firms' suppliers and distributors are in other countries. Thus, self-managed teams may share market information across national boundaries. The government may encourage the networking of teams, and government coordinators may assist such projects.

---

**FIGURE | 9.7**

**Types of Organizations**
Each form of organization has its advantages and disadvantages.

|  | Advantage | Disadvantage |
|---|---|---|
| **Line** | • Clearly defined responsibility and authority<br>• Easy to understand<br>• One supervisor for each person | • Too inflexible<br>• Few specialists to advise<br>• Long lines of communication<br>• Unable to handle complex questions quickly |
| **Line and Staff** | • Expert advice from staff to line personnel<br>• Establishes lines of authority<br>• Encourages co-operation and better communication at all levels | • Potential overstaffing<br>• Potential overanalyzing<br>• Lines of communication can get blurred<br>• Staff frustrations because of lack of authority |
| **Matrix** | • Flexible<br>• Encourages co-operation among departments<br>• Can produce creative solutions to problems<br>• Allows organization to take on new projects without adding to the organizational structure<br>• Provides for more efficient use of organizational resources | • Costly and complex<br>• Can confuse employees<br>• Requires good interpersonal skills and co-operative managers and employees<br>• Difficult to evaluate employees and to set up reward systems |
| **Self-Managed Teams** | • Greatly increases interdepartmental coordination and co-operation<br>• Quicker response to customers and market conditions<br>• Increased employee motivation and morale | • Some confusion over responsibility and authority<br>• Perceived loss of control by management<br>• Difficult to evaluate employees and to set up reward systems<br>• Requires self-motivated and highly trained workers |

In that case, cross-functional teams break the barriers between government and business. The use of cross-functional teams is only one way in which businesses have changed to interact with other companies. In the next section of this chapter we look at other ways that organizations manage their various interactions.

## Progress Assessment

- What is the difference between line and staff personnel?
- What management principle does a matrix-style organization challenge?
- What may hinder the development of self-managed teams?

## MANAGING INTERACTIONS AMONG FIRMS

Whether it involves customers, suppliers and distributors, or the government, **networking** is using communications technology and other means to link organizations and allow them to work together on common objectives.[18] Organizations are so closely linked by the Internet that each can find out what the others are doing in real time. **Real time** simply means the present moment or the actual time in which something takes place. Internet data are available in real time because they are sent instantly to various organizational partners as they are developed or collected. The net effect is a rather new concept called transparency. **Transparency** occurs when a company is so open to other companies working with it that the once-solid barriers between them become see-through and electronic information is shared as if the companies were one. Because of this integration, two companies can now work as closely together as two departments once did in traditional firms. One approach to this transparency is seen in how Pistachio works with their suppliers as described in the Green Box.

Can you see the implications for organizational design? Most organizations are no longer self-sufficient or self-contained. Rather, many modern organizations are part of a vast network of global businesses that work closely together. An organization chart showing

**networking**
Using communications technology and other means to link organizations and allow them to work together on common objectives.

**real time**
The present moment or the actual time in which something takes place; data sent over the Internet to various organizational partners as they are developed or collected are said to be available in real time.

**transparency**
A concept that describes a company being so open to other companies working with it that the once-solid barriers between them become see-through and electronic information is shared as if the companies were one.

## GreenBOX

### Ethical Consumerism

The primary mandate of retail chain, Pistachio (owned by Indigo Books), is to provide products that last and don't take from the natural resources of the earth. They want to create, use, and reuse things intelligently. They do this through being environmentally caring and holding suppliers accountable to their standards.

All of their products (in the following categories: stationery and invitations, health and beauty, and gifts) are certified for authenticity as to having the least possible impact on the Earth. Where applicable, every item sold in their stores is processed without chlorine, uses soy or vegetable inks, doesn't involve animal testing, is government-certified organic, is biodegradeable, is fair trade, is made from post-consumer waste, or is recyclable.

They have a list of criteria they apply to each one of their suppliers. Their suppliers must be committed to ethical sourcing, producing locally hand-made products. Supplier's missions must also include improving working and environmental conditions. Part of the accountability is addressed with third-party certifications on products they buy, including, where appropriate, such designations as "Forest Stewardship Council," "USDA approved," and "Made in Canada."

Pistachio also demonstrates a commitment to social responsibility by supporting the development of a local environmental community centre by contributing a percentage of each store's sales.

Sources: Heidi Sopinka, "Our Philosophy Is to Buy Better, Buy Less and Buy Forever," *The Globe and Mail*, 22 November 2008, http://www.epistachio.com.

**virtual corporation**
A temporary networked organization made up of replaceable firms that join and leave as needed.

To review the possible scope of operations of VANOC, visit their Web site at www.vancouver2010.com.

what people do within any one organization is simply not complete, because the organization is part of a much larger system of firms. A modern organization chart would show people in different organizations and indicate how they are networked. This is a relatively new concept, however, so few such charts are yet available.

The organization structures tend to be flexible and changing. That is, one company may work with a design expert from a different company in Italy for a year and then not need that person anymore. Another expert from another company in another country may be hired next time for another project. Such a temporary networked organization, made up of replaceable firms that join and leave as needed, is called a **virtual corporation** (see Figure 9.8). Hosting the 2010 Winter Olympics is a dramatic example of a situation requiring a temporary networked organization. This may sound confusing because it is so different from traditional organization structures, and in fact, traditional managers do often have trouble adapting to the speed of change and the impermanence of relationships

The Vancouver Organizing Committee (VANOC) is responsible for the planning, organizing, financing, and staging of the 2010 Olympic and Paralympic Winter Games. With an operating budget of $1.6 billion and a capital budget of $580 million, the VANOC will employee and utilize 25,000 volunteers.

**FIGURE | 9.8**

**A Virtual Corporation**
A virtual corporation has no permanent ties to the firms that do its production, distribution, legal, and other work. Such firms are very flexible and can adapt to changes in the market quickly.

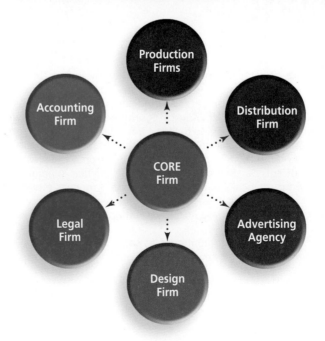

that have come about in the age of networking. We discuss adaptation to change in the final section of this chapter; first, though, we describe how organizations are using benchmarking and outsourcing to manage their interactions with other firms.

## Benchmarking and Core Competencies

Traditionally, organizations have tried to do all functions themselves. That is, each organization had a separate department for accounting, finance, marketing, production, and so on. Today's organizations are looking to other organizations to help them in areas where they are not able to generate world-class quality. **Benchmarking** (also referred to as best practices) involves comparing an organization's practices, processes, and products against the world's best.[19] For example, K2 is a company that makes skis, snowboards, in-line skates, and related products. It studied the compact-disc industry and learned to use ultraviolet inks to print graphics on skis. It went to the aerospace industry to get Piezo technology to reduce vibration in its snowboards (the aerospace industry uses the technology for wings on planes). Finally, it learned from the cable TV industry how to braid layers of fibre-glass and carbon, and adapted that knowledge to make skis. Suncor, one of Canada's largest emitters of greenhouse gases, continually benchmarks "best-of-class" companies in terms of sustainability reporting.[20] By doing so, they are able to evaluate their performance in reducing their carbon footprint.

Benchmarking is also used in a more directly competitive way. For example, Zellers may compare itself to Walmart to see what, if anything, Walmart does better. Zellers would then try to improve its practices or processes to become even better than Walmart. Sam Walton used to do competitive benchmarking regularly. He would visit the stores of competitors and see what, if anything, the competitor was doing better. When he found something better—say, a pricing program—he would come back to Walmart and make the appropriate changes.

Benchmarking has become a significant activity in Canada. Governments and large and small companies are all involved in procedures to discover and apply the best practices available. Industry Canada and Statistics Canada have accumulated extensive statistics on the use of benchmarking in a variety of industries. Some examples are breweries, flour mixing and cereal production, electronic computing, paperboard manufacturing, musical instruments, and the recording industry.

If an organization can't do as well as the best in any particular area, such as shipping, it often will try to outsource the function to an organization that is the best (e.g., FedEx). You may recall from Chapter 1 that outsourcing involves assigning various functions (e.g., production, legal work) to outside organizations. We have already discussed some problems associated with outsourcing, especially when companies outsource functions to other countries. Jobs are lost in Canada and this has a negative impact on our economy. Some functions, such as information management and marketing, may be too important to assign to outside firms. In that case, the organization should benchmark on the best firms and restructure its departments to try to be equally good.

An article titled "Offshore Outsourcing Seen Reshaping the Tech Sector" highlights this growing trend. The article states the following points:

> *Increasing global competition to decrease prices has led technology players to find low-cost partners or contract out work, according to Ramalinga Raju, chairman of Satyam Computer Services Ltd, a tech provider based in India. "Competition is something you cannot wish away. More often than not, offshore delivery has meant an offset in costs." Potential savings are dramatic. In Canada, the average computer programmer with two to three years experience earns between $33,000 and $65,000 annually. In comparison, programmers in India earn between $8,000 and $13,000 annually. Canadian partners include document management software maker Hummingbird Ltd. of Toronto and business intelligence software provider Cognos Inc. of Ottawa.*

**benchmarking**
Comparing an organization's practices, processes, and products against the world's best.

SME Direct (http://strategis.ic. gc.ca/epic/internet/indir-ect. nsf/en/h_uw00000e.html) is a Web site designed specifically for small and medium-sized businesses (SMEs). The government has collected numerous diagnostic and benchmarking tools, links to informative Web sites, relevant databases, and a wealth of other resources to assist in decision making.

## DEALING with CHANGE

### Hurd to the Rescue at Hewlett-Packard Company

Few managers have received more attention in the last few years than Carleton (Carly) Fiorina. She led the fight to unite her company, Hewlett-Packard (HP), with Compaq Computer. The news media and the stock market experts all expected the attempt to fail, but the integration took place and Fiorina had the task of reorganizing the two companies into one.

Fiorina had to get rid of duplicate products and eliminate some employees to realize the cost savings that the integration made available. She hoped to cut costs by $3 billion annually. The 2002 stock market crash occurred in the middle of her reorganization attempt, and made the process more difficult. Eventually, Fiorina was ousted from the firm and Mark Hurd took over. Hurd came from NCR, a much smaller firm, where he was known as a cost cutter and strong operations manager. In other words, he was more involved in the day-to-day operations of the firm.

Experts have suggested that Hurd adopt a decentralized form of management at first, especially with consumer products with which he had no experience at NCR. They also suggest that he restructure the sales force and focus more on innovation, especially in the printer business. Finally, Hurd has been advised to restore the old corporate culture, which emphasized simple objectives, enlightened business practices, and trust in employees to make the right decisions (empowerment). Results from the past three years would seem to indicate a successful turnaround has happened. In 2009, Hewlett-Packard Company is the largest technology company in the world with revenue of over $100 billion. They are the largest seller in the world of personal computers. In 2008 they completed the acquisition of Electronic Data Systems, thus filling a void in technology services. Making organization change is never easy, but it is especially difficult for a large firm, in a highly competitive market, growing its business through acquisitions—the latter requiring a reconciliation of different corporate cultures.

Sources: Peter Burrows and Ben Elgin, "Memo to: Mark Hurd," *Business Week*, 11 April 2005, 38–39; Michael S. Malone, "What's the Hurd Instinct?" *The Wall Street Journal*, 19 May 2005, A14; and "Hewlett-Packard," *Wikipedia, The Free Encyclopedia*, http://en.wikipedia.org/w/index.php?title=Hewlett-Packard&oldid=322884558.

*In addition to lower costs, outsourcing frees up financial resources for better use, reports ATI Technologies Inc. of Markham, Ontario. All of the company's graphics chips are made for it by low-cost manufacturers in Taiwan, allowing the company to invest more heavily in research and development.*[21]

**core competencies**
Those functions that an organization can do as well as or better than any other organization in the world.

When a firm has completed its outsourcing process, the remaining functions are the firm's core competencies. C. K. Prahalad and Gary Hamel believe that businesses need to organize around their core competencies. **Core competencies** are those functions that the organization can do as well as or better than any other organization in the world. For example, Nike is great at designing and marketing athletic shoes. Those are its core competencies. It outsources the manufacturing of those shoes, however, to other companies that can make shoes better and less expensively than Nike itself can. Similarly, Dell is best at marketing computers and outsources most other functions, including manufacturing and distribution, to others. Celestica and Nortel have also outsourced most of their manufacturing functions.

## ADAPTING TO CHANGE

Once you have structured an organization, you must be prepared to adapt that structure to changes in the market. That is not always easy to do. Over a number of years, it is easy for an organization to become stuck in its ways. Employees have a tendency to say, "That's the way we've always done things. If it isn't broken, don't fix it." Managers also get stuck in their ways. Managers may say that they have 20 years' experience when the truth is that they've had one year's experience 20 times. Introducing change into an organization is thus one of the hardest challenges facing any manager. Nonetheless, that is what is happening to companies around the country and around the world. Traditional companies are used to operating in traditional ways. Such ways are often no longer appropriate. But change is hard. You have old facilities that are no longer efficient and you have to get rid of them. That's exactly what Ford and other companies are doing. You may have to cut your labour force to lower costs. Again, that is what companies are doing. They hope to rehire those people in the future when the reorganization results in a faster-growing firm.

Several companies have been cited in the business literature as having difficulty reinventing themselves in response to changes in the competitive environment. They include Polaroid and the Bay. New cameras (digital) and new kinds of film brought about the downfall of Polaroid, which filed for bankruptcy and was later sold. The Bay has attempted to re-establish itself in the very competitive merchandising business after more than one recent change in ownership. New managers at firms experiencing such challenges face tremendous hurdles as they try to revive the companies. Mergers and acquisitions pose special challenges in adapting to change. That's why so many mergers of big corporations fail. The Dealing With Change box discusses the new management at HP, and the challenges facing Mark Hurd, its CEO. He is dealing with issues of decentralization, empowerment, and corporate culture, all subjects of this chapter.

## Restructuring for Empowerment

To implement the empowerment of employees, firms often must reorganize dramatically. Sometimes that may mean restructuring the firm to make front-line workers the most important people in the organization. **Restructuring** is redesigning an organization so that it can more effectively and efficiently serve its customers.[22] Until recently, front-desk people in hotels, clerks in department stores, and tellers in banks hadn't been considered key personnel. Instead, managers were considered key people, and they were responsible for directing the work of the front-line people. The organization chart in a typical firm looked something like the traditional organization pyramid shown in Figure 9.9.

A few service-oriented organizations have turned the traditional organization structure upside down. An **inverted organization** has contact people at the top and the chief executive officer at the bottom. There are few layers of management, and the manager's job is to assist and support front-line people, not boss them around. Figure 9.9 illustrates the difference between an inverted and a traditional organizational structure.

A good example of an inverted organization is NovaCare, a provider of rehabilitation care.[23] At its top are some 5,000 physical, occupational, and speech therapists. The rest of the organization is structured to serve those therapists. Managers consider the therapists to be their bosses, and the manager's job is to support the therapists by arranging contacts with nursing homes, handling accounting and credit activities, and providing training.

**restructuring**
Redesigning an organization so that it can more effectively and efficiently serve its customers.

**inverted organization**
An organization that has contact people at the top and the chief executive officer at the bottom of the organization chart.

**FIGURE** | **9.9**

**Comparison of a Traditional Organization Structure and an Inverted Organization Structure**

Traditional Organization

- Top management
- Middle management
- Supervisory management
- Front-line workers

Inverted Organization

- Empowered front-line workers (often in teams)
- Support personnel
- Top management

Companies based on this organization structure support front-line personnel with internal and external databases, advanced communication systems, and professional assistance. Naturally, this means that front-line people have to be better educated, better trained, and better paid than in the past. It takes a lot of trust for top managers to implement such a system—but when they do, the payoff in customer satisfaction and in profits is often well worth the effort. In the past, managers controlled information—and that gave them power. In more progressive organizations, everyone shares information, often through an elaborate database system. Today, that information sharing is among firms as well as within firms. Organizations have formed close alliances with other firms (for example, one firm may design the product and the other firm produces it). The communication among such firms is often just as close and personal as within a single firm.

## Focusing on the Customer

No matter what organizational model you choose or how much you empower your employees, the secret to successful organization change is to focus on customers and give them what they want. That's what Ford is now doing. Former CEO Bill Ford has introduced a new program called "The Way Forward." "True customer focus means that our business decisions originate from our knowledge of what the customer wants," Ford says. He confessed that product plans in the past were "defined by our capacity" and vehicles were designed to use plant capacity "sometimes at the expense of creativity."[24]

One thing Ford and other auto manufacturers have learned is that customers today want more fuel-efficient (usually smaller) cars or hybrids.[25] GM, Ford, and Chrysler have lost billions of dollars over the last few years selling their gas-guzzling trucks and SUVs. Sometimes it is hard for such large companies to adapt to market changes, such as higher gas prices, but eventually they *do* change, or they go out of business.

## The Restructuring Process

It's not easy to move from an organization dominated by managers to one that relies heavily on self-managed teams. How you restructure an organization depends on the status of the present system. If the system already has a customer focus, but isn't working well, a total quality management approach may work.

**Total quality management (TQM)** is the practice of striving for maximum customer satisfaction by ensuring quality from all departments. TQM calls for *continual improvement of present processes*. Processes are sets of activities strung together for a reason, such as the process for handling a customer's order. The process may consist of getting the order in the mail, opening it, sending it to someone to fill, putting the order into a package, and sending it out. In Chapter 10 we will review the importance of quality control in operations management.

**Continuous improvement (CI)** means constantly improving the way the organization does things so that customer needs can be satisfied. Many of the companies spotlighted in this book practise it. For example, if you visit Celestica's Web site, you will read how continuous improvement underpins everything that the company does to provide value to its customers, empower its employees to innovate, and respond to customer and competitive requirements. The key focus elements for continuous improvement at Celestica are customer satisfaction, defect prevention and elimination, and process management and control. Continuous improvement provides the framework to achieve and maintain technology leadership and set the benchmark for product quality.[26]

---

**total quality management (TQM)**
Striving for maximum customer satisfaction by ensuring quality from all departments.

**continuous improvement (CI)**
Constantly improving the way the organization does things so that customer needs can be better satisfied.

Creation Technologies is a Canadian-based, world-class electronic manufacturing services provider to original equipment manufacturers. They build premier customer relationships, in part, through continuous improvement. All of their divisions have received ISO 9001 certification, as well as medical certification under ISO13485. For more information about this dynamic company go to www.creationtech.com.

It's possible, in an organization with few layers of management and a customer focus, that new computer software and employee training could lead to a team-oriented approach with few problems. In bureaucratic organizations with many layers of management, however, TQM is not useful. Continual improvement doesn't work when the whole process is being done incorrectly. When an organization needs dramatic changes, only re-engineering will do.

**Re-engineering** is the fundamental rethinking and radical redesign of organizational processes to achieve dramatic improvements in critical measures of performance. Note the words *radical redesign* and *dramatic improvements*. At IBM's credit organization, for example, the procedure for handling a customer's request for credit once went through a five-step process that took an average of six days. By completely re-engineering the customer-request process, IBM cut its credit request processing time from six days to four hours! In re-engineering, narrow, task-oriented jobs become multidimensional. Employees who once did as they were told now make decisions on their own. Functional departments lose their reason for being. Managers stop acting like supervisors and instead behave like coaches. Workers focus more on the customers' needs and less on their bosses' needs. Attitudes and values change in response to new incentives. Practically every aspect of the organization is transformed, often beyond recognition.

Can you see how re-engineering is often necessary to change a firm from a managerial orientation to one based on self-managed teams? Re-engineering may also be necessary to adapt an organization to fit into a virtual network. Remember, re-engineering involves radical redesign and dramatic improvements. Not all organizations need such dramatic change. In fact, because of the complexity of the process, many re-engineering efforts fail. In firms where re-engineering is not feasible, restructuring may do. As discussed earlier in this chapter, restructuring involves making relatively minor changes to an organization in response to a changing environment. For example, many firms have added an Internet marketing component to the marketing department. That is a restructuring move, but it is not drastic enough to be called re-engineering.

**re-engineering**
The fundamental rethinking and radical redesign of organizational processes to achieve dramatic improvements in critical measures of performance.

## Creating a Change-Oriented Organizational Culture

Any organizational change is bound to cause some stress and resistance among members of the firm. Firms adapt best when they have a change-oriented culture. **Organizational (or corporate) culture** may be defined as widely shared values within an organization that provide unity and co-operation to achieve common goals. It's obvious from visiting any McDonald's restaurant that effort has been made to maintain a culture that emphasizes quality, service, cleanliness, and value. Each restaurant has the same feel, the same look, the same atmosphere. In short, each has a similar organizational culture.

An organizational culture can also be negative. Have you ever been in an organization where you feel that no one cares about service or quality? The clerks may seem uniformly glum, indifferent, and testy. The mood seems to pervade the atmosphere so that patrons become unhappy or upset. It may be hard to believe that an organization, especially a profit-making one, can be run so badly and still survive. When searching for a job, therefore, it is important to study the organizational culture to see if you will thrive in the present culture.[27]

Mintzberg notes that culture affects the way in which employees are chosen, developed, nurtured, interrelated, and rewarded. The kinds of people attracted to an organization and the way they can most effectively deal with problems and each other are largely a function of the culture a place builds and the practices and systems that support it.[28]

**organizational (or corporate) culture**
Widely shared values within an organization that provide coherence and co-operation to achieve common goals.

Canadian Tire Financial Services has an annual Shadow Day when children of employees join their parents for a morning at work. At a BBQ lunch, scholarships for post-secondary education are presented. What are some benefits of working for a company that provides such a positive organizational culture?

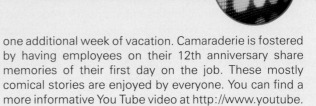

## SPOTLIGHT ON **Small Business**

### Getting the Word Out

One of the top three employers, according to the 2008 Great Place to Work Institute, is Environics Communication Inc. You may have seen their name, as they offer marketing comunications and public-relations services for businesses. They build credibility by instilling with each employee the over-arching goal of doing the right thing. Respect is fostered by ensuring that full credit is always given to those who initiate winning concepts. After five years, each employee receives $4,000 toward a holiday, plus one additional week of vacation. Camaraderie is fostered by having employees on their 12th anniversary share memories of their first day on the job. These mostly comical stories are enjoyed by everyone. You can find a more informative You Tube video at http://www.youtube.com/watch?v=_v3O84qMwMI.

Source: "Great Places to Work in Canada," *The Globe and Mail*, 28 April 2008, http://resources.greatplacetowork.com/news/pdf/2008_best_workplaces_in_canada_feature.pdf.

The very best organizations have cultures that emphasize service to others, especially customers.[29] The atmosphere is one of friendly, concerned, caring people who enjoy working together to provide a good product at a reasonable price. Those companies that have such cultures have less need for close supervision of employees, not to mention policy manuals, organization charts, and formal rules, procedures, and controls. The key to a productive culture is mutual trust. You get such trust by giving it. The very best companies stress high moral and ethical values such as honesty, reliability, fairness, environmental protection, and social involvement. One such example is TD Bank Financial Group. Creating contented workers isn't all about cash, says Teri Currie, executive vice-president of human resources. "We've found that it's really about pride," Currie says. "Making that goodwill sustainable means helping your people achieve their own definition of success. They stay because they're proud to be here." One of the best ways that TD has found to instill that sense of pride, Currie says, is by actively supporting volunteerism. Here again, it's not just about the money: not only did the bank give $27.5 million to charities in 2005, but it encourages employees to get involved by allowing paid time off—over and above vacation days—for volunteer activities.[30]

Nortel Networks has undergone major changes over the last ten years in terms of organizational structure. One key ingredient in recreating Nortel is its new customer-oriented mission of Business Made Simple.[31] According to president and CEO Mike Zafirovski, "It is our mantra for driving cultural change internally and it will come to life through our behaviour and actions. The premise is simple: We are simplifying our own business, making it easier for customers to do business with us and making our products simpler and more intuitive."[32] The Spotlight on Small Business box looks at how one small organization successfully implemented a team-oriented culture.

Thus far, we've been talking as if organizational matters were mostly controllable by management. The fact is that the formal organization structure is just one element of the total organizational system. In the creation of organizational culture, the informal organization is of equal or even greater importance. Let's explore this notion next.

**formal organization**
The structure that details lines of responsibility, authority, and position; that is, the structure shown on organization charts.

**informal organization**
The system of relationships and lines of authority that develops spontaneously as employees meet and form power centres; that is, the human side of the organization that does not appear on any organization chart.

## The Informal Organization

All organizations have two organizational systems. One is the **formal organization**, which is the structure that details lines of responsibility, authority, and position. It's the structure shown on organization charts. The other is the **informal organization**, which is the system of relationships that develops spontaneously as employees meet and form power centres. It consists of the various cliques, relationships, and lines of authority that develop outside the formal organization. It's the human side of the organization that doesn't show on any organization chart.

No organization can operate effectively without both types of organization. The formal system is often too slow and bureaucratic to enable the organization to adapt quickly. However, the formal organization does provide helpful guides and lines of authority to follow in routine situations.

The informal organization is often too unstructured and emotional to allow careful, reasoned decision making on critical matters. It's extremely effective, however, in generating creative solutions to short-term problems and providing a feeling of camaraderie and teamwork among employees.

In any organization, it's wise to learn quickly who the important people are in the informal organization. Typically, there are formal rules and procedures to follow for getting certain supplies or equipment, but those procedures may take days. Who in the organization knows how to obtain supplies immediately without following the normal procedures? Which administrative assistants should you see if you want your work given first priority? These are the questions to answer to work effectively in many organizations.

The informal organization's nerve centre is the grapevine (the system through which unofficial information flows between and among managers and employees). The key people in the grapevine usually have considerable influence in the organization.

In the old "us-versus-them" system of organizations, where managers and employees were often at odds, the informal system often hindered effective management. In the new, more open organizations, where managers and employees work together to set objectives and design procedures, the informal organization can be an invaluable managerial asset that often promotes harmony among workers and establishes the corporate culture. That's a major advantage, for example, of self-managed teams.

Michael Sabia, the former CEO of Bell Canada said, "A formal organization is responsive to the exertion of power, but an informal organization is responsive to persuasion. It's changed the way I think about management." In 2002, Michael took over the reins of a struggling 122 year-old company that needed to banish its monopolist mentality to compete. Traditional approaches weren't changing the culture. Working with an outside consultant, Jon Katzenbach, a plan was developed to work from within, using the informal organization. Read about the plan and its success at www.katzenbach.com/Work/News/NewsInstance/tabid/60/Default.aspx?Entity_ID=551.

As effective as the informal organization may be in creating group co-operation, it can still be equally powerful in resisting management directives. Employees may form unions, go on strike together, and generally disrupt operations.[33] Learning to create the right corporate culture and to work within the informal organization is a key to managerial success.

## Progress Assessment

- What is an inverted organization?
- Why do organizations outsource functions?
- What is organizational culture?

# SUMMARY

**LO ▸ 1** Explain the historical organizational theories of Henri Fayol and Max Weber.

1. Until the twentieth century, most businesses were rather small, the processes of producing goods were rather simple, and organizing workers was fairly easy. Not until the 1900s and the introduction of mass production did businesses become complex. During this era, business theorists emerged.

   **What concepts did Fayol and Weber contribute?**
   Fayol introduced principles such as unity of command, hierarchy of authority, division of labour, subordination of individual interests to the general interest, authority, clear communication channels, order, and equity. Weber added principles of bureaucracy such as job descriptions, written rules and decision guidelines, consistent procedures, and staffing and promotions based on qualifications.

**LO ▸ 2** Discuss the various issues involved in structuring organizations.

2. Issues involved in structuring and restructuring organizations include (1) centralization versus decentralization, (2) span of control, (3) tall versus flat organization structures, and (4) departmentalization.

   **What are the basics of each issue?**
   The problem with tall organizations is that they slow communications. The trend is to eliminate managers and flatten organizations. The span of control becomes larger as employees become self-directed. Departments are often being replaced or supplemented by matrix organizations and cross-functional teams. Use of cross-functional teams results in decentralization of authority.

   **How do inverted organizations fit into these concepts?**
   An inverted organization usually results from a major re-engineering effort because the changes are dramatic in that employees are placed at the top of the hierarchy and are given much training and support, while managers are at the bottom and are there to train and assist employees.

**LO ▸ 3** Describe and differentiate the various organizational models.

3. Organizational design is the coordinating of workers so that they can best accomplish the firm's goals. New forms of organization are emerging that enable firms to be more responsive to customers.

   **What are the traditional forms of organization and their advantages?**
   The two traditional forms of organization explored in the text are (1) line organizations and (2) line-and-staff organizations. A line organization has the advantages of having clearly defined responsibility and authority, being easy to understand, and providing one supervisor for each person. Most organizations have benefited from the expert advice of staff assistants in areas such as safety, quality control, computer technology, ethics counselling, human resource management, and investing.

   **What are the alternative forms of organization?**
   The alternatives are matrix organizations and self-managed teams.

   **How do they differ?**
   Matrix organizations involve temporary assignments (projects) that give flexibility to managers in assigning people to projects and encourage interorganizational co-operation and teamwork. Self-managed teams are long term and have all the benefits of the matrix style.

**LO ▸ 4** Understand how organizations are connecting with their external environment

4. Networking is using communications technology and other means to link organizations and allow them to work together on common objectives.

   **What is a virtual corporation?**
   A virtual corporation is a networked organization made up of replaceable firms that join the network and leave it as needed.

**Why do firms outsource some of their functions?**

Some firms are very good at one function, for example, marketing. Competitive benchmarking tells them that they are not as good as some companies at production or distribution. The company may then outsource those functions to companies that can perform them more effectively and efficiently. The functions the company retains are called the firm's core competencies.

5. Organizational culture may be defined as widely shared values within an organization that provide coherence and co-operation to achieve common goals.

**LO ▶ 5** Explain how restructuring, organizational culture, and informal organizations can help businesses adapt to change.

**How do inverted organizations fit into these concepts?**

An inverted organization usually results from a major restructuring effort because the changes are dramatic in that employees are placed at the top of the hierarchy and are given much training and support while managers are at the bottom and are there to train and assist employees.

**How can organizational culture and the informal organization hinder or assist organizational change?**

The very best organizations have cultures that emphasize service to others, especially customers. The atmosphere is one of friendly, concerned, caring people who enjoy working together to provide a good product at a reasonable price. Companies with such cultures have less need than other companies for close supervision of employees, policy manuals, organization charts, and formal rules, procedures, and controls. This opens the way for self-managed teams.

## KEY TERMS

benchmarking 281

bureaucracy 267

centralized authority 269

chain of command 267

continuous improvement (CI) 284

core competencies 282

decentralized authority 269

departmentalization 272

economies of scale 265

economies of scope 266

flat organization structure 272

formal organization 286

hierarchy 267

informal organization 286

inverted organization 283

line organization 275

line personnel 275

matrix organization 276

networking 279

organizational (or corporate) culture 285

real time 279

re-engineering 285

restructuring 283

self-managed teams 278

span of control 270

staff personnel 275

tall organization structure 271

total quality management (TQM) 284

transparency 279

virtual corporation 280

## CRITICAL THINKING

Now that you have learned some of the basic principles of organization, pause and think about when you have already applied such concepts yourself or have been involved with an organization that did.

1. Did you find that a division of labour was necessary and helpful?

2. Were you assigned specific tasks or were you left on your own to decide what to do?

3. Were promotions based strictly on qualifications, as Weber suggested? What other factors may have been considered?

4. How can the informal organization help or impede an organization's effectiveness?

Businesses are now trying to redesign their structures to optimize skill development while increasing communication among employees in different departments. The goal, remember, is to better serve customers and to win their loyalty.

1. What kind of skills and attributes might you need to prepare yourself to work in such an organization?

2. What can you do to increase your personal ability to feel comfortable with change in your work setting?

## DEVELOPING WORKPLACE SKILLS

1. There is no better way to understand the effects of having many layers of management on communication accuracy than to play the game of Message Relay. Choose seven or more members of the class and have them leave the classroom. Then choose one person to read the following paragraph and another student to listen. Call in one of the students from outside and have the "listener" tell him or her the information contained in the paragraph. Then bring in another student and have the new listener repeat the information to him or her. Continue the process with all those who left the room. Do not allow anyone in the class to offer corrections as each listener becomes the storyteller in turn. In this way, all students can hear how the facts become distorted over time. The distortions and mistakes are often quite humorous, but they are not so funny in organizations such as Ford, which once had 22 layers of management.

   Here's the paragraph:

   *Dealers in the Maritimes have received more than 130 complaints about steering on the new Commander and Roadhandler models of our minivans. Apparently, the front suspension system is weak and the ball joints are wearing too fast. This causes slippage in the linkage and results in oversteering. Mr. Berenstein*

   *has been notified, but so far only 213 of 4,300 dealers have received repair kits.*

2. Describe some informal groups within an organization with which you are familiar (at school, at work, etc.). What have you noticed about how those groups help or hinder progress in the organization?

3. Imagine that you are working for Kitchen Magic, an appliance manufacturer that produces, among other things, dishwashers for the home. Imagine further that a competitor introduces a new dishwasher that uses sound waves to clean dishes. The result is a dishwasher that cleans even the worst burnt-on food and sterilizes the dishes and silverware as well. You need to develop a similar offering fast, or your company will lose the market. Write an e-mail to management outlining the problem and explaining your rationale for recommending the use of a self-managed team to respond quickly and what type of skills you need.

4. Divide the class into teams of five. You are a producer of athletic shoes. Identify all of main functional areas of your business. Looking at your list, identify which ones you view as your core competencies, and why? For those that are not part of your competencies, how would you go about outsourcing them?

## TAKING IT TO THE NET

www.mcgrawhillconnect.ca

### Purpose

To describe Ford Motor Company's formal and informal organizational structures.

### Exercise

When you think of how Ford Motor Company is organized, you may think of it in terms of its brands (Mercury, Lincoln, and Volvo) or its businesses (Automotive Operations, and Ford Credit). However, the company serves all of its brands and businesses through what it calls career programs. Learn more about this practice by going to www.mycareer.ford.com/OurCompany.asp.

1. How are Ford's career programs organized?

2. Click on the link of one of the career programs. What types of positions does this function provide? What are the preferred qualifications of the candidates Ford would like to find to fill these positions?

3. Describe Ford's unique hiring process. If you've applied for jobs before, how does Ford's hiring process differ from what you've experienced? What could this process tell you about Ford's organizational culture? How does the process help Ford find employees who will fit into its culture?

## ANALYZING MANAGEMENT DECISIONS

### IBM Is Both an Outsourcer and a Major Outsource for Others

Few companies are better known for their manufacturing expertise than IBM. Nonetheless, even IBM has to adapt to today's dynamic marketplace. In the area of personal computers, for example, IBM was unable to match the prices or speed of delivery of mail-order firms such as Dell Computer. Dell built machines after receiving orders for them and then rushed the computers to customers. IBM, in contrast, made machines ahead of time and hoped that the orders would match its inventory.

To compete against firms like Dell, IBM had to custom-make computers for its business customers, but IBM was not particularly suited to do such work. However, IBM did work with several distributors that were also having problems. The distributors were trying to custom-make IBM machines but were forced to carry a heavy inventory of parts and materials to do so. Distributors were also tearing IBM computers apart and putting them back together with other computer companies' parts to produce custom-made computers.

IBM decided to allow its distributors to store parts and materials and then custom-make computers to customer demand. In other words, IBM outsourced about 60 percent of its commercial PC business. Distributors such as Inacom Corporation became profitable, and IBM was able to offer custom-made PCs competitive in price with those of Dell and other direct-mail companies.

More recently, IBM has begun selling its technology—tiny disk drives, speedy new chips, and more—to its former competitors! For some of these new partners, IBM will design their new products and let them explore its labs. In short, IBM is doing a bit of reverse outsourcing in that it is offering itself as a search and product development company ready to work with others. Thus, IBM will sell networking chips to Cisco Systems and not compete with that company any more. And it will likewise sell disk drives to EMC. IBM benchmarked its final products against these companies and saw that it was not winning. The winning strategy, it decided, was to join them and become an even better team. IBM's long-range strategy is to move away from hardware toward software development. It acquired PricewaterhouseCoopers to put more emphasis on services rather than hardware.

Sources: Michael Useem and Joseph Harder, "Leading Laterally in Company Outsourcing," *Sloan Management Review*, Winter 2000, 25–36; Daniel Eisenberg, "There's a New Way to Think @ Big Blue," *Time*, 20 January 2003, 49–53; and Alison Overholt, "In the Hot Seat," *Fast Company*, January 2003, 46.

### Discussion Questions

1. What does it say about today's competitive environment when leading companies such as IBM give up competing and decide to work with competitors instead?

2. What effects will outsourcing have on trade relationships among countries?

3. If more Canadian companies unite their technologies, what will that do to competitors in other countries? Should foreign companies do more uniting with Canadian companies themselves? What about Canadian companies uniting with foreign companies?

4. How much influence will the Internet have on world trade and outsourcing among countries? What does the Internet provide that wasn't available before?

## CHAPTER 10

# Producing World-Class Goods and Services

PROFILE

## LEARNING OBJECTIVES

**AFTER YOU HAVE READ AND STUDIED THIS CHAPTER, YOU SHOULD BE ABLE TO:**

**LO ▶ 1** Define operations management and explain what types of firms use it.

**LO ▶ 2** Describe the operations management planning issues involved in both the manufacturing and the service sectors, including facility location, facility layout, and quality control.

**LO ▶ 3** Discuss the problem of measuring productivity in the service sector, and tell how technology is leading to productivity gains in service companies.

**LO ▶ 4** Explain how manufacturing processes can be used in the manufacturing sector.

**LO ▶ 5** Describe seven manufacturing techniques that have improved the productivity of companies.

## PROFILE

### Getting to Know Pierre Beaudoin of Bombardier Inc.

After many ups and downs, in September 2009, Bombardier employed 60,000 people in 29 countries, had a market value of $1 billion, and is the world's No. 1 passenger train maker and No. 3 civil aircraft manufacturer. The company designs and manufactures a portfolio of rail vehicles and aviation products. Their competition includes Embraer, a state-owned aircraft manufactured from Brazil.

If you know anything about Bombardier, the one person who's name would come up is Laurent Beaudoin. He was the President and CEO for 35 years, the son-in-law of its founder, Joseph-Armand Bombardier. Laurent oversaw the development of this goliath—by Canadian standards—manufacturing company. So, who is Pierre Beaudoin, the 47-year-old who studied business administration and industrial relations at McGill and became President and CEO in June of 2008? Back in 1985, while Pierre was working for a sporting goods company, his father, Laurent, asked him to help develop the Sea-Doo. Pierre started as test driver for the first few prototypes of the Sea-Doo, and for the next 16 years he worked in various capacities for Bombardier Recreational Products. In 2001, he was appointed President of Bombardier Aerospace, and then in 2004 he was appointed Executive Vice President of Bombardier Inc.

In his short tenure as President of the parent company, Pierre has had to lead the company through both some very bad and good times. With the collapse of the global economy in the second half of 2008 and into 2009, which lead to a significant slowdown. However, Bombardier remained profitable in this difficult time and also committed to invest for the long term in research and development programs such as the *CSeries* commercial aircraft, the *Learjet 85* business jet, and the very high speed train, to prepare for the next economic cycle.

Pierre has supported a Code of Ethics and Business Conduct that addresses employee ethical conduct and business practices and relationships with external stakeholders. He has publicly supported the development of sustainable transportation systems including more fuel-efficient aircraft that have targeted a 20 percent reduction of carbon dioxide emissions, and rail products to increase energy efficiency by up to 50 percent (these commitments were included in their first Corporate Social Responsibility report, which was released in December 2008). Bombardier is an official supporter of the Vancouver 2010 Olympic and Paralympic Games, with total annual donations of $10 million. Pierre is a twenty-first-century leader of a truly world-class, Canadian-based manufacturer.

Sources: Joe Castaldo, "Laurent Beaudoin Interview, Déjà vu," *Canadian Business Magazine*, 7 August 2008; "Bombardier Signs Airline for Five Q400 NextGen Airliners," *Market Wire*, 3 August 2009; "Bombardier Signs 225 Million USD Contracts to Supply, Operate and Maintain an Automated People Mover System in Phoenix, USA," CCNMatthews, 14 July 2009; and www.bombardier.com.

# CANADA TODAY

Canada is a large industrial country with many major industries. We are one of the largest producers of forest products in the world, with plants in nearly all provinces turning out a vast array of wood, furniture, and paper products. There are giant aluminum mills in Quebec and British Columbia, automotive-related manufacturing plants in Ontario and Quebec, and aircraft plants in Ontario, Quebec, and Manitoba. Oil, natural gas, and coal are produced in Alberta, Saskatchewan, Newfoundland and Labrador, Nova Scotia, and British Columbia, and are processed there or in other provinces; a vast array of metals and minerals come from all parts of Canada. These are only some of the thousands of components, products, and natural resources produced or processed in Canada.

Canada is facing some serious challenges to its ability to remain a modern, competitive industrial country. Today's business climate is characterized by constant and restless change and dislocation, as ever-newer technologies and increasing global competition force companies to respond quickly to these challenges. Many factors account for our difficulties in the world's competitive race. Among them are inadequate improvement in productivity and unrelenting competition from the United States, Japan, Germany, and more recently from India, China, and other Southeast Asian countries; inadequate education and retraining programs for our workforce; our "branch plant economy," whereby many subsidiaries are owned by foreign parent companies and profits are mostly returned to these foreign-based companies rather then invested in Canada; and not enough money spent on research and development. Where once a Canadian dollar was worth US$0.65, values closer to parity are forcing Canadian manufactures to improve productivity to remain competitive. Figure 10.1 lists these and other challenges.

Despite these challenges, Canada still ranks fairly well in world competitiveness, as discussed in Analyzing Management Decisions in Chapter 3. However, one cannot expect this to continue, as other countries are becoming stronger and more competitive. In response, the federal government's innovation strategy will, among other areas, focus on research and development as a way to improve our competitiveness. Let us look at research and development next.

**FIGURE** | **10.1**

**Management Issues Survey**
The Canadian Manufacturers & Exporters asked manufacturers to identify current and future challenges that will fundamentally change the nature of their business over the next five to ten years. For more information on each of these issues, visit http://cme-mec.ca/pdf/cme08.pdf.

Source: Courtesy Canadian Manufacturers & Exporters, http://cme-mec.ca/pdf/cme08.pdf, "Most Pressing Challenges," p. 11.

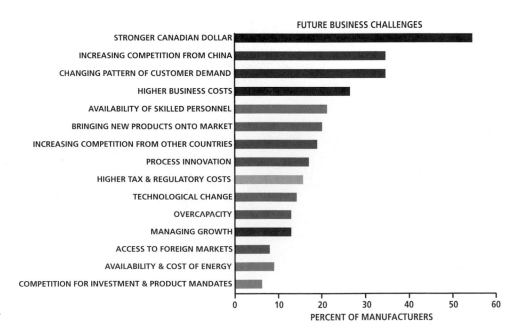

# Research and Development

According to the *Canadian Oxford Dictionary*, **research and development (R&D)** is defined as work directed toward the innovation, introduction, and improvement of products and processes. When evaluating why some companies are more competitive than others, the terms *technology* and *innovation* often come up. What do these terms mean?

The Centre for Canadian Studies at Mount Allison University, in co-operation with the Canadian Heritage Canadian Studies Programme, produces the *About Canada* series. Innovation in Canada is the focus of one of these documents.

> *Technology is know-how, knowing how to make and use the tools for the job. It's the combination of technology with markets that creates innovation and gives a competitive edge. An innovation is a new product or process that can be purchased. Put another way, an idea may lead to an invention, but it cannot be called an innovation until it is commercialized. When technological know-how is developed, sold, distributed, and used, then it becomes an innovation.*[1]

In the Survey of Innovation conducted by Statistics Canada, respondents indicated that the three most important objectives of innovation are to improve product quality, to increase production capacity, and to extend product range. Since that time, the Science, Innovation, and Electronic Information Division (SIEID) of Statistics Canada has piloted more surveys that focus on the importance of innovation. SIEID believes that innovation and the adoption and dissemination of innovative technologies and processes are vital to economic growth and development. It continues to elaborate by stating that, through innovation, new products are introduced in the market, new production processes are developed and introduced, and organizational changes are made. Through the adoption of newer, more advanced technologies and practices, industries can increase their production capabilities, improve their productivity, and expand their lines of new goods and services.[2]

Private industry, Canadian universities, hospitals, and government laboratories were expected to expend $29 billion on R&D in 2007.[3] The federal government alone— considered the principal source of R&D funds in Canada—spent an estimated $9.5 billion in 2007/2008 on science and technology.[4] Figure 10.2 outlines Canada's top ten corporate R&D spenders. Corporate spending on R&D continued to decline in 2006.[5] As you may note, four of the top 10 spenders were organizations that are part of the communications/telecommunications equipment and aerospace industries. Without the expenditures of Nortel, the decline in spending would have been even worse. A review of the corporate R&D spenders reflected that more companies spent more than $100 million while the largest spenders historically spent less. Such expenditures clearly show that relatively smaller companies understand that R&D is a critical component in ensuring their growth and competitiveness both domestically and internationally.

Based on its research, what does RE$EARCH Infosource Inc. forecast? "...in the 5 years (2002–2006) have seen an increase in corporate mergers...Brand name Canadian companies have disappeared, and this surely does not bode well for R&D investment, as their new owners inevitably rationalize company-wide R&D spending. For another, economic growth is being driven by the oil & gas and mineral and metals section, industries that have traditionally low levels of R&D spending. And manufacturing —which is typically a hotbed of R&D investment—has been hit hard by the fall of the U.S. dollar, squeezing profit margins and leaving fewer funds available for R&D, precisely at a time when more investment in innovation is needed."[6]

**research and development (R&D)**
Work directed toward the innovation, introduction, and improvement of products and processes.

## FIGURE | 10.2

**Canada's Top Corporate R&D Spenders 2008**

| Rank 2007 | Rank 2006 | Company | R&D Expenditures FY2007 $000 | R&D Expenditures FY2006 $000 | R&D Expenditures % Change 2006–2007 | Revenue FY2007 $000 | Research Intensity R&D as % of Revenue** | Industry |
|---|---|---|---|---|---|---|---|---|
| 1 | 1 | Nortel Networks Corporation* | $1,851,880 | $2,199,020 | −15.8 | $11,766,910 | 15.7 | Comm/telecom equipment |
| 2 | 2 | Bell Canada | $1,260,000 | $1,459,000 | −13.6 | $17,822,000 | 7.1 | Telecommunications services |
| 3 | 3 | Magna International Inc.* | $725,490 | $652,108 | 11.3 | $28,016,812 | 2.6 | Automotive |
| 4 | 4 | Pratt & Whitney Canada Corp.(fs) | $444,000 | $481,000 | −7.7 | $3,300,000 | 13.5 | Aerospace |
| 5 | 6 | IBM Canada Ltd.(fs) | $377,000 | $360,000 | 4.7 | nd | | Software and computer services |
| 6 | 8 | Atomic Energy of Canada Limited | $288,982 | $246,144 | 17.4 | $554,113 | 52.2 | Energy/oil and gas |
| 7 | 11 | Research in Motion* | $253,839 | $178,767 | 42 | $3,264,278 | 7.8 | Comm/telecom equipment |
| 8 | 10 | Alcatel-Lucent(fs) | $236,000 | $187,167 | 26.1 | nd | | Comm/telecom equipment |
| 9 | | Sanofi-aventis Group++(fs) | $207,156 | $216,987 | −4.5 | $660,769 | 31.4 | Pharmaceuticals/ biotechnology |
| 10 | 12 | Apotex Inc. | $181,818 | $178,757 | 1.7 | $1,021,900 | 17.8 | Pharmaceuticals/ biotechnology |

NOTES:

We have attempted, wherever possible, to provide gross R&D expenditures before deduction of investment tax credits or government grants. FY2006 R&D expenditure figures may have been adjusted, as more accurate information became available.

Canadian-owned company results include worldwide R&D expenditures; foreign subsidiaries (fs) include R&D expenditures for Canadian operations only.

We have attempted, wherever possible, to provide revenue figures net of interest and investment income.

* = Converted to CDN$ at average 2007 = $1.0748, 2006 = $1.1341 (Bank of Canada)

++ = Includes sanofi-aventis Canada Inc. and Sanofi Pasteur Limited

** = $1 million or more of revenue

fs = Foreign subsidiary (includes R&D expenditures for Canadian operations only)

nd = Not disclosed

Source: RE$EARCH Infosource Inc., www.researchinfosource.com.

# CANADA'S EVOLVING MANUFACTURING AND SERVICES BASE

Over the previous two decades, foreign manufacturers captured huge chunks of the North American market for basic products such as steel, cement, machinery, and farm equipment using the latest in production techniques. That competition forced companies to greatly alter their production techniques and managerial styles. Many firms are now as good as or better than competitors anywhere in the world. What have Canadian manufacturers done to regain a competitive edge? They've emphasized the following:

- focusing on customers
- maintaining close relationships with suppliers and other companies to satisfy customer needs
- practising continuous improvement
- focusing on quality
- saving on costs through site selection
- relying on the Internet to unite companies
- adopting production techniques such as enterprise resource planning, computer-integrated manufacturing, flexible manufacturing, and lean manufacturing

As you may recall from Figure 1.5 in Chapter 1, the manufacturing sector employs slightly over 7 percent of Canada's working population. Manufacturing not only is important in employing Canadians, but is also critical to our economy, as manufacturers perform 75 percent of private-sector R&D. They have also been increasing their use of advanced production technologies at an average annual rate of more than 20 percent over the last several years.[7]

As we progress through this chapter, you'll see that operations management has become a challenging and vital element of Canadian business. The growth of Canada's manufacturing base will likely remain a major business issue in the near future. There will be debates about the merits of moving production facilities to foreign countries. Serious questions will be raised about replacing workers with robots and other machinery. Major political decisions will be made regarding protection of Canadian manufacturers through quotas and other restrictions on free trade. Concerns about the impact of manufacturing on our environment will result in the development of new technologies as discussed in the Green Box. Regardless of how these issues are decided, however, there will be many opportunities along the way.

The service sector will also continue to get attention as it continues to become a larger part of the overall economy. Service productivity is a real issue, as is the blending of service and manufacturing through the Internet. Since many of tomorrow's graduates will likely find jobs in the service sector, it is important to understand the latest operations management concepts for this sector.

Each year companies discover new ways of automating that eliminate the need for human labour. This photo shows an automated apparatus known as a Flipper. It can pour a dozen pancakes and flip them when needed on one griddle while, at the same time, flipping burgers on another grill. Are any restaurants in your area already using equipment like this?

## From Production to Operations Management

**Production** is the creation of goods and services using the factors of production: land, labour, capital, entrepreneurship, and knowledge. Production has historically been associated with manufacturing, but the nature of business has changed significantly in the last

**production**
The creation of finished goods and services using the factors of production: land, labour, capital, entrepreneurship, and knowledge.

## GreenBOX

### Carbon Capture and Storage

One of Canada's primary resources is its fossil fuels. Abundant supplies of oil, natural gas, and coal make this country one of the world's most attractive energy centres for continuing investment and development. However, with this economic opportunity comes a challenge, to mitigate greenhouse gas (GHG) emissions and their impact on climate change. More and more evidence is being gathered by the scientific community that global emissions growth could bring rapid climate change. The challenge is to reduce GHG emissions while continuing economic progress.

Carbon dioxide capture and storage (CCS) is one way to address the carbon challenge. With CCS, carbon dioxide emissions from large industrial facilities are separated from the plant's process or exhaust system, compressed, and injected deep underground.

CCS can be built as an add-on to existing fossil energy infra-structure or incorporated into new and future facilities. The main components of this operation are: capture, transportation, and storage. Once the carbon dioxide is captured at a plant, it needs to be transported to a location with the appropriate geological formation. These stable sedimentary rock formations, that securely held vast oil and gas reserves, can now be used to hold carbon dioxide, which will be injected into these formations.

Both the federal and a number of provincial governments are financially supporting the development of CCS and bringing forward legislation to reduce GHG emissions or the carbon footprint.

Carbon dioxide is also being used for enhanced oil recovery by companies including Encana. Since 2000, Encana has been injecting existing oil reserves with carbon dioxide to extract more resource.

Source: The Canadian $CO_2$ Capture and Storage Technology Network, Natural Resources Canada, www.CO$_2$network.gc.ca; and Racel Pulfer, "Burying King Coal," *Canadian Business*, 28 April 2008, 21–22.

---

20 years or so. The service sector, including Internet services, has grown dramatically, and the manufacturing sector has not grown much at all. As discussed in Chapter 1, Canada is a service economy—that is, one dominated by the service sector. This can be a benefit to future graduates because many of the top-paying jobs are in legal services, medical services, entertainment, broadcasting, and business services such as accounting, finance, and management consulting.

**production management**
The term used to describe all of the activities that managers do to help their firms create goods.

**Production management** has been the term used to describe all of the activities that managers do to help their firms create goods. To reflect the change in importance from manufacturing to services, the term *production* often has been replaced by *operations* to reflect both goods and services production. **Operations management**, then, is a specialized area in management that converts or transforms resources (including human resources) into goods and services. It includes inventory management, quality control, production scheduling, follow-up services, and more. In an automobile plant, operations management transforms raw materials, human resources, parts, supplies, paints, tools, and other resources into automobiles. It does this through the processes of fabrication and assembly. In a school, operations management takes inputs—such as information, professors, supplies, buildings, offices, and computer systems—and creates services that transform students into educated people. It does this through a process called education.

**operations management**
A specialized area in management that converts or transforms resources (including human resources) into goods and services.

Some organizations—such as factories, farms, and mines—produce mostly goods. Others—such as hospitals, schools, and government agencies—produce mostly services. Still others produce a combination of goods and services. For example, an automobile manufacturer not only makes cars but also provides services such as repairs, financing, and insurance. And at Harvey's you get goods such as hamburgers and fries, but you also get services such as order taking, order filling, and cleanup.

As this chapter's profile mentions, Bombardier is a Canadian-based, world-class manufacturing organization, which also earns substantial revenue from their service businesses. Bombardier Aerospace also is involved in fractional ownership, aircraft charter and management, aircraft maintenance, and pilot training.

## Manufacturers Turn to a Customer Orientation and Services for Profit

Many manufacturers have spent an enormous amount of money on productivity and quality initiatives. Companies that have prospered and grown—General Electric and Dell, to name just a couple—have taken a similar road to success. They've expanded operations management out of the factory and moved it closer to the customer, providing services such as custom manufacturing, fast delivery, credit, installation, and repair.[8]

Another example of the growing importance of services is in the area of corporate computing. The average company spends only one-fifth of its annual personal computer budget on purchasing hardware. The rest (80 percent) goes to technical support, administration, and other maintenance activities. Because of this, IBM has shifted from its dependence on selling computer hardware to becoming a major supplier of computer services, software, and technology components.[9] Its purchase of Pricewaterhouse-Coopers' tech consulting affiliate was intended to increase its presence in the service sector. General Electric is doing the same; it generates more than $5 billion a year in worldwide revenues from Internet transactions.[10]

Companies such as Celestica and Ford have outsourced much of their production processes and are focusing more on building customer relationships and brand images.[11] As you can see, operations management has become much more focused on services, because by redirecting corporate thinking towards satisfying customer needs better than the competition, they retain their customers.

### Progress Assessment

- What are some challenges that Canada is facing in its ability to remain a competitive country?
- How is innovation related to research and development?
- Explain the difference between production management and operations management.

# OPERATIONS MANAGEMENT PLANNING

Operations management planning involves many of the same issues in both the service and manufacturing sectors. These issues include facility location, facility layout, and quality control. The resources used may be different, but the management issues are similar.

## Facility Location

**facility location**

The process of selecting a geographic location for a company's operations.

Companies today are making strategic decisions when establishing, operating, and closing facilities. **Facility location** is the process of selecting a geographic location for a company's operations. In keeping with the need to focus on customers, one strategy in facility location is to find a site that makes it easy for consumers to access the company's service and to maintain a dialogue about their needs. For example, Hewlett-Packard (Canada) Company opened a new computer manufacturing facility in Toronto in a bid to speed new machines to Canadian business customers as fast as archrival Dell Incorporated. In doing so, HP became the only major computer vendor active in Canada to actually assemble machines here.[12] Flower shops and banks are putting facilities in supermarkets so that their products are more accessible than they are in freestanding facilities. You can find a Second Cup inside some Home Depot stores and there are Tim Hortons outlets in some gas stations. Customers can buy gas and their meals, all in one location. Of course, the ultimate in convenience is never having to leave home to get services. That's why there is so much interest in Internet banking, Internet car shopping, Internet education, and so on. For brick-and-mortar businesses (e.g., retail stores) to beat such competition, they have to choose good locations and offer outstanding service to those who do come. Study the location of service-sector businesses—such as hotels, banks, athletic clubs, and supermarkets—and you will see that the most successful ones are conveniently located.

### Facility Location for Manufacturers

A major issue of the recent past has been the shift of manufacturing organizations from one city or province to another in Canada, or to other foreign sites. In 2005, Gildan, a Canadian company and one of the world's largest manufacturers of T-shirts, closed two plants in Canada, transferring production to North Carolina.[13] Such shifts sometimes result in pockets of unemployment in some geographic areas and lead to tremendous economic growth in others that benefit from these shifts. The Making Ethical Decisions box considers some of the issues surrounding such moves.

Why would companies spend millions of dollars to move their facilities from one location to another? Issues that influence site selection include labour costs; availability of resources, such as labour; access to transportation that can reduce time to market; proximity to suppliers; proximity to customers; low crime rates; quality of life for employees; a lower cost of living; and the ability to train or retrain the local workforce.

One of the most common reasons for a business move is the availability of inexpensive labour or the right kind of skilled labour. Even though labour cost is becoming a smaller percentage of total cost in some highly automated industries, the low cost of labour remains a key reason that many producers move their plants. For example, low-cost labour is one reason why some firms are moving to Malaysia, Mexico, and other countries with low wage rates. Some of these firms have been charged with providing substandard working conditions and/or exploiting children in the countries where they have set up factories. Others, such as Grupo Moraira (Grupo M), a real estate construction and sales company in the Dominican Republic, are being used as role models for global manufacturing. Grupo M provides its employees with higher pay relative to local businesses, transportation to and from work, daycare centres, discounted food, and health clinics. Its operations are so efficient that it can compete in world markets and provide world-class services to its employees.

Inexpensive resources are another major reason for moving production facilities. Companies usually need water, electricity, wood, coal, and other basic resources. By moving

## Making Ethical Decisions

### Financial Support or Not?

In early 2009, both General Motors and Chrysler approached the federal and Ontario governments, along with their unions, looking for financial support and major concessions. Both companies indicated that without this support, they would be forced to close their Canadian operations. They claimed they were unable to compete with the lower wage costs of non-North American owned facilities. Closure of their operations would result in tens of thousands of job losses between their plants and their suppliers' operations. They sought billions of dollars from the governments to cover losses and update their production facilities while labour leaders had to agree to re-negotiate labour contracts significantly reducing labour costs. Do you think the governments and unions should have agreed to the demands of General Motors and Chrysler? What could have been the consequences if they didn't? What would you have chosen to do?

to areas where natural resources are inexpensive and plentiful, firms can significantly lower costs—not only the cost of buying such resources but also the cost of shipping finished products. Often the most important resource is people, so companies tend to cluster where smart and talented people are. Witness the Ottawa area, also known as Silicon Valley North.

Reducing time to market is another decision-making factor. As manufacturers attempt to compete globally, they need sites that allow products to move through the system quickly, at the lowest costs, so that they can be delivered rapidly to customers.[14] Access to various modes of transportation (such as highways, rail lines, airports, water, and the like) is thus critical. Information technology (IT) is also important to quicken response time, so many firms are seeking countries with the most advanced information systems.

Another way to work closely with suppliers to satisfy your customers' needs is to locate your production facilities near supplier facilities. That cuts the cost of distribution and makes communication easier.[15]

Many businesses are building factories in foreign countries to get closer to their international customers. That's a major reason why the U.S. automaker General Motors builds cars in Windsor, Ontario, and Japanese automaker Toyota builds cars in Cambridge, Ontario. Japanese-based automaker Honda opened an engine factory plant in Alliston, Ontario, in 2008, close to its two assembly plants. Honda Canada president Hiroshi Kobayashi told a news conference that this site selection "supports Honda's global strategic manufacturing focus of bringing manufacturing and sales operations to the local market."[16] When firms select foreign sites, they consider whether they are near airports, waterways, and highways so that raw materials and finished goods can be moved quickly and easily.

Businesses also study the quality of life for workers and managers. Quality-of-life questions include these: Are there good schools nearby? Is the weather nice? Is the crime rate low? Does the local community welcome new businesses? Do the chief executive and other key managers want to live there? Sometimes a region with a high quality of life is also an expensive one, which complicates the decision. In short, facility location has become a critical issue in operations management. The Dealing with Change box looks at how a major natural disaster can affect manufacturing and service organizations within the region and beyond. Nothing challenges firms more.

## Outsourcing

The previous chapter noted that many companies now try to divide their production between core competencies, work they do best in-house, and outsourcing, letting outside companies service them by doing what they are experts at. The result sought is the best-quality products at the lowest possible costs.

Outsourcing goods and services has become a hot practice in North America. Software development, call-centre jobs, and back-office jobs have been moving to developing

With average labour costs about one-fortieth of those in Canada, China is now a leading manufacturer of not only textiles and consumer products, but also increasingly sophisticated electronic equipment, software, and other technologies. It is competing increasingly on the basis of high-end value-added products, as well as costs, using some of the world's best technologies and drawing from a pool of highly skilled talent.

countries for some time. The range of jobs now shifting to these countries includes accounting, financial analysis, medicine, architecture, aircraft maintenance, law, film production, and banking activities.[17] One estimate puts the current value of outsourced goods and services around the world at a whopping US$6 trillion a year.[18] Macadamian, an Ottawa-based software firm, estimates that by 2009, 90 percent of companies will outsource their software R&D, while only a quarter outsourced it in 2004.[19] Keep in mind that while outsourcing may look good on paper financially, if a company does not do its homework, outsourcing can become a problem due to language and cultural differences, differences in expectations, etc. A Canadian organization, the Centre for Outsourcing Research and Education (CORE), has been formed to provide organizations with the knowledge and skills to manage outsourcing activities.[20] CORE has released a report on new trends affecting companies outsourcing activities. More than just a cost-saving tool, outsourcing is being used as a strategic tool for focusing scarce human capital on core business activities.

One outsourcing model that is working involves the software company mentioned above, Macadamian Technologies Inc. Using software engineers in eastern Europe and India, Macadamian uses a distributed model with completely transparent communication. Using wikis, every small iteration on a project is reviewed by the rest of the team members, who then post comments. A project manager gets the final say. Everyone shares their work resulting in clients getting more flexibility and quicker turnaround.

Keep in mind that Canadian companies are also benefiting from other countries' outsourcing. For example, Procter & Gamble's bar soap for North America is now manufactured by Newmarket-based Trillium Health Care Products. This contract makes Trillium—already the leader in making private-label soap for retailers—the second- or third-largest bar soap maker on the continent.[21] Canada is one of the top IT outsourcing destinations in the world, especially for the United States. Reasons noted for why U.S. companies will outsource to Canada include: availability of highly skilled IT professionals, stable workforce without high attrition rates, similar culture and language, familiarity with American business processes, same time zones allowing for real time communication, and an excellent communication system between the two countries.[22]

There can be instances, however, when jobs do not need to be lost to foreign locations. When the Bank of Montreal (BMO) outsourced its human resources processing services to California-based Exult Inc., it negotiated an unusual condition: Take our business, take our people. As part of this $75-million-a-year contract for the next ten years, more than 100 former BMO employees now work for Exult in the same office

## DEALING with CHANGE

### Responding to a Major Disaster

Hurricane Katrina has been called "the largest natural disaster in American history." So what do you do if you have your corporate headquarters in New Orleans, where almost the whole city was flooded, and your only factory is in Long Beach, Mississippi, where the devastation was enormous? If you are Thomas Oreck, you plan to resume manufacturing in just two weeks. Here was the situation: The vacuum cleaner factory in Long Beach had no phone service, no electricity, and no water. Roads in and out of town were blocked. Hundreds of employees had lost their homes, and hundreds more were missing. The list of things needed to restart was long: diesel fuel, generators, food, water, and housing. One team of workers went looking for generators while another team searched for mobile homes.

Arrangements were made with United Parcel Service to distribute the vacuum cleaners and bring in food and water. The grounds around the manufacturing facility became a campus of sorts, with housing, health clinics, and offices. Web sites were established so that workers could contact each other and family members. The company was operating again as soon as it possibly could.

Businesses responded to the disaster in many ways. Getting old factories started again was a major contribution because it renewed old jobs and created some

hope. Hurricane Katrina closed 126 Walmart facilities, but all but 14 were operating again within a couple of weeks. Hundreds of businesses did what they could to help, and they responded quickly. Springs Industries of Fort Mill, South Carolina, sent sheets, blankets, and comforters. Anheuser Busch sent 2.5 million cans of drinking water *per week*! Bristol-Myers Squibb sent many cartons of baby formula. Eli Lilly sent 40,000 vials of insulin. Kellogg sent seven truckloads of crackers and cookies. Pfizer sent $2 million and a lot of medicine. The other pharmaceutical companies were equally or more generous. Amgen, for example, sent $2.5 million and offered to match any contributions made by employees. The list goes on and on.

Change management means more than adjusting to day-to-day challenges. It also means adjusting to catastrophic disasters, and reacting quickly. That is true for both manufacturing firms such as Oreck and service firms such as Walmart.

Sources: Jeffrey H. Birnbaum, "Stepping Up," *The Washington Post*, 4 September 2005, F1, F4; Jonathan Eig, "Manufacturer Finds More Than Vacuums At Stake in Recovery," *The Wall Street Journal*, 9 September 2005, B1, B5; Susan Morse, "A Tide of Giving," *The Washington Post*, 13 September 2005, F3.

---

tower. Exult sees this as an excellent opportunity to expand its business in Canada, and these new employees have a mandate to bring in more Canadian clients.[23] Unfortunately, examples such as this are not the norm.

**Canada's Auto Industry[24]**   The auto industry is critical to Canada's manufacturing economy. According to the Canadian Vehicle Manufacturers' Association, the auto sector is Canada's biggest contributor to manufacturing Gross Domestic Product (GDP) and its largest manufacturing employer, employing one out of every seven Canadians. The industry supports jobs across Canada in 13 assembly plants, more than 540 parts manufacturers, 3,900 dealerships, and many other related industries.

It is no wonder that this industry is Canada's largest, both domestically and in exports (recall the value of these exports from Chapter 3). As well, it should be of no surprise that this industry has also faced increased competition from international players. In recent years, faced with relatively high labour and pension costs, plants have closed, eliminating thousands of jobs. Other than Toyota in Cambridge and Woodstock, and Honda in Alliston (all these locations are in Ontario), plant expansion projects have gone south of the border.

To potential investors, Canada offers cost advantages due to our public medicare program and, until a few years ago, a low currency. However, southern U.S. states such as

**Auto plants, auto jobs.**

**Don't let them fade away.**

CAW ✦ TCA
CANADA

**Fax your MP at www.caw.ca**

The Canadian Auto Workers (CAW) has a Manufacturing Matters Campaign. Over 25,000 jobs have been lost in the last three to five years, due, in part, to incentives and cheaper wages offered in other countries. What other factors may influence companies to relocate?

A video called *The Toyota Production System* provides a very informative presentation of how this company has positioned itself as a leading global manufacturing entity. Go to www.toyota.ca, click on the "Company Info" tab, then "Toyota Motor Manufacturing Canada," then "How We Build" to find the video.

Alabama, Georgia, and Mississippi are luring billions of dollars' worth of auto industry assembly plants with more attractive incentives, including land and training. These incentives are also starting to be offered to parts makers. To respond to the decreasing trend in new auto investments, a joint industry–government council was established. A major goal of the Canadian Automotive Partnership Council (CAPC) is to improve the future of the assembly industry. The Council has acknowledged tax cuts and provincial government support for investment in environmental research as important to the survival of this industry in Canada. Time will tell if such initiatives will improve the industry's health.

## Taking Operations Management to the Internet

Many of today's rapidly growing companies do very little production themselves. Instead, they outsource engineering, design, manufacturing, and other tasks to other companies that specialize in those functions. Furthermore, companies are creating whole new relationships with suppliers over the Internet, so that operations management is becoming an inter-firm process in which companies work together to design, produce, and ship products to customers. Coordination among companies today can be as close as coordination among departments in a single firm was in the past.

Many of the major manufacturing companies (e.g., Microsoft) are developing new Internet-focused strategies that will enable them and others to compete more effectively in the future.[25] These changes are having a dramatic effect on operations managers as they adjust from a one-firm system to an inter-firm environment, and from a relatively stable environment to one that is constantly changing and evolving. This linking of firms is called *supply chain management*. We will briefly introduce you to this concept later in the chapter.

## Facility Location in the Future

Developments in information technology (computers, modems, email, voice mail, teleconferencing, etc.) are giving firms and employees more flexibility than ever before in choosing locations while staying in the competitive mainstream. As we noted in Appendix A, telecommuting (working from home via computer and modem) is a major trend in business.[26] Companies that no longer need to locate near sources of labour will be able to move to areas where land is less expensive and the quality of life may be nicer.

One big incentive to locate or relocate in a particular city or province is the tax situation and degree of government support. Those with lower taxes, such as Alberta, may be more attractive to companies. Some provinces and local governments have higher taxes than others, yet many engage in fierce competition by giving tax reductions and other support, such as zoning changes and financial aid, so that businesses will locate there. The Reaching Beyond Our Borders box explores how one company has handled the complex role of handling production facilities all over the world.

## Facility Layout

**facility layout**
The physical arrangement of resources (including people) in the production process.

**Facility layout** is the physical arrangement of resources (including people) in the production process. The idea is to have offices, machines, storage areas, and other items in the best possible position to enable workers to produce goods and provide services for customers. Facility layout depends greatly on the processes that are to be performed. For services, the layout is usually designed to help the consumer find and buy things. More and more, that means helping consumers find and buy things on the Internet. Some stores have added kiosks that enable customers to search for goods on the Internet and then place orders in the store. The store also handles returns and other customer-contact functions. In short, services are becoming more and more customer oriented in how they design their stores and their Internet services. Some service-oriented organizations, such as hospitals, use layouts that improve the efficiency of the production process, just as manufacturers do. For manufacturing plants, facilities layout has become critical because the possible cost savings are enormous.

## Reaching Beyond Our Borders

### Lockheed Martin Goes Global

Can you imagine how hard it would be to manage the construction of a combat jet airplane? Now try to imagine how hard it would be if the plane was being built by 80 different suppliers in 187 different locations. Furthermore, while the plane is being constructed, the U.S. Air Force, Navy, and Marines; the British Ministry of Defence; and eight other U.S. allies will be watching the progress, making comments, and changing the plans if necessary. What kind of person could pull all of that together?

The man responsible for this huge project is Dain Hancock of Lockheed Martin. One of his successes at Lockheed was to consolidate three operating units into a single company. Now he has the responsibility, with the help of others, of uniting some 80 companies into a single production unit. To do that, Lockheed and its partner companies will be using a system of 90 Web software tools to share designs, track the exchange of documents, and keep an eye on progress. The Internet enables people from different companies with incompatible computer systems to meet on Web sites and speak a common language. They will be able to talk via their computers while looking at shared documents. They can also use electronic white boards on which two or more people can draw pictures or charts, in real time, as others watch and comment.

Hancock and other managers are taking operations management beyond the control of one plant to the control of multiple plants in multiple locations, often in multiple countries. The Internet has changed business in many ways, but none other may be as dramatic as this.

Many companies are moving from an *assembly line layout*, in which workers do only a few tasks at a time, to a *modular layout*, in which *teams* of workers combine to produce more complex units of the final product.[27] For example, there may have been a dozen or more workstations on an assembly line to complete an automobile engine in the past, but all of that work may be done in one module today. A *process layout* is one in which similar equipment and functions are grouped together. The order in which the product visits a function depends on the design of the item. This allows for flexibility. When working on a major project, such as a bridge or an airplane, companies use a *fixed-position layout* that allows workers to congregate around the product to be completed. Figure 10.3 illustrates typical layout designs.

## Quality Control

**Quality** is consistently producing what the customer wants while reducing errors before and after delivery to the customer. Before, quality control was often done by a quality control department at the end of the production line. Products were completed *and then tested*. This resulted in several problems:

1. There was a need to inspect other people's work. This required extra people and resources.

2. If an error was found, someone would have to correct the mistake or scrap the product. This, of course, was costly.

3. If the customer found the mistake, he or she might be dissatisfied and might even buy from someone else thereafter.

Such problems led to the realization that quality is not an outcome; it is a never-ending process of continually improving what a company produces. Therefore, quality control should be part of the operations management planning process rather than simply an end-of-the-line inspection.

Companies have turned to the use of modern quality control standards, such as six sigma. **Six sigma quality** (just 3.4 defects per million opportunities) detects potential problems

The Igus manufacturing plant in Cologne, Germany, can shrink or expand in a flash. Its flexible design keeps it competitive in a fast-changing market. Because the layout of the plant changes so often, some employees use scooters in order to more efficiently provide needed skills, supplies, and services to multiple workstations. A fast-changing plant needs a fast-moving employee base to achieve maximum productivity.

**quality**
Consistently producing what the customer wants while reducing errors before and after delivery to the customer.

**six sigma quality**
A quality measure that allows only 3.4 defects per million events.

**FIGURE | 10.3**

**Typical Layout Designs**

**A. ASSEMBLY-LINE LAYOUT**
Used for repetitive tasks.

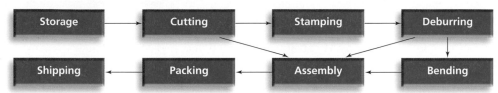

**B. PROCESS LAYOUT**
Frequently used in operations that serve different customers' different needs.

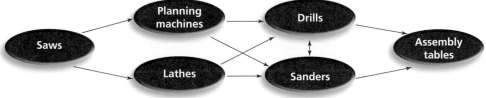

**statistical quality control (SQC)**
The process that some managers use to continually monitor all phases of the production process to ensure that quality is being built into the product from the beginning.

**C. MODULAR LAYOUT**
Can accommodate changes in design or customer demand.

**statistical process control (SPC)**
The process of taking statistical samples of product components at each stage of the production process and plotting those results on a graph. Any variances from quality standards are recognized and can be corrected if beyond the set standards.

**D. FIXED POSITION LAYOUT**
A major feature of planning is scheduling work operations.

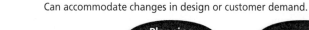

What happens when you combine the zeal of technical innovators with the six sigma discipline of a large company like General Electric? You get a medical breakthrough. Janet Burki and her 280-person operations team developed the world's fastest CT scanner. It works ten times faster than other systems and produces clear 3-D images of the beating heart. Can you see how efforts to build in quality lead to better (and faster) products?

to prevent their occurrence. The Spotlight on Small Business box explores how small businesses can apply six sigma to their operations.

**Statistical quality control (SQC)** is the process that some managers use to continually monitor all phases of the production process to ensure that quality is being built into the product from the beginning. **Statistical process control (SPC)** is the process of taking statistical samples of product components at each stage of the production process and plotting those results on a graph. Any variances from quality standards are recognized and can be corrected if beyond the set standards. Ensuring that products meet standards all along the production process eliminates or minimizes the need for having a quality control inspection at the end. Any mistakes would have been caught much earlier in the process. SQC and SPC thus save companies much time and many dollars. Some companies call such an approach to quality control the Deming cycle (after W. Edwards Deming, the father of the movement toward quality).[28] The cycle steps are: Plan, Do, Check, Act (PDCA). Again, the idea is to find potential errors *before* they happen. Deming's approach, including implementing standards, was used for many years before the International Organization for Standardization (ISO), which we will talk about shortly, came into being.

The customer is ultimately the one who determines what the standard for quality should be. Businesses are getting serious about providing top customer service, and many are already doing it. Service organizations

## SPOTLIGHT ON Small Business

### Meeting the Six Sigma Standard

Six sigma is a quality measure that allows only 3.4 defects per million opportunities. It is one thing for Motorola or General Electric (GE) to reach for such standards, but what about a small company like Dolan Industries? Dolan is a 41-person manufacturer of fasteners. It spent a few years trying to meet ISO 9000 standards, which are comparable to six sigma.

Once the company was able to achieve six sigma quality itself, it turned to its suppliers and demanded six sigma quality from them as well. Dolan had to do that because its customers were demanding that level of quality. Companies such as Honeywell, Motorola, and Nortel Networks Corp. are all seeking six sigma quality. In his first conference call, Mike Zafirovski, president and CEO of Nortel, announced his intention to introduce the six sigma program in an attempt to improve performance via decreased costs and improved quality and process. Other benefits include increases in product performance and, more important, happy customers—and profit growth.

Here is how six sigma works: If you can make it to the level of one sigma, two out of three products will meet specifications. If you can reach the two sigma level, then more than 95 percent of products will qualify. But when you meet six sigma quality, as we've said, you have only 3.4 defects in a million opportunities (which means that 99.99966 percent of your products will qualify). The bottom line is that small businesses are being held to a higher standard, one that approaches perfection. Service organizations are also adopting six sigma standards.

So, how can a small business learn about such processes quickly? The answer is to use TRIZ. TRIZ is a Russian acronym for Theory of Inventive Problem Solving. The ideas are these: (1) Somebody, someplace, has already solved your problem or one similar to it. Creativity means finding that solution and adapting it to the current problem, and (2) Do not accept compromises; eliminate them. For example, farmers learned how to process manure to remove the water from studying the orange juice industry (that's how it makes concentrated orange juice). The pharmaceutical industry learned to manage foam in the production process by studying the beer industry. You get the idea. Today, searching for answers on the Internet is critical to a company's success. You might look at some of the sources below for examples.

Sources: Ellen Domb, "Enhance Six Sigma Creativity with TRIZ," *Quality Digest*, February 2004; Ellen Domb, "Think TRIZ for Creative Problem Solving," *Quality Digest*, August 2005, 35–40; www.TRIZ-journal.com, 2005; and Andrew Wahl, "Nortel's New Game Plan: Canada Telecom," *Canadian Business*, March 27–April 9, 2006, http://www.canadianbusiness.com/technology/companies/article.jsp;jsessionid=JGFKAOIDBBDD?content=20060327_75509_75509.

The National Quality Institute is working to help companies understand and apply a focus on excellence through the adoption of the Canadian Framework for Business Excellence. This approach will help companies reduce rework, waste, and costs while improving productivity and competitiveness. Do you see how this framework incorporates principles discussed in this textbook?

are finding it difficult to provide outstanding service every time because the process is so labour intensive. Physical goods (e.g., a gold ring) can be designed and manufactured to near perfection. However, it is hard to reach such perfection when designing and providing a service experience such as a dance on a cruise ship or a cab drive through Vancouver.

## Quality Award: The Canada Awards for Excellence[29]

The National Quality Institute (NQI), an independent, Canadian, not-for-profit organization, is the leading authority in Canada on workplace excellence based on quality systems and healthy workplace criteria. The Canada Awards for Excellence (CAE) are presented annually to private, public, and not-for-profit organizations that have displayed outstanding performance in the areas of quality and healthy workplace. The award has honoured hundreds of Canadian organizations, including the British Columbia Transplant Society, Delta Hotels, Statistics Canada, and the College of Physicians & Surgeons of Nova Scotia. Recent recipients include 3M Canada Company, Vincent Massey School, the City of Kamloops, and Manulife Financial. Other CAE awards include Healthy Workplace, Customer Service, and Health Care. For more information, visit www.nqi.ca.

## ISO 9000 and ISO 14000 Standards

The International Organization for Standardization (ISO) is a worldwide federation of national standards bodies from more than 140 countries that set the global measures for the quality of individual products. ISO is a non-governmental organization established in 1947 to promote the development of world standards to facilitate the international exchange of goods and services. (ISO is not an acronym. It comes from the Greek word *isos*, meaning oneness.) **ISO 9000** is the common name given to quality management and assurance standards. The latest standards are called ISO 9004:2000.[30] The standards require that a company must determine what customer needs are, including regulatory and legal requirements. The company must also make communication arrangements to handle issues such as complaints. Other standards involve process control, product testing, storage, and delivery. Improving quality is an investment that can pay off in better customer relations and higher sales.[31]

**ISO 9000**

The common name given to quality management and assurance standards.

It is important to know that ISO did not start as a quality certification, the way many people think. In the beginning, it simply meant that your process was under control. In short, it looked to see that companies were consistently producing the same products each time. There is a difference between consistency (flawed products every time) and quality (products free from defects). Today, ISO has developed over 17,000 international standards and 1,100 new standards are published every year.[32]

Lange Con Custom Homes Inc. has been building custom homes since 1983. It first obtained ISO 9001 certification in 2000, which it continues to maintain. Its processes are regularly reviewed to ensure high standards of quality, which supports its leadership position in the export of manufactured housing.

What makes ISO 9000 so important is that the European Union (EU) is demanding that companies that want to do business with the EU be certified by ISO standards. Some major Canadian companies are also demanding that suppliers meet these standards. There are several accreditation agencies in Europe and in North America whose function is to certify that a company meets the standards for all phases of its operations, from product development through production and testing to installation. SNC-Lavalin Group Inc. (www.snclavalin.com), one of the leading groups of engineering and construction companies in the world, has met such standards. It provides engineering, procurement, construction, project management, and project financing services to a variety of industry sectors in more than 120 countries. The Quality Policy at SNC-Lavalin is to "achieve client satisfaction through the careful management of our work processes, with due attention to value creation through scope, schedule, cost control, and with emphasis on safety and the environment." To best serve its various stakeholders, the company has implemented

Client Satisfaction and Continual Improvement Programs in every division, business unit, geographic office, and subsidiary. These programs are based on the applicable requirements of ISO 9001 International Standard for Quality Management Systems.[33]

**ISO 14000** is a collection of the best practices for managing an organization's impact on the environment. It does not prescribe a performance level. ISO 14000 is an environmental management system (EMS). The requirements for certification include having an environmental policy, having specific improvement targets, conducting audits of environmental programs, and maintaining top management review of the processes. Certification in both ISO 9000 and ISO 14000 would show that a firm has a world-class management system in both quality and environmental standards. In the past, firms assigned employees separately to meet both standards. Today, ISO 9000 and ISO 14000 standards have been blended so that an organization can work on both at once. ISO is now working on ISO 26000 standards, which are designed to give guidance on social responsibility.[34]

## Supply Chain Management

Before we discuss this next topic, it is important to introduce some terms. **Logistics** involves those activities that focus on getting the right amount of the right products or services to the right place at the right time at the lowest possible cost. A **supply chain** is a sequence of firms that perform activities required to create and deliver a good or service to consumers or industrial users. Some companies have been successful in attracting more customers due to their supply chain management efficiencies. **Supply chain management** is the integration and organization of information and logistics activities *across* firms in a supply chain for the purpose of creating and delivering goods and services that provide value to customers.

Facilities included in supply chain management include: factories, processing centres, warehouses, distribution centres, and retail outlets. Functions and activities included are: forecasting, purchasing, inventory management, information management, quality assurance, scheduling, production, delivery, and customer service. Today, the major factors contributing to the importance of supply chain management include the need for improvement to remain competitive, the increase in outsourcing, shorter product life cycles and increased customization, increase in globalization, the growth of technology and e-commerce, the increase in complexity through just-in-time inventory (which will be talked about later in the chapter), and the need for better management of inventories. When implementing supply chain management, firms are trying to improve quality, reduce costs, increase flexibility and speed, improve customer service while reducing the number of suppliers used. Two examples are as follows:

- Canadian National Railway (CN) purchased supply chain management planning software from i2 Technologies to manage its intermodal business. CN has 10,000 freight cars and 7,000 containers that it owns, along with equipment belonging to shippers and other railways. While implementing this software is still a work in progress, CN expects to increase the level of speed and reliability of hauling containers and truck trailers from ports and major cities across North America.[35]

- Only Canada's Armed Forces surpasses the Cirque du Soleil in terms of the level of supply chain and logistics planning required to deploy large amounts of equipment, supplies, and people all over the world. According to Guy Migneron, director of international headquarters operations for Cirque du Soleil, "We use computers for a lot of what we do." The planning and logistics work for each performance begins 12 to 18 months before the first act enters the tent.[36]

# OPERATIONS MANAGEMENT IN THE SERVICE SECTOR

Operations management in the service industry is all about creating a good experience for those who use the service. For example, in a Four Seasons hotel, operations management includes restaurants that offer the finest in service, elevators that run smoothly, and

**ISO 14000**
A collection of the best practices for managing an organization's impact on the environment.

**logistics**
Those activities that focus on getting the right amount of the right products or services to the right place at the right time at the lowest possible cost.

**supply chain**
The sequence of firms that perform activities required to create and deliver a good or service to consumers or industrial users.

**supply chain management**
The integration and organization of information and logistics activities *across* firms in a supply chain for the purpose of creating and delivering goods and services that provide value to customers.

Purolator Courier provides a video about Purolator's global supply services called "Connected to the World," concerning emerging worldwide manufacturing sectors and supply chain management. Go to http://purolator.com and click on "Purolator Global Supply Chain Services," then select "Connected to the World" from the list of available videos.

a front desk that processes people quickly. It may include placing fresh-cut flowers in the lobbies and dishes of fruit in every room. More important, it may mean spending thousands of dollars to provide training in quality management for every new employee.

Operations management in luxury hotels is changing with today's new executives. As customers in hotels, executives are likely to want in-room Internet access and a help centre with toll-free telephone service. Also, when an executive has to give a speech or presentation, he or she needs video equipment and a host of computer hardware and other aids. Foreign visitors would like multilingual customer-support services. Hotel shops need to carry more than souvenirs, newspapers, and some drugstore and food items to serve today's high-tech travellers. The shops may also carry laptop computer supplies, electrical adapters, and the like. Operations management is responsible for locating and providing such amenities to make customers happy. In short, delighting customers by anticipating their needs has become the quality standard for luxury hotels, as it has for most other service businesses. But knowing customer needs and satisfying them are two different things. That's why operations management is so important: It is the implementation phase of management.

Information Mapping Canada helps leading organizations focus on improving performance through better written communication. Clients including Xerox Canada have increased productivity through better management of customer complaints. What types of measures could you implement to track how good a job was being done in managing customer complaints?

## Measuring Quality in the Service Sector

There's strong evidence that productivity in the service sector is rising, but productivity measures don't capture improvements in quality. In an example from health care, positron emission tomography (PET) scans are much better than X-rays, but the quality difference is not reported in productivity figures. The traditional way to measure productivity involves tracking inputs (worker hours) compared to outputs (dollars). Notice that there is no measure for quality improvement. When new information systems are developed to measure the quality improvement of goods and services—including the speed of their delivery and customer satisfaction—productivity in the service sector will go up dramatically.

Using computers is one way in which the service sector is improving productivity, but not the only one. Think about labour-intensive businesses such as hospitals and fast-food restaurants, where automation plays a big role in controlling costs and improving service. Today, at Burger King, for example, customers fill their own drink cups from pop machines, which allows workers to concentrate on preparing the food. And because the people working at the drive-up window now wear headsets instead of using stationary mikes, they are no longer glued to one spot and can do four or five tasks while taking an order.

Most of us have been exposed to similar productivity gains in banking. For example, people in most cities no longer have to wait in long lines for tellers to help them deposit and withdraw money. Instead, they use automated teller machines (ATMs), which usually involve little or no waiting and are available 24 hours a day.

Another service that was once very slow was grocery store checkout. The system of marking goods with universal product codes (UPC) enables computerized checkout and allows cashiers to be much more productive than before. Now, many stores have set up automated systems that enable customers to go through the checkout process on their own. Some grocery chains, such as Longo's, are implementing Internet services that allow customers to place orders online and receive home delivery. The potential for productivity gains in this area are enormous.

In short, operations management has led to tremendous productivity increases in the service sector but still has a long way to go. Also, service workers are losing jobs to machines just as manufacturing workers did. The secret to obtaining and holding a good job is to acquire appropriate education and training. Such education and training must go on for a lifetime to keep up with the rapid changes that are happening in all areas of business. That message cannot be repeated too frequently.

International SOS is the world's leading provider of medical assistance, international health care, security services, and outsourced customer care. Customers include individuals, companies, and government agencies. As one of its many services, International SOS provides full support service to companies requiring 24/7 on-call and online services. This includes medical assistance and evacuation (as noted in this picture). Do you see how critical it is for service providers to respond in a timely manner?

## Services Go Interactive

The service industry has always taken advantage of new technology to increase customer satisfaction. Jet travel enabled Purolator to deliver goods overnight. Cable TV led to pay-per-view services. And now interactive computer networks are revolutionizing services. Interactive services are already available from banks, stockbrokers, travel agents, and information providers of all kinds. More individuals may soon be able to participate directly in community and national decision making via telephone, cable, and computer networks.

eBay, an online auction and shopping Web site, is a huge phenomena. Revenues are between $5 and $10 billion. People and businesses buy and sell products and services worldwide. Regardless of what is being sold, however, the success of service organizations in the future will depend greatly on establishing a dialogue with consumers so that the operations managers can help their organizations adapt to consumer demands faster and more efficiently. Such information systems have been developed and should prove highly useful.

### Progress Assessment

- Can you name and define three functions that are common to operations management in both the service and the manufacturing sectors?
- What are the major criteria for facility location?
- What is involved in implementing each of the following: six sigma, SQC, SPC, ISO 9000, and ISO 14000?

# OPERATIONS MANAGEMENT IN THE MANUFACTURING SECTOR

Common sense and some experience have already taught you much of what you need to know about production processes. You know what it takes to write a term paper or prepare a dinner. You need money to buy the materials, you need a place to work, and you need

**FIGURE** | **10.4**

**The Production Process**
The production process consists of taking the factors of production (land, etc.) and using those inputs to produce goods, services, and ideas. Planning, routing, scheduling, and the other activities are the means to accomplish the objective—output.

**form utility**
The value added by the creation of finished goods and services.

to be organized to get the task done. The same is true of the production process in industry. It uses basic inputs to produce outputs (see Figure 10.4). Production adds value, or utility, to materials or processes. **Form utility** is the value added by the creation of finished goods and services, such as the value added by taking silicon and making computer chips or putting services together to create a vacation package. Form utility can exist at the retail level as well. For example, a butcher can produce a specific cut of beef from a whole cow or a baker can make a specific type of cake out of basic ingredients.

To be competitive, manufacturers must keep the costs of inputs down. That is, the costs of workers, machinery, and so on must be kept as low as possible. Similarly, the amount of output must be relatively high. The question today is: How does a producer keep costs low and still increase output? This question will dominate thinking in the manufacturing and service sectors for years to come. In the next few sections, we explore production processes and the latest technology being used to cut costs.

## Production Processes

There are several different processes that manufacturers use to produce goods. Andrew S. Grove, chairman of computer chip manufacturer Intel, uses a great analogy to explain production:

> *To understand the principles of production, imagine that you're a chef and that your task is to serve a breakfast consisting of a three-minute soft-boiled egg, buttered toast, and coffee. Your job is to prepare and deliver the three items simultaneously, each of them fresh and hot.*

Grove goes on to say that the task here encompasses the three basic requirements of production: (1) to build and deliver products in response to the demands of the customer at a scheduled delivery time, (2) to provide an acceptable quality level, and (3) to provide everything at the lowest possible cost.

**process manufacturing**
That part of the production process that physically or chemically changes materials.

Using the breakfast example, it's easy to understand two manufacturing terms: *process* and *assembly*. **Process manufacturing** physically or chemically changes materials. For example, boiling physically changes the egg. (Similarly, process manufacturing turns sand into glass or computer chips.) The **assembly process** puts together components (eggs, toast, and coffee) to make a product (breakfast). Cars are made through an assembly process that puts together the frame, engine, and other parts.

**assembly process**
That part of the production process that puts together components.

In addition, production processes are either continuous or intermittent. A **continuous process** is one in which long production runs (lots of eggs) turn out finished goods over time. As the chef in our diner, you could have a conveyor belt that lowers eggs into boiling water for three minutes and then lifts them out on a continuous basis. A three-minute egg would be available whenever you wanted one. (A chemical plant, for example, is run on a continuous process.)

**continuous process**
A production process in which long production runs turn out finished goods over time.

It usually makes more sense when responding to specific customer orders to use an **intermittent process**. This is an operation where the production run is short (one or two eggs) and the machines are changed frequently to make different products (such as the oven in a bakery where you could make different types of bread). Manufacturers of custom-designed furniture would use an intermittent process.

**intermittent process**
A production process in which the production run is short and the machines are changed frequently to make different products.

As an example of a company that uses both long and short production runs, for the first time in nine years, Kodiak boots are being produced in Canada:

*"At the end of the day, we're going to service customers a lot better through this core Canadian production," says Kevin Huckle, president of Kodiak Group Holdings Inc., which plans to do a third of its production in Canada. Domestic production offers quick, efficient service for Canadian retailers, who may require only small numbers of boots, but need them in a hurry. With Asian production, he has to contract for long production runs—more than 1,200 pairs—and has to carry a lot of inventory. With domestic manufacturing, the plant keeps enough materials around for relatively short runs. Because of automation and location, it can turn around Canadian production orders in 21 days, compared with 90 days for orders in Asia.*[37]

Today, many new manufacturers use intermittent processes. Computers, robots, and flexible manufacturing processes allow firms to turn out custom-made goods almost as fast as mass-produced goods were once turned out.[38] We'll discuss how they do that in more detail in the next few sections as we explore advanced production techniques and the latest technology being used to cut costs.

## Progress Assessment

- What are three basic requirements of production?
- Define and differentiate the following: process manufacturing, assembly process, continuous process, and intermittent process.

# MODERN PRODUCTION TECHNIQUES

The ultimate goal of manufacturing and process management is to provide high-quality goods and services instantaneously in response to customer demand. As we have stressed throughout this book, traditional organizations were simply not designed to be so responsive to the customer. Rather, they were designed to make goods efficiently (inexpensively). The whole idea of mass production was to make a large number of a limited variety of products at very low cost.

Over the years, low cost often came at the expense of quality and flexibility. Furthermore, suppliers didn't always deliver when they said they would, so manufacturers had to carry large inventories of raw materials and components. Such inefficiencies made companies less competitive than foreign competitors that were using more advanced production techniques.

As a result of global competition, companies have had to make a wide variety of high-quality, custom-designed products at very low cost. Clearly, something had to change on the production floor to make that possible. Seven major developments have radically changed the production process: (1) materials requirement planning, (2) just-in-time inventory control, (3) purchasing, (4) flexible manufacturing, (5) lean manufacturing, (6) mass customization, and (7) computer-aided design and manufacturing.

## Materials Requirement Planning (MRP)

**Economic order quantity** (also known as the Wilson EOQ Model, or simply the EOQ Model) is a model that defines the optimal quantity to order to minimize total variable costs required to order and hold inventory.[39] The theory gained wide acceptance in the early 1980s due to the benefits that such a model would generate. However, a major drawback was that businesses did not always understand the trade-off between ordering costs and holding costs. Another drawback was that the theory assumed that shortages or stockouts did not occur and it was difficult to guarantee this when demand was not always known (another assumption of the theory). Since this time, businesses and technology have become more sophisticated in the area of planning.

**economic order quantity**
A model that defines the optimal quantity to order to minimize total variable costs required to order and hold inventory.

Enterprise Resource
Planning

| Multifirm Functions | Computer Software | System Output |
|---|---|---|
| Requirement planning | | Manufacturing resource plan |
| Finance | | Master production schedule |
| Human resources | | Financial report |
| Order fulfillment | | Distribution plan |

**materials requirement
planning (MRP)**
A computer-based production
management system that
uses sales forecasts to make
sure that needed parts and
materials are available at the
right time and place.

**enterprise resource
planning (ERP)**
A computer application that
enables multiple firms to
manage all of their operations
(finance, requirements planning,
human resources, and order
fulfillment) on the basis of
a single, integrated set of
corporate data.

**Materials requirement planning (MRP)** is a computer-based operations management system that uses sales forecasts to ensure that needed parts and materials are available at the right time and place *in a specific company*. In our diner, for example, we could feed the sales forecast into the computer, which would specify how many eggs and how much coffee to order and then print out the proper scheduling and routing sequence. The same can be done with the seats and other parts of an automobile. In the next section, you will read how just-in-time inventory control has a similar objective.

The newest version of MRP is **enterprise resource planning (ERP)**. ERP is a computer application that enables *multiple* firms to manage all of their operations (finance, requirements planning, human resources, and order fulfillment) on the basis of a single, integrated set of corporate data (see Figure 10.5). The result is shorter time between orders and payment, less staff to do ordering and order processing, reduced inventories, and better customer service for all firms involved. By entering customer and sales information in an ERP system, a manufacturer can generate the next period's demand forecast, which in turn generates orders for raw materials, production scheduling, and financial projections.

ERP software enables the monitoring of quality and customer satisfaction as it is happening. ERP systems are going global now that the Internet is powerful enough to handle the data flows. At the plant level, dynamic performance monitoring enables plant operators to monitor the use of power, chemicals, and other resources and to make needed adjustments. In short, flows to, through, and from plants have become automated.

Some firms are providing a service called sequential delivery. These firms are suppliers that provide components in an order sequenced to their customers' production process. For example, Ford's seat supplier loads seats onto a truck such that, when off-loaded, the seats are in perfect sequence for the type of vehicle coming down the assembly line.

While ERP can be an effective tool, it also can have its problems. The Royal Canadian Mint was having difficulties extracting and manipulating data. Departments were operated independently, and because it took so long to produce reports for analysis, employees did not trust the reliability of the information once it was in their hands. "Anyone who has used an ERP system knows that reporting can be problematic," says Azfar Ali Khan, director of operations and systems at the Mint's sales and marketing departments. "They're wonderful transactional engines, but getting the richness of the data in front of the people in a context they can understand is particularly challenging."[40]

Information technology (IT) has had a major influence on the entire production process, from purchasing to final delivery. Many IT advances have been add-ons to ERP. To solve its difficulties, the Mint turned to Cognos (www.cognos.com) for its enterprise solution. Cognos's Analytic Applications solution made it possible for users to access data right to the day, as well as to create new reporting opportunities. The Mint's self-service, web-enabled, enterprise-wide solution has allowed it to act quickly and thereby improve customer service. According to Ali

One of the biggest providers of Enterprise Resources Planning (ERP) software is SAS. Their business analytics software supports customers making better decisions faster through spending less time looking for data.

Khan, "Buying a prepackaged solution and customizing it to our own unique business requirements has saved us a lot of time and a lot of money."[41]

## Just-in-Time Inventory Control

One major cost of production is holding parts, motors, and other items in storage for later use. Storage not only subjects such items to obsolescence, pilferage, and damage but also requires construction and maintenance of costly warehouses. To cut such costs, many companies have implemented a concept called **just-in-time (JIT) inventory control**. JIT systems keep a minimum of inventory on the premises and parts, supplies, and other needs are delivered just in time to go on the assembly line. To work effectively, however, the process requires excellent coordination with carefully selected suppliers. Sometimes the supplier builds new facilities close to the main producer to minimize distribution time.

JIT runs into problems when suppliers are farther away. Shipments may be delayed due to poor weather, worker strikes, and events such as the power outage in Ontario in August 2003. With more than $1.9 billion in goods and more than 300,000 people moving across the Canada–U.S. border each day, the efficient flow of products and people is vital to Canada's economy.[42] Any delays require that companies adjust their JIT schedules. Today, the longer delays at borders due to increased traffic and security measures have forced companies to do just that. Other limitations are that JIT works best with standard products, demand needs to be high and stable to justify the cost and savings, and suppliers need to be extremely reliable.

Here's how it works: A manufacturer sets a production schedule (using ERP) to determine what parts and supplies will be needed. Suppliers are connected electronically, so they know immediately what will be needed and when. The suppliers must then deliver the goods *just in time* to go on the assembly line. Naturally, this calls for more effort (and more costs) on the suppliers' part. The manufacturer maintains efficiency by linking electronically to the suppliers so that the suppliers become more like departments in the firm than separate businesses.

JIT systems ensure that the right materials are at the right place at the right time at the cheapest cost to meet both customer and production needs. That's a key step in modern production innovation. Part of that process is rethinking the purchasing process. We shall explore that issue next.

Huge warehouses such as the one depicted in the photo would become a thing of the past if all companies implemented just-in-time (JIT) inventory control. What are the advantages and disadvantages of having large amounts of inventory available?

**just-in-time (JIT) inventory control**
A production process in which a minimum of inventory is kept on the premises and parts, supplies, and other needs are delivered just in time to go on the assembly line.

## Purchasing

**Purchasing** is the functional area in a firm that searches for quality material resources, finds the best suppliers, and negotiates the best price for quality goods and services. In the past, manufacturers tended to deal with many different suppliers with the idea that, if one supplier or another couldn't deliver, materials would be available from someone else. Today, however, manufacturers are relying more heavily on one or two suppliers because the firms share so much information that they don't want to have too many suppliers knowing their business. The Hudson's Bay Company shifted to single merchandise buyers for a growing number of departments at its Bay, Zellers, and Home Outfitters chains. This move was designed to help improve product selection and save money through less duplication and larger purchase orders.[43] The relationship between suppliers and manufacturers is thus much closer than ever before.[44]

The Internet has transformed the purchasing function in recent years. For example, a business looking for supplies can contact an Internet-based purchasing service and

**purchasing**
The functional area in a firm that searches for quality material resources, finds the best suppliers, and negotiates the best price for goods and services.

find the best supplies at the best price. Similarly, a company wishing to sell supplies can use the Internet to find all companies looking for such supplies. The cost of purchasing items has thus been reduced tremendously.

## Flexible Manufacturing

**flexible manufacturing**
Designing machines to do multiple tasks so that they can produce a variety of products.

**Flexible manufacturing** involves designing machines to do multiple tasks so that they can produce a variety of products. Flexible manufacturing (also known as flex) not only leads to improved productivity, but it may also result in cost savings. Frank Gourneau, plant manager at Ford Motor Company of Canada Ltd., calls the $1-billion Oakville complex "a game changer" and a "jewel" with all the latest advances in auto technology. The first phase of the plant started production in 2006. According to Gourneau, "Undergoing major model changes in traditional plants means weeks of downtime and millions spent on new tooling and equipment. Once a flexible body shop is installed, downtime is reduced dramatically and the equipment changes consist mainly of reprogramming robots. The point is to be able to cease assembly of one model on a Friday and start a new one on a Monday, instead of six, eight or 10 weeks later."[45] Gourneau estimates productivity will improve at least 20 percent in the new plant and the company expects to achieve $2 billion in production cost savings alone during the next decade.[46]

Allen-Bradley (part of Rockwell Automation), a maker of industrial automation controls, uses flexible manufacturing to build motor starters. Orders come in daily, and within 24 hours the company's 26 machines and robots manufacture, test, and package the starters—which are untouched by human hands. Allen-Bradley's machines are so flexible that a special order, even a single item, can be included in the assembly without slowing down the process. Did you notice that these products were made without any labour? One way to compete with cheap labour is to have as few workers as possible.

## Lean Manufacturing

**lean manufacturing**
The production of goods using less of everything compared to mass production.

**Lean manufacturing** is the production of goods using less of everything compared to mass production: less human effort, less manufacturing space, less investment in tools, and less engineering time to develop a new product. A company becomes lean by continuously increasing its capacity to produce high-quality goods while decreasing its need for resources.[47] That's called "increasing productivity." You can see how technological improvements are largely responsible for the increase in productivity and efficiency of Canadian plants. That makes labour more productive and makes it possible to pay higher rates.

General Motors (GM) uses lean manufacturing. To make the Saturn automobile, for example, GM abandoned its assembly-line production process. The fundamental purpose of restructuring was to dramatically cut the number of worker hours needed to build a car. GM made numerous changes, the most dramatic of which was to switch to modular construction. GM suppliers pre-assemble most of the auto parts into a few large components called modules. Workers are no longer positioned along kilometres of assembly line. Instead, they're grouped at various workstations, where they put the modules together. Rather than do a few set tasks, workers perform a whole cluster of tasks. Trolleys carry the partly completed car from station to station. Compared to the assembly line, modular assembly takes up less space and calls for fewer workers—both of which are money-saving factors.

**robot**
A computer-controlled machine capable of performing many tasks requiring the use of materials and tools.

Finally, GM greatly expanded its use of robots in the manufacturing process. A **robot** is a computer-controlled machine capable of performing many tasks requiring the use of materials and tools. Robots, for example, spray-paint cars and do welding. Robots usually are fast, efficient, and accurate. Robots and other machines perform routine, repetitive jobs quickly, efficiently, and accurately. This provides opportunities for workers to be more creative.

# Mass Customization

To *customize* means to make a unique good or provide a specific service to an individual. Although it once may have seemed impossible, **mass customization**, which means tailoring products to meet the needs of a large number of individual customers, is now practised widely. The National Bicycle Industrial Company in Japan, for example, makes 18 bicycle models in more than 2 million combinations, with each combination designed to fit the needs of a specific customer. The customer chooses the model, size, colour, and design. The retailer takes various measurements from the buyer and faxes the data to the factory, where robots handle the bulk of the assembly. Thus, flexible manufacturing (discussed earlier) is one of the factors that makes mass customization possible. Given the exact needs of a customer, flexible machines can produce a customized good as quickly as mass-produced goods were once made.

More and more manufacturers are learning to customize their products. For example, some General Nutrition Center (GNC) stores feature machines that enable shoppers to custom-design their own vitamins, shampoo, and lotions. Other companies produce custom-made books with a child's name inserted in key places, and custom-made greeting cards have appeared on the market. The Custom Foot stores use infrared scanners to precisely measure each foot so that shoes can be crafted to fit perfectly. Adidas can make each shoe fit perfectly for each customer.[48] InterActive Custom Clothes offers a wide variety of options in custom-made jeans, including four different rivet colours. You can even buy custom-made M&Ms.[49]

Mass customization can be used in the service sector as well. Health clubs offer unique fitness programs for individuals, travel agencies provide vacation packages that vary according to individual choices, and some schools allow students to design their own majors. Actually, it is much easier to custom-design service programs than it is to custom-make goods, because there is no fixed tangible good that has to be adapted. Each customer can specify what he or she wants, within the limits of the service organization—limits that seem to be ever widening.

**mass customization**
Tailoring products to meet the needs of individual customers.

**computer-aided manufacturing (CAM)**
The use of computers in the manufacturing of products.

**computer-aided design (CAD)**
The use of computers in the design of products.

# Computer-Aided Design and Manufacturing

The one development in the recent past that appears to have changed production techniques and strategies more than any other has been the integration of computers into the design and manufacturing of products. The first thing computers did was help in the design of products; this is called **computer-aided design (CAD)**. The latest CAD systems allow designers to work in three dimensions. The next step was to involve computers directly in the production process; this is called **computer-aided manufacturing (CAM)**.

CAD/CAM (the use of both computer-aided design and computer-aided manufacturing) made it possible to custom-design products to meet the needs of small markets with very little increase in cost. A manufacturer programs the computer to make a simple design change, and that change can be incorporated directly into the production line. For example, CAD and CAM are used in the clothing industry. A computer program establishes a pattern and cuts the cloth automatically. Today, a person's dimensions can be programmed into the machines to create custom-cut clothing at little additional cost. In food service, CAM is used to make cookies in fresh-baked cookie shops. On-site, small-scale, semi-automated, sensor-controlled baking makes consistent quality easy to achieve.

CAD has doubled productivity in many firms. However, it's one thing to design a product and quite another to set the specifications

This photo shows computer-aided design (CAD) in operation. When linked with computer-aided manufacturing (CAM), these software systems can greatly improve the design and production process. What advantages might this technology offer to smaller manufacturing companies? What types of industries would benefit most from CAD/CAM?

**computer-integrated manufacturing (CIM)**
The uniting of computer-aided design with computer-aided manufacturing.

to make a machine do the work. The problem in the past was that CAD machines couldn't talk to CAM machines directly. Today, however, software programs unite CAD with CAM: the result is **computer-integrated manufacturing (CIM)**. The software is expensive, but it cuts as much as 80 percent of the time needed to program machines to make parts. The printing company JohnsByrne uses CIM in its Niles, Illinois, plant. The company noticed a decreased cost in overhead, reduced outlay of resources, and fewer errors. You can consult the *International Journal of Computer-Integrated Manufacturing* for other examples.

## Progress Assessment

- What is the difference between materials resource planning (MRP) and enterprise resource planning (ERP)?
- What is just-in-time inventory control?
- How does flexible manufacturing differ from lean manufacturing?
- What are CAD, CAM, and CIM?

# PREPARING FOR THE FUTURE

Canada is a major industrial country, but competition is growing stronger each year. This means that there are tremendous opportunities for careers in operations management as companies fight to stay competitive.

Today, relatively few graduates have majored in production and operations management, inventory management, and other areas involving manufacturing and operations management in the service sector. That means more opportunities for those students who can see the future trends and have the skills (e.g., high-level math) to own or work in tomorrow's highly automated, efficient factories, mines, service facilities, and other production locations. Students will need to keep a broad mind and seek information from a variety of sources to help them anticipate and plan for changes in the future.

# SUMMARY

**LO ▶ 1** Define operations management and explain what types of firms use it.

1. Operations management is a specialized area in management that converts or transforms resources (including human resources) into goods and services.

**What kinds of firms use operations managers?**
Firms in both the manufacturing and the service sectors use operations managers.

**LO ▶ 2** Describe the operations management planning issues involved in both the manufacturing and the service sectors, including facility location, facility layout, and quality control.

2. Functions involved in both the manufacturing and the service sectors include facility location, facility layout, and quality control.

**What is facility location and how does it differ from facility layout?**
Facility location is the process of selecting a geographic location for a company's operations. Facility layout is the physical arrangement of resources (including people) to produce goods and services effectively and efficiently.

**Why is facility location so important, and what criteria are used to evaluate different sites?**
The very survival of manufacturing depends on its ability to remain competitive, and that means either making inputs less costly (reducing costs of labour and land)

or increasing outputs from present inputs (increasing productivity). Labour costs and land costs are two major criteria for selecting the right sites. Other criteria include whether (1) resources are plentiful and inexpensive, (2) skilled workers are available or are trainable, (3) taxes are low and the local government offers support, (4) energy and water are available, (5) transportation costs are low, and (6) the quality of life and quality of education are high.

### What are the latest quality control concepts?

Six sigma quality (just 3.4 defects per million products) detects potential problems before they occur. Statistical quality control (SQC) is the process that some managers use to continually monitor all processes in production to ensure that quality is being built into the product from the beginning. Statistical process control (SPC) is the process of taking statistical samples of product components at each stage of the production process and plotting those results on a graph. Any variances from quality standards are recognized and can be corrected.

### What quality standards do firms use in Canada?

International standards that Canadian firms strive to meet include ISO 9004:2000 (ISO 9000) and ISO 14000. The first is a European standard for quality and the second is a collection of the best practices for managing an organization's impact on the environment.

3. There's strong evidence that productivity in the service sector is rising, but this is difficult to measure.

**LO ▸ 3** Discuss the problem of measuring productivity in the service sector, and tell how technology is leading to productivity gains in service companies.

### Why is productivity so hard to measure?

The traditional way to measure productivity involves tracking inputs (worker hours) compared to outputs (dollars). Quality improvements are not weighed. New information systems must be developed to measure the quality of goods and services, the speed of their delivery, and customer satisfaction.

### How is technology creating productivity gains in service organizations?

Computers have been a great help to service employees, allowing them to perform their tasks faster and more accurately. ATMs make banking faster and easier; automated checkout machines enable grocery clerks (and customers) to process items more quickly. In short, operations management has led to tremendous productivity increases in the service sector but still has a long way to go.

4. There are several different processes that manufacturers use to produce goods.

**LO ▸ 4** Explain how manufacturing processes can be used in the manufacturing sector.

### What is process manufacturing, and how does it differ from assembly processes?

Process manufacturing physically or chemically changes materials. Assembly processes put together components.

### Are there other production processes?

Production processes are either continuous or intermittent. A continuous process is one in which long production runs turn out finished goods over time. An intermittent process is an operation where the production run is short and the machines are changed frequently to produce different products.

5. Companies are using seven production techniques to become more profitable: (1) materials requirement planning, (2) just-in-time inventory control, (3) purchasing, (4) flexible manufacturing, (5) lean manufacturing, (6) mass customization, and (7) computer-aided design and manufacturing.

**LO ▸ 5** Describe seven manufacturing techniques that have improved the productivity of companies.

### What relationship does enterprise resource planning (ERP) have with the production process?

ERP is a computer application that enables multiple firms to manage all of their operations (finance, requirements planning, human resources, and order fulfillment) on the basis of a single, integrated set of corporate data. The result is shorter time between orders and payment, less staff to do ordering and order processing, reduced inventories, and better customer service for all firms involved. It is an advanced form of materials requirement planning.

### What is just-in-time (JIT) inventory control?

JIT involves having suppliers deliver parts and materials just in time to go on the assembly line so they don't have to be stored in warehouses.

### How have purchasing agreements changed?

Purchasing agreements now involve fewer suppliers who supply quality goods and services at better prices in return for getting the business. Many new Internet companies have emerged to help both buyers and sellers complete the exchange process more efficiently.

### What is flexible manufacturing?

Flexible manufacturing involves designing machines to produce a variety of products.

### What is lean manufacturing?

Lean manufacturing is the production of goods using less of everything compared to mass production: less human effort, less manufacturing space, less investment in tools, and less engineering time to develop a new product.

### What is mass customization?

Mass customization means making custom-designed goods and services for a large number of individual customers. Flexible manufacturing makes mass customization possible. Given the exact needs of a customer, flexible machines can produce a customized good as fast as mass-produced goods were once made.

### How do CAD/CAM systems work?

Design changes made in computer-aided design (CAD) are instantly incorporated into the computer-aided manufacturing (CAM) process. The linking of the two systems—CAD and CAM—is called computer-integrated manufacturing (CIM).

## KEY TERMS

assembly process  312

computer-aided design (CAD)  317

computer-aided manufacturing (CAM)  317

computer-integrated manufacturing (CIM)  318

continuous process  312

economic order quantity  313

enterprise resource planning (ERP)  314

facility layout  304

facility location  300

flexible manufacturing  316

form utility  312

intermittent process  312

ISO 9000  308

ISO 14000  309

just-in-time (JIT) inventory control  315

lean manufacturing  316

logistics  309

mass customization  317

materials requirement planning (MRP)  314

operations management  298

process manufacturing  312

production  297

production management  298

purchasing  315

quality  305

research and development (R&D)  395

robot  316

six sigma quality  305

statistical process control (SPC)  306

statistical quality control (SQC)  306

supply chain  309

supply chain management  309

## CRITICAL THINKING

1. People on the manufacturing floor are being replaced by robots and other machines. On the one hand, that is one way in which companies compete with cheap labour from other countries. No labour at all is less expensive than cheap labour. On the other hand, automation eliminates many jobs. Are you concerned that automation may increase unemployment or under-employment in Canada and around the world? Why?

2. Computer-integrated manufacturing (CIM) has revolutionized the production process. Now everything from cookies to cars can be designed and manufactured much more cheaply than before. Furthermore, customized changes can be made with very little increase in cost. What will such changes mean for the clothing industry, the shoe industry, and other fashion related industries? What will they mean for other consumer and industrial goods industries? How will you benefit as a consumer?

3. One way to create new jobs in Canada is to have more innovation. Much innovation comes from new graduates from engineering and the sciences. What could Canada do to motivate more students to major in those areas?

## DEVELOPING WORKPLACE SKILLS

1. Choosing the right location for a manufacturing plant or a service organization is often critical to its success. Form small groups and have each group member pick one manufacturing plant or one service organization in town and list at least three reasons why its location helps or hinders its success. If its location is not ideal, where would be a better one?

2. In teams of four or five, discuss the need for better operations management at clothing stores. Have the team develop a three-page report listing (1) problems that team members have encountered when clothes shopping, and (2) suggestions for improving operations so such problems won't occur in the future.

3. Discuss some of the advantages and disadvantages of producing goods overseas using inexpensive labour. Summarize the moral and ethical issues of this practice.

4. Think of any retail outlet (e.g., bookstore or food outlet) or service centre (e.g., library, copy centre) at your school and redesign the layout (make a pencil drawing placing people and materials) so that the facility could more effectively serve its customers and so that the workers would be more effective and efficient.

## TAKING IT TO THE NET 1

www.mcgrawhillconnect.ca

### Purpose

To illustrate production processes.

### Exercise

Take a virtual tour of the Hershey Foods Corporation's chocolate factory by going to www.hersheys.com/discover/tour_video.asp.

1. Does Hershey use process manufacturing or the assembly process? Is the production of Hershey's chocolate an example of an intermittent or continuous production process? Justify your answers.

2. What location factors might go into the selection of a manufacturing site for Hershey's chocolate?

# TAKING IT TO THE NET 2

### Purpose

To understand the extent and importance of research and development (R&D) spending in Canada.

### Exercise

RE$EARCH Infosource Inc. publishes an in-depth report on Canadian R&D trends. The top 100 R&D spending firms can be found by visiting www.researchinfosource.com/top100.shtml.

1. How has this ranking changed from last year's ranking?

2. What are the top ten R&D-intensive firms?

3. What is the future expectation for R&D spending in Canada?

# ANALYZING MANAGEMENT DECISIONS

## Why Big Companies Fail to Innovate

Matthew Kiernan, based in Unionville, Ontario, is a management consultant whose views command attention. He has a PhD degree in strategic management from the University of London and was a senior partner with an international consulting firm, KPMG Peat Marwick. Subsequently, he founded his own firm, Innovest Group International, with a staff operating out of Geneva, London, and Toronto. He was also a director of the Business Council for Sustainable Development based in Geneva.

His book *Get Innovative or Get Dead* took aim at big corporations for their poor record on innovation. Any five-year-old could tell you that companies must innovate to survive, he said, so what's the problem? According to Kiernan, it's one thing to understand something in your head but quite another thing to really feel it in your gut. This is further complicated by the difficulty of getting a big company to shift gears, to turn its culture around so that innovation becomes the norm rather than the special effort.

Kiernan called for a company to develop a style and atmosphere that favours individual risk-taking, the intra-preneurial approach discussed in Chapter 7. That means

that if a team tries something that doesn't work, you don't shoot it down. Encouraging innovation, which inevitably involves taking risks with the unknown, means accepting the fact that it may take two or three attempts before something useful is developed. Recently, Matthew has applied this principle to sustainable development, including the topic of carbon finance.

The 3M company is often used as a great example of a company that encourages creativity. Its policy dictates that 30 percent of annual sales come from products less than four years old. However, 3M wasn't always that progressive. When the now legendary Post-it Notes were first developed by an employee, he had a hard time getting the company to see the potential in his idea. This ultimately triggered a major change in the company's policy. Kiernan pointed out that most companies give lip service to the necessity of innovation but do not act in a credible way as far as their employees are concerned. If you mean business, you must take that "bright guy out of the basement, [the one] everybody knows is a genius, but whose last two enterprise efforts came to grief, and visibly promote him."

## Discussion Questions

1. Do large companies find it difficult to innovate because they resist change? Is it because they are big or because they are afraid of the unknown? Why is that?

2. Do smaller companies do better at innovation because they are not so risk-averse? Is that because most of

them are private companies and not accountable to outside stakeholders?

3. If you were a vice-president in charge of operations management at a big corporation, how would you encourage innovation?

## RUNNING CASE

## Requisite Organization at Canadian Tire Financial Services (CTFS)

*Requisite organization* is a term created by Dr. Elliott Jaques. It is a scientific approach to the effective management of work systems. The word *requisite* is defined as "required by nature." The ideas in a requisite organization flow from the nature of things—the nature of tasks, work, and human behaviour. These systems include structure, leadership processes, and human resources.

The *structure*, which considers the total number of layers (or strata) in an organization, should be based on the complexity of the work to be performed. Work and accountability cascade downward in successive layers, and a system of organizational strata is formed. These strata comprise a series of levels in the organization with specified work to be done in each stratum. Jaques states that effective leadership in large corporations requires only seven layers (strata), including the CEO. Business units inside corporations, such as Canadian Tire Financial Services (formerly known as Canadian Tire Acceptance Limited), generally need five strata. At CTFS, the five levels are president, vice-presidents, associate vice-presidents, managers, and individual contributors.

A requisite structure, or any structure, in itself will not guarantee the success of an organization in meeting its business strategy. This is why the second major component of a requisite organization is to ensure that *competent individuals are performing work at each organizational level*. Once an assessment is made of the complexity of work to be performed, staffing of the role requires an individual who can manage the complexity.

The third key component of a requisite organization is that it sets a context for *human resource practices and procedures* that are fully integrated and supportive of the business strategy. A few of the key practices and procedures include assigning accountabilities and authority for decisions at the correct level and, as part of job design/job evaluation, determining the level of work for a role.

Jaques demonstrated in a wide variety of organizations that organizational effectiveness and efficiency (through gains in productivity and morale) could be increased by 20 to 50 percent by designing organizational structure and choosing people in ways consistent with those principles. Canadian companies that have implemented, in varying degrees, requisite practices include Essar Steel Algoma, Ontario Hydro, Sunoco, Health Canada, and the Public Service Commission. CTFS has been following this approach for almost over 20 years. Periodically, the structure is revisited to ensure that it is still efficient and effective.

Sources: Rich Morgan, "An Overview of Requisite Organization," Canadian Tire Acceptance Limited, December 1995; Marco Marrone, President, Canadian Tire Financial Service, in-person interview, 10 March 2006; Sharon Patterson, Vice-President Human Resources, Canadian Tire Financial Services, in-person interview, 5 April 2006; Requisite Organization International Institute, http://www.requisite.org/main.html, 6 November 2006; and Ken Shepard, "The Rigour of Requisite Organization," Queen's University iRC, http://irc.queensu.ca/articles/the-rigour-of-requisite-organization.

### Discussion Questions

1. If a company wishes to implement a requisite organization structure, how would this process apply to each of the four management functions?

2. From your understanding of a requisite organization, what is the optimal span of control?

3. What role and accountabilities might a manager have within a requisite organization?

# PART 4

# CHAPTER 11

# Motivating Employees

PROFILE

## LEARNING OBJECTIVES

**AFTER YOU HAVE READ AND STUDIED THIS CHAPTER, YOU SHOULD BE ABLE TO:**

**LO ▶ 1** Relate the significance of Taylor's scientific management and the Hawthorne studies to management.

**LO ▶ 2** Identify the levels of Maslow's hierarchy of needs, and relate their importance to employee motivation.

**LO ▶ 3** Distinguish between the motivators and hygiene factors identified by Herzberg.

**LO ▶ 4** Explain how job enrichment affects employee motivation and performance.

**LO ▶ 5** Differentiate between McGregor's Theory X and Theory Y.

**LO ▶ 6** Describe the key principles of goal setting, expectancy, reinforcement, and equity theories.

**LO ▶ 7** Explain how open communication builds teamwork, and describe how managers are likely to motivate teams in the future.

## PROFILE

## Getting to Know Catherine Daw of SPM Group Ltd.

Catherine Daw is president and co-founder of SPM Group Ltd., a leading management consulting firm that focuses on strategic project management. In her role, Daw provides the vision and leadership needed to evolve the firm. With more than 25 years of experience, she has worked in a variety of public- and private-sector companies, holding progressively higher positions in both information technology and business areas. Daw's approach has always been to deliver results within a foundation of integrity and open communication and with a strong understanding of the link between strategy and projects.

When asked why she pursued her own business versus working for someone else, Daw responded: "I started a family and didn't want to work full-time. My employer at the time was not interested in part-time or job-sharing options. So, I started initially doing freelance work through my network. Then in 1992, my husband had an opportunity to branch out from his organization and we decided to start this company."

There are three ways that SPM helps its clients to become more effective: translate client strategies into executable initiatives, help clients set up end-to-end infrastructure for Initiative Management, and assist clients overcome the roadblocks created by traditional silo-based cultures and reward systems. SPM does this by providing consulting, training, and resourcing services. When you put it all together, SPM enables the Effective Enterprise. This gives clients the agility to seize opportunities and respond to changes.

In recognition of its work, SPM has won the National Award for Small Business Skills Development, which recognizes outstanding achievement in developing employees' skills in small business environments. The resulting competencies are expected to enable employees to contribute to growing the small business in which they work. "SPM Group recognizes that its long-term growth and sustainability depends on its ability to innovate and bring fresh thinking to its clients," said Michael Bloom, Executive

Director, Education and Learning, and Strategic Projects and Initiatives. "SPM's Learning Solutions model is a unique way of understanding the potential of people, leveraging their individual strengths, and building additional competencies." More recently, Daw has been named (for the fourth year in a row) to the 10th annual *PROFIT* W100 list which showcases 100 enterprising women entrepreneurs who are delivering world-class products and services—and reaping the rewards.

Thousands of books and articles have been written about how to motivate a workforce. Not surprisingly, there are many conflicting points of view. Peter Drucker, considered by many to be the "father of management," believed that many workers are knowledge workers. Therefore, to motivate them, employees need autonomy and continual innovation and learning, which should be built into the job. Clearly, employees feel this under the leadership of Catherine Daw. In this chapter, you will be introduced to some motivation theories. Motivated workers are critical, as they contribute to the success of an organization. Some, like Catherine Daw, are self-motivated, and they create opportunities for themselves and others. As you read through this chapter, consider situations in which you have been involved. Did you witness some of the theories being applied? Looking back, could some of these situations have been handled differently to better motivate the audience?

Sources: "Catherine Daw Named to the 10th Annual PROFIT 100W," SPM Group Ltd., 21 October 2008, http://www.spmgroup.ca/AboutUs/News/tabid/91/articleType/ArticleView/articleId/37/Default.aspx; "Let's Talk Interviews—Catherine Daw," Women Can Do Anything Inc., [2006?], http://www.womencandoanything.com/interviews/564_catherinedaw.htm; and "SPM Group Wins First National Award for Small Business Skills Development," The Conference Board of Canada, 29 November 2005, http://www.conferenceboard.ca/press/2005/RBC_awards.asp.

# THE IMPORTANCE OF MOTIVATION

**motivation**

A person's internal drive to act.

"If work is such fun, how come the rich don't do it?" quipped comedian Groucho Marx. Well, the rich do work—Bill Gates didn't make his billions playing computer games. And workers can have fun—if managers make the effort to motivate them. **Motivation** is a person's internal drive to act.[1] One of the most challenging skills of a manager is the ability to induce motivation in employees so that they will be committed and productive employees.[2] The importance of workforce satisfaction cannot be overstated. Happy workers lead to happy customers, and happy customers lead to successful businesses.[3]

On the opposite side, unhappy workers are likely to leave the company, and when this happens, the company usually loses out. The cost associated with losing an employee fluctuates wildly, depending on who you ask: some say it's as low as 25 percent of the departing person's salary while others peg it as high as 200 percent.[4] As the following will illustrate, turnover costs include many variables.

Direct costs include the time it takes to hire the replacement (e.g., process the paperwork, interview candidates, moving costs, and signing/referral bonuses) and costs related to onboarding (e.g., orientation, training, and new material and equipment). The indirect costs are harder to quantify, but they can be substantial as these include loss of productivity. This can be of the outgoing employee, but also on the part of the team or departmental level, on the part of the colleagues who have to fill in once the employee has departed, and on the part of the new hire while he or she gets up to speed. Besides productivity, "some organizations will think about what they've invested in the person in terms of training, knowledge, and skills development that the person is now going to walk out the door with," said David Sissons, Toronto-based vice-president of HR consulting firm Hay Group. "That's a more difficult item to quantify because where do you begin—the last year, the last two years, or the last five years?"[5]

The "soft" costs are even greater: loss of intellectual capital, decreased morale, increased employee stress, and a negative reputation. Motivating the right people to join and remain with the organization is a key function of managers.

**intrinsic reward**

The good feeling you have when you have done a job well.

People are willing to work, and work hard, if they feel that their work makes a difference and is appreciated. People are motivated by a variety of things, such as recognition, accomplishment, and status.[6] An **intrinsic reward** is the personal satisfaction you feel when you perform well and achieve goals. The belief that your work makes a significant contribution to the organization or society is a form of intrinsic reward. An **extrinsic reward** is something given to you by someone else as recognition for good work. Such things as pay increases, praise, and promotions are examples of extrinsic rewards. Although ultimately motivation—the drive to satisfy a need—comes from within an individual, there are ways to stimulate people that bring out their natural drive to do a good job.

**extrinsic reward**

Something given to you by someone else as recognition for good work; extrinsic rewards include pay increases, praise, and promotions.

As an example, Canadian Tire Financial Services Ltd. designates "Customers for Life" awards to its employees that have gone above and beyond the requirements of their jobs. The award is a way to recognize and reward employees (through a presentation, plaque, and day off) who have demonstrated superior customer service. Candidates are nominated based on outstanding conduct witnessed by fellow employees or customer feedback. The award criteria include direct customer contact, positive customer perception of experience, and an experience that meets World Class Customer Service Standards and upholds the company's values and mission statement.

The purpose of this chapter is to help you understand the concepts, theories, and practices of motivation. The most important person to motivate, of course, is yourself. One way to do that is to find the right job in the right organization—one that enables you to reach your goals in life. The job of a leader is to find that commitment, encourage it, and focus it on some common goal.

This chapter begins with a look at some of the traditional theories of motivation. You will learn about the Hawthorne studies because they created a new interest in worker satisfaction and motivation. Then you'll look at some assumptions about employees that

Marco Marrone, President of Canadian Tire Financial Services Ltd., presents a Customers for Life award to Maureen Ethier. Maureen suggested some nearby accommodations for a customer and her passengers that had called in for roadside assistance. This is not a service offered by the plan or requested by the customer, but was done to make the situation easier. Would being recognized in an award ceremony motivate you?

come from the traditional theorists. You will see the names of these theorists over and over in business literature and courses: Taylor, Mayo, Maslow, Herzberg, and McGregor. Finally, you will learn the modern applications of motivation theories and the managerial procedures for implementing them.

# FREDERICK TAYLOR: THE FATHER OF SCIENTIFIC MANAGEMENT

Several books in the nineteenth century presented management principles, but not until the early twentieth century did there appear any significant works with lasting implications. One of the most well known, *The Principles of Scientific Management*, was written by American efficiency engineer Frederick Taylor and published in 1911. This book earned Taylor the title "father of scientific management." Taylor's goal was to increase worker productivity to benefit both the firm and the worker. The way to improve productivity, Taylor thought, was to scientifically study the most efficient ways to do things, determine the one "best way" to perform each task (all the way down to how long a step to take, how often to break, how much water to drink, etc.), and then teach people those methods.[7] This became known as **scientific management**. Three elements were basic to Taylor's approach: time, methods, and rules of work. His most important tools were observation and the stopwatch. Taylor's thinking is behind today's measures of how many burgers McDonald's expects its flippers to flip and how many callers the phone companies expect operators to assist.

A classic Taylor story involves his study of men shovelling rice coal and iron ore with the same type of shovel. Taylor felt that different materials called for different shovels. He proceeded to test a number of different shovel lengths and capacities with seasoned shov-

**scientific management**
Studying workers to find the most efficient ways of doing things and then teaching people those techniques.

**time-motion studies**
Studies, begun by Frederick Taylor, of which tasks must be performed to complete a job and the time needed to do each task.

elers and, with stopwatch in hand, measured output over time in what were called time-motion studies. **Time motion studies** were studies of the tasks performed to complete a job and the time needed to do each task. Sure enough, an average person could shovel more (in fact, from 25 to 35 tons more per day) using the most efficient motions and the proper shovel. This finding led to time-motion studies of virtually every factory job. As the most efficient ways of doing things were determined, efficiency became the standard for setting goals.[8]

Taylor's scientific management became the dominant strategy for improving productivity in the early 1900s. Hundreds of time-motion specialists developed standards in plants throughout the country. One follower of Taylor was Henry L. Gantt, who developed charts by which managers plotted the work of employees a day in advance down to the smallest detail. Engineers Frank and Lillian Gilbreth used Taylor's ideas in a three-year study of bricklaying. They developed the **principle of motion economy**, which showed that every job could be broken down into a series of elementary motions. They then analyzed each motion to make it more efficient.

**principle of motion economy**
Theory developed by Frank and Lillian Gilbreth that every job can be broken down into a series of elementary motions.

Some critics of Taylor's approach compared people largely to machines that needed to be properly programmed.[9] There was little concern for the psychological or human aspects of work. While Taylor did not use this comparison, he had very precise ideas about how to introduce his system: "It is only through enforced standardization of methods, enforced adoption of the best implements and working conditions, and enforced cooperation that this faster work can be assured. And the duty of enforcing the adoption of standards and enforcing this cooperation rests with management alone."[10] A crusader for better working conditions and pay for the working class, Taylor believed that the resulting improved productivity should then benefit both the workers and the company.

Some of Taylor's ideas are still being implemented. Some companies still place more emphasis on conformity to work rules than on creativity, flexibility, and responsiveness.[11] For example, UPS tells drivers how fast to walk (three feet per second), how many packages to pick up and deliver per day (average of 400), and how to hold their keys (teeth up, third finger). Drivers even wear "ring scanners," electronic devices on their index fingers wired to a small computer on their wrists that shoot a pattern of photons at a bar code on a package to let a customer using the Internet know exactly where his or her package is at any given moment.

The benefits of relying on workers to come up with solutions to productivity problems have long been recognized, as we shall discover next.

# ELTON MAYO AND THE HAWTHORNE STUDIES

One of the studies that grew out of Frederick Taylor's research was conducted at the Western Electric Company's Hawthorne plant in Cicero, Illinois. The study began in 1927 and ended six years later. Let's see why it was one of the major studies in management literature.

Elton Mayo and his colleagues from Harvard University came to the Hawthorne plant to test the degree of lighting associated with optimum productivity. In this respect, theirs was a traditional scientific management study; the idea was to keep records of the workers' productivity under different levels of illumination. However, the initial experiments revealed what seemed to be a problem: The productivity of the experimental group compared to that of other workers doing the same job went up regardless of whether the lighting was bright or dim. This was true even when the lighting was reduced to about the level of moonlight. These results confused and frustrated the researchers, who had expected productivity to fall as the lighting was dimmed.

A second series of experiments was conducted. In these, a separate test room was set up where temperature, humidity, and other environmental factors could be manipulated. In the series of 13 experimental periods, productivity went up each time; in fact, it increased by 50 percent overall. When the experimenters repeated the original condition (expecting productivity to fall to original levels), productivity increased yet again. The experiments were considered a total failure at this point. No matter what the experimenters did, productivity went up. What was causing the increase?

Mayo believed that some human or psychological factor was involved. He and his colleagues then interviewed the workers, asking them about their feelings and attitudes toward the experiment. The researchers' findings began a profound change in management thinking that has had repercussions up to the present. Here is what they concluded:

- The workers in the test room thought of themselves as a social group. The atmosphere was informal, they could talk freely, and they interacted regularly with their supervisors and the experimenters. They felt special and worked hard to stay in the group. This motivated them.

- The workers were involved in the planning of the experiments. For example, they rejected one kind of pay schedule and recommended another, which was used. The workers felt that their ideas were respected and that they were involved in managerial decision making. This, too, motivated them.

- No matter what the physical conditions were, the workers enjoyed the atmosphere of their special room and the additional pay they got for more productivity. Job satisfaction increased dramatically.

Researchers now use the term **Hawthorne effect** to refer to the tendency for people to behave differently when they know they're being studied.[12] The Hawthorne studies' results encouraged researchers to study human motivation and the managerial styles that lead to greater productivity. The emphasis of research shifted away from Taylor's scientific management and toward Mayo's new human-based management.

Mayo's findings led to completely new assumptions about employees. One of those assumptions, of course, was that pay was not the only motivator. In fact, money was found to be a relatively ineffective motivator. That change in assumptions led to many theories about the human side of motivation. One of the best-known motivation theorists was Abraham Maslow, whose work we discuss next.

Elton Mayo and his research team forever changed managers' fixed assumptions about what motivates employees. Mayo and his team gave birth to the concept of human-based motivation after conducting studies at the Western Electric Hawthorne plant (pictured here). Before the studies at Hawthorne, workers were often programmed to behave like human robots.

**Hawthorne effect**
The tendency for people to behave differently when they know they are being studied.

# MOTIVATION AND MASLOW'S HIERARCHY OF NEEDS

Psychologist Abraham Maslow believed that to understand motivation at work, one must understand human motivation in general. It seemed to him that motivation arises from need. That is, people are motivated to satisfy unmet needs; needs that have been satisfied no longer provide motivation. He thought that needs could be placed on a hierarchy of importance.

Figure 11.1 shows **Maslow's hierarchy of needs**, whose levels are as follows:

- *Physiological Needs*. Basic survival needs, such as the need for food, water, and shelter.

- *Safety Needs*. The need to feel secure at work and at home.

- *Social Needs*. The need to feel loved, accepted, and part of the group.

- *Esteem Needs*. The need for recognition and acknowledgement from others, as well as self-respect and a sense of status or importance.

- *Self-Actualization Needs*. The need to develop to one's fullest potential.

**Maslow's hierarchy of needs**
Theory of motivation that places different types of human needs in order of importance, from basic physiological needs to safety, social, and esteem needs to self-actualization needs.

**FIGURE** | **11.1**

**Maslow's Hierarchy of Needs**
Maslow's hierarchy of needs is based on the idea that motivation comes from need. If a need is met, it's no longer a motivator, so a higher-level need becomes the motivator. Higher-level needs demand the support of lower-level needs. This chart shows the various levels of need.

When one need is satisfied, another, higher-level need emerges and motivates the person to do something to satisfy it. The satisfied need is no longer a motivator. For example, if you just ate a full-course dinner, hunger would not (at least for several hours) be a motivator, and your attention may turn to your surroundings (safety needs) or family (social needs). Of course, lower-level needs (e.g., thirst) may emerge at any time they are not met and take your attention away from higher-level needs such as the need for recognition or status.

Most of the world's workers struggle all day simply to meet the basic physiological and safety needs. In developed countries, such needs no longer dominate, and workers seek to satisfy growth needs (social, esteem, and self-actualization).

To compete successfully, firms must create a work environment that motivates the best and the brightest workers. That means establishing a work environment that includes goals such as social contribution, honesty, reliability, service, quality, dependability, and unity.

## Applying Maslow's Theory

Andrew Grove, Senior Advisor of Intel Corporation (and former CEO and Chairman), observed Maslow's concepts in action in his firm.[13] One woman, for example, took a low-paying job that did little for her family's standard of living. Why? Because she needed the companionship her work offered (social/affiliation need). One of Grove's friends had a mid-life crisis when he was made a vice-president. This position had been a lifelong goal, and when the man reached it he felt unsettled because he had to find another way to motivate himself (self-actualization need). People at a research and development lab were motivated by the desire to know more about their field of interest, but they had little desire to produce marketable results and thus little was achieved. Grove had to find new people who wanted to learn not just for the sake of learning but to achieve results as well. Once managers understand the need level of employees, it is easier to design programs that will trigger self-motivation.[14]

### Progress Assessment

- What are the similarities and differences between Taylor's time-motion studies and Mayo's Hawthorne studies?
- How did Mayo's findings influence scientific management?
- Can you draw a diagram of Maslow's hierarchy of needs? Label and describe the parts.

# HERZBERG'S MOTIVATING FACTORS

Another direction in managerial theory is to explore what managers can do with the job itself to motivate employees (a modern-day look at Taylor's research). In other words, some theorists ask: Of all the factors controllable by managers, which are most effective in generating an enthusiastic work effort?

The most discussed study in this area was conducted in the mid-1960s by psychologist Frederick Herzberg. He asked workers to rank various job-related factors in order of importance relative to motivation. The question was: What creates enthusiasm for workers and makes them work to full potential? The results showed that the most important motivating factors were the following:

1. Sense of achievement
2. Earned recognition
3. Interest in the work itself
4. Opportunity for growth
5. Opportunity for advancement
6. Importance of responsibility
7. Peer and group relationships
8. Pay
9. Supervisor's fairness
10. Company policies and rules
11. Status
12. Job security
13. Supervisor's friendliness
14. Working conditions

Herzberg noted that the factors receiving the most votes were clustered around job content. Workers like to feel that they contribute to the company (sense of achievement was number one). They want to earn recognition (number two) and feel that their jobs are important (number six). They want responsibility (which is why learning is so important) and want recognition for that responsibility by having a chance for growth and advancement. Of course, workers also want the job to be interesting.

Herzberg believed that motivational factors such as recognition increase worker performance. How do you think Herzberg's motivational factors encourage workers to a higher level of performance on the job?

**Herzberg's Motivators and Hygiene Factors**
There's some controversy over Herzberg's results. For example, sales managers often use money as a motivator. Recent studies have shown that money can be a motivator if used as part of a recognition program.

| Motivators | Hygiene (Maintenance) Factors |
|---|---|
| (These factors can be used to motivate workers.) | (These factors can cause dissatisfaction, but changing them will have little motivational effect.) |
| Work itself | Company policy and administration |
| Achievement | Supervision |
| Recognition | Working conditions |
| Responsibility | Interpersonal relations (co-workers) |
| Growth and advancement | Salary, status, and job security |

**motivators**

In Herzberg's theory of motivating factors, job factors that cause employees to be productive and that give them satisfaction.

**hygiene (maintenance) factors**

In Herzberg's theory of motivating factors, job factors that can cause dissatisfaction if missing but that do not necessarily motivate employees if increased.

Herzberg noted further that factors having to do with the job environment were not considered motivators by workers. It was interesting to find that one of those factors was pay. Workers felt that the absence of good pay, job security, friendly supervisors, and the like could cause dissatisfaction, but the presence of those factors did not motivate them to work harder; they simply provided satisfaction and contentment in the work situation.

The conclusions of Herzberg's study were that certain factors, called **motivators**, did cause employees to be productive and gave them a great deal of satisfaction. These factors mostly had to do with job content. Herzberg called other elements of the job **hygiene factors** (or **maintenance factors**). These had to do mostly with the job environment and could cause dissatisfaction if missing but would not necessarily motivate employees if increased. See Figure 11.2 for a list of both motivators and hygiene factors.

Considering Herzberg's motivating factors, we come up with the following conclusion: The best way to motivate employees is to make the job interesting, help them achieve their objectives, and recognize that achievement through advancement and added responsibility.

## Applying Herzberg's Theories

Improved working conditions (such as better wages or increased security) are taken for granted after workers get used to them. This is what Herzberg meant by hygiene (or maintenance) factors: their absence causes dissatisfaction, but their presence (maintenance) does not motivate. The best motivator for some employees is a simple and sincere "Thanks, I really appreciate what you're doing."

Mediacorp Canada Inc. annually publishes a list of Canada's Top 100 Employers. Companies are ranked based on seven key areas: community involvement; work atmosphere and social culture; vacation; performance management; health, financial and family benefits; training and skills development; and physical workspace.[15] The following example illustrates why Canadian Pacific Railway Ltd. has been noted on this list for its workforce planning and community involvement. Community involvement, it turns out, is one of the biggest things that draws employees to work for a firm. In the case of Canadian Pacific, every year the company sends out its Spirit Train to support local food banks as it rattles through the communities where it operates. The company is also highly involved with the United Way and encourages its employees to take part in various initiatives throughout the year. The unique geographic spread of the company—from Vancouver to Montreal—means employees can literally work in communities across Canada. The perks don't hurt, either. The company offers tuition subsidies up to $10,000, a flexible health benefits program including retirees, a diverse range of working environments and roles within the firm, and its very own training facility for conductors and engineers. Mobility is what the company is all about. "You can start with this company in human resources and end up in operations, finance, public affairs—a career within a career within this railway," says Patti Clarkson, an employment advisor at the company.[16]

Mars Canada, the Canadian manufacturer of Mars and Snickers candy bars, was also cited on this list for offering benefits that include products at cost to employees at its onsite store, three weeks of paid vacation to start, weekly visits from a Wellness Coordinator who provides one-on-one fitness training, operating an onsite fitness facility with free employee memberships, and rewarding employees with a generous bonus (up to $1,500) when they recommend a friend who gets hired.[17] Its employee engagement program is rated as exceptional. Employees receive individual performance reviews every six months and the company recognizes exceptional performance through two formal programs. One program (called Aspire) is for part-time employees who are awarded performance "points" that are redeemable for a selection of merchandise, and the "Difference is You Award" recognizes employee innovation and initiative. Through this second program, individual and group winners travel to Washington for a chance to compete for Mars Inc. Global Awards.[18]

The Green Box highlights Vancity, an organization that has also been recognized as one of Canada's Top 100 Employers. Here you will learn about some of its climate change initiatives.

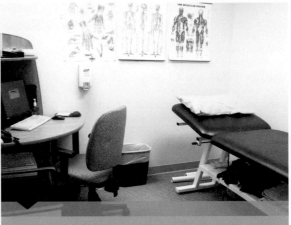

Back in Motion (BiM), a full-service rehabilitation and disability management company, has been cited as one of Canada's top employers. The company offers profit-sharing, an annual education allowance, flexible hours, and a policy of promoting from within. Cynthia Abbott, a vocational coach, recalls being shocked when, accompanying her first raise, she received a handwritten note from the CEO praising her accomplishments.

Many surveys conducted to test Herzberg's theories have supported his finding that the number-one motivator is not money but a sense of achievement and recognition for a job well done.[19] If you're skeptical about this, think about the limitations of money as a motivating force. Most organizations review an employee's performance only once a year and allocate raises at that time. To inspire and motivate employees to perform at their highest level of capability, managers must recognize their achievements and progress more than once a year.

"Employees are most productive when they feel their contributions are valued and their feedback is welcomed by management," said Max Messmer, chairman of Accountemps and author of *Motivating Employees for Dummies*. "The reverse is also true—an unsupportive atmosphere can lead to reduced performance levels and higher turnover for businesses."[20] According to a recent Accountemps report, 48 percent of executives cited that better communication was the best remedy for low employee spirits, with other results such as recognition programs (19 percent), monetary awards for exceptional performance (13 percent), team-building events or meetings (5 percent), and additional days off (3 percent) lagging much farther behind. When asked what factors play a role in affecting employee morale negatively, again the top reason, was a lack of open, honest communication (33 percent). Other reasons included failure to recognize employee achievements (19 percent), micromanaging employees (17 percent), excessive workloads for extensive periods (16 percent), and fear of job loss (14 percent).[21]

Look back at Herzberg's list of motivating factors and identify the ones that tend to motivate you. Rank them in order of importance to you. Keep these factors in mind as you consider jobs and careers. What motivators do your job opportunities offer to you? Are they the ones you consider important? Evaluating your job offers in terms of what's really important to you will help you make a wise career choice.

A review of Figure 11.3 shows that there is a good deal of similarity in Maslow's hierarchy of needs and Herzberg's theory of factors.

## GreenBOX

### Vancity's Climate Change Solutions

Vancouver City Savings Credit Union (Vancity) is Canada's largest credit union with $14.1 billion in assets, 400,000 members, and 59 branches throughout Greater Vancouver, the Fraser Valley, Victoria, and Squamish. Vancity also owns Citizens Bank of Canada, which serves members across the country by telephone, ATM, and the Internet.

Vancity is committed to supporting ways to find positive solutions to climate change. There are many individual and easy, everyday changes that can be made to reduce the impact on the environment including recycling, using less energy, and alternative forms of daily transportation. To be part of the climate change solution, here are some initiatives that are supported at Vancity:

- *Financing Member Action.* To encourage members to take action, Vancity offers an enviro-VISA and financing for activities that reduce energy use or that shift to cleaner energy. Activities include the purchase of hybrid and natural gas vehicles, energy-efficient home renovations, and financing green energy alternatives such as the Furry Creek small-scale hydro project.
- *Funding Community Action.* Numerous organizations have been funded for activities like sustainable transportation, greening spaces, sustainable urban form, and green energy. One example is its three-year commitment to reduce vehicle trips to the University of British Columbia and Simon Fraser University by sponsoring the student U-Pass program for transit access on buses, SkyTrain, and SeaBus.
- *Encouraging Sustainable Transportation.* Employee incentive programs offer priority parking for carpoolers and reduced-rate transit passes. Branches located close to public transit have bike racks and the head office has a secure bike room, lockers, and shower facilities. Today, over 50 percent of employees take alternative transportation.
- *Leading the Way in Energy Management.* Dozens of initiatives have been undertaken to make operations more energy efficient. As a result, more than $1.16 million has been saved in electricity costs. This has reduced energy use by 27 percent per square metre and decreased greenhouse gas emissions by 223 tonnes.

Vancity is committed to a further 10 percent reduction in total energy use over the next three years and it has set a goal to rank among the top 10 percent of organizations in energy efficiency within its industry. Would you like to work for an organization that is so committed to climate change?

Source: "Climate Change Solutions," Vancouver City Savings Credit Union, 4 January 2009, https://www.vancity.com/AboutUs/OurValues/CorporateSocialResponsibility/ClimateChangeSolutions/, used with permission of Vancity.

---

**FIGURE 11.3**

**Comparison of Maslow's Hierarchy of Needs and Herzberg's Theory of Factors**

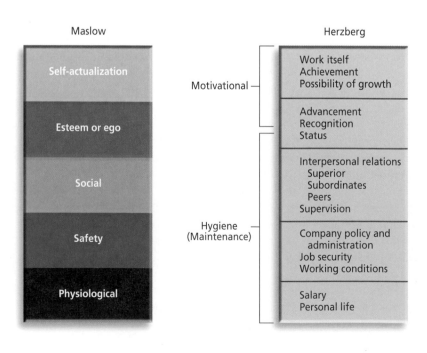

# JOB ENRICHMENT

Both Maslow's and Herzberg's theories have been extended by job enrichment theory. **Job enrichment** is a motivational strategy that emphasizes motivating the worker through the job itself. Work is assigned to individuals so that they have the opportunity to complete an identifiable task from beginning to end. They are held responsible for successful completion of the task. The motivational effect of job enrichment can come from the opportunities for personal achievement, challenge, and recognition.

J. Richard Hackman and Greg R. Oldham proposed the Job Characteristics Model, which is widely used as a framework to study how particular job characteristics influence work outcomes (i.e., job satisfaction, absenteeism, work motivation, etc.).[22] The five characteristics of work that are important in affecting individual motivation and performance are as follows:

1. *Skill Variety*. The extent to which a job demands different skills.

2. *Task Identity*. The degree to which the job requires doing a task with a visible outcome from beginning to end.

3. *Task Significance*. The degree to which the job has a substantial impact on the lives or work of others in the company.

4. *Autonomy*. The degree of freedom, independence, and discretion in scheduling work and determining procedures.

5. *Feedback*. The amount of direct and clear information that is received about job performance.

Variety, identity, and significance contribute to the meaningfulness of the job. Autonomy gives people a feeling of responsibility, and feedback contributes to a feeling of achievement and recognition.

Job enrichment is what makes work fun. The word *fun* can be misleading. We're not talking about having parties all the time. For example, Roger Sant, founder of AES Corporation, one of the world's largest global companies, said that what makes working at AES fun is that people are fully engaged: "They have total responsibility for decisions. They are accountable for results. What they do every day matters to the company, and it matters to the communities we operate in. We do celebrate a lot—because lots of great things are happening. We just did a billion-dollar deal, for instance, and that called for a party. But it's what happens before the celebrations that's really fun."[23]

Job enrichment is based on Herzberg's higher motivators such as responsibility, achievement, and recognition. It stands in contrast to *job simplification*, which produces task efficiency by breaking down a job into simple steps and assigning people to each of those steps.

Another type of job enrichment used for motivation is **job enlargement**, which extends the work cycle by adding related tasks to the job description.[24] An example might be to involve the workers in cleaning and maintaining their own plant, as well as obtaining their own materials from a central store, thereby doing tasks that were once done by service departments.[25] **Job rotation** also makes work more interesting and motivating by moving employees from one job to another. One problem with job rotation, of course, is having to train employees to do several different operations. However, the resulting increase in employee motivation and the value of having flexible, cross-trained employees offsets the additional costs.[26]

Job enrichment is one way to ensure that workers enjoy responsibility and a sense of accomplishment. The Spotlight on Small Business box offers advice on using job enrichment strategies in small businesses.

**job enrichment**
A motivational strategy that emphasizes motivating the worker through the job itself.

**job enlargement**
A job enrichment strategy that extends the work cycle by adding related tasks to the job description.

**job rotation**
A job enrichment strategy that involves moving employees from one job to another.

## Small Businesses Can Motivate Without Big Costs

Often, small businesses cannot offer their employees the financial incentives that larger business can. So, how can they motivate their workers to perform their best? Celine Rattray of Plum Pictures, a small independent movie production company, says that you must offer employees something that money can't buy. "On a small-budget film, you offer typecasted actors different roles. You offer crew members a position above what they're used to doing—the makeup assistant might be the lead makeup artist. And we compensate writers by including them more in the production. We paid nothing for one script; a studio might have paid $10,000. The writer is helping choose a director and a cast. It's an exchange."

According to Rhonda Abrams, author of *Wear Clean Underwear: Business Wisdom from Mom*, the surest way to get the best value from your employees is to treat them with respect: "When you allow your employees to think about how to solve problems, not just carry out specific tasks, you can unleash an amazing amount of creativity and energy. To do so, however, they'll need information, patience, and a sense they won't be 'punished' if they make an honest mistake."

To help your employees be more productive, Abrams recommends that you:

- *Train your employees to do a wide variety of tasks.* In a small business, employees have to pitch in on many jobs, so instead of teaching them specific tasks, you need to teach them about the whole business and encourage problem solving.
- *Communicate frequently.* You could hold frequent brief motivation sessions in which employees compliment each other for recent behaviours, both minor and major. Then each person could share something they've done well. These meetings raise individual self-esteem and set the tone for the rest of the day. According to Abrams, "Giving people positive feedback isn't just about building their self-esteem or empty flattery, it's about creating a strong, productive, atmosphere."
- *Empower your employees to make decisions.* Let them use their brains, not just their backs.
- *Acknowledge their contributions.* The least productive thing you can say is "I don't need to thank employees; I pay them." We all need to be thanked and recognized.

It's important for small-business owners to make every employee feel valued, included, and respected. As your employees grow, your business is more likely to grow.

Sources: Lucas Conley and Rhonda Abrams, "Twenty Years Reaps Many Entrepreneurial Lessons," Gannett News Service, 26 January 2006; Danielle Sacks, "A Plum Partnership," *Fast Company*, March 2005, 39; and Rhonda Abrams, "Say It with Compliments," Gannett News Service, 11 February 2005.

# McGREGOR'S THEORY X AND THEORY Y

The way in which managers go about motivating people at work depends greatly on their attitudes toward workers. Management theorist Douglas McGregor observed that managers' attitudes generally fall into one of two entirely different sets of managerial assumptions, which he called Theory X and Theory Y. His research found that the assumptions of the manager provided a self-fulfilling prophecy about the behaviour of those he or she managed.

## Theory X

The assumptions of Theory X management are as follows:

- The average person dislikes work and will avoid it if possible.
- Because of this dislike, workers must be forced, controlled, directed, or threatened with punishment to make them put forth the effort to achieve the organization's goals.
- The average worker prefers to be directed, wishes to avoid responsibility, has relatively little ambition, and wants security.
- Primary motivators are fear and money.

The natural consequence of such attitudes, beliefs, and assumptions is a manager who is very "busy" and who watches people closely, telling them what to do and how to do it. Motivation is more likely to take the form of punishment for bad work rather than reward for good work. Theory X managers give workers little responsibility, authority, or flexibility. It was assumed that workers needed to be trained and carefully watched to see that they conformed to the standards that had been established as being the most efficient and effective.

Theory X management still dominates some organizations. These managers and entrepreneurs still suspect that employees cannot be fully trusted and need to be closely supervised. No doubt you have seen such managers in action. How did this make you feel? Were these managers' assumptions accurate regarding the workers' attitudes?

## Theory Y

Theory Y makes entirely different assumptions about people. They are as follows:

Theory X managers come in all sizes and shapes. Such managers may have an in-your-face style. Would you prefer to work for a Theory X or a Theory Y manager?

- Most people like work; it is as natural as play or rest.

- Most people naturally work toward goals to which they are committed.

- The depth of a person's commitment to goals depends on the perceived rewards for achieving them.

- Under certain conditions, most people not only accept but also seek responsibility.

- People are capable of using a relatively high degree of imagination, creativity, and cleverness to solve problems.

- People are motivated by a variety of rewards. Each worker is stimulated by a reward unique to that worker (e.g., time off, money, recognition, etc.).

Rather than emphasize authority, direction, and close supervision, Theory Y emphasizes a relaxed managerial atmosphere in which workers are free to set objectives, be creative, be flexible, and go beyond the goals set by management. (Figure 11.4 compares both Theories X and Y.) A key technique in meeting these objectives is empowerment. Empowerment gives employees the ability to make decisions and the tools to implement the decisions they make. For empowerment to be a real motivator, management should follow these three steps:

1. Find out what people think the problems in the organization are.

2. Let them design the solutions.

3. Get out of the way and let them put those solutions into action.

| Theory X | Theory Y |
|---|---|
| 1. Employees dislike work and will try to avoid it. | 1. Employees view work as a natural part of life. |
| 2. Employees prefer to be controlled and directed. | 2. Employees prefer limited control and direction. |
| 3. Employees seek security, not responsibility. | 3. Employees will seek responsibility under proper work conditions. |
| 4. Employees must be intimidated by managers to perform. | 4. Employees perform better in work environments that are non-intimidating |
| 5. Employees are motivated by financial rewards. | 5. Employees are motivated by many different needs. |

**FIGURE** 11.4

**A Comparison of Theories X and Y**

At Mini Maids, the emphasis is on teamwork and employee empowerment to deal with on-the-job problems that arise. The company values the principles of Theory Y management where employees are looked on as partners. What businesses do you feel can most appropriately use the principles of Theory Y management?

Often employees complain that although they're asked to become involved in company decision making, their managers fail to actually empower them to make decisions. Have you ever worked in such an atmosphere? How did that make you feel?

The trend in many businesses is toward Theory Y management. One reason for this trend is that many service industries are finding Theory Y helpful in dealing with on-the-spot problems. Dan Kaplan of Hertz Rental Corporation would attest to this. He empowers his employees in the field to think and work as entrepreneurs. Leona Ackerly of Mini Maid, Inc., agrees: "If our employees look at our managers as partners, a real team effort is built."

## Progress Assessment

- Explain the difference between Herzberg's motivators and hygiene factors.
- Relate job enrichment to Herzberg's motivating factors.
- Briefly describe the managerial attitudes behind Theories X and Y.

# GOAL-SETTING THEORY AND MANAGEMENT BY OBJECTIVES

**goal-setting theory**
The idea that setting ambitious but attainable goals can motivate workers and improve performance if the goals are accepted, accompanied by feedback, and facilitated by organizational conditions.

**Goal-setting theory** is based on the idea that setting ambitious but attainable goals can motivate workers and improve performance if the goals are accepted, accompanied by feedback, and facilitated by organizational conditions. All members of an organization should have some basic agreement about the overall goals of the organization and the specific objectives to be met by each department and individual. It follows, then, that there should be a system to involve everyone in the organization in goal setting and implementation.

Notice that goal-setting potentially improves employee performance in two ways: (1) by stretching the intensity and persistence of effort, and (2) by giving employees clearer role perceptions so that their effort is channelled toward behaviours that will improve work performance.[29] At Montreal-based The Messaging Architects Inc., CEO Pierre Chamberland agrees that employees need to be involved in setting company goals. "It's total disclosure, and it works to build a culture of ownership within the organization," says Chamberland. With a clearer understanding of how business works, employees can participate, whether it's asking questions or setting targets. "They are more motivated to achieve targets because they set their own," says Chamberland.[27]

**management by objectives (MBO)**
A system of goal setting and implementation that involves a cycle of discussion, review, and evaluation of objectives among top- and middle-level managers, supervisors, and employees.

Peter Drucker developed such a system in the 1960s. Drucker asserted: "Managers cannot motivate people; they can only thwart people's motivation because people motivate themselves." Managers, he believed, can only create the proper environment for the seed to grow. Thus, he designed his system to help employees motivate themselves. Called **management by objectives (MBO)**, it is a system of goal setting and implementation that involves a cycle of discussion, review, and evaluation of objectives among top- and middle-level managers, supervisors, and employees. MBO calls on managers to formulate goals in co-operation with everyone in the organization, to commit employees to those goals, and then to monitor results and reward accomplishment.[28]

MBO is most effective in relatively stable situations in which long-range plans can be made and implemented with little need for major changes. It is also important to MBO that managers understand the difference between helping and coaching subordinates. Helping means working with the subordinate and doing part of the work if necessary. Coaching means acting as a resource—teaching, guiding, and recommending—but not helping (that is, not participating actively or doing the task). The central idea of MBO is that employees need to motivate themselves.

Problems can arise when management uses MBO as a strategy for forcing managers and workers to commit to goals that are not really agreed on mutually but are instead set by top management. Employee involvement and expectations are important.[29]

Victor Vroom identified the importance of employee expectations and developed a process called expectancy theory. Let's examine this concept next.

## MEETING EMPLOYEE EXPECTATIONS: EXPECTANCY THEORY

According to Victor Vroom's **expectancy theory**, employee expectations can affect an individual's motivation. Therefore, the amount of effort employees exert on a specific task depends on their expectations of the outcome.[30] Vroom contends that employees ask three questions before committing maximum effort to a task: (1) Can I accomplish the task? (2) If I do accomplish it, what's my reward? (3) Is the reward worth the effort? (See Figure 11.5 for a summary of this process.)

Performance feedback is crucial for the motivation of employees. The feedback session is also ideal for setting goals.

**expectancy theory**
Victor Vroom's theory that the amount of effort employees exert on a specific task depends on their expectations of the outcome.

Recall from the start of the chapter when it was stated that motivation comes from within when you consider this next example. Think of the effort you might exert in your class under the following conditions: Your instructor says that to earn an A in the course you must achieve an average of 90 percent on coursework plus jump two metres high. Would you exert maximum effort toward earning an A if you knew you could not possibly jump two metres high? Or what if your instructor said that any student can earn an A in the course but you know that this instructor has not awarded an A in 25 years of teaching? If the reward of an A seems unattainable, would you exert significant effort in the course? Better yet, let's say that you read in the newspaper that businesses actually prefer hiring C-minus students to hiring A-plus students. Does the reward of an A seem worth it? Now think of the same types of situations that may occur on the job.

Expectancy theory does note that expectation varies from individual to individual. Employees therefore establish their own views in terms of task difficulty and the value of the reward. Researchers David Nadler and Edward Lawler modified Vroom's theory and suggested that managers follow five steps to improve employee performance:[31]

1. Determine what rewards are valued by employees.
2. Determine each employee's desired performance standard.
3. Ensure that performance standards are attainable.
4. Guarantee rewards tied to performance.
5. Be certain that rewards are considered adequate.

**FIGURE** | **11.5**

**Expectancy Theory**
The amount of effort employees exert on a task depends on their expectations of the outcome.

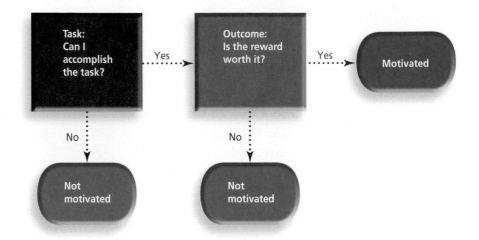

Now that we have covered several theories, you may have realized that they try to explain all behaviour, by all people, all of the time. But this is impossible given the complexity of human behaviour. The value of being briefly introduced to different theories (you will discuss these theories in more detail in an Organizational Behaviour course) is that each theory offers some piece of the puzzle. No theory is complete, as people are very complex and our attempts to theorize about behaviour will never be complete. Successful leaders are sensitive to the differences between their employees and what motivates them. A starting point is understanding these theories.

# REINFORCING EMPLOYEE PERFORMANCE: REINFORCEMENT THEORY

**reinforcement theory**
Theory that positive and negative reinforcers motivate a person to behave in certain ways.

**Reinforcement theory** is based on the idea that positive and negative reinforcers motivate a person to behave in certain ways. In other words, motivation is the result of the carrot-and-stick approach (reward and punishment). B.F. Skinner asserted that positive reinforcement is more effective at changing and establishing behaviour than punishment and that the main thing people learn from being punished is how to avoid punishment.[32] Put another way, individuals act to receive rewards and avoid punishment. Positive reinforcements are rewards such as praise, recognition, or a pay raise. Negative reinforcement includes reprimands, reduced pay, and layoff or firing. A manager might also try to stop undesirable behaviour by not responding to it. This is called *extinction*, because the hope is that the unwanted behaviour will eventually become extinct. Figure 11.6 illustrates how a manager can use reinforcement theory to motivate workers.

# TREATING EMPLOYEES FAIRLY: EQUITY THEORY

**equity theory**
The idea that employees try to maintain equity between inputs and outputs compared to others in similar positions.

**Equity theory** deals with the questions "If I do a good job, will it be worth it?" and "What's fair?" It has to do with perceptions of fairness and how those perceptions affect employees' willingness to perform. The basic principle is that employees try to maintain equity between inputs and outputs compared to others in similar positions. Equity comparisons are made from the information that is available through personal relationships, professional organizations, and so on.[33]

When workers do perceive inequity, they will try to re-establish equitable exchanges in a number of ways. For example, suppose that you compare the grade you earned on a

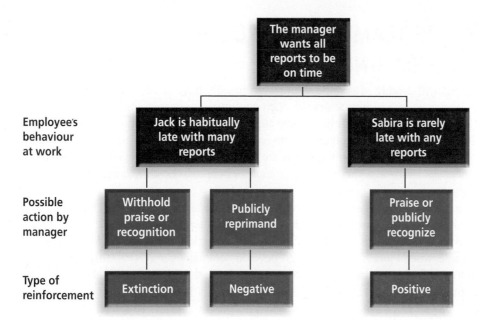

**FIGURE** | **11.6**

**Reinforcement Theory**
A manager can use both positive and negative reinforcement to motivate employee behaviour.

term paper with your classmates' grades. If you think you received a lower grade compared to the students who put out the same effort as you, you will probably react in one of two ways: (1) by reducing your effort on future class projects, or (2) by rationalizing. The latter may include saying, "Grades are overvalued anyway!" If you think that your paper received a higher grade than comparable papers, you will probably (1) increase your effort to justify the higher reward in the future, or (2) rationalize by saying, "I'm worth it!" In the workplace, inequity may lead to lower productivity, reduced quality, increased absenteeism, and voluntary resignation.

Remember that equity judgments are based on perceptions and are therefore subject to errors in perception. When workers overestimate their own contributions—as happens often—they are going to feel that any rewards given out for performance are inequitable. Sometimes organizations try to deal with this by keeping employee salaries secret, but secrecy may make things worse; employees are likely to overestimate the salaries of others in addition to overestimating their own contribution.[34] In general, the best remedy is clear and frequent communication. Managers must communicate as clearly as possible both the results they expect and the outcomes that will occur when those results are achieved or when they are not.

If you attend class regularly but do not do well on your first midterm exam, how do you react? Do you stop going to class regularly as you do not think that it is worthwhile? Or, do you go and speak with your instructor to find out how to improve for the next exam?

## Progress Assessment

- Explain goal-setting theory.
- Evaluate expectancy theory. Can you think of situations in which expectancy theory could apply to your efforts or lack of effort?
- Explain the principles of equity theory.

# BUILDING TEAMWORK THROUGH OPEN COMMUNICATION

Companies with highly motivated workforces usually have several things in common. Among the most important factors are open communication systems and self-managed teams.[35] Open communication helps both top managers and team members understand the objectives and work together to achieve them. Communication must flow freely throughout the organization when teams are empowered to make decisions—they can't make these decisions in a vacuum. It is crucial for people to be able to access the knowledge they need when they need it.

Having teams creates an environment in which learning can happen, because most learning happens at the peer level—peers who have an interest in helping each other along. Empowerment works when people volunteer to share their knowledge with their colleagues. For example, when Flora Zhou, a business development manager at AES Corporation, was putting together a bid to the Vietnam government, she sent a detailed email about what she was planning to bid and why to about 300 people within the company. She asked for and received a lot of advice and comments. Most people thought her proposal was fine, but Sarah Slusser, a group manager in Central America, sent Zhou a three-page response that contained a wealth of information about a similar situation she had encountered with a plant in the Yucatan. Slusser told Zhou what technology issues she needed to pay attention to. A few days later, Zhou made the bid. It was the lowest bid by two-tenths of a percent. Did Slusser tell Zhou the exact dollar to bid? No, but she and many others, including plant leaders and board members, gave her the best information and judgments they had to help her make her decision. They shared everything they knew with her.

Teamwork does not happen by itself. The entire organization must be structured to make it easy for managers and employees to talk to one another. Procedures for encouraging open communication include the following:[36]

- *Create an organizational culture that rewards listening.* Top managers must create places to talk, and they must show employees that talking with superiors counts—by providing feedback, adopting employee suggestions, and rewarding upward communication—even if the discussion is negative. Employees must feel free to say anything they deem appropriate. This is evident at the Vancouver-based Great Little Box Company Ltd. (GLBC), a leading manufacturer of custom and stock corrugated boxes and point-of-purchase display. To keep employees up-to-date, GLBC hosts monthly meetings (with catered lunches) that include frank discussions about all financial matters relating to the business. Uniquely, the private company opens its books for all employees every month and splits 15 percent of its profits, distributed equally every month. Employees can also provide direct feedback through a traditional suggestion box.[37]

- *Train supervisors and managers to listen.* Most people receive no training in how to listen, either in school or anywhere else, so organizations must do such training themselves or hire someone to do it.

- *Remove barriers to open communication.* Having separate offices, parking areas, bathrooms, and dining rooms for managers and workers only sets up barriers in an organization. Other barriers are different dress codes and different ways of addressing one another (e.g., calling workers by their first names and managers by their last). Removing such barriers may require imagination and willingness on the part of managers to give up their special privileges.

- *Actively undertake efforts to facilitate communication.* Large lunch tables at which all organization members eat, conference rooms, organizational picnics, organizational athletic teams, and other such efforts all allow managers to mix with each other and with workers.

## DEALING with CHANGE

### Applying Open Communication in Self-Managed Teams

In 2008, Rob Ashe sold Ottawa-based software business Cognos to IBM, the world's largest IT company, for $5 billion. With this sale, he swapped his President and CEO title for that of General Manager and took on the task of integrating his team of 3,500 into IBM's workforce. In his opinion, the biggest challenge facing the company was talent. If the company attracts the right talent, innovation will flow from that. As a result, a lot of time was spent on thinking and strategizing as to how to attract and keep talent. To attract talent, the company tries to make it a very exciting place to be. Employees are rallied around a vision and there is a lot of communication about the vision and company strategy.

To promote innovation, employees are kept close to customers to keep innovation relevant. Customer feedback and customer involvement are part of development activities. Every quarter, there is a staff meeting for the development team. Customers are brought in to talk about how they're using the products so the developers stay close to the usage of the product.

Innovation is also evident in the creation of Cognos Labs. Cognos Labs is an interactive environment where anybody who's got an idea about a potential product or solution can register it in the collaborative Web site. Other people can start looking at it and give comments on it. Groups of people will start to participate and develop the idea further. There are more than 100 projects on the go in the site and the first Cognos Labs project is heading into the product phase.

To get talent, the company needs talent that thinks it can contribute and participate and be part of decisions. And so a team environment has been created where people can contribute. There's a very open, accessible environment at the company. Ashe is talking to employees down many levels of the organization all the time, as is his management team. In his opinion, it creates a sense of accessibility. Accessibility creates a sense of people feeling that they can contribute and say what's on their mind. This allows management to really deal with the truth and get it out on the table. Part of getting people engaged is giving them access to the decision-making through a lot of open communication, which, again, creates accessibility.

You can see elements of theories that we have discussed already being successfully applied by the company. Employees can make a difference when they are respected (e.g., Theory Y), involved in the process (e.g., goal-setting theory), and enjoy their jobs (e.g., job enrichment). The result is a sense of achievement (e.g., Herzberg motivators). Before you think that teamwork is all positive, as in many management practices, there are negatives as well. Take a few minutes to consider what these might have been in this example. Consider teamwork that you have experienced. What went well? What didn't?

Source: "6 Questions: One-on-One with Rob Ashe, GM, Cognos products, Software Group Division, IBM," *Canadian Business Online*, 17 July 2008, http://www.canadianbusiness.com/innovation/article.jsp?content=20 080624_143756_948. Used with permission.

In the Dealing With Change box, you will learn how one organization has addressed the challenge of open communication in teams.

To implement self-managed teams, managers at most companies must reinvent work. This means respecting workers, providing interesting work, rewarding good work, developing workers' skills, allowing autonomy, and decentralizing authority. In the process of reinventing work, it is essential that managers behave ethically toward all employees. The Making Ethical Decisions box illustrates a problem managers may face when filling temporary positions.

## MOTIVATION IN THE FUTURE

What can you learn from all the theories and companies discussed in this chapter? You should have learned that people can be motivated to improve productivity and quality of work if managers know which technique to use and when. You should now be aware that:

- The growth and competitiveness of businesses in general depends on a motivated, productive workforce. To sustain competitive advantage in the global marketplace a company's workforce must be engaged in continual improvement and innovation. Only motivated employees can achieve improvement and innovation as normal methods of operations.

## Making Ethical Decisions

### Motivating Temporary Employees

Say that you work as a manager for the hypothetical Highbrow's, a rather prestigious department store. Each year, to handle the large number of holiday shoppers, you must hire temporary employees. Because of store policy and budget constraints, all temporaries must be discharged on January 10. As you interview prospective employees, however, you give the impression that the store will hire at least two new full-time retail salespeople for the coming year. You hope that this will serve to motivate the temporary workers and even foster some competition among them. You also instruct your permanent salespeople to reinforce the falsehood that good work during the holiday season is the path to full-time employment. Is this an ethical way to try to motivate your employees? What are the dangers of using a tactic such as this?

- Motivation is largely internal, generated by workers themselves; giving employees the freedom to be creative and rewarding achievement when it occurs will release their energy.

- The first step in any motivational program is to establish open communication among workers and managers so that the feeling generated is one of co-operation and teamwork. A family-type atmosphere should prevail.

Today's customers expect high-quality, customized goods and services. This means that employees must provide extensive personal service and pay close attention to details. Employees will have to work smart as well as hard. No amount of supervision can force an employee to smile or to go the extra step to help a customer. Managers need to know how to motivate their employees to meet customer needs.

Tomorrow's managers will not be able to use any one formula for all employees. Rather, they will have to get to know each worker personally and tailor the motivational effort to the individual. As you have learned in this chapter, different employees respond to different managerial and motivational styles. This is further complicated by the increase in global business and the fact that managers now work with employees from a variety of cultural backgrounds. Different cultures experience motivational approaches differently; therefore, the manager of the future will have to study and understand these cultural factors in designing a reward system. The Reaching Beyond Our Borders box describes how a company dealt with cultural issues within global teams.

Cultural differences are not restricted to groups of people from various countries. Such differences also exist between generations raised in the same country. Canadian demographer David Foot has studied the importance of demographic groups on business. He has categorized groups as follows:[38]

- Baby boomers (those born between 1947 and 1966)

- Generation X (those born between 1961 and 1966), a subgroup of the baby boomers

- The baby bust (those born between 1967 and 1979)

- The baby-boom echo (those born between 1980 and 1995)

- The millennium busters (those born between 1996 and 2010).

Note that in your general readings you may encounter different categories of generations, depending on the source. For example, U.S. demographers often define generations as follows: baby boomers (those born between 1946 and 1964), Generation X (those born between 1965 and 1980), and Generation Y (those born between 1981 and 1994). For this discussion, we will use the Canadian demographic groups coined by David Foot.

Back to generational differences, members in each generation are linked through shared life experiences in their formative years—usually the first ten years of life. The

## Global Teamwork

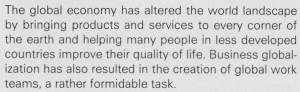

The global economy has altered the world landscape by bringing products and services to every corner of the earth and helping many people in less developed countries improve their quality of life. Business globalization has also resulted in the creation of global work teams, a rather formidable task.

Even though the concept of teamwork is nothing new, building a harmonious global work team is a new task and can be complicated. Global companies must recognize differing attitudes and competencies in the team's cultural mix and the technological capabilities among team members. For example, a global work team needs to determine whether the culture of its members is high context or low context. In a high-context team culture, members build personal relationships and develop group trust before focusing on tasks. In the low-context culture, members often view relationship building as a waste of time that diverts attention from the task. Koreans, Thais, and Saudis (high-context cultures), for example, often view American team members as insincere due to their need for data and quick decision making.

When Digital Equipment Corporation (now a part of Hewlett-Packard) decided to consolidate its operations at six manufacturing sites, the company recognized the need to form multicultural work teams. Realizing the challenge that it faced, the company hired an internal organization development specialist to train the team in relationship building, foreign languages, and valuing differences. All team members from outside the United States were assigned American partners and invited to spend time with their families. Digital also flew the flags of each employee's native country at all of its manufacturing sites. As communication within the teams increased, the company reduced the time of new-product handoffs from three years to just six months.

Understanding the motivational forces in global organizations and building effective global teams is still new territory for most companies. Developing group leaders who are culturally astute, flexible, and able to deal with ambiguity is a challenge businesses must face in the twenty-first century.

Sources: Katherine Sima, "Global Design Focuses on Regional Needs," *Plastics News*, 2 January 2006; and Patricia Sellers, "Blowing in the Wind: To Build a Better Wind Turbine, General Electric Built a Global Team of Researchers in Germany, China, India, and the U.S.," *Fortune*, 25 July 2005, http://money.cnn.com/magazines/fortune.

---

beliefs that you gather as a child affect how you view risk and challenge, authority, technology, relationships, and economics. If you are in a management position, they can affect even whom you hire, fire, or promote. Some generalities apply to these different groups. Baby boomers were raised in families that experienced unprecedented economic prosperity, parents with secure jobs, and optimism about the future. On the other hand, baby busters were raised in dual-career families with parents who focused on work. As children, they attended day care or became latchkey kids. Their parents' successive layoffs added to their insecurity about a lifelong job. Read next how these generational differences affect motivation in the workplace.

## Baby Boom Perspective

Boomer managers will need to be flexible with their baby bust employees or they will lose them. For baby bust employees, it means that they will need to use their enthusiasm for change and streamlining to their advantage. Although many baby busters are unwilling to pay the same price for success that their parents and grandparents did, concern about undue stress and long work hours does not mean that they lack ambition. Rather than focusing on job security, baby busters tend to focus on career security. As they look for opportunities to expand their skills and grow professionally, they are willing to change jobs to do it.[39]

## Baby Bust Perspective

Many baby busters are now or soon will be managers themselves and they will be responsible for motivating other employees. In general, they will be well equipped to motivate people. They understand that there is more to life than work, and they think that a big part of motivating people is letting them know you recognize that fact. As a result, these

There's no magic formula to successfully motivating every worker. Each generation of employees has different attitudes about what's important to them in seeking a balance between a successful career and happy private life. What expectations do you have of your potential supervisor and company?

managers may tend to focus more on results than on hours in the workplace. They will be flexible and good at collaboration and consensus building. They tend to think in broader terms than their predecessors because, through the media, they have been exposed to a lot of problems around the world. They may have a great impact on their team members because they will likely give the people working for them the goals and the parameters of the project and then leave them alone to do their work. Perhaps their best asset might be their ability to give their employees feedback, especially positive feedback. One reason they may be better at providing feedback is that they expect more of it themselves. Managers will need to realize that young workers demand performance reviews and other forms of feedback more than once or twice a year.

## Baby-Boom Echo Perspective

Those that are part of the baby-boom echo are entering the professional workforce now. As a group, they tend to share a number of common characteristics. They are considered impatient, skeptical, blunt and expressive, image driven, and inexperienced. Like any generation, what may make this newer generation difficult to deal with on the job is also what could make it uniquely skilled. For example, a number of talents and tendencies dominate this group: They are adaptable, tech savvy, able to grasp new concepts, practised at multi-tasking, efficient, and tolerant. Perhaps the most surprising attribute that many share is a sense of commitment.

In his book, *Not Everyone Gets A Trophy: How to Manage Generation Y*, Bruce Tulgan shares how the corporate world can recruit and retain workers in this age group. He disproves dozens of myths, including that young employees have no sense of loyalty, won't do grunt work, won't take direction, want to interact only with computers, and are only about money. To motivate them he suggests that their expectations be managed (i.e., don't downplay negative aspects of the job), focus on how each job will improve their skill sets, and recognize that they require balance as their personal life is most important.[40]

One thing in business is likely to remain constant, though. Motivation will come from the job itself rather than from external punishments or rewards. Managers will need to give workers what they require to do a good job: the right tools, the right information, and the right amount of co-operation.

Motivation doesn't have to be difficult. It begins with acknowledging a job well done. You can simply tell those who do such a job that you appreciate them—especially if you make this statement in front of others. After all, as we said earlier in this chapter, the best motivator is frequently a sincere "Thanks, I really appreciate what you're doing."

## Progress Assessment

- What are several steps firms can take to increase internal communications and thus motivation?
- What problems may emerge when trying to implement participative management?
- Why is it important today to adjust motivational styles to individual employees?

# SUMMARY

1. Human efficiency engineer Frederick Taylor was one of the first people to study management. He did time-motion studies to learn the most efficient way of doing a job and then trained workers in those procedures.

LO ▶ 1 Relate the significance of Taylor's scientific management and the Hawthorne studies to management.

**What led to management theories that stress human factors of motivation?**
The greatest impact on motivation theory was generated by the Hawthorne studies in the late 1920s and early 1930s. In these studies, Elton Mayo found that human factors such as feelings of involvement and participation led to greater productivity gains than did physical changes in the workplace.

2. Abraham Maslow studied basic human motivation and found that motivation was based on needs. He said that a person with an unfilled need would be motivated to satisfy it and that a satisfied need no longer served as motivation.

LO ▶ 2 Identify the levels of Maslow's hierarchy of needs, and relate their importance to employee motivation.

**What were the various levels of need identified by Maslow?**
Starting at the bottom of Maslow's hierarchy of needs and going to the top, the levels of need are physiological, safety, social, esteem, and self-actualization.

**Can managers use Maslow's theory?**
Yes, they can recognize what unmet needs a person has and design work so that it satisfies those needs.

3. Frederick Herzberg found that some factors are motivators and others are hygiene (or maintenance) factors. Hygiene factors cause job dissatisfaction if missing but are not motivators if present.

LO ▶ 3 Distinguish between the motivators and hygiene factors identified by Herzberg.

**What are the factors called motivators?**
The work itself, achievement, recognition, responsibility, growth, and advancement are motivators.

**What are hygiene (maintenance) factors?**
Factors that do not motivate but must be present for employee satisfaction, such as company policies, supervision, working conditions, interpersonal relations, and salary, are examples of hygiene factors.

4. Job enrichment describes efforts to make jobs more interesting.

LO ▶ 4 Explain how job enrichment affects employee motivation and performance.

**What characteristics of work affect motivation and performance?**
The job characteristics that influence motivation are skill variety, task identity, task significance, autonomy, and feedback.

**Name two forms of job enrichment that increase motivation.**
Job enrichment strategies include job enlargement and job rotation.

5. Douglas McGregor held that managers will have one of two opposing attitudes toward employees. They are called Theory X and Theory Y.

LO ▶ 5 Differentiate between McGregor's Theory X and Theory Y.

**What is Theory X?**
Theory X assumes that the average person dislikes work and will avoid it if possible. Therefore, people must be forced, controlled, and threatened with punishment to accomplish organizational goals.

**What is Theory Y?**
Theory Y assumes that people like working and will accept responsibility for achieving goals if rewarded for doing so.

LO ▶ 6 Describe the key principles of goal setting, expectancy, reinforcement, and equity theories.

6. Goal-setting theory is based on the notion that setting ambitious but attainable goals will lead to high levels of motivation and performance if the goals are accepted, accompanied by feedback, and facilitated by organizational conditions.

### What is management by objectives (MBO)?

MBO is a system of goal setting and implementation that involves a cycle of discussion, review, and evaluation by objectives among top and middle-level managers, supervisors, and employees.

### What are the key elements involved in expectancy theory?

Expectancy theory centres on three questions employees often ask about performance on the job: (1) Can I accomplish the task? (2) If I do accomplish it, what's my reward? and (3) Is the reward worth the effort?

### What are the variables in reinforcement theory?

Positive reinforcers are rewards such as praise, recognition, or pay raises that a worker might strive to receive after performing well. Negative reinforcers are punishments such as reprimands, pay cuts, or firing that a worker might be expected to try to avoid.

### According to equity theory, employees try to maintain equity between inputs and outputs compared to other employees in similar positions. What happens when employees perceive that their rewards are not equitable?

If employees perceive that they are under-rewarded, they will either reduce their effort or rationalize that it isn't important. If they perceive that they are over-rewarded, they will either increase their effort to justify the higher reward in the future or rationalize by saying, "I'm worth it!" Inequity leads to lower productivity, reduced quality, increased absenteeism, and voluntary resignation.

LO ▶ 7 Explain how open communication builds teamwork, and describe how managers are likely to motivate teams in the future.

7. Companies with highly motivated workforces often have open communication systems and self-managed teams.

### Why is open communication so important in building effective self-managed teams?

Open communication helps both top managers and team members understand the objectives and work together to achieve them. Teams establish an environment in which learning can happen because most learning happens at the peer level.

### How are baby bust managers likely to be different from their baby-boomer predecessors?

Baby boomers are willing to work long hours to build their careers and often expect their subordinates to do likewise. Baby busters strive for a more balanced lifestyle and are likely to focus on results rather than on how many hours their teams work. Baby busters are better than previous generations at working in teams and providing frequent feedback. They are not bound by traditions that may constrain those who have been with an organization for a long time. Baby busters are willing to try new approaches to solving problems.

## KEY TERMS

equity theory  340

expectancy theory  339

extrinsic reward  326

goal-setting theory  338

Hawthorne effect  329

hygiene (maintenance) factors  332

intrinsic reward  326

job enlargement  335

job enrichment  335

job rotation  335

management by objectives (MBO)  338

Maslow's hierarchy of needs  329

motivation  326

motivators  332

principle of motion economy  328

reinforcement theory  340

scientific management  327

time-motion studies  328

## CRITICAL THINKING

1. The textbook introduced you to the theory of scientific management. What do you think are problems that would arise as a result of breaking jobs into a series of discrete steps and treating people as cogs in a wheel? How can you motivate employees if this is how they are managed?

2. Look over Maslow's hierarchy of needs and try to determine where you are right now on the hierarchy. What needs of yours are not being met? How could a company go about meeting those needs and thus motivate you to work better and harder?

## DEVELOPING WORKPLACE SKILLS

1. Talk with several of your friends about the subject of motivation. What motivates them to work hard or not work hard on projects in teams? How important is self-motivation to them?

2. Speak to a manager in the workplace. Find out what this manager does to motivate his/her direct reports.

3. Think of all of the groups with which you have been associated over the years—sports groups, friendship groups, and so on—and try to recall how the leaders of those groups motivated the group to action. What motivational tools were used, and to what effect?

4. Herzberg concluded that pay was not a motivator. If you were paid to get better grades, would you be motivated to study harder? In your employment experiences, have you ever worked harder to obtain a raise or as a result of receiving a large raise? Do you agree with Herzberg?

## TAKING IT TO THE NET 1

### Purpose

To assess your personality type using the Keirsey Character Sorter and to evaluate how well the description of your personality type fits you.

### Exercise

Sometimes understanding differences in employees' personalities helps managers determine how to motivate them. Find out about your personality by going to the Keirsey Temperament Sorter Web site (www.keirsey.com) and answer the 70-item Keirsey Temperament Sorter-II questionnaire. (Disclaimer: The Keirsey test, like all other personality tests, is only a preliminary and rough indicator of personality.)

1. After you complete the steps, you will receive your free Custom Temperament Report. In your opinion, how well or how poorly does the identified personality type fit?

2. Sometimes a personality test does not accurately identify your personality, but it may give you a place to start looking for a portrait that fits. After you have read the Report, ask a good friend or relative for feedback on the results.

3. Based on this information, how do you think a manager can best motivate you?

## TAKING IT TO THE NET 2

### Purpose

To learn why some companies have made it to Canada's Top 100 Employers list.

### Exercise

Canada's Top 100 Employers is an annual competition to recognize Canada's best places to work. The report identifies the companies and organizations that lead their industries in attracting and retaining employees. Visit www.canadastop100.com and find the list of companies that have made it on the most recent list.

1. Choose five companies and read how each one tries to attract and retain employees.

2. What are some non-monetary rewards that are offered to motivate employees and recognize their contributions?

3. Would you want to work for any of these companies? Explain.

## ANALYZING MANAGEMENT DECISIONS

### Motivation Tips for Tough Times

With company cutbacks, layoffs, and economic uncertainty weighing heavily on everybody, it's no wonder some employees are dragging their feet into work. But according to Steven Stein, Toronto-based psychologist and entrepreneur, there are ways to lift and maintain motivation, even in tough times. In *Make Your Workplace Great: The 7 Keys to an Emotionally Intelligent Organization*, he offers these valuable tips for motivating employees.

- *What motivates your workers.* You may be surprised to discover how small changes, such as those in job design or reporting systems, can motivate certain

people. It might not take much, but the only way to discover what your employees want, and how they react to change, is to ask them.

- *Offer ongoing feedback.* No time is better than now to open up lines of communication with your employees, if you haven't already. Whether you offer feedback formally or informally, it's important to let your staff know how they are doing, where they are performing well and where there is room for improvement on a regular basis.

- *Emphasize personal accountability.* Self-management can be highly motivating, and if you're short-staffed, it can make a lot of sense, too. Most people will work much harder for their own sense of accomplishment than they will because they were told to do something.

- *Involve everyone in decision-making.* By involving workers in certain company decisions, especially those that involve them directly, you are much more likely to get support for your initiatives. And you may even get some creative input along the way: your frontline staff might have better knowledge about the impact of certain decisions that you may not be aware of.

- *Be flexible.* Time is an important commodity for people today, especially if they're taking on more work than usual. By giving your employees the opportunity to juggle their time around critical personal or family events and responsibilities, you will increase their motivation.

- *Celebrate employee and company success.* It's important to stop and recognize successes, whether individual, team, or organizational. Let everybody see that hard work is recognized and worth carrying out.

Source: "Great Ideas: Motivation Tips for Tough Times," *PROFIT*, 4 June 2009, http://www.canadianbusiness.com/entrepreneur/human_resources/article.jsp?content=20090603_115416_7820.

## Discussion Questions

1. What other suggestions might you add to this list?

2. If you are employed now (or have been in the past), how has your supervisor motivated you? If you have never been employed before, how can a supervisor motivate you?

3. Apply each one of these tips to group work. How might you implement these suggestions so that group members, including yourself, are motivated to do well in the assigned work?

## CHAPTER 12

# Human Resource Management: Finding and Keeping the Best Employees

## LEARNING OBJECTIVES

**AFTER YOU HAVE READ AND STUDIED THIS CHAPTER, YOU SHOULD BE ABLE TO:**

**LO ▶ 1** Explain the importance of human resource management as a strategic contributor to organizational success, and summarize the five steps in human resources planning.

**LO ▶ 2** Describe methods that companies use to recruit new employees, and explain some of the issues that make recruitment challenging.

**LO ▶ 3** Outline the five steps in selecting employees, and illustrate the use of various types of employee training and development methods.

**LO ▶ 4** Trace the six steps in appraising employee performance, and summarize the objectives of employee compensation programs.

**LO ▶ 5** Describe the ways in which employees can move through a company: promotion, reassignment, termination, and retirement.

**LO ▶ 6** Illustrate the effects of legislation on human resource management.

## PROFILE

## Getting to Know Janice M. Wismer, Global Vice-President of Human Resources, McCain Foods Limited

Janice Wismer started her career at Bell Canada and settled in at Suncor Energy, where she spent fifteen years in human resources (HR) and operations management in locations across Canada. Wismer joined Canadian Tire Corporation Ltd. in 1995, in the financial services division, and moved to the retail division in 1999. In October 2000, she was promoted to Officer of Canadian Tire Corporation. Prior to leaving Canadian Tire Corporation to join McCain Foods Limited, she was Senior Vice-President, Human Resources. At Canadian Tire, Wismer played a lead role in establishing a learning centre and implementing progressive development, pay, and performance management systems.

McCain Foods Limited is a privately owned Canadian multinational manufacturer of frozen and non-frozen food products with 55 plant operations on six continents and annual sales of over $6 billion. McCain Foods is the world's largest producer of french fries and potato specialties, and a manufacturer of pizza, appetizers and snack foods, vegetables, juices and beverages, entrées, oven meals, desserts, and other quality products.

As Global Vice-President of Human Resources for McCain Foods Limited, Wismer is responsible for designing and implementing global human resource programs and systems to maximize individual and organizational capabilities and performance. She believes that business today offers a wide range of opportunities that can appeal to a wide range of skill sets. For example, on one day she is working with a "usability expert" (there are only 10,000 such professionals in the world) to design a company Web site. On another day, she is recruiting a president for the company's transportation business or facilitating an executive leadership development program.

Working for a global company has its own challenges. At the top of the list is working across time zones. There is also the challenge of staying connected. Technology is a wonderful support, but Wismer believes that it can never replace a good old-fashioned face-to-face conversation. She travels extensively to stay close to the business and the people, and through her travels, she learns many things that she would never know by sitting in her office. By visiting plants and offices around the world and listening to people, she learns a great deal about what is working for the business and its people and what is not working. "There is a feel in the business you can only get by being out there," says Wismer.

For those considering a career in business, Wismer encourages individuals to pay attention to what they love to do and seek work that allows them to do just that. "I often say that human resources work is really very basic; get people in jobs they love with clear, aligned goals and get out of the way. It takes a diversity of talents to produce an optimal outcome. For example, some people love retailing and the thrill of filling shelves and being face to face with customers every day. A customer is very lucky to be served by someone who has identified a passion for retail and who has built the skill to do it well!

Simply put, do what you love and do it with purpose, and never stop learning."

If you are considering a career in HR, Wismer shares some words of wisdom from a mentor. He said, "I've come to the conclusion that human resources work, when done well, is the most complex work! In your profession, you not only have to understand the economics and dynamics of running a successful business but you also must understand the subtleties and idiosyncrasies of human behaviour and the value of great leadership. The profession is not for the faint of heart but the rewards are far reaching."

In this chapter, you will be introduced to human resource management. Human resources managers face many challenges as they strive to recruit, hire, train, evaluate, and compensate the best people to accomplish the objectives of their organizations. Let us look at this topic next.

Sources: Janice Wismer, Global Vice-President of Human Resources, McCain Foods Ltd., interview, 20 November 2008; and "Our Company," McCain Foods Ltd., 2008, http://www.mccain.com/company/Pages/default.aspx.

# WORKING WITH PEOPLE IS JUST THE BEGINNING

Students have been known to say they want to go into human resource management because they want to "work with people." It is true that human resources managers work with people, but they are also deeply involved in planning, record keeping, and other administrative duties. To begin a career in human resource management, you need to develop a better reason than "I want to work with people."

This chapter will discuss various aspects of human resource management. **Human resource management (HRM)** is the process of determining human resources needs and then recruiting, selecting, developing, motivating, evaluating, compensating, and scheduling employees to achieve organizational goals. Janice Wismer, Global Vice-President of Human Resources for McCain Foods Limited, believes that human resources (HR) professionals can do a lot to develop people to fulfill roles that contribute to organizational success and individual happiness. According to Wismer, "The ripple effect on our society from the way we lead and govern organizations is remarkable. In the HR profession we are not only of service to an organization, but we are also of service to the very society of which we are all a part. I can't think of a profession where we can make more of a difference. Healthy organizations are like oxygen to a vibrant community and family unit—there is an inextricable link between what happens in organizations and the prosperity of a country."[1]

Figure 12.1 illustrates the activities associated with HRM. Let's explore the changing role of this very important function.

**human resource management (HRM)**
The process of determining human resource needs and then recruiting, selecting, developing, motivating, evaluating, compensating, and scheduling employees to achieve organizational goals.

**FIGURE** | **12.1**

**Human Resource Management**
As this figure shows, human resource management is more than hiring and firing personnel. All activities are designed to achieve organizational goals within the laws that affect human resource management. (Note that human resource management includes motivation, as discussed in Chapter 11, and employee–management relations, which will be discussed in Chapter 13.)

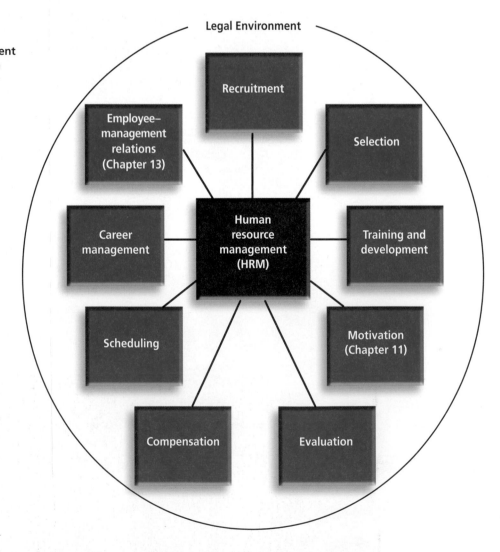

Legal Environment

Recruitment

Employee–management relations (Chapter 13)

Selection

Human resource management (HRM)

Career management

Training and development

Scheduling

Motivation (Chapter 11)

Compensation

Evaluation

## Developing the Ultimate Resource

One reason why human resource management is receiving increased attention is the major shift from traditional manufacturing industries to service and high-tech manufacturing industries that require highly technical job skills. This shift means that many workers must be retrained for new, more challenging jobs.

Some people have called employees the "ultimate resource," and when you think about it, nothing could be truer. People develop the ideas that eventually become the products that satisfy consumers' wants and needs. Take away their creative minds and large leading firms such as Research In Motion, Bombardier, Cirque du Soleil, and Celestica would be nothing. This would also be the case if you are a smaller business or an emerging growth company such as model-train manufacturer Rapido Trains or online auction management firm Auctionwire.[2] The problem is that in the past human resources were relatively plentiful, so there was little need to nurture and develop them. If you needed qualified people, you simply went out and hired them. If they didn't work out, you fired them and found others. But qualified employees are scarcer today, and that makes recruiting more difficult.

Historically, most firms assigned the job of recruiting, selecting, training, evaluating, compensating, motivating, and, yes, firing people to the various functional departments. For years, the personnel department was more or less responsible for clerical functions such as screening applications, keeping records, processing the payroll, and finding people when necessary.

Today the job of human resource management has taken on an entirely new role in the firm.[3] In a survey conducted by DBM, an HR consulting firm, Canadian human resources professionals expect that by 2013 at least 50 percent of their HR departments' roles will be involve providing strategic input and less time and energy will be spent on HR administration.[4] This survey reinforces what David Weiss, a partner of GSW consultants, communicated in his best selling book *Higher Performance HR: Leveraging Human Resources for Competitive Advantage*. He states that as companies are beginning to shed outdated processes and unprofitable lines of business, HR is in danger of extinction if it continues to rely solely on recruiting, employee relations, and compensation and training. In his book, Weiss examines how HR should instead streamline its core responsibilities and align its efforts with the company's vision and customer needs. This alignment will allow HR to take advantage of unique qualifications that will enable it to provide strategic value to the company and the company's customers.[5]

In the future HR may become *the* most critical function, in that it will be responsible for dealing with all aspects of a business's most critical resource—people. In fact, the human resources function has become so important that it is no longer the responsibility of just one department; it is a responsibility of all managers. Most human resources functions are shared between the professional human resources manager and the other managers. What are some of the challenges in the human resources area that managers face? We'll outline a few of those challenges next.

The Certified Human Resources Professional (CHRP) designation is a nationally recognized level of achievement within the field of HR. If you are considering such a career in HR, you may learn more about this designation at www.cchra.ca/Web/certification/content.aspx?f=29789.

## The Human Resources Challenge[6]

The changes in the business environment that have had the most dramatic impact on the workings of the free enterprise system are the changes in the labour force. The ability of businesses to compete in international markets depends on new products and services, and new levels of productivity. In other words, on people with good ideas.

The World Federation of Personnel Management Associations, the Boston Consulting Group, and the Canadian Council of Human Resources Associations partnered to conduct a world study. In preparation of the study, titled *Creating People Advantage: How to Address HR Challenges Worldwide Through 2015*, more than 4,700 executives worldwide were surveyed on seventeen topics in HRM. The survey found that managing talent was the number one human resources challenge worldwide and there were predictions

that it would remain at or near the top of executive agendas for the foreseeable future. In Canada, executives also identified other critical challenges: managing demographics (the Dealing with Change box discusses the implications of an aging workforce), improving leadership development, managing work-life balance, and transforming HR into a strategic partner. To create people advantage and overcome some of the human resource challenges identified, the report suggested five major steps to be taken by companies: (1) understand the external environment, (2) understand the internal environment, (3) select the most critical human resource topics and set priorities, (4) initiate projects with dedicated teams, and (5) secure support from top management.

Wismer believes that the three greatest opportunities facing HR professionals today are to be relentless in ensuring that every undertaking is well sponsored and has positive business impact, to be a catalyst for constructive change by building on the strengths of the organization, and to build integrated and aligned people systems that differentiate the organization in the marketplace and that can be self-managed. Given the issues mentioned, and others that are sure to develop, you can see why HRM has taken a more central position in management thinking than ever before. While the HR challenges are greater than ever before, so too are the opportunities for companies to excel through their HR strategies.

The Canadian Charter of Rights and Freedoms allows and encourages Canadians to maintain their mother tongue, traditions, and culture. However, some workers still experience harassment. What can an employer do to create a respectful environment?

# DETERMINING YOUR HUMAN RESOURCES NEEDS

All management, including human resource management, begins with planning. Five steps are involved in the human resources planning process:

**job analysis**
A study of what is done by employees who hold various job titles.

**job description**
A summary of the objectives of a job, the type of work to be done, the responsibilities and duties, the working conditions, and the relationship of the job to other functions.

**job specifications**
A written summary of the minimum qualifications required of workers to do a particular job.

1. *Preparing a human resources inventory of the organization's employees.* This inventory should include ages, names, education (e.g., languages spoken), capabilities, training, specialized skills, and other information pertinent to the specific organization. Such information reveals whether the labour force is technically up to date, thoroughly trained, and so forth.

2. *Preparing a job analysis.* A **job analysis** is a study of what is done by employees who hold various job titles. Such analyses are necessary to recruit and train employees with the necessary skills to do the job. The result is two written statements: job descriptions and job specifications. A **job description** specifies the objectives of the job, the type of work to be done, the responsibilities and duties, the working conditions, and the relationship of the job to other functions. **Job specifications** are a written summary of the minimum qualifications (e.g., education and skills) required of workers to do a particular job. In short, job descriptions are statements about the job, whereas job specifications are statements about the person who does the job. See Figure 12.2 for hypothetical examples of a job description and job specifications.

3. *Assessing future human resources demand.* Because technology changes rapidly, training programs must be started long before the need is apparent. Human resources managers who are proactive—that is, who anticipate the organization's requirements identified in the forecasting process—ensure that trained people are available when needed.

4. *Assessing future human resources supply.* The labour force is constantly shifting: getting older, becoming more technically oriented, attracting more women, and so forth. There are likely to be increased shortages of some workers in the future (e.g., computer and robotic repair workers) and an oversupply of others (e.g., assembly line workers).

## DEALING with CHANGE

### Replacing the Old Guard

Wine connoisseurs believe that most great wines get better with age. Unfortunately, the decision makers of most industrialized countries don't see it that way when evaluating people. It is anticipated that one in three Canadians will be 55 and over by 2021. By 2050, the average age of the world's population is expected to rise from 26 to 36. This aging of the population presents huge economic implications. Who will do the work in geriatric societies? Who will support the increasing number of pensioners? What will happen to economic growth with a declining labour force?

Eliminating age, gender, and cultural barriers could add 1.6 million Canadians to the workforce and increase personal incomes by $174 billion, according to a report from RBC Economics titled *The Diversity Advantage: A Case for Canada's 21st Century Economy*. The report's recommendations range from tax and policy reform, increased immigration levels, and ways in which the country should capitalize on cultural, gender, and age diversity. "With an aging population, fertility rates well below the 2.1 rate that is necessary to sustain population levels, and one in five manufacturers unable to find skilled labour, Canada needs to have an effective long-range economic strategy to ensure a successful twenty-first century economy and society," said Derek Holt, assistant chief economist at RBC. "Without a talented workforce, Canadian businesses will be unable to achieve corporate strategies for innovation and growth."

The report suggests that immigrants, women, and baby boomers approaching retirement will need to play more significant roles in the country's workforce, as Canada needs to capitalize on the broader economic benefits that a more diverse population has to offer. "To replace retiring baby boomers and maintain our current economic performance, Canada will need an additional 2.75 million workers over the next 20 years... If immigrants and women were employed at their level of education and skills training, and earning equal pay to men born in Canada, personal incomes in Canada would increase by 21 percent or $174 billion, and 1.6 million more working-age Canadians would be employed."

As critical as the impending labour shortage is, most companies seem more concerned about the brain drain caused by experienced, knowledgeable workers taking their irreplaceable knowledge with them as they retire. Mentoring is one way that companies are working to transfer knowledge. Other companies, such as Hewlett-Packard (HP), use online communities of different professional groups, such as sales and software engineering. "They're online knowledge repositories for people who do the same kind of work. They post how they do things, solutions, and experience," explains James R. Malanson, an HP human resources executive.

Many industries and businesses are trying to keep potential retirees for as long as possible by offering consultant positions, flexible work schedules, job sharing, and gradual retirement. The challenge is to keep mature workers on the job— at least until they've shared their knowledge with their younger colleagues.

Sources: Susannah Patton, "Beating the Boomer Brain Drain Blues," *CIO*, 15 January 2006; Derek Holt, "Capitalizing on Canada's Diversity Is Key to Nation's Future Prosperity," Canada NewsWire, 20 October 2005, http://global.factiva.com/ha/default.aspx; Kathryn Tyler, "Training Revs Up," *HRMagazine*, 1 April 2005; Statistics Canada, "The Canadian Labour Market at a Glance," 2005, http://www.statcan.ca/english/freepub/71-222-XIE/71-222-XIE2006001.pdf;. Anne Fisher, "How to Battle the Coming Brain Drain," *Fortune*, 21 March 2005; Marguerite Smith, "Aging Workers: Overlooked No More?" *Public Management*, 1 January 2005; and http://www.chrc-ccdp.ca/publications/diversity-en.asp.

5. *Establishing a strategic plan.* The plan must address recruitment, selection, training and development, evaluation, compensation, scheduling, and career management for the labour force. For this plan to have impact, the HR department must have upper management support for its acceptance and implementation. Because the previous four steps lead up to this one, this chapter will focus on these elements of the strategic human resources plan.

Some companies use advanced technology to perform this human resources planning process more efficiently. For example, IBM manages its global workforce by using software and a database that catalogues employee skills, experiences, schedules, and references. IBM uses the system to match employee skills with the jobs needed. For example, if a client in Nova Scotia has a month-long project that needs a consultant who can speak English and French, has an advanced degree in engineering, and has experience with Linux programming, the IBM system can search the database to find the best-suited consultant available and arrange for the employee to contact the client.[7]

FIGURE | 12.2

**Job Analysis**
A job analysis yields two important statements: job descriptions and job specifications. Here you have a job description and job specifications for a sales representative.

## Job Analysis

Observe current sales representatives doing the job.

Discuss job with sales managers.

Have current sales reps keep a diary of their activities.

| Job Description | Job Specifications |
|---|---|
| Primary objective is to sell company's products to stores in Territory Z. Duties include servicing accounts and maintaining positive relationships with clients. Responsibilities include:<br><br>• introducing the new products to store managers in the area<br>• helping the store managers estimate the volume to order<br>• negotiating prime shelf space<br>• explaining sales promotion activities to store managers<br>• stocking and maintaining shelves in stores that wish such service | Characteristics of the person qualifying for this job include:<br><br>• two years sales experience<br>• positive attitude<br>• well-groomed appearance<br>• good communication skills<br>• high-school diploma and two years of post-secondary credit |

**recruitment**
The set of activities used to obtain a sufficient number of the right people at the right time.

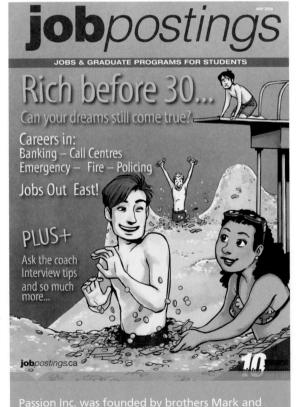

Passion Inc. was founded by brothers Mark and Nathan Laurie from their student residence with $500 in savings and the dream of graduating from Dalhousie University debt free. Today, one of the company's three divisions is jobpostings (jobpostings.ca), which helps students find jobs through print and online media. Have you seen this magazine on campus?

# RECRUITING EMPLOYEES FROM A DIVERSE POPULATION

**Recruitment** is the set of activities used to obtain a sufficient number of the right people at the right time. The end result is to have a pool of qualified applicants. One would think that with a continuous flow of new people into the workforce recruiting would be easy. On the contrary, recruiting has become very difficult, for several reasons:

• Some organizations have policies that demand promotions from within, operate under union contracts, or offer low wages, which makes recruiting and keeping employees difficult or subject to outside influence and restrictions.

• There are legal guidelines that surround hiring practices. The Canadian Human Rights Act requires that employers provide equal employment opportunities. For example, a human rights complaint could be made if an employer said that he would not hire a woman or a visible minority for a particular job, regardless of that person's competency. The Canadian Human Rights Act protects those that work for federally regulated organizations or service providers (e.g., chartered banks and airlines). The rest of employees are protected by provincial or territorial jurisdiction.

• The emphasis on corporate culture, teamwork, and participative management makes it important to hire people who not only are skilled but also fit in with the culture and leadership style of the organization.[8]

• Sometimes people with the necessary skills are not available; in this case, workers must be hired and then trained internally.[9]

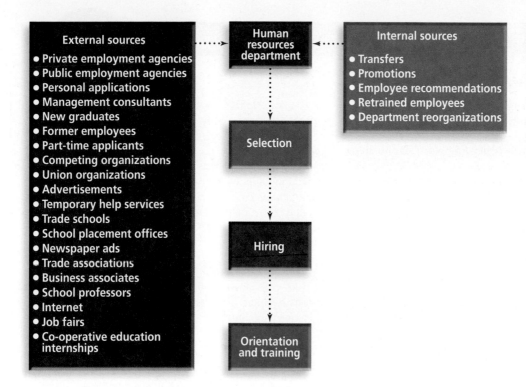

**External sources**
- Private employment agencies
- Public employment agencies
- Personal applications
- Management consultants
- New graduates
- Former employees
- Part-time applicants
- Competing organizations
- Union organizations
- Advertisements
- Temporary help services
- Trade schools
- School placement offices
- Newspaper ads
- Trade associations
- Business associates
- School professors
- Internet
- Job fairs
- Co-operative education internships

**Human resources department**

**Internal sources**
- Transfers
- Promotions
- Employee recommendations
- Retrained employees
- Department reorganizations

Selection

Hiring

Orientation and training

**FIGURE | 12.3**

**Employee Sources**
Internal sources are often given first consideration. So it's useful to get a recommendation from a current employee of the firm for which you want to work. School placement offices are also an important source. Be sure to learn about such facilities early so that you can plan an employment strategy throughout your academic career.

Because recruiting is a difficult chore that involves finding people who are an appropriate technical and social fit, human resources managers turn to many sources for assistance. Figure 12.3 highlights examples of sources used by organizations. These sources are classified as either internal or external. Internal sources include employees who are already within the firm (and may be transferred or promoted) and employees who can recommend others to hire. Using internal sources is less expensive than recruiting outside the company. The greatest advantage of hiring from within is that it helps maintain employee morale. It isn't always possible to find qualified workers within the company, however, so human resources managers must use external recruitment sources such as advertisements, public and private employment agencies, school placement offices, management consultants, professional organizations, referrals, and walk-in applications. While most external sources are straightforward, some may involve difficult decisions. The Making Ethical Decisions box presents questions about recruiting employees from competitors.

Recruiting qualified workers may be particularly difficult for small businesses that do not have enough staff members to serve as internal sources and may not be able to offer the sort of competitive compensation that attracts external sources. The Spotlight

## Making Ethical Decisions

### Recruiting Employees from Competitors

As the human resources director for Technocrat, Inc., it is your job to recruit the best employees. Your most recent human resource inventory indicated that Technocrat currently has an abundance of qualified designers and that several lower-level workers will soon be eligible for promotions to designer positions. Despite the surplus of qualified designers within the firm, you are considering

recruiting a designer who is now with a major competitor. Your thinking is that the new employee will be a source of information about the competition's new products. What are your ethical considerations in this case? Will you lure the employee away from the competition even though you have no need for a designer? What will be the consequences of your decision?

## SPOTLIGHT ON Small Business

### Attracting Qualified Employees

It is difficult for small-business owners to find qualified employees. Small businesses want top talent but often cannot afford corporate-level benefits or expensive recruiters to hunt down the best people. Despite the hurdles, small-business management consultants say that there are many ways to lure desirable workers:

- *Transform ads into promotional tools.* For example, Ecoprint, a small print shop, brags in its advertisements about the benefits of working for this collegial company.

- *Post job openings on the Internet.* Running a 30-day job posting on an online service such as Monster.ca costs $695. A job posting (where approximately 30 to 40 words would fit within a 3.5 inch by 2 inch box) in the national Careers section of *The Globe and Mail* newspaper for three days costs $3,056.13.

- *Let your staff help select hires.* The more staff people involved in the interview process, the better chance you have to find out who has the personality and skills to fit in.

- *Create a dynamic workplace to attract local, energetic applicants.* Sometimes word of mouth is the most effective recruiting tool.

- *Test-drive an employee.* Hiring temporary workers can allow you to test candidates for a few months before deciding whether to make an offer.

- *Hire your customer.* Loyal customers sometimes make the smartest employees.

- *Check community groups and local government agencies.* Don't forget to check out provincial- or territory-run employment agencies. Programs may turn up excellent candidates that you can train.

- *Lure candidates with a policy of promotions and raises.* Most employees want to know that they can move up in the company. Give employees an incentive for learning the business.

- *Outsource fringe benefit management to a professional employer organization (PEO).* PEOs may be able to offer lower insurance rates for benefit programs because of greater economies of scale. While this may not bring a small business's benefits program all the way up to the level of those offered by most large companies, it may help close the gap and therefore help attract qualified workers.

Sources: "Buy a Job Posting," 15 February 2009, http://hiring.monster.ca/recruitment/Job-Postings.aspx; *The Globe and Mail – Classifieds Department (1-866-999-9237),* 18 February 2009; Anne Field, "Hire Right," *Registered Rep,* 1 February 2006; Debra Morrill, "How to Tackle the Looming Labor Shortage," *Wisconsin State Journal,* 1 February 2006; J. Holly Dolloff, "Companies Compete For Shrinking Work Force Pool," *Nashville Business Journal,* 22 July 2005; and Heather Gooch, "Aspire to Hire: Little Things Go a Long Way in Attracting and Retaining Loyal Employees," *Pest Control,* 1 January 2005.

on Small Business box outlines some ways in which small businesses can address their recruiting needs. The first Taking It to the Net exercise near the end of this chapter lists some popular recruiting Internet services such as Workopolis.com and Monster.ca.

### Progress Assessment

- What is human resource management?
- What are the five steps in human resources planning?
- What factors make it difficult to recruit qualified employees?

## SELECTING EMPLOYEES WHO WILL BE PRODUCTIVE

**selection**
The process of gathering information and deciding who should be hired, under legal guidelines, for the best interests of the individual and the organization.

**Selection** is the process of gathering information and deciding who should be hired, under legal guidelines, for the best interests of the individual and the organization. Selecting and training employees have become extremely expensive processes in some firms. Think of what's involved: interview time, medical exams in some instances, training costs, unproductive time spent learning the job, moving expenses, and so on. Calculating the cost-per-hire can get extremely complicated and numbers vary, depending on the source. The latest Compensation Planning Outlook published by the Conference Board of Canada calculates the average cost-per-hire as follows: Executive—$43,000; Management/Professional—$17,000; Technical—$13,300; and Clerical/Support—$3,300.[10] Keep in mind that these are average numbers and that selection expenses can vary widely depending on the position and job expectations. What is clear is that the selection process is an important element of any human resource program. A typical selection process involves five steps:

1. *Obtaining complete application forms.* Once, this was a simple procedure with few complications. Today, however, legal guidelines limit the kinds of questions that may appear on an application form. Nonetheless, such forms help the employer discover the applicant's educational background, past work experience, career objectives, and other qualifications directly related to the requirements of the job. Canada's Wonderland receives over 18,000 applications for seasonal employment each year. With only 4,000 positions to fill, a stringent screening process has been developed to select and hire candidates. All applications are individually screened and only those qualified will be granted an opportunity to move on to the interview stage of the process. Candidates who submit an application online receive an automated email response that confirms that their application has been successfully transmitted.[11]

2. *Conducting initial and follow-up interviews.* A staff member from the human resources department often screens applicants in a first interview. If the interviewer considers the applicant a potential employee, the manager who will supervise the new employee interviews the applicant as well. It's important that managers prepare adequately for the interview to avoid selection decisions they may regret.[12] This includes asking all candidates the same questions so as to be able to fairly compare answers. Always keep in mind that certain questions, no matter how innocent the intention, could later be used as evidence if that applicant files discrimination charges.[13] For example, asking an applicant about his or her family background, children, and family planning are prohibited. In the past, an employer might have asked if the applicant had children to determine whether the applicant could work shift work or on weekends. Today, the applicant would be asked if working shift work or on weekends would be a problem (without asking about children), as this is a relevant job-related question.

Depending on the job, it is not uncommon to be involved in several interviews, one of which might include a panel interview. How would you prepare differently if this was the case?

3. *Giving employment tests.* Organizations use tests to measure basic competencies in specific job skills (e.g., word processing) and to help evaluate applicants' personalities and interests.[14] In using employment tests, it's important that they be directly related to the job. Many companies test potential employees in assessment centres, where applicants perform actual tasks of the real job. Such testing is likely to make the selection process more efficient and will generally satisfy legal requirements.

4. *Confirming background information.* Most organizations now confirm a candidate's work record, school record, credit history, and references more carefully than they have in the past.[15] It is simply too costly to hire, train, and motivate people only to lose them and have to start the process over. Background checks help an employer identify which candidates are most likely to succeed in a given position. Web sites such as QuickReferenceCheck and PeopleWise allow prospective employers to not only conduct speedy background checks of criminal records, driving records, and credit histories, but to also verify work experience and professional and educational credentials.

   Be aware that more hiring managers and recruiters are visiting social networking Web sites such as Facebook and MySpace to gather background information as a way to eliminate candidates.[16] A few examples of the types of things that might cause concern

QuickReferenceCheck.com was founded by Benjamin Slaney in Halifax after researching the idea for nearly a year. The company is known for its quick turnaround time with its reports (consider the company name), and a high level of customer service.

and raise questions for employers can include one's recreational activities (e.g., if one appears drunk or out of control or engaged in behaviour that may be considered offensive) as exhibited by photos on one's profile and friends' profiles; comments about employment situations (e.g., "I hate my boss?" or "I was late again for work today. I just can't get out of bed."); or religious, political, or sexual activities or views that vary significantly from the mainstream.[17] What do you think you can do to protect yourself from embarrassment or lost employment opportunities?

5. *Establishing trial (probationary) periods.* Often, an organization will hire an employee conditionally. This enables the person to prove his or her worth on the job. After a specified probationary period (perhaps three months or a year), the firm may either permanently hire or discharge that employee on the basis of evaluations from supervisors. Although such systems make it easier to fire inefficient or problem employees, they do not eliminate the high cost of turnover.[18]

The selection process is often long and difficult, but it is worth the effort to select new employees carefully because of the high costs of replacing workers. The process helps ensure that new employees meet the requirements in all relevant areas, including communication skills, education, technical skills, experience, personality, and health. Finally, where a company has a collective labour agreement (a union contract with its employees) the selection process must also follow the provisions of that agreement. This is discussed in more detail in the next chapter.

## Hiring Contingent Workers

**contingent workers**
Workers who do not have regular, full-time employment.

When more workers are needed in a company, human resources managers may want to consider finding creative staffing alternatives rather than simply hiring new full-time employees. A company with varying needs for employees—from hour to hour, day to day, week to week, and season to season—may find it cost-effective to hire contingent workers. **Contingent workers** are defined as workers who do not have regular, full-time employment. Such workers include part-time workers (according to Statistics Canada, this would be anyone who works less than 30 hours per week), temporary workers (workers paid by temporary employment agencies), seasonal workers, independent contractors, interns, and co-op students.

A varying need for employees is the most common reason for hiring contingent workers. Companies may also look to hire contingent workers when full-time employees are on some type of leave (such as maternity leave), when there is a peak demand for labour, or when quick service to customers is a priority. Companies in areas where qualified contingent workers are available, and in which the jobs require minimum training, are most likely to consider alternative staffing options.

Contingent workers receive few benefits; they are rarely offered health insurance, vacation time, or private pensions. They also tend to earn less than permanent workers do. The cachet of a job with the CBC (Canadian Broadcasting Corporation) is one of the reasons the Crown corporation is able to employ 30 percent of its workforce of 5,500 on contracts as freelancers, temporary workers, or casuals.[19] The voices you hear reporting from around the city and around the world often belong to stringers and freelancers hoping to make an impression and land a permanent position.[20] Some companies see using temporary workers as a way of weeding out poor workers and finding good hires. Because temporary workers are often told that they may, at some point, be hired as permanent workers, they are often more productive than those on the permanent payroll. "We're seeing ... temporary workers with the motivation to become full timers," said Joe Jotkowitz, senior consultant with Communication Development Associates, a human resources consulting firm. "They go out of their way because they're trying to impress."[21]

Many people find that temporary work offers them a lot more flexibility than permanent employment. For example, student Daniel Butrym found that the transition from student to temp worker was not difficult. Butrym says, "You come back in town. You don't have to interview. You don't have to waste a lot of time looking for a job. The first time you walk into the temporary staffing office, they meet you, sit you down and they find out your skills. Once you're in their computer, they have all your stats, they know what you can do and you're done. [Later] I can call from school, say 'I'm going to be home for spring break, I need some money.'" As soon as Butrym calls, he's put into the system for work assignments.

Butrym is not alone. Andy Williams of Randstad North America, the staffing services giant, welcomes students. "A lot of the students are computer-literate, and they are familiar with many of the popular software programs that the companies use. And, they are quick to get up to speed on [any] proprietary software an employer might use.... Every customer is different. Some assignments are for one day. Some assignments are for weeks or for the whole summer," Williams says.[22]

In an era of downsizing and rapid change, educated or highly skilled contingent workers have even found that temping can be more secure than full-time employment.

# TRAINING AND DEVELOPING EMPLOYEES FOR OPTIMUM PERFORMANCE

Because employees need to learn how to work with new equipment—such as word processors, computers, and robots—companies are finding that they must offer training programs that often are quite sophisticated. Employers find that spending money on training is usually money well spent. A quality training program could lead to higher retention rates, increased productivity, and greater job satisfaction among employees.[23] **Training and development** include all attempts to improve productivity by increasing an employee's ability to perform. Training focuses on short-term skills, whereas development focuses on long-term abilities. But both training and development programs include three steps: (1) assessing the needs of the organization and the skills of the employees to determine training needs; (2) designing training activities to meet the identified needs; and (3) evaluating the effectiveness of the training. Some common training and development activities are employee orientation, on-the-job training, apprentice programs, off-the-job training, online training, vestibule training, and job simulation. Management development will be discussed in a separate section.

**Employee orientation** is the activity that initiates new employees to the organization, to fellow employees, to their immediate supervisors, and to the policies, practices, values, and objectives of the firm. Orientation programs include everything from informal talks to formal activities that last a day or more. They may involve such activities as scheduled visits to various departments and required reading of handbooks.[24] For example, all new Canadian Tire Financial Services (CTFS) employees attend Canadian Tire University, Niagara campus. During their orientation employees learn about the company; they are introduced to the differences between the Canadian Tire Corporation divisions, and to what CTFS does. This includes CTFS's structure, vision, purpose, and team values.

**On-the-job training** is the most fundamental type of training. The employee being trained on the job immediately begins his or her tasks and learns by doing, or watches others for a while and then imitates them, right at the workplace. Salespeople, for example,

**training and development**
All attempts to improve productivity by increasing an employee's ability to perform. Training focuses on short-term skills, whereas development focuses on long-term abilities.

**employee orientation**
The activity that introduces new employees to the organization; to fellow employees; to their immediate supervisors; and to the policies, practices, values, and objectives of the firm.

**on-the-job training**
Training in which the employee immediately begins his or her tasks and learns by doing, or watches others for a while and then imitates them, all right at the workplace.

**apprentice programs**
Training programs involving a period during which a learner works alongside an experienced employee to master the skills and procedures of a craft.

**off-the-job training**
Training that occurs away from the workplace and consists of internal or external programs to develop any of a variety of skills or to foster personal development.

**online training**
Training programs in which employees "attend" classes via the Internet.

**vestibule training**
Training done in schools where employees are taught on equipment similar to that used on the job.

**job simulation**
The use of equipment that duplicates job conditions and tasks so that trainees can learn skills before attempting them on the job.

are often trained by watching experienced salespeople perform (often called *shadowing*). Naturally, this can be either quite effective or disastrous, depending on the skills and habits of the person being watched. On-the-job training is obviously the easiest kind of training to implement when the job is relatively simple (such as clerking in a store) or repetitive (such as collecting refuse, cleaning carpets, or mowing lawns). More demanding or intricate jobs require a more intense training effort. Intranets and other new forms of technology are leading to cost-effective on-the-job training programs available 24 hours a day, all year long. Computer systems can monitor workers' input and give them instructions if they become confused about what to do next. Such an intranet system helped Big Boy Restaurants realize training cost savings at an average of 2 to 4 percent per year.[25] The Web allows greater flexibility, but most companies believe its greatest advantage is the ability to make changes and updates in real time.[26]

**Apprentice programs** involve a period during which a learner works alongside an experienced employee to master the skills and procedures of a craft. Some apprenticeship programs also involve classroom training. Many skilled crafts, such as bricklaying and plumbing, require a new worker to serve as an apprentice for several years. Trade unions often require new workers to serve apprenticeships to ensure excellence among their members as well as to limit entry to the union. Workers who successfully complete an apprenticeship earn the classification of *journeyman*. In the future, there are likely to be more but shorter apprenticeship programs to prepare people for skilled jobs in changing industries. For example, auto repair will require more intense training as new automobile models include advanced computers and other electronic devices.[27]

**Off-the-job training** occurs away from the workplace and consists of internal or external programs to develop any of a variety of skills or to foster personal development. Training is becoming more sophisticated as jobs become more sophisticated. Furthermore, training is expanding to include education (e.g., an MBA) and personal development. Subjects may include time management, stress management, health and wellness, physical education, nutrition, and even art and languages.

**Online training** offers an example of how technology is improving the efficiency of many off-the-job training programs. In such training, employees "attend" classes via the Internet. These can be courses that have been created in-house or *distance learning* courses (because the students are separated by distance from the instructor or content source) that are offered by colleges and universities. Online training gives employers the ability to provide consistent content that is tailored to specific employee training needs, at convenient times, to a large number of employees.

Some employers are also creating online bulletin boards, email discussion lists, blogs, or other intranet forums for employees to share best practices and ask for help.[28] At 1-800-GOT-JUNK?, there is an active discussion bulletin board where the company hosts the site and monitors the forum, but the discussions are between franchise owners.[29]

**Vestibule training** (near-the-job training) is done in classrooms where employees are taught on equipment similar to that used on the job. Such classrooms enable employees to learn proper methods and safety procedures before assuming a specific job assignment in an organization. Computer and robotics training is often completed in a vestibule classroom.

**Job simulation** is the use of equipment that duplicates job conditions and tasks so that trainees can learn skills before attempting them on the job. Job simulation differs from vestibule training in that the simulation attempts to duplicate the exact combination of conditions that occur on the job. Such training simulations are used because the potential cost of real-world mistakes is huge. This is the kind of training given to astronauts, airline pilots, operators, ship captains, and others who must learn difficult procedures off the job.

Training and development can include a combination of activities such as off-the-job training and online training.

# Management Development

Managers need special training. To be good communicators, they especially need to learn listening skills and empathy. They also need time management, planning, and human relations skills.

**Management development**, then, is the process of training and educating employees to become good managers and then monitoring the progress of their managerial skills over time. Management development programs have sprung up everywhere, especially at colleges, universities, and private management development firms. Managers participate in role-playing exercises, solve various management cases, view films, and attend lectures.

**management development**
The process of training and educating employees to become good managers and then monitoring the progress of their managerial skills over time.

Management development is increasingly being used as a tool to accomplish business objectives. Most management training programs also include several of the following:

- *On-the-job coaching.* A senior manager will assist a lower-level manager by teaching him or her needed skills and generally providing direction, advice, and helpful feedback.
- *Understudy positions.* Job titles such as undersecretary and assistant are part of a relatively successful way of developing managers. Selected employees work as assistants to higher-level managers and participate in planning and other managerial functions until they are ready to assume such positions themselves.
- *Job rotation.* So that they can learn about different functions of the organization, managers are often given assignments in a variety of departments. Through job rotation, top managers gain the broad picture of the organization necessary to their success.
- *Off-the-job courses and training.* Managers periodically go to schools or seminars for a week or more to hone their technical and human relations skills. You may recall the example of Hamburger University (McDonald's) in Chapter 6 where managers and potential franchise owners attend courses to develop their skills.

Management development can include on-the-job and off-the-job training. The activities will vary depending on the person being developed and the purpose of the program.

On a final note, both training and development budgets and initiatives need to be reviewed regularly to ensure that maximum impact is being achieved and that organizations of all sizes are getting the best return on their investments. Jerry Gratton, director of learning and development for 1-800-GOT-JUNK?, used to spend several weeks a year on the road bringing training to franchise employees, sometimes visiting eight cities in two weeks. He has replaced that travel-heavy schedule with frequent telephone-based training. For less money, he now reaches more employees and has wider impact throughout North America and Australia.[30] When the economy takes a downturn, training budgets often get slashed, which is why in-house initiatives (e.g., online training) are used more heavily to fill in the gaps and generate greater impact.[31]

# Empowering Workers

Historically, many managers gave explicit instructions to workers, telling them what to do to meet the goals and objectives of the organization. The term for such an approach is *directing*. In traditional organizations, directing involves giving assignments, explaining routines, clarifying policies, and providing feedback on performance. Many organizations still follow this model, especially in firms such as fast-food restaurants and small retail establishments where the employees don't have the skills and experience needed to work on their own, at least at first.

Progressive managers, such as those in many high-tech firms and Internet companies, are less likely than traditional managers to give specific instructions to employees.

Rather, they're more likely to empower employees to make decisions on their own. Empowerment means giving employees the *authority* (the right to make a decision without consulting the manager) and *responsibility* (the requirement to accept the consequences of one's actions) to respond quickly to customer requests. Managers are often reluctant to give up the power they have to make such decisions; thus, empowerment is often resisted. In those firms that are able to implement the concept, the manager's role is becoming less that of a boss and director and more that of a coach, assistant, counsellor, or team member.

**Enabling** is the term used to describe giving workers the education and tools they need to make decisions. Clearly, enabling is the key to the success of empowerment. Without the right education, training, coaching, and tools, workers cannot assume the responsibilities and decision-making roles that make empowerment work. At WestJet, employees are encouraged through regular training sessions to resolve issues with WestJet customers. "From handing out flight credits to sending out for hamburgers to feed stranded passengers, they take care of things up front," says Don Bell, co-founder. "That kind of commitment comes from hiring the right people, aligning their interests to the company, and hooking the success of the business to their pocketbooks."[32]

**enabling**
Giving workers the education and tools they need to make decisions.

# Networking

**Networking** is the process of establishing and maintaining contacts with key managers in one's own organization and in other organizations and using those contacts to weave strong relationships that serve as informal development systems. Of equal or greater importance to potential managers is a **mentor**, a corporate manager who supervises, coaches, and guides selected lower-level employees by introducing them to the right people and generally being their organizational sponsor. In reality, an informal type of mentoring goes on in most organizations on a regular basis as older employees assist younger workers. However, many organizations use a formal system of assigning mentors to employees considered to have strong potential.[33]

**networking**
The process of establishing and maintaining contacts with key managers in one's own organization and other organizations and using those contacts to weave strong relationships that serve as informal development systems.

Networking is important at all levels of an organization and also through professional associations and organizations. Vancouver-based Absolute Software Corporation is a small company that used its senior executives to talk to top executives at Apple Computer by attending the National Education Conference in Philadelphia. John Livingston, CEO of Absolute Software, sees great value in networking: "Industry functions provide an opportunity to make contacts, but ... networking works only when you have something to say that's of interest."[34]

**mentor**
An experienced employee who supervises, coaches, and guides lower-level employees by introducing them to the right people and generally being their organizational sponsor.

When considering your career, Janice Wismer of McCain Foods suggests that you talk to people who are doing what you would like to do. Seek them out, learn from them, and thereby make choices that line up with your energy. Engage them to help you refine your vision. These connections will help you to succeed.[35]

Networking and mentoring can go beyond the business environment. For example, school is a perfect place to begin networking. Associations you nurture with instructors, with business people through internships, and especially with your classmates might provide you with a valuable network you can turn to for the rest of your career.

# Diversity in Management Development

As women moved into management, they also learned the importance of networking and of having mentors. But since many older managers are male, women often have more difficulty than men do in finding mentors and entering the network. More and more, women are now entering established networking systems or, in some instances, creating their own.[36] As mentioned in Chapter 7, some examples of organizations include Canadian Women's Business Network (www.cdnbizwomen.com), Women Entrepreneurs of Canada (www.wec.ca), and Canadian Association of Women Executives & Entrepreneurs (www.cawee.net).

Other ethnic groups are networking as well. For example, Mark Shir, a financial and computer specialist from Taiwan, felt that he would never get ahead in the companies he had worked in for ten years. When he joined Monte Jade, an association that helps Taiwanese and Chinese assimilate in American business, he met people who helped him start his own successful hardware-packaging company.[37]

Companies that take the initiative to develop female and minority managers understand three crucial principles: (1) grooming women and minorities for management positions isn't about legality or morality; it is about bringing more talent in the door—the key to long-term profitability; (2) the best women and minorities will become harder to attract and retain, so the companies that start now will have an edge later; and (3) having more women and minorities at all levels means that businesses can serve their female and minority customers better. If you do not have a diverse workforce, how are you going to satisfy your diverse customers?

## Progress Assessment

- What are the five steps in the selection process?
- What are contingent workers? Why do companies hire such workers?
- Can you name and describe four training and development techniques?

# EVALUATING EMPLOYEE PERFORMANCE TO GET OPTIMUM RESULTS

Managers must be able to determine whether their workers are doing an effective and efficient job. This is critical if an organization is to achieve its goals. Managers determine this by using performance appraisals. A **performance appraisal** is an evaluation in which the performance level of employees is measured against established standards to make decisions about promotions, compensation, additional training, or firing. One way to look at the performance appraisal process is to consider these six steps:

1. *Establishing Performance Standards.* This is a crucial step. Standards must be understandable, subject to measurement, and reasonable. They must be accepted by both the manager and subordinate.

2. *Communicating Standards.* Often managers assume that employees know what is expected of them, but such assumptions are dangerous at best. Employees must be told clearly and precisely what the standards and expectations are and how they are to be met.

3. *Evaluating Performance.* If the first two steps are done correctly, performance evaluation is relatively easy. It is a matter of evaluating the employee's behaviour to see if it matches standards.

4. *Discussing Results.* Most people will make mistakes and fail to meet expectations at first. It takes time to learn a new job and do it well. Discussing an employee's successes and areas that need improvement can provide managers with an opportunity to be understanding and helpful and to guide the employee to better performance. Additionally, the performance appraisal can be a good source of employee suggestions on how a particular task could be better performed.

5. *Taking Corrective Action.* As an appropriate part of the performance appraisal, a manager can take corrective action or provide corrective feedback to help the employee perform his or her job better. Remember, the key word is performance. The primary purpose of conducting this type of appraisal is to improve employee performance if possible.

**performance appraisal**
An evaluation in which the performance level of employees is measured against established standards to make decisions about promotions, compensation, additional training, or firing.

**FIGURE** | **12.4**

**Conducting Effective
Appraisals and Reviews**

1. **DON'T** attack the employee personally. Critically evaluate his or her work.

2. **DO** allow sufficient time, without distractions, for appraisal. (Take the phone off the hook or close the office door.)

3. **DON'T** make the employee feel uncomfortable or uneasy. Never conduct an appraisal where other employees are present (such as on the shop floor).

4. **DO** include the employee in the process as much as possible. (Let the employee prepare a self-improvement program.)

5. **DON'T** wait until the appraisal to address problems with the employee's work that have been developing for some time.

6. **DO** end the appraisal with positive suggestions for employee improvement.

6. *Using the Results to Make Decisions.* Decisions about promotions, compensation, additional training, or firing are most often based on performance evaluations. (Be aware that sometimes new hires and promotions are also influenced by other factors such as a family connection or whether the employee is particularly liked by his or her supervisor. You may have heard the phrase that "it is who you know.") Keep in mind that an effective performance appraisal system is a way of satisfying certain legal conditions concerning such decisions.

Effective management means getting results through top performance by employees. That is what performance appraisals are for—at all levels of the organization. Even top-level managers benefit from performance reviews made by their subordinates. One of the latest forms of performance appraisal is called the 360-degree review because it calls for feedback from all directions in the organization. Instead of an appraisal based solely on the employee's and the supervisor's perceptions, opinions are gathered from those under, above, and on the same level as the worker. The goal is to get an accurate, comprehensive idea of the worker's abilities. Figure 12.4 illustrates how managers can make performance appraisals more meaningful.

## Progress Assessment

- What is the primary purpose of a performance appraisal?
- What are the six steps in a performance appraisal?
- Why do employers and employees find the appraisal process so difficult?

# COMPENSATING EMPLOYEES: ATTRACTING AND KEEPING THE BEST

Companies don't just compete for customers; they also compete for employees. Compensation is one of the main marketing tools that companies use to attract (and retain) qualified employees, and it is one of the largest operating costs for many organizations. The long-term success of a firm—perhaps even its survival—may depend on how well it can control employee costs and optimize employee efficiency. For example, service organizations such as hospitals, airlines, and banks have recently struggled with managing high employee costs. This is not unusual since these firms are considered labour intensive; that is, their primary cost of operations is the cost of labour. Manufacturing firms in the auto, airline, and steel industries have asked employees to take reductions in wages to make the firms more competitive (as was seen, for example, during the restructuring of Air Canada). Many employees have agreed, even union employees who have traditionally resisted such cuts. They know that not to do so is to risk going out of business and losing their jobs forever. In other words, the competitive environment is such that compensation and benefit packages are being given special attention. In fact, some experts believe that determining how best to pay people has replaced downsizing as today's greatest human resources challenge.

A carefully managed compensation and benefits program can accomplish several objectives:

- Attracting the kinds of people needed by the organization, and in sufficient numbers.

- Providing employees with the incentive to work efficiently and productively.

- Keeping valued employees from leaving and going to competitors, or starting competing firms.

- Maintaining a competitive position in the marketplace by paying competitively and by keeping costs low through high productivity from a satisfied workforce.

- Providing employees with some sense of financial security through insurance and retirement benefits.

## Pay Equity[38]

**Pay equity** refers to equal pay for work of equal value. It compares the value of male and female jobs by objectively evaluating the jobs in terms of four neutral factors: skill, effort, responsibility, and working conditions. If a female job is approximately equal in value to a higher-paying job done mainly by men, the female job gets the same wages as the male job.

**pay equity**
Equal pay for work of equal value.

You may be asking, so what is the problem? According to Statistics Canada, almost 63 percent of all working-age women now participate in the labour force. What you may not know is that, on average, Canadian women earn less than men. Despite the increased focus on this form of discrimination, women working full-time still earn 70.5 percent of men's salaries regardless of age, occupation, or education. For women of colour, Aboriginal women, and women with a disability, the wage gap is even greater.

There are many historical reasons for this large wage gap. Men and women tended to work in different jobs, and the traditional women's jobs—teachers, nurses, and secretaries—have tended to pay poorly. But there has also been evidence of outright salary discrimination in other types of jobs. Today, women are more educated, they are working in greater numbers and for longer hours, they are having fewer children, and they are taking less time away from work. Despite these changes, women's hourly wages continue to fall below men's wages at all levels of education. Generally speaking, the wage gap between men and women has been narrowing as education level rises. Figure 12.5 considers the wage gap in different occupations.

**FIGURE | 12.5**

**Average Hourly Wages, by Occupation and Sex, 2007**

Source: "The Canadian Labour Market at a Glance," Statistics Canada – CANSIM table 282-0070, 25 November 2008, http://www.statcan.gc.ca/pub/71-222-x/2008001/sectionj/j-hourly-horaire-eng.htm.

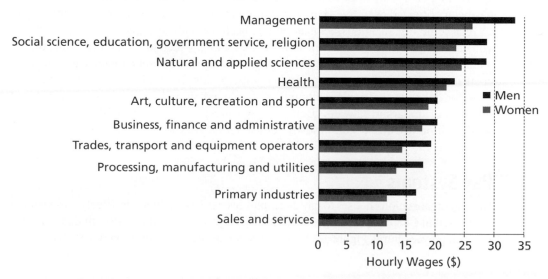

When evaluating pay equity, studies have shown that women's jobs with the same value as men's work are underpaid. To get the conversation started, the Canadian Labour Congress has produced this pay equity sales coupon. How receptive do you think an employer would be to this topic if presented with this coupon?

Canada has a variety of pay equity laws and policies, depending on where one works. If one works in a federally-regulated industry (e.g., banking, telecommunications, transportation, or the federal government), one is covered by federal labour and human rights laws. Only Ontario and Quebec have proactive pay equity laws that cover both the public and private sectors. Other provinces enacted pay equity legislation that covered only the public sector. Still other jurisdictions, including the territories, have provisions in their human rights laws that depend on an individual filing an official complaint against her employer. In response to pressure from women's groups and trade unions (to be discussed in Chapter 13), the federal government set up a Task Force to review how pay equity could be more effectively implemented. Extensive consultations took place across the country with stakeholders that included employees, employers, trade unions, researchers, and pay equity experts. The Task Force reviewed the current pay equity framework and made recommendations in 2004 to improve the system. Despite widespread support for the implementation of the recommendations, the federal government has been criticized even five years later for taking no action to implement them.

For some organizations, legislation has been difficult to implement. First, how do you define equal (or comparable) value? For example, which job has more value, that of a nurse or that of a trash collector? As well, officials cite budget cutbacks and the huge costs of making up for past inequitable compensation to female employees as the reasons for delaying the implementation of this legislation. After 14 years in court and millions of dollars in lawyers, Bell Canada Enterprises agreed in 2006 to pay up to $100 million to almost 5,000 mostly female employees who worked for the company during the 1990s. As you can see, this is not an issue that can easily be resolved.

## Pay Systems

How an organization chooses to pay its employees can have a dramatic effect on motivation (discussed in Chapter 11) and productivity. Managers want to find a system that compensates employees fairly. Figure 12.6 outlines some of the most common pay systems.

**FIGURE** | **12.6**

**Pay Systems**

Some of the different pay systems are as follows:

- **Salary:** Fixed compensation computed on weekly, bi-weekly, or monthly pay periods (e.g., $1,500 per month or $400 per week). Salaried employees do not receive additional pay for any extra hours worked.

- **Hourly Wage or Daywork:** Wage based on number of hours or days worked, used for most blue-collar and clerical workers. Often employees must punch a time clock when they arrive at work and when they leave. Hourly wages vary greatly. This does not include benefits such as retirement systems, which may add 30 percent or more to the total package.

- **Piecework System:** Wage based on the number of items produced rather than by the hour or day. This type of system creates powerful incentives to work efficiently and productively.

- **Commission Plans:** Pay based on some percentage of sales. Often used to compensate salespeople, commission plans resemble piecework systems.

- **Bonus Plans:** Extra pay for accomplishing or surpassing certain objectives. There are two types of bonuses: monetary and cashless. Money is always a welcome bonus. Cashless rewards include written thank-you notes, appreciation notes sent to the employee's family, movie tickets, flowers, time off, gift certificates, shopping sprees, and other types of recognition.

- **Profit-Sharing Plans:** Annual bonuses paid to employees based on the company's profits. The amount paid to each employee is based on a predetermined percentage. Profit-sharing is one of the most common forms of performance-based pay.

- **Gain-Sharing Plans:** Annual bonuses paid to employees based on achieving specific goals such as quality measures, customer satisfaction measures, and production targets.

- **Cost-of-Living Allowances (COLAs):** Annual increases in wages based on increases in the Consumer Price Index. This is usually found in union contracts.

- **Stock Options:** Right to purchase stock in the company at a specific price over a specific period of time. Often this gives employees the right to buy stock cheaply despite huge increases in the price of the stock. For example, if over the course of his employment a worker received options to buy 10,000 shares of the company stock at $10 each and the price of the stock eventually grows to $100, he can use those options to buy the 10,000 shares (now worth $1 million) for $100,000.

Many companies still use the pay system devised by Edward Hay for General Foods. Known as the Hay system, this compensation plan is based on job tiers, each of which has a strict pay range. In some firms, you're guaranteed a raise after 13 weeks if you're still working for the company. Conflict can arise when an employee who is performing well earns less than an employee who is not performing well simply because the latter has worked for the company longer.

John Whitney, author of *The Trust Factor*, believes that companies should begin with some base pay and give all employees the same percentage merit raise. Doing so, he says, sends out the message that everyone in the company is important. Fairness remains the issue. What do you think is the fairest pay system?

According to Hewitt Associates, a global human resources services firm, most organizations are using variable pay plans (performance-related award programs that must be re-earned each year) as a way to attract and retain rather than simply reward their employees. A majority of companies (90 percent) have at least one type of broad-based variable pay plan. Among the various types of awards, signing bonuses are the most commonly offered by employers (65 percent), followed by business incentives (63 percent), special recognition awards (56 percent), individual performance awards (41 percent), and retention bonuses (39 percent).[39] In an economic downturn, as was the case in the late 2000s, changes to base salary spending, variable pay spending, or both, were planned by at least 42 percent of companies surveyed.[40]

## Compensating Teams

Thus far we've talked about compensating individuals. What about teams? Since you want your teams to be more than simply a group of individuals, would you compensate them as you would individuals? If you can't answer that question immediately, you are not alone. While most managers believe in using teams, fewer are sure about how to pay them. This suggests that team-based pay programs are not as effective or as fully developed as managers would hope. Measuring and rewarding individual performance on teams while at the same time rewarding team performance can be tricky. Nonetheless, it can be done. Football players are rewarded as a team when they go to the playoffs and to the Super Bowl, but they are paid individually as well. Companies are now experimenting with and developing similar incentive systems.

Jay Schuster, co-author of an ongoing study of team pay, found that when pay is based strictly on individual performance, it erodes team cohesiveness and makes it less likely that the team will meet its goals as a collaborative effort. Schuster recommends basing pay on team performance. Skill-based pay and profit-sharing are the two most common compensation methods for teams.

*Skill-based pay* (also known as "pay for knowledge") is related to the growth of both the individual and the team. Base pay is raised when team members learn and apply new skills. For example, Eastman Chemical Company rewards its teams for proficiency in technical, social, and business knowledge skills. A cross-functional compensation policy team defines the skills. There are drawbacks of the skill-based pay system: the system is complex, training costs can be high, and it is difficult to correlate skill acquisition and bottom-line gains.

In most gain-sharing systems, bonuses are based on improvements over a previous performance baseline. For example, Behlen Manufacturing, a diversified maker of agricultural and industrial products, calculates its bonuses by dividing quality pounds of product by worker hours. Quality means no defects; any defects are subtracted from the total. Workers can receive a monthly gain-sharing bonus of up to $1 an hour when their teams meet productivity goals.

It is important to reward individual team players also. Outstanding team players—those who go beyond what is required and make an outstanding individual contribution to the firm—should be separately recognized for their additional contribution.[41] Recognition can include cashless as well as cash rewards. A good way to avoid alienating recipients who feel that team participation is uneven is to let the team decide which members get what type of individual award. After all, if you really support the team process, you need to give teams the freedom to reward themselves.

## Fringe Benefits

**fringe benefits**

Benefits such as sick-leave pay, vacation pay, pension plans, and health plans that represent additional compensation to employees beyond base wages.

**Fringe benefits** are benefits that provide additional compensation to employees. They may be divided into three categories. One group derives from federal or provincial legislation (which varies somewhat from province to province) and requires compulsory deductions from employees' pay cheques, employer contributions, or both. These include the Canada/Quebec Pension Plan, employment insurance, and income tax. You have probably seen some of these deductions on your pay stub. The second group consists of legally required benefits, including vacation pay, holiday pay, time and a half or double time for overtime, and unpaid maternity leave with job protection. The third category includes all other benefits and stems from voluntary employer programs or from employer–union contracts. Some are paid by the employer alone and others are jointly paid by the employer and employee. Among the most common are bonuses, company pension plans, group insurance, sick leave, termination pay, and paid rest periods.

Fringe benefits in recent years grew faster than wages. In fact, employee benefits can't really be considered "fringe" anymore. The list of benefits is long and has become quite significant. Fringe benefits can include everything from paid vacations to health care programs, pension plans, recreation facilities, company cars, country club memberships, discounted massages, special home-mortgage rates, paid and unpaid sabbaticals, day care services, and executive dining rooms.[42] Employees want packages to include dental care, mental health care, elder care, legal counselling, eye care, and short workweeks. It is important to note that some firms offer very little in the way of benefits, especially small firms. According to Statistics Canada, health-related benefits (e.g., medical and dental plans, and life or disability insurance) remain the most common form of non-wage benefit (40.6 percent had access to at least one). The rate of access to non-wage benefits was higher among workers who were unionized (88.5 percent versus 68.6 percent for the non-unionized) or employed full time (78.9 percent versus 47.4 percent for part time).[43] Research reveals that in Canada benefits seldom rank among the top five factors in an employee's decision of whether or not to stay with an organization, with the exception of employees with disabilities, and that if benefits do not meet employees' needs, or they don't understand what the program consists of or how it works, benefit plans can *prevent* employee engagement.[44]

Benefits plans have become a bigger expense in the last decade, with costs increasing two to three times faster than the rate of inflation. According to KPMG and the Conference Board of Canada, group health benefits costs (which are just one component of the overall benefits package) were an estimated 7.3 percent of payroll in 2006. Health care costs—particularly drug and dental care costs—are expected to continue to rise. Our population is aging, and as employees age, they spend more on health care. The government, which already spends a large percentage of its revenue on health care, will likely continue to shift costs to private plans by limiting and eliminating health services. Practitioners are increasingly recommending more expensive procedures, and patients are also asking for and receiving them.[45] Such outlays are a major and growing cost of doing business, and if this trend continues, total benefits and services could amount to over one-half of most firms' payroll costs in the near future.[46] As a result, employers are trying to control costs in various ways and are making cuts where possible: "Traditionally, you had post-retirement benefits, but employers are trying to get out of these. Telecommunications giant Bell Canada, for example, announced that it would be phasing out all post-retirement benefits by 2012 for retirees over the age of 55 and it would eliminate all post-retirement benefits for those retiring post-2017."[47]

Understanding that it takes many attractions to retain the best employees, companies offer so-called soft benefits. *Soft benefits* help workers maintain the balance between work and family life that is as important to hardworking employees as the nature of the job itself. These perks include things such as onsite haircuts and shoe repair, concierge services, and free breakfasts.[48] Freeing employees from spending time on errands and chores gives them more time for family—and work.

*Canada's Top 100 Employers* list shares some examples of soft benefits: Toyota Motor Manufacturing Canada Inc. received special praise for its physical amenities such as an onsite fitness facility, lounge and rest areas, and an exceptional benefits plan; Bayer CropScience Inc. got top marks for training and an exceptional performance management program with rewards for outstanding employees; Ernst & Young LLP is one of the top ten family-friendly employers, with an exceptional maternity leave and parental leave program and flexible work hours; and Co-operators General Insurance Co. was exceptional in health and family benefits, employee communications, and community involvement, which included each employee getting money to donate to a charity of his or her own choice.[49] As you can see, there are a variety of employee benefits that companies can consider.

Published annually, *Canada's Top 100 Employers* (www.canadastop100.com), highlights employers that lead their industries in providing the best benefits and working conditions. You can also read about Canada's top employers for young people (http://www.canadastop100.com/young_people/). Would you consider this resource when looking for a job?

## GreenBOX

### Canada's Most Earth-Friendly Employers, 2008

Officially launched in 2007, the Canada's Most Earth-Friendly Employers competition is organized by the editors of *Canada's Top 100 Employers*. This designation recognizes the employers that lead the country in creating a culture of environmental awareness in their organizations. These employers have developed exceptional earth-friendly initiatives and are attracting people to their organizations because of their environmental leadership. Some of the 2008 winners are briefly highlighted below:

- **Golder Associates Ltd. (Burnaby, British Columbia):** For excellence in training employees for its environmental consulting engineering practice. The firm sets aside one percent of its net revenues for a fund that employees can use to pay for courses and degree programs at outside educational institutions.

- **New Flyer Industries Canada ULC (Winnipeg, Manitoba):** For supporting skilled trades workers by providing full salary to machinist, tool-and-die, and millwright apprentices while they train to work on some of North America's most environmentally-friendly mass transit bus designs.

- **EPCOR Utilities Inc. (Edmonton, Alberta):** For providing excellent career opportunities to people who are interested in working on environmentally-responsible energy projects, such as the company's new methane and wind-power generation facilities.

- **Toyota Motor Manufacturing Canada Inc. (Cambridge, Ontario):** For exceptional leadership in the automotive industry by working with employees to create an automotive assembly operation that sends absolutely no waste to landfills and offers greatly reduced chemical emissions.

"These employers are setting the standard for integrating environmental values into their organizational cultures," said Richard Yerema, Managing Editor of the *Canada's Top 100 Employers* project. "Employees increasingly look at how their employers address the issue of environmental stewardship—and these organizations are attracting people who identify with these values."

Sources: "Canada's Most Earth-Friendly Employers," Mediacorp Canada Inc., 2009, http://www.canadastop100.com/environmental/; and "Environmental Values at Work: Canada's Most Earth-Friendly Employers (2008)," CNW Group, 22 April 2008, http://www.newswire.ca/en/releases/archive/April2008/22/c8160.html.

One factor driving better employment practices is a population that's getting older. Michael Fitzgibbon, a partner at Borden Ladner Gervais specializing in employment law, says that some of the best employers are adopting new programs in response to Canada's dramatically changing demographics. In less than a decade, as boomers age, the workforce will be dominated by people between the ages of 45 and 64. "Older people have to be part of the business plan," he says. "The best employers are taking proactive steps now to deal with the demographic shift." Among practices designed for workers approaching retirement are compressed workdays and part-time jobs.[50]

The environmental movement is also having an effect on employee benefits. The Green Box shares some examples of Canada's most earth-friendly employers. This competition is organized by the editors of *Canada's Top 100 Employers*.

**cafeteria-style benefits (flexible benefits plan)**
Benefit plans that allow employees to choose which benefits they want up to a certain dollar amount.

To counter these growing demands, **cafeteria-style benefits** plans (also known as **flexible benefits plans**), in which employees can choose the benefits they want up to a certain dollar amount, continue to grow in popularity. About 33 percent of employers now offer some sort of flexibility within benefits.[51] Choice is the key to these flexible plans. At one time, most employees' needs were similar. Today, employees are more varied and more demanding. Some employees may need childcare benefits, whereas others may need relatively large pension benefits. Rather than giving all employees identical benefits, managers can equitably and cost-effectively meet employees' individual needs by allowing employees some choice.[52] After an internal survey showed dissatisfaction with its benefits plan, Wardrop Engineering Inc., a mid-sized, Winnipeg-based firm, dumped it—and created a whole new package. "The old package was a standard one, average for our industry," says James Popel, Wardrop's vice-president of human resources. The new one allows

## Reaching Beyond Our Borders

### Working Worldwide

Human resources people who manage a global workforce begin by understanding the customs, laws, and local business needs of every country in which the organization operates.

Varying cultural and legal standards can affect a variety of human resources functions:

- *Compensation.* Salaries must be converted to and from foreign currencies. Often employees with international assignments receive special allowances for relocation, children's education, housing, travel, or other business-related expenses.

- *Health and Pension Standards.* Human resources managers must consider the different social contexts for benefits in other countries. For example, in the Netherlands, the government provides retirement income and health care.

- *Paid Time Off.* Cultural differences can be quite apparent when it comes to paid time off. Employees in other countries enjoy more vacation time than those in Canada. For example, four weeks of paid vacation is the standard of many European employers. But other countries do not have the short-term and long-term absence policies we have in Canada. They do not have sick leave, personal leave, or family and medical leave. Global companies need a standard definition of what time off is.

- *Taxation.* Different countries have varying taxation rules, and the payroll department is an important player in managing immigration information.

- *Communication.* When employees leave to work in another country, they often feel a disconnection from their home country. Wise companies use their intranet and the Internet to help these faraway employees keep in direct contact.

Human resources policies will be influenced more and more by conditions and practices in other countries and cultures. Human resources managers will need to move away from the assumed dominance and/or superiority of domestic business practices and sensitize themselves and their organizations to the cultural and business practices of other nations.

Sources: "Proposed Hong Kong Law Gives Business Shudders," *Agence France Presse English*, 19 January 2006; Anthony Kshanika, "Managing Globally: Managing a Diverse, Global Environment Is Critical Today—How You Do It Depends on Where You Are," *HR Magazine*, 1 August 2005; and "How To Prepare Your Expatriate Employees for Cross-Cultural Work Environments," *Managing and Training Development*, 1 February 2005.

employees to opt into or out of different benefits, and to increase or decrease their level of coverage. "It's not rocket science. We just listened to the employees," Popel says. "If you can do it without increasing costs *and* improve employee morale, it's a gold mine."[53]

Managing the benefits package will continue to be a major human resources issue in the future. The cost of administering benefits programs has become so great that a number of companies outsource this function—that is, they are hiring outside companies to run their employee benefits plans.[54] IBM, for example, decided to spin off its human resources and benefits operation into a separate company, Workforce Solutions, which provides customized services to each of IBM's independent units. The new company saves IBM $45 million each year. Workforce Solutions also handles benefits for other organizations such as the National Geographic Society.

Managing benefits can be especially complicated when employees are located in other countries. The Reaching Beyond Our Borders box discusses some of the new human resources challenges faced by global businesses. To put it simply, benefits are as important to wage negotiations and recruitment now as salary. In the future, benefits may become even more important than salary.

# SCHEDULING EMPLOYEES TO MEET ORGANIZATIONAL AND EMPLOYEE NEEDS

By now, you are quite familiar with the trends occurring in the workforce that result in managers' and workers' demands regarding companies' flexibility and responsiveness. From these trends, some companies offer alternative work arrangements such as flextime, telework, and job sharing.

# Flextime Plans

**flextime plan**
Work schedule that gives employees some freedom to choose when to work, as long as they work the required number of hours.

A **flextime plan** gives employees some freedom to choose when to work, as long as they work the required number of hours. The most popular plans allow employees to come to work between 7 and 9 a.m. and leave between 4 and 6 p.m. Usually, flextime plans will incorporate what is called *core time*. Core time refers to the period when all employees are expected to be at their job stations. For example, an organization may designate core time as between 9:30 and 11:00 a.m. and between 2:00 and 3:00 p.m. During these hours, all employees are required to be at work (see Figure 12.7).

Flextime plans are designed to allow employees to adjust to the demands of the times, including two-income families. For example, the stress of juggling work and family usually falls more heavily on women, says Sonya Kunkel, director for Canada of Catalyst, a North American research and advisory group working to advance women in business. Catalyst has completed two studies on work-life balance in Canadian law firms, underwritten by several large firms. Kunkel says that there is a clear business case for being more accommodating of lawyers' personal lives generally, even beyond child-rearing concerns. "When associates are evaluating a workplace, work-life balance is a key issue," she says of the results of the Catalyst studies. "The younger generation of workers [has] a greater appetite around greater options and flexibility." Losing lawyers also hits the bottom line: Catalyst studies show an associate's departure costs a firm about $315,000 in recruiting, training, salaries, overhead, severance and outplacement—not including hiring a replacement.[55]

**compressed workweek**
Work schedule that allows an employee to work a full number of hours per week but in fewer days.

There are some real disadvantages to flextime as well. Flextime is certainly not for all organizations. For example, it cannot be offered in assembly line processes, where everyone must be at work at the same time. It also is not effective for shift work. Another disadvantage to flextime is that managers often have to work longer days to assist and supervise employees. Some organizations operate from 6 a.m. to 6 p.m. under flextime—a long day for supervisors. Flextime also makes communication more difficult; certain employees may not be there when others need to talk to them. Furthermore, if not carefully supervised, some employees could abuse the system, and that could cause resentment among others. You can imagine how you'd feel if half the workforce left at 3 p.m. on Friday and you had to work until 6 p.m.

**FIGURE** **12.7**

**A Flextime Chart**
At this company, employees can start work anytime between 6:30 and 9:30 a.m. They take a half hour for lunch anytime between 11:00 a.m. and 2:00 p.m., and can leave between 3:00 and 6:30 p.m. Everyone works an eight-hour day. The blue arrows show a typical employee's flextime day.

Another popular option is a **compressed workweek**. That means that an employee works a full number of hours in less than the standard number of days. For example, an employee may work four 10-hour days and then enjoy a long weekend instead of working five 8-hour days with a traditional weekend. There are the obvious advantages of working only four days and having three days off, but some employees get tired when working such long hours, and productivity could decline. Many employees find such a system of great benefit, however, and are quite enthusiastic about it.

Although many companies offer flexible schedules, few employees take advantage of them. Most workers report that they resist using the programs because they fear it

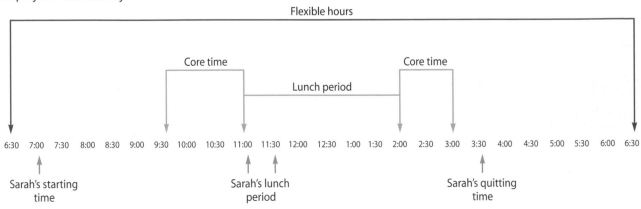

will hurt their careers. Managers signal (directly or indirectly) that employees who change their hours are not serious about their careers.

While there are several options that employers can offer, Statistics Canada communicates what is actually happening in the Canadian marketplace.

- The most common form of alternative work arrangement is flexible hours (36.6 percent of all employees), followed by weekend work (27.99 percent).

- The incidence of flexible hours is more common among workers in the retail trade and consumer services industries (44.6 percent). About six in ten employees in these industries usually worked weekends.

- The incidence of various work arrangements is also related to the educational attainment of workers. For example, the university educated reported the greatest incidence of flexible hours (43.5 percent), but seldom had regularly scheduled weekend work (17 percent).

- Reduced work weeks (e.g., job-sharing and work-sharing) and compressed work-weeks are not widespread, with each being reported by fewer than one in ten workers. The age, occupation, and industry groups with the highest incidence of reduced work weeks were youth (19.5 percent), marketing/sales (15.5 percent), and retail trade and consumer services (13.7 percent).[56]

So, what does this mean to you? Clearly, there are different plans that employers can consider. The choice of plans will be affected by the type of job you have, your employer's needs, your age and needs, and possibly your level of education.

## Telework (Telecommuting)[57]

In Appendix A, you were briefly introduced to the concept of telework. Telework, also known as telecommuting, occurs when paid workers reduce their commute by carrying out all, or part, of their work away from their normal place of business. Rising gas prices, leading-edge technology, and pushes for work-life flexibility have all contributed to an increase in telework across Canada. An estimated 1.4 million Canadians are involved in such an arrangement with the norm being a day or two per week. The number of teleworkers is expected to increase in the next five years.

Increased productivity and improved retention and morale were cited as the greatest benefits among firms that allow telework. The ability to balance work and personal life is the most critical factor in employee decisions to stay with their jobs. Home-based workers can choose their own hours, interrupt work for child care and other tasks, and take time out for various personal reasons. Working at home isn't for everyone, however. Recall from Chapter 7 that to be successful, a home-based worker must have the discipline to stay focused on the work and not be easily distracted.

Telework can also be a cost saver for employers. For example, IBM used to have a surplus of office space, maintaining more offices than it had employees. Now the company has cut back on the number of offices, with employees telecommuting, "hotelling" (being assigned to a desk through a reservations system), and "hot-desking" (sharing a desk with other employees at different times). Other companies are hiring call agents rather than using more expensive in-house operators or less-qualified offshore call centres. For example, Office Depot says that it saves 30 or 40 percent on the cost of each call because it's not providing work space or benefits for its home-based call-centre workers.

Some young new moms, whose careers are not as established, are choosing to stay home because day care is expensive. If more companies offered alternative work arrangements, do you think that this might change?

While telework is not for everyone, for every job, or for every organization, even if it applies only to a small percentage of employees and new hires, it represents a significant tool in the ability to attract and retain the "best of breed."

## Job-Sharing Plans

**job sharing**

An arrangement whereby two part-time employees share one full-time job.

**Job sharing** is an arrangement whereby two part-time employees share one full-time job. The concept has received great attention as more and more women with small children have entered the labour force. Job sharing enables parents to work only during the hours their children are in school. It has also proved beneficial to others with special needs, such as students and older people who want to work part time before fully retiring. The benefits include:

- employment opportunities for those who cannot or prefer not to work full-time
- a high level of enthusiasm and productivity
- reduced absenteeism and tardiness
- ability to schedule people into peak demand periods (e.g., banks on payday) when part-time people are available
- retention of experienced employees who might have left otherwise

Disadvantages include having to hire, train, motivate, and supervise twice as many people and to prorate some fringe benefits. Nonetheless, most firms that were at first reluctant to try job sharing are finding that the benefits outweigh the disadvantages.

### Progress Assessment

- Can you name and describe five alternative compensation systems?
- What advantages do compensation plans such as profit-sharing offer an organization?
- What are the benefits and challenges of flextime? Telework? Job sharing?

# CAREER MANAGEMENT: UP, OVER, AND OUT

Employees don't always stay in the position they were initially hired to fill. They may excel and move up the corporate ladder or fail and move out the front door. In addition to being moved through promotion and termination, employees can be moved by reassignment and retirement. Of course, employees can choose to move themselves by quitting and going to another company.

## Promoting and Reassigning Employees

Many companies find that promotion from within the company improves employee morale. Promotions are also cost-effective in that the promoted employees are already familiar with the corporate culture and procedures and do not need to spend valuable time on basic orientation.

Due to the prevalence of flatter corporate structures, there are fewer levels for employees to reach now than there were in the past. Therefore, it is more common today for workers to move *over* to a new position than to move *up* to one. Such transfers allow employees to develop and display new skills and to learn more about the company overall. This is one way of motivating experienced employees to remain in a company with few upward advancement opportunities.

## Terminating Employees

Downsizing and restructuring, increasing customer demands for greater value, and the relentless pressure of global competition and shifts in technology have human resources managers struggling to manage layoffs and firings. In the case of layoffs, older employees are often offered early retirement packages (to be discussed soon). Companies may counsel other laid-off employees to enable them to better cope with the loss of their jobs and to help them find new jobs. Some set up in-house outplacement facilities so that employees can get counselling on how to obtain a new job. For senior managers, companies usually pay for private-agency career counselling.

For those that remain, the job losses and the threat of future job losses has introduced strong feelings that may include fear, insecurity, and uncertainty; frustration, resentment, and anger; sadness, depression, and guilt; and unfairness, betrayal, and distrust.[58] Insecurity undermines motivation, so HRM must deal with this issue. According to Wayne Cascio, author on numerous books on organizational restructuring and the economic impact of HR activities, "They're very worried about their own future: 'What is this going to mean for me?' So, they don't want to stick their necks out and take risks." Yet companies need to engage in risk-taking to generate new products, markets, and customers, he says. Cascio adds, "Taking the same amount of work and just loading it onto fewer workers has long-term effects in terms of stress." This stress, he says, often intensifies four to six months after the downsizing, resulting in increased absenteeism and higher turnover.[59] Keeping employees fully informed and having a clear policy on termination pay helps to remove some insecurity.

Even companies that regain financial strength, however, are hesitant to rehire new full-time employees. Why? One reason is that the cost of terminating employees is prohibitively high. The cost of firing comes from lost training costs as well as damages and legal fees paid in wrongful discharge suits. (This is why is it critical to have a good system of verbal and written notices, and record-keeping, to deal with poorly-performing employees.) To save money, many companies are either using contingent workers or outsourcing certain functions.

## Retiring Employees

In addition to layoffs, another tool used to downsize companies is to offer early retirement benefits to entice older (and more expensive) workers to retire. Such benefits usually involve financial incentives such as one-time cash payments, known in some companies as *golden handshakes*. The advantage of offering early retirement benefits over laying off employees is that early retirement offers increase the morale of the surviving employees. Retiring senior workers also increases promotion opportunities for younger employees.

## Losing Employees

In spite of a company's efforts to retain talented workers by offering flexible schedules, competitive salaries, and attractive fringe benefits, some employees will choose to pursue opportunities elsewhere. Learning about their reasons for leaving can be invaluable in preventing the loss of other good people in the future. One way to learn the real reasons that employees leave is to have an independent third party (not the employee's direct manager) conduct an exit interview. Many companies contract with outside vendors to conduct exit interviews. Outsiders can provide confidentiality and anonymity features that can result in honest feedback that employees may feel uncomfortable giving in face-to-face interviews with their supervisors. Today there are Web-based exit interview management systems that capture, track, and statistically analyze employee exit interview data and generate reports that identify retention trouble areas. Such programs can also coordinate exit interview data with employee satisfaction surveys to predict which departments should expect turnover to occur.[60] The **turnover rate** measures the percentage of employees that leave the firm each year. The most reliable way to use turnover rates is to compare an organization against itself over time, says Ken Strom, senior consultant at Watson Wyatt Worldwide.[61]

**turnover rate**
A measure of the percentage of employees that leave a firm each year.

# LAWS AFFECTING HUMAN RESOURCES MANAGEMENT[62]

The Charter of Rights and Freedoms, which is part of the Constitution, guarantees equality before the law for every Canadian. The Human Rights Act seeks to provide equal employment opportunities without regard to people's race, national or ethnic origin, colour, religion, age, sex, sexual orientation, marital status, family status, disability, or conviction for an offense for which a pardon has been granted. Human rights legislation requires that every employer ensure equal opportunities and that there is no discrimination. This legislation affects nearly every human resource function (which includes planning, recruiting, selection, training, compensation, and labour relations) and it has made managing these activities more complicated. This is true in both a non-union environment, which is governed by these laws and regulations, and a union environment, which must also reflect the conditions outlined in the labour contract (to be discussed in Chapter 13).

Since Canada is a confederation of provinces and territories, jurisdiction over many aspects of our lives is divided between the federal and provincial governments. As noted in Chapter 4, the federal government legislates on national issues such as employment insurance. The federal government also has jurisdiction over certain types of businesses that are deemed to be of a national nature. Banks, insurance companies, airlines, railways, shipping companies, telephone, radio, TV, cable companies, and others are subject to federal law, as are all federal employees. However, fewer than 10 percent of all Canadian employees are subject to federal legislation.

The provinces have jurisdiction over most provincial matters. This includes employment standards in areas such as minimum wage, hours of work, overtime, statutory holidays, parental leave, employment of people under 18 years of age, and as noted earlier in this chapter, discrimination in the workplace.

What all of this means is that there are literally hundreds of laws and regulations, federal and provincial, which apply to all aspects of HRM. Furthermore, these laws are constantly being revised because of social pressure or rulings by human rights commissions or courts. One of the most regulated areas involves discrimination.

## Employment Equity

A well-known 1980s case of discrimination highlights a major problem and how it was solved. A group of women accused the Canadian National Railway (CNR) of not hiring them because they were women. The CNR, like many other companies, did not hire women for jobs that were thought to be traditional men's jobs, those for which heavy physical labour was required. In this case, the jobs involved maintenance and repairs of the tracks. The Canadian Human Rights Commission ruled in favour of the women. The CNR appealed and the courts ruled against it all the way to the Supreme Court of Canada.

**Employment equity** refers to employment activities designed to increase employment opportunities for certain groups, given past discrimination toward these groups. As a result, the Employment Equity Act was introduced in 1986 to ensure that federally-regulated employers with 100 or more employees "achieve equality in the workplace so that no person shall be denied employment opportunities or benefits for reasons unrelated to ability and, in the fulfillment of that goal, to correct the conditions of disadvantage in employment experienced by women, aboriginal peoples, persons with disabilities and members of visible minorities by giving effect to the principle that employment equity means more than treating persons in the same way but also requires special measures and the accommodation of differences."[63] This means that in the CNR example, CNR had to develop a plan that would result in more women than men being hired for such jobs until the balance was more even. The result is that when a man and a woman are equally qualified, the woman must be given preference. This would occur for a period of time until the balance of male and female workers was adjusted more equally.

Visit http://www.chrc-ccdp.ca/media_room/jurisprudence/jurisprudence-en.asp to learn of cases and decisions where the Canadian Human Rights Commission has played a role and/or that established jurisprudence in the area of Canadian human rights.

**employment equity**
Employment activities designed to "right past wrongs" by increasing opportunities for minorities and women.

Interpretation of the employment equity law eventually led employers to actively recruit and give preference to women and minority group members. Employment equity, for many employers, has become mostly a reporting function. They keep track of numbers of employees that belong to these groups, and they try to remove any discrimination from hiring procedures, including trying to advertise positions more widely. As you might expect, interpretation of the law is often controversial and enforcement is difficult. Questions persist about the effect the program could have in creating a sort of reverse discrimination in the workplace.

**Reverse discrimination** refers to the unfairness that unprotected groups (say, whites or males) may perceive when protected groups receive preference in hiring and promotion. Charges of reverse discrimination have occurred when companies have been perceived as unfairly giving preference to women or minority group members in hiring and promoting. The Canadian Charter of Rights and Freedoms specifically allows for employment equity as a method to overcome long-standing discrimination against specific groups. Therefore, the courts accept it as being non-discriminatory in the legal sense. Be aware that this continues to be a controversial issue today.

The Employment Equity Act promotes equitable representation for women, Aboriginal peoples, persons with disabilities, and visible minorities who work in federally-regulated workplaces. Would you seek employment in such a workplace if you belonged to one of these groups?

## Laws That Protect the Disabled

Legislation protects people with disabilities. Businesses cannot discriminate against people on the basis of any physical or mental disability. Employers are required to give disabled applicants the same consideration for employment as people without disabilities. It also requires that businesses make "reasonable accommodations" for people with disabilities. Accommodation may include modifying equipment or widening doorways. Reasonable accommodations are not always expensive. For example, a company can provide an inexpensive headset that allows someone with cerebral palsy to talk on the phone and write at the same time. Equal opportunity for people with disabilities promises to be a continuing issue into the next decade.

**reverse discrimination**
The unfairness that unprotected groups (say, whites or males) may perceive when protected groups receive preference in hiring and promotion.

## Laws That Protect Older Employees

In the years to come, labour shortages are forecast due to the retirement of aging baby boomers. While there is no law in Canada that requires retirement at age 65 (Nova Scotia was the last province to eliminate mandatory retirement, effective 2009), some workplaces may mandate it. For example, the Supreme Court of Canada ruled against a New Brunswick miner who challenged his company's right to compel him to retire at age 65 as a requirement of his employee pension plan. While the province's act prohibits mandatory retirement, it includes a provision allowing companies to enforce mandatory retirement under the terms or conditions of any retirement or pension plan. The Supreme Court of Canada has stated that unless there is evidence that the pension plan as a whole is not legitimate, it will be protected by the province's Human Rights Act "from the conclusion that a particular provision compelling retirement at a certain age constitutes age discrimination."[64]

Generally speaking, employees are guaranteed protection against age discrimination in the workplace. Courts have ruled against firms in unlawful-discharge suits where age appeared to be the major factor in dismissal. (An exception was noted above.) In addition, the federal government and the provinces protect over-65 workers in their labour or human rights legislation. Changes to the ban on mandatory retirement age provide opportunities for companies to retain workers who wish to work past age 65.[65]

## Progress Assessment

- Name three areas of HRM responsibility that are affected by government legislation.
- Explain what employment equity is and give one example of it.
- Why should HRM be concerned about legislation or court rulings when terminating employees?

## Effects of Legislation

Clearly, laws and regulations affect all areas of HRM. It should be apparent that a career in HRM offers a challenge to anyone willing to put forth the effort. Figure 12.8 lists some sites that you may consult to learn about some of the topics discussed in this chapter. In summary:

- Employers must know and act in accordance with the legal rights of their employees or risk costly court cases.
- Legislation affects all areas of HRM, from hiring and training to compensating employees.
- Managers must be sensitive not only to legal requirements, but also to union contracts and social standards and expectations, which can be even more demanding.
- Court cases have made it clear that it is sometimes legal to go beyond providing equal rights for minorities and women to provide special employment (employment equity) and training to correct past discrimination.
- New court cases and legislation change HRM almost daily. The only way to keep current is to read business literature and become familiar with the issues.

**FIGURE** | **12.8**

**Human Resources Information Sites**

| Organization | URL |
| --- | --- |
| Canadian Council of Human Resources Associations | http://www.cchra.ca/ |
| Canadian HR Reporter | http://www.canadianhrreporter.com/ |
| Canadian Human Rights Commission | http://www.chrc-ccdp.ca/ |
| Canadian Human Rights Reporter | http://www.cdn-hr-reporter.ca/ |
| Conference Board of Canada | http://www.conferenceboard.ca/ |
| Employee Benefit News Canada | http://ebnc.benefitnews.com/ |
| Government of Canada | http://www.canada.gc.ca/ |
| HR Council for the Voluntary & Non-profit Sector | http://www.hrcouncil.ca/ |
| Pay Equity Commission | http://www.payequity.gov.on.ca/ |
| Provincial and Territorial Government Sites | http://www.canada.gc.ca/othergov-autregouv/prov-eng.html |
| Society for Human Resource Management | http://www.shrm.org/Pages/default.aspx |
| Statistics Canada | http://www.statcan.gc.ca/ |

# SUMMARY

1. Human resource management is the process of evaluating human resource needs, finding people to fill those needs, and getting the best work from each employee by providing the right incentives and job environment, all with the goal of meeting organizational objectives. Like all other types of management, human resource management begins with planning.

**LO ▶ 1** Explain the importance of human resource management as a strategic contributor to organizational success, and summarize the five steps in human resources planning.

### What are the steps in human resources planning?
The five steps are (1) preparing a human resources inventory of the organization's employees; (2) preparing a job analysis; (3) assessing future demand; (4) assessing future supply; and (5) establishing a strategic plan for recruitment, selection, training and development, evaluation, compensation, scheduling, and career management for the labour force.

2. Recruitment is the set of activities used to obtain a sufficient number of the right people at the right time.

**LO ▶ 2** Describe methods that companies use to recruit new employees, and explain some of the issues that make recruitment challenging.

### What methods do human resources managers use to recruit new employees?
Recruiting sources are classified as either internal or external. Internal sources include hiring from within the firm (e.g., transfers and promotions) and employees who recommend others to hire. External recruitment sources include advertisements, public and private employment agencies, school placement offices, management consultants, professional organizations, referrals, walk-in applications, and the Internet.

### Why has recruitment become more difficult?
Legal restrictions complicate hiring practices. Finding suitable employees can also be made more difficult if companies are considered unattractive workplaces.

3. Selection is the process of gathering and interpreting information to decide which applicants should be hired.

**LO ▶ 3** Outline the five steps in selecting employees, and illustrate the use of various types of employee training and development methods.

### What are the five steps in the selection process?
The steps are (1) obtaining complete application forms; (2) conducting initial and follow-up interviews; (3) giving employment tests; (4) confirming background information; and (5) establishing a trial period of employment.

### What are some of the activities used for training?
After assessing the needs of the organization and the skills of the employees, training programs are designed that may include the following activities: employee orientation, on-the-job training, apprenticeship programs, off-the-job training, online training, vestibule training, and job simulation. The effectiveness of the training is evaluated at the conclusion of the activities.

### What methods are used to develop managerial skills?
Management development methods include on-the-job coaching, understudy positions, job rotation, and off-the-job courses and training.

### How does networking fit in this process?
Networking is the process of establishing contacts with key managers within and outside the organization to get additional development assistance.

4. A performance appraisal is an evaluation of the performance level of employees against established standards to make decisions about promotions, compensation, additional training, or firing.

**LO ▶ 4** Trace the six steps in appraising employee performance, and summarize the objectives of employee compensation programs.

### How is performance evaluated?

The steps are (1) establish performance standards; (2) communicate those standards; (3) evaluate performance; (4) discuss results; (5) take corrective action when needed; and (6) use the results for decisions about promotions, compensation, additional training, or firing.

### What kind of compensation systems are used?

They include salary systems, hourly wages, piecework, commission plans, bonus plans, profit-sharing plans, and stock options.

### What types of compensation systems are appropriate for teams?

The most common are profit-sharing and skill-based compensation programs. It is also important to reward outstanding individual performance within teams.

### What are fringe benefits?

Fringe benefits include such items as sick leave, vacation pay, pension plans, and health plans that provide additional compensation to employees beyond base wages. Many firms offer cafeteria-style fringe benefits plans, in which employees can choose the benefits they want, up to a certain dollar amount.

**LO ▶ 5** Describe the ways in which employees can move through a company: promotion, reassignment, termination, and retirement.

5. Employees often move from their original positions in a company.

### How can employees move within a company?

Employees can be moved up (promotion), over (reassignment), or out (termination or retirement) of a company. Employees can also choose to leave a company to pursue opportunities elsewhere.

**LO ▶ 6** Illustrate the effects of legislation on human resource management.

6. There are many laws that affect human resources planning.

### What are those laws?

Some important areas discussed include employment equity, laws that protect the disabled, as well as laws that protect older employees. This is an important subject for future managers to study.

## KEY TERMS

apprentice programs  364

cafeteria-style benefits
(flexible benefit plans)  374

compressed workweek  376

contingent workers  362

employee orientation  363

employment equity  380

enabling  366

flextime plan  376

fringe benefits  372

human resource management
(HRM)  354

job analysis  356

job description  356

job sharing  378

job simulation  364

job specifications  356

management development  365

mentor  366

networking  366

off-the-job training  364

online training  364

on-the-job training  363

pay equity  369

performance appraisal  367

recruitment  358

reverse discrimination  381

selection  360

training and development  363

turnover rate  379

vestibule training  364

## CRITICAL THINKING

1. Given the complex situations you'd be addressing, does human resource management seem like a career area that interests you? What have been your experiences in dealing with people who work in human resource management?

2. Why should you be interested in the subject matter of human resources management, even if you are not majoring in this field?

3. What problems can arise when family members work together in the same firm?

4. Do you think that most vacancies in firms are filled through a competitive process?

5. Performance appraisals are often done poorly for different reasons. For example, people may not like to complete them or have them done to them. The company's perspective also affects the effectiveness of this process. Is the appraisal conducted so employees can be assessed and corrected (some might say punished) or so that the collective can do better? What can a company do to ensure that appraisals are effectively conducted?

6. Imagine that you must fire an employee. What effect might the employee's dismissal have on your other workers? Explain how you would tell the employee and your remaining subordinates.

## DEVELOPING WORKPLACE SKILLS

1. Look through the classified ads in your local newspaper or on the Internet and find at least two positions that you might like to have when you graduate. List the qualifications specified in each of the ads. Identify methods that the companies might use to determine how well applicants meet each of those qualifications.

2. Secure a blank performance-appraisal form from any company and for any category of entry-level employment. State specifically what dimensions of work performance are being measured and how the dimensions are measured.

3. Consider these occupations: car salesperson, computer software developer, teacher, and assembly-line worker. Identify the method of compensation that you think is appropriate for determining the wages for each of these workers. Explain your answer.

4. Imagine that you are the human resources manager at your company. You get a call from a company doing a reference check for a former employee. This former employee is being considered for a position. During the call, you are asked to provide information on the employee's medical history and his marital status. You have recently reviewed changes to the privacy laws for your province/territory through the Office of the Privacy Commissioner of Canada (http://www.privcom.gc.ca/). What do you tell this person on the phone?

5. List the three groups of fringe benefits and include benefits under each group. Speak with a local HR professional and find out what the employee and employer cost is for each benefit, on a monthly basis, for an entry-level position that a graduate might consider.

## TAKING IT TO THE NET 1

### Purpose

To use job-search Web sites to identify employment opportunities and to compare the services offered by several recruiting-related sites.

### Exercise

There are many recruiting-related sites on the Internet. Examples include:

- canadiancareers.com
- monster.ca
- workopolis.com
- jobloft.com
- canada.plusjobs.com
- cooljobscanada.com

The Government of Canada has created several sites that provide information on jobs, workers, training, and careers. They include Human Resources and Skills Development Canada (www.hrsdc.gc.ca/en/gateways/individuals/menu. shtml), Service Canada's Job Futures site (www.job futures.ca), and the Federal Student Work Experience Program (http://jobs-emplois.gc.ca/fswep-pfete/index-eng.htm).

1. Access these job information sites and examine what they contain. Do you find any important differences?

2. Do you see any positions that might interest you on a part-time or full-time basis?

## TAKING IT TO THE NET 2

### Purpose

The purpose of this exercise is twofold. From a manager's perspective, the purpose is to illustrate the types of questions managers typically ask during interviews. From an applicant's perspective, the purpose is to practise answering such questions in a safe environment.

### Exercise

Go to http://www.monstertrak.com/career-guide. This may be a useful site if you are looking for an internship or entry-level position, but don't know the next steps or even where to start. Career advice, job seeker guidance, or the necessary tools to differentiate you from others can be accessed.

1. What are some interview suggestions that are made on this site?

2. Reviewing the Career Development link, what suggestions did you find surprising?

## ANALYZING MANAGEMENT DECISIONS

### Dual-Career Planning

Carey Moler is a 32-year-old account executive for a communications company. She is married to Mitchell Moler, a lawyer. Carey and Mitchell did not make any definite plans about how to juggle their careers and family life until Carey reached age 30. Then they decided to have a baby, and career planning took on a whole new dimension. A company named Catalyst talked to 815 dual-career couples and found that most of them, like the Molers, had not made any long-range career decisions regarding family lifestyle.

From the business perspective, such dual-career families create real concerns. There are problems with relocation, with child care, and so on that affect recruiting, productivity, morale, and promotion policies.

For a couple such as the Molers, having both career and family responsibilities is exhausting. But that is just one problem. If Carey is moving up in her firm, what happens if

Mitchell gets a terrific job offer a thousand kilometres away? What if Carey gets such an offer? Who is going to care for the baby? What happens if the baby becomes ill? How do they plan their vacations when there are three schedules to balance? Who will do the housework? Dual careers require careful planning and discussion, and those plans need to be reviewed over time. A couple that decides at age 22 to do certain things may change their minds at age 30. Whether or not to have children, where to locate, how to manage the household—all such issues and more can become major problems if not carefully planned.

The same is true for corporations. They too must plan for dual-career families. They must give attention to job sharing, flextime, parental leave policies, transfer policies, nepotism rules (i.e., rules about hiring family members), and more.

### Discussion Questions

1. What are some of the issues you can see developing because of dual-career families? How is this affecting children in such families?

2. What kind of corporate policies need changing to adapt to these new realities?

3. What are the advantages of dual careers? Disadvantages? What can newlywed couples do to minimize the problems of dual careers? How can a couple achieve the advantages?

# CHAPTER 13

# Understanding Employee– Management Issues and Relations

## LEARNING OBJECTIVES

**AFTER YOU HAVE READ AND STUDIED THIS CHAPTER, YOU SHOULD BE ABLE TO:**

**LO ▶ 1** Trace the history of organized labour in Canada.

**LO ▶ 2** Discuss the major legislation affecting trade unions.

**LO ▶ 3** Understand the collective bargaining process.

**LO ▶ 4** Outline the objectives of trade unions.

**LO ▶ 5** Describe the negotiation tactics used by labour and management during conflicts, and discuss the role of unions in the future.

**LO ▶ 5** Explain some of today's employee–management issues.

## Getting to Know Gerry Varricchio, Director of Organizing for Central and Eastern Canada for the Labourers' International Union of North America (LIUNA)

Gerry Varricchio is a labour organizer and first contract negotiator. He specializes in the construction industry in the Province of Ontario, though he regularly runs campaigns in the industrial sector and negotiates the first collective agreements in both sectors. To successfully administer organizing drives through the application process, and in the industrial sector the vote process, a low profile is essential. One does not conduct successful organizing drives if employers see it coming. For this reason, Varricchio's picture is missing from in this profile.

As the Director of Organizing for Central and Eastern Canada for the Labourers' International Union of North America (LIUNA), Varricchio works for the international office, and reports directly to Joseph S. Mancinelli, International Vice-President for Central and Eastern Canada. Varricchio runs the Central and Eastern Canada Organizing Fund (CECOF), and has over sixty organizers reporting directly to him. This is a highly motivated and powerful unit dedicated to organizing the unorganized and levelling the playing field to preserve work for its members and keep management competitive. Varricchio's vision encompasses a joint co-operative effort between labour and management to achieve that goal. Since 1993, the LIUNA organization has grown from having one regional organizer (Varricchio) to having over 65 regional organizers in 2008, with Varricchio at the helm.

Varricchio started his working life on the tools, first as a carpenter, and then as a member of LIUNA Local 1089 in his hometown of Sarnia, working in "Chemical Valley." He was elected to the LIUNA Local 1089 Executive board and as a delegate to the LIUNA Ontario Provincial District Council in 1985, and re-elected every four years subsequently. Experiencing his own health issues as a result of chemical spills in the workplace, Varricchio was very aware of the difficulties faced in the work environment, including health and safety issues. He recognized early on that some of the major protections for workers are accessible only thorough unionization. Consequently, when offered a job in 1987 by the LIUNA Ontario Provincial District Council as an organizer, Varricchio jumped at the chance. In addition to all of his organizing duties on behalf of LIUNA, he also serves as a Trustee on the Local 1089 Training and Rehabilitation Trust Fund and on the Benefits Trust Fund. One accomplishment is that he pioneered the first and only Union Benefit Plan that integrates a Registered Educational Scholarship Plan for members and their children into a Union Benefit Trust Plan as part of the standard benefit package.

In the past twenty years, Varricchio has adapted to the demands of the workplace. He was at the forefront in introducing the process of "top-down" organizing, a system of engaging the employer in the initial stages of organizing, with the intent of levelling the playing field for all of the employers in the industry. This reassures individual employers who believe that the presence of a union in the workplace will lead to inequalities in terms of bid power and limit their access to future contracts. Varricchio has expressed this as follows: "Unions have a dual responsibility—to ensure that their members are getting the best wage and benefit packages and working conditions available in the marketplace, and equally as important, to ensure that their contractual employers not only remain competitive, but have a labour partner that can assist them in expanding their business and market share."

As a result of LIUNA's organizing initiatives through CECOF and Varricchio, the organization has the distinct honour of being the most prolific of union organizers in the entire province of Ontario. The statistics for the fiscal year ending in 2007 show that LIUNA submitted over 167 applications for certification to the Ontario Labour Relations Board (OLRB), far in excess of the 40 applications sent in by the runner-up union. Of these 167 applications submitted to the OLRB, 130 were successful and only 17 were lost. Due to prolonged OLRB proceedings, 20 applications carried over into 2008; of those, 13 were successful. These figures do not include the additional 151 companies that voluntarily recognized LIUNA through top-down organizing initiatives during the same period. It is expected that 2008 will tell a similar story.

Managers in both profit-seeking and non-profit organizations address labour-relations challenges every day. This chapter discusses some of these employee–management

relations and issues. When asked what his thoughts are for the future of labour-management relations, Varricchio points out that the labour-management community is at the mercy of the political climate, both federally and provincially. The Conservative Party of Canada is not labour friendly and a continuation of the erosion of workers' rights in that jurisdiction is expected throughout Prime Minister Harper's second term. Ontario is somewhat more fortunate in the provincial arena however, with gradual progress being made by Ontario Premier McGuinty's government with respect to workers' rights. However, the economy suffered a tremendous blow in 2008, with sky-rocketing unemployment resulting from plant closures. It is even more important in these times for labour and management to partner together to achieve common goals and look out for each other's interests. "Perhaps in spite of the adversarial beginnings between unions and employers and the prejudices that evolved over time," says Varricchio, "the true business value of unions will be recognized and utilized when it is most needed."

Source: Gerry Varricchio, Director of Organizing for Central and Eastern Canada, The Labourers' International Union of North America, interview, 16 February 2009.

**union**

An employee organization that has the main goal of representing members in employee–management bargaining over job-related issues.

# EMPLOYEE–MANAGEMENT ISSUES

The relationship between management (representing owners or stockholders) and employees has never been very smooth. Management has the responsibility of producing a profit through maximum productivity. Thus, managers have to make hard decisions that often do not win them popularity contests. Labour (the collective term for non-management workers) is interested in fair and competent management, human dignity, decent working conditions, a reasonable share in the wealth that its work generates, and assurance that the conditions of the contract and government labour laws will not be ignored. Many issues affect the relationship between managers and labour, including union activity, executive compensation, and child care and elder care.

Like other managerial challenges, employee–management issues must be worked out through open discussion, goodwill, and compromise. How management and labour adapt to the changing business environment will determine our economic and political well-being in the years ahead. To make a reasoned decision, it is important to know both sides of an issue.

Canadian companies have been trying to compete more effectively under the demands of a sagging economy, improved technology, and world competitiveness. While coping with a changing economy, management has been laying off employees, automating operations, and demanding more flexibility in how it uses its remaining workforce. Management should consider what can be done to become more competitive (e.g., adopt the most advanced technological methods, simplify and thin out organizational structure, increase productivity, etc.).

Over the years, these pressures on companies have led to numerous layoffs, plant closings, and the loss of thousands of jobs. Skilled employees with 15, 20, or 25 years of experience have found themselves without a job. As more traditional labour-intensive jobs are lost due to technology and competition from lower-wage countries, the issues of job security and retraining for the new information-age jobs have become key concerns for unions and the people they represent.

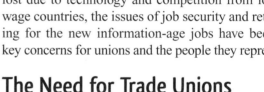

In the late 2000s, it seemed like almost every week another plant shut its doors, filed for bankruptcy or announced its intention to move its operations out of Canada. As part of its campaign to stop this trend, the Canadian Auto Workers union called on all levels of government to adopt Buy Canadian policies for all public purchases. Do you think that such policies save jobs and build stronger communities?

## The Need for Trade Unions

Any discussion of employee–management relations in Canada should begin with a discussion of unions. A **union** (known as a *trade union* in British English or a *labor union* in U.S. English) is an employee organization that has the main goal of representing members in employee–management bargaining over job-related issues.[1] Workers originally formed unions to protect themselves from intolerable work conditions and unfair treatment. They also united to secure some say in the operation of their jobs. As the number of union members grew, workers gained more negotiating power with managers and more political power as well.

Historically, employees turned to unions for assistance in gaining specific workplace rights and benefits. Trade unions were largely responsible for the establishment of minimum-wage laws, overtime rules, workers' compensation, severance pay, child-labour laws, job safety regulations, and more. In recent decades, however, union strength has waned. Business observers suggest that global competition, shifts from manufacturing to service and high-tech industries, growth in part-time work, and changes in management philosophies are some of the reasons for labour's decline. Some analysts also contend that the decline is related to labour's success in seeing the issues it championed become law.[2]

Some labour analysts forecast that unions will regain strength as companies become more involved in practices such as outsourcing; others insist that unions have seen their brightest days. Few doubt that the role and influence of unions—particularly in selected regions—will continue to arouse emotions and opinions that contrast considerably. Let's briefly look at trade unions and then analyze other key issues affecting employee–management relations.

# TRADE UNIONS FROM DIFFERENT PERSPECTIVES

Are trade unions essential in the Canadian economy today? This is a very political subject with strongly-held opposing positions. An electrician carrying a picket sign in Sudbury would say yes and elaborate on the dangers to a free society if employers continue to try to bust, or break apart, authorized unions. A small manufacturer would likely embrace a different perspective and complain about having to operate under union wage and benefit obligations in an increasingly competitive global economy.

Historians generally agree that today's unions are an outgrowth of the economic transition caused by the Industrial Revolution of the nineteenth and early twentieth centuries. Workers who once toiled in the fields, dependent on the mercies of nature for survival, suddenly became dependent on the continuous roll of the factory presses and assembly lines for their living.[3] Breaking away from an agricultural economy to form an industrial economy was quite difficult. Over time, workers learned that strength through unity (unions) could lead to improved job conditions, better wages, and job security.

Thousands of Canadian Auto Workers union members and retirees protested at Queen's Park on 23 April 2009. They were demanding that the Ontario government guarantee pensions from General Motors amid bankruptcy speculation for the company. Do you think such actions influence political decisions?

According to Gerry Varricchio, "In a perfect world, labour and management partner together to achieve common goals and look out for each other's interests. Unfortunately, human nature being what it is, greed, incompetence, and self-serving interests of players from one side or the other, or both, can supersede the common good thereby creating conflict and negative perceptions about unions. In any market, competing on a level playing field is extremely important to the success and future growth of a business. The most effective vehicle for competing businesses to utilize in creating and sustaining a level playing field, in their respective markets, is a union. Through the union structure and the collective bargaining process, employers can level off labour costs across entire markets and create optimum standards in training and health and safety practices that can be properly enforced through their collective agreements."[4] He also believes that because of the adversarial beginnings between unions and employers, and the subsequent prejudices that have evolved over time, the true business value of unions remains largely untapped.[5]

Critics of organized labour maintain that few of the inhumane conditions that once dominated industry still exist in the workplace. They charge that organized labour has in fact become a large industrial entity in itself and that the real issue of protecting workers has become secondary. That is, unions can be bureaucratic, resistant to change, and political, whereby some union leaders may be self-serving and act counter to a union's best interests. Critics also maintain that the current legal system and changing management philosophies minimize the chances that the sweatshops (workplaces with unsatisfactory and often unsafe or oppressive labour conditions) of the late nineteenth and early twentieth centuries will reappear.[6] A short discussion of the history of trade unions will cast a better light on the issues involved.

## The Early History of Organized Labour

The presence of formal labour organizations in Canada dates back to the 1800s. Early unions on the wharves of Halifax, St. John's, and Quebec during the War of 1812 existed to profit from labour scarcity. Others, such as the Montreal shoemakers or the Toronto printers of the 1830s, were craft unions. A **craft union** is an organization of skilled specialists in a particular craft or trade. These unions were formed to address fundamental work issues of pay, hours, conditions, and job security—many of the same issues that dominate labour negotiations today. By forming a union, these skilled workers hoped to protect their craft and status from being undermined.

**craft union**
An organization of skilled specialists in a particular craft or trade.

Many of the early labour organizations were local or regional in membership. Also, most were established to achieve some short-range goal (e.g., a pay increase) and disbanded after attaining a specific objective. This situation changed dramatically in the late nineteenth century with the expansion of the Industrial Revolution. The nineteenth century witnessed the emergence of modern industrial capitalism. The system of producing the necessities of society in small, home-based workplaces gave way to production in large factories driven by steam and later electricity. Enormous productivity increases were gained through mass production and job specialization. However, this brought problems for workers in terms of productivity expectations, hours of work, wages, and unemployment.

Workers were faced with the reality that production was vital. Anyone who failed to produce lost his or her job. People had to go to work even if they were ill or had family problems. Accidents were frequent and injured workers were simply thrown out and replaced by others. Over time, the increased emphasis on production led firms to expand the hours of work. The length of the average workweek in 1900 was 60 hours, but an 80-hour workweek was not uncommon.[7] Wages were low and the use of child labour was widespread. For example, small boys worked long hours in mines, in areas that were inaccessible to adults, for a few cents an hour. Minimum-wage laws and unemployment benefits were non-existent, which meant that periods of unemployment were hard on families who earned subsistence wages. As you can sense, these were not short-term issues that would easily go away. The workplace was ripe for the emergence of labour organizations.

The struggle for more humane working conditions and wages was not an easy one, because before 1872 it was illegal to attempt to form a union in Canada. The pioneers in the early struggles were treated as common criminals. They were arrested, beaten, and often shot. In 1919, for example, two protesting strikers were shot and killed by police during the Winnipeg General Strike. This was followed by 428 strikes across the country.[8]

As the years progressed, more unions were formed and more employees joined them. Other union types—such as industrial unions—were created to represent certain workers. An **industrial union** is one that consists of unskilled and semi-skilled workers in mass-production industries such as automobile manufacturing and mining.

Long after it was no longer illegal, the idea of workers forming unions to protect their interests was still regarded with suspicion by employers and governments in Canada. Democratic rights for all was still a weak concept, and the idea of people getting together to fight for their rights was not accepted as it is today. The union movement was greatly influenced by immigrants from Europe (especially Britain), who brought with them the ideas and experiences of a more advanced and often more radical background. The growing union movement in the United States also influenced Canada. Many Canadian unions started as locals of American unions, and this relationship persists today. As democracy gradually gained strength, the union movement grew with it. Its participation, in turn, helped democracy sink deeper, wider roots in Canada.

A legal holiday since 1894, Labour Day is a celebration of workers and their families. It was inspired by the first significant workers demonstration in 1872, where, accompanied by four bands, unionists marched through the streets of Toronto. Leaders demanded better conditions for all workers, as well as the release of 24 union members who were imprisoned for going on strike. About 10,000 Torontonians turned out to see the parade and listen to the speeches.

**industrial union**
Consists of unskilled and semi-skilled workers in mass-production industries such as automobile manufacturing and mining.

# THE STRUCTURE AND SIZE OF TRADE UNIONS IN CANADA

The organization structure of unions in Canada is quite complex. The most basic unit is the *union local* (also called a local or local union). One local usually represents one school, government office, or a specific factory or office of a company. However, that local can also cover several small companies or other work units.

While a local can be an independent organization within a specific geographic area, it is usually part of a larger structure, namely one that is provincial or regional in focus, or a *national* (a union that charters locals in only one country) or *international body*. For example, a local of the Ford plant in Windsor, Ontario, is part of the Canadian Auto Workers (CAW) union, which is a national body. A local of the U.S. Steel Canada plant in Hamilton is part of the United Steel Workers (USW) union, which is an international body based in the United States.

In addition, union locals typically belong to *union centrals*. The main functions of these union centrals has been to coordinate the activities of member unions when representing the interests of labour to local, provincial, and federal governments as well as to organized labour on the world scene.[9] As a rule, union centrals in Canada have had limited authority over their affiliates, except in jurisdictional matters.[10] Some of the larger bodies in Canada include the Canadian Labour Congress (CLC) and the Quebec-based Confédération des Syndicats Nationaux/Confederation of National Trade Unions (CSN/CNTU).

The CLC is the largest union central in Canada and it promotes itself as "bringing together the majority of unions in Canada in a unified, national voice." Through its over 3 million worker members, the CLC represents Canada's national and international unions,

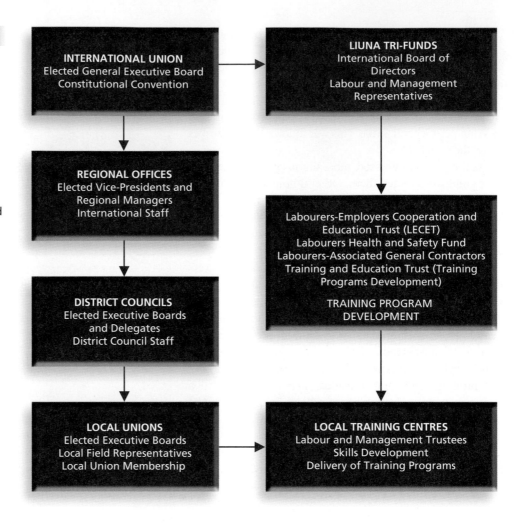

**FIGURE** **13.1**

**The Structure of the Labourers' International Union of North America (LIUNA)**

Elections are extremely democratic at LIUNA, as members vote for representation at each level of the union's structure. Members at the union local elect their local's executive board and officers. Each local then elects a district council delegate. These delegates elect the district council's executive board. Local union members also elect the international vice-president and regional managers for their regional office. At the international union, each local member elects the general president of the union (the equivalent of a CEO) and the general secretary treasurer (the equivalent of a CFO).

the provincial and territorial federations of labour, and 130 district labour councils.[11] Among other issues, the CLC promotes decent wages and working conditions and improved health and safety laws. It lobbies the government on a wide range of topics including improving Canada's Employment Insurance program, better enforcing our existing health and safety legislation, fair taxes, and strong social programs, including child care, medicare, and pensions.

Figure 13.1 charts the structure of LIUNA. LIUNA is structured under a governing Constitution, which is reviewed and amended every five years at a constitutional convention, bringing together elected delegates from every local union and district council in North America. Along with constitutional resolutions, the convention also elects the General Executive Board, composed of the general president, general secretary treasurer, and ten regional vice-presidents. The international union issues and holds the charters of all local unions and district councils that operate under the rule of the LIUNA Constitution. District councils are composed of elected delegates from local unions within a state, states, province, or provinces. District councils are responsible for collective bargaining and are the holders of "bargaining rights" on behalf of LIUNA members. LIUNA also has established national labour management funds that are responsible for training, health and safety, and promotion of unionized construction. The funds are referred to as the Tri-Funds. These unique funds, which are supported by joint contributions, provide a broad range of services to both labour and management.

# Size of Trade Unions in Canada

**Union density** measures the percentage of workers who belong to unions. In 2009, unions represent almost 32 percent (approximately 4.4 million) of all workers.[12] To contrast, when unions were most powerful, in 1984, they represented almost 42 percent of workers.[13] You can see that while union membership has been increasing, this has not always been reflected in an increase in union density. Why do you think that this is so? Figure 13.2 summarizes union membership and coverage by selected characteristics.

Before we discuss labour legislation, let us briefly look at two unions that are often in the news.

**union density**
A measure of the percentage of workers who belong to unions.

## The Canadian Union of Public Employees (CUPE)[14]

Formed in 1963, CUPE is Canada's largest union, with approximately 590,000 members. The union represents workers in sectors that include health care, education, municipalities, transportation, emergency services, and airlines. CUPE members are service providers, white-collar workers, technicians, labourers, skilled tradespeople, and professionals. More than half are women, and about one-third work part time. CUPE, like other unions, lobbies the government on a number of issues. For example, the Green Box highlights some of CUPE's suggestions on what the federal government should do to protect the environment.

**To learn more about CUPE (www.cupe.ca) and CAW (www.caw.ca), visit their Web sites.**

## The Canadian Auto Workers (CAW)[15]

The CAW was founded in 1985 after the Canadian members of the U.S.-based United Auto Workers (UAW) decided to form their own Canadian-controlled union. Today, the CAW is the largest private-sector union in Canada, representing 225,000 workers in all major sectors of the economy, as noted in Figure 13.3. Given the plant closings and restructuring over the past few years, it should not be surprising that the auto and vehicle manufacturing sectors represent 24 percent of union membership. Members are organized into approximately 266 local unions and 1,930 bargaining units.

| | | | |
|---|---|---|---|
| Public sector | 74.5 | Workplace size: Less than 100 employees | 23.1 |
| Private sector | 18.7 | Workplace size: 100 or more employees | 47.6 |
| Aged 15 to 24 | 15.0 | With same employer: Less than five years | 21.6 |
| Aged 25 and over | 35.0 | With same employer: More than five years | 43.9 |
| Full-time employee | 33.0 | Quebec | 39.7 |
| Part-time employee | 24.5 | Newfoundland and Labrador | 37.7 |
| Education: High school graduate or less | 25.7 | Alberta | 23.8 |
| Education: Post-secondary diploma | 36.1 | | |

**FIGURE 13.2**

**Union Density by Membership and Coverage by Selected Characteristics, 2007**

Source: Adapted from Statistics Canada publication *The Canadian Labour Market at a Glance*, Catalogue 71-222-XWE, issue 2007, release date: 25 November 2008, http://www.statcan.gc.ca/pub/71-222-x/2008001/c-g/desc/desc-k4-eng.htm.

## GreenBOX

### Protect the Environment

According to the Climate Change Performance Index 2008, Canada now ranks 53rd out of 56 countries. The Canadian Union of Public Employees (CUPE) feels that the federal Conservative government is to blame for this global ranking. Some of the government actions (and inactions) that have contributed to this standing are cited as follows: (1) federal climate change programs and initiatives to help low-income Canadians increase energy efficiency and reduce energy costs were slashed; (2) Canada has failed to meet its legal commitments under the Kyoto Protocol; (3) an effective plan to cut greenhouse gas emissions has not been developed; and (4) the Alberta oil sands developments have been allowed to grow unfettered, poisoning the air, natural landscape, water and drinking supply of communities in the process.

Some of CUPE's suggestions for federal government action that can be taken to improve Canada's ranking are noted below:

- Develop a climate change plan that will reach emissions reduction targets in line with what is called for by the international community.

- Impose a broad-based price on carbon to prompt greenhouse gas reductions.

- Pass meaningful regulations on industry and business to cut greenhouse gases.

- End federal government subsidies to the oil sands and implement comprehensive energy conservation programs and support for clean and renewable sources of energy.

- Create an aggressive green jobs strategy to develop new types of work, supported by a fair transition program for workers displaced by an evolving green and low-carbon economy.

- Invest in green technologies and innovation.

What do you think? Does such lobbying have an impact on government policies? Do you think that the suggestions are realistic given the economic and political climate?

Source: "Protect the Environment," Canadian Union of Public Employees, 1 October 2008, http://cupe.ca/2008-federal-election/Protect-the-environm.

---

**FIGURE  13.3**

**Canadian Auto Workers Sector Breakdown**

Source: "Facts - Sector Breakdown," Canadian Auto Workers, [2009?], http://www.caw.ca/en/media-centre-facts.htm. Used with permission.

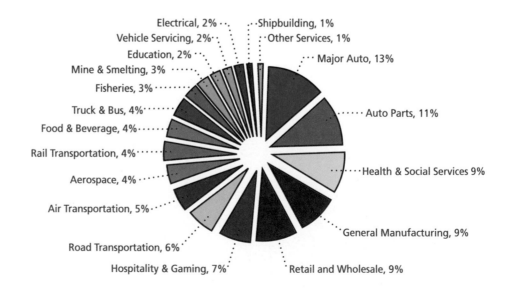

Electrical, 2% — Shipbuilding, 1%
Vehicle Servicing, 2% — Other Services, 1%
Education, 2% — Major Auto, 13%
Mine & Smelting, 3%
Fisheries, 3%
Truck & Bus, 4% — Auto Parts, 11%
Food & Beverage, 4%
Rail Transportation, 4%
Aerospace, 4% — Health & Social Services 9%
Air Transportation, 5%
Road Transportation, 6% — General Manufacturing, 9%
Hospitality & Gaming, 7% — Retail and Wholesale, 9%

### Progress Assessment

- Why were unions originally formed?
- List three reasons why union membership has been declining.
- Describe the structure of unions. Why would a union local affiliate itself with the CLC?

# LABOUR LEGISLATION

The growth and influence of organized labour in Canada have depended primarily on two major factors: the law and public opinion.

As with other movements for greater fairness and equity in our society—such as women's right to vote, equal rights for minorities and women, and protection for children—when support for employees' rights became widespread in Canada, laws were passed to enforce them. Today we have laws establishing minimum wage, paid minimum holidays and vacation, maximum hours, overtime pay, health and safety conditions, workers' compensation, employment insurance, the Canada/Quebec Pension Plan, and a host of other rights. It is strange to realize that at one time or another, these were all on the agenda of unions and were opposed by employers and governments for many years. They often denounced these demands as radical notions.

The effect of unions goes far beyond their numbers. Companies that want to keep unions out often provide compensation, benefits, and working conditions that match or exceed those found in union plants or offices. Thus, the levels established by unions spill over to non-union companies. Read the Spotlight on Small Business box for a look at some of the challenges associated with unionizing small businesses.

## SPOTLIGHT ON Small Business

### Unionizing in a Challenging Sector

Union coverage is lower in businesses that have fewer than 100 employees (23.1 percent) than for large businesses that have more than 100 employees (47.6 percent). As you read on, you will see why in some sectors creating a union is particularly challenging.

The very first Tim Hortons franchise opened in Hamilton, Ontario, in 1964. Today, the chain has 3,437 systemwide restaurants across Canada and the United States, and a handful of them are unionized. One such location is the first Tim Hortons franchise in Quebec, where in 2003 about 40 employees received union accreditation with Local 500R of the United Food and Commercial Workers. The majority of the 40 workers were women between the ages of 20 and 45. A spokesperson for the Quebec Federation of Labour stated that the approval was granted quickly due to a reform of the Quebec Labour Code. Gains under the employees' first collective agreement, which took a year to negotiate, included recognition of seniority, improved working conditions, and fairer shift allotments, said Quebec Federation of Labour spokesman Louis Fournier. "The negotiations were long because it was a first contract." The other two unionized Tim Hortons locations are in London, Ontario.

The organizing victory is a breakthrough of sorts for the workers, because unionizing restaurants is difficult. Unions often cite the high turnover among young workers as the main reason why there are few successful union drives in the sector. For example, about 75 percent of workers in Quebec's restaurant sector are younger than 20, according to Tony Filato, secretary-treasurer of UFCW 500R. They're not paid very well, and they don't stay in one place for too long. Consequently, organizing them is extremely challenging.

Sources: "Corporate Profile," Tim Hortons, 2008, http://www.timhortons.com/ca/en/about/profile.html; "Union Coverage Rates for Selected Job and Employee Characteristics, 2007," Statistics Canada, 25 November 2008, http://www.statcan.gc.ca/pub/71-222-x/2008001/c-g/desc/desc-k4-eng.htm; "First Union at a Tim Hortons in Quebec Gets Labour Relations Board Approval," *Foodservice News*, 14 August 2003, www.foodservice.com/news_homepage_expandtitle_fromhome.cfm?passid!E7238; "Do Workers Looking for Unions Need a BUB?" *MFS*, 3 September 2003, http://www.ufcw.net/articles/docs/2003-09-03_do_workers_need_a_bub.html; and "Employees Sign First Contract at Tim Hortons Only Union Store in Quebec," Canadian Press NewsWire, 11 August 2004, http://proquest.umi.com/pqdweb.

As indicated in Chapter 4, the federal government has control over specified fields of activity that are national in nature. In Chapter 12, it was mentioned that such activities apply to approximately 10 percent of Canadian workers. They work for banks, railways, airlines, telephone and cable systems, and radio and broadcasting companies. The federal government also has jurisdiction over many First Nations activities. Therefore, federal legislation applies to unions and labour–management relations in these businesses as well as to all federal Crown corporations and federal civil servants. The major legislation that governs labour–management relations for these employees is the Canada Labour Code, which is administered by Human Resources and Social Development Canada. It is also responsible for the Employment Equity Act as well as other legislation on wages and working conditions.

Provincial or territorial laws apply to the other 90 percent of the Canadian workforce. As you can imagine, these laws vary and it is the responsibility of businesses to know the rights of their workers and vice versa.

Employees can visit WorkRights (www. workrights.ca) to find out about work-related issues, including finding a job, getting paid, health and safety topics, and the work environment.

## Workplace Laws[16]

There are also various workplace laws in Canada that protect all workers. Be aware that they differ in detail in each province and territory.

One workplace law is the *right to know about workplace hazards*. By knowing about workplace hazards, workers can ensure that employers make work safer, provide protection to workers, and give training so that workers can work with the smallest possibility of injury or illness. Unfortunately, and in spite of some of the best workplace health and safety laws in the world, over 1,000 Canadian workers die each year due to an unsafe workplace. Employers have to do more work to enforce these laws and to protect their workers if this increasing trend is going to be reversed.

Another example is the *right to refuse unsafe work*, which entitles a worker to step away from work that he or she believes is unsafe. This right allows the worker to have the refused work investigated, and repaired if it's dangerous. During this time, the worker receives pay and is protected from an employer's possible reprisal, since it's illegal for an employer to fire or discipline a worker who refuses work that she or he believes is unsafe.

In 2006, workers at a Walmart store in St-Jean-Sur-Richelieu, Quebec, were ordered by management to help police search for a bomb, even though police recommended to company officials that the store should be completely evacuated. "This was a pretty sad message about how much value Walmart puts on the lives of its workers," said Wayne Hanley, national director of United Food and Commercial Workers (UFCW) Canada. "It makes you wonder what kind of information Walmart gives its employees about the labour laws."[17]

## Labour Relations Boards[18]

A labour relations board (LRB) is a quasi-judicial body consisting of representatives from government, labour, and business. It functions more informally than a court but it has the full authority of the law.

For example, the federal government has created the Canada Industrial Relations Board (CIRB). Its mandate is to contribute to and promote effective industrial relations in any work, undertaking, or business that falls within the authority of the Parliament of Canada. The CIRB plays an active role in helping parties resolve their disputes through mediation (to be discussed soon) and alternative dispute resolution approaches. It also undertakes a wide range of industrial relations activities, including the following:

- certifying trade unions
- investigating complaints of unfair labour practices
- issuing cease and desist orders in cases of unlawful strikes and lockouts
- rendering decisions on jurisdictional issues

The provincial governments have their own boards that oversee their specific legislation. The laws, regulations, and procedures vary from province to province.

# THE COLLECTIVE BARGAINING PROCESS

The Labour Relations Board (LRB) oversees **collective bargaining**, which is the process whereby union and management representatives negotiate a contract for workers. Collective bargaining includes how unions are selected, the period prior to a vote, certification, ongoing contract negotiations, and behaviour while a contract is in force and during a breakdown in negotiations for a renewal of contract. **Certification** is a formal process whereby a union is recognized by the LRB as the bargaining agent for a group of employees. **Decertification** is the process by which workers can take away a union's right to represent them.

The whole bargaining process and the important certification procedure are shown in detail in Figure 13.4. As you can see, the process is quite regulated and controlled so that employers and employees as well as unions have to follow a strict procedure to ensure that everybody is playing by the rules. For example, did you know that it is illegal for employers to fire employees for union activities? This process is also democratic, and as in any election, the minority has to accept the majority's decision.

The actual contract is quite complex, covering a wide range of topics. We will look at some of the major ones shortly.

## Objectives of Organized Labour

The objectives of unions frequently change because of shifts in social and economic trends. For example, in the 1970s the primary objective of unions was to obtain additional pay and benefits for their members. Throughout the 1980s, objectives shifted toward issues related to job security and union recognition. In the 1990s and early 2000s, unions again focused on job security, but the issue of global competition and its effects often took centre stage. Unions were a major opponent of NAFTA, passed by Parliament in 1994. They feared that their members would lose their jobs to low-wage workers in other countries. Today, we are seeing increasing emphasis on skills upgrading as the basis of job security. In some industries, union jobs have been declining due to outsourcing. Unions recognize that they must work closely with management if jobs are going to be kept within our borders. Having a skilled and productive workforce is one major way to do this. The Dealing with Change box shares what both management and labour may expect at the bargaining table given what is happening in the business environment.

According to Gerry Varricchio, Director of Organizing for Central and Eastern Canada for LIUNA, "Unions have a dual responsibility—to ensure that their members are getting the best wage and benefit packages and working conditions available in the marketplace, and equally as important, to ensure that their contractual employers not only remain competitive, but have a labour partner that can assist them in expanding their businesses and market share. In any market, competing on a level playing field is extremely important to the success and future growth of a business. The most effective vehicle for competing businesses to utilize in creating and sustaining a level playing

**collective bargaining**
The process whereby union and management representatives negotiate a contract for workers.

**certification**
Formal process whereby a union is recognized by the Labour Relations Board (LRB) as the bargaining agent for a group of employees.

**decertification**
Process by which workers can take away a union's right to represent them.

**FIGURE** | **13.4**

**Steps in Collective Bargaining**

Employees interested in joining a union contact a union representative.

The union campaigns for employees to sign union membership cards.

When enough cards are signed (each province/territory and the federal government has laws outlining the exact percentage of workers who must sign), an application to represent the employees is made by the union to the LRB.

The LRB reviews the application and will either order a vote or certify the union automatically, depending on the province/territory.

If employees vote for the union (each province/territory and the federal government has laws outlining the exact percentage of workers who must accept), it becomes the sole bargaining agent for that group of employees. This is known as certification.

A union local is established and members elect officers who appoint a negotiating committee to negotiate a contract with the employer.

Members vote to accept or reject the negotiated contract.

If accepted by the majority, the contract governs all of the working conditions during the contract. Strikes or lockouts are illegal while the contract is in force.

A grievance committee is set up with members from both sides to handle any contract violation complaints.

If a new contract is not negotiated before existing one expires, it still remains in force until various LRB conciliation procedures have been followed.

If disagreement persists, a strike or lockout is then legal; should either occur, the contract then lapses.

If the majority votes against the union, it is not certified and workers cannot reapply for another vote for six months or a year.

A large company may have several locations and the union local may be part of a larger unit that bargains with the employer on behalf of all employees, negotiating a master contract.

If rejected, the negotiating committee must try to renegotiate and come up with a contract that a majority of members will accept.

If an acceptable contract is not negotiated and the LRB conciliation procedures fail, then a strike or lockout may take place.

field, in their respective markets, is a union. Through the union structure and the collective bargaining process, employers can level off labour costs across entire markets and create optimum standards in training and health and safety practices that can be properly enforced through their collective agreements."[19]

The **negotiated labour–management agreement**, more informally referred to as the **labour contract**, clarifies the terms and conditions and sets the tone under which management and organized labour will function over a specific period. "Common sense and good business practice dictates the importance of having a binding written contract between parties engaged in a business transaction, thereby protecting the interests of all parties involved," says Varricchio. "Such a contract spells out the responsibilities and obligations of both parties, itemizes the compensation package agreed to for services rendered or products purchased, and identifies a mechanism to be employed to settle differences in the event either party violates the terms of the mutually agreed to contract. How much more important then is it to have such a contract between an employer and his/her employees that protects the interests of everyone, especially in an environment where the interaction between personalities could negatively impact the productivity of the workforce and the business?"[20] Figure 13.5 provides an abbreviated list of topics commonly negotiated by labour and management during contract talks, which often take a long time to complete.

## DEALING with CHANGE

### Industrial Relations Outlook: Managing Expectations in Uncertain Times

Over much of the last decade, the Canadian economy has enjoyed a "virtuous" economic cycle (e.g., low interest rates and inflation; an increase in employment, disposable income, and corporate profits; and a significant increase in consumption, investment, government spending, and net exports. But, those days are past. The state of the global financial markets, which has led to the near collapse of many economies and sapped consumer confidence, will significantly affect labour relations in 2009 and beyond.

Labour and management must manage their expectations while remaining focused on workplace issues that require ongoing attention. During past recessions, power shifted to management and labour paid the price. Firms are now powerless as the markets for their goods and services disintegrate and profits decline. Organizations in the hardest-hit sectors will be driven by the need to stay in business.

In the short and medium terms, unions, management, and government must address pension access and security concerns, as well as benefits issues for older workers. For employers and unions going to the bargaining table in 2009, there will be downward pressure on wage settlements until there is evidence of a global economic recovery. Private-sector industries will suffer until consumer demand and exports pick up. Public-sector settlements will be constrained by declining revenue and higher infrastructure spending, although wages might rise in sectors where workers are scarce, such as nursing.

Employers will focus on containing costs and improving productivity, while unions will struggle to save jobs. Negotiating issues such as pensions will be challenging, given their cost to the employers and the employees' need for long-term income security. However, in most cases, the economic threat to business will likely enable them to reach agreements without resorting to work stoppages. Negotiations in the public sector may be concluded with little fanfare, because governments have made it clear that their spending priorities are on developing infrastructure and funding the private sector, where appropriate.

Source: Used with permission of the Conference Board of Canada 2009.

1. Management rights
2. Union recognition
3. Union security clause
4. Strikes and lockouts
5. Union activities and responsibilities
   a. Dues checkoff
   b. Union notices
   c. Shop stewards on the floor
6. Wages
   a. Wage structure
   b. Shift differentials
   c. Wage incentives
   d. Bonuses
   e. Piecework conditions
   f. Tiered wage structures
7. Hours of work and time-off policies
   a. Regular hours of work
   b. Holidays
   c. Vacation policies
   d. Overtime regulations
   e. Leaves of absence
   f. Break periods
   g. Flextime
   h. Mealtime allotments
8. Job rights and seniority principles
   a. Seniority regulations
   b. Transfer policies and bumping
   c. Promotions
   d. Layoffs and recall procedures
   e. Job bidding and posting
9. Discharge and discipline
   a. Suspension
   b. Conditions for discharge
10. Grievance procedures
    a. Arbitration agreement
    b. Mediation procedures
11. Employee benefits, health, and welfare

**FIGURE 13.5**

**Issues in a Negotiated Labour–Management Agreement**
Labour and management often meet to discuss and clarify the terms that specify employees' functions within the company. The topics listed in this figure are typically discussed during these meetings.

**negotiated labour–management agreement (labour contract)**
Agreement that clarifies the terms and conditions and sets the tone under which management and labour agree to function over a period of time.

**union security clause**
Provision in a negotiated labour–management agreement that stipulates that employees who benefit from a union must either officially join or at least pay dues to the union.

**closed shop**
A workplace in which all new hires must already be union members.

**union shop**
A workplace in which the employer is free to hire anybody, but the recruit must then join the union within a short period, perhaps a month.

**agency shop (Rand formula)**
A workplace in which a new employee is not required to join the union but must pay union dues.

**open shop**
A workplace in which employees are free to join or not join the union and to pay or not pay union dues.

**check-off clause**
A contract clause requiring the employer to deduct union dues from employees' pay and remit them to a union.

Trade unions generally insist that contracts contain a **union security clause**, which stipulates that employees who reap benefits from a union must either officially join or at least pay dues to the union. There are basically four types of clauses:

1. The clause favoured by unions is called a **closed shop**, which means that all new hires must be union members. In effect, hiring is done through the union. Unemployed members of the union register for employment or show up daily at a union hiring hall.

2. One step down is a union shop. In a **union shop**, the employer is free to hire anybody but the recruit must then join the union within a short period, perhaps a month.

3. One of the most common conditions is an **agency shop**, which is based on the **Rand formula** that was devised by Supreme Court Justice Rand in 1946. The new employee is not required to join the union but must pay union dues. The argument for this requirement is that all employees who benefit from a contract signed by the union should help pay for the costs of maintaining that union—its officers, union expenses, negotiating committee, shop stewards, and so forth.

4. The hiring condition least popular with unions and the one favoured by employers is the **open shop**, where employees are free to join or not join the union and to pay or not pay union dues.

Regardless of which hiring condition prevails, the contract usually contains a **check-off clause** requiring the employer to deduct union dues from employees and pay and remit them to the union (except for non-members in an open shop). It would obviously be a lot harder to collect union dues individually.

How successful have trade unions been in negotiating improved wages and benefits for their members? Figure 13.6 summarizes some of the advantages of joining a union. This figure supports that higher average hourly wages and benefits are indeed one of the major benefits of joining a union.

In the future, the focus of union negotiations will most likely shift as issues such as child and elder care, worker retraining, two-tiered wage plans, outsourcing, employee empowerment, and even integrity and honesty testing further challenge union members' rights in the workplace. Unions also intend to carefully monitor immigration policies and global agreements to ensure that Canadian jobs are not lost.

Trade unions play a key workplace role in countries other than Canada as well. In Europe, organized labour is a major force throughout the continent. The Reaching Beyond Our Borders box discusses a formidable challenge the European unions face due to changing global markets.

**FIGURE | 13.6**

**Wage and Benefit Coverage Advantages of Joining a Union**

| Criteria | Union Employees | Non-Union Employees | Union Advantage |
|---|---|---|---|
| **WAGES** | | | |
| Full-time | $20.29 | $17.22 | $3.07 |
| Part-time | $17.31 | $10.60 | $6.71 |
| **BENEFIT COVERAGE** | | | |
| Pension Plan/Group RRSP | 83% | 33% | Yes |
| Better Paid Vacation Leave | 84% | 65% | Yes |
| Supplemental Health Care | 84% | 45% | Yes |
| Dental Plan | 77% | 45% | Yes |
| **HEALTH AND SAFETY COMPLIANCE** | 79% | 54% | Yes |

Source: "Why Join a Union," Alberta Federation of Labour, 2009, http://www.afl.org/need-a-union/why-join.cfm. Used with permission.

## Reaching Beyond Our Borders

### Are the Good Times Really Over for Good?

Over the past 30 years, European unions have been the envy of organized labour in North America. Powerful unions such as IG Metall (the leading labour union in Germany) negotiated some of the most worker-friendly contracts imaginable. For example, in Germany, the workweek for union workers was typically 35 hours per week; workers also received paid vacations ranging from five to nine weeks each year. Unions also had considerable control in the company boardrooms. The system of "co-determination" gave labour 50 percent of the seats on corporate boards, which laid the foundation for labour peace but limited the power of the management team. In France, the situation was similar. According to a law passed in 1998, French workers could only be required to work a maximum of 35 hours per week; of course, jobs were complemented by generous vacation benefits. It looks as if the life of a union worker in Europe is pretty good. Well, maybe.

As Bob Dylan once sang, "the times they are a-changin'." European unions, like their North American counterparts, are getting accustomed to givebacks. For example, unions at DaimlerChrysler agreed to scrap a pay raise and increase the workweek to 39 hours in exchange for a promise that 6,000 auto workers' jobs would remain in Germany for the next eight years. A similar agreement was reached at the Siemens factories, where workers agreed to a 40-hour workweek if the company agreed not to move jobs to Hungary. Similarly, union workers in Lyon, France, agreed to expand their workweek if the company promised not to relocate to the Czech Republic.

Managers feel that the establishment of the euro laid bare comparative wage costs across Europe. The problem for the unions is that the hourly wage rate varies greatly among the member countries of the European Union (EU). Wages in low-labour-cost countries such as Poland and the Czech Republic are about 20 percent of those in France or Germany; workers in those countries also spend about 500 more hours on the job each year. These realities have convinced many companies to move their operations to countries in Eastern Europe; some have even talked of moving to China. Talk has also surfaced to end "co-determination" in Germany. The high unemployment rates in Germany and France are also issues that work against the unions.

Unions promise to fight to protect the strength they built over the past three decades. Nonetheless, the draw of low-cost operations and declining public opinion may be too strong to fight off. One thing is for certain, the notoriously rigid labour markets of a few years back are most likely a thing of the past.

Sources: Matt Moore, "Germany's IG Metall Wants 5 Percent Wage Increase For Its 3.4 Million Members in 2006," AP Worldstream, 29 January 2006; Richard Milne, "German Steel Workers Close to Strike Over Pay," *Financial Times*, 10 May 2005, 3; and Jack Ewing and Justin Hibbard, "The Bell Tolls for Germany, Inc.," *Business Week*, 15 August 2005, 40–41.

## Resolving Labour–Management Disputes

The rights of labour and management are outlined in the negotiated labour–management agreement. Upon acceptance by both sides, the agreement becomes a guide to work relations between union members and managers. However, signing the agreement doesn't necessarily end the employee–management negotiations. There are sometimes differences concerning interpretations of the labour–management agreement. For example, managers may interpret a certain clause in the agreement to mean that they are free to select who works overtime. Union members may interpret the same clause to mean that managers must select employees for overtime on the basis of *employee seniority*. If controversies such as this cannot be resolved between the two parties, employees may file a grievance.

A **grievance** is a formal protest by an individual employee, with the support of the union, when they believe that management is not abiding by or fulfilling the terms of a labour contract. Companies in which relations between management and union are poor or deteriorating usually have a backlog of unresolved grievances. This is not good for the morale of the employees and, if allowed to continue for any length of time, will ultimately result in lower productivity. Where relations are good, there are few grievances and those that arise are quickly settled. Overtime rules, promotions, layoffs, transfers, job assignments, and so forth are generally sources of employee grievances.

**grievance**
A formal protest by an individual employee, with the support of the union, when they believe that management is not abiding by or fulfilling the terms of a labour contract.

**FIGURE** | **13.7**

**Stages in Processing Grievances**

| | Management | Union |
|---|---|---|
| **Stage 1** | First-level supervisor | Shop steward |
| **Stage 2** | Second-level supervisor | Chief steward |
| **Stage 3** | Plant manager | Chief grievance officer |
| **Stage 4** | Director of industrial relations | National or international union official |
| **Stage 5** | CEO or President | President of union or central labour body |
| **Stage 6** | Dispute goes to arbitration (quite rare) | |

**shop stewards**
Union officials who work permanently in an organization and represent employee interests on a daily basis.

Handling such grievances demands a good deal of contact between union officials and managers. Grievances, however, do not imply that the company has broken the law or the labour agreement. In fact, the vast majority of grievances are negotiated and resolved by **shop stewards** (union officials who work permanently in an organization and represent employee interests on a daily basis) and supervisory-level managers. However, if a grievance is not settled at this level, formal grievance procedures will begin.

Figure 13.7 indicates all steps, specified by the contract for a plant, in the processing of a grievance. Typically there are five or six levels in this procedure. If the grievance cannot be settled at one level, it moves up to the next level. The final step is an outside arbitrator or arbitration board (arbitration will be discussed after mediation). In practice, this is quite rare. Many complaints are settled informally and never put in writing.

## Conciliation, Mediation, and Arbitration

**bargaining zone**
Range of options between the initial and final offer that each party will consider before negotiations dissolve or reach an impasse.

During the negotiation process, there is generally what's called a **bargaining zone**, which is a range of options between the initial and final offer that each party will consider in reaching an agreement through collective bargaining. If labour–management negotiators aren't able to agree on alternatives within this bargaining zone, and negotiations dissolve or reach an impasse, conciliation is the next necessary step.

**conciliation**
A process by which a trade union or an employer must use the government's services (via the Ministry of Labour) for help in resolving their differences so that they can reach a collective agreement.

**Conciliation** is a process by which a trade union or an employer must use the government's services (via the Ministry of Labour) for help in resolving their differences so that they can reach a collective agreement.[21] If conciliation fails and both parties cannot reach an agreement, the Minister of Labour would then issue a "*no board*," which is a notice informing both parties that the Minister "does not consider it advisable to appoint a conciliation board." Conciliation boards are exceedingly rare and have not been appointed since the 1960s.[22] Once conciliation fails, the union is then in a legal position to strike and the employer is also free to declare a lockout (both will be discussed soon). After a "no board" is issued, the Ministry will also suggest mediation and offer to provide this service.

**mediation**
The use of a third party, called a mediator, who encourages both sides in a dispute to continue negotiating and often makes suggestions for resolving the dispute.

**Mediation** is the use of a third party, called a *mediator*, who encourages both sides in a dispute to consider negotiating and often makes suggestions for resolving the dispute. However, it's important to remember that mediators evaluate facts in the dispute and then make suggestions, not decisions.[23] Elected officials (current and past), attorneys, and professors are often called on to serve as mediators in labour disputes. For example, the Northwest Territories Power Corporation and its employees had been without a collective agreement for more than a year and, among other issues, the union wanted employees to receive the same salary as people who do similar work for the Northwest Territories government. The two parties required mediation to settle the contract.[24]

**arbitration**
An agreement to bring in an impartial third party (a single arbitrator or a panel of arbitrators) to render a binding decision in a labour dispute.

A more extreme approach used to resolve conflict is arbitration. **Arbitration** is an agreement to bring in an impartial third party (a single arbitrator or a panel of arbitrators) to render a binding decision in a labour dispute. Arbitration may be voluntary; both sides decide to submit their case to an arbitrator. Arbitration may also be compulsory; imposed by the government or by Parliament or a provincial legislature. Compulsory arbitration usually occurs in a major or prolonged strike with serious consequences for the public. Usually, non-grievance arbitration (say, for contract disputes) is voluntary and grievance arbitration is compulsory. Employees who are designated as having essential positions (e.g., police, firefighters, and hospital employees) don't have the right to strike as stated in their collective agreements and their disputes must be settled through binding arbitration.[25] This topic will be briefly discussed later on in the chapter.

It should be noted that both mediation and arbitration can be difficult, lengthy, and costly procedures, especially when both sides are locked into rigid positions. That is why negotiators from both sides usually try to settle their differences before resorting to these steps.

## Progress Assessment

- How do labour relations boards regulate labour–management relations?
- In the collective bargaining process, what happens after certification?
- What is the difference between conciliation, mediation, and arbitration?

# NEGOTIATION TACTICS

If labour and management cannot reach an agreement through collective bargaining and negotiations break down, either side or both sides may use specific tactics to enhance their negotiating position and perhaps sway public opinion. Keep in mind that today the great majority of labour negotiations end successfully without the disruption of a strike or lockout. Remember that mediation and arbitration are always available to the parties in dispute. They may take advantage of these procedures before, during, or after any of these tactics are exercised. Let us look at some examples next.

## Union Tactics

The primary tactics used by organized labour are strikes and boycotts. Unions might also use picketing and work slowdowns to get desired changes.

### Strikes

Strikes have historically been the most potent tactic that unions use to achieve their objectives in labour disputes. A **strike** occurs when workers collectively refuse to go to work. Strikes can attract public attention to a labour dispute and at times cause operations in a company to slow down or totally cease.

**strike**
A union strategy in which workers refuse to go to work.

Prior to the actual strike, union leaders call for a *strike vote*, which is a secret ballot authorizing the union leadership to call a strike. This democratic vote is necessary if a potential strike is to be considered legal. If the union gets a strong mandate—say, more than 80 percent in favour of a strike—it can use this as a lever to convince management to accept its demands without actually going on strike.

Union tactics include rotating strikes—on and off or alternating among different plants or cities—rather than a full-fledged strike in which all employees are off the job for the duration. With rotating strikes, employees still get some pay, which is not the case in an all-out strike. Many unions build up a strike fund from union dues and use it to give their members strike pay, but that's usually a fraction of their normal wages. Sometimes, in important or long-lasting strikes, other unions will give moral or financial aid.

Strikes sometimes lead to the resolution of a labour dispute; however, they also have generated violence and extended bitterness. Often after a strike is finally settled both labour and management remain openly hostile toward each other and mutual complaints of violations of the negotiated labour–management agreement continue.

**wildcat strike**
An unauthorized (by the union) work stoppage while a labour contract is still in effect.

A **wildcat strike** is an unauthorized (by the union) work stoppage while a labour contract is still in effect.[26] An example of this occurred as the result of increasing tension between Toronto Transit Commission (TTC) workers and the TTC. Maintenance workers, angered at being forced into permanent overnight shifts, were quickly joined by drivers, who had their own safety concerns, for a one-day wildcat strike in May 2006. Eric Lascelles, a strategist at Toronto-Dominion Bank, estimated that the strike could cost the local economy roughly $10 million in lost productivity as 800,000 commuters were forced to find alternate modes of transportation. The Ontario Labour Relations Board issued a cease and desist order to force employees back to work. Bob Kinnear, president of the Amalgamated Transit Union, warned that the relationship between union and management could get worse and "the problems have not gone away."[27]

## Boycotts

**primary boycott**
When a union encourages both its members and the general public not to buy the products of a firm involved in a labour dispute.

Unions can use boycotts as a means to obtain their objectives in a labour dispute. A **primary boycott** occurs when organized labour encourages both its members and the general public not to buy the products or services of a firm involved in a labour dispute. Such was the case when striking employees at the Browning Harvey Ltd. bottling plant in St. John's took their pickets to retail stores, encouraging consumers not to buy Pepsi products for as long as the dispute lasted.[28] A **secondary boycott** is an attempt by labour to convince others to stop doing business with a firm that is the subject of a primary boycott. For example, a union can initiate a secondary boycott against a supermarket chain because the chain carries goods produced by a company that is the target of a primary boycott.

**secondary boycott**
An attempt by labour to convince others to stop doing business with a firm that is the subject of a primary boycott.

## Picketing

Strikers may also picket the company, which means that they walk around the outside of the organization carrying signs and talking with the public and the media about issues in the labour dispute. Picket obstruction is illegal, but by slowing down anyone or anything from entering or leaving, strikers ensure that things are not "business as usual" for the company with the hope that negotiations will continue. Unions also use picketing as an informational tool before going on strike. The purpose is to alert the public to an issue that is stirring labour unrest, even though no strike has been voted.

**Diamonds produced in Canada's Arctic by BHP Billiton at the Ekati diamond mine are being marketed as a "conflict-free" alternative to diamonds from war-torn countries.**

But today Canadian AURIAS™ and CanadaMark™ diamonds are being produced in a conflict – behind a **picket line** set up by 385 diamond mine workers who have been on strike at Ekati for over two months to win a first contract.

The Ekati workers, many of them aboriginal people from Canada's north, are only asking for fair treatment.

But **BHP Billiton** – an Australian multinational that made US$6.5 billion in profits last year – won't negotiate a reasonable deal.

And BHP Billiton is using **strikebreakers** to operate the Ekati diamond mine despite the strike by workers represented by the Public Service Alliance of Canada/Union of Northern Workers.

Ekati workers **urgently** need your help.

**PLEASE SEND BHP BILLITON A MESSAGE – tell them you support a fair first contract with Ekati workers – and that you don't want BHP Billiton's dirty diamonds from Canada!**

SEND BHP BILLITON A MESSAGE:
**No to AURIAS™ Dirty Diamonds from Canada!**

To send BHP Billiton a message and for more information on the Ekati diamond mine strike please go to our websites:
**www.unw.ca. www.psacnorth.com**

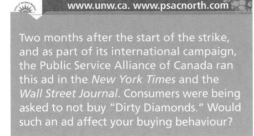

Two months after the start of the strike, and as part of its international campaign, the Public Service Alliance of Canada ran this ad in the *New York Times* and the *Wall Street Journal*. Consumers were being asked to not buy "Dirty Diamonds." Would such an ad affect your buying behaviour?

## Other Tactics[29]

*Sabotage*, where workers damage their machines; *sit-ins*, where they occupy the workplace and refuse to move; or *work-to-rule*, where they follow the operating rules of the workplace in every detail to slow down the work, are other tactics that have been used by union members. About 15,000 unionized employees at TELUS, after having been without a contract for nearly five years, began a work-to-rule campaign. Among other suggestions by the union executive, employees were encouraged to plan the safest route to their next job site (which may not be the shortest route), take all scheduled breaks, and provide "super service" by making sure that customer needs were fully met and that Telus workers take the time to explain all options to customers. What would the implications be to the company as a result of these suggestions?

## Management Tactics

Like labour, management also uses specific tactics to achieve its workplace goals. Management may announce layoffs or a shortened workweek and blame it on declining business. It may say the company is having trouble competing due to high labour costs. Quite often, management may continue to work and try to do some of the tasks formerly done by the striking workforce. Let us look briefly at how management also considers the use of lockouts, injunctions, and strikebreakers.

## Lockouts

A **lockout** is an attempt by managers to put pressure on union workers by temporarily closing the business. It may seem less costly to close down and cease paying wages than to put up with slowdowns, rotating strikes, or work-to-rule union tactics, all of which can be very disruptive. This tactic may force the union to reduce its demands if individual members cannot do without an income for very long or if there is a weak strike-vote majority. The high-profile lockout of National Hockey League (NHL) players that caused the cancellation of the entire 2004–2005 season is just one example of this tactic being exercised.

Clearly, a strike is a weapon of last resort for unions, to be used when all else fails. Similarly, management is reluctant to lock out its employees and call a halt to operations. Without products and services, there are no profits.

## Injunctions

An **injunction** is a court order directing someone to do something or to refrain from doing something. Management has sought injunctions to order striking workers back to work, limit the number of pickets that can be used during a strike, or otherwise deal with actions that could be detrimental to the public welfare. For a court to issue an injunction, management must show a "just cause," such as the possibility of violence or the destruction of property. The use of strikebreakers has been a particular source of hostility and violence in labour relations.

TELUS workers staged a walkout to protest an attempt by the company to eliminate many restrictions on the contracting out of work in its contract. TELUS immediately locked out the 12,500 workers, retained the services of professional strikebreakers, and sought injunctions to limit picketing. The lockout lasted for almost three months.

## Strikebreakers

Sometimes, a company may try to bring in replacement workers. These workers, also known as **strikebreakers** (called *scabs* by unions), are workers who are hired to do the jobs of striking employees until the labour dispute is resolved. This often leads to violence. Picketers mass in large numbers to block buses carrying these strikebreakers, threats are uttered, articles are thrown, vehicles may be attacked, and so on.

British Columbia and Quebec have legislation banning the use of replacement workers in their provinces. At the time this chapter was written, there was no federal legislation that would put an end to the use of replacement workers during strikes and lockouts in workplaces covered by the Canada Labour Code. Supporters of such legislation cite fewer days lost due to strikes and lockouts and a quick and peaceful settlement of disputes as benefits if such legislation were to be passed.[30] Be sure to read the Making Ethical Decisions box on this issue for further insight.

## Battle for Public Support

In major cases where the public is affected—the postal service, nurses, doctors, teachers, transportation, telecommunication, and civil servants at all levels—each side plays a propaganda game to win the public to its side. It can be difficult for those not directly involved to sort out the issues. Sometimes management, if it thinks that the public is on its side and the union is perhaps not well organized or lacks strong support, will provoke the union into an unsuccessful strike, weakening the union's bargaining position.

# Legislation

Essential services have traditionally been those provided 24 hours a day, 7 days a week, 365 days a year, such as health care, police officers, and firefighters.[31] Under the Labour

**lockout**
An attempt by management to put pressure on unions by temporarily closing the business.

**injunction**
A court order directing someone to do something or to refrain from doing something.

**strikebreakers**
Replacement workers hired to do the jobs of striking employees until the labour dispute is resolved.

## Making Ethical Decisions

### Crossing the Line or Double-Crossing?

Assume that you read over the weekend that More-4-Less, a grocery chain in your town, is seeking workers to replace members of the Commercial Food Workers Union who are currently on strike against the company. Some of the students at your school are employed at More-4-Less and are supporting the strike, as are several people employed by the company in your neighbourhood. More-4-Less argues that its management has made a fair offer to the union and that the demands of the workers are clearly excessive and could ruin the company. More-4-Less is offering an attractive wage rate and flexible schedules to workers willing to cross the picket line and work during the strike. As a student, you could certainly use the job and the extra money for tuition and expenses. What would you do? What will be the consequences of your decision? Is your choice ethical? What are the ethical dilemmas faced by unions? Give some examples. How do these differ from those faced by management?

Relations Code, essential services legislation restricts the right to strike of various levels of civil servants and quasi-government employees such as hospital workers and electric and telephone utility workers. The provinces and the federal government forbid some employees under their jurisdiction from striking. In other cases, certain minimum levels of service must be provided.

Federal or provincial governments have the power to end a particular strike by passing back-to-work legislation. **Back-to-work legislation** orders an end to a labour–management dispute that has escalated to a strike or lockout, in an industry that the government decides is essential to the operation of the economy.[32] Such legislation has been used to end strikes by teachers, nurses, postal workers, bus drivers, and others. Governments pass back-to-work legislation when they believe they have enough support among the population for such action because of serious hardship to businesses or individuals. Such was the case when the Ontario legislature passed back-to-work legislation in early 2009 mandating that the almost 3,300 contract professors and teaching, graduate and research assistants at York University (who had been bargaining for improved job security for contract staff, and more funding for graduate students, among other issues) return to work.[33] For three months about 45,000 students had been out of class and mediation had failed to resolve the issues.[34]

**back-to-work legislation**
Legislation that orders an end to a labour–management dispute that has escalated to a strike or lockout, in an industry that the government decides is essential to the operation of the economy.

Do you recall reading about the York University strike? Would this have impacted your decision to apply to York University if you had been considering this school?

Union supporters believe that back-to-work legislation is a denial of the legal right to strike, therefore to a certain extent it is a restriction of the democratic rights of individuals. Consequently, there is often much controversy about such legislation. It is rarely used to deal with strikes against private businesses. If union members remain on strike after they have been legislated back to work, they are engaging in an illegal strike and are subject to punishment (e.g., substantial fines), as are all lawbreakers.

# THE FUTURE OF UNIONS AND LABOUR– MANAGEMENT RELATIONS

As mentioned earlier, many new issues have emerged that have affected union–management relations. They include increased global competition, advancing technology, outsourcing, and the changing nature of work. To save jobs, many unions have granted concessions, or **givebacks**, to management. In such acts, union members give back previous gains from labour negotiations. For example, in 2003 the CAW Local 2002 agreed to $150 million in payroll savings over each of the next six years to give Air Canada the funding relief it needed to complete its restructuring.[35] The Air Canada flight attendants, members of CUPE's Airline Division, also agreed to concessions that would save the airline $1.1 billion a year for six years.[36] Review the Analyzing Management Decisions discussion near the end of the chapter for a longer discussion on this topic.

**givebacks**
Concessions made by union members to management; previous gains from labour negotiations are given up to help employers remain competitive and thereby save jobs.

It's safe to assume that unions in the twenty-first century are likely to be quite different than in the past.[37] Union members understand that companies must remain competitive with foreign firms, and organized labour must do its best to maintain Canada's competitiveness.[38] (So too, must businesses.) Many unions have already taken on a new role in assisting management in training workers, redesigning jobs, and assimilating the changing workforce. They are also helping to recruit and train foreign workers, unskilled workers, and any others who need special help in adapting to the job requirements of the new economy. For co-operating with management, unions can expect improved job security, profit-sharing, and sometimes increased wages. Management can expect a productive, dedicated workforce to handle the challenges of growing competition.[39]

Joseph S. Mancinelli, International Vice-President for Central and Eastern Canada of LIUNA, understands these challenges and opportunities. According to Mancinelli, "Pensions, level of skills, quality of work, productivity, and safety in the workplace have become our new challenges. These challenges cannot be met through adversarial conflict, but in a new era of unionism, through good relations with our employer partners. Good relations are paramount in ensuring such progress and evolution. Working closely with our employer partners can produce more benefits for our members, our employers, and the entire construction industry. In recognition of this fact, LIUNA has established a labour– employer co-operation trust specifically set up for both parties to work together, outside of the bargaining table, every day of the year to find creative and innovative solutions and initiatives that result in an ongoing win-win scenario for both labour and management. Concurrently, LIUNA has actively pursued public-private partnerships. Through the Labourers' Pension Fund of Central and Eastern Canada, sound, financially viable partnerships have evolved resulting in a doubly viable result: excellent returns on pension fund dollars and employment opportunities for our members across the country. An example of this relationship is LIUNA joining numerous construction companies to build several hospitals throughout the province of Ontario."[40]

PARTNERSHIP. THE FOUNDATION OF STRENGTH

Through the open and ongoing cooperation of Labour and Management, LIUNA and its contractor partners across Ontario are increasing market share, training for efficient work practices and discovering new technologies that revolutionize the construction industry.

LIUNA's employee–employer relationships embrace new technologies that advance the industry and provide a trained workforce for an ever-changing construction market.

How other trade unions and management groups handle such challenges may well define the future of trade unions in Canada. After the Progress Assessment, we will look at other issues facing employees and managers in the twenty-first century.

---

## Progress Assessment

- Why do the objectives of unions change over time?
- What are the major tactics used by unions and by management to assert their power in contract negotiations?
- When is back-to-work legislation used?

---

# CURRENT EMPLOYEE–MANAGEMENT TOPICS

This is an interesting time in the history of employee–management relations. Organizations are involved in global expansion, outsourcing, and technology changes. The government has eliminated some social benefits to workers. For example, employment insurance eligibility requirements overall are stricter today than they were ten years ago. In other instances, the government is taking a more active role in mandating what benefits and assurances businesses must provide to workers. The extension of maternity leave benefits from six months to one year in 2001 and the implementation of a new compassionate care program in 2004 are just two such instances.

It is important to note that all employees are protected under the Employment Standards Act. Recall that this Act covers issues such as minimum wage, holiday pay, and so on. In a non-union environment, if an employer violates the Act, it is up to the employee to file a complaint. An employee may seek advice and assistance from an officer of the Ministry of Labour in the province where he or she works. The employee can also contact the Canadian Human Rights Commission or a Human Resources and Skills Development Canada office, where he or she can talk to a federal government labour affairs officer.

Union supporters point out that a labour contract would further protect workers, as the union would represent the employee if there were a breach of the Act or the labour contract. If an employee is not part of a trade union, there is no legal contract with the employer. Keep in mind that official legal protection isn't very meaningful without effective enforcement.

Employees today are raising questions about fairness and workplace benefits. They are looking increasingly at company policies as they apply to workplace discrimination (e.g., wages and sexual orientation), sexual harassment, and mandatory testing (e.g., HIV, alcohol, and drug testing). Three other areas that are increasingly in the news are executive compensation, child care, and elder care. Let us briefly look at each of these areas.

The Canadian Human Rights Commission is empowered to investigate and try to settle complaints of discrimination in employment and in the provision of services within federal jurisdiction. The Commission is also mandated to develop and conduct information and discrimination prevention programs.

www.chrc-ccdp.gc.ca

CANADIAN
HUMAN RIGHTS
COMMISSION

Canadä

# Executive Compensation

Is it out of line for some of Canada's top executives to make tens of millions of dollars in annual compensation? Consider the total direct compensation (which includes salary, bonus, and stock incentives) received by some of Canada's top executives in 2007: William Doyle (CEO of Potash Corporation of Saskatchewan Inc.) received approximately $320.4 million; executives James Balsillie and Michael Lazaridis (Research in Motion Ltd.) were paid approximately $178.5 million; and Gerald Schwartz (Onex Corporation) took home approximately $61.7 million.[41] According to research conducted by the Canadian Centre for Policy Alternatives (CCPA), individual total compensation packages in 2007 for the top 100 CEOs at publicly-listed Canadian companies increased an average of 22 percent to $10.4 million. This compared to a pay hike of 3.2 percent to $40,237 for the average Canadian worker during 2007. Between 1998 and 2007, the average compensation of top CEOs increased by 147 percent, adjusted for inflation. This compared with a 3 percent decline in inflation-adjusted weekly wages for average Canadians and a 6 percent rise for those paid the minimum wage.[42]

In Chapter 2, we explained that the free-market system is built on incentives that allow top executives to make such large amounts—or more. Today, however, the government, boards of directors, shareholders, unions, and employees are challenging this principle and arguing that executive compensation has gotten out of line. In fact, way out of line.

In times past, CEO compensation and bonuses were determined by the firm's profitability or an increase in its stock price.[43] The logic of this assumption was that as the fortunes of a company and its stockholders grew, so would the rewards of the CEO. Today, however, executives generally receive *stock options* (the ability to buy company stock at a set price at a later date) and *restricted stock* (stock issued directly to the CEO that cannot be sold for about three or four years) as part of their compensation.[44] Many believe that a problem arises when executives are so compensated even when the company does not meet expectations. There are some exceptions. For example, Loblaw Cos. Ltd. chairman Galen Weston and then-president John Lederer declined to accept bonuses for 2005 after the Canadian supermarket chain's profit fell for the first time in 13 years.[45] What's even more frustrating to some people, however, is when a CEO whose poor performance forced him or her to resign walks away with a large compensation.[46] Many CEOs are also awarded fat retainers, consulting contracts, and lavish perks when they retire.[47]

The late management consultant Peter Drucker criticized executive pay levels and he suggested that CEOs should not earn more than 20 times the salary of the company's lowest-paid employee. Many companies have clearly ignored this advice. For example, in 2007, Canada's top 50 CEOs earned 398 times more than the average worker compared with 85 times in 1995.[48] As global competition intensifies, it's worth noting that American CEOs typically earn two to three times as much as executives in Canada and Europe.[49] In European countries such as Germany, workers account for 50 percent of the seats on the boards of directors of major firms according to a process called codetermination.[50] Since boards set executive pay, this could be a reason why the imbalance in pay is less for European executives than for their American counterparts. Graef Crystal, a pay consultant and expert on corporate governance, has long suggested a link between CEO compensation and executive-friendly boards of directors that are often paid well for a modest amount of work.[51]

Pressure from government and dissatisfied shareholders for full disclosure concerning executive compensation promises to put boards of directors on notice that they are not there simply to enrich CEOs.[52] While the federal government has no immediate plans to put caps or restrictions on the pay of chief executives (like those seen in the United States and the United Kingdom), it has welcomed the voluntary return of bonuses: "Many of the top 100 publicly-traded Canadian companies include Canada's big bank CEOs, who recently received billions in federal government bailout money to purchase mortgage loans. Gordon Nixon, CEO of The Royal Bank of Canada, was the first to announce he was returning $5 million of his bonus. The rich gesture of some of the bank CEOs underlines the heightened sensitivity of bank chiefs to a brewing political backlash following a crisis in the banking system that continues to weaken the global economy and force governments to intervene."[53]

It's important to recognize, however, that many executives are responsible for multi-billion-dollar corporations and work 70-plus hours a week. Many can show that their decisions turned potential problems into success and rewards for employees and share-holders as well as themselves.[54] Clearly, there is no easy answer to the question of what constitutes fair compensation for executives, but it's a safe bet that the controversy will not go away.

## Child Care

Child care became an increasingly important workplace issue as questions involving responsibilities for child-care subsidies, child-care programs, and even parental leave have spurred much debate in the private and public sectors of the economy. Many workers strongly question workplace benefits for parents, and argue that single workers and single-income families should not subsidize child care for dual-income families. Although men are increasingly shouldering child-care responsibility, most of that responsibility still falls on women. This often leads to greater stress and absenteeism in the workplace. Employers are increasingly concerned as businesses lose millions annually in lost productivity. Employee child care also raises the controversial workplace question of who should pay for child-care services.

The number of companies that offer child care as an employee benefit is growing. *Working Mother* magazine highlighted companies such as Colgate-Palmolive, IBM, and General Mills as being particularly sympathetic to working mothers.[55] Other large firms that offer extensive child-care programs include Johnson & Johnson, American Express, and Campbell Soup. A few companies even provide emergency child-care services for employees whose children are ill or whose regular child-care arrangements are disrupted.

As the number of single-parent and two-income households continues to grow in the twenty-first century, child care is certain to remain a hotly debated employee–management issue. However, a new workplace storm is brewing over an issue employees and managers have not faced in times past: elder care. Let's look at this next.

## Elder Care

The workforce in Canada is aging. While baby boomers will not have to concern themselves with finding child care for their children, they will confront another problem: how to care for older parents and other relatives. In the future, more workers are expected to be involved in the time-consuming and stressful task of caring for an aging relative. Current estimates suggest that companies are seeing reduced productivity, and increased absenteeism and turnover from employees who are responsible for aging relatives.[56] Denise Talbot-White, a gerontology specialist for MetLife Mature Market Institute, suggests that elder care is the child care of the new millennium.

Employees with elder-care responsibilities need information on medical, legal, and insurance issues, as well as the full support of their supervisors and company. This issue may require some employees to switch to flextime, telecommuting, part-time employment, or job sharing.[57] Some firms have reacted to the effect of elder care on their workforce. At Boeing and AT&T, employees are offered elder-care programs that include telephone hotlines that workers can call to seek help or counselling for older relatives. Unfortunately, few companies (large, medium, or small) now provide any type of elder-care programs or benefits.

Andrew Scharlach, a professor of aging at the University of California—Berkeley, expects costs to companies to rise even higher as more and more experienced and high-ranking employees become involved in caring for older parents and other relatives. His arguments make sense. Since the jobs older workers hold are often more critical to a company than those held by younger workers (who are most affected by child-care problems), many businesses will see the cost of elder care skyrocket. Already, many firms note that transfer and promotion decisions are especially difficult for employees whose elderly parents need ongoing care. Unfortunately, as Canadians age, the elder-care situation will grow considerably worse. With an aging workforce, this employee–management issue promises to persist well into the twenty-first century.

## YOU AND UNIONS

Do you think that unions are still necessary? We are fortunate to be living in a democratic country where free and private enterprise is the vital feature of our economic system. We believe that all citizens have the right to do what they can, within legal and ethical limits, to better themselves. Improving your financial situation is an admired goal, and those who do so are usually seen as good examples.

If you select the entrepreneurial route, you will try to build a successful company by providing a necessary service or product in a manner that your customers appreciate. If you are successful, you will ultimately accumulate profits and personal wealth and financial security for yourself and your family. One of the costs of doing business that you will be keeping an eye on is wages, salaries, and benefits paid to employees. Will you want a well-trained, smart workforce capable of keeping up with the rapid pace of technological advances, or will you want your employees to work "cheap"? Will you consider unions nothing but a hindrance?

Suppose that you do not see yourself as an entrepreneur and instead go the employee route. Imagine yourself ten years down the road: you have a partner and two children and are now a computer specialist working for a large company in a non-managerial role. Will you seek the best salary you can possibly get? How about working hours? Your partner also works and you need flexible arrangements to be able to spend time with your children and deliver them to school and various other activities. How about overtime demands on the job that cut into time with your children? Will you have adequate, affordable child care?

Can you and your co-workers arrange these and a host of other issues—bonuses, sick leave, termination pay, pensions, retraining, holidays, and more—on a personal basis? Or are you better off with an organization, such as the CAW union, to represent all of you in making proper contractual arrangements with your employer so that your rights and obligations, as well as the employer's, are clearly spelled out?

What about all of the workers who are less skilled than you are? Some are illiterate and others did not graduate from high school. Thousands of employees have lost their jobs in the past decade through no fault of their own. Do they need a strong union to protect their interests? Hopefully this chapter has given you an understanding of the importance of employee–management issues.

In summary, firms that have healthy employee–management relations have a better chance to prosper than those that do not. As managers, taking a proactive approach is the best way to ensure workable employee–management environments. The proactive manager anticipates potential problems and works toward resolving those issues before they get out of hand—a good lesson to remember.

The CAW union is lobbying the government to improve the standards under which employees provide care for seniors with nursing services, personal care, or rehabilitation. The union believes that the decline in quality care for patients runs parallel to a decline in working conditions for care providers. Would you support such a campaign?

## Progress Assessment

- How does top-executive pay in Canada compare with top-executive pay in other countries?

- What are some of the issues related to child care and elder care, and how are companies addressing those issues?

# SUMMARY

**LO ▶ 1** Trace the history of organized labour in Canada.

1. Organized labour in Canada dates back to the 1800s. Early unions on the wharves of Halifax, St. John's, and Quebec existed during the War of 1812 to profit from labour scarcity. Craft unions represented shoemakers and printers. Many of the early labour organizations were local or regional in nature.

**Describe some of the main objectives of labour and whether they were achieved.**
Unions hoped to improve workers' poor conditions and wages by forming unions that would fight for workers' rights. This has largely been achieved, and many early demands are now entrenched in law.

**Describe some of the unions in existence today.**
The Canadian Union of Public Employees (CUPE) and the Canadian Auto Workers (CAW) are two of the largest unions in Canada. They represent workers from different sectors in the economy. Many unions in Canada are national in nature. Many also belong to international organizations. The Canadian Labour Congress, which represents over 3 million unionized workers, is the national voice of the labour movement in Canada.

**LO ▶ 2** Discuss the major legislation affecting trade unions.

2. Much labour legislation has been passed by federal and provincial governments.

**What is the major piece of labour legislation?**
The Canada Labour Code outlines labour legislation as it applies to federal government employees, who represent approximately 10 percent of all workers in Canada. Each provincial jurisdiction in Canada has its own labour legislation and employment standards that apply to workers within its borders.

**LO ▶ 3** Understand the collective bargaining process.

3. Collective bargaining is the process by which a union represents employees in relations with their employer.

**What is included in collective bargaining?**
Collective bargaining includes how unions are selected, the period prior to a vote, certification, ongoing contract negotiations, and behaviour while a contract is in force.

**What are the steps in the collective bargaining process?**
Refer to Figure 13.4 for the steps in the collective bargaining process.

**LO ▶ 4** Outline the objectives of trade unions.

4. The objectives of trade unions shift in response to changes in social and economic trends.

**What topics typically appear in labour–management agreements?**
Labour–management agreements may include issues such as management rights, union security clauses, hours of work, vacation policies, job rights and seniority principles, and employee benefits. See Figure 13.5 for a more exhaustive list.

**LO ▶ 5** Describe the negotiation tactics used by labour and management during conflicts, and discuss the role of unions in the future.

5. If negotiations between labour and management break down, either or both sides may use certain tactics to enhance their position or sway public opinion.

**What are the tactics used by unions and management in conflicts?**
Unions can use strikes, boycotts, and picketing. Management can use lockouts, injunctions, and strikebreakers.

**What will unions have to do to cope with declining membership?**
To grow, unions will have to adapt to an increasingly white-collar, female, and culturally diverse workforce. To help keep businesses competitive in international markets, unions must soften their historical "us-versus-them" attitude and build a new "we" attitude with management.

6. Some employee–management issues are executive compensation, child care, and elder care.

**LO ▶ 6** Explain some of today's employee–management issues.

**What is a fair wage for managers?**

The market and the businesses in it set managers' salaries. What is fair is open to debate.

**How are some companies addressing the child care issue?**

Responsive companies are providing child care on their premises, discounts with child-care chains, vouchers to be used at the employee's chosen care centre, and referral services.

**What is elder care, and what problems do companies face with regard to this growing problem?**

Workers with older parents or other relatives often need to find some way to care for them. Elder care is becoming a problem that will perhaps outpace the need for child care. Workers who need to care for dependent parents are generally more experienced and vital to the mission of the organization than younger workers are. The cost to business is very large and growing.

## KEY TERMS

| | | |
|---|---|---|
| agency shop (Rand formula)  402 | decertification  399 | primary boycott  406 |
| arbitration  404 | givebacks  409 | secondary boycott  406 |
| back-to-work legislation  408 | grievance  403 | shop stewards  404 |
| bargaining zone  404 | industrial union  393 | strike  405 |
| certification  399 | injunction  407 | strikebreakers  407 |
| check-off clause  402 | lockout  407 | union  390 |
| closed shop  402 | mediation  404 | union density  395 |
| collective bargaining  399 | negotiated labour–management agreement (labour contract)  400 | union security clause  402 |
| conciliation  404 | | union shop  402 |
| craft union  392 | open shop  402 | wildcat strike  406 |

## CRITICAL THINKING

1. Do you believe that union shop agreements are violations of a worker's freedom of choice in the workplace?

2. Why are unionization rates much higher in the public sector than in the private sector?

3. Do businesses and government agencies have a duty to provide additional benefits to employees beyond fair pay and good working conditions? Does providing benefits such as child care and elder care to some employees discriminate against those who do not require such assistance? Propose a benefits system that you consider fair and workable for both employees and employers.

4. What are the disadvantages of joining a union?

5. Do you agree that back-to-work legislation is a denial of the legal right to strike, therefore to a certain extent it is a restriction of the democratic rights of individuals?

# DEVELOPING WORKPLACE SKILLS

1. Debate the following statement with several classmates: Non-union firms are better managed (or perform better) than unionized firm. To get a better feeling for the other side's point of view, take the opposite side of this issue from the one you normally would. Include information from outside sources to support your position.

2. Top executives' high pay creates tremendous incentives for lower-level executives to work hard to get those jobs. Their high pay also creates resentment among workers, shareholders, and members of the general public. Debate the following in class: Business executives receive a total compensation package that is far beyond their value. They should not earn more than twenty times the compensation of the lowest-paid worker at the firm. Take the opposite side of the issue from your normal stance to get a better feel for the other point of view.

3. Find the latest information on federal and provincial legislation related to child care, parental leave, and elder care benefits for employees. In what direction are the trends pointing? What will be the cost to businesses for these new initiatives? Do you favour such advancements in workplace legislation? Why or why not?

4. Examine an actual collective agreement and identify the constraints set upon workers and management by its provisions.

## TAKING IT TO THE NET 1

### Purpose

To learn more about a Government of Canada resource that highlights labour topics.

### Exercise

The Department of Human Resources and Skills Development Canada develops labour policies through one of its programs, the Labour Program. Visit this site at http://www.hrsdc.gc.ca/eng/labour/index.shtml.

1. What are some of the topics that are covered on this site? (Hint: Look at the tabs on the left-hand side of the page.) Search through each of these topics to learn more about them.

2. Input 'union membership' in the Search box. Looking at Table 1, what is the trend in union membership in Canada? In Table 2, state the top five organizations that have the largest membership. Have you heard of these organizations?

3. Visit the Newsroom tab and search for recent News Releases that relate to Labour. What is in the news right now?

## TAKING IT TO THE NET 2

### Purpose

To understand some of the issues being promoted by the Canadian Labour Congress (CLC).

### Exercise

The CLC represents over 3 million unionized workers in Canada. Visit the CLC Web site at www.clc-ctc.ca. Navigate through the site.

1. What are some of the social and economic policy issues being reviewed by the CLC? Pick one and discuss it with your classmates.

2. What are some of the campaigns being supported by the CLC?

3. Click on the Environmental Issues and review some of the links (e.g., unsafe conditions). Does this information concern you when you consider the employer's responsibility to create a safe work environment?

# ANALYZING MANAGEMENT DECISIONS

## Plant Closings, Unions, and Concessions

The first decade of the twenty-first century has been challenging for hundreds of thousands of Canadian employees, especially in the manufacturing sector. Plants and offices have laid off thousands of people or closed because of bankruptcy, consolidation, or transfer of operations to other lower-wage countries. Employment in the manufacturing sector alone continued to decline in 2008, falling by about 84,800 to 1.7 million workers. In some cases, management advised unions that the only way that they could avoid closing would be substantial concessions in wages and other changes in existing contracts.

For example, Air Canada came out of bankruptcy protection in 2004 after receiving concessions from its unions as part of its restructuring conditions. Speculation in 2009 is that the company may once again file for bankruptcy. Since the end of 2000, Air Canada has reduced its total full-time equivalent staff by 47 percent, resulting in a loss of over 20,000 jobs (from almost 45,000 jobs to 23,600 today). The company is now urging the government to relax pension contribution regulations, which otherwise would force it to increase its contributions as its $3.2 billion pension deficit grows. Its "discussions have focused on seeking support from its unions for a moratorium and other conditions on funding its pension deficit so as to establish financial certainty over the next several years."

Keep in mind that non-unionized employees also saw tens of thousands of jobs eliminated. At the start of 2001, Nortel Networks Corporation had more than 90,000 employees worldwide. By 2006, the company had cut its workforce by two-thirds as it restructured several times in an attempt to regain profitability. In the first two months of 2009, an additional 5,000 jobs were eliminated as the company filed for bankruptcy protection. No employees are safe as companies try to remain competitive in the marketplace.

Union leaders and their members are in a quandary when faced with such decisions. Sometimes they think management is bluffing. Sometimes they are reluctant to give up contract conditions they fought long and hard for. Accepting wage cuts or benefit reductions when the cost of living continues to rise is not easy. Agreeing to staff reductions to save other jobs is also a tough decision. Unions worry about where these concessions will end. Will there be another round of layoffs or even worse in a few months? Such was the case with concessions the Canadian Auto Workers union made with General Motors of Canada Ltd. This cost-cutting deal, a condition for GM receiving government bailout money, included cutting hourly labour costs and freezing wages and pensions until 2012. Despite such concessions, thousands of jobs are expected to be lost in the years to come.

These examples highlight some of the dilemmas facing unions. The business environment demands that companies become more efficient and productive. However, this will not happen unless there is mutual respect between management and labour.

Sources: Brent Jang, "Air Canada, Union at Odds Over Proposed Moratorium on Pension Payments," *The Globe and Mail*, 5 May 2009, http://www.theglobeandmail.com/servlet/story/LAC.20090505.RAIR CANADA05ART1908/TPStory/Business; "Study: The Year in Review in Manufacturing," Statistics Canada, 29 April 2009, http://www.statcan.gc.ca/daily-quotidien/090429/dq090429b-eng.htm; Paul Kunert, "Nortel Networks Lays off 3,200 Staff," *Computer Weekly*, 26 February 2009, http://www.computerweekly.com/Articles/2009/02/26/235029/nortel-networks-lays-off-3200-staff.htm; "Air Canada: Fly it Right!," Canadian Auto Workers Union, 2009, http://www.caw.ca/en/7423.htm; Garry Marr, "GM Deal Freezes Wages, Pensions," *National Post*, 9 March 2009, http://www.ottawacitizen.com/cars/deal+freezes+wages+pensions/1369798/story.html; and "Nortel Rebuilding and Hiring Again: CEO," CBC News, 29 September 2006, http://www.cbc.ca/money/story/2006/09/29/zafirovski-nortel.html.

## Discussion Questions

1. What would you recommend to union workers whose employer is threatening to close down unless they agree to wage or other concessions?

2. Is there some alternative to cutting wages or closing down? What is it?

3. Union workers often feel that the company is bluffing when it threatens to close. How can such doubts be settled so that more open negotiations can take place?

4. Does government have a right to interfere with organizations (i.e., union and employer) that have already negotiated a collective agreement and force them to renegotiate?

## RUNNING CASE

### Attraction, Retention, and Engagement at Canadian Tire Financial Services (CTFS)

Canada's population will undergo considerable aging in the twenty-first century. This, along with a fertility rate below replacement and increased life expectancy due to improvements in public health, will create challenges and opportunities for Canadian companies to attract, retain, and engage high-performing employees.

At Canadian Tire Financial Services (CTFS), being an employer of choice is no accident. One advantage that CTFS has is that it can draw on the strong brand image of its parent company, Canadian Tire Corporation, Limited. But this is only the beginning. To be attractive to candidates, companies need to evaluate recruiting channels (e.g., speak with recruiters), research the competition, conduct informal focus groups, and review existing employee opinion data.

Employees usually choose to pursue opportunities elsewhere because they are dissatisfied with their pay, with their career development, with management, or with a combination of these. To retain and engage employees, efforts are made to differentiate pay (base and variable) to keep key talent. In addition, profit-sharing, stock purchase, and long-term incentives (e.g., stock options plan) may be offered.

Career development efforts include formal training and development programs, job enrichment, and succession planning. Participation in performance management programs, mentoring, and sharing 360-degree feedback are other examples of how CTFS effectively applies some of the techniques discussed in Chapter 12.

Senior managers at CTFS are expected to model their behaviour on CTFS's core values (enterprise-wide core beliefs) of honesty, integrity, dignity, and respect. These managers not only need to understand the business strategy and business drivers, but they must also know the impact of their own role in the business. To achieve their performance metrics, they need to inspire the trust of their subordinates and, in turn, motivate them to succeed. Company values, a well-communicated business strategy, strong leadership, and alignment with human resources practices all contribute to a performance culture. In the words of Lou Gerstner, retired chairman of IBM, "Culture isn't just one aspect of the game. It is the game."

Sources: Sharon Patterson, Vice-President Human Resources, Canadian Tire Financial Services, in-person interview, 5 April 2006; and Sharon Patterson, "Why Culture and Human Resources Practices Are a Competitive Advantage," Canadian Tire Financial Services, 6 November 2003.

### Discussion Questions

1. At what step of the selection process might new hires be surveyed about their level of satisfaction?

2. Consider Maslow's hierarchy of needs. What level of needs are unmet if employees leave because they are dissatisfied with their career development?

3. Efforts are made to decrease the level of dissatisfaction as an attempt to retain and engage employees. What theorist tried to answer the question, "What creates enthusiasm for workers and makes them work to full potential?"

# PART 5

# CHAPTER 14

# Marketing: Building Customer and Stakeholder Relationships

## LEARNING OBJECTIVES

AFTER YOU HAVE READ AND STUDIED THIS CHAPTER, YOU SHOULD BE ABLE TO:

**LO ▶ 1**  Define marketing and explain how the marketing concept applies to both for-profit and non-profit organizations.

**LO ▶ 2**  List and describe the four Ps of marketing.

**LO ▶ 3**  Describe the marketing research process, and explain how marketers use environmental scanning to learn about the changing marketing environment.

**LO ▶ 4**  Explain how marketers meet the needs of the consumer market through market segmentation, relationship marketing, and the study of consumer behaviour.

**LO ▶ 5**  List ways in which the business-to-business market differs from the consumer market.

## PROFILE

### Getting To Know Erica Van Kamp, Sales Director, Mattel Canada, Inc.

When Erica Van Kamp graduated with a Bachelor of Science degree in biology in 1992, little did she know that she would one day be working with toys. Her marketing career began as an Assistant Brand Manager at Good Humor-Breyers in 1997. Over the next two years, she launched seven new products. During this time, she also issued monthly market research reports and managed budgets for advertising, research, public relations, and consumer and trade promotions. In marketing, as in other functional areas of business, teamwork is a part of most positions. Working with the company's advertising agency, Van Kamp was involved in developing creative television commercials. In another group effort, Van Kamp led a packaging optimizing team. These initiatives led to improved product placement and increased store inventory levels.

Building on this experience, Van Kamp started at Mattel Canada, Inc. (the Canadian subsidiary of parent company Mattel, Inc.) in June 1999 as the Product Manager on the Barbie brand. Mattel, Inc. is the worldwide leader in the design, manufacture, and marketing of toys and family products. The Mattel family is comprised of such best-selling brands as Barbie®, the most popular fashion doll ever introduced, Hot Wheels®, Matchbox®, American Girl®, Radica® and Tyco® R/C, as well as Fisher-Price® brands, including Little People®, Power Wheels® and a wide array of entertainment-inspired toy lines. Mattel, Inc. employs approximately 30,000 people in 43 countries and territories and sells products in more than 150 nations. Mattel's vision is to be the world's premier toy brand—today and tomorrow.

The year 2000 proved to be an exciting one in Van Kamp's career. Not only did she complete her part-time MBA, but she also received several promotions. Early in 2000, Van Kamp was promoted to Senior Product Manager on the Barbie brand, where she was responsible for the $100-million-plus brand. In September 2000, a promotion to Marketing Manager followed where her responsibilities for the $150-million-plus category included seven brands and seven sub-brands.

In her current role as the Director of Sales, Van Kamp works across sales and marketing and strives to align the two with respect to strategic account planning and strategic brand planning. Her focus is to ensure that the two areas build and support each other. The typical day varies—especially in sales! There are always account issues that touch all functional areas. The issue can come from finance and accounting, supply chain, customer service, as well as the sales and marketing teams. Generally, she strives to keep things moving to ensure the company sticks to the plan and most importantly, delivers the plan. When asked what advice she would give to students who are interested in a career in marketing, Van Kamp responds that there are so many ways to get involved in this area as it touches almost every aspect of the organization. "Try to learn from every business opportunity you come across, observe transactions as they go on around you and try to see how everything fits together. If it is marketing, consider all of the fundamental elements, look for one that excites you and go after it!"

In this chapter, you will be introduced to the importance of marketing. Like Mattel Canada, Inc., businesses must conduct an environmental scan to discover opportunities and threats in their industry. Customers demand a four-P marketing mix (to be introduced in this chapter) that will meet their expectations. With a greater customer relationship management (CRM) focus today, marketers need to reach their customers wherever they may be.

Sources: Erica Van Kamp, Sales Director, Mattel Canada, Inc., interview, 13 March 2009; and "Mattel Listed Among 100 Best Corporate Citizens in 2009, Ranks #7," Mattel, Inc., 10 March 2009, http://investor.shareholder.com/mattel/releasedetail.cfm?ReleaseID=370003.

# WHAT IS MARKETING?

**marketing**
The process of determining customer needs and wants and then developing goods and services that meet or exceed these expectations.

Many people think of marketing as "selling" or "advertising." Yes, selling and advertising are part of marketing, but marketing involves more.[1] **Marketing** is the process of planning and executing the conception, pricing, promotion, and distribution of goods and services to facilitate exchanges that satisfy individual and organizational objectives.

The main term in marketing is market. Recall that a market is defined as a group of people with unsatisfied wants and needs who have the resources and the willingness to buy products. A market is, therefore, created as a result of this demand for goods and services. What marketers do at any particular time depends on what needs to be done to fill customers' needs. These wants and needs continually change. For example, today we see an increasing focus on **green marketing**, which refers to marketing efforts to produce, promote, and reclaim environmentally-sensitive products. In response to this trend, and as an alternative to plastic water bottles that are hazardous to the environment, Onebottle (www.onebottle.ca) has developed a reusable and recyclable stainless steel water container. One dollar from every Onebottle sold is donated to World Wildlife Fund Canada's conservation efforts.

**green marketing**
Marketing efforts to produce, promote, and reclaim environmentally-sensitive products.

Let's take a brief look at how changes have influenced the evolution of marketing.

## The Evolution of Marketing

The evolution of marketing involved four eras: (1) production, (2) sales, (3) marketing concept, and (4) customer relationship.

### The Production Era

From the time the first European settlers arrived in Canada until the start of the 1900s, the general philosophy of business was to produce as much as possible. Given the limited production capabilities and the vast demand for products in those days, such a production orientation was both logical and profitable, as demand exceeded supply. Manufacturers focused on production, as most goods were bought as soon as they became available. The greatest marketing need was for distribution and storage.

Many successful Canadian entrepreneurs suggest that their success was based on the "find a need and fill it" concept. This was the case for Brenda Carriere when she purchased a Curves International franchise in Saint John, New Brunswick. Curves, targeted to mostly overweight women 30 years and older, many using a gym for the first time, provides a no-frills approach to exercise: there are no showers, therapeutic massages, or fresh-fruit smoothies. Facilities are 1,200 to 1,500 square feet and can be profitable with as few as 200 members.

### The Sales Era

By the 1920s, businesses had developed mass production techniques (e.g., automobile assembly lines) and production capacity often exceeded the immediate market demand. Therefore, the business philosophy turned from an emphasis on production to an emphasis on *selling*. Most companies emphasized selling and advertising in an effort to persuade consumers to buy existing products. Few offered service after the sale.

### The Marketing Concept Era

After the Second World War ended in 1945, there was a tremendous demand for goods and services among the returning soldiers who were starting new careers and beginning families. Those postwar years launched the baby boom (a sudden increase in the birth rate) and a boom in consumer spending. Competition for the consumer's dollar was fierce. Organizations recognized the need to be responsive to consumers if they wanted to get their business, and a philosophy called the marketing concept emerged in the 1950s.

The **marketing concept** had three parts:

1. *A customer orientation.* Find out what consumers want and provide it for them. (Note the emphasis on meeting consumer needs rather than on promotion or sales.)

2. *A service orientation.* Ensure that everyone in the organization has the same objective: customer satisfaction. This should be a total and integrated organizational effort. That is, everyone from the president of the firm to the delivery people should be customer oriented.[2]

3. *A profit orientation.* Focus on those goods and services that will earn the most profit and enable the organization to survive and expand to serve more consumer wants and needs.

It took a while for businesses to implement the marketing concept. That process went slowly during the 1960s and 1970s. During the 1980s, businesses began to apply the marketing concept more aggressively than they had done over the preceding 30 years. That led to the focus on customer relationship management (CRM) that has become so important today.[3] We shall explore that concept next.

### The Customer Relationship Era

Starting in the 1990s, managers extended the marketing concept by adopting the concept of customer relationship management. **Customer relationship management (CRM)** is the process of learning as much as possible about customers and doing everything you can to satisfy them—or even exceed their expectations—with goods and services over time.[4] The idea is to enhance customer satisfaction and stimulate long-term customer loyalty. For example, most airlines offer frequent-flier programs that reward loyal customers with free flights.[5]

# No Ifs, Ands or Buts.

Truth is an essential part of any successful ad campaign. Smart advertisers have known this for years. That's why the advertising industry created the *Canadian Code of Advertising Standards* more than 40 years ago. Since then the *Code* has set the standards for acceptable advertising in Canada. It helps ensure that the ads you see and hear are truthful, fair and accurate. Check it out for yourself. Because the more you know about advertising, the more you get out of it.

Learn about the *Code* at:
**www.adstandards.com**

ASC Advertising Standards Canada

Advertising Standards Canada (ASC), a non-profit organization, is committed to ensuring the integrity and viability of advertising in Canada through responsible industry self-regulation. Would you complain to ASC if you saw an ad that you thought was unacceptable?

# Non-Profit Organizations Prosper from Marketing

Even though the marketing concept emphasizes a profit orientation, marketing is a critical part of all organizations, whether for-profit or non-profit. Charities use marketing to raise funds or to obtain other resources. For example, when Canadian Blood Services was faced with the challenge of recruiting 80,000 new blood donors to meet the ongoing need for blood for patients in Canada, it turned to marketing. A direct-response television campaign was developed to promote the emotional benefit of donating blood, coupled with a very strong call to action to the organization's national call centre and to www.blood.ca. According to Steve Harding, Executive Director of Marketing and External Communications, "The not-for-profit category is one of the most competitive segments in the Canadian marketplace. It is of paramount importance that non-profit organizations utilize the key brand building and customer management strategies to break through and succeed. The stakes are so much greater when lives are at stake!"[6]

Churches use marketing to attract new members and to raise funds. Politicians use marketing to get votes. Provinces use marketing to attract new businesses and tourists. Some provinces, for example, have competed to get automobile companies from other countries to locate plants in their area. Schools use marketing to attract new students. Other organizations, such as arts groups and social groups, also use marketing.

**marketing concept**
A three-part business philosophy:
(1) a customer orientation,
(2) a service orientation, and
(3) a profit orientation.

**customer relationship management (CRM)**
The process of learning as much as possible about customers and doing everything you can to satisfy them—or even exceed their expectations—with goods and services over time.

# THE MARKETING MIX

Pleasing customers has become a priority for marketers. Much of what marketing people do has been conveniently divided into four factors, called "the four Ps" to make them easy to remember and implement. They are:

1. Product
2. Price
3. Place
4. Promotion

**marketing mix**

The ingredients that go into a marketing program: product, price, place, and promotion.

Managing the controllable parts of the marketing process, then, involves (1) designing a want-satisfying *product*, (2) setting a *price* for the product, (3) putting the product in a *place* where people will buy it, and (4) *promoting* the product. These four factors are called the **marketing mix** because they are blended together in a marketing program. A marketing manager designs a marketing program that effectively combines the ingredients of the marketing mix (as highlighted in Figure 14.1). The Dealing with Change box discusses how the automobile industry is adjusting to the market using the four Ps.

## Applying the Marketing Process

The four Ps are a convenient way to remember the basics of marketing, but they don't include everything that goes into the marketing process. One of the best ways to understand the entire marketing process is to take a product and follow the process that led to its development and sale. Figure 14.2 outlines some of these steps. In Chapter 15, we will investigate each of the Ps in more detail.

Imagine, for example, that you and your friends want to start a money-making business near your school. You have noticed that there are a lot of vegetarians among your friends. You do a quick survey in a couple of dorms and other campus clubs and find that there are many vegetarians—and other students who like to eat vegetarian meals once in a while.[7] Your preliminary research indicates that there may be some demand for a vegetarian restaurant nearby. You check the fast-food stores in the area and find that it is very difficult to find more than one or two vegetarian meals at any one restaurant. In fact, most don't have any vegetarian options except salads and some soups.

Further research indicates that there are a number of different kinds of vegetarians. Some eat dairy products and eggs (lacto-ovo). Others eat dairy products, but no eggs (lacto-vegetarian). Vegans eat no eggs, dairy products, or any other animal products. Fruitarians eat mostly raw fruits, grains, and nuts. You conclude that a vegetarian restaurant would have to appeal to all kinds of vegetarians to be a success. Without consciously knowing it, you are performing the first couple of steps in the marketing process. You notice an opportunity (a need for vegetarian food near campus). You also do some pre-

**FIGURE** | **14.1**

**Marketing Managers and the Marketing Mix**
Marketing managers must choose how to implement the four Ps of the marketing mix: product, price, place, and promotion. The goals are to please customers and make a profit.

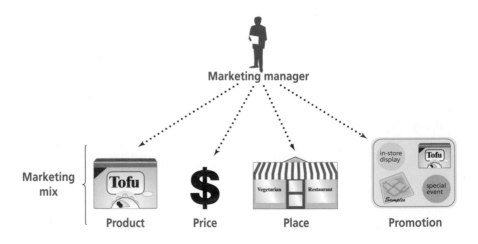

liminary research to see whether your idea has any merit. And then you identify groups of people who may be very interested in your product. They will be your target market (the people you will try to persuade to come to your restaurant). Without clearly understanding your target market (e.g., needs, characteristics, etc.), the marketing mix is of little value.

## Designing a Product to Meet Needs

Once you have researched consumer needs and found a target market (to be discussed later) for your product, the four Ps of marketing begin. You start by developing a product. A **product** is any physical good, service, or idea that satisfies a want or need plus anything that would enhance the product in the eyes of consumers, such as the brand. Many products today are not pure goods or pure services. Figure 14.3 illustrates the service continuum, which is a range from the tangible to the intangible or good-dominant to service-dominant offerings.[8]

In this case, your proposed product is a vegetarian restaurant that would serve different kinds of vegetarian meals to appeal to anyone looking for a vegetarian meal as opposed to a normal fast-food meal with hamburgers, chicken, or the like. It's a good idea at this point to do *concept testing*. That is, you develop an accurate description of your product and ask people, in person or online, whether the concept (the idea of the restaurant and the kind of meals you intend to offer) appeals to them. If it does, you might go to a supplier, such as Amy's Kitchen (found at Loblaws and natural and health food stores throughout Canada), that makes vegetarian meals to obtain samples of products that you then take to consumers to test their reactions.[9] The process of testing products among potential users is called **test marketing**.

If consumers like the product and agree that they would buy it, you have the information you need to find investors and a convenient location to open a restaurant. You will have to think of a catchy name for the restaurant. (Stop for a minute and try to think of a clever name.) We'll use Very Vegetarian in this text.

**FIGURE | 14.2**

**The Marketing Process with the Four Ps**

| |
|---|
| Find |
| Conduct research |
| Identify a target market |

**Product** — Design a product to meet the need based on research and then conduct product testing

Determine a brand name and design a package

**Price** — Set a price

**Place** — Select a distribution system

**Promotion** — Design a promotional program

Build a relationship with customers

**FIGURE | 14.3**

**Service Continuum**

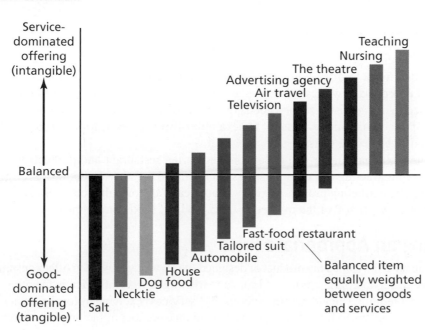

**product**
Any physical good, service, or idea that satisfies a want or need.

**test marketing**
The process of testing products among potential users.

## DEALING with CHANGE

### The Four Ps Drive Marketing

You can see the four Ps of marketing in action if you review some of the changes that are occurring in the automobile industry. Due to the poor financial situation of many car manufacturers, higher fuel prices, and tightening credit, product decisions are being re-evaluated. For example, Chrysler cut low-volume models such as the Chrysler PT Cruiser convertible. Ford will focus on a growing line of small cars such as a North American version of the Fiesta in 2010 and the redesigned Focus for 2011. These cars will meet market demand for fuel-efficient, low-cost transportation in nice packages.

As they continue to listen to customers, car manufacturers are adding new features to cars such as massaging seats, satellite radio, drowsiness alerts for drivers, and eventually a seamless transition between personal communication devices in the home and the car. Ford Motor Company plans to make a new device called MyKey standard equipment on all of its vehicles. Parents of teenagers will be able to program a top speed for the car (129 kilometres an hour) and also keep the music a little less loud by limiting the sound system to 44 percent of its total volume. The special key can be programmed to remind young drivers every six seconds for five minutes to put on their seat belts and will actually keep the audio system mute until the seat belt is fastened.

When it comes to pricing, consumers have even more options to price shop than ever before. For US$29.95, the *Consumer Reports New Car Price Report* gives the optimal price to use as the starting point when negotiating the price for a new car. This *Report* includes behind-the-scenes dealer incentive information as well as customer rebate and incentive amounts. Sites such as cars4u. com and usedcarscanada.com provide product and price information and dealer referrals. Customers can determine the best price before going to a dealership. Some dealers also offer automobiles at employee prices.

While one can go to a traditional dealership, getting cars to a place that is convenient for customers is also being done via sites such as autobytel.com and usedcars canada.com. These services help customers find the dealer closest to them that will offer the best price for the automobile they want.

Promotion for new and used cars is also changing. Some dealers are trying low-pressure sales tactics because they know that customers are now armed with much more information than in the past. Consumers can go on the Internet and learn about various cars and their features, pick which features they want, get the best price available, and order the car. This is all without leaving their homes. Online, you can also learn about special promotions through sites such as www.redflags. ca. For example, Toyota's Graduate Rebate offer ranged from $500 to $1,000 depending on the vehicle.

In such a business atmosphere, the marketing task shifts from helping the seller sell to helping the buyer buy. Today, consumers have more choice than ever before and successful marketers must develop marketing mixes that will meet, if not exceed, the needs of their customers.

Sources: Melissa Anderson, "New Model Launch Interruptions—or Not," *Automotive Design & Production*, Volume 120, Issue 12, 11 December 2008; Greg Keenan, "Ford Helps Parents Control Teen's Driving," *The Globe and Mail*, 6 October 2008, http://global.factiva.com/ha/default.aspx; Kate Musgrove, "Graduate Rebates from Car Manufacturers," RedFlagDeals. com, 19 August 2008, http://www.redflagdeals.com/deals/main.php/ articles/graduate_rebates/; and "New Car Price Service," Consumers Union of U.S., Inc., 2008, http://crcanadacars.org/default.asp?EXTKEY =cana2CROAP.

---

**brand name**
A word, device (design, shape, sound, or colour), or combination of these used to distinguish a seller's goods or services from those of competitors.

You may want to offer some well-known brand names to attract people right away. A **brand name** is any word, device (design, shape, sound, or colour), or combination of these used to distinguish a seller's goods or services from those of competitors.[10] Brand names of vegetarian meals include, for example, Tofurky Feast, Mori-Nu Silken Soft Tofu, and Yves Veggie Cuisine.

In the next chapter, we will follow the vegetarian restaurant and products to show you how all marketing and other business decisions tie together. For now, we're simply sketching the marketing process to give you an idea of the overall picture. So far, we've only covered the first P of the marketing mix: product. Next comes price.

## Setting an Appropriate Price

**price**
The money or other consideration (including other goods and services) exchanged for the ownership or use of a good or service.

After you have developed the product or designed the service you want to offer consumers, you have to set appropriate prices.[11] From a marketing viewpoint, **price** is the money or other consideration (including other goods and services) exchanged for the ownership or use of a good or service.[12] These prices depend on a number of factors.[13] For example, in the restaurant business, the price could be close to what other restaurants charge to

Marketers try to develop promotional campaigns that are eye-catching and memorable. Seeing this advertisement, would you be interested in visiting this retailer? What is the message being communicated?

stay competitive. Or you might charge less to attract business, especially at the beginning.[14] Or, you may charge more and offer high-quality products for which customers are willing to pay a little more (à la Starbucks).[15] You also have to consider the costs involved in producing, distributing, and promoting the product.

## Getting the Product to the Right Place

Once you have opened your restaurant, you have to decide how best to get your products to the consumer, which is the focus of place. Of course, you can always have them sit down and eat in the restaurant, but that is not the only alternative, as you have seen with pizza. You could deliver the food to their dorms, rooming houses, and other dwelling places. Remember, place is the third P in the marketing mix. In addition to having a restaurant, you may want to sell your products to supermarkets or health food stores, or you may want to sell them through organizations that specialize in distributing food products. Such organizations, called intermediaries, are in the middle of a series of organizations that distribute goods from producers to consumers. (The more traditional word for such companies is middlemen.) Getting the product to consumers when and where they want it is critical to market success.[16]

## Developing an Effective Promotional Strategy

The last of the four Ps of marketing is promotion. **Promotion** consists of all of the techniques sellers use to inform people and motivate them to buy their goods or services. They include advertising, personal selling, public relations, and various sales promotion efforts, such as coupons and samples.

This last step in the marketing process often includes relationship building with customers. That includes responding to suggestions consumers may make to improve the products or their marketing (including price and packaging).[17] Post-purchase, or after-sale, service may include refusing payment for meals that weren't satisfactory and making other adjustments to ensure consumer satisfaction. Marketing is an ongoing process. To remain competitive, companies must continually adapt to changes in the market and to changes in consumer wants and needs. Customers will likely recommend that you stock other vegetarian products that they would like. Listening to customers and responding to their needs is the key to marketing.[18] You do not have to decide on every product to carry; your customers will tell you what they want through what they buy and what they request.

**promotion**
All of the techniques sellers use to motivate customers to buy their products.

> ## Progress Assessment
>
> - Define marketing.
> - State each marketing era and the emphasis for each.
> - What are the three parts of the marketing concept?
> - What are the four Ps of the marketing mix?

# PROVIDING MARKETERS WITH INFORMATION

**marketing research**
The analysis of markets to determine opportunities and challenges, and to find the information needed to make good decisions.

Every step in the marketing process depends on information that is used to make the right decisions. **Marketing research** is the analysis of markets to determine opportunities and challenges, and to find the information needed to make good decisions.

Marketing research helps determine what customers have purchased in the past and what situational changes have occurred to alter not only what consumers want now but also what they're likely to want in the future. In addition, marketers conduct research on business trends, the ecological impact of their decisions, international trends, and more. Businesses need information to compete effectively, and marketing research is the activity that gathers that information. Note, too, that in addition to listening to customers, marketing researchers should pay attention to what employees, stockholders, dealers, consumer advocates, media representatives, and other stakeholders have to say.

## The Marketing Research Process

A simplified marketing research process consists of at least four key steps:

1. Defining the question (problem or opportunity) and determining the present situation
2. Collecting data
3. Analyzing the research data
4. Choosing the best solution and implementing it

The following sections look at each of these steps.

## Defining the Question and Determining the Present Situation

Marketing researchers should be given the freedom to help discover what the present situation is, what the problems or opportunities are, what the alternatives are, what information is needed, and how to go about gathering and analyzing data.

## Collecting Data

**secondary data**
Information that has already been compiled by others and published in journals and books or made available online.

Obtaining usable information is vital to the marketing research process. Research can become quite expensive, so some trade-off must often be made between the need for information and the cost of obtaining that information. Normally the least expensive method is to gather information that has already been compiled by others and published in journals and books or made available online. Such existing data are called **secondary data** since you aren't the first one to gather them. Figure 14.4 lists the principal sources of secondary marketing research information. Despite its name, secondary data should be gathered first to avoid incurring unnecessary expense. To collect secondary data about vegetarians, go on the Internet and see what you can find.

**primary data**
Data that you gather yourself (not from secondary sources such as books and magazines).

Often, secondary data do not provide all of the information managers need to make important decisions. To gather additional, in-depth information, marketers must do their own research. The results of such *new* studies are called primary data. **Primary data** are facts, figures, and opinions that you have gathered yourself.

One primary research technique is *observation*. This occurs when trained people observe and record the actions of potential buyers. For example, companies have followed

| Primary Sources | |
|---|---|
| Observation | Personal interview |
| Survey/questionnaire | Focus group |

| Secondary Sources | |
|---|---|
| **Statistics Canada Publications** | **Trade Sources** |
| *Canada Year Book* | A.C. Nielsen |
| *Canadian Economic Observer* | Conference Board of Canada |
| *Family Expenditure Guide* | Dun & Bradstreet Canada |
| *Market Research Handbook* | Direct Marketing Association |
| *Statistics Canada Catalogue* | Retail Council of Canada |
| | |
| **Newspapers** | **General Internet Sites** |
| *The Toronto Star* | Industry Canada—www.ic.gc.ca |
| *The Globe and Mail* | Statistics Canada—www.statcan.gc.ca |
| *The National Post* | Track market news, industries, annual reports, |
| Local newspapers (*e.g., Calgary Herald* | etc.—ca.finance.yahoo.com |
| and *The Chronicle Herald*) | |
| | **Periodicals** |
| **Internal Sources** | *Canadian Business* |
| Company records | *Journal of Marketing* |
| Financial statements | *Maclean's* |
| Prior research reports | *Marketing Magazine* |
| | *PROFIT* |
| **Indexes and Directories** | |
| Business Periodical Index | **Databases** |
| Canadian Business Index | ABI/Inform |
| Canadian Statistics Index | CANSIM (Statistics Canada) |
| Scott's Directories | Canadian Business and Current Affairs (CBCA) |
| Standards Periodical Directory | Factiva |
| | LexisNexis Academic |

**FIGURE** **14.4**

**Sources of Selected Primary and Secondary Information**

For a list of local and national Canadian newspapers, visit **www.world-newspapers. com/canada.html.** On this site, you will also find some news sites.

customers into supermarkets to record their purchasing behaviours for products such as meat, bread, and laundry detergent. These marketers may observe that consumers do not bend to look at products, that they compare prices, and that they touch the product to see how heavy it is. Observation may provide insight into behaviours that consumers do not even know they exhibit while shopping.

Primary data can also be gathered by developing a list of questions and conducting a survey (also known as a questionnaire). Telephone surveys, mail surveys, and online surveys are the most common forms. Surveys are best completed by independent third parties so that the information gathered and the results reported can be as objective as possible. You can use the information to understand behaviours, perceptions, preferences, and opinions. While the information gathered is useful, there are some disadvantages to this method. Not everyone who is approached may be willing to answer your questions, respondents may not be truthful, and (for written surveys) not everyone can read and write. What do you think would be the best way (e.g., online) to survey students about your potential new restaurant? Would you conduct a different kind of survey after you have been open for a few months? One question that researchers pay close attention to is this: Would you recommend this product to a friend?

To increase the response and accuracy rate, marketers use personal interviews. *Personal interviews* are a face-to-face opportunity to ask consumers prepared questions. While this research method can be more expensive than surveys, the interviewer has the opportunity to observe reactions and to dig a little deeper with the questions if the respondent wishes to add more information.

A **focus group** is a small group of people (8 to 14 individuals, for example) who meet under the direction of a discussion leader to communicate their opinions about an organization, its products, or other issues. These questions should be free of bias and participants should be encouraged to answer questions honestly without being influenced by the responses of others in the focus group. This textbook is updated periodically using many focus groups made up of faculty and students. They tell the authors what subjects and examples they like and dislike, and the authors consider their suggestions when making changes.

**focus group**
A small group of people who meet under the direction of a discussion leader to communicate their opinions about an organization, its products, or other issues.

## Analyzing the Research Data

The data collected in the research process must be turned into useful information. Careful, honest interpretation of the data collected can help a company find useful alternatives to specific marketing challenges. For example, by doing primary research, Fresh Italy, a small Italian pizzeria, found that its pizza's taste was rated superior compared to the larger pizza chains. However, the company's sales lagged behind the competition. Secondary research on the industry revealed that free delivery (which Fresh Italy did not offer) was more important to customers than taste. Fresh Italy now delivers—and has increased its market share.

## Choosing the Best Solution and Implementing It

After collecting and analyzing the data, market researchers determine alternative strategies and make recommendations as to which strategy may be best and why. This final step in a research effort involves following up on the actions taken to see if the results were as expected. If not, the company can take corrective action and conduct new studies in the ongoing attempt to provide consumer satisfaction at the lowest cost. You can see that marketing research is a continuous process of responding to changes in the marketplace and changes in consumer preferences.

In today's customer-driven market, ethics is important in every aspect of marketing. Ideally, companies should therefore do what's right as well as what's profitable. This step could add greatly to the social benefits of marketing decisions. See the Making Ethical Decisions box for such an example.

# The Marketing Environment

**environmental scanning**
The process of identifying the factors that can affect marketing success.

Marketing managers must be aware of the surrounding environment when making marketing mix decisions. **Environmental scanning** is the process of identifying the factors that can affect marketing success. As you can see in Figure 14.5, those factors include global, technological, sociocultural, competitive, and economic influences. We discussed these factors in some detail in Chapter 1, but it is helpful to review them strictly from a marketing perspective as well.

## Global Factors

The most dramatic global change in recent years is probably the growth of the Internet.[19] Now businesses can reach many of the consumers in the world relatively easily and carry on a dialogue with them about the goods and services they want. The Reaching Beyond Our Borders box shares how the Canadian Tourism Commission is trying to promote Canada as a destination for global travellers.

This globalization of marketing puts more pressure on those whose responsibility it is to deliver products. Many marketers outsource that function to companies such as Purolator, which has a solid reputation for delivering goods quickly. Are there any food delivery firms in your area that you could use to distribute your vegetarian products and meals?

## Making Ethical Decisions

### No Kidding

Marketers have long recognized that children can be an important influence on their parents' buying decisions. In fact, many direct appeals for products are focused on children. Let's say that you've experienced a great response to a new high-fibre, high-protein cereal among health-conscious consumers. The one important group you haven't been able to attract is children. Therefore, the product development team is considering introducing a child-oriented brand to expand the product line.

The new children's cereal may have strong market potential if you follow two recommendations of the research department. First, coat the flakes generously with sugar (significantly changing the cereal's nutritional benefits). Second, promote the product exclusively on

children's TV programs. Such a promotional strategy should create a strong demand for the product, especially if you offer a premium (a toy or other "surprise") in each box. The consensus among the research department is that kids will love the new taste and parents will agree to buy the product because of their positive impression of your best-selling brand. The research director commented, "The chance of a parent actually reading our label and noting the addition of sugar is nil."

Would you introduce the children's cereal following the recommendations of your research department? What are the benefits of doing so? What are the risks involved in following these recommendations? What would you do if you were the marketing manager for this product?

## Technological Factors

The most important technological changes also involve the Internet and the growth of consumer databases. Using consumer databases, companies can develop products and services that closely match the needs of consumers. As you read in Chapter 10, it is now possible to produce customized goods and services for about the same price as mass-produced goods. Thus, flexible manufacturing and mass customization are also major influences on marketers. You can imagine, for example, whipping up custom-made fruit mixes and various salads for your vegetarian customers.

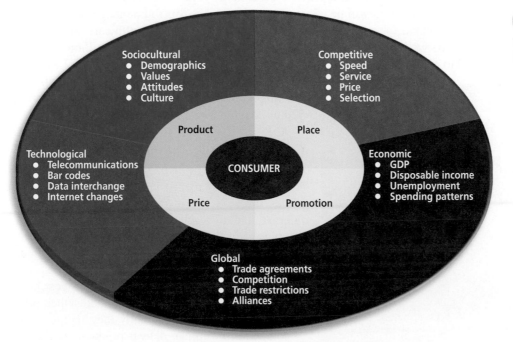

**FIGURE** | **14.5**

**The Marketing Environment**

## Reaching Beyond Our Borders

### Canada—Your Vacation Destination

In just two short years, FutureBrand has moved Canada from the world's 12th most respected country brand to No. 2. "It's proof the 'Canada. Keep Exploring' tourism brand, developed four years ago in collaboration with Canada's tourism sector, is sound, solid and working," said Michele McKenzie, Canadian Tourism Commission (CTC) president and CEO. In addition to the FutureBrand ranking, the influential Lonely Planet guide book publisher recently named Canada one of the Top 10 Countries for 2009, describing it as a place of "life-changing experiences, festivals and events, and cosmopolitan, cultured and foodie-filled cities."

The CTC's 2009 global marketing strategy focuses on inspiring travellers to choose Canada as their next vacation destination. CTC is showcasing the emotion of real travellers having profound personal Canadian travel experiences, and is bringing these to life in its first-ever global TV and Internet campaign. The centrepiece is a series of video clips shot by actual visitors to Canada. Great moments include an adventure-seeker "ziplining"

above a raging creek in Whistler, British Columbia (home to several events during the Vancouver 2010 Olympic and Paralympic Winter Games), and awestruck nature lovers watching a collapsing iceberg off Newfoundland. The CTC has started airing the 15-second clips as broadcast TV spots and online videos in selected markets. The videos are designed to "create a movie about Canada" in the viewers' minds.

The Canadian tourism industry will be the greatest beneficiary of the Vancouver 2010 Olympic and Paralympic Winter Games when more than 3 billion viewers around the world tune in. With a $26 million federal investment, the CTC is leveraging the international exposure to drive tourism to Canada through innovative strategies such as this 2009 campaign.

Source: Margaret Nevin, "Canada Jumps 10 Spots to Become World's No. 2 Ranked Country Brand as CTC Launches New Global Marketing Strategy," Canadian Tourism Commission, 10 November 2008, Used with permission.

## Sociocultural Factors

There are a number of social trends that marketers must monitor to maintain their close relationship with customers. Population growth and changing demographics are examples of social trends that can affect sales.

The fastest-growing segment of the Canadian population is baby boomers. By 2031, one in four Canadians will be 65 years or older, and as this segment ages there will be growing demand for recreation, travel, continuing education, health care, and nursing homes.[20] As well, opportunities exist for firms that target Canada's 2.5 million "tweens" (ages 9 to 14); according to the YTV Tween Report, in addition to spending $2.9 billion of their own money on food, entertainment, and clothing each year, tweens also influence another $20 billion in household purchases.[21]

## Competitive Factors

Of course, marketers must pay attention to the dynamic competitive environment. Many brick-and-mortar companies must be aware of new competition on the Internet, including companies that sell automobiles, insurance, music videos, and clothes. In the book business, Indigo is competing with Amazon.ca's huge selection of books at good prices. Now that consumers can literally search the world for the best buys through the Internet, marketers must adjust their pricing policies accordingly. Similarly, they have to adjust to competitors who can deliver products quickly or provide excellent service. Can you see any opportunities to sell vegetarian food over the Internet?

Since 1984, TLN Telelatino Network has been providing programming in Italian, Spanish, and English to 10 million Canadians coast to coast. Are you aware of any other ethnic segments that are targeted by television channels?

## Economic Factors

As we began the new millennium, Canada was experiencing unparalleled growth and customers were eager to buy expensive automobiles, watches, and vacations. But as the economy slowed, marketers had to adapt by offering products that were less expensive and more tailored to consumers with modest incomes. Scotiabank chief economist Warren Jestin predicts the global economy won't begin to recover until 2010 and then the revival will be "gradual and in some cases disappointing." Most developed countries will see "virtually no economic gain" until 2011 or 2012, he said, with "slower growth in the developed world the reality."[22]

You can see, therefore, that environmental scanning is critical to a company's success during rapidly changing economic times. What economic changes are occurring around your school that might affect a new restaurant?

## Legal and Regulatory Factors[23]

Governments enact laws and regulations to protect consumers and businesses. Businesses must be aware of how these may impact their practices. For example, the Supreme Court of Canada dismissed Great Glasses founder Bruce Bergez's two applications to appeal a contempt ruling and more than $46 million in fines. Bergez had been fined $1 million in 2006—the largest fine for a civil contempt case in Canadian history—and a further $50,000 a day for every day since that he hasn't been in compliance with Ontario legislation. The legislation requires that eyeglasses and contact lenses be dispensed by a registered optician based on a prescription supplied either by an optometrist or a physician. Great Glasses was dispensing glasses based on eye tests conducted on a computerized machine without a proper prescription. On top of this, the Supreme Court also ordered Bergez to pay unspecified costs to Ontario's College of Optometrists.

**consumer market**
All individuals or households that want goods and services for personal consumption or use.

## Two Different Markets: Consumer and Business-to-Business (B2B)

Marketers must know as much as possible about the market they wish to serve. There are two major markets in business: the consumer market and the business-to-business market. The **consumer market** consists of all individuals or households that want goods and services for personal consumption or use and have the resources to buy them. The **business-to-business (B2B) market** consists of all individuals and organizations that want goods and services to use in producing other goods and services or to sell, rent, or supply goods to

**business-to-business (B2B) market**
All individuals and organizations that want goods and services to use in producing other goods and services or to sell, rent, or supply goods to others.

Legislation not only needs to be in place to protect consumers and businesses, but it must also be enforced. What can be done to force companies to stop illegal activities immediately? Is this realistic?

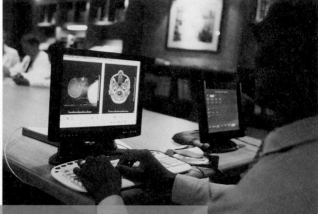

Many goods could be classified as consumer goods or B2B goods, based on their uses. For example, a computer that a person uses at home for personal use would clearly be a consumer good. But that same computer used in a commercial setting, such as an accounting firm or a manufacturing plant, would be classified as a B2B good. What difference does it make how a good is classified?

others. Oil-drilling bits, cash registers, display cases, office desks, public accounting audits, and corporate legal advice are examples of B2B goods and services.[24] Traditionally, they have been known as industrial goods and services because they are used in industry.

The important thing to remember is that the buyer's reason for buying—that is, the end use of the product—determines whether a product is considered a consumer product or a B2B product. For example, a cup of yogurt for a family's breakfast is considered a consumer product. However, if the Golden Griddle purchased the same cup of yogurt to sell to its breakfast customers, this yogurt would then be considered a B2B product. The following sections will outline in more detail consumer and B2B markets.

## Progress Assessment

- What are the steps in the marketing research process?
- What is environmental scanning?
- Can you define the terms consumer market and business-to-business market?

# THE CONSUMER MARKET

The total potential consumer market consists of more than 6 billion people in global markets. Because consumer groups differ greatly in age, education level, income, and taste, a business usually cannot fill the needs of every group. Therefore, it must first decide which groups to serve and then develop products and services specially tailored to their needs.

**market segmentation**
The process of dividing the total market into groups whose members have similar characteristics.

**target marketing**
Marketing directed toward those groups (market segments) an organization decides it can serve profitably.

The process of dividing the total market into several groups whose members have similar characteristics is called **market segmentation**. Selecting which groups (market segments) an organization can serve profitably is called **target marketing**. For example, a shoe store may choose to sell only women's shoes, only children's shoes (e.g., Kiddie Kobbler), or only athletic shoes. The issue is finding the right target market (the segment that would be most profitable to serve) for the new venture. For example, the B.C. Lions, a Vancouver-based football team, is the first Canadian professional sports franchise to have its own beer brand—B.C. Lions Lager—as a result of its partnership with the Russell Brewing Company.[25] "Beer and football are pretty synonymous. They've got the same demographics," said Brian Harris, CEO at the small Surrey, B.C.-based microbrewery, adding the target market for the brewery and the football team is males, aged 25–40.[26]

# Segmenting the Consumer Market

There are several ways a firm can segment the consumer market, as outlined in Figure 14.6. For example, rather than trying to sell a product throughout Canada, you might try to focus on just one or two regions of the country where you might be most successful. Dividing the market by geographic area (cities, counties, provinces, etc.) is called **geographic segmentation**. A few years ago, HSBC Bank Canada pursued an expansion strategy in Canada by building branches in growing suburban communities, as this is where HSBC's target customers live. Lindsay Gordon, CEO of HSBC Bank Canada, is a big believer in the "bricks and clicks" strategy: "With more customers doing their banking online, branches are becoming a destination for financial services and advice, rather than basic transactions."[27]

Alternatively, you could aim your product's promotions toward people aged 25 to 45 who have some post-secondary training and have above-average incomes. Automobiles such as Lexus are often targeted to this audience. Segmentation by age, income, and education level are ways of **demographic segmentation**. Also included are religion, ethnic origin, and profession. This is the most used segmentation variable, but it is not necessarily the best, as the information gathered is just a starting point.

Marketers use **psychographic segmentation** when they segment markets according to personality or lifestyle (activities, interests, and opinions).[28] For example, if you decide to target teenagers, you would do an in-depth study of their values and interests. Such research reveals which TV shows they watch and which actors they like the best. That information could then be used to develop advertisements for those TV shows using those stars. PepsiCo did such a segmentation study for its Mountain Dew brand. The resulting promotion dealt with teenagers living life to the limit.

**Behavioural segmentation** divides the market based on behaviour with or toward a product.[29] Let us examine questions that you might ask while considering different variables of this segmentation strategy as it applies to your vegetarian restaurant:

- *Benefits Sought*—What benefits of vegetarianism and your food might you discuss? What should you emphasize (e.g., freshness, heart-healthiness, taste, etc.)? The Green Box highlights some concerns that consumers have raised about "green" advertising claims.

- *Usage Rate*—In marketing, the 80/20 rule says that 80 percent of your business is likely to come from just 20 percent of your customers. Determine who are the big eaters of vegetarian food. Does your restaurant attract more men or women, more students or faculty members?

- *User Status*—You may be surprised to find that repeat customers come from the local community or are commuters.

**geographic segmentation**
Dividing the market by geographic area.

**demographic segmentation**
Dividing the market by age, income, and education level.

**psychographic segmentation**
Dividing the market according to personality or lifestyle (activities, interests, and opinions).

**behavioural segmentation**
Dividing the market based on behaviour with or toward a product.

Canadian television personalities Brad Pattison and Gail Vaz-Oxlade both host popular TV shows, namely *At the End of My Leash* and *Til Debt Do Us Part*. When considering viewers for these shows, what segmentation variables are being applied? Have you seen these shows? If so, do you think that you are part of the primary target market?

**Market Segmentation**
This table shows some of the methods marketers use to divide the market. The aim of segmentation is to break the market into smaller units.

| Main Dimension | Sample Variables | Possible Segments |
|---|---|---|
| **City or Country Size** | | |
| | Region | British Columbia, Prairies, Nunavut, Eastern Quebec, Sydney, St. John's |
| | City or Country Size | under 5,000; 5,000–20,000; 20,001–50,000; 50,001–100,000; 100,001–250,000; 250,001–500,000; 500,001–1,000,000; 1,000,000+ |
| | Density | urban; suburban; rural |
| **Demographic Segmentation** | | |
| | Gender | male; female |
| | Marital Status | single; married; widowed; divorced |
| | Age | 0–5; 6–11; 12–17; 18–24; 25–34; 35–49; 50–64; 65+ |
| | Education Attainment | some education; high school graduation certificate; trades certificate or diploma; college certificate or diploma; university certificate or diploma below bachelor level; bachelor's degree; university certificate or diploma above bachelor level; medical degree; master's degree; earned doctorate |
| | Ethnic Origin | Canadian; English; French; Scottish; Irish; German; Italian; Chinese; Ukrainian; North American Indian; Dutch; Polish; East Indian; Jewish; Russian; American; Jamaican; Vietnamese; other |
| | Occupation | professional; technical; clerical; sales supervisor; farmer; homemaker; self-employed; student; unemployed; retired; other |
| | Religion | Catholic; Protestant; Christian Orthodox; other Christian; Muslim; Jewish; Buddhist; Hindu; Sikh; Eastern religions; other; no affiliation |
| **Psychographic Segmentation** | | |
| | Personality | gregarious; compulsive; extroverted; aggressive; ambitious |
| | Social Class | lower lowers; upper lowers; working class; middle class; upper middles; lower uppers; upper uppers |
| **Behavioural Segmentation** | | |
| | Benefits Sought | quality; service; low price; luxury; safety; status |
| | Usage Rate | light user; medium user; heavy user |
| | User Status | non-user; ex-user; prospect; first-time user; regular user |
| | Loyalty Status | none; medium; strong |

## GreenBOX

### When Green Is Not Really Green

Concerns about the environment and global warming are in the public's mind as never before, and advertisements that include environmental claims are becoming more and more prevalent. In their desire to convince consumers that a product causes no harm and may even benefit the environment, making claims that don't exaggerate a product's benefit or minimize its negative impact must seem to many advertisers to be like a high-wire act without a safety net.

Advertising Standards Canada (ASC) has created an Advisory that is intended to provide guidance to advertisers and the public about circumstances in which "green" advertising claims may raise issues under the Canadian Code of Advertising Standards. While ASC has only recently been hearing complaints from consumers about advertisements they believe make misleading environmental claims, this issue is not new.

In Canada, in most cases, allegedly misleading environmental claims are evaluated under Clause 1 (Accuracy and Clarity) of the Canadian Code of Advertising Standards. Whether any particular "green" claim actually raises an issue under Clause 1 depends on various factors. These include:

1. Does the environmental benefit claimed for the product appear to be supported by science-based evidence?
2. Is the scientific evidence that is being used to substantiate the claim generally well-recognized and accepted by authorities on the subject?
3. Is the advertisement unbalanced by singling out one environmentally positive attribute of the product while ignoring other characteristics or issues that may be harmful to the environment?
4. Does the advertisement make absolute and unqualified claims, such as "environmentally friendly" or "not harmful to the environment"? Or does the advertiser qualify its claims by appropriately communicating a product's limitations?

Consumers have a difficult time finding reliable information on which to base buying decisions about products that make claims about environmental benefits. "Green" advertising is a useful way to communicate important information to consumers who want to make responsible and environmentally-conscious choices between competing products that claim to respect the environment. Following the advice and comments in this Advisory can help advertisers make "green" claims that are truthful, fair, accurate and in compliance with the Code.

Source: © Advertising Standards Canada.

Once you know who your customer base is, you can design your marketing mix to appeal to that specific group or groups.

Usually, the best segmentation strategy is to use a combination of these bases to come up with a consumer profile (a target market or more) that is *sizable*, *reachable*, and *profitable*. For example, Shoppers Drug Mart Corp. uses multiple bases when it offers a selection of seasonal goods that cater to local ethnic populations. At holiday time, some stores stock Hanukkah items along with those for Christmas. This combination of geographic and demographic segmentation is an attempt to steal business from grocery chains, discounters, and department stores.[30]

When you consider the best segmentation strategy, it could be not segmenting the market at all and instead going after the total market (everyone). On the other hand, it could be going after smaller and smaller segments. Let us discuss this next.

## Reaching Smaller Market Segments

**Niche marketing** is the process of finding small but profitable market segments and designing or finding products for them. *Vita* magazine, for example, is sold in Quebec and it includes content that is relevant to French-Canadian women in their forties.[31]

**One-to-one (individual) marketing** means developing a unique mix of goods and services for each *individual customer*. Travel agencies often develop such packages, including airline reservations, hotel reservations, rental cars, restaurants, and admission to museums and other attractions for individual customers. Dell provides a unique computer system for each customer. Can you envision designing special menu items for individual customers?

**niche marketing**
The process of finding small but profitable market segments and designing or finding products for them.

**one-to-one (individual) marketing**
Developing a unique mix of goods and services for each individual customer.

# Moving Toward Relationship Marketing

**mass marketing**
Developing products and promotions to please large groups of people.

In the world of mass production following the Industrial Revolution, marketers responded by practising mass marketing. **Mass marketing** means developing products and promotions to please large groups of people. That is, there is little segmentation. The mass marketer tries to sell products to as many people as possible. That means using mass media, such as TV, radio, and newspapers. Although mass marketing led many firms to success, marketing managers often got so caught up with their products and competition that they became less responsive to the market.

**relationship marketing**
Marketing strategy with the goal of keeping individual customers over time by offering them products that exactly meet their requirements.

**Relationship marketing** tends to lead away from mass production and toward custom-made goods and services. The goal is to keep individual customers over time by offering them new products that meet their requirements exactly. The Spotlight on Small Business box shows how a small business can compete with larger firms by using relationship marketing.

The latest in technology enables sellers to work with individual buyers to determine their wants and needs and to develop goods and services specifically designed for them, such as hand-tailored shirts and unique vacations. One-way messages in mass media give way to a personal dialogue among participants. Relationship marketing combined with enterprise resource planning (ERP) links firms in a smooth customer-oriented system. Customer relationship management software such as Maximizer CRM (www.maximizer.com/) and ACT! (www.act.com/) can help keep track of client information. Businesses can consider such software to more effectively and efficiently market to their customers.

Airlines, rental car companies, and hotels have frequent-user programs through which loyal customers can earn special services and rewards. For example, a traveller can earn bonus "miles" good for free flights on an airline through a loyalty program such as the Aeroplan program. A customer can also earn benefits at a car rental agency (which includes no stopping at the rental desk—just pick up a car and go) and special services

## SPOTLIGHT ON Small Business

### Marketing Helps Small Firms Compete

Putting into practice old marketing techniques has enabled small retailers to compete with the giants such as Walmart and Sears. Zane's Cycles is a good example. Chris Zane, the owner, began the shop when he was still a teenager. Early on, he learned that to keep customers a store has to offer outstanding service and more. The principle behind such service is a concept now called customer relationship management (CRM). Long before such a concept emerged, however, small stores knew that the secret to long-term success against giant competitors is to provide superior service.

Most large stores focus on making the sale and give follow-up service little thought. Their goal is to make the transaction, and that is the end of it; thus, such an approach is called *transactional marketing*.

With CRM, in contrast, the goal is to keep a customer for life. Zane's Cycles attracts customers by setting competitive prices (and providing free coffee). Chris Zane keeps customers by giving them free lifetime service on their bicycles. He also sells helmets at cost to young people to encourage safety.

Zane keeps a database on customers so that he knows what they need and when they will need it. For example, if he sells a bicycle with a child's seat, he knows that soon the customer who purchased that bike may be buying a regular bicycle for the child—and he can send out an appropriate brochure at just the right time. Zane encourages customers to give him their names, addresses, and other such information by offering to make exchanges without receipts for those whose transaction information is in the database.

Zane also establishes close community relationships by providing scholarships for local students. Because of Zane's competitive prices, great service, and community involvement, his customers recommend his shop to others. No large store can compete with Zane's in the areas of friendly service and personal attention to each customer. That is what the new style of marketing is all about.

Are there stores in your area that offer such great service and that can compete successfully with giant department stores and national chains?

at a hotel, including faster check-in and check-out procedures, flowers in the room, free breakfasts, and free use of exercise rooms. Can you imagine having a loyalty program at your restaurant? What kind of "specials" might you offer?

Relationship marketing depends greatly on understanding consumers and responding quickly to their wants and needs. Therefore, knowing how consumers make decisions is important to marketers. An understanding of the consumer decision-making process helps marketers adapt their strategies in reaching customers and developing lasting relationships.

## The Consumer Decision-Making Process

A major part of the marketing discipline is called consumer behaviour. Figure 14.7 shows the consumer decision-making process and some of the outside factors that influence it. The five steps in the process are often studied in courses on consumer behaviour. Problem recognition may occur when your washing machine breaks down. This leads to an information search—you look for ads about washing machines and read brochures about them. You may even consult a secondary data source such as *Consumer Reports* or other information sources. And, most likely, you will seek advice from other people who have purchased washing machines. After compiling this information, you evaluate alternatives and make a purchase decision. But the process does not end there. After the purchase, you may ask the people you spoke to previously about how their machines perform and then do other comparisons. Marketing researchers investigate consumer thought processes and behaviour at each stage to determine the best way to facilitate marketing exchanges.

Consumer behaviour researchers also study the various influences that affect consumer behaviour. Figure 14.7 shows several such influences: marketing mix variables (the four Ps); psychological influences, such as perception and attitudes; situational influences, such as the type of purchase and the physical surroundings; and sociocultural influences, such as reference groups and culture. Other factors important in

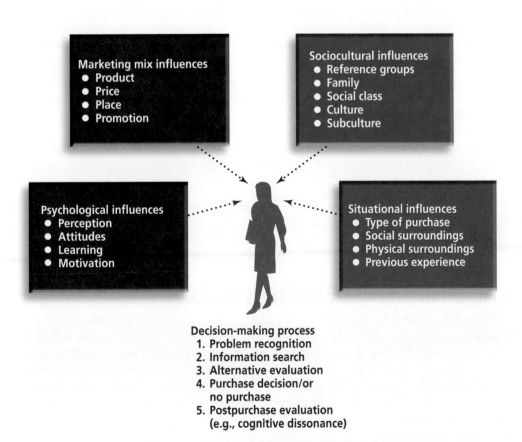

Marketing mix influences
- Product
- Price
- Place
- Promotion

Sociocultural influences
- Reference groups
- Family
- Social class
- Culture
- Subculture

Psychological influences
- Perception
- Attitudes
- Learning
- Motivation

Situational influences
- Type of purchase
- Social surroundings
- Physical surroundings
- Previous experience

Decision-making process
1. **Problem recognition**
2. **Information search**
3. **Alternative evaluation**
4. **Purchase decision/or no purchase**
5. **Postpurchase evaluation (e.g., cognitive dissonance)**

**FIGURE | 14.7**

**The Consumer Decision-Making Process and Outside Influences**
There are many influences on consumers as they decide which goods and services to buy. Marketers have some influence, but it's not usually as strong as sociocultural influences. Helping consumers in their information search and their evaluation of alternatives is a major function of marketing.

Research indicates that Canadians are becoming increasingly health-conscious, creating opportunities for marketers that can develop products to address this change in buying behaviour. Do you think that baby boomers are driving this demand, or is it being driven by people of all ages?

the consumer decision-making process whose technical definitions may be unfamiliar to you include the following:

- *Learning* involves changes in an individual's behaviour resulting from previous experiences and information. For example, if you've tried a particular brand of shampoo and you don't like it, you may never buy it again.

- *Reference group* is the group that an individual uses as a reference point in the formation of his or her beliefs, attitudes, values, or behaviours. For example, a student who carries a briefcase instead of a backpack may see business people as his or her reference group.

- *Culture*, as you may recall from Chapter 3, refers to the set of values, beliefs, rules, and institutions held by a specific group of people.[32] These are transmitted from one generation to another in a given society. Some of the changing attitudes and values in Canada include more women working outside of the home, time poverty (i.e., the increasing need for convenient products due to having less time), and attitudes toward health.[33] Consider how your restaurant can benefit from healthy takeout food that is quickly prepared.

- *Subculture* is the set of values, attitudes, and ways of doing things that results from belonging to a certain ethnic group, religious group, or other group with which one closely identifies (e.g., teenagers). The subculture is one small part of the larger culture. Your subculture may prefer rap and hip-hop music, while your parents' subculture may prefer light jazz.

- *Cognitive dissonance* is a type of psychological conflict that can occur after a purchase. Consumers who make a major purchase may have doubts about whether they got the best product at the best price. Marketers must therefore reassure such consumers that they made a good decision after the sale. An auto dealer, for example, may send the customer positive press articles about the particular car purchased. The dealer may also offer product guarantees and provide certain free services to the customer.

Consumer behaviour courses are a long-standing part of a marketing curriculum. Today, school offerings in marketing include courses in business-to-business marketing. The following section will give you some insight into that important area.

## THE BUSINESS-TO-BUSINESS MARKET

B2B marketers include manufacturers, intermediaries such as retailers, institutions (e.g., hospitals, schools, and charities), and the government. The B2B market is larger than the consumer market because items are often sold and resold several times in the B2B process before they are sold to the final consumer. The marketing strategies often differ from those in consumer marketing because business buyers have their own decision-making process. Several factors make B2B marketing different; some of the more important ones are as follows:

1. *The number of customers in the B2B market is relatively few.* That is, there are far fewer construction firms or mining operations compared to the more than 33 million potential customers in the Canadian consumer market.

2. *The size of business customers is relatively large.* That is, a few large organizations account for most of the employment and production of various goods and services. Nonetheless, there are many small- to medium-sized firms in Canada that together make an attractive market.

3. *B2B markets tend to be geographically concentrated.* For example, diamonds tend to be concentrated in Canada's territories. Consequently, marketing efforts may be concentrated in a particular geographic area and distribution problems can be minimized by locating warehouses near industrial centres.

4. *Business buyers are generally thought to be more rational (as opposed to emotional) than ultimate consumers in their selection of goods and services.* They use specifications and often more carefully weigh the total product offer, including quality, price, and service.

5. *B2B sales tend to be direct.* Manufacturers sell products, such as tires, directly to auto manufacturers but tend to use intermediaries, such as wholesalers and retailers, to sell to ultimate consumers.

6. *There is much more emphasis on personal selling in B2B markets than in consumer markets.* Whereas consumer promotions are based more on advertising, B2B sales are based on personal selling. That is because there are fewer customers who demand more personal service, and the quantities being purchased justify the expense of a sales force.

Figure 14.8 shows some of the differences between buying behaviour in the B2B market and the consumer market.

**FIGURE 14.8**

**Comparing Business-to-Business and Consumer Buying Behaviour**

| | Business-To-Business Market | Consumer Market |
|---|---|---|
| **Market structure** | Relatively few potential customers | Many potential customers |
| | Larger purchases | Smaller purchases |
| | Geographically concentrated | Geographically dispersed |
| **Products and Services** | Require technical, complex products | Require less technical products |
| | Frequently require customization | Sometimes require customization |
| | Frequently require technical advice, delivery, and after-sale service | Sometimes require technical advice, delivery, and after-sale service |
| **Buying procedures** | Buyers are trained | No special training for buyers |
| | Negotiate details of most purchases | Accept standard terms for most purchases |
| | Follow objective standards | Use personal judgment |
| | Formal process involving specific employees | Informal process involving members |
| | Closer relationships between marketers and buyers | Impersonal relationships between marketers and consumers |
| | Buy from pre-approved suppliers (in-suppliers) | Often buy from multiple sources |

## Progress Assessment

- Can you name and describe four ways to segment the consumer market?
- What is niche marketing and how does it differ from one-to-one marketing?
- List the five steps in the decision-making process.
- What are six key factors that make the business-to-business market different from the consumer market?

# Your Prospects in Marketing

There is a wider variety of careers in marketing than in most business disciplines. You could become a manager in a retail store. You could conduct marketing research or get involved in product management. You could go into selling, advertising, sales promotion, or public relations. You could get involved in transportation, storage, or international distribution. You could design interactive Web sites to implement CRM. These are just a few of the possibilities. As you read Chapter 15, consider whether a marketing career would interest you.

# SUMMARY

**LO ▸ 1**  Define marketing and explain how the marketing concept applies to both for-profit and non-profit organizations.

1. Marketing is the process of determining customer wants and needs and then providing customers with goods and services that meet or exceed these expectations.

**How has marketing changed over time?**
During the *production era*, marketing was largely a distribution function. Emphasis was on producing as many goods as possible and getting them to markets. By the early 1920s, during the *sales era*, the emphasis turned to selling and advertising to persuade customers to buy the existing goods produced by mass production. After the Second World War, the tremendous demand for goods and services led to the *marketing concept era*, during which businesses recognized the need to be responsive to customers' needs. During the 1990s, marketing entered the *customer relationship era*. The idea became one of trying to enhance customer satisfaction and stimulate long-term customer loyalty.

**What are the three parts of the marketing concept?**
The three parts of the marketing concept are (1) a customer orientation, (2) a service orientation, and (3) a profit orientation (that is, market goods and services that will earn the firm a profit and enable it to survive and expand to serve more customer wants and needs).

**What kinds of organizations are involved in marketing?**
All kinds of organizations use marketing, both for-profit and non-profit organizations. Examples of non-profit organizations include the provinces and other government agencies, charities (e.g., churches), politicians, and schools.

**LO ▸ 2**  List and describe the four Ps of marketing.

2. The marketing mix consists of the four Ps of marketing: product, price, place, and promotion.

**How do marketers implement the four Ps?**
The idea is to design a product that people want, price it competitively, place it in a location where consumers can find it easily, and promote it so that consumers know it exists. While this chapter briefly outlined these Ps, they will be discussed in more detail in Chapter 15.

3.  Marketing research is the analysis of markets to determine opportunities and challenges and to find the information needed to make good decisions.

    **What are the steps to follow when conducting marketing research?**
    (1) Define the problem or opportunity and determine the present situation, (2) collect data, (3) analyze the research data, and (4) choose the best solution and implement it.

    **What are different methods used to gather research?**
    Research can be gathered through secondary data (information that has already be compiled by others) and published in sources such as journals, newspapers, directories, databases, and internal sources. Primary data (data that you gather yourself) includes observation, surveys, interviews, and focus groups.

    **What is environmental scanning?**
    Environmental scanning is the process of identifying the factors that can affect marketing success. Marketers pay attention to all environmental factors that create opportunities and threats.

    **What are some of the more important environmental trends in marketing?**
    The most important global and technological change is probably the growth of the Internet. An important technological change is the growth of consumer databases. Using consumer databases, companies can develop products and services that closely match the needs of customers. There are a number of social trends that marketers must monitor to maintain their close relationship with customers—population growth and shifts, for example. Of course, marketers must also monitor the dynamic competitive environment and pay attention to the economic environment.

    **LO ▶ 3** Describe the marketing research process, and explain how marketers use environmental scanning to learn about the changing marketing environment

4.  The process of dividing the total market into several groups whose members have similar characteristics is called market segmentation.

    **What are some of the ways that marketers segment the consumer market?**
    Geographic segmentation means dividing the market into different regions. Segmentation by age, income, and education level are methods of demographic segmentation. We could study a group's personality or lifestyle (activities, interests, and opinions) to understand psychographic segmentation. Behavioural segmentation divides the market based on behaviour with or toward a product. Different variables of behavioural segmentation include benefits sought, usage rate, and user status. The best segmentation strategy is to use as many of these segmentation bases as possible to come up with a consumer profile (a target market) that's sizable, reachable, and profitable.

    **LO ▶ 4** Explain how marketers meet the needs of the consumer market through market segmentation, relationship marketing, and the study of consumer behaviour

    **What is the difference between mass marketing and relationship marketing?**
    Mass marketing means developing products and promotions to please large groups of people. Relationship marketing tends to lead away from mass production and toward custom-made goods and services. Its goal is to keep individual customers over time by offering them goods or services that meet their needs.

    **What are some of the factors that influence the consumer decision-making process?**
    See Figure 14.7 for some of the major influences on consumer decision making. Some other factors in the process are learning, reference group, culture, subculture, and cognitive dissonance.

5.  The B2B market consists of manufacturers, intermediaries such as retailers, institutions (e.g., hospitals, schools, and charities), and the government.

    **LO ▶ 5** List ways in which the business-to-business market differs from the consumer market.

    **What makes the business-to-business market different from the consumer market?**
    The number of customers in the B2B market is relatively small, and the size of business customers is relatively large. B2B markets tend to be geographically concentrated, and industrial buyers generally are more rational than ultimate consumers in their selection of goods and services. B2B sales tend to be direct, and there is much more emphasis on personal selling in B2B markets than in consumer markets.

## KEY TERMS

behavioural segmentation  435

brand name  426

business-to-business (B2B) market  433

consumer market  433

customer relationship management (CRM)  423

demographic segmentation  435

environmental scanning  430

focus group  430

geographic segmentation  435

green marketing  422

market segmentation  434

marketing  422

marketing concept  423

marketing mix  424

marketing research  428

mass marketing  438

niche marketing  437

one-to-one (individual) marketing  437

price  426

primary data  428

product  425

promotion  427

psychographic segmentation  435

relationship marketing  438

secondary data  428

target marketing  434

test marketing  425

## CRITICAL THINKING

1. Do you agree that individual consumers are not rational decision makers? Are you aware of marketers' efforts, and in some cases success, in targeting you for goods and services?

2. When businesses buy goods and services from other businesses, they usually buy in large volumes. Sales-people in the B2B area usually are paid on a commission basis. Do you agree that it is more professionally rewarding for employees to be engaged in B2B marketing/sales?

3. Retailers such as Hudson's Bay Company (HBC Rewards) and Canadian Tire Corporation (Canadian Tire money) offer loyalty programs. Are you encouraged to visit these retailers more often as a result of such programs? Do you buy more products as a result of programs? Do you buy more products as a result of

such programs? Many retailers also offer incentives to use their credit cards. For example, you may get 10 percent off your purchase if you open an HBC credit card account. Points that you accumulate on your Canadian Tire Options® MasterCard® can be redeemed for Canadian Tire merchandise, auto parts, or auto labour. Do you feel that companies are trying to bribe you to support their businesses, or do you think that these are good business practices? Explain.

4. What environmental changes are occurring in your community? What environmental changes in marketing are most likely to change your career prospects in the future? How can you learn more about those changes? What might you do to prepare for them?

## DEVELOPING WORKPLACE SKILLS

1. Think of an effective marketing mix for one of the following products: a new electric car, an easy-to-use digital camera, or a car wash for your neighbourhood. Be prepared to discuss your ideas in class.

2. Working in teams of five (or on your own if class size is a problem), think of a product that your friends want but cannot get on or near campus. You might ask your friends at other schools what is available there. What kind of product would fill that need? Discuss your results in class and determine how you might go about marketing that new product.

3. Relationship marketing efforts include frequent-flier deals at airlines, special discounts for members at certain supermarkets (e.g., Sobeys), and Web sites that remember your name and what you've purchased in the past and recommend new products that you may like (e.g., Amazon.ca). Evaluate any one of these programs. (If you have no personal experience with them, look up such programs on the Internet.) What might they do to increase your satisfaction and loyalty? Be prepared to discuss these programs in class.

4. Working in teams of four or five, list as many brand names of pizza as you can. Merge your list with those from other groups. Then try to identify the "target market" for each brand. Do they all seem to be after the same market, or are there different brands for different markets? What are the separate appeals?

5. Imagine that you are starting up a company but have a shoe-string budget (i.e., very little money). How would you market your company and its products and services? If applicable for promotion, you may wish to consider newer forms such as mobile advertising, etc. Justify your decisions.

## TAKING IT TO THE NET 1

www.mcgrawhillconnect.ca

### Purpose

To understand some aspects of the Canadian population.

### Exercise

Visit the Statistics Canada Web site at www.statcan.gc.ca and click on Find Statistics by Subject. Then click on Population and Demography, then Summary Tables (in the left-hand column).

1. Type in the key words Family Income, by Family Type. What is the median total income?

2. Type in the key words Immigrant Population by Place of Birth, by Province and Territory. What are the top three places of birth for Canadian immigrants?

3. Type in the key words Population by Marital Status and Sex. What percentage of Canadians are single, married, widowed, and divorced? If you were considering a mass marketing campaign, which segment would be the largest?

4. Type in the key words Population by Mother Tongue, by Province and Territory. What are the top three languages spoken in Canada? Where do you fall within these categories?

# TAKING IT TO THE NET 2

## Purpose

To find out how much car you can afford.

## Exercise

This handy tool provides you with an easy way to help determine the price range of car that might be most affordable for you. See for yourself at http://www.cars4u.com/calculators/. Choose "How much car can I afford?" and then fill in the fields with your information.

1. What is your monthly payment?

2. Play around with the income and expenses fields. For example, if you were making $45,000 per year and had expenses of $1,000 (housing—$800 and student loan—$200), what could you afford?

3. Based on this information, how likely is it that you will own a car in five years? What factors are likely to change in the next five years that will allow you to purchase a car?

# ANALYZING MANAGEMENT DECISIONS

## Applying Customer-Oriented Marketing Concepts at Thermos

Thermos is the company made famous by its Thermos bottles and lunch boxes. Thermos also manufactures cookout grills. Its competitors include Sunbeam and Weber. To become a world-class competitor, Thermos completely reinvented the way it conducted its marketing operations. By reviewing what Thermos did, you can see how new marketing concepts affect organizations.

First, Thermos modified its corporate culture. It had become a bureaucratic firm organized by function: design, engineering, manufacturing, marketing, and so on. That organizational structure was replaced by flexible, cross-functional, self-managed teams. The idea was to focus on a customer group—for example, buyers of outdoor grills—and build a product development team to create a product for that market.

The product development team for grills consisted of six middle managers from various disciplines, including engineering, manufacturing, finance, and marketing. They called themselves the Lifestyle Team because their job was to study grill users to see how they lived and what they were looking for in an outdoor grill. To get a fresh perspective, the company hired Fitch, Inc., an outside consulting firm, to help with design and marketing research. Team leadership was rotated based on needs of the moment. For example, the marketing person took the lead in doing field research, but the R&D person took over when technical developments became the issue.

The team's first step was to analyze the market. Together, team members spent about a month on the road talking with people, videotaping barbecues, conducting focus groups, and learning what people wanted in an outdoor grill. The company found that people wanted a nice-looking grill that didn't pollute the air and was easy to use. It also had to be safe enough for apartment dwellers, which meant that it had to be electric.

As the research results came in, engineering began playing with ways to improve electric grills. Manufacturing kept in touch to ensure that any new ideas could be produced economically. Design people were already building models of the new product. R&D people relied heavily on Thermos's strengths. The company's core strength was the vacuum technology it had developed to keep hot things hot and cold things cold in Thermos bottles. Drawing on that strength, the engineers developed a domed lid that contained the heat inside the grill.

Once a prototype was developed, the company showed the model to potential customers, who suggested several changes. Employees also took sample grills home and tried to find weaknesses. Using the input from potential customers and employees, the company used continuous improvement to manufacture what became a world-class outdoor grill.

No product can become a success without communicating with the market. The team took the grill on the road, showing it at trade shows and in retail stores. The product was such a success that Thermos is now using self-managed customer-oriented teams to develop all of its product lines.

## Discussion Questions

1. How could the growth of self-managed cross-functional teams affect marketing departments in other companies? Do you believe that would be a good change or not? Explain.

2. How can Thermos now build a closer relationship with its customers using the Internet?

3. What other products might Thermos develop that would appeal to the same market segment that uses outdoor grills?

## CHAPTER 15

# Managing the Marketing Mix: Product, Price, Place, and Promotion

## LEARNING OBJECTIVES

**AFTER YOU HAVE READ AND STUDIED THIS CHAPTER, YOU SHOULD BE ABLE TO:**

**LO ▶ 1** Explain the concept of a total product offer and the functions of packaging.

**LO ▶ 2** Describe the differences between a brand name and a trademark, and explain the concepts of brand equity and brand loyalty.

**LO ▶ 3** List the various pricing objectives and strategies, and explain why non-pricing strategies are growing in importance.

**LO ▶ 4** Explain the concept of marketing channels and the value of marketing intermediaries.

**LO ▶ 5** Discuss retailing and explain the various kinds of non-store retailing.

**LO ▶ 5** Define promotion and list the five traditional tools that make up the promotion mix.

## Getting to Know Ron Foxcroft of Fox 40 International Inc.

For successful Canadian entrepreneur and inventor Ron Foxcroft, it all started in 1982 when he purchased Fluke Transport, a Southern Ontario trucking business. The company slogan—If It's On Time…It's A "FLUKE"—was soon recognized throughout North America. Over the years, Foxcroft diversified into new ventures and the Foxcroft Group of Companies now includes Fluke Transportation Group, Hamilton Terminals Inc., Foxcroft Capital Group, and Fox 40 International Inc.

The formation of Fox 40 International Inc. is the result of a dream for a pealess whistle. When Foxcroft began developing the Whistle, he was motivated by his knowledge and experience as an international basketball referee. Frustrated with faulty pea whistles, he spent three years of development with design consultant Chuck Shepherd, resulting in the creation of the Fox 40® Classic Whistle (named for Foxcroft and that he was 40 when his invention was being developed). Introduced in 1987, this finely tuned precision instrument doesn't use a pea to generate sound. In fact, there are no moving parts whatsoever. There is nothing to obstruct sound, nothing to stick, freeze, or fail. The patented design moves the air blast through three tuned chambers. Fox 40® Whistles are 100 percent constructed of high-impact ABS plastic so they are 100 percent impervious to moisture. A quick rinse in disinfectant eliminates bacteria. Every time, they deliver on faultless performance (e.g., loudness) and they never fail.

Foxcroft pledged to Shepherd that he would continue to make the Whistle better and the company has done just that by introducing new Whistles and product lines. (You can read about the newest product in the Analyzing Management Decisions Case.) Foxcroft credits his customers and employees for the design, marketing, and improvements to the original Whistle. In his words, "When you are the best, you need to be better." As a result, the company is the world leader in pealess Whistle design and innovation, with thousands of Fox 40® Whistles produced per day for shipment to more than 140 countries. These Whistles can be heard in arenas, stadiums, and gymnasiums and it is estimated that 98 percent of all referees around the world use a Fox 40® Whistle. It is the sanctioned Whistle for referees and officials in several professional and amateur sports leagues including the NBA, NFL, NHL, FIFA, and the NCAA. Fox 40® Whistles are also used by fire and rescue professionals around the world (including the Royal Life Saving Society of Canada, the U.S. Coast Guard, and NATO forces), lifeguards, school crossing guards, boaters, and for individual safety use.

Ron Foxcroft's philosophy of "be the best at what you do" has contributed to his success both on and off the basketball courts. In 2007, he was chosen by *REFEREE* magazine to be one of the 52 most influential persons in North American Officiating of all time. *PROFIT* magazine voted him to be one of the top ten Canadian businessmen in the 1990s. Today, he continues his active role as Founder and CEO of Fox 40 International Inc. and Chairman and CEO of Fluke Transportation. On the courts, he is in his sixth season as an Evaluator for the National Basketball Association.

When asked where he next plans to target his Whistles, Foxcroft responds that he does not know where the new markets are but that the eyes and ears of employees are open. "There is no data to say we are not in every market," he says. "There must be markets that we are not hitting as we will not accept that we are in every market."

Foxcroft's story illustrates that marketing begins with watching people to understand their needs. It then involves developing products and services that customers might want. Those products and services need to be perfected and tested in the marketplace. One must develop a marketing mix that will resonate with the target market. Making such decisions is challenging, but if you are successful, you can make a lot of customers very happy. This is what marketing is all about.

Sources: "Catching the Ear of the World!" Fox 40 International Inc., 2008, http://www.fox40world.com/index.cfm?pagepath=ABOUT_US/Corporate&id =4099; Ron Foxcroft, Founder and Chairman of Fox 40 International Inc., in-person interviews, 12 February 2008 and 10 December 2007; REFEREE Staff, "Not An Inadvertent Whistle," *REFEREE Magazine*, July 2007, 45-47; Global TV, "Ron Foxcroft," Summit of Life, Summer 2005; and "Ron Foxcroft," Famous, Should Be Famous, and Infamous Canadians, 21 April 2002, http://www.famouscanadians.net/name/f/foxcroftron.php.

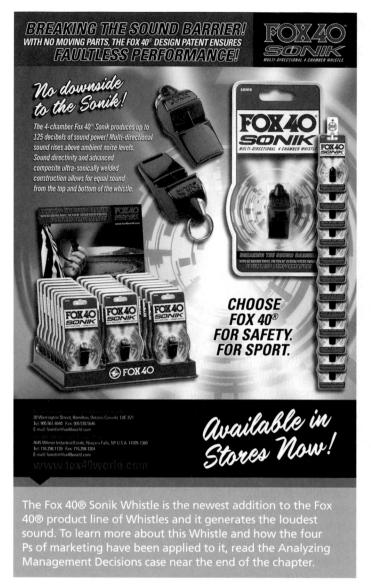

The Fox 40® Sonik Whistle is the newest addition to the Fox 40® product line of Whistles and it generates the loudest sound. To learn more about this Whistle and how the four Ps of marketing have been applied to it, read the Analyzing Management Decisions case near the end of the chapter.

**product differentiation**
The creation of real or perceived product differences.

# Product Differentiation

**Product differentiation** is the creation of real or perceived product differences. Actual product differences are sometimes quite small, so marketers must use a creative mix of pricing, advertising, and packaging (value enhancers) to create a unique and attractive image. Various bottled water companies, for example, have successfully attempted product differentiation. These companies made their bottled waters so attractive through pricing and promotion that restaurant customers often order water by brand name instead of other popular cola drinks such as Coke.

There's no reason why you couldn't create an attractive image for Very Vegetarian, your vegetarian restaurant. It would be easy to differentiate such a restaurant from the typical burger joint. Small businesses can often win market share with creative product differentiation. For example, yearbook photographer Charlie Clark competes with other yearbook photographers by offering multiple clothing changes, backgrounds, and poses along with special allowances, discounts, and guarantees. This is just one more example of how small businesses may have the advantage of being more flexible than big businesses in adapting to customer wants and needs and providing attractive product differences. How could you be equally creative in responding to the consumer wants of vegetarians?

# Packaging Changes the Product

Consumers evaluate many aspects of the total product offer, including the brand. It's surprising how important packaging can be in such evaluations.[7] Companies have used packaging to change and improve their basic product. Thus, we have squeezable ketchup bottles that stand upside down on their caps for easier pouring, toothpaste pumps, packaged dinners that can be cooked in a microwave oven, and so forth. In each case, the package changed the product in the minds of consumers and opened large markets.

Packaging can also help make a product more attractive to retailers. For example, the Universal Product Codes (UPCs) on many packages help stores control inventory; the UPC is the combination of a bar code (those familiar black and white lines) and a preset number that gives the retailer information about the product (price, size, colour, etc.). In short, packaging changes the product by changing its visibility, usefulness, or attractiveness.

Today, packaging carries more of the promotional burden than in the past. Many products that were once sold by salespeople are now being sold in self-service outlets, and the package has been given more sales responsibility. The package communicates information about the contents and the benefits of the product. It can also give some indication of price, value, and uses.

Services can also be packaged. For example, Virgin Airlines includes door-to-door limousine service and in-flight massages in its total package. Financial institutions are offering everything from financial advice to help in purchasing insurance, stocks, bonds, mutual funds, and more. When combining goods or services into one package, it's important not to include so much that the price becomes too high. It's best to work with customers to develop value enhancers that meet their individual needs.

---

## Progress Assessment

- What's the difference between a product line and a product mix?
- What functions does packaging now perform?
- What value enhancers may be included in a total product offer?

# BRANDING AND BRAND EQUITY

Closely related to packaging is branding. Recall from Chapter 14 that the word brand is sufficiently comprehensive to include practically all means of identification of a product. Brand names you may be familiar with include Air Canada, Roots, and President's Choice. Such brand names give products a distinction that tends to make them attractive to consumers.[8] For the buyer, a brand name assures quality, reduces search time, and adds prestige to purchases. For the seller, brand names facilitate new-product introductions, help promotional efforts, add to repeat purchases, and differentiate products so that prices can be set higher.

A **trademark** is a brand that has been given exclusive legal protection for both the brand name and the pictorial design. Trademarks such as the Quebec Winter Carnival's Bonhomme Carnaval mascot, the National Hockey League's Stanley Cup, and the Nike swoosh are widely recognized. Trademarks need to be protected from other companies that may want to trade on the trademark holder's reputation and image. Companies often sue other companies for too closely matching brand names. This was the case when Mattel, Inc., owner of the Barbie doll registered trademark, tried to stop Barbie's, a small chain of Montreal restaurants, from registering the word "Barbie's" as a trademark for use with restaurant services. However, the Supreme Court of Canada ruled in favour of the restaurant chain as "there was no evidence that adult consumers would consider a doll manufacturer to be a source of good food."[9] In another example, the Victoria School of Business and Technology Inc. (VSBT) received a cease and desist letter from Apple Inc. claiming that the School's logo "reproduces, without authority, our client's Apple design logo which it widely uses. By doing so, you are infringing Apple's rights, and further, falsely suggesting that Apple has authorized your activities."[10] In this case, what are the School's options? Which one would you pursue?

## Generating Brand Equity and Loyalty

A major goal of marketers in the future is to leverage their companies' and products' brand equity. **Brand equity** is the combination of factors—such as awareness, loyalty, perceived quality, images, and emotions—that people associate with a given brand name. The core of brand equity is brand loyalty. **Brand loyalty** is the degree to which customers are satisfied, enjoy the brand, and are committed to further purchases. A loyal group of customers represents substantial value to a firm.[11] Canadian brand names with the highest brand values—that is, how much profit the brands are likely to generate for their owners—are RBC Financial Group ($5.05 billion), TD Canada Trust ($3.39 billion), Manulife Financial ($3.19 billion), and BCE ($3.13 billion).[12] To learn about the best global brands, including the top Canadian brands, complete the Taking It To The Net exercise near the end of this chapter.

**Brand awareness** refers to how quickly or easily a given brand name comes to mind when a product category is mentioned. Advertising helps build strong brand awareness. Event sponsorship, such as the Rogers Cup tennis tournament and the RONA MS Bike Tour, can contribute to brand awareness.

## Brand Management

A **brand manager** (known as a *product manager* in some firms) has direct responsibility for one brand or one product line. This responsibility includes all elements of the marketing mix. Thus, the brand manager might be thought of as president of a one-product firm.

**trademark**
A brand that has been given exclusive legal protection for both the brand name and the pictorial design.

Do you agree that people would confuse the VSBT logo with the Apple logo?

**brand equity**
The combination of factors—such as awareness, loyalty, perceived quality, images, and emotions—that people associate with a given brand name.

**brand loyalty**
The degree to which customers are satisfied, enjoy the brand, and are committed to further purchase.

**brand awareness**
How quickly or easily a given brand name comes to mind when a product category is mentioned.

**brand manager**
A manager who has direct responsibility for one brand or one product line; called a product manager in some firms.

Many large consumer product companies created the position of brand manager to have greater control over new-product development and product promotion.[13] Some companies have brand management *teams* to bolster the overall effort.

Typically, brand managers make marketing decisions (as they apply to the four Ps) throughout the life cycle of each product and service. For example, what do you do with a product that has a well-known brand name but fading sales? One solution may be to reinvent the product to satisfy the needs of loyal customers in the form of a new and improved version of the original product. Companies also need to introduce new products and services to satisfy customers' needs or risk having competitors steal their business. For example, Gillette introduced its Fusion Power Phenon razor that directly competes with its other razors, including the Mach3 brand. The Fusion Power Phenon razor is promoted as offering "more comfort and less irritation than the Mach3 razor." In other instances, the decision may be made to abandon the product or service and focus on other areas. This was the case when IBM sold its personal computer unit in favour of focusing on offering technology and consulting services.[14] You will learn more about such decision-making in an Introduction to Marketing course.

## Progress Assessment

- What's the difference between a brand name and a trademark?
- What are the key components of brand equity?
- Explain the role of brand managers.

# COMPETITIVE PRICING

Pricing is the only element of the four Ps that generates revenue. It is one of the most difficult of the four Ps for a manager to control. This is important because price is a critical ingredient in consumer evaluations of the product. In this section, we'll explore price both as an ingredient of the total product offer and as a strategic marketing tool.

## Pricing Objectives

A firm may have several objectives in mind when setting a pricing strategy. When pricing a new vegetarian offering, we may want to promote the product's image. If we price it high and use the right promotion, maybe we can make it the Evian of vegetarian meals. We also might price it high to achieve a certain profit objective or return on investment. We could also price such a product lower than its competitors, as low pricing may discourage competition because the profit potential is less in this case. A low price may also help us capture a larger share of the market. The point is that a firm may have several pricing objectives over time, and it must formulate these objectives clearly before developing an overall pricing strategy. Popular objectives include the following:

1. *Achieving a target return on investment or profit.* Ultimately, the goal of marketing is to make a profit by providing goods and services to others. Naturally, one long-run pricing objective of almost all firms is to optimize profit.[15]

2. *Building traffic.* Supermarkets often advertise certain products at or below cost to attract people to the store. These products are called *loss leaders*. The long-run objective is to make profits by following the short-run objective of building a customer base. Yahoo! once provided an auction service for free to compete with eBay. Why give such a service away for free? To increase advertising revenue on the Yahoo! site and attract more people to Yahoo!'s other services.

3. *Achieving greater market share.* The auto industry is in a fierce international battle to capture and hold market share. One way to capture a larger part of the market is to offer low finance rates (e.g., zero-percent financing), low lease rates, or rebates.

4. *Creating an image.* Certain watches (e.g., Rolex), perfumes, and other socially visible products are priced high to give them an image of exclusivity and status.

5. *Furthering social objectives.* A firm may want to price a product low so that people with little money can afford the product. The government often gets involved in pricing farm products so that everyone can get basic needs such as milk and bread at a low price.

Note that a firm may have short-run objectives that differ greatly from its long-run objectives. Both should be understood at the beginning and put into the strategic marketing plan. Pricing objectives should be influenced by other marketing decisions regarding product design, packaging, branding, distribution, and promotion. All of these marketing decisions are interrelated.

## Major Approaches to Pricing

People believe intuitively that the price charged for a product must bear some relation to the cost of producing the product. In fact, we'd generally agree that prices are usually set somewhere above cost. But as we'll see, prices and cost aren't always related. Let us consider three major approaches to pricing strategy.

### Cost-Based Pricing

Producers often use cost as a primary basis for setting price. They develop elaborate cost accounting systems to measure production costs (including materials, labour, and overhead), add in some margin of profit, and come up with a price. The question is whether the price will be satisfactory to the market as well. In the long run, the market—not the producer—determines what the price will be. Pricing should take into account costs, but it should also include the expected costs of product updates, the objectives for each product, and competitor prices.

### Demand-Based Pricing

This strategy considers factors underlying customer tastes and preferences when selecting the price. This can include bundling, psychological pricing, and target costing.

**Bundling** means grouping two or more products together and pricing them as a unit. For example, a store might price a unit of a washer and a dryer at a cheaper price than if they were each purchased separately. **Psychological pricing** means pricing goods and services at price points that make the product appear less expensive than it is. For example, a house might be priced at $299,000 with the idea that it sounds like a lot less than $300,000.

**Target costing** means designing a product so that it satisfies customers and meets the profit margins desired by the firm. Target costing makes the final price an input to the product development process, not an outcome of it. You estimate the selling price people would be willing to pay for a product and subtract the desired profit margin. The result is the target cost of production. Japanese companies such as Isuzu Motors, Komatsu Limited, and Sony have used target costing.

### Competition-Based Pricing

**Competition-based pricing** is a strategy based on what all the other competitors are doing. The price can be at, above, or below competitors' prices. Pricing depends on customer loyalty, perceived differences, and the competitive climate. **Price leadership** is the procedure by which one or more dominant firms set the pricing practices that all competitors in an industry follow. You may have noticed this practice among oil and cigarette companies.

Lakeport Brewing started the value beer category in Ontario and it was the first brewer to offer "24 for $24." Positioned as a great beer at value prices, what is the pricing objective?

**bundling**
Grouping two or more products together and pricing them as a unit.

**psychological pricing**
Pricing goods and services at price points that make the product appear less expensive than it is.

**target costing**
Designing a product so that it satisfies customers and meets the profit margins desired by the firm.

**competition-based pricing**
A pricing strategy based on what all the other competitors are doing. The price can be set at, above, or below competitors' prices.

**price leadership**
The procedure by which one or more dominant firms set the pricing practices that all competitors in an industry follow.

Bundle pricing is based on the idea that consumers value the package more than the individual items. Maxxim Vacations offers concert and theatre getaway packages in addition to vacation experiences. Can you think of other examples of bundle pricing?

*Atlantic Canada* ✺
**VACATION PLANNER 2009**

Newfoundland and Labrador
Nova Scotia
Prince Edward Island
New Brunswick

*Creating Memorable Experiences*

## Break-Even Analysis

Before you begin selling a new vegetarian sandwich, it may be wise to determine how many sandwiches you'd have to sell before making a profit. You'd then determine whether you could reach such a sales goal. **Break-even analysis** is the process used to determine profitability at various levels of sales. The break-even point is the point where revenue from sales equals all costs. The formula for calculating the break-even point is as follows:

**break-even analysis**
The process used to determine profitability at various levels of sales.

$$\text{Break-even point (BEP)} = \frac{\text{Total fixed cost (FC)}}{\text{Price of one unit (P)} - \text{Variable cost (VC) of one unit}}$$

**total fixed costs**
All expenses that remain the same no matter how many products are made or sold.

**Total fixed costs** are all expenses that remain the same no matter how many products are made or sold. Among the expenses that make up fixed costs are the amount paid to own or rent a factory or warehouse and the amount paid for business insurance. **Variable costs** change according to the level of production. Included are the expenses for the materials used to make products and the direct costs of labour used to make those goods.

**variable costs**
Costs that change according to the level of production.

To produce a specific product, let's say you have a fixed cost of $200,000 (for mortgage interest, real estate taxes, equipment, and so on). Your variable cost (e.g., labour and materials) per item is $2. If you sold the product for $4, the break-even point would be 100,000 items. In other words, you wouldn't make any money selling this product unless you sold more than 100,000 of it:

$$\text{BEP} = \frac{\text{FC}}{\text{P} - \text{VC}} = \frac{\$200,000}{\$4.00 - \$2.00} = \frac{\$200,000}{\$2.00} = 100,000 \text{ boxes}$$

Air Canada plans to reduce aircraft weight in an attempt to save fuel have included measures such as tightening weight limits on the checked-luggage allowance, only partly filling water tanks, disposing of empty wine bottles at the arrival city instead of flying them back to the departure site, and replacing glass wine bottles with Tetra Paks.[16] Would these measures be targeted at decreasing fixed costs or variable costs?

## Pricing Strategies for New Products

Let's say that a firm has just developed a new line of products, such as high-definition television (HDTV) sets. The firm has to decide how to price these sets at the introductory stage of the product life cycle. A **skimming price strategy** is one in which a new product is priced high to make optimum profit while there's little competition. Of course, those large profits will attract competitors.

A second strategy would be to price the new TV low. A **penetration price strategy** is one in which the product is priced low to attract more customers and discourage competitors. Nintendo consciously chose a penetration strategy when it originally introduced its GameCube video game console (predecessor to Nintendo's Wii) by choosing a price substantially lower than Microsoft's Xbox and Sony's PlayStation consoles.[17] What are disadvantages of such a strategy?

## Retailer Pricing Strategies

Several pricing strategies are used by retailers. One is called **everyday low pricing (EDLP)**, the pricing strategy used by Home Depot and Walmart. Such stores set prices lower than competitors and usually do not have many special sales. The idea is to have consumers come to those stores whenever they want a bargain rather than waiting until there is a sale, as they do with most department stores.[18]

Department stores and other retailers most often use a **high–low pricing strategy**. The idea is to have regular prices that are higher than those at stores using EDLP but also to have many special sales in which the prices are lower than those of competitors. The problem with such pricing is that it teaches consumers to wait for sales, thus cutting into profits.[19] As the Internet grows in popularity, you may see fewer stores with a high–low strategy, because consumers will be able to find better prices on the Internet and begin buying more and more from online retailers.

## How Market Forces Affect Pricing

Recognizing the fact that different consumers may be willing to pay different prices, marketers sometimes price on the basis of consumer demand rather than cost or some other calculation. That's called *demand-oriented pricing* and it's reflected by movie theatres with low rates for children and by department stores, such as Zellers, that offer discounts to senior citizens if they shop there on certain days.

Marketers are facing a new pricing problem: customers can now compare prices of many goods and services on the Internet. For example, you may want to check out deals on sites such as Travelocity.ca or Hotels.ca. Priceline.com introduced consumers to a "demand collection system," in which buyers post the price they are willing to pay and invite sellers to either accept or decline that price. Consumers can get great prices on airlines, hotels, and other products by naming the price they are willing to pay. You can also buy used goods online. Have you or any of your friends bought or sold anything on eBay.ca, Kijiji.ca, or Craigslist.ca? Clearly, price competition is going to heat up as consumers have more access to price information from around the world. As a result, non-price competition is likely to increase.

## NON-PRICE COMPETITION

In spite of the emphasis placed on price in microeconomic theory, marketers often compete on product attributes other than price. You may have noted that price differences are small with products such as gasoline, men's haircuts, candy bars, and even major products such as compact cars. Typically, you will not see price used as a major promotional appeal. Instead, marketers tend to stress product image and consumer benefits such as comfort, style, convenience, and durability.

**skimming price strategy**
A strategy in which a new product is priced high to make optimum profit while there's little competition.

**penetration price strategy**
A strategy in which the product is priced low to attract many customers and discourage competitors.

**everyday low pricing (EDLP)**
Setting prices lower than competitors and then not having any special sales.

**high–low pricing strategy**
Set prices that are higher than EDLP stores, but have many special sales where the prices are lower than competitors.

The Home Depot offers free Know-How Workshops on everything from laying tile to installing a toilet to how to save money on your energy bills. What other retailers use non-price competition?

Organizations of all sizes promote the services that accompany basic products rather than price to be competitive. The idea is that good service will enhance a relatively homogeneous product. Often marketers emphasize non-price differences because prices are so easy to match. However, few competitors can match the image of a friendly, responsive, consumer-oriented company. Other strategies to avoid price wars include adding value (e.g., home delivery from a drugstore), educating consumers on how to use the product, and establishing relationships. Customers will pay extra for goods and services when they have a friendly relationship with the seller. The services aren't always less expensive, but they offer more value.

## Progress Assessment

- Can you list two short-term and two long-term pricing objectives? Can the two be compatible?
- What's a disadvantage of using a cost-based pricing strategy?
- Can you calculate a product's break-even point if producing it costs $10,000 and revenue from the sale is $20?
- Why is increasing focus being placed on non-price competition?

**marketing intermediaries**
Organizations that assist in moving goods and services from producers to business and consumer users.

**channel of distribution**
A set of marketing intermediaries, such as agents, brokers, wholesalers, and retailers, that join together to transport and store goods in their path (or channel) from producers to consumers.

**agents and brokers**
Marketing intermediaries that bring buyers and sellers together and assist in negotiating an exchange but don't take title to the goods.

**wholesaler**
A marketing intermediary that sells to other organizations.

**retailer**
An organization that sells to ultimate consumers.

# THE IMPORTANCE OF CHANNELS OF DISTRIBUTION

There are thousands of marketing intermediaries whose job it is to help move goods from the raw-material state to producers and then on to consumers. **Marketing intermediaries** are organizations that assist in moving goods and services from producers to business and consumer users. They're called intermediaries because they're in the middle of a whole series of organizations that join together to help distribute goods from producers to consumers. A **channel of distribution** consists of a set of marketing intermediaries, such as agents, brokers, wholesalers, and retailers, that join together to transport and store goods in their path (or channel) from producers to consumers.

**Agents and brokers** are marketing intermediaries that bring buyers and sellers together and assist in negotiating an exchange, but don't take title to the goods—that is, at no point do they own the goods. A **wholesaler** is a marketing intermediary that sells to other organizations, such as retailers, manufacturers, and institutions (e.g., hospitals). They are part of the business-to-business (B2B) system. A **retailer** is an organization that sells to ultimate consumers (that is, people like you and me) who buy for their own use. For consumers to receive the maximum benefit from marketing intermediaries, the various organizations must work together to ensure a smooth flow of goods and services to the customer.

Channels of distribution ensure communication flows and the flow of money and title to goods. They also help ensure that the right quantity and assortment of goods will be available when and where needed.[20] Figure 15.2 depicts selected channels of distribution for both consumer and industrial (or B2B) goods.

FIGURE 15.2

**Selected Channels of Distribution for Industrial and Consumer Goods and Services**

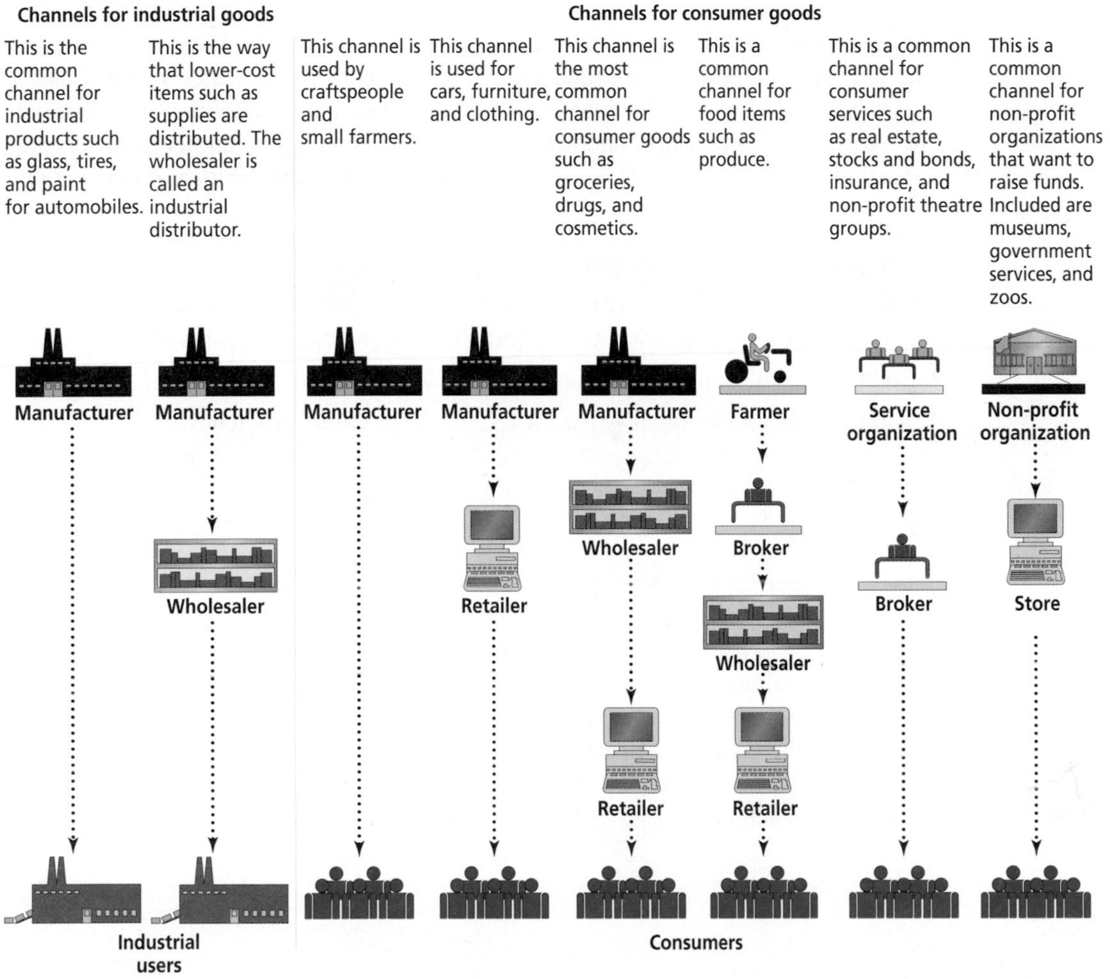
Channels for industrial goods
Channels for consumer goods
This is the common channel for industrial products such as glass, tires, and paint for automobiles.
This is the way that lower-cost items such as supplies are distributed. The wholesaler is called an industrial distributor.
This channel is used by craftspeople and small farmers.
This channel is used for cars, furniture, and clothing.
This channel is the most common channel for consumer goods such as groceries, drugs, and cosmetics.
This is a common channel for food items such as produce.
This is a common channel for consumer services such as real estate, stocks and bonds, insurance, and non-profit theatre groups.
This is a common channel for non-profit organizations that want to raise funds. Included are museums, government services, and zoos.
Manufacturer
Manufacturer
Manufacturer
Manufacturer
Manufacturer
Farmer
Service organization
Non-profit organization
Wholesaler
Retailer
Wholesaler
Broker
Broker
Store
Wholesaler
Retailer
Retailer
Industrial users
Consumers

## Why Marketing Needs Intermediaries: Creating Exchange Efficiency

Manufacturers don't always need marketing intermediaries to sell their goods to consumer and business buyers.[21] Figure 15.2 shows that some manufacturers sell directly to buyers. So why have marketing intermediaries at all? The answer is that intermediaries perform certain marketing tasks—such as transporting, storing, selling, advertising, and relationship building—faster and cheaper than most manufacturers could.[22] A simple analogy is this: You could deliver packages in person to people anywhere in the world, but usually you don't. Why not? Because it's usually cheaper and faster to have them delivered by Canada Post or a private firm such as Purolator.

Similarly, you could sell your home by yourself, or buy stock directly from other people, but you probably wouldn't do so. Why? Again, because there are specialists (agents and brokers) who make the process more efficient and easier than it would be otherwise. Agents and brokers are marketing intermediaries. They facilitate the exchange process.

The benefits of using marketing intermediaries can be illustrated rather easily. Suppose that five manufacturers of various food products each tried to sell directly to five retailers. The number of exchange relationships that would have to be established is 5 times 5, or 25. But picture what happens when a wholesaler enters the system. The five manufacturers would contact one wholesaler to establish five exchange relationships. The wholesaler would have to establish contact with the five retailers. That would also mean five exchange relationships. Note that the number of exchanges is reduced from 25 to only 10 by the addition of a wholesaler.

Some economists have said that intermediaries add costs and need to be eliminated. Marketers say that intermediaries add value and that the *value greatly exceeds the cost*. While marketing intermediaries can be eliminated, their activities cannot if consumers are to have access to products and services. Intermediary organizations have survived because they have performed marketing functions faster and cheaper than others could.

## Progress Assessment

- What is a channel of distribution, and what intermediaries are involved?
- Why do we need intermediaries?
- Can you illustrate how intermediaries create exchange efficiency?

# RETAILING

Perhaps the most useful marketing intermediaries, as far as you're concerned, are retailers. Remember that retailers sell to ultimate consumers. They're the ones who bring goods and services to your neighbourhood and make them available day and night. Retailing is important to our economy. In 2008, retail trade generated approximately $426 billion in its employment of almost 1.9 million Canadians.[23] These numbers do not include sales generated via the Internet.

Figure 15.3 lists, describes, and gives examples of various kinds of retailers. Have you shopped in each kind of store? What seems to be the advantage of each?

**FIGURE | 15.3**

**Types of Retail Stores**

| Type | Description | Example |
|------|-------------|---------|
| Department store | Sells a wide variety of products (clothes, furniture, housewares) in separate departments | Sears, The Bay |
| Discount store | Sells many different products at prices generally below those of department stores | Giant Tiger, Dollar Store |
| Supermarket | Sells mostly food with other non-food products such as detergent and paper products | Metro, Sobeys, Provigo |
| Warehouse club | Sells food and general merchandise in facilities that are usually larger than supermarkets and offer discount prices; membership may be required | Costco Wholesale, Real Canadian Wholesale Club |
| Convenience store | Sells food and other often-needed items at convenient locations; may stay open all night | Mac's, 7-Eleven |
| Category killer | Sells a huge variety of one type of product to dominate that category of goods | Indigo Books & Music, Sleep Country Canada, Staples |
| Outlet store | Sells general merchandise directly from the manufacturer at a discount; items may be discontinued or have flaws ("seconds") | Nike, Rockport, Liz Claiborne |
| Specialty store | Sells a wide selection of goods in one category | Jewellery stores, shoe stores, bicycle shops |
| Supercentre | Sells food and general merchandise at discount prices; no membership required | Loblaws (some locations), Walmart (some locations) |

## Retail Distribution Strategy

A major decision that marketers must make is selecting the right retailers to sell their products. Different products call for different retail distribution strategies.

**Intensive distribution** puts products into as many retail outlets as possible, including vending machines. Products that need intensive distribution include convenience goods such as candy, cigarettes, gum, and popular magazines.

**Selective distribution** is the use of only a preferred group of the available retailers in an area. Such selection helps assure producers of quality sales and service. Manufacturers of shopping goods (appliances, furniture, and clothing) usually use selective distribution.

**Exclusive distribution** is the use of only one retail outlet in a given geographic area. The retailer has exclusive rights to sell the product and is therefore likely to carry a large inventory, give exceptional service, and pay more attention to this brand than to others. Auto manufacturers usually use exclusive distribution, as do producers of specialty goods such as skydiving equipment or fly-fishing products.

## Non-Store Retailing

Non-store retailing categories include electronic retailing; telemarketing; vending machines, kiosks, and carts; and direct selling. Small businesses can use non-store retailing to open up new channels of distribution for their products.

### Electronic Retailing

**Electronic retailing** consists of selling products to ultimate consumers (e.g., you and me) over the Internet. But getting customers is only half the battle. The other half is delivering the goods, providing helpful service, and keeping your customers. When electronic retailers fail to have sufficient inventory or fail to deliver goods on time (especially during busy periods), customers give up and go back to brick-and-mortar stores.

Most Internet retailers now offer e-mail confirmation. But sometimes electronic retailers are not so good at handling complaints, taking back goods that customers don't like, and providing personal help. Some Web sites are trying to improve customer service by adding help buttons that lead customers to almost instant assistance from a real person.

Traditional brick-and-mortar stores are rapidly going online also. The result, sometimes called a bricks-and-clicks store, allows customers to choose which shopping technique suits them best.[24]

### Telemarketing

**Telemarketing** is the sale of goods and services by telephone. Telemarketing is used to supplement or replace in-store selling and to complement online selling. Many telemarketers send a catalogue to consumers and let them order by calling a toll-free number. As we noted, many electronic retailers provide a help feature online that serves the same function. Telemarketing is a $4 billion industry in Canada.[25] If you wish to reduce the number of telemarketing calls you receive, you may register your residential, wireless, fax, or VoIP telephone number(s) on the National Do Not Call List at https://www.lnnte-dncl.gc.ca/insnum-regnum-eng.[26]

### Vending Machines, Kiosks, and Carts

A vending machine dispenses convenience goods when consumers deposit sufficient money in the machine. Vending machines carry the benefit of location—they're found in airports, schools, service stations, and other areas where people want convenience items.

**intensive distribution**
Distribution that puts products into as many retail outlets as possible.

**selective distribution**
Distribution that sends products to only a preferred group of retailers in an area.

**exclusive distribution**
Distribution that sends products to only one retail outlet in a given geographic area.

**electronic retailing**
Selling goods and services to ultimate customers (e.g., you and me) over the Internet.

**telemarketing**
The sale of goods and services by telephone.

Registration on the Do Not Call List will not eliminate all telemarketing calls as there are some exemptions. Examples include calls for or on behalf of Canadian registered charities and persons collecting information for a survey of members of the public.

Kiosks and carts have lower overhead costs than stores do; therefore, they can offer lower prices on items such as T-shirts and umbrellas. You often see vending carts outside stores on the sidewalk or along walkways in malls. Mall owners love them because they're colourful and create a marketplace atmosphere. Kiosk workers often dispense coupons and provide all kinds of helpful information to consumers, who tend to enjoy the interaction. Many kiosks serve as a gateway to the Internet, so consumers can shop at a store and still have access to all of the products available on the Internet in one place.

## Direct Selling

**direct selling**
Selling to consumers in their homes or where they work.

**Direct selling** involves selling to consumers in their homes or where they work. Major users of this category include Avon, Amway, and Electrolux. Trying to emulate the success of those companies, other businesses are now venturing into direct selling. Lingerie, artwork, and plants are just a few of the goods now sold at "house parties" sponsored by sellers.[27]

Because so many women work outside the home, companies that use direct selling are sponsoring parties at workplaces or in the evenings and on weekends. Some companies, such as those in encyclopedia sales, have dropped most of their direct selling efforts in favour of Internet selling.

# Choosing the Right Distribution Mode

A primary concern of supply-chain managers is selecting a transportation mode that will minimize costs and ensure a certain level of service. (*Modes*, in the language of distribution, are the various means used to transport goods, such as by truck, train, plane, ship, and pipeline.) Generally speaking, the faster the mode of transportation, the higher the cost. Today, supply chains involve more than simply moving products from place to place; they involve all kinds of activities such as processing orders and taking inventory of products. In other words, logistics systems involve whatever it takes to see that the right products are sent to the right place quickly and efficiently.

The job of the supply-chain manager is to find the most efficient combination of these forms of transportation. Figure 15.4 shows the advantages and disadvantages of each mode.

**FIGURE** | **15.4**

**Comparing Transportation Modes**
Combining trucks with railroads lowers cost and increases the number of locations reached. The same is true when combining trucks with ships. Combining trucks with airlines speeds goods long distances and gets them to almost any location.

## Progress Assessment

- What are some of the ways in which retailers compete?
- What kinds of products would call for each of the different distribution strategies: intensive, selective, exclusive?
- Give five examples of non-store retailing and describe each.
- Which transportation mode is fastest, which is cheapest, and which is most flexible?

| Mode | Cost | Speed | On-Time Dependability | Flexibility Handling Products | Frequency of Shipments | Reach |
|------|------|-------|----------------------|-------------------------------|-----------------------|-------|
| Railroad | Medium | Slow | Medium | High | Low | High |
| Trucks | High | Fast | High | Medium | High | Most |
| Pipeline | Low | Medium | Highest | Lowest | Highest | Lowest |
| Ships (water) | Lowest | Slowest | Lowest | Highest | Lowest | Low |
| Airplane | Highest | Fastest | Low | Low | Medium | Medium |

# PROMOTION AND THE PROMOTION MIX

Recall from Chapter 14 that *promotion* consists of all techniques that sellers use to motivate customers to buy their products. Marketers use many different tools to promote their products and services. Traditionally, as shown in Figure 15.5, those tools included advertising, personal selling, public relations, sales promotion, and direct marketing. The combination of promotional tools an organization uses is called its **promotion mix**. The product is shown in the middle of the figure to illustrate the fact that the product itself can be a promotional tool (e.g., through giving away free samples).

Each target group calls for a separate promotion mix. For example, large homogeneous groups of consumers (i.e., groups whose members share specific similar traits) are usually most efficiently reached through advertising. Large organizations are best reached through personal selling.

**Integrated marketing communication (IMC)** combines all promotional tools into one comprehensive and unified promotional strategy. The idea is to use all promotional tools and company resources to create a positive brand image and to meet the strategic marketing and promotional goals of the firm.[28] Lately, companies have been including a lot of Internet promotions in that mix.[29] An ongoing challenge for marketers is to develop a mix that will break through the clutter of the over 3,000 daily marketing messages that consumers receive.[30] Let us briefly explore each of the promotional tools.

## Advertising: Fighting to Keep Consumer Interest

**Advertising** is paid, non-personal communication through various media by organizations and individuals who are in some way *identified in the advertising message*. There are various categories of advertising, including product advertising, online advertising, and comparison advertising, which is advertising that compares competitive products.

The public benefits from advertising expenditures. First, ads are informative. For example, newspaper advertising is full of information about products, prices, features, and more. Advertising not only informs us about products but also provides us with free TV, community newspapers, and radio programs: The money advertisers spend for commercial time pays for the production costs. Advertising also covers the major costs of producing newspapers and magazines. When we buy a magazine, we pay mostly for mailing or promotional costs. Figure 15.6 discusses the advantages and disadvantages of various advertising media to the advertiser. According to the Canadian Marketing Association, advertising spending in Canadian media will increase from $19 billion in 2007 to more than $23.3 billion in 2011. Moreover, every dollar spent on advertising will directly result in nearly $9 of economic activity in Canada, with overall direct sales from advertising campaigns expected to reach $203 billion by 2011.[31]

Marketers must choose which media can best be used to reach the audience they desire. Radio advertising, for example, is less expensive than TV advertising and often reaches people when they have few other distractions, such as driving in their cars. Radio is especially good, therefore, for selling services that people don't usually read about in print media— services such as banking, mortgages, continuing education, and the like. On the other

**promotion mix**
The combination of promotional tools an organization uses.

**integrated marketing communication (IMC)**
A technique that combines all promotional tools into one comprehensive and unified promotional strategy.

**advertising**
Paid, non-personal communication through various media by organizations and individuals who are in some way identified in the advertising message.

Friends4friends.ca is a multi-faceted media campaign that includes an interactive Web site providing young adults with strategies to recognize and help friends who may have gambling problems. Posters are distributed to campuses and bars, and advertising has run in cinemas, youth-oriented publications, and transit systems.

**FIGURE | 15.6**

**Advantages and Disadvantages of Various Advertising Media**
The most effective media are often very expensive. The inexpensive media may not reach your market. The goal is to use the medium that can reach your desired market most efficiently.

| Medium | Advantages | Disadvantages |
|---|---|---|
| Newspapers | Good coverage of local markets; ads can be placed quickly; high consumer acceptance; ads can be clipped and saved. | Ads compete with other features in paper; poor colour; ads get thrown away with paper (short lifespan). |
| Television | Uses sight, sound, and motion; reaches all audiences; high attention with no competition from other material. | High cost; short exposure time; takes time to prepare ads; digital video recorders skip over ads. |
| Radio | Low cost; can target specific audiences; very flexible; good for local marketing. | People may not listen to ad; depends on one sense (hearing); short exposure time; audience can't keep ad. |
| Magazines | Can target specific audiences; good use of colour; long life of ad; ads can be clipped and saved. | Inflexible; ads often must be placed weeks before publication; cost is relatively high. |
| Outdoor | High visibility and repeat exposures; low cost; local market focus. | Limited message; low selectivity of audience. |
| Direct Mail | Best for targeting specific markets; very flexible; ad can be saved. | High cost; consumers may reject ad as junk mail; must conform to Post Office regulations. |
| Yellow Pages–type advertising | Great coverage of local markets; widely used by consumers; available at point of purchase. | Competition with other ads; cost may be high for very small businesses. |
| Internet | Inexpensive global coverage; available at any time; interactive. | Relatively low readership in the short term, but growing rapidly. |

hand, radio has become so commercial-ridden that some people are switching to Sirius XM Radio or some other commercial-free offer.[32] See the Spotlight on Small Business box, which highlights an organization that focuses on word of mouth advertising.

## Global Advertising

Global advertising involves developing a product and promotional strategy that can be implemented worldwide. Certainly, global advertising would save companies money in research and design. However, other experts think that promotions targeted at specific countries or regions may be much more successful than global promotions since each country or region has its own culture, language, and buying habits.

The evidence supports that promotional efforts specifically designed for individual countries often work best since problems arise when one campaign is used in all countries. For example, Canadians may have difficulty with Krapp toilet paper from Sweden. Clairol introduced its curling iron, the Mist Stick, to the German market, not realizing that mist in German can mean "manure." As you can see, getting the words right in international advertising is tricky and critical. So is understanding the culture.

Even in Canada we have regional differences that are important enough to constitute separate market segments. Each province has its own history and culture. The large metropolitan areas such as Vancouver, Toronto, and Montreal are different from the rest of the provinces in which they are located. All require their own promotions and advertising.

In short, much advertising today is moving from globalism (one ad for everyone in the world) to regionalism (specific ads for each country or for specific groups within a country). In the future, marketers will prepare more custom-designed promotions to reach smaller audiences—audiences as small as one person.

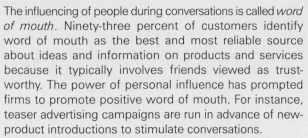

## Have You Been "Buzzed"?

The influencing of people during conversations is called *word of mouth*. Ninety-three percent of customers identify word of mouth as the best and most reliable source about ideas and information on products and services because it typically involves friends viewed as trustworthy. The power of personal influence has prompted firms to promote positive word of mouth. For instance, teaser advertising campaigns are run in advance of new-product introductions to stimulate conversations.

Increasingly, companies are working hard to stimulate positive consumer word of mouth about their products and services. Agent Wildfire was founded in 2004 by Sean Moffitt after having spent 15 years in senior client and agency marketing and innovation roles for some of Canada's most-loved brands. Over the years, he has established himself as one of Canada's leading marketing innovators and the thought leader in the word of mouth industry. He applies his unique hybrid of brand management, digital, social media, strategic planning and innovation and word of mouth marketing philosophy to client objectives. He has authored over 500+ posts on the subject at his popular blog, Buzz Canuck, and is a frequent consultant, commentator, and speaker on new media and marketing subjects.

The key to successful *buzz marketing*—popularity created by consumer word of mouth—is to find the quarterbacks of buzz. (The electronic or online version of word of mouth is viral marketing.) As part of its word of mouth campaigns, Agent Wildfire operates Canada's first and only dedicated Influencer community. The Influencers constitute thousands of qualified Canadians who adopt earlier, know more, connect more, and influence others across 25 different categories of interest. They help start, seed, and spread news, discoveries, and campaigns among Canada's chattering social classes and key tribes. As a result of this community, Agent Wildfire helps launch word of mouth campaigns and narrowcast media for buzzable brands, new products, retailers, events, and causes.

"Transparency is essential for word-of-mouth advertising," says Moffitt, noting that campaigns perceived as being misrepresentative drew virulent backlash and compromised the advertiser. For example, fake online blogs, which are made to appear as if written by consumers instead of advertisers, have been created by McDonalds, Sony, and other companies. Now advertising agencies, the Canadian Marketing Association, the Federal Trade Commission, and the Word of Mouth Marketing Association recommend that disclosure be used in any marketing strategy. Apart from disclosure being ethical, it actually makes the campaign more effective, says Dave Balter, the founder of BzzAgent Inc., one of the top word-of-mouth marketers in North America. He referred to a study by Northeastern University in Boston that showed "word of mouth that is being communicated through disclosure travels nearly twice as far than when people don't disclose."

What do you think? Is this form of advertising ethical, regardless if there has been disclosure?

Sources: "The Agent Wildfire Story," Agent Wildfire, 2 January 2009, http://www.agentwildfire.com/how_we_work/our_story; Frederick G. Crane et al., *Marketing*, 7th Canadian ed. (Toronto: McGraw-Hill Ryerson, 2008), 128–129; and Bonnie Staring, "Word-of-Mouth Marketing—Smart or Sneaky?" Homemakers.com, 2008, http://www.homemakers.com/Life&Times/reallives/word-of-mouth-marketing--smart-or-sneaky-n247176p3.html.

# Personal Selling: Providing Personal Attention

**Personal selling** is the face-to-face presentation and promotion of goods and services. It also involves the search for new prospects and follow-up service after the sale. Effective selling isn't simply a matter of persuading others to buy. In fact, it's more accurately described today as helping others satisfy their wants and needs.

Given that perspective, you can see why salespeople are starting to use the Internet, portable computers, paging devices, fax machines, and other technology. They can use this technology to help customers search the Internet, design custom-made products, compare prices, and generally do everything it takes to complete the order. The benefit of personal selling is that there is a person there to help you complete a transaction. The salesperson can listen to your needs, help you reach a solution, and do all that is possible to make accomplishing that solution smoother and easier.

It is costly to provide customers with personal attention, especially since some companies are replacing salespeople with Internet services and information. Therefore, those companies that retain salespeople must train them to be especially effective, efficient, and helpful.

**personal selling**
The face-to-face presentation and promotion of goods and services.

## The Business-to-Consumer (B2C) Sales Process

Most sales to consumers take place in retail stores, where the role of the salesperson differs somewhat. It is important to understand as much as possible about the type of people who shop at a given store. One thing is certain, though: a salesperson needs to focus on the customer and refrain from talking to fellow salespeople—or, worse, talking on the phone to friends—while customers are around.

The first formal step in the B2C sales process, then, is the *approach*. Too many salespeople begin with a line like "May I help you?" That is not a good opening, because the answer too often is no. A better approach is "What may I help you with?" or simply "How are you today?" The idea is to show the customer that you are there to help and that you are friendly and knowledgeable. Also, you need to discover what the customer wants.

According to what the customer tells you, you then make a *presentation*. You show customers how the products meet their needs. You answer questions that help them choose the products that are right for them. The more you learn about the customers' specific wants, the better you are able to help them choose the right product or products to meet those wants.

Next comes the *trial close*. "Would you like me to put that on hold?" or "Will you be paying for that with your store credit card?" are two such efforts. A store salesperson walks a fine line between being helpful and being pushy. Selling is an art, and a salesperson must learn just how far to go. Often individual buyers need some time alone to think about the purchase. The salesperson must respect that need and give them time and space, but still be clearly available when needed.

*After-sale follow-up* is an important but often neglected step in B2C sales. If the product is to be delivered, the salesperson should follow up to be sure it is delivered on time. The same is true if the product has to be installed. There is often a chance to sell more merchandise when a salesperson follows up on a sale. Figure 15.7 shows the B2C selling process.

**FIGURE | 15.7**

**Steps in the Business-to-Consumer (B2C) Selling Process**

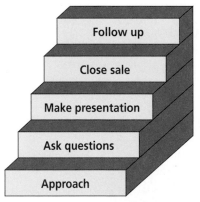

Follow up

Close sale

Make presentation

Ask questions

Approach

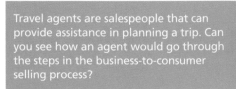

Travel agents are salespeople that can provide assistance in planning a trip. Can you see how an agent would go through the steps in the business-to-consumer selling process?

## Progress Assessment

- What are the five traditional elements of the promotion mix?
- Define integrated marking communication and explain why it is important.
- Define advertising and explain why advertising today is moving from globalism to regionalism.
- What are the five steps in the B2C selling process?

# Public Relations: Building Relationships

**Public relations (PR)** is the management function that evaluates public attitudes, changes policies and procedures in response to the public's requests, and executes a program of action and information to earn public understanding and acceptance. It is the responsibility of the PR department to maintain close ties with the media, community leaders, government officials, and other corporate stakeholders.[33] The idea is to establish and maintain a dialogue with all stakeholders so that the company can respond to inquiries, complaints, and suggestions quickly.[34] Such was the case with this next example where Maple Leaf Foods CEO, Michael McCain, was named Newsmaker of the Year for his response to the listeriosis outbreak that killed 20 Canadians:[35]

> *Shortly after dozens of cases of listeriosis were linked to cold cuts produced at Maple Leaf's Toronto plant, McCain appeared in a television ad to issue a candid and abject apology for the outbreak. "We have an unwavering commitment to keeping your food safe with standards well beyond regulatory requirements, but this week our best efforts failed and we are deeply sorry," a weary and upset-looking McCain said. His apology could not have seemed more personal or heartfelt. And he was widely praised at the time for promptly recalling any products produced at the plant, even if they hadn't been linked to listeriosis. It is estimated the outbreak and recall cost the company between \$25 million and \$30 million, plus another \$15 million in lost sales.*

Review the Green Box which highlights the activities one PR agency is implementing to become carbon neutral.

**public relations (PR)**
The management function that evaluates public attitudes, changes policies and procedures in response to the public's requests, and executes a program of action and information to earn public understanding and acceptance.

# Publicity: The Talking Arm of PR

**Publicity** is the talking arm of public relations. Publicity is any information about an individual, product, or organization that's distributed to the public through the media and that's not paid for, or controlled, by the seller. You might prepare a publicity release describing Very Vegetarian and the research results showing that consumers love it, and send it to the various media. What might your vegetarian restaurant do to help the community and thus create more publicity?

Much skill is involved in writing such releases so that the media will want to publish them. You may need to write different stories for different media. One may talk about the new owners. Another may talk about the unusual product offerings. If the stories are published, release of the news about your store will reach many potential consumers (and investors, distributors, and dealers), and you may be on your way to becoming a wealthy marketer. Publicity works only if the media find the material interesting or newsworthy. The idea, then, is to write publicity that meets those criteria.

Besides being free, publicity has several further advantages over other promotional tools, such as advertising. For example, publicity may reach people who wouldn't read an ad. It may appear on the front page of a newspaper or in some other prominent position, or be given air time on a television news show. Perhaps the greatest advantage of publicity is its believability. When a newspaper or magazine publishes a story as news, the reader treats that story as news—and news is more believable than advertising. Review the Making Ethical Decisions box for a dilemma that you might face as a marketer when you consider publicity.

**publicity**
Any information about an individual, product, or organization that's distributed to the public through the media and that's not paid for or controlled by the seller.

## GreenBOX

### The Greenest PR Shop in Canada

Environics Communications is trimming its carbon emissions in an effort to become "the greenest" PR agency in North America. The full-service public relations firm, with offices in Toronto, Montreal, Washington, and New York, is making moves to reduce its environmental footprint by becoming carbon neutral. According to Bruce MacLellan, President of Environics Communications, "Everyone on our team is contributing ideas and taking action to make this possible...Going green is the right thing for the planet and also allows us to be more knowledgeable partners on this important topic with our clients...We can help clients distinguish between genuinely going green and 'green-washing,'" he added.

The company's four offices are expected to follow the reduce/reuse/recycle approach that includes turning off lights and computers when they aren't in use, using energy-saving light bulbs in desk lamps, and recycling printer and fax machine cartridges. The company now gets most of its electricity from producers that use wind and water instead of coal and oil, will provide a $250 subsidy for each employee towards the purchase of a bicycle, and water coolers at large offices are out, replaced by re-usable, non-toxic personal water bottles for each employee to fill up on tap water.

Environics has partnered up with the Pembina Institute to help measure its greenhouse gas emissions from air travel, electricity usage, paper usage, and staff commuting so that sufficient carbon offset credits can be purchased.

Source: Kristin Laird, "Environics Goes Really Green," *Marketing Magazine*, 6 February 2008, http://www.marketingmag.ca/english/news/agency/article.jsp?content=20080206_777333_2237.

There are several disadvantages to publicity. For example, marketers have no control over how, when, or if the media will use the story. The media aren't obligated to use a publicity release, and most are thrown away. Furthermore, the story may be altered so that it's not so positive. Also, once a story has run, it's not likely to be repeated. Advertising, in contrast, can be repeated as often as needed. One way to see that publicity is handled well by the media is to establish a friendly relationship with media representatives, being open with them when they seek information. Then, when you want their support, they're more likely to co-operate.

## Making Ethical Decisions

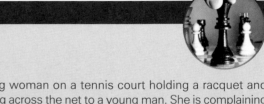

### Is the Ad as Honest as the Product?

You are producing a high-fibre, nutritious cereal called Fiberrific and are having a modest degree of success. Research shows that your number of customers, or market segment, is growing but is still a relatively small percentage of breakfast cereal buyers. Generally, Fiberrific appeals mostly to health-conscious people aged 25 to 60. You are trying to broaden the appeal of your cereal to the under-25 and over-60 age groups. You know that Fiberrific is a tasty and healthy product that is good for customers. Joan, one of your managers, suggests that you stretch the truth a bit in your advertising and publicity material so that it will attract more consumers in the age groups you are targeting. After all, your product can't hurt anybody and is actually good for them.

Joan's idea is to develop two ads, each with two segments. The first segment of one ad would show a young woman on a tennis court holding a racquet and talking across the net to a young man. She is complaining that she seems to tire easily. The next segment would show the same two people, with the woman looking lively and saying that she tried this new breakfast cereal, Fiberrific, for two weeks and feels so energized, like a new person. A similar ad would be used to show two senior citizens walking uphill and talking. The first segment would show the man wondering why he tires so easily and the second one would show the same scene, with one man now a little ahead of the other, looking lively and stating that he is amazed at the improvement in his energy and endurance after eating Fiberrific for only two weeks. Would you go along with Joan's suggestion? What is your decision based on? Explain.

## Progress Assessment

- What is the responsibility of the public relations department?
- What are the advantages and disadvantages of publicity versus advertising?

# Sales Promotion: Getting a Good Deal

**Sales promotion** is a promotional tool that stimulates consumer purchasing and dealer interest by means of short-term activities. Sales promotion programs are designed to supplement personal selling, advertising, and public relations efforts by creating enthusiasm for the overall promotional program. See Figure 15.8 for a list of sales promotion techniques.

Sales promotion can take place both internally (within the company) and externally (outside the company). Often it's just as important to generate employee enthusiasm about a product as it is to attract potential customers. The most important internal sales promotion efforts are directed at salespeople and other customer-contact people, such as complaint handlers and clerks. Internal sales promotion efforts include (1) sales training; (2) the development of sales aids such as flip charts, portable audiovisual displays, and videotapes; and (3) participation in trade shows where salespeople can get leads.

After generating enthusiasm internally, it's important to get distributors and dealers involved so that they too are eager to help promote the product. Trade shows are an important sales promotion tool because they allow marketing intermediaries to see products from many different sellers and make comparisons among them. Today, virtual trade shows—trade shows on the Internet—enable buyers to see many products without leaving the office. Furthermore, the information is available 24/7.

After the company's employees and intermediaries have been motivated with sales promotion efforts, the next step is to promote to final consumers using samples, coupons, store demonstrations, rebates, displays, and so on. Sales promotion is an ongoing effort to maintain enthusiasm, so different strategies must be used over time to keep the ideas fresh. You could put displays of various dishes in your Very Vegetarian store to show customers how attractive the products look. You could also sponsor in-store cooking demonstrations to attract new vegetarians.

**sales promotion**
The promotional tool that stimulates consumer purchasing and dealer interest by means of short-term activities.

## Sampling Is a Powerful Sales Promotion Tool

One popular sales promotion tool is **sampling**—letting consumers have a small sample of the product for no charge. Because many consumers won't buy a new product unless they've had a chance to see it or try it, grocery stores often have people handing out small portions of food and beverage products in the aisles. Sampling is a quick, effective way of demonstrating a product's superiority at a time when consumers are making a purchase decision. Standing outside Very Vegetarian and giving out samples would surely attract attention.

**sampling**
A promotional tool in which a company lets consumers have a small sample of a product for no charge.

| Business-to-Business | |
|---|---|
| Trade shows | Catalogues |
| Portfolios for salespeople | Conventions |
| Deals (price reductions) | Event sponsorship |
| **Consumer Sales** | |
| Coupons | Bonuses (buy one, get one free) |
| Cents-off promotions | Catalogues |
| Sampling | Demonstrations |
| Premiums | Special events |
| Sweepstakes | Lotteries |
| Contests | In-store displays |

**FIGURE  15.8**

**Business-to-Business and Consumer Sales Promotion Techniques**

Coupons such as these can be mailed to your home. Alternatively, some retailers offer coupons in-store and online. Do you use coupons? If yes, under what circumstances? Do they have to offer a certain monetary value before you choose to use them?

## How New Technologies Are Affecting Promotion

As people purchase products and services on the Internet, companies keep track of those purchases and gather other facts and figures about those consumers. Over time, companies learn who buys what, when, and how often. They can then use that information to design catalogues and brochures specifically tailored to meet the wants and needs of individual consumers as demonstrated by their actual purchasing behaviour. So, for example, a flower company may send you a postcard reminding you that your partner's birthday is coming up soon and that you bought a particular flower arrangement for him or her last year. The company then may recommend a new arrangement.

Because so much information about consumers is now available, companies are tending to use the traditional promotional tools (e.g., advertising) less than before and are putting more money into direct mail and other forms of direct marketing (to be discussed below), including catalogues and the Internet. Consumers are reacting favourably to such promotions, so you can expect the trend toward direct sales and Internet sales to accelerate. Promotional programs will change accordingly.

New technology offers consumers a continuous connection to the Internet and enables marketers to send video files and other data to them faster than ever before. Using such connections, marketers can interact with consumers in real time. That means that you can talk with a salesperson online and chat with other consumers about their experiences with products and services. You can also search the Internet for the best price (e.g., hotels) and find any product information you may want in almost any form you desire, such as copy, sound, or video.

Such technology gives a great deal of power to consumers like you. You no longer have to rely on advertising or other promotions to learn about products. You can search the Internet on your own and find as much information as you want, when you want it. (For example, if you are thinking of trying a new restaurant, you may visit www.restaurantica.com to see how other diners have rated the restaurant.) If the information is not posted, you can request it and get it immediately. Thus, promotion has become much more interactive than ever before.

## Direct Marketing[36]

**direct marketing**
Uses direct communication with consumers to generate a response in the form of an order, a request for further information, or a visit to a retail outlet.

**Direct marketing** includes any activity that directly links manufacturers or intermediaries with the ultimate consumer. It uses direct communication with consumers to generate a response in the form of an order, a request for further information, or a visit to a retail outlet. The communication can take many forms including face-to-face selling, direct mail, catalogues, telephone solicitation (e.g., telemarketing), and direct response advertising on television, radio, print, online, or over mobile communications devices. Direct marketing has become popular because shopping from home or work is more convenient

## Reaching Beyond Our Borders

### Reach High with lululemon athletica

After 20 years in the surf, skate, and snowboard business, founder Chip Wilson took his first commercial yoga class in Vancouver and found the result exhilarating. The post-yoga feeling was so close to surfing and snowboarding that he began to build a business with a yoga focus. At the time, cotton clothing was being used for sweaty, stretchy power yoga and seemed completely inappropriate to Wilson, whose passion lay in technical athletic fabrics. From this, a design studio was born that became a yoga studio at night to pay the rent. Clothing was offered for sale and an underground yoga clothing movement was born.

Founded in 1998, lululemon athletica is a yoga-inspired athletic apparel company for both women and men. By producing products that help keep people active and stress free, lululemon believes that the world will be a better place. Setting the bar in technical fabrics and functional designs, lululemon works with yogis and athletes in local communities for continuous research and product feedback.

The company's first real store opened in the beach area of Vancouver, called Kitsilano, in November of 2000. The idea was to have the store be a community hub where people could learn and discuss the physical aspects of healthy living from yoga and diet to running and cycling as well as the mental aspects of living a powerful life of possibilities. Unfortunately for this concept, the store became so busy that it was impossible to help the customer in this way in addition to selling the product. So the focus of training shifted solely to the lululemon educator or staff person.

Styles and colours are constantly updated within each season. Photos and information on the company's newest products can be reviewed and purchased on the company's online Web site, www.lululemon.com. Customers can interact with staff at lululemon athletica and learn about the full benefits and technical features of the products. lululemon is also available via wholesale partners in yoga, Pilates, and fitness studios.

lululemon currently has over 100 stores across Canada, the United States, and Australia. Work is done with factories in Canada, the United States, China, Taiwan, South Korea, Peru, Israel, Cambodia, Thailand, and Vietnam that share the company's commitment to quality and ethics. It is vital for lululemon to keep a manufacturing base in Vancouver for security and speed-to-market of its core designs. Future expansion will centre on corporate stores only.

Sources: © Lululemon Athletica 2008, www.lululemon.com.

for consumers than going to stores. People can "shop" in catalogues and freestanding advertising supplements in the newspaper and then buy by phone, mail, or computer. It is estimated that in 2011, almost $31 billion in goods and services will be purchased as the result of marketing offers over the telephone compared to $27 billion in 2007. More than half (53 percent) of the sales will originate as the result of business-to-business telemarketing calls. Popular consumer catalogue companies that use direct marketing include Lee Valley and Victoria's Secret. The Reaching Beyond Our Borders box highlights a company that chooses not to produce catalogues as its products change frequently.

While direct marketing has been one of the fastest-growing forms of promotion, it has several disadvantages. First, most forms of direct marketing require a comprehensive and up-to-date database with information about the target market. Developing and maintaining the database can be expensive and time-consuming. In addition, growing concern about privacy has led to a decline in response rates among some customer groups. The Dealing with Change box highlights a piece of legislation that was enacted to protect consumer privacy. Companies with successful direct marketing programs are sensitive to these issues and often use a combination of direct marketing alternatives together, or direct marketing combined with other promotional tools, to increase value for customers.

primarily the distributor that would offer the promotion. Distributor site visits around the world are also an ongoing aspect of the personal selling element of the promotion mix. These efforts are used to maintain and build long-term and profitable relationships with global distributors.

Increasingly, company attention is focusing on direct marketing. Customer information is continuously being updated in the company's database. Customer information collected at trade shows is purchased and subsequently downloaded as well. Customers are categorized in the database according to their market (e.g., marine, outdoor, etc.). With this information, personalized letters were created and sent out to current and prospective customers. Personal communication followed to confirm if a sale could be generated.

Fox 40 International Inc. also runs a promotional products division. Approximately 65 percent of all Whistles sold have another organization's logo on them. According to Juliana Child, since the Fox 40® brand is so well established, it can effectively be directed to promotional sales. This co-branding is another opportunity to link the Fox 40® brand with a company brand that is meaningful to the receiver of the Whistle. Given the different package and imprint capabilities, the company can quickly fill personalized orders.

Sources: Dave Foxcroft, Executive Vice President and COO, Fox 40 International Inc., interview, 24 June 2008; Kelley Horton, Vice President Sales, Fox 40 International Inc., interview, 24 June 2008; Juliana Child, Manager, Marketing & Events, Fox 40 International Inc., interview, 24 June 2008; and "Not An Inadvertent Whistle," *REFEREE*, July 2007, 45–47.

## Discussion Questions

1. What new product pricing strategy did Fox 40 International Inc. use for the Fox 40® Sonik Whistle?

2. What retail distribution strategy do you think is used for the Fox 40® Sonik Whistle?

3. Which promotional strategy is the most effective when selling the Fox 40® Sonik Whistle? Explain.

## RUNNING CASE

### Canadian Tire Financial Services' Gas Advantage™ MasterCard®

Canadian Tire Financial Services (CTFS) is the second-largest MasterCard franchise in Canada based on dollar volume. The introduction of the Gas Advantage™ MasterCard® allowed CTFS to add value with the parent company's (Canadian Tire Corporation, Limited) petroleum division, while at the same time leveraging its MasterCard franchise by expanding its offering to customers. It was expected that this in turn would contribute to the increase of volume growth for its credit card business.

The Gas Advantage™ MasterCard® was introduced in Guelph on a four month trial in May 2005. The pilot was so successful that it was expanded to the rest of the province of Ontario. Once the loyalty program was restructured to improve the return on portfolio, it was expanded across Canada. While this product is sold nationally, the marketing focus is from Ontario to Eastern Canada as this is where the majority of the company's 274 Gas Bars are located.

You may be wondering, "Why was the product introduced in Ontario?" There were several reasons. First of all, the company needed to be close to the expertise; the software companies that work on the petroleum system are located in Toronto. About half of Canadian Tire Corporation's petroleum sales are in Ontario, so if the model did not work in Ontario, it was unlikely to work elsewhere. Ease of pilot management was another consideration. As well, the marketing expertise, technical expertise, and execution required close proximity to the market, especially when changes needed to be made. As a result, Ontario was the best choice given that CTFS's two offices are located in Welland and Burlington.

You have been introduced to the four Ps of marketing. Here is how the product works. The more you spend on the plastic credit card, the higher your discount. You save at least 2 cents and up to 10 cents off per litre of gas you purchase at participating Canadian Tire Gas Bars. For example, if you spend less than $200 this month on your card, your savings next month will be 2 cents per litre. If you spend $2,000 or more this month, your savings next month will be 10 cents per litre. When you are at the Canadian Tire Gas Bar, you swipe the card and watch the litre price turn back INSTANTLY – up to 10 cents per litre. By 2010, the Gas Advantage™ MasterCard® will also be chip-enabled.

Price is related to the rewards associated with using the Gas Advantage™ MasterCard®. Research has shown that 56 percent of consumers are loyalty driven and 30 percent are driven by the credit card rate. When your card is used in Canadian Tire stores, you earn your gas discount two times faster. Those that are sensitive to gas prices are also rewarded based on their overall purchases. The amount of discount per litre will be deducted automatically from the price at the pump and shown on the receipt. For those that are price-conscious, another feature is that there is no annual fee for the credit card.

When considering place, customers can use the credit card everywhere and these purchases will contribute to the month's balance. This balance will influence the following month's gas discount. For the 40 percent of Canadians that shop at Canadian Tire every week, filling up on gas can be part of the shopping experience.

When the Gas Advantage™ MasterCard® was first piloted, promotional efforts included having field representatives in Canadian Tire Gas Bars and stores sign up customers. Representatives were also available in kiosks and over the phone to sign up new customers. In eight weeks, 10 percent of households in Guelph had signed up. Radio spots were used to introduce the card and share its features and benefits. Print materials included banners advertising gas sales for the day of ten cents a litre. Inter-ested customers could also sign up through the company's Web site at https://www.ctfs.com/Products/CreditCards/GasAdvantageMasterCard/.

Today, the Retail and Petroleum divisions continue to work together to drive sales. A customer may be intercepted by a salesperson in the store or by a gas station attendant. Both are working to promote the card. Limited-time, deep discount promotions on products continue to attract customers to the Gas Bar where an offer is made for the card. Other examples of promotional efforts include radio and site ads that are used for remote sales (e.g., from 6–8 a.m., get 20 cents off per litre) and weekly flyers are used to drive customers to buy online.

From an interrelated business point of view, the Gas Advantage™ MasterCard® is a perfect product. It leverages the Canadian Tire brand and it encourages customers to support the company's different divisions. From a customer point of view, it provides value in the form of lower gas prices. The result of all these efforts is a petroleum lift due to loyal customers that keep coming back.

Sources: Jim Kozack, Vice President of Credit Card Marketing and Customer Acquisition, Canadian Tire Financial Services, interview, 13 November 2008; and "Gas Advantage Mastercard," Canadian Tire Financial Services, 10 November 2008, https://www.ctfs.com/Products/CreditCards/GasAdvantageMasterCard.

## Discussion Questions

1. What marketing era concept is evident with the introduction of the Gas Advantage™ MasterCard®?

2. Describe the market segmentation dimensions that were used with this product.

3. How was non-store retailing used to encourage this product's adoption?

# PART 6

# CHAPTER 16

# Understanding Accounting and Financial Information

## LEARNING OBJECTIVES

**AFTER YOU HAVE READ AND STUDIED THIS CHAPTER, YOU SHOULD BE ABLE TO:**

**LO▶1** Describe the importance of accounting and financial information.

**LO▶2** Define and explain the different areas of the accounting profession.

**LO▶3** List the steps in the accounting cycle, distinguish between accounting and bookkeeping, and explain how computers are used in accounting.

**LO▶4** Explain how the major financial statements differ.

**LO▶5** Describe the role of amortization, LIFO, and FIFO in reporting financial information.

**LO▶6** Explain the importance of ratio analysis in reporting financial information.

## PROFILE

## Getting to Know Michelle Waldorf of Shell Canada

Over the past two decades, hiring and firing at oil and gas companies in Canada has gone in cycles, through restructuring and downsizing and other market challenges that made employment anything but a sure thing. However, now, with the demand for oil growing at a fast pace and prices spiking ever higher, money is available to drive major expansions and substantial job growth.

Most of the focus in the media has been on the growth of jobs on the operational side: maintenance workers and technical engineers. However, with competition booming and regulatory requirements expanding apace, the heat is on for companies to attract strong accounting talent. One CMA we spoke to recently has an intimate understanding of what that means.

Michelle Waldorf, CMA, has been rising in the ranks of Shell Canada ever since she joined the company ten years ago, straight out of university as part of the firm's New Graduates Program.

Waldorf is now the manager of Shell's Exploration and Production marketing accounting group. "We look after the financials for several businesses—natural gas, sulphur, liquefied petroleum gases (ethane, propane, and butane), condensate, bitumen, and asphalt," she notes. But she's involved in more than the accounting side of the business. As part of her role, Waldorf is also part of Shell's campus recruiting team for the finance function.

"When I started at Shell, the purse strings were closed," she recalls. "We were reducing staff and operating costs, and natural gas was our primary revenue contributor. Now growth is a word used on a daily basis, and Shell is back to being both a gas and oil company. At the same time, compliance is a big watchword throughout the organization, and something we need good people to tackle."

"At Shell, we are actively recruiting business co-op and summer students from universities across the country," says Waldorf. "The students take on 4–8 month assignments in various areas of the company, from supply chain management to tax. Through this type of program we're able to see the students in action and, in turn, they are able to evaluate us. Presently it is difficult to find enough staff to fill all of our vacancies. We're even hiring for unspecific jobs, knowing that by the time the staff arrive we'll have a position for them. The oil sands business unit is planning on growing from the production of 150,000 barrels a day to up to 500,000 barrels a day. This is going to be a challenge."

Growth is only part of the story, of course. Shell, like many other companies, will face a demographic crunch in a few years as many baby boomers retire, and management wants to be ready to face that with young, capable replacements. In addition, Sarbanes-Oxley compliance and increasingly complex accounting standards are also playing a role in HR needs.

"We continually monitored LNG (liquefied natural gas), Mackenzie Delta, and Alaska project developments to assess potential impacts on our existing and future business strategies. I strongly believe these types of roles make you a stronger accountant because you develop an appreciation for the broader external environment and how that translates to the numbers."

"There is a huge market for sulphur, particularly in China, and our Canadian production accounts for 15–20 percent of internationally traded sulphur. We ship in excess of 4 million tonnes per year or 11,300 tonnes per day. Shipping the product throughout North America and overseas is a significant logistics challenge. Our job in accounting is to work closely with our marketing and logistics counterparts to capture all revenue and costs accurately and provide them with timely profitability measures that help them assess performance of their business."

Waldorf considers her CMA designation an important part of her continued success at Shell. "The program taught me the important leadership skills I need to do my job," she notes.

Controlling costs, managing cash flows, understanding profit margins and taxes, and reporting financial results accurately are keys to survival for both profit-seeking and non-profit organizations. This chapter will introduce you to the accounting fundamentals and financial information critical to business success. As you read in this profile, accounting serves a vital link in supplying key information to decision makers. The chapter also briefly explores the financial ratios that are essential in measuring business performance.

Source: Robert Colman, "Tapping into Vital Resources," *CMA Management*, August/September 2005, 39–42.

# THE IMPORTANCE OF ACCOUNTING AND FINANCIAL INFORMATION

Small and sometimes large businesses falter or even fail because they do not follow good financial procedures. Financial information is the heartbeat of competitive businesses. Accounting information keeps the heartbeat stable.

You have to know something about accounting if you want to succeed in business. The simple truth is that learning some basic accounting terms is mandatory. You also have to understand the relationship of bookkeeping to accounting and how accounts are kept. It's almost impossible to run a business without being able to read, understand, and analyze accounting reports and financial statements; they reveal as much about a business's health as pulse rate and blood pressure readings tell us about a person's health. The purpose of this chapter is to introduce you to basic accounting principles and the important financial information obtained from accounting. By the end of this chapter, you should have a good idea of what accounting is, how it works, and why it is important. You should also know some accounting terms and understand the purpose of accounting statements. While it's important to understand how accounting statements are constructed, it's even more important to know what they mean to the business. A few hours invested in learning this material will pay off handsomely as you become more involved in business or simply in understanding what's going on in the world of business and finance.

## What Is Accounting?

Financial information is primarily based on information generated from accounting. **Accounting** is the recording, classifying, summarizing, and interpreting of financial events to provide management and other interested parties with the information they need to make good decisions. Financial transactions can include such specifics as buying and selling goods and services, acquiring insurance, paying employees, and using supplies. Once the business's transactions have been recorded, they are usually classified into groups that have common characteristics. For example, all purchases are grouped together, as are all sales transactions. The method used to record and summarize accounting data into reports is called an accounting system (see Figure 16.1).

A major purpose of accounting is to help managers evaluate the financial condition and the operating performance of the firm so that they can make well-informed decisions. Once a decision is made, future activities will result in a new set of accounting information, which leads to another set of decisions. Another major purpose is to report financial information to people outside the firm such as owners, creditors, suppliers, employees, investors, and the government (for tax purposes). In basic terms, accounting is the measurement and reporting of financial information to various users (inside and outside the organization) regarding the economic activities of the firm (see Figure 16.2). Accounting work is divided into several major areas. Let's look at those areas next.

**accounting**
The recording, classifying, summarizing, and interpreting of financial events to provide management and other interested parties the information they need to make good decisions.

**FIGURE | 16.1**

**The Accounting System**
The inputs to an accounting system include sales documents and other records. The data are recorded, classified, and summarized. They're then put into summary financial statements such as the income statement and balance sheet.

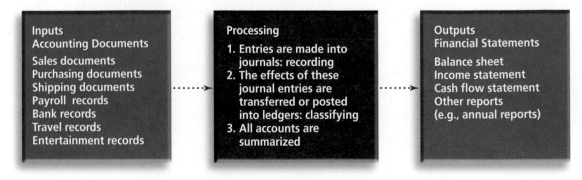

| Inputs<br>Accounting Documents | Processing | Outputs<br>Financial Statements |
|---|---|---|
| Sales documents<br>Purchasing documents<br>Shipping documents<br>Payroll records<br>Bank records<br>Travel records<br>Entertainment records | 1. Entries are made into journals: recording<br>2. The effects of these journal entries are transferred or posted into ledgers: classifying<br>3. All accounts are summarized | Balance sheet<br>Income statement<br>Cash flow statement<br>Other reports<br>(e.g., annual reports) |

| Users | Type of Report |
|---|---|
| Government taxing authorities (e.g., Canada Revenue Agency) | Tax returns |
| Government regulatory agencies | Required reports |
| People interested in the organization's income and financial position (e.g., owners, creditors, financial analysts, suppliers) | Financial statements found in annual reports (e.g., income statement, balance sheet, cash flow statement) |
| Managers of the firm | Financial statements and various internally distributed financial reports |

**FIGURE 16.2**

**Users of Accounting Information and the Required Reports**
Many types of organizations use accounting information to make business decisions. The reports needed vary according to the information each user requires. An accountant must prepare the appropriate forms.

# AREAS OF ACCOUNTING

Accounting has been called the language of business. Without closer scrutiny, you may think that accounting is only for profit-seeking firms. Nothing could be further from the truth. It is also the language used to report financial information about non-profit organizations such as churches, schools, hospitals, and government agencies. The accounting profession is divided into five key working areas: managerial accounting, financial accounting, compliance (auditing), tax accounting, and governmental and not-for-profit accounting. All five areas are important, and all create career opportunities for students who are willing to put forth the effort to study accounting.[1]

## Managerial Accounting

**Managerial accounting** is used to provide information and analyses to managers within the organization to assist them in decision making. Often this data reflects segments that these managers have responsibility for. While financial accounting is heavily focused on historical information, management accounting also provides much forward looking data in the form of budgets.

Analysis of the accounts receivable will help in evaluating the credit policies of a company. Monitoring profit margins, unit sales, travel expenses, cash flow, inventory turnover, and other such data is critical to the success of a firm. Management decision making is based on such data.

Some of the questions that managerial accounting reports are designed to answer include:

- What goods and services are selling the most and what promotional tools are working best?
- How quickly is the firm selling what it buys?
- Which are the most profitable products?
- What is the appropriate allocation of expenses between products?
- Which expenses change with changes in revenue?
- How much tax is the firm paying, and how can it minimize that amount?
- Will the firm have enough cash to pay its bills? If not, has it made arrangements to borrow that money?

In all cases, results are compared with plans to see if the results are achieving the targets set for the month, for the quarter, and for the year. When they do not, management must figure out how performance can be improved. Results are also compared with those of the particular industry to see that they are in line with, or better than, the results in competing firms. Finally, trends that the results may reveal are carefully examined to ensure that good trends are continued and unfavourable ones are reversed. This prevents negative activities from continuing unnoticed until they create serious problems. You can see how important such information is. That is why accounting is a good subject to learn.

**managerial accounting**
Accounting used to provide information and analyses to managers within the organization to assist them in decision making.

Assembling a marine diesel engine involves many tools, parts, raw materials, and other components. Keeping these costs at a minimum and setting realistic production schedules is critical to industry survival. Management accountants team with managers from production, marketing, and other areas to ensure company competitiveness.

# Financial Accounting

**financial accounting**
Accounting information and analyses prepared for people outside the organization.

**Financial accounting** differs from managerial accounting in that the information and analyses it generates are for people *outside* the organization. The information goes to owners and prospective owners, creditors and lenders, employee unions, customers, suppliers, government agencies, and the general public. These external users are interested in the organization's profits, its ability to pay its bills, and other important financial information. Within organizations, management must also be knowledgeable about the financial accounting information, as they often have to deal with external parties. Accounting staff will be required to discuss financial information with a potential lender when applying for a loan. Much of the information derived from financial accounting is contained in the company's **annual report**, a yearly statement of the financial condition, progress, and expectations of an organization. Various quarterly reports (every three months) keep the users more current. These reports are required by law for the shareholders of all public corporations. As pressure builds from stakeholders, companies are pouring more information than ever into their annual reports.[2]

**annual report**
A yearly statement of the financial condition, progress, and expectations of an organization.

Financial accounting reports provide the information that allows readers to answer questions such as:

- Has the company's income been satisfactory? Should we invest in this company?
- Should we lend money to this company? Will it be able to pay it back?
- Are the company's costs getting out of control?
- Is the company financially strong enough to stay in business to honour product warranties?
- Should we sell to this company? Will it be able to pay its bills?

We hope you are getting the idea that accounting is critical to business and to anyone who wants to understand business. You may want to know more about accounting firms, the people who prepare these reports, and how you can be sure that they know what they are doing.

## GreenBOX

### Annual Sustainability Report

More and more companies are committing to reporting of their "green" initiatives. Mountain Equipment Co-op (MEC) has just completed their Second Annual Accountability Report.

The report informs stakeholders of their social, environmental, and economic sustainability. They discuss selecting and designing products with a significant sustainability feature. They are continually looking for ways to reduce petrochemical derivatives in their products. They have a significant repair program in place for their products, and facilitate gear swaps and donations, along with a product take-back program to recycle polyester clothing. Sustainability audits of their mills are an annual occurrence.

MEC comments on many green initiatives in their facilities, reducing their output of energy and greenhouse gases to a point lower than what is produced by transporting products to their retail outlets. Some of these initiative include reducing the level of solid waste, greenhouse gas emissions, and paper usage, and using greater amounts of certified green power.

They also reported on reducing their carbon footprint through switching to rail instead of road transportation, better inventory planning, greening employee commuting through the provision of bike racks at their offices and providing employee showers, along with having all their facilities near transit routes.

In terms of product sustainability, they reported on a targeted use of 50 percent organic cotton, recycled polyester, and PVC-free inputs. In terms of ethical sourcing, they select factories that aspire to fair labour practices, working with their suppliers to improve working conditions.

Source: www.mec.ca, Sustainability Report.

Every public company is required to provide financial information. Users can access this information either from the company's Web site or from a service provided from sites like www.sedar.com. This information varies from a quarterly set of financial statements, with accompanying notes, to annual reports with a breadth of financial information.

**Chartered accountant (CA)**
An accountant who has met the examination, education, and experience requirements of the Canadian Institute of Chartered Accountants.

**certified management accountant (CMA)**
An accountant who has met the examination, education, and experience requirements of the Society of Management Accountants of Canada.

**certified general accountant (CGA)**
An accountant who has met the examination, education, and experience requirements of the Certified General Accountants Association of Canada.

**private accountant**
An accountant who works for a single firm, government agency, or non-profit organization.

**public accountant**
An accountant who provides his or her accounting services to individuals or businesses on a fee basis.

# Accounting Designations

A prestigious professional accounting designation is that of chartered accountant. A **chartered accountant (CA)** is an accountant who has met the examination, education, and experience requirements of the CA profession, which includes the Uniform Evaluation (UFE), widely recognized as one of the most rigorous professional examinations in the world. Chartered Accountants are widely recognized as the leading financial and accounting professionals in Canada.

If you are a business major, it is almost certain you will be required to take a course in managerial accounting. You may even elect to pursue a career as a certified management accountant. A **certified management accountant (CMA)** is a professional accountant who has met certain educational and experience requirements, passed a qualifying exam in the field, participated in a two year professional development program, and been certified by the Society of Management Accountants of Canada (CMA Canada). With growing emphasis on global competition, company rightsizing, outsourcing, and organizational cost-cutting, managerial accounting may be one of the most important areas you study in your school career.

The Certified General Accountants Association of Canada (CGA-Canada) also trains and certifies accountants. **Certified general accountants (CGAs)** are those who have met the examination, education, and experience requirements of CGA-Canada. CGAs offer expertise in taxation, finance, information technology, and strategic business management.[3]

Accountants work in all areas of business. One third of chartered accountants work in industry; another third are sole practitioners or work for accounting firms, and the rest primarily work in government and education; managerial accountants generally choose to get a CMA designation. Many CGAs are employed by different levels of government, while others are in public practice.

# Private and Public Accountants

It's critical for firms to keep accurate financial information. Because of this, many organizations employ **private accountants**, who work for a single firm, government agency, or non-profit organization. However, not all organizations want or need a full-time accountant. Therefore, they hire independent public accounting firms to maintain their financial records.

An accountant who provides his or her services to individuals or businesses on a fee basis is called a **public accountant.** Through independent firms, public accountants can provide a variety of services including accounting, compliance (to be discussed in another section), and other professional advice. Professional services can include designing an accounting system for a firm, helping select the correct computer and software to run the system, analyzing the financial strength of an organization, and providing consulting services.[4] Large accounting and auditing firms operate internationally to serve large transnational companies.

It is vital for the accounting profession to assure users of financial information that the information provided is accurate. Accountants must follow a set of generally accepted accounting principles (GAAP).[5] If financial reports are prepared in accordance with GAAP, users can expect that the information is reported according to standards agreed upon by accounting professionals.[6] We will discuss GAAP later in this chapter. In the early 2000s, the accounting profession suffered through perhaps the darkest period in its his-

**Decisions Matter.**   CA   www.cica.ca

- Prohibits accounting firms from providing certain non-auditing work (such as consulting services) to companies they audit.
- Strengthens the protection for whistleblowers who report wrongful actions of company officers.
- Requires company CEOs and CFOs to certify the accuracy of financial reports and imparts strict penalties for any violation of securities reporting (e.g., earnings misstatements).
- Prohibits corporate loans to directors and executives of the company.
- Establishes the five-member Public Company Accounting Oversight Board under the Securities and Exchange Commission (SEC) to oversee the accounting industry.
- Stipulates that altering or destroying key audit documents will result in felony charges and significant criminal penalties.

**FIGURE 16.3**

**Key Provisions of the Sarbanes-Oxley Act**

tory.[7] Accounting scandals involving high-profile companies such as Enron, WorldCom, and Tyco raised public suspicions and led to the downfall of one of the big five accounting firms: Arthur Andersen.[8] Andersen was convicted of obstruction of justice for its actions in the Enron case (the conviction was later reversed by the U.S. Supreme Court).[9] Canadian companies are not immune either; Nortel and Biovail have been investigated for their accounting practices. Scrutiny of the accounting industry intensified and culminated with the passage of the Sarbanes-Oxley Act by the U.S. Congress.[10] This legislation created new government reporting standards for publicly-traded companies.[11] Figure 16.3 lists a few of the major provisions of Sarbanes-Oxley. This Act also applies to any Canadian public company wishing to have their shares traded on an American stock exchange. In Canada, the Ontario Securities Commission introduced Bill 198. CEOs and CFOs of public companies are now required to certify reports. Auditors are now also required to be part of the Canadian Public Accountability Board Oversight Program, which reviews the audited financial statements of public companies. In addition, standards for the independence and education experience of Audit Committees were defined. A relatively new area of accounting that focuses its attention on fraudulent activity is **forensic accounting**. This field of accounting gathers evidence for presentation in a court of law. This evidence comes from a review of financial and other records.

**forensic accounting**
A relatively new area of accounting that focuses its attention on fraudulent activity.

## Compliance

The job of reviewing and evaluating the records used to prepare a company's financial statements is referred to as **compliance**. Private accountants within the organization often perform internal audits to ensure that proper accounting procedures and financial reporting are being carried out within the company.[12] Public accountants also conduct independent audits of accounting and related records. Financial auditors today not only examine the financial health of an organization but also look into operational efficiencies and effectiveness.[13]

The most important function and income generator for public accounting firms is performing independent audits (examinations) of the books and financial statements of companies. An **independent audit** is an evaluation and unbiased opinion about the accuracy of a company's financial statements. All stakeholders, including the public, governments, financial institutions, and shareholders (owners) are interested in the results of these audits. This audit is required by law for all public corporations in Canada. A firm's annual report often includes a written opinion by an auditor that is important to read for useful information.[14]

**compliance**
The job of reviewing and evaluating the records used to prepare a company's financial statements.

**independent audit**
An evaluation and unbiased opinion about the accuracy of a company's financial statements.

## Tax Accounting

Taxes are the price we pay for roads, parks, schools, police protection, the military, and other functions provided by government. Federal and provincial governments require submission of tax returns that must be filed at specific times and in a precise format. A tax accountant is trained in tax law and is responsible for preparing tax returns or developing tax strategies. Since governments often change tax policies according to specific needs

## DEALING with CHANGE

### Elementary, Mr. Auditor, Elementary!

Having problems with an audit that's gone awry? Think there's some hidden debt buried in a far corner of your company's books? Who are you going to call? Ghost-busters? No, it's time to call the accounting industry's version of Sherlock Holmes: the forensic accountant.

According to ex–RCMP chief Norman Inkster, president of the Inkster Group, forensic accounting is the gathering of accounting information for presentation as evidence in a court of law. "In today's burgeoning global village, time and distance are no longer relevant," he said, "and even language and cultural differences do not count as before. Greater complexity now marks many business deals and with it comes more possibilities for wrongdoing."

Forensic accountants have a somewhat sexy job in the normally quiet world of accounting. Forensic accountant Bill Kauppila sums it up well: "Our job is coming up with the story behind the story." Many companies found out the hard way that even the slightest whiff of accounting irregu-larities can be detrimental to the firm's health. Unfor-tunately, the pressure to meet earnings expectations caused some companies to play fast and loose with their financial reporting. Enter the accounting supersleuths.

Stealthily uncovering paper trails left behind by company rogues starts the detailed forensic work. Mining computer hard drives, financial papers, and bank records in a search for a smoking gun consumes the attention of the forensic accountant. However, forensic accountants also see part of their job as behavioural, meaning they get out and listen to employees who have concerns about supervisors encouraging them to "cook the books" or "hide some costs." Larry Crumbley, editor of the *Journal of Forensic Accounting*, compares looking for accounting fraud through forensic analysis to taking a metal detector to a garbage dump to find rare coins: "You're going to find a lot of junk out there." As pressures mount on companies to provide accurate financial information, we can expect forensic accountants to stay busy.

If you are interested in this career, according to Inkster a forensic accountant needs the following skills: a CA designation, knowledge of the business, an enquiring mind, puzzle-solving ability, writing skills, and the ability to tell the story in court.

Sources: Bill Cramer, "Fraud Squad," *CFO*, April 2003, 36–44; Stan Lomax, "Cooking the Books," *Business and Economics Review*, April–June 2003, 3–8; William Poe, "Forensic Accounting," *St. Louis Commerce*, March 2002, 44–45; Edward Iwata, "Accounting Detectives in Demand," *USA Today*, 28 February 2003, 3B; and "Challenges in the Global Village," University of Waterloo, Fall 1997, retrieved from www.accounting.uwaterloo.ca/accnews/fall97/forensic.htm.

---

or objectives, the job of the tax accountant is certainly challenging. Also, as the burden of taxes grows in the economy, the role of the tax accountant becomes increasingly important to the organization or entrepreneur.[15]

## Governmental and Not-for-Profit Accounting

Governmental and not-for-profit accounting involves working for organizations whose purpose is not generating a profit but serving ratepayers, taxpayers, and others according to a duly approved budget. The different levels of government require an accounting system that satisfies the needs of their information users. The primary users of govern-ment accounting information are citizens, special interest groups, legislative bodies, and creditors. These users want to ensure that government is fulfilling its obligations and making the proper use of taxpayers' money. For example Canada's auditor general, Sheila Fraser, is a CA. Her office regularly audits the federal government.

Not-for-profit organizations also require accounting professionals. In fact, not-for-profit organizations have a growing need for trained accountants since contributors to non-profits want to see exactly how and where the funds they contribute are being spent. Charities (such as the Canadian Cancer Society and the United Way of Canada), universities and colleges, hospitals, and trade unions all hire accountants to show how the funds they raise are being spent.

As you can see, managerial and financial accounting, compliance, tax accounting, and governmental and not-for-profit accounting each require specific training and skill. Yet some people are confused about the difference between an accountant and a book-keeper. We'll clarify that difference right after the Progress Assessment.

**Progress Assessment**

- Could you define accounting to a friend so that he or she would clearly understand what's involved?
- Can you explain the difference between managerial and financial accounting?
- Describe the three accounting designations.
- What's the difference between a private accountant and a public accountant?

# THE ACCOUNTING CYCLE

The **accounting cycle** is a six-step procedure that results in the preparation and analysis of the major financial statements (see Figure 16.4). The accounting cycle generally involves the work of both the bookkeeper and the accountant. **Bookkeeping** involves the recording of business transactions and is an important part of financial reporting. Accounting, however, goes far beyond the mere recording of financial information. Accountants classify and summarize financial data provided by bookkeepers and then interpret the data and report the information to management. They also suggest strategies for improving the financial condition and progress of the firm and are especially important in financial analysis and income tax preparation.

A bookkeeper's first task is to divide all of the firm's transactions into meaningful categories such as sales documents, purchasing receipts, and shipping documents. Bookkeepers then record financial data from the original transaction documents (sales slips and so forth) into a record book called a journal. It's interesting that the word *journal* comes from the French word *jour*, which means "day." A **journal** is where the day's transactions arc kept.

## The Fundamental Accounting Equation

The practice of having every transaction affect at least two accounts is called **double-entry bookkeeping**. **Accounts** are different types of assets, liabilities, and owners' equity (which will be discussed later). This practice is consistent with the **fundamental accounting equation**: Assets = Liabilities + Owners' equity.

In accounting, this equation must always be balanced. For example, suppose that you have $50,000 in cash and decide to use that money to open a small coffee shop. Your business has assets of $50,000 and no debts. The accounting equation would be:

$$\text{Assets} = \text{Liabilities} + \text{Owners' equity}$$
$$\$50,000 = \$0 + \$50,000$$

Remember, with each business transaction there is a recording of at least two entries. Each entry is either a debit or a credit. Debits or credits on their own are neither good nor bad, simply a mechanism for maintaining the balance of the accounting equation.

**accounting cycle**
A six-step procedure that results in the preparation and analysis of the two major financial statements: the balance sheet and the income statement.

**bookkeeping**
The recording of business transactions.

**journal**
The record book or computer program where accounting data are first entered.

**double-entry bookkeeping**
The concept of every business transaction affecting at least two accounts.

**accounts**
Different types of assets, liabilities, and owners' equity

**fundamental accounting equation**
Assets = liabilities + owners' equity; this is the basis for the balance sheet.

**FIGURE | 16.4**

**Steps in the Accounting Cycle**

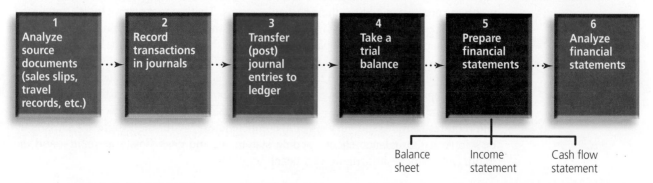

| 1 Analyze source documents (sales slips, travel records, etc.) | 2 Record transactions in journals | 3 Transfer (post) journal entries to ledger | 4 Take a trial balance | 5 Prepare financial statements | 6 Analyze financial statements |

Balance sheet    Income statement    Cash flow statement

" I'LL TELL YOU HARRIS, THEY DON'T MAKE ACCOUNTANTS LIKE THEY USED TO. THOSE I HAD IN THE 1990's NEVER BROUGHT ME FIGURES LIKE THESE."

The integrity of a firm's financial statements is vital. Accounting irregularities that occurred at firms like Livent, Nortel, and Parmalat made the companies look stronger than they actually were. Accountants are now committed to regaining the trust and respect their profession enjoyed in the past. What part should the government play in overseeing the accounting industry?

**ledger**
A specialized accounting book in which information from accounting journals is accumulated into accounts and posted so that managers can find all of the information about a specific account in one place.

**trial balance**
A summary of all of the data in the account ledgers to show whether the figures are correct and balanced.

You have $50,000 cash and $50,000 owners' equity (the amount of your investment in the business—sometimes referred to as net worth). However, before opening the business, you borrow $30,000 from a local bank; the equation now changes. You have $30,000 of additional cash, but you also have a debt (liability) of $30,000.

Your financial position within the business has changed. The equation is still balanced but is changed to reflect the transaction:

$$\text{Assets} = \text{Liabilities} + \text{Owners' equity}$$
$$\$80,000 = \$30,000 + \$50,000$$

One more bookkeeping tool is used. Let's suppose that a business wanted to determine how much it paid for office supplies in the first quarter of the year. Even with accurate accounting journals, to answer that question you have to review all journal entries and summarize those that included office supplies. Therefore, bookkeepers make use of a specialized accounting book called a **ledger** in which information from accounting journals is recorded into specific accounts and posted so that managers can find all of the information about a specific account in one place.

The next step is to prepare a trial balance. A **trial balance** is a summary of all of the accounts in the ledger to check whether the figures are correct and balanced. If the information in the accounts is not accurate, it must be corrected before the firm's financial statements are prepared. The accountant then prepares the financial statements, including a balance sheet, income statement, and cash flow statement according to generally accepted accounting principles. From the information in the financial statement, the accountant analyzes and evaluates the financial condition of the firm.

# Using Computers in Accounting

Computers and accounting software have simplified this process considerably.[16] Today, computerized accounting programs post information from journals instantaneously so that financial information is readily available whenever the organization needs it. Because computers can rapidly handle large amounts of financial information, accountants are freed up to do more important tasks such as financial analysis.[17] Computerized accounting programs have been particularly helpful to small-business owners who often lack the strong accounting support within their companies that larger firms enjoy.[18] Many accounting packages, such as Simply Accounting and Quicken, address the specific needs of small business, which are often significantly different from the needs of a major corporation. Yet business owners should understand exactly what computer system and which programs are best suited for their particular needs. That's one reason why it's suggested that before entrepreneurs get started in a small business, they should hire or consult with an accountant to identify the particular needs of their proposed firm. Then, a specific accounting system can be developed using the accounting software that's been chosen.[19]

A computer is a wonderful tool for business people and it helps ease the monotony of bookkeeping and accounting work, but it's important to remember that no computer has been programmed to make good financial decisions by itself. The work of an accountant requires training and very specific competencies.[20] After the Progress Assessment, let's look at the balance sheet, income statement, and cash flow statement—and the important financial information that each provides.

## Progress Assessment

- Can you explain the difference between accounting and bookkeeping?
- What's the difference between an accounting journal and a ledger?
- Why does a bookkeeper prepare a trial balance?
- What key advantages do computers provide businesses in maintaining and compiling accounting information?

# UNDERSTANDING KEY FINANCIAL STATEMENTS

A **financial statement** is a summary of all of the transactions that have occurred over a particular period. Financial statements indicate a firm's financial health and stability and are a key factor in management decision making. That's why shareholders (the owners of the firm), bondholders and banks (people and institutions that lend money to the firm), labour unions, employees, and the Canada Revenue Agency are all interested in a firm's financial statements. The following are the key financial statements of a business:

1. The balance sheet, which reports the firm's financial position at the end of a period.
2. The income statement, which summarizes revenues, cost of goods, and expenses (including taxes) for a specific period of time and highlights the total profit or loss the firm experienced during a period.
3. The cash flow statement, which provides a summary of money coming into and going out of the firm during a period.

The differences among the financial statements can be summarized this way: The balance sheet details what the company owns and owes on a certain day; the income statement shows what a firm sells its products for and what its selling costs are over a specific period; and the cash flow statement highlights the difference between cash coming in and cash going out over a specific period. To fully understand important financial information, you must be able to understand the purpose of an organization's financial statements. To help you with this task, we'll explain each statement in more detail next.

## The Balance Sheet

The fundamental accounting equation is the basis for the balance sheet. As Figure 16.5 (a sample balance sheet for Very Vegetarian, the hypothetical restaurant we introduced in Chapter 14) highlights, on the balance sheet you list assets first, followed by liabilities and owners' (or shareholders') equity. The assets are equal to or are balanced with the liabilities and owners' (or shareholders') equity. It's that simple. What's often complicated is determining what is included in the asset accounts and what is included in the liabilities and owners' equity accounts. It's critical that business people understand the important financial information on the balance sheet, so let's take a closer look.

A **balance sheet** is the financial statement that reports a firm's financial condition at a specific time. It's composed of three major groups of accounts: assets, liabilities, and owners' equity.[21] The balance sheet is so named because it shows a *balance* between two figures: the company's assets on the one hand, and its liabilities plus owners' equity on the other. (These terms will be defined fully in the next sections.) Note that the income statement reports on changes *over a period* and the balance sheet reports conditions *at the end of that period*. The following analogy will help explain the idea behind the balance sheet.

Let's say that you want to know what your financial condition is at a given time. Maybe you want to buy a new house or car and therefore need to calculate your available resources. One of the best measuring sticks is your balance sheet. First, you would add up everything you own—cash, property, money owed you, and so forth (assets). Subtract

**financial statement**
A summary of all of the transactions that have occurred over a particular period.

**balance sheet**
The financial statement that reports a firm's financial condition at a specific time.

**FIGURE 16.5**

Sample Very Vegetarian Balance Sheet

① Current assets: Items that can be converted to cash within one year.

② Capital assets: Items such as land, buildings, and equipment that are relatively permanent.

③ Intangible assets: Items of value such as patents and copyrights that don't have a physical form.

④ Current liabilities: Payments that are due in one year or less.

⑤ Long-term liabilities: Payments not due for one year or longer.

⑥ Shareholders' equity: The value of what shareholders own in a firm (also called owners' equity).

**VERY VEGETARIAN**
**Balance Sheet**
**December 31, 2010**

**Assets**

① **Current assets**

| | | |
|---|---:|---:|
| Cash | $ 15,000 | |
| Accounts receivable | 200,000 | |
| Notes receivable | 50,000 | |
| Inventory | 335,000 | |
| Total current assets | | $600,000 |

② **Capital assets**

| | | | |
|---|---:|---:|---:|
| Land | | $40,000 | |
| Building and improvements | $200,000 | | |
|    Less: Accumulated amortization | −90,000 | | |
| | | 110,000 | |
| Equipment and vehicles | $120,000 | | |
|    Less: Accumulated amortization | −80,000 | | |
| | | 40,000 | |
| Furniture and fixtures | $26,000 | | |
|    Less: Accumulated amortization | −10,000 | | |
| | | 16,000 | |
| Total fixed assets | | | 206,000 |

③ **Intangible assets**

| | | |
|---|---:|---:|
| Goodwill | $20,000 | |
| Total intangible assets | | 20,000 |
| **Total assets** | | **$826,000** |

**Liabilities and Owners' or Shareholders' Equity Liabilities**

④ **Current liabilities**

| | | |
|---|---:|---:|
| Accounts payable | $40,000 | |
| Notes payable (due June 2011) | 8,000 | |
| Accrued taxes | 150,000 | |
| Accrued salaries | 90,000 | |
| Total current liabilities | | $288,000 |

⑤ **Long-term liabilities**

| | | |
|---|---:|---:|
| Notes payable (due Mar. 2013) | $ 35,000 | |
| Bonds payable (due Dec. 2018) | 290,000 | |
| Total long-term liabilities | | 325,000 |
| **Total liabilities** | | **$613,000** |

⑥ **Shareholders' equity**

| | | |
|---|---:|---:|
| Common stock (1,000,000 shares) | $100,000 | |
| Retained earnings | 113,000 | |
| Total shareholders' equity | | 213,000 |
| **Total liabilities & shareholders' equity** | | **$826,000** |

from that the money you owe others—credit card debt, IOUs, car loan, student loan, and so forth (liabilities)—and you have a figure that tells you your net worth (equity). This is fundamentally what companies do in preparing a balance sheet; follow the procedures set in the fundamental accounting equation. In that preparation, however, it's important to follow generally accepted accounting principles (GAAP).

## Assets

**Assets** are economic resources (things of value) owned by a firm. Assets include productive, tangible items (e.g., equipment, buildings, land, furniture, fixtures, and motor vehicles) that help generate income, as well as intangibles with value (e.g., patents, trademarks, copyrights, or goodwill).[22] Think, for example, of the value of brand names such as Roots, WestJet, and Canadian Tire. Intangibles such as brand names can be among the firm's most valuable assets.[23] Goodwill is the value that can be attributed to factors such as reputation, location, and superior products.[24] It is included on the balance sheet when a firm acquiring another firm pays more than the value of that firm's tangible assets. Not all companies, however, have intangible assets.

Assets are listed on the firm's balance sheet according to their liquidity. **Liquidity** refers to how fast an asset is expected to be converted into cash. For example, an account receivable is an amount of money owed to the firm that it expects to be paid within one year. Accounts receivable are considered liquid assets. However, the longer a firm takes to collect its receivables, the less collectible they become. Land, however, is typically owned for many years; thus, land is a long-term asset (an asset expected to last more than one year) and not considered liquid. Thus, assets are divided into three categories according to how quickly they can be turned into cash:

1. **Current assets** are items that can or will be converted into cash within one year. Current assets include cash, accounts receivable, and inventory.

2. **Capital assets** are items that are relatively permanent goods, such as land and buildings, acquired to produce products for a business. They are not bought to be sold but to generate revenue. (These assets are also referred to as fixed assets or property, plant, and equipment.)

3. **Intangible assets** are long-term assets that have no real physical form but do have value. Patents, trademarks, copyrights, and goodwill are examples of intangible assets.

## Liabilities and Owners' Equity Accounts

Another important accounting term is *liabilities*. **Liabilities** are what the business owes to others (debts). Current liabilities are debts due in one year or less; long-term liabilities are debts not due for one year or longer. The following are common liability accounts recorded on a balance sheet (refer to Figure 16.5):

1. *Accounts payable* are current liabilities involving money owed to others for merchandise or services purchased on credit but not yet paid. If you have a bill you haven't paid, you have an account payable. The longer you take to pay, the greater the risk that a supplier will no longer grant you credit.

2. *Notes payable* can be short-term or long-term liabilities (e.g., loans from banks) that a business promises to repay by a certain date.

3. *Bonds payable* are long-term liabilities that represent money lent to the firm that must be paid back. (We will discuss bonds in depth in Chapters 17 and 18.)

4. *Taxes payable* include sales taxes and GST collected, and income tax payable.

As the fundamental accounting equation highlighted earlier, the value of things you own (assets) minus the amount of money you owe others (liabilities) is called equity. The value of what shareholders own in a firm (minus liabilities) is called shareholders' equity (or stockholders' equity).

The **owners' equity** in a company consists of all that the owners have invested in the company plus all profits that have accumulated since the business commenced but that have not yet been paid out to them. This figure always equals the book value of the assets minus the liabilities of the company.

---

**assets**
Economic resources (things of value) owned by a firm.

**liquidity**
How fast an asset can be converted into cash.

**current assets**
Items that can or will be converted into cash within one year.

**capital assets**
Assets that are relatively permanent, such as land, buildings, and equipment.

**intangible assets**
Long-term assets (e.g., patents, trademarks, copyrights) that have no real physical form but do have value.

**liabilities**
What the business owes to others (debts).

**owners' equity**
The amount of the business that belongs to the owners minus any liabilities owed by the business.

In a partnership, owners' equity is called partners' equity or capital. In a sole proprietorship, it is called owner's or proprietor's equity or capital. In a corporation, it is called shareholders' equity and is shown in two separate accounts. The amount the owners (shareholders) invest is shown in one account, called common stock; the accumulated profit that remains after dividends have been paid to shareholders is shown in an account called retained earnings. We will discuss dividends in Chapter 17. Take a few moments to review Figure 16.5 and see what facts you can determine about Very Vegetarian from its balance sheet.

## Progress Assessment

- What is the formula for the balance sheet? What do we call this formula?
- What does it mean to list various assets by liquidity?
- What goes into the liabilities accounts?
- What is owners' equity and how is it determined?

## The Income Statement

**income statement**
The financial statement that shows a firm's profit after costs, expenses, and taxes; it summarizes all of the resources that have come into the firm (revenue), all of the resources that have left the firm, and the resulting net income.

The financial statement that shows a firm's bottom line—that is, its profit after costs, expenses, and taxes—is the **income statement** (at one time called the profit and loss statement). The income statement summarizes all of the resources (called revenue) that have been earned by the firm from operating activities, resources that were used up, expenses incurred in doing business, and the resources left after all costs and expenses, including taxes, were incurred. The resources (revenue) left over are referred to as **net income or net loss** (see Figure 16.6).

The income statement reports the firm's financial operations over a particular period of time, usually a year, a quarter of a year, or a month.[25] It's the financial statement that reveals whether the business is actually earning a profit or not. The income statement includes valuable financial information for shareholders, lenders, investors (or potential investors), and employees. Because of the importance of this financial report, let's take a moment to look at the income statement and learn what each step means. Before we start, however, take a quick look at how the income statement is arranged (for a company that sells a product) according to generally accepted accounting principles (GAAP), which we will discuss later in the chapter:

**net income or net loss**
Revenue left over after all costs and expenses, including taxes, are paid.

$$
\begin{array}{l}
\text{Revenue} \\
- \text{ Cost of goods sold} \\
\hline
\text{Gross profit (gross margin)} \\
- \text{ Operating expenses} \\
\hline
\text{Net income before taxes} \\
- \text{ Taxes} \\
\hline
\text{Net income or loss}
\end{array}
$$

## Revenue

**revenue**
The value of what is received for goods sold, services rendered, and other financial sources.

**Revenue** is the value of what is received for goods sold, services rendered, and other financial sources. Note that there is a difference between revenue and sales. Most revenue comes from sales, but there could be other sources of revenue, such as rents received, money paid to the firm for use of its patents, and interest earned, that's included in reporting revenue. Be careful not to confuse the terms *revenue* and *sales*, or to use them as if they were synonymous. Also, a quick glance at the income statement shows you that gross sales are the total of all sales the firm completed. Net sales are gross sales minus returns, discounts, and allowances.

**VERY VEGETARIAN**
**Income Statement**
**For the Year Ended December 31, 2010**

| | | | |
|---|---|---|---|
| ① Revenues | | | |
| Gross sales | | $720,000 | |
| Less: Sales returns and allowances | $12,000 | | |
| Sales discounts | 8,000 | −20,000 | |
| Net sales | | | $700,000 |
| ② Cost of goods sold | | | |
| Beginning inventory, Jan. 1 | | $200,000 | |
| Merchandise purchases | $400,000 | | |
| Freight | 40,000 | | |
| Net purchases | | 440,000 | |
| Cost of goods available for sale | | $640,000 | |
| Less ending inventory, Dec. 31 | | −230,000 | |
| Cost of goods sold | | | −410,000 |
| ③ Gross profit | | | $290,000 |
| ④ Operating expenses | | | |
| Selling expenses | | | |
| Salaries for salespeople | $90,000 | | |
| Advertising | 18,000 | | |
| Supplies | 2,000 | | |
| Total selling expenses | | $110,000 | |
| General expenses | | | |
| Office salaries | $67,000 | | |
| Amortization | 1,500 | | |
| Insurance | 1,500 | | |
| Rent | 28,000 | | |
| Light, heat, and power | 12,000 | | |
| Miscellaneous | 2,000 | | |
| | | 112,000 | |
| Total operating expenses | | | 222,000 |
| Net income before taxes | | | $68,000 |
| Less: Income tax expense | | | 19,000 |
| ⑤ Net income after taxes | | | $49,000 |

**FIGURE | 16.6**

**Sample Very Vegetarian Income Statement**

① **Revenues:** Value of what's received from goods sold, services rendered, and other financial sources.

② **Cost of goods sold:** Cost of merchandise sold or cost of raw materials or parts used for producing items for resale.

③ **Gross profit:** How much the firm earned by buying or selling merchandise.

④ **Operating expenses:** Cost incurred in operating a business.

⑤ **Net income after taxes:** Profit or loss over a specific period after subtracting all costs and expenses including taxes.

# Cost of Goods Sold (Cost of Goods Manufactured)

The **cost of goods sold** (or **cost of goods manufactured**) is a measure of the cost of merchandise sold or cost of raw materials and supplies used for producing items for resale. It's common sense to calculate how much a business earned by selling merchandise over the period being evaluated, compared to how much it spent to buy, or produce, the merchandise. The cost of goods sold includes the purchase price plus any freight charges paid to transport goods (or all the costs associated with producing the merchandise). In other words, all of the costs of buying (making) are included in the cost of goods sold. It's critical that companies accurately report and manage this important income statement item.

When you subtract the cost of goods sold from net sales, you get what is called gross profit or gross margin. **Gross profit (gross margin)** is how much a firm earned by buying (or making) and selling merchandise. In a service firm, it's possible there may be no

**cost of goods sold (or cost of goods manufactured)**
A measure of the cost of merchandise sold or cost of raw materials and supplies used for producing items for resale.

**gross profit (gross margin)**
How much a firm earned by buying (or making) and selling merchandise.

cost of goods sold; therefore, net revenue could equal gross profit. In either case (selling goods or services), the gross profit doesn't tell you everything you need to know about the financial performance of the firm. The financial evaluation of an income statement also includes determining the net profit or loss a firm experienced. To get that, you must subtract the business's expenses.

## Operating Expenses

**operating expenses**
Costs involved in operating a business, such as rent, utilities, and salaries.

In the process of selling goods or services, a business experiences certain expenses. **Operating expenses** are the costs involved in operating a business. Obvious operating expenses include rent, salaries, supplies, utilities, insurance, research, and even amortization of equipment. (We will look at amortization a little later.) Operating expenses can generally be classified into two categories: selling expenses and general expenses. Selling expenses are expenses related to the marketing and distribution of the firm's goods or services (such as salaries for salespeople, advertising, and supplies). General expenses are administrative expenses of the firm (such as office salaries, amortization, insurance, and rent). Accountants are trained to help you record all applicable expenses and find other relevant expenses you need to deduct as part of doing business.

## Net Profit or Loss

After all expenses are deducted, the firm's net income before taxes is determined (refer to Figure 16.6). After allocating for taxes, we get to what's called the bottom line, which is the net income (or perhaps net loss) the firm incurred from revenue minus sales returns, costs, expenses, and taxes.[26] It answers the question: How much did the business earn or lose in the reporting period? Net income can also be referred to as net earnings or net profit.

The terms associated with the balance sheet and income statement may seem a bit confusing to you at this point, but you actually use similar accounting concepts all the time. For example, you know the importance of keeping track of costs and expenses when you prepare your own budget. If your expenses (e.g., rent and utilities) exceed your revenues (how much you earn), you are in trouble. If you need more money (revenue), you may need to sell some of the things you own to pay your expenses. The same is true in business. Companies need to keep track of how much money is earned and spent, how much cash they have on hand, and so on. The only difference is that companies tend to have more complex problems and a good deal more information to record than you as an individual do.

Users of financial statements are very interested in handling the flow of cash into and the flow of cash out of a business. Some very profitable businesses have experienced serious cash flow problems. Keep this fact in mind as we look at the cash flow statement in the next section.

## The Cash Flow Statement

**cash flow statement**
Financial statement that reports cash receipts and disbursements related to a firm's three major activities: operations, investing, and financing.

The **cash flow statement** reports cash receipts and disbursements related to the three major activities of a firm:

- operations: cash transactions associated with running the business
- investing: cash used in or provided by the firm's investing activities (normally including capital assets)
- financing: cash raised from the issuance of new debt or equity capital or cash used to repay loans or company dividends. We will discuss these terms in Chapter 17.

Accountants analyze all of the cash changes that have occurred from operating, investing, and financing, and determine the firm's net cash position. The cash flow statement also gives the firm some insight into how to handle cash better so that no cash flow problems (e.g., having no cash on hand) occur.

**VERY VEGETARIAN**
**Cash Flow Statement**
**For the Year Ended December 31, 2010**

| | | |
|---|---:|---:|
| ① Cash flows from operating activities | | |
| Cash received from customers | $150,000 | |
| Cash paid to suppliers and employees | (90,000) | |
| Interest paid | (5,000) | |
| Income tax paid | (4,500) | |
| Interest and dividends received | 1,500 | |
| Net cash provided by operating activities | | $52,000 |
| ② Cash flows from investing activities | | |
| Proceeds from sale of plant assets | $4,000 | |
| Payments for purchase of equipment | (10,000) | |
| Net cash provided by investing activities | | (6,000) |
| ③ Cash flows from financing activities | | |
| Proceeds from issuance of short-term debt | $3,000 | |
| Payment of long-term debt | (7,000) | |
| Payment of dividends | (15,000) | |
| Net cash inflow from financing activities | | (19,000) |
| Net change in cash and equivalents | | $27,000 |
| Cash balance (beginning of year) | | (2,000) |
| Cash balance (end of year) | | $25,000 |

**FIGURE 16.7**

**Sample Very Vegetarian Cash Flow Statement**

① Cash receipts from sales, commissions, fees, interest, and dividends. Cash payments for salaries, inventories, operating expenses, interest, and taxes.

② Includes cash flows that are generated through a company's purchase or sale of long-term operational assets, investments in other companies, and its lending activities.

③ Cash inflows and outflows associated with the company's own equity transactions or its borrowing activities.

Figure 16.7 shows a cash flow statement, again using the example of Very Vegetarian. As you can see, this financial statement answers such questions as: How much cash came into the business from current operations? That is, how much cash came into the firm from buying and selling goods and services? Was cash used to buy stocks, bonds, or other capital assets? Were some investments sold that brought in cash? How much money came into the firm from issuing stock?

These and other financial transactions are analyzed to see their effect on the cash position of the firm. Understanding cash flow can mean the success or failure of any business. We will analyze cash flow a bit more in depth in the next section.

## The Importance of Cash Flow Analysis

Cash flow, if not properly managed, can cause a business much concern. Cash flow analysis is really rather simple to comprehend.[27] Let's say that you borrow $100 from a friend to buy a used bike and agree to pay your friend back at the end of the week. In turn, you sell the bike for $150 to someone else, who also agrees to pay you in a week. Unfortunately, at the end of the week, the person who bought the bike from you does not have the money as promised. This person says that he will have to pay you next month. Meanwhile, your friend wants the $100 you agreed to pay her by the end of the week! What seemed like a great opportunity to make an easy $50 profit is a real cause for concern. Right now, you owe $100 and have no cash. What do you do when your friend shows up at the end of the week and demands to be paid? If you were a business, this might cause you to default on the loan and possibly go bankrupt, even though you had profits.

It is very possible that a business can increase sales and profits, and still suffer greatly from cash flow problems. **Cash flow** is simply the difference between cash coming in and cash going out of a business. A common mistake among start-ups is to focus on the product and not the running of the business, explained Blair Davidson, KPMG partner in the Financial Advisory Services Group, at a recent York Technology Association and Canadian

**cash flow**
The difference between cash coming in and cash going out of a business.

Technology Network breakfast speech. "Business can be viewed as a triangle of operations: making, selling, and scorekeeping. If you devote yourself only to production and neglect the other sides, the imbalance will show up in the bottom line and shake the confidence of potential investors in the future," he said.[28]

Cash flow is a constant challenge for businesses of all sizes. Consider how critical this is for seasonal businesses (such as ski resorts) in which the flow of cash into the business is sporadic. Accountants sometimes face tough ethical challenges in reporting the flow of funds into a business. Read the Making Ethical Decisions box to see how such an ethical dilemma can arise. Sometimes, very large companies are forced to sell off one or more of their profitable subsidiaries to raise cash because of a recession or other unexpected development. This is the problem that caused Lehman Brothers to go bankrupt in 2008. Sometimes, a company can nearly be destroyed by cash flow problems. This was evident when Air Canada had to restructure its operations under the Companies' Creditors Arrangement Act (CCAA) in 2003. To improve its cash flow, General Electric's corporate finance division granted Air Canada more than $1 billion in financing.[29]

What often happens to a business is that, to meet the demands of customers, the business buys more and more goods on credit (no cash is involved). Similarly, more and more goods are sold on credit (no cash is involved). If their customers delay in paying, all of the credit it has with its lenders will get used. When the firm requests more money from its bank to pay a crucial bill, the bank refuses the loan because the credit limit has been reached. All other credit sources refuse funds as well. The company desperately needs funds to pay its bills, or it could be forced into bankruptcy. Unfortunately, all too often, the company does go into bankruptcy because there was no cash available when it was most needed.

An online learning object about the financial statements at www.baruch. cuny.edu/tutorials/statements provides you with an interactive experience to further your understanding

Cash flow analysis also points out clearly that a business's relationship with its banker(s) is critical. Maintaining a working relationship with a bank is a path to preventing cash flow problems that often develop. The value that accountants provide to businesses in dealing with cash flow is also critical. Accountants can advise the firm on whether it needs cash and, if so, how much. They can also offer advice on how a company is managing its cash position, and provide key insights into how, when, and where finance managers can get the money a firm needs.

---

## Making Ethical Decisions

### On the Accounting Hot Seat

You are the only accountant employed by a small manufacturing firm. You are in charge of keeping the books for the company, which has been suffering from an economic downturn that shows no signs of lightening in the near future.

You know that your employer is going to ask the bank for an additional loan so the company can continue to pay its bills. Unfortunately, the financial statements for the year will not show good results, and your best guess is that the bank will not approve a loan increase on the basis of the financial information you will present.

Your boss approaches you in early January before you have closed the books for the preceding year and suggests that perhaps the statements can be "improved" by treating the sales that were made at the beginning of

January as if they were made in December. He also asks you to do a number of other things that will cover up the trail so that the auditors will not discover the padding of the year's sales.

You know that these results go against the professional rules, and you argue with your boss. Your boss tells you that, if the company does not get the additional bank loan, there's a very good chance the business will close. That means you and everyone else in the firm will be out of a job. You believe your boss is probably right and you know that, with the current economic downturn, finding a job will be tough for you and almost impossible for others in the company. What are your alternatives? What are the likely consequences of each alternative? How will jobs be affected? What will you do?

# APPLYING ACCOUNTING KNOWLEDGE IN BUSINESS

If accounting consisted of nothing more than repetitive functions of gathering and recording transactions and preparing financial statements, the tasks could be assigned solely to computers. In fact, most medium and large firms as well as growing numbers of small businesses have done just that. The Internet has initiated a new way of managing a firm's finances: online accounting. But the truth is that how you record and report financial data is also critically important.

## Generally Accepted Accounting Principles

Business transactions require certain guidelines that help accountants make proper and consistent decisions. These guidelines are called generally accepted accounting principles (GAAP). They are published in the handbook of the Canadian Institute of Chartered Accountants, along with many other important guidelines. This handbook is the ultimate authority of the accounting profession. Bankers, financial analysts, and others also refer to it. From time to time (and after much discussion) it is updated or modified.

There are about a dozen important accounting principles, which provide options for how certain financial events are recorded. Every audited set of financial statements includes a series of notes explaining how these principles have been applied, as well as a report by the auditors that GAAP have been used. This makes it possible for financial statements to be compared from one year to the next as well as from one company to another.

Like other business disciplines, accounting is subject to change. Currently, the accounting profession is feeling the impact of the global market. The Reaching Beyond Our Borders box discusses a movement to globalize accounting procedures.

## Reaching Beyond Our Borders

### The Accounting Shot Heard Around the World

You have read throughout this text about the tremendous impact of the global market on business. Companies like Coca-Cola and Nestlé earn more than 50 percent of their revenues from global markets, helping them grow but creating a number of accounting headaches. Multinationals must adapt their accounting reporting to the rules of multiple countries, since no global system of accounting exists. However, that situation could soon change. As a growing number of countries have adopted the International Financial Reporting Standards (IFRS), the International Accounting Standards Board (IASB) has pushed to make them the clear accounting authority worldwide.

The European Union, Australia, and New Zealand have already adopted these standards. Canada, China, Japan, India, and South Korea have agreed to implement these standards in 2011. In total, over 100 countries are in the process of adopting the IFRS. In Canada, crown and public organizations are required to convert. Requirements for all other types of organizations are still being determined. Converting to the IFRS may take up to two years for well-established, large organizations. Those corporations

that are converting have in some instances already started the process. The United States has yet to agree to implementing IFRS. There, debate is ongoing as to how these new standards will impact the quality of reporting. Regardless of if or when the United States changes, the adoption of these new standards is having a big impact on accounting globally.

Many others believe, however, that the accounting profession still needs to resolve some questions: Do international standards produce the same quality of reporting as GAAP? Would application and enforcement of international standards in the United States be as rigorous as they have been for GAAP? Professor Sue Haka of Michigan State University also points out that accounting exams and textbooks must be ready for implementation of IFRS. Stay tuned for the possibility of big changes on the accounting front.

Sources: David Katz , "Global Standards: Jilted at the Altar," CFO.com, 5 August 2008; Edward Iwata , "Will Going Global Extend to Accounting?" *USA Today*, 6 January 2009; and Alix Stuart , "Which One When?" *CFO*, February 2009.

# Amortization, LIFO, and FIFO

Take a look at Figures 16.5 and 16.6 again. Note that in Figure 16.5, Very Vegetarian lists accumulated amortization on its property, plant, and equipment, and in Figure 16.6, Very Vegetarian lists amortization as a general expense. What exactly does this mean, and how does it affect the company's financial position? **Amortization** is the systematic write-off of the cost of a tangible asset over its estimated useful life. These assets, including buildings, equipment, and furniture and fixtures, are used for a number of years to help a business earn revenues. Therefore, their cost needs to be matched against the revenues earned from using these assets, over this time period, to properly determine the profits.

Subject to certain technical accounting rules (set by GAAP and the Canada Revenue Agency) that are beyond the scope of this chapter, a firm may use one of several different techniques for calculating amortization. The key thing to understand right now is that different amortization techniques could result in a different net income for the firm. Accountants are able to offer financial advice and recommend ways of legally handling questions regarding amortization, as well as other accounts such as inventory, where different valuation methods can affect a firm's financial performance. Let's look briefly at how accountants can value inventory.

The valuation of a firm's inventory presents another interesting accounting application. Inventories are a key part of many companies' financial statements and are important in determining a firm's cost of goods sold (or manufactured) on the income statement. Look again at Very Vegetarian's income statement in Figure 16.6. When a firm sells merchandise from its inventory, it can calculate the cost of that item in different ways. In financial reporting, it doesn't matter when a particular item was actually placed in a firm's inventory, but it does matter how an accountant records the cost of the item when it was sold. Two common accounting treatments are **first in, first out (FIFO)** and **last in, first out (LIFO)**. Sound a bit confusing? See the Spotlight on Small Business box for an example of how different inventory valuation methods can affect the numbers in an income statement.

What's important to understand about amortization and inventory valuation is that generally accepted accounting principles (GAAP) can permit an accountant to use different methods of amortizing a firm's long-term assets and valuing a firm's inventory. That's why companies provide readers of their financial statements with complete information concerning their financial operations.[30]

## SPOTLIGHT ON Small Business

### Accounting for What's Coming and Going in a Small Business

A bookstore maintains stock in a certain introductory-level textbook all year. In late December, when the bookstore orders 50 additional copies of a text to sell for the coming term, the publisher's price has increased from $70 to $80 a copy due to inflation and other costs. The bookstore now has in its inventory 100 copies of the same textbook from different purchase cycles. If it sells 50 copies to students at $100 each at the beginning of the new term, what's the bookstore's cost of the book for accounting purposes? It depends.

The books are identical, but the accounting treatment is different. If the bookstore uses a method called first in, first out (FIFO), the cost of goods sold is $70 for each textbook, because the textbook the store bought first—the first in—cost $70. The bookstore could use another method, however. Under last in, first out (LIFO), its last purchase of the textbooks, at $80 each, determines the cost of each of the 50 textbooks sold. If the book sells for $100, what is the difference in gross margin between using FIFO and using LIFO? Eventually, when all 100 copies are sold the cumulative net income will be the same regardless of whether FIFO or LIFO is used. The choice between the two methods solely affects the timing of when the net income is realized.

## Progress Assessment

- What is the formula for the income statement?
- What is the difference between revenue and income on the income statement?
- What is the connection between the income statement and the balance sheet?
- Why is the cash flow statement important in evaluating a firm's operations?
- What is the difference between LIFO and FIFO inventory valuation? How could the use of these methods change financial results?

# ANALYZING FINANCIAL STATEMENTS: RATIO ANALYSIS

Accurate financial information from the firm's financial statements forms the basis of the financial analysis performed by accountants inside and outside the firm. **Ratio analysis** is the assessment of a firm's financial condition and performance through calculations and interpretation of financial ratios developed from the firm's financial statements. Financial ratios are especially useful in analyzing the actual performance of the company compared to its past performance, current financial objectives, and compared to other firms within its industry.[31] At first glance, ratio analysis may seem complicated; the fact is that most of us already use ratios quite often. For example, in basketball, the number of shots made from the foul line is expressed by a ratio: shots made to shots attempted. A player who shoots 85 percent from the foul line is considered an outstanding foul shooter, and suggestions are to not foul him or her in a close game.

Whether ratios measure an athlete's performance or the financial health of a business, they provide a good deal of valuable information. Financial ratios provide key insights on changes in a firm's performance over time and how a firm compares to other firms in its industry in the important areas of liquidity (speed of changing assets into cash), debt (leverage), profitability, and business activity. Understanding and interpreting business ratios is a key to sound financial analysis. Let's look briefly at four key types of ratios that businesses use to measure financial performance.

**ratio analysis**
The assessment of a firm's financial condition and performance through calculations and interpretations of financial ratios developed from the firm's financial statements.

## Liquidity Ratios

As explained earlier, the word *liquidity* refers to how fast an asset can be converted to cash. Liquidity ratios measure a company's ability to turn assets into cash to pay its short-term debts (liabilities that must be repaid within one year).[32] These short-term debts are of particular importance to creditors of the firm, who expect to be paid on time. Two key liquidity ratios are the current ratio and the acid-test ratio.

The current ratio is the ratio of a firm's current assets to its current liabilities. This information can be found on the firm's balance sheet. Look back at Figure 16.5, which details Very Vegetarian's balance sheet. Very Vegetarian lists current assets of $600,000 and current liabilities of $288,000. The firm therefore has a current ratio of 2.08, which means Very Vegetarian has $2.08 of current assets for every $1 of current liabilities. See below:

$$\text{Current ratio} = \frac{\text{Current assets}}{\text{Current liabilities}} = \frac{\$600,000}{\$288,000} = 2.08$$

An obvious question to ask is: How well positioned financially is Very Vegetarian for the short term (less than one year)? It depends! Usually a company with a current ratio of 2 or better is considered a safe risk for granting short-term credit since it has over two times more current assets (that when converted to cash) will be available to pay their current liabilities. However, it's important to compare Very Vegetarian's current ratio to that of competing firms in its industry. It's also important for the firm to compare its current ratio with the same ratio from the previous year to note any significant changes.

Another key liquidity ratio, called the acid-test or quick ratio, measures the cash, marketable securities (such as stocks and bonds), and receivables of a firm, compared to its current liabilities:

$$\text{Acid test ratio} = \frac{\text{Cash} + \text{Accounts receivable} + \text{Marketable securities}}{\text{Current liabilities}}$$

$$= \frac{\$265,000}{\$288,000} = .92$$

This ratio is particularly important to firms with relatively large inventory, which can take longer than other current assets to convert into cash. It helps answer such questions as the following: What if sales drop off and we can't sell our inventory? Can we still pay our short-term debt? Though ratios vary among industries, an acid-test ratio of between .50 and 1.0 is usually considered satisfactory, but a ratio under 1.0 could also be a hint of some cash flow problems. Therefore, Very Vegetarian's acid-test ratio of .92 could raise concerns that perhaps the firm may not meet its short-term debt and may therefore have to go to a high-cost lender for financial assistance.

## Leverage (Debt) Ratios

Leverage (debt) ratios measure the degree to which a firm relies on borrowed funds in its operations. A firm that takes on too much debt could experience problems repaying lenders or meeting promises made to shareholders. The debt to owners' equity ratio measures the degree to which the company is financed by borrowed funds that must be repaid. Again, we can use Figure 16.5 to measure Very Vegetarian's level of debt:

$$\text{Debt to owner's equity} = \frac{\text{Total liabilities}}{\text{Owner's equity}} = \frac{\$613,000}{\$213,000} = 287\%$$

A ratio above 1 (above 100 percent) shows that a firm has more debt than equity. With a ratio of 287 percent, Very Vegetarian has a rather high degree of debt compared to its equity, which implies that the firm may be perceived as quite risky to lenders and investors. However, it's always important to compare a firm's debt ratios to those of other firms in its industry because debt financing is more acceptable in some industries than it is in others. Comparisons with past debt ratios can also identify trends that may be occurring within the firm or industry.

## Profitability (Performance) Ratios

Profitability (performance) ratios measure how effectively a firm is using its various resources to achieve profits. Company management's performance is often measured by the firm's profitability ratios. Three of the more important ratios used are earnings per share, return on sales, and return on equity.

Companies report their quarterly earnings per share in two ways: basic and diluted. The basic earnings per share (basic EPS) ratio helps determine the amount of profit earned by a company for each share of outstanding common stock. The diluted earnings per share (diluted EPS) ratio measures the amount of profit earned by a company for each share of outstanding common stock, but this ratio also takes into consideration stock options, warrants, preferred stock, and convertible debt securities, which can be converted into common stock. For simplicity's sake, we will compute only the basic earnings per share (EPS). Continued earnings growth is well received by both investors and lenders. The basic EPS ratio calculated for Very Vegetarian is as follows:

$$\text{Basic earnings per share} = \frac{\text{Net income after taxes}}{\text{Average number of common stock shares outstanding}}$$

$$= \frac{\$49,000}{1,000,000} = \$.049 \text{ per share}$$

Another reliable indicator of performance is obtained by using a ratio that measures the return on sales. Firms use this ratio to see how their current performance compares to past performance and if they are doing as well as the companies they compete against in generating income from the sales they achieve. Return on sales is calculated by comparing a company's net income to its total sales: Very Vegetarian's return on sales is 7 percent, a figure that must be measured against competing firms in its industry to judge its performance.

$$\text{Return on sales} = \frac{\text{Net income}}{\text{Net sales}} = \frac{\$49,000}{\$700,000} = 7\% \text{ (return on sales)}$$

Risk is a market variable that concerns investors. The higher the risk involved in an industry, the higher the return investors expect on their investment. Therefore, the level of risk involved in an industry (which the debt ratio measures) and the return on investment of competing firms is important in comparing the firm's performance. Return on equity measures how much was earned for each dollar invested by owners. It's calculated by comparing a company's net income to its total owners' equity. Very Vegetarian's return on equity looks reasonably sound:

$$\text{Return on equity} = \frac{\text{Net income}}{\text{Average total owner's equity}} = \frac{\$49,000}{\$213,000} = 23\% \text{ (return on equity)}$$

It's important to remember that profits help companies like Very Vegetarian grow. Therefore, these and other profitability ratios are considered vital measurements of company growth and management performance.

When calculating profitability ratios you need to take into consideration the time periods involved. The EPS and return on equity ratios compare the income earned over a period of time with the number of shares outstanding and owners' equity, respectively. The latter two amounts come from the balance sheet, which provides amounts at a point of time. To deal with these timing differences, each ratio uses an average of the balance sheet amounts using balance sheets at the beginning and end of the period covered by the net income. For the above calculations, only one set of balance sheet figures is all the information we were given in Figure 16.5. You will see this approach repeated in the discussion of activity ratios.

## Activity Ratios

Converting the firm's resources to profits is a key function of management. Activity ratios measure the effectiveness of a firm's management in using the assets that are available.

The inventory turnover ratio measures the speed of inventory moving through the firm and its conversion into sales. Inventory sitting by idly in a business costs money. Think of the fixed cost of storing inventory in a warehouse as opposed to the revenue available when companies sell (turn over) inventory. The more efficiently a firm manages its inventory, the higher the return. The inventory turnover ratio for Very Vegetarian is measured as follows:

$$\text{Inventory turnover} = \frac{\text{Cost of goods sold}}{\text{Average inventory}} = \frac{\$410,000}{\$215,000} = 1.9 \text{ times}$$

Note that the average inventory is calculated by adding the beginning and ending inventories and dividing by two.

A lower-than-average inventory turnover ratio for a firm in an industry often indicates obsolete merchandise on hand or poor buying practices. A higher-than-average ratio may signal lost sales because of inadequate stock. An acceptable turnover ratio is generally determined industry by industry.

Faucets, faucets, and more faucets. Home Depot stores stock more than 36,000 items that cover 130,000 square feet of floor space. Maintaining such an enormous inventory is no small task. What financial ratios would help Home Depot make sure it is managing its inventory efficiently?

Managers need to be aware of proper inventory control and expected inventory turnover to ensure proper performance. Have you ever worked as a food server in a restaurant? How many times did your employer expect you to turn over a table (keep changing customers at the table) in an evening? The more times a table turns, the higher the return to the owner.

Accountants and other finance professionals use several other specific ratios, in addition to the ones we have discussed, to learn more about a firm's financial condition. The key purpose here is to acquaint you with what financial ratios are, the relationship they have with the firm's financial statements, and how business people—including investors, creditors, lenders, and managers—use them. If you can't recall where the accounting information used in ratio analysis comes from, see Figure 16.8 for a quick reference. It's also important for you to keep in mind that financial analysis begins where the accounting statements end.

We hope that you can see from this chapter that there is more to accounting than meets the eye. It can be fascinating and is critical to the firm's operations. It's worth saying one more time that, as the language of business, accounting is a worthwhile language to learn.

An online learning object about ratio analysis www. bized.co.uk/compfact/ratios/ index.htm provides you with an interactive experience to further your understanding.

**FIGURE | 16.8**

**Accounts in the Balance Sheet and Income Statement**

| BALANCE SHEET ACCOUNTS | | | INCOME STATEMENT ACCOUNTS | | | |
|---|---|---|---|---|---|---|
| Assets | Owners' Liabilities | Shareholders' Equity | Revenues | Cost of Goods Sold | Expenses | |
| Cash | Accounts payable | Capital stock | Sales revenue | Cost of buying goods | Wages | Interest |
| Accounts receivable | Notes payable | Retained earnings | Rental revenue | | Rent | Donations |
| Inventory | Bonds payable | Common stock | Commissions revenue | Cost of storing goods | Repairs | Licences |
| Investments | Taxes payable | | Royalty revenue | | Travel | Fees |
| Equipment | | | | | Insurance | Supplies |
| Land | | | | | Utilities | Advertising |
| Buildings | | | | | Entertainment | Taxes |
| Motor vehicles | | | | | Storage | Research |
| Goodwill | | | | | | |

## Progress Assessment

- How do financial ratios benefit stakeholders?
- What are the four main categories of financial ratios?

## SUMMARY

1. Financial information is critical to the growth and development of an organization. Accounting provides the information necessary to measure a firm's financial condition.

**LO ▶ 1** Describe the importance of accounting and financial information.

### What is accounting?
Accounting is the recording, classifying, summarizing, and interpreting of financial events and transactions that affect an organization. The methods used to record and summarize accounting data into reports are called an accounting system.

2. The accounting profession covers five major areas: managerial accounting, financial accounting, compliance, tax accounting, and governmental and not for profit accounting.

**LO ▶ 2** Define and explain the different areas of the accounting profession.

### How does managerial accounting differ from financial accounting?
Managerial accounting provides information (often of segments of a business) for planning and control purposes to managers within the firm to assist them in decision making. Financial accounting provides information in the form of the three basic financial statements to managers and external users of data such as creditors and lenders.

### What is the job of an auditor?
Auditors review and evaluate the standards used to prepare a company's financial statements. An independent audit is conducted by a public accountant and is an evaluation and unbiased opinion about the accuracy of a company's financial statements.

### What is the difference between a private accountant and a public accountant?
A public accountant provides services for a fee to a variety of companies, whereas a private accountant works for a single company. Private and public accountants do essentially the same things, with the exception of independent audits. Private accountants do perform internal audits, but only public accountants supply independent audits.

3. Many people confuse bookkeeping and accounting.

**LO ▶ 3** List the steps in the accounting cycle, distinguish between accounting and bookkeeping, and explain how computers are used in accounting.

### What is the difference between bookkeeping and accounting?
Bookkeeping is part of accounting and includes the mechanical part of recording data. Accounting also includes classifying, summarizing, interpreting, and reporting data to management.

### What are journals and ledgers?
Journals are original-entry accounting documents. This means that they are the first place that transactions are recorded. Summaries of journal entries are recorded (posted) into ledgers. Ledgers are specialized accounting books that arrange the transactions by homogeneous groups (accounts).

### What are the six steps of the accounting cycle?
The six steps of the accounting cycle are (1) analyzing documents; (2) recording information into journals; (3) posting that information into ledgers; (4) developing a trial balance; (5) preparing financial statements (the balance sheet, income statement, and cash flow statement); and (6) analyzing financial statements.

### How can computers help accountants?

Computers can record and analyze data and provide financial reports. Software is available that can continuously analyze and test accounting systems to be sure that they are functioning correctly. Computers can help decision making by providing appropriate information, but they cannot make good financial decisions independently. Accounting applications and creativity are still human traits.

**LO ▶ 4**   Explain how the major financial statements differ.

4. Financial statements are a critical part of the firm's financial position.

### What is a balance sheet?

A balance sheet reports the financial position of a firm on a particular day. The fundamental accounting equation used to prepare the balance sheet is Assets = Liabilities + Owners' equity.

### What are the major accounts of the balance sheet?

Assets are economic resources owned by the firm, such as buildings and machinery. Liabilities are amounts owed by the firm to others (e.g., creditors, bondholders). Owners' equity is the value of the things the firm owns (assets) minus any liabilities; thus, owners' equity equals assets minus liabilities.

### What is an income statement?

An income statement reports revenues, costs, and expenses for a specific period of time (e.g., for the year ended December 31, 2009). The formula is Revenue − Cost of goods sold = Gross margin; Gross margin − Operating expenses = Net income before taxes; and Net income before taxes − Taxes = Net income (or net loss).

### What is a cash flow statement?

Cash flow is the difference between cash receipts (money coming in) and cash disbursements (money going out). The cash flow statement reports cash receipts and disbursements related to the firm's major activities: operations, investing, and financing.

**LO ▶ 5**   Describe the role of amortization, LIFO, and FIFO in reporting financial information.

5. Applying accounting knowledge makes the reporting and analysis of data a challenging occupation. Amortization is a key account that accountants evaluate. Two accounting techniques for valuing inventory are known as LIFO and FIFO.

### What is amortization?

Amortization is the systematic matching of the cost of a tangible asset against the revenue earned from the use of this asset over the asset's estimated useful life. Amortization must be noted on both the balance sheet and the income statement.

### What are LIFO and FIFO?

LIFO and FIFO are methods of valuing inventory. FIFO means first in, first out; LIFO means last in, first out. The method an accountant uses to value inventory, FIFO or LIFO, can affect its net income.

**LO ▶ 6**   Explain the importance of ratio analysis in reporting financial information.

6. Financial ratios are a key part of analyzing financial information.

### What are the four key categories of ratios?

There are four key categories of ratios: liquidity ratios, leverage (debt) ratios, profitability (performance) ratios, and activity ratios.

### What is the major value of ratio analysis to the firm?

Ratio analysis provides the firm with information about its financial position in key areas compared to similar firms in its industry and its past performance.

## KEY TERMS

accounting 482

accounting cycle 489

accounts 489

amortization 500

annual report 484

assets 493

balance sheet 491

bookkeeping 489

capital assets 493

cash flow 497

cash flow statement 496

certified general accountant (CGA) 486

certified management accountant (CMA) 486

chartered accountant (CA) 486

compliance 487

cost of goods sold (or cost of goods manufactured) 495

current assets 493

double-entry bookkeeping 489

financial accounting 484

financial statement 491

first in, first out (FIFO) 500

forensic accounting 487

fundamental accounting equation 489

gross profit (gross margin) 495

income statement 494

independent audit 487

intangible assets 493

journal 489

last in, first out (LIFO) 500

ledger 490

liabilities 493

liquidity 493

managerial accounting 483

net income or net loss 494

operating expenses 496

owners' equity 493

private accountant 486

public accountant 486

ratio analysis 501

revenue 494

trial balance 490

## CRITICAL THINKING

1. In business, hundreds of documents are received or created every day, so you can appreciate the valuable role an accountant plays. Can you see why most businesses have to hire people to do this work? Would it be worth the owners' time to do all the paperwork? Can you understand why most accountants find it easier to do this work on a computer?

2. As a potential investor in a firm or perhaps the buyer of a business, would you be interested in evaluating the company's financial statements? Why or why not? What would be the key information you would seek from a firm's financial statements?

3. Why is it important that accounting reports be prepared according to specific procedures (GAAP)? Would it be advisable to allow businesses some flexibility or creativity in preparing financial statements?

## DEVELOPING WORKPLACE SKILLS

1. Visit, telephone, or e-mail a professional accountant from a local company in your area, or talk with one in your school's business department. Ask what challenges, changes, and opportunities he or she foresees in the accounting profession in the next five years. List the forecasts on a sheet of paper and then compare them with the information in this chapter.

2. Obtain the most recent annual report for a Canadian company of your choice. *The Globe and Mail* has a free annual reports service; order a report at http://globeinvestor.ar.wilink.com/v5/index.asp?cp_code=A169&. Many companies post their annual reports on their Web sites. Hints: Look over the company's financial statements and see if they coincide with the information in this chapter. Read the opinion of the auditing firm (usually at the beginning of the report). Write down important conclusions the auditors have made about the company's financial statements.

3. Place yourself in the role of a small-business consultant. One of your clients, Be Pretty Fashions, is considering opening two new stores. Their industry experiences continuous style changes that occur in the fashion industry. Prepare a formal draft memo to Be Pretty Fashions explaining the difficulties a firm experiences when it encounters the cash flow problems that typically occur in this industry. Think of a business option that Be Pretty Fashions could try to avoid cash flow problems.

4. Using the annual report you obtained in problem 2 above, try your hand at computing financial ratios. Compute the current ratio, debt to owners' equity ratio, and return on sales for the firm. Next, obtain an annual report of one of the company's competitors and compute the same ratios for that company; then compare the differences.

## TAKING IT TO THE NET 1

### Purpose

To research careers in accounting.

### Exercise

Go to the Web site for Workopolis (www.workopolis.com) and investigate a mid-level accounting position.

Browse through the advertisement and:

1. Summarize the duties and responsibilities for the position.

2. List the skills required.

## TAKING IT TO THE NET 2

### Purpose

To calculate and analyze current ratios and quick (acid-test) ratios.

### Exercise

Two large Canadian retailers, RONA and Shoppers Drug Mart, are applying for a loan. To evaluate the loan applications, information from the balance sheet of each company needs to be analyzed. Go to www.sedar.com to find the most recent balance sheets for both companies, access "Company Profiles" after you have logged onto the Sedar site. Answer the following questions:

1. Calculate the current ratio for each company. Comparing the ratios, which company is more likely to get the loan? Why?

2. The quick (acid-test) ratio is considered an even more reliable measure of a business's ability to repay loans than the current ratio. Because inventory is often difficult to liquidate, the value of the inventory is subtracted from the total current assets. Calculate the quick ratio for each business. Based on this additional information, do you think either business will get the loan? Why?

## ANALYZING MANAGEMENT DECISIONS

### Getting Through the Hard Times at Hard Rock

In the mid-1990s, the theme-dining business seemed like a path lined with gold. With regularity, celebrity stargazers, enthusiastic press from around the globe, and hungry customers gathered at the openings of theme restaurants such as Planet Hollywood and Motown Cafe.

Unfortunately, the situation changed. In the late 1990s and early 2000s, Planet Hollywood filed for bankruptcy protection and Motown Cafe closed units across the country. Consumer boredom, a slowing economy, and a saturated market were blamed.

The changing "entertainment" market raised eyebrows at the granddaddy of theme restaurants, the Hard Rock Cafe (HRC). HRC knew that its market position was shaky due to increased competition and shifting consumer attitudes. The company also felt growing financial pressures and speculated that a change in financial management might be needed. HRC had operated with a traditional, competent accounting department that ensured that the company paid its bills, had money left at the end of the day, and could state how much it was earning. The problem was that HRC lacked the ability to analyze its financial information fully and use it to improve operations. To address these concerns, the company recruited a new chief financial officer (CFO) and dedicated itself to changing the financial reporting and information structure at the company.

Hard Rock Cafe believed that it had a tremendous undervalued asset—a premium global brand. The company dedicated itself to protecting and expanding that asset. However, it was evident that, without revenue, brand loyalty doesn't matter. Hard Rock's CFO was astonished to find that HRC sold $180 million per year in merchandise (primarily its well-known T-shirts) in addition to food, yet could not explain exactly how these individual items contributed to the firm's profit. It was then that the company realized that Hard Rock Cafe's accounting and financial management had to change.

To begin, the company piloted a food and beverage management system to track usage and item profitability. This system included information such as daily and seasonal buying patterns, profitability of one menu versus another, average weekly guest counts per restaurant, and specific cost of sales and profit margins per item. The company then shifted the responsibility of the firm's accountants. Instead of being responsible for profit-and-loss statements for a certain number of restaurants, company accountants now were responsible for one major financial category only, such as cost of goods sold, for all of the company's operations. The objective was to compile companywide information for sound financial decision making.

Hard Rock Cafe also broke down the barriers that existed between the finance and accounting departments and operations, merchandising, and marketing. Today, financial information is shared directly with managers who can execute the recommendations at the restaurant level. Still, the company realized that this was not going to be a quick fix but rather an ongoing challenge. Last year, 27 million people visited one of 103 Hard Rock Cafe locations. Even so, competitors such as Rainforest Cafe promise to make the fight for entertainment customers an interesting one.

Sources: Larry Bleiberg. "Cafe Quest Has Retiree on a Roll," *Dallas Morning News*, 15 March 2000, 12G; "Rank Is Betting on Another Good Year," *Birmingham (UK) Post*, 1 March 2003, 15; and Jon Griffin, "Rank Is Backing a Winner," *Evening Mail (UK)*, 28 February 2003, 26.

## Discussion Questions

1. Why is it important for Hard Rock Cafe to know how different products contribute financially to overall company profits?

2. Do you think that Hard Rock Cafe's focus on improved financial reporting helped its company planning capabilities? How?

3. Would a company like Hard Rock Cafe be most likely to use a FIFO or a LIFO form of inventory valuation? Why?

## CHAPTER 17

# Financial Management

## LEARNING OBJECTIVES

**AFTER YOU HAVE READ AND STUDIED THIS CHAPTER, YOU SHOULD BE ABLE TO:**

**LO ▶ 1** Describe the importance of finance and financial management to an organization, and explain the responsibilities of financial managers.

**LO ▶ 2** Outline the financial planning process, and explain the three key budgets in the financial plan.

**LO ▶ 3** Explain the major reasons why firms need funds, and identify various types of financing that can be used to obtain these funds.

**LO ▶ 4** Identify and describe different sources of short-term financing.

**LO ▶ 5** Identify and describe different sources of long-term financing.

## Getting to Know Cynthia Devine, CFO of Tim Hortons

Very few brands enjoy the emotional ties and customer loyalty that Tim Hortons has earned. The company has spent the past 42 years building one of the most unique and successful brands in the highly competitive quick-service restaurant industry. On 24 March 2006, after ten very successful years as part of the Wendy's International organization, Tim Hortons completed an initial public offering (IPO) on the New York and Toronto stock exchanges. The offering of 33 million shares—or 17 percent of the company—raised net proceeds of $843 million and gave investors the opportunity to own part of this household name. On 29 September 2006, the remaining 83 percent of the company was divided out to Wendy's shareholders, launching Tim Hortons as a stand-alone public company. In September 2009, a merger and reorganization were approved by an overwhelming majority of the shareholders which resulted in Tim Hortons once again becoming a Canadian public company.

Cynthia Devine is the chief financial officer of Tim Hortons, where she is responsible for financial reporting, business planning and analysis, tax, and information technology. She has built an extensive 20-year financial career with some of the most established consumer product brands in Canada.

Devine began her career at Ernst & Young, where she obtained her chartered accountant designation. She then spent almost ten years in a variety of finance-related positions with Pepsi Canada. Her involvement in many initiatives at Pepsi helped her become chief financial officer of Pepsi-Cola Canada Ltd. During her term at Pepsi, Devine was heavily involved on the Canadian side with the spinoff of both the restaurant division and the bottling operations. This experience proved invaluable for her role at Tim Hortons during the IPO and ultimate spinoff. Prior to joining Tim Hortons, Devine held a senior financial position at Maple Leaf Foods, where she was very involved in all aspects of the business within the consumer products division. During her time at Maple Leaf, Devine was part of the team that completed the acquisition of Schneiders. This experience helped expand her knowledge of mergers and acquisition activity.

In late 2003, Devine joined Tim Hortons as chief financial officer and guided the company through its IPO and the building of a financial organization to become a stand-alone public company and support the ongoing needs of the business. Despite a busy workload, Devine enjoys spending time with her husband and two children.

In May 1964, Tim Horton, a National Hockey League All-Star defenceman, opened his first coffee and dough-nut shop on Ottawa Street in Hamilton, Ontario. In 1967, Ron Joyce, then the operator of three Tim Hortons restaurants, became partners with Tim Horton, and together they opened 37 new restaurants over the next seven years. In the early 1990s, Tim Hortons and Wendy's entered into a partnership to develop real estate and combination restaurants containing both brands under the same roof.

Tim Hortons has always had a focus on top-quality, always-fresh product, value, exceptional service, and community leadership. This has allowed the chain to grow into the largest quick-service restaurant chain in Canada, specializing in always-fresh coffee, baked goods, and homestyle lunches. By January 2009, there were more than 3,400 stores across Canada, and more than 500 locations in key markets in the United States. Tim Hortons has a diversified base of revenue and operating income generated from franchisee royalties and fees, rental income, warehouse sales, and company-operated stores. In fiscal 2008, it had total revenues of $2 billion, operating income of $444 million, and net income of $284 million.

Tim Hortons' commitment to maintaining a close relationship with franchisees and the communities in which it operates has helped generate immense customer loyalty and build Tim Hortons into one of the most widely recognized consumer brands in Canada. Tim Hortons was recognized as the best managed brand in Canada, according to annual surveys published by *Canadian Business* magazine in 2004 and 2005. It was also named one of Canada's most admired corporate cultures in 2005 by *Canadian Business*.

Risk, complexity, and uncertainty clearly define the role of financial management, especially in fast-growing companies such as Tim Hortons. Add to these challenges fluctuations in interest and exchange rates, expectations of investors and lenders, budgeting, and managing funds, and the job of the financial manager takes on even more intensity. In this chapter, you'll explore the role of finance in business, and learn about the tools that financial managers use to seek financial stability and future growth.

Source: Cynthia Devine, interview; Tim Hortons Web site, www.timhortons. com; Sharon Patterson, Vice President Human Resources, interview, 5 April 2006; and www.ctfs.com, 6 November 2006.

# THE ROLE OF FINANCE AND FINANCIAL MANAGERS

**finance**
The function in a business that acquires funds for the firm and manages those funds within the firm.

The central goal of this chapter is to answer two major questions: "What is finance?" and "What do financial managers do?" **Finance** is the function in a business that acquires funds for the firm and manages those funds within the firm. Finance activities include preparing budgets; doing cash flow analysis; and planning for the expenditure of funds on such assets as plant, equipment, and machinery. **Financial management** is the job of managing a firm's resources so it can meet its goals and objectives. Without a carefully calculated financial plan, the firm has little chance for survival, regardless of its product or marketing effectiveness.

**financial management**
The job of managing a firm's resources so it can meet its goals and objectives.

An accountant could be compared to a skilled laboratory technician who takes blood samples and other measures of a person's health and writes the findings on a health report (in business, the equivalent of a set of financial statements).[1] A financial manager of a business is the doctor who interprets the report and makes recommendations to the patient regarding changes that will improve the patient's health. In short, **financial managers** examine the financial data prepared by accountants and make recommendations to top executives regarding strategies for improving the health (financial strength) of the firm. Refer to the Dealing with Change box for a description of how financial managers are doing major restorative work on a troubled Canadian organization.

**financial managers**
Managers who make recommendations to top executives regarding strategies for improving the financial strength of a firm.

It should be clear that financial managers can make sound financial decisions only if they understand accounting information. That's why we examined accounting thoroughly in Chapter 16. Similarly, a good accountant needs to understand finance. It's fair to say that accounting and finance go together like peanut butter and jelly. In large and medium-sized organizations, both the accounting and the finance functions are generally under the control of a chief financial office or a vice-president of finance.

Figure 17.1 highlights a financial manager's tasks. As you can see, a key responsibility is to obtain money and then control the use of that money effectively. Financial managers are responsible for seeing that the company pays its bills. Finance functions such as buying merchandise on credit (accounts payable) and collecting payment from customers (accounts receivable) are responsibilities of financial managers. Therefore, financial managers are responsible for paying the company's bills at the appropriate time and for collecting overdue accounts receivable to make sure that the company does not lose too much money to bad debts (people or firms that don't pay their bills). While these functions are critical to all types of businesses, they are particularly critical to small- and medium-sized businesses, which typically have smaller cash or credit cushions than large corporations. The role of advising top management on financial matters has become even more

| **FIGURE** | **17.1** |

**What Financial Managers Do**

## DEALING with CHANGE

### Financial Restructuring for Canwest Global Communications

Canwest Global Communications and a number of affiliated companies have just applied for creditor protection under the Company's Creditors Arrangement Act (CCAA). This is a court-approved arrangement in which a major restructuring plan is submitted to and then hopefully approved by the shareholders and creditors.

In most cases, creditor protection is sought to provide a company with the time to develop a recapitalization plan. However, in this particular situation, Canwest entered creditor protection with what is called a prepackaged recapitalization plan, which has the support of its major debt holders and was backed up by up to $100 million in debtor in possession (DIP) financing to carry the businesses through the restructuring process.

This plan was developed in concert with the major debt holders to minimize business disruption and preserve the value of the business operations. It provides the time and the stability for Canwest to implement a controlled and orderly and consensual financial restructuring while continuing all its day-to-day operations. Because it is consensual the company is able to immediately begin to restructure its balance sheet, enabling it to emerge more quickly, providing a renewed financial outlook for the business units and putting them on a stronger, more stable footing for the future.

Creditor protection is normally approved by the Court based on the perception that the fundamental business of a company is viable. In the case of Canwest, the business operations of Global Television Network, three smaller specialty television channels, were generating operating profits even with recessionary level revenues. The National Post, originally part of the filing, has since been transitioned over into the Canwest publishing group (Canwest Limited Partnership) which is not part of this filing.

Over the past few years, Canwest undertook a massive expansion plan including the purchase of its publishing group from Conrad Black, a stable of 17 industry leading specialty channels from Alliance Atlantis, and radio operations in the United Kingdom and Turkey. They wanted to establish themselves as a global media heavyweight, and indeed are the largest media company in Canada. They choose to finance this growth with debt, and at the time of their filling, owed over $3.8 billion. The severe economic downturn over the past year resulted in an unprecedented decline in advertising revenue, which resulted in Canwest being unable to service their large debt.

During this time of restructuring, their financial managers have and will undertake to improve the operations of the companies through a combination of selling off non-core assets, closing unprofitable operations, and reducing operating expenses. The current net value of these companies is virtually zero and the restructuring plan calls for the conversion of a substantial portion of the debt into new equity. Operating under the CCAA will provide stability for the company while the financial managers complete all the complicated negotiations with the current shareholders and debtors.

Time will tell if all the efforts put into this restructuring will result in the emergence of Canwest as a far trimmer, healthier business organization.

You can access an audio presentation from the C.E.O., Leonard Asper, on the financial restructuring plans at www.canwestmediaworks.com/about/restructuring.asp.

Source: "About Us: Business and Financial Restructuring," CanWest Global Communications Web site, www.canwestmediaworks.com/about/restructuring.asp. Used with permission of CanWest Global Communications Corp.

important in recent years as risk has increased. Appendix D, immediately following this chapter, is devoted to the subject of Financial Risk.

As you may remember from Chapter 7, financing a small business is a difficult but essential function if a firm expects to survive those important first five years. The following are three of the most common ways for a firm to fail financially: (1) undercapitalization (lacking funds to start and run the business), (2) poor control over cash flow, and (3) inadequate expense control. Firms in a growth mode can often find themselves with large increases in their working capital as accounts receivable and inventory grow. Therefore, the need for careful financial management goes well beyond the first five years and remains a challenge that a business, large or small, must face throughout its existence.

## The Importance of Understanding Finance

You can see the issues involved with all three of the items listed above when you consider the financial problems encountered by a small organization called Parsley Patch. Two friends, Elizabeth Bertani and Pat Sherwood, started the company on what can best be described as a shoestring budget. It began when Bertani prepared salt-free seasonings for her husband, who was on a no-salt diet. Her friend Sherwood thought the seasonings were good enough to sell. Bertani agreed, and Parsley Patch Inc. was born.

The business began with an investment of $5,000, which was rapidly eaten up for a logo and a label design. Bertani and Sherwood quickly learned the importance of capital in getting a business going. Eventually, the two women personally invested more than $100,000 to keep the business from experiencing severe undercapitalization.

The partners believed that gourmet shops would be an ideal distribution point for their product. Everything started well, and hundreds of gourmet shops adopted the product line. But when sales failed to meet expectations, the women decided that the health-food market offered more potential than gourmet shops, because salt-free seasonings were a natural for people with restricted diets. The choice was a good one. Sales soared and approached $30,000 a month. Still, the company earned no profits.

Bertani and Sherwood were not trained in monitoring cash flow or in controlling expenses. In fact, they had been told not to worry about costs, and they hadn't. They eventually hired a chartered accountant (CA) and an experienced financial manager, who taught them how to compute the costs of the various blends they produced and how to control their expenses. The financial specialists also offered insight into how to control cash coming in and out of the company (cash flow). Soon Parsley Patch earned a comfortable margin on operations that ran close to $1 million a year. Luckily, the owners were able to turn things around before it was too late.

If Bertani and Sherwood had understood finance before starting their business, they may have been able to avoid the problems they encountered. The key word here is *understood*. You do not have to pursue finance as a career to understand finance, which is important to anyone who wants to start a small business, invest in stocks and bonds (to be discussed later in this chapter), or plan a retirement fund.

Also, it's vital that financial managers in any business stay abreast of changes or opportunities in finance and prepare to adjust to them. For example, tax payments represent an outflow of cash from the business. Therefore, financial managers have become increasingly involved in tax management, and must keep abreast of changes in tax law. Financial managers also carefully analyze the tax implications of various managerial decisions in an attempt to minimize the taxes paid by the business.[2] It's critical that businesses of all sizes concern themselves with managing taxes.

Another responsibility of the firm's finance department, internal audit, checks on the journals, ledgers, and financial statements prepared by the accounting department. Another purpose of an internal audit is to safeguard assets, including cash. In short, finance and accounting are two areas everyone involved in business needs to study. Since accounting was discussed in Chapter 16, let's look more closely at what financial management is all about. Let's start by looking at financial planning.

# FINANCIAL PLANNING

Financial planning is a key responsibility of the financial manager in a business. Planning has been a recurring theme of this book. We've stressed planning's importance as a managerial function and offered insights into planning your career. Financial planning involves analyzing short-term and long-term money flows to and from the firm. The overall objective of financial planning is to optimize the firm's profitability and make the best use of its money.[3] The quality of a financial plan improves based on lived experiences. A start-up company's plan is of necessity, hopeful expectation, that can become more precise with experience and a track record.

Financial planning involves three steps: (1) forecasting both short-term and long-term financial needs, (2) developing budgets to meet those needs, and (3) establishing financial control to see how well the company is doing what it set out to do (see Figure 17.2). Let's look at each step and the role these steps play in improving the financial health of an organization.

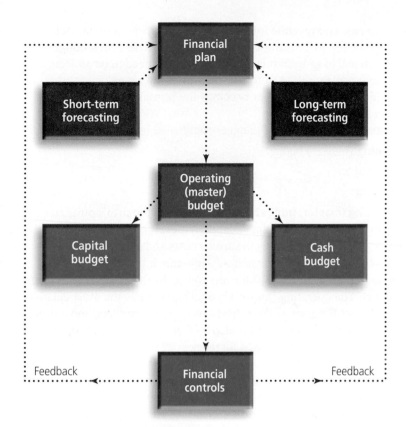

**FIGURE | 17.2**

**Financial Planning**
Note the close link between
financial planning and
budgeting.

## Forecasting Financial Needs

Forecasting is an important part of any firm's financial plan. A **short-term forecast** predicts revenues, costs, and expenses for a period of one year or less. This forecast is the foundation for most other financial plans, so its accuracy is critical. Part of the short-term forecast may be in the form of a **cash flow forecast**, which predicts the cash inflows and outflows in future periods, usually months or quarters. The inflows and outflows of cash recorded in the cash flow forecast are based on expected sales revenues and on various costs and expenses incurred and when the cash will be collected and costs will need to be paid.[4] The company's sales forecast estimates the firm's projected sales for a particular period. A business often uses its past financial statements as the starting point for projecting expected sales and various costs and expenses.[5]

A **long-term forecast** predicts revenues, costs, and expenses for a period longer than one year, and sometimes as far as five or ten years into the future. This forecast plays a crucial part in the company's long-term strategic plan, which asks questions such as these: What business are we in? Should we be in it five years from now? How much money should we invest in technology and new plant and equipment over the next decade? Will there be cash available to meet long-term obligations? Today, innovations in software assist financial managers in dealing with these long-term forecasting questions.

The long-term financial forecast gives top management, as well as operations managers, some sense of the income or profit potential possible with different strategic plans. Additionally, long-term projections assist financial managers with the preparation of company budgets.

## Working with the Budget Process

The budgeting process depends on the accuracy of the firm's financial statements. Put simply, a budget is a financial plan.[6] Specifically, a **budget** sets forth management's expectations for revenues and, on the basis of those expectations, allocates the use of specific resources throughout the firm. The key financial statements —the balance sheet, income statement, and the cash flow statement—form the basis for the budgeting process. Often,

**short-term forecast**
Forecast that predicts
revenues, costs, and
expenses for a period
of one year or less.

**cash flow forecast**
Forecast that predicts the
cash inflows and outflows
in future periods, usually
months or quarters.

**long-term forecast**
Forecast that predicts revenues,
costs, and expenses for a period
longer than one year, and
sometimes as far as five or
ten years into the future.

**budget**
A financial plan that sets forth
management's expectations,
and, on the basis of those
expectations, allocates the
use of specific resources
throughout the firm.

businesses use cost and revenue information, derived from past financial statements, as the starting point for forecasting company budgets.[7] The firm's budgets are compiled from short-term and long-term financial forecasts that need to be as accurate as possible. Since budgeting is clearly tied to forecasting, financial managers must take forecasting responsibilities seriously. A budget becomes the primary guide for the firm's financial operations and financial needs.

There are usually several types of budgets established in a firm's financial plan:

- An operating (master) budget
- A capital budget
- A cash budget

**operating (master) budget**
The budget that ties together all of a firm's other budgets; it is the projection of dollar allocations to various costs and expenses needed to run or operate the business, given projected revenues.

The **operating (master) budget** ties together all of the firm's other budgets and summarizes the business's proposed financial activities. It can be defined more formally as the projection of dollar allocations to various costs and expenses needed to run or operate a business, given projected revenues.[8] How much the firm will spend on supplies, travel, rent, advertising, research, salaries, and so forth is determined in the operating (master) budget. The operating (master) budget is generally the most detailed (firms will prepare this budget for each of their divisions/departments) and most used budget that a firm prepares (see the following discussion on financial controls). Most firms will prepare an operating budget on a monthly basis for the next 12 months. Typically, those responsible for the activities reflected within the operating budget(s) will be involved in its preparation. Ultimately the firm's board of directors is responsible for approving all budgets. Often the entire budget process can take months and involve a significant amount of time.

**capital budget**
A budget that highlights a firm's spending plans for major asset purchases that often require large sums of money.

A **capital budget** highlights a firm's spending plans for major asset purchases that often require large sums of money. The capital budget primarily concerns itself with the purchase of such assets as property, buildings, and equipment.

**cash budget**
A budget that estimates a firm's projected cash inflows and outflows that the firm can use to plan for any cash shortages or surpluses during a given period.

A **cash budget** estimates a firm's projected cash inflows and outflows that the firm can use to plan for any cash shortages or surpluses during a given period (e.g., monthly, quarterly). Cash budgets are important guidelines that assist managers in anticipating borrowing, debt repayment, operating expenses, and short-term investments.[9] A sample cash budget for our continuing example company, Very Vegetarian, is provided in Figure 17.3.

When first looking at the collection of sales, typically they occur over more than the month of sale. Sales, especially made in the latter part of a given month, will not be collected until the following month. The monthly cash collections in Figure 17.3 are based on collecting 20% of the current months sales and 80% of the prior month's sales. When forecasting the cash budget, not only do you want to identify the projected increase or decrease in cash for the month, but you also want to ensure that you maintain a minimum cash balance (a safety level). For planning purposes, you need to know when your projected cash balance may fall below the minimum, so that you can change how you will manage either your cash collections or your cash payments.

For example, when putting together the monthly cash budget in Figure 17.3, if the original payments schedule had projected salaries of $15,000, then February's cash budget would have ended up with total cash of $3,000. As such, after subtracting the minimum cash balance the excess cash would have had a balance of −$3,000. This amount would not be acceptable and therefore changes would have to be made to some of the assumptions. The other option would be to arrange for short-term financing to cover an expected shortfall.

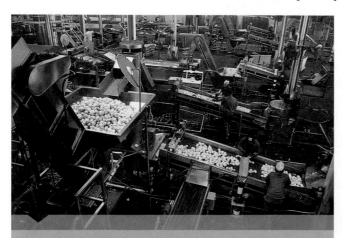

Special processing equipment turns an average potato into the chips and fries we consume. The firm's capital budget is the financial tool that controls business spending for expensive assets such as this processing equipment. Such major assets are referred to as capital assets or property, plant, and equipment. What items are in your school's capital budget?

**FIGURE** 17.3

**A Sample Cash Budget for Very Vegetarian**

| VERY VEGETARIAN<br>Monthly Cash Budget | January | February | March |
|---|---|---|---|
| Sales forecast | $50,000 | $45,000 | $40,000 |
| Collections | | | |
|    Cash sales (20%) | | $9,000 | $8,000 |
|    Credit sales (80% of past month) | | $40,000 | $36,000 |
| Monthly cash collection | | $49,000 | $44,000 |
| Payments schedule | | | |
|    Supplies and material | | $11,000 | $10,000 |
|    Salaries | | 12,000 | 12,000 |
|    Direct labour | | 9,000 | 9,000 |
|    Taxes | | 3,000 | 3,000 |
|    Other expenses | | 7,000 | 6,000 |
| Monthly cash payments | | $42,000 | $40,000 |
| Cash budget | | | |
|    Cash flow | | $7,000 | $5,000 |
|    Beginning cash | | −1,000 | 6,000 |
|    Total cash | | $6,000 | $11,000 |
|      Less minimum cash balance | | −6,000 | −6,000 |
| Excess cash to market securities | | $0 | $5,000 |
| Loans needed for minimum balance | | 0 | 0 |

Conversely, you should manage cash surpluses by planning for short-term investments (as illustrated in March in Figure 17.3) given the time value of money (which we will discuss later in this chapter). Regardless of how comfortable you are with your planning, investing your excess cash with fraudulent financiers like Bernie Madoff can have a devastating impact on your ability to carry on your business.

Clearly, financial planning plays an important role in the operations of the firm. This planning often determines what long-term investments are made, when specific funds will be needed, and how the funds will be generated. Once a company has forecast its short-term and long-term financial needs and established budgets to show how funds will be allocated, the final step in financial planning is to establish financial controls. We will discuss this topic in a moment. But first, the Spotlight on Small Business box challenges you to check your personal financial planning skill by developing a monthly budget for "You, Incorporated."

# Establishing Financial Controls

**Financial control** is a process in which a firm periodically compares its actual revenues, costs, and expenses with its budget. Most companies hold at least monthly financial reviews as a way to ensure financial control. Such control procedures help managers identify variances to the financial plan and allow them to take corrective action if necessary. Financial controls also provide feedback to help reveal which accounts, which departments, and which people are varying from the financial plans. Finance managers can judge if such variances may or may not be justified, allowing them to make some financial adjustments to the plan when needed. The Making Ethical Decisions box details a situation a manager can face related to financial control. After the Progess Assessment, we will explore specific reasons why firms need to have funds readily available.

**financial control**
A process in which a firm periodically compares its actual revenues, costs, and expenses with its projected ones.

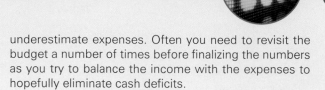

## SPOTLIGHT ON  Small Business

### You, Incorporated, Monthly Budget

Let's develop a monthly budget for You, Inc. Be honest and think of everything that needs to be included for an accurate monthly budget for You! Much like a small business, when putting the monthly budget together, remember that the norm is to overestimate income and underestimate expenses. Often you need to revisit the budget a number of times before finalizing the numbers as you try to balance the income with the expenses to hopefully eliminate cash deficits.

|  | Expected | Actual | Difference |
|---|---|---|---|
| **Monthly income:** | | | |
| Wages (net pay after taxes) | | | |
| Savings account withdrawal | | | |
| Family support | | | |
| Other sources | | | |
| **Total monthly income** | | | |
| **Monthly expenses:** | | | |
| **Fixed expenses** | | | |
| Rent or mortgage | | | |
| Car payment | | | |
| Life insurance | | | |
| Tuition or fees | | | |
| Other fixed expenses | | | |
| **Subtotal of fixed expenses** | | | |
| **Variable expenses** | | | |
| Food | | | |
| Clothing | | | |
| Entertainment | | | |
| Transportation | | | |
| Phone | | | |
| Utilities | | | |
| Publications | | | |
| Internet connection | | | |
| Cable television | | | |
| Other expenses | | | |
| **Subtotal of variable expenses** | | | |
| **Total expenses** | | | |
| **Total income − Total expenses = Cash on hand/(Cash deficit)** | | | |

## Making Ethical Decisions

### Playing It Safe

Suppose that you are the chairperson of the business administration department at a local community college. Like many other colleges, your campus has been affected financially by cuts in federal and provincial support and increasing expenses. As the end of the college's fiscal year approaches, you review your departmental budget and note that some unused travel funds, which you lobbied very hard to get for this year, are still available for faculty and staff development. The faculty and staff have not seemed interested in using the travel money for development purposes throughout the year, even though it has been readily available. You fear that if the funds are not spent this year, there's a good chance the college's chief financial officer will recommend cutting your travel budget for next year. That means if faculty and staff wish

to travel for staff development next year and the needed funds are not available, you will have to limit the number of people who get to use the travel funds.

You consider telling faculty and staff that this money is available for about any type of travel or staff development they desire on a first-come, first-served basis, with no extensive justification needed concerning the educational benefit the college would receive from the travel requested. It's almost certain your superior will not contest any request you make for travel funds, and you can certainly be a hero in the eyes of your faculty and staff. However, you could also simply return the unused funds to the dean's office for disbursement to the college's general fund and risk what may happen next year. What will you do? What could result from your decision?

## Progress Assessment

- Name three finance functions important to the firm's overall operations and performance.
- What are the three primary financial problems that cause firms to fail?
- In what ways do short-term and long-term financial forecasts differ?
- What is the organization's purpose in preparing budgets? Can you identify three different types of budgets?

# THE NEED FOR FUNDS

In business, the need for funds never seems to cease. That's why sound financial management is essential to all businesses. Like our personal financial needs, those of a business change over time. For example, as a small business grows, its financial requirements shift considerably. (Remember the example of Parsley Patch.) The same is true with large corporations such as Barrick Gold Corporation, Irving Oil, and McCain Foods. As they venture into new product areas or markets, their capital needs increase, causing a need for funds for different reasons. In virtually all organizations, there are certain needs for which funds must be available. Key areas include:

- Managing day-to-day needs of the business
- Controlling credit operations
- Acquiring needed inventory
- Making capital expenditures

Let's look at the financial needs that affect both the smallest and the largest of businesses.

## Managing Day-to-Day Needs of the Business

If workers expect to be paid on Friday, they don't want to have to wait until Monday for their paycheques. If tax payments are due on the fifteenth of the month, the government expects the money on time. If the payment on a business loan is due on the thirtieth, the

# GreenBOX

## Environmental Credits, Cap and Trade

In the late 1990s global leaders met in Kyoto, Japan, to address growing concern about the state of our environment. One of the initiatives coming out of these meeting was the Kyoto Protocol (an international agreement linked to the United Nations Framework Convention on Climate Change). The Protocol was a mechanism that would hopefully reduce global levels of greenhouse emissions (GHG). Starting in 2005, one of the ways countries could meet their respective targets was through the trading of carbon credits.

Carbon credits are meant to reduce greenhouse gas emissions and fight climate change through the use of carbon offsets. One popular form in Canada for carbon offsets involves tree planting. In the past few years, environmentalists and green-minded civilians have been jumping on board the carbon credit bandwagon, calculating their personal emissions and purchasing credits to neutralize the pollution they contribute to the atmosphere by the simple act of driving to work or running the dishwasher.

Carbon credits correspond to a determined tradable quantity of greenhouse gas (GHG) emissions. They are normally quoted in metric tonnes of carbon dioxide equivalent, and are used to offset emissions from the combustion of fossil fuels in any process that uses energy that emits GHGs, whether in industry, transportation, or the household.

In August of 2008, the province of British Columbia was the first Canadian jurisdiction to pass legislation dealing with climate change. They passed the Western Climate Initiative, which requires B.C. businesses to begin reducing their GHG emissions to 33 percent below their 2005 levels. If these greenhouse gases can't be reduced, companies will be required to offset their pollution via a new form of environmental currency, the carbon credit.

The city of Maple Ridge, British Columbia, and Shell Canada have had an agreement in place whereby a third party is planting trees in Maple Ridge, at no cost to the city, and selling the carbon credits to Shell Canada, who is then applying them to their Fort MacMurray operations. Companies (such as Planetair, a not-for-profit service offered by the Unieféra International Centre) have been created to help individuals, corporations, and institutions reduce their climate footprint by raising awareness of how day-to-day activities impact global climate and supporting initiatives like the trading of carbon credits.

In 2007 the trading of carbon credits globally amounted to $30 billion. Many organizations now have to provide funds specifically for the purchase of these credits.

There's no shortage of carbon-neutral suppliers to choose from, but prices can vary. While some companies charge as little as US$5.50 per metric tonne of carbon dioxide, the price can go as high as US$13.00 per tonne.

Sources: Planetair Home Page, http://planetair.ca; and "Kyoto Protocol," United Nations Framework Convention on Climate Change, http://unfccc.int/kyoto_protocol/items/2830.php.

Collecting accounts receivable form some customers can be time-consuming and costly. Accepting credit cards like Visa, MasterCard, or American Express simplifies transactions, guarantees payment, and provides convenience for both customers and businesses at minimal cost. For what sort of purchases do you regularly use a credit card?

lender doesn't mean the first of the next month. Refer to the Green Box for a discussion of funding needs associated with an environmental issue. As you can see, funds have to be available to meet all operational costs of the business.

The challenge of sound financial management is to see that funds are available to meet these daily cash needs. Money has what is called a *time value*. In other words, if someone offered to give you $200 today or $200 one year from today, you would benefit by taking the $200 today. Why? It's very simple. You could invest the $200 you receive today, start collecting interest, and over a year's time your money would grow. The same thing is true in business; the interest gained on the firm's investments is important in maximizing the profit the company will gain. That's why financial managers encourage keeping a firm's cash expenditures to a minimum.[10] By doing this, the firm can free up funds for investment in interest-bearing accounts. It's also not unusual for finance managers to suggest that a company pay its bills as late as possible (unless a cash discount is available) but try to collect what's owed to it as fast as possible. This way, they maximize the investment potential of the firm's funds. Efficient cash management is particularly important to small firms in conducting their daily operations because their access to capital is generally much more limited than that of larger businesses.[11]

## Controlling Credit Operations

Financial managers know that making credit available helps keep current customers happy and attracts new customers. In today's highly competitive business environment, many businesses would have trouble surviving without making credit available to customers.

The major problem with selling on credit is that a large percentage of a non-retailer's business assets could be tied up in its credit accounts (accounts receivable). At the same time the firm needs to pay the costs incurred for the making or provision of goods or services already sold to customers, who bought on credit. Financial managers in such firms must develop efficient collection procedures. For example, businesses often provide cash or quantity discounts to buyers who pay their accounts by a certain time. Also, finance managers carefully scrutinize old and new credit customers to see if they have a favourable history of meeting their credit obligations on time.[12] In essence, the firm's credit policy reflects its financial position and its desire to expand into new markets.

One way to decrease the time, and therefore expense, involved in collecting accounts receivable is to accept bank credit cards such as MasterCard or Visa.[13] This is convenient for both the customer and the business. The banks that issue such credit cards have already established the customer's creditworthiness, and have the expertise to manage credit. Businesses must pay a fee to accept credit cards, but the fees are generally not excessive compared to the benefits the cards provide. Accepting credit cards will enhance sales and a business no longer incurs the cost of running a credit department.

## Acquiring Inventory

As we noted earlier in the text, effective marketing implies a clear customer orientation. This focus on the customer means that high-quality service and availability of goods are vital if a business expects to prosper in today's markets.[14] Therefore, to satisfy customers, businesses must maintain inventories that often involve a sizable expenditure of funds. Although it's true that firms expect to recapture their investment in inventory through sales to customers, a carefully constructed inventory policy assists in managing the firm's available funds and maximizing profitability. For example, Take-a-Dip, a neighbourhood ice cream parlour, ties up more funds in inventory (ice cream) in the summer than in the winter. It's obvious why. Demand for ice cream goes up in the summer.

Innovations such as just-in-time inventory (discussed in Chapter 10) help reduce the amount of funds a firm must tie up in inventory. Also, by carefully evaluating its inventory turnover ratio (discussed in Chapter 16), a firm can better control its outflow of cash for inventory. It's important for a business of any size to understand that a poorly managed inventory system can seriously affect cash flow and drain its finances dry.

## Making Capital Expenditures

**Capital expenditures** are major investments in either tangible long-term assets such as land, buildings, and equipment, or intangible assets such as patents, trademarks, and copyrights. In many organizations, the purchase of major assets—such as land for future expansion, manufacturing plants to increase production capabilities, research to develop new-product ideas, and equipment to maintain or exceed current levels of output—is essential. As you can imagine, these expenditures often require a huge portion of the organization's funds.

Expansion into new markets can cost large sums of money with no guarantee that the expansion will be commercially successful. Therefore, it's critical that companies weigh

**capital expenditures**
Major investments in either tangible long-term assets such as land, buildings, and equipment, or intangible assets such as patents, trademarks, and copyrights.

all possible options before committing what may be a large portion of their available resources.[15] Long-term financing could be used, as this type of expenditure should benefit a business for many years to come. For this reason, financial managers and analysts evaluate the appropriateness of such purchases or expenditures. Consider the situation in which a firm needs to expand its production capabilities due to increases in customer demand. One option is to buy land and build a new plant. Another option would be to purchase an existing plant or consider renting. Can you think of financial and accounting considerations that would come into play in this decision?

Obviously, the need for funds raises several questions in any firm: How does the firm obtain funds to finance operations and other business necessities? Will specific funds be needed by the firm in the long term or short term? How much will it cost to obtain these needed funds? Will these funds come from internal or external sources? Let's address these questions next.

**debt financing**
Funds raised through various forms of borrowing that must be repaid.

**equity financing**
Funds raised from operations within the firm or through the sale of ownership in the firm.

**short-term financing**
Borrowed funds that are needed for one year or less.

**long-term financing**
Borrowed funds that are needed for a period longer than one year.

## Alternative Sources of Funds

Earlier in the chapter, you learned that finance is the function in a business that is responsible for acquiring and managing funds within the firm. Determining the amount of money needed and finding out the most appropriate sources from which to obtain these funds are fundamental steps in sound financial management. A firm can seek to raise needed capital through borrowing money (debt), selling ownership (equity), or earning profits (retained earnings). **Debt financing** refers to funds raised through various forms of borrowing that must be repaid. **Equity financing** is money raised from within the firm (from operations) or through the sale of ownership in the firm (e.g., the sale of stock). Firms can borrow funds either short-term or long-term. **Short-term financing** refers to funds needed for one year or less. In contrast, **long-term financing** refers to funds needed for a period longer than one year (usually two to ten years). Figure 17.4 summarizes the sources that can be used to acquire these needed short-term and long-term funds.

We'll explore the different sources of short-term and long-term financing fully in the next sections. For now it's important to know that businesses can use different methods of raising money. Before we go on, however, pause to check your understanding of what you just read by completing the Progress Assessment.

**FIGURE  17.4**

Sources of Short-Term and Long-Term Financing

| Short-Term Financing | Long-Term Financing |
|---|---|
| Trade credit | **A. Debt Financing** |
| Promissory notes | Lending institutions (e.g., loan) |
| Family and friends | Selling bonds |
| Financial institutions (e.g., line of credit) | **B. Equity Financing** |
| Short-term loans | Retained earnings |
| Factoring | Venture capital |
| Commercial paper | Selling stock |

## Progress Assessment

- Money is said to have a time value. What does that mean?
- Why are accounts receivable a financial concern to the firm?
- What is the primary reason that an organization spends a good deal of its available funds on inventory and capital expenditures?
- What is the difference between debt financing and equity financing?

# OBTAINING SHORT-TERM FINANCING

The bulk of a finance manager's job does not involve obtaining long-term funds. In fact, in small businesses, long-term financing is often out of the question. Instead, the day-to-day operation of the firm calls for the careful management of short-term financial needs. Firms need to borrow short-term funds to purchase additional inventory or to meet bills that come due. Also, as we do in our personal lives, a business sometimes needs to obtain short-term funds when the firm's cash reserves are low. This is particularly true, again, of small businesses.

Most small businesses are primarily concerned with just staying afloat until they are able to build capital and creditworthiness. Until a small business gets to that point, normally a lender will require some form of security for a loan. The security would typically be in the form of collateral (to be discussed later), or a personal guarantee. Firms can obtain short-term financing in several different ways. Let's look at the major forms of short-term financing and what's meant by secured and unsecured financing with regard to different ways of obtaining needed funds.

## Trade Credit

The most widely used source of short-term funding, trade credit (an account payable), is the least expensive and most convenient form of short-term financing. **Trade credit** is the practice of buying goods or services now and paying for them later. For example, when a firm buys merchandise, it receives an invoice (a bill) much like the one you receive when you buy something with a credit card. As you will see, however, the terms that businesses receive are often different.

**trade credit**
The practice of buying goods and services now and paying for them later.

It is common for business invoices to contain items such as *2/10, net 30*. This means that the buyer can take a 2 percent discount if the invoice is paid within 10 days. The total bill is due (net) in 30 days if the purchaser does not take advantage of the discount. Finance managers need to pay close attention to such discounts because they create opportunities to reduce the firm's costs. Think about it for a moment: If the discount offered to the customer is 2/10, net 30, the customer will pay 2 percent more by using trade credit for an extra 20 days to pay the invoice.

Uninformed business people feel that 2 percent is insignificant, so they pay their bills after the discount period. By doing that, however, such firms lose a tremendous opportunity to save money—and it's much more than 2 percent! In the course of a year, 2 percent for 20 days adds up to a 36 percent interest rate (because there are eighteen 20-day periods in the year). If the firm is capable of paying within ten days, it is needlessly (and significantly) increasing its cost of financing by not doing so.

Some suppliers hesitate to give trade credit to organizations with a poor credit rating, no credit history, or a history of slow payment. In such cases, the supplier may insist that the customer sign a promissory note as a condition for obtaining credit. A **promissory note** is a written contract with a promise to pay a supplier a specific sum of money at a definite time. Promissory notes can be sold by the supplier to a bank at a discount (the amount of the note less a fee for the bank's services in collecting the amount due).

**promissory note**
A written contract with a promise to pay.

## Family and Friends

Many small firms obtain short-term funds by borrowing money from family and friends. Because such funds are needed for periods of less than a year, friends or relatives are sometimes willing to help and the normal steps to obtain this type of funding are minimal. Such loans can create problems, however, if the firm does not understand cash flow.[16] As we discussed earlier, the firm may suddenly find itself having several bills coming due at the same time with no sources of funds to pay them. It is better, therefore, not to borrow from friends or relatives; instead, go to a commercial bank that fully understands the business's risk and can help analyze your firm's future financial needs.

Entrepreneurs appear to be listening to this advice. According to the National Federation of Independent Business, entrepreneurs today are relying less on family and friends as a source of borrowed funds than they have in the past. If an entrepreneur does, however, decide to ask family or friends for financial assistance, it's important that both parties (1) agree on specific loan terms, (2) put the agreement in writing, and (3) arrange for repayment in the same way they would for a bank loan. Such actions help keep family relationships and friendships intact.[17]

## Commercial Banks and Other Financial Institutions

Banks are highly sensitive to risk and are often reluctant to lend money to small, relatively new, businesses. Nonetheless, a promising and well-organized venture may be able to get a bank loan. If a business is able to get such a loan, a small- or medium-sized business should have the person in charge of the finance function keep in close touch with the bank. It's also wise to see a banker periodically (as often as once a month) and send the banker all of the firm's financial statements and other required information so that the bank continues to supply funds when needed.

If you try to imagine the different types of business people who go to banks for a loan, you'll get a better idea of the role of financial management. Picture, for example, a farmer going to the bank to borrow funds for seed, fertilizer, supplies, and other needs. The farmer may buy these items in the spring and pay for them after the fall harvest. Now picture a local toy store buying merchandise for holiday-season sales. The store may borrow the money for such purchases in the summer and pay it back after the holidays. Restaurants may borrow funds at the beginning of the month and pay by the end of the month. It's evident that how much a business borrows and for how long often depends on the kind of business it is and how quickly the merchandise purchased with a bank loan can be resold or used to generate funds.

You can also imagine how important it is for specialists in a company's finance and accounting departments to do a cash flow forecast. Unfortunately, small-business owners generally lack the luxury of such specialists and must monitor cash flow themselves or look for outside help. By anticipating times when many bills will come due, a business can begin early to seek funds or sell other assets to prepare for a possible financial crunch. Often unplanned for events will happen and so it's important for a business person to keep friendly and close relations with his or her banker.[18] An experienced banker may spot cash flow problems early or be more willing to lend money in a crisis if a business person has established a strong, friendly relationship built on openness, trust, and sound management practices. It's important to remember that your banker

'Tis the season to shop. Ever wonder how retailers get the money to buy all of the items available during the holiday season? Department stores and other large retailers make extensive use of commercial banks and other lenders to borrow the money needed to buy merchandise to stock their shelves.

wants you to succeed almost as much as you do, so that the banker can earn interest as part of the repayment of loans. Bankers can be an invaluable support to any business, but especially to small, growing businesses.

## Different Forms of Short-Term Loans

Banks and other financial institutions offer different types of loans to customers. A **secured loan** is a loan that's backed by something valuable, such as property. The item of value is called collateral. If the borrower fails to pay the loan, the lender may take possession of the collateral. For example, an automobile loan is a secured loan. If the borrower fails to pay the loan, the lender will repossess (take back) the car. Collateral takes some of the risk out of lending money.

Accounts receivable are assets that are often used by businesses as collateral for a loan; the process is called *pledging*. Some percentage of the value of accounts receivables pledged (usually about 75 percent) is advanced to the borrowing firm. As customers pay off their accounts, the funds received are forwarded to the lender in repayment of the funds that were advanced.[19] Inventory such as raw materials (e.g., coal, steel) can also be used as collateral or security for a business loan. Other assets that can be used as collateral include buildings, machinery, and company-owned stocks and bonds (to be discussed next).

The most difficult kind of loan to get from a bank or other financial institution is an unsecured loan. An **unsecured loan** doesn't require a borrower to offer the lending institution any collateral to obtain the loan. In other words, the loan is not backed by any assets. Normally, a lender will give unsecured loans only to highly regarded customers (e.g., long-standing customers or customers considered financially stable), who are seen as less risky.

If a business develops a good relationship with a bank, the bank may open a line of credit for the firm. A **line of credit** is a given amount of unsecured funds a bank will lend to a business. In other words, a line of credit is not guaranteed to a business. The primary purpose of a line of credit is to speed the borrowing process so that a firm does not have to go through the process of applying for a new loan every time it needs funds. The funds are generally available as long as the credit rating is satisfactory. As businesses mature and become more financially secure, the amount of credit often is increased, much like the credit limit on your credit card. Some firms will even apply for a **revolving credit agreement**, which is a line of credit that's guaranteed. However, banks usually charge a fee for guaranteeing such an agreement. Both lines of credit and revolving credit agreements are particularly good sources of funds for unexpected cash needs.

If a business is unable to secure a short-term loan from a bank, a financial manager may obtain short-term funds from **commercial finance companies**. These non-deposit-type organizations (often called non-banks) make short-term loans to borrowers who offer tangible assets (e.g., property, plant, and equipment) as collateral. Since commercial finance companies accept higher degrees of risk than commercial banks, they usually charge higher interest rates than banks. Commercial finance companies often make loans to individuals and businesses (e.g., General Electric loaned money to Air Canada as the airline restructured its business) that cannot get funds elsewhere.

## Factoring Accounts Receivable

One relatively expensive source of short-term funds for a firm is **factoring**, which is the process of selling accounts receivable for cash. Factoring dates as far back as 4,000 years, during the days of ancient Babylon. Today, the Internet can help businesses find factors quickly so that they can solicit bids on a firm's accounts receivable promptly.[20] Here's how it works: Let's say that a firm sells many of its products on credit to consumers and other businesses, creating a number of accounts receivable. Some of the buyers may be slow to pay their bills, causing the firm to have a large amount of money due to it. A factor is a market intermediary (usually a financial institution such as a commercial bank or commercial finance company) that agrees to buy the accounts receivable from the firm,

**secured loan**
A loan backed by something valuable, such as property.

**unsecured loan**
A loan that's not backed by any specific assets.

**line of credit**
A given amount of unsecured funds a bank will lend to a business.

**revolving credit agreement**
A line of credit that is guaranteed by the bank.

**commercial finance companies**
Organizations that make short-term loans to borrowers who offer tangible assets as collateral.

**factoring**
The process of selling accounts receivable for cash.

at a discount, for cash. The discount rate charged depends on the age of the accounts receivable, the nature of the business, and the condition of the economy. The factor then collects and keeps the money that was owed the firm when it collects the accounts receivable.

Even though factoring can be an expensive way of raising cash, it is popular among small businesses. Factoring is very common in the clothing and furniture business, and is popular in financing a growing number of global trade ventures. What's important for you to note is that factoring is not a loan; factoring is the sale of an asset (accounts receivable). And while it's true that discount rates charged by factors are usually higher than loan rates charged by banks or commercial finance companies, remember that many small businesses cannot qualify for a loan. A company can reduce the cost of factoring if it agrees to reimburse the factor for slow-paying accounts, and it can reduce them even further if it assumes the risk of those people who don't pay at all.

## Commercial Paper

**commercial paper**
Unsecured promissory notes of $100,000 and up that mature (come due) in 365 days or less.

Sometimes a large corporation needs funds for just a few months and wants to get lower rates of interest than those charged by banks. One strategy is to sell commercial paper. **Commercial paper** consists of unsecured promissory notes, in amounts of $100,000 and up, that mature (come due) in 365 days (366 days in a leap year) or less. Commercial paper states a fixed amount of money that the business agrees to repay to the lender (investor) on a specific date. The interest rate for commercial paper is stated in the agreement.

Still, because it is unsecured, only financially stable firms (mainly large corporations with excellent credit reputations) are able to sell commercial paper.[21] For these companies, it's a way to get short-term funds quickly and for less than the interest charged by commercial banks. Since most commercial paper matures in 30 to 90 days, it's also an investment opportunity for buyers who can afford to put up cash for short periods to earn some interest on their money at rates higher than they could earn by leaving surplus funds in their bank account. However, in late 2008 and into 2009, the ability for any large credit worthy corporation to sell commercial paper was significantly curtailed by the world-wide credit crunch.

## Credit Cards

Letitia Mulzac seemed to have things going her way as she planned to open an imported gift and furniture shop. She had a great location and reliable business contacts lined up in India, Indonesia, and Morocco. Unfortunately, she didn't have enough money in her savings to start the business.[22] She did, however, have a Small Business Visa card with a high credit limit. Letitia was able to use her credit card to pay for the stock to start her business. Credit cards provide a readily available line of credit to a business that can save time and the likely embarrassment of being rejected for a bank loan. Of course, in contrast to the convenience that credit cards offer, they are extremely risky and costly. For example, interest rates can be exorbitant. There are also considerable penalties users must pay if they fail to make their payments on time. Credit cards are an expensive way to borrow money and are probably best used as a last resort. The recent credit problems were do in part to the excessive use of credit cards and the resulting inability of borrowers to make even the minimum monthly payments.

### Progress Assessment

- What does the term "2/10, net 30" mean?
- What's the difference between trade credit and a line of credit at a bank?
- What's the difference between a secured loan and an unsecured loan?
- What is factoring? What are some of the considerations involved in establishing a discount rate in factoring?

# OBTAINING LONG-TERM FINANCING

Forecasting helps the firm to develop a financial plan. This plan specifies the amount of funding the firm will need over longer time periods and the most appropriate sources for obtaining those funds. In setting long-term financing objectives, financial managers generally ask three major questions:

1. What are the organization's long-term goals and objectives?

2. What are the financial requirements needed to achieve these long-term goals and objectives?

3. What sources of long-term capital are available, and which will best fit our needs?

In business, long-term capital is used to buy capital assets such as plant and equipment, to develop new products, and to finance expansion of the organization. In major corporations, decisions involving long-term financing normally involve the board of directors and top management, as well as finance and accounting managers. Take pharmaceutical giant Pfizer, for example. Pfizer spends more than $8 billion a year researching and developing new products.[23] The actual development of a new innovative medicine can sometimes take ten years and cost close to $1 billion in company funds before the product is ever introduced in the market. It's easy to see why long-term financing decisions involve high-level managers at Pfizer. In small- and medium-sized businesses, it's also obvious that the owners are always actively involved in analyzing long-term financing opportunities that affect their company.

As we noted earlier in the chapter, long-term funding comes from two major types of financing: debt financing and equity financing. Let's look at these two important sources of long-term financing next. But first check out the Reaching Beyond Our Borders box to learn why a source of long-term funding is raising eyebrows in the financial community.

## Reaching Beyond Our Borders

### Sharing the Wealth?

When a nation's government has a budget surplus, it usually has many ways to invest the extra cash back into the country. But sometimes the surplus is too great to distribute immediately, so the country puts the money away in a sovereign wealth fund (SWF), where it can hold the excess assets for future investment.

For years, oil rich nations like United Arab Emirates (UAE) and Kuwait have been blessed with enormous budgetary surpluses, causing their SWFs to swell with capital. Kuwait's SWF boasts an impressive value of $200 billion, while UAE's fund Abu Dhabi Investment Authority (ADIA) is valued at an unbelievable $875 billion. With so much capital at their fingertips, these countries have started to run out of investment opportunities within their own borders, sending them on a search for foreign businesses to support, and their biggest target is the United States.

Though SWFs provide both distressed companies and those looking for significant investment capital with much-needed funds, the presence of foreign governments in the domestic business world concerns some who think SWFs will try to use their financial footholds to influence or even dictate government policy; some concerns have

also been expressed about the business acumen possessed by the managers of these funds. Despite such concerns, investment continues, and the United States and Canada remain an ideal investment target for foreign governments flush with funds.

For example, in 2007, a Chinese SWF invested billions of dollars in Morgan Stanley, a giant in the investment community. Similarly, ADIA dropped $7.5 billion in Citigroup, the largest bank in the United States, and bought out high-end retailer Barneys New York for $875 million. Resource-rich Canada has also attracted the interest of these funds. In 2009, a Chinese SWF invested $1.5 billion in Teck Resources. The huge funding requirements for the oil sands have also attracted a significant amount of interest.

Sources: Geoff Colvin, "America for Sale," *Fortune*, 18 February 2008; Emily Thornton and Stanley Reed, "A Power Player Emerges in the Gulf," *BusinessWeek*, 23 June 2008; Daniel Gross, "Exec Desperately Seeks SWF," *Newsweek*, 7 January 2008; and Bob Davis, "U.S. Pushes Sovereign Funds to Open to Outside Scrutiny," *The Wall Street Journal*, 26 February 2008.

# Debt Financing

Debt financing involves borrowing money that the company has a legal obligation to repay. Firms can borrow funds by either getting a loan from a lending institution or issuing bonds.

## Debt Financing by Borrowing Money from Lending Institutions

Firms that establish and develop rapport with a bank, insurance company, pension fund, commercial finance company, or other financial institution often are able to secure a long-term loan. Long-term loans are usually repaid within 3 to 7 years but may extend to 15 or 20 years. For such loans, a business must sign what is called a term-loan agreement. A **term-loan agreement** is a promissory note that requires the borrower to repay the loan in specified instalments (e.g., monthly or yearly). A major advantage of a business using this type of financing is that the interest paid on the long-term debt is tax deductible.

Sometimes the debt financing may result from selling an asset already owned to a financing company and then leasing the asset back. Ferries and railway rolling stock are two examples of assets that could be sold and leased back. The firm selling this type of asset immediately receives some cash and their future lease will be provided from the revenue earned from these assets.

Because they involve larger amounts of funding, long-term loans are often more complex than short-term loans. Also, since the repayment period could be quite long, lenders are not assured that their capital will be repaid in full. Therefore, most long-term loans require collateral, which may be in the form of real estate, machinery, equipment, stock, or other items of value. Lenders will also often require certain restrictions on a firm's operations to force it to act responsibly in its business practices. The interest rate for long-term loans is based on the adequacy of collateral, the firm's credit rating, and the general level of market interest rates. The greater the risk a lender takes in making a loan, the higher the rate of interest a lender requires. This principle is known as the **risk/return trade-off**.

## Debt Financing by Issuing Bonds

If an organization is unable to obtain its long-term financing needs by getting a loan from a lending institution, it may try to issue bonds. A **bond** is a long-term debt obligation of a corporation or government. A company that issues a bond has a legal obligation to make regular interest payments to investors and to repay the entire bond principal amount at a prescribed time, called the maturity date.

Bonds can be issued by large organizations including different levels of government, government agencies, corporations, and foreign governments and corporations. Maybe your community is building a new stadium or cultural centre that requires selling municipal bonds. Potential investors (individuals and institutions) measure the risk involved in purchasing a bond against the return (interest) the bond promises to pay and the company's ability to repay the bond when promised. **Institutional investors** are large organizations—such as pension funds, mutual funds, insurance companies, and banks—that invest their own funds or the funds of others.

Interest is paid to the holder of the bond until the principal amount is repaid. Thus, in this context, **interest** is the payment the issuer of the bond makes to the bondholders for use of the borrowed money.

Like long-term loans, the interest rate paid on a bond varies according to factors such as the general level of market rates, the reputation of the company issuing the bond, and the going interest rate for government bonds or bonds of similar companies. Once an interest rate is set for a corporate bond issue (except in the case of what's called a floating-rate bond), it cannot be changed.

Bonds of all types are evaluated (rated) in terms of their risk to investors by independent rating firms such as Dominion Bond Rating Service (www.dbrs.com) and Standard & Poor's (www2.standardandpoors.com). Bond ratings can range from high quality to

---

**term-loan agreement**
A promissory note that requires the borrower to repay the loan in specified instalments.

**risk/return trade-off**
The principle that the greater the risk a lender takes in making a loan, the higher the interest rate required.

**bond**
A corporate certificate indicating that a person has lent money to a firm.

**institutional investors**
Large organizations—such as pension funds, mutual funds, insurance companies, and banks—that invest their own funds or the funds of others.

**interest**
The payment the issuer of the bond makes to the bondholders for use of the borrowed money.

bonds considered junk (which we discuss later in this chapter). Naturally, the higher the risk associated with the bond issue, the higher the interest rate the organization must offer investors. Investors should not assume high levels of risk if they don't feel that the potential return is worth it.

Bonds are issued with a denomination, which is the amount of debt represented by one bond. (Bonds are almost always issued in multiples of $1,000.) The principal is the face value of a bond. The issuing company is legally bound to repay the bond principal to the bondholder in full on the **maturity date**. For example, if Very Vegetarian issues a $1,000 bond with an interest rate of 5 percent and a maturity date of 2025, the company is agreeing to pay a bondholder a total of $50 in interest each year until a specified date in 2025, when the full $1,000 must be repaid. Though bond interest is quoted for an entire year, it is usually paid in two instalments (semi-annually). Maturity dates for bonds can vary. For example, firms such as Disney and Coca-Cola have issued bonds with 50-year maturity dates.

**maturity date**
The exact date the issuer of a bond must pay the principal to the bondholder.

**Advantages and Disadvantages of Issuing Bonds**   Bonds offer several long-term financing advantages to an organization. The decision to issue bonds is often based on advantages such as the following:

- Bondholders are creditors, not owners, of the firm and seldom have a vote on corporate matters; thus, management maintains control over the firm's operations.
- Interest paid on bonds is tax deductible to the firm issuing the bond.
- When bonds are repaid the debt obligation is eliminated.
- Bonds can be repaid before the maturity date if they contain a call provision. Some may also be converted to common shares (which is discussed later in this chapter).

But bonds also have their drawbacks:

- Bonds increase debt (long-term liabilities, an additional risk) and may adversely affect the market's perception of the firm.
- Paying interest on bonds is a legal obligation. If interest is not paid, bondholders can take legal action to force payment.
- The face value (denomination) of bonds must be repaid on the maturity date. Without careful planning, this repayment can cause cash flow problems when the bonds come due.

**Different Classes of Bonds**   Corporations can issue two different classes of corporate bonds. The first class is unsecured bonds, which are not backed by any collateral (such as equipment). These bonds are usually referred to as **debenture bonds**. Generally, only well-respected firms with excellent credit ratings can issue debenture bonds, since the only security the bondholder has is the reputation and credit history of the company.

The second class of bonds is *secured bonds*, which are backed by some tangible asset (collateral) that is pledged to the bondholder if bond interest isn't paid or the principal isn't paid back when promised. For example, a mortgage bond is a bond secured by company assets such as land and buildings. In issuing bonds, a company can choose to include different features in the various bond issues. Let's look at some possible special bond features.

**debenture bonds**
Bonds that are unsecured (i.e., not backed by any collateral such as equipment).

**Special Bond Features**   By now you should understand that bonds are issued with an interest rate, are unsecured or secured by some type of collateral, and must be repaid at their maturity date. This repayment requirement often leads companies to establish a reserve account called a **sinking fund**, whose primary purpose is to ensure that enough money will be available to repay bondholders on the bond's maturity date. Firms issuing sinking-fund bonds periodically retire (set aside) some part of the bond principal prior to maturity so that enough capital will be accumulated by the maturity date to pay off

**sinking fund**
A reserve account in which the issuer of a bond periodically retires some part of the bond principal prior to maturity so that enough capital will be accumulated by the maturity date to pay off the bond.

the bond. Sinking funds can be attractive to issuing firms and potential investors for several reasons:

- They provide for an orderly retirement (repayment) of a bond issue
- They reduce the risk the bond will not be repaid
- The market price of the bond is supported because the risk of the firm not repaying the principal on the maturity date is reduced

Another special feature that can be included in a bond issue is a call provision. A *callable bond* permits the bond issuer to pay off the bond's principal (i.e., call the bond) prior to its maturity date. Call provisions must be included when a bond is issued, and bondholders should be aware of whether a bond is callable. Callable bonds give companies some discretion in their long-term forecasting. For example, suppose that Very Vegetarian issued $50 million in 20-year bonds in 2010 with an interest rate of 10 percent. The yearly interest expense would be $5 million ($50 million times 10 percent). If market conditions change in 2014, and bonds issued of the same quality are only paying 7 percent, Very Vegetarian would be paying 3 percent, or $1.5 million ($50 million times 3 percent), in excess interest yearly. Obviously, Very Vegetarian could benefit if it could call in (pay off) the old bonds and issue new bonds at the lower interest rate. If a company calls a bond before maturity, investors in the bond are often paid a price above the bond's face value.

Another feature sometimes included in bonds is convertibility. A *convertible bond* is a bond that can be converted into common shares in the issuing company.[24] This feature is often an incentive for an investor to buy a bond. Why, you may ask, would bond investors want to convert their investment to shares? That's easy. If the value of the firm's common shares grows sizably over time, bondholders can compare the value of continued bond interest with the possible sizable profit they could gain by converting to a specified number of common shares. When we discuss common shares in the next section, this advantage will become more evident to you.

## Progress Assessment

- What are the major forms of debt financing available to a firm?
- What role do bond rating services play in the bond market?
- What does it mean when a firm states that it is issuing a 9 percent debenture bond due in 2025?
- What are advantages and disadvantages of bonds?
- Why do companies like callable bonds? Why might investors dislike them?
- Why are convertible bonds attractive to investors?

# Equity Financing

Rather than obtaining a long-term loan from a lending institution, or selling bonds to investors, a firm may look for long-term funding from equity financing. Equity financing comes from the owners of the firm. Therefore, equity financing involves selling ownership in the firm in the form of stock, or using earnings that have been retained by the company to reinvest in the business (retained earnings). A business can also seek equity financing by selling ownership in the firm to venture capitalists. Figure 17.5 compares debt and equity financing options.

## Equity Financing by Selling Stock

There usually comes a time when a firm needs additional funds. One way to obtain such funds is to sell stock to private investors. **Stocks** represent ownership in a company. Both common and preferred shares (to be discussed soon) form the company's capital stock, also known as equity capital.[25]

**stocks**
Shares of ownership in a company.

| | TYPE OF FINANCING | |
|---|---|---|
| | **Debt** | **Equity** |
| Management influence | There's usually none unless special conditions have been agreed on. | Common shareholders have voting rights. |
| Repayment | Debt has a maturity date. Principal must be repaid. | Stock has no maturity date. The company is never required to repay equity. |
| Yearly obligations | Payment of interest is a contractual obligation. | The firm isn't usually legally liable to pay dividends. |
| Tax issues | Interest is tax deductible. | Dividends are paid from after-tax income and aren't deductible. |

**FIGURE 17.5**

**Differences Between Debt and Equity Financing**

The purchasers of stock become owners in the organization. The number of shares of stock that will be available for purchase is generally decided by the organization's board of directors. The first time a corporation offers to sell new stock to the general public is called an **initial public offering (IPO)**.

**initial public offering (IPO)**
The first public offering of a corporation's stock.

## Equity Financing from Retained Earnings

Have you ever heard a business person say that he or she reinvests the firm's profits right back into the business? You probably remember from Chapter 16 that the profits the company keeps and reinvests in the firm are called retained earnings. Retained earnings often are a major source of long-term funds, especially for small businesses, which have fewer financing alternatives, such as selling bonds or stock, than large businesses do. However, large corporations also depend on retained earnings for needed long-term funding. In fact, retained earnings are usually the most favoured source of meeting long-term capital needs, since a company that uses them saves interest payments, dividends (payments for investing in stock), and any possible underwriting fees for issuing bonds or stock. Also, if a firm uses retained earnings, there is no new ownership created in the firm, as occurs with selling stock.

Unfortunately, many organizations do not have sufficient retained earnings on hand to finance extensive capital improvements or business expansion. If you think about it for a moment, it makes sense. What if you wanted to buy an expensive personal asset such as a new car? The ideal way to purchase the car would be to go to your personal savings account and take out the necessary cash. No hassle! No interest! Unfortunately, few people have such large amounts of cash available. Most businesses are no different. Even though they would like to finance long-term needs from retained earnings, few have enough to accomplish this.

## Equity Financing from Venture Capital

The hardest time for a business to raise money is when it is just starting or moving into early stages of expansion. A start-up business typically has few assets and no market track record, so the chances of borrowing significant amounts of money from a bank are slim. Recall from Chapter 7 that venture capitalists are a potential source of funds. **Venture capital** is money that is invested in new or emerging companies that are perceived as having great profit potential. Venture capital firms are a possible source of start-up capital for new companies or companies moving into expanding stages of business.

**venture capital**
Money that is invested in new or emerging companies that are perceived as having great profit potential.

An entrepreneur or finance manager must remember that venture capitalists invest in a company in return for part ownership of the business. Venture capitalists concede that they expect higher-than-average returns and competent management performance for their investment. Therefore, venture capital firms are careful when choosing a firm to invest in.

**stock certificate**

Evidence of stock ownership
that specifies the name of
the company, the number of
shares it represents, and the
type of stock being issued.

**dividends**

Part of a firm's profits that may
be distributed to shareholders
as either cash payments or
additional shares of stock.

A **stock certificate** is evidence of stock ownership that specifies the name of the company, the number of shares it represents, and the type of stock being issued (see Figure 17.6). Today, stock certificates are generally held electronically for the owners of the stock. Certificates sometimes indicate a stock's *par value*, which is a dollar amount assigned to each share of stock by the corporation's charter. Since par values do not reflect the market value of the stock, most companies issue "no-par" stock. **Dividends** are part of a firm's profits that may be distributed to shareholders as either cash payments or additional shares of stock. Dividends are declared by a corporation's board of directors and are generally paid quarterly. Although it's a legal obligation for companies that issue bonds to pay interest, companies that issue stock are not usually required to pay dividends.[26]

**Advantages and Disadvantages of Issuing Stock**   The following are some advantages to the firm of issuing stock:

- As owners of the business, shareholders never have to be repaid.

- There's usually no legal obligation to pay dividends to shareholders; therefore, income (retained earnings) can be reinvested in the firm for future financing needs.

- Selling stock has no risk since issuing stock creates no debt. (A corporation may also buy back its stock to improve its balance sheet and make the company appear stronger financially.)

Disadvantages of issuing stock include the following:

- As owners, shareholders (usually only common shareholders) have the right to vote for the company's board of directors. Typically one vote is granted for each share of stock. Hence, the direction and control of the firm can be altered by the sale of additional shares of stock.

- Dividends are paid out of profit after taxes and thus are not tax deductible.[27]

- Management's decisions can be affected by the need to keep stockholders happy.

Companies can issue two classes of shares: common and preferred. Let's see how these two forms of equity financing differ.

**Issuing Common Shares**   **Common shares** are the most basic form of ownership in a firm. In fact, if a company issues only one type of stock, it must be common. Holders of common stock have the right (1) to vote for company board directors and important issues affecting the company, and (2) to share in the firm's profits through dividends, if approved by the firm's board of directors. Having voting rights in a corporation allows common shareholders to influence corporate policy since the elected board chooses the firm's top management and makes major policy decisions. Common shareholders also have what is called a pre-emptive right, which is the first right to purchase any new common shares the firm decides to issue. This right allows common shareholders to maintain a proportional share of ownership in the company.

**common shares**
The most basic form of ownership in a firm; it confers voting rights and the right to share in the firm's profits through dividends, if offered by the firm's board of directors.

**Issuing Preferred Shares**   Owners of **preferred shares** enjoy a preference (hence the term *preferred*) in the payment of dividends; they also have a prior claim on company assets if the firm is forced out of business and its assets are sold. Normally, however, preferred shares do not include voting rights in the firm. Preferred shares are frequently referred to as a hybrid investment because they have characteristics of both bonds and stocks. To illustrate this, consider the treatment of preferred share dividends.

Preferred share dividends differ from common share dividends in several ways. Preferred shares are generally issued with a par value that becomes the base for the dividend the firm is willing to pay. For example, if a preferred share's par value is $100 a share and its dividend rate is 4 percent, the firm is committing to a $4 dividend for each share of preferred stock the investor owns (4 percent of $100 = $4). An owner of 100 shares of this preferred stock is promised a fixed yearly dividend of $400. In addition, the preferred shareholder is also assured that this dividend must be paid in full before any common share dividends can be distributed.[28]

Preferred shares are therefore quite similar to bonds; both have a face (or par) value and both have a fixed rate of return. Also, like bonds, rating services rate preferred shares according to risk. So how do bonds and preferred shares differ? Remember that companies are legally bound to pay bond interest and to repay the face value (denomination) of the bond on its maturity date. In contrast, even though preferred share dividends are generally fixed, they do not legally have to be paid; also shares (preferred or common) never have to be repurchased. Though both bonds and stock can increase in market value, the price of stock generally increases at a higher percentage than bonds. Of course, the market value of both could also go down. Figure 17.7 compares features of bonds and stock.

**preferred shares**
Stock that gives its owners preference in the payment of dividends and an earlier claim on assets than common shareholders if the company is forced out of business and its assets are sold.

| | Bonds | Common Share | Preferred Share |
|---|---|---|---|
| **Interest or Dividends** | | | |
| Must be paid | Yes | No | Depends |
| Pays a fixed rate | Yes | No | Usually |
| Deductible from payor's income tax | Yes | No | No |
| Canadian payee is taxed at reduced rate | | (if payor company is Canadian) | |
| | No | Yes | Yes |
| **Stock or bond** | | | |
| Has voting rights | No | Yes | Not normally |
| May be traded on the stock exchange | Yes | Yes | Yes |
| Can be held indefinitely | No | Yes | Depends |
| Is convertible to common shares | Maybe | No | Maybe |

**FIGURE 17.7**

**Comparison of Bonds and Stock of Public Companies** The different features help both the issuer and the investor decide which vehicle is right for each of them at a particular time.

**Special Features of Preferred Shares**   Preferred shares can have special features that do not apply to common shares. For example, like bonds, preferred shares can be callable. This means that preferred shareholders could be required to sell back their shares to the corporation. Preferred shares can also be convertible to common shares. Another important feature of preferred shares is that they can often be cumulative. That is, if one or more dividends are not paid when promised, the missed dividends will be accumulated and paid later to a cumulative preferred shareholder. This means that all dividends, including any back dividends, must be paid in full before any common share dividends can be distributed. Figure 17.8 lists some optional features of preferred shares.

**FIGURE | 17.8**

**Optional Features Available with Preferred Shares**
Each feature holds some attraction for the potential investor.

| Preferred Share Feature | Description |
|---|---|
| Convertible | The shares may be exchanged after a stated number of years for common shares at a preset rate, at the option of the shareholder. |
| Cumulative | If the dividend is not paid in full in any year, the balance is carried forward (accumulates). The cumulative unpaid balance must be paid before any dividends are paid to common shareholders. |
| Callable | The company that issued the shares has the right after a stated number of years to call them back by repaying the shareholders their original investment.* |
| Redeemable | After a stated number of years, the investor may return the stock and ask for repayment of his or her investment.* |

*If the shares are also cumulative, all dividend arrears must be paid as well.

## Progress Assessment

- What are the major forms of equity financing available to a firm?
- Name at least two advantages and two disadvantages of issuing stock as a form of equity financing.
- What are the major differences between common shares and preferred shares?
- In what ways are preferred shares similar to bonds? How are they different?

## SUMMARY

1. Finance comprises those functions in a business responsible for acquiring funds for the firm, managing funds within the firm (e.g., preparing budgets and doing cash flow analysis), and planning for the expenditure of funds on various assets.

   **What are the most common ways in which firms fail financially?**
   The most common financial problems are (1) undercapitalization, (2) poor control over cash flow, and (3) inadequate expense control.

   **What do financial managers do?**
   Financial managers plan, budget, control funds, obtain funds, collect funds, audit, manage taxes, and advise top management on financial matters.

   **LO ▸ 1** Describe the importance of finance and financial management to an organization, and explain the responsibilities of financial managers.

2. Financial planning involves forecasting short-term and long-term needs, budgeting, and establishing financial controls.

   **What are the three budgets of finance?**
   The operating (master) budget summarizes the information in the other two budgets; it projects dollar allocations to various costs and expenses given various revenues. The capital budget is the spending plan for expensive assets, such as property, plant, and equipment. The cash budget is the projected cash inflows and outflows for a period and the balance at the end of a given period.

   **LO ▸ 2** Outline the financial planning process, and explain the three key budgets in the financial plan.

3. During the course of a business's life, its financial needs shift considerably.

   **What are the major financial needs for firms?**
   Businesses have financial needs in four major areas: (1) managing day-to-day needs of the business, (2) controlling credit operations, (3) acquiring needed inventory, and (4) making capital expenditures.

   **What's the difference between short-term and long-term financing?**
   Short-term financing refers to funds that will be repaid in less than one year, whereas long-term financing refers to funds that will be repaid over a specific time period of more than one year.

   **What's the difference between debt financing and equity financing?**
   Debt financing refers to funds raised by borrowing (going into debt), whereas equity financing is raised from within the firm (through retained earnings) or by selling ownership in the company to venture capitalists or by issuing shares to other investors.

   **LO ▸ 3** Explain the major reasons why firms need operating funds, and identify various types of financing that can be used to obtain these funds.

4. Sources of short-term financing include trade credit, promissory notes, family and friends, commercial banks and other financial institutions, factoring, and commercial paper.

   **Why should businesses use trade credit?**
   Trade credit is the least expensive and most convenient form of short-term financing. Businesses can buy goods today and pay for them sometime in the future.

   **What's a line of credit?**
   It is an agreement by a bank to lend up to a specified amount of money to the business at any time, as long as certain conditions are met. A revolving credit agreement is a line of credit that guarantees a loan will be available—for a fee.

   **What's the difference between a secured loan and an unsecured loan?**
   An unsecured loan has no collateral backing it. Secured loans have collateral pledged as security such as accounts receivable, inventory, or other property of value.

   **LO ▸ 4** Identify and describe different sources of short-term financing.

**Is factoring a form of secured loan?**

No, factoring means selling accounts receivable at a discounted rate to a factor (an intermediary that pays cash for those accounts).

**What's commercial paper?**

Commercial paper is a corporation's unsecured promissory note maturing in 365 days or less.

**LO ▶ 5** Identify and describe different sources of long-term financing.

5. One of the important functions of a finance manager is to obtain long-term financing.

**What are the major sources of long-term financing?**

Debt financing involves the sale of bonds and long-term loans from banks and other financial institutions. Equity financing is obtained through the sale of company stock, from the firm's retained earnings, or from venture capital firms.

**What are the two major forms of long-term financing?**

Debt financing comes from two sources: selling bonds and borrowing from individuals, banks, and other financial institutions. Bonds can be secured by some form of collateral or can be unsecured. The same is true of loans.

# KEY TERMS

bond 528
budget 515
capital budget 516
capital expenditures 521
cash budget 516
cash flow forecast 514
commercial finance companies 525
commercial paper 526
common shares 533
debenture bonds 529
debt financing 522
dividends 532
equity financing 522

factoring 525
finance 512
financial control 517
financial management 512
financial managers 512
initial public offering (IPO) 531
institutional investors 528
interest 528
line of credit 525
long-term financing 522
long-term forecast 515
maturity date 529
operating (master) budget 516
preferred shares 533

promissory note 523
revolving credit agreement 525
risk/return trade-off 528
secured loan 525
short-term financing 522
short-term forecast 514
sinking fund 529
stock certificate 532
stocks 530
term-loan agreement 528
trade credit 523
unsecured loan 525
venture capital 531

# CRITICAL THINKING

1. Budgets are designed to keep decision-makers informed of progress compared to company plans. An important theme of this book is the need for managers to be flexible so that they can adapt quickly to rapidly changing conditions. This often means modifying previous plans. Do you see any conflict between budgets and such flexibility? How do managers stay within the confines of budgets when they must shift gears to accommodate a rapidly changing world? Which forecasts are more affected by these problems, short-term or long-term? Why?

2. Considering the disadvantages and advantages of different forms of raising funds, which method would you adopt if you had to make that decision in your company? How would your decision be affected in a high-interest year? If your company was doing well, what would you do for short-term financing? For long-term financing? How would you justify your choices?

## DEVELOPING WORKPLACE SKILLS

1. Visit a local bank lending officer. Ask what the current interest rate is and what rate small businesses pay for short-term and long-term loans. Ask for blank forms that borrowers use to apply for loans. Share these forms with your class, and explain the types of information they ask for.

2. Use information from Standard & Poor's and Dominion Bond Rating Service to find their evaluation of the bonds of three large Canadian companies. Ask the librarian what similar references are available. Report what you find to the class.

3. Many businesses try to raise funds through initial public offerings (IPOs). Access your library and use the services of Proquest, or visit securities dealers' Web sites such as www.bmonesbittburns.com and www.tdwaterhouse.ca. Find two IPOs that have been offered during the past six months. Track the performance of each IPO from its introduction to its present price.

4. Analyze the risks and opportunities of investing today in bonds and stock. Assume that your great-aunt Hildi just left you $10,000. Since you and your parents have already saved enough money to cover your education bills, you decide to invest the money so that you can start your own business after you graduate. How will you invest your money? Why? Name specific investments.

## TAKING IT TO THE NET 1

www.mcgrawhillconnect.ca

### Purpose

To research the current lending practices between banks and small businesses.

### Exercises

1. Check out the Web site of the Canadian Bankers Association (www.cba.ca) to see if you can find information on the trend of lending to small businesses. What was the rate of refusal of loans to small businesses during the last few years? Is the refusal rate rising, declining, or unchanged?

2. Look through the Web site of the Business Development Bank of Canada (BDC) at www.bdc.ca to see how helpful it is. If you were starting a small business, would the information lead you to apply for a loan with the BDC? Is there anything you were looking for that you could not find? Is there much information for those wanting to start an Internet-based company?

## TAKING IT TO THE NET 2

www.mcgrawhillconnect.ca

### Purpose

To learn how small-business owners can obtain support for financing from the federal government.

### Exercise

The Canada Small Business Financing Program (www.ic.gc.ca/eic/site/csbfp-pfpec.nsf/eng/home) seeks to increase the availability of loans and capital leases for establishing, expanding, modernizing, and improving small businesses. Visit the site and answer the following questions.

1. How does this financing program work?

2. Which financial institutions participate in the program?

3. What are the restrictions on which type of businesses can participate in the program?

4. What type of purchase is eligible for financing, what percentage of the purchase can be financed, and what is the maximum amount that can be financed?

## ANALYZING MANAGEMENT DECISIONS

### Making Dreams Come True

Carlos Galendez had big dreams but very little money. He had worked more than ten years washing dishes and then as a cook for two major restaurants. Finally, his dream to save enough money to start his own Mexican restaurant came true. Galendez opened his restaurant, Casa de Carlos, with a guaranteed loan. His old family recipes and appealing Hispanic decor helped the business gain immediate success. He repaid his small-business loan within 14 months and immediately opened a second location, and then a third. Casa de Carlos became one of the largest Mexican restaurant chains in the area.

Galendez decided that the company needed to go public to help finance expansion. He believed that continued growth was beneficial to the company, and that offering ownership was the way to bring in loyal investors. Nevertheless, he wanted to make certain that his family maintained a controlling interest in the firm's stock. Therefore, in its initial public offering (IPO), Casa de Carlos offered to sell only 40 percent of the company's available shares to investors. The Galendez family kept control of the remaining 60 percent.

As the public's craving for Mexican food grew, so did the fortunes of Casa de Carlos, Inc. By early 2007, the company enjoyed the enviable position of being light on debt and heavy on cash. But the firm's debt position changed dramatically when it bought out Captain Ahab's Seafood Restaurants and, two years later, expanded into full-service wholesale distribution of seafood products with the purchase of Ancient Mariner Wholesalers.

The firm's debt increased, but the price of its stock was up and all of its business operations were booming. Then tragedy struck the firm when Carlos Galendez died suddenly from a heart attack. His oldest child, Maria, was selected to take control as chief executive officer. Maria Galendez had learned the business from her father, who had taught her to keep an eye out for opportunities that seemed fiscally responsible. Even so, the fortunes of the firm began to shift. Two major competitors were taking market share from Casa de Carlos, and the seafood venture began to flounder (pun intended). Also, consumer shifts in eating habits and the slight recession in 2008 encouraged consumers to spend less, causing the company some severe cash flow problems. It was up to Maria Galendez as CEO to decide how to get the funds the firm needed for improvements and other expenses. Unfortunately, several local banks wouldn't expand the firm's credit line, so she considered the possibility of a bond or stock offering to raise capital for the business. Her decision could be crucial to the future of the firm.

### Discussion Questions

1. What advantages do bonds offer a company such as Casa de Carlos? What disadvantages do bonds impose?

2. What would be the advantages and disadvantages of the company's offering new stock to investors?

3. Are any other options available to Maria Galendez?

4. What choice would you make and why?

# APPENDIX D
# Risk Management

## UNDERSTANDING BUSINESS RISKS

The management of risk is a major issue for businesses throughout the country.[1] Almost every day you hear about a hurricane, earthquake, flood, fire, airplane crash, riot, or car accident that destroyed property or injured someone. An accident that involves a major personality may be front-page news for weeks. Such reports are so much a part of the news that we tend to accept these events as part of everyday life. But events involving loss mean a great deal to the business people involved. They must pay to restore the property and compensate those who are injured.

After two wars (Afghanistan and Iraq), corporate and government scandals, several major hurricanes and tornadoes, and the threat of terrorists and a pandemic flu, it is no surprise that risk management is getting more attention.[2] The risks of serious information security failures are manifold. Computer hackers and computer viruses have become a real threat, and identity theft has become commonplace.[3]

In addition to the newsmaking stories, thousands of other incidents involve business people in lawsuits. Lawsuits in recent years have covered everything from job-related accidents to product liability. In some provinces, insurance is not available or is too expensive for high-risk businesses. New legislation has been passed in some areas to lessen some of these risks so that companies can obtain insurance coverage again at a reasonable price.[4]

The outbreak of listeriosis in the late summer of 2008 claimed many lives. The financial impact on Maple Leaf Foods both in terms of lost sales and lawsuits was significant. Real financial risk relates to the variability of costs and revenues resulting in the inability to cover off all obligations. The future cannot be predicted but the financial risk that arises from uncertainty can be managed. Business needs to identify, measure, and appreciate the consequences of financial risk, and then take action to transfer or mitigate it. Financial risk management and risk taking are two sides of the same coin. Risk management is the process of understanding, costing, and efficiently managing unexpected levels of variability in the financial outcomes for a business. Risk management is about firms actively selecting the type and level of risk that is appropriate for them to assume. What current resources are sacrificed for future uncertain returns? Problems can arise when risk factors suddenly begin to act together.[5] Risk management is all about minimizing the losses from unexpected events.

## How Rapid Change Affects Risk Management

Changes are occurring so fast in the business world that it is difficult to keep up with the new risks involved. For example, who in the organization can evaluate the risks of buying or selling products over the Internet or what the price of a barrel of oil will be six months from now? As companies reach global markets over the Internet, who in the company watches for fluctuations in the world's currencies and how they may affect profits? Will global warming affect weather conditions? How will climate change affect farms and cattle raising? What would happen to the economy if there were a series of terrorist attacks on the country? What would happen if a flu pandemic were to occur?[6] As you can see, risk management is getting more complex and more critical for all businesses. Those who do business in other countries face increasing risk from social unrest—think of the ongoing strife in the Middle East, Africa, and other third world countries.

The last 10 years have seen significant growth in new institutions that are in the business of taking and managing risks (hedge funds). Credit derivatives have been used to redistribute part or all of a company's credit-risk exposures, which if properly dispersed should minimize the shocks to the overall economic system. This thinking was turned on its head in the Fall of 2008. Derivative markets have made it easier to take on large amounts of risks, but as we saw in 2008, a "lemming" mentality can take over after a crisis gets underway, which increases market volatility. These problems might also be due to regulators who have colluded with the financial community to incorrectly value risky assets when the stakes are very high. Let's explore how companies go about managing risk. We'll begin by going over a few key terms.

# MANAGING RISK

The term **risk** refers to the chance of loss, the degree of probability of loss, and the amount of possible loss. There are two different kinds of risk:

- **Speculative risk** involves a chance of either profit or loss. It includes the chance a firm takes to make extra money by buying new machinery, acquiring more inventory, and making other decisions in which the probability of loss may be relatively low and the amount of loss is known.[7] An entrepreneur takes speculative risk on the chance of making a profit.[8] In business, building a new plant is a speculative risk because it may result in a loss or a profit.[9]

- **Pure risk** is the threat of loss with no chance for profit. Pure risk involves the threat of fire, accident, or loss. If such events occur, a company loses money; but if the events do not occur, the company gains nothing.[10]

**risk**
The chance of loss, the degree of probability of loss, and the amount of possible loss.

**speculative risk**
A chance of either profit or loss.

**pure risk**
The threat of loss with no chance for profit.

The risk that is of most concern to businesspeople is pure risk. Pure risk threatens the very existence of some firms. Once such risks are identified, firms have several options:

1. Reduce the risk
2. Avoid the risk
3. Self-insure against the risk
4. Buy insurance against the risk

We'll discuss the option of buying insurance in detail later. In the next sections, we will discuss each of the other alternatives for managing risk. These steps should be taken to lower the need for outside insurance.

## Reducing Risk

A firm can reduce risk through internal controls and by establishing loss-prevention programs such as fire drills, health education, safety inspections, equipment maintenance, accident prevention programs, and so on. Many retail stores, for example, use mirrors, video cameras, and other devices to prevent shoplifting. Water sprinklers and smoke detectors are used to minimize fire loss. In industry, most machines have safety devices to protect workers' fingers, eyes, and so on.

Product recalls can also reduce risk. A classic example is the highly publicized decision by Johnson & Johnson Company to pull its Tylenol pills off the shelves across the country when sabotaged capsules killed several people. As mentioned already, the Listeriosis outbreak resulted in Maple Leaf Foods recalling all its production from their Toronto facility.[11]

Employees as well as managers can reduce risk. For example, truck drivers can wear seat belts to minimize injuries from accidents, operators of loud machinery can wear earplugs to reduce the chance of hearing loss, and those who lift heavy objects can wear back braces. The beginning of an effective risk management strategy is a good loss-prevention program. However, high insurance rates have forced some people to go beyond merely preventing risks to the point of avoiding risks, and in extreme cases by going out of business.

## Avoiding Risk

Many risks cannot be avoided. There is always the chance of fire, theft, accident, or injury. But some companies are avoiding risk by not accepting hazardous jobs and by outsourcing shipping and other functions.[12] The threat of lawsuits has driven away some drug companies from manufacturing vaccines, and some consulting engineers refuse to work on hazardous sites. Some companies are losing outside members of their boards of directors for lack of liability coverage protecting them from legal action against the firms they represent.

## Self-Insuring

**self-insurance**
The practice of setting aside money to cover routine claims and buying only "catastrophe" policies to cover big losses.

Many companies, municipalities, and other not-for-profit organizations have turned to self-insurance because they either can't find or can't afford conventional property/casualty policies. Such firms set aside money to cover routine claims and buy only "catastrophe" insurance policies to cover big losses. **Self-insurance**, then, lowers the cost of insurance by allowing companies to take out insurance only for larger losses.

Self-insurance is most appropriate when a firm has several widely distributed facilities or where many similar organizations, like universities, self-insure as a group. The risk from fire, theft, or other catastrophe is then more manageable. Firms with huge facilities, in which a major fire or earthquake could destroy the entire operation, usually turn to insurance companies to cover the risk.

## Buying Insurance to Cover Risk

Although well-designed, consistently enforced risk-prevention programs reduce the probability of claims, accidents do happen. Insurance is the armour individuals, businesses, and non-profit organizations use to protect themselves from various financial risks. For this protection, such organizations spend about 10 percent of gross domestic product (GDP) on insurance premiums. Some insurance protection is provided by governments (see Figure D.1), but most risks must be covered by individuals and businesses on their own.[13] We will continue our discussion of insurance by identifying the types of risks that are uninsurable, followed by those that are insurable.

### What Risks Are Uninsurable?

**uninsurable risk**
A risk that no insurance company will cover.

Not all risks are insurable, even risks that once were covered by insurance. An **uninsurable risk** is one that no insurance company will cover. Examples of things that you cannot insure include market risks (e.g., losses that occur because of price changes, style changes, or new products that make your product obsolete); political risks (e.g., losses from war or government restrictions on trade); some personal risks (such as loss of a job); and some risks of operation (e.g., strikes or inefficient machinery).

| Type of Insurance | What It Does |
|---|---|
| Canadian Public Health Care | Provides all Canadians with free basic health care, free doctor visits, free hospital ward care, free surgery, and free drugs and medicine while in hospital. |
| Employment Insurance | Provides financial benefits, job counselling, and placement services for unemployed workers. |
| Old Age Security /Canada Pension Plan | Provides retirement benefits and life insurance. |
| Canada Mortgage Housing Corporation (CMHC) | Provides mortgage insurance to lenders to protect against default by home buyers. |
| Canada Deposit Insurance Corporation | Provides re-imbursement of up to $100,000 for funds held in banks, trusts, and loan companies that fail. |
| Provincial Auto Insurance (Manitoba, Saskatchewan, British Columbia) | Provides all citizens in these provinces with standard automobile insurance including collision, liability, and accident benefits. |

**FIGURE D.1**

**Public Insurance**
Provincial or federal government agencies that provide insurance protection.

## What Risks Are Insurable?

An **insurable risk** is one that the typical insurance company will cover. Generally, insurance companies use the following guidelines when evaluating whether or not a risk is insurable:

1. The policyholder must have an **insurable interest**, which means that the policyholder is the one at risk to suffer a loss. You cannot, for example, buy fire insurance on your neighbour's house and collect if it burns down.
2. The loss should be measurable.
3. The chance of loss should be measurable.
4. The loss should be accidental.
5. The risk should be dispersed; that is, spread among different geographical areas so that a flood or other natural disaster in one area would not bankrupt the insurance company.
6. The insurance company can set standards for accepting the risk.

**insurable risk**
A risk that the typical insurance company will cover.

**insurable interest**
The possibility of the policyholder to suffer a loss.

# UNDERSTANDING INSURANCE POLICIES

An **insurance policy** is a written contract between the insured (an individual or organization) and an insurance company that promises to pay for all or part of a loss. A **premium** is the fee charged by the insurance company or, in other words, the cost of the insurance policy.

Like all other private businesses, an insurance company is designed to make a profit. Insurance companies therefore gather data to determine the extent of various risks. What makes the acceptance of risk possible for insurance companies is the law of large numbers.

The **law of large numbers** states that if a large number of people or organizations are exposed to the same risk, a predictable number of losses will occur during a given period of time. Once the insurance company predicts the number of losses likely to occur, it can determine the appropriate premiums for each policy it issues. The premium is supposed to be high enough to cover expected losses and yet earn a profit for the firm and its stockholders. Today, many insurance companies are charging high premiums not for past risks but for the anticipated costs associated with the increasing number of court cases and high damage awards.

Insurance companies can also earn revenue from investing the premiums they collect. Premiums are usually collected at the beginning of a policy period. Until policy claims need to be paid out, premiums can be placed in very secure interest paying investments.

**insurance policy**
A written contract between the insured and an insurance company that promises to pay for all or part of a loss.

**premium**
The fee charged by an insurance company for an insurance policy.

**law of large numbers**
Principle that if a large number of people are exposed to the same risk, a predictable number of losses will occur during a given period of time.

## Rule of Indemnity

The **rule of indemnity** says that an insured person or organization cannot collect more than the actual loss from an insurable risk. One cannot gain from risk management; one can only minimize losses. One cannot, for example, buy two insurance policies and collect from both for the same loss. If a company or person carried two policies, the two insurance companies would calculate the loss and divide the reimbursement between them.

## Types of Insurance Companies

There are two major types of insurance companies. A **stock insurance company** is owned by stockholders, just like any other investor-owned company. A **mutual insurance company** is owned by its policyholders. A mutual insurance company, unlike a stock company, does not earn profits for its owners. It is a non-profit organization, and any excess funds (over losses, expenses, and growth costs) go to the policyholders in the form of dividends or premium reductions.

# INSURANCE COVERAGE FOR VARIOUS KINDS OF RISK

As we have discussed, risk management consists of reducing risk, avoiding risk, self-insuring, and buying insurance. There are many types of insurance that cover various losses: property and liability insurance, health insurance, and life insurance. Property losses result from fires, accidents, theft, or other perils. Liability losses result from property damage or injuries suffered by others for which the policyholder is held responsible. Let's begin our exploration of insurance by looking at health insurance.

## Health Insurance

Canada provides universal health care for every citizen. The description of the coverage provided is found in Figure D.1. Above and beyond this insurance, individuals can be covered by benefit plans usually provided through their employer or a group the individual is affiliated with. Coverage typically includes dental, extended health care, survivors' benefits, worldwide travel benefits, income continuance, and pensions.

Dental coverage can vary from basic preventative care through to major procedures (e.g., dentures). Extended health care can cover prescription drugs, a number of paramedical services (e.g., massage), vision care, and upgraded hospital accommodation, normally up to a semi-private room. Worldwide travel benefits cover expenses that are the result of an accident or unexpected illness incurred while on business or vacation in a foreign country. Eligible expenses may include hospital accommodation and private duty nursing. Survivor benefits can include a death benefit (lump sum payment) for a spouse and dependent children, as well as a pension. Income continuance provides for both short- and long-term disability. Pensions will provide monthly income for a retired employee.

Over the past few years, the cost of benefit plans have increased significantly. As a result, coverage limits have been reduced, and a greater share of the cost has become the responsibility of the insured.

## Disability Insurance

Disability insurance replaces part of your income (50 to 70 percent) if you become disabled and thus unable to work. There usually is a period during which you must be disabled (e.g., 60 days) before you can begin collecting. Many employers provide this type of insurance (as described above), but some do not. In either case, insurance experts recommend that you get disability insurance because the chances of becoming disabled by a disease or accident when young are much higher than the chance of dying. The premiums for such insurance vary according to age, occupation, and income.

## Workplace Safety and Insurance

Provincial Workplace Safety and Insurance Boards guarantee payment of wages, medical care, and rehabilitation services (e.g., retraining) for employees who are injured on the job. Employers in all provinces and territories are required to provide this insurance. This insurance also provides benefits to the survivors of workers who die as a result of work-related injuries. The cost of insurance varies in relation to the company's safety record, its payroll, and the types of hazards faced by workers. For example, it costs more to insure a steelworker than an accountant.

## Liability Insurance

*Professional* liability insurance covers people who are found liable for professional negligence. For example, if a lawyer gives advice carelessly and the client loses money, the client may then sue the lawyer for an amount equal to that lost which the insurance would cover. Professional liability insurance is also known as malpractice insurance. While you may think of doctors and dentists when you hear that term, the fact is that many professionals, including accountants, are buying professional liability insurance because of large lawsuits their colleagues have faced.

*Product* liability insurance covers liability arising out of products sold. (You may recall the product liability discussion in Appendix B.) If a person is injured by, say, a ladder or some other household good, he or she may sue the manufacturer for damages. Insurance usually covers such losses.

*Personal* liability insurance covers liability of any individual through a negligent act either at work or at home.

*Premises* liability insurance would cover claims resulting from an accident occurring either at a place of work or personal residence.

# OTHER BUSINESS INSURANCE

This introductory course cannot discuss in detail all the insurance coverage that businesses may buy. Naturally, businesses must protect themselves against property damage, and they must buy car and truck insurance and more. Figure D.2 will give you some idea of the types of insurance available. Many businesses were happy that they had business interruption insurance after a major ice storm in Quebec and the 2003 blackout in Ontario.

The point to be made in this appendix is that risk management is critical in all firms. That includes the risk of investing funds and the risk of opening your own business (speculative risk). Remember from Chapter 1, though, that risk is often matched by opportunity and profits. Taking on risk is one way for an entrepreneur to prosper. Regardless of how careful we are, however, we all face the prospect of death, even entrepreneurs. To ensure that those left behind will be able to continue the business, entrepreneurs often buy life insurance that will pay partners and others what they will need to keep the business going.

## Key Employee Insurance

A significant risk for businesses relates to the loss of a key employee. The best kind of insurance to cover executives in the firm is term insurance, but dozens of new policies with interesting features now exist.

## Insurance Coverage for Home-Based Businesses

Homeowner's policies usually don't have adequate protection for a home-based business. For example, they may have a limit of $2,500 for business equipment. For more coverage, you may need to add an *endorsement* (sometimes called a rider) to your homeowners insurance. For about $25 a year, you can increase the coverage to $10,000.

**FIGURE**  **D.2**

**Private Insurance**

| Types of Insurance | What It Does |
|---|---|
| **Property and Liability** | |
| Fire | Covers losses to buildings and their contents from fire. |
| Automobile | Covers property damage, bodily injury, collision, fire, theft, vandalism, and other related vehicle losses. |
| Homeowners | Covers the home, other structures on the premises, home contents, expenses if forced from the home because of an insured peril, third-party liability, and medical payments to others. |
| Computer coverage | Covers loss of equipment from fire, theft, sometimes spills, power surges, and accidents. |
| Professional liability | Covers court-awarded losses stemming from mistakes made or bad advice given in a professional context. |
| Business interruption | Provides compensation for loss due to fire, theft, or similar disasters that close a business. Covers lost income, continuing expenses, and utility expenses. |
| Nonperformance loss protection | Protects from failure of a contractor, supplier, or other person to fulfill an obligation. |
| Criminal loss protection | Protects from loss due to theft, burglary, or robbery. |
| Commercial credit insurance | Protects manufacturers and wholesalers from credit losses due to insolvency or default. |
| Public liability insurance | Provides protection for businesses and individuals against losses resulting from personal injuries or damage to the property of others for which the insured is responsible. |
| Extended product liability insurance | Covers potentially toxic substances in products; environmental liability; and, for corporations, director and officer liability. |
| Fidelity bond | Protects businesses from employee dishonesty. |
| Surety bond | Covers losses resulting from a second party's failure to fulfill a contract. |
| Title insurance | Protects buyers from losses resulting from errors in title to property. |
| **Health Insurance** | |
| Extended health care | Pays a percentage of prescription drug costs, dental care, vision care, and paramedical services. |
| Disability income insurance | Pays income while the insured is disabled as a result of accident or illness. |
| **Life Insurance** | |
| Group life insurance | Covers all the employees of a firm or members of a group. |
| Owner or key executive insurance | Enables businesses of sole proprietors or partnerships to pay bills and continue operating, saving employee jobs if the owner or a key executive dies. Enables corporations to hire and train or relocate another manager with no loss to the firm. |
| Retirement and pension plans | Provides employees with supplemental retirement and pension plans. |
| Credit life insurance | Pays the amount due on outstanding credit (e.g., loan, line of credit, etc.) if the debtor dies. |

If clients visit your office or if you receive deliveries regularly, you may need home-office insurance. It costs around $150 a year, but it protects you from slip-and-fall lawsuits and other risks associated with visitors. For more elaborate businesses, such as custom cabinetry shops and other types of manufacturing or inventory-keeping businesses, a business-owner policy may be needed which costs $300 a year or more. Unless you are an expert on insurance, you will need to consult an insurance agent about the best insurance for your home-business needs.

## The Risk of Damaging the Environment

The risk of environmental harm reaches international proportions in issues such as global warming. The 1986 explosion at the Chernobyl nuclear power plant in what was then the Soviet Union caused much concern throughout the world. Due to high safety standards, Ontario nuclear power plants are closely watched for safety violations. Yet since coal-fired power plants are said to cause acid rain (and global warming), and other inexpensive fuel sources haven't been fully developed, nuclear power plants are still considered by some to be a necessity. However nuclear power plants also pose environment concerns.

Many people feel there is a need for a more careful evaluation of environmental risks than currently is done. How much risk is there in global warming? We don't know all the details yet, but the risks may be substantial.[14] Therefore, many companies are going out of their way to protect the environment.[15]

Clearly, risk management now goes far beyond the protection of individuals, businesses, and non-profit organizations from known risks. It means the evaluation of worldwide risks such as global warming.[16] It also means prioritizing these risks so that international funds can be spent where they can do the most good. No insurance company can protect humanity from such risks. These risks are the concern of businesses and governments throughout the world, with the assistance of the international scientific community.[17] They should also be your concern as you study risk management in all its dimensions.

## SUMMARY

1. Risk management is becoming a critical part of management in most firms.

   **What changes have made risk management more important?**
   Global warming, terrorist threats, natural disasters, war, and an unstable economy have all contributed to additional risk and the need for more risk management.

   **LO ▸ 1** Discuss the environmental changes that have made risk management more important.

2. There are several ways of handling risk.

   **What are the four major ways of managing risk?**
   The major ways of avoiding risk are: (1) reduce risk, (2) avoid risk, (3) self-insure, and (4) buy insurance.

   **LO ▸ 2** Explain the four ways of managing risk.

3. Some risks are insurable and others are not.

   **What's the difference between insurable and uninsurable risk?**
   Uninsurable risk is risk that no insurance company will cover. Examples of things that you cannot insure include market risks, political risks, some personal risks (such as loss of a job); and some risks of operation (e.g., strikes or inefficient machinery). An insurable risk is one that the typical insurance company will cover. Generally, insurance companies use the following guidelines when evaluating whether or not a risk is insurable: (1) the policyholder must have an insurable interest, (2) the loss should be measurable, (3) the chance of loss should be measurable, (4) the loss should be accidental, (5) the risk should be dispersed, and (6) the insurance company can set standards for accepting risks.

   **LO ▸ 3** Distinguish between insurable and uninsurable risk.

**LO ▶ 4** Explain the rule of indemnity.

4. There are some things one should know about insurance company rules.

**What is the rule of indemnity?**

The rule of indemnity says that an insured person or organization cannot collect more than the actual loss from an insurable risk.

**What are the two kinds of insurance companies?**

A stock insurance company is owned by stockholders, just like any other investor-owned company. A mutual insurance company is owned by its policyholders.

**LO ▶ 5** Discuss the various types of insurance that businesses may buy.

5. There are insurance policies to cover all different kinds of risk.

**What kind of policy covers health risks?**

Individuals can obtain benefit plans that cover dental care, extended health care, survivors' benefits, income continuance, and pensions. These coverages are over and above the universal health care system that operates in Canada. The cost of benefit plans has increased significantly in recent years. To manage these costs, coverage limits have been reduced and deductibles have been raised.

**LO ▶ 6** Explain why businesses must carry workers' compensation insurance.

6. Businesses must explore many kinds of insurance.

**What kinds of insurance do most businesses have?**

Workers' compensation insurance guarantees payment of wages, medical care, and rehabilitation services (e.g., retraining) for employees who are injured on the job. Employers in all provinces and territories are required to provide this insurance. Professional liability insurance covers people who are found liable for professional negligence. Product liability insurance provides coverage against liability arising out of products sold. If a person is injured by a ladder or some other household good, he or she may sue the manufacturer for damages. Personal and premises liability insurance provides coverage for individuals based on their negligent acts or an accident occurring. Most businesses also have some kind of life insurance for the executives. If you conduct business from home, you should also have some form of home-office insurance to cover certain risks.

**LO ▶ 7** Tell others why businesses cannot manage environmental damage on their own.

7. There is much discussion in the news about whether or not businesses are ruining the environment.

**What are businesses doing to cover the risks of harming the environment?**

Many businesses are doing what they can to minimize damage to the environment. Such risks, however, are often beyond what businesses can manage. They are the concern of governments around the world.

## KEY TERMS

insurable interest  543
insurable risk  543
insurance policy  543
law of large numbers  543
mutual insurance company  544

premium  543
pure risk  541
risk  541
rule of indemnity  544

self-insurance  542
speculative risk  541
stock insurance company  544
uninsurable risk  542

## CRITICAL THINKING

1. Are you self-insuring your apartment (or where you live) and your assets? What have you done to reduce the risk? Have you done anything to avoid risk? How much would it cost to buy insurance for your dwelling and the contents?

2. What risks do you take that cannot be covered by insurance?

3. What actions have you taken to avoid risk?

4. What can you do to lower the risk of natural disasters such as floods, hurricanes, and tornadoes?

## DEVELOPING WORKPLACE SKILLS

1. Write a one-page paper about ways you could reduce risk in your life (e.g., drive more slowly). Form into small groups and share what you have written. Then discuss everything that you and your classmates might do to reduce the risk of loss or harm.

2. You cannot insure yourself against speculative risk. However, you can minimize the risks you take when investing. Compare and contrast the risks of investing in stocks versus bonds for the long term. Be prepared to discuss your results in class.

3. Much of risk management is observing the behaviour of others and then acting to reduce risky behaviour. What kind of risky behaviour have you observed among college students? What is being done, if anything, to inform them of such risks and to minimize them?

What has been the response? What can you learn from such observation? Discuss the merits of having a risk manager for education facilities.

4. Form into small groups and discuss liability insurance, automobile insurance, renter's insurance, life insurance, and disability insurance. Develop a list of questions to discuss openly in class so that everyone is more informed about these issues.

5. Write a short (two-page) essay on the perceived risks of a terrorist attack, a natural disaster, or a major health disaster such as bird flu. Which risk do you perceive as most likely? Most dangerous? Discuss what you could do to warn others of such risks and motivate them to do something about them.

## TAKING IT TO THE NET

www.mcgrawhillconnect.ca

### Purpose

To learn about insurance for your dwelling and property, and to examine the issue of liability.

### Exercise

Go to Insurance-Canada at www.insurance-canada.ca. Explore the site and then answer the following questions:

1. What is homeowner's insurance?

2. What is in a standard policy?

3. What different types of homeowner's policies are there?

4. What is renter's insurance?

# CHAPTER 18

# The Financial Services Industry in Canada

## LEARNING OBJECTIVES

### AFTER YOU HAVE READ AND STUDIED THIS CHAPTER, YOU SHOULD BE ABLE TO:

**LO ▸ 1** Describe the importance of the financial services industry in Canada.

**LO ▸ 2** Explain what money is and how its value is determined.

**LO ▸ 3** Discuss the role that banks play in providing services.

**LO ▸ 4** Discuss the nature and impact of insurance.

**LO ▸ 5** List the five key criteria when selecting investment options.

**LO ▸ 6** Explain the opportunities in mutual funds as investments and the benefits of diversifying investments.

## PROFILE

### Getting to Know Marco Marrone, President of Canadian Tire Financial Services Limited

Marco Marrone is the president of Canadian Tire Financial Services (CTFS), a wholly owned subsidiary of Canadian Tire Corporation, Ltd. As the financial arm of Canadian Tire, CTFS is primarily engaged in financing and managing the Canadian Tire Options® MasterCard to more than 4 million card members. CTFS also offers personal loans, markets a variety of insurance and warranty products to more than 6 million customers, and offers emergency roadside assistance through the Canadian Tire Auto Club.

CTFS originated in 1961 as Midland Shoppers Credit Limited, a small financial services company offering third-party credit processing for local retailers. During the 1960s, the Canadian Tire Associate Stores became clients. In 1968, Midland became a subsidiary of Canadian Tire Corporation and was renamed Canadian Tire Acceptance Limited (CTAL). In the decades that followed, CTAL continued to provide credit processing. In 1995, it became the first non–deposit-taking financial institution worldwide to launch a MasterCard. In 2000, it expanded the Canadian Tire "Money" loyalty program by launching Canadian Tire "Money" on the card. Card members could accumulate Canadian Tire Money by using their MasterCard anywhere in the world and then redeem it in any Canadian Tire store for merchandise, auto parts, or auto labour. In 2002, CTAL's name was changed to Canadian Tire Financial Services Limited to better reflect the company's stronger and broader position within the financial services industry. In 2003, CTFS established Canadian Tire Bank to enable greater marketing flexibility for its card operations and to facilitate continued expansion into the high-growth bank card market. Operating the credit card business under Canadian Tire Bank enables the company to offer customers credit card services consistently across the country.

Marrone is an example of a business person who has excelled and adapted to opportunities within the financial services business sector. During the 20 years at CTFS that preceded his current role, he held key management positions in finance, credit risk management, information technology, marketing, and operations. He was instrumental in many of the organization's most significant strategies. These include his role as vice-president of customer development with responsibility for the conversion of the company's retail card portfolio to Options® MasterCard, and the creation of Canadian Tire Bank, which he has led as chief operating officer (COO). As COO, he has had strategic and operational responsibility for the development of the credit card and personal loan businesses.

Marrone's ongoing education has contributed to his professional growth. Since becoming a certified management accountant, he has completed his MBA at McMaster University and the Leadership Development Program at the International Institute for Management Development in Switzerland. He is also a graduate of the McMaster University College for Corporate Directors. He is an officer of Canadian Tire, a member of the Canadian Tire Bank board of directors, a member of the MasterCard Advisory Board, and he serves in the community as the chair of the Niagara Health Systems Foundation board.

Today, CTFS is the second-largest MasterCard franchise in Canada, including the Options® MasterCard, the Gas Advantage MasterCard, and Commercial Link. The credit card portfolio has grown through adding new cards and features, including: Pay Pass, exclusive offers, product protector, credit protector, identity watch, line of credit, and road side assistance. While approximately 32 percent of Canadian Tire's overall earnings are generated through this division's activities, this contribution is expected to increase as new opportunities are explored. Under Marrone's leadership, initiatives will surely be in line with the company's purpose: "We build lifetime customer relationships by providing financial services which add trust and value to the Canadian Tire Brand." There are plans to expand CTFS's financial services products and services. Some of the products being piloted in select markets, include high-interest savings accounts, mortgages, and guaranteed investment certificates.

Sources: Marco Marrone, President, Canadian Tire Financial Services, interview, 10 March 2006; Rita Trichur, "Canadian Tire's Q2 Profit Rises 12% to $103.3 Million, Firm Raises Guidance," Canadian Press NewsWire, July 2008; and "2008 Investor Fact Sheet," Canadian Tire Corporation Ltd., http://investorrelations.canadiantire.ca.

# THE FINANCIAL SERVICES INDUSTRY IN CANADA

Back in Chapter 17 we talked about the role financial institutions play in supporting the financial needs of businessses. Now we focus our attention on all the product offered by the actual institutions: money, banking, investing, insurance, financing, and financial planning. Every day across the country, consumers, businesses, and governments depend on the products provided by financial institutions. In addition, the ever-changing environment in the financial services industry is supported by a number of new features provided by the Financial Consumer Agency of Canada, including:

- Model credit card application form
- Cost of banking guide
- Ten tips you need to know before signing any contract.[1]

According to this same agency, the financial services sector plays an important role in the Canadian economy, as it:

- Employs more than 600,000 Canadians
- Provides a yearly payroll of more than $35 billion
- Represents 6 percent of Canada's GDP, exceeded only by the manufacturing sector
- Yields more than $13 billion in tax revenue to all levels of government
- Is widely recognized as one of the safest and healthiest in the world[2]

Until the middle of the 1980s, the financial services industry in Canada was termed a "four-pillar system." These four pillars were banks, trust companies, insurance companies, and securities dealers. Regulation was designed to foster competition within each pillar, but not among them. When the government permitted commercial banks to acquire securities firms in 1987, this segregation of functions began to erode.

Since that time, changes in regulations have eliminated many of the old barriers that prohibited financial institutions from competing in each other's business. Today, it is increasingly difficult to distinguish firms by type of function, as this industry has become highly competitive. For example, a life insurance company can now own a bank, and vice versa. As a result of Bill C-8 (in force since October 2001), important changes were made to federal financial institutions legislation and how the financial services industry is regulated. Among other changes, ownership and organization rules for banks were loosened. Consequently, we see non-traditional financial services providers—such as Canadian Tire Financial Services (mentioned in the chapter-opening profile)—taking advantage of changes in the regulatory environment to offer new products and build on their customer base.

## Participants in the Financial Services Industry

**credit unions**
Non-profit, member-owned financial co-operatives that offer a full variety of banking services to their members.

**trust company**
A financial institution that can administer estates, pension plans, and agency contracts, in addition to other activities conducted by banks.

**non-banks**
Financial organizations that accept no deposits but offer many services provided by regular banks.

Canada's financial services industry consists of traditional banks (also called commercial banks), credit unions, caisses populaires, and trust companies. **Credit unions** are non-profit, member-owned financial co-operatives that offer a full variety of banking services to their members. Caisses populaires, a form of credit unions, are located predominantly in Quebec. A **trust company** is a financial institution that conducts activities like a bank. However, because of its fiduciary role, a trust company can administer estates, pension plans, and agency contracts, which banks cannot do. As a result of changes in legislation, we have seen instances of banks acquiring trust companies, such as Scotiabank's acquisition of Montreal Trust and National Trust.

There are also a variety of other institutions that traditionally have been called non-banks. **Non-banks** are financial organizations that accept no deposits but offer many services provided by regular banks. Examples include pension funds, insurance companies, commercial finance companies, consumer finance companies, and brokerage houses. We will discuss brokerage houses soon.

**Pension funds** are amounts of money put aside by corporations, non-profit organizations, or unions to cover part of the financial needs of their members when they retire. Contributions to pension funds are made either by employees, by employers, or by both employees and employers.

Life insurance companies provide financial protection for policyholders, who periodically pay premiums. In addition, insurers invest the funds they receive from policyholders in a variety of vehicles, including corporate and government bonds. More insurance companies have begun to provide long-term financing for real estate development projects.

Commercial and consumer finance companies offer short-term loans to businesses or individuals who either cannot meet the credit requirements of regular banks or have exceeded their credit limit and need more funds. Typically, these finance companies' interest rates are higher than those of regular banks. The primary customers of these companies are new businesses and individuals with no credit history. One should be careful when borrowing from such institutions, because the interest rates can be quite high. Corporate financial systems established at major corporations such as General Electric, Sears, General Motors, and American Express offer considerable financial services to customers.

In the past, they were often called non-banks because they did not accept deposits but offered many of the services provided by regular banks. As competition among these organizations and banks has increased, the dividing line between banks and non-banks has become less and less apparent. Today, many of these non-banks offer select banking products, including taking deposits, making loans, and issuing credit cards.[3] Review Figure 18.1 to get an idea of the range of suppliers of financial services in Canada.

Since all of these financial institutions have one thing in common—money—we will discuss the importance of money to the economy. This will be followed by an introduction to three main players in the overall financial services industry: the banking industry, the securities industry, and the mutual fund industry. But first, let us briefly review how this industry is regulated.

| FIGURE | 18.1 |
| --- | --- |

**The Canadian Financial Services Industry**

- 70 domestic and foreign-owned banks
- 35 trust companies
- 70 life insurance companies
- 1,000 credit unions and caisses populaires
- 200 finance companies

Also, there are over 100 bank account packages and 96% of Canadians have an account with a financial institution.

Source: Courtesy of Canadian Bankers Association.

**pension funds**
Amounts of money put aside by corporations, non-profit organizations, or unions to cover part of the financial needs of their members when they retire.

# How the Financial Services Industry Is Regulated[4]

Because of its important role in the economy, the financial industry is one of the most regulated sectors in the country. Regulation is designed to ensure the integrity, safety, and soundness of financial institutions and markets. Legislative, self-regulatory, and other initiatives help minimize crises and company failures. In addition, they protect investors, depositors, and policyholders. These detailed and varied compliance requirements take a considerable amount of time and money for companies in this industry to complete.

In Canada, there is no single body that regulates the entire industry. It's a responsibility shared among different organizations and levels of government. To start with, financial institutions may be regulated at either the federal or the provincial level, or jointly. For example, banks are federally regulated. Securities dealers, credit unions, and caisses populaires are provincially regulated. Insurance, trust and loan companies, and co-operative credit associations may be federally and/or provincially regulated, depending on the jurisdiction under which the company is incorporated or registered.

For institutions under federal responsibility, the Department of Finance is charged with overseeing their overall powers—in other words, what they can and cannot do. The Department of Finance relies on three federal agencies to supervise the ongoing operations of these institutions and their compliance with legislation:

- The Office of the Superintendent of Financial Institutions (www.osfi-bsif.gc.ca) monitors the day-to-day operations of institutions with respect to their financial soundness.

- Overseeing the deposit insurance system is the Canada Deposit Insurance Corporation (www.cdic.ca), which protects deposits that Canadians have in their federal financial institutions. CDIC will be discussed below.
- The Financial Consumer Agency of Canada (www.fcac-acfc.gc.ca) monitors financial institutions to ensure that they comply with federal consumer protection measures, which range from disclosure requirements to complaint-handling procedures.

For institutions under provincial jurisdiction, the province(s) in which a company is incorporated or registered is (are) responsible for regulating the company's overall powers. As at the federal level, provinces are supported by agencies and organizations that supervise the ongoing operations of these institutions.

### The Canada Deposit Insurance Corporation[5]

The Canada Deposit Insurance Corporation (CDIC) is a federal Crown corporation that was created in 1967 to provide deposit insurance and contribute to the stability of Canada's financial system. CDIC insures eligible deposits at member institutions (e.g., banks and trust companies) against these institutions' failure or collapse. CDIC guarantees deposits up to $100,000 (principal and interest) in each member institution. It is funded primarily by premiums paid by banks and trust companies that belong to this program.

Keep in mind that CDIC does not cover all types of deposits. For example, foreign currency accounts, term deposits with a maturity of greater than five years, and investments in mortgages, stocks, and mutual funds are not covered.

To date, CDIC has provided protection to depositors in 43 member institution failures. As of April 2008, CDIC had insured some $477 billion in deposits.

---

### Progress Assessment

- What components of the financial services industry were known as the four pillars?
- Describe some changes to the industry as a result of Bill C-8.
- Contrast credit unions and caisses populaires, and list some non-bank competitors.
- Describe the responsibilities of three federal agencies that oversee financial institutions.
- What deposits are not secured by CDIC?

---

## WHY MONEY IS IMPORTANT

The Canadian economy depends heavily on money: its availability and its value relative to other currencies. Economic growth and the creation of jobs depend on money. Money is so important to the economy that many institutions have evolved to manage money and to make it available to you when you need it. Today, you can easily get cash from an automated teller machine (ATM) almost anywhere in the world, but in many places cash isn't the only means of payment you can use. Most organizations will accept a cheque, credit card, debit card, or smart card for purchases.[6] Behind the scenes of this free flow of money is a complex system of banking that makes it possible for you to do all of these things.

The complexity of the banking system has increased as the electronic flow of money from country to country has become as free as that from province to territory. Each day, more than $1.5 trillion is exchanged in the world's currency markets. Therefore, what happens to any major country's economy has an effect on the Canadian economy and vice versa. Looking back on the fall of 2008, the global inter-connnectivity of banking systems resulted in a widespread liquidity crisis which lead to major government interventions. Clearly, there's more to money and its role in the economies of the world than meets the eye. There's no way to understand the Canadian economy without understanding global money exchanges and the various institutions involved in the creation and management of money.

## What Is Money?

**Money** is anything that people generally accept as payment for goods and services. In the past, objects as diverse as salt, feathers, stones, rare shells, tea, and horses have been used as money. In fact, until the 1880s, cowrie shells were one of the world's most abundant currencies. **Barter** is the trading of goods and services for other goods and services directly; though barter may sound like something from the past, many people have discovered the benefits of bartering online. Others still barter goods and services the old-fashioned way—face to face. For example, in Siberia, two eggs have been used to buy one admission to a movie, and employees of Ukraine's Chernobyl nuclear plant have been paid in sausages and milk. Some of the trade in Russia over recent years has been done in barter.

The problem is that eggs and milk are difficult to carry around. People need some object that's portable, divisible, durable, and stable so that they can trade goods and services without carrying the actual goods around with them. One answer to that problem over the years was to create coins made of silver or gold. Coins met all of the standards of a useful form of money:

- *Portability*. Coins are a lot easier to take to market than are pigs or other heavy products.
- *Divisibility*. Different-sized coins could be made to represent different values. Because silver is now too expensive, today's coins are made of other metals, but the accepted values remain.
- *Stability*. When everybody agrees on the value of coins, the value of money is relatively stable.
- *Durability*. Coins last for thousands of years, even when they've sunk to the bottom of the ocean, as you've seen when divers find old Roman coins in sunken ships.
- *Uniqueness*. It's hard to counterfeit, or copy, elaborately designed and minted coins. But with the latest colour copiers, people are able to duplicate the look of paper money relatively easily. Thus, the government has had to go to extra lengths to ensure that real dollars are readily identifiable. That's why some denominations have raised print or raised ink, watermarks, and fine-line patterns.[7]

When coins and paper money become units of value, they simplify exchanges. Most countries have their own coins and paper money, and they're all equally portable, divisible, and durable. However, they're not always equally stable. For example, the value of money in Russia is so uncertain and so unstable that other countries won't accept Russian money (rubles) in international trade.

Electronic cash (e-cash) is the latest form of money.[8] In addition to being able to make online bill payments using software programs such as Quicken or Microsoft Money, you can e-mail e-cash to anyone using Web sites such as PayPal.com (owned by eBay). Recipients get an e-mail message telling them that they have several choices for how they can receive the money: automatic deposit (the money will be sent to their bank), e-dollars for spending online, or a traditional cheque in the mail.

**money**
Anything that people generally accept as payment for goods and services.

**barter**
The trading of goods and services for other goods and services directly.

Some of the security features on the $5 note include a holographic stripe, watermark, see-through number, and windowed security thread. Additional features include raised ink, iridescent maple leaves, the hidden number 5, fine-line patterns printing, fluorescence, and a tactile feature. Do you check your notes for security features?

## What Is the Money Supply?

The **money supply** is the amount of money the Bank of Canada (introduced in Chapter 4) makes available for people to buy goods and services. The money supply can be measured in a number of different ways. Some of these different measures, called monetary aggregates, are described in Figure 18.2.

M1 represents money that can be accessed quickly and easily. M2, M2+, and M2++ are even broader measures of the money supply. Before we consider how the Bank of Canada controls the money supply, let us first consider why the money supply needs to be controlled and its impact on the global exchange of money.

## Why Does the Money Supply Need to Be Controlled?

Imagine what would happen if governments or non-governmental organizations were to generate twice as much money as exists now. There would be twice as much money available, but there would be the same amount of goods and services. What would happen to prices in that case? Think about the answer for a minute. (Hint: Remember the laws of supply and demand from Chapter 2.) The answer is that prices would go up because more people would try to buy goods and services with their money and would bid up the price to get what they wanted. This is called inflation. That is why some people define inflation as "too much money chasing too few goods."

Now think about the opposite: What would happen if the Bank of Canada took some of the money out of the economy? What would happen to prices? Prices would go down because there would be an oversupply of goods and services compared to the money available to buy them; this is called deflation.[9] If too much money is taken out of the economy, a recession might occur. That is, people would lose jobs and the economy would stop growing.

Now we come to a second question about the money supply: Why does the money supply need to be controlled? The money supply needs to be controlled because doing so allows us to manage the prices of goods and services somewhat. And controlling the money supply affects employment and economic growth or decline.

## The Global Exchange of Money

A falling dollar value means that the amount of goods and services you can buy with a dollar decreases.[10] A rising dollar value means that the amount of goods and services you can buy with a dollar goes up.

What makes the dollar weak (falling dollar value) or strong (rising dollar value) is the position of the Canadian economy relative to other economies. When the economy

**FIGURE 18.2**

**Measures of Money—Canada's Money Supply**

| Measures of Money (Monetary Aggregates) | Definition of the Monetary Aggregates |
| --- | --- |
| M1 | The currency (bank notes and coins) in circulation plus personal chequing accounts and current accounts at banks. |
| M2 | Includes personal savings accounts and other chequing accounts, term deposits, and non-personal deposits requiring notice before withdrawal, in addition to M1. |
| M2+ | Includes all deposits at non-bank deposit-taking institutions, money-market mutual funds, and individual annuities at life insurance companies, in addition to M2. |
| M2++ | Includes all types of mutual funds and Canada Savings Bonds, in addition to M2+. |

Source: Bank of Canada, "Canada's Money Supply," January 2000, www.bankofcanada.ca/en/backgrounders/bg-m2.htm.

is strong, the demand for dollars is high, and the value of the dollar rises. As commodity prices rose from 2007 through 2008, the value of the Canadian dollar rose dramatically. After years of the exchange rate of a Canadian dollar being below par compared to a U.S. dollar, the exchange rate rose above parity. When the economy is perceived as weakening, however, the demand for dollars declines, and the value of the dollar falls. The value of the dollar thus depends on a strong economy. Clearly, control over the money supply is important. In the following section, we'll discuss briefly how the money supply is controlled.

## Control of the Money Supply[11]

You already know that money plays a huge role in the world economies. Therefore, it's important to have an organization that controls the money supply to try to keep the economy from growing too fast or too slow. Theoretically, with proper monetary policy you can keep the economy growing without causing inflation. As mentioned in Chapter 4, the organization in charge of monetary policy is the Bank of Canada.

The Bank of Canada monitors the money supply. Indicators such as M1 provide useful information about changes that are occurring in the economy. The availability of money and credit must expand over time, and the Bank of Canada is responsible for ensuring that the rate at which more money is introduced into the economy is consistent with long-term stable growth.

The bank's economic research indicates that the growth of M1 provides useful information on the future level of production in the economy. The growth of the broader monetary aggregates is a good leading indicator of the rate of inflation.

The objective of the Bank of Canada's monetary policy is to support a level of spending by Canadians that is consistent with the Bank's goal of price stability. This is defined as keeping inflation within the inflation-control target range (of 1 to 3 percent). By influencing the rate at which the supply of money and credit is growing, total spending on goods and services in the economy can be stabilized.

The Bank of Canada manages the rate of money growth indirectly through the influence it exercises over short-term interest rates. When these rates change, they carry other interest rates—such as those paid by consumers for loans from commercial banks—along with them. When interest rates rise, consumers and businesses are apt to hold less money, to borrow less, and to pay back existing loans. The result is a slowing in the growth of M1 and the other broader monetary aggregates.[12]

The Bank of Canada has an influence on very short-term interest rates through changes in its target for the overnight rate. The target for the overnight rate is the main tool used by the Bank of Canada to conduct monetary policy. It tells major financial institutions the average interest rate the Bank of Canada wants to see in the marketplace where they lend each other money for one day, or "overnight." When the Bank changes the target for the overnight rate, this change usually affects other interest rates charged by commercial banks. The **prime rate** is the interest rate that banks charge their most creditworthy customers.

When the Bank changes the target for the overnight rate, this sends a clear signal about the direction in which it wants short-term interest rates to go. These changes usually lead to moves in the prime rate at commercial banks. The prime rate serves as a benchmark for many of their loans. These changes can also indirectly affect mortgage rates, and the interest paid to consumers on bank accounts, term deposits, and other savings.

When interest rates go down, people and businesses are encouraged to borrow and spend more, boosting the economy. But if the economy grows too fast, it can lead to inflation. The Bank may then raise interest rates to slow down borrowing and spending, putting a brake on inflation.

In choosing a target for the overnight rate, the Bank of Canada picks a level that it feels will keep future inflation low, stable, and predictable. Keeping inflation low and stable helps provide a good climate for sustainable economic growth, investment, and job creation.[13]

**prime rate**
The interest rate that banks charge their most creditworthy customers.

## Progress Assessment

- What are the characteristics of useful money?
- What is the money supply and why is it important?
- What are the various ways in which the Bank of Canada controls the money supply?

# THE BANKING INDUSTRY

Following legislative changes in 1992, banks were allowed to own insurance, trust, and securities subsidiaries. Today, most of Canada's large banks have subsidiaries in these areas. As major players in Canada's financial industry, the banks serve millions of customers. They include individuals, small- and medium-sized businesses, large corporations, governments, institutional investors, and non-profit organizations. The major banks offer a full range of banking, investment, and financial services. They have extensive nationwide distribution networks and also are active in the United States, Latin America, the Caribbean, Asia, and other parts of the world. Close to half of their earnings are generated outside of Canada.

Figure 18.3 outlines Canada's six largest banks. Strong players in the Canadian economy, Canada's banks are were extremely profitable until the fall of 2008. These financial results have garnered criticism by some who believe that the banks are taking advantage of customers by charging high service charges. The reality is that bank revenues are increasingly being generated from international activities. As well, banks distribute a good portion of their net income to their shareholders. Most Canadians own bank shares, whether they know it or not; bank shares form a large part of many major mutual funds (to be discussed later in this chapter) and pension funds.[14] In 2007, Canada's banks distributed $8.7 billion of dividends to their shareholders, which represented 44 percent of the banks' net earnings.[15]

Some of the major banks have been trying to merge for several years. They believe that if they were permitted to merge, they would be able to take advantage of economies of scale and be more efficient. They argue that they are not big players globally (see Figure 18.4), and that they are increasingly being forced to look outside Canada for more opportunities due to the laws and regulations that control their domestic activities. Shareholders continue to demand good returns, and the banks are under more pressure to continue to

| FIGURE | 18.3 |
| --- | --- |

**Canada's Six Largest Banks**

| Bank Name | Total Assets | Total Loans | Net Income for Fiscal Year Ended October 31, 2008 |
| --- | --- | --- | --- |
| | | | ($ millions) |
| RBC Financial Group | 723,859 | 334,236 | 4,555 |
| Scotiabank | 507,625 | 304,888 | 3,140 |
| TD Bank Financial Group | 563,214 | 262,049 | 3,833 |
| BMO Financial Group | 416,050 | 205,678 | 1,978 |
| CIBC | 353,930 | 207,072 | (2,060) |
| National Bank of Canada | 129,332 | 59,608 | 776 |
| Total 6 Banks | 2,694,010 | 1,373,529 | 12,222 |

Source: Courtesy of Canadian Bankers Association.

## The Banking Crisis Goes Global

The banking crisis has become a global phenomenon, even in countries that appeared to be doing well, such as China. Even though the Chinese government could force banks to make loans, it is reluctant to do so now that capitalism seems to be working. Because banks began holding on to their money, some 67,000 small businesses in China went into bankruptcy in the first half of 2008.

Even some larger state-owned businesses felt the effects of the crisis. Pakistan recently went to China to borrow funds but could not get them and turned to the International Monetary Fund (IMF) for help. Several Eastern and Central European countries and former Soviet republics are also in trouble. The IMF has agreed to lend Ukraine over $16 billion and Hungary over $15 billion.

Turkey could need as much as $90 billion. Other countries are in similar straits. Even oil-rich Bahrain is suffering from the crisis.

Should the IMF and World Bank continue to give funds to countries suffering financial crises? Where do those funds come from? Should the United States and Canada, along with other G8 countries, continue to help provide money for such loans as it has pledged to do?

Sources: "Back in Business," *The Wall Street Journal*, 30 October 2008; David Stringer, "Struggling Nations Depleting IMF's Bailout," *Washington Times*, 29 October 2008; Ariana Eunjung Cha and Maureen Fan, "China Unveils $586 Billion Stimulus Plan," *The Washington Post*, 10 November 2008; and Chip Cummins, "Bahrain Credit Outlook Is Downgraded," *The Wall Street Journal*, 7 January 2009.

---

deliver, year after year. This is an issue that will not go away in the years to come. However, all the aggressive growth over the past few years has been stalled by the banking crisis that started at the end of 2008. The Reaching Beyond Our Borders box talks about the global nature of this banking crisis.

## Commercial Banks

A **commercial bank** is a profit-seeking organization that receives deposits from individuals and corporations in the form of chequing and savings accounts and then uses some of these funds to make loans. Commercial banks have two types of customers: depositors and borrowers (those who take out loans). A commercial bank is equally responsible to both types of customers. Commercial banks try to make a profit by efficiently using the funds that depositors give them. In essence, a commercial bank uses customer deposits as inputs (on which it pays interest) and invests that money in interest-bearing loans to other customers (mostly businesses). Commercial banks make a profit if the revenue generated by loans exceeds the interest paid to depositors plus all other operating expenses.

**FIGURE | 18.4**

**Worldwide Bank Rankings, 2008**

| Rank | Bank | Assets (Cad$ Billions) |
|------|------|------------------------|
| 1 | Royal Bank of Scotland | 4,287 |
| 33 | Royal Bank of Canada | 883 |
| 47 | Toronto-Dominion Bank | 384 |
| 48 | Scotiabank | 614 |
| 53 | Bank of Montreal | 504 |
| 60 | CIBC | 428 |
| 116 | National Bank of Canada | 160 |
| 125 | Desjardins Group | 152 |

Source: Courtesy of Canadian Bankers Association.

## Some Services Provided by Banks

Individuals and corporations that deposit money in a *chequing account* have the privilege of writing personal cheques to pay for almost any purchase or transaction. Typically, banks impose a service charge for cheque-writing privileges or demand a minimum deposit. Banks might also charge a small handling fee for each cheque written. For business depositors, the amount of the service charge depends on the average daily balance in the chequing account, the number of cheques written, and the firm's credit rating and credit history.

In addition to chequing accounts, commercial banks offer a variety of savings account options. As for the chequing accounts, each individual needs to evaluate the different features of each account as they differ from institution to institution.

A *term deposit* (also known as a guaranteed investment certificate or a certificate of deposit) is a savings account that earns interest to be delivered at the end of the specified

**commercial bank**
A profit-seeking organization that receives deposits from individuals and corporations in the form of chequing and savings accounts and then uses some of these funds to make loans.

## Making Ethical Decisions

### To Tell the Teller or Not?

You have been banking at the same bank for some time, but the tellers at the bank keep changing, so it is difficult to establish a relationship with any one teller. You do not like using the automated teller machine because the bank has decided to charge for each transaction. Therefore, you are working with a teller and withdrawing $300 for some expenses you expect to incur. The teller counts out your money and says: "Okay, here's your $300." Before you leave the bank, you count the money once more. You notice that the teller has given you $350 by mistake. You return to the teller and say, "I think you have made a mistake in giving me this money." She replies indignantly, "I don't think so. I counted the money in front of you."

You are upset by her quick denial of a mistake and her attitude. You have to decide whether to give her back the overpayment of $50. What are your alternatives? What would you do? Is that the ethical thing to do?

The Canadian Bankers Association has a series of free publications on a variety of financial topics. Some examples are Getting Started in Small Business, Small Business Financing, Getting Value for Your Service Fees, Investing Your Dollars, Managing Money, and Planning for Retirement. For more details, visit www.cba.ca.

period. The depositor agrees not to withdraw any of the funds in the account until the end of the specified term (e.g., one year). The longer the term deposit is to be held by the bank, the higher the interest rate for the depositor.

Banks also offer a variety of other products. Some examples of credit products for creditworthy customers include credit cards, lines of credit, loans, mortgages, and overdraft protection on chequing accounts. Additional products are access to automated teller machines (ATMs), life insurance coverage on credit products, brokerage services, financial counselling, telephone and Internet bill payment options, safe-deposit boxes, registered retirement accounts, and traveller's cheques. Visit a local bank branch to find out the details for all of these types of products. It is up to each individual to compare the different features on each type of account or service as they vary from institution to institution. Features and rates are competitive. The Making Ethical Decisions box highlights a human error that can easily be made.

ATMs give customers the convenience of 24-hour banking at a variety of outlets such as supermarkets, department stores, and drugstores, in addition to the bank's regular branches. Depositors can—almost anywhere in the world—transfer funds, make deposits, and get cash at their own discretion with the use of a computer-coded personalized plastic access card. Beyond all that, today's ATMs are doing even more. New ATMs can dispense maps and directions, phone cards, and postage stamps. They can sell tickets to movies, concerts, sporting events, and so on. They can even show movie trailers, news tickers, and video ads. Some can take orders for flowers and DVDs, and download music and games.[16] The convenience store chain 7-Eleven is testing machines that cash cheques and send wire transfers.[17] What will be next?

## Services to Borrowers

In addition to other financial services firms and government agencies (such as the Business Development Bank of Canada), banks offer a variety of services to individuals and corporations in need of a loan. Generally, loans are given on the basis of the recipient's

## SPOTLIGHT ON Small Business

### How the Banking Crisis Affected Small Business

One of the consequences of the banking crisis of 2008–2009 was that it became more difficult to get a loan from a bank, especially if you ran a small business. It used to be that small businesses could get an "air-ball loan," that is, a loan based more on the borrower's personal relationship with the banker than on his or her assets. Today, however, banks are more reluctant to give out loans. Sometimes the bank will demand that the borrower make a "substantial" deposit—up to half the loan amount—to get a loan. Some banks have even cut lending to new customers to conserve available funds for existing customers. While the scope of the crisis has not been quite as severe in Canada compared to the United States, small business has found it more and more difficult to borrow from banks. Because borrowing from a bank has become so difficult, you might have to look to alternative sources of funds. For example, if you are buying equipment, you might ask the vendor for financing.

In Canada, banks have wanted to reduce their risk, so they have been advocating for more government guarantees for small business loans. There has also been talk about the governments providing a pool of funds to offset the decrease in loans being made by the banks, and the drying up of other credit options for small business.

Some small businesses use credit cards to get started, but the fees can be extremely high if the bills are not paid promptly. Many small-business owners turn to friends and family for loans, but that too can be dicey if the business does not do well. What other sources of funds are available? Angel investors are wealthy individuals who use their own money to fund start-up companies at the early stages of their development. They usually seek out high-growth companies in fields like technology and biotech that might issue stock or get profitably bought out in a few years. Local companies like restaurants, roofers, and deck cleaners usually cannot get a hearing, much less a loan. In short, banks and nonbanks are often reluctant to loan money to small businesses. Small business has to be far more diligent in searching out sources of funding as they try to expand their operations.

Sources: Norm Brodsky, "What the Financial Crisis Means to You," *Inc.*, November 2008; Binyamin Appelbaum and David Cho, "Small Banks, Tight Credit," *The Washington Post*, 27 August 2008; C. J. Prince, "Something to Bank On," *Entrepreneur*, August 2008; and Bob Seiwert, "Borrowing Trouble," *Black Enterprise*, January 2009.

creditworthiness. Banks want to manage their funds effectively and are supposed to screen loan applicants carefully to ensure that the loan plus interest will be paid back on time. Small businesses often search out banks that cater to their needs. The Spotlight on Small Business box discusses the new relationship between small businesses and banks after the 2008–2009 banking crisis.

## Managing Your Personal Finances

A major reason for studying business is that it prepares you for finding and keeping a good job. You already know that one of the secrets to finding a well-paying job is to have a good education. With your earnings, you can take vacations, raise a family, make investments, buy the products you want, and give generously to others.

Money management, however, is not easy. You have to earn the money in the first place. Then you have to learn how to save money, spend money wisely, and insure yourself against any financial and health risks. While these topics are important from a personal perspective, they are outside the scope of this chapter. However, given their importance, you can visit the Online Learning Centre for an introduction to managing your personal finances. Starting with the six steps of learning to control your assets, we discuss ways to build a financial asset base, explain how to buy the appropriate insurance, and outline a strategy for retiring with enough money to last a lifetime.

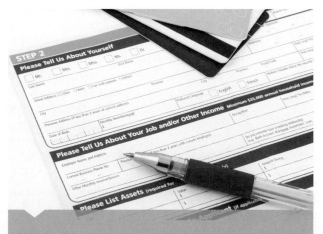

Many consumers, especially first-time credit card owners, are unable to properly manage their money and often end up with severely damaged credit ratings—or worse, in bankruptcy. That's why it may be a good idea for you to pass up the free T-shirt or other offer made by credit card companies.

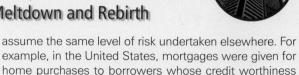

### The Internet—Its Support for the Financial Meltdown and Rebirth

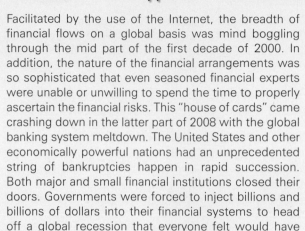

Facilitated by the use of the Internet, the breadth of financial flows on a global basis was mind boggling through the mid part of the first decade of 2000. In addition, the nature of the financial arrangements was so sophisticated that even seasoned financial experts were unable or unwilling to spend the time to properly ascertain the financial risks. This "house of cards" came crashing down in the latter part of 2008 with the global banking system meltdown. The United States and other economically powerful nations had an unprecedented string of bankruptcies happen in rapid succession. Both major and small financial institutions closed their doors. Governments were forced to inject billions and billions of dollars into their financial systems to head off a global recession that everyone felt would have been unprecedented in its scope and severity.

While the United States, in particular, and other countries to a lesser extent, has taken many months to try to deal with their problems, Canada has escaped the blood bath relatively unscathed. Our banking system has become the envy of the world due to its unwillingness to assume the same level of risk undertaken elsewhere. For example, in the United States, mortgages were given for home purchases to borrowers whose credit worthiness was questionable.

Given their relatively strong position, Canadian banks are looking for opportunities to expand globally by making sound investments at rock bottom prices. Many highly qualified investment bankers have been hired away from struggling firms in the United States and elsewhere. These individuals have supported expansion planning by all five major Canadian banks into countries that are viewed as having the greatest growth potential in the rebounding economy. Acquisitions or the opening of offices have been completed or are planned for China, India, Brazil, and Russia.

Sources: Daniel Fairlamb and Stanley Reed, "Uber Bank," *BusinessWeek*, 20 March 2000, 52–53; "The Global Giants," *The Wall Street Journal*, 14 October 2002, R10, R11; Stephanie Miles, "What's a Check?" *The Wall Street Journal*, 21 October 2002, R5; and Erik Portanger and Paul Beckett, "Banks Vie for Europe's Consumers," *The Wall Street Journal*, 24 February 2003, C1, C5.

# Electronic Banking on the Internet

Not only have banking, insurance, and brokerage services been combined by financial service companies, but they are also available online. All of Canada's top banks allow customers to have access to their accounts online, and all have bill-paying capacity. Thus, you are now able to do all of your financial transactions from home, using your telephone or your computer. That includes banking transactions such as transferring funds from one account to another (e.g., savings to chequing), paying your bills, and finding out how much is in your various accounts.[18] In some instances, you can apply for a loan online and get a response almost immediately. The company can check your financial records and give you a reply while you wait. Buying and selling stocks and bonds is equally easy. The Dealing with Change box discusses how the Internet contributed to the financial crisis that started in late 2008.

Internet banks (such as ING) have been created that offer branchless banking. Such banks can offer high interest rates and low fees because they do not have the costs of physical overhead that traditional banks have. While many consumers are pleased with the savings and convenience, not all are entirely happy with the service they receive from Internet banks. Why are they dissatisfied? First, they are nervous about security. People fear putting their financial information into cyberspace, where others may see it. Despite all of the assurances of privacy, people are still concerned. Furthermore, some people want to be able to talk to a knowledgeable person when they have banking problems. They miss the service, the one-on-one help, and the security of local banks.

Because of these issues, the future seems to be with organizations like TD Bank Financial Group and BMO Financial Group, which are traditional banks that offer both online services and brick-and-mortar facilities.[19] Combined online and brick-and-mortar banks not only offer online services of all kinds but also have automated teller machines (ATMs), places to go to deposit and get funds, and real people to talk to in person.

## Progress Assessment

- Why are banks interested in merging?
- List some services provided by commercial banks.
- What are some benefits of electronic banking to users?

# THE INSURANCE INDUSTRY

Over the past few years, we seem to continually hear stories of natural disasters causing damages totalling in the billions of dollars. Where does the money come from to pay for these damages? How can we seem to deal with these huge costs so relatively easily? Insurance has served a vital role in dealing with the repairs and rebuilding.

The general insurance industry in Canada provides insurance protection for most homes, motor vehicles, and commercial enterprises throughout Canada.[20] Most general insurance is provided by private insurance companies, which are subject to either provincial or federal regulations. Auto insurance is provided through a combination of private and government-owned auto insurers. The latter exist in British Columbia, Saskatchewan, and Manitoba. Another major category of general insurance is liability or business interruption insurance. Liability insurance provides protection in the event that the insured causes bodily injury or property damage to others for which the insured is liable. In 2007, insurance sales totalled more than $38 billion, while insurance companies controlled assets of more than $116 billion.[21]

The idea of insurance is to share risk with others. Instead of having to set aside significant cash reserves to deal with possible losses that may arise, an ongoing, relatively small insurance premium allows those insured to have piece of mind that, in the event of a major catastrophe, their losses will be covered. Insurance companies collect insurance premiums from literally thousands of clients, using them to pay for the cost of the relatively few catastrophes that will inevitably occur.

Ever wonder why we typically have to pay insurance premiums at the start of an insurance period? Often, in a given year, the amount of claims paid out, in combination with the cost of running the insurance business, exceeds the premiums collected (we will get back to this anomaly shortly). The insurance industry is able to cover this shortfall with the interest it earns on the premiums it collects—it collects premiums before it has to pay out claims. Claims include theft, liability, natural disasters including hail and wind, water damage, and fire.

In most businesses, the selling price is set once all costs are determined. In the insurance industry, the exact opposite happens. Insurance premiums (the selling price) are set before the actual claims are paid out (the most significant cost). In setting premiums for the upcoming renewal period, an insurance company estimates the number and cost of current and future claims and the amount of investment income it will earn.

In recent years, skyrocketing claims costs have greatly increased the premiums for auto insurance, and in some instances even the availability of insurance. Costs for all forms of insurance have also increased significantly due to insurance crime, which results when individuals inflate the cost of a claim for a stolen item or when highly organized rings bilk insurers out of millions of dollars. In addition, liability claims, as awarded by courts, have increased dramatically.

From a consumer standpoint, we need to budget for premiums for at least auto and property insurance. From an employment standpoint, the insurance industry offers many opportunities.

# THE CANADIAN SECURITIES INDUSTRY[22]

**securities dealer**
A firm that trades securities for its clients and offers investment services.

A **securities dealer** (also known as an investment dealer or brokerage house) is a firm that trades securities for its clients and offers investment services. Such firms also assist companies in raising all forms of capital for new and expanding businesses. As a result, this industry allows investors to trade in open capital markets. In 2003, there were 207 firms that employed more than 37,000 people. Since 1987, when federally regulated financial institutions were permitted to own securities firms, most of Canada's large, full-service securities firms have been bank-owned. Some examples are noted in Figure 18.5.

More Canadians are turning to the securities industry to ensure their financial security. The past decade has seen extraordinary growth in the number of individuals participating in Canadian capital markets. Roughly half of all working Canadians are directly and indirectly invested in the equities market. In the ten years prior to 2003, investors' holdings of shares have more than doubled to more than $660 billion. Ten years ago, 20 percent of the average investor's financial assets (bank accounts, registered retirement savings plans, pension, insurance, etc.) were stocks. Today, this ratio has grown to 27 percent. Not only are individuals choosing to invest more and more in the equities market, but so are companies and government agencies. Insurance companies will invest all of the excess of premiums they collect at the beginning of a policy year, over operating and claim costs. Pension plans, including the Canada Pension Plan, are investing a greater portion of their reserves. In all cases, investors want to increase their returns, but with increased risks.

Recently, increases in maximum foreign holdings of registered retirement savings plans have been granted in recognition of how proportionately small, on a global basis, the Canadian securities market is. The Canadian securities market is less than 3 percent of total world markets.

## Securities Regulations[23]

**prospectus**
A condensed version of economic and financial information that a company must make available to investors before they purchase a security.

As mentioned earlier in the textbook, one of the reasons why private corporations become public corporations is to raise capital to expand their existing operations. In recent times, companies such as Tim Hortons Inc., Sleep Country Canada, and the Brick became publicly traded companies following the successful completion of their first IPO.

Companies seeking public financing must issue a prospectus. A **prospectus** is a condensed version of economic and financial information that a company must make available to investors before they purchase the security. The prospectus must be approved by the securities commission in the province where the public funding is being sought. The **securities commission** is a government agency that administers provincial securities legislation.[24] For example, the mandate of the Ontario Securities Commission is to "protect investors from unfair improper and fraudulent practices, foster fair and efficient

**securities commission**
A government agency that administers provincial securities legislation.

| FIGURE | 18.5 |
| --- | --- |

**Canada's Bank-Owned Securities Firms**

| Firm | Majority owner |
| --- | --- |
| BMO Nesbitt Burns | Bank of Montreal |
| CIBC World Markets | Canadian Imperial Bank of Commerce |
| National Bank Financial | National Bank |
| RBC Dominion Securities | Royal Bank of Canada |
| Scotia Capital | The Bank of Nova Scotia |
| TD Securities | The Toronto-Dominion Bank |

Source: Department of Finance Canada, "Canada's Securities Industry," January 2005, http://www.fin.gc.ca/toc/2005/cansec05_-eng.asp.

capital markets and maintain public and investor confidence in the integrity of those markets." Recently, stock promoter Stevens Demers was found guilty of multiple counts of securities violations.[25]

Canada's ten provinces and three territories are responsible for the securities regulations within their respective borders. The Canadian Securities Administrators (CSA) is a forum for these securities regulators to coordinate and harmonize regulation of the Canadian capital markets. The CSA brings provincial and territorial securities regulators together. The focus of these meetings is to share ideas, work at designing policies and regulations that are consistent across the country, and ensure the smooth operation of Canada's securities industry. By collaborating on rules, regulations, and other programs, the CSA helps avoid duplication of work and streamlines the regulatory process for companies seeking to raise investment capital and others working in the investment industry. However perceptions exist in capital markets that the level of enforcement of regulations varies from one jurisdiction to another.

Canada's regulatory framework has been reviewed over the past number of years. Successive Ministers of Finance have continued to encourage a solution that would address the problems of a costly, cumbersome regulatory framework. A steering committee made up of ministers from six provinces agreed in the summer of 2003 to try to fix Canada's patchwork regulatory system. In 2004, this steering committee recommended a national securities regulator. Quebec, Alberta, and British Columbia were opposed to giving up their control over securities regulations. Today, a national body has yet to be created to oversee all securities activities.

# THE FUNCTION OF SECURITIES MARKETS

A **stock exchange** is an organization whose members can buy and sell (exchange) securities for companies and investors. A security is a transferable certificate of ownership of an investment product such as a stock or bond.[26] The Toronto Stock Exchange and the Montreal Exchange are just two examples of securities markets in Canada. These institutions serve two major functions: First, they assist businesses in finding long-term funding to finance capital needs, such as beginning operations, expanding their businesses, or buying major goods and services. Second, they provide private investors with a place to buy and sell securities (investments), such as stocks, bonds, and mutual funds (to be discussed later in this chapter) that can help them build their financial future.

Securities markets are divided into primary and secondary markets. Primary markets handle the sale of new securities. This is an important point to understand. Corporations make money on the sale of their securities only once—when they are first sold on the primary market through an IPO.[27] After that, the secondary market handles the trading of securities between investors, with the proceeds of a sale going to the investor selling the stock, not to the corporation whose stocks are sold. For example, if you, the owner of Very Vegetarian, offer 2 million shares of stock in your company at $15 a share, you would raise $30 million at this initial offering. However, if Shareholder Jones sells 100 shares of her Very Vegetarian stock to Investor Smith, Very Vegetarian collects nothing from this transaction. Smith bought the stock from Jones, not from Very Vegetarian. However, it's possible for companies like Very Vegetarian to offer additional shares to raise additional capital.

**stock exchange**
An organization whose members can buy and sell (exchange) securities for companies and investors.

The Toronto Stock Exchange and the TSX Venture Exchange are not the only fish in the stock exchange sea. Exchanges like the London Exchange (pictured here) are located throughout the world, even in former communist-bloc countries like Poland and Hungary. If you think a foreign company is destined to be the next Magna or Bombardier, call a broker and get in on the opportunity.

The importance of long-term funding to businesses cannot be overemphasized. Unfortunately, many new companies start without sufficient capital, and many established firms fail to do adequate long-term financial planning. If given a choice, businesses normally prefer to meet long-term financial needs by using retained earnings or by borrowing from a lending institution (bank, pension fund, insurance company). However, if such types of long-term funding are not available, a company may be able to raise funds by issuing corporate bonds (debt) or selling stock (ownership). Recall from Chapter 17 that issuing corporate bonds is a form of debt financing and selling stock in the corporation is a form of equity financing. These forms of debt financing or equity financing are not available to all companies, especially small businesses. However, many firms use such financing options to meet long-term financial needs.

## Progress Assessment

- Describe the Canadian securities industry. Why are more Canadians turning to this industry?
- What is the role of the Canadian Securities Administrators?
- What is the primary purpose of a stock exchange? Can you name a stock exchange in Canada?

# HOW TO INVEST IN SECURITIES

**stockbroker**

A registered representative who works as a market intermediary to buy and sell securities for clients.

Investing in bonds, stocks, or other securities is not very difficult. First, you decide what bond or stock you want to buy or that you have to sell. After that, it's necessary to use a registered representative authorized to trade stocks and bonds who can call a member of the stock exchange to execute your order. A **stockbroker** is a registered representative who works as a market intermediary to buy and sell securities for clients. Stockbrokers place an order with a stock exchange member, who goes to the place at the exchange where the bond or stock is traded and negotiates a price. After the transaction is completed, the trade is reported to your broker, who notifies you to confirm your purchase. Large brokerage firms like RBC Capital Markets and BMO Nesbitt Burns maintain automated order systems that allow their brokers to enter your order the instant you make it. Seconds later, the order can be confirmed.

A broker can be a valuable source of information about what stocks or bonds would best meet your financial objectives. It's important, however, that you learn about and follow stocks and bonds on your own, because investment analysts' advice may not always meet your specific expectations and needs.[28]

## Investing Online

Investors can also use online trading services to buy and sell stocks and bonds in place of using traditional brokerage services.[29] BMO Investorline (www.bmoinvestorline.com), TD Waterhouse (www.tdwaterhouse.ca), and iTrade Canada (https://www.scotiaitrade.com) are a few of the leading providers of web-based stock trading services. The commissions charged by these trading services are far less than those of regular stockbrokers. Trades that used to cost hundreds of dollars with full-service brokerage firms may cost as low as $5 each on the Web.

Today, customers interested in online trading services are primarily investors willing to do their own research and make their own investment decisions without the assistance of a broker. The leading online services, however, do provide important market information such as company financial data, price histories of a stock, and consensus analysts' reports.

Whether you decide to trade stocks and bonds using an online broker or decide to invest through a traditional stockbroker, it is important to remember that investing means committing (and risking) your money with the expectation of making a profit.[30] As the market downturn in the fall of 2008 highlighted, investing is certainly a risky business. Therefore, the first step in any investment program is to analyze such factors as desired income, cash requirements, growth prospects, level of risk, and hedging against inflation. You are never too young or too old to get involved in investments, so let's look at some alternatives and questions you should consider before investing.

## Choosing the Right Investment Strategy

As you might suspect, investment objectives change over the course of a person's life. Key investment decisions often centre on personal objectives such as growth and income. For example, a young person can afford more high-risk investment options (such as stocks) than a person nearing retirement. Often young investors are looking for significant growth in the value of their investments over time. Therefore, if stocks go into a tailspin and decrease in value, the younger person has time to wait for stocks to rise again. An older person, perhaps on a fixed income, doesn't have the luxury of waiting, and might be prone to invest in bonds that offer a steady return as a protection against inflation.

Inherent in any investment strategy is the risk/return trade-off. That's why it's important for investors to consider five key criteria when selecting investment options:

1. *Investment risk*—the chance that an investment will be worth less at some future time than it's worth now.

2. *Yield*—the expected rate of return on an investment, such as interest or dividends, usually over a period of one year.

3. *Duration*—the length of time your money is committed to an investment.

4. *Liquidity*—how quickly you can get back your invested funds if you want them or need them.

5. *Tax consequences*—how the investment will affect your tax situation.

Setting investment objectives such as growth or income should clearly set the tone for your investment strategy. Bonds, stocks, and mutual funds all offer opportunities for investors to enhance their financial future. We will look first at the potential of bonds as an investment, then move on to stocks and mutual funds.

## INVESTING IN BONDS

For investors who desire low risk and guaranteed income, government bonds are a secure investment because these bonds have the financial backing and full faith and credit of the government. In recent history no government bond issue in Canada has been defaulted on. Corporate bonds are a bit more risky and challenging. However, bond interest is fully taxable in the hands of the bond holder, while dividend income qualifies for tax credits.

One question often bothers first-time corporate bond investors: If I purchase a corporate bond, do I have to hold it until the maturity date? The answer is no, you do not have to hold a bond until maturity. Bonds are bought and sold daily on major securities exchanges. However, if you decide to sell your bond to another investor before its maturity date, you are not guaranteed to get the face value of the bond (usually $1,000). For example, if your bond does not have features that make it attractive to other investors, you may be forced to sell your bond at a discount; that is, a price less than the bond's face value. But if your bond is highly valued by other investors, you may be able to sell it at a premium; that is, a price above its face value. Remember that with most bonds the interest rate is fixed throughout the term of the bond. Therefore, after the bond is first issued, more often than not, there is a difference between the bond interest rate and the market interest rate. Therefore, bond prices generally fluctuate inversely with current market interest rates. As market interest rates go up, bond prices fall, given that the bond interest rate remains constant, and vice versa. Thus, like all investments, bonds have a degree of risk.

Investors will invest in a bond that is considered risky only if the potential return to them is high enough. It's important to remember that investors have many investment options besides bonds. One such option is to buy stock.

# INVESTING IN STOCKS

Buying stock makes the investor an owner of the firm. Stocks provide investors with an opportunity to participate in the success of emerging or expanding companies if the share price rises. In fact, since 1925, the average annual return on stocks has been about 12 percent, the highest return of any popular investment. This return is made up both of increases in the share price and of dividends that may be paid. For a discussion of dividends, refer to Chapter 17. As owners, however, stockholders can also lose money if a company does not do well or if the overall stock market is declining. The market fall of 2008 was proof of that. Again, it's up to investors to choose the investment that best fits their overall investment objectives.

According to investment analysts, the market price (and growth potential) of a common share depends heavily on the overall performance of the corporation in meeting its business objectives. If a company reaches its stated objectives, there are great opportunities for capital gains. **Capital gains** are the positive difference between the price at which you bought a stock and what you sell it for. For example, a $1,000 investment made in Microsoft when its stock was first offered to the public would be worth more than $1 million today. Stocks can be subject to a high degree of risk, however. While the late 1990s and early 2000s witnessed significant drops in the stock market, from 2004 to 2008 the Canadian stock market rose significantly as a result of the worldwide escalating demand for all types of natural resources. However, a financial crisis in the fall of 2008 drove markets down by close to 50 percent.

Stock investors are often called bulls or bears depending on their perceptions of the market. *Bulls* are investors who believe that stock prices are going to rise, so they buy stock in anticipation of the increase. When overall stock prices are rising, the market is called a bull market. *Bears* are investors who expect stock prices to decline. Bears sell their stocks in anticipation of falling prices. When the prices of stocks decline steadily, the market is called a bear market.[31]

As we discussed previously, setting investment objectives such as growth, income, inflation protection, or cash can set the tone for your investment strategy. Investors may select several different investment opportunities in stock depending on their strategy. Growth stocks, for example, are stocks of corporations (often technology, biotechnology, or Internet-related firms) whose earnings are expected to grow at a rate faster than other stocks in the market. While often considered very risky, such stocks offer investors the potential for high returns. Another option is income stocks. These are stocks that offer investors a rather high dividend yield on their investment. Public utilities are often considered good income stocks that will generally keep pace with inflation.

The stock of high-quality companies such as Petro-Canada and Canadian National (CN) are referred to as *blue-chip stocks*. These stocks pay regular dividends and generally experience consistent growth in the company's stock price. Investors can even invest in a type of stock called a penny stock. *Penny stocks* are

**capital gains**
The positive difference between the purchase price of a stock and its sale price.

Crystal Hanlan started with Home Depot as a cashier several years ago. She began buying shares in the company as part of an employee ownership plan and is now worth over a million dollars. There are over a million other employees who got to be millionaires the same way. Are you getting the idea that it is a good idea to participate in such ownership programs and to put the maximum you can into such accounts?

stocks that sell for less than $2 (some analysts say less than $5).[32] Such stocks frequently represent ownership in firms, such as mining or oil exploration companies, that compete in high-risk industries. Suffice it to say, penny stocks are considered very risky investments.

Investors who buy stock have more options for placing an order than investors buying and selling bonds. Stock investors, for example, can place a market order, which tells a broker to buy or to sell a stock immediately at the best price available. This type of order can be processed quickly, and the trade price can be given to the investor almost instantaneously. A limit order tells the broker to buy or to sell a particular stock at a specific price, if that price becomes available. Let's say, for example, that a stock is selling for $40 a share; you believe that the price will go up eventually but that it might drop a little before it goes higher. You could place a limit order at $36. The broker will buy the stock for you at $36 if the stock drops to that price. If the stock never falls to $36, the broker will not purchase it. See Figure 18.6 for a summary of some transactions. Which investments generated a capital gain (excluding any commissions) of more than $0.50 per share based on the closing price from the previous day?

## Stock Indexes

Stock indexes measure the trend of different stock exchanges. Every country with a stock exchange has such indexes. In Canada, there are several thousand companies listed, and the prices of their shares fluctuate constantly. Some may be rising over a certain period and others may be falling. Various indexes have been developed to give interested parties useful information about significant trends. More and more indexes are being continually developed. Another use of an index is as an investment vehicle. Investors who do not have the time or expertise to actively manage their investments are choosing to be passive investors by investing in index funds.

In Canada, the largest index is the S&P/TSX Composite Index. There is no requirement for the index to hold a certain number of companies. The number of stocks that make up the index will vary over time and will be included in the index if they qualify (based on size and liquidity) after quarterly reviews.[33]

Staying abreast of what is happening in the market will help you decide what investments seem most appropriate to your needs and objectives. However, it's important to remember two key investment realities: (1) your personal financial objectives will change over time, and (2) markets can be volatile.

## Buying on Margin

**Buying on margin** means you purchase securities by borrowing some of the cost from your broker, who holds them as collateral security until you pay the balance due. In effect, the broker lends you the money and charges you interest. Provincial regulatory agencies, such as the Ontario Securities Commission, control all aspects of this industry, including what minimum percentage of the purchase price must be paid in cash. For example, if the current rate is 50 percent for shares and 10 percent for bonds, you would have to invest a minimum of $4 to buy an $8 share (plus commissions to the broker), and $97 for a bond selling for $970.

Buying on margin is risky. If the stock or bond drops in price, you will get a margin call from your broker. This means that you will have to make a payment to your broker to maintain the margin of collateral protection that the broker is obligated to observe. In this case, the loan cannot exceed 50 percent of the stock value, or 90 percent of the bond value.

**buying on margin**
Purchasing securities by borrowing some of the cost from the broker.

## Stock Splits

As the price of a stock rises, the number of potential owners falls. Companies and brokers usually don't like to see this happen. If such a situation is happening to a given company, they may declare a **stock split**; that is, they issue two or more shares for every share of stock that's currently outstanding. For example, if Very Vegetarian stock were selling for

**stock split**
An action by a company that gives shareholders two or more shares of stock for each one they own.

**FIGURE** | **18.6**

**Daily Stock Transactions**
This is a small segment of the list of stocks traded on the Toronto Stock Exchange, as reported on 27 October 2006, in *The Globe and Mail*.

Here is an explanation of what the column headings mean:

A & B: highest and lowest price in the last year

C: abbreviated name of the company

D: the symbol used to identify the company for trading purposes

E: annual dividend per share

F, G, & H: highest, lowest, and closing price for that day

I: change in closing price from the previous day

J: number of shares traded that day in hundreds (e.g., first line is 5,500 shares)

K: *yield* refers to the estimated percent income your investment would yield if you bought at closing price and kept the stock for a year. It is the ratio of annual dividend to closing price. There is no yield for those companies that show no dividend paid.

L: *P/E ratio* refers to ratio of closing price to estimated earnings per share (which is not shown but is known). Where no ratio is shown it means either that the company is not making any profits or that no estimate of earnings is available.

| A | B | C | D | E | F | G | H | I | J | K | L |
|---|---|---|---|---|---|---|---|---|---|---|---|
| **365-day** | | | | | | | | | **vol.** | | **p/e** |
| **high** | **low** | **stock** | **sym** | **div** | **high** | **low** | **close** | **chg** | **(100s)** | **yield** | **ratio** |
| 1.80 | 0.75 | Lab Intl | LAB | | 0.85 | 0.75 | 0.80 | | 2731 | | |
| 4.50 | 3.55 | Lab Researc | LRI | | 4.30 | 4.05 | 4.10 | −0.20 | 144 | | |
| 10.95 | 3.75 | ♣ Labopharm | DDS | | 5.55 | 5.40 | 5.50 | | 2482 | | |
| 2.65 | 1.21 | Lake Shore | LSG | | 1.45 | 1.38 | 1.43 | +0.06 | 2840 | | |
| 29.50 | 16.21 | Laperriere | GLV.A | | 25.30 | 24.50 | 24.80 | +0.30 | 419 | | 14.4 |
| 8.50 | 4.06 | Laramide | LAM | | 7.75 | 7.25 | 7.37 | −0.16 | 3711 | | |
| 36.72 | 28.01 | Laurentn Bk | LB | 1.16 | 29.15 | 28.97 | 29.10 | +0.10 | 268 | 4.0 | 12.0 |
| 27.05 | 25.24 | Lauren | LB.PR.B | 1.50 | 26.30 | 26.04 | 26.20 | +0.09 | 103 | 5.7 | |
| 27.85 | 24.70 | Laurenti | LB.PR.E | 1.312 | 26.68 | 26.60 | 26.60 | +0.05 | 12 | 4.9 | |
| 59.40 | 36.00 | Le Chatea | CTU.A | 1.00 | 43.10 | 43.00 | 43.00 | −0.45 | 82 | 2.3 | 12.4 |
| 158.00 | 92.85 | Legg Masn | LMI | .944 | 101.00 | 99.38 | 101.00 | +3.36 | 32 | 0.09 | 22.1 |
| 46.50 | 35.00 | Leons Furnit | LNF | 1.00 | 46.25 | 45.75 | 45.75 | +0.25 | 39 | 2.2 | 15.8 |
| 14.72 | 14.00 | Life & B | LBS | 1.20 | 14.72 | 14.50 | 14.51 | −0.07 | 747 | 8.3 | |
| 10.68 | 10.35 | Life & B | LBS.PR.A | | 10.63 | 10.56 | 10.57 | +0.01 | 1140 | | |
| 16.74 | 10.81 | Linamar | LNR | 0.24 | 13.40 | 13.05 | 13.18 | +0.14 | 220 | 1.8 | 8.9 |
| 7.76 | 3.15 | Linear Gold | LRR | | 5.35 | 5.00 | 5.00 | −0.25 | 225 | | |
| 9.46 | 4.62 | LionOre | LIM | | 9.46 | 9.11 | 9.26 | +0.11 | 36528 | | |
| 7.45 | 2.80 | Liquidatin | LQW | | 6.60 | 6.45 | 6.60 | +0.05 | 89 | | 17.8 |
| 68.22 | 45.22 | Loblaw Cos | L | 0.84 | 46.38 | 46.00 | 46.30 | +0.15 | 4133 | 1.8 | 17.5 |
| 0.49 | .215 | Lorus | LOR | | 0.24 | 0.23 | 0.23 | −0.01 | 3498 | | |
| 1.54 | 0.21 | Lumina Res | LUR | | 1.45 | 1.38 | 1.43 | +0.02 | 1030 | | |
| 43.92 | 11.75 | Lundin Min | LUN | | 41.22 | 40.19 | 41.00 | +1.55 | 1703 | | 17.2 |
| 0.38 | 0.03 | Luxell Tech | LUX | | .055 | 0.05 | 0.05 | −0.01 | 427 | | |
| 8.65 | 6.22 | ♣ MCM | MUH.A | 1.20 | 7.53 | 7.52 | 7.52 | | 60 | 16.0 | 5.0 |
| 16.05 | 15.14 | ♣ MCM | MUH.PR.A | .866 | 15.30 | 15.30 | 15.30 | | 6 | 5.7 | |
| 23.20 | 18.25 | MDS Inc | MDS | 0.13 | 19.70 | 19.27 | 19.33 | −0.15 | 1738 | 0.7 | 64.4 |
| 42.48 | 34.90 | MI Dev | MIM.A | .674 | 42.25 | 41.57 | 41.79 | −0.21 | 159 | 1.6 | 60.6 |
| 3.50 | 1.90 | MKS | MKX | 0.09 | 2.77 | 2.65 | 2.70 | +0.05 | 183 | 3.3 | 13.5 |
| 52.49 | 33.00 | MacDonld | MDA | | 42.29 | 41.19 | 41.61 | −0.74 | 1844 | — | 21.6 |
| 3.34 | 2.11 | Magellan | MAL | | 2.76 | 2.68 | 2.68 | −0.10 | 233 | | |
| 92.10 | 75.88 | Magna Intl | MG.A | 1.71 | 86.52 | 84.34 | 85.86 | +0.73 | 1853 | 2.0 | 12.5 |
| 8.00 | 2.05 | Mahalo Enr | CBM | | 3.15 | 2.85 | 2.85 | −0.07 | 809 | | 47.5 |
| 11.50 | 4.85 | Mainstreet | MEQ | | 11.25 | 11.00 | 11.12 | −0.13 | 48 | | |
| 30.16 | 15.73 | ♣ Major Dril | MDI | | 23.25 | 21.60 | 22.59 | +0.48 | 763 | | 12.0 |
| 50.24 | 36.61 | Manitob Tl | MBT | 2.60 | 46.05 | 45.76 | 45.90 | −0.09 | 2853 | 5.7 | 30.2 |
| 37.55 | 29.70 | Manulife Fi | MFC | 0.70 | 36.89 | 36.48 | 36.62 | −0.01 | 38050 | 1.9 | 16.3 |
| 27.74 | 25.60 | Manuli | MFC.PR.A | 1.025 | 26.84 | 26.83 | 26.83 | | 92 | 3.8 | |
| 25.80 | 24.25 | Manuli | MFC.PR.B | 1.162 | 25.26 | 25.14 | 25.26 | −0.02 | 102 | 4.6 | |
| 25.05 | 23.77 | Manuli | MFC.PR.C | 1.125 | 24.98 | 24.76 | 24.81 | +0.06 | 179 | 4.5 | |
| 17.15 | 11.00 | Maple Leaf | MFI | 0.16 | 12.58 | 12.00 | 12.40 | −0.10 | 3067 | 1.3 | 45.9 |
| 42.00 | 16.85 | March Netwo | MN | | 26.84 | 25.48 | 26.00 | +0.85 | 746 | | 9.5 |
| 9.99 | 7.18 | Marsulex | MLX | | 8.65 | 8.65 | 8.65 | +0.15 | 6 | | 66.5 |
| 9.90 | 4.82 | Martinrea | MRE | | 9.40 | 9.10 | 9.40 | +0.20 | 1226 | | 17.4 |
| 7.90 | 4.01 | Maxin Pow | MXG | | 4.59 | 4.45 | 4.58 | +0.08 | 1052 | | 22.9 |
| 2.37 | 0.91 | Medicure | MPH | | 1.70 | 1.51 | 1.57 | −0.06 | 2448 | | |
| 29.75 | 20.25 | Mega Brands | MB | | 25.39 | 24.81 | 24.85 | −0.05 | 738 | | 13.6 |
| 5.625 | 1.255 | Mega Urani | MGA | | 4.90 | 4.65 | 4.90 | +0.28 | 8347 | | |
| 22.25 | 9.80 | Melcor Dev | MRD | 0.30 | 20.61 | 20.25 | 20.61 | +0.56 | 206 | 1.5 | 12.8 |
| 3.15 | 0.82 | Mercator Min | ML | | 2.70 | 2.64 | 2.69 | +0.06 | 668 | | 40.1 |
| 42.30 | 21.44 | MeridinGl | MNG | | 28.19 | 27.27 | 27.45 | −0.13 | 5476 | | |

$100 a share, you could declare a two-for-one stock split. Investors who owned one share of Very Vegetarian would now own two shares; each share, however, would now be worth only $50 (half the value before the split). As you can see, there is no change in the firm's ownership structure and no change in the investment's value after the stock split.[34] Investors, however, generally approve of stock splits because often the demand for the stock at $50 per share may be greater than the demand at $100 per share. Thus, the $50 stock price may go up in the near future.

---

## Progress Assessment

- What is the key advantage to online investing? What do investors need to remember if they decide to do their investing online?
- What is a stock split? Why do companies sometimes split their stock?
- What is meant by buying on margin?

---

# INVESTING IN MUTUAL FUNDS

A **mutual fund** is a fund that buys a variety of securities and then sells units of ownership in the fund to the public. A mutual fund company is similar to an investment company that pools investors' money and then buys stocks or bonds in many companies in accordance with the specific purpose of the fund. Mutual fund managers are experts who pick what they consider to be the best securities.

Investors can buy shares of the mutual funds and thus take part in the ownership of many different companies that they may not have been able to afford to invest in individually or may not have had the time to thoroughly analyze. Thus, for a fee, mutual funds provide professional investment management and help investors diversify. So for the investor, they consider the trade-off between the fees paid for mutual fund management against the return earned by the mutual fund. The return over and above an index is expected to exceed all the fees paid.

Funds available range in purpose from very conservative funds that invest only in government securities or secure corporate bonds to others that specialize in emerging high-tech firms, Internet companies, foreign companies, precious metals, and other investments with greater risk. A number of mutual funds invest only in indexes (refer to the earlier discussion on stock indexes). Some mutual funds even invest exclusively in socially responsible companies. See the Green Box for a discussion of socially responsible investing.

In Canada, mutual fund companies fall under the jurisdiction of the provincial securities commissions. Some examples of companies that manage mutual fund assets include Investors Group, AIM Funds Management, Mackenzie Financial, and TD Asset Management. According to the Investment Funds Institute of Canada, total assets under administration were just less than $600 billion at the end of October 2008.[35]

With mutual funds, investors benefit from diversification. **Diversification** involves buying several different investment alternatives to spread the risk of investing. Consequently, a mutual fund investor is not 100 percent invested in only one company. So, if one company's shares decrease, hopefully there will be increases in the value of other companies' shares. This is also applicable if a mutual fund holds bonds.

One key advantage of mutual funds is that you can buy some funds directly and save any fees or commissions. The Internet has made access in and out of mutual funds easier than ever. A true no-load fund is one that charges no commission to investors to either buy or sell its shares. A load fund would charge a commission to investors to buy shares in the fund or would charge a commission when investors sell shares in the fund.

**mutual fund**
A fund that buys stocks and bonds and then sells units of ownership in the fund to the public.

**diversification**
Buying several different investment alternatives to spread the risk of investing.

## GreenBOX

### Socially Responsible Investing

Also known as sustainable investing, Social Responsible Investing (SRI) is an investment strategy that seeks to achieve both financial return and social good. One of the focuses for SRI is environmental stewardship, including sustainability. Specifically, investment should be channeled away from companies that are perceived to negatively impact climate change.

On a global basis, by 2003, 200 SRI mutual funds existed, with assets over $160 billion. The proportion of mutual funds focused on SRI continues to grow exponentially. Shareholder activism has played an important role in either implementing a screening process that will exclude mutual funds from owning shares in certain companies, or divesting themselves of investment in other companies—with the latter being companies causing ethical objections. Government-controlled pension funds face growing pressure to undertake SRI.

A Canadian organization, Social Investment Organization, is mandated to promote the practice of SRI. They do this by taking a leadership role in supporting social and environmental criteria for investing decisions, raising public awareness of SRI, raising the case for environmental/social analysis with other investment organizations, and providing a forum for SRI. This organization sponsors a biennial conference, a list-serve (with data on the performance of SRI funds), a listing of financial advisors knowledgeable about SRI, a Web site and media relations activities. For more information, see their Web site at www.socialinvestment.ca.

Source: "Socially-Responsible Investing," http://en.wikipedia.org/wiki/Socially_responsible_investing.

Sprott Asset Management, with assets under management of nearly $4.4 billion, was founded by Eric Sprott. Recognized as a very good stock picker, he was recognized as the Fund Manager of the Year in 2007. A public offering of stock in his company made Eric Canada's newest billionaire in 2008.

It's important to check the costs involved in a mutual fund, such as fees and charges imposed in the managing of a fund, because these can differ significantly. It's also important to check the long-term performance record of the fund's management.[36] Some funds, called open-end funds, will accept the investments of any interested investors. Closed-end funds offer a specific number of shares for investment; once a closed-end fund reaches its target number, no new investors can buy into the fund.

Most financial advisers put mutual funds high on the list of recommended investments for small or beginning investors. Figure 18.7 evaluates bonds, stocks, and mutual funds according to risk, income, and possible investment growth (capital gain).

We hope you have enjoyed the discussion of investing in this chapter. It's critical for you to know that there's no such thing as easy money or a sure thing. Investing is a challenging and interesting field that's always changing.

### Progress Assessment

- What is a mutual fund and what is the role of mutual fund managers?
- How do mutual funds benefit small investors?
- Describe the degree of risk, expected income, and possible growth one can expect with mutual funds.

| Investment | Degree of risk | Expected income | Possible growth (capital gain) |
| --- | --- | --- | --- |
| Bonds | Low | Secure | Little |
| Preferred shares | Medium | Steady | Little |
| Common shares | High | Variable | Good |
| Mutual funds | Medium | Variable | Good |

**FIGURE 18.7**

**Comparing Investments**

# SUMMARY

1. Figure 18.1 briefly lists the variety of financial organizations that comprise this industry.

   **Why is this industry important to Canada?**

   The financial services industry employs more than 1 million Canadians, directly or indirectly. Its activities represent 5 percent of Canada's GDP. On a yearly basis, more than $9 billion in tax revenue to all levels of government is generated. Nearly $50 billion of services are exported annually. Because of its important role in the economy, the financial industry is one of the most regulated sectors in the country. Regulation is designed to ensure the integrity, safety, and soundness of financial institutions and markets.

   **LO ▶ 1** Describe the importance of the financial services industry in Canada.

2. Money is anything that people generally accept as payment for goods and services.

   **How is the value of money determined?**

   The value of money depends on the money supply; that is, how much money is available to buy goods and services. Too much money in circulation causes inflation. Too little money causes deflation, recession, and unemployment.

   **LO ▶ 2** Explain what money is and how its value is determined.

3. As major players in Canada's financial industry, banks serve millions of customers.

   **Who benefits from the services offered by banks?**

   Bank customers include individuals, small- and medium-sized businesses, large corporations, governments, institutional investors, and non-profit organizations. The major banks offer a full range of banking, investment, and financial services.

   **LO ▶ 3** Discuss the role that banks play in providing services.

4. Insurance is big business and a key component of the financial services industry.

   **What is the role of insurance as part of the financial services industry?**

   Everyone who drives a vehicle is required to have auto insurance. All businesses typically carry a mix of insurance coverage from property, to liability, to crime, to business interruption insurance.

   **LO ▶ 4** Discuss the nature and impact of insurance.

5. The risk/return trade-off is inherent in any investment strategy.

   **What are the key criteria when selecting investment options?**

   Five key criteria are investment risk (the chance that an investment will be worth less at some future time than it's worth now); yield (the expected rate of return on an investment over a period of time); duration (the length of time your investment is committed to an investment); liquidity (how quickly you can get your money back if you need it); and tax consequences (how the investment will affect your tax situation).

   **LO ▶ 5** List the five key criteria when selecting investment options.

**LO ▶ 6** Explain the opportunities in mutual funds as investments and the benefits of diversifying investments.

6. Diversification means buying several different types of investments (e.g., government bonds, preferred shares, common shares, etc.) with different degrees of risk. The purpose is to reduce the overall risk an investor would assume by investing in just one type of security.

**How can mutual funds help individuals diversify their investments?**

A mutual fund is a fund that buys a variety of securities and then sells units of ownership in the fund to the public. Individuals who buy shares in a mutual fund are able to invest in many different companies they could not afford to invest in otherwise.

## KEY TERMS

barter  555

buying on margin  569

capital gains  568

commercial bank  559

credit unions  552

diversification  571

money  555

money supply  556

mutual fund  571

non-banks  552

pension funds  553

prime rate  557

prospectus  564

securities commission  564

securities dealer  564

stockbroker  566

stock exchange  565

stock split  569

trust company  552

## CRITICAL THINKING

1. In the past few years, we have seen significant swings in the exchange rate of the Canadian dollar. The value of the Canadian dollar rose from as low as $.62 to over $1.00 and then back down to under $.80 (relative to the U.S. dollar). What have been some of the major contributors to the swings? What have been the impacts on the Canadian economy with both the rising and then the falling of the Canadian dollar's exchange rate?

2. The financial services marketplace is growing, changing, and becoming more competitive. Bill C-8 allowed more players into the marketplace. Despite increased competition, Canada's banks believe that they are still restricted in the business decisions they can make to achieve the size and scale they need to compete in the international marketplace. Do you agree with the claim that banks make that they are denied the opportunity to pursue legitimate strategies for growth, including insurance retailing and mergers? Do you believe that banks should be allowed to merge? (Note that at the time of this writing, no mergers had been approved.) Do you believe that consumers and businesses will suffer if bank mergers are permitted? Explain your position.

## DEVELOPING WORKPLACE SKILLS

1. In a small group, discuss the following: What services do you use from banks? Does anyone use Internet banking? What seem to be the pros and cons of online banking? Use this opportunity to compare the rates and services of various local banks. compare the services at each (interest rates given on accounts, the services available, and the loan rates). If anyone uses an online service, see how those rates compare. If no one uses a credit union or online bank, discuss the reasons.

2. Poll the class to see who uses banks and who uses a credit union or caisse populaire. Have class members

3. Break up into small groups and discuss when and where you use cheques versus credit cards and cash.

Do you often write cheques for small amounts? Would you stop doing that if you calculated how much it costs to process such cheques? Discuss your findings with others in the class.

4. Write a one-page paper on the role of the World Bank and the International Monetary Fund in providing loans to countries. Is it important for Canadian citizens to lend money to people in other countries through such organizations? Why or why not? Be prepared to debate the value of these organizations in class.

## TAKING IT TO THE NET 1

www.mcgrawhillconnect.ca

### Purpose

To learn about how financial institutions combat money laundering, terrorist financing, and threats to the security of Canada.

### Exercise

Visit the Financial Transactions and Reports Analysis Centre of Canada (www.fintrac.gc.ca) and answer the following questions.

1. Who is obligated to report suspicious transactions?

2. What types of transactions would qualify as suspicious?

3. What is it about terrorist financing that is more "legitimate" than money laundering?

## TAKING IT TO THE NET 2

www.mcgrawhillconnect.ca

### Purpose

To learn about services that are available to help consumers make educated financial decisions.

### Exercise

Visit "For Consumers" at the Financial Consumer Agency of Canada (www.fcac-acfc.gc.ca/eng/consumers/default.asp) and answer the following questions.

1. What information must you receive when you open a bank account?

2. What do you do if you find unauthorized transactions on your credit card account?

3. What are some suggestions for protecting yourself against debit card fraud?

4. What information must a financial institution provide on a monthly basis, if you have a line of credit?

5. If you have a complaint or problem with a federally regulated financial institution, what are the steps that you need to follow?

## ANALYZING MANAGEMENT DECISIONS

### Becoming Financially Secure

Mike and Priscilla Thomas are a married couple with two incomes and no children. Their cars are both paid for. They've saved enough money to buy a new house without selling their old one. (Real estate is typically a sound investment.) They're renting out their townhouse for added income. They hope to buy more rental property to use as an income producer so that they can both retire at age 50!

Priscilla runs a company called Cost Reduction Services and Associates. It advises small firms on ways to cut overhead expenses. The couple also owned a window-washing business when they were in university. Priscilla loves being in business for herself because, she says, "When you own your own business, you can work hard and you get paid for your hard work." Mike is a pharmaceutical salesperson.

How did the Thomases get the money to start their own businesses and buy a couple of homes? They committed themselves from the beginning of their marriage to live on Mike's income and to save Priscilla's income. Further-more, they decided to live frugally. The goal of early retirement was their incentive. They "lived like university kids" for five years, clipping coupons and saving every cent they could. They don't often go out to eat, and they rent movies for their VCR instead of going to the movie theatre.

Mike puts the maximum amount into his company's pension plan. It's invested in a very aggressive growth fund: half Canadian stocks and half international stocks. Now that the couple is financially secure, they're planning to have children.

Source: *Marketplace*, July 31, 2002.

## Discussion Questions

1. When considering investment risk, where would you rank real estate relative to stocks, bonds, and mutual funds?

2. How can a financial services firm help a person develop a budget in order to achieve one's goals?

3. Do you agree with how Mike has allocated his pension plan contributions? Explain.

4. Can you see why money management is one of the keys to both entrepreneurship and personal financial security?

# RUNNING CASE

## Risk Management at Canadian Tire Financial Services

In 1995, Canadian Tire Financial Services (CTFS) became the first non-bank to receive a MasterCard® licence. While the company had experience with its retail card business (the card could be used in Canadian Tire stores only), the ultimate goal was to convert retail card users to the company's new Options® MasterCard®. Both cards are loyalty cards that encourage retail spending at Canadian Tire stores. The advantage of the Options® MasterCard® is huge growth potential, as the market now includes worldwide purchases (MasterCard is accepted at more than 24 million shops and services worldwide) rather than simply purchases in Canadian Tire stores. Thus, Options® MasterCard® holders generate more loyalty benefits through the increased use of this card. Before this could happen, a model had to be established to understand how the company could mitigate its risk.

The initial launch of the credit card was followed by the introduction of the Gas Advantage MasterCard in selected regions in 2006, followed by a full national roll-out in 2008. This credit card allows cardholders to earn discounts on gas purchases at all Canadian Tire Petroleum locations. The Gas Advantage MasterCard is a key initiative supporting interrelated businesses within Canadian Tire Corporation. Also in 2008, there was a re-issue of the entire Options MasterCard base incorporating new PayPass technology.

After changes to the Bank Act in 2001, CTFS launched Canadian Tire Bank in 2003. New controls had to be established to ensure compliance with regulatory require-ments. Canadian Tire Bank had to ensure its documen-tation and reporting met the requirements of federal organizations (such as the Office of the Superintendent of Financial Institutions and the Financial Consumer Agency of Canada) and incorporate privacy legislation controls and anti–money laundering checks. In 2007 the Canadian Tire One and Only Account was launched. This product combines a customer's mortgage, chequing and savings accounts, loans, and credit card balances in one account.

Because of the Enron scandal and the increasing focus on ethics, organizational risk management has become even more critical within organizations. This became key as CTFS reviewed its operations under the new structure, which included Canadian Tire Bank. Risk had to be assessed across the organization. As a result, a team was created that was responsible for identifying, quantifying, and consolidating risk across the organization. This coordinated effort resulted in a disciplined approach to risk management. For example, when considering the credit risk function, policies and procedures were developed to ensure that the amount of credit risk-taking (that is, how much was loaned to a customer based on his or her creditworthiness or ability to repay) was within defined limits and subject to appropriate procedural controls. Such controls are critical for organizations to mitigate risk. To further manage their risk, in late 2007 Canadian Tire Bank began selling GICs through brokers as an alternative funding source to the securitization of credit card receivables, at reasonable and cost-effective interest rates, to fund operations.

This focus on risk management has resulted in an increasing level of complexity and rigour. Complex accounting and finance knowledge is required for employees to understand the increasing number of rules (e.g., SOX-like Canadian financial certification requirements) and how they are to be implemented, applied, and followed within the organization. The CEO and the CFO are now required to personally certify the accuracy of CTFS's financial statements, the design and effectiveness of disclosure controls and procedures, and the internal controls over financial reporting.

Sources: Dean McCann, Vice-President Finance, Canadian Tire Financial Services, interview, 13 April 2006; Gregory Craig, Vice-President Finance and Chief Financial Officer, Canadian Tire Bank, interview, 10 December 2008; and www.ctfs.com, 31 December 2008.

## Discussion Questions

1. What are some of the operational needs that face CTFS? How would this differ for smaller organizations?

2. Conduct some research on the Internet. What are some additional products and services that have been introduced by CTFS, through Canadian Tire Bank, since this textbook was published?

3. Visit www.ctfs.com/Products/CreditCards/Options MasterCard/. What are the loyalty benefits of using the Options® MasterCard®? What is the purpose of the Pay Pass feature? What other features of this credit card help with personal security?

# Video Cases

Several themes were introduced in this first chapter, including the importance of entrepreneurship to the success of the overall economy, the need for entrepreneurs to take risks (and the greater the risk, the higher the profit may be), and the dynamic business environment and the challenges it presents. Few organizations in today's society are more indicative of the new challenges than *Cirque du Soleil*.

First, Guy Laliberté took a huge risk by challenging the established circus tradition. The elaborate shows are expensive to start, and the talent must be the best in the world. But the risk paid off big time with sales of almost a billion dollars per year. *Cirque du Soleil* creates thousands of new jobs and contributes greatly to the communities it serves. It does this not only through the taxes it pays, but also through community outreach programs. Because of its entertainment value, *Cirque* contributes to both the standard of living (through the taxes it pays) and the quality of life (the fun it provides for citizens of all ages).

Like all organizations, *Cirque du Soleil* has many stakeholders. They include the owners, the employees, and the local community. The organization is especially focused on the stakeholder group called customers. It wants to put on the best show possible, and that means providing the best talent in the best locations. To reach as many people as possible, many of the shows go on the road. You can even watch some of the shows on TV.

The business environment presents many challenges for *Cirque du Soleil*, as it does for all businesses. The economic and legal environment of Canada greatly supports entrepreneurs like Laliberté.

The technological environment in Canada and the United States is also supportive of new business ventures. No circus in the past came close to the elaborate technological devices used by *Cirque du Soleil*. The stage for one of the *Cirque* productions in Las Vegas, for example, is a huge pool that delights the audience with its ability to change from a place where the actors can seem to walk on water to one where they can dive from many feet above it.

The social environment is also conducive to new businesses. The diversity of the Canadian population has contributed greatly to the ability of the circus to find diverse acts and to recruit such acts from around the world. The ability of the organization to adapt to many cultures is shown by its success in various cities throughout the world.

Of course, success is likely to breed much competition, and *Cirque* has its share. Even traditional circuses are tending to offer more exciting programs that reflect what *Cirque* has been doing for years. Competition is good for business, as it prompts all businesses to offer the best products possible.

One of the best things about this video is that it allows you to see part of *Cirque du Soleil* in action. If you have never seen the show, search it out—if only on TV. It is exciting and fun, and it shows that entrepreneurship is alive and well and providing wonderful new services. The result is profits for the owners and a better quality of life for us.

## Discussion Questions

1. What lessons can you take from Guy Laliberté about how to be a successful entrepreneur?

2. What are some of the challenges and opportunities you can identify for *Cirque du Soleil* in today's dynamic business environment?

3. How would you compare the excitement and fun of working for a new entrepreneurial venture like *Cirque du Soleil* with working for a large, traditional business? What are the risks? The rewards? The challenges?

# CHAPTER 2   Bank of Canada: Not Your Average Bank

The Bank of Canada contributes to the well-being of the Canadian economy through the implementation of monetary policy, its role in the Canadian financial system, and its management of Canada's bank notes. (Some of these topics will be further discussed in Chapters 3 and 4.) Located in Ottawa, the Bank of Canada is our country's central bank. It is not a commercial bank and it does not offer banking services to the public. Its principal role, as defined in the Bank of Canada Act, is "to promote the economic and financial welfare of Canada." The Bank was founded in 1934 as a privately owned corporation. In 1938, it became a Crown corporation belonging to the federal government.

The Currency Museum houses Canada's national currency collection. The museum provides a glimpse into the history and evolution of money. Until the 1930s, bank notes were printed by private banks, municipal and provincial governments, as well as the federal government. When the Bank of Canada was established, it was given the sole authority to issue bank notes in Canada and to preserve the value of money. As Canada's central bank, the Bank of Canada and other federal agencies contribute to the safety and soundness of the Canadian financial system. Currently, there is more than $40 billion worth of Canadian bank notes in circulation.

Bank of Canada employees analyze the world and Canadian financial markets. They then monitor the impact of financial developments on the real economy in which Canadians work and run businesses. Regional offices play an important role in analyzing economic and financial developments. Bank employees visit businesses and organizations in each region to gather information about local economic conditions. This information helps staff assess where things are going in the economy.

The Bank of Canada's main job is to direct monetary policy, which involves setting the interest rates that people pay when they borrow money. The Bank's objective is to influence interest rates so that the economy can remain healthy and create jobs. A healthy and stable economy helps families and businesses adapt to the changing conditions in the world economy.

Economists use the word *inflation* to describe the rate of price increases. While Canada has enjoyed relatively low and stable interest rates over the last 15 years, this has not always been the case. Inflation can sometimes get out of control. When inflation rates were in excess of 10 percent, this created uncertainty with consumers and investors. Those periods of high inflation were followed by economic recessions, which undermined the economy's ability to create long-lasting growth and jobs.

In 1991, the Bank of Canada and the federal government agreed to try to keep the rate of inflation within a specific target range. Since 1995, the target range has been between 1 and 3 percent. The Bank works to keep inflation within this range by targeting the 2 percent midpoint. This helps reduce the uncertainty that all consumers and businesses face when planning for the future.

Canada has had a flexible exchange rate for more than 30 years, determined by supply and demand conditions in the international currency markets. The Bank of Canada does not target any particular level for the exchange rate. The bank changes interest rates to ensure that domestic inflation stays low and stable.

A sound financial system is the backbone of a modern economy. Every day, Canada's major financial institutions exchange more than $150 billion in electronic and cheque payments among themselves. This exchange happens through two payment systems: the Large Value Transfer System and the Automated Clearing and Settlement System.

While the Bank of Canada oversees activities domestically, it also recognizes the importance of understanding and influencing global activities. It is active in many international organizations, such as the International Monetary Fund and the G-20. Since Canada is an open economy (i.e., we depend more on international trade and capital flows than many other countries), it is important to understand the global economic environment as well.

Sources: Bank of Canada, "Who We Are," 2006, http://www.bankofcanada.ca/en/video_corp/videos.html; and www.bankofcanada.ca, September 18, 2006.

## Discussion Questions

1. Why is the Bank of Canada called the banker's bank?

2. How does the Bank of Canada try to keep the future rate of inflation close to 2 percent?

3. How is too much or too little demand bad for the economy? What actions does the Bank of Canada take to correct for this?

4. What accounts for movements in the exchange rate? What can the Bank of Canada do to influence the exchange rate?

## CHAPTER 3    The Mouse That Doesn't Come with a Computer

Who has not heard of Mickey Mouse? M I C, K E Y, M O U S E! How would you say that in French or Chinese or Spanish? Would it have the same meaning, the same appeal? Those are the questions Disney faced when planning to take the Disneyland experience overseas. Would the "Happiest Place on Earth" be equally happy for people who hadn't been exposed since birth to Mickey Mouse, Donald Duck, and the other Disney characters?

Walt Disney Imagineering is the creative arm of the Walt Disney Company. The people in Imagineering come up with solutions to the questions posed above. The problem may be easier to solve than you imagine, because people all over the world have similar likes, fears, and imaginations. Just because they come from a different culture and speak a different language doesn't mean that they won't be equally enchanted by Cinderella, Snow White, and Mickey Mouse. On the other hand, there may be huge differences in the way people react. So, what can you do to minimize the potential for disharmony? One answer is to hire local people to help in every phase of the project. They know the culture. They know the language. And they know what people like and dislike—in each specific country or town or village.

Taking Disney to China would have many positive benefits for both countries. It would create jobs in China and bring new entertainment to the people there. A Chinese Disneyland would create a more favourable balance of trade for the United States and possibly lead the way to more trade with China. Chinese labour is less expensive than U.S. labour, so a Disney park could perhaps be built for less—if local architects, engineers, and set designers were used. Everything would have to be planned with a Chinese audience in mind.

The same would be true in other countries. For example, in Japan, people like to shop for gifts, so the gift shop might be bigger and have more clerks. In France, people may prefer to drink wine instead of Coke. Local laws and local tastes must be considered. In short, taking a business overseas is a real challenge. It means listening to what locals have to say and then adapting your offerings accordingly.

Many questions need to be answered. For example, would people in other countries be willing to spend the same amount of money to enter the parks? Are there alternative ways to charge for the experience? Which of the Disney characters would appeal the most to people from China? How would you find out?

### Discussion Questions

1. Working in another country can be a fun and challenging experience. If you had to choose one country to live in other than Canada, what would it be? What Canadian companies are located there?

2. What products have you bought lately that were made in a different country? What countries produced them?

Did you have any difficulty accepting the fact that the product came from there? Did you have any difficulty with the directions or the follow-up service? What does that tell you about global marketing and global business?

## CHAPTER 4    Creating a Buzz: Red Bull

In this chapter, you were introduced to the ways in which government activities can affect businesses. Let us consider how the creation of laws and regulations, one of the six government activities discussed, can create an opportunity for the sale of a product that some believe is dangerous to one's health.

Developed in Austria, Red Bull is an energy drink with high caffeine content. It is creating quite a buzz, literally. It is promoted to people who need an energy boost. Last year, people in 120 countries drank 2 billion cans of this trendy energy drink.

Health Canada (www.hc-sc.gc.ca) is the federal department responsible for helping Canadians maintain and improve their health, while respecting individual choices and circumstances. Health Canada created new legislation for health products, regulating everything from vitamins to herbal remedies. With this new legislation, Red Bull was approved as a health product, with many warnings. These warnings include the following: Red Bull is not recommended for children, for pregnant women or those who are breastfeeding, or for caffeine-sensitive persons. It is not to be mixed with alcohol and people should not consume more than 500 mL of it per day.

Some believe that Red Bull should not have been approved for sale in Canada as a health product. Too much consumption of Red Bull can be dehydrating. Despite allegations to the contrary, there is no evidence to date supporting the claim that Red Bull negatively affects people's hearts. Very simply, there is no long-term research on how the combination of ingredients in this product interacts with the body. Regardless, some countries—Norway, Denmark, and France—are so concerned that they have banned Red Bull. The governments in Sweden and Iceland have also voiced concerns.

In addition to other marketing activities, Red Bull sponsors extreme sporting events. The product can be purchased in a variety of locations across Canada, including bars and local variety stores. In fact, it is a number-one seller in 7-Eleven variety stores, which are easily accessible to children. The video shows how Red Bull representatives are promoting their product throughout Canada and encouraging participants to try it. From the footage shown, it does not appear that they are consistently communicating the warnings on the label, including that Red Bull should not be mixed with alcohol.

The company plans to spend $10 million on a Canadian marketing campaign over the next few months to further promote this product.

Source: "Raging Bull," *Marketplace*, February 6, 2005.

## Discussion Questions

1. What ingredients are found in Red Bull?
2. Why did Health Canada approve the sale of Red Bull even when other countries have banned the sale of this product?
3. Do you agree that people must take responsibility for their own health, including reading labels and following instructions? In your opinion, should Health Canada be doing more? Explain.
4. Have you tasted Red Bull? If so, did you like it? If not, are you curious to try it?

# CHAPTER 5  If It Isn't Ethical, It Isn't Right

Cancer affects the lives of millions of people each year. While significant progress has been made toward fighting the disease, finding a cure is considered by many to be the "holy grail" of medicine. For most of the twentieth century, cancer-fighting drugs were like Second World War bombers. They'd drop thousands of bombs, hoping that a few would get lucky and hit the target. Since the drugs couldn't tell the difference between a cancer cell and a healthy cell, they killed them both. But new generations of drugs are more precise and target individual disease cells, leaving healthy cells unharmed.

Unfortunately, developing effective new treatments for cancer is a lengthy and costly process. Every step in the process of developing a new drug calls for ethical decision making. The temptation may be to rush the process and cut corners to minimize costs and maximize profits. Does the drug violate a patent that already exists? How far should a company go in testing the effectiveness and the side effects of the new product? Should the drug be tested on animals? Should it be tested on humans? How much should a company charge for the drug? What should the company say in its promotions?

Jennie Mather founded a company called Raven Biotechnologies to develop solutions to the most serious cancer illnesses. She understood from the beginning that ethical decisions are based on ethical management. She used the latest monoclonal technology because it enabled her company to target and attack a single disease cell such as a cancer cell. This is a much safer and ethical way of solving the problem because it dramatically reduces the serious side effects caused by "shotgun" treatments. Because of these precautions, such drugs tend to make it through the government screening process faster and easier.

Mather hires employees who have the same ethical approach to business and the same kind of scientific approach that she has. She knows that management sets the ethical parameters, but that employees must maintain those standards. Business people today are conscious of the fact that the public is very sensitive to ethical practices because of companies, such as Enron, that violated ethical principles. The public is particularly sensitive to issues surrounding pharmaceutical companies. One popular movie focused on the ethics of product testing. Should drugs be tested on humans? If so, how should people taking the test drugs be treated? Is it right to give some people the test medicine and others a placebo (a fake medicine)?

Another fundamental issue is price. It costs a lot of money to develop a new drug, and companies cannot come up with new solutions to illnesses without recouping those huge costs. On the other hand, people without health insurance and people in developing countries simply cannot afford high prices for drugs. Who should bear the cost of providing life-saving drugs to those people?

It's comforting to know that people like Mather are willing to take the entrepreneurial risks demanded by a pioneering company such as Raven Biotechnologies. It is even more comforting to know that Mather and her

employees take an ethical approach to everything they do. Everyone looks forward to the day when there are effective drugs for pancreatic cancer, colorectal cancer, and other serious illnesses. We look to science to solve those problems, and we look to ethical managers to apply the science in the right way.

### Discussion Questions

1. What ethical issues concern you most about the development and sale of pharmaceutical drugs? Does Raven Biotechnologies address all of your concerns?

2. One of the major issues involving pharmaceutical drugs is their high cost. Do you understand why drug companies have to charge such high prices? Should

they charge lower prices in countries where the people cannot afford expensive drugs?

3. Is the need for high ethical standards more or less important in the pharmaceutical industry? Why? What could be done to assure the public that the highest standards are being used?

## CHAPTER 6   SONIC Is Booming

Entrepreneurship is the path to success throughout the world. More millionaires come from the ranks of entrepreneurs than from any other place. Because the work is so hard, however, fewer people than you would imagine are willing to take the plunge.

One major decision an entrepreneur must make is what form of business to use: sole proprietorship, partnership, corporation, franchise? SONIC is a large chain of fast-food restaurants with more than 3,000 drive-in locations. It began as a sole proprietorship, evolved into a partnership, later added many franchises, and eventually became a publicly traded corporation. This is not an unusual progression for a business, but SONIC did it relatively quickly and effectively.

Troy Smith started the first SONIC in 1954. It was a sole proprietorship that took the form of a drive-in restaurant, much like other drive-ins of that era. Smith brought in a partner in 1956, and the business began to grow. The partner shared profits and liability with Smith. When his partner died, Smith found many other people who were interested in becoming franchisees. The company grew even faster then.

Cody Barnett's father owned seven SONIC franchises. Barnett eventually took over those franchises and added 15 more. There is much to learn about buying and

running a number of franchises, and Barnett schooled himself in the managerial techniques and strategies that he would need. Like most franchisors, SONIC was a big help in that regard.

Clearly, understanding the various forms of business is key to both getting started in business and then growing the business later. If you plan to franchise the business, it is critical to find franchisees such as the Barnetts who understand that the business is their own and also understand the value of having the foundation of a well-known brand name and a ready customer base.

One thing that franchisees learn quickly is that running your own business takes a lot of work. At first, you have to be there whenever the business is open. That means long, long hours at work—and away from the family. That is true of many businesses, and balanced living is one of the most important skills a business owner must learn.

You don't have to go very far in most towns to see the results of franchising. On every corner, there is a fast-food restaurant of some franchise that is serving the local population and travellers. Many are obviously very successful. SONIC is one of them. But, as you can see in this video, that success does not come easily. It takes a lot of time and hard work.

### Discussion Questions

1. SONIC started as a sole proprietorship and gradually evolved to a partnership, then to a corporation, and finally to a franchisor. Do you think that SONIC would have grown as large as it is today if it had remained a sole proprietorship? Why or why not?

2. What were the advantages and disadvantages to SONIC of each form of business ownership?

3. There have been many drive-in and fast-food restaurants over time. In your opinion, what makes SONIC and other major franchises more successful than the others?

## CHAPTER 7 The Frozen Empire

In this chapter, you learned that Canada's 2.5 million self-employed people represent approximately 15 percent of all employed workers in the Canadian economy.

Entrepreneurs employ 49 percent of the private workforce, and they contribute more than 40 percent to the Gross Domestic Product.

Many people, however, are reluctant to start their own businesses because there is too much risk and uncertainty. One person who did assume this risk is Morrie Baker. Like all entrepreneurs, Baker saw a marketing opportunity—in his case, opening the first Ben & Jerry's ice cream shop in Canada. After graduating from university, and after months of perseverance, he convinced Ben Cohen and Jerry Greenfield, the founders of Ben & Jerry's, to give him this opportunity. Seventeen years later, Baker had three scoop shops in Montreal.

Prior to 2000, ice cream supply problems meant that no more Canadian shops could be opened. But the 2000 sale of Ben & Jerry's to Unilever, a huge multinational organization with a distribution network across Canada, meant that this could change. Now, Baker is betting that he can scoop up something much bigger. He and his partner, Gary Lackstein, a real-estate developer, have the rights to build 100 Ben & Jerry's shops across Canada over the next ten years.

This will be the biggest expansion in company history, as Baker and Lackstein try to turn a successful American brand into a Canadian chain. With this venture, they are investing more than $1 million of their own money. They are assuming a huge amount of risk by borrowing money and investing in cities where they do not live.

There are many reasons to start a small business; that is, to become an entrepreneur. They include the freedom to do your own thing and see it to completion, to follow your passion, and, of course, to make a lot of money. Baker's mantra is to shoot for the sun and maybe land on the moon. His goal is to have his business become the number one ice cream brand in Canada. For the next decade, he knows what he will be doing: summers spent scooping and winters spent searching for real estate.

Today, Baker owns 20 shops. "It's my destiny," he says of his quest for a frozen empire. "I was put on the planet earth to do this project."

### Discussion Questions

1. Morrie Baker started Canadian franchises of American-based Ben & Jerry's. Do you think that he works as hard as entrepreneurs who start their own business without the benefit of a well-known brand name?

2. Does this story encourage you to be an entrepreneur someday? Where might you begin? Whom might you seek out for help?

3. What do you see as the advantages and disadvantages of working for others rather than starting your own business?

## CHAPTER 8 How Bad Is Your Boss?

No matter where you work, no matter how important you think you are, you can't escape the boss. Some are demanding, some are out of touch, and they are creating stress in the workplace.

Shaun Belding, author of *Winning with Bosses from Hell*, shares the seven deadly sins of bosses. You will hear from former employees examples of bad boss behaviour that contributed to a negative work environment. In many instances, employees quit their jobs as a result of poor management styles.

Business people who have risen through the ranks share some of their insights based on years of experience. In one instance, you will hear how treating workers well can boost the bottom line: good management is important for the health of an organization and the individual, while poor management makes organizations and people unhealthy. One former executive believes that employees are asking for reality, clarity, and opportunity in the workplace, and that this is what executives need to deliver.

In this chapter, you read about changes occurring in the areas of management and leadership. Most managers today are flexible and open to new ideas. They tend to give their workers more responsibility and authority and act more like leaders than bosses who tell their workers what to do. Robert Lemieux is a young executive at the Delta Chelsea in Toronto, Canada's biggest hotel. He is the director of sales, with a staff of 50. In order to become president or vice-president, he knows that he has to become a great boss. To help him avoid becoming a bad boss, he agrees to work with Lindsay Sukornyk, founder of North Star Coaches, an executive coaching firm. As part of the process, she helps identify those things he does well as a boss and those things he needs to do better. The result is that in addition to his positive traits, Lemieux learns that there is a perception that he over-promises and under-delivers with his employees as he becomes too involved in projects. In a discussion with his employees, he shares this feedback and solicits their advice on how he can change his approach in order to become a better supervisor. Such open communica- tion is reflective of his strong leadership and the care that he demonstrates for his employees.

When you consider your answers to the seven ques- tions posed in the video, it is important to recognize that not everyone can be perfect all of the time. However, if you said yes to between three and six questions, you have (or have had) a bad boss. If you are in this situation now, you may need to take action to change the situa- tion, but be careful if you confront your boss. After all, you are the subordinate and such a discussion would require a high degree of tact.

If you have limited work experience, this video is still of value to you. One day you likely will hold a manage- ment position, and hopefully you will remember some of these points as you move up the corporate ladder.

## Discussion Questions

1. What are the seven deadly sins of bosses?
2. Do you believe that people can be coached to be bet- ter managers? Explain.
3. What leadership style should Robert Lemieux use to be considered more effective by his staff?
4. What can workers do to protect themselves from a bad boss?

## CHAPTER 9   One Smooth Stone

David slew Goliath with a single smooth stone, and thus was born the name of the company One Smooth Stone (OSS). It's an unusual name for an unusually interesting company. OSS is in the business of providing materials for big corporate events: sales meetings, client meet- ings, and product presentations. Most people in the industry have attended many such meetings, so keeping them entertained is a major challenge. And that's where OSS comes in: It uses project teams to come up with original and captivating presentations for its customers.

You read about the history of organizational design in this chapter. You learned, for example, about Fayol and his principles of organization. The first principle is unity of command (every worker is to report to one, and only one, boss). Other principles include order, equity, and esprit de corps. This video shows that OSS understands the importance of esprit de corps. It is a fun and interesting place to work, and employee turn- over is very low. The company does not follow many of Weber's principles dealing with written rules and con- sistent procedures. Quite the contrary: OSS is structured to be flexible and responsive to its clients. There are no set rules, and the company is certainly not consistent with its projects. Everything is custom-made to the needs of each client.

OSS uses a flat organization structure. There are a few project managers, who have workers under them, but they don't look over the employees' shoulders telling them what to do or how to do it. That means there is decentralized authority. Whereas many companies are structured by department—design, engineering, market- ing, finance, accounting, and so forth—OSS is structured using project teams. Each team is structured to meet the needs of an individual client. For example, the company hires people with specific skills as they are needed. The term for this is outsourcing, and OSS outsources many of its tasks to freelance professionals. Together, these pro- fessionals work as self-managed teams. The teams focus on client needs. There are some staff workers to help with personnel, legal, and other such services.

The company is not keen on making strategic plans because its environment changes so rapidly that such plans are obsolete as soon as they are made. Therefore, the company engages in "strategic improvising." Although OSS sounds less structured and more informal than most companies, it still focuses on total quality and practises continuous improvement.

In addition, the company is particularly concerned about its corporate culture. It has three values: smart, fast, and kind. It works smart, responds quickly, and is always kind to others, including its own workers. Because of its culture and responsiveness, the company has been able to capture big accounts such as Motorola, Sun Microsystems, and International Truck and Engine.

The long-run success of the firm, however, is based on its project management teams. They carefully listen to what clients are trying to accomplish and then come up with solutions to their problems. You can see their creativity in this video. Clearly, OSS has been able to impress the Goliaths of big business with its presentations.

## Discussion Questions

1. What have you learned from this video about the use of teams as an organizational tool versus the traditional line or line-and-staff forms of organization?

2. Does working at OSS look like more or less fun than working for a company with a more traditional approach to organizational structure and operations? Why?

3. From what you saw in the video, what do you think the core competencies of the company might be?

## CHAPTER 10    Reality on Request: Digital Domain

As chairman and CEO of Digital Domain, Scott Ross runs one of the largest digital production studios in the world. His studio won an Academy Award for simulating the sinking of the *Titanic* in the movie of the same name. It also created the digital waves that wiped out the horsemen in *The Lord of the Rings*.

Operations management is unique at Digital Domain because no two projects are ever the same. One day the company may be making a digital cow (*O Brother, Where Art Thou?*), on another a digital spaceship (*Apollo 13*), and on still another digital waves (*Titanic*). Digital Domain is both a production and a service provider. How so? In addition to producing digital scenes for movies, the company advises movie producers as to what is possible to accomplish digitally. Still, certain activities, such as facility location and facility layout, are common to both service organizations and production firms.

Since many movies are made in Los Angeles, it's important for Digital Domain to be close to the city. Actors are often chosen from that area, as are workers and specialists at Digital. The company's most important resource, however, is its workers. Thus, facilities layout is designed to make workers' jobs easier yet efficient. For example, there's a combination conference room and cafeteria. Given the company's passion for *quality*, everything is designed to be clean and logical. Facility layout assists workers in developing the highest-quality product possible given time and money constraints.

Materials requirement planning (MRP) is a computer-based operations management system that uses sales forecasts to make needed parts and materials available at the right time and place. Since Digital's primary resource is people, the company lists 54 key disciplines in its database, so it's easy to find the right person for the right job. For example, a project may come up on Wednesday that demands resources be available the next Monday. People have to be contacted and hired just in time to keep the project on time and within budget.

The company does much of its purchasing on the Internet. It also uses *flexible manufacturing*. To keep costs down, Digital also uses *lean manufacturing*, the production of goods using less of everything: less human effort, less manufacturing space, less investment in tools, and less engineering time for a given project. To keep costs down, the company does a lot of previsualizing—simulating projects to determine the best way to proceed.

Of course, *mass customization* is basically what Digital Domain is all about: creating new and different scenes that cannot be duplicated. However, once the company learns to create artificial waves or some other image, it is easier to duplicate a similar image next time. Since film is very expensive, many ideas are created using pen and pencil first. From such "primitive" tools, the company goes on to use *computer-aided design*.

Making movies is expensive. Everything needs to be done as planned. Scott Ross knows it's show *business*, and that making a profit is vital. For this reason, getting things done right and on time is the hallmark at Digital Domain.

## Discussion Questions

1. Do you have an appreciation for operations management now that you've seen how exciting such a job can be at a company like Digital Domain?

2. Mass customization is critical in the production of movies and special effects. As a consumer, what benefits do you see in being able to buy custom-made shoes, clothes, automobiles, and more?

3. What lessons did you learn from this video that you could apply at any job you might get?

4. This video points out that certain workers are very focused on quality, and that there comes a time when you have to stop improving things because time has a cost. Have you had to make a trade-off between perfection and "good enough"? What were the consequences?

## CHAPTER 11    Motivation Is a Hot Topic

We all have witnessed retail employees who seem indifferent at best to customer satisfaction. They are as likely to be talking to one another as to customers—sometimes on the phone. It doesn't take a retailing expert to know that such employees do not contribute to the success of the firm. So, how do firms get retail employees to be passionate about their work? To answer that question, consider Hot Topic Incorporated.

Hot Topic stores sell clothing and accessories that appeal to the alternative culture. Emphasis is on the latest music trends and the fashions that accompany them. Employees, therefore, need to be familiar with the newest bands and the latest music. That means going to concerts and observing what people wear and becoming very familiar with the cultural trends within those groups.

Torrid is another store run by the same company. It caters to an entirely different audience: more mature women who are looking for fashionable plus sizes. Hot Topic Incorporated runs both stores. The CEO of the company is Betsy McLaughlin. She has learned how to motivate the employees at both stores using well-established managerial techniques outlined in this chapter.

There is much emphasis in this text on employee empowerment. At Hot Topic, that means that employees are paid to attend music concerts where they not only have a good time, but also learn more about the culture of the people they will be serving. Since promotions come from within, that culture carries over into headquarters. There are none of the usual offices that designate hierarchy. Instead, all employees are encouraged to make decisions on their own, within reason, and to be responsive to customer needs. As you read in this chapter, Herzberg says that employees have certain needs that are not motivating but result in dissatisfaction (and possible poor performance) if not present. They include salary and other benefits. Thus, the salary and benefits at both stores have to be competitive.

Employees feel good about their work when they are empowered to do what it takes to please customers. Empowerment often demands some in-house training to teach employees the skills they need to be responsive to customer demands. All of this falls under the concepts of Theory Y, which states that people are willing to work hard if given the freedom and opportunity to do so. Such freedom is what Hot Topic Incorporated is all about.

## Discussion Questions

1. What motivators identified by Herzberg are used at Hot Topic?

2. How do you think Hot Topic employees would react if the company gave them each a small raise, but stopped paying them to attend music concerts? Would they be more or less motivated to please customers? Why?

3. How well would a Theory X manager perform at Hot Topic? Why?

# CHAPTER 12   Surf's Up at Patagonia!

Human resource management (HRM) can be one of the most exciting and enjoyable parts of a firm, depending on management commitment to workers' needs. No company reflects this commitment better than Patagonia. Patagonia's HRM doesn't have to worry about where it's going to get its next worker, as people are lined up to get a job with the company. Why? Because this is a firm with passion—passion for making the best products possible, passion for making its employees happy, and passion about the environment.

Patagonia believes that a great business begins with great products. Who could argue with that? Great products meet the needs of customers. In this case, that means that they will be long-lasting and are backed by a full guarantee. But great products do more than satisfy consumers; they also have a minimal impact on the environment.

Workers at Patagonia are pleased that the company's commitment to the environment is not just a slogan. Ten percent of its pre-tax profit goes to environmental groups of all kinds. Employees are encouraged to get to know these groups and to participate in selecting the groups that receive the company's donations. If an environmental group is not familiar with best business practices, such as writing a business plan, Patagonia will give it that training.

Given that thousands of people are willing to work for Patagonia, how does the HRM department choose which ones to hire? They are looking for people who are as passionate as they are. What kind of passion do they require? Any kind: a passion for cooking, for cleaning, for life. When employees have passion, they will stick with an employer. That's why the turnover rate at Patagonia is a low 4 percent per year. Some businesses have a turnover rate approaching 100 percent per year. These businesses have to train and retrain their employees constantly. Patagonia can put all of that effort into satisfying the needs of employees who want to stay.

What does the company do for its employees that makes it stand out from other companies? For one thing, Patagonia knows that parents often feel uncomfortable leaving their children with child-care centres. Patagonia provides onsite daycare—and they did so long before other companies even dreamed about offering such a benefit. Children thus become part of the company's atmosphere. There are children everywhere, and the parents feel comfortable having them nearby.

All employees experience days when the sun is shining and nature is calling. You simply can't get your work done because you are dreaming about fishing or golfing or mountain climbing or whatever. How would you like it if your manager said, "Go ahead, take off. Have fun!" How can a company do that? One way is to have a flexible work schedule. With such a schedule, workers can take off early or come in late when the "surf's up"—that is, when recreation calls. Patagonia's top managers have a passion for sports and sports equipment—the kind that Patagonia sells. Since they expect their employees to have the same passion, that means letting them go when they need to go. That employee passion is communicated to customers, who buy more. It's a win–win deal for the company. Employees are happy with the freedom they have, and the company is happy with the productivity that such freedom creates.

What other company offers surfing lessons to its employees? Few companies let their employees leave when the surf's up, but many other companies offer employees flexible work schedules and other incentives that allow them to balance their work and personal lives. These companies also have workers who are passionate about the company and their work. Who organizes all of these activities for workers? HRM!

## Discussion Questions

1. Patagonia stresses the importance of hiring employees with passion—a passion for anything, not just sports. Why does it place such importance on passion? Why would it think that someone with a passion for something unrelated to sports (i.e., cooking) might be an excellent employee?

2. What effect do Patagonia's practices of providing child care and donating to environmental groups have on employee productivity and retention? Why?

3. Can you see the potential for possible abuses of a flextime program? What could a company do to prevent such abuses before they occur?

# CHAPTER 13    Young Blood

The labour movement could use a hotshot marketing department, as it is not what it used to be. At a labour convention in Ottawa, one focus is on the importance of young workers to the labour movement. In short, labour needs a transfusion of young blood. In the next 10 to 15 years, a huge percentage of the workforce will be retiring, so the unions are trying to encourage the active participation of young people so that they will be experienced when they become involved in labour–management negotiations.

Based on the way in which businesses are operating today, the video's participants believe that union representation will benefit workers. The challenge is how to accomplish this, as the workforce is growing faster than unions are organizing.

The labour movement has made great strides in the areas of pensions and collective bargaining for benefits. Today, there is a focus on safety in the workplace, and it is suggested in the video that many young people organize because they want dignity in the workplace. Do you agree?

## Discussion Questions

1. In what sectors do young people work? Based on your experience or on what you have heard from friends, have attempts been made to unionize some of these sectors?

2. How should unions approach young people if they want to earn their support? What are some concerns that young people have about their work environment?

3. Are you supportive of the union movement? How do you think a union might benefit you, if at all? Explain.

# CHAPTER 14    MTV Goes Everywhere

Marketing begins and ends with the customer. Nowhere is that more true than at MTV. The company serves many market segments, but two of the most important are the high school audience and the post-secondary audience. These two groups are very dynamic; they adopt new ideas and new products faster than movie stars change spouses. That's why MTV has people on campuses listening to and responding to the latest trends, wants, and needs. One result is Urge, an online music subscription service for pre-college students. Another online subscription service, University, does many of the same things as Urge, but targets university students. The competition is stiff, so MTV has to offer the right kinds of music and be ready to react to new trends. The four Ps of marketing—product, place, promotion, and price—all come into play.

The product is not fixed. Students can develop their own products and work with MTV to make them available to others. The best place to be is everywhere. Today, that means online, but it also includes offering a cable channel, mtvU.com, and various events. The most effective promotions include word-of-mouth marketing, or viral marketing as it's known today. The price has to be competitive, and that's a moving target. Right now, you can buy tracks for 99 cents each, buy an album, or subscribe to a service that provides whatever you want.

Music marketers must understand consumer behaviour better than most marketers because the market is so specialized. That means understanding the cultures of high school listeners, the cultures of post-secondary listeners, and the cultures that exist in different parts of the country and in different areas within a city. Sometimes it is easier to let each group make its own videos and music and then help them spread that new material to different audiences. That's exactly what MTV does. Students like to explore, and MTV provides the means to do that.

This chapter emphasizes relationship building. MTV does everything it can to establish and maintain a close relationship not only with its customers but also with its performers. There are many stakeholders in the music business, and MTV must listen and respond to all of them. That includes performers, young listeners, post-secondary customers, parents, and people throughout the world.

Like the authors of this text, the people at MTV conduct periodic focus groups to determine how well they are serving their customers. When a new idea like the Digital Incubator comes up, there is a need to work with various groups to get the service right. When you give

$25,000 to a group to create something new, you want the product to be one that people will enjoy. That means listening, responding, and listening again.

MTV provides composition courses to teach young people how to create music. By establishing relationships with the music producers of tomorrow, MTV assures itself of being relevant for years to come. When exploring the dynamic world of marketing, no company provides a better example of relationship marketing than MTV. Many students dream of working in the music industry when they graduate. They may find, however, that there are equally interesting marketing jobs in other industries. That includes sports marketing and event marketing of all kinds.

## Discussion Questions

1. There are many ways that MTV tries to reach the post-secondary audience. What are some ways in which members of your class have interacted with the company?

2. Does the move to selling music digitally rather than as a physical product represent a change that will affect other industries? What trends do you see on campus that affect the music industry, and other industries as well?

3. On a scale of 1 to 10, how would you rate the efforts that MTV has made to reach you and your friends? What mistakes are they making, if any? Are there other stakeholders whose needs are not being met?

# CHAPTER 15    Promotion Gets a Big Push

Students today are witnessing a major revolution in promotion. They have seen radio change from standard broadcasting to commercial-free satellite radio. They have watched families blank out TV commercials with TiVo and other digital video recording devices. Students spend less time reading newspapers and magazines and more time talking on the phone, playing video games, and listening to their iPods. More entertainment options are available today and there are more distractions from traditional promotional tools.

Today's students also have a wonderful opportunity to reinvent promotion, changing it from a one-way stream of sales pitches to an interactive dialogue among promoters and consumers. Traditional promotional tools—selling, advertising, public relations, and sales promotion—have always provided fun and interesting careers. The challenge today is to create promotions for the new realities of the marketplace. That means, for one thing, creating advertising and other promotions on the Internet. One of the cutting-edge advertising agencies in this regard is Night Agency, which has become an integral part of the marketing process for the firms it serves. It does everything from helping in the design of the product to working with the company to develop a winning brand name, effective packaging, and fast distribution.

A company like Night Agency has to promote itself to other businesses. Like most firms, Night Agency relies heavily on word of mouth to spread its name. Publicity in the form of articles written about the company is another powerful promotional tool. Night Agency teaches other firms how to use public relations and publicity to educate the public about the good things the firms do and to give the firm's side of the story during controversies. Think of the public relations challenge that oil companies have had over high gas prices at the pump.

Often, promotional efforts begin inside a company. Salespeople, clerks, and other customer-contact people (and that means almost everyone in the firm, because all workers contact other people) often don't understand everything they need to know about the products they make and sell. That means using internal promotions to keep employees informed. That may take the form of videos, brochures, meetings, charts, and more. Full-function advertising agencies get involved in such internal promotions as well as the more traditional external promotions that you are more used to seeing.

One of the more innovative products from Night Agency is interactive web games and demonstrations. Such promotions get potential customers more deeply involved in promotions than they have been in the past. However, such promotions need to be measured like any other promotional tool to ensure that they are seen, remembered, and followed. One of the more memorable of Night Agency's efforts was the Darfur Digital Activist Contest, which was designed to increase awareness of the desperate need for aid among the people in Darfur, Sudan. It is exciting and rewarding to use promotional tools to make a difference in the world, and doing what you can to end world hunger, poverty, disease, and war is part of that challenge.

## Discussion Questions

1. What kinds of promotions have led you to buy the items you have purchased recently? These items include the school you attend (what prompted you to go there?), the clothes you wear, the music you listen to, the restaurants you go to, and so on.

2. What differences, if any, did you notice between what Night Agency does and what you are used to seeing in promotions?

3. What has been your reaction thus far to Internet promotions? Do you pay any attention to them? Are they getting better? If so, in what way?

# CHAPTER 16    When the Goal Line Meets the Bottom Line

There are a lot of statistics to gather in any sport. Football is no exception. There are those that the average fan follows most closely, such as win-loss records and the number of passes completed given the number of tries. For the Chicago Rush of the Arena Football League, the regular-season statistics were not so wonderful in 2006. The team won only seven games and lost nine. Nonetheless, that record was good enough to win them a wildcard spot in the playoffs. Much to their credit, the team went on to win the Foster Trophy.

There are other important statistics for a football team to follow. You can't keep playing unless you make enough money to pay the players and keep the games going. Therefore, like all companies, the Chicago Rush has to keep careful accounting records. At the top of the income statement, revenues are a key. Winning a championship should improve that number and, after all costs and expenses are deducted, that bigger number should carry right down to the bottom line—profit after taxes.

A new team in a relatively new sport can't expect the bottom line to be huge. Investing in a team can be a major commitment. So the bottom-line score is often as important as the scores on the field. And the person keeping those scores is a major player. That person at the Chicago Rush is Maggie Wirth. She goes through the same six-step accounting process outlined in this chapter.

Accounting can be an interesting and challenging occupation when you consider how important it is to the team and all of its owners, players, and fans. When it comes time to be paid, the players are interested in whether the cash flow is sufficient. Costs and expenses have to be kept in line—and that includes player salaries. What seem like mere data to the average person turn out to be more important in the long run than wins and losses and championships won. Without the money, the game is over.

With increased revenue comes the opportunity to increase marketing. There are many competing sports in Chicago, and many teams have been around for years. To attract fans, the Rush must consistently provide exciting games and fun entertainment during those games. As in any sports program, the team is looking for revenue from all sorts of sources: parking, food concessions, team merchandise, and more. Growth often is accompanied by more expenses, including higher-cost players. Going international adds its own expenses, for airline fees, hotels, and related items.

Keeping track of revenues, expenses, and other details may seem a rather remote part of team planning, but, as you can see from this case, such details are at the heart of the enterprise. Just as the offence and the defence need to have their plans and their appraisals over time, the fiscal health (profit and loss) of the team must be measured as well. And, just as there is a football team, there is a financial team. Keeping score is more than keeping track of first downs and touchdowns. In the background are people keeping score of how many fans are attending games versus last year, how many hot dogs and drinks were sold, and how much it cost to clean the uniforms and the stadium. Boring statistics? Hardly. They determine whether the team can stay in business. Many people rely on the results. The same is true in all businesses. The managers, employees, investors, and others are all following the accounting scores as closely as whatever scorekeeping the company does (usually sales or profit).

## Discussion Questions

1. Does accounting seem more interesting and important when analyzed in the context of a major sport?

2. Player salaries are a major expense to a sports team. What role might accounting play in helping managers and coaches talk to the players about salaries?

Does the fact that arena football is a relatively new sport have anything to do with such negotiations?

3. Do different groups, such as managers and stockholders and players and fans, want different figures compiled by the accounting department? What are those differences?

# CHAPTER 17    It's My Money

Entrepreneurs tend to be an independent bunch of people, but few are as independently minded as Todd McFarlane. He started out working for others as a cartoonist and eventually started his own firm. Now he focuses more on making toys; that is, collectibles of sports personalities, musicians, movie heroes, and the like. You can see in the video that McFarlane takes a rather casual approach to business. That doesn't mean, however, that he is not constantly aware of his need for financing. Nor does it mean that he doesn't know everything he needs to know about financing options.

Of course, the number-one financing option is to put up your own money. The advantage of doing that is that no one can tell you what to do. And that means a lot to McFarlane. But usually your own money won't pay for everything that you need. In that case, you have to go to the banks and other sources to get funding. It helps to have a financial expert on board to determine what funds are needed, to budget those funds, and to keep track of spending. Steve Peterson is that guy for McFarlane. Nonetheless, McFarlane has trained himself to be able to read reports and keep track of everything that's going on in the finance area. All entrepreneurs could learn from his example.

McFarlane knows that it is easy to spend too much money on something—and to lose a lot of money in the bargain. That means being wise in both long-term and short-term financing. Usually, McFarlane stays away from investors, but that isn't possible when funding a major project such as a movie. Furthermore, when you get into ownership financing, you also lose some control over the project. Normally, McFarlane doesn't like to lose such control, but in some cases, such as making an animated movie, it's necessary.

One way to keep loan costs down is to be a good customer of the bank. If you repay your loans in time, you can get lower interest rates. But McFarlane also knows the benefit of having a budget and sticking to it. That's as true in your personal finances as it is in business. If you make $25,000, you need to spend less than $25,000. And if you make $1 million, you have to spend less than $1 million. It's the same principle.

Sometimes people spend money for a passion. In McFarlane's case, that means baseball. He once paid several million dollars for a home-run ball hit by one of the home-run leaders. The problem was that that player didn't remain the leader very long, and the ball was not worth nearly as much money. So? The publicity that McFarlane received for buying the ball—and losing millions—made up for the loss. It earned him licensing agreements with many ball clubs, and the right to make the images he sells. He expects to make millions from the investment in the long run.

So, what do you do with your money when you have millions more than you need? For McFarlane, it means giving money to the ALS Association, which fights Lou Gehrig's disease. Again, the publicity that McFarlane receives from investing in home-run balls attracts more donors to the cause.

So, what can we learn from this video? Every entrepreneur needs to understand finance to be successful in the long run. You can be as casual as you want about business, but when it comes to finance, you had better know what you're doing. And the money you make is yours to spend. You can have a good time buying what you want, but you can also make a difference in the world by helping a favourite cause to raise money.

## Discussion Questions

1. Why do you suppose a free thinker like McFarlane tries to avoid getting other investors involved in his business? What is the advantage, in this instance, of debt financing?

2. What is the advantage of having a line of credit at the bank? What can a business do to keep loan charges at a minimum?

3. Do business people have a special obligation to give some of their money to charity? What famous business people have been in the news because of their giving? Should others follow their example?

# CHAPTER 18   Would You Like Banking with That Insurance?

It's not unusual to hear employees at a fast-food restaurant ask, "Would you like fries with that?" But you don't expect your banker to ask, "Would you like insurance while we are taking care of your banking needs?" Nonetheless, that's exactly what is happening at the major banks in Canada. This chapter is all about money and banking, and the latest trends in banking. One of those trends is to combine banking with insurance, as you will see in this video.

Recent changes in legislation have allowed banks to start selling insurance, either directly or through an insurance company they own (the Toronto Dominion bank owns Meloche, Monnex). In the United States, an example of these combined services is State Farm Insurance. State Farm also operates a virtual bank; that is, an online bank. At State Farm Bank, you can get regular banking services such as chequing accounts, loans, short term investments, and more.

So, how does State Farm offer such services? State Farm Insurance agents will handle any of your banking needs. But, like most online banks, you can do most of your banking online via the Internet. Customer service is available 24 hours a day. Any remaining questions can be directed to a State Farm agent.

This chapter talked about banks. State Farm has its deposits, insured much like we have deposits insured in Canada, through the Canadian Deposit Insurance Corporation. State Farm, however, does not have strategic partnerships with car dealerships or other firms like General Motors Acceptance Corporation does.

Because it is in the health and banking business, State Farm offers products such as health insurance plans that are low cost and high deductible. Although State Farm's insurance and banking operations have been integrated, that integration was not as easy as might be imagined. Two different corporate cultures had to be merged, but that merger has gone relatively smoothly. Now, when a customer suffers a major loss because of a flood, hurricane, or something similar, the bank can easily respond and adjust insurance payments and house payments accordingly.

Like all corporations, State Farm has ethical issues to confront. For example, agents ensure that customers understand that they can buy insurance and not get involved in banking, and vice versa. The whole idea is to listen to customers to determine their wants and needs. If they want to buy a new car, financing can be made available—and insurance, too. Because of their good products and good service, State Farm mostly relies on word of mouth to promote its products. Of course, there are highly trained salespeople to help customers as well.

## Discussion Questions

1. What advantages and disadvantages do you see with doing both insurance and banking with the same company?

2. Are you as comfortable doing banking online as with a clerk in a brick-and-mortar bank? Would it help to be able to work with your insurance agent instead of a banking clerk?

3. What kind of services do you get from a brick-and-mortar bank (such as ATMs) that you might not get as easily from an online bank?

# Endnotes

## Chapter 1

1. Luisa Kroll, Matthew Miller, and Tatiana Serafin, "The World's Billionaires," Forbes.com, 11 March 2009, http://www.forbes.com/2009/03/11/worlds-richest-people-billionaires-2009-billionaires_land.html.
2. "#1 William Gates III," Forbes.com, 11 March 2009, http://www.forbes.com/lists/2009/10/billionaires-2009-richest-people_William-Gates-III_BH69.html.
3. "Key Small Business Statistics," Industry Canada, July 2008, http://www.ic.gc.ca/epic/site/sbrp-rppe.nsf/vwapj/KSBS_July2008_Eng.pdf/$FILE/KSBS_July2008_Eng.pdf.
4. Small Business Quarterly, "Business Insolvencies," Industry Canada, May 2008, http://www.ic.gc.ca/epic/site/sbrp-rppe.nsf/vwapj/SBQ_May2008_Eng.pdf/$FILE/SBQ_May2008_Eng.pdf.
5. Pete Engardio, "The Future of Outsourcing," BusinessWeek, 30 January 2006, 50–58.
6. John R. Baldwin and Wulong Gu, "Outsourcing and Offshoring in Canada," Statistics Canada, May 2008, http://www.statcan.ca/english/research/11F0027MIE/11F0027MIE2008055.pdf.
7. Erin White, "Smaller Companies Join the Outsourcing Trend," The Wall Street Journal, 8 May 2006, B3.
8. Baldwin and Gu, "Outsourcing and Offshoring in Canada."
9. Pete Engardio and Bruce Einhorn, "Outsourcing Innovation," BusinessWeek, 21 March 2005, 84–94.
10. Ibid.
11. Gary N. Bowen, "Nearshore? Farshore? Which Shore for CRM?" Everest Group, March 2005, http://www.outsourcing-journal.com/mar2005-canada.html.
12. William Foster and Jeffrey Bradach, "Should Nonprofits Seek Profits?" Harvard Business Review, February 2005, 92–100.
13. Steve Case, "Purpose and Profit Go Together," The Wall Street Journal, 10 May 2005, B2.
14. Amanda Bower, "Meet the Hard-Nosed Do-Gooders," Time Inside Business, January 2006, A24.
15. "Welcome to CharityVillage.com," Charity Village, 15 August 2008, http://www.charityvillage.com/.
16. John Gray et al., "It's A Rich Life," Canadian Business, Winter 2007/2008, 22.
17. Ibid.
18. "Corporate Profile," Tim Hortons, 24 July 2009, http://www.timhortons.com/en/about/profile.html.
19. Grant Robertson, "Boom Has Tech Grads Mulling Their Options," The Globe and Mail, 14 March 2006, B1.
20. Brook Manville and Josiah Ober, "Beyond Empowerment," Harvard Business Review, January 2003, 48–53.
21. "Competition Act C-34," Department of Justice Canada, 11 August 2008, http://laws.justice.gc.ca/en/showdoc/cs/C-34//20080816/en?command=home&caller=SI&search_type=all&shorttitle=competition%20act&day=16&month=8&year=2008&search_domain=cs&showall=L&statuteyear=all&lengthannual=50&length=50.
22. "Definitions: Understanding Legal Words," Manitoba Courts, 23 October 2006, http://www.manitobacourts.mb.ca/index.html.
23. "CEO Justice," The Wall Street Journal, 16 March 2005, A24.
24. "Conrad Black Complains Appeal Judges Don't Understand Case," CBC News, 10 June 2008, http://www.cbc.ca/world/story/2008/06/10/conrad-black-email.html; "Conrad Black's Lawyers File Appeal of his Conviction, CBC News, 14 March 2008, http://www.cbc.ca/world/story/2008/03/14/blackappeal.html.
25. "'Sense of Urgency,' as Premiers Meet with Central Banker," CBC News, 18 July 2008, http://www.cbc.ca/canada/saskatchewan/story/2008/07/18/premiers-economy.html.
26. Frederick G. Crane et al., Marketing, 7th Canadian ed., (Toronto: McGraw-Hill Ryerson Ltd., 2008), 81.
27. Ibid.
28. Paul Sloan, "Retail Without the Risk," Business 2.0, March 2006, 118.
29. "Talent Technology Corp.," PROFIT 100—Canada's Fastest Growing Companies, 2008 http://list.canadianbusiness.com/rankings/profit100/2008/DisplayProfile.aspx?profile=17.
30. "E-BUSINESS," Webster's Online Dictionary, 2009, http://www.websters-online-dictionary.org/definition/e-business.
31. "Introduction to e-Business," Kioskea.net, 16 October 2008, http://en.kioskea.net/contents/entreprise/e-business.php3.
32. Department of Justice Canada, "Competition Act C-34."
33. Mike Richman, "The Quest for Zero Defects," Quality Digest, April 2005, 40–43.
34. Crane et al., Marketing, 84–85.
35. David Foot with Daniel Stoffman, Boom Bust & Echo 2000 (Toronto: Macfarlane Walter & Ross, 1998), 24–31.
36. "Boom, Bust & Echo, Profiting from the Demographic Shift in the 21st Century," Footwork Consulting Inc., 2008, http://www.footwork.com/21c.asp.
37. "Immigration Trends in Canada," Statistics Canada, 11 September 2007, http://www12.statcan.ca/english/census06/reference/lmm_trends_Canada.cfm; "Immigration in Canada: A Portrait of the Foreign-Born Population, 2006 Census: Highlights," Statistics Canada, 30 November 2007, http://www12.statcan.ca/english/census06/analysis/immcit/highlights.cfm.
38. "About Us—Careers," NAV CANADA, 2008, http://www.navcanada.ca/NavCanada.asp?Language=en&Content=ContentDefinitionFiles\AboutUs\Careers\ValuingDiversity\default.xml.
39. "Family Portrait: Continuity and Change in Canadian Families and Households in 2006: Highlights," Statistics Canada, 5 September 2007, http://www12.statcan.ca/english/census06/analysis/famhouse/highlights.cfm.
40. "Will Globalization Survive?" Washington Times, 10 April 2005, B2.
41. "Mobilizing Science and Technology to Canada's Advantage," Government of Canada, May 2007, http://www.ic.gc.ca/epic/site/ic1.nsf/vwapj/S&Tstrategy.pdf/$file/S&Tstrategy.pdf.
42. Associated Press, "Wardrobe Malfunction Joins the Credit Crunch," Toronto Star, 16 August 2008, http://www.thestar.com/article/478662.
43. "Manufacturing Our Future," Canadian Manufacturing Coalition, [2007?], http://www.cme-mec.ca/pdf/CMECoalitionFINAL.pdf.

## Appendix A

1. Beth Stackpole, "Virtually Flawless?" CIO, 15 May 2005, 58–64; Allan Holmes, "The Changing CIO Role: The Dual Demands of Strategy and Execution," CIO, 1 January 2006.
2. Christopher Koch, "Who's Minding the Store?" CIO, 15 May 2005, 52–56; Marianne Kolbasuk McGee and Chris Murphy, "Facing the Challenge," Informationweek, 28 March 2005, 22–24; Jaime Capella, "The CIO's First 100 Days," Optimize, March 2006.
3. Daniel McGinn, "Movies on the Move," Newsweek, 17 October 2005, E4; Michael Hastings, "A Click Away: Internet TV," Newsweek, 31 January 2005, E10; Rana Foroohar, "Hi! The Net Is Calling," Newsweek, 31 January 2005, E4; Steven Levy, "Life Isn't Just as You Want It? Remix It!" Newsweek, 28 March 2005, 17; Karen Breslau and Daniel McGinn, "A Movie Classic for a New Age," Newsweek, 17 October 2005, E6–E10; "Google Enters Video-on-Demand Domain," Screen Digest, 1 January 2006.
4. Steve Hamm, "A Virtual Revolution," Businessweek, 20 June 2005, 98–102; Robert L. Mitchell, "Virtualization's REAL IMPACT," Computerworld, 13 March 2006.

5.  David George-Cosh, "Analysts Slam Defence of Text-Message Fees Deny Services Overload System," *Winnipeg Free Press*, 5 August 2008, B6.

6.  Ibid.

7.  Meridith Levinson, "The Brain Behind the Big, Bad Burger," *CIO*, 15 March 2005, 49–58; Meridith Levinson, "Business Intelligence: Not Just for Bosses Anymore," *CIO*, 15 January 2006.

8.  "Operational BI Comes of Age," *Businessweek*, 23 May 2005, S2–S10; Jennifer McAdams and Heather Havenstein, "WHAT'S NEXT: Business Intelligence," *Computerworld*, 2 January 2006.

9.  Rick Whiting and Charles Babcock, "Integrate or Disintegrate," *Informationweek*, 21 March 2005, 20–22; Alan Cane, "Super-Fast Blue Gene Looks for Answers," *Financial Times*, 6 May 2005, 10.

10. Glover Ferguson, Sanjay Mathur, and Baiju Shah, "Evolving from Information to Insight," *MIT Sloan Management Review*, Winter 2005, 51–58.

11. Grant Buckler, "It's About Time," *tq Magazine*, Spring 2008, 9.

12. Ibid.

13. Glover Ferguson, Sanjay Mathur, and Baiju Shah, "Evolving from Information to Insight," *MIT Sloan Management Review*, Winter 2005, 51–58.

14. Terence Belford, "How the Mailman Pushed the Envelope," *tq Magazine*, Spring 2006, 16–17.

15. Accenture Technology Labs, "Sentiment Monitoring Services," case study, www.accenture.com.

16. Robert D. Hof, "The Future of Tech," *BusinessWeek*, 20 June 2005, 73–82; Steven Levy, "Ma Bell's Kids Will Live on the Net," *Newsweek*, 28 February 2005, 14; Richard Waters, "It's the Internet, But Not as We Know It," *Financial Times*, 30 April 2005, 1.

17. Michael V. Copeland, "How to Ride the Fifth Wave," *Business 2.0*, July 2005, 78–85.

18. "Japan Tests Super Fast Satellite Broadband," CBC.ca, 13 May 2008, http://www.cbc.ca/technology/story/2008/05/13/tech-japan.html.

19. "About Us," Internet2, 2008, http://www.internet2.edu/membership/index.cfm.

20. Ian Harvey, "Talkin' 'Bout A Revolution," *tq Magazine*, Spring 2008, 16.

21. Ibid.

22. Jay Greene, "Combat Over Collaboration," *BusinessWeek*, 18 April 2005, 64–66; Brad Foss, "Telecommuters Tout Perks of Lifestyle," AP Online, 14 March 2006.

23. Ian Harvey and Ian Johnson, "By the End of the Decade, There Will Be an Estimated 850 Million Mobile Workers Across the Globe," *tq Magazine*, Spring 2006, 22.

24. Ibid.

25. Cliff Edwards, "Wherever You Go, You're on the Job," *BusinessWeek*, 20 June 2005, 87–96; Roger Fillion, "Doing Homework. Telecommuting Jobs Benefit Workers, Help Companies Cut Costs," *Rocky Mountain News*, 6 February 2006.

26. Matt Hartley, "Legitimate Websites Face New Threats," *The Globe and Mail*, 29 July 2008, http://www.theglobeandmail.com/servlet/story/RTGAM.20080729.wrsecurity29/BNStory/specialComment/http://www.theglobeandmail.com/servlet/story/RTGAM.20080729.wrsecurity29/BNStory/specialComment/.

27. Mike Richman, "The Quest for Zero Defects," *Quality Digest*, April 2005, 40–43; Ted Kritsonis, "They Used to Attack Your Computer System Just for the Thrill of It. Now the Thieves Are After Your Money," *tq Magazine*, Summer 2006, 21.

28. Hartley, "Legitimate Websites Face New Threats."

20. Brian Grow, "New Sharks in the Web Surf," *BusinessWeek*, 28 March 2005, 14; Joan Caplin, "That Smell? Something Truly Phishy," *Money*, January 2005, 28; Steven Marlin, "Phishers Try to Reel in Small Businesses," *Informationweek*, 21 March 2005, 78–79; Scott Berinato, "How to Save the Internet," *CIO*, 15 March 2005, 70–80; Phyllis Furman, "Don't Get Hooked by Phishing Scam," *New York Daily News*, 30 March 2006.

30. Michael Sivy, Pat Regnier, and Carolyn Bigda, "What No One Is Telling You about Identity Theft," *Money*, July 2005, 95–99; Julie Tripp, "Stolen Pins Expose Debit Cards to Fraud; Hundreds of Thousands Were Taken, Unlocking Access to Victims' Bank Accounts," *The Post-Standard*, 23 March 2006.

31. Kritsonis, "They Used to Attack Your Computer System Just for the Thrill of It," 20.

32. Treena Hein, "Barbarians Inside the Gates," *tq Magazine*, Summer 2006, 28.

33. Ibid.

34. Michael Myser, "Invasion of the Corporate Spyware," *Business 2.0*, March 2005, 30; Stephen H. Wildstrom, "Fighting Spyware: Microsoft to the Rescue?" *BusinessWeek*, 7 February 2005, 22; Martin J. Garvey, "Uncovering Spyware," *Informationweek*, 21 March 2005, 45–48; "Spyware Companies Beware: New Consumer Protection Initiative to Combat Spyware and Other 'Badware'," *US Newswire*, 25 January 2006.

35. "Platform for Privacy Preferences (P3P) Project," World Wide Web Consortium, 20 November 2007, www.w3.org/P3P.

## Chapter 2

1.  "Index of Economic Freedom, China," The Heritage Foundation, 2008, http://www.heritage.org/research/features/index/country.cfm?id=China; "Index of Economic Freedom, Switzerland," The Heritage Foundation, 2008, http://www.heritage.org/research/features/index/country.cfm?id=Switzerland.

2.  Justin Gillis, "Old Laws, New Fish," *Washington Post*, 15 January 2003, E1.

3.  "Transportation," Burnaby: Ballard Power Systems, 2004, http://www.ballard.com/tC.asp?pgid_44.

4.  Anne Underwood, "Designing the Future," *Newsweek*, 16 May 2005, 40–45.

5.  Kristin Ohlson, "Burst of Energy," *Entrepreneur*, February 2006, 46–47.

6.  "Net Is Cast for Fish Farms," *Washington Times*, 4 April 2005, A8.

7.  "Quirky Causes," *Forbes*, 28 March 2005, 172.

8.  "Charitable Donations," Canadian Bankers Association, 2007, http://www.cba.ca/en/content/stats/DB%20283%20Eng%20(New)%202007.pdf.

9.  "Foundation Fact Sheet," Bill & Melinda Gates Foundation, 30 June 2008, http://www.gatesfoundation.org/MediaCenter/FactSheet/; Amanda Ripley and Amanda Bower, "From Riches to Rags," *Time*, December–January 2006, 72–88.

10. Marilyn Chase, "Gates to Donate Extra $250 Million for Health Grants," *The Wall Street Journal*, 17 May 2005, D7.

11. Frederick G. Crane et al. *Marketing*, 7th Canadian ed. (Toronto: McGraw-Hill Ryerson Limited, 2008), 84.

12. "Bill Gates No Longer Tops World's-Richest List," *The Chronicle of Philanthropy*, 6 March 2008, http://philanthropy.com/news/philanthropytoday/4105/bill-gates-no-longer-tops-worlds-richest-list.

13. "About Us, History of Our Citizenship Action," Cirque du Soleil, 2008, http://www.cirquedusoleil.com/CirqueDuSoleil/en/cirquecitoyen/about/history.htm.

14. Richard Rahn, "Weapons of Mass Disinformation," *Washington Times*, 21 March 2005, A15.

15. Brian M. Carney, "Europe Hasn't Outgrown 'That '70s Show,'" *The Wall Street Journal*, 9 May 2005, A23.

16. Mark Henricks, "The New China?" *Entrepreneur*, February 2006, 17–18; Dexter Roberts, "How Rising Wages Are Changing the Game in China," *BusinessWeek*, 27 March 2006, 32–35.

17. Laura D'Andrea Tyson, "How Europe Is Revving Its Engine," *BusinessWeek*, 21 February 2005, 24.

18. Eric J. Savitz, "Look Who's Storming the Net," *Smart Money*, June 2005, 40–48.

19. "Latest Indicators, Population Estimate (January 2009)," Statistics Canada, 26 March 2009, http://www.statcan.gc.ca/start-debut-eng.html.

20. Matthew Coutts, "Complacency Hurts Nation: Think-Tank; Quality of Life Declining, Report Warns," *National Post*, 30 June 2008, A4.

21. Ibid.

22. "Health Care Spending to Reach $160 Billion This Year," Canadian Institute for Health Information, 13 November 2007, http://secure.cihi.ca/cihiweb/dispPage.jsp?cw_page=media_13nov2007_e.

23. "Provincial and Territorial Economic Accounts Review," Statistics Canada, 27 April 2009, http://www.statcan.gc.ca/pub/13-016-x/13-016-x2009001-eng.pdf.

24. "Country Report, Canada," The Economist Intelligence Unit, May 2009, http://portal.eiu.com.

25. "Country Profile 2005," The Economist Intelligence Unit, 1 September 2005, http://portal.eiu.com.

26. Richard S. Dunham, "The Struggle to Sell the Economy's Sizzle," *BusinessWeek*, 23 January 2006, 43.

27. Steven Gray, "Coffee on the Double," *The Wall Street Journal*, 12 April 2005, B1.

28. "Economic Concepts—Unemployment Rate," Government of Canada, 4 May 2007, http://canadianeconomy.gc.ca/english/economy/unemployment2.html.

29. Ibid.

30. Armine Yalnizyan, "Recession packs biggest wallop since 1930s: Study," Canadian Centre for Policy Alternatives, 28 April 2009.

31. Government of Canada, "Economic Concepts—Unemployment Rate."

32. "Study: The year in review in manufacturing," Statistics Canada, 29 April 2009, http://www.statcan.gc.ca/daily-quotidien/090429/dq090429b-eng.htm; "Study: The year in review in manufacturing," Statistics Canada, 29 April 2008, http://www.statcan.ca/Daily/English/080429/d080429a.htm.

33. David Pilling, "Japan Still in Grip of Deflation as Prices Fall," *Financial Times*, 27 April 2005, 7.

34. E. S. Browning, "Stagflation Fear Puts a Chill into Blue Chips," *The Wall Street Journal*, 29 April 2005, C1 and C4.

35. "Latest Release from the Consumer Price Index," Statistics Canada, 20 May 2009, http://www.statcan.gc.ca/subjects-sujets/cpi-ipc/cpi-ipc-eng.htm.

36. Ibid.

37. Victor Zarnowitz and Dara Lee, "Can U.S. Business Cycles Still Be Dated by Monthly Coincident Indicators Alone?" *Business Cycle Indicator*, March 2005, 3–4.

38. "Business Cycle," Wikimedia Foundation Inc., 18 August 2008, http://en.wikipedia.org/wiki/Business_cycle.

39. "Economic Concepts Business Cycle," Government of Canada, 4 May 2007, http://www.canadianeconomy.gc.ca/english/economy/business_cycle.html.

40. Lakshman Achuthan, "How Anyone Can Forecast Booms and Busts," *Bottom Line Personal*, 1 June 2005, 3–4.

## Chapter 3

1. "Latest Indicators, Population Estimate (January 2009)," Statistics Canada, 26 March 2009, http://www.statcan.gc.ca/start-debut-eng.html; "World POPClock Projection," U.S. Census Bureau, 7 January 2009, http://www.census.gov/ipc/www/popclockworld.html; Matt Rosenberg, "Capitals of Every Independent Country," About.com, 25 March 2009, http://geography.about.com/od/countryinformation/a/capitals.htm.

2. "Current World Population," Nations Online, 2008, http://www.nationsonline.org/oneworld/world_population.htm.

3. "Developed Countries—Population, Births, and Deaths," French National Institute of Demographic Studies, 3 April 2008, http://www.ined.fr/en/pop_figures/developed_countries/population_births_deaths/. This percentage was calculated by adding up the 51 developed countries listed on this site and then dividing by the 195 countries on earth.

4. "Scotiabank Reaches Agreement to Buy E*TRADE Canada," CNW Group, 14 July 2008, http://www.newswire.ca/en/releases/archive/July2008/14/c4216.html.

5. "Canada's Fastest-Growing Companies—LIJA," *Profit*, June 2008, 50–51.

6. "Hargrove calls for help from feds after another round of Chrysler cuts," CBC.ca, 24 July 2008, http://www.cbc.ca/canada/story/2008/07/24/chrysler-caw.html; Nicolas Van Praet, "Polywheels grinds to halt in Oakville," *Financial Post*, 10 July 2008, http://network.nationalpost.com/np/blogs/fpposted/archive/2008/07/10/polywheels-grinds-to-halt-in-oakville.aspx; "2,000 jobs lost as auto-parts plants close," The Canadian Press, 3 July 2008, http://www.cbc.ca/canada/toronto/story/2008/07/03/plant-closure.html.

7. Erin White, "Future CEOs May Need to Have Broad Liberal-Arts Foundation," *The Wall Street Journal*, 12 April 2005, B4.

8. Guy DeJonquieres, "Going Global Is Always a Risky Business," *Financial Times*, 8 March 2005, 15; Christine Hall, "Understanding Culture Is Key to Global Mindset," *Houston Business Journal*, 13 January 2006.

9. Frank Vargo, "U.S. Trade Policy: Free Trade Agreements Level the Playing Field for Everyone," *Rubber & Plastics News*, 2 May 2005; "Free Trade Winds in the Mideast," *The Wall Street Journal*, 11 January 2006.

10. Dave Abler, "Glossary—Absolute Advantage," Penn State University, 2008, http://450.aers.psu.edu/glossary_search.cfm?letter=a.

11. "Absolute Advantage," Wikimedia Foundation, Inc., 22 July 2008, http://en.wikipedia.org/wiki/Absolute_advantage.

12. "Key Small Business Statistics," Industry Canada, July 2008, http://www.ic.gc.ca/epic/site/sbrp-rppe.nsf/vwapj/KSBS_July2008_Eng.pdf/$FILE/KSBS_July2008_Eng.pdf ; "Canada's State of Trade—Trade and Investment Update 2008, Export Establishments by Employee Size," Foreign Affairs and International Trade Canada, 8 May 2008, http://www.international.gc.ca/eet/trade/sot_2008/sot-2008-en.asp.

13. "Anticipating Needs, Delivering Results, EDC in an Evolving Trade Environment," Export Development Canada, May 2008, http://www.edc.ca/english/docs/LegReview_2008_e.pdf.

14. "Canada's State of Trade: Trade and Investment Update—2009," Foreign Affairs and International Trade Canada, 2009, http://www.international.gc.ca/economist-economiste/assets/pdfs/DFAIT_SoT_2009_en.pdf.

15. Ibid.

16. Ibid.

17. Ibid.

18. Ibid.

19. "Canada's State of Trade: Trade and Investment Update—2009," Foreign Affairs and International Trade Canada, 2009, http://www.international.gc.ca/economist-economiste/assets/pdfs/DFAIT_SoT_2009_en.pdf; "Seizing Global Advantage: A Global Commerce Strategy for Securing Canada's Growth & Prosperity," Foreign Affairs and International Trade Canada, 2008, http://www.international.gc.ca/commerce/assets/pdfs/GCS-en.pdf; "A Global Commerce Strategy for Securing Canada's Growth and Prosperity, A Message from the Minister," Foreign Affairs and International Trade Canada, 12 August 2008, http://www.international.gc.ca/commerce/strategy-strategie/minister-ministre.aspx; Jim Middlemiss, "Canada Readying to Ride the Tiger," *Financial Post*, 28 May 2008, http://www.financialpost.com/reports/legal/story.html?id=546037; "International Science and Technology Partnerships Program—ISTPP," Foreign Affairs and International Trade Canada, 5 June 2007, http://www.infoexport.gc.ca/science/istpp-en.htm.

20. "Tokyo Disney Parks Operator Sees Sales, Profit Fall," *Kyodo World News Service*, 9 May 2005.

21. "Workers in Contract Factories," Nike, 2007, http://www.nike.com/nikebiz/nikeresponsibility/pdfs/color/3_Nike_CRR_Workers_C.pdf.

22. "FouFou Dog," *PROFIT*, 2009, http://list.canadianbusiness.com/rankings/hot50/2008/DisplayProfile.aspx?profile=32; Jerry Langton, "Canine Couture," *Toronto Star*, 17 November 2008, http://www.thestar.com/Business/SmallBusiness/article/538014; "About Us," FouFou Dog, 2009, http://www.foufoudog.com/about.html.

23. "In a joint venture, Lotus and Jaguar are developing a new engine called Omnivore," Auto123.com, 12 August 2008, http://www.auto123.com/en/news/car-news/in-a-joint-venture-lotus-and-jaguar-are-developing-a-new-engine-called-omnivore?artid=100249.

24. Lee Hawkins Jr. and Joann S. Lublin, "Emergency Repairman: GM's Wagoner Aims to Make Auto Company More Global," *The Wall Street Journal*, 6 April 2005, B1; "Shanghai Automotive Industry Corporation Guide to China's Auto Market," *Automotive News*, 9 March 2005; Martin Strathnairn, "SAIC Car Sales to Get Boost from GM," *Birmingham Post*, 9 January 2006.

25. Kenneth Fox, "Seeing the Invisible," *Business & Economics Review*, April–June 2005, 17.

26. Haig Simonian, "A Case of Two Heads Being Better Than One," *Financial Times*, 4 March 2005, 9.

27. Brent Jang, "Air Canada, Continental join forces; Move Counters WestJet-Southwest deal," *The Globe and Mail*, 25 July 2008, B3.

28. Ibid.

29. "GroupM and Consilient Form Alliance to Expand Mobile Email Advertising in Asia Pacific," Consilient Technologies Corporation, 10 April 2008, http://www.consilient.com/media/press/groupm-consilient-alliance.php.

30. Ibid.

31. Foreign Affairs and International Trade Canada, "Canada's State of Trade: Trade and Investment Update—2009."

32. Kim Shiffman, "HOT 50 Overview: Canada's hottest startups," *PROFIT*, October 2007, http://rankings.canadianbusiness.com/hot50/article.asp?pageID=article&year=2007&content=overview&type=overview.

33. "The World of Nestle," Nestlé S.A., [2009?], http://www.nestle.com/Resource.axd?Id=602C42FE-04D6-4669-BEE1-1027492FE5E8; Tom Wright, "Nestlé Focuses on Health to Fatten Its Profit-Bucking Global Trend," *International Herald Tribune*, 9 April 2005.

34. Mark Srite, "Levels of Culture and Individual Behavior: An Integrative Perspective," *Journal of Global Information Management*, 1 April 2005.

35. Eric Bellman and Kris Hudson, "Wal-Mart Trains Sights on India's Retail Market," *The Wall Street Journal*, 18 January 2006, A9.

36. Steve H. Hanke, "The Strong Dollar Charade," *Forbes*, 3 February 2003, 122.

37. Ed Zwirn, "Dollar Doldrums," *CFO*, May 2005, 35–38.

38. Matt Krantz, "Regulators Look Closely at Bartering," *USA Today*, 21 May 2002, 35.

39. Alan O. Sykes, "New Directions in Law and Economics," *American Economist*, 1 April 2002, 10.

40. Peter Fritsch and Timothy Mapes, "In Indonesia, a Tangle of Bribes Creates Trouble for Monsanto," *The Wall Street Journal*, 5 April 2005, A1–A6.

41. "The 2007 Results," Transparency International, 26 September 2007, http://www.transparency.org/news_room/latest_news/press_releases/2007/2007_09_26_cpi_2007_en.

42. Ibid.

43. Alma Olaechea, "Globalization Is Best for All," *University Wire*, 13 February 2002.

44. "Washington to Fight New Tariffs on U.S. Corn," CBC News, 6 December 2005, http://www.cbc.ca/story/business/national/2005/12/16/corn-051216.html.

45. "China Delays WTO Probe on Auto Part Tariffs," CBC.ca, 28 September 2006, http://www.cbc.ca/money/story/2006/09/28/chinawto.html.

46. "WTO Rules Against China Over Auto Parts Dispute," Xinhua News Agency, 19 July 2008, http://news.xinhuanet.com/english/2008-07/19/content_8573630.htm.

47. "About the Export and Import Controls Bureau (EICB) Controlled Goods," Foreign Affairs and International Trade Canada, 3 January 2007, http://www.dfait-maeci.gc.ca/eicb/eicbintro-en.asp.

48. "Important Information Related to Canada's Sanctions Against Burma," Foreign Affairs and International Trade Canada, 7 July 2008, http://www.international.gc.ca/international/Sanctions_Burma-Birmanie.aspx.

49. John Zarocostas, "WTO to Focus on Barriers," *Footwear News*, 10 January 2005; Evan Ramstad, "Tech Companies Push for Tariff Overhauls as Products Converge," *The Wall Street Journal*, 15 December 2005.

50. Chester Dawson, "A China Price for Toyota," *BusinessWeek*, 21 February 2005, 50–51; Clay Chandler, "Full Speed Ahead," *Fortune*, 7 February 2005, 79–84.

51. "Mad Cow in Canada: The Science and the Story," CBC.ca, 13 March 2006, http://www.cbc.ca/news/background/madcow/.

52. "Members and Observers," World Trade Organization, 23 July 2008, http://www.wto.org/english/thewto_e/whatis_e/tif_e/org6_e.htm; Elizabeth Wasserman, "Happy Birthday WTO," *Inc.*, January 2005, 21–23; Julian Morris, "The Future of World Trade," *The Wall Street Journal*, 20 December 2005.

53. "Developing Countries," World Trade Organization, 2008, http://www.wto.org/english/res_e/doload_e/inbr_e.pdf.

54. "The WTO Launches World Trade Report 2008: Trade in a Globalizing World," World Trade Organization, 15 July 2008, http://www.wto.org/english/news_e/pres08_e/pr534_e.htm.

55. "North American Free Trade Agreement," Wikimedia Foundation, Inc., 30 August 2008, http://en.wikipedia.org/wiki/NAFTA.

56. "European Union," Wikimedia Foundation, Inc., 2 June 2009, http://en.wikipedia.org/wiki/European_union.

57. "Europa, Key Facts and Figures about Europe and the Europeans," EUROPA [2008?], http://europa.eu/abc/keyfigures/index_en.htm; Graham Bowley, "Enlarged EU Portrayed as a 'Job Machine,'" *International Herald Tribune*, 21 May 2005; Paul Ames, "EU Mulls Plan to Create Rival to MIT in Bid to Counter Trans-Atlantic Brain Drain," *AP Worldstream*, 13 January 2006.

58. "EU Ready to Negotiate New Trade Deal with Canada," CBC News, 27 April 2009, http://www.cbc.ca/world/story/2009/04/27/eu-trade.html.

59. *The 2005 CIA World Fact Book* (www.cia.gov/cia/publications/factbook); "Exporting an Uber-Brand," *BusinessWeek*, 4 April 2005, 74.

60. Joe Studwell, "China's Boom Has Led to Only Partial Change," *Financial Times*, 4 April 2005, 15.

61. Frederik Balfour, "Fakes," *BusinessWeek*, 7 February 2005, 54–64.

62. Peter Mandelson, "India's New Leadership Role: An Economic Giant," *International Herald Tribune*, 15 January 2005; Foster Klug, "Lawmaker Says Tour of China and India a 'Reality Check on Asia's Growing Economies,'" *AP Worldstream*, 6 January 2006.

63. Mary Dejevsky, "Forget the China Story, Russia Offers a Greater Prize for Western Investors," *Independent*, 22 April 2005.

64. Pete Engardio, "The Future of Outsourcing," *BusinessWeek*, 30 January 2006, 50–58.

65. Anne Fisher, "Offshoring Could Boost Your Career," *Fortune*, 24 January 2005, 36.

## Chapter 4

1. "Alberta Heritage Savings Trust Fund 2008–09 Third Quarter Update, February 26, 2009," Government of Alberta, 6 April 2009, http://www.finance.alberta.ca/business/ahstf/index.html.

2. "Assets Under Management," Caisse de Dépôt et Placement du Québec, 2009, http://www.lacaisse.com/en/chiffres/chiffres/Pages/faits-saillants.aspx.

3. "Sources of Canadian Law," Department of Justice Canada, 24 April 2003, http://canada.justice.gc.ca/en/dept/pub/just/CSJ_page7.html.

4. Eugene A. Forsey, *How Canadians Govern Themselves*, 6th ed., Government of Canada, 2005, http://www.parl.gc.ca/information/library/idb/forsey/index-e.asp.

5. Campbell Clark and Rheal Seguin, "Ottawa Pushes for New Chapter in Free Trade with U.S.," *The Globe and Mail*, 4 June 2009, A1.

6. "Price-Fixing Is Bad, No Matter Who Does It," *The Montreal Gazette*, 23 July 2008, A18.

7. Matt Hartley, "Competition Watchdog reviewing Google's Yahoo deal," *The Globe and Mail*, 28 August 2008, B2.

8. Forsey, *How Canadians Govern Themselves*.

9. James Daw, "High Interest, Bad Job Market Make Repaying Loans That Much Harder," *Toronto Star*, 30 May 2009, http://www.thestar.com/article/642879; "Elimination of Loan Interest Delights Students," CBC News, 27 March 2009, http://www.cbc.ca/canada/newfoundland-labrador/story/2009/03/27/student-loan-budget.html.

10. Forsey, *How Canadians Govern Themselves*.

11. "Research in Motion Opens Technical Support Centre in Halifax," Canadian Press, 21 April 2006, http://finance.sympatico.msn.ca/content/investing/other/P40361.asp.

12. Alan Reynolds, "Improvements . . . and Horror Replays," *Washington Times*, 12 January 2003, B8.

13. "The Federal Debt," Statistics Canada, 26 August 2004, http://142.206.72.67/03/03a/03a_055d_e.htm.

14. "Federal Debt," Government of Canada, 2 June 2009, http://canadianeconomy.gc.ca/english/economy/#top.

15. Presentation by the Honourable John Manley, P.C., M.P. to the House of Commons Standing Committee on Finance, Department of Finance Canada, 3 November 2003, http://www.fin.gc.ca/ec2003/speeche.html; Sandra Cordon, "Strong Growth Forecast," *Montreal Gazette*, 20 May 1999, A1; "Sheltered from the Global Storm," *ScotiaPlus*, Spring/Summer 1999, 5.

16. "Budget Deficit in 2009–10, Flaherty Confirms," CBC News, 17 December 2008, http://www.cbc.ca/canada/story/2008/12/17/finance-meeting.html; "Top TD Economist Sees Lingering Canadian Deficits," Reuters, 2 June 2009, http://finance.sympatico.msn.ca/investing/news/breakingnews/article.aspx?cp-documentid=20169426.

17. Richard S. Dunham, "The Struggle to Sell the Economy's Sizzle," *BusinessWeek*, 23 January 2006, 43.

18. "Glossary: Vocabulary for a Financial Crisis," CBC News, 24 March 2009, http://www.cbc.ca/money/story/2008/10/24/f-econoglossary.html; "Canada's Banks: Admired Worldwide for their Management—and Cash," CBC News, 3 March 2009, http://www.cbc.ca/money/story/2009/03/03/f-canada-banks.html; "$25B Credit Backstop for Banks 'Not a Bailout': Harper," CBC News, 10 October 2008, http://www.cbc.ca/canada/story/2008/10/10/flaherty-banks.html; Michel Chossudovsky, "Canada's 75 Billion Dollar Bank Bailout," Global Research, 25 January 2009, http://www.globalresearch.ca/index.php?context=va&aid=12007; Stefan Theil, "Europe's Bank Bailout: Is It Enough?" *Newsweek*, 13 October 2008, http://blog.newsweek.com/blogs/ov/archive/2008/10/13/europe-bank-bailout-is-it-enough.aspx; Kimberly Amadeo, "Understanding the Subprime Mortgage Crisis," About.com, 2008, http://useconomy.about.com/od/economicindicators/tp/Subprime-Mortgage-Primer.htm; Joel Schlesinger, "Why the Bank of Canada Is Doing What It's Doing," *Winnipeg Free Press*, 31 May 2009, http://www.winnipegfreepress.com/business/making-the-money-move-46566862.html?viewAllComments=y.

19. "Canadian Subsidy Directory," Canadian Publications, 2008, http://www.mgpublishing.net/grants-and-loans.htm#CSD.

20. "'Tolerable Risk' in Giving $34M Bailout Loan to Discovery Air: Miltenberger," CBC News, 3 February 2009, http://www.cbc.ca/canada/north/story/2009/02/03/discovery-loan.html.

21. "Nfld. Announces $18-million Aid for Crab Workers," Canadian Press Newswire, 28 June 2005, http://proquest.umi.com/pqdweb.

22. "U.S. Takes Dim View of Government Aid to Bombardier," CBC.ca, 11 August 2008, http://www.cbc.ca/money/story/2008/08/11/bombardier-aid.html.

23. L. Ian MacDonald, "Harper Had No Choice," *The Gazette*, 3 June 2009, http://www.montrealgazette.com/Business/Harper+choice/1657861/story.html.

24. "Ocean Choice Buys Polar Foods," PEI.CBC.CA 24 March 2004. Retrieved from http://pei.cbc.ca/regional/servlet/View?filename_pe_oceanbuys20040324.

25. "Equalization Program," Department of Finance Canada, 22 July 2008, http://www.fin.gc.ca/FEDPROV/eqpe.html; "A New Framework for Equalization and Territorial Formula Financing," Department of Finance Canada, 27 March 2006, http://www.fin.gc.ca/toce/2004/eq_tff-e.html; "Equalization Payments," Department of Finance Canada, 11 May 2009, http://www.fin.gc.ca/fedprov/eqp-eng.asp; Kate Yule, "Ontario Receives First Equalization Payment," CFRA.com, 14 April 2009, http://www.cfra.com/?cat=3&nid=64463; "Have-not Is No More: N.L. Off Equalization," 3 November 2008, CBC News, http://www.cbc.ca/canada/newfoundland-labrador/story/2008/11/03/have-not.html.

26. "Just the Facts," National Research Council Canada, 10 September 2007, http://www.nrc-cnrc.gc.ca/aboutUs/facts_e.html.

27. "Trade and Investment at 10," Foreign Affairs and International Trade Canada, 10 July 2007, http://www.dfait-maeci.gc.ca/canada-magazine/issue24/06-title-en.asp.

28. Glossary of Key Terms: Minority Government," British Columbia Referendum Office, 2009, http://www.gov.bc.ca/referendum_info/first_past_the_post_bc_stv/glossary.html.

29. "Thousands of Forestry Workers Protest in Ottawa," CBC News, 2 June 2009, http://www.cbc.ca/canada/ottawa/story/2009/06/02/forestry-demonstration-ottawa002.html.

## Chapter 5

1. Brent Jang, "WestJet Admits Spying," globeandmail.com, 29 May 2006, http://www.theglobeandmail.com/servlet/story/RTGAM.20060529.waircanada0529/BNStory/Business.

2. Ibid.

3. Auditor General's Report 2004, CBC News, 11 February 2004, http://www.cbc.ca/news/background/auditorgeneral/report2004.html.

4. "Lotto 6/49 Bonus Rounds Coincided with Lottery Scandals," CBC News, 30 May 2007, http://www.cbc.ca/canada/toronto/story/2007/05/30/lotto649-bonus-rounds.html.

5. Ibid.

6. Pallavi Guniganti, "Ethics' Place in Education," *University Wire*, 16 April 2002.

7. Kenneth Blanchard and Norman Vincent Peale, *The Power of Ethical Management* (New York: William Morrow, 1996); Shoshana Zuboff, "A Starter Kit for Business Ethics," *Fast Company*, 1 January 2005.

8. "Generosity in Canada and the United States: The 2008 Generosity Index," The Fraser Institute, December 2008, http://www.fraserinstitute.org/Commerce.Web/product_files/Generosity_Index_2008.pdf.

9. Product Specialist, iParadigms, LLC, E-mail interview, 27 October 2008, reqtii@turnitin.com; Jennifer Smith Richards, "OSU Sniffing Out Cheaters: Penalties Being Stiffened, More Cases Being Pursued in University Crackdown," *Columbus Dispatch*, 17 January 2006; Alicia Shepherd, "Psst . . . What's the Answer?" *People Weekly*, 24 January 2005; Camille Breland, "U. Mississippi Business School Warns Prospective Cheaters," *University Wire*, 21 January 2005.

10. David F. Martin, "Plagiarism and Technology: A Tool for Coping with Plagiarism," *Journal of Business Education*, 1 January 2005.

11. Blanchard and Peale, *The Power of Ethical Management*.

12. "Small Business Owners Doing Little to Promote Ethics," *Ascribe Newswire*, 25 June 2002.

13. Booz Allen Hamilton, "New Study Finds Link Between Financial Success and Focus on Corporate Values," *Business Wire*, 3 February 2005.

14. Craig Savoye, "Workers Say Honesty Is Best Company Policy," *Christian Science Monitor*, 15 June 2000, 3; Andrea Kay, "Tread Carefully Before Becoming a Whistleblower," *Gannett News Service*, 21 February 2002.

15. Alison Maitland, "How Ethics Codes Can Be Made to Work," *Financial Times*, 7 March 2005, 9.

16. Stephen Spector, "SOX and SOX North, Part 3 The Impact of SOX," Professional Development Network, https://www.cga-pdnet.org/Non_VerifiableProducts/ArticlePublication/SOX_E/SOX_part_3.pdf; "What is SOX?" Metso Corporation, 10 March 2006, http://www.metso.com/corporation/home_eng.nsf/FR?ReadForm&ATL=/corporation/articles_eng.nsf/WebWID/WTB-050704-2256F-A1200; Curtis Verschoor, "Is This the Age of Whistleblowers?" *Strategic Finance*, 1 February 2005; Guillermo Contreras, "San Antonio Whistleblower Doubly Rewarded in Exposing HealthSouth Fraud," *San Antonio Express News*, 14 January 2005; Paul K. Mcmasters, "Inside the First Amendment: Blowing the Whistle Can Also Blow a Career," *Gannett News Service*, 16 January 2006.

17. Larry Brown, "The Case for Whistleblowing Legislation in Canada," 3 November 2003, Nepean: National Union of Public and General Employees, http://www.nupge.ca/news_2003/n06no03a.htm; "Whistleblowing and Bill C-11," Public Service Commission of Canada, 11 January 2006, http://www.psc-cfp.gc.ca/speech/2005/whistleblowing_e.htm; "Submission to the Standing Committee on Government Operations and Estimates," Public Service Integrity Office, 30 November 2004, http://www.psio-bifp.gc.ca/media/speech-discours/2004-11-30/part-2_e.php?printversion=1; "Reporting Abuses, Whistleblower Protection Policy," Petro-Canada, 21 March 2006, http://www.petro-canada.ca/eng/investor/9334.htm; Michele Brill-Edwards, Brian McAdam and David Hutton, "Whistleblower Legislation Might Have Prevented Listeriosis Outbreak, Say Activists," *The Hill Times*, 6 October 2008, http://fairwhistleblower.ca/news/articles/2008-10-06_Whistleblower_legislation_might_have_prevented_listeriosis_outbreak.html; "1 Year Later, Tory-Touted Accountability Act Scores 'D' Grade: Watchdog," CBC News, 12 December 2007, http://www.cbc.ca/canada/story/2007/12/12/accountabiliy-report.html; "Federal Accountability Act Becomes Law," Treasury Board of Canada Secretariat, 12 December 2006, http://www.tbs-sct.gc.ca/media/nr-cp/2006/1212-eng.asp; "The Lobbying Act and You," Government of Canada, 7 August 2007, http://www.faa-lfi.gc.ca/index-eng.asp.

18. John S. McClenahen, "Defining Social Responsibility," *Industry Week*, 1 March 2005.

19. Milton Friedman, "The Social Responsibility of Business is to Increase its Profits," *The New York Times Magazine*, 13 September 1970, http://www.colorado.edu/studentgroups/libertarians/issues/friedman-soc-resp-business.html.

20. "Canadian Tire Jumpstart®," The Canadian Tire Foundation for Families, 2009, http://www.canadiantire.ca/jumpstart/about.html.

21. William Damon, "Saints and Sinners in Business," *Security Management*, 1 January 2005.

22. "Trading Places," M2 Presswire, 31 January 2005.

23. "Empower Employees to be active in their communities" [n.d.], Redmond: Microsoft Corporation, http://www.microsoft.com/canada/ican/communityfocus/employees.mspx.

24. "Corporate Social Responsibility," Wikimedia Foundation, Inc., 5 June 2009, http://en.wikipedia.org/wiki/Corporate_social_responsibility.

25. Anita Lienhart, "She Drove, He Drove Mercedes C320," Gannett News Service, 9 January 2001; Menke-Gluckert, "Baby Benz Faces the Moose," *Europe*, 2 February 1998, 40–44; Earle Eldridge, "Luxury Sales Up: 'Move Up' Market Strong," *Edmonton Sun*, 21 June 2002, DR16.

26. "Nortel May Lose NYSE Listing," CBC News, 11 December 2008, http://www.cbc.ca/mobile/text/story_news- technology.html?/ept/html/story/2008/12/11/nortellisting.html; "Trustee Sues Madoff's Wife for $45M," CBS News, 29 July 2009, http://www.cbsnews.com/stories/2009/07/29/business/main5196249.shtml?source=related_story&tag=related; Sidhartha Banerjee, "Disgraced Financier Lived Lavishly," The Canadian Press, 30 July 2009, http://www.thestar.com/news/canada/article/673888; Robert Kuttner, "Dishonest Capitalism Won't Go Unpunished," *BusinessWeek*, 23 May 2005, 32; RBC Financial Group Voted Most Respected Corporation," KPMG LLP, 30 January 2006, http://www.mostrespected.ca/en/mrpr01.html.

27. Steven Skurka, "Black vs. Drabinsky: Two Trials, Two Very Different Systems," *National Post*, 4 June 2009, http://network.nationalpost.com/np/blogs/fullcomment/archive/2009/06/04/steven-skurka-on-black-vs-drabinsky-two-trials-two-very-different-systems.aspx; "Livent Sentencing Hearing Postponed," The Canadian Press, 3 June 2009, http://www.thestar.com/article/644834; Joe Schneider, "Livent Founders Convicted of C$500 Million Fraud (Update3)," Bloomber.com, 25 March 2009, http://www.bloomberg.com/apps/news?pid=20601082&sid=aBkY_Qtnf9y8&refer=canada.

28. "Former RBC Dominion Securities Exec Faces Insider Trading Charges," CBC News, 5 February 2004, http://www.cbc.ca/stories/2004/02/04/rankin040204; Nancy Carr, "Daniel Duic to Pay $1.9M, Stop Trading in Ont., Testify at Rankin Trial: OSC," Canoe Money, 3 March 2004, http://money.canoe.ca/News/Other/2004/03/03/369029-cp.html; Tara Perkins, "Andrew Rankin Gets 6 Months in Canada's 1st Stock-Tipping Conviction," CBC News, 10 April 2005, http://www.cbc.ca/cp/business/051027/b1027100.html.

29. "Background Checks—Know Who You Are Hiring," Hiring Smart, http://www.hiringsmart.ca/bc_stats.jsp.

30. Vicki O'Brien, "Hands in Your Pocket," BC Business Online, 1 August 2007, http://www.bcbusinessonline.ca/bcb/top-stories/2007/08/01/hands-your-pockets.

31. Ibid.

32. Ibid.

33. Jared Gilbert, "Alcoa Does Its Bit for the World—and Its Own Image—with Earthwatch Projects," *Workforce Management*, 1 March 2005; Katherine Mangu-Ward, "The Age of Corporate Environmentalism: Surprise—Big Business Has Learned That It's Pretty Easy Being Green," *Reason*, 1 February 2006.

34. Colin Perkel, "Harris Apologizes for Government's Role in Tragedy," 18 January 2002, Canoe C-Health, http://www.canoe.ca/EcoliTragedy/020118_report-cp.html.

35. Jim MacDonald, "Syncrude Charged After 500 Ducks Perished on Oilsands Pond," The Canadian Press, 9 February 2009, http://www.thestar.com/article/584719; "Tar Ponds in Sydney, Nova Scotia," PageWise Inc., 2002, http://tntn.essortment.com/tarpondssydney_rhxq.htm; "Sydney Nova Scotia Tar Ponds Move Closer to Cleanup" Ellicott, http://www.dredge.com/casestudies/enviro8.htm; "Our Site Overview," Province of Nova Scotia: Sydney Tar Ponds Agency, 2004, http://www.gov.ns.ca/stpa; "The Great Lakes Atlas," The United States Environmental Protection Agency, 2003, www.epa.gov/glnpo/atlas; Pat Currie, "All's Not Well in This Valley," *Lake Ontario Waterkeeper*, 3 April 2004, http://www.waterkeeper.ca/lok; Chris Sebastian, "Canada Getting Tough on Spills," *Times Herald*, 12 May 2004, http:www. thetimesherald.com/news/stories/20040512/localnews/403633.html; "Home," Jantzi Research, 2005, http://www.jantziresearch.com; "About Imagine—Who We Are," Imagine Canada, http://www.imagine.ca/content/about_imagine/who_we_are.asp?section=about.

36. Elizabeth Laurienzo, "Calvert Social Index Quarterly Adjustments," PR Newswire, 17 March 2005; "Corporate Social Concerns: Are They Good Citizenship, or a Rip-Off for Investors?" *The Wall Street Journal*, 6 December 2005.

37. "Triple Bottom Line," Wikipedia, 13 December 2008, http://en.wikipedia.org/wiki/Triple_bottom_line.

38. "What Is the Triple Bottom Line?" SustainAbility Ltd., http://www.sustainability.com/downloads_public/news/TBL.pdf.

39. Ibid.

40. "Defining Sustainability," Sustainability Reporting Program, 2000, http://www.sustreport.org/background/definitions.html; "Introducing Revive," Green Solutions North American, Inc., 2009, http://revive-d.com/revive_overview.cfm; "Loblaws, Sobeys put a wrap on plastic bags," The Canadian Press, 27 November 2008, http://www.cbc.ca/consumer/story/2008/11/27/loblaw-sobeys-bags.html.

41. Aaron Bernstein, "A Major Swipe at Sweatshops," *BusinessWeek*, 23 May 2005, 98–100; "Stamping Out Sweatshops," *BusinessWeek*, 23 May 2005, 136; Mari Herreras, "Recent Court Cases Might Help Rewrite Company Policies: Employment Law Update," *Wenatchee Business Journal*, 1 January 2006.

42. "Workers in Contract Factories," Nike, 2008, http://nikeresponsibility.com/pdfs/color/3_Nike_CRR_Workers_C.pdf.

43. Karl Schoenberger, "U.S. Companies Must Follow U.S. Anti-Corruption Law Abroad," San Jose Mercury News, 13 March 2005.

## Chapter 6

1. "Proprietorship," Canadian Tax and Financial Information, Taxtips.ca, 2008, http://www.taxtips.ca/smallbusiness/incorporate.htm.

2. Ibid.

3. Elswick, "Loaded Statements: Web-Based Total Compensation Statements Keep Employees in the Know," *Employee Benefit News*, 1 May 2005.

4. Canadian Tax and Financial Information, "Proprietorship."

5. Ibid.

6. "Partnership," Canadian Tax and Financial Information, Taxtips.ca, 2008, http://www.taxtips.ca/glossary.htm#P.

7. Jeff Opdyke, "When Business and Friendship Don't Mix," *The Wall Street Journal*, 17 March 2005; Paulette Thomas, "One Sweet Solution to a Sour Partnership," *The Wall Street Journal*, 23 March 2005.

8. Canadian Tax and Financial Information, "Partnership."

9. Ibid.

10. "Corporations," Canadian Tax and Financial Information, Taxtips.ca, 2008, http://www.taxtips.ca/smallbusiness/incorporate.htm.

11. Ibid.

12. "Federal Budget," H&R Block, 2006, http://www.hrblock.ca/resources/fed_budget.asp.

13. "McCain Business Empire has Deep Roots," CBC.ca, 19 March 2004, http://www.cbc.ca/stories/2004/03/19/mccainbiz_040319.

14. "Professional Advantage: New Rules Spell Tax Breaks for Ontario Professionals," Visa, June 2003, http://www.visa.ca/smallbusiness/articles/article.cfm?articleID=189&catID=90; "Incorporation: Is It Right for You?" Newfoundland and Labrador Medical Association, Winter 2003, http://www.nlma.nf.ca/nexus/issues/winter_2003/articles/article_12.html; "Professional Corporation," Business Centre, 2005, http://www.corporationcentre.ca/docen/pinc/home.asp?t=incpr; "Incorporation Rules Expanded for Ontario Doctors and Dentists," BDO Dunwoody LLP, December 2005, http://www.bdo.ca/en/library/publications/taxpub/fastfacts/IncorporationRulesExpandedRevised.cfm.

15. "The Basics of Corporate Structure," Investopedia.com, 2008, http://www.investopedia.com/articles/basics/03/022803.asp.

16. Janet McFarland, "Business Gets Better at the Business of Disclosure," *The Globe and Mail*, 26 November 2007, http://www.theglobeandmail.com/servlet/story/RTGAM.20071125.wrbgmain26/BNStory/boardgames2007/home.

17. Ibid.

18. Ibid.

19. Sean Silcoff, "Old Dutch Buys Humpty Dumpty," *National Post*, 22 March 2006, FP1.

20. Ibid., FP3.

21. Thomas D. Scholtes, "Board Guidance for Going Private," *Directors & Boards*, 22 March 2005.

22. "Company Overview" and "Divisions," Cara Operations Limited, 2001, http://www.cara.com.

23. Matthew Benjamin, "Deal Mania," *U.S. News & World Report*, 18 April 2005.

24. "Interesting Facts," CANAM Franchise Development Group, 2008, http://www.canamfranchise.com/interestingfacts.cfm.

25. Ibid.

26. "Food Restaurants—Boston Pizza International," Canadian Franchise Association, 2006, http://www.cfa.ca/members/food_restaurants.html#boston_pizza_international.

27. Tiesha Higgins, "Franchising Not Just for Fast Food Anymore," *Gazette Business*, 5 January 2005, A31; Ed Duggan, "Playing the Franchising Game Can Be a Risky Business," *South Florida Business Journal*, 13 May 2005.

28. "Kumon Franchise," Occasionfranchise.ca, 2008, http://canada.occasionfranchise.ca/brochure/43/Kumon-franchise.html.

29. "Franchise FAQ," The Keg Steakhouse & Bar, 2008, http://en.kegsteakhouse.com/franchise/faq#1.

30. Julie Bennett, "A Franchiser's Path to International Success Is Often Paved with Pitfalls," *The Wall Street Journal*, 7 April 2005, D7; Anne Fisher, "Hidden Risk," *Fortune*, 26 December 2005.

31. "About Us," Yogen Früz, 2008, http://www.yogenfruz.com/home/about-us; "Our Company," Couche-Tard, 2008, http://www.couche-tard.com/the-network.html; "Beavertails Pastry," *World Franchising*, 2004, http://www.worldfranchising.com/profiles/BeaverTail.htm; "Taco Chain Heads East," *Canadian Business Franchise*, 2006, http://www.cgb.ca/hotnews1.html.

32. "Cooperatives in Canada," Coop Zone, [2008?], http://www.coopzone.coop/en/coopsincda; "About Co-ops in Canada," Government of Canada, 22 August 2008, http://www.agr.gc.ca/rcs-src/coop/index_e.php?s1=info_coop&page=intro; "About Cooperatives," Canadian Co-Operative Association, 2008, http://www.coopscanada.coop/aboutcoop/.

## Chapter 7

1. "Key Small Business Statistics," Industry Canada, January 2009, http://www.ic.gc.ca/eic/site/sbrp-rppe.nsf/vwapj/KSBS-PSRPE_Jan2009_eng.pdf/$FILE/KSBS-PSRPE_Jan2009_eng.pdf; "Latest Release from the Labour Force Survey," Statistics Canada, 5 September 2008, http://www.statcan.ca/english/Subjects/Labour/LFS/lfs-en.htm; Tiana Velez, "New Generation of High-Tech Entrepreneurs Gathers Steam," *Arizona Daily Star*, 31 January 2005; "A Definition of Entrepreneurship," Internet Center for Management and Business Administration, Inc., 19992007, http://www.quickmba.com/entre/definition/.

2. "Entrepreneurship vs. Small Business," Internet Center for Management and Business Administration, Inc., 1999–2007, http://www.quickmba.com/entre/definition/; "Entrepreneurship vs. Small Business," Ryerson University, 2008, http://www.ryerson.ca/career/jobsearch/searchjob/entrepreneurship/.

3. Retrieved 16 June 2009 from the following company Web sites: http://www.jimpattison.com, and http://www.jeancoutu.com. Retrieved 27 May 2004 from the following company Web sites: www.leons.ca/history/default.asp, www2.canadiantire.ca/CTenglish/h_ourstory.html, www.sobeys.ca, http://www.leons.ca/history/default.asp, and http://www.irvingoilco.com/aboutus.htm.

4. "About Us," Travel CUTS, 2008, http://www.travelcuts.com/en/01%20Home/About%20Us.asp.

5. "The Museum," Anne of Green Gables Store, [n.d.], http://www.annesociety.org/anne/index.cfm?id=206.

6. "Lessons from the Leaders," *PROFIT*, June 2008, 31; Samuel Fromartz, "Newbiz: Entrepreneurs Not Braking for Economic Slowdown," *Reuters Business Report*, 20 March 2002; Kathy Wagstaff, "Pointers Offered for Small Businesses," *Atlanta Journal and Constitution*, 30 May 2002, J3; Sarah Kwak, "Students Succeed as Entrepreneurs," *University Wire*, 3 June 2005; Karen E. Klein, "Rekindling an Entrepreneur's Passion," BusinessWeek Online, 15 December 2005; Pallavi Gogoi, "Startup Secrets of the Successful," BusinessWeek Online, 18 January 2006; Ben Whitney, "Alumni Profile: Extreme Success," queensbusiness.ca, Winter 2006, https://business.queensu.ca/alumni/docs/inqw06_profile_rechichi.pdf.

7. Industry Canada, "Key Small Business Statistics;" "CIBC Report Predicts Canada Will Be Home to One Million Women Entrepreneurs by 2010," Canada NewsWire, 28 June 2005, http://proquest.umi.com/pqdweb.

8. Virginia Galt, "CAREER COACH; Before Blaming the Boss, Expert Advises You Take Stock of Your Situation," *The Globe and Mail*, 11 March 2006, B11.

9. Thomas M. Cooney, "What Is An Entrepreneurial Team?" International Small Business Journal, 1 June 2005, "Management Advisory Group to Advise Paxson," *South Florida Business Journal*, 16 January 2006.

10. Helle Neergaard, "Networking Activities in Technology-Based Entrepreneurial Teams," *International Small Business Journal*, 16 January 2005.

11. Industry Canada "Key Small Business Statistics."

12. Ibid.

13. Dan Strempel, "UConn Mulls Stamford Tech Incubator," *Fairfield County (Connecticut) Business Journal*, 11 April 2005; Emily Le Coz, "Incubators Provide Tools for Entrepreneurs," *Northeast Mississippi Daily Journal*, 6 January 2006; Nancy Cambria, "'Incubator' Loan Program Will Foster Small Businesses," *St. Louis Post-Dispatch*, 19 January 2006.

14. Sammi King, "Internet a Boon to Home-Based Businesses," *Arlington Heights (Illinois) Daily Herald*, 22 February 2005; Steve Jones, "Home Businesses Can Be Path to Freedom," *Myrtle Beach (South Carolina) Sun News*, 15 May 2005; Kristen Millares Bolt, "Moms Setting Up Online Businesses," *Seattle Post-Intelligencer*, 5 February 2005.

15. Deb Gruver, "Small-Business Owners Face Pros, Cons of Home-Based Enterprises," *Wichita Eagle*, 3 June 2005; Deb Gruver, "Home-Based Businesses Need to Use Caution with Deductions," *Wichita Eagle*, 18 March 2005; "Parenting, Work-at-Home Experts Join to Author Book Series for Busy Moms," *PR Newswire*, 31 January 2005; Janel Stephens, "Disciplined Commute from Bed to Home Office," *Sarasota Herald Tribune*, 17 March 2005.

16. "E-Commerce Sales Now over $60B," Canwest News Service, 25 April 2008, http://www.canada.com/theprovince/news/money/story.html?id=6919a090-7616-4f8e-bd75-f6bb13de52b6&k=3365.

17. Ibid.

18. Simon Avery, "Pioneers of E-Commerce," *Cincinnati Post*, 6 August 2005.

19. Larry Olmsted, "Nonstop Innovation: How One Company Transforms Its Employees into Entrepreneurs," *Inc.*, July 2005, 34; Alan Deutschman, "Building a Better Skunk Works," *Fast Company*, March 2005, 68–73; Nicole Marie Richardson, "What It Takes to Be a Successful Intrapreneur," *Black Enterprise*, 1 December 2005.

20. Phil Bishop, "Strengthening the Innovation Chain," *Electronic Business*, 1 December 2004; Robert D. Ramsey, "Gaining the Edge over the Competition," *Supervision*, 1 May 2005.

21. "Business Incubation," Canadian Association of Business Incubation 2008, http://www.cabi.ca/business-incubation.php; "How Many Business Incubators Are There?," National Incubation Association, 22 August 2008, http://www.nbia.org/resource_center/bus_inc_facts/index.php; "Canada Business—About Us," Government of Canada, 8 December 2005, http://www.cbsc.org/servlet/ContentServer?cid=1063391060815&pagename=CBSC_FE/CBSC_WebPage/CBSC_WebPage_Temp&lang=eng&c=CBSC_WebPage; "Aboriginal Business Service Network," Government of Canada, 5 August 2003, http://www.cbsc.org/servlet/ContentServer?cid=1091626045548&pagename=ABSN_FE%2FCBSC_WebPage%2FCBSC_WebPage_

Temp&lang=en&c=CBSC_WebPage; "Business Incubation," Canadian Association of Business Incubation, 2006, http://www.cabi.ca/page_05.htm; "Business Incubation FAQ," National Incubation Association, 31 March 2006, http://www.nbia.org/resource_center/bus_inc_facts/index.php; Jean-Pierre Trudel, "Laval's Biotech City Adds Two New Biotech Development Centres to Its Complex," *LifeSciencesWorld*, 26 April 2003, http://www.biotecfind.com/pages/articles_eg/laval/laval.htm.

22. Industry Canada, "Key Small Business Statistics,".

23. Ibid.

24. Ibid.

25. Andy Holloway, "Fill Your Shoes: Small-Business Succession," *Canadian Business*, March 27–April 9, 2006, http://www.canadianbusiness.com/managing/strategy/article.jsp?content=20060327_75741_75741.

26. "Governance for the Family Business," KPMG in Canada, 2008, http://www.kpmg.ca/en/services/enterprise/issuesGrowthGovernance.html.

27. "BBB Tips Give Entrepreneurs the Inside Track on Small Business Start-Up," *Business Wire*, 24 August 2005, Perri Capell, "Typical Funding Mistakes That You Should Avoid," *The Wall Street Journal*, 12 April 2005.

28. "Where Does the Money Come From?," Canadian Bankers Association, 2008, http://www.cba.ca/en/viewDocument.asp?fl=6&sl=111&tl=&docid=251&pg=1.

29. "Venture Capitalists Invested $4.63 Billion During the First Three Months of 2005," *Purchasing*, 19 May 2005; Amanda Fung, "Startups Find Few VC Funds," *Crain's New York Business*, 1 August 2005; Tricia Bishop, "Fewer Venture Capital-Funded Companies Go Public in 2005," *Baltimore Sun*, 4 January 2006.

30. Jim Melloan, "Angels with Angles," *Inc.*, July 2005, 93–104; Lee Gomes, "Angel Investors Return and They Are Serious," *The Wall Street Journal*, 12 April 2005; Kevin Allison, "Angel Investing Takes Flight Again," *Financial Times*, 3 May 2005, 12; Arlene Weintraub, "Where VCs Fear to Tread," *BusinessWeek*, 7 March 2005, 86–87.

31. "Canada's Venture Capital Industry in 2008," Thomas Reuters, 2009, http://www.cvca.ca/files/Downloads/Final_English_Q4_2008_VC_Data_Deck.pdf.

32. Rick Spence, "2006 Financing Guide: Get cash now," *PROFIT*, August 2007, http://www.canadianbusiness.com/entrepreneur/financing/article.jsp?content=20060210_145411_1560.

33. John Canter, "How *and Why I Hired My Tax Accountant*," *The Wall Street Journal*, 25 February 2005.

34. Megan Harman, "Angel Investors: Spreading Your Wings," *Canadian Business*, 17 March 2008, http://www.canadianbusiness.com/managing/strategy/article.jsp?content=20080226_198715_198715.

35. "The Amazing Race: Cervélo Cycles," *PROFIT*, May 2006, http://www.canadian business.com/entrepreneur/managing/article.jsp?content=20060404_153018_5420.

36. Keith Lowe, "Why You Need an Accountant," Entreprenuer.com, 3 June 2002.

37. "Welcome Note," The Forzani Group Ltd., 2006, http://www.forzanigroup.com/home_forzani_group.aspx.

## Chapter 8

1. Jack Welch and Suzy Welch, "How to Be a Good Leader," *Newsweek*, 4 April 2005, 45–48.

2. Greg Thompson, "Great Expectations, the Secret to Coaching," *CMA Magazine*, April 2008, 22–23.

3. Gary Hamel, "The Why, What, and How of Management Innovation," *Harvard Business Review*, February 2006, 72–84.

4. Peter Cappelli and Monika Hamori, "The New Road to the Top," *Harvard Business Review*, January 2005, 25–32.

5. Marcus Buckingham, "What Great Managers Do," *Harvard Business Review*, March 2005, 70–79.

6. Elizabeth Fenner, "Happiness," *Fortune*, 21 February 2005, 36.

7. Kenneth R. Brousseau, Michael J. Driver, Gary Hourihon, and Rikard Larsson. "The Seasoned Executive's Decision-Making Style," *Harvard Business Review*, February 2006, 111–121.

8. John E. West, "Listening to the Customer," *Quality Digest*, February 2006, 16.

9. Jack Welch, "It's All in the Sauce," *Fortune*, 18 April 2005, 138–144.

10. Sholnn Freeman, "What Drives Them," *Washington Post*, 11 January 2006, D1 and D3.

11. Jonathan Fahey, "Hydrogen Gas," *Forbes*, 25 April 2005, 78–83.

12. Bill Breen, "The Clear Leader," *Fast Company*, March 2005, 65–67.

13. Janel M. Radtke, "How to Write a Mission Statement," *TCCI Magazine Online*, 2005.

14. Giovanni Gavetti and Jan W. Rivkin, "How Strategists Really Think," *Harvard Business Review*, April 2005, 54–63.

15. Neal E. Boudette, "Powerful Nostalgia," *The Wall Street Journal*, 10 January 2006, B1.

16. Michael C. Mankins and Richard Steele, "Stop Making Plans: Start Making Decisions," *Harvard Business Review*, January 2006, 76–84.

17. Robert J. Samuelson, "No Joke: CEOs Do Some Good," *Newsweek*, 18 April 2005, 49.

18. Andrew Nikiforuk, "Avian Flu—Winging It?" *Canadian Business*, 24 April–7 May 2006, 57.

19. "The Next Pandemic?" CBC News Online, 21 March 2006, http://www.cbc.ca/news/background/avianflu/.

20. Public Health Agency of Canada, "The Public Health Agency of Canada's Pandemic Preparedness Activities," 27 March 2006, http://www.phac-aspc.gc.ca/influenza/pha-asp-prep_e.html.

21. Ibid.

22. "The New Contingency Plan—Health-Related Emergencies," 27 May 2003, Toronto: Morneau Sobeco. Retrieved from http://www.morneausobeco.com/PDF/SARSCommuniqué_E.pdf.

23. Roma Luciw, "Is Your Company Ready for a Sisaster?" *The Globe and Mail*, 21 June 2006, http://www.theglobeandmail.com/servlet/story/RTGAM.20060621.wdisaster0621/BNStory/Business.

24. Ibid.

25. Gary Silverman, "How May I Help You?" *Financial Times*, 4/5 February 2006, W1 and W2.

26. Paul Rogers and Marcia Blenko, "Who Has the D?" *Harvard Business Review*, January 2006, 53–61.

27. Chris Penttila, "Musical Chairs," *Entrepreneur*, April 2006, 24.

28. "Making Loblaw Best Again", 27 November 2007, www.loblaw.ca/en/inv_analyst_materials.html

29. Andreas Priestland and Robert Hanig, "Developing First-Level Leaders," *Harvard Business Review*, June 2005, 113–120.

30. Robert Kutz, "Skills of an Effective Administrator," Harvard Business Review, Sept – Oct 1974, 90-101.

31. Anthony Davis, "Sky High," *PROFIT Guide*, March 2004, http://www.profitguide.com/shared/print.jsp?content_20040213_171556_4580.

32. P. Fraser Johnson and Robert D. Klassen, "E-Procurement," *MIT Sloan Management Review*, Winter 2005, 7–10.

33. WestJet Airlines Limited, "2005 Annual Report," http://www.westjet.com/pdffile/WestJet2005AR.pdf.

34. Mahender Singh, "Supply Chain Reality Check," *MIT Sloan Management Review*, Spring 2005, 96.

35. Murray Johannsen, "Nine Characteristics of Successful Entrepreneurs and Business Leaders," http://www.legacee.com/Info/Leadership/LeadershipEntrepreneurial.html.

36. Murray Johannsen, "Nine Spheres of Leadership Influence' http://www.legacee.com/Info/Leadership/Influence.html.

37. "Transformational Leadership," Changingminds.org, http://changingminds.org/disciplines/leadership/styles/transformational_leadership.

38. Chris Sorensen, "WestJet Apologizes to Air Canada for Snooping," *Financial Post*, 30 May 2006, http://www.canada.com/nationalpost/financialpost/story.html?id=6ca8461a-fb61-4bcc-be49-002f092c337f&p=2.

39. Ibid.

40. Bertrand Marotte, "Management Guru Assails Excessive CEO Salaries," *The Globe and Mail*, 8 May 2003, B7.

41. Virginia Galt, "Anything but Middling," *The Globe and Mail*, 11 April 2003, C1.

42. H. James Harrington, "Knowledge Management Takes Us from Chance to Choice," *Quality Digest*, April 2003, 14–16.

43. Laura Bogomolny, "Most Innovative Exec/Canadian Tire—Janice Wismer," Canadian Business, 2004, http://www.canadianbusiness.com/allstars/best_innovative_exec.html.

44. Joy Riggs, "Empowering Workers by Setting Goals," *Nation's Business*, January 1995, 6.

## Chapter 9

1. Linda Teschler, "Is Your Company up to Speed?" *Fast Company*, June 2003, 81–111.
2. Robert J. Samuelson, "The World Is Still Round," *Washington Post*, 22 July 2005, A23.
3. Fred Reichheld, "The Microeconomics of Customer Relations," *MIT Sloan Management Review*, Winter 2006, 73–78.
4. Charles Forelle, "IBM Restructuring, Job Cuts," *The Wall Street Journal*, 5 May 2005, A3.
5. Henry Mintzberg and James Brian Quinn, *The Strategy Process: Concepts and Contexts* (New Jersey: Prentice Hall Inc., 1992).
6. Henry Mintzberg, *Managers not MBAs* (San Francisco: Berrett-Koehler Publishers, 2004).
7. Jim Clemmer, "How to Make Empowerment Work," *The Globe and Mail*, classroom edition, April 1993, 17.
8. Pui-Wing Tam, "H-P Net Rises on Gains Across Units," *The Wall Street Journal*, 16 February 2006, A3.
9. Magna International, "Magna 2005 Annual Report," 2006, http://www.magna.com/magna/en/investors/governance/documents/pdf/Annual%20Report%202005.pdf.
10. Steven Gray, "Beyond Burgers," *The Wall Street Journal*, 18–19 February 2006, A1 and A7.
11. Harry Maurer, "News You Need to Know," *BusinessWeek*, 6 February 2006, 32.
12. Mark Athitakis, "How to Make Money on the Net," *Business 2.0* May 2003, 83–90.
13. Ron Adner, "Innovation Ecosystem," *Harvard Business Review*, April 2006, 98–107.
14. Jon R. Katzenbach and Douglas K. Smith, "The Discipline of Teams," *Harvard Business Review*, July–August 2005, 162–71.
15. Jeff Weiss and Jonathan Hughes, "Want Collaboration?" *Harvard Business Review*, March 2005, 93–101.
16. Bill Fischer and Andy Boynton, "Virtuoso Teams," *Harvard Business Review*, July–August 2005, 117–21.
17. John E. (Jack) Wert, "Listening to the Customer," *Quality Digest*, February 2006, 16.
18. Philip Evans and Bob Wolf, "Collaboration Rules," *Harvard Business Review*, July–August 2005, 96–104.
19. Jerker Denrell, "Selection Bias and the Perils of Benchmarking," *Harvard Business Review*, April 2005, 114–19.
20. Jeff Sanford, "Clean and Green, Suncor Uses Sustainability Performance to Track Business," *Canadian Business*, 22 February 2006.
21. Pip Coburn, "China's Magic Number," *Red Herring*, February 2003, 67.
22. Amy Barrett, "Man with Scalpel," *BusinessWeek*, 18 April 2005, 42.
23. David Ernst and James Bamford, "Your Alliances Are Too Stable," *Harvard Business Review*, June 2005, 133–141.
24. Jean Halliday, "Ford Puts Consumers at Center of 'Rebirthing,'" *Advertising Age*, 30 January 2006, 31.
25. Keith Naughton, "Detroit Hoping for a Small Victory," *Newsweek*, 6 February 2006, 10.
26. Celestica, "Capabilities," http://www.celestica.com/capabilities/Excellence.asp
27. Erin White, "Savvy Job Hunters Research Office Culture," The Wall Street Journal Online, 12 April 2005.
28. Henry Mintzberg and James Brian Quinn, *The Strategy Process: Concepts and Contexts* (New Jersey: Prentice Hall Inc., 1992).
29. Steven Watters, "The Organization Woman," *Business 2.0*, April 2006, 106–110.
30. Andrew Wahl, Zena Olijnyk, Peter Evans, Andy Holloway, and Erin Pooley, "Best Workplaces 2006: Lessons from Some of the Best," *Canadian Business*, 10–23 April 2006, http://www.canadianbusiness.com/managing/employees/article.jsp?content=20060410_76257_76257&page=2.
31. Nortel Networks, "2005 Annual Report," (2006), http://www.nortel.com/corporate/investor/reports/collateral/nnc_annual_report_2005.pdf
32. Ibid.
33. "Will CEO Pain Lead to Labor Gains?" *Business Week*, 16 September 2002, 6.

## Chapter 10

1. "Innovation in Canada," Sackville: Centre for Canadian Studies at Mount Allison University, http://www.mta.ca/faculty/arts/canadian_studies/english/about/innovation/.
2. *Innovation Analysis Bulletin*, Vol. 6, No. 1, March 2004, http://www.statcan.gc.ca/pub/88-003-x/88-003-x2004001-eng.pdf.
3. "Spending on research and development," *The Daily*, 20 December 2007, Statscan.ca/Daily/English/071220/d071220b.htm.
4. Statistics Canada "Science Statistics," December 2007, http://www.statcan.gc.ca/pub/88-001-x/88-001-x2007007-eng.pdf.
5. "Business Research and Development Spending Slumps in 2006, According to Canada's Top 100 Corporate R&D Spenders List," Re$earch Infosource, Inc, press release, 22 October 2007, http://researchinfosource.com/pressroom/20071022/top100_gen.pdf.
6. "Canada's Top 100 Corporate R&D Spenders List 2007 Analysis," Re$earch Infosource, Inc., 2007, Researchinfosource.com/2007analysis.pdf.
7. Canadian Manufacturers & Exporters, "Canada's Manufacturing Industry Drives Our Economy," 2004, http://www.cme-mec.ca/national/template_na.asp?p=4.
8. Kathryn Jones, "The Dell Way," *Business 2.0*, February 2003, 61–66.
9. Spencer E. Ante, "The New Blue," *Business Week*, 17 March 2003, 80–88.
10. Daniel Eisenberg, "There's a New Way to Think @ Big Blue," *Time*, 20 January 2003, 49–53.
11. Pete Engardio, Aaron Bernstein, and Manjeet Kripalani, "Is Your Job Next?" *Business Week*, 3 February 2003, 50–60.
12. David Atkin, "HP Toronto Plant Aimed at Dell," *The Globe and Mail*, 14 November 2003, B1.
13. "Hoover's Profile: Gilden Activewear, Inc.," Answers.com, http://www.Answers.com/topic/gildan-activewear-inc.
14. Richard Wilding, "The Ghost in the Machine," *Financial Times*, 7 April 2006, p. 5 of a section called "Mastering Uncertainty."
15. Gordon Pitts, "Kodiak Comes Home," *The Globe and Mail*, 15 May 2006, B5.
16. Douglas M. Lambert and A. Michael Knemeyer, "We're in This Together," *Harvard Business Review*, December 2004, 114–22.
17. Gary Norris, "Honda Putting New Assembly Plant in U.S.; Ontario Gets $154M Engine Factory," Canadian Business Online, 17 May 2006, http://www.canadianbusiness.com/markets/headline_news/article.jsp?content=b051777A.
18. David Crane, "We've Got to Use Our Brains More than Our Brawn," *Toronto Star*, D2.
19. CBC News Online, "Outsourcing: Contracting Out Becomes Big Business," 7 March 2006, http://www.cbc.ca/news/background/economy/outsourcing.html.
20. CORE Centre for Outsourcing Research and Education, www.core-outsourcing.org
21. Gordon Pitts, "Small Producer Cleans Up Making Soap," *The Globe and Mail*, 28 July 2003, B1.
22. "IT Outsourcing to Canada," IMEX Systems, Inc., www.imexsystems.com/pdf/Outsourcing_USA.pdf.
23. Virginia Galt, "Take Our Business, Take Our People: BMO," *The Globe and Mail*, 19 May 2003, B1.
24. Canadian Vehicle Manufacturers Association, "The Automotive Industry in Canada," 2006, http://www.cvma.ca/eng/industry/industry.cfm.
25. Richard Waters, "Manufacturing Glitches Dent Xbox Sales," *Financial Times*, 27 January 2006, 17.
26. Michelle Conlin, "Call Centers in the Rec Room," *BusinessWeek*, 23 January 2006, 76–77.
27. Janet Bealer Rodie, "Brückner, M-Tec Partner to Provide Carpet Solutions," *Textile World*, 1 May 2005.
28. Davis Balestracci, "When Processes Moonlight as Trends," *Quality Digest*, June 2005, 18.
29. "More about NQI" and "Canada Awards for Excellence," Toronto: National Quality Institute, http://www.nqi.ca.
30. John E. (Jack) West, "Continuous Improvement and Your QMS," *Quality Digest*, April 2006, 16.
31. Scott M. Paton, "The Cost of Quality," *Quality Digest*, January 2006, 128.
32. "ISO Standards," International Organization for Standardization, www.iso.org/iso/iso_catalogue.htm.

33. SNC-Lavalin Group Inc., "Quality Policy," http://www.snclavalin.com/en/6_0/6_10.aspx.
34. "Extensive debate improves consensus on future ISO 26000 standard on social responsibility," International Organization for Standardization, 4 June 2009, http://www.iso.org/iso/pressrelease.htm?refid=Ref1229.
35. "Grocery Chain in Drive to Improve," *National Post*, 31 October 2001, JV3.
36. "The Juggling Act Behind the Cirque," *National Post*, 31 October 2001, JV4.
37. Gordon Pitts, "Kodiak Comes Home," *The Globe and Mail*, 15 May 2006, http://www.theglobeandmail.com/servlet/story/LAC.20060515.RKODIAK15/TPStory/?query=kodiak.
38. Robyn Waters, "The Secret of Feel-Good Shopping," *Kiplinger's*, January 2006, 20–22.
39. Wikimedia Foundation Inc., "Economic Order Quantity," 3 May 2006, http://en.wikipedia.org/wiki/Economic_order_quantity.
40. "Royal Canadian Mint," September 2003, Cognos, http://www.cognos.com/products/applications/success.html.
41. Ibid.
42. Centre for Research and Information on Canada, "Background," 11 May 2006, http://www.cric.ca/en_html/guide/border/border.html#faqs.
43. Daren Fonda, "Why the Most Profitable Cars Made in the U.S.A. are Japanese and German," *Time*, June 2003, A9–A13.
44. Horst-Henning Wolf, "Making the Transition to Strategic Purchasing," *MIT Sloan Management Review*, Summer 2005, 17–24.
45. Greg Keenan, "Ford's New Maxim: Flex Manufacturing; New Oakville Plant Should Be Able to Switch Models in Days, not Weeks," *The Globe and Mail*, 10 May 2006, B3.
46. Ibid.
47. Derrell S. James, "Using Lean and Six Sigma in Project Management," *Quality Digest*, August 2005, 49–55; Bill Ritsch, "Breaking the Bottleneck," *Quality Digest*, March 2006, 41.
48. Julia Boorstin, "Adidas Expands Its Footprint," *Fortune*, 30 May 2005, 33.
49. Robyn Waters, "The Secret of Feel-Good Shopping," *Kiplinger's*," January 2006, 20–22.

## Chapter 11

1. Hermann Schwind et al, *Canadian Human Resource Management, A Strategic Approach*, 8th ed. (Toronto: McGraw-Hill Ryerson, 2007), 398.
2. Ibid.
3. "How Employee Satisfaction and Motivation Are Tied to Customer Satisfaction," *Managing Training & Development*, 1 January 2005; Michael Skapinker, "Measures of Success Must Go Beyond Financial Results," *Financial Times*, 2 March 2005; "Employee Retention and Succession Programs Lead to Higher Retention, Increased ROI, Says AberdeenGroup," *Business Wire*, 9 January 2006.
4. "What's the Real Cost of Turnover?" go2 Tourism Society, 2008, http://www.go2hr.ca/ForbrEmployers/Retention/StaffTurnover/WhatstheRealCostofTurnover/tabid/1624/Default.aspx.
5. Ibid.
6. Michael Wilson, "The Psychology of Motivation and Employee Retention," *Maintenance Supplies*, 1 July 2005; Jeff Kirby, "Light Their Fires: Find Out How to Improve Employee Motivation and Increase Overall Company Productivity," *Security Management*, 1 June 2005; Michael Arndt, "Nice Work If You Can Get It," *BusinessWeek*, 9 January 2006.
7. Jane Gaboury, "Tension Invention," *Industrial Engineer*, 1 July 2005; "Hawthorne Studies," Analytic Technologies, http://www.analytictech.com/mb021/handouts/bank_wiring.htm.
8. Richard DiPaolo, "Ergonomically Inclined," *Maintenance Supplies*, 1 June 2005.
9. David Montgomery, *The Fall of the House of Labor: The Workplace, the State, and American Labor Activism*, 1865–1925, (New York: Cambridge University Press, 1987); "Frederick Winslow Taylor," Wikimedia Foundation, Inc., 15 December 2008, http://en.wikipedia.org/wiki/Frederick_Winslow_Taylor#cite_note-8.
10. Jay Velury, "Empowerment to the People," *Industrial Engineer*, 1 May 2005.

11. Horst Brand, "Working in the Digital Age," *Monthly Labor Review*, 1 January 2005.
12. Steven Bratman, "The Double-Blind Gaze," *Altadena (California) Skeptic*, 1 January 2005.
13. John A. Byrne, "The 21st Century Corporation: Back to the Future: Visionary vs. Visionary," *BusinessWeek*, 28 August 2000, 210; Richard S. Tedlow, "The Education of Andy Grove," *Fortune*, 12 December 2005.
14. Pamela Babcock, "Find What Workers Want," *HRMagazine*, 1 April 2005.
15. Derek Sankey, "CP Railway Offers Best Overall Package," *Financial Post*, 22 October 2008, http://www.financialpost.com/working/story.html?id=899342.
16. Ibid.
17. "Employer Review: Mars Canada Inc.," Eluta Inc., 2008, http://www.eluta.ca/top-employer-mars-canada.
18. Ibid.
19. Michael Wilson, "The Psychology of Motivation and Employee Retention," *Maintenance Supplies*, 1 July 2005; Jeff D. Opdyke, "Money Can't Buy Job Happiness," *The Wall Street Journal*, 19 April 2005; "Incentives on the Rise," *Financial & Insurance Meetings*, 1 January 2006.
20. Career Connection, "Getting Along with Your Boss?" 12 March 2003, http://www.canoe.ca/CareerConnectionNews/031203_flash2.html.
21. "Boosting Morale from an Employer's Perspective," Training + Development Blog, 18 November 2008, http://tdblog.typepad.com/td_blog/surveys/.
22. "Job Satisfaction," Psychology Wikia, 2008, http://psychology.wikia.com/wiki/Job_satisfaction#cite_note-5.
23. "Organizing for Empowerment: An Interview with AES's Roger Sant and Dennis Bakke," *Harvard Business Review*, 1 January 1999, 110; Dave Hemsath, "301 More Ways to Have Fun at Work," *HRMagazine*, 1 July 2005; Sandy McCrarey, "Motivating the Workforce with a Positive Culture," Franchising World, 1 March 2005; Linda F. Jarrett, "Helping Drive Enterprise," *St. Louis Commerce*, March 2005, 14–21; Alan Schwarz, "How I Did It," *Inc.*, April 2005, 116–18; Mark Dominiak, "Use Creative Tactics to Retain Staff; Management Rewards Such as Outings, Time Off, Group Activities Can Revitalize Hard-Working Employees," *TelevisionWeek*, 16 January 2006.
24. "Ergonomics Glossary: Job Enlargement," CAE Association of Canadian Ergonomists/Association canadienne d'ergonomie, 2008, http://www.ace-ergocanada.ca/index.php?command=buildBlock&contentid=245#[J].
25. Ibid.
26. Margaret Heffernan, "The Morale of the Story," *Fast Company*, March 2005, 79–81.
27. Deena Waisberg, "Simple Steps to Super Growth: Open the Books," *PROFIT*, 2003, www.profitguide.com/profit100/2003/article.asp?ID=1265.
28. Richard A. Roberts, "Success Means Change," *Supervision*, 1 April 2005; Dawn Sagario, "With a Plan, Delusional Office Slackers Can Be Put Back on Track," *Gannett News Service*, 30 June 2005.
29. Patricia M. Buhler, "Managing in the New Millennium: Human Resources," *Supervision*, 1 January 2005; Jena McGregor, "The Struggle to Measure Performance," *BusinessWeek*, 9 January 2006.
30. Karen van Dam, "Employee Attitudes Toward Job Changes," *Journal of Occupational and Organizational Psychology*, 1 June 2005; Goutam Challagalla, "Adapting Motivation, Control, and Compensation Research to a New Environment," *Journal of Personal Selling & Sales Management*, 22 March 2005.
31. David Nadler and Edward Lawler, "Motivation—A Diagnostic Approach," in *Perspectives on Behavior in Organizations* (New York: McGraw-Hill, 1977).
32. "B.F. Skinner," Wikimedia Foundation, Inc., 3 January 2009, http://en.wikipedia.org/wiki/B.F._Skinner.
33. Rebecca M. Chory-Assad, "Motivating Factors: Perceptions of Justice and Their Relationship with Managerial and Organizational Trust," *Communication Studies*, 1 March 2005; Christine A. Henle, "Predicting Workplace Deviance from the Interaction Between Organizational Justice and Personality," *Journal of Managerial Issues*, 22 June 2005.

34. Dean B. McFarlin, "Wage Comparisons with Similar and Dissimilar Others," *Journal of Occupational and Organizational Psychology*, 1 March 2005; Katherine Reynolds Lewis, "If You Think You're Underpaid, Think Again," Post-Standard, 18 January 2006.

35. Holly J. Payne, "Reconceptualizing Social Skills in Organizations: Exploring the Relationship Between Communication Competence, Job Performance, and Supervisory Roles," *Journal of Leadership & Organizational Studies*, 1 January 2005.

36. John E. Guiniven, "Making Employee Communication Work," *Journal of Employee Assistance*, 1 March 2005; Dean A. Hill, "Communication Strategy: Conquer the Hurdles That Are Inhibiting Dialogue with Your Employees," *Detroiter*, 1 January 2005; Mark Faircloth, "Eight Strategies for Building a Sales Culture," *Community Banker*, 1 August 2005; "Communications Q&A," *Pensions Management*, 1 August 2005; Mark Henricks, "The Truth? Your Employees Can Handle It, So Just Communicate with Them, Already," *Entrepreneur*, 1 July 2005.

37. "Employer Review: Great Little Box Company Ltd., The," Eluta Inc., 2008, http://www.eluta.ca/top-employer-great-little-box-company.

38. David K. Foot, *Boom Bust & Echo 2000* (Toronto: Macfarlane Walter & Ross, 1998), 24–31.

39. Ellen Goldhar, "How to Manage Gen X Workers," *London Free Press*, 19 August 2002, 7; Ellen Goldhar, "Gen-Xers Require Whole New Management Style," *The Toronto Sun*, 14 August 2002, C8; Lisi de Bourbon, "Business Watercooler Stories," AP Online, 22 January 2002; "Overtime: When Generations Collide," *United Press International*, 21 May 2002; Andrea Sachs, "Generation Hex? A New Book Identifies Four Age Groups Warring at Work," *Time*, 11 March 2002, Y22; Toddi Gutner, "Businessweek Investor: A Balancing Act for Gen X Women," *Business Week*, 21 January 2002, 82.

40. Bruce Tulgan, *Not Everyone Gets A Trophy: How to Manage Generation Y*, (Wiley, 2009), http://ca.wiley.com/WileyCDA/WileyTitle/productCd-0470256265.html.

## Chapter 12

1. "Janice Wismer," *Canadian Business*, 2004, http://www.canadianbusiness.com/allstars/best_innovative_exec.html.

2. Kara Aaserud, "Canada's Hottest Startups," *PROFIT*, September 2008, http://list.canadianbusiness.com/rankings/hot50/2008/overview/article.aspx?id=20080909_131914_28700.

3. Sally Coleman Selden, "Human Resource Management in American Counties," *Public Personnel Management*, 1 April 2005; Robert Rodriguez, "HR's New Breed," *HR Magazine*, 1 January 2006.

4. David Brown, "HR and the Workforce 10 Years from Now," *Canadian HR Reporter*, 20 October 2003, 2.

5. Susan Carr and Lydia Morris Brown, "People Perfect", *Business of Management*, http://learning.indiatimes.com/bm/features/books/book2.htm.

6. "What's New," Canadian Council of Human Resources Associations, 2008, http://www.cchra.ca/Web/CCHRA/content.aspx?f=29943; Jean-Michel Caye, Andrew Dyer, Michael Leicht, Anna Minto, and Rainer Strack, Creating People Advantage: How to Address HR Challenges Worldwide Through 2015," The Boston Consulting Group, Inc. and World Federation of Personnel Management Associations, 14 April 2008, http://www.bcg.com/impact_expertise/publications/files/Creating_People_Advantage_Summary_May_2008.pdf; Janice M. Wismer, Global Vice-President of Human Resources, McCain Foods Ltd., interview, 20 November 2008.

7. Elena Malykhina, "Supplying Labor to Meet Demand," *Informationweek*, 21 March 2005, 69–72.

8. Anthony R. Wheeler, "Post-Hire Human Resource Management Practices and Person-Organization Fit: A Study of Blue-Collar Employees," *Journal of Managerial Issues*, 22 March 2005.

9. "What to Do Now That Training Is Becoming a Major HR Force," HR Focus, 1 February 2005.

10. Alan Davis, "Calculating the Cost-per-Hire," CharityVillage Ltd., 14 January 2008, http://www.charityvillage.com/cv/research/rhr33.html

11. "Our Hiring Process,"Cedar Fair Entertainment Company, 2009, http://www.canadaswonderland.com/jobs/jobs_benefits.cfm?et_id=1.

12. Liz Kislik, "A Hire Authority," *Catalog Age*, 1 April 2005; "HR by Numbers: How to Hire the Right People and Then Lead Them to Success," Prosales, 1 January 2006.

13. Marcela Creps, "What Not to Ask Applicants at a Job Interview," *Bloomington (Indiana) Herald-Times*, 31 May 2005.

14. Tara Pepper, "Inside the Head of an Applicant," *Newsweek*, 21 February 2005; "Personality Assessment Tests," PR Newswire, 12 April 2005.

15. David Hench, "Maine Overwhelmed as Background Checks Balloon," *Portland (Maine) Press Herald*, 18 April 2005; Carol Hymowitz, "Add Candidate's Character to Boards' Lists of Concerns," *The Wall Street Journal*, 17 March 2005; James Swann, "Guarding the Gates with Employee Background Checks," *Community Banker*, 1 August 2005; Carol Patton, "To Tell the Truth: It's an Institution's Duty to Ensure that New Hires Are Who They Say They Are," *University Business*, 1 January 2006; Mary Jane Maytum, "Look a Little Closer: Investigators Say Employers Can Thwart Value of Background Checks; Some Should Dig Deeper," *Business First*, 27 January 2006.

16. "Reference Check: Is Your Boss Watching? Privacy and Your Facebook Profile," Office of the Information and Privacy Commissioner of Ontario, 2008, http://www.ipc.on.ca/images/Resources/up-facebook_refcheck.pdf.

17. Ibid.

18. Deborah J. Myers, "You're Fired! Letting an Employee Go Isn't Easy for Any Manager," *Alaska Business Monthly*, 1 May 2005.

19. "9 Years on Contracts and No Full-Time Job in Sight," *Toronto Star*, 4 December 2008, http://www.thestar.com/News/GTA/article/548153.

20. Ibid.

21. "Why HR Must Act as a Strategic Gatekeeper for Contingent Staffing," *Human Resource Department Management Report*, 1 January 2005; Shelly Garcia, "Use of Temporary Workers May Be Permanent Solution for Businesses," *San Fernando Valley Business Journal*, 22 November 2004; H. Lee Murphy, "Temps Are Back, and Cheaper," *Crain's Chicago Business*, 14 February 2005; "Temp Jobs' Climb Hints at Broader Growth to Come," *Washington Post*, 16 January 2006.

22. Maria Mallory White, "Student Gives Temp Work 'A' Experience, Pay Found Rewarding," *Atlanta Journal and Constitution*, 14 July 2002, R1.

23. Alison Maitland, "Employers Nurse the Stress Bug," *Financial Times*, 19 April 2005, 12.

24. Robert Green, "Effective Training Programs: How to Design In-House Training on a Limited Budget," *CADalyst*, 1 March 2005; Lynne M. Connelly, "Welcoming New Employees," *Journal of Nursing Scholarship*, 22 June 2005.

25. "Big Boy Restaurants Launches National Online Training Program for Employees," *Business Wire*, 28 March 2005.

26. Sunwoo Kang, "Perceived Usefulness and Outcomes of Intranet-Based Learning," *Journal of Instructional Psychology*, 1 March 2005.

27. Patrick J. Sauer, "The Problem: Magnetech Wants to Triple Its Workforce," *Inc.*, January 2005, 38–39.

28. Kathryn Tyler, "15 Ways To Train on the Job," *HR Magazine*, September 2008, 108.

29. Ibid.

30. Ibid., 105.

31. Ibid.

32. Anthony Davis, "Sky High," *PROFIT Guide*, March 2004, http://www.profitguide.com/shared/print.jsp?content_20040213_171556_4580.

33. Anne Fisher, "How to Network—and Enjoy It," *Fortune*, 4 April 2005, 38; Daisy Wademan, "The Best Advice I Ever Got," *Harvard Business Review*, January 2005, 35–38; E. R. 'Bud' Giesinger, "A Formal Mentoring Program Puts Informal Goodwill to Work," *Houston Business Journal*, 6 January 2006.

34. John Worsley Simpson, "All Great Networkers Are Successful," *National Post*, 22 March 2006, WK5.

35. Janice Wismer," *Canadian Business*, 2004, http://www.canadianbusiness.com/allstars/best_innovative_exec.html.

36. "The Puzzle of the Lost Women," *Financial Times*, 1 March 2005, 10.

37. "Networking Should Cross Ethnic Lines," *Orange County Register*, 18 August 2005; Dean Takahashi, "Ethnic Network Helps Immigrants Succeed," *The Wall Street Journal Interactive Edition*, 28 July 1999; Benita Newton, "National Networking Event Makes Its Way to Virginia for First Time," Norfolk, (Virginia) *Virginian-Pilot*, 21 July 2005.

38. "Women's Economic Equality Campaign," Canadian Labour Congress, 2009, http://www.canadianlabour.ca/en/womens_economic_equa; "Labour Force and Participation Rates by Sex and Age Group," Statistics Canada, 8 January 2009, http://www40.statcan.gc.ca/l01/cst01/labor05-eng.htm; "Status Report on Pay Equity Laws in Canada," Canadian Labour Congress, 10 November 2008, http://canadianlabour.ca/en/status-report-pay-equity-laws-canada;"Working Women: Still a Long Way from Equality," Canadian Labour Congress, 3 March 2008, http://canadianlabour.ca/sites/clc/files/updir/WorkingWomenEn.txt; "Pay Equity and Women in Canada," Canadian Feminist Alliance for International Action, 1 January 2007, http://www.fafia-afai.org/en/pay_equity_and_women_in_canada; Colin Freeze, "Bell Settles Pay Equity Dispute," *The Globe and Mail*, 16 May 2006, A5.

39. "Hewitt Study Finds Salaries Will Remain Constant Despite Faltering Economy," Hewitt Associates, 2 September 2009, http://www.hewittassociates.com/Intl/NA/en-US/AboutHewitt/Newsroom/PressReleaseDetail.aspx?cid=5526.

40. "Hewitt Point of View: How to Manage Compensation Costs Proactively in a Changing Economy," Hewitt Associates, November 2008, http://www.hewittassociates.com/_MetaBasicCMAssetCache_/Assets/Articles/2008/hewitt_pov_comp%20costs.pdf.

41. Glen Fest, "Incentive Pay: Compensating for Good Relationships," *Bank Technology News*, 1 June 2005.

42. Christine Larson, "Time Out," *U.S. News & World Report*, 28 February 2005; Lynda V. Mapes, "Two Local Companies Are Proving It Pays to Do Well by Workers," *Seattle Times*, 31 January 2005; Danielle Sacks, "Not the Retiring Sort," *Fast Company*, May 2005; "Baby Boomer and Generation X Workers Agree When It Comes to Voluntary Benefits, Says Aon Consulting," PR Newswire, 31 January 2006.

43. "The Canadian Labour Market at a Glance: Employees Participating in Selected Non-Wage Benefits," Statistics Canada, 25 November 2008, http://www.statcan.gc.ca/pub/71-222-x/2008001/sectionl/k-emp-eng.htm.

44. Linda M. Byron, "Strategic Benefit Plan Design to Meet Demographic Change," *Canadian Benefits & Compensation Digest*, December 2008, 10.

45. Jim Pearse, "Premium Value," *Benefits Canada*, 1 May 2008, http://www.benefitscanada.com/benefit/health/article.jsp?content=20080529_110610_4324.

46. Hermann Schwind, Hari Das and Terry Wagar, *Canadian Human Resource Management — A Strategic Approach*, 8th ed. (Toronto: McGraw-Hill Ryerson, 2007), 414.

47. Sarah Coles, "Canada's Crunch," *Employee Benefits*, January 2009, 28; Brooke Smith, "Out of Reach," *Benefits Canada*, 23 May 2007, http://www.benefitscanada.com/benefit/health/article.jsp?content=20070523_150213_6320.

48. Michael Hayes, "Outrageous Employee Benefits," *Journal of Accountancy*, 1 May 2005.

49. "Toyota, Dalsa, Manulife Among Canada's Top Employers; Nine Companies with Ties to Area Make MediaCorp's Top 100 list," *The Kitchener Record*, 18 March 2006, http://web.lexis-nexis.com/universe.

50. Katherine Macklem, "Top 100 Employers," Macleans.ca, 20 October 2003, http://www.macleans.ca/webspecials/article.jsp?content=20031020_67488_67488.

51. Coles, "Canada's Crunch."

52. Leah Carlson, "Businesses Decry Proposed Tax on Flex Benefits," *Employee Benefit News*, 1 May 2005.

53. Macklem, "Top 100 Employers."

54. "What Role Will HRIS Be Playing This Year?" *Human Resource Department Management Report*, 1 January 2005; "Outsourcing Benefits Administration?" *Payroll Manager's Report*, 1 February 2005.

55. Sarah Dougherty, "Flex Schedules Save Money," *Financial Post*, 3 May 2006, http://web.lexis-nexis.com/universe/.

56. "The Canadian Labour Market at a Glance: Alternative Work Arrangements," Statistics Canada, 25 November 2008, http://www.statcan.gc.ca/pub/71-222-x/2008001/sectionl/l-work-travail-eng.htm.

57. "Canadian Studies on Telework, etc." InnoVisions Canada, 2009, http://www.ivc.ca/studies/canada/index.htm; Sarah Dougherty, "Flex Schedules Save Money," *Financial Post*, 3 May 2006, http://web.lexis-nexis.com/universe/; Michelle Conlin, "Call Centers in the Rec Room," *BusinessWeek*, 23 January 2006; InnoVisions Canada, "Telework: Recruitment, Retention and Jobs," InnoVisions Canada, 2006, http://www.ivc.ca/jobs/index.html.

58. Susan J. Wells, "Layoff Aftermath," *HR Magazine*, November 2008, 38.

59. Ibid.

60. "How New Style Exit Interviews Can Help You Reduce Turnover," *Human Resource Department Management Report*, 1 April 2005; Lee Conrad, "Hated Working Here? Log On and Vent," *Bank Technology News*, 1 April 2005; Robert Half, "Enlightening Departures," *NZ Business*, 1 August 2005.

61. Uyen Vu, "What's Our Turnover Rate?" *Canadian HR Reporter*, 20 October 2003, 5.

62. Schwind, Das, and Wagar, *Canadian Human Resource Management*, 163.

63. "Employment Equity Act," Department of Justice Canada, 3 March 2006, http://laws.justice.gc.ca/en/E-5.401/238505.html#rid-238508.

64. "Top Court Rules Against N.B. Miner in Mandatory Retirement Case," CBC News, 18 July 2008, http://www.cbc.ca/canada/story/2008/07/18/scoc-retirement.html.

65. "Retiring Mandatory Retirement," CBC News Online, 9 December 2005, http://www.cbc.ca/news/background/retirement/mandatory_retirement.html.

## Chapter 13

1. "Labor union," Wikipedia, 1 February 2004, http://en.wikipedia.org/wiki/Labor_union.

2. John Hoerr, "Lucky Strike," *Harper's*, 1 June 2005; Kris Maher, "Share of the U.S. Work Force in Unions Held Steady in 2005," *The Wall Street Journal*, 21 January 2006.

3. Paolo Quattrone, "Is Time Spent, Passed, or Counted? The Missing Link Between Time and Accounting History," *Accounting Historian's Journal*, 1 June 2005; Paula Dobbyn, "Alaska High in Union Tally," *Anchorage Daily News*, 21 January 2006.

4. Gerry Varricchio, Director of Organizing for Central and Eastern Canada for the Labourers' International Union of North America (LIUNA), interview, 16 February 2009.

5. Ibid.

6. Danielle Welty, "U. Nebraska Student Plans Mock Sweatshop to Raise Student Awareness," University Wire, 21 March 2005.

7. Marlon Manuel, "Warped Speed: Where Has All the Time Gone?" *Atlanta Journal and Constitution*, 12 May 2002, A1.

8. "Labour Unions," Statistics Canada, 19 March 2004, http://142.206.72.67/02/02e/02e_011_e.htm.

9. "Union Centrals, National," The Canadian Encyclopedia, 2006, http://www.thecanadianencyclopedia.com/index.cfm?PgNm=TCE&Params=A1ARTA0008214.

10. Ibid.

11. "Welcome," Canadian Labour Congress, 2009, http://canadianlabour.ca/en/welcome.

12. "Average Hourly Wages of Employees by Selected Characteristics and Profession, Unadjusted Data, by Province (Monthly)," Statistics Canada, 9 April 2009, http://www40.statcan.gc.ca/l01/cst01/labr69a-eng.htm.

13. D.W. Livingston and M. Raykov, "Union Influence on Worker Education and Training in Canada in Tough Times," *Just Labour*, Vol. 5 (Winter 2005), http://www.justlabour.yorku.ca/Livingstone_Raykov.pdf.

14. "Welcome to Canada's Largest Union," Canadian Union of Public Employees, 17 March 2006, http://cupe.ca/about/Welcome_to_Canadas_l.

15. "Facts," Canadian Auto Workers, 2007, http://www.caw.ca/en/media-centre-facts.htm.

16. "Over 1,000 Canadian Workers Die Each Year Due to an Unsafe Workplace," The Canadian Labour Congress, 27 April 2009, http://canadianlabour.ca/en/canadian-labour-congress-action-centre/over-1000-canadian-workers-die-each-year-due-unsafe-workplace; "Safe Workplaces: The Right to a Safe and Healthy Workplace," Workrights.ca, http://www.workrights.ca/Health+and+Safety/Safe+Workplaces.htm; "Workplace Dangers (Right to Know About Workplace Dangers)," Workrights.ca, http://www.workrights.ca/Health+and+Safety/Workplace+dangers.htm.

17. "Life Is Cheap at Wal-Mart: Company Orders 40 Employees to Search for a Bomb," United Food and Commercial Workers Canada., 11 July 2006, http://www.ufcw.ca/Default.aspx?SectionId=af80f8cf-ddd2-4b12-9f41-641ea94d4fa4&LanguageId=1&ItemId=d11797a6-5cc1-4a82-ac07-ccb922d6fa83.

18. "The Board's Role," Canada Industrial Relations Board, 23 October 2003, htttp://www.cirb-ccri.gc.ca/about/role_e.html.

19. Varricchio, interview, 16 February 2009.

20. Ibid.

21. "What is Conciliation?" Government of Ontario, 27 September 2005, http://www.labour.gov.on.ca/english/lr/faq/lr_faq2.html.

22. Ibid.

23. "National Mediation Board Puts UPS Talks with IPA in Recess," Business Wire, 23 June 2005; Paul Monies, "Settlements Offered in DHL-Teamsters Dispute," Daily Oklahoman, 6 January 2006.

24. "N.W.T. Power Employees Holding Strike Vote," CBC News, 6 April 2006, http://www.cbc.ca/north/story/nor-power-mediation.html.

25. "Essential Services," CBC News, 6 May 2008, http://www.cbc.ca/news/background/strike/.

26. "Definition—Wildcat Strike," WebFinance Inc., 2005, http://www.investorwords.com/5316/wildcat_strike.html.

27. Tavia Grant, "TTC Strike Could Cost Toronto," The Globe and Mail, 29 May 2006, http://www.theglobeandmail.com/servlet/story/RTGAM.20060529.wttceco0529/BNStory/Business/home; "TTC Strike Is Over, but More Trouble Could Lie Ahead," CBC News, 30 May 2006, http://www.cbc.ca/toronto/story/toTTCstrike0060530.html.

28. "Boycott Pepsi, Strikers Tell Consumers," CBC News, 30 May 2006, http://www.cbc.ca/nl/story/nf-pepsi-strike-20060530.html.

29. "Strikes and Lockouts," The Canadian Encyclopedia, 2006, http://www.thecanadianencyclopedia.com/index.cfm?PgNm=TCE&Params=J1ARTJ0007754; "Telus Workers Launch Work-to-Rule," CBC News, 20 June 2005, http://www.cbc.ca/story/business/national/2005/06/20/telus-050620.html.

30. "Essential Services Legislation Undermines Public Education," British Columbia Teachers' Federation, http://www.bctf.ca/bargain/rights/EssentialServices.html.

31. "Back-to-Work Legislation: When Negotiations Fail," CBC News Online, 13 October 2005, http://www.cbc.ca/news/background/strike/backtowork.html.

32. "CAW Reaches Pension Funding Agreement with Air Canada," Canadian Auto Workers, 19 February 2004, http://www.caw.ca/news/newsnow/news.asp?art10_369.

33. "Ontario Legislature Ends York University Strike," CBC News, 29 January 2009, http://www.cbc.ca/canada/toronto/story/2009/01/29/york-strike.html.

34. Ibid.

35. Allan Swift, "Storm Gathers over Sky-High Compensation for Top Air Canada Executives," Canoe, 16 November 2003, http://money.canoe.ca/News/Sectors/Consumer/AirCanada/2003/11/16/pdf-259744.html.

36. Norm Brodsky, "Why the Union Can't Win," Inc., March 2005, 55–56.

37. Hoyt N. Wheeler, "The Third Way," Business & Economic Review, January–March 2005, 6–8.

38. Jeffrey Pfeffer, "In Praise of Organized Labor," Business 2.0, June 2005, 80.

39. "Labour Laws and Human Rights," CIC Canada, www.cic.gc.ca/english/newcomer/welcome/wel-10e.html.

40. Joseph S. Mancinelli, International Vice-President for Central and Eastern Canada for the Labourers' International Union of North America (LIUNA), interview, 16 February 2009.

41. "CEO Scorecard 2008," Financial Post, 2009, http://www.financialpost.com/magazine/ceo/scorecard/index.html#120.

42. Alia McMullen, "CEO Pay in Canada to Come Under Spotlight," Financial Post, 2 January 2009, http://www.financialpost.com/story.html?id=1134977.

43. Jeffrey Pfeffer, "The Pay-for-Performance Fallacy," Business 2.0, July 2005, 64.

44. Michael Sisk, "Taking Stock," Inc., April 2005, 34.

45. "Loblaw Executives Forgo 2005 Bonuses," The Globe and Mail, 18 March 2006, B3.

46. William F. Buckley, "Capitalism's Boil," National Review, 23 May 2005, 58; David Barkholz, "Delphi Compensation Plan Troubles Lenders; Banks Want to Base Pay on Performance," Automotive News, 9 January 2006.

47. Louis Lavelle, "Consulting Even Beyond the Grave," BusinessWeek, 28 February 2005, 14.

48. McMullen, "CEO Pay in Canada."

49. Blanca Torres, "Pace of Chief Executive Compensation Continues Rapid Rise," Baltimore Sun, 15 May 2005.

50. Jack Ewing and Justin Hibbard, "The Bell Tolls for Germany Inc.," BusinessWeek, 15 August 2005, 40–41.

51. Georrfrey Colvin, "CEO Knockdown," Fortune, 5 April 2005, 19-20.

52. Kate O'Sullivan, "Targeting Executive Pay," CFO, March 2005, 15; Becky Yerak, "SEC Wants Executive Pay, Perks Spelled Out," Chicago Tribune, 18 January 2006.

53. Eoin Callan, "Clark's Pay Rekindles Compensation Debate," Financial Post, 20 February 2009, http://www.financialpost.com/story.html?id=1310188.

54. Robert J. Samuelson, "No Joke: CEOs Do Some Good," Newsweek, 18 April 2005, 49.

55. Ann Merrill, "General Mills Lauded for Aid to Working Mothers," Minneapolis Star Tribune, 24 September 2002, 1D.

56. Laura Koss-Feder, "Providing for Parents the 'Sandwich Generation' Looks for New Solutions," Time, 17 March 2003, G8.

57. Stephen Barr, "Elder Care Becoming Major Issue for Many Workers," Washington Post, 20 August 2002, B2.

## Chapter 14

1. George Potts, "Deconstructing the M Word," Inc., January 2006, 16–17.

2. Jena McGregor, "Would You Recommend Us?" BusinessWeek, 30 January 2006, 94–95.

3. V. Kumar, Rajkumar Venkatesan, and Werner Reinartz, "Knowing What to Sell, When, and to Whom," Harvard Business Review, March 2006, 131–137.

4. Michael Lowenstein, "What Do Customers Want?" Deliver, March 2006, 17.

5. Joseph C. Nunes and Xavier Dréze, "Your Loyalty Program Is Betraying You," Harvard Business Review, April 2006, 124–131.

6. Steve Harding, Executive Director of Marketing and Communications, Canadian Blood Services, interview, 26 June 2006.

7. Daniel Yee, "Students Demand Veggies," Washington Times, 12 January 2006, A2.

8. Frederick G. Crane et al., Marketing, 7th Canadian ed. (Toronto: McGraw-Hill Ryerson, 2008), 310.

9. Lora Kolodny, "Things I Can't Live Without: Andy Berliner," Inc., July 2005, 64.

10. Crane et al., Marketing, 287.

11. "Priced to Sell," Entrepreneur, February 2006, 100.

12. Crane et al., Marketing, 329.

13. Geoff Williams, "Name Your Price," Entrepreneur, September 2005, 108–15.

14. Peter Lattman, "Cheapskates," Forbes, 4 July 2005, 76–77.

15. Rafi Mohammed, "Pick the Right Price Point to Pull in Profits," Entrepreneur, January 2006, 27.

16. Geoffrey Colvin, "The FedEx Edge," Fortune, 3 April 2006, 77–84.

17. Stephanie Clifford, "Running Through the Legs of Goliath," *Inc.*, February 2006, 103–9.

18. John E. (Jack) West, "Listening to the Customer," *Quality Digest*, February 2006, 16.

19. Steven Levy and Brad Stone, "The New Wisdom of the Web," *Newsweek*, 3 April 2006, 47–53.

20. Lynda Hurst, "How the Boomers Will Go Bust," *Toronto Star*, 23 September 2000, A20.

21. "Kidfluence," YTV Media, 2008, http://www.corusmedia.com/ytv/research/index.asp#TWEEN.

22. "Outlook Continues to Darken with Dismal New Data and Predictions," *Toronto Star*, 17 December 2008, http://www.thestar.com/article/555293.

23. Steve Buist, "Great Glasses Appeal Dismissed by Supreme Court of Canada," *The Burlington Post*, 17 June 2009, http://www.burlingtonpost.com/news/article/261941.

24. Steve Hamm, "An eBay for Business Software," *BusinessWeek*, 19 September 2005, 78–79.

25. Eve Lazarus, "B.C. Lions Brew Up New Brand Extension," *Marketing Magazine*, 27 August 2008, http://www.marketingmag.ca/english/news/marketer/article.jsp?content=20080827_145922_31268.

26. Ibid.

27. Omar El Akkad, "For HSBC, It's All About Location," *The Globe and Mail*, 6 May 2006, B3.

28. Crane et al., *Marketing*, 233.

29. Ibid.

30. "Shoppers Moves to Localize Merchandise, Boost Marketing," *The Globe and Mail*, 2 May 2006, B10.

31. Paul Brent, "The Best of '08 Media Players: Transcontinental Media," *Marketing Magazine*, 24 November 2008, http://www.marketingmag.ca/english/news/media/article.jsp?content=20081218_110059_17612.

32. Crane et al., *Marketing*, 76.

33. Ibid.

## Chapter 15

1. Michael D. Lemonick, "Are We Losing Our Edge?," *Time*, 13 February 2006, 22–31.

2. Avery Johnson, "Hotels Take 'Know Your Customer' to New Level," *The Wall Street Journal*, 7 February 2006, D1 and D3.

3. Paul Taylor, "Can There Be Any Future for Traditional Telephony?" *Financial Times*, 22 February 2006, 1.

4. Mike Hogan, "Go the Distance," *Entrepreneur*, April 2006, 57.

5. Jeremy Grant, "Golden Arches Bridge Local Tastes," *Financial Times*, 9 February 2006, 10.

6. Jeremy Grant, "Appetite for Plastic Makes Fast Food a Short Order," *Financial Times*, 3 January 2006, 17.

7. Pascal Zachary, "Evolution of an Envelope," *Business 2.0*, April 2006, 70.

8. Paul Kaihla, "Sexing Up a Piece of Meat," *Business 2.0*, April 2006, 72–76.

9. Eric Swetsky, "Barbie's Rule," *Marketing Magazine*, 3 July 2006, http://www.marketingmag.ca/magazine/current/top_mind/article.jsp?content=20060703_68651_68651.

10. "No Apple for Vancouver Island School, Says Computer Corporation," CBC News, 6 October 2008, http://www.cbc.ca/technology/story/2008/10/06/bc-school-apple-logo.html.

11. Michele Kayal, "Brand Quest: This Summer, Aston Hotels Will Rebrand as ResortQuest Hawaii," *TravelAge West*, 30 May 2005.

12. John Gray, "Canada's Top 50 Brands," Canadian Business Online, 18 June 2007, http://www.canadianbusiness.com/managing/strategy/article.jsp?content=20070619_131518_5568.

13. Niraj Dawar, "What Are Brands Good For?" *Sloan Management Review*, Fall 2004, 31–37.

14. "IBM to Sell PC Unit: Report," CBC News, 3 December 2004, http://www.cbc.ca/money/story/2004/12/03/ibm-sale041203.html.

15. Alison Stein Wellner, "Boost Your Bottom Line by Taking the Guesswork Out of Pricing," *Inc.*, June 2005, 72–82.

16. Brent Jang, "Air Canada Goes Off the Bottle," *The Globe and Mail*, 20 April 2006, A6.

17. "Nintendo GameCube Set at Mass Market Price of $199.95," Encyclopedia.com, 21 May 2001, http://www.encyclopedia.com/

doc/1G1-74824260.html; "Dedicated Gameplay System Launches November 5, 2001, with Six First-Party Titles Prices at $49.95," Nintendo of America, *Inc.*, 21 May 2001, http://www.nintendoworldreport.com/newsArt.cfm?artid=5963.

18. Julian Hunt, "Losing Their Religion? Julian Hunt Finds Worshipers at the Altar of EDLP Are Having Their Faith Challenged," *Grocer*, 12 March 2005.

19. John Springer, "Better Pricing, Promotions Required, Speakers Say," *Supermarket News*, 9 May 2005.

20. Rob Carter, "The FedEx Edge," *Fortune*, 3 April 2006, 77–84.

21. Kyle Cattani, Hans Sebastian Heese, Wendell Gilland, and Jayashankar Swaminathan, "When Manufacturers Go Retail," *MIT Sloan Management Review*, Winter 2006, 9.

22. Daniel Nissanoff, "Futureshop," *Fast Company*, January–February 2006, 103.

23. "Retail Trade, by Industry," Statistics Canada, 22 June 2009, http://www40.statcan.gc.ca/l01/cst01/trad15a-eng.htm; "Employment, Payroll Employment, by Industry (Retail Trade)," Statistics Canada, 20 May 2009, http://www40.statcan.gc.ca/l01/cst01/labr71g-eng.htm.

24. Greg Holden, "Fast Forward," *Entrepreneur*, May 2006, 63–69.

25. Sarah Schmidt, "'Do Not Call List' Has Telemarketers Worried About Hackers Eliminating Entire Phone Book," *The Vancouver Sun*, 19 March 2008, http://www.canada.com/vancouversun/news/story.html?id=5c2c11b6-6fa3-470f-8351-c4291cbf57fa.

26. "National Do Not Call List," Canadian Radio-television and Telecommunications Commission, 22 November 2008, https://www.lnnte-dncl.gc.ca/insnum-regnum-eng.

27. Alan Farnham, "The Party That Crashed Retailing," *Forbes*, 1 November 2005, 80–81.

28. Randall Rothenberg, "Despite All the Talk, Ad and Media Shops Aren't Truly Integrated," Advertising Age, 27 March 2006, 24.

29. Stephen Baker, "Wiser About the Web," *BusinessWeek*, 27 March 2006, 54–58.

30. "Behind the Scenes," Rubicon Consulting, 2 March 2007, http://rubiconconsulting.com/nilofer/view/2007/03/3000-marketing-messages-per-da/.

31. "Canadian Ad Spend Across All Media Signals Strong Growth to 2011: CMA," Canadian Marketing Association, 12 November 2007, http://www.the-cma.org/?WCE=C=47%7CK=227708.

32. Westin Renehart, "What Your Targets Are Saying," *Advertising Age*, 28 March 2005, 94; "Sirius XM Set to Launch 'Best of Both' Programming on October 6th," Digital Home Canada, 11 September 2008, http://www.digitalhome.ca/content/view/2821/281/.

33. Paul Holmes, "Senior Marketers Are Sharply Divided About the Role of PR in the Overall Mix," *Advertising Age*, 24 January 2005, C1 and C2.

34. Clark S. Judge, "PR Lessons from the Pentagon," *The Wall Street Journal*, 1 April 2003, B2.

35. Kristine Owram, "Maple Leaf Foods CEO Michael McCain Named Business Newsmaker of the Year," The Canadian Press, 2 January 2009, http://www.fftimes.com/node/218140.

36. Frederick G. Crane et al., *Marketing*, 7th Canadian ed. (Toronto: McGraw-Hill Ryerson, 2008), 430; "Canadian Ad Spend," Canadian Marketing Association; Lawrence M. Kimmel, "Direct Marketing Can't Get Lost in the Mail," *Advertising Age*, 16 January 2006, 15.

## Chapter 16

1. Ellen Heffes, "Accounting: Trends Affecting the Next Generation of Accountants," *Financial Executive*, 1 September 2005.

2. Mike McNamee, "Finance: Annual Reports: Still Not Enough Candor," *Business Week*, 24 March 2003, 74.

3. "Become a CGA," CGA-Canada, www.cga-canada.org/eng/designation/cga-become.htm.

4. Michael Connor, "Accountants Group Sees Continued Role," *Reuters Business*, 20 March 2003.

5. David Henry, "The Business Week 50: Investing for Growth: Cleaning Up the Numbers," *Business Week*, 25 March 2003, 126.

6. David Henry and Robert Berner, "Finance: Accounting: Ouch! Real Numbers," *Business Week*, 24 March 2003, 72.

7. Greg Farrell, "CPAs Look for an Ad Agency to Rebuild Images," *USA Today*, 26 February 2003, 2B.

8. Paul Craig Roberts, "Unintended Consequences of Earlier Reforms Bit Market Hard," *Washington Times*, 16 March 2003.

9. Mary Flood, "Andersen Document Shredding Conviction Overturned," *Houston Chronicle*, 1 June 2005; Elwin Green, "Scandal also Brought Arthur Andersen Down," *Pittsburgh Post-Gazette*, 31 January 2006.

10. J. Bonasia, "Deloitte Going Against the Grain in 'Mixing' Accounting, Consulting," *Investors Business Daily*, 24 February 2005, A4.

11. Steve Hamm, "Death, Taxes, & Sarbanes-Oxley," *BusinessWeek*, 17 January 2005, 28–32; Terence O'Hara, "Excavations in Accounting; To Monitor Internal Controls, Firms Dig Ever Deeper into Their Books," *Washington Post*, 30 January 2006.

12. Stacy A. Teicher, "Job of 'Policing' Companies May Fall More to Auditors," *Christian Science Monitor*, 31 March 2003, 18.

13. Carrie Johnson Washington, "Corporate Audit Panels to Gain Power; SEC Passes New Rules," *Washington Post*, 2 April 2003, E2.

14. Matt Krantz, "More Annual Reports Delayed," *USA Today*, 2 April 2003, 1B; McNamee, "Still Not Enough Candor."

15. Floyd Norris, "How KPMG Was Given a Lesson in Humility," *International Herald Tribune*, 30 August 2005; Celia Whitaker, "Bridging the Book-Tax Accounting Gap," Yale Law Journal, 1 December 2005.

16. Jeffrey Battersby, "QuickBooks Pro 5.0," *MacWorld*, 1 April 2003, 34.

17. Randy Johnston, "Management & Compliance: Accounting Software Is Morphing to Business Management Software," *CPA Technology Advisor*, 1 August 2005.

18. Nicole Torres, "Count Me In: Scared of Numbers? With These Accounting Tips You Won't Be," *Entrepreneur*, 1 April 2005.

19. Randy Johnston, "Your Accounting Software Should Have Business Management & Analytics," *CPA Technology Advisor*, 1 September 2005; Gregory L. LaFollette, "The Dream Team: Meet America's Tax and Accounting Technology Dream Team," *CPA Technology Advisor*, 1 January 2006.

20. Barbara Hagenbaugh, "Rules Spur Demand for Accountants," *USA Today*, 18 January 2005, B1; "Back to Basics Necessitated by Law," *USA Today*, 1 December 2005.

21. Mike Vorster, "Balance Sheet Basics," *Construction Equipment*, 1 February 2005; Joseph S. Eastern, "How to Read a Balance Sheet," *Family Practice News*, 1 January 2006.

22. Samuel Greengard, "Get a Grip on Assets," *Business Finance*, January 2002, 39–42.

23. David Whelan, "Beyond the Balance Sheet: Hot Brand Values," *Forbes*, 20 June 2005, 113–15.

24. Kenneth Dogra, "Accounting for Goodwill: Why Are Firms Willing to Pay So Much for Takeovers When the Goodwill Burden Is Onerous?" *Financial Management*, 1 May 2005; Greg Paeth, "Scripps Weighs Sale of Channel," *Cincinnati Post*, 3 February 2006.

25. Jennifer Heebner, "Snapshot of an Income Statement," *Jewelers Circular Keystone*, 1 May 2005; "Here's a Sweet Lesson on Income Statements," *The Bergen County (New Jersey) Record*, 14 April 2005.

26. Elizabeth MacDonald, "The EBITDA Folly," Forbes, 17 March 2003, 165.

27. Virginia Munger Kahn, "Beating the Cash Crunch," *BusinessWeek Small Biz*, Spring 2005; Kenneth L. Parkinson, "Cash Flow Forecasting: Do It Better and Save," *Financial Executive*, 1 January 2006; John S. McClenahen and Traci Purdum, "Cash Flow Is King," *Industry Week*, 1 February 2006.

28. "Warning! How to Tell if You Are Having Cash Flow Problems Before It's Too Late," Visa Canada, www.visa.ca/smallbusiness/article.cfm?cat_3&subcat_95&articleID_101.

29. Jason Kirby, "Mr. Moneybags," *Canadian Business*, 15 March 2004, www.canadianbusiness.com/columns/article.jsp?content_20040315_59015_59015.

30. McNamee, "Still Not Enough Candor," 74.

31. Sativa Ross, "All in the Numbers: Does Your Income Statement and Balance Sheet Provide a Winning Combination?," *Aftermarket Business*, 1 May 2005.

32. Tom Judge, "Liquidity Ratio Can Help Spot Cash Gap," *Powersports Business*, 14 March 2005.

## Chapter 17

1. Jane von Bergen, "Calling All Accountants," *Philadelphia Enquirer*, 12 October 2005; David Simanoff, "Accountants Can Count on More Job Offers," *Tampa Tribune*, 26 June 2005; Mike Allen, "Supply and Demand Works in Accountants' Favor: Firms Are Desperately Seeking Skilled CPAs," *San Diego Business Journal*, 16 January 2006.

2. Nanette Byrnes and Louis Lavelle, "The Corporate Tax Game," *BusinessWeek*, 31 March 2003, 78–83.

3. Gary McWilliams, "Dell Puts Cash Flow to Work," *The Wall Street Journal*, 25 April 2005, C3.

4. Michael Hunstad, "Better Forecasting: Know Your Cash Flows," *Financial Executive*, 1 May 2005; Kenneth L. Parkinson, "Cash Flow Forecasting: Do It Better and Save," *Financial Executive*, 1 January 2006.

5. Patrick Kilts, "Effective Cash Flow Management Improves Investment Outlook," *Crain's Cleveland Business*, 19 September 2005; Bruce Perryman, "Grow with the Flow," *Stitches Magazine*, 1 January 2005; Andi Gray, "The Optimum Growth Model," *Fairfield County Business Journal*, 30 January 2006.

6. Tim Reason, "Budgeting in the Real World," *CFO*, July 2005, 43–48.

7. Mara Der Hovanesian, "Cash: Burn, Baby, Burn," *BusinessWeek*, 28 April 2003, 82–83.

8. Jordan I. Shifrin, "All Boards Must Grapple with Budget Issues," *Daily Herald*, 4 June 2005.

9. Charles Mulford, "A Best Practices Approach to Cash Flow Reporting: Implications for Analysis," *Business Credit*, 1 January 2005.

10. Anne Tergesen, "Cash-Flow Hocus-Pocus," *BusinessWeek*, 16 July 2002, 130–32.

11. Paul Katzeff, "Manage Accounts Receivable Upfront Before There's a Problem," *Investors Business Daily*, 27 January 2003, A4.

12. Krissah Williams Washington, "How Stores Play Their Cards: They'll Give Discounts and Awards to Get Interest and Bigger Sales," *Washington Post*, 2 February 2003, H5.

13. Linda Stern, "Credit Card Issuers Offer Some Good Deals," *Reuters Business*, 1 March 2003.

14. Lisa McLaughlin, "New Brew on the Block," *Time*, 20 January 2003, 143.

15. Courtney McGrath, "Bankers You Can Love," *Kiplinger's*, April 2003, 46–48.

16. Susan C. Thompson, "Mixing Personal, Business Funds Is a Formula for Bankruptcy," *St. Louis Post-Dispatch*, 5 August 2005; Carolyn M. Brown, "Borrowing from Dad: Financing from Relatives and Friends Has Risks and Rewards," *Black Enterprise*, 1 January 2005.

17. Kate Ashford, "Lend to a Friend (Without Regret): Four Things to Do When a Pal Asks for a Loan," *Money*, 1 November 2005.

18. Janice Revell, "How Debt Triggers Can Sink a Stock," *Fortune*, 18 March 2002, 147–51.

19. John M. Berry, "Low Interest Rates Are Allowing Corporations to Boost Profit," *Washington Post*, 19 April 2003, D12.

20. Liza Casabona, "Origins of Factoring Come Full Circle," *WWD*, 19 September 2005; "Texas Oil Drill Bit Manufacturer Taps into a $1 Million Factoring Credit Line," *PR Newswire*, 1 February 2006.

21. Toni Clarke and Jed Stelzer, "Merck Profit Rises on Higher Drug Sales," *Reuters Business*, 21 April 2003.

22. Jean Ende, "Card Issuers Charge After Owners," *Crain's New York Business*, 18 July 2005.

23. Amy Barrett, "Pfizer's Funk," *BusinessWeek*, 28 February 2005; Jennifer Bayot, "Pfizer's Pain Inflamed by Weak Sales," *International Herald Tribune*, 6 April 2005.

24. The Canadian Securities Course 1993 (Toronto: The Canadian Securities Institute, 1992), 63.

25. Justin Fox, "Show Us the Money," *Fortune*, 3 February 2003, 76–78.

26. Walter Updegrave, "Dividend Mania, What the Bush Dividend Plan Would Really Mean for You," *Money*, 1 March 2003, 69–74.

27. "The Preferred Route to Income Preferred Stocks Offer the Most Sumptuous Dividend Payments Around," *Money*, 1 March 2003, 54B.

28. Michael Barbaro, "Primus Agrees to Sell Convertible Preferred Stock," *Washington Post*, 1 January 2003, E5.

## Appendix D

1. Nitin Nohria, "Risk, Uncertainty, and Doubt," *Harvard Business Review*, February 2006, 39–40.
2. Andrew Jack, "The Bird Flu Issue Has Landed," *Financial Times*, 10 January 2006, 8.
3. Eric Schoeniger, "How to Plug the $13 Billion Leak," *BusinessWeek*, 20 March 2006, 2–5; M. Eric Johnson, "A Broader Context for Information Security," a special section in *Financial Times* called "Mastering Risk," 16 September 2005, 1–12.
4. Charlie Ross, "Jackson Action," *The Wall Street Journal*, 15 September 2005, A21.
5. Michel Crouhy, Dan Galai, and Robert Mark, *The Essentials of Risk Management*, (New York: McGraw Hill, 2006), 1–11.
6. James Altucher, "Living with Bird Flu, Sharks and Hurricanes," *Financial Times*, 4 April 2006, 10.
7. Deborah Wince-Smith, "Innovate at Your Own Risk," *Harvard Business Review*, May 2005, 25.
8. Keith Goffin and Rick Mitchell, "The Risks of Innovation," a special section in *Financial Times* called "Managing Risk," 30 September 2005, 1–12.
9. Norm Brodsky, "How Much Risk Can You Take?," *Inc.*, December 2005, 73–74.
10. Maggie Urry, "Business Stands By and Sees Profits Go to Blazes," *Financial Times*, 25 April 2006, 4.
11. Tamsyn Burgmann and Joan Bryden, "Health Officials Tie Listeria Outbreaks to Maple Leaf Meats," *The Globe and Mail*, 23 August 2008, www.theglobeandmail.com/servlet/story/RTGAM.20080823.wmapleleaf0823/BNStory/National.
12. Erin White, "Smaller Companies Join the Outsourcing Trend," *The Wall Street Journal*, 8 May 2006, B3. 15. Jack Kemp, "How Congress Stalks the Economic Upturn," *Washington Times*, 4 August 2005, p. A17.
13. Amy Borrus, Mike McNamee, and Howard Gleckman, "Up to His Neck in the Risk Pool," *BusinessWeek*, 6 June 2005, 109–11; Andrea Siedsma, "Insurance Well Spent," *Hispanic Business*, March 2006, 48–50.
14. Jeffrey Kluger, "Global Warming," *Time*, 3 April 2006, 28–42; Thomas G. Donlan, "Take the Hot Air Out of Global Warming," Barron's, 5 December 2005, 47.
15. David Ignatius, "Corporate Green," *Washington Post*, 11 May 2005, A17.
16. Holman W. Jenkins, "A Global Warming Worksheet," *The Wall Street Journal*, 1 February 2006, A15.
17. Chip Giller and David Roberts, "Green Gets Going," *Fast Company*, March 2006, 73–78.

## Chapter 18

1. Financial Consumer Agency of Canada, "About the Financial Services Sector," 22 February 2009, www.fcac-acfc.gc.ca.
2. Financial Consumer Agency of Canada, "About the Financial Services Sector—Facts & Figures," 22 February 2009, www.fcac-acfc.gc.ca/eng/media/facts/default.asp.
3. Canadian Bankers Association, "Competition in the Canadian Financial Services Sector," May 2004, www.cba.ca/en/content/stats/fastfacts/040528_Competitionffact.pdf.
4. Financial Consumer Agency of Canada, "How the Industry Is Regulated," 22 February 2009, www.fcac-acfc.gc.ca/eng/industry/actsregs/default.asp.
5. The Canada Deposit Insurance Corporation, 29 January 2004, www.cdic.ca.
6. Evan I. Schwartz, "How You'll Pay," *Technology Review*, January 2003, 50–56.
7. Bank of Canada, "Counterfeit Detection," www.bankofcanada.ca/en/banknotes/counterfeit/security/index100b.html.
8. Catherine Siskos, "Cash in a Flash," *Kiplinger's*, October 2002, 30–31.
9. "Deflation Warning," *Washington Times*, 14 May 2003, A20.
10. Patrick Barta and Michelle Higgins, "Dollar's Fall Could End Many Bargains," *The Wall Street Journal*, 9 January 2003, D1, D4.

11. Bank of Canada, "Canada's Money Supply," January 2000, www.bankofcanada.ca/en/backgrounders/bg-m2.htm; Bank of Canada, "Target for the Overnight Rate," July 2001, www.bankofcanada.ca/en/backgrounders/bg-p9.htm.
12. Bank of Canada, "Canada's Money Supply."
13. Bank of Canada, "Target for the Overnight Rate."
14. Canadian Bankers Association, "Bank Earnings," April 2003, www.cba.ca/en/ViewDocument.asp?fl_6&sl_111&tl_&docid_420.
15. Canadian Bankers Association, "Income Statement—Net Income," February 2009, www.cba.ca/en/content/stats/DB251-2007-eng updated.pdf.
16. Julie Rawe, "A Mini-Mall in Your ATM," *Time*, 8 April 2002, 61.
17. Michelle Higgins, "ATMs to Go Far Beyond Cash," *The Wall Street Journal*, 6 June 2002, D1, D2.
18. Stephanie Miles, "What's a Check?" *The Wall Street Journal*, 21 October 2002, p. R5.
19. Pallavi Gogoi, "The Hot News in Banking: Bricks and Mortar," *BusinessWeek*, 21 April 2003, 83–84.
20. Insurance Bureau of Canada, "Facts on the General Insurance Industry in Canada," www.ibc.ca/pdffiles/publications/brochures/consumer/FactsBook2005.html.
21. Insurance Bureau of Canada, "Facts of the General Insurance Industry of Canada," www.ibc.ca/en/need_more_info/documents/facts book 2009_eng.pdf.
22. Financial Consumer Agency of Canada, "Financial Consumer Agency of Canada Glossary—Investment Dealer Definition," 26 February 2004, www.fcac-acfc.gc.ca/eng/glossary.asp; Investment Dealers Association of Canada, "Canadian Securities IndustryProfile," www.ida.ca/IndIssues/IndProfile_en.asp; Department of Finance Canada., "The Canadian Securities Industry—The Canadian Financial System—June 2000," 5 September 2003, www.fin.gc.ca/toce/2000/cansec_e.html.
23. Bertrand Marotte, "Regulator Assails Plan for National Stock Watchdog," *The Globe and Mail*, 22 January 2004, B6; Karen Howlett and Heather Scoffield, "Consensus Elusive over Regulator," *The Globe and Mail*, 20 January 2004, B6; "What Is the CSA?" and "Who Are the Canadian Securities Administrators?" June 2001: Canadian Securities Administrators, www.csa-acvm.ca/html_CSA/about_who_are_csa.html and www.csa-acvm.ca/html_CSA/about.html.
24. Financial Consumer Agency of Canada, "Financial Consumer Agency of Canada Glossary—Securities Commission Definition," 26 February 2004, www.fcac-acfc.gc.ca/eng/glossary.asp.
25. "Demen Found Guilty of Securities Violations," *The Gazette*, 30 September 2008, www.canada.com/montrealgazette/news/business/story.html?id=dc8f3467-0591-490f-bf65-ea5b76b732d2.
26. Financial Consumer Agency of Canada, "Financial Consumer Agency of Canada Glossary—Security Definition," 26 February 2004, www.fcac-acfc.gc.ca/eng/glossary.asp.
27. "The Case for Going Private: Corporate Ownership," *The Economist*, 25 January 2003, 67.
28. Ben White and Kathleen Day, "SEC Approves Wall Street Settlement; Conflict of Interest Targeted," *Washington Post*, 29 April 2003, A1.
29. Mara Der Hovanesian, "The Market's Closed—Wake Up," *BusinessWeek*, 3 March 2003, 132.
30. Ben White, "A Crisis of Trust on Wall Street," *Washington Post*, 4 May 2003, F1.
31. Eric Troseth, "Finding a Rally in Bearish Times," *Christian Science Monitor*, 5 May 2003, 14.
32. Jyoti Thottam, "Are Penny Stocks Worth a Look?" *Time*, 12 August 2002, 46.
33. "Hillsdale Hedge Funds Prepared for May 1st S&P/TSE Composite Index Changes," Hillsdale Investment Management, February 2002, www.hillsdaleinv.com/research/pdf/tse_change.pdf.
34. Matt Krantz, "Microsoft Stock Splits into 10 Billion Shares," *USA Today*, 19 February 2003, 1B.
35. The Investment Funds Institute of Canada, "Industry Statistics," October 2008, www.ific.ca/eng/home/index.asp.
36. John Rekenthaler, "When Mutual Funds Die, Companies Bury Their Mistakes, Distorting Returns," *Money*, April 2003, 49–53.

# Glossary

**Absolute advantage (p. 72)** The advantage that exists when a country has the ability to produce a particular good or service using fewer resources (and therefore at a lower cost) than another country.

**Accounting (p. 482)** The recording, classifying, summarizing, and interpreting of financial events and transactions to provide management and other interested parties the information they need to make good decisions.

**Accounting cycle (p. 489)** A six-step procedure that results in the preparation and analysis of the two major financial statements: the balance sheet and the income statement.

**Accounts (p. 489)** Different types of assets, liabilities, and owners' equity.

**Acquisition (p. 184)** One company's purchase of the property and obligations of another company.

**Administrative agencies (p. 129)** Federal or provincial institutions and other government organizations created by Parliament or provincial legislatures with delegated power to pass rules and regulations within their mandated area of authority.

**Advertising (p. 463)** Paid, non-personal communication through various media by organizations and individuals who are in some way identified in the advertising message.

**Agency shop (Rand formula) (p. 402)** A workplace in which a new employee is not required to join the union but must pay union dues.

**Agents and brokers (p. 458)** Marketing intermediaries that bring buyers and sellers together and assist in negotiating an exchange but don't take title to the goods.

**Amortization (p. 500)** The systematic writeoff of the cost of a tangible asset over its estimated useful life.

**Angel investors (p. 222)** Private individuals who invest their own money in potentially hot new companies before they go public.

**Annual report (p. 484)** A yearly statement of the financial condition, progress, and expectations of an organization.

**Apprentice programs (p. 364)** Training programs involving a period during which a learner works alongside an experienced employee to master the skills and procedures of a craft.

**Arbitration (p. 404)** An agreement to bring in an impartial third party (a single arbitrator or a panel of arbitrators) to render a binding decision in a labour dispute.

**Articles of incorporation (p. 184)** A legal authorization from the federal or provincial/territorial government for a company to use the corporate format.

**Assembly process (p. 312)** That part of the production process that puts together components.

**Assets (p. 493)** Economic resources (things of value) owned by a firm.

**Autocratic leadership (p. 251)** Leadership style that involves making managerial decisions without consulting others.

**Baby-boom echo (p. 18)** A demographic group of Canadians that were born in the period from 1980 to 1995: the children of the baby boomers.

**Baby boomers (p. 18)** A demographic group of Canadians that were born in the period from 1947 to 1966.

**Back-to-work legislation (p. 408)** Legislation that orders an end to a labour-management dispute that has escalated to a strike or lockout, in an industry that the government decides is essential to the operation of the economy.

**Balance of payments (p. 75)** The difference between money coming into a country (from exports) and money leaving the country (for imports) plus money flows from other factors such as tourism, foreign aid, military expenditures, and foreign investment.

**Balance of trade (p. 75)** A nation's ratio of exports to imports.

**Balance sheet (p. 491)** The financial statement that reports a firm's financial condition at a specific time.

**Bankruptcy (p. 135)** The legal process by which a person, business, or government entity unable to meet financial obligations is relieved of those obligations by a court that divides any assets among creditors, allowing creditors to get at least part of their money and freeing the debtor to begin anew.

**Bargaining zone (p. 404)** Range of options between the initial and final offer that each party will consider before negotiations dissolve or reach an impasse.

**Barter (p. 555)** The trading of goods and services for other goods and services directly.

**Behavioural segmentation (p. 435)** Dividing the market based on behaviour with or toward a product.

**Benchmarking (p. 281)** Comparing an organization's practices, processes, and products against the world's best.

**Bond (p. 528)** A corporate certificate indicating that a person has lent money to a firm.

**Bookkeeping (p. 489)** The recording of business transactions.

**Brainstorming (p. 244)** Coming up with as many solutions to a problem as possible in a short period of time with no censoring of ideas.

**Brand awareness (p. 453)** How quickly or easily a given brand name comes to mind when a product category is mentioned.

**Brand equity (p. 453)** The combination of factors—such as awareness, loyalty, perceived quality, images, and emotions—that people associate with a given brand name.

**Brand loyalty (p. 453)** The degree to which customers are satisfied, enjoy the brand, and are committed to further purchase.

**Brand manager (p. 453)** A manager who has direct responsibility for one brand or one product line; called a product manager in some firms.

**Brand name (p. 426)** A word, device (design, shape, sound, or colour), or combination of these used to distinguish a seller's goods or services from those of competitors.

**Breach of contract (p. 133)** When one party fails to follow the terms of a contract.

**Break-even analysis (p. 456)** The process used to determine profitability at various levels of sales.

**Broadband technology (p. 34)** Technology that offers users a continuous connection to the Internet and allows them to send and receive mammoth files that include voice, video, and data much faster than ever before.

**Budget (p. 515)** A financial plan that sets forth management's expectations, and, on the basis of those expectations, allocates the use of specific resources throughout the firm.

**Bundling (p. 455)** Grouping two or more products together and pricing them as a unit.

**Bureaucracy (p. 267)** An organization with many layers of managers who set rules and regulations and oversee all decisions.

**Business (p. 4)** Any activity that seeks to provide goods and services to others while operating at a profit.

**Business cycles (economic cycles) (p. 62)** The periodic rises and falls that occur in all economies over time.

**Business environment (p. 11)** The surrounding factors that either help or hinder the development of businesses.

**Business establishment (p. 211)** Has at least one paid employee, annual sales revenue of $30,000, or is incorporated and has filed a federal corporate income tax return at least once in the previous three years.

**Business law (p. 128)** Rules, statutes, codes, and regulations that are established to provide a legal framework within which business may be conducted and that are enforceable by court action.

**Business plan (p. 220)** A detailed written statement that describes the nature of the business, the target market, the advantages the business will have in relation to competition, and the resources and qualifications of the owner(s).

**Business-to-business (B2B) market (p. 433)** All individuals and organizations that want goods and services to use in producing other goods and services or to sell, rent, or supply goods to others.

**Buying on margin (p. 569)** Purchasing securities by borrowing some of the cost from the broker.

**Cafeteria-style benefits (flexible benefits plans) (p. 374)** Benefit plans that allow employees to choose which benefits they want up to a certain dollar amount.

**Capital assets (p. 493)** Assets that are relatively permanent, such as land, buildings, and equipment.

**Capital budget (p. 516)** A budget that highlights a firm's spending plans for major asset purchases that often require large sums of money.

**Capital expenditures (p. 521)** Major investments in either tangible long-term assets such as land, buildings, and equipment, or intangible assets such as patents, trademarks, and copyrights.

**Capital gains (p. 568)** The positive difference between the purchase price of a stock and its sale price.

**Capitalism (p. 48)** An economic system in which all or most of the factors of production and distribution are privately owned and operated for profit.

**Cash budget (p. 516)** A budget that estimates a firm's projected cash inflows and outflows that the firm can use to plan for any cash shortages or surpluses during a given period.

**Cash flow (p. 497)** The difference between cash coming in and cash going out of a business.

**Cash flow forecast (p. 514)** Forecast that predicts the cash inflows and outflows in future periods, usually months or quarters.

**Cash flow statement (p. 496)** Financial statement that reports cash receipts and disbursements related to a firm's three major activities: operation, investing, and financing.

**Centralized authority (p. 269)** An organization structure in which decision-making authority is maintained at the top level of management at the company's headquarters.

**Certification (p. 399)** Formal process whereby a union is recognized by the Labour Relations Board (LRB) as the bargaining agent for a group of employees.

**Certified general accountant (CGA) (p. 486)** An accountant who has met the examination, education, and experience requirements of the Certified General Accountants Association of Canada.

**Certified management accountant (CMA) (p. 486)** An accountant who has met the examination, education, and experience requirements of the Society of Management Accountants of Canada.

**Chain of command (p. 267)** The line of authority that moves from the top of a hierarchy to the lowest level.

**Channel of distribution (p. 458)** A set of marketing intermediaries, such as agents, brokers, wholesalers, and retailers, that join together to transport and store goods in their path (or channel) from producers to consumers.

**Chartered accountant (CA) (p. 486)** An accountant who has met the examination, education, and experience requirements of the Canadian Institute of Chartered Accountants.

**Check-off clause (p. 402)** A contract clause requiring the employer to deduct union dues from employees' pay and remit them to a union.

**Civil law (p. 128)** Legal proceedings that do not involve criminal acts.

**Closed shop (p. 402)** A workplace in which all new hires must already be union members.

**Collective bargaining (p. 399)** The process whereby union and management representatives negotiate a contract for workers.

**Command economy (p. 55)** An economy in which the government largely decides what goods and services are produced, who gets them, and how the economy will grow.

**Commercial bank (p. 559)** A profit-seeking organization that receives deposits from individuals and corporations in the form of chequing and savings accounts and then uses some of these funds to make loans.

**Commercial finance companies (p. 525)** Organizations that make short-term loans to borrowers who offer tangible assets as collateral.

**Commercial paper (p. 526)** Unsecured promissory notes of $100,000 and up that mature (come due) in 365 days or less.

**Common law (p. 129)** The body of law that comes from decisions handed down by judges; also referred to as unwritten law.

**Common market (trading bloc) (p. 90)** A regional group of countries that have a common external tariff, no internal tariffs, and a coordination of laws to facilitate exchange.

**Common shares (p. 533)**   The most basic form of ownership in a firm; it confers voting rights and the right to share in the firm's profits through dividends, if offered by the firm's board of directors.

**Communism (p. 54)**   An economic and political system in which the state (the government) makes all economic decisions and owns almost all of the major factors of production.

**Comparative advantage theory (p. 72)**   Theory that states that a country should sell to other countries those products that it produces most effectively and efficiently, and buy from other countries those products that it cannot produce as effectively or efficiently.

**Competition-based pricing (p. 455)**   A pricing strategy based on what all other competitors are doing. The price can be set at, above, or below competitors' prices.

**Compliance (p. 487)**   The job of reviewing and evaluating the records used to prepare a company's financial statements.

**Compliance-based ethics codes (p. 146)**   Ethical standards that emphasize preventing unlawful behaviour by increasing control and by penalizing wrongdoers.

**Compressed workweek (p. 376)**   Work schedule that allows an employee to work a full number of hours per week but in fewer days.

**Computer-aided design (CAD) (p. 317)**   The use of computers in the design of products.

**Computer-aided manufacturing (CAM) (p. 317)**   The use of computers in the manufacturing of products.

**Computer-integrated manufacturing (CIM) (p. 318)**   The uniting of computer-aided design with computer-aided manufacturing.

**Conceptual skills (p. 247)**   Skills that involve the ability to picture the organization as a whole and the relationship among its various parts.

**Conciliation (p. 404)**   A process by which a trade union or an employer must use the government's services (via the Ministry of Labour) for help in resolving their differences so that they can reach a collective agreement.

**Conglomerate merger (p. 185)**   The joining of firms in completely unrelated industries.

**Consideration (p. 132)**   Something of value; consideration is one of the requirements of a legal contract.

**Consumer market (p. 433)**   All individuals or households that want goods and services for personal consumption or use.

**Consumer price index (CPI) (p. 62)**   Monthly statistic that measures the pace of inflation or deflation.

**Consumerism (p. 134)**   A social movement that seeks to increase and strengthen the rights and powers of buyers in relation to sellers.

**Contingency planning (p. 242)**   The process of preparing alternative courses of action that may be used if the primary plans don't achieve the organization's objectives.

**Contingent workers (p. 362)**   Workers who do not have regular, full-time employment.

**Continuous improvement (CI) (p. 284)**   Constantly improving the way the organization does things so that customer needs can be better satisfied.

**Continuous process (p. 312)**   A production process in which long production runs turn out finished goods over time.

**Contract (p. 132)**   A legally enforceable agreement between two or more parties.

**Contract law (p. 132)**   Set of laws that specify what constitutes a legally enforceable agreement.

**Contract manufacturing (p. 79)**   A foreign country's production of private-label goods to which a domestic company then attaches its brand name or trademark; also called outsourcing.

**Controlling (p. 238)**   A management function that involves establishing clear standards to determine whether or not an organization is progressing toward its goals and objectives, rewarding people for doing a good job, and taking corrective action if they are not.

**Cookies (p. 40)**   Pieces of information, such as registration data or user preferences, sent by a Web site over the Internet to a Web browser that the browser software is expected to save and send back to the server whenever the user returns to that Web site.

**Co-operative (p. 193)**   An organization that is owned by members and customers, who pay an annual membership fee and share in any profits.

**Copyright (p. 131)**   A form of intellectual property that protects a creator's rights to materials such as books, articles, photos, and cartoons.

**Core competencies (p. 282)**   Those functions that an organization can do as well as or better than any other organization in the world.

**Corporate governance (p. 182)**   The process and policies that determine how an organization interacts with its stakeholders, both internal and external.

**Corporate philanthropy (p. 150)**   Dimension of social responsibility that includes charitable donations.

**Corporate policy (p. 151)**   Dimension of social responsibility that refers to the position a firm takes on social and political issues.

**Corporate responsibility (p. 151)**   Dimension of social responsibility that includes everything from hiring minority workers to making safe products.

**Corporate social initiatives (p. 151)**   Dimension of social responsibility that includes enhanced forms of corporate philanthropy that are more directly related to the company's competencies.

**Corporate social responsibility (CSR) (p. 150)**   A business's concern for the welfare of society as a whole.

**Corporation (p. 170)**   A legal entity with authority to act and have liability separate from its owners.

**Cost of goods sold (or cost of goods manufactured) (p. 495)**   A measure of the cost of merchandise sold or cost of raw materials and supplies used for producing items for resale.

**Countertrading (p. 86)**   A complex form of bartering in which several countries may be involved, each trading goods for goods or services for services.

**Craft union (p. 392)**   An organization of skilled specialists in a particular craft or trade.

**Credit unions (p. 552)**   Non-profit, member-owned financial co-operatives that offer a full variety of banking services to their members.

**Criminal law (p. 128)**   Defines crimes, establishes punishments, and regulates the investigation and prosecution of people accused of committing crimes.

**Crisis planning (p. 243)**   Involves reacting to sudden changes in the environment.

**Crown corporation (p. 103)** A company that is owned by the federal or provincial government.

**Culture (p. 84)** The set of values, beliefs, rules, and institutions held by a specific group of people.

**Current assets (p. 493)** Items that can or will be converted into cash within one year.

**Customer relationship management (CRM) (p. 423)** The process of learning as much as possible about customers and doing everything you can to satisfy them—or even exceed their expectations—with goods and services over time.

**Damages (p. 133)** The monetary settlement awarded to a person who is injured by a breach of contract.

**Database (p. 16)** An electronic storage file where information is kept; one use of databases is to store vast amounts of information about customers.

**Debenture bonds (p. 529)** Bonds that are unsecured (i.e., not backed by any collateral such as equipment).

**Debt financing (p. 522)** Funds raised through various forms of borrowing that must be repaid.

**Decentralized authority (p. 269)** An organization structure in which decision-making authority is delegated to lower-level managers more familiar with local conditions than headquarters management could be.

**Decertification (p. 399)** Process by which workers can take away a union's right to represent them.

**Decision making (p. 244)** Choosing among two or more alternatives.

**Deficit (p. 113)** Occurs when a government spends over and above the amount it gathers in taxes for a specific period of time (namely, a fiscal year).

**Deflation (p. 62)** A situation in which prices are declining.

**Demand (p. 49)** The quantity of products that people are willing to buy at different prices at a specific time.

**Demographic segmentation (p. 435)** Dividing the market by age, income, and education level.

**Demography (p. 18)** The statistical study of the human population with regard to its size, density, and other characteristics such as age, race, gender, and income.

**Departmentalization (p. 272)** Dividing an organization into separate units.

**Depression (p. 63)** A severe recession.

**Deregulation (p. 136)** Government withdrawal of certain laws and regulations that seem to hinder competition.

**Devaluation (p. 86)** Lowering the value of a nation's currency relative to other currencies.

**Direct marketing (p. 470)** Uses direct communication with consumers to generate a response in the form of an order, a request for further information, or a visit to a retail outlet.

**Direct selling (p. 462)** Selling to consumers in their homes or where they work.

**Disinflation (p. 62)** A situation in which price increases are slowing (the inflation rate is declining).

**Diversification (p. 571)** Buying several different investment alternatives to spread the risk of investing.

**Dividends (p. 532)** Part of a firm's profits that may be distributed to shareholders as either cash payments or additional shares of stock.

**Double-entry bookkeeping (p. 489)** The concept of every business transaction affecting at least two accounts.

**Dumping (p. 87)** Selling products in a foreign country at lower prices than those charged in the producing country.

**E-business (p. 15)** Any information system or application that empowers business processes.

**E-commerce (p. 15)** The buying and selling of goods and services over the Internet.

**Economic order quantity (p. 313)** A model that defines the optimal quantity to order to minimize total variable costs required to order and hold inventory.

**Economics (p. 44)** The study of how society chooses to employ resources to produce goods and services and distribute them for consumption among various competing groups and individuals.

**Economies of scale (p. 265)** The situation in which companies can reduce their production costs if they can purchase raw materials in bulk; the average cost of goods goes down as production levels increase.

**Economies of scope (p. 266)** Efficiencies associated with the demand side of a business where more products are promoted or a broader media is used to increase the potential customers reached with each dollar spent.

**Electronic retailing (p. 461)** Selling goods and services to ultimate customers (e.g., you and me) over the Internet.

**Embargo (p. 88)** A complete ban on the import or export of a certain product or the stopping of all trade with a particular country.

**Employee orientation (p. 363)** The activity that introduces new employees to the organization; to fellow employees; to their immediate supervisors; and to the policies, practices, values, and objectives of the firm.

**Employer business (p. 211)** Meets one of the business establishment criteria and usually maintains a payroll of at least one person, possibly the owner.

**Employment equity (p. 380)** Employment activities designed to "right past wrongs" by increasing opportunities for minorities and women.

**Empowerment (p. 17)** Giving front-line workers the responsibility, authority, and freedom to respond quickly to customer requests.

**Enabling (p. 366)** Giving workers the education and tools they need to make decisions.

**Enterprise resource planning (ERP) (p. 314)** A computer application that enables multiple firms to manage all of their operations (finance, requirements planning, human resources, and order fulfillment) on the basis of a single, integrated set of corporate data.

**Entrepreneur (p. 4)** A person who risks time and money to start and manage a business.

**Entrepreneurial team (p. 206)** A group of experienced people from different areas of business who join together to form a managerial team with the skills needed to develop, make, and market a new product.

**Entrepreneurship (p. 200)** Accepting the challenge of starting and running a business.

**Environmental scanning (p. 430)** The process of identifying the factors that can affect marketing success.

**Equalization (p. 119)** A federal government program for reducing fiscal disparities among provinces.

**Equity financing (p. 522)** Funds raised from operations within the firm or through the sale of ownership in the firm.

**Equity theory (p. 340)** The idea that employees try to maintain equity between inputs and outputs compared to others in similar positions.

**Ethics (p. 142)** Standards of moral behaviour; that is, behaviour that is accepted by society as right versus wrong.

**Ethnocentricity (p. 84)** An attitude that one's own culture is superior to all others.

**Everyday low pricing (EDLP) (p. 457)** Setting prices lower than competitors and then not having any special sales.

**Exchange rate (p. 85)** The value of one nation's currency relative to the currencies of other countries.

**Exclusive distribution (p. 461)** Distribution that sends products to only one retail outlet in a given geographic area.

**Expectancy theory (p. 339)** Victor Vroom's theory that the amount of effort employees exert on a specific task depends on their expectations of the outcome.

**Exporting (p. 71)** Selling goods and services to another country.

**Express warranties (p. 131)** Specific representations by the seller that buyers rely on regarding the goods they purchase.

**External customers (p. 256)** Dealers, who buy products to sell to others, and ultimate customers (or end users), who buy products for their own personal use.

**Extranet (p. 33)** A semi-private network that uses Internet technology and allows more than one company to access the same information or allows people on different servers to collaborate.

**Extrinsic reward (p. 326)** Something given to you by someone else as recognition for good work; extrinsic rewards include pay increases, praise, and promotions.

**Facility layout (p. 304)** The physical arrangement of resources (including people) in the production process.

**Facility location (p. 300)** The process of selecting a geographic location for a company's operations.

**Factoring (p. 525)** The process of selling accounts receivable for cash.

**Factors of production (p. 9)** The resources used to create wealth: land, labour, capital, entrepreneurship, and knowledge.

**Federal budget (p. 115)** A comprehensive report that reveals government financial policies for the coming year.

**Finance (p. 512)** The function in a business that acquires funds for the firm and manages those funds within the firm.

**Financial accounting (p. 484)** Accounting information and analyses prepared for people outside the organization.

**Financial control (p. 517)** A process in which a firm periodically compares its actual revenues, costs, and expenses with its projected ones.

**Financial management (p. 512)** The job of managing a firm's resources so it can meet its goals and objectives.

**Financial managers (p. 512)** Managers who make recommendations to top executives regarding strategies for improving the financial strength of a firm.

**Financial statement (p. 491)** A summary of all of the transactions that have occurred over a particular period.

**First in, first out (FIFO) (p. 500)** An accounting method for calculating cost of inventory; it assumes that the first goods to come in are the first to go out.

**Fiscal policy (p. 113)** The federal government's effort to keep the economy stable by increasing or decreasing taxes or government spending.

**Flat organization structure (p. 272)** An organization structure that has few layers of management and a broad span of control.

**Flexible manufacturing (p. 316)** Designing machines to do multiple tasks so that they can produce a variety of products.

**Flextime plan (p. 376)** Work schedule that gives employees some freedom to choose when to work, as long as they work the required number of hours.

**Focus group (p. 430)** A small group of people who meet under the direction of a discussion leader to communicate their opinions about an organization, its products, or other issues.

**Foreign direct investment (FDI) (p. 82)** The buying of permanent property and businesses in foreign nations.

**Foreign subsidiary (p. 82)** A company owned in a foreign country by the parent company.

**Forensic accounting (p. 487)** A relatively new area of accounting that focuses its attention on fraudulent activity.

**Form utility (p. 312)** The value added by the creation of finished goods and services.

**Formal organization (p. 286)** The structure that details lines of responsibility, authority, and position; that is, the structure shown on organization charts.

**Franchise (p. 187)** The right to use a specific business's name and sell its goods or services in a given territory.

**Franchise agreement (p. 187)** An arrangement where-by someone with a good idea for a business sells the rights to use the business name and sell its goods and services in a given territory.

**Franchisee (p. 187)** A person who buys a franchise.

**Franchisor (p. 187)** A company that develops a product concept and sells others the rights to make and sell the products.

**Free-market economy (p. 55)** An economy in which the market largely determines what goods and services are produced, who gets them, and how the economy grows.

**Free-rein (laissez-faire) leadership (p. 252)** Leadership style that involves managers setting objectives and employees being relatively free to do whatever it takes to accomplish those objectives.

**Free trade (p. 71)** The movement of goods and services among nations without political or economic obstruction.

**Fringe benefits (p. 372)** Benefits such as sick-leave pay, vacation pay, pension plans, and health plans that represent additional compensation to employees beyond base wages.

**Fundamental accounting equation (p. 489)** Assets = liabilities + owners' equity; this is the basis for the balance sheet.

**General Agreement on Tariffs and Trade (GATT) (p. 89)** A 1948 agreement that established an international forum for negotiating mutual reductions in trade restrictions.

**General partner (p. 173)** An owner (partner) who has unlimited liability and is active in managing the firm.

**General partnership (p. 173)** A partnership in which all owners share in operating the business and in assuming liability for the business's debts.

**Geographic segmentation (p. 435)** Dividing the market by geographic area.

**Givebacks (p. 409)** Concessions made by union members to management; gains from previous labour negotiations are given up to help employers remain competitive and thereby save jobs.

**Goals (p. 239)** The broad, long-term accomplishments an organization wishes to attain.

**Goal-setting theory (p. 338)** The idea that setting ambitious but attainable goals can motivate workers and improve performance if the goals are accepted, accompanied by feedback, and facilitated by organizational conditions.

**Goods (p. 21)** Tangible products such as computers, food, clothing, cars, and appliances.

**Green marketing (p. 422)** Marketing efforts to produce, promote, and reclaim environmentally-sensitive products.

**Grievance (p. 403)** A formal protest by an individual employee, with the support of the union, when they believe that management is not abiding by or fulfilling the terms of a labour contract.

**Gross domestic product (GDP) (p. 58)** The total value of goods and services produced in a country in a given year.

**Gross profit (gross margin) (p. 495)** How much a firm earned by buying (or making) and selling merchandise.

**Hawthorne effect (p. 329)** The tendency for people to behave differently when they know they are being studied.

**Hierarchy (p. 267)** A system in which one person is at the top of the organization and there is a ranked or sequential ordering from the top down of managers who are responsible to that person.

**High-low pricing strategy (p. 457)** Set prices that are higher than EDLP stores, but have many special sales where the prices are lower than competitors.

**Horizontal merger (p. 184)** The joining of two firms in the same industry.

**Human relations skills (p. 247)** Skills that involve communication and motivation; they enable managers to work through and with people.

**Human resource management (HRM) (p. 354)** The process of determining human resource needs and then recruiting, selecting, developing, motivating, evaluating, compensating, and scheduling employees to achieve organizational goals.

**Hygiene (maintenance) factors (p. 332)** In Herzberg's theory of motivating factors, job factors that can cause dissatisfaction if missing but that do not necessarily motivate employees if increased.

**Identity theft (p. 16)** Obtaining personal information about a person and using that information for illegal purposes.

**Implied warranties (p. 131)** Guarantees legally imposed on the seller.

**Import quota (p. 88)** A limit on the number of products in certain categories that a nation can import.

**Importing (p. 71)** Buying goods and services from another country.

**Income statement (p. 494)** The financial statement that shows a firm's profit after costs, expenses, and taxes; it summarizes all of the resources that have come into the firm (revenue), all the resources that have left the firm, and the resulting net income.

**Incubators (p. 210)** Centres that provide hands-on management assistance, education, information, technical and vital business support services, networking resources, financial advice, as well as advice on where to go to seek financial assistance.

**Independent audit (p. 487)** An evaluation and unbiased opinion about the accuracy of a company's financial statements.

**Industrial design (p. 131)** A form of intellectual property that protects the owner's exclusive right to use the visible features of a finished product that identify it.

**Industrial policy (p. 122)** A comprehensive, coordinated government plan to guide and revitalize the economy.

**Industrial union (p. 393)** Consists of unskilled and semi-skilled workers in mass-production industries such as automobile manufacturing and mining.

**Inflation (p. 62)** A general rise in the prices of goods and services over time.

**Informal organization (p. 286)** The system of relationships and lines of authority that develops spontaneously as employees meet and form power centres; that is, the human side of the organization that does not appear on any organization chart.

**Information technology (IT) (p. 28)** Technology that helps companies change business by allowing them to use new methods.

**Initial public offering (IPO) (p. 531)** The first public offering of a corporation's stock.

**Injunction (p. 407)** A court order directing someone to do something or to refrain from doing something.

**Insider trading (p. 154)** An unethical activity in which insiders use private company information to further their own fortunes or those of their family and friends.

**Institutional investors (p. 528)** Large organizations—such as pension funds, mutual funds, insurance companies, and banks—that invest their own funds or the funds of others.

**Insurable interest (p. 543)** The possibility of the policyholder to suffer a loss.

**Insurable risk (p. 543)** A risk that the typical insurance company will cover.

**Insurance policy (p. 543)** A written contract between the insured and an insurance company that promises to pay for all or part of a loss.

**Intangible assets (p. 493)** Long-term assets (e.g., patents, trademarks, copyrights) that have no real physical form but do have value.

**Integrated marketing communication (IMC) (p. 463)** A technique that combines all of the promotional tools into one comprehensive and unified promotional strategy.

**Integrity-based ethics codes (p. 146)** Ethical standards that define the organization's guiding values, create an environment that supports ethically sound behaviour, and stress a shared accountability among employees.

**Intensive distribution (p. 461)** Distribution that puts products into as many retail outlets as possible.

**Interest (p. 528)** The payment the issuer of the bond makes to the bondholders for use of the borrowed money.

**Intermittent process (p. 312)** A production process in which the production run is short and the machines are changed frequently to make different products.

**Internal customers (p. 256)** Individuals and units within the firm that receive services from other individuals or units.

**International Monetary Fund (IMF) (p. 89)** An international bank that makes short-term loans to countries experiencing problems with their balance of trade.

**Internet2 (p. 34)** The new Internet system that links government supercomputer centres and a select group of universities; it runs more than 22,000 times faster than today's public infrastructure and supports heavy-duty applications.

**Intranet (p. 33)** A companywide network, closed to public access, that uses Internet-type technology.

**Intrapreneurs (p. 209)** Creative people who work as entrepreneurs within corporations.

**Intrinsic reward (p. 326)** The good feeling you have when you have done a job well.

**Inverted organization (p. 283)** An organization that has contact people at the top and the chief executive officer at the bottom of the organization chart.

**Invisible hand (p. 46)** A phrase coined by Adam Smith to describe the process that turns self-directed gain into social and economic benefits for all.

**Involuntary bankruptcy (p. 135)** Bankruptcy procedures filed by a debtor's creditors.

**ISO 9000 (p. 308)** The common name given to quality management and assurance standards.

**ISO 14000 (p. 309)** A collection of the best practices for managing an organization's impact on the environment.

**Job analysis (p. 356)** A study of what is done by employees who hold various job titles.

**Job description (p. 356)** A summary of the objectives of a job, the type of work to be done, the responsibilities and duties, the working conditions, and the relationship of the job to other functions.

**Job enlargement (p. 335)** A job enrichment strategy that extends the work cycle by adding related tasks to the job description.

**Job enrichment (p. 335)** A motivational strategy that emphasizes motivating the worker through the job itself.

**Job rotation (p. 335)** A job enrichment strategy that involves moving employees from one job to another.

**Job sharing (p. 378)** An arrangement whereby two part-time employees share one full-time job.

**Job simulation (p. 364)** The use of equipment that duplicates job conditions and tasks so that trainees can learn skills before attempting them on the job.

**Job specifications (p. 356)** A written summary of the minimum qualifications required of workers to do a particular job.

**Joint venture (p. 80)** A partnership in which two or more companies (often from different countries) join to undertake a major project or to form a new company.

**Journal (p. 489)** The record book or computer program where accounting data are first entered.

**Just-in-time (JIT) inventory control (p. 315)** A production process in which a minimum of inventory is kept on the premises and parts, supplies, and other needs are delivered just in time to go on the assembly line.

**Knowledge management (p. 253)** Finding the right information, keeping the information in a readily accessible place, and making the information known to everyone in the firm.

**Last in, first out (LIFO) (p. 500)** An accounting method for calculating cost of inventory; it assumes that the last goods to come in are the first to go out.

**Law of large numbers (p. 543)** Principle that if a large number of people are exposed to the same risk, a predictable number of losses will occur during a given period of time.

**Leading (p. 237)** Creating a vision for the organization and guiding, training, coaching, and motivating others to work effectively to achieve the organization's goals and objectives.

**Lean manufacturing (p. 316)** The production of goods using less of everything compared to mass production.

**Ledger (p. 490)** A specialized accounting book in which information from accounting journals is accumulated into accounts and posted so that managers can find all of the information about one account in the same place.

**Leveraged buyout (LBO) (p. 186)** An attempt by employees, management, or a group of investors to purchase an organization primarily through borrowing.

**Liabilities (p. 493)** What the business owes to others (debts).

**Liability (p. 170)** For a business, it includes the responsibility to pay all normal debts and to pay because of a court order or law, for performance under a contract, or payment of damages to a person or property in an accident.

**Licensing (p. 78)** A global strategy in which a firm (the licensor) allows a foreign company (the licensee) to produce its product in exchange for a fee (a royalty).

**Limited liability (p. 173)** The responsibility of a business's owners for losses only up to the amount they invest; limited partners and shareholders have limited liability.

**Limited partner (p. 173)** An owner who invests money in the business but does not have any management responsibility or liability for losses beyond the investment.

**Limited partnership (p. 173)** A partnership with one or more general partners and one or more limited partners.

**Line of credit (p. 525)** A given amount of unsecured funds a bank will lend to a business.

**Line organization (p. 275)** An organization that has direct two-way lines of responsibility, authority, and communication running from the top to the bottom of the organization, with all people reporting to only one supervisor.

**Line personnel (p. 275)** Employees who are part of the chain of command that is responsible for achieving organizational goals.

**Liquidity (p. 493)** How fast an asset can be converted into cash.

**Lockout (p. 407)** An attempt by management to put pressure on unions by temporarily closing the business.

**Logistics (p. 309)** Those activities that focus on getting the right amount of the right products or services to the right place at the right time at the lowest possible cost.

**Long-term financing (p. 522)** Borrowed funds that are needed for a period longer than one year.

**Long-term forecast (p. 515)** Forecast that predicts revenues, costs, and expenses for a period longer than one year, and sometimes as far as five or ten years into the future.

**Loss (p. 4)** When a business's expenses are more than its revenues.

**Macroeconomics (p. 45)** The part of economic study that looks at the operation of a nation's economy as a whole.

**Management (p. 236)** The process used to accomplish organizational goals through planning, organizing, leading, and controlling people and other organizational resources.

**Management by objectives (MBO) (p. 338)** A system of goal setting and implementation that involves a cycle of discussion, review, and evaluation of objectives among top and middle-level managers, supervisors, and employees.

**Management development (p. 365)** The process of training and educating employees to become good managers and then monitoring the progress of their managerial skills over time.

**Managerial accounting (p. 483)** Accounting used to provide information and analyses to managers within the organization to assist them in decision making.

**Market (p. 223)** People with unsatisfied wants and needs who have both the resources and the willingness to buy.

**Market price (p. 50)** The price determined by supply and demand.

**Market segmentation (p. 434)** The process of dividing the total market into groups whose members have similar characteristics.

**Marketing (p. 422)** The process of determining customer needs and wants and then developing goods and services that meet or exceed these expectations.

**Marketing boards (p. 107)** Organizations that control the supply or pricing of certain agricultural products in Canada.

**Marketing concept (p. 423)** A three-part business philosophy: (1) a customer orientation, (2) a service orientation, and (3) a profit orientation.

**Marketing intermediaries (p. 458)** Organizations that assist in moving goods and services from producers to industrial and consumer users.

**Marketing mix (p. 424)** The ingredients that go into a marketing program: product, price, place, and promotion.

**Marketing research (p. 428)** The analysis of markets to determine opportunities and challenges, and to find the information needed to make good decisions.

**Maslow's hierarchy of needs (p. 329)** Theory of motivation that places different types of human needs in order of importance, from basic physiological needs to safety, social, and esteem needs to self-actualization needs.

**Mass customization (p. 317)** Tailoring products to meet the needs of individual customers.

**Mass marketing (p. 438)** Developing products and promotions to please large groups of people.

**Materials requirement planning (MRP) (p. 314)** A computer-based production management system that uses sales forecasts to ensure that needed parts and materials are available at the right time and place.

**Matrix organization (p. 276)** An organization in which specialists from different parts of the organization are brought together to work on specific projects but still remain part of a line-and-staff structure.

**Maturity date (p. 529)** The exact date the issuer of a bond must pay the principal to the bondholder.

**Mediation (p. 404)** The use of a third party, called a mediator, who encourages both sides in a dispute to continue negotiating and often makes suggestions for resolving the dispute.

**Mentor (p. 366)** An experienced employee who supervises, coaches, and guides lower-level employees by introducing them to the right people and generally being their organizational sponsor.

**Merger (p. 184)** The result of two firms forming one company.

**Microeconomics (p. 45)** The part of economic study that looks at the behaviour of people and organizations in particular markets.

**Micro-enterprise (p. 207)** A small business defined as having fewer than five employees.

**Micropreneurs (p. 207)** Small-business owners with fewer than five employees who are willing to accept the risk of starting and managing the type of business that remains small, lets them do the kind of work they want to do, and offers them a balanced lifestyle.

**Middle management (p. 246)** The level of management that includes general managers, division managers, and branch and plant managers, who are responsible for tactical planning and controlling.

**Mission statement (p. 239)** An outline of the fundamental purposes of an organization.

**Mixed economies (p. 55)** Economic systems in which some allocation of resources is made by the market and some by the government.

**Monetary policy (p. 115)** The management of the money supply and interest rates.

**Money (p. 555)** Anything that people generally accept as payment for goods and services.

**Money supply (p. 556)** The amount of money the Bank of Canada makes available for people to buy goods and services.

**Monopolistic competition (p. 51)** The market situation in which a large number of sellers produce products that are very similar but that are perceived by buyers as different.

**Monopoly (p. 52)** A market in which there is only one seller for a product or service.

**Motivation (p. 326)** A person's internal drive to act.

**Motivators (p. 332)** In Herzberg's theory of motivating factors, job factors that cause employees to be productive and that give them satisfaction.

**Multinational corporation (p. 83)** An organization that manufactures and markets products in many different countries and has multinational stock ownership and multinational management.

**Mutual fund (p. 571)**   A fund that buys stocks and bonds and then sells shares in those securities to the public.

**Mutual insurance company (p. 544)**   A type of insurance company owned by its policyholders.

**National debt (federal debt) (p. 113)**   The accumulation of government surpluses and deficits over time.

**National Policy (p. 103)**   Government directive that placed high tariffs on imports from the United States to protect Canadian manufacturing, which had higher costs.

**Negligence (p. 130)**   In tort law, behaviour that does not meet the standard of care required and causes unintentional harm or injury.

**Negotiable instruments (p. 132)**   Forms of commercial paper (such as cheques) that are transferable among businesses and individuals and represent a promise to pay a specified amount.

**Negotiated labour–management agreement (labour contract) (p. 400)**   Agreement that clarifies the terms and conditions and sets the tone under which management and labour agree to function over a period of time.

**Net income or net loss (p. 494)**   Revenue left over after all costs and expenses, including taxes, are paid.

**Network computing system (client/server computing) (p. 35)**   Computer systems that allow personal computers (clients) to obtain needed information from huge databases in a central computer (the server).

**Networking (p. 366)**   The process of establishing and maintaining contacts with key managers in one's own organization and other organizations and using those contacts to weave strong relationships that serve as informal development systems.

**Networking (p. 279)**   Using communications technology and other means to link organizations and allow them to work together on common objectives.

**Niche marketing (p. 437)**   The process of finding small but profitable market segments and designing or finding products for them.

**Non-banks (p. 552)**   Financial organizations that accept no deposits but offer many services provided by regular banks.

**Non-profit organization (p. 7)**   An organization whose goals do not include making a personal profit for its owners or organizers.

**North American Free Trade Agreement (NAFTA) (p. 90)**   Agreement that created a free-trade area among Canada, the United States, and Mexico.

**Objectives (p. 239)**   Specific, short-term statements detailing how to achieve the organization's goals.

**Off-the-job training (p. 364)**   Training that occurs away from the workplace and consists of internal or external programs to develop any of a variety of skills or to foster personal development.

**Offshoring (p. 6)**   Sourcing part of the purchased inputs outside of the country.

**Oligopoly (p. 51)**   A form of competition in which just a few sellers dominate the market.

**One-to-one (individual) marketing (p. 437)**   Developing a unique mix of goods and services for each individual customer.

**Online training (p. 364)**   Training programs in which employees "attend" classes via the Internet.

**On-the-job training (p. 363)**   Training in which the employee immediately begins his or her tasks and learns by doing, or watches others for a while and then imitates them, all right at the workplace.

**Open shop (p. 402)**   A workplace in which employees are free to join or not join the union and to pay or not pay union dues.

**Operating (master) budget (p. 516)**   The budget that ties together all of a firm's other budgets; it is the projection of dollar allocations to various costs and expenses needed to run or operate the business, given projected revenues.

**Operating expenses (p. 496)**   Costs involved in operating a business, such as rent, utilities, and salaries.

**Operational planning (p. 242)**   The process of setting work standards and schedules necessary to implement the company's tactical objectives.

**Operations management (p. 298)**   A specialized area in management that converts or transforms resources (including human resources) into goods and services.

**Organization chart (p. 245)**   A visual device that shows the relationships among people and divides the organization's work; it shows who is accountable for the completion of specific work and who reports to whom.

**Organizational (or corporate) culture (p. 285)**   Widely shared values within an organization that provide coherence and co-operation to achieve common goals.

**Organizing (p. 237)**   A management function that includes designing the structure of the organization and creating conditions and systems in which everyone and everything work together to achieve the organization's goals and objectives.

**Outsourcing (p. 6)**   Assigning various functions, such as accounting, production, security, maintenance, and legal work, to outside organizations.

**Owners' equity (p. 493)**   The amount of the business that belongs to the owners minus any liabilities owed by the business.

**Participative (democratic) leadership (p. 251)**   Leadership style that consists of managers and employees working together to make decisions

**Partnership (p. 170)**   A legal form of business with two or more parties.

**Partnership agreement (p. 175)**   Legal document that specifies the rights and responsibilities of each partner.

**Patent (p. 130)**   A form of intellectual property that gives inventors exclusive rights to their inventions for 20 years.

**Pay equity (p. 369)**   Equal pay for work of equal value.

**Penetration price strategy (p. 457)**   A strategy in which the product is priced low to attract many customers and discourage competitors.

**Pension funds (p. 553)**   Amounts of money put aside by corporations, non-profit organizations, or unions to cover part of the financial needs of their members when they retire.

**Perfect competition (p. 51)**   The market situation in which there are many sellers in a market and no seller is large enough to dictate the price of a product.

**Performance appraisal (p. 367)** An evaluation in which the performance level of employees is measured against established standards to make decisions about promotions, compensation, additional training, or firing.

**Personal selling (p. 465)** The face-to-face presentation and promotion of goods and services.

**Phishing (p. 39)** E-mails embellished with a stolen logo for a well-known enterprise (often from financial institutions) that make the messages look authentic, but which are used to collect personal data and use it to commit fraud.

**Planning (p. 237)** A management function that includes anticipating trends and determining the best strategies and tactics to achieve organizational goals and objectives.

**PMI (p. 244)** Listing all of the pluses for a solution in one column, all of the minuses in another, and the implications in a third column.

**Precedent (p. 129)** Decisions that judges have made in earlier cases that guide the handling of new cases.

**Preferred shares (p. 533)** Stock that gives its owners preference in the payment of dividends and an earlier claim on assets than common shareholders if the company is forced out of business and its assets are sold.

**Premium (p. 543)** The fee charged by an insurance company for an insurance policy.

**Price (p. 426)** The money or other consideration (including other goods and services) exchanged for the ownership or use of a good or service.

**Price leadership (p. 455)** The procedure by which one or more dominant firms set the pricing practices that all competitors in an industry follow.

**Primary boycott (p. 406)** When a union encourages both its members and the general public not to buy the products of a firm involved in a labour dispute.

**Primary data (p. 428)** Data that you gather yourself (not from secondary sources such as books and magazines).

**Prime rate (p. 557)** The interest rate that banks charge their most creditworthy customers.

**Principle of motion economy (p. 328)** Theory developed by Frank and Lillian Gilbreth that every job can be broken down into a series of elementary motions.

**Private accountant (p. 486)** An accountant who works for a single firm, government agency, or non-profit organization.

**Private corporation (p. 177)** Corporation that is not allowed to issue stock to the public, so its shares are not listed on stock exchanges; it is limited to 50 or fewer shareholders.

**Privatization (p. 104)** The process of governments selling Crown corporations.

**Problem solving (p. 244)** The process of solving the everyday problems that occur. Problem solving is less formal than decision making and usually calls for quicker action.

**Process manufacturing (p. 312)** That part of the production process that physically or chemically changes materials.

**Producers' cartels (p. 90)** Organizations of commodity-producing countries that are formed to stabilize or increase prices to optimize overall profits in the long run.

**Product (p. 425)** Any physical good, service, or idea that satisfies a want or need.

**Product differentiation (p. 452)** The creation of real or perceived product differences.

**Product liability (p. 130)** Part of tort law that holds businesses liable for harm that results from the production, design, sale, or use of products they market.

**Product line (p. 451)** A group of products that are physically similar or are intended for a similar market.

**Product mix (p. 451)** The combination of product lines offered by a manufacturer.

**Production (p. 297)** The creation of finished goods and services using the factors of production: land, labour, capital, entrepreneurship, and knowledge.

**Production management (p. 298)** The term used to describe all of the activities that managers do to help their firms create goods.

**Productivity (p. 15)** The amount of output that is generated given the amount of input.

**Productivity (p. 59)** The total output of goods and services in a given period divided by the total hours of labour required to provide them.

**Profit (p. 4)** The amount a business earns above and beyond what it spends for salaries and other expenses.

**Promissory note (p. 523)** A written contract with a promise to pay.

**Promotion (p. 427)** All of the techniques that sellers use to motivate customers to buy their products.

**Promotion mix (p. 463)** The combination of promotional tools an organization uses.

**Prospectus (p. 564)** A condensed version of economic and financial information that a company must make available to investors before they purchase a security.

**Psychographic segmentation (p. 435)** Dividing the market according to personality or lifestyle (activities, interests, and opinions).

**Psychological pricing (p. 455)** Pricing goods and services at price points that make the product appear less expensive than it is.

**Public accountant (p. 486)** An accountant who provides his or her accounting services to individuals or businesses on a fee basis.

**Public corporation (p. 177)** Corporation that has the right to issue shares to the public, so its shares may be listed on a stock exchange.

**Public domain software (freeware) (p. 36)** Software that is free for the taking.

**Public relations (PR) (p. 467)** The management function that evaluates public attitudes, changes policies and procedures in response to the public's requests, and executes a program of action and information to earn public understanding and acceptance.

**Publicity (p. 467)** Any information about an individual, product, or organization that's distributed to the public through the media and that's not paid for or controlled by the seller.

**Purchasing (p. 315)** The functional area in a firm that searches for quality material resources, finds the best suppliers, and negotiates the best price for goods and services.

**Pure risk (p. 541)** The threat of loss with no chance for profit.

**Quality (p. 305)** Consistently producing what the customer wants while reducing errors before and after delivery to the customer.

**Quality of life (p. 59)** The general well-being of a society in terms of political freedom, a clean natural environment, education, health care, safety, free time, and everything else that leads to satisfaction and joy.

**Ratio analysis (p. 501)** The assessment of a firm's financial condition and performance through calculations and interpretations of financial ratios developed from the firm's financial statements.

**Real time (p. 279)** The present moment or the actual time in which something takes place; data sent over the Internet to various organizational partners as they are developed or collected are said to be available in real time.

**Recession (p. 62)** Two or more consecutive quarters of decline in the GDP.

**Recruitment (p. 358)** The set of activities used to obtain a sufficient number of the right people at the right time.

**Re-engineering (p. 285)** The fundamental rethinking and radical redesign of organizational processes to achieve dramatic improvements in critical measures of performance.

**Regulations (p. 12)** Rules or orders made by government to carry out the purposes set out in statutes.

**Reinforcement theory (p. 340)** Theory that positive and negative reinforcers motivate a person to behave in certain ways.

**Relationship marketing (p. 438)** Marketing strategy with the goal of keeping individual customers over time by offering them products that exactly meet their requirements.

**Research and development (R&D) (p. 395)** Work directed toward the innovation, introduction, and improvement of products and processes.

**Resource development (p. 45)** The study of how to increase resources and the creation of the conditions that will make better use of those resources (e.g., recycling).

**Resources (p. 236)** A general term that incorporates human resources, natural resources, and financial resources.

**Restructuring (p. 283)** Redesigning an organization so that it can more effectively and efficiently serve its customers.

**Retailer (p. 458)** An organization that sells to ultimate consumers.

**Revenue (p. 4)** The total amount of money a business takes in during a given period by selling goods and services.

**Revenue (p. 494)** The value of what is received for goods sold, services rendered, and other financial sources.

**Reverse discrimination (p. 381)** The unfairness that unprotected groups (say, whites or males) may perceive when protected groups receive preference in hiring and promotion.

**Revolving credit agreement (p. 525)** A line of credit that is guaranteed by the bank.

**Risk (p. 5)** The chance an entrepreneur takes of losing time and money on a business that may not prove profitable.

**Risk (p. 541)** The chance of loss, the degree of probability of loss, and the amount of possible loss.

**Risk/return trade-off (p. 528)** The principle that the greater the risk a lender takes in making a loan, the higher the interest rate required.

**Robot (p. 316)** A computer-controlled machine capable of performing many tasks requiring the use of materials and tools.

**Rule of indemnity (p. 544)** Rule saying that an insured person or organization cannot collect more than the actual loss from an insurable risk.

**Sales promotion (p. 469)** The promotional tool that stimulates consumer purchasing and dealer interest by means of short-term activities.

**Sampling (p. 469)** A promotional tool in which a company lets consumers have a small sample of a product for no charge.

**Scientific management (p. 327)** Studying workers to find the most efficient ways of doing things and then teaching people those techniques.

**Secondary boycott (p. 406)** An attempt by labour to convince others to stop doing business with a firm that is the subject of a primary boycott.

**Secondary data (p. 428)** Information that has already been compiled by others and published in journals and books or made available online.

**Secured loan (p. 525)** A loan backed by something valuable, such as property.

**Securities commission (p. 564)** A government agency that administers provincial securities legislation.

**Securities dealer (p. 564)** A firm that trades securities for its clients and offers investment services.

**Selection (p. 360)** The process of gathering information and deciding who should be hired, under legal guidelines, for the best interests of the individual and the organization.

**Selective distribution (p. 461)** Distribution that sends products to only a preferred group of retailers in an area.

**Self-insurance (p. 542)** The practice of setting aside money to cover routine claims and buying only "catastrophe" policies to cover big losses.

**Self-managed teams (p. 278)** Groups of employees from different departments who work together on a long-term basis.

**Services (p. 23)** Intangible products (i.e., products that can't be held in your hand) such as education, health care, insurance, recreation, and travel and tourism.

**Shareware (p. 36)** Software that is copyrighted but distributed to potential customers free of charge.

**Shop stewards (p. 404)** Union officials who work permanently in an organization and represent employee interests on a daily basis.

**Short-term financing (p. 522)** Borrowed funds that are needed for one year or less.

**Short-term forecast (p. 514)** Forecast that predicts revenues, costs, and expenses for a period of one year or less.

**Sinking fund (p. 529)** A reserve account in which the issuer of a bond periodically retires some part of the bond principal prior to maturity so that enough capital will be accumulated by the maturity date to pay off the bond.

**Six sigma quality (p. 305)** A quality measure that allows only 3.4 defects per million events.

**Skimming price strategy (p. 457)** A strategy in which a new product is priced high to make optimum profit while there's little competition.

**Small and medium-sized enterprises (SMEs) (p. 205)** Refers to all businesses with fewer than 500 employees.

**Small business (p. 211)** A business that is independently owned and operated, is not dominant in its field, and meets certain standards of size in terms of employees or annual revenues.

**Social audit (p. 157)** A systematic evaluation of an organization's progress toward implementing programs that are socially responsible and responsive.

**Socialism (p. 53)** An economic system based on the premise that some, if not most, basic businesses should be owned by the government so that profits can be evenly distributed among the people.

**Sole proprietorship (p. 170)** A business that is owned and operated by one person, without forming a corporation.

**Span of control (p. 270)** The optimum number of subordinates a manager supervises or should supervise.

**Speculative risk (p. 541)** A chance of either profit or loss.

**Staff personnel (p. 275)** Employees who advise and assist line personnel in meeting their goals.

**Stagflation (p. 62)** A situation in which the economy is slowing but prices are going up regardless.

**Stakeholders (p. 5)** All of the people who stand to gain or lose by the policies and activities of a business.

**Standard of living (p. 59)** The amount of goods and services people can buy with the money they have.

**Statistical process control (SPC) (p. 306)** The process of taking statistical samples of product components at each stage of the production process and plotting those results on a graph. Any variances from quality standards are recognized and can be corrected if beyond the set standards.

**Statistical quality control (SQC) (p. 306)** The process that some managers use to continually monitor all phases of the production process to ensure that quality is being built into the product from the beginning.

**Statutory law (p. 129)** Federal and provincial legislative enactments, treaties of the federal government, and bylaws/ordinances—in short, written law.

**Stock certificate (p. 532)** Evidence of stock ownership that specifies the name of the company, the number of shares it represents, and the type of stock being issued.

**Stock exchange (p. 565)** An organization whose members can buy and sell (exchange) securities for companies and investors.

**Stock insurance company (p. 544)** A type of insurance company owned by stockholders.

**Stock split (p. 569)** An action by a company that gives shareholders two or more shares of stock for each one they own.

**Stockbroker (p. 566)** A registered representative who works as a market intermediary to buy and sell securities for clients.

**Stocks (p. 530)** Shares of ownership in a company.

**Strategic alliance (p. 81)** A long-term partnership between two or more companies established to help each company build competitive market advantages.

**Strategic planning (p. 240)** The process of determining the major goals of the organization and the policies and strategies for obtaining and using resources to achieve those goals.

**Strict product liability (p. 130)** Legal responsibility for harm or injury caused by a product regardless of fault.

**Strike (p. 405)** A union strategy in which workers refuse to go to work.

**Strikebreakers (p. 407)** Replacement workers hired to do the jobs of striking employees until the labour dispute is resolved.

**Supervisory management (p. 247)** Managers who are directly responsible for supervising workers and evaluating their daily performance.

**Supply (p. 49)** The quantity of products that manufacturers or owners are willing to sell at different prices at a specific time.

**Supply chain (p. 309)** The sequence of firms that perform activities required to create and deliver a good or service to consumers or industrial users.

**Supply chain management (p. 309)** The integration and organization of information and logistics activities across firms in a supply chain for the purpose of creating and delivering goods and services that provide value to customers.

**Surplus (p. 114)** An excess of revenues over expenditures.

**Sustainable development (p. 159)** Implementing a process that integrates environmental, economic, and social considerations into decision making.

**SWOT analysis (p. 240)** A planning tool used to analyze an organization's strengths, weaknesses, opportunities, and threats.

**Tactical planning (p. 242)** The process of developing detailed, short-term statements about what is to be done, who is to do it, and how it is to be done.

**Tall organization structure (p. 271)** An organization structure in which the pyramidal organization chart would be quite tall because of the various levels of management.

**Target costing (p. 455)** Designing a product so that it satisfies customers and meets the profit margins desired by the firm.

**Target marketing (p. 434)** Marketing directed toward those groups (market segments) an organization decides it can serve profitably.

**Tariff (p. 87)** A tax imposed on imports.

**Technical skills (p. 247)** Skills that involve the ability to perform tasks in a specific discipline or department.

**Technology (p. 14)** Inventions or innovations from applied science or engineering research.

**Telecommuting (telework) (p. 38)** Occurs when paid workers reduce their commute by carrying out all, or part, of their work away from their normal place of business.

**Telemarketing (p. 461)** The sale of goods and services by telephone.

**Term-loan agreement (p. 528)** A promissory note that requires the borrower to repay the loan in specified instalments.

**Test marketing (p. 425)** The process of testing products among potential users.

**Time-motion studies (p. 328)** Studies, begun by Frederick Taylor, of which tasks must be performed to complete a job and the time needed to do each task.

**Top management (p. 246)** Highest level of management, consisting of the president and other key company executives who develop strategic plans.

**Tort (p. 130)** A wrongful act that causes injury to another person's body, property, or reputation.

**Total fixed costs (p. 456)** All of the expenses that remain the same no matter how many products are made or sold.

**Total product offer (value package) (p. 450)** Everything that consumers evaluate when deciding whether to buy something; also called a value package.

**Total quality management (TQM) (p. 284)** Striving for maximum customer satisfaction by ensuring quality from all departments.

**Trade credit (p. 523)** The practice of buying goods and services now and paying for them later.

**Trade deficit (unfavourable balance of trade) (p. 75)** Occurs when the value of a country's imports exceeds that of its exports.

**Trade protectionism (p. 87)** The use of government regulations to limit the import of goods and services.

**Trademark (p. 131, 453)** A brand that has been given exclusive legal protection for both the brand name and the pictorial design.

**Training and development (p. 363)** All attempts to improve productivity by increasing an employee's ability to perform. Training focuses on short-term skills, whereas development focuses on long-term abilities.

**Transfer payments (p. 119)** Direct payments from governments to other governments or to individuals.

**Transparency (p. 279)** A concept that describes a company being so open to other companies working with it that the once-solid barriers between them become see-through and electronic information is shared as if the companies were one.

**Trial balance (p. 490)** A summary of all of the data in the account ledgers to show whether the figures are correct and balanced.

**Triple-bottom line (TBL, 3BL, or People, Planet, Profit) (p. 157)** A framework for measuring and reporting corporate performance against economic, social, and environmental parameters.

**Trust company (p. 552)** A financial institution that can administer estates, pension plans, and agency contracts, in addition to other activities conducted by banks.

**Turnover rate (p. 379)** A measure of the percentage of employees that leave a firm each year.

**Unemployment rate (p. 60)** The percentage of the labour force that actively seeks work but is unable to find work at a given time.

**Uninsurable risk (p. 542)** A risk that no insurance company will cover.

**Union (p. 390)** An employee organization that has the main goal of representing members in employee–management bargaining over job-related issues.

**Union density (p. 395)** A measure of the percentage of workers who belong to unions.

**Union security clause (p. 402)** Provision in a negotiated labour–management agreement that stipulates that employees who benefit from a union must either officially join or at least pay dues to the union.

**Union shop (p. 402)** A workplace in which the employer is free to hire anybody, but the recruit must then join the union within a short period, perhaps a month.

**Unlimited liability (p. 172)** The responsibility of business owners for all of the debts of the business.

**Unsecured loan (p. 525)** A loan that's not backed by any specific assets.

**Value (p. 450)** Good quality at a fair price. When consumers calculate the value of a product, they look at the benefits and then subtract the cost to see if the benefits exceed the costs.

**Values (p. 238)** A set of fundamental beliefs that guide a business in the decisions they make.

**Variable costs (p. 456)** Costs that change according to the level of production.

**Venture capital (p. 531)** Money that is invested in new or emerging companies that are perceived as having great profit potential.

**Venture capitalists (VCs) (p. 222)** Individuals or companies that invest in new businesses in exchange for partial ownership of those businesses.

**Vertical merger (p. 184)** The joining of two companies involved in different stages of related businesses.

**Vestibule training (p. 364)** Training done in schools where employees are taught on equipment similar to that used on the job.

**Virtual corporation (p. 280)** A temporary networked organization made up of replaceable firms that join and leave as needed.

**Virtual private network (VPN) (p. 33)** A private data network that creates secure connections, or "tunnels," over regular Internet lines.

**Virtualization (p. 29)** Accessibility through technology that allows business to be conducted independent of location.

**Virus (p. 39)** A piece of programming code inserted into other programming to cause some unexpected and, for the victim, usually undesirable event.

**Vision (p. 238)** An encompassing explanation of why the organization exists and where it's trying to head.

**Voluntary bankruptcy (p. 135)** Legal procedures initiated by a debtor.

**Whistleblowers (p. 146)** People who report illegal or unethical behaviour.

**Wholesaler (p. 458)** A marketing intermediary that sells to other organizations.

**Wildcat strike (p. 406)** An unauthorized (by the union) work stoppage while a labour contract is still in effect.

**World Bank (International Bank for Reconstruction and Development) (p. 90)** An autonomous United Nations agency that borrows money from the more prosperous countries and lends it to less-developed countries to develop their infrastructure.

**World Trade Organization (WTO) (p. 89)** The international organization that replaced the General Agreement on Tariffs and Trade, and was assigned the duty to mediate trade disputes among nations.

# Photo Credits

## Chapter 1

p. 3 © Used with permission of Research In Motion; p. 4 © image 100/ Corbis; p. 7 Used with permission of Canadian Blood Services 2009; p. 9 Courtesy of Sequel Naturals Ltd.; p. 13 AP/Wide World Photos; p. 16 CP/ Toronto Star (Colin McConnell); p. 19 Yellow Dog Productions; p. 22 Keith Weller/US Department of Agriculture.

## Chapter 2

p. 43 Photo by Ojo Newspaper/Getty Images; p. 44 Maria Teijeiro / age footstock; p. 45 Used with permission of Fisheries and Oceans Canada. Reproduced with the permission of Her Majesty the Queen in Right of Canada, 2009; p. 48 top: Photodisc; p. 52 © Lonnie Ganz; p. 54 left: Francis Dean/The Image Works, right: National Geographic/Getty Images; p. 57 Dynamic Graphics/Jupiter Images; p. 60 Used with permission of the Conference Board of Canada 2009.

## Chapter 3

p. 69 Courtesy of Portfolio Entertainment; p. 72 CP/Adrian Wyld; p. 73 CP/ Aaron Harris; p. 77 Tetra Images; p. 79 Yoshikazu Tsuno/AFP/Getty Images; p. 80 CP PHOTO (Steve White); p. 83 Courtesy of Bombardier Transportation; p. 88 Bruce Heinemann/Getty Images; p. 89 © The McGraw-Hill Companies/ Barry Barker, photographer; p. 91 Mark Gabrenya/Shutterstock.

## Chapter 4

p. 101 Melody Dover — President & Creative Director, Fresh Media Inc.; p. 103 top: Federal Student Work Experience Program (FWSEP): www.jobs-emplois. gc.ca/fswep-pfete/student/index_e.htm Aug 22, 2006. Reproduced with the permission of the Staffing and Assessment Services Branch, Public Service Commission of Canada 2009, bottom: Tim Stevens Photography; p. 105 Courtesy of Petro-Canada; p. 106 McGraw-Hill Ryerson (Alison Derry); p. 107 © Library of Parliament/Bibliothèque du Parlement; p. 117 Bank of Canada; p. 118 Ford of Canada Public Affairs; p. 121 National Research Council.

## Chapter 5

p. 139 Photo of Mary Dawson. Reproduced with the permission of the Office of the Conflict of Interest and Ethics Commissioner, 2009; p. 140 Crowle Art Group; p. 142 © Corbis/Veer; p. 147 © CTV; p. 150 Flickr.com Timhortonsmktg; p. 152 Dick Hemingway; p. 156 © Todd Selby; p. 160 © Deanne Fitzmaurice/San Francisco Chronicle/CORBIS.

## Chapter 6

p. 169 Courtesy of BDC; p. 171 © What's Up Yukon; p. 178 The Canadian Press/ CPI (Mario Beauregard); p. 183 Royalty-Free/CORBIS; p. 187 © Supperworks 2009; p. 190 CP/Steve White; p. 192 InterContinental Hotels Group; p. 193 Used with permission of Mountain Equipment Co-op © 2009.

## Chapter 7

p. 199 Marlene Ross, Marlene Ross Design; p. 201 Courtesy McCain Foods (Canada); p. 202 Courtesy of Company's Coming; p. 205 © National Post/ Peter J. Thompson; p. 207 THE CANADIAN PRESS/Aaron Harris; p. 209 © Bill Varie/CORBIS; p. 210 National Research Council Canada; p. 216 Co-Founder and President, Tal Delatiar. MBAs Without Borders — www. mbaswithoutborders.org; p. 222 Courtesy of Canadian Broadcasting Corporation.

## Chapter 8

p. 235 THE CANADIAN PRESS/Jeff McIntosh; p. 237 LWA; p. 238 Courtesy of Monster; p. 239 Used with permission of Sears Canada Inc.; p. 248 Kaz Mori; p. 249 Big Cheese Photo/JupiterImages.

## Chapter 9

p. 263 Courtesy of Indigo Books and Music, Inc.; p. 264 © Hulton-Deutsch Collection/CORBIS; p. 267 Courtesy of German Information Center, NY; p. 275 McGraw-Hill Ryerson; p. 280 THE CANADIAN PRESS/Larry MacDougall; p. 284 Courtesy of Creation Technologies; p. 285 Courtesy of Canadian Tire Financial Services; p. 287 THE CANADIAN PRESS/Ian Barrett.

## Chapter 10

p. 293 Bombardier Inc.; p. 297 Courtesy of Demetria Giannisis; p. 299 THE CANADIAN PRESS/Graham Hughes; p. 302 THE CANADIAN PRESS/ Richard Jones / Rex Features; p. 303 Courtesy CAW; p. 305 Courtesy of Reuner Holz; p. 306 Jeff Sciortino; p. 307 National Quality Institute (416)251-7600 www.nqi.ca; p. 308 Brand X / Fotosearch; p. 310 Nyul/Dreamstime.com/ GetStock.com; p. 311 Keith Brofsky/Getty Images; p. 314 Courtesy of SAS Institute; p. 315 Ryan McVay/Getty Images; p. 317 CORBIS.

## Chapter 11

p. 325 Courtesy of Catherine Daw SPM Group; p. 327 © Canadian Tire Financial Services; p. 329 Courtesy AT&T Corporate Archives; p. 331 © Digital Vision; p. 333 Back in Motion Rehab Inc. Located in British Columbia, Back in Motion is a full-service rehabilitation, disability management and employment solutions company; p. 337 Bruce Ayres; p. 338 Courtesy of Mini Maid; p. 339 Purestock; p. 341 © Stockbyte/Getty Images; p. 346 Getty Images.

## Chapter 12

p. 353 Richard Bell; p. 356 Source: Prevent Discrimination — Cultivate Diversity poster URL: http://www.chrc-ccdp.ca/publications/diversity-en.asp Author/Organization: Canadian Human Rights Commission. Reproduced with the permission of the Ministry of Public Works and Government Services, 2009; p. 358 Published by Nathan and Mark Laurie, co-founders of jobpostings Magazine (est. 1998) and www.jobpostings.ca; p. 361 fStop; p. 362 Yuri Arcurs/Getty Images; p. 364 © Photodisc/Getty Images; p. 365 Keith Brofsky/Getty Images; p. 370 Courtesy of Canadian Labour Congress; p. 373 © 2010 Mediacorp Canada Inc. Canada's Top 100 Employers logo used with permission; p. 377 © Royalty-Free Corbis; p. 381 ColorBlind Images.

## Chapter 13

p. 389 James Hardy/PhotoAlto; p. 390 Courtesy of Canadian Auto Workers; p. 391 Jenna-Lee Mainse; p. 393 City of Toronto Archives (Fonds 1568, Item 314).; p. 398 Courtesy UFCW Canada; p. 406 Ad courtesy of the Public Service Alliance of Canada. The ad was created by West Star Communications and Working Design for a boycott campaign during a strike at BHP Billiton's Ekati diamond mine in the Northwest Territories in June 2006.; p. 407 THE CANADIAN PRESS/Edmonton Sun/Walter Tychnowicz; p. 408 Toronto Star/ GetStock.com; p. 409 Cosmo Mannella, Director of LIUNA's Canadian Tri-Funds (416) 245-9520; p. 410 Source: CHRC Bookmark URL: http://www. chrc-ccdp.ca/publications/bookmark_commission_signet-en.asp Author/ Organization: Canadian Human Rights Commission. Reproduced with the permission of the Ministry of Public Works and Government Services, 2009.; p. 413 Courtesy of Canadian Auto Workers.

## Chapter 14

p. 421 Erica Van Kamp; p. 422 Curves International Inc.; p. 423 © Advertising Standards Canada; p. 427 The McGraw-Hill Companies, Inc./LarsNiki, photographer; p. 432 Courtesy Telelatino; p. 433 Siri Stafford/Getty Images; p. 434 left: © age fotostock/SuperStock right: © Comstock/Superstock; p. 435 left: Courtesy of Brad Pattison "The End of My Leash" right: Courtesy of Frantic Films and Gail Vax-Oxlade "Till Debt Do Us Part"; p. 440 BECEL is a registered trade-mark owned by Unilever Canada Inc. HEART & STROKE FOUNDATION is a trade-mark of Heart and Stroke Foundation of Canada. Both marks are used with permission.

## Chapter 15

p. 449 Whistle designs and trademarks used with permission of Fox 40 International Inc.; p. 451 right: © Christopher Kerrigan; p. 452 Whistle designs and trademarks used with permission of Fox 40 International Inc.; p. 453 Courtesy of Victoria School of Business; p. 435 Courtesy of Lakeport Brewing LP; p. 456 Newfoundland and Labrador Tourism; p. 458 Courtesy of The Home Depot Canada; p. 461 Image Source/Getty Images; p. 463 © Responsible Gambling Council 2009; p. 466 Verge Cover © Verge Magazine Inc. Cover Photo: J Duggan; p. 470 Jack Star/PhotoLink/ Getty Images; p. 471 © Lululemon Athletica 2008.

## Chapter 16

p. 481 Reproduced by permission of Certified Management Accountants of Canada. Photo by Bob Hewitt (mhphoto.com); p. 484 Michael Rosefeld/ Getty Images; p. 485 © Stockbyte/PunchStock; p. 486 Reproduced with the permission of the Canadian Institute of Chartered Accountants; p. 490 Harvard Business Review, 2002; p. 504 Courtesy of the Home Depot.

## Chapter 17

p. 511 Bob Chambers, Bochsler Creative Solutions; p. 516 Jeff Greenbert/ PhotoEdit; p. 520 Comstock Images; p. 524 Vic Bider/PhotoEdit.

## Chapter 18

p. 551 Courtesy of Canadian Tire Financial Services; p. 555 THE CANADIAN PRESS/Paul Chiasson; p. 560 Boris Lyubner/Getty Images; p. 561 Gvictoria/ Dreamstime.com; p. 565 Christian Lagereek/Getty Images; p. 568 AP WideWorld Photo; p. 572 Courtesy of Sprott Asset Management.

# Organization Index

# Subject Index

# URL Index